W9-BYU-331

ALTERNATIVE PAPERS

ALTERNATIVE PAPERS

Selections from the Alternative Press, 1979-1980

Edited by

Elliott Shore

Patricia J. Case

Laura Daly

WITH THE HELP OF

Sandy Berman

Paul Buhle

James P. Danky

John DeMott

John Jackson

Ann Pride

Daniel Tsang

Celeste West

Temple University Press
Philadelphia

Temple University Press, Philadelphia 19122
© 1982 by Temple University. All rights reserved
Published 1982
Printed in the United States of America

Library of Congress Cataloging in Publication Data

Main entry under title:

Alternative papers.

  Includes index.
  I. Shore, Elliott, 1951-   II. Case, Patricia J.
  III. Daly, Laura.
  AC5.A49   081   82-3250
  ISBN 0-87722-243-6   AACR2
  ISBN 0-87722-244-4 (pbk.)

Alternative Cataloging in Publication Data

Shore, Elliott, 1951-   editor.
  Alternative papers: selections from the
alternative press, 1979-1980. Edited by Elliott
Shore, Patricia J. Case, and Laura Daly. Temple
Univ. Press, copyright 1982.
  Cover subtitle: Stories, events, and issues that
the mass media ignored, distorted, buried, or
missed altogether, selected from alternative
magazines, newspapers, journals, and sporadicals.

  PARTIAL CONTENTS: The Press. -Nukes. -
Appropriate technology. - Third World. -
Corporate connections. - Repression. - Women. -
Lesbians and gay men. - Work. - Directory.
  1. Alternative press publications—Excerpts.
2. Alternative press—Directories. 3. Radicalism.
4. Social change. 5. Social problems. 6. Nuclear
power. 7. Third World. 8. Corporate
accountability. 9. Repression. 10. Feminism.
11. Gays. I. Title. II. Case, Patricia J.,
editor. III. Daly, Laura, editor. IV. Title:
Alternative press selections, 1979-1980. V. Title:
Stories, events, and issues that the mass media
ignored, distorted, buried, or missed altogether,
selected from alternative magazines, newspapers,
journals, and sporadicals.

081 or 301.23

Contents

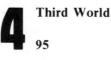

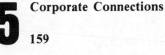

5 Corporate Connections
159

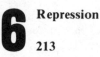

8 Lesbians and Gay Men 307

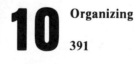

11   The Movement
437

Introduction

Alternative Papers is a selection of articles from the English-language alternative press. It offers a view of reality that differs both in scope and emphasis from that presented by the corporate media, without claiming to represent all aspects of the alternative press or even to be an accurate cross section. There are specific assumptions that have governed the editing and development of this book, and outlining them here will help to orient the reader approaching the alternative press for the first time, as well as the reader looking for a clearer perspective on the 1979-1980 period.

What the mass media tell us about our society conditions our experience, narrows our choices, and channels our responses. Because of the bias inherent in their perspective, their power can be particularly dangerous. Television, radio, and the daily and weekly press depend in one way or another on industry and government, which inevitably trade in conservative information. They therefore present a version of reality designed to reinforce rather than challenge the social and political consensus. Reports of corruption, social misery, and injustice blame powerful individuals, human nature, or an unlucky sequence of miscalculations instead of questioning the basic nature of our society. And even while implicitly assuming our society's continued inability to provide a decent life for many of its citizens, they consider tinkering and fine-tuning through laws, government regulations, and individual decisions better than radical change.

Leaders have always recognized the importance of managing information. Technological advances such as the printing press and movable type, which helped to make mass publication possible, also led to sophisticated methods of control. Writing in *One Big Union Monthly* in September 1920, Ralph Winstead attacked the corporate press in accounting for the failure of political democracy in America's industrial society. Winstead pointed out that large-scale printing technology in the early twentieth century had created a daily and periodical press that could "standardize social thought." And, Winstead added, that press was owned, "with pitifully few exceptions, by the capitalist class." For Winstead, a press controlled by the same interests that controlled the industrial life of the community gave those interests "a power never held by any ancient tyrant." It was the power to mold thinking, to define boundaries of informed discussion, and to channel perceptions.

Now we are confronted by more powerful electronic forms of communication that offer the possibility of even greater centralization and more persuasive and subtle methods of influence. For example, the advertising of Time, Inc., asks the consumer to read the whole company: *Sports Illustrated, Life Magazine, People, Fortune, Discover, Money,* and, of course, *Time.* And there is more to Time, Inc.: the Pioneer Press newspaper chain in the Chicago area, TV stations, film and video companies, Home Box Office, and the paper it killed, the *Washington Star.* Or take, for example, Gulf and Western, which distributes Harlequin Romances and produces books under the Simon and Schuster imprint, as well as fifteen other brands.

Celeste West, writing sixty years after Winstead, echoes his charges and voices the fear that the independent publisher is a vanishing species. In *Where Have All the Publishers Gone? Gone to Conglomerates Every One . . .* (Booklegger Press, 1981) she documents the emergence through corporate mergers of a "Literary-Industrial Complex." Even the biggest presses are threatened. She sees them being absorbed by multinational corporations that will consider publishing secondary to the other goods and services they provide.

But the "pitifully few exceptions" still fight the battle. Today's alternative press began with the explosive growth of the alternative press in the 1960s that corresponded to the growth of the anti-Vietnam War movement. The underground press of the sixties provided news and information that was unavailable in the corporate-controlled media. The *Berkeley Barb, Black Panther, East Village Other,* and *Rat* helped to affirm the existence of the anti-war movement and the counterculture and provide a much-needed forum for self-expression.

That counterculture and anti-war movement, viewed through the lens of the corporate media, has died. In its place, we are told, have come complacency, apathy, the "Me" decade, and the dress-for-success generation that seeks a remunerative place in the system and the pleasures that relative affluence can provide. In the eyes of our reporters and advertising executives, the women's movement, as well as the other progressive parts of the 1960s movement, has become a field for selling new goods. The liberated woman of the 1980s wears eighties clothes, plays eighties games, is a complete mother and consumer. Hippie garb, ten years later, is designer jeans. Seen through the media, equality for oppressed minorities has been taken care of through programs such as affirmative action, which can now be quietly dropped or conveniently abused. To protest now is to complain, to annoy, to be a nuisance, or to be a really serious nuisance, a terrorist. More people are seen as unwilling, even if not satisfied, to make the effort to change the system or even to protest it in an effective way.

But the alternative movement persists and grows. It does so removed from the view of the mass media. It no longer—or better, much less often—makes the kind of news that appeals to the commercial press, although the press in the past decade has enjoyed the slightly mocking tone that it can take when finding another "leader" of the 1960s who has gone over to the establishment or who has embraced Jesus. Readers of *Newsweek* and *Time* and their less respectable counterparts in the popular press will be familiar with this kind of writing. It implies that the anti-war and attendant movements relied upon leaders, colorful ones, and if they have been co-opted, then of course their supporters must have followed. These articles reinforce the popular image of the counterculture as kids who have now learned their lesson after becoming dissatisfied with their privileged lot and rebelling against their parents. That they have passed the test can be shown through the numbers of them who are now corporate executives and/or dutiful parents in nuclear families. They may retain nostalgic connections to their youth by choosing, for example, to renovate an inner-city dwelling, but of course that is also a shrewd business move. They may even continue to eat well and take care of their bodies, but that is another good investment. And it fits into the prevailing ideology of individualism.

Beneath the veneer of happy-talk news, all-news radio stations, maxi- and mini-cams, instant analysis, in-depth interviews, and constant updates, we can see evidence that the movement has grown and not been completely engulfed by the redefined American Dream. One of the indicators is the growth of the alternative press.

The alternative, or movement, press has changed and grown considerably since the late sixties. Tabloids like the *Barb* and the *Great Speckled Bird* have disappeared or undergone drastic alterations. Papers that address more specific issues and constituencies have emerged in their place. Questions and problems that the movement press of the sixties confronted only on occasion and in haste are now in the chief subjects of such papers as the *Waste Paper, Science for the People, Gay Community News,* and *Union W.A.G.E.* Today, the number and diversity of independent publications is impossible to estimate—many publications have developed in response to local issues and have never tried to reach a larger public. In 1980, *Alternatives in Print,* a reference work on the independent press, listed fourteen hundred periodicals. There undoubtedly are many more.

The important stories for these papers, and for the many people who buy and read them, differ either in focus or in content from stories in the corporate media. For example, in 1979 and 1980, the nuclear power question, the Iranian "crisis," and the presidential election dominated the attention of the mass media. But the alternative press represented here took a very different perspective on nuclear power and ignored the "crisis" and the election. Managed media events, like the hostage situation, are not the concern of much of the alternative press, despite *Newsweek's* designation of 1980 as the year of the hostage. Questions about the effects of the Iranian revolution on the structure of life in that country are the concern of these papers. Elections that offer no choice, such as the Carter-Reagan race, are important only in what they say about the nature of politics in the United States, as voters, by largely ignoring the election, seemed to agree. The concerns of 1979 and 1980 in the alternative press represented here include alternative energy sources, apartheid, violence against women, institutional racism, multinational corporations, union busting, and the anti-draft movement.

It could be said that the papers included in this book were in fact more vital in the 1970s than the established media. Investigative reporting was the rule rather than the exception. Many of these papers consistently offered alternative perspectives on stories that might otherwise have gone the way of yesterday's weather. They consistently raised questions about public events not raised in the mass media for months, or years, or, in some cases, ever. If one could read through a selection of them for a given period of time, one's perspective on "the news" would be radically different. But these papers are not usually offered for sale on newsstands. Nor are they available in most libraries. *Alternative Papers* was conceived as a way of offering that different perspective for the years 1979-1980, when many issues seemed to come into focus.

The more than ninety-papers represented in this collection cover a wide range of opinion, but there is much they share in outlook. Most of the editors and writers here would agree that they write to promote progressive social change and to advance the interests of their own groups, interests that they actively and openly support, unlike editors and writers in the established press, whose "objectivity" turns out to be support for the consensus. These writers and editors believe that information is a powerful tool that can be used to educate for action. Many would support these specific contentions: nuclear power is an inefficient and dangerous source of energy; our lives are threatened by increasing corporate power; nonhierarchical structures should prevail in government, the workplace, and personal life. Most view American society as racist, sexist, and violent. And all would agree that war is not a human option.

There are differences in opinion too. Most would probably be found in the extent to which the writers and editors of each paper would blame the economic system for the problems they address. But the range of political analysis represented in these papers does not exhaust the possibilities. The alternative press voices all varieties of radicalism. We have chosen to concentrate on the pacificist Left; the various strains of anarchism and its allied libertarian and decentralist movements; democratic socialism; feminist, gay, anti-corporate, anti-nuclear, racial, peoples' liberation, and rank and file labor movements; alternative life style and energy movements; and an occasional voice from the more orthodox Marxist Left. Our definition of radical or alternative may differ from other people's. But it most closely follows the spirit of the 1960s movement and, one could argue for the U.S. papers, is in the most genuine American radical tradition.

While we do not pretend that this collection is representative of all points of view on the left, or that, taken together, the articles here exhaust the riches of the alternative press, we have tried to represent as broad a cross section of perspectives as possible on the issues that appeared to dominate in the two years covered by this book. We looked for articles that both address important issues and give a sense of the general positions of their writers or of the papers in which they appeared. We frequently chose articles of considerable length, but length is another characteristic that distinguishes alternative press articles from those of the established media. Alternative press articles tend to be as long as they need to be, rather than to be subject to rigid space requirements.

The two hundred articles here—only a fraction of the total dissident output—represent English-language material published mainly in the United States, though some Canadian and British material will be found in these pages as well. Some alternative papers, such as *Mother Jones,* are not represented because of their availability to a larger public. All the papers here have a circulation below twenty thousand and most hover between five hundred and two thousand subscribers. Eight papers provided much material: *Seven Days* (which ceased publication in April 1980), *In These Times, WIN, Southern Africa, Northern Sun News, off our backs, Gay Community News,* and *Undercurrents.* These are among the most widely read in the independent press movement. We have included articles from another eighty or so journals that have smaller circulations and focus on more specific issues. Space limitations and difficulty in obtaining permission forced us to eliminate many additional articles from these and other publications that we would have liked to include. All but a handful of articles are reprinted by permission of the publisher and/or the author. In spite of determined effort, we were unable to contact all of the authors represented here. If you are an author whom we haven't talked to, please get in touch with us.

Most of the papers we used to construct the book are in the archives of the Contemporary Culture Collection at Temple University and the Alternative Press Collection at the University of Connecticut at Storrs. The graphics throughout the volume come from the Liberation News Service (LNS), which has provided the alternative press with stories and illustrative material for fifteen years. A board of advisors, assembled to help put the book together, provided papers not available from those sources and guided us to others.

Putting the book together was a collective activity. The advisory board, comprised of librarians and publishers, some of whom have been reading or writing for the alternative press for fifteen years, met regularly to discuss the contents of the book, its organization, and its thematic structure. All fundamental decisions were made in consultation with members of the board, although the final configuration of the book was the responsibility of the primary editors.

We have organized the selections in eleven topical categories. Within each section we tried to group articles to form subsections. For example, Section 6 covers several types of repression: patriotism, police terrorism, racism, "intelligence" agencies, prisons, and right-wing extremism. Each section opens with a short summary of its contents.

The articles have been reprinted here as they appeared in the alternative papers. No attempt has been made to edit them for length, content, or style, aside from correcting obvious typographical, spelling, or punctuation errors. In four instances authors have made slight corrections in their published work.

This book will be news to some readers. We hope that it will awaken them to the existence of other points of view and other philosophies. The book is also a record of how a variety of groups not represented in official bodies and publications in the United States and elsewhere feel about the direction in which the nation and the world are going. In some ways, this book is a manifesto, an announcement that homogeneity has not triumphed and that there is still hope for a society organized on just grounds.

The readership of the alternative press is probably much smaller than it could be. This is, perhaps, the price it must pay for its integrity. Because it depends on its readership rather than corporate advertising for support, it does not need to pass corporate approval. But the noncommercial nature of the independent press limits its availability, or at least its visibility, since mass distribution is controlled mostly by the same corporate forces that control the mass media. All of the articles included here were contributed by publishers and authors who received no payment other than the knowledge that their writing might reach a wider audience. This anthology is our attempt to broaden the readership and support for the alternative press. We have provided a directory, including subscription information and statements of purpose for all the publications represented here, so that you can subscribe to the papers of your choice.

Alternative Papers is a result of collaboration among a number of people. The idea for an independent press review came from John Jackson, editor and publisher of one of the first alternative papers of the 1960s, *Graffiti,* published in Philadelphia in 1966-1967. He is now publishing *Afro-American Affairs,* a review quarterly. David Bartlett, director of Temple University Press, and Joseph A. Boissé, director of Temple University Libraries, developed and encouraged the idea. Their support was crucial to the success of this work. John DeMott, formerly at the Temple University Department of Journalism, kindly shared his insight into the alternative press. Paul Buhle, an underground press veteran and social historian, helped to provide a framework for choosing and grouping the articles. Celeste West, a leading critic of the mass media and supporter of the independent press, inspired the effort and offered constructive criticism. Tom Whitehead, head of the Special Collections Department at the Temple University Library, was generous with staff and resources. Yvette Davis and Joyce Good at Temple University and Ellen Embardo at Storrs helped put the manuscript together. Eva Maria Swidler at Temple University contributed with skill and vigor to the polishing and final editing of the manuscript.

A number of people shared the difficult work of selection: Jim Danky, Newspapers and Periodicals librarian at the State Historical Society of Wisconsin and one of the leading authorities on the alternative press, helped considerably, as did Anne Pride, editor and publisher of *Motheroot* and founder of Know, Inc., a feminist clearinghouse in Pittsburgh. Daniel Tsang contributed expertise derived from his experience as a librarian working with the alternative press and from his publishing experiences, most recently with the *Gay Insurgent.* Sandy Berman, head cataloger at the Hennepin County Library in Minnesota, not only chose some of the most delightful articles, but prepared the index to this volume. Sandy has been the leading advocate of the alternative press in libraries for close to two decades. His abiding commitment to the freedom of all peoples is evident in his work. Kenneth Arnold, editor-in-chief at Temple University Press, spent hours selecting articles with the editors. His invaluable enthusiasm for this volume helped bring it to fruition.

Zachary Simpson's careful work as our editor at Temple improved the volume immeasurably and helped it to see the light of print.

Laura Daly, who began working with this project as a student at Temple, saw it through with determination and hard work, contributing to the selection and proofreading and coordinating the graphics used in the volume. She immersed herself in the material and became one of the best-read people in the alternative press. Pat Case, at the Alternative Press Collection of the University of Connecticut, bore a major amount of selection work, compiled the directory, and provided the energy to see the project to conclusion. Her keen sense of the value of the alternative press has been essential to *Alternative Papers.*

Our most lasting debt, however, is to the editors, publishers, illustrators, and authors of the independent press. Their publications are issued from the thick of the conflict, and reflect the involvement and intensity of their contributors. These men and women have literally taken the presses into their own hands, insisting on being active participants in their society in an age when alienation and apathy are the rule. They are de facto guardians of our first amendment freedoms, and to them this book is dedicated.

Elliott Shore
Philadelphia
August 1981

1 THE PRESS

Alternative press publications are advocacy publications. Their commitment as well as their size, their absence in standard channels of distribution, and their not-for-profit status distinguishes them from commercial publications. They are often bold and make no claim to impartiality. Their constituency is often a community rather than an audience. They strive to be responsive to that community and to serve its information needs. To that end the editors and publishers of the alternative press often solicit suggestions and criticism and frequently editorialize on their mission and effectiveness. In the process of this introspection, they have produced some of the most vital and insightful analysis of the alternative press available.

Therefore we have chosen to have the alternative press introduce itself. The editors of the *Fifth Estate* begin the introduction by reflecting on their history, their impetus for publishing, and their painful transition through the seventies, proving, despite the title of their editorial, that they do indeed still have something to say. David Armstrong pays tribute to one of the first undergrounds, the *Berkeley Barb*. Chip Berlet reminisces about the intensity of the movements of the late sixties and early seventies and the trials and triumphs of their presses.

The articles reprinted in this volume are from alternative press publications that are veterans of or successors to the underground newspapers and other publications generated by the civil rights, counterculture, and New Left movements. The passage of the seventies has wrought fundamental changes in focus, style, tone, and content. The publications excerpted in this volume are apolitical community newspapers, autonomous feminist, lesbian, and gay publications, publications from radical professional associations, movement organizations working for peace and grassroots change, and alternative life style and energy advocates. Consequently, we complete our introduction with articles from two of the most prolific genres of contemporary alternative press publishing—the independent socialist and feminist presses. An editorial from *In These Times* discusses the nature, value, and vulnerability of the alternative press. Frances Doughty interviews Charlotte Bunch on the mission and processes that distinguish the feminist press.

—PJC

From *Fifth Estate* 14, no. 2
(April 18, 1979): 4-5, 20

On Having Nothing to Say

The long delay between this issue and the last one published at the end of January resulted from our being confronted by a bout of cerebral paralysis which left us feeling empty of words and ideas. We mostly articulated this feeling to one another by stating rather aimlessly that perhaps "we no longer had anything to say," which carried with it the vague suggestion that maybe we should even close up shop.

It's not that we were bereft of the concepts or desires that had motivated us in the past, but rather that we wanted to continue to meet the criteria we have somewhat rigorously always demanded of ourselves. We've always felt that if we aren't involved in continually turning over new ground and challenging our old assumptions, maybe we should pack it in and leave the propaganda work and political glad-handing to others.

In fairness to ourselves, however, we should state that the last two issues seemed quite decent to us and met at least part of the criteria just mentioned. Hence it would be easy to see these current doldrums as just episodic, since we have published some real stinkers in the past without ever having come to the conclusion that we had run entirely out of steam. What is different at this juncture, is that we have reached a critical period; one which we are just beginning to realize has been developing for a long time.

Even while we were describing history we failed to recognize our role in the contemporary process of creating it in a period when it would have been crucial for us to have done so. The beginnings of what we are now faced with trace back to the origins of our project long before the involvement of the current staff.

New Left Origins

For most of its existence (beginning in 1965) the *Fifth Estate* was a quintessen-

tially New Left publication, but the period which gave rise to it was in a severe eclipse by 1974-75 as was the newspaper itself when we first began to function with it, first as the Eat the Rich Gang and then as the staff. It was evident to us at that time that we were in a period of declining political activity and disintegrating forms of rebellion which had typified the aforegoing period. Yet we were bright with enthusiasm about our new project, and the host of recently discovered ideas we had just come across—such as situationism, anarchism, and council communism—animated us all the more.

We felt we were the inheritors of the '60s but now armed with a much more potent formula for revolution than the statist and authoritarian muck which had been previously carried. Ultimately, we thought we were at the beginning of things, not at their end.

We were soon dispossessed of that optimism as the disintegration continued and now, almost at the '80s, any continuity with that previous period has been broken. All that was "the Movement" seems now only fit subject matter for TV specials, leaving us back at ground zero suddenly truncated from our past or any tradition of rebellion.

Invasion of the Body Snatchers

This appears as most striking when witnessing the travels of many of our former comrades and *FE* staffers who drifted out of a movement which called for world revolution and a "total assault on the culture" and into the prescribed pursuits of

middle and working class America. Many of them have embraced the world of professions, business and conventional politics with such an uncanny vigor that we are led to suspect that a sort of "Invasion of the Body Snatchers" syndrome has occurred with the vital, lively bodies of our friends being inhabited by lifeless aliens leaving only a slightly recognizable outer shell.

Of course, our ultimate concern isn't so much with them as with ourselves, because it becomes harder and harder to distinguish our lives from theirs. Our ideas, we continually assert, are different, but much of our activity is almost identical—work, sports, consumption of entertainment, etc.

One of the ways we try to show that we haven't entirely bought capital's program on such a wholesale level is through projects like the *Fifth Estate*, but communication on any level presupposes receptors. So, perhaps the problem isn't so much with us not having anything to say as a problem of what we have to say becoming understood by an ever decreasing number of people. Most of us still continue to get excited upon hearing plans for new projects or when we are confronted with new ideas, and each new abuse by authority still makes us bristle, but previously all of that emotional energy appeared to be part of a larger dynamic that contained the desire and the possibility for a revolutionary transformation and was seen similarly by those around us.

Now we get the distinct impression that at best we are conceived of as having a slightly arcane hobby ("politics," and weird politics at that) and at worst are thought to be quite rude and self-righteous for continuing to evoke a set of values stemming from activity already long exhausted. If, in the midst of a polite conversation that has oscillated between cooking, running and movies, one of us should happen to inject

Ruis/LNS

something such as you might find in the pages of the *FE*, everyone else sort of drifts off, hopes you will finish soon and then returns to what was under discussion previously.

No one has yet kicked us out of their house, since much of what we are saying contains recognizable buzz-words like "capitalism," "domination," "critique" (seemingly prima facie evidence that something important must be being said), but given the reception and lack of response, there is progressively less willingness on our part to even say those things. By this silence, we find ourselves, too, becoming agents of recuperation: conformists.

Lest this all be seen as just us crying the blues about not being recognized as hot-shot politicos any longer, some exploration of what is happening on the contemporary scene to *all of us* should be attempted.

Capital and Domestication

Even in our marxist and leftist days we knew something hideous and inhuman was afoot in a society dominated by capital. Since entering a stage in our thinking when those theories of domination began to stretch ever backwards to encompass the entire breadth of what we call civilization, we have become even more aware of what has been done to the species since emerging from the jungles and the savannas into *history*. All the while stating that the configurations of domination have become increasingly pernicious and have accelerated tremendously within the epoch of capital, we, again, have stood (or so we thought) ahistorically aside, possessed of the foolish assumption that those who look thoughtfully at the processes of society (and who note them down in a systematic manner) are somehow themselves exempt from the results which affect everyone else.

A good case in point is when we first came across the reinvigorated marxist concept of the "real domination of capital." Its appeal to us lay, of course, in its seeming validity although many have been critical of it because of its apparent "pessimism"— if capital dominates all institutions, modes of thought, the culture, it would follow that no resistance, let alone destruction of capital's domination, appears possible. Well, that's what it would mean, we smugly said, contending that our small project kept us at least partially out of the path of the Juggernaut we were describing. And to some extent projects and personal resistance and

collective activity do keep you out from under the wheels, but not for long if those activities are diminishing rather than expanding and linking up with the activity of others. Without specific forms of resistance, and (even more importantly) a community of resistance, we are left awash in the same currents which are sweeping over everyone else whether there is an awareness of what is happening or not.

Culture of Capital

And what has been happening is the total collapse of the social infrastructure* of rebellion which had been created during the '60s (flawed as it may have been), leaving all of us as individuals to face the staggering cultural might of the administrative state. Without structures of resistance in which to organize collective projects and our own lives as rebels, capital steps in to organize our energy around wage work and other activity ordained by official society.

Again, with all of its serious and perhaps fatal flaws, the culture and politics of the '60s were an attempt to back away from institutionalized boredom and official amorality and to pose lives based on a code of high morality, face-to-face interaction and self-activity.

Its collapse, however, provided the breathing space needed for a society under sharp attack. Capital quickly recuperated what the defeated forces had advocated and transformed an increasingly unworkable mode of rule into a new variant of domination accompanied by a culture vaguely shaped on the radical forms it imitated. (Women, blacks and youth were taken into the middle levels of political rule, the concerns of ecology, equal rights, and peace are enunciated by those in power, rock and roll and casual dress become the accepted fashion, etc.)

These transmogrified values and ideals in their congealed and matured form now appear as independent of their radical

---

*The stiff and academic term "social infrastructure" should in no way be construed as a desire for any formal organization of "revolutionaries." It is used here as a synonym for community which has been a buzz-word for so long as to almost have become devoid of its intended meaning. A radical infrastructure would/could include an informal network of people involved in projects, self-activity, living arrangements, etc. occupying a definable geographical space and whose inhabitants subscribe to values and activity which place them in opposition to this society.

origins and present themselves in the popular media as clichés about the "Me Generation" in which victory has been achieved and nothing remains but to enjoy life through consumerism. Still, this banalization represents more than what appears on the surface; they are the popular expressions of fundamentally different ways in which we live our lives, and conceive of ourselves and the world which we inhabit. A quick look at the period just preceding that decade of activism and transition should serve to make the point.

The matrix of values that appeared to be at the heart of the American century at its apex (1945-1960)—nationalism, rabid anti-communism, the family, pride of job, neighborhood and ethnic loyalty, etc.— suddenly came under attack, and with the onslaught of the '60s, disappeared just as suddenly as determinant concepts, and were easily replaced in the popular imagination with new and more "modern" ones.

What becomes ever more clear is that the rule of capital continues through its material mode of production and is capable of erecting codes of domination into a cultural and political superstructure dependent upon the needs of a given epoch. The entrenched and on-going processes of the circulation of capital continue whether or not there is a specific class of men in control in the form of a bourgeoisie, whether an authoritarian family exists or not (Reich notwithstanding) or whether the society cloaks its activities in the mystifications of democracy, fascism or state communism.

Bourgeois Revolution

The social process developing today is in a large part the final (or perhaps more cautiously, the current) phase of the bourgeois revolutions that began 300 years ago and are still in a dynamic form today regardless of what ignorant leftists say. Concomitant with the establishment of the rule of capital, these revolutions brought about the political and ethical demand for the eradication of privilege. Beginning with an assault on the hereditary power of the aristocracy, the battlelines with capital have always been toward a leveling of society—to end the domination of one class over another, one race over the other, and within our personal lives, the domination of men over women and the destruction of the authority of the patriarchal family.

None of these are sham battles; all of the

aforegoing were genuine struggles (and *are*; the battles for those reforms not being yet won). Each victory, however, whether it is decent wages for a section of the working class, or jobs for some blacks and women, has always meant an extension and affirmation of a society that is resilient enough to understand viscerally, even if its reigning lieutenants always don't, that if people come knocking hard enough, they have to be let in.

And once inside, it's not so much that they get "bought off" in the popular sense, but they suffer from the same malaise that all of those that have been inside all along suffer from—social vertigo; if you look up or down you get dizzy, so best to embrace what is.

Eventually, all forms of domination operational on the terrain of capital become subject to demands for equality and eventually the culture of domination begins to bend at its most odious points, but only when a particular institution can be relinquished due to antiquation or replacement. For instance, the code concerns itself naught with who administers, a capitalist class or socialist bureaucrats, blacks or whites, men or women, as long as its administration is assured. Or, the work ethic—long thought to be a lynchpin of our society, but now a cultural lag hanging on from an era when sacrifice to the job was necessary for the period of the early accumulation of capital in the 19th century—has been replaced by an ethic of consumption which doesn't care whether you love or hate your job, whether you buy new homes and cars or backpacks and dope paraphernalia, just as long as you keep buying.

Consumption and Passivity

And buy we do, all of us, if for no other reason than to attempt to compensate for the lack of generalized gratification and the collapsing state of our personal lives. Consumption and passive reception of spectacles have become the signature of our era to the point where even the popular culture reflects the wide-spread alienation and contemporary anguish. But the current gush of pop approaches to the malaise fails to comprehend what the total process is bringing about.

What we are faced with at this time is the final shattering of all forms of human association that at once precisely defined us as human beings for some eons (a collective and reciprocal sociability) and at

1970's COMMEMORATIVE STAMPS
OFFICIAL ISSUE

ACCELERATION OF CAPITALIST DISINTEGRATION ?

the same time gave us sustenance outside of official society. All the statistics of social disintegration—high divorce rate, destruction of traditional communities, frequent moving, the average of persons in a living unit slipping below two, increasing social rootlessness, the seeming universal disaster of achieving gratifying personal relationships—eventually lead to the creation of the monad—the individual unit of society, reduced from tribe to clan to extended family to nuclear family to the lone human: easily manageable, completely domesticated to capital, who experiences a world of things only through mediated activity, e.g. wage work and the consumption of commodities, spectacles and entertainment.

The smiling, well-dressed and coiffed face from the disco or condominium is the face of the future, who only thinks and acts in terms that are programmed into him/ her. After the final fragmentation of what formerly was interconnected human activity comes, in Adorno's words, the totally administered society. Without humans linked together through ancient forms of association, capital and the administrative state move in to fill the gaps. It raises children, cares for the blind and infirm, counsels the anxious, cures the sick, protects the harassed, puts out fires and picks up garbage, and so totally takes command of the processes of life that were once organized informally that if the

individual were asked for alternative possibilities, most likely none would be forthcoming as everything has or will become a question of complex administering. No one will love being administered, but without extensive patterns and traditions of self-activity/self-help, there will be no other choices. (No one will even have memory of anything different.)

In the United States the process of the new domination seems complete—vestiges of the nuclear family, religion, patriotism, ethnicity and the like remain, and from time to time raise their forces in valiant but doomed rearguard actions, but all of these domains of privilege and irrationality no longer serve the function they once did. With the pervasiveness of television capable of instilling instant values in people, the family and religion seem hopelessly inflexible, irrelevant and condemned by all that is "modern." The patriotic love of country or one's ethnic group seems at best sentimental in a period when U.S. multinational corporations owe their allegiance nowhere and have larger GNS's than many nations. So all of it is dumped by the wayside like last year's platform shoes. But gone with them are the last remaining private moments and transcendental properties these institutions embraced, albeit in the most flawed of forms. In fact, it was for these very qualities that they could command such allegiance over so long a period no matter how grotesque they appear from

FREE THE THREE MILE ISLAND HOSTAGES DAY 365 — PLUS FOR THE TMI THOUSANDS!

Cindy Fredrick/LNS

Cindy Fredrick/L.N.S.
With Thanks to PICASSO

the outside. The desire for blood and tribal connections, a longing to be immersed in something larger than one's own life, seems almost at the level of instincts. All of it, even the ugly forms, has been disposed of.

The new mode of rule—a soft authoritarianism (no cops needed except for the flip-outs)—leaves people with no intense, internal belief structure, just an imposed, external, cool one, passively absorbed from capital and its culture.

Still, this is not to say that all is tranquil in Flatland. It's difficult to believe that people have been so robotized that they still don't possess a volatileness born of the desire for belief in something meaningful and that is one's own; for a life of intensity; for something that interconnects one human with another. And there are malfunctions among the manipulated.

On the level of personal disintegration, statistics of mental illness, skyrocketing tranquilizer usage, alcoholism, drug addiction, etc., announce in dramatic fashion a socially and individually immiserated population. Also, spasmodic minority uprisings, youth revolts, wild-cat strikes and random violence suggest all is not well for the totally administered society.

Yet all of these "aberrations" will remain at the level of personalized disorders or collective tantrums easily brought back under control unless a self-conscious conception of both what the revolt is against and what we have for a personal and collective vision of our future emerges. Without these expressions which, above all, *carry a confidence in ourselves*, we confront the massive culture of domination with empty hands.

Language of Resistance

To even think about creating a social infrastructure of rebellion, a language of resistance has to be maintained and nurtured. Total control of the language is a primary goal of all ruling apparatuses as social power ultimately is the ability to define the social code and have the administrative control to make it act accordingly. Without us taking a hold of the language to make meaningful examinations of the current state of human affairs and a firm (although generalized; no programs please) vision, we will soon see an erosion of human communication to the point where we will suffer a total inability to be understood.

As it is, the destruction of language is progressing at a rapid rate along the lines of an odd variant of Newspeak. In Orwell's *1984*, language was purposely being reduced by the Party to continually eliminate words and phrases from speech with the end of eventually eradicating proscribed concepts from human intelligence. Almost the reverse process is at work within this culture, so that all language is permissible and produced at such a torrent that a banalization and equalization takes place making words totally lacking in any emotive force.

Orwell's frightening image of the Thought Police watching everyone through ubiquitous TV monitors has been reversed now to where everyone willingly watches the Thought Police on TV and remains just as compliant as desired by *1984's* Party. As the prime source of values for the dominant code (having replaced mass education) television allows, and in fact, encourages an appearance of immense diversity but actually reduces all language and concepts to equals—entertainment to be passively consumed (what did the SLA do in the Neilsen ratings?).

It is difficult not to end abruptly as all of the foregoing has been so inadequate and incomplete, but a larger, extensive investigation properly occupies many pages not possible here. Suffice it to say we are faced with a real, not simply theoretical, question of our survival as humans in the face of the destruction of the individual as an historical subject. Unless some dramatic undertaking reverses this, there is no reason to think that this process will not include the last holdouts as well. Nothing, at this moment, announces itself as a way to regain our humanity, but if we truly have "nothing to say," we are as lost as those we have so vividly described. If we have only momentarily lost our voice, we had better find it.

Free For All

From *Free For All* 8, no. 15
(July 23, 1980): 5

Barb Folds After 15 Years

by David Armstrong

(FFA)—The *Berkeley Barb*, the oldest survivor of the underground press era, died near San Francisco after a long illness. The *Barb* was just six weeks shy of its fifteenth birthday when the paper's last issue rolled off the presses on July 3. The official cause of death was financial anemia. Probably the most influential underground paper in the United States at its peak, the *Barb* was selling only 2,000 biweekly copies when it folded—down from about 90,000 in 1969.

It was a dizzying descent for a paper that exemplified a once-popular press movement. The underground press spearheaded opposition to the Vietnam war and promoted the once-radical embrace of sex, drugs, rock music and communal living. There were some 400 underground papers, with a combined circulation of five million in the late sixties. Like the *Barb*, most are gone now; but, like the *Barb*, they helped draw the contours of recent history.

I have a personal interest in the rise and fall of the *Barb*. I edited the *Barb* from 1975-1976.

Since then, I watched five editors—one of whom lasted nine days—try to resuscitate the paper without success. Despite our best efforts, the *Barb* belonged to the days when women were chicks, cops were pigs and everyone knew which side of the barricades they were on. When the hazy seventies came into view, the *Barb* seemed unable to maintain a clear editorial focus.

Shannon Bryony, the *Barb's* last editor, attributes the paper's long goodbye to the rise of the right and the apathy of former radicals "who have lost their vigor, the belief that their convictions can actually be practiced." Bryony was sad that the *Barb* was folding, but defiant, too—proud, she said, that the paper didn't water down its content with entertainment guides and

---

celebrity puff pieces. "We're making a political statement by choosing to go under instead of whoring after money."

The *Berkeley Barb* was born on a Friday the 13th in August 1965, the progeny of a bar owner and lawyer named Max Scherr, who started the paper to cover an early antiwar demonstration. The *Barb* maintained its antiwar commitment through issue number 735, its last, when the paper printed a critical analysis of Pentagon plans for intervention in the Middle Eastern oilfields.

When the counterculture began to take form, Scherr was among the first journalists to align himself with it. The *Barb* gave early and empathetic coverage to Haight-Ashbury, picked up a column by Timothy Leary called "Turn On, Tune In, Drop Out," and published rock criticism by the manager of Country Joe and the Fish, Berkeley's resident drugs and revolution band. The *Barb* also introduced a column called "Dr. Hippocrates," written by Eugene Schoenfeld, a medical doctor, that gave many young readers their first accurate, nonjudgemental information on drugs and sex. "Dr. Hip" was later syndicated to a number of daily papers, where it prompted other writers to deal more forthrightly with those sensitive topics.

Early in its history, the *Barb* began running news and features on nude beaches and the Sexual Freedom League—and page after page of increasingly raunchy personal classified ads. Display ads for porno movies and massage parlors began finding their way into the *Barb*, too. In a few years, they would comprise nearly all the ads and give the *Barb* a well-deserved reputation for sexism; but at first they were defended as important breaks with sexual repression and easy sources of income for The Revolution.

The *Barb* was never an elegant paper. Thick, sludgy headlines, overexposed

Berkeley Barb

photos and crazy-quilt pages that looked as though they were pasted up in a day care center made the paper unspeakably ugly. But the *Barb* had a rough vitality and a knack for anticipating what was going to happen—and for helping to make it happen.

"We'd plant small articles in the paper saying, 'There's a rumor going around that something is going to happen on Telegraph Avenue at two o'clock,'" remembered Scherr. "So people would show up Friday at two to see what would happen, someone would say, 'Hey, let's close off the street,' and something *would* happen."

The *Barb* sprinted to center stage in 1969, when Berkeley radicals, including several *Barb* regulars, seized a muddy, vacant lot owned by the University of California and transformed it into a "people's park," complete with transplanted turf, flowers and a pond. In the police assault that retook the park, one person was killed and another was blinded, setting off street fighting that lasted for fifteen days and resulting in martial law. After California Governor Ronald Reagan singled out the *Barb* by name for subverting law and order, the paper's weekly circulation soared to 93,000. About 30,000 of those copies were sold outside the United States—in Canada, Western Europe, even in Vietnam, where the *Barb* was read avidly by American GIs.

Then things fell apart. Staff members, who were seeing plenty of blood-and-guts action, but little money, walked out to start their own paper, the *Tribe*. Scherr had a heart attack and sold the *Barb*, then won it back in a court case and gave the paper to a charitable trust in 1973. The trust, in turn, sold the *Barb* that same year to a group of tax lawyers who managed the paper so badly, staffers suspected them of using the *Barb* as a tax write-off.

To make matters worse, the *Barb* had declined terribly as a new newspaper. It was marred by endemic sloppiness and mired in political rhetoric. What had once been fresh was now formulaic. Something had to be done to drag the *Barb* into the seventies.

That's where I came in—or tried to. Feeling like the paper was starting to read like the *Pyongyang Times*, I decided to stop reflexively printing, in their sleep-inducing entirety, the many turgid communiques the paper received from radical underground groups. That almost got us killed. Between enraged bombardiers, who were convinced the *Barb* had betrayed them, and remnants of the Manson family, who threatened us for reasons of their own, things got tense enough to require posting an armed guard in the office.

Ah, yes, the *Barb* office—dank and dark, with cardboard partitions to separate staffers' cubicles, and battered typewriters that barely pecked. I was able to remove the psychedelic day-glo murals that flanked the front door, but I couldn't do much about the chickenwire in the windows or—worse!—the compost that organic gardeners spread out back in the summertime.

Despite all that, the *Barb* published some good material. The paper ran an interview with Sara Jane Moore three months before she attempted to assassinate Gerald Ford, in which Moore revealed, for the first time anywhere, that she had been an FBI informer. The *Barb* also printed some of the first press reports of covert CIA involvement in the Angolan civil war of 1975-76. Several writers on film, poetry, music and theatre contributed excellent work.

Unfortunately, the sometimes-fine reporting and cultural coverage in the *Barb* was neutralized by the paper's long-standing reputation for stridency and its continuing reproduction of sexual stereotypes in the adult ads. When I became editor, I was told the sex ads would be gone in six months. They lasted a lot longer than that, and a lot longer than I did. I left after a year, convinced the *Barb* had painted itself into a corner and would soon fold.

It took four painful years. Years in which the editor's swivel chair turned into a revolving door. Years in which amputation of the editorial budget became a way of life. Years in which drops in staff morale paced circulation losses.

In 1978, the *Barb* switched to a free, biweekly format and the sex ads were shunted into a new weekly paper called *The Spectator*. *The Spectator* made money from the first, and still does. But it was too late for the *Barb*. The guides to restaurants and wine had been done, and done better, by a variety of publications in the San Francisco area. Six months ago, the *Barb* went back to paid circulation and adopted more of a grassroots political slant. The few issues edited by Shannon Bryony were among the *Barb*'s best, but virtually no one read them.

The *Barb*'s quiet demise was of a piece with a trend that accelerated throughout the seventies: namely, the replacement of underground papers by the alternative press. Local and regional in focus where papers like the *Barb*, were cosmic; more often than not liberal where the *Barb* was radical; professional where the *Barb*, in its prime, was staffed by inspired amateurs, the alternative press produces a very different kind of journalism than did the underground.

The *Barb* was disdainful of many alternative papers and was, in turn, disdained by them. Considered sexist, sloppy, and shrill by the alternative press, the *Barb* characterized alternative papers as bland sell-outs. "An underground paper," said Scherr, "is part of the action and is definitely interested in making things happen. An alternative primarily reports what has happened and analyzes it. Both things serve a function, but one's duller than the other."

According to *Barb* publisher Tom Meehan, efforts to find a suitable—i.e., politically active—buyer for the *Barb* were unsuccessful. Meehan insists the *Barb* was "not for sale at any price" to would-be buyers who wouldn't honor the paper's radical tradition. He also hinted that publication may be resumed "if there is a demand for the *Barb* again. Let's have four

years of Ronald Reagan, fundamentalism and rearmament, and see how people feel then." The fact that the *Barb*'s old enemy is knocking on the White House door just as the *Barb* is knocking on heaven's door is an ironic historical twist.

The *Barb* was a maddening, exciting paper, more visceral than cerebral in its impact, and wildly uneven in its execution. Never a great newspaper, the *Barb* was an important one, particularly in its halcyon days. "The history of the sixties," wrote Morris Dickstein in *Gates of Eden*, "was written as much in the *Berkeley Barb* as in the *New York Times*."

The *Barb* is survived by its founder, Max Scherr; its notorious sex ads; a raft of ex-staffers and writers and a few thousand orphaned readers.

ALTERNATIVE MEDIA

From *Alternative Media* 11, no. 1 (1979): 5, 6, 7

How the Muckrakers Saved America

by Chip Berlet

For me, the most glorious period for the underground press was when the up-against-the-wall-motherfucker attitude towards "official" reality merged with the techniques of investigative advocacy journalism.

The years 1968 to 1973 saw the underground press highlight its role as political muckraker. From the early sixties until roughly 1967, the emphasis had been on cultural shock treatment and metaphysical

Reprinted with permission from *Alternative Media*.

alternatives to plasticized consumerist materialism. After 1973 the trend was towards community newspapers seeking a broader audience; although the political viewpoint remained progressive, there was no longer a mass movement centered around anti-war and anti-Nixon issues and a certain sense of urgency was lost.

It is no coincidence that Richard M. Nixon was President during the height of underground press muckraking—Nixon was the perfect target for the cynical anti-authoritarian journalists who drifted towards underground newspapers. It wasn't just that Nixon was a liar, but he was a bad liar, and a humorless asshole to boot. And boot we did.

In the course of baiting Nixon and his clones throughout government, the underground press uncovered some of the most dramatic stories of the decade. These stories were generally ignored but for those of us involved in researching and publishing them there was a sense of excitement and pride that made me thank the day I discovered the underground press and decided it was where I belonged.

It was the Fall of 1967 and I was a senior in high school. The move toward political versus cultural coverage was already causing staff splits on underground newspapers, and in Washington, D.C., Ray Mungo and Marshall Bloom were moving down Church Street to set up Liberation News Service after being fired from College Press Service for being too radical.

I learned about the creation of Liberation News Service and the mysterious world of the underground press as a token youth delegate to the National Council of Churches' Conference on Church and Society in riot-torn Detroit. The topic wasn't on the agenda, but a group of seamy-looking underground writers had stopped at the meeting while returning to San Francisco from the exorcism of the Pentagon in Washington, D.C. They talked about a tumultuous meeting where Liberation News Service and the Underground Press Syndicate had vied for support from underground newspapers.

The underground writers hung out with some of the more unusual ministers and nuns, and had the peculiar habit of passing their cigarettes back and forth during meetings. Everyone thought it was exemplary how they shared things. The clique that formed around the writers included those conference delegates that challenged policies and forced heated debate on issues during every meeting. They were articulate and outrageous at the same time. Nothing was too sacred to be profaned. I was fascinated.

One night a huge Black dude stepped on the elevator as my friends and I headed for bed. He smoked a large gnarled pipe and wore a Cheshire Cat grin. As a fledgling pipe smoker myself I asked in all innocence what blend of tobacco he smoked. "It's a special blend," he said slowly after inspecting me for several seconds. "If you would like to try some, follow me," he said between puffs. "Some of us are having a little party."

Thus began my descent into evil drugs, subversion of authority, sinful sex, communism and the underground press, topics I was to find both totally interrelated and immensely enjoyable. That night I got stoned for the first time and was taken on a tour of Detroit's *Fifth Estate*. We were met at the door to the paper by a gun-toting editor who suspected another police raid, but instead found several old friends from the San Francisco underground scene accompanied by some very straight-looking teenagers.

That night I decided that the underground press was the most exciting occupation in the world; and for many people in the late '60s and early '70s it really was. There was a sense of immediacy and danger that seems almost naive today, and it is difficult for many people to appreciate the threat to authority posed by underground press coverage of issues such as the war, draft resistance, racism, repression, sex, drugs, and mysticism.

The underground press was a solvent dissolving the cement of lies by which the Nixon administration was trying to hold together American society for a final plunge into open fascism. Many of the stories appearing in the underground press that were denounced as paranoid ravings were later to appear in corporate newspapers as the "startling revelations" that led to the resignation of Nixon. The role of the underground press in alerting the public to the situation in Vietnam, the erosion of liberties, the spying by the FBI, and a dozen other topics has been consistently downgraded by historians and straight journalists.

A classic example is the story about the CIA's role in smuggling heroin out of Southeast Asia. In February of 1971 College Press Service held its annual conference in Hollywood, California. One of the workshops was led by Michael Aldrich, Professor of Psychedelics at the California Institute of the Arts. Aldrich told the assembled editors about research he and Allan Ginsberg had conducted showing links between the CIA, the Saigon regime, and the opium smuggling of Meo tribespeople in Laos.

Allan Ginsberg had stumbled across the story while sorting his massive newspaper clipping file. He noticed that when arranged chronologically, clippings reporting that American and South Vietnamese forces controlled the Golden Triangle opium-growing area in Southeast Asia were followed a few months later by a significant increase in clippings detailing a rise in heroin overdose deaths in American cities.

I attended Aldrich's session and, along with several other college and underground editors, put together enough money to purchase one-time reprint rights for Aldrich's manuscript. We agreed to print the story in early March and my college newspaper, *The Denver Clarion*, became the first U.S. publication to run a story about the CIA-heroin connection.

I was also working with College Press Service at the time, and one night at the Hollywood conference I sat down with Aldrich, Carl Nelson and Barry Holtzclaw of CPS, and former CPS writer Frank Browning who was an editor at *Ramparts* magazine. Talk turned to the Aldrich story and the CPS editors were hot to run the story if some information holes could be filled in. Browning suggested that *Ramparts* research the story and that CPS wait and release the text of the *Ramparts* article timed to coincide with the magazine hitting the newsstands. An agreement was struck and Browning enlisted Banning Garret of the Pacific Studies Center to co-author the piece.

The May 1971 issue of *Ramparts* featured the story on its cover with the headline "Marshal Ky: The Biggest Pusher in the World." CPS mailed out the text one week before the magazine was released and told its subscribers, "News of the story has already stirred considerable interest among Capitol Hill doves, and both Sen. George McGovern and Rep. Ronald Dellums say they will announce it in press conferences at the end of this week and press for hearings on the issues raised in their respective houses of Congress. In light of President Nixon's claims for a new worldwide effort to fight the international drug trade, the revelations in this story easily point out U.S. hypocrisy."

The story was a well-documented blockbuster, but the straight press virtually ignored it. There were a few column inches about Congressional hearings being called for, and then the story vanished for months until Senator Albert Gruening of Alaska opened hearings. Suddenly the story was "discovered" by the *Washington Post* and NBC News. However, after the hearings, the story received continued coverage only through alternative sources such as the Dispatch News Service International, which ran articles on the subjects by T.D. Allman and D. Gareth Porter, who also wrote for CPS from Vietnam.

The story added one more straw to the pile of revelations that eventually broke the back of public support for the U.S. role in southeast Asia. Score another uncredited victory for the underground and alternative press.

An interesting anecdote about the CIA heroin story is that just before publication, CPS editor Carl Nelson took a copy of the

PEOPLES HISTORY FOR APRIL & MAY '79

APRIL 17, 1773: SLAVES PETITION THE LEGISLATURE FOR EQUAL RIGHTS AND FREEDOM AFTER THE REVOLUTIONARY WAR.

APRIL 20, 1769: CHIEF PONTIAC OF THE OTTAWA PEOPLE KILLED BY A PAID ASSASSIN.

APRIL 29, 1961: DEMONSTRATION AGAINST NUCLEAR WEAPONS IN LONDON, 826 ARRESTED.

MAY 1, 1763: BEGINNING OF CHIEF PONTIAC'S WAR, WHICH DESTROYED EVERY BRITISH FORT WEST OF THE NIAGRA.

MAY 7, 1882: CHINESE EXCLUSION ACT PASSED. MOST CHINESE HAD TO CARRY ID'S AND COULDN'T BECOME U.S. CITIZENS.

MAY 19, 1925: MALCOLM X BORN.

MAY 22, 1978: TOKYO-NARITA AIRPORT OPENS OFFICIALLY AFTER A PROTRACTED FIGHT BY PEASANTS AND STUDENTS TO SAVE FARMLAND.

MAY 31, 1779: GEORGE WASHINGTON ORDERS THE GENOCIDE OF THE IRIQUOIS PEOPLE—"NOT MERELY OVERRUN, BUT DESTROYED."

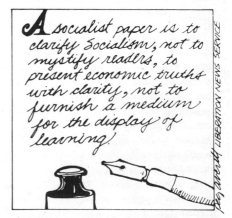

FROM A LETTER TO THE EDITOR OF THE SOCIAL DEMOCRAT, MAY 14, 1901.

Peg Averill/LNS

story to his father to see what his reaction would be. His father was deputy assistant director of the CIA. Typical of CIA compartmentalization of information, Carl's father was astounded by the story, and at first simply didn't believe a word of it.

Another example of an underground press scoop was the Louis Tackwood story. Tackwood was an undercover agent and informer for the Los Angeles Police Department who had flipped out and revealed to a group of alternative writers some details about a plot to disrupt the San Diego Republican Convention in 1972 and blame it on radical groups. The conspirators planned to use the event to legitimize repression against leftists and gain sympathy for Nixon and other conservative politicians.

Unbeknownst to the alternative press, it had stumbled onto the first evidence of a "dirty tricks" campaign being orchestrated out of the White House.

Alternative Features Service covered the breaking story on the West Coast and rushed a release into the mail. Recognizing the importance of the story, AFS phoned their subscribers, including the Denver underground *Chinook*, which alerted College Press Service upstairs in the same building. *Chinook* and CPS decided to cooperate in further researching the story. After a quick briefing from AFS, CPS patched into a live press conference with Tackwood on the coast through a hook-up with a Pacifica radio station in Houston.

Meanwhile, CPS's Carl Nelson in Washington was collecting vehement denials from various government officials. Nelson also slipped into the *Washington Post* with the help of a friend in the newsroom, and he read the *Post* article on Tackwood over the phone to CPS in Denver.

Down the Wire

Working all night, CPS and *Chinook* writers managed to piece together a lengthy story. I condensed the article for CPS and we had a release in the mail by morning. Then we moved over to a local college typesetting collective and with some help from a sympathetic *Denver Post* editor, *Chinook* staffers re-wrote the story for a special edition. We missed our press deadline and the printers called to say they were going home; after a few minutes of negotiations on the price of the bribe, the printers agreed to stay open, and *Chinook* hit the streets with the first version of the story to appear in print. We even beat the *Washington Post*.

The *Chicago Journalism Review* praised both the CPS and AFS for their handling of the story, saying the two alternative services "acted truer to the tenets of good journalism than the most established services."

It was frustrating to have your stories ignored and even more frustrating to have a straight publication steal your research or story ideas without credit. There were compensations, however, including zany escapades that seem improbable in retrospect.

While covering the 1972 Democratic convention for *Straight Creek Journal*, which had been formed by merging *Chinook* and *Boulder Magazine*, I decided the demonstrators needed their own newspaper; so when I drove back to Miami Beach for the Republican convention I loaded up a VW bus with the CPS mimeograph machine and 20,000 sheets of paper expropriated from the Colorado McGovern campaign.

Publishing the *Flamingo Park Gazette* was a group effort by assorted alternative journalists, and it became quite popular, especially on the last night of the convention when we went mobile and issued hourly updates for the demonstrators who were being chased all over the island by enraged police firing tear gas. For some reason our van, with *Flamingo Park Gazette* signs posted all over the sides and roof, was allowed through the police lines.

We would dash through a line of police then fling leaflets through the windows telling demonstrators to regroup with Dave Dellinger at the Doral hotel for a sit-in, or that the Zippies were heading back to the park. One clever but useless leaflet was our map of fountains and water hoses to aid demonstrators in washing the mace and tear gas out of their eyes. When they needed the information they couldn't read the map. One idea that worked better was our Special Incarceration Supplement of poetry for people busted during the

demonstrations. Included was a page of the prison poetry of Ho Chi Minh.

In Miami I re-established ties with the Underground Press Syndicate through Tom Forcade and Ron Lichty and when I moved to Washington, D.C. in late 1972 to run the CPS office there, I started writing for UPS. Both Lichty and Forcade came to Washington in May 1973 to attend the second A.J. Leibling Counter-Convention sponsored by *More* magazine, the trendy journalism review that recently folded.

The year before the underground press had terrorized and guilt-tripped the gathering into scheduling a workshop on the alternative media. Writing in the *Underground Press Review*, Lichty and Forcade described the meeting:

The alternative media workshop offered a sharp visual contrast to the others, if nothing else. Instead of having the 'panelists' on a stage addressing the 'audience' thru microphones, the chairs were rearranged in a circle, and the panelists sat in the audience, indistinguishable from anyone else. While the smell of Bolivian reefer permeated the large ballroom, the gathering resembled a revival meeting in spirit as the underground writers laid out their trip. Rex Weiner of UPS non-moderated. Beryl Epstein of LNS patiently and precisely explained how LNS functions collectively, what it means to be a radical news service, and so on. Frances Chapman from *off our backs* explained the goals of a women's paper. Steve Foeher of *Straight Creek Journal* delved into some of the changes the underground press has been through. Roger Cranz from *All You Can Eat* contrasted the straight press with the underground press, and rather harshly. Jack Schwartz, formerly of Albany's *Sweetfire*, spoke of the problems of underground papers in small towns. Art Kunkin of the *L.A. Free Press* held the audience spellbound as he reeled off long lists of stories of national importance that had first broken in the underground press, proving it with copies of the papers.

Enlisted Times/LNS

Individual alternative journalists raised criticisms at other panels but the overwhelming impression was that although some of the journalists attending the conference had a greater respect for the alternative media, they were not about to challenge official reality themselves. As Paul Krassner put it: "The underground press has its force and impact because it began with the supposition that the government is corrupt and writes from there."

The summer of 1973 saw the last meeting of the underground press in both name and form. The Boulder conference was sponsored by *Straight Creek Journal*, itself showing the signs of transition that marked so many other underground newspapers. There was a move towards community focus and firm advertising bases that confused some of the older "movement" journalists. As Rex Weiner of UPS pointed out, however, the mere fact that "over fifty papers and 150 people gathered in Boulder was in itself affirmation of purpose . . . the Alternative Press remains as the one viable institution created from the counter culture of the '60s."

At the Boulder conference a group of us argued that the name underground was a dinosaur and suggested changing the name of UPS to the Alternative Press Syndicate. The vote in favor of the change was overwhelming.

The Boulder conference was a line of demarcation between two eras in alternative journalism. Many alternative publications still carry on the traditions of muckraking and exposé that characterized the underground press during the Nixon years; but for those of us who still long for the days of barricade journalism, things will never be quite the same.

IN THESE TIMES

From *In These Times* 4, no. 30
(July 16-29, 1980): 14

Editorial: Recession Imperils Small Press

The demise of 130-year-old *Harper's Magazine* has deservedly prompted questions about the relationship between the world of business and the world of ideas. *Harper's* had no lack of readers—over 300,000—but it didn't have the kind of well-defined upper-income ("upscale") audience that advertisers are looking for. Its fall, like that of *Look, Life,* the *Saturday Evening Post,* or *New Times,* had little to do with the quality or use-value of its product.

The 1980 recession will exact an even greater toll on small political journals, magazines and newspapers like *In These Times. Seven Days* has already gone under. *Socialist Review* had to issue a plea for funds to pay its payroll taxes. The 15-year-old *WIN* announced that the current issue may be its last. The NACLA *Report on the Americas* warned its readers it might soon suspend publication. And *In These Times* has had to go to its readers with an emergency appeal.

Reprinted with permission from *In These Times: The Independent Socialist Newspaper.*

The small press is in an even worse position than magazines like *Harper's.* Because its readership is relatively small, regionally dispersed, and, from a Madison Avenue standpoint, heterogeneous, it has no chance of gaining substantial revenues from advertising. Instead, it has to derive its income from circulation.

Its circulation income is, in turn, largely limited to subscriptions, acquired primarily through direct-mail. Newsstand sales, which are at the mercy of large-scale distributors, hardly ever merit the cost. Mass-market publications often do their own distribution, and besides that, they don't have to make money on circulation. They only have to compile impressive figures.

The small press must also seek subscriptions under special handicaps. Because it cannot offset its circulation costs by advertising revenue, it cannot offer the kind of discounts the larger publications offer. (It is possible to get discount subscriptions to *The New Yorker, Newsweek,* and *Time* at less cost than a year's subscription to *In These Times* or *The Nation.*)

The small press is also more dependent than the larger media on the post office, which since its reorganization in 1971 has been pushing its rates ever upward. It now costs 200 percent more to mail an issue of *In These Times* than it did four years ago when we began. And mailing costs are much higher for publications that do not have regional distribution points.

In other words, the small press must rely on the least profitable source of publishing revenue, and must do so at a distinct disadvantage to its larger cousins. For this reason alone, small publications like *In These Times* always run large annual deficits. The 115-year-old *Nation* and the 71-year-old *Progressive* have rarely if ever been in the black. Even *National Review,* which would stand to benefit by the recent fortunes of the right, ran a $500,000 deficit last year.

Given this structural weakness, the small press has been in a poor position to withstand the current combination of high interest rates, spiralling inflation, and growing unemployment. Readers increasingly doubt whether their budgets can include a subscription to *In These Times,* even though its price is less than a family outing to the movies.

But inflation and the credit crunch have even more insidious effects on the small press. Printing, postal, and supply costs have gone up about 10 percent annually without publications being able to increase their prices accordingly.

The Federal Reserve's credit crunch caused suppliers, printers, mailing houses, and the ever-wonderful Post Office to demand 30-day payment rather than 60 or 120 days and, in some cases, like that of the Chicago post office, to demand cash payment. This wiped out most publications' cash reserves.

David Hausman/1199 News/cpf/LNS

If you were black and born in South Africa, this could be you.
Stop Apartheid!

But if it is so hard for the small press to exist, why not just shut them down? Do they make any contribution beyond that of the major news media? It is undeniable that the small magazines and newspapers, no less than public radio and television and off-Broadway theater and dance, have often been dull, pretentious, irrelevant, or otherwise unworthy of support or respect. But it can also be argued that amidst the current conglomerate-dominated world of movies, television, magazine, newspapers and book publishing, the small presses provide a particularly invaluable function.

The Ironies of Capitalism

As Pauline Kael points out in a recent *New Yorker* article on "Why Are Movies So Bad?" the '70s have been a particularly dismal time for mass-produced art and ideas. Movies, book-publishing and magazines have increasingly come under the sway of conglomerates like Transamerica, which have no intrinsic interest in the use or quality of the products they produce.

The new conglomerate-dominated media are obsessed with ratings and sales. They prefer proven formulas. They would rather fund a consumer-targetted magazine like *The Runner* than a diffuse political rag like *New Times*. In the news, they are more concerned with what is visually dramatic than with what is genuinely informative. (They are more interested in gondola rides down the Venice canals than the comings and goings of oil companies and international bankers that underlie much of the current Western economic malaise.)

Small presses, public television and radio, live theater, and independent movie producers are often the only places where art and ideas can flourish. They are the only places where, in Herbert Gans' terms, news is considered a "utility" rather than a "commodity," and where art is valued for its ability to test and not simply entertain an audience.

The political small press has an additional function. With the political parties having long ago foregone any role in educating the public and with the public dialogue polluted by sloganeers and pollsters, the small press is the only medium where serious analysis and programs can be presented and discussed, and where the germs of future movements can be nourished.

American corporate leaders have always understood this, and for this reason they have generously supported journals like *Foreign Affairs* and *Foreign Policy*. The right wing also has publications like

OPEC: Oil Producing and Exploiting Companies

Conrad/Daily World/LNS

Human Events and *National Review*. The program of the Barry Goldwater candidacy in 1964 sprung out of the pages of the limited-readership *National Review*. One hopes that the program and perspective of a new American left will likewise be discussed and discovered within *In These Times, The Progressive, The Nation,* and other similar publications.

But it may not be. The same recession that has thrown into question the viability of capitalism has also thrown into question the survival of the small left press. It is a cruel irony that capitalism might destroy both the confidence of people in its own viability and the means to forge any alternative.

ſINIſTER WIſDOM

From *Sinister Wisdom,* no. 13 (Spring 1980), pp. 71-78

Frances Doughty Talks to Charlotte Bunch About Women's Publishing

transcribed and edited by the Boston staff

F: Will you talk about why you think reading and writing—which some think are

First published in *Sinister Wisdom.* Reprinted with permission.

becoming obsolete arts these days—may be more important than television, speeches, tours, and other kinds of media?

C: My interest in print per se grows out of my sense that the basic tools of thinking, for being able to think imaginatively, for being able to think for yourself, grow out of people being able to read and write. I think it's not surprising that most revolutionary movements have always seen literacy as one of the tools of revolution because the first process of literacy enables people, in this case women, to understand what our situation is; it also gives us words for our experience and helps us to figure out what we want to do and how things could be different.

The stories that we all grew up with are

still very true—the stories of women who grew up in environments where reading was their only access to any other reality than the one they lived in. And their ability to imagine that their life could be different was based on what they could get to read. Now occasionally you can get 15 minutes on TV. But if you get 15 minutes on TV, it goes on when they want it on, and there's no way that an ordinary woman can have that for herself to repeat. It's not permanent, and it's not under the woman's control. One thing that's nice about the printed medium is that once we get out our books and our magazines, the women who have them can do whatever they want with them. We have control in producing books and magazines that we don't have in other mediums. And we also have control in using them that the other mediums don't lend themselves to as well. There's very little equipment, very little expense involved in the printed word compared to other media, so it's accessible to a wider range of women from different backgrounds. I think the other media lend themselves to controlling people much more completely, and that our whole sense of existence is tied up with the ability of people to think differently than what the mass culture tells them. The ability to create your own reality, to create new space—print is very important to that. It's also important to theory, which requires the process of thinking through and putting out ideas. You can do films, you can do art that's based on that same set of ideas and communicate them in a different fashion, but I still think that we need the ABC process of reading and writing as the basis for taking other mediums and developing them further.

F: So you would say that print is our primary vehicle for the development of an educated feminist movement, educated in the sense of being able to reach conclusions for oneself, being able to digest different messages, interpret them, and see what they lead to, in both action and theory?

C: I think that other vehicles may be primary to first reaching someone with an idea. But print is still the primary vehicle for the development of that and expansion of it.

F: For those of us who weren't directly involved in it, the Women in Print Conference has a legendary aura about it as a place where many important things happened, but I'm not sure what they are.

C: For background, the Women in Print Conference was held in Omaha, Nebraska, at a Campfire Girls' campsite in August of 1976. It was the vision of June Arnold that women involved in publishing, including presses, journals, newspapers, bookstores, and distributors—all aspects of women in print—should come together from around the country and discuss what we had learned and how we could cooperate better. She took the initiative and was the driving force to get the rest of us to help organize and make it happen. It was a real landmark—slightly over 100 women came from around the country. We spent a week together with the grasshoppers and the duststorms. You can't say there is any one result because the emphasis of the conference was on what is now called networking with each other and developing resources for cooperating more. A lot of the people who were there are no longer working in print and some of the groups no longer exist, which in itself isn't an important statement. But one of the things the conference did was to end the isolation a lot of people felt in their own particular work, and it enabled us to see how mammoth the women-in-print movement was. It was a magnificent feeling you had—that early women's liberation sense of everybody finding each other, finding the people who had the same problems and were working on the same issues you were. Most of the people who came were working on projects that, on the average, had four to six people in them. Most of the projects survived by a very small number of people sticking together over a long time to work very long hours in underpaid conditions to create whatever part of the process they were doing in print. You become so involved in the survival of the project you're doing that without special effort you can also begin to feel it's you against the world and to lose track of the fact that you're a part of a larger movement and that the problems you face are not yours alone and are not because you're failing to do it right. It's funny that in 1976, after years with women's liberation ideology in which we learned that the society oppressed us, in which we learned that society was a capitalist patriarchy, that big business and multinational corporations control, that small businesses were, in fact, on the way out, we nonetheless all still felt that if we just worked harder, if we just did it better, our projects would survive. Some of that mythology broke down at the Women in Print Conference because when we sat down and talked about some of the problems in getting out a journal—things like the fact that no matter what price you set your journal at, even though you kept thinking it cost too much, you still couldn't make it financially—we learned that no publication survived solely on selling its product—that they're all either subsidized by major corporations or they're subsidized by universities or they're publications of organizations whose membership subsidizes them. We had a lot to learn about publishing in America.

F: Did you find that discovery liberating, energizing, depressing? What effect did it have on you?

C: It liberated us from individual guilt. I don't know whether it was energizing. It was energizing to look for other solutions. In another way it was like reality crashing in on you. It was not going to get better just by working hard for a couple of more years. The mythical break-even point where this particular bad period would be

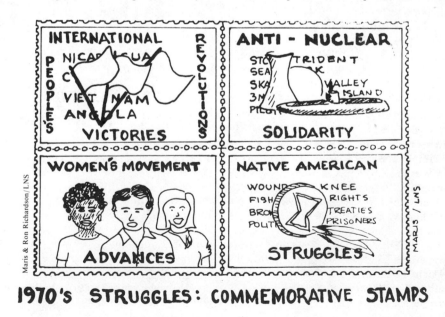

Maris & Ron Richardson/LNS

1970's STRUGGLES: COMMEMORATIVE STAMPS

over was never going to come. I think it meant that each of us had to make more realistic decisions about what we were going to do. Some of the realistic decisions were for some publications and groups to close and to stop trying. Others began to develop other structures to try to survive. Or to accept, as a couple of the journals and newspapers have, the less standardized version of reality as an OK way to be: that if you didn't come out four times a year, but you still produced interesting issues that were valuable, it was OK—that we didn't have to meet the standards of the main culture's publishing world to still be a valuable enterprise.

A turning point for me was that I faced the limitation of the small press world much more harshly than I had been willing to before that. I had to realize that we were not going to become *the* press instead of the alternate press. Some of the exciting, idealistic theory we had put forward was simply not true. If I was going to continue to work in that press, I would have to work there because it was still what I wanted to do and not with the illusion that it would reach the masses of people or become the popular culture. If I wanted to reach the popular culture in that way, I would have to be more willing than I had been up until that time to deal with some of the mainstream presses and publications, although not necessarily to the exclusion of women's presses, but in addition to that. I think that was a clear choice that I began to see—I think other people did too—from that experience.

F: So when you're talking about popular culture, you're talking about mainstream American popular culture. I've been wondering whether within the lesbian feminist world we're also developing some kind of split between popular lesbian feminist culture and a somewhat less widely spread culture of people who are more interested in theory than in, say, music. Did you feel any of that kind of split when you were working with *Quest*?

C: Definitely. *Quest* started at the same time that Olivia Records started, for example. We were friends. We both started in Washington. A few of us were ex-Furies members. It was very interesting to me to observe the difference in the development of those two projects which came out of relatively similar politics and yet took two very different media to develop. It was sometimes hard to watch Olivia Records— which I liked and I was glad to see succeed—take off in the popular culture of the lesbian movement in the way that

theory did not. Yes, there are those divisions. I think that we at *Quest* have had to keep reaffirming that the ideas you work on in a small place do begin to spread out in other ways and in other forms. That was one division. The other division is with the mainstream culture. For me, joining the mainstream is to write in *Ms* Magazine, yet *Ms* Magazine is still not the mainstream.

I made a decision that I would try to write for more of the mainstream women's movement, for *Ms* Magazine and for *NOW Times*, which reaches 100,000 NOW members, I would try to take what we were developing in the women-in-print subculture into at least the broader sphere of the organized established women's groups. The next step which I haven't taken personally but I would consider is how to take that into the popular culture beyond those places. Certainly Kathy Barry's article in *Redbook* which took some of the themes she had developed in *Chrysalis* a few years before was a good example of that. I think we need more of that because otherwise what we end up having is a set of professional feminist writers who haven't had the experience of the women's press movement. If no one from the feminist press ever does that, then the division will become greater and greater.

F: How have you seen the women's presses go on since the Women in Print Conference?

C: I don't think any of us that week realized the effect that being there was going to have on us. I didn't realize the implications for the questions I was concerned with. At the end of the Women in Print Conference we were on a high. But the seeds had been sown for a more realistic assessment that came after that. For example, Women In Distribution (WIND) was a distribution network that had been started by a couple of women. They found themselves a year and a half after the Women in Print Conference further in debt than they had been when they started. They did a very careful financial analysis whereby they were able to project that in the next year or two they would not be able to break even. Furthermore, if they went out of existence at that moment, they would owe everybody a certain amount of money, but if they kept on they would owe more money, and therefore would have taken more money away from women's presses and that they couldn't do that. There were two central issues. One was that they had not chosen to involve more people in the project, so they didn't really have a new group to take over. The other was that

financially they couldn't see any way out— any way that they could responsibly go on existing, that wouldn't take so much energy and money from so many women. They went out of existence.

The other real thing that a lot of us did after Women in Print was to recognize that we couldn't go on at the same standards we had wanted. We began to scale down our operations in terms of the quality of paper, in terms of the amount of money we spent on production, such as one-color or no-color covers instead of three-color covers, or newsprint instead of nicer paper. All of which were goals a lot of us had set out with: to create products that looked the way the society expected them to look.

I think the real question that has never been answered is do feminists consider the existence of their own presses and publications important enough to subsidize them? Because unless the women's movement does subsidize those, most of them will not go on existing. Most of them are right now subsidized by a small group of people giving volunteer labor and money. Most of the presses survive on the money that comes from people working outside jobs. A lot of presses now do pay a small token salary, but to live off those salaries you usually have to have had some savings or have a lover or friends who are willing to help you get by.

So there's a number of different ways we're indirectly subsidizing the presses and the publications. But we have to decide if they're important enough to become more systematic about subsidies so it isn't simply the ones with the best hustling ability or the best connections or the most endurance who can do it—which is what determines it now in most cases.

F: Not only are women making 57 cents to the men's dollar these days, but many women have children to support. When you're talking about trying to subsidize feminist presses you're also talking about a much smaller pool for the money to come from than there is in the mainstream society, which is one of those things that's both liberating and depressing at the same time. I think what I'm hearing is not so much that the vision failed, but that the realities got it.

C: You've put it in a nutshell. I don't think the vision failed at all. The heart of the vision was that in order to build a movement and bring change we have to have some kind of vehicle for our own words, our own expression, our own graphics, our art, our own institutions. The vision of both producing our own institu-

C.S./Daily World/LNS

tions and particularly the importance of producing them in the area of publishing as a tool for communication as well as for developing ideas—all of that vision has not failed. The vision that we would be able to do it better if we controlled it ourselves is still true. Certainly the brief experiences I've had in publishing situations that are not primarily controlled by feminists have led me to believe that we were absolutely right about the kind of indirect censorship, the slight distortion of your ideas that goes on, and that that's still true. The part of the vision that failed was the part of the vision that had to do with reality. It had to do with, what does it take to make that vision possible? At Omaha, in an indirect way, we faced the fact that our vision that we would become the main culture was probably not realistic.

F: I think one thing it does is let us see ourselves, instead of going back to that total invisibility from which we emerged with such a struggle. Print in particular is important for that sense that there is a community out there beyond individual problems.

C: Right, for example you walk into any library and see the amount of feminist work that is available. It's a real high. I walk into your study and even though I know these books exist, just seeing them, seeing the magazines piled up, it still can give me a lift. And that's even more important in more isolated places than Brooklyn, NY. I've now seen it on an international scale. I've worked with women who're putting out a radical feminist magazine in India. One of the women from that magazine came to NY a few weeks ago. I wanted to give her everything I could. I wanted to send her back with brief cases full because every single publication, every single book she saw gave her such a thrill. And there is that visible product sense of your reality that is

even more important when times are bad and even more important to women who are very isolated. In my traveling the dog-eared copies I've seen of the things we sometimes take for granted have been a good reminder, not to speak of Barbara Grier's library which can inspire all of us to realize that we continued to exist through the 30's, 40's, 50's and we didn't even know it. The history of our existence . . . The Lesbian Herstory Archives—the vision does become slightly different in the 80's, and it has to be more of the vision of what it means to survive with economic realities.

We also have to recycle our energy. We have to recognize much more than we did in the 70's the necessary process of what I call moving in and out. Each of us has to have that both individually and as a movement.

For example, I see myself moving out into a popular culture place. I felt isolated; I felt at a certain point that the subculture was stifling me in what I needed to know about making change. I had to get out there and interact more with women who were not committed feminists, but who were at least friendly. I had to get out in the world and see what we were up against in a different way and try my ideas out in more hostile environments. That wasn't just my missionary impulse to go out and convert them, which is also always at work, but it was because my own work was suffering from lack of that exposure. I think that it's time, and I think we need to allow each feminist more space for her own rhythm, more space to say, "This is the period where I am consolidating my ideas within the subculture, and this is the period when I'm trying them out in the popular culture," whether that's in writing, or in projects, or in activism in all different forms.

F: Something I've been wishing we could get written for people to think about is a developmental psychology of being in the movement because I think we really need it. I think we need an overt recognition of things we all know, that people's chronological age or even the period of the movement at which you enter determine a lot of things, but also some things seem to be determined by a natural life rhythm that takes place once you're in the movement. There's a burst of energy and a lot of commitment, then a pulling back. I think

that's the place where a lot of people drop out. I think if we recognized that that was an ongoing life process and made space for people to do that instead of saying, "Oh forget her, she's not working this year," I think we'd have a much wider base of movement and a lot longer life.

C: I think that also affects projects, that there's a cycle for projects as well. There are new presses, Persephone Press, for example, that have come up and are taking the role that say Diana or Daughters Press had five years ago, of being the new press willing to experiment, to hold the vision up. Perhaps they'll do it more realistically, but even if they're not more realistic, even if they simply do it for a while, I'm beginning to see that a particular project or group or person or even country may carry the forward edge of feminism at a given moment, while the rest of us may be doing something that keeps it alive.

F: Do you have any last words for the future or the past or our current readers?

C: I think my last words for the future are to draw from the past—which is giving me a lot more sustenance lately. When I think about some of the hard times that we seem to be in for in the 80's, I'm always sustained by remembering not only our heroines of the past, the Gertrude Steins and the Eleanor Roosevelts that we've dug up, but perhaps even more by remembering the Daughters of Bilitis, starting their organizations in the 50's during the McCarthy era and particularly—when we're talking about print—starting the publication *The Ladder* which existed from 1956 to 1972—years during which very little existed for lesbians to read, but they kept that alive for all of us. They could go out of existence in 1972 because of the present wave of feminism and lesbian writing, but without their existence I don't know that we would have had the present wave of lesbian writing. My final words are to remember that history and our own work ebb and flow, but that keeping alive the core of what we are about through those hard times has been done by women in our past and they can serve as guideposts for us in facing the future.

F: Sometimes I think of us as a river. And sometimes we're flowing underground and sometimes we're getting out there in public.

2 NUKES

The anti-nuclear power movement has been alive since the 1940s. But it took the accident at the Three Mile Island plant to dramatize the position that radical activists have been taking for years: nuclear power is dangerous, expensive, and wasteful. Moreover, it both supports and depends upon a forty-year connection between big government and industry that threatens our liberty as well as our health and wealth. The first three articles in this section maintain that the government, the utility companies, and the media distorted and covered up the actual sequence of events at Three Mile Island as well as hiding the real dangers of the situation.

The next article, from *No Nuclear News,* is about another landmark event in the history of the anti-nuclear movement—the attempt to halt the construction of the Seabrook nuclear power plant. "*Seven Days* Homemade H-Bomb Recipe" which follows, humorously but accurately, describes not only how to make a nuclear bomb but also the threats and dangers inherent in each step of the process.

"Inside the Nuclear Industry's Heart" examines the attitudes of workers involved in the construction of a nuclear power plant towards the safety regulations and precautions set up by the utility company. "Labor Crusades for Safe Energy" approaches the issue of workers and nuclear power from the opposite angle of workers and unions uninvolved in the nuclear industry but nevertheless concerned with a number of nuclear power issues—not only safety but also jobs and the U.S. economy.

Stressing the international nature of both the nuclear industry and the anti-nuclear movement, Anna Gyorgy's article, "Europeans Oppose Nukes," describes an array of movements and political struggles from Denmark, Sweden, Germany, and Switzerland to France, Austria, Italy, Australia, and Namibia.

A hypothetical scenario of one of the many dangers that opponents of the nuclear industry fear is outlined in "Spent Fuel Accident Devastating: Can Millions Be Evacuated?" An equally frightening threat to our safety comes from nuclear weapons. Two articles about nuclear weapons are included, "The Trident/Seafarer Connection" and "Nuclear Weapons: A Cancer in the Earth." In these articles we see the connection between the power plants, once euphemistically sold to the world as "Atoms for Peace," and the arms race, which threatens us even if the weapons are never used. The last group of articles explores some of the physical effects of radiation from fallout, nuclear accidents, and nuclear waste disposal, and even the possibility of an anti-nuclear diet!

—ES

Green Revolution

From *Green Revolution* 36, no. 3 (April 1979): 8-9

Three Mile Island

by Rarihokwats

The sirens started wailing as we took advantage of early-Spring warmth to spade our large hilltop garden of raised beds arranged in ever-increasing concentric circles. At first, no one said anything. But as the wails continued to wave out across the land, we began to ask ourselves, and then each other: "What does that mean?"

Finally, we walked down to the house for a drink of fresh spring water, and to check out the radio. "Citizens are urged to remain calm," a male voice slowly and carefully intoned. "Prepare for evacuation. Close your windows. Turn off your appliances. Have your eye-glasses and prescription medicine ready. This is not a notice to evacuate, but you should be prepared. Do not worry about leaving your house. It will be protected in your absence. Stay calm. Stay calm. Stay calm."

Other radio stations told what this was all about: "There has been an incident at Three Mile Island Nuclear Reactor. Officials say the situation is well under control, and there is no cause for alarm. However, kindergarten classes will remain at schools and children will be fed there. Afternoon kindergarten is cancelled."

We returned to the garden to continue spading. We had made that promise to the Earth, that we would prepare her for planting, and that we would try to live over the next year on the food which she provided us. As I worked the soil, I thought of this issue on Community which was just taking shape.

Some friends and neighbors had heard the announcement and had jumped in their cars and left, grabbing undiapered babies and a few treasured possessions. Others stayed anxiously by their radios and televisions. By changing stations, one could be sure to obtain a report to fit one's mood. "The situation is improving," one would say. "There has been a change and officials fear the worst," the next would announce. The Nuclear Regulatory Commission officials would be quoted one way, followed by a Metropolitan Edison official saying the opposite about the reactor which Met Ed operates.

Through the nights and the following days, ears stayed close to the radio and TV, and normal living came to a halt. As the possibility of a China Syndrome-type meltdown became apparent, more people left their homes. Then came the announcement that perhaps a population of over a half-million people might have to be evacuated. When would they return to their homes? No one knew. Where would they go? No one knew. "Just check into a motel," the Harrisburg mayor told an anxious woman on a 2 a.m. call-in broadcast. "The insurance will pay for it." Another woman was advised that it would be all right to leave behind a dairy-barn full of cows "because cows won't be affected by the radiation."

In a crisis of this sort, where could people turn? Generally, it seemed, most thought of themselves and immediate family. If there were those who worried about the sick and elderly and shut-in and confused, they did not make their concern known. Civil Defense and rescue operations were not besieged with callers offering to help in the emergency.

And with such grave, life-threatening circumstances, one might think that people might turn to their churches, finding strength in their faith, or prayer. However, most clergymen reported few calls, and on Sunday, the previously-announced sermons were delivered on schedule even though the churches, like the streets and shopping centers, were fairly quiet and almost deserted.

Although the little valley we call home is just eight miles from Three Mile Island, there were some who decided not to leave.

Reprinted with permission from *Green Revolution: A Voice for Decentralization and Balanced Living.*

Johanna Vogelsang/Off Our Backs/LNS

Others had already gone, and it seemed a correct decision for them to have made. And yet we who stayed seemed to feel comfortable with our decision too.

Where is there to run away to anymore? An alert for strong radioactivity was issued in southeastern Maine days after radioactive gases were released from Three Mile Island's flooded, explosive deadly puzzle. Nuclear plants seem to be almost everywhere now, and quirks of fate could make a place near Three Mile, but upwind, perhaps one of the safest places around—after all is said and done, it may be one of the few areas *without* an operating nuclear plant.

And how far should we run? Those who fled to Philadelphia sometimes found a note on the door saying their hoped-for hosts had fled down to Virginia. Somehow, it seems, no direction and no distance was safe.

It's sort of like the anti-nuke protesters in Hannover, Germany, who carried signs reading, "We All Live In Pennsylvania." Where in the world was there to go?

Friends called from California, urging us to evacuate, saying the situation was worse than we were being told. Others called to suggest that we test radioactivity in our water and air—but with what could we do that? The most gratifying call came from upstate New York, where local residents were willing to provide home for one hundred evacuated families, one of the few offers of tangible help of all those who phoned.

I thought of my promise to the Earth to plant. And I thought of the trees and the birds with whom I had been making friends. We humans who had built the horror were going to be the only ones to escape? To abandon the earth in this way may mean that she would cease to recognize us as her children, and would cease to give us the necessaries of life. No, there comes a time when moving along is only a self-serving and temporary solution, I thought, as it applied to myself. There comes a time when I would have to dig in my heels and fight from where I was, and this seemed to be the time.

"Besides, if I'm going to die, I want to die happy. I'm not going anywhere," a teenaged companion said, reaffirming my thought. And so we took care of the cows and chickens and continued to prepare the hilltop for planting.

Nuclear problems, in a sense, have been caused by our failure to assume our human responsibilities. Cities enable us to live evading our responsibilities—to flush our wastes out of sight without worrying about where they are going; to give our children purchased foods without worrying about how they are raised and by what labor; to be anonymous in most of our daily conduct, and able to leave for distant cities when our irresponsibility causes an unpleasantness. Communities do not long permit irresponsibility.

Nuclear power will not disappear until there are social changes on the American scene. The "public," individualized to the point of powerlessness, dependent upon Reddy Kilowatt for water, food, and every necessity of life, collected into massive metropolitan areas and without access to land, supporting corporate giants in return for paychecks with which to "pay the bills," is in the hands of the utilities and vested interests, victims of a systematic blackmail. With oil running out, and energy demands still on the increase, power companies will before long announce brown-outs here and there, factories will shorten hours and lay off workers, a heavy advertising campaign will hit at emotional soft-spots, and before long, the "public" will be *demanding* more nuclear power. That is, unless there are basic changes making this scenario unlikely.

Thus any campaign against nuclear energy is going to have to address itself simultaneously with alternative lifestyles and decentralization. Now that the myth of reliable nuclear power is temporarily shattered (despite Energy Secretary Schlesinger's twisted logic that "the Three Mile Island incident proves the safety of nuclear power by showing how infrequently this sort of thing happens"), now is the time for a massive educational campaign in neighborhoods, churches, schools, city hall, union hall. There is a hunger for information—Three Mile Island made it clear that we all were lied to.

Maybe now the few serious anti-nuclear movement people will be joined by millions of informed supporters. Those who aren't interested in putting their lives on the line to end nuclear power now will have forfeited the right to run when the Three Mile Island syndrome visits their local reactor.

The Waste Paper

From *The Waste Paper,*
June/July 1979, pp. 1, 4–5

Harrisburg Accident: Once in 17,000 Years?

EDITOR'S NOTE: Maybe you've read enough about the reactor accident at Three Mile Island. The news coverage has certainly been heavy. But we at *The Waste Paper* believe that the basic analysis of the accident, how it happened and what is still to come, has not yet been adequately presented. The news media cannot be entirely faulted, however. Reactors are complicated machines and not even the owners, Metropolitan Edison, nor the Nuclear Regulatory Commission, knew what was happening. It was like the blind leading the blind. In the words of Walter Creitz, president of Met Ed, "When this thing occurred, none of us knew the extent of the accident at the very beginning. The unfortunate thing is, we didn't know the total extent of the

Reprinted with permission from *The Waste Paper* and the Sierra Club Radioactive Waste Campaign.

accident until several days later. From what I understood, the situation was completely under control." They didn't know what was happening, yet the situation was completely under control. No wonder the news media was in the dark. But the readers of *The Waste Paper*, the public, and not the Walter Creitzes, are the energy decision-makers in this post-Harrisburg era, and it is for you we have written this article. You need this information.

The Harrisburg accident, the most serious reactor accident to date, began eleven years ago, sometime before April, 1968, the date on which Metropolitan Edison applied for a construction permit from the Atomic Energy Commission. An operating license was issued February, 1978, despite strong opposition by public interest environmental groups. The groups charged that "Three Mile Island is an accident waiting to happen." But by now, too much money had been poured into the plant to turn back. In March, 1978, the plant went "critical," and testing started. Despite failures in the cooling system which caused *five* shutdowns during the month of December alone, the company raced to full power production by December 30, 1978.

The company wanted to claim a full year's depreciation on income tax returns. As the *St. Louis Post Dispatch* inquired, "What was Metropolitan Edison's principal concern in rushing the unit into service, profits or the public's safety and welfare?" Only two weeks after start-up, on Jaunary 15, 1979, the plant was shut down two weeks because of mechanical malfunctions. Then, on March 28, 1979, the most serious reactor accident to date occurred, putting the reactor out of operation for several years, perhaps forever. How long will not be known until the reactor can be opened and inspected. One billion dollars and ten years after the issuance of a construction permit, the reactor sits idle.

The accident at Three Mile Island (TMI) began at 3:54 AM on March 28. A combination of design problems and operator error almost led to a meltdown and a major release of radioactivity to the environment. Luck played a part in averting a more serious accident.

For the first three hours of the accident see the box.

After this early morning three-hour sequence of design defects and operator errors, Three Mile Island and the nuclear industry will never be the same again.

Wednesday Continues

Radiation levels outside of the plant are beginning to increase. The steam which spurted out of the stuck valve on the pressurizer becomes water several feet deep within the containment building. A sump pump transfers this water to a supposedly sealed container within a second building. However—third design defect—the container leaks the radioactive water into the second building, where the ventilation system vents the radioactive air to the environment. At 8:45 AM the NRC dispatches a dozen inspectors and technicians to the site and notifies the White House of the crisis. Radiation levels of 20 mrem/hr are being recorded on the TMI site.

Temperatures at the top and center of the core are above boiling. *The Waste Paper* believes that these parts of the core were not covered with water, and were cooled only by steam. This section of the core continues to heat up. At 1:50 PM, about 10 hours after the initiation of the accident, a small explosion takes place. *The Waste Paper* believes that the explosion was caused by an interaction between the cladding and the steam which leads to destruction of fuel cladding at the top of the core, and the release of hydrogen

and fission products. The radiation levels in the coolant increase from 600 mr/hr to 1,000 rems/hr. A large hydrogen bubble forms at the top of the reactor vessel. According to the NRC, "there is evidence of severe damage to the nuclear fuel." Samples of primary coolant containing high levels of radioiodine and instruments in the core indicate high fuel temperatures in some of the fuel bundles.

As of 3:30 PM, the plant is being cooled down at 3°F/hr, with pressure at 450 psi. It was thought that it would take 15 to 18 hours to reach 350°F and 350 psi pressure. However, the purification filters, which remove radioactive particle contamination, are somewhat plugged, causing resistance to the flow. There is concern that the large bubble in the reactor vessel may grow if the pressure is dropped.

Thursday, March 29

At 5 PM two Met Ed employees take a 100 ml sample of the primary coolant system. The workers receive a 3 rem dose in 11 seconds. In 1/6th of a minute, the workers have received their maximum quarterly dose! From the temperature assessment of the core, the NRC estimates that core damage has occured in 1/4 of the 177 fuel assemblies and generally in the center of the core. The core continues to cool throughout the day. A case of extraordinary luck. The reactor has only operated for a few weeks, and limited radioactivity has built up in the fuel. With each day's operation of a nuclear reactor, the levels of Sr-90 and Cs-137 and other radionuclides build up. The presence of these hot elements would have made the cool-down extremely difficult. Had the accident happened two and a half years later, a major meltdown, with catastrophic releases, probably would have occurred. Pennsylvania residents are lucky. New Jerseyites and New Yorkers are lucky. Met Ed officials remain blandly reassuring. "There is presently no danger to the public health or safety. We didn't injure anybody. We didn't overexpose anybody. And we certainly didn't kill anybody. The radiation off-site was absolutely minuscule." Nevertheless, inexplicably Met Ed pulls all its radiation monitors (thermoluminescent dosimeters) from 17 fixed positions located within a 15 mile radius of the site. The highests readings were 4 times above the background dose for the quarterly period. Met Ed released 50,000 gallons of "slightly contaminated" industrial wastes into the Susquehanna River. Apparently the reactor is not cooling down as rapidly as

previously thought. Met Ed tells the NRC at 11:00 PM it will require another 24 hours to cool down the reactor.

Friday, March 30

The reassurances by Met Ed officials are premature. There are intermittent "uncontrolled" releases of radioactivity into the atmosphere from the primary coolant system. The levels are as high as 20 to 25 mrem/hr near the site. This is 1/5th of natural background radiation for a year *in one hour*. At 11:15 AM, President Carter calls the Governor. According to the *New York Times*, the President is deeply concerned about all the confusion. An NRC official, Harold Denton, is dispatched to the scene, and special phones are installed by the Army. The release of information about the reactor is now being controlled. At 11:30 AM another radiation burst occurs. Apparently the reactor is not being cooled down as easily or as rapidly as originally had been hoped.

Hendrie, the Chairman of the Nuclear Regulatory Commission, complains that the Pennsylvania governor and he are operating "almost totally in the blind. . . . It's like a couple of blind men staggering around making decisions."

The NRC team is increased to 83. The NRC officials understand the seriousness of the problem. A badly damaged core, a hydrogen bubble at the top of the reactor. The bubble may explode, ripping open the reactor, or it may expand, further exposing the fuel elements. At 2:50 PM another gaseous release occurs. Since Met Ed has removed the radiation monitors, only helicopter flights record the drift of radioactive gasses.

The NRC determines that the pressure must remain high while the reactor cools in order to restrict the size of the hydrogen bubble at the top of the reactor.

Saturday, March 31

There are no surprises that we know of on Saturday. The fuel, apparently now covered with water, continues to cool.

Sunday, April 1

The President and Rosalynn arrive at 12:45 PM and stay in the control room long enough for a picture to be taken. Jimmy's purpose is to reassure the American public and to protect the nuclear industry. A cold shutdown of the reactor is reached on April 27, one day short of a full month after the initiation of the accident.

Wednesday, March 28

3:54 AM — Pump in secondary cooling loop fails. → Stand-by pump does not kick on. → **1st Operator Error** The pump does not kick on because a valve is closed. This is an operator error. The valve had been closed two weeks earlier during an inspection.

Without the pump, there is no water in the secondary loop. Without water there is no steam. The electric generating turbine turns off. The control rods fall into place shutting off the nuclear reaction.

The nuclear fuel is still searing hot and will self-melt without steam or water cooling.

With secondary cooling loop *not* functioning, the water in reactor heats up. **Pressure builds up. Water in reactor is boiling.** → Pressurizer valve opens and allows steam to escape, but → **1st Design Defect** Valve on pressurizer stays open. Plant operators do not know that valve is stuck open for 2 1/2 hours.

Water in reactor continues to boil. ECCS kicks on automatically, replacing water that is boiling off.

Water, condensed from the escaping steam, begins to collect on floor of containment vessel. Operator, aware of excess water, shuts off the ECCS. → **2nd Design Defect** The B and W reactors have no reliable instruments which determine actual water level in the reactor core. → **2nd Operator Error** Reactor operator bypasses the automatic system and shuts off the ECCS. As a result, not enough water is delivered to the hot reactor core.

3:59 AM — With ECCS off and pressurizer valve open, water level in reactor drops. *Fuel is exposed to air.* Temperature in fuel assemblies rises. Cladding around fuel pellets starts to deteriorate. This is the beginning of a meltdown.

Design defect and operator error repeated. Operator starts up ECCS again, then shuts it down because of improper instrument reading. Operators still do not know water level in the core.

6:10 AM — Finally, the stuck pressurizer valve is discovered and forced shut.

The Waste Paper believes that at least one quarter of the core was uncovered from 4:00 AM to 1:50 PM. At 7:00 AM, high radioactivity levels were noted in the reactor coolant—readings of about 600 mr/hr. These levels indicate that fuel cladding damage was occurring. As radiation began to leave the TMI site, a site emergency was declared and at 7:45 AM, *three hours* after the initiation of the accident, the NRC is notified.

Harrisburg Syndrome

Meanwhile, the message has gotten through to the public. Nuclear reactors are not so safe as the industry has led us to believe. The famous Rasmussen report which calculates the probability of an accident occurring has been shown to be nothing more than nuclear industry public relations. The probability of this type of accident occurring is 1 in 17,000 reactor years. It is highly unlikely for such an accident to occur once in 500 reactor years. The "Harrisburg Syndrome" has set in: a meltdown of confidence in public officials and the nuclear industry.

The Nuclear Regulatory Commission is in a quandary. Should the remaining B & W reactors be shut down for safety improvements? The Duke Power Company threatens the Nuclear Regulatory Commission with the thought of a 23% rate increase and rotational blackouts throughout the summer. The NRC comes to a compromise agreement on April 26. Duke Power can be allowed to operate two of their Occonee reactors providing a reactor technician is stationed at all times near the auxiliary pumps to make sure that the valves are opened when the pumps kick on. Will there be a string around the technician's toe? Another senior operator, capable of dealing with Pennsylvania-type accidents, will be located in the control room at all times.

The safety devices to be installed include improved reliability and speed of auxiliary pumps. Another system would shut down the reactor immediately if there is a water supply problem in the secondary loop. This would shut down the reactor before it overheated and over-pressurized. It is our understanding that this will cause increased down time of the B & W reactor. If any utility is still buying a B & W reactor.

The TMI reactor is in a shutdown mode. It may stay this way for a year, as the radioactivity and temperature cool down. Eventually, it will be opened. *The Waste Paper* conjectures that considerable fuel cladding damage has occurred, primarily at the top, and in the center of the reactor core. The fuel cladding will be broken and brittle. Under ordinary circumstances, the fuel would be lifted with a crane by a grapple at the top of each fuel assembly. It is not clear what will be done to remove the fuel elements in this case. Perhaps entirely new equipment will have to be designed to extract the fuel assemblies. The radioactive water will have to be disposed of somewhere. It is highly likely that the reactor metal structure that holds the fuel assemblies is itself damaged. The costs to clean up and repair the reactor may equal the original price of the reactor due to inflation and increased safety equipment. It seeems unlikely that the TMI reactor will ever operate again.

No decommissioning fund has been established. Who will pay the costs of the management decision to build a B & W nuclear reactor? Who will pay the costs to clean up the reactor? Met Ed, the utility, says that the ratepayers will have to pay or the company will go bankrupt. The public, the taxpayers, will have to pay for the private decision of the company to go nuclear. If the company goes bankrupt, the large bondholders, the banks, will pay for the management decision to go nuclear.

Bailout

With bankruptcy a possibility, with increasing pressure to close down the nuclear industry, it is no wonder the *New York Times* is urging calm: "It may turn out that the facts of the accident, once understood, will impel a temperate response from the public—maintaining the nuclear option though with more stringent safety protections." The American public will be asked to pay more for the "clean, safe energy of the atom," but will the real promotors of nuclear power and their supporters in the news media be forced to pay their share? It seems, on the contrary, the more the public understands TMI, the *less* temperate the response. At a packed April 19 rate hearing in Harrisburg, the possibility that Met Ed might go bankrupt was welcomed with shouts of "Good." It looked like utility rate payers might not tolerate more bailouts of the peaceful atom.

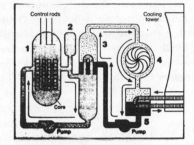

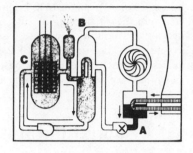

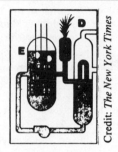

What Went Wrong
Normally water in the reactor is heated (1) by the radioactive core (2) and pressurized to prevent boiling. (3) Its heat—but not its radioactivity—is transferred through coils in the steam generator and the hot water recirculates. (4) Steam turns the turbine blades, (5) is cooled and condensed back into water, and recirculated.

In the accident, the condensate pump failed (A), depriving the steam generator of its ability to draw heat out of the reactor's water system. As the water from the core overheated, pressure was relieved (B) by venting the pressurizer and rods were dropped into the core (C) to control the chain reaction.

The situation worsened because the vent (D) did not close, and in the absence of pressure, water in the core boiled. As it did, (E) steam bubbles in the core deprived the fuel assembly of necessary coolant and damaged it.

Seven Days

From *Seven Days* 3, no. 5 (April 27, 1979): 9-10

We Almost Lost Pennsylvania

by Michio Kaku

The tragic events at Harrisburg, which almost resulted in the evacuation of the entire state of Pennsylvania, demonstrate once again the readiness of the utilities and the government to resort to cover-ups, distortions, and half-truths to protect nuclear power. It's hardly an accident, after all, that they waited almost 11 hours before informing the general public that massive amounts of radiation had been released at the Unit #2 reactor site.

In fact, we came closer to a genuine "Maximum Credible Accident"—a Class 9 accident—than has been so far revealed in the media. First of all, the hydrogen bubble in the reactor core was dangerously close to being explosive. The hydrogen gas content of the bubble was growing at the rate of 1 percent a day (at 4 percent, hydrogen gas becomes flammable; at 8 percent it becomes explosive). The bubble—10-feet across—had an initial hydrogen gas content of 2.6 percent: In 6 days it would have been explosive.

Its explosion would almost certainly have ruptured the steam pipes, releasing vast amounts of radioactive steam into the air. And there's a chance its explosion could have been sufficiently powerful to blow off the stud bolts on the inner core. Had that happened, up to *100 tons* of uranium dioxide could have been pulverized and scattered all over Pennsylvania—

a Class 9 accident. According to the government's own estimates (published in two earlier reports, *WASH* 740 and *WASH* 1400*) up to 90,000 casualties, between $14- and $17-billion of property damage, and contamination of 600,000 square miles (an area about the size of Pennsylvania) would have been the result of such an accident.

Radiation and temperature levels were so high that the gauges and dials at the core were blasted off scale within the first five minutes of the initial hydrogen gas explosion (which released fission products such as iodine-131 into the air) at four in the morning. Radiation levels measured

*[Theoretical Possibilities and Consequences of Major Accidents in Large Nuclear Power Plants, (Washington, D.C.: Division of Civilian Application, Atomic Energy Commission, 1957). Report no. WASH-740, 112 pp. And *Reactor Safety Study: An Assessment of Accident Risks in U.S. Commercial Nuclear Power Plants.* (Washington, D.C.: Nuclear Regulatory Commission; Springfield, Va.: National Technical Information Service, 1975). Report nos. WASH-1400 and NUREG-75/014, 12 v. in 8. Final report of a study originally sponsored by the Atomic Enegy Commission. Commonly known as The Rasmussen Report.—eds., *Alternative Papers.*]

30,000 rads per hour at the site within 24 hours of the first gas explosion (at 200 rads, a human becomes dangerously sick, suffering vomiting and extreme cell damage; at 500 rads, death is inevitable; 30,000 rads is thus about 60 times the lethal dose). Workers in radiation suits couldn't even get near the site: That's why engineers were forced to rely on clumsy and time-consuming methods, using sonar on the pipes, using known gas-liquid equations, etc., in measuring the bubble.

In areas surrounding the site, radiation levels were much higher than the Nuclear Regulatory Commission was willing to admit. Independent measurements showed that people near the site were receiving the full maximum yearly dose of radiation (500 millirems) every few hours. People in the city of Middletown were receiving the equivalent of several chest x-rays every few hours. Radiation levels beyond 30 miles were extremely small (not much above cosmic-ray background, or 100 millirems per year), but by April 7 samples of milk in New York City showed iodine-131 at levels of up to 10 picocuries per quart. (See box, "Forget the milk . . . ")

Even though the reactor is now decommissioned, it will be at least four years before much of the radioactive core can be dismantled. (By way of contrast, it took

about a year to dismantle the Fermi-I reactor, which suffered a partial meltdown in October 1966, almost requiring the evacuation of the city of Detroit.) During those four years, the core will leak radiation into the surrounding area. No one is sure what cancer rates will look like in the near future, but it is known that people living near the Shippingport reactor, also in Pennsylvania, experienced a 180 percent increase in cancer rates over a 10 year period. (A reactor normally spews radioactive argon-41, xenon-133, krypton-85, etc., into the air through its smokestack, because the utilities find these gases too expensive to dispose of safely.) Property values plummeted, people and businesses slowly left the area, and there have been

strange changes in the animal and plant life surrounding the reactor. We can expect even more significant changes in Middletown.

The utility companies have been protesting that, if anything, the disaster at Three Mile Island proves how effective the "fail-safe" methods are in preventing a general meltdown. But utilities like Metropolitan Edison only tell half-truths. The first back-up system (the SCRAM, which plunges control rods into the uranium core) did function at the site, but not before the uranium turned white-hot and partially melted. About one ton of uranium (360 out of 36,000 fuel rods) melted in the first explosion. The second backup system, the Emergency Core Cooling System (ECCS),

Forget the Milk and Cookies, Kids . . .

Once most of us living in New York and its environs decided not to leave the city (friends did go, rather than believe the pap the Nuclear Regulatory Commission was putting out), our next concern was the dairy products, meat, and vegetables coming from the central Pennsylvania area. Ten days after the accident began, the government announced that radioactive-iodine levels of 10 picocuries per quart were being found in New York's milk. Panic once again.

Did this mean we shouldn't drink milk for weeks, months, years? What about other substances, such as strontium-90, which have a much longer half-life than iodine-131 (half-life, 8 days)? What about all the people living near the plant who've been told it's safe to return? We at *Seven Days* wish we could tell people what to do to protect themselves from radioactive elements in the food supply. We can't, because even the antinuke scientists just aren't sure what has been released, or whether the figures being given out by the government are correct.

Ten picocuries equal 10-billionths of a curie. At levels of one-millionth of a curie, radioactive iodine is considered potentially dangerous in the food chain. Thus, you would have to drink 100 **quarts of milk containing 10 picocuries** per quart to ingest a potentially dangerous amount of radioactive iodine. But Professor Kaku nevertheless warns, "You drink the milk at a risk," cautioning that real levels may be higher than **the government reports and that no** one really knows if the millionth-of-a-curie danger level is correct. If past

experience with government-approved radiation levels is any guide, it's probably too high.

Other scientists we talked to were equally unsure of the effects of the Harrisburg incident. Henry Kendall, of the Union of Concerned Scientists, told *Seven Days* that at the publicly announced levels of radiation, there would be no severe health problems. But since there are no recordings of the radiation released in the first two-and-a-half days, Kendall does expect the health of people within five or ten miles of the site to be affected. "There'll be birth defects ranging from grotesque monsters incapable of survival to children with congenital deafness or blindness," Kendall said, adding that there'll undoubtedly be an increase in the number of cases of cancer.

Government sources told the public that potassium iodide could be taken to prevent the thyroid from absorbing iodine-131; on the other hand, Dr. Helen Caldicott, of Boston's Children's Hospital and author of *Nuclear Madness*, points out there's no way to protect yourself from strontium-90, which can cause bone cancer and leukemia, or from cesium-137 which is responsible for muscle cancer. Fetuses, young children, and the aged are most susceptible to the effects of all of these substances.

Both Dr. Caldicott and Dr. Kaku took the same position when we asked what was the best protection: "Fight nuclear power," they said. "That's the only protection there is."

—Gloria Jacobs

...and I'd like to say a couple of words about nuclear power's potentially GREATEST contribution to mankind... OUTRAGEOUS PROFITS!

Peg Averill/Win/LNS

WIN/LIBERATION NEWS SERVICE

which dumps tons of water on the reactor core, was actually *turned off* twice during the initial meltdown by the nervous radiation workers at the site.

In general, the history of the fail-safe mechanisms is far from reassuring. The Indian Point I Reactor 23 miles north of New York City operated for 13 years without an ECCS. Computer simulations of the ECCS have almost always failed. A "successful" test of the ECCS last December (the Loss of Fluid Test—LOFT) was carried out using a scale model, not the real thing. The Brown's Ferry TVA reactor in Alabama came within a hair's-breadth of a complete meltdown when a fire gutted all the cables and electronics at the reactor, crippling both the SCRAM and ECCS. Luckily, local firemen arrived on the scene and doused the core before a meltdown occurred.

Moreover the events at the Harrisburg reactor show that any fail-safe system, no matter how reliable, can always be nullified by human error. For example, the Atomic Energy Commission (AEC) admitted that in 1969 a 3,000 gallon radioactive water coolant tank at one reactor site was accidentally hooked up to the drinking water fountain! Workers at that plant were drinking radioactive water. "The coupling of a contaminated system with a potable water system is considered poor practice in general . . . ," the AEC dead-panned.

The nuclear industry, indeed, sustains over *800* small accidents a year. Most of these are not considered newsworthy, but many of them are potentially significant. Control rods are put in backwards. Radioactive waste is left lying around the reactor yard. (A few years ago, one worker accidentally poured out pure radioactive waste liquid left lying around and was exposed to the largest lethal dose of radiation yet recorded under measurable conditions. Over the next 15 hours, the worker literally disintegrated, as every cell in his body was blasted apart, into carbon and liquids.) Radioactive plutonium catches fire (as it did at the Rocky Flats installation and at the Cimmarron plant, where Karen Silkwood worked) and it gets into the lungs of workers. Examples of "minor mishaps" are simply too numerous to list.

Because of the current economic crisis, we can expect speed-ups, corner cutting, falsification of safety records, sloppy supervision of construction, to increase enormously. Harrisburg is not the final act, but a sneak preview of things to come.

The Harrisburg incident now takes its

place beside meltdowns in Idaho Falls (1955, 1961), in England (1957), and in Detroit (1966) in a lengthening list of nuclear disasters: Fifty tons of uranium dioxide lies melted and fused into a twisted hulk at Middletown—a monument to the nuclear industry's furious grab for profits and quick energy.

NO NUCLEAR NEWS

From *No Nuclear News* 3, no. 8 (mid-April/May 1980): 10

Seabrook May 24, 1980: Occupation/ Blockade

For the second time in less than eight months, anti-nuclear activists from across the United States converged on the Seabrook nuclear plants under construction in New Hampshire. Repression came early from the State. Shuffling for a good public image, politicians alternated between expressions of remorse at having to spend much needed welfare money to defend the corporate property of Public Service Co. of New Hampshire (owners-builders of the plant) and violence-baiting of the Coalition for Direct Action at Seabrook in the media. Further harassment of Seabrook supporters who offered land to the anti-nuclear groups, and instigation for an unconstitutional anti-assembly/anti-camping ordinance in the town of Seabrook filled out the State's strategy of appearing lawful and reasonable, yet tough and invincible.

Ultimately, threats by local supporters to defy the assembly/camping ordinances and CDAS' back-up plans (including strategies which anticipated the complete absence of staging land) contributed to Seabrook town Selectmen agreeing to camping health, fire, and permits for nearly 1600 people. Other CDAS groups camped on semi-public lands.

Activists from 28 states and more than 60 anti-nuclear groups arrived in Seabrook for a single purpose that weekend: to take direct action against construction of the Seabrook nuclear plants through Occupation and Blockade of the site. This was to culminate months of anti-nuclear organizing, and participation by CDAS groups in

No Nuclear News: A Monthly Cooperative Clipping Service, c/o Boston Clam, 595 Massachusetts Ave., Cambridge, MA 02139.

a variety of activities geared towards expanding the anti-nuclear movement.

Using a 64-page handbook filled with information to enable people to participate democratically in the action, CDAS remained committed to providing as much information as possible to anyone who was interested in taking direct action.

The strategy for May 24 was broadened over October's occupation attempts to include a simultaneous Blockade of access roads to the construction site. For the first time anti-nuclear forces planned on creating actual barricades in an effort to shut down a nuclear plant— further experimentation with tactics that are applicable at many nuclear sites.

Beginning Saturday at 12 noon and continuing through Monday groups of Occupiers, wearing protective gear like gas-masks, helmets, or goggles attempted to gain access to the site from at least 5 principal points around its perimeter. Whole sections of fence were removed as occupiers worked in teams using wooden shields to protect people weakening fences with large boltcutters, followed by others who attached grappling hooks and "carabiniers" on ropes and chains to tear down the fence. At each breech police using clubs, Mace, dogs, and firehoses were able to overwhelm and force back occupiers. Protective clothing helped keep injuries down in the face of police violence, and gas masks and the wind once again often made police use of gas ineffective.

The numbers of people who actually went to the fences increased dramatically

STOP NUCLEAR POWER

over the October action at Seabrook as did the effectiveness of fence take-down tactics. But clearly the overall numbers of occupiers, about 2000, were no match for the hundreds of police and national guard called up to protect PSCo.'s nuclear plant. (Estimates range from 500 to 900 police and guards). In spite of this massive police presence occupiers remained collectively steadfast in confrontations, chanting and linking arms to quell police assaults. Numerous arrests were thwarted by group rescues and tight organization.

Simultaneously, a few hundred people built barricades of scrounged dead trees and trash against the 2 main gates along Route 1 (the gates are about 3/4 of a mile apart). This tactic worked well initially taking the authorities by surprise and heat off occupying groups. However, the lack of numbers took its toll here as well—while most barricades were built high, they were not very thick or solid in construction. When the company brought out an earthmover to tear them down other barricades were built further out from the gate and on Rt. 1 itself. These tactics were generally uncoordinated, and needed more planning, but Blockade tactics seem to be especially viable in light of the authorities' limitations in extending their perimeter too far from a nuclear site. Meanwhile, a smaller number of people continually created a sit-in at the Rocks Rd. gate near Rt. 1, though they were sometimes violently driven off by police.

During these days of siege against the Seabrook plants supporters from throughout New England arrived to picket and march on Rt. 1 adding to the numbers of people who supported direct action tactics. On Saturday, for example, about 500 assembled and marched up Rt. 1, where they were joined by additional supporters along the way to the gates. They set up moving pickets in support of the occupation/blockade.

Organizationally, the May 24th actions covered some interesting ground. New forms of organization attempted to help us take action. "Clusters" of affinity groups were the basic decision-making and tactical unit of the May action. This change raised the level of involvement from simply 5 or 15 people in an isolated affinity group to coordination of 50 to 150 people in many ag's* working together. Decisions were made by Cluster Representatives and, generally, were arrived at more quickly than in most past nuclear actions. Clusters

*[affinity groups—eds., *Alternative Papers*.]

were substantial enough to make significant tactical decisions during the action in order to adjust strategy or manoevre.

Was it a success or failure? Obviously, the largest goal—that of permanently shutting down Seabrook—was not realized. Failure as a *completed direct action* can be clearly attributed to limited numbers, since tactics aimed at the site were diverse (i.e. occupation, blockade, support) and appeared viable. A more fundamental question could be: What should direct action groups do to increase their numbers?

One success was apparent early on: May 24-27 were days of community and strengthened commitment between anti-

nuclear activists from across the country. Many clusters still exist, and regional organizing and educational projects continue.

Will Seabrook die of its own weight? It's not enough to rely on an unjust and oppressive system to close down nuclear power. Exxon-controlled solar energy or a PSCo/State-owned coal plant at Seabrook are certainly not solutions. While much work remains and many questions must be resolved about the movement's future, actions like May in Seabrook will continue to be part of the anti-nuclear strategy because they involve people in actually creating solutions.

Seven Days

From *Seven Days* 3, no. 4 (April 13, 1979): 3, 15-21

Seven Days Homemade H-Bomb Recipe

by the staff

LETTER FROM THE STAFF

A Funny Thing Happened on the Way to the Printer

This issue almost did not reach you at all. The reason is instructive, because it tells us something about the probable consequences of Judge Robert Warren's precedent-setting decision barring *The Progressive* from printing its article on the hydrogen bomb. In order to dramatize our support of *The Progressive's* spirited resistance to official censorship, we prepared our own mock H-bomb recipe, entitled "How to Make Your Own H-Bomb."

When our stripper (the man who makes the film which the printer uses) saw the article he was scared. He decided to call the U.S. Attorney's office in New York and was told "Don't touch it." The U.S. Attorney had not even read the article in question. When our lawyers remonstrated, they were told we could go ahead only if we provided the government with assurances

that (a) our article was not *The Progressive's* article (b) it contained no portions of *The Progressive* article (c) it contained no classified information.

After due deliberation, we refused to provide this information, and informed the U.S. attorney's office that we were looking for a new stripper and planned to go ahead as scheduled. In our view, the government's demand represented prior restraint, pure and simple. At this point, the U.S. attorney's office could have sought a temporary restraining order and then an injunction aimed at preventing us from publishing the story until they had a chance to review it.

We were fully prepared for a court battle, but the government backed down. They notified the stripper that they had exceeded their authority when they told him "not to touch" the article, and that whether or not he proceeded was up to his own "discretion." The stripper chose not to, a classic example of the "chilling" effect of government action on civil liberties. The U.S. attorney also informed our lawyer, "as a service to his clients," of various laws pertaining to the dissemination of restricted data, violation of any one of which could land us in jail. This was another, not-very-subtle attempt to discourage us from publishing an article they hadn't even seen.

Our brush with the law ended relatively happily, but it is a clear intimation of things to come if the present trend is not reversed. By invoking "national security," the government can force the press to submit for approval, in advance of publication, any material it wishes to examine. One day it may be a story on the H-bomb; the next it may be a list of CIA agents; the next it may be a story on the growing Carter Family peanut loan scandal that is embarrassing to the Administration. Once we embark on the slippery slope to prior restraint, it's hard to stop before we reach intellectual darkness. *Seven Days* has put its little foot on the brake, as *The Progressive* has courageously in a much bigger case. Without all our efforts there could come a time when mentioning a free press will raise more eyebrows than word of a nuclear power plant accident near Harrisburg.

HOW TO MAKE YOUR OWN H-BOMB

A Message from The Progressive

Four days after the government restrained *The Progressive* from publishing an article on hydrogen-bomb secrecy, I was sitting with two other editors of *The Progressive* reading a censored version of Howard Morland's manuscript—a version which the government had told us we could publish. The Department of Energy had deleted a sentence or two from a paragraph here and there; in some cases only a word or two had been removed. The deleted terms, which I am not allowed to mention in this article, are all terms with which I am very familiar, though I have had only a few college-level physics courses.

The government had even cut out of the manuscript a few concepts which one of our senior editors had inserted. That editor's primary claim to scientific expertise is a close reading of popular newspaper and magazine articles on scientific subjects.

Even if Idi Amin gets to see a copy of Howard Morland's article, there's no reason to fear that he will soon be able to build his own bomb. I suspect most government officials and scientists are fully aware of this fact. To build a bomb Amin would need an elaborate, sophisticated, and costly technological and economic infrastructure. This might explain why, despite their rhetoric in court, no representative of the government has shown any concern about the members of our staff who saw the Morland manuscript before we were restrained from publishing it.

Yet if United States security really isn't endangered by the Morland article, what possible motive could the government have in its gargantuan effort to suppress the piece?

The myth that there are fundamental secrets serves political and economic elites in this country. Since the beginning of the nuclear age, government scientists and military leaders have fostered the notion that nuclear policy must be the preserve of experts because (1) they alone are familiar with these abstruse mysteries; and (2) those who have been given "national security clearance" are the only ones who can be trusted not to give the secrets to our enemies.

Defining the issue in terms of secrecy has thus allowed the government to engage in continuous surveillance and repression of dissident groups which might give the "secret" away.

The effect of the secrecy mythology—the notion that there are vital decisions which only a select few can and must make—is to keep information needed for intelligent public policy out of the public domain. For example, weapons builders have argued for years against a comprehensive nuclear test ban treaty on grounds that continued underground testing is essential. But they have never explained why, insisting that the relevant information is classified. Morland's article explains the reasons for testing, so that citizens can assess the validity of the weapon builders' claims. The mystique of secrecy and expertise fosters a passive or fatalistic attitude among citizens who might otherwise question these policies. Such fatalism shields from criticism economic and military elites who have a huge stake in the arms race.

John Buell, Associate Editor, *The Progressive*

Part I
MAKING YOUR ATOM BOMBS

Making and owning an H-bomb is the kind of challenge real Americans seek. Who wants to be a passive victim of nuclear war, when, with a little effort, you can be an active participant? Bomb shelters are for losers. Who wants to huddle together underground, eating canned Spam? Winners want to push the button themselves. Making your own H-bomb is a big step in nuclear-assertiveness training—it's called Taking Charge. We're sure you'll enjoy the risks and the heady thrill of playing nuclear chicken.

Introduction

When the feds clamped down on *The Progressive* magazine for attempting to publish an article on the manufacture of the hydrogen bomb, it piqued our curiosity. Was it really true that atomic- and hydrogen-bomb technology was so simple you could build an H-bomb in your own kitchen? *Seven Days* decided to find out. Food editor Barbara Ehrenreich, investigative reporter Peter Biskind, photographer Jane Melnick and nuclear scientist Michio Kaku were given three days to cook up a workable H-bomb. They did, and we have decided to share their culinary secrets with you.

Not that *Seven Days* supports nuclear terrorism. We don't. We would prefer to die slowly from familiar poisons like low-level radiation, microwaves, DDT, DBCP, aflatoxins, PBBs, PBCs, or food dyes, rather than unexpectedly—say, as hostage to a Latvian nationalist brandishing a homemade bomb.

In our view, the real terrorists are the governments—American, Soviet, French, Chinese, and British—that are hoarding H-bombs for their own use, and, worse still, those governments (U.S., French, and German) that are eagerly peddling advanced nuclear technology to countries like South Africa, Brazil, and Argentina so that they can make their own bombs. When these bombs are used, and they will be, it will be the world's big-time nuclear peddlers, along with corporate suppliers like General Electric, Westinghouse, and Gulf Oil, that we can thank for it. Gagging *The Progressive* will do no more for national security than back-yard bomb shelters, because, like it or not, the news is out.

The heart of the successful H-bomb is the successful A-bomb. Once you've got your A-bombs made, the rest is frosting on the cake. All you have to do is set them up so that when they detonate they'll start off a hydrogen-fusion reaction.

1. Getting the Ingredients

Uranium is the basic ingredient of the A-bomb. When a uranium atom's nucleus splits apart, it releases a tremendous amount of energy (for its size). And it emits neutrons which go on to split other near-by uranium nuclei, releasing more energy, in what is called a "chain reaction." (When atoms split, matter is converted into energy according to Einstein's equation $E = mc^2$. What better way to mark his centennial than with your own atomic fireworks?)

There are two kinds (isotopes) of uranium, the rare U-235, used in bombs, and the more common, heavier, but useless U-238. Natural uranium contains less than 1 percent U-235, and in order to be usable in bombs it has to be "enriched" to 90 percent U-235 and only 10 percent U-238. Plutonium-239 can also be used in bombs as a substitute for U-235.

Ten pounds of U-235 (or slightly less plutonium) is all that is necessary for a bomb. Less than ten pounds won't give you a critical mass.

So, purifying or enriching naturally occurring uranium is likely to be your first big hurdle. It is infinitely easier to steal ready-to-use, enriched uranium or plutonium than to enrich some yourself. And stealing uranium is not so hard as it sounds.

There are at least three sources of enriched uranium or plutonium. Enriched uranium is manufactured at a gaseous-diffusion plant in Portsmouth, Ohio. From there it is shipped in 10-liter bottles, by airplane and trucks, to conversion plants that turn it into uranium oxide or uranium metal. Each 10-liter bottle contains 7 kilograms of U-235, and there are 20 bottles in a typical shipment. Conversion facilities exist at Hematite, Missouri; Apollo, Pennsylvania; and Erwin, Tennessee. The Kerr-McGee plant at Crescent, Oklahoma, where Karen Silkwood worked, was a conversion plant that "lost" 40 lbs of plutonium. Enriched uranium can be stolen from these plants or from fuel-fabricating plants, like those in New Haven, San Diego, or Lynchburg, Virginia. (A former Kerr-McGee supervisor, James V. Smith, when asked at the Silkwood trial [see *Seven Days*, March 16] if there were any security precautions at the plant to prevent theft, testified that "There was none of any kind—no guards, no fences, no nothing.")

Plutonium can be obtained from places like United Nuclear, in Pawling, New York; Nuclear Fuel Services, in Erwin, Tennessee; General Electric, in Pleasanton, California; Westinghouse, in Cheswick, Pennsylvania; Nuclear Materials and Equipment Corporation (NUMEC), in Leechburg, Pennsylvania; and plants in Hanford, Washington, and Morris, Illinois. According to *Rolling Stone* magazine, the Israelis were involved in the theft of plutonium from NUMEC.

Finally, you can steal enriched uranium or plutonium while it's en route from conversion plants to fuel-fabricating plants. It is usually transported (by air or truck) in the form of uranium oxide, a brownish powder resembling instant coffee, or as a metal, coming in small chunks called "broken buttons." Both forms are shipped in small cans stacked in 5-inch cylinders braced with welded struts in the center of ordinary 55-gallon steel drums. The drums weigh about 100 pounds and are clearly marked "Fissile Material" or "Danger: Plutonium." A typical shipment might go from the enrichment plant at Portsmouth, Ohio, to the conversion plant in Hematite, Missouri, then to Kansas City by truck where it would be flown to Los Angeles, and then trucked down to the General Atomic plant in San Diego. The plans for the General Atomic plant are on file at the Nuclear Regulatory Commission's reading room at 1717 H Street, NW, Washington. A Xerox machine is provided for the convenience of the public.

If you can't get hold of any enriched uranium, you'll have to settle for commercial grade (20 percent U-235). This can be stolen from university reactors of a type called TRIGA Mark II, where security is even more casual than at commercial plants.

If stealing uranium seems too tacky, you can buy it. Unenriched uranium is available at any chemical supply house for $23 a pound. Commercial-grade (3 to 20 percent enriched) is available for $40 a pound from Gulf Atomic. You will have to enrich it further yourself. Quite frankly, this can be something of a pain in the ass. You'll need to start with a little more than 50 pounds of commercial-grade uranium (it's only 20 percent U-235 at best, and you need 10 pounds of U-235, so . . .). But, with a little kitchen-table chemistry you'll be able to convert the solid uranium oxide you've purchased into a liquid form. Once you've done that, you'll be ready to separate the U-235 you'll need from the U-238.

First pour a few gallons of concentrated hydrofluoric acid into your uranium oxide, converting it to uranium tetrafluoride. (*Safety note*: Concentrated hydrofluoric acid is so corrosive that it will eat its way through glass, so store it only in plastic. Used 2-gallon plastic milk containers will do.) Now you have to convert your uranium tetrafluoride to uranium hexafluoride—the gaseous form of uranium, which is convenient for separating out the isotope U-235 from U-238.

To get the hexafluoride form, bubble fluorine gas into your container of uranium tetrafluoride. Fluorine is available in pressurized tanks from chemical-supply firms. Be careful how you use it though, because fluorine is several times more deadly than chlorine, the classic World War I poison gas. Chemists recommend that you carry out this step under a stove hood (the kind used to remove unpleasant cooking odors).

If you've done your chemistry right, you should now have a generous supply of uranium hexafluoride ready for enriching. In the old horse-and-buggy days of A-bomb manufacture, the enrichment was carried out by passing the uranium hexafluoride through hundreds of miles of pipes, tubes, and membranes, until the U-235 was eventually separated from the U-238. This gaseous-diffusion process, as it was called is difficult, time-consuming, and expensive. Gaseous-diffusion plants cover hundreds of acres and cost in the neighborhood of $2-billion each. So forget it. There are easier and cheaper ways to enrich your uranium.

First transform the gas into a liquid by subjecting it to pressure. You can use a bicycle pump for this. Then make a simple, home centrifuge: Fill a standard-size bucket one-quarter full of liquid uranium hexafluoride. Attach a six-foot rope to the bucket handle. Now swing the rope (and attached bucket) around your head as fast as possible. Keep this up for about 45 minutes. Slow down gradually, and very gently put the bucket on the floor. The U-235, which is lighter, will have risen to the top, where it can be skimmed off like cream.

Repeat this step until you have the required 10 pounds of uranium. (*Safety note*: Don't put all your enriched uranium hexafluoride into one bucket. Use at least two or three buckets and keep them in separate corners of the room. This will prevent the premature build-up of a critical mass.)

Now it's time to convert your enriched

uranium back to metal form. This is easily enough accomplished by spooning several ladlefuls of calcium (available in tablet form from your drugstore) into each bucket of liquid uranium. The calcium will react with the uranium hexafluoride to produce calcium fluoride, a colorless salt which can be easily separated from your pure, enriched uranium metal.

A few precautions: Uranium is not dangerously radioactive in the amounts you'll be handling. If you plan to make more than one bomb, it might be wise to wear gloves and a lead apron, the kind you can buy in dental supply stores. Plutonium is one of the most toxic substances known. If inhaled, a thousandth of a gram can cause massive fibrosis of the lungs, a painful way to go. Even a millionth of a gram in the lungs will cause cancer. If eaten, plutonium is metabolized like calcium. It goes straight to the bones, where it gives out alpha particles, preventing bone marrow from manufacturing red blood cells. The best way to avoid inhaling plutonium is to hold your breath while handling it. If this is too difficult, wear a mask. To avoid ingesting plutonium orally, follow this simple rule: Never make an A-bomb on an empty stomach. If you find yourself dozing off while you're working or if you begin to glow in the dark, it might be wise to take a blood count. Prick your finger with a sterile pin, place a drop of blood on a microscope slide, cover it with cover slip, and examine under a microscope (a low power kid's microscope should do). If you count much over 0.3 percent white cells, call a doctor.

2. Stuffing Your A-bomb

You will now have three or four bowls of uranium metal. Keep the bowls covered—you don't want your silvery white uranium to tarnish. Now take about five pounds of the uranium and pack it into a hemispheric steel bowl (a stainless-steel salad bowl should do). Uranium is malleable—like gold—so you should have no trouble hammering it into the bowl to get a good fit. Take another five-pound hunk of uranium and fit it into a second stainless steel bowl.

These two bowls of U-235 are the "subcritical masses," which when brought together forcefully will provide the critical mass that makes your A-bomb go. Keep them a respectful distance apart while working, because you don't want them to "go critical" on you . . . at least not yet.

Now hollow out the body of an old vacuum cleaner and place your two hemispherical bowls inside, open ends facing each other, no less than seven inches apart, using masking tape to set them up in position. The reason for the steel bowls and the vacuum cleaner, in case you're wondering, is that these help reflect neutrons back into the uranium for a more efficient explosion. "A loose neutron is a useless neutron," as the A-bomb pioneers used to say.

As far as the A-bomb goes, you're almost done. The final problem is to figure out how to get the two U-235 hemispheres to smash into each other with sufficient force to set off a truly effective fission reaction. Almost any type of explosive can be used to drive them together. Gunpowder, for example, is easily made at home from potassium nitrate, sulfur, and carbon. Or, you can get some blasting caps or TNT: Buy them or steal them from a construction site. Best of all is C4 plastic explosive. You can mold it around your bowls, and it's fairly safe to work with (but it might be wise to shape it around an extra salad bowl in another room and then fit it to your stainless-steel bowls). Once the explosives are in place, all you need to do is to hook up a simple detonation device with a few batteries, a switch, and some wire. Remember, though, it is essential that the two charges, one on each side of the casing, go off at once.

Now put the whole thing in the casing of an old Hoover vacuum cleaner, and you're finished with this part of the process. The rest is easy.

A word to the wise about wastes: After your A-bomb is completed, you'll have a pile of moderately fatal radioactive wastes like U-238. These are not dangerous, but you do have to get rid of them. You can flush leftovers down the toilet (don't worry about polluting the ocean; there is already so much radioactive waste there, a few more bucketfuls won't make waves), or if you're the fastidious type—the kind who never leaves gum under their seat at the movies—you can seal the nasty stuff in coffee cans and bury it in the back yard—just like Uncle Sam does. If the neighbors' kids have a habit of trampling the lawn, tell them to play over by the waste. You'll soon find that they're spending most of their time in bed.

Going first-class: If you're like us, you're feeling the economic pinch, and you'll want to make your bomb as inexpensively as possible, consonant of course with reasonable yield. The recipe we've given is for a budget-pleasing H-bomb—no frills, no fancy flourishes, just your basic 5-megaton bomb, capable of wiping out the New York metropolitan area, the Bay Area, or Boston. But, don't forget, your H-bomb will only be as good as the A-bombs in it. If you want to spend a little more money you can punch-up your A-bomb considerably. Instead of centrifuging your uranium by hand, you can buy a commercial centrifuge (Fisher Scientific sells one for about $1,000). You also might want to be fussier about your design. The Hiroshima bomb, a relatively crude one, only fissioned 1 percent of its uranium and yielded only 13 kilotons. In order to fission more of the uranium, the force of your explosive "trigger" has got to be evenly diffused around the sphere: The same pressure has to be exerted on every point of the sphere simultaneously. (It was a technique for producing this sort of simultaneous detonation by fashioning the explosives into lenses that the government accused Julius and Ethel Rosenberg of trying to steal.)

3. Make Three More A-bombs, Following the Directions Above

Part 2
PUTTING YOUR H-BOMB TOGETHER

The heart of the H-bomb is the fusion process. Several A-bombs are detonated in such a way as to create the extremely high temperature (100,000,000° C.) necessary to fuse lithium deuteride (LiD) into helium. When the lithium nucleus slams into the deuterium nucleus, two helium nuclei are created, and if this happens to enough deuterium nuclei rapidly enough the result is an enormous amount of energy, the energy of the H-bomb.

And, you don't have to worry about stealing lithium deuteride; it can be purchased from any chemical-supply house. It costs $1,000 a pound. If your budget won't allow it, you can substitute lithium hydride at $40 a pound. You will need at least 100 pounds: It's a corrosive and toxic powder, so be careful. Place the lithium deuteride or hydride in glass jars and surround it with four A-bombs in their casings. Attach each one to the same detonator so that they will go off simultaneously. The container for the whole thing is no problem. They can be placed anywhere (inside an old stereo console, a discarded refrigerator, etc.). When the detonator sets off the four A-bombs, all eight hemispheres of fissionable material will slam into each other at the same time, creating four critical masses and four detonations. This will raise the temperature of the lithium deuteride to 100,000,000°C. fast enough (a few billionths of a second) so that the lithium will not be blown all over the neighborhood before the nuclei have time to fuse. The result: at least 1,000 times the punch of the puny A-bomb that leveled Hiroshima (20,000,000 tons of TNT vs 20,000 tons).

WHAT TO DO WITH YOUR BOMB

Now that you have a fully assembled H-bomb housed in an attractive console of your choice, you may be wondering. What should I do with it? Every family will have to answer this question according to its own tastes and preferences, but you may want to explore some possibilities which have been successfully pioneered by the American government:

1. Sell Your Bomb and Make a Pile of Money

In these days of rising inflation, rising unemployment, and an uncertain economic outlook, few businesses make as much sense as weapons production. If your career forecast is cloudy, bomb sales may be the only sure way to avoid the humiliation of receiving welfare or unemployment. At any income level, a home H-bomb business can be an invaluable income supplement—and certainly a profitable alternative to selling Tupperware or pirated Girl Scout cookies.

Unfortunately for the family bomb business, big government has already cornered a large part of the world market. But this does not mean that there is a shortage of potential customers. The raid at Entebbe was the Waterloo of hijacking,

and many nationalist groups are now on the alert for new means to get their message across. They'd jump at the chance to get hold of an H-bomb. Emerging nations that can't ante up enough rice or sugar to buy themselves a reactor from G.E. or Westinghouse are also shopping around. You may wonder about the ethics of selling to nations or groups whose goals you disapprove of. But here again, take a tip from our government: Forget ideology. It's cash that counts.

And remember, H-bomb sales have a way of escalating, almost like a chain reaction. Suppose you make a sale to South Yemen which you believe to be a Soviet puppet. Well, within a few days, some discrete inquiries from North Yemen and possibly the Saudis, the Egyptians and the Ethiopians as well can be expected. Similarly, a sale to the IRA will generate a sale to the Ulster government; a sale to the Tanzanians will bring the Ugandans running, and so forth. It doesn't matter which side you're on, only how many sides there are.

Don't forget about the possibility of repeat sales to the same customer. As the experience of the US and the USSR has shown, each individual nation has a potentially infinite need for H-bombs. No customer, no matter how small, can ever have too many.

2. Use Your Bomb at Home

Many families are attracted to the H-bomb simply as a *deterrent*. A discrete sticker on the door or on the living room window saying "This Home Protected by H-Bomb" will discourage IRS investigators, census takers and Jehovah's Witnesses. You'll be surprised how fast the crime rate will go down and property values will go up. And, once the news gets out that you are a home H-bomb owner you'll find that you have unexpected leverage in neighbor-

hood disputes over everything from parking places and stereo noise levels to school-tax rates.

So relax, and enjoy the pride and excitement of home H-bomb ownership!

IS IT FOR YOU?

Let's be honest. The H-bomb isn't for everyone. Frankly, there are people who can't handle it. They break out in hives at the very mention of megadeaths, fallout, radiation sickness. The following quiz will help you find out whether you have what it takes for home H-bomb ownership. If you can answer "yes" to six or more of these questions, then you're emotionally eligible to join the nuclear club. If not, a more conventional weapon may be more your cup of tea: Try botulism toxin, laser rays, or nerve gas. Here's the quiz:

1. I have learned to say "no" to the unfair demands of others.

2. I subscribe to one or more of the following: *Soldier of Fortune, Hustler, Popular Mechanics, Self.*

3. Though I have many interesting acquaintances, I am my own best friend.

4. I know what to say after you say "Hello," but I am seldom interested in pursuing the conversation.

5. I have seen the movie *The Deer Hunter* more than once.

6. I know that everyone can be a winner if they want to, and I resent whiners.

7. I own one or more of the following: handgun, video game, trash compactor, snowmobile.

8. I am convinced that leukemia is psychosomatic.

9. I am aware that most vegetarians are sexually impotent.

10. I have read evidence that solar energy is a Communist conspiracy.

THE HARLEQUIN SYNDROME

BUT SERIOUSLY, GUYS — WHO IS THE EXPERT ?

MYTHS ABOUT NUCLEAR WAR

Ever since the first mushroom cloud over Hiroshima ushered in the atomic age a small group of nay sayers and doommongers has lobbied, campaigned, and demonstrated to convince Americans that H-bomb ownership, along with nuclear power, is dangerous and unhealthy. Using their virtual stranglehold over the media, these people have tried to discredit everything nuclear, from energy to war. They have vastly overrated the risks of nuclear bombs and left many Americans feeling demoralized and indecisive, not sure where the truth lies. Well, here are the myths, and here are the facts.

Myth: After a nuclear exchange, the earth will no longer be suitable for human habitation.

Fact: This is completely false. According to one scientist (quoted in John McPhee's *The Curve of Binding Energy*), "The largest bomb that has ever been exploded anywhere was 60 megatons, and that is one-thousandth the force of an earthquake, one-thousandth the force of a hurricane. We have lived with earthquakes and hurricanes for a long time." Another scientist adds: "It is often assumed that a full-blown nuclear war would be the end of life on earth. That is far from the truth. To end life on earth would take at least a thousand times the total yield of all the nuclear explosives existing in the world, and probably a lot more." Even if humans succumbed, many forms of life would survive a nuclear free-for-all: cockroaches, certain forms of bacteria, and lichens.

Myth: Radiation is bad for you.

Fact: Everything is bad for you if you have too much of it. If you eat too many bananas, you'll get a stomachache. If you get too much sun, you can get sunburned (or even skin cancer). Same thing with radiation. Too much may make you feel under the weather, but nuclear industry officials insist that there's no evidence that low-level radiation has any really serious adverse effects. And, high-level radiation may bring unexpected benefits. It speeds up evolution by weeding out unwanted genetic types and creating new ones. (Remember the old saying, "Two heads are better than one.") Nearer home, it's plain that radiation will get rid of pesky crab grass and weeds, and teen-agers will find that brief exposure to a nuclear burst vaporizes acne and other skin blemishes. (Many survivors of the Hiroshima bomb found they were free from skin, and its attendant problems, forever.)

LETTER FROM THE STAFF

For once, neither we nor the U.S. Postal Service was responsible for your belated receipt of our last issue. The culprit was our Justice Department.

Shortly after writing our last *Letter from the Staff* (with its optimistic assumption that we were about to go to press), we received word from our printer that he, like our stripper, had doubts about going ahead with our parody on how to build an H-bomb unless we got an okay from a U.S. Attorney. *The Progressive* case was mentioned as well as our problems with the stripper and the possibility of government penalties. We remained adamant: The article could not be shown to any government official, since this would mean we accepted the validity of prior restraint on the right to publish.

Negotiations went on through the weekend. After a great deal of discussion, we decided to go to court. On a hectic Sunday, with the help of our own legal advisers, Marty Stolar and Rick Wagner, aided by William Kunstler, we prepared for a court appearance and a press conference on Monday.

After sending out a jury deciding a cocaine case, the federal judge whose name we drew from the barrel agreed to hear our plea for a temporary restraining order against the government, the printer, and the stripper that afternoon—a sign that he thought our sense of urgency was justified.

While these legal efforts were in motion, our printer called in to say that he had decided to go ahead and put the magazine on the press without obtaining government approval. Elated and relieved, but still nervous, we explained our position at the press conference and returned to court at 2:15 to tell the judge that the magazine would be printed. Persuaded by the argument that we couldn't be sure our problems were over until all our copies of the H-bomb parody went through the post offices and distributors, he did not dismiss the case even though he deemed that no immediate emergency required his hearing it then and there.

We find it galling that our tax dollars went to pay for a delay in the publication of *Seven Days*, but there is little we can do about it. Suing the government for damages costs thousands of dollars, and the court might well rule that the doctrine of "sovereign immunity" prevents us from suing without the government's permission—which we are unlikely to get. Our first foray into the courts has already cost us a great deal of money that we don't have. Nevertheless, we are not at all sorry that we went; the First Amendment seems to entice mice to nibble away at it more frequently than it tempts snakes to try to swallow it whole.

From *Seven Days* 3, no. 13 (October 26, 1979): 7-10

Inside the Nuclear Industry's Heart: Construction Workers Talk About the Monster They're Building at Shoreham

by Gloria Jacobs

"This construction site has to be, without a doubt, the world's biggest flea market. It makes no difference what you have to sell, what you have to give, what you're looking for—it's there. Drugs. There's a constant underground throughout the entire complex. Horse racing, numbers. There are even sexual pleasures you could receive on your lunch hour. It's a casino. It's a circus."

The worker telling this story wasn't describing the construction site at an Atlantic City gambling palace. Or a Times Square porno emporium. He was talking about the Shoreham nuclear power plant, the world's most expensive nuclear reactor, now rising beside a pretty inlet on eastern Long Island.

The Long Island Lighting Company

(LILCO) has been building Shoreham for over three years now with few complaints from the workers. They're mostly glad to have the jobs, because ever since the '74 recession sliced through Long Island's building boom, there hasn't been much work. With the pay on this sometimes rising as high as $2,000 a week, and the boss telling workers to shut up or get out, there are few gripes. Anyone who talks and gets found out by the union or the contractor will never work in the Northeast again.

But Three Mile Island changed a few workers' minds about remaining silent. When 15,000 people came to demonstrate at Shoreham on June 3, someone got up on the stage and called Shoreham "the biggest lemon of them all"—these guys knew it was true. In June I heard about an engineer working at Shoreham who told a friend he planned to be "a thousand miles away when the plant comes on line," but wouldn't talk to reporters. I spent all summer fruitlessly looking for a "Deep Throat" at Shoreham. But in September, one phone call led to another, and suddenly I had eight men eager to reveal what was going on. Barbara Ehrenreich, another *Seven Days* editor, and I spent a few days driving up and down Long Island to meet these people in union halls and at their homes.

We talked to five construction workers, a quality-control engineer, an operator at one of LILCO's nonnuclear plants, and a union leader. Everyone, except the engineer, said he had finally made the decision to discuss Shoreham publicly because he worried about what they were building in their own back yards. The engineer, on the other hand, wanted to talk to us because he really does believe in nuclear power as a transition to solar energy; he wanted to explain that nuclear power is not as dangerous as most people think it is. "My only concern is the wastes," he says. "The plant is safe."

From the stories I've heard about Shoreham in the last few weeks, that's like saying Frankenstein's monster had bad breath. The fact is, the situation is out of control and a lot of people are going to pay a heavy price unless Shoreham is stopped.

Most of the men we spoke with were angry, and fearful about talking. They'd already tried to tell LILCO about construction problems, but word was out on the site that "tattlers" were looking for trouble. Our informants' greatest fear was that others working at the Shoreham site would discover who had been passing informa-tion. "If it ever got out I was talking to you," a LILCO employee told Barbara and me, "my life would be on the line, because I'm threatening someone else's job. All they gotta do is drop one piece of metal and you're dead." That's why only one person is named in this article, and there are no descriptions or clues which could be used to identify the others.

LILCO first announced plans to build the Shoreham reactor 11 years ago, when its projected cost was $271 million. Now, at $1.54 billion and still growing, it's set a world record. In the mid-'60s LILCO had dreams for Long Island; they were going to turn the eastern end into a nuclear "park" with power to spare—and to sell. Long Island journalist Karl Grossman (see page 5)* has reported on these plans, but somehow the stories never make it from the local weekly papers to the big-city dailies which, nevertheless, continue to express "interest" in them.

"Suffolk [County] will be a place for clusters of nuclear plants, making use of the water that surrounds us for coolant and our relatively low population in the event of a catastrophe," Grossman wrote in *The Smithtown News* last spring. LILCO has already proposed its next addition to the "park," two nuclear reactor units at Jamesport by the end of the '80s. Jamesport is about ten miles from Shoreham as the crow flies—if it could survive the trip—and both sites are between seventy and eighty miles from New York City. Jamesport's units will be about 1,100 megawatts each, compared to Shoreham's approximately 800. That's a lot of wattage for an area whose business and housing construction are in a slump.

In view of the bungling which is coming to light at Shoreham. LILCO's plans smack of a Strangeloveian mania for nukes at any price. Of the one-and-a-half-billion dollars already spent on this financial behemoth, a staggering amount pays for doing many of the jobs several times over, because somebody didn't get it right the first time.

"I saw them weld a seam on one of the structures near the turbine," a mechanic told us. "Then the whole thing had to be done a second time. Then they decided the metal was too thin from being rewelded, so

*[Karl Grossman, "Shoring Up Shoreham: Long Island's Nuclear Interlock Has Big Plans, Leaky Pipes," *Seven Days* 3, no. 12 (October 26, 1979): 5-6.—eds. *Alternative Papers*.]
they had to put another metal plate over it."

It's not just sheer incompetence that causes the constant revisions. LILCO got a good deal on a different kind of nuclear core than its plans called for and ended up building a different unit than the one its engineers put on paper. The core, a boiling-water type, was originally built by General Electric for the New York State Electric and Gas Company (NYSEG) in the mid-'60s, but community opposition forced NYSEG to put up a coal-fired plant instead. GE, stuck with this 800-megawatt reactor, offered it to LILCO, probably at a very good price. The only problem was, LILCO had designed a smaller nuclear unit; taking the larger meant that all the specifications for the dome, the secondary housing, the turbines, and the cooling system had to be enlarged. Somehow work started on the plant without all the changes being made. "You've got to understand," the engineer said in defense of the plant, "some of those specifications are for a different core. There are modifications that have to be made as the work goes along."

"Most people are under the impression that you don't build a nuclear plant until you've got the whole process figured out," I responded. "You're saying that if some-thing doesn't work it gets altered on the spot?"

"Well, it's still subject to careful controls, but it's just not possible to foresee every problem. That's how a construction site is," he shrugged.

But the outmoded specifications aren't the only problem created by LILCO's decision to go with a bargain-basement reactor core. Work on the core was started over ten years ago, at a time when regulation of the nuclear industry was even more lax than it is now. The core has never been tested to see if it fulfills the require-ments on the books today—or if it has been tested, nobody's releasing that informa-tion. A group of Long Island environment-alists, led by attorney Irving Like, has been trying to get a copy of *any* test results for a long time, without any luck.

But the problems at Shoreham go way beyond the complications surrounding the core. There's also a great deal of sheer incompetence, corruption, and as one worker put it, "lackadaisical attitudes."

One night a group of three construction workers got together and spent a few hours describing their jobs to us. They could have been working on the Tower of Babel. "Most of the time, especially in the beginning, you went in and you just hid somewhere for seven hours. Then the next day you worked, and someone else hid. The contractor was padding the payroll, and we had more guys than we needed."

"You just get lost in the crowd," another man interrupted. "I can walk around all day with the same 2x4 on my shoulder, and there's no one standing in the same place watching me."

The real issue for these men was not what they could get away with—although it surprised them—but the poor quality of the work they were being forced to do. One of them told this story:

"We were passing pipes through plates that were supposed to hold them in place. The contractor told us one man should be able to take a pipe and push it in with one hand, and after it was in you had to be able to turn it with one hand. But little by little, it changed. They said you could use two hands. Pretty soon it was two guys that had to be able to turn it. And then it got down to where a few of us with pipe wrenches could turn it. But as long as it would turn, they left it."

"Was anyone besides the contractor checking the work?" we asked.

"Sure they were. It's totally impossible to miss it."

Then there's the condenser-box story, told to us by a union leader. The condenser box contains about 100,000 tubes which hold sea water for secondary cooling. Like the too-tightly mounted pipes, they are supposed to fit through a series of plates. Apparently none of the plates were aligned, so workers were told to bend the tubes to get them through each opening. And for the tubes that still didn't fit, there were a bunch of men standing by with pieces of lumber, 4x4s, pounding them in.

The man who told us that story is Bill Koenig, the only person we spoke to who's taking a chance on letting us use his name. Koenig is president of Local 101 of the International Brotherhood of Craftsmen, Professionals and Allied Trades, in Brentwood, Long Island. He says he decided to go public with his accusations against the nuclear industry because nobody would respond to him when he used the normal channels. "I talked to the NRC [Nuclear Regulatory Commission]. I called OSHA [Office of Occupational Safety and Health]. Nobody wanted to talk to me, so now I'm talking to the press," he said when we met him in his office.

The men from Koenig's union don't work at Shoreham. They do mostly "decon" work (see page 11)* in the Northeast at plants like Indian Point, 25 miles up the Hudson River from New York City, and at Millstone in Connecticut, just a few miles across the Long Island Sound from Shoreham.

Koenig used to be a member of the Boilermaker's Union, which is still represented at Shoreham, but he was thrown out after challenging his boss, business agent George Boylan, for the union's leadership. Boylan was convicted last month on charges of income tax evasion and of accepting payoffs from contractors—some of whom are still doing work at Shoreham.

According to the trial transcripts, Champion Construction, the original contractor for the condenser box, was involved in some of these payoffs. "They worked on the condenser box three years," Koenig says, "and had to redo it a couple of times. The company ended up going bankrupt, and the contract was awarded to a successor company—run by the same management as Champion. And LILCO okayed them to come back to Shoreham, even though the company was shown to be incompetent.

"Now, I don't know how important that condenser box is," Koenig continued. "But it seems to me that if a tube breaks, there's a possibility of a radioactive spill."

We asked him, as well as several of the other men we talked to, why LILCO would allow such bad construction methods. Even if careful oversight is expensive, utilities are allowed to pass their costs on to customers; the company isn't paying. Some people think LILCO really doesn't know what's going on, others that the company just wants to get the job over with, at a cost the public will accept.

None of the men we talked to are anti-nuke. They're convinced that following the rules would make nuclear plants safe, but

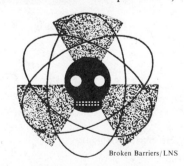

Broken Barriers/LNS

---

*[Bill Koenig and Decon, "Nuclear Power's Bottom Line: A Worker at Indian Point Explains that After the Party Someone Has to Clean Up," *Seven Days* 3, no. 12 (October 26, 1979): 11-12, 33.—eds., *Alternative Papers*.]

they've seen incredible mismanagement on the job. They say they know they can do the job right, but nobody seems to care how the work is done, nobody even seems to know who's there each day. Security at the construction site is so lax that two people from *Seven Days* drove right through the gate up to the workers' parking lot and began taking pictures of the complex from the roof of their car. None of the guards asked them what they were doing.

There are thousands of workers at Shoreham, and because each job is contracted out and the contractors bring in their own people to do the work, very few of them have been hired by the same office. Generally, the people who get the work are the "good" guys who follow orders and keep their mouths shut—if they're quiet enough, they don't even have to know how to do the job.

"I've seen welders teaching guys how to do the job—while they're working," one of the carpenters told us. "They were teaching them as they went along, how to hold the rod and everything. I heard they hired some of these guys because they were friends of the boss."

When we told the engineer that particular story, he insisted it was impossible for an unqualified worker to get on the site. "Everybody takes a test," he said. "You take it right on site and can't fake the results." That's what *he* thinks.

One of the men we talked to said he'd seen someone at a test who obviously didn't know how to use all the tools. "There was one job he apparently couldn't do, so when the inspector walks away, the guy steps out of this booth, his friend comes in and does the job for him. The kid's working at Shoreham now."

The engineer had good reason to defend procedures at the plant and ignore our stories, since his job requires that he inspect every stage of the work. If what we were telling him was true, then he wasn't doing his job right. He's young, about twenty-two, earning his B.A. in mechanical engineering by going to school at night. This is supposed to be a job with a great future for him. If 16 million lives weren't at stake, I might even feel sorry for him.

LILCO hired him when it decided too many questions were being directed at Stone and Webster, the engineering firm on the job. So, to ease the pressure, LILCO added another layer to its already overstuffed bureaucracy by creating UNICO—Unified Command.

Inspections seem to work something like

this: First the contractor inspects the work. Depending on his personal integrity, and who's stuffing his pocket, he may or may not pay much attention. Then UNICO comes in and okays the work, passing its approval to Stone and Webster, which then tells LILCO everything is fine. LILCO in turn tells the NRC inspector who comes around once a month that, yes indeed, everything is going just according to plan. Or if it isn't according to plan, they're working on it, and the place is under control.

But what *really* happens could be straight out of the *China Syndrome*. Remember the scene where Jack Lemmon sits staring at a series of x-rays of pipe welds, hoping to find the weak link? Suddenly, he places each x-ray on top of the other and discovers they all match up exactly. It's the same picture being used for all the welds. Well, we talked to someone who reports that quality-control workers used to come around before an inspection and mark the welds they were going to x-ray, so the contractor only had to send his best men over to redo the marked spots: Presto! perfect x-rays next day. The x-rays were then passed on to Stone and Webster which gave them to LILCO and so on down the line. We talked to someone else who said quality control—or UNICO—didn't realize that the contractor knew which pipes would be x-rayed, but such naïveté is no more comforting than willful deceit.

So what do these men think, who know the x-rays are faked, who know the pipes are bent, the welds are weak, and the tubes don't turn? How do they feel about the fact that they built it, and someday, somebody is going to flick the switch and this great big thing will heave into life—or will it? None of the men thinks the plant can be stopped, not with litigations or exposure; it cost too much, and LILCO is too powerful. On whether the plant will actually work, the men we talked to are divided into two camps. One side believes so many little things will go wrong first, the reactor will probably be shut down before it has a chance to blow up. The other side says it'll blow the minute it's turned on. And they figure there's nothing much they can do about it.

"I'll probably go lay down on the bed and watch TV and wait for it to come and hope it's fast," says one. "What're you gonna do? There's no sense in running because there's no way you're going to get off the Island."

The only way off Long Island short of swimming out to sea is a series of highways. All of them eventually merge into either the Long Island Expressway or the Brooklyn-Queens Expressway, both of which lead into the traffic jams of Manhattan. The only other possible escape route is over the Verrazano Bridge from the Brooklyn-Queens Expressway to the city's outer borough of Staten Island, and then into the industrialized areas of northern New Jersey. But the NRC isn't worried about the logistics of emptying Long Island. Its evacuation report on Shoreham postulates a calm, orderly row of 10,000 people per lane of traffic per hour on the highway nearest the reactor. Anyone riding Long Island's expressways on normal workdays—as I have while writing this article—knows they can't accommodate their daily traffic now, let alone the entire population fleeing an "incident" at Shoreham. Even if everyone could make it off Long Island, that would leave the majority of them trying to shove their way out of Manhattan—which the NRC admits cannot be evacuated if an accident occurs.

If you're a journalist you can, at least, find out what the NRC's evacuation scheme is. An operator and shop steward at a LILCO fossil-fuel plant told us that when he asks the company what its evacuation plans are the answer is always, "Who wants to know?"

Despite all this, every time we asked someone if he'd work on another power plant should the job arise, he answered yes.

"You're asking me if I'd like to make money and be happy," said one.

Another replied, "You know, I watched the demonstration at Shoreham on television. I'm watching these people, and I can almost see myself going to the fence, climbing the fence . . . but then, they're taking away my job. How can I say, 'No more nukes'?"

Several said they thought Shoreham could be shut down as a nuclear plant and turned into a fossil-fuel generator. "There's a lot more work for us on coal plants. But what're you gonna do? They're building nukes."

They're building nukes, and no one knows why. No one can figure out why sane people, cognizant of the consequences, would allow work on this plant to continue, let alone plan for and work on more of them. After all, LILCO executives live on Long Island too, and profits don't have any value for the dead. One gets the feeling that blind optimism, not hubris, will turn out to be the fatal flaw of the human race. Somehow everyone with the authority to stop building Shoreham seems to believe the whole mess will hold together instead of exploding. It's almost a pagan belief in the mysteries of the atom, as though human error cannot affect nuclear reaction, as though construction errors are mere petty irritations in the face of this, the greatest of humanity's achievements. The guys who build it say they know better, but nobody's listening to them.

This article is based on research and interviews by Barbara Ehrenreich and Gloria Jacobs.

From *WIN* 16, no. 20 (December 1, 1980): 12-13

Labor Crusades for Safe Energy

by Sharon Tracy

The anti-nuclear movement hit a new peak this fall when nearly 1000 trade unionists and supporters gathered in Pittsburgh at

the First National Conference for Safe Energy and Full Employment. Work by labor and anti-nuclear activists has been slow but productive in building a bridge between the two movements, creating a dynamic force to stimulate both.

Sponsored by 10 international unions, including the International Association of Machinists (IAM), the United Auto Workers (UAW) and the United Mine Workers (UMW), the conference was attended by members of 57 different trade unions from 32 states. All told, more than 800 people attended, far more than expected.

"This weekend we are here to challenge the myth that working people don't care about the environment," said Jerry Gordon, chair of the conference and coordinator of the Labor Committee for Safe Energy and Full Employment, another sponsor of the October 11-12 weekend event held at the Pittsburgh Hilton.

The spirit of that comment was heard throughout the Friday night rally, the weekend's speeches, workshops, parties and music. A resolution to wage an education campaign at all levels of the union structure, to raise the nuclear power debate on the factory floor, in union meetings and labor newspapers was introduced by the sponsoring unions and passed unanimously at the end of the conference.

Despite the gathering's unity on the nuclear power issue, the conference was not without controversy. The opening rally was the scene of a counter-demonstration by approximately 150 members of the International Brotherhood of Electrical Workers' (IBEW) building trades local constructing the atomic reactors at nearby Beaver Valley. They carried signs which read, among other things, "Anti-Nukes are Kooks," "No Power, No Employment," and "Nuclear Power Is Safe, People Are Not," drawing prolonged chants of "No Nukes" from the ralliers. They left after about 40 minutes. They maintained their presence during the weekend with a picket line Saturday and Sunday, giving faces to pro-nuke opponents in labor and clarifying the tasks ahead. "In a way their presence was energizing," said Richard Grossman of the Washington-based Environmentalists for Full Employment (EFFE) and one of the conference organizers. "It got everybody's blood flowing," he said.

Twice the number of participants expected by organizers came. "It's a five-year dream come to fruition," said Gail Daneker, a founder of EFFE. Indeed, it was, in part, EFFE's years of research, production and distribution of educational material which made the conference a reality. In 1976 EFFE published the pamphlet *Jobs and Energy*, a valuable resource for anti-nuclear workers, showing there are more and safer jobs in alternative energy than in nuclear power.

The theme was a thread running through all the speeches and discussion. "Working people are told they have a choice between jobs and safe energy," said Rosemary Trump of the Coalition of Labor Union Women and international vice president of Service Employees International Union (SEIU) in the opening speech Saturday.

Michael Scurato/LNS

"It's like being told we have a choice between drinking mercury or arsenic—both will kill you. Why not have jobs *and* safe energy? We have the muscle and the know-how. Continued reliance on nuclear power leads us down the path of no return," she said.

Sam Church, International president of the UMW spoke against war to enormous applause and declared coal an immediate answer to America's energy problems. Referring to a possible Middle East war to get US control of dwindling oil supplies, he said, "American history is full of examples of people dwelling on problems, and inevitably we have found ourselves in a war somewhere. War is not a solution. It is just destruction."

"For too long," Church said, "decisions have been made by the energy elite concerned only for profits. They have made the US a country of petroleum junkies, saying 'Trust us, when you need a fix, we'll be there.' Now we're going through withdrawal, and the oil companies did nothing for the pain, they just jacked up the price."

"In the 50s there was a promise that nuclear power would provide a never-ending supply of energy so cheap we wouldn't need meters," he explained. "But they gave us meters, Three Mile Island, tons of nuclear waste, and most of all, lies."

Church voiced the opinions of the many miners present when he said, "If you are painting an energy picture, you must use the colors available. And by far the most available color is coal black. Coal can be mined and burned safely and cleanly," he said. "It's not dirty, merely black."

The fiery president of the IAM, William Winpisinger, followed Church on the podium, spelling out an alternative energy scenario. "The US can cut its energy needs by 40% through more efficient energy use," he said. "Solar space and water heating are competitive now. If we maximize energy diversification, we maximize jobs." Winpisinger warned, however, that big oil is trying to control solar. "Energy companies

are getting a corner on the copper market (a prime ingredient of solar), they are buying up small solar companies and cutting back on uranium mining," he said. "It is our right and duty to demand public support be given to alternative energy. This country will stay in trouble until the nuclear monster is put on a diet."

The anti-nuclear work of union locals around the country is the bedrock of labor's participation in the energy debate. Local and regional unions have passed anti-nuclear/safe energy resolutions and are taking action against atomic power. Their work has gone far in dispelling the rumor, promoted by the energy industry that labor is pro-nuke.

Maine's recent referendum vote to shut down Maine Yankee, the state's only nuke, got 40% of the vote and had substantial labor backing, while the pro-nuke side had virtually none. The Maine state AFL-CIO took a neutral stand on the issue, a daring move since the national leadership is notoriously conservative on that point. The secretary-treasurer of the state AFL-CIO publicly favored shutdown, and 25 labor leaders sent a letter to all union locals in the state recommending the plant be closed.

Perhaps the most dramatic event during the referendum campaign were the arrests just two days before the vote, of three shoe factory workers on the floor of their workplace. Two women and a man said they wouldn't leave work after being told to do so by the bosses when they refused to remove buttons they were wearing and a leaflet from the union bulletin board supporting shutdown of the nuke. They were arrested for criminal trespass. Peter Kellman, president of Amalgamated Clothing and Textile Workers Union (ACTWU) Local 82 at the factory and one of those arrested, humorously noted, "The difference between environmentalists who oppose nuclear power and labor people who do is that environmentalists have to go to a nuclear plant to get arrested. We can get arrested right in our workplace." He added in a more serious tone, "Before the referendum we thought we had freedom of speech in the workplace. Now we know what to fight for."

The Bailly 1 nuclear plant under construction by the Northern Indiana Public Service Company (NIPSCO) is under attack by a number of powerful unions, among them United Steelworkers (USW) Local 1010 headed by Joe Franz, a longtime nuclear foe. The 6000 members of USW Local 6787 at the Inland Steel Mill,

500 feet from the nuke, are also not enthusiastic about it, especially when they discovered someone would have to remain behind if an accident occurred at Bailly 1. "The ovens would self-destruct if they aren't tended," said Robin Rich, an assistant griever for the union. "So if there's an accident at the plant, the company is going to expect a 'suicide squad' to stay behind."

Employees of NIPSCO itself have been engaged in a bitter strike since last May 31, refusing to accept take-backs out of their contract. "We think part of the reason they're taking such a hard line is that they're trying to save some of the money they've wasted on Bailly," said Jerry Phelps, vice-president of USW Local 12775, representing 3000 of the NIPSCO workers. The Bailly Alliance, an anti-nuclear group, has provided strike support including donations of food and money.

An Oregon campaign for public ownership of power has heavy union participation, as does a move in Washington state to prevent nuclear waste storage there.

Organizing the unorganized was one of the resolutions passed at the Sunday morning session, as was union control of pension funds and employee ownership of closing plants. The gathering opposed the closing of the Pullman National Standard Car Division, the last US-owned manufacturer of passenger rail cars. A resolve was made to support Native American treaty rights and self-determination. Coalition building with women's, minority and environmental groups was stressed.

Participants left the conference stronger in their determination to, in Winpisinger's words, "Carve a new direction for energy and economic policies this country needs to take."

Sharon Tracy is an anti-nuclear activist and a staff member of New Roots *magazine.*

NO NUCLEAR NEWS

From *No Nuclear News* 3, no. 5 (January 1980): 48

Scoreboard

Where	Worker Contami-nation	Environ-mental / Nation Contam.	Nuclear Plant Shut-downs	Trans-port Accidents	Waste Acci-dents	Miscel-laneous Mishaps	Bomb Away
MI Donald C. Cook Nuclear Plant, Bridgman, Michigan	12.3 ONE WORKER CUT						
JAPAN Genkai Atomic Plant, Genkai, Saga Prefecture, Japan		12.4 LEAK IN VALVES IN CONTAINMENT VESSEL					
AL Brown's Ferry Unit 3 – improperly secured hatch on 12.6 to 12.9, Athens, Alabama					1.4 $29,000		
MA Pilgrim I, Plymouth, Massachusetts			JAN: REPAIRS TO ECCS NOZZLES DURING REFUELING				
CT Millstone I, Waterford, Connecticut			1.4 CRACKS IN CONCRETE SUPPORT — 40% CAPACITY				
NJ Salem I, Lower Alloways Creek, New Jersey			1.5 COOLING SYSTEM VALVE LEAK WHILE SHUT DOWN				
OR Trojan, Portland, Oregon			1.6 AIRLINE LEAK – CONDENSER (started up 1.5 after 2 mos offline)				
CA Three water wells found contaminated, Lathrop, California		1.10 REPORT OCCIDENTAL CHEM. CO.					
CT Connecticut Yankee – violating worker radiation standards, Haddam, Connecticut					1.10 REPORT $27,500		
MT Homes built near old uranium mines, Butte, Montana		1.10 REPORT RADON GAS↑					
SD Homes built over uranium mill site, Edgemont, South Dakota		1.11 REPORT RADON: 12 TIMES HAZARD LEVEL					
U.K. 2 nuclear reactors (unspecified), Southeast England			1.13 WELDING DEFECTS IN COOLING GAS PRESSURE CIRCUITS				
CA Rancho Seco Plant, Rancho Seco, California			1.14 COOLING WATER LOSS – INVENTORY SHOWED SHORT				
PA Tractor-trailer carrying cobalt pellets, Dubois, Pennsylvania				1.14 CRASH IN ICE STORM			
WEST GERMY Ohu Nuclear Plant, near Landshut, West Germany			1.14 REPORT: 1-YR. SHUT-DOWN FOR NEW PARTS				
CA San Onofre Plant, San Onofre, California			1.16 ACCIDENTLY TRIPPED VALVE SUDDEN LOSS OF COOLING WATER				
NY Near Indian Point, Peekskill, New York						1.17 LEVEL 3 TREMOR	

No Nuclear News: A Monthly Cooperative Clipping Service, c/o Boston Clam, 595 Massachusetts Ave., Cambridge, MA 02139.

-SC	SAVANNAH RIVER REPROCESSING PLANT COLUMBIA, SOUTH CAROLINA		1·17 '75-'78: 145 KILOS PL MISSING
-PA	BEAVER VALLEY STATION NW of PITTSBURGH, PENNSYLVANIA	1·20 REPORT STEAM LEAK	
-NJ	SALEM STATION LOWER ALLOWAYS CREEK, NEW JERSEY	1·22 2 gal/hr FUEL ROD POOL	
-VT	VERMONT YANKEE VERNON, VERMONT	1·23 SHORT CIRCUIT IN TRANSFORMER	
-CA	LAWRENCE LIVERMORE LABORATORY LIVERMORE, CALIFORNIA	1·24 LEAK AFTER QUAKE	
-MA	MILLSTONE I WATERFORD, CONNECTICUT	1·28 SHUT-DOWN EXTENDED - FURTHER STRUCTURAL DAMAGE	
-NV	BEATTY DUMP - LEAKY SHIPMENT FROM BEATTY, NEVADA SW NUCLEAR CORP.		1·28 REPORT LEVELS > 3 TIMES ↑

BROADSIDE

From *Broadside*, no. 141 (January-June 1979), p. 12

The Energy Game

by Della Valle, DiGiuseppe, Van Pelt

(Music: "The Patriot Game" words: Ray Zirblis)

I might be from Boston, or from the Mid-West
I am a ratepayer and I want to protest.
I was told all my lifetime, I did not have to save.
I could always get more from the Energy Game.

But then came the seventies, and the famed oil drought.
We were in a big hole. Could the Nukes get us out?
We did not know then we were set up for gain
By the people who profit from the Energy Game.

We were told Nukes were safe and efficient and clean.
What layman could question such a complex machine?
They said there'd be jobs to construct and maintain
Those fancy creations of the Energy Game.

So the problem was "solved" and the crisis was won,

And few stopped to question just what they had done.
I got my 'lectricity, paid my bill when it came,
And I trusted the experts in the Energy Game.

Soon rumours were spreading, they weren't so safe,
From Uranium mining to disposal of waste.
The Scientists were quitting, their reasons the same;
They would not be pawns in the Energy Game.

They've emergency plans if the darn things should "go"

But they never have drills and they don't really know
What the effects would be of a nuclear rain.
They might lose a few pieces in their Energy Game.

Now they keep telling us "Father" knows best.
They're passing a law soon so no one can protest
And the jobs that were promised, they finally came.
They need guards and police for their Energy Game.

This song has more verses than I wanted it to.
Like the anti-nuke movement, it grew and it grew.
We're people not pieces and we're here to complain.
And knock the board over on their Energy Game.

From *Clamshell Alliance News* [4], no. 3 (February/March 1980): 8

Europeans Oppose Nukes

by Anna Gyorgy

Across the ocean, Europeans are opposing the existence and continued development of nuclear power. Although most European countries are more conscious and sparing of energy than here, nuclear power is still seen as crucial to future economic growth. In most countries the major trade unions are solidly behind nuclear expansion. With reprocessing plants operating in Scotland (Windscale), France (La Hague), and a huge reprocessing-waste storage facility proposed for the West German village of Gorleben that would—the government hopes—"solve" the problem of high-level radioactive waste storage, European countries are in some ways "ahead" of the U.S. in terms of completing the nuclear fuel cycle. But pro-nuclear policies have been met with opposition throughout the 1970's.

The '80s promise still broader and more sophisticated opposition, as activists make the connections between nuclear plants and atomic weapons, oppose exports to Third World countries, and work with trade union members. A new awareness of the dangers of low-level radiation has been aided by visits from Sr. Rosalie Bertell and Dr. Helen Caldicott.

There are quite different nuclear situations in each European country and a variety of approaches being taken in opposition.

The 1975-77 Wyhl nuclear power plant site occupation (in southwestern Germany) was non-violent and successful. It had strong local and regional grass-roots support. And these groups continue to be active. (Right now they are raising $40,000 to fight the state government's appeal of the court decision that prevented construction.) But later occupation attempts against nuclear plants already under construction ended in violent confrontations: at Brokdorf (W. Germany) in '76, at Grohnde (W. Germany) in '77 and near the fast breeder under construction at Malville, France in '78. These battles of armies vs. demonstrators revealed the violent police-state nature of the pro-nuclear French and German governments, but also alienated much of the general public from the anti-nuclear movement. The German government and press criminalized the movement, passing restrictive laws; anti-nuclear activists could not hold any state-supported jobs, including teaching and social work.

There continue to be direct actions against nuclear power, but these are smaller and more localized. For instance there have been several non-violent road blockades trying to prevent trucks from entering the Gorleben site for test drilling. Last fall Gorleben women organized a picnic in woods about to be felled for construction work. As the picnic ended, people climbed trees to protect them. The trees were cut down with demonstrators still in them—but resistance to the project still goes on. This summer a group of activists from Berlin and West Germany came to the U.S. specifically to learn ways of organizing non-violent civil disobedience demonstrations.

Since 1978 the French and German activists have turned away from large

Seven Days/LNS

occupation-style actions to mass rallies. In the past year there have been two big German demonstrations. On March 30, during the accident at Three Mile Island, more than 100,000 people marched in Hannover, Northern Germany, against the Gorleben waste reprocessing/storage plant, and on Nov. 14 a similar crowd turned out for a rally in Bonn against the entire German nuclear program and export policies. That rally emphasized the international aspects of the nuclear problem, with Native Americans and a woman from Harrisburg among the speakers.

As many groups turned from confrontation at plant sites to smaller actions, large marches and rallies, opposition continued to be expressed through isolated acts of sabotage against nuclear plants and facilities. For example, on Nov. 2-3, a weather tower was blown up at the newly opened Swiss nuke at Goesgen, cutting electrical lines and shutting off power for 45 minutes. A group called "Do It Yourself-007" claimed the action, writing to the Swiss government to protest nuclear construction. A Swiss activist said, "We don't want to isolate these people. . . . I can understand why people are doing this, but it's wrong and it's counter-productive. . . . It's good for the enemy because he is able then to make more and more police, and to make the repression harder." In the middle of October '79 he had been part of a blockade—quickly organized by phone trees—to block transport of a transformer to a planned nuclear plant. He felt that this action reached and mobilized people, although it was unable to prevent the transformer's delivery.

The first successful national ban on nuclear power came in a close but successful vote Nov. 5, 1978 in Austria. Voters there rejected an expensive utility campaign and voted NO against start-up of Austria's first and only nuke—the fully completed Zwentendorf plant. The victory followed long and active organizing all over the country. Having successfully prevented the opening of Zwentendorf, Austrian activists are now turning their attention to the German and Czech borders, where planned nukes threaten them across political frontiers.

A major vote was lost last spring in Switzerland. There were several reasons for this. The initiative was drawn up by only part of the Swiss movement, without consulting the many groups needed to organize to get it passed. Also the wording was confusing, resulting in mistaken "pro-" votes.

A LAS CENTRALAS ATOMICAS
Ralph Miller/LNS

The next big national vote will be in Sweden, on March 23rd. A "no" vote there will mean a stop to continued nuclear development and a phase-out of existing plants over 10 years.

There have been anti-nuclear ecology candidates in elections for several years. The largest campaign in 1979 was for delegates to the first European Parliament, an international although fairly powerless forum. Ecologists ran on a unified international European slate. Because of restrictive delegate laws only ecologists from Denmark and Italy were actually elected, although ecology candidates attracted more than 3% of the vote in Germany.

The June 10th Parliamentary elections showed that European ecologists have enough support to challenge the larger pronuclear parties of both left and right by gaining a small percentage that can act as a "swing" vote. After the 3.2% vote in the European elections, a 5.1% vote in state elections in Bremen and 11.7% in the local elections of the university town of Tuebingen, the Greens have decided to enter the national German fall elections.

All over Europe there is increased awareness of the international aspects of the nuclear fuel cycle. Exports are being opposed by grass-roots local groups. Winona La Duke, a Native American, in October joined other native peoples fighting uranium mining at a conference in Copenhagen. There aboriginals from Australia, natives from Greenland, representatives of SWAPO (Southwest Africa People's Organization) in Nambia—all people threatened by uranium exploitation by multi-nationals—met to coordinate information and ideas.

On September 15-16, more than a thousand women met in Cologne, West Germany, for a "Women's Congress Against Nuclear Power and Militarism." Their meeting ended with a "die-in" before the historic Cologne Cathedral, as they lay down in simulation of a nuclear accident.

The European religious holiday of Whitsun saw peace marches all through the 1960's. Now it has become the date of anti-nuclear actions in many countries. Last June 2-4, more than 300,000 people participated in demonstrations all over the world. This year there will be demonstrations on May 25-26, coordinated through the International Conference of Coordination Postbox 231 CH-4015 Basel, Switzerland.

The Waste Paper

From *The Waste Paper*, August/ September 1979, pp. 1, 8-9

Spent Fuel Accident Devastating: Can Millions Be Evacuated?

A semi pulls out of the Indian Point reactor at noon. It is a hot, sunny day with a mild wind. The trailer is an open rectangular frame made up of heavy metal beams with a radiation symbol on the side. Inside the latticework is a metal cylinder about three feet in diameter and 18 feet long. The cylinder contains one spent fuel assembly approximately 13 feet long from the Indian Point reactor. The hot spent fuel assembly is immersed in water inside the cask. The gross weight of the semi is close to 35 tons.

The truck wheels onto highway U.S. 9, heading north out of Peekskill. The truck is on its way to West Valley, New York. Just outside of town, for some unknown reason, the truck swerves into a bridge abutment.

The collision with the unyielding abutment sprawls the truck across the highway. Both drivers are knocked unconscious. The truck catches fire. Traffic is stopped. Within 15 minutes the County Sheriff arrives. A tow truck, ambulance and volunteer fire company are called. Passersby stop and gawk at the flaming wreckage. The ambulance and tow truck arrive after 15 long minutes. The sheriff and tow truck operator, braving searing flames, wrench the still unconscious drivers from the wreckage. The ambulance takes away the drivers. More tow trucks and the State Police arrive. The State Police are the first on the scene to note the radiation symbol. They call the State radiation hot line asking

for advice. Thirty-five minutes have passed since the start of the accident.

The State hot line has been looking for the truck since communication was broken off. Because of new security rules, the truck was to be in constant communication with the dispatcher. Sirens blasting, the volunteer fire company arrives. Hoses douse the flames from the spilled diesel fuel. The two trucks have difficulty moving the semi. Several of the tires are flat, deflated by the heat from the fire. Two others are flat even though the fire never reached them. The truck had blow-out tires to prevent hijacking.

The State hot line tells the State Police to keep people away from the truck until a radiation survey is made of the area. It is a long wait. The truck sits. Traffic is tied up. The police and Sheriff move the curiosity-seekers about 100 yds. away. The highway is now wet with water from fire hoses. No one has thought to call Con Ed. Helicopters are enroute from Washington. Finally, they arrive about three hours after the accident.

In white space suits and wearing masks, the Washington emergency assistance crew does a survey. The Geiger counters record deadly amounts of radiation 100 yards from the truck. Because a flood of water was released to put out the fire, a leak from the cask has gone unnoticed until now. Three hours have passed since the initiation of the accident. The cask is now hissing ominously. Steam from an unseated pressure relief valve is escaping. The steam contains Cesium (Cs). Apparently the crash shattered part of the cladding around the reactor fuel. This cladding had become brittle during reactor operation. Con Ed had shipped one of their hottest spent fuel assemblies, cooled only 150 days.

Following the radiation survey, the helicopter crew tell the police to evacuate immediately a one mile radius from the accident, including a local high school. The hissing sound increases. The radiation levels in the area of the cordoned-off truck increase. Only the emergency crew has protective clothing but it offers no protection against gamma rays coming from the cesium. The cask begins to deform. Because of high radiation levels, the fire trucks cannot get close enough to hose down the cask in an attempt to cool it off.

Ten hours into the accident, about 10% of the Cs has been released. An explosion takes place. The cask is ripped open near the top. The radiation levels go off scale. Massive amounts of Ruthenium, Strontium, Cesium, Cecium and alpha-emitting actinides are released. Persons one mile downwind have an intense burning sensation in the lungs. All died of cancer, most of lung cancer. Many die within days but a veritable epidemic of lung and bone cancer and leukemia occur in the following years. Eventually, a 31-mile sector will have to be evacuated including Yonkers and upper

Auth/Guardian/LNS

'Nuclear waste problem? I don't know about you, but I don't want my kids growing up in a world where there weren't any problems left to solve!'

Manhattan. Editor's Note: This accident has not happened but our research indicates that it can.

Analysis: The Waste Paper analysis of this accident follows. For several reasons, the NRC believes that this accident cannot happen. They are misguided.

Can the cask leak coolant? Each spent fuel shipping cask contains a pressure relief valve. Under a fire or collision, the valve may unseat. According to a reference on this subject, ("Siting of Fuel Reprocessing Plants and Waste Management Facilities," ORNL 4451, p. 5-4),* "If a cask that has been designed for a water coolant is involved in a fire, it is unlikely that the outer cask seal can be maintained. Generally, such a cask contains a pressure relief valve. Once this valve is actuated, it is extremely difficult to reseat; therefore we must postulate that all the coolant will be lost in a fire." Editor's Note: Only casks cooled by water have been used to date.

In an accident where the water leaks out of the pressure relief valve, the remaining water will steam up and the cladding and fuel pellets will rise in temperature.

The NRC has stated that the cask has shock absorbing fins which will absorb the energy of the collision. However, the cladding becomes embrittled during reactor operation and can easily shatter.

NRC accident analyses assume a low number of fatalities due to a loss of coolant accident. The NRC assumes that the noble gases, Xenon and Krypton, will be released, but not the more "serious" radionuclides such as Cesium (Cs). *The Waste Paper* analysis shows that some of the radionuclides will not remain in the fuel pellets during reactor operation, but will be vaporized and located in the gap between the pellets and fuel cladding. The vaporization temperature of Cs is 1240° F, easily attained in reactors which reach 3600° F. If the cladding breaks, the water-soluble Cs mixes with the water and steam. We assume during this initial phase of the accident that 10% of the Cs will be released with the steam.

With 10% of the Cs released over a ten-hour period, the dose at 100 yds. from the cask is very large. *The Waste Paper* calculates a dose of 36 rads/min to the lungs due entirely to this 10% Cs release. It is not possible to stay at 100 yds. for longer than 10 to 15 minutes without receiving a

*[*Siting of Fuel Reprocessing Plants and Waste Management Facilities* (Oak Ridge, Tenn.: Oak Ridge National Laboratory, 1970), Report no. ORNL-4451, 415 pp.—eds., *Alternative Papers.*]

large lung dose. In addition, the Cs deposits on the ground and clothes and radiates "groundshine." The dose closer than 100 yds. is higher, of course. We estimate that the police and volunteer firemen will die in several days. In addition to a lung dose due to inhaled radioactivity the Cs will enter the blood stream and provide a whole-body dose. Also, the passing Cs gamma-emitting cloud will provide a whole-body dose.

The NRC has stated that the cask will withstand a crash into a wall at 80 mph. However, the cask involved in the test had no heat producer within the cask, therefore, and no testing of the pressure relief valve. This accident assumes that the

pressure relief valve will be jarred loose due to the shock of the accident, or to the pressure within due to the 1/2 hr. fire. As the leakage continues, and radiation builds up to the point where persons cannot approach the cask, the major release due to the Zr reaction follows.

The cask accident is similar to the Three Mile Island (TMI) accident, where an explosion took place 10 hours into the accident (see June/July, *The Waste Paper*).* The loss of water causes the interior of the cask to heat up. There is no

*["Harrisburg Accident: Once in 17,000 Years?" *The Wastepaper* (June/July 1979): 1, 4-5. Reprinted in Nukes section, p. 28.—eds., *Alternative Papers.*]

Radionuclides released during loss of coolant spent fuel shipping accident

radionuclide	Ci/PWR assembly [a]	Phase 1 steam % release	Phase 2 Zr reaction % release
Kr-85	5.04×10^5	100	100
Sr-89	4.32×10^4	0	5
Sr-90	3.45×10^4	0	90
Ru-106	1.85×10^5	10	90
Cs-134	9.59×10^4	10	
Cs-137	4.77×10^4		
Ce-144	3.47×10^5		
I-131	0.977	100	100
Actinides ( )[b]	1.15×10^4	0	1

(a) Assumes PWR spent fuel assembly, burn up of 33,000 MWD/MT, 150 days cooling period.
(b) Actinides ( ) are PU-238, -239 and -240, Am-241 and Cm-242 and -244. Note that Cm-242 and -244 decay to Pu-238 and Pu-240, respectively.

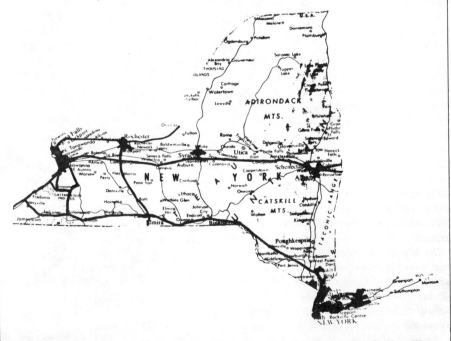

These routes have been used in the past to ship highly radioactive spent nuclear fuel into West Valley. If the site is re-opened as an Away-From-Reactor spent fuel station facility the dangerous shipments will begin again.

ventilation and circulation in the cask to retard the process. As the spent fuel cladding increases in temperature, an interaction between the zirconium alloy cladding and steam takes place at about 1700°F. The Indian Point spent fuel assembly normally puts out 9.14 Kw of heat, while the zirconium water heat output is 106 Kw, more than ten times hotter. The heat within the cask vaporizes the fuel pellets. Within seconds, an explosive mixture of hydrogen gas similar to the TMI bubble is formed.

The cask cannot withstand the pressure of the reaction and splits open the lid, leading to a major release of radioactivity. The numbers for radionuclide release are presented in the Table.

Assuming the releases in the Table, and using standard cloud diffusion models (*Meteorology and Atomic Energy, 1968,* by D.H. Slade, Editor, Atomic Energy Commission) and NRC values for the dose due to the ingestion, immersion or inhalation of selected radionuclides (*Reactor Safety Study*, NUREG 75/104, The Rasmussen Report, Appendix VI, 1975), *The Waste Paper* has calculated the doses received by bystanders in the spent fuel shipping accident. We assume stable weather conditions and a slow wind of 4.5 mph (2 meters/sec).

The short-term lung dose is very high one mile from the accident, and this is primarily due to Ruthenium-106. *The Waste Paper* calculates a lung dose of 3720 rems, within the first two days following the accident. This dose is sufficient to kill everyone within 1 mile of lung cancer, if not killed by another type of cancer first. Much of the radioactive material will remain in the lung and continue to radiate those who do not die immediately. The NRC would say that only 5% of the Ru-106 will be volatilized because the Ru has a high volatilization temperature. While this is true of the Ru volatilization temperature, Ru will be in the form of oxides RuO_2, RuO_3 and RuO_4. The latter two oxides have a very low volatilization temperature, while RuO_2 will volatilize after the Zr reaction.

The Waste Paper calculates the marrow dose, over a 30 year period, due to inhaled radionuclides at 1 mile from the accident will be 1967 rems. With almost certainty, this will cause leukemia in every individual exposed. Within the first two days, the dose to the bone skeleton will be 40,700 rems. The 30 year dose to bone skeleton is *extremely high*—100 million rems—due to the actinides and Sr-90.

A large section of land will be contaminated by the accident. *The Waste Paper* has performed calculations due only to the deposition of Cs, and to the consequent groundshine (gamma radiation) only. We do not account for other radionuclides, contaminated produce and milk, and the resuspension of the radioactive material. Assuming stable weather and a wind speed of 2.5 mph (2 meters/sec), the Cs will deposit itself within 31 miles, in a narrow wedge shaped formation. The whole body dose will be 43.5 rems/y, or about 350 times background. The NRC regulations require that no person receive more than 0.5 rems per year. It would take 194 years before the Cs contamination decayed to safe levels; the land must be evacuated for this period of time.

The Zr-reaction produces the major release of radioactivity and can be avoided by transporting old fuel, rather than fuel aged a mere 150 days. However, there is no regulation that presently requires this action on the part of utilities. Since rail casks will hold about 10 times the amount of a truck cask, an accident with a rail cask leading to an explosion could take place for fuel aged longer than 150 days. In any case, the 10% Cs release would occur first.

Just as the NRC allows the public the opportunity to comment on the Draft Environmental Impact Statements they issue, we welcome comments by the Nuclear Regulatory Commission on this analysis. We would hope to consider their comments more seriously than they consider ours.

Copies of the calculations underlying this analysis are available from The Waste Paper *for a charge of $50 to utilities and the agencies NRC and DOE, and $5 to any public interest or environmental group. Send to the AC RWC, Box 64, Station 6, Buffalo, New York 14213.*

Nukelessness

From *Nukelessness*, no. 2 (March/April 1979), pp. 4-5

The Trident/ Seafarer Connection

by Ken Lans of the Arbor Alliance

If the Navy has its way, by the year 2000 the United States will have a fleet of perhaps thirty Trident submarines, each potentially armed with nuclear warheads capable of destroying 408 cities or military installations with a blast five times more powerful than the Hiroshima explosion. Each Trident will be 560 feet long, 4 stories high, capable of housing 24 missiles with seventeen 100-kiloton nuclear warheads, each independently deliverable over 6000 miles with 30-foot accuracy.

Trident is the latest in the line of U.S. nuclear subs (each sub and missile more lethal than its predecessor) designed to replace the existing Polaris and Poseidon systems in the 1980's. The system was dreamed up for a Pentagon "contest" in 1967. The competition was an opportunity for defense system engineers to submit various proposals for their "ideal weapon." Trident won.

Reprinted with permission from *Nukelessness*.

The Trident concept was made public in 1971, with the first sub to be built and delivered by the Electric Boat Company of Groton, Connecticut, in 1979. Cost overruns and production difficulties have postponed that date to 1981. Eventually, up to 4 Trident bases will be built by the time the 29 subs are operational. Two bases will be in the United States: the base in Bangor, Washington on Puget Sound is already under construction and the Environmental Impact Statement for the second, at Kings Bay, Georgia has already been written. The other two will be in the Third World: Palau (islands near the Philippines) and Diego Garcia (an island in the Indian Ocean).

Trident is the most expensive weapons system ever—almost $2 billion per sub (or $58 billion for the 29 ship fleet now planned. That's a lot of money for National Insecurity. Money that could go for alternatives in energy, housing, agriculture, and other human needs, all providing more and better jobs than Trident.

A First Strike System

Trident represents, along with the neutron bomb, the MX, and the cruise missiles, a new generation of nuclear weapons developed for first-strike use and for "limited" nuclear war. They represent a drastic and costly escalation in the arms race, making nuclear war more "thinkable"—more likely.

The Pentagon sees other possible uses for nuclear weapons besides massive retaliation to a Soviet attack. One such use is described by the "flexibility" doctrine. In the case of a Societ strike or in the case of a large-scale non-nuclear conflict in Europe or elsewhere in the world, the Pentagon argues that the U.S. must be able to hit Soviet targets such as troop concentrations or missile sites selectively and accurately. In this way, it is claimed, the U.S. could use its nuclear firepower without sparking total war. For the Pentagon, the Trident system is justified by this doctrine, since its missiles will be accurate to within 30 feet, but, there is little acceptance of this argument, outside of the Pentagon, as there is little acceptance of the idea of a "limited" nuclear war.

Such accuracy is one necessary factor for a United States first strike aimed at destroying enough Soviet weapons to make damage sustained in the U.S. from a return Soviet attack "acceptable." Robert Aldridge, a former weapons designer working on the Trident missile before he resigned from Lockheed, and Daniel Ellsberg, at one time a top official in the State Department, believe that at least some elements in the Pentagon are indeed contemplating a first strike. They argue that the U.S. is currently developing the technology, including accurate missiles like those slated for the Trident subs and anti-satellite, anti-submarine, and anti-ballistic missile systems, which at some point in the future would give the U.S. the capacity to begin nuclear war on the supposition that it could survive in an acceptable fashion.

The Trigger Finger

The Trident/Seafarer connection? Seafarer is the trigger finger necessary for this first-strike capability whose only use can be seen as sending the bombs away to the Trident subs.

Since 1958, the Navy has had various extra low frequency (ELF) communication systems on the drawing board because the public has refused to buy them; Wisconsin, then Texas, and now Michigan have refused to permit the Navy to build. The Navy refuses to accept the public's verdict and continues to spend millions on an unwanted project.

Despite campaign promises to the contrary, President Carter asked for $13.4 million to fund Project ELF for this year and an additional $30 million for the year after. Project ELF, a one-way communica-

tions system for the Trident sub and missile system, would consist of radio transmitters and a 130 mile underground grid of cables situated near Sawyer Air Force base in the U.P. In 1976, Carter promised Michigan residents, "If I am elected, Project Seafarer will not be built on the Upper Peninsula against the wishes of its citizens." Shortly thereafter, the residents in all the affected counties in the Upper Peninsula voted "no" against Seafarer by a margin of 4 to 1.

So they just changed the name, but the game remained the same. Now called ELF, a supposed much-scaled-down version, it would emit extremely low frequency radio waves in the range of 45-80 cycles per second. The safety and health effects of these microwaves is seriously questionable. ELF radio waves can penetrate the ocean to several hundred feet. Present systems force the submarines to surface for communications and thus expose them to detection and destruction in times of danger. Upper Michigan would serve as a suitable location for Seafarer because it has an underlying rock formation (the Laurentian Shield) that greatly assists transmission.

The Navy described Seafarer as a "soft" (vulnerable to destruction) ELF system. This stands in contrast to an earlier Navy proposal, Project Sanguine, which would have laced 22,500 square miles (41%) of Wisconsin with buried cables. This was a "hardened" ELF antenna because it was designed to survive a bombing. Because of this and because of its extremely slow transmission, Seafarer would not be effective as a retaliatory system. Rather it could only be used in a first-strike capacity, to launch a nuclear attack.

The Navy maintains that Project ELF is not Seafarer, since it is so much smaller. Governor Milliken, who originally opened the door by inviting the Navy to conduct an EIS of Seafarer in 1975, vetoed the Navy's "compromise," contending that the small system was a "foot in the door" he could not accept. His contention was validated later in press releases as well as *Science* magazine; the Navy admitted they wanted to connect the Sawyer Air Force Base system with an old test facility they had built earlier—in Clam Lake, Wisconsin. "The three test antennas would be integrated into a full-scale system."

Live Without Trident

Resistance to the Trident system began in 1971 with the formation of Concerned About Trident in the Bangor, Washington area, the site of the proposed first sub base.

Opposition has continued to grow, centered around the Bangor base, the Groton, CT. sub construction facility, the Seafarer grid, and the missile assembly site near San Francisco. Last May 22-23, in an action set to coincide with the United Nations' first formal discussion of nuclear disarmament, over 260 people were arrested after occupying the Bangor base two days in a row, the second time carrying a banner declaring the area Bangor National Park. They are basing their appeals on necessity and international law arguments, the latter based on the Trident's design as a first-strike nuclear weapon illegal under international law.

Further actions against the Trident system are planned nationwide for 1979. Live Without Trident will feature a Trident Monster march on Tax Day, April 15 and a Gathering of Thousands is planned for August 6. The Trident Monster is a 560-foot rope (as long as the sub) with 408 black pennants (one for each warhead). The Pacific Life Community and the Abalone Alliance in Northern California are mapping further strategies aimed at the Lockheed weapons facility. In addition, the first Trident sub will be "launched" sometime the end of March. This is purely a publicity stunt, however, and the sub will be put right back in drydock as it is nowhere near ready to go to sea. The Trident Conversion Campaign will stage a protest at the launching and the Trident Monster will make an appearance.

For further information contact:
STOP SANGUINE/ELF COMMITTEE, Box 474, Mellen, Wisconsin 54546.
LIVE WITHOUT TRIDENT, 1305 N.E. 45th St., Rm. 210, Seattle, Washington 98105.
TRIDENT CONVERSION CAMPAIGN, RD 1, Box 430, Voluntown, Connecticut 06384.

MORE: Recommended, excellent articles on the subjects of the arms race and disarmament:
• "The Doomsday Strategy," Sidney Lens, *The Progressive*, February, 1976.
• "The Russians Are Coming Again," George McGovern, *The Progressive*, May, 1977.
• *Sojourners*, special issue on disarmament, February, 1977.

Fallout Forum

From *Fallout Forum* 2, no. 4 (July/August 1979): 3, 12

Nuclear Weapons: A Cancer in the Earth

by Charles Scheiner

The United States is now the proud owner of 35,000 nuclear bombs, each of which can wreak havoc a hundredfold more devastating than the worst reactor meltdown scenario. We build three new ones every day. Defense Department studies show that 200-400 H-bombs could totally destroy Russia, but we now have a hundred times that many, an arsenal with over 600,000 times the explosive power of the "Little Boy" bomb which murdered Hiroshima. We can kill the world's people more than thirty times over. The Russians are a little behind us—they can only annihilate humanity twenty times.

It was the Hiroshima and Nagasaki nuclear tests, with their 200,000 fatalities, which proved that there is no safe level for the biologically damaging effects of low-level radiation. Today, a third of a century later, seven people still die every day from cancer, leukemia, and genetic damage caused by that experiment. Many of the victims weren't even born in 1945.

The nuclear menace is a cancer which threatens all life on this planet. The cancerous growth has now spread throughout the world, with six nations having publicly tested nuclear weapons and several dozen who could develop them by 1985.

The Atoms for Peace program, begun in 1953, was an effort to disguise the new technology as benign. But now after it has imitated its parent and proliferated across the planet, nuclear energy has proven hardly less dangerous than its malignant source.

Many people are aware of the problems involved with nuclear power, so a brief recap should suffice here:

• The danger of a catastrophic accident threatens thousands of lives. The Atomic Energy Commission's WASH-740 study projects 43,000 casualties, billions of dol-

lars worth of property damage, and the contamination of an area "the size of the State of Pennsylvania" from a nuclear accident.*

• In normal operation, nuclear facilities continually emit low-level radiation. Any exposure to such radiation, no matter how slight, increases your odds of getting cancer or leukemia and makes birth defects more likely.

• Nuclear waste (spent fuel) is highly radioactive and must be kept from the environment for hundreds of thousands of years. No proven method for long-term storage or safe disposal of nuclear waste exists.

• Although a nuclear plant has a maximum operating life of only thirty years, no commercial-scale reactor has ever been decommissioned. Reactors which are out of service are simply sealed off and ignored—although their residual radiation will be dangerous for centuries—because no one knows how to dismantle them.

• The world's limited supply of nuclear fuel will lead the nuclear industry inevitably to breeder reactors within two decades. Breeders use plutonium as fuel and would require its frequent shipment between reactors and reprocessing plants. As little as twenty pounds of plutonium can be made into an atomic bomb, and there are no technological problems in building a bomb once you have the plutonium. A police state will be required, in a plutonium economy, to keep this material from getting into the wrong hands.

• Similarly, the export of nuclear reactors around the world fuels the proliferation of nuclear weapons. Even non-breeders can be used to produce weapons-grade material; India made her nuclear bomb from plutonium made with a Canadian-supplied "research" reactor.

• Money spent on nuclear reactors (and other high-technology, capital-intensive projects) aggravates unemployment and inflation. It creates few jobs because money is spent on materials instead of wages and because salaries are higher (more skilled

workers), and it removes dollars from circulation.

• Energy corporations, utilities, and government agencies work together in a world apart from the needs and health of people. Their collusion and priorities make a sham of our "democracy" and "free enterprise" system.

These are the observable symptoms of nuclear cancer. Its terminal state, the ultimate metastasis of nuclear effects throughout the body of the planet, is nuclear war. This tumor has been growing since 1945, awaiting its time to annihilate all higher forms of life on earth. As we put bandaids on the effects of nuclear power (all of which are also symptoms of nuclear weapons production and testing programs), the cancer continues to grow.

Recent studies by Ernest Sternglass, Professor of Radiology at the University of Pittsburgh, indicate that all people born between 1953 and 1964 may be victims of nuclear weapons tests. He attributes the drop in average SAT scores and similar measures over the last decade to lower intelligence caused by exposure of fetuses and infants to radioactive fallout from H-bomb tests. We can only wait a few more years, until children born after the atmospheric test ban went into effect take their SATs, to see if he is right.

Nuclear MADness

Mutual Assured Destruction became superpower nuclear policy in the mid-sixties. Each government holds the people of the other country hostage in return for their own government's nuclear restraint. Neither will initiate a nuclear war because of the certainty of massive retaliation. Each side has dozens of nuclear-powered, nuclear-armed submarines circling under the oceans, doomsday machines which wait for the signal telling them that their family, friends, and country have been killed so that they can do the same to the offender. This precarious balance of terror kept us alive through the sixties and seventies.

It was simple before MAD arrived—when air-raid drills and fallout shelters would save us and when nuclear energy promised electricity that would be too cheap to meter. Weapons would keep us secure, and the American monolith would be invulnerable.

Weapons technology improved, however, and the prospect of winning a nuclear war became impossible—even the "survivors" would be condemned by high radioactivity levels to live underground on

---

*[*Theoretical Possibilities and Consequences of Major Accidents in Large Nuclear Power Plants* (Washington, D.C.: Division of Civilian Application, Atomic Energy Commission, 1957), Report no. WASH-740, 112 pp.—eds, *Alternative Papers*.]

Reprinted with permission from *Fallout Forum,* the newsletter of the SHAD Alliance.

canned food for generations. It became clear that the luckiest ones in the nuclear holocaust would be those directly hit by bombs; at least they wouldn't know what happened. We turned to new rationales for our security, and MAD became U.S. policy. We didn't even pretend to be able to survive a nuclear war any more. Both superpowers promised that they would not develop a first-strike capability (the power to destroy the enemy's retaliatory strength in an initial attack), and the balance appeared stable.

Enter Counterforce

But MAD was boring. It offered no chance for new strategies, little opportunity for generals and engineers to play with new weapons, few lucrative defense contracts. America's forswearance of a first-strike policy prevented us from reasserting our masculinity after the humiliations of Vietnam and Watergate.

In 1975, President Ford and Defense (now Energy) Secretary Schlesinger announced a change in the rules. The U.S. will, under certain circumstances, be the first country to use nuclear weapons. A new policy of "limited nuclear war" (a fictional concept) is in effect, and military strategists again have something to play with. They plot scenarios of "counterforce," where a "surgical strike" by American H-bombs would prevent the enemy from striking back. If the U.S. or an American ally is attacked, even with conventional weapons, we maintain the option of nuclear retaliation. This is a direct reversal of the pledge of every President since Harry Truman that, Hiroshima and Nagasaki forgotten, we would never be the first country to use nuclear weapons.

Peg Averill/War Resisters League/LNS

The Carter-Brown team has continued the new policy, developing plans for limited nuclear war in Europe (the neutron bomb) and for giving Americans the option of a slow death (through evacuation and fallout shelters) instead of the euthanasia provided when the bombs explode. Carter's recently announced budget, with a 3% military expenditure growth after inflation accompanied by cutbacks in domestic programs, is clear evidence of his escalatory policies.

The Soviet Union, however, has not made the policy shift. By adhering to this no first use position, they have no need for tactical (battlefield) nuclear warheads and haven't built any. If attacked by small nuclear weapons, they can only respond with big ones which will take the "limits" off the war. The metastasis will quickly be fatal to the entire human species.

We've got the big bombs too, and we're developing a host of new weapons which aim for a first-strike capability. Some, like the cruise missile, fly low enough to avoid detection by enemy radar and are ideal for surprise first strikes. Others, such as the submarine-based Trident or the mobile, land-based MX (each crowned by a dozen highly accurate, independently targetable H-bombs) can put thousands of warheads simultaneously on Soviet targets with an accuracy of 300 feet after an 8,000 mile flight. Such accuracy is useless for destroying cities, but it is invaluable for wiping out hardened missile silos. Since it makes little sense to destroy empty silos, we must assume that the enemy missiles will not yet have been launched when the warheads get there—clearly a first-strike scenario.

The Russians have over 20,000 H-bombs. If our counterforce eliminates 99.5% of them (which seems implausible but is part of Pentagon planning), the 100 which still get through will kill about 30 million Americans. These "acceptable casualties" assume, of course, that the Soviets have given us three days notice in which to evacuate our cities. The recent flurry of public pronouncements about American civil defense are preparing the way for the new policy.

Nuclear Realities

All this pragmatism is a charade, more hypnotism to keep us from noticing the spreading cancer. It's hard to conceive that anyone would want to survive in a world which underwent the equivalent of ten million meltdowns, but military strategists are planning for it. The world is being inherited by a new generation of leaders, people whose entire adult life has been since Hiroshima. If you've never known a world free from the threat of annihilation, that annihilation is plausible to consider.

In 1962, when I was twelve, I would wake up in terror upon hearing a low-flying plane at night, waiting for the blinding flash which would signal the end of the world. I sleep more soundly now; it's hard to stay terrified for decades. Maintaining your sanity requires repressing the idea of a nuclear war actually happening, but the repression of the thought makes the fact more likely. We must begin to deal with the cancer among us.

U.S. and Soviet politicians have recently been offering a new form of psychological treatment. Arms control talks pretend to slow down the spread of the malignancy, but actually further its growth. Not one single nuclear weapon has ever been dismantled as a result of arms control agreements. Every pact, from the atmospheric test ban through Vladivostok, has been an agreement not to do what we weren't going to do anyway. They have served as excuses for additional military escalation, even as the Carter Administration now rubs SALT II in our wounds by authorizing new weapons programs such as the first-strike MX Missile in return for Senate votes for the treaty.

Radical Surgery Needed Quickly

The only way to deal with cancer is to surgically remove all of the malignancy. It is not enough simply to stop building nuclear weapons (although that would be chemotherapy, a necessary step before we can move forward); the tumor must be excised. True security can come only through universal, total, worldwide, nuclear disarmament. The United States, which unilaterally initiated the nuclear arms race and remains ahead in every aspect, must begin to rid itself of the cancerous material. When we have dismantled 99% of our warheads, and still are able to destroy the Soviet Union, we can look to see if they are reciprocating.

As disarmament progresses, so will other aspects of our society. The removal of the nuclear cancer will pump new life into our economy as the $130 billion spent annually on the military becomes available for human needs. Unemployment and inflation will ease, and a new sense of hope will emerge. As we stop selling arms around the world (the U.S. is by far the leading merchant of death), people of other nations will share in our new-found health. Technical expertise and resources will become available to address needs of people—food, housing, transportation, and safe, cheap, renewable, decentralized energy.

Addressing the Basic Disease

The cure of this cancer lies with the people of the world, especially those who live in the United States and the Soviet Union. For it is only we who have the potential influence with our governments to reverse the spiral toward annihilation.

In America, a new emergence of political activism has developed around the issue of nuclear power, a resurgence reminiscent of the civil rights and anti-war movements of the 1960's. The anti-nuclear movement must broaden its focus to encompass the entire nuclear malignancy. Not to do so would be to address a skin cancer while ignoring the lung cancer which is spreading throughout the body. Military uses of nuclear technology share the symptoms of their civilian offspring—the same health hazards, waste, and accident risks exist. We must use our awareness of these effects to awaken people to the real nature of the cancer, much as Vietnam taught us our role in the world (and kept us out of Angola—if we remember the lesson it will get us out of South Africa).

Serious malpractice is being committed while the anti-nuclear movement by-passes the weapons issue. Disarmament may appear to be an unpopular cause, but any meaningful political activity will antagonize some people—those with vested interests—and activism for a worthwhile goal will eventually attract widespread support. If people only worked on what was popular, and not what was important, there would have been no anti-war movement, no civil rights movement in the South, no American Revolution. Politically aware people must work to teach others what they know, not choose safe issues which already have a popular consensus.

The obvious symptoms of nuclear power have already convinced most Americans (and people worldwide) that it is not the way to go; a quick look at reactor order cancellations proves that, as does the opposition from more and more establishment people. We must now build on that awareness toward a broader view of the nuclear cancer.

If we do not confront the true nature of the nuclear weapons malignancy, it will surely be terminal.

From *Environmental Action* 12, no. 1 (June 1980): 22-25

Human Fallout from the Atomic Age

by William Sweet

"I'd like it to be known that the Veterans Administration does its best to render substantial justice, on a case by case basis, to each individual veteran who comes to us for assistance."

—J.C. Peckarsky,
Director of Compensation,
Veterans Administration

A large number of people are beginning to think they got cancer or other serious diseases from exposure to radiation, and

with their claims mounting rapidly, the government is finding itself in a serious bind. If it ignores their plight, then it will be seen as callous and unfeeling. But if it admits some may have suffered from radiation, then it also will have to admit that levels of radiation it always claimed were safe were not so safe after all. The implications for the nuclear industry, both civilian and military, could be devastating.

The radiation "problem" involves cold cash and lots of it. If the government were to grant compensation to some radiation victims, then it might well find itself besieged by everybody who has been exposed to radiation. Since there is no sure way of proving whether an individual got cancer from radiation or some other source, the government would have no basis for rejecting claims.

Roughly 250,000 people are thought to have participated in atomic bomb tests during the 1940s, 50s and 60s. About 400,000 people have worked in nuclear

facilities operated by the Department of Energy or its predecessor agencies. Another 20,000 to 30,000 people, many of them Native Americans, have mined uranium in the Southwest. All told, close to a million Americans may have been exposed to radiation.

People who are worried about what radiation may have done to them are beginning to get in touch with one another, and last month they had a chance to discuss their experiences at the National Citizens' Hearing for Radiation Victims, an event organized by members of the Environmental Policy Center and the American Friends Service Committee. Such diverse groups as atomic workers, test veterans and American Indians sponsored the event, which took place April 11 to 14 in Washington, D.C.

The organizers and sponsors hoped to dramatize the difficulties people who are worried about radiation have had in getting the government to pay them heed. Regrettably, the national media gave the hearings little or no coverage, though some local radio stations did broadcast the proceedings live.

Admittedly, a great deal has been known for a long time about some groups represented at the hearings, among them uranium miners, who have suffered extraordinarily high lung cancer rates (*EA*, June 1979).* Even so, the miners still have received little help, and there are other people whose problems are only beginning to emerge. Among these, the veterans of Hiroshima and Nagasaki occupation forces stand out as perhaps the single most shocking example of abuse and neglect.

Most of the people who testified at the hearings appeared to have one thing in common. They had been contaminated to some extent or another by radioactive particles or dust. That dust, it is beginning to seem, may be very much more lethal than experts once supposed.

People who work in nuclear power plants are not exposed to radioactive dust under normal working conditions, since the fuel is contained in the reactor core. Most of the radiation emitted into the environment by power plants consists of highly penetrating beta and gamma rays. Like x-rays these pass easily through the human body, and if the dose is kept small enough, then it seems reasonable to assume

---

*[Dede Feldman, "The Yellowcake Connection: Or How Nuclear Power Ties Suburban Long Island to a Tiny Town 2000 Miles Away," *Environmental Action* 11, no. 1 (June 1979): 5-9.—eds., *Alternative Papers*.]

individual cells and organs will escape serious damage. This is the basis for the industry's claim that nuclear power is safe.

What the industry likes to overlook, however, is the plight of those who work directly with nuclear materials outside power plants. Miners, fuel processors and builders of nuclear weapons, like atomic test veterans, may be exposed to alpha-emitting particles that have attached themselves to dust in the working environment. While less penetrating than beta and gamma rays, alpha radiation is much more damaging to unprotected tissue. Even the tiniest alpha-contaminated particle, if it attaches itself to an organ such as the stomach or lung, can continue to emit damaging radiation for a period of years.

According to Dr. Thomas Martell, an expert on radiation health hazards who was exposed to radiation while studying the effects of atomic fallout, the risks associated with alpha emitters may increase exponentially with the level of exposure. Double the amount of radiation, he suggests, and the health risks quadruple. Quadruple the radiation, and the incidence of certain diseases becomes 16 times greater.

Martell believes that he personally contracted all the symptoms of multiple sclerosis from exposure to radiation. In a sense he is lucky, because his symptoms come and go in a mysterious fashion, leaving him at times with his faculties intact. Many others, judging from the testimony at the Citizens' Hearings, see their health deteriorate with horrifying speed once the first symptoms begin to appear.

It was the same story, again and again. Originally people were told that their work would not involve exposure to dangerous levels of radiation. Frequently, because of the sensitive nature of their work, they'd be told not to discuss it with friends or family. Periodically, their film badges which measure radiation would be sent off somewhere for evaluation, and generally that would be the end of it. But sometimes a person would be abruptly transferred, without explanation, to a new line of work.

This was the beginning of a new era, and bizarre experiences were far from uncommon. The first troops sent into Hiroshima and Nagasaki could not have been fully prepared for the destruction they encountered, even one month after the blasts had occurred. Troops participating in bomb tests during the 50s saw through their arms when they shielded their faces, and some reported seeing a companion's skull illuminated as though in an x-ray. Workers in fuel plants noticed signs of premature aging or an alarming number of defects among their newborn infants. But the nation's security and the workers' incomes were at stake, and so generally the rule of silence prevailed.

Then, after 15 or 20 or 25 years, more alarming signs would appear: cancer of the lung, digestive organs or bone marrow, rare nervous disorders, a sudden and drastic deterioration of general health. Then the individual might remember, and discuss for the first time with friends and family, the time he drove a bulldozer in Nagasaki, or the time he crawled under a vehicle in the center of the crater the day after the nuclear blast, or the time he ate lunch in a room filled with uranium dust. The search for medical confirmation, and for financial assistance, would begin.

Requests for copies of radiation records would go unanswered, and finally the records would turn out to be lost. Local doctors would be sympathetic, but they also would be fearful of jeopardizing their position in the company town, be it Oak Ridge, the towns near the Nevada test site, or the desolate mining communities of New Mexico. The daughter of a uranium enrichment worker in Paducah, Ky. reported that the doctors would "say you had radiation damage, but they wouldn't put it on paper."

Individuals began to appeal to higher authorities—to members of Congress, to the Veterans Administration, to the President—but that would only produce more frustration. A veteran who asked Justice Department officials which of his experiences he could discuss in public was told he'd just have to take his chances: under the provisions of the 1954 Atomic Energy Act they didn't have to specify what was secret, but if he goofed and illegally divulged a secret, then they'd be in touch . . . .

Experiences of this kind eventually gave rise to organizations such as the Committee for Veterans of Hiroshima and Nagasaki and the National Association of Atomic Veterans. And the growth of those organizations led finally to the Citizens' Hearings, an event where you felt out of place if you didn't have crutches, or an eye patch, or funny balding patches on a visibly shrunken head.

Those were the outward manifestations of a turmoil the radiation victims sought to express and explain. "If you could take the feelings on our insides and put them on our outsides," said Oscar Thomas Weeks, a Nevada test site veteran, "you wouldn't recognize us as human beings."

The government's reaction to the growing anxiety about radiation has been cautious, to say the least. Generally, the agency which would have to pay in the event damage is found is given the job of deciding whether damage occurred. President Carter has set up committee upon committee

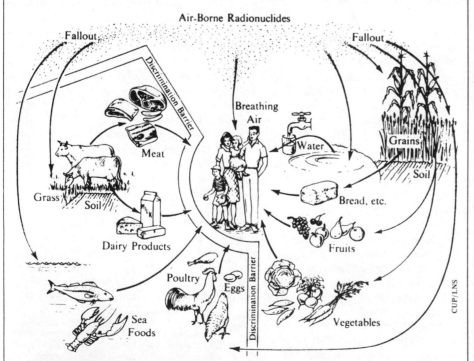

PATHWAYS OF RADIATION . . . various ways it reaches the human body

to coordinate radiation research and to study the compensation problem, but most research funds remain concentrated in the Departments of Energy and Defense, and the Justice Department official who is responsible for preparing a report on "fair and effective" compensation measures is the very same person who would defend the government against compensation claims.

For some groups, such as the Native Americans, this treatment comes as no surprise. Lakota Harden, a representative of the Black Hills Alliance and the Women of All Red Nations, pointed out at the Citizens' Hearings that this is just another generation of Indians coming to Washington to talk to the government in vain. "They're not going to do anything for us. We've been going through this for 200 years."

But for other groups, such as the veterans of Hiroshima and Nagasaki, the government's attitude is unintelligible and utterly galling. Many of them, having survived the grueling Pacific campaign only to be struck down in middle age by diseases like multiple myeloma and Hodgkin's disease, find it hard to believe that the government for which they fought is now turning a deaf ear to their requests for help.

During the past year or so, the number of compensation claims filed by veterans of the Hiroshima and Nagasaki occupation forces has grown from a handful to over a hundred. Estimates of the total number of American soldiers who were at the two cities range from 1,000 to 2,000, on up to 20,000. Considering that this total population is quite small it would seem a study of all the Americans who went into the two cities is called for.

In ruling on the claims, the Veterans Administration (VA) relies heavily on evaluations prepared by the Defense Nuclear Agency—the branch of government that is responsible for testing and maintaining the country's nuclear weapons. According to this agency's public relations chief, government scientists have found *no* danger from inhalation or ingestion of radioactive dust.

J. C. Peckarsky, the VA's director of compensation, reports that none of the Hiroshima and Nagasaki claimants have received compensation. Peckarsky sees no reason to believe that these people suffered specifically from radiation exposure, since 16 percent of Americans die from cancer anyway, and since the exposure of the Hiroshima and Nagasaki veterans is "known" to have been low.

When asked whether the VA was making any effort to investigate the whole group of Hiroshima and Nagasaki veterans, Peckarsky said there would be "no way to do it." Instead, the Defense Nuclear Agency is spending $24 million to find out whether the 250,000 veterans of all nuclear explosions are dying in abnormal numbers. If, after this four-year study is completed, abnormal numbers of deaths are found, then presumably another study will be started to find out why they are dying. Then perhaps there will be another study to figure out how to find the victims and compensate them. All that can be done, certainly, but it is impossible according to Peckarsky, to round up 1,000 to 20,000 people to find out whether they are suffering from certain extremely unusual diseases in excessive numbers.

Very high rates of multiple myeloma have turned up not only among the U.S. veterans of Hiroshima and Nagasaki but also among Japanese survivors and among workers at the Lawrence Livermore Nuclear Weapons Laboratory in California. Nonetheless, Peckarsky sees no point in doing a Hiroshima-Nagasaki study, because even if abnormally high cancer rates turned up, there still would be no way to sort out the service related cancers from the ones that would have occurred anyway. Either the VA would have to compensate everybody, which would be hopelessly expensive and "unfair to the taxpayer," or it would have to select some percentage of the veterans "by lot" and arbitrarily restrict compensation to them. Peckarsky concluded that veterans' claims could be reasonably handled only on a case by case basis.

Upon further questioning, Peckarsky agreed that there is no consensus among scientists about how dangerous radiation is, even when the exact exposure is known, and he agreed that it can never be proved conclusively that an individual contracted cancer specifically from one radiation incident. He sees no reasonable alternative, however, to the case by case approach.

The Senate Veterans Committee, chaired by Alan Cranston (D-Calif.), has successfully pushed for reforms which some believe will lead to fairer treatment of radiation claims by the VA. The burden of proof has been shifted somewhat to favor the claimant, and the VA is now required to explain its reasons for rejecting claims.

If the VA continues to consider radiation claims on a case by case basis, it would consider how much—and what kind of—radiation the person was exposed to, what other carcinogens the person was exposed to during his or her lifetime and whether the person's disease is characteristic of other people who were exposed to radiation at that time. It is, however, difficult to see how the VA can know what diseases are characteristic of people exposed to radiation during nuclear explosions until it studies the whole group.

Considering the absence of knowledge about what the effects of Hiroshima-Nagasaki exposure actually were and considering almost all individuals are exposed to carcinogens during their lifetime, the case by case approach would appear to be a convenient ruse for simply rejecting all claims. Many suspect that political pressure from the top, spurred by a desire to protect both the nuclear

D.C. Gazette/LNS

industry and the military establishment, is responsible for the VA approach.

Veterans Committee staff member Molly Milligan expects that the committee's reforms will substantially improve VA procedures. Even so, she believes the Carter administration is missing a chance to address widespread fears and doubts about radiation dangers. In refusing to do the kind of epidemiological study of Hiroshima and Nagasaki victims that could resolve some of these concerns, the administration has fed suspicions that telling the whole truth about radiation dangers would deal the nuclear industry a mortal blow. At the same time, Milligan says, the administration has seemed "willing to let people suffer and die thinking their government is screwing them."

What to do: The Citizens' Hearings suggest three steps for people interested in the radiation health issue.

• Become informed. The Citizens' Hearings office, 317 Pennsylvania Ave., SE, Washington, D.C. 20003, has information on this subject.

• There may be radiation victims in your area who need support and help. The Citizens' Hearings can tell you where to find them.

• Support bills which have been proposed in Congress to help radiation victims win compensation and protect future generations from radiation hazards. For a list of this legislation, contact the Citizens' Hearings.

William Sweet is a staff writer with the Editorial Research Reports, *a division of* Congressional Quarterly.

NO NUKES NEWS
Citizens Against Nuclear Power

From *No Nukes News*, September 1979, p. 2

The Duke Is Nuked

by Joe Barr

America's film hero, John "Duke" Wayne, died a victim of radiation from U.S. atomic fallout. His death and the deaths of his co-stars in the movie "The Conqueror," have been linked to an open-air atomic test explosion in 1953. The explosion took place shortly before the movie was filmed in St. George, Utah, the site of the nation's worst radiation fallout.

Wayne, co-star Susan Hayward, Agnes Moorehead, Dick Powell, and the bulk of the top production people of the movie have all fallen to forms of cancer following film work near the Nevada open-air testing range.

The cancer and death rate is also very high for other people who worked on the film. The victims include members of an Indian tribe hired to work on the movie.

The location of the movie, which was based upon Genghis Khan's conquests in Asia, was in the main fallout zone of one of America's first nuclear accidents—an explosion known as "Dirty Harry." "Dirty Harry" was one of 87 open-air nuclear tests conducted in the nearby Nevada test range between 1951 and 1962.

A sudden wind change before detonation at 5:05 a.m. on May 19, 1953 sent clouds of radiation over St. George and the cast of "The Conqueror."

The radiation levels at St. George, were the highest ever recorded in a populated area, surpassing measurements in Japan after the delivery of two nuclear weapons during World War II.

Although "Dirty Harry" was detonated atop a 300 foot tower, at 5:05 a.m., documents show that test officials ordered no precautions for local residents until 9:25, hours after the fallout had settled on the area. Most people in the area were never warned at all because "it would create a disturbance" and "it would not take much to start wild rumors," according to Atomic Energy Commission memos obtained recently through the Freedom of Information Act by newspapers.

The link of Wayne's death comes at a time when 700 longtime residents of St. George are filing lawsuits against the federal government over the effects of the radiation fallout on the community between 1951 and 1962.

In the years since the blasts, studies have uncovered a marked increase in leukemia, thyroid cancer, birth defects and other radiation-related illness.

Erna Thomas, grandmother and local resident of St. George, has become a vocal critic of the government's neglect and an advocate of compensation for the victims.

"When too many people seemed to be dying around me from cancer, I decided to do a check of neighbors in just a one-block radius of my home. I was surprised when the figure got to nine. Now the number is 30, either with cancer or dead from it," she reports.

Like the people of St. George, the cast of "The Conqueror" were unaware of the atomic tests. One of the few surviving co-stars, veteran Western actor Lee Van Cleef, said that, "We never talked about it at all. Nobody really knows what causes these things [sic] but I guess if I was going to get it, I would have it by now. It has been some time since I had a cancer check, but maybe I ought to get one now."

Ironically, the producers of the film not only selected a site contaminated by radioactivity, but transported tons of the red earth back to a Hollywood set where work on the movie continued for two more years.

"I remember them bringing all that red earth back to the Hollywood set where a lot of the scenes were shot," says Van Cleef.

A promotional brochure for the movie boasts about the tragic miscalculation, saying "The caravan of big trucks and trailers began rolling in, unloading and going back to the studio for more props for the sets. But they didn't return to Hollywood empty—they went back with tons of Utah's red earth to be used to make exterior scenes filmed at the studio."

A check of the major stars and crew of the six million dollar Howard Huges/RKO Radio production epic shows the common, tragic legacy. John Wayne fell to his second bout with cancer this year despite the best efforts of modern medicine and Wayne's courageous fight.

Susan Hayward succumbed to a malignant brain tumor in March, 1975.

Dick Powell was claimed by a malignant brain tumor in October, 1963.

Agnes Moorehead, like Hayward and Powell, was stricken by a malignant brain tumor and died in April, 1974.

Character actor Pedro Armendariz committed suicide in June, 1963 at UCLA Medical Center after learning he had acute lymph gland cancer. Art director Carroll Clark died of emphysema in 1973, but his widow said he had prostate cancer also. Production manager Harold Lewis was taken by cancer as was his wife, who accompanied him on location. One newspaper reported that it was difficult to identify any deaths of the cast and crew that were not cancer-related.

Calculation of the tragedy may never be complete, since "The Conquerer," a Hollywood epic, boasted a cast of thousands.

The DC Gazette

AN ALTERNATIVE JOURNAL

From *The DC Gazette* 10, no. 9 (December 1979): 5, 11

Is There an Anti-Nuclear Diet?

by Mary Claire Blakeman

Brown Rice, miso soup, bean sprouts, seaweed, green vegetables, fruit and sunflower seeds. It may not sound very appetizing to most American palates, but according to a growing number of health activists in the anti-nuclear movement, such a diet may be the best culinary response to the post-Harrisburg nuclear age.

Though the medical establishment puts little stock in the connection between what people eat and their ability to withstand nuclear radiation, some scientists are beginning to take a serious look at the possibilities. What they have found is intriguing, and tends to support some of the non-scientific evidence.

The notion that diet may have a protective or rehabilitative effect on persons exposed to nuclear radiation first surfaced among Japanese survivors of the bombing of Hiroshima and Nagasaki. In the current issue of the *East-West Journal*, Dr. Tatshichiro Akizuki attributes his survival and that of his patients in Nagasaki to a diet which included the combination of brown rice, salt and miso soup, and which strictly eliminated sugar. Miso is a form of fermented soy beans which has a high mineral content.

"I had fed my co-workers brown rice and miso soup for some time before the bombing. None of them suffered from atomic radiation," Dr. Akizuki says, "I believe this is because they had been eating miso soup."

"The radioactivity may not have been a fatal dose," he adds, "but I, and other staff members and in-patients kept on living on the lethal ashes of the bombed ruins.

"It was thanks to this salt mineral method that all of us . . . survived the disaster free from severe symptoms of radioactivity."

Others who lived through the bombing of Hiroshima say their traditional macrobiotic diet, which emphasized whole grains and vegetables, helped them to survive. However, no one has collected conclusive data to show that people on macrobiotic diets had a higher survival rate than others.

What is known is that certain foods act as "chelators" to help remove radioactive material from the body. Chelators combine with radioactive elements to form stable compounds in the body which then can be eliminated.

A British study, published in the *International Journal of Radiation Biology* in 1971, showed that kelp effectively removed strontium 90 from the body. "The alginate preparation (OG1) reduced the absorption and retention of strontium about 4-fold," the report states.

Annalisa Kennedy, an anti-nuclear activist with Oregon's Trojan Decommissioning Alliance, says that kelp can be used daily, like salt, in salads and cooking. "The best way to protect yourself is to join the anti-nuclear movement," she says, "but kelp and other seaweeds like dulse provide an abundant source of minerals—iodine, potassium, calcium—which can help protect the body and limit the absorption of radioactive elements. People can also protect themselves by avoiding smoking and stress and other things that trigger cancer."

Pectin in foods such as fruit and sunflower seeds has also exhibited an effect on strontium. During the early 1960s, Russian scientists reported that pectin extracted from sunflower seeds reduced the absorption and deposition of strontium 90 in skeletons of test animals.

An earlier report by the US Army Quartermaster Food and Container Institute showed that supplementing the diet of guinea pigs with green vegetables such as cabbage or broccoli "enhanced the survival of irradiated animals while the use of beets did not." The 1958 study concluded that "feeding of cabbage both before and after radiation exposure produced the greatest amount of protection."

This apparent protective ability of green plants is also attributed to sprouted seeds, such as alfalfa or wheat, which are high in chlorophyll. Wheat grass, which is grown

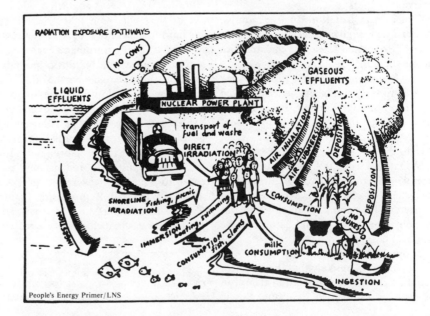

RADIATION EXPOSURE PATHWAYS

People's Energy Primer/LNS

by sprouting wheat berries, is gaining attention from unorthodox health circles and established doctors alike for its beneficial effects—which seem to include protection from radiation.

Dr. Chiu-Nan Lai of the University of Texas System Cancer Center reported in *Science News* that "extracts of wheat sprouts exhibit antagonistic activity toward carcinogens."

Advocates of natural substances as protection from radiation point out that the use of certain foods is most effective when incorporated into the regular diet—not as a quick fix remedy. While there is some evidence to support their claims, most medical doctors remain skeptical about the correlation between diet and radiation.

"Getting the necessary vitamins and minerals is important," says Dr. Roy Thompson, senior staff scientist at Battelle Memorial Institute in Richland, Wash. "But I don't know of any substantial scientific evidence that any of these things have an effect on radiation except for the fact that it could make you more healthy. And a healthy animal is more resistant to outside insult than an unhealthy one." Despite the skepticism regarding natural foods, medical science puts great store in chemical substances which act as effective chelators in certain high exposure cases.

One such case is that of Harold McClusky, a former chemical operator at the Hanford Nuclear Reservation in Washington, who was exposed to radioactive contamination in an explosion at the plant in 1976. He breathed the highest recorded human dose of the isotope americium 242— 400 times what an average adult might receive in a lifetime.

Kept in near isolation for five months, McClusky was given specially produced zinc DTPA, which acted as a chelator with the americium.

His levels of radiation finally were lowered to the point where he was allowed to return home. His doctor, Bruce Britenstein, reports that the 67-year-old McClusky stopped the DTPA treatments last March.

"As far as we can tell, the treatment has been 95 percent effective," Dr. Britenstein says, "but he still has a large burden of americium. He's doing reasonably well, but we don't know what could happen in the future."

In the McClusky case, DTPA proved useful—but it is unlikely that the chemical would be given to the population at large in the event of radioactive exposure. Public

health officials are much more likely to turn to potassium iodide as a precaution against radioactive iodine-131.

Iodine-131 is considered especially hazardous since the thyroid gland has a special affinity for the element, and it can endanger growing children.

"Since iodine concentrates in the thyroid, we can prevent the concentration of radioactive iodine by saturating the gland with nonradioactive iodine," explains Dr. Sidney Marks, associate manager for environmental health and safety at Battelle. "The result of the gland being saturated is that it can't pick up additional iodine."

But whether one pops a pill or turns to a macrobiotic diet, the chances of warding off the effects of high level radiation through chelators is a hedge, at best. Much more important, says Richard Penberthy, project director of the Center for International Environment Information in Washington DC is to know the nature and seriousness of the hazard.

Power plants can release an array of different isotopes which pose various health threats. A variety of responses could be appropriate. They range from evacuation to the quarantining of food and distribution of potassium iodide.

"You have to know the exact nature of the exposure," Penberthy says, "and the best way for people to protect themselves is to make demands on the operator of the nuclear facility to report exactly the percentage of release and what kind of release it is.

"You've got to demand a warning system, demand an evacuation if necessary, and demand that civil defense tell you how to clean up."

Mary Claire Blakeman is an Associate Editor with Pacific News Service.

---

spare Rib

From *Spare Rib*, no. 91 (February 1980), pp. 6-7

Nuclear Power: It'll Cost the Earth

by Sheryl Crown, Lesley Merryfinch, Bee Pooley, Rosie and Jola, and Jill Sutcliffe

It's hard to believe that nuclear power is as bad as it is. That governments encourage—indeed, finance with billions of pounds—an industry that could have the same effect on our health as did the atomic bombs on Hiroshima and Nagasaki. Even now, babies are being born with defects and people are dying from the radiation created there in 1945. Nuclear power is creating radioactive substances; for instance, compared to a natural background level of 12 'curies', Windscale Reprocessing Plant in Cumbria will let out 230 *million* curies of a radioactive gas in its lifetime, according to

---

Reprinted with permission from *Spare Rib*, a monthly women's liberation magazine, 27 Clerkenwell Close, London EC1R OAT, England. Subscription details upon request.

The Ecologist. Even when they're functioning "normally" nuclear plants cause increases in leukaemia—700% according to one West German study, and a report in the doctors' journal *The Lancet* in September, gives evidence connecting an increase of leukaemia in Lancashire with the nuclear plants on the Cumbrian coast. Nuclear power stations are being operated with serious defects, like those that led to the accident at Three Mile Island in the USA, when the whole of Pennsylvania came near to being poisoned. The industry is dumping radioactive wastes into the sea, and they're coming back up again . . . think of that next time you eat 'sea-fresh' fish.

And the "experts" are deliberately lying to us about these dangers. At Three Mile Island, spokesmen for the company said that the releases of radiation were only at the level you'd get through a dentist's x-ray—and yet workmen on the site later testified that so much radioactivity was let off that the dials all went off the scale. Even while the government denied there was a problem, it evacuated all pregnant women and children. Research scientists have lost their funding, and even their jobs, for speaking out about radiation hazards.

All the decisions about nuclear power have been made by a handful of men, industrialists and politicians—and many of the facts are covered by official secrets acts. Yet it's a matter of life and death for us all. There have been serious explosions at nuclear installations, such as the one in the Russian Urals in 1957, and there will certainly be more. But what threatens all of us, even if we don't live near nuclear reactors, is the amount of radioactive substances transported around the country and around the world, that are mined under land where people are living and created in nuclear power stations, that are dumped or buried or simply released into the countryside.

Recent research has shown that women are twice as likely as men to get cancer from radiation, because we are more prone to thyroid and breast cancers that are particularly triggered by it. (Cancer is already the biggest single cause of death for women over 35.) Foetuses and young children are even more affected, as growing cells are so susceptible to radiation damage. Radiation also affects egg and sperm cells, so that mutations show up in future generations. And there's *no* safe level of exposure to radioactive substance —any increase will cause a corresponding increase in the number of miscarriages, deformed babies and people who die from cancer, according to the latest evidence.

And still the present government plans to expand the nuclear programme as fast as possible . . .

The use of nuclear power to produce electricity arose from and is still connected to, military development. The world's first commercial nuclear power station, opened by the Queen in 1956 at Calder Hall in Cumbria, was intended primarily to supplement the production of plutonium for the British weapons programme. Before that, the sole purpose of reactors was to make plutonium for bombs. The more nuclear power stations there are, the more plutonium can be extracted from the used fuel and used for bombs. What is more, dropping an ordinary bomb on a nuclear reactor would be just as effective as an atomic bomb elsewhere.

No government invests in science out of a pure thirst for knowledge. The Western nations make a great deal of money from exporting nuclear technology to other countries, despite a 'non-proliferation' treaty—the Canadians to India, for instance, and the West Germans to Brazil and South Africa, against the interests of the majority of people in those countries.

The "experts" said it wasn't possible to make atomic bombs solely by reprocessing the waste of a reactor—until India managed it in 1974 . . . The West makes money, and an increasing number of governments get nuclear weapons. The Stockholm Peace Research Institute has predicted that the world will suffer its first nuclear war within 24 years, as the nuclear capacity spreads to somewhere between 40 and 60 nations; already over 30 have atomic weapons. There is no such thing as 'peaceful' atomic energy.

Overcapacity

The nuclear power programme in this country has been based on predictions of growth in the use of electricity; these were made some years ago, at a time of ridiculous economic optimism and before there was any official recognition that much energy is simply wasted by inefficient use. Since then growth in consumption has slowed down considerably, but the electricity boards have not substantially revised their plans. The South of Scotland Electricity Board already has the capacity to generate 86% more electricity than it ever needs at once, but it still intends to go ahead with a new Advanced Gas-Cooled Reactor (AGR) at Torness. The only answer the industry has found to over-production is overconsumption; they are pushing the equation that happiness depends on high living standards which depend on high energy consumption.

The 'Think Electric' campaign would have us invest in consumer non-durables such as electric potato peelers and toothbrushes. Women, forced back into the thrilling confines of the nuclear family when they lose their jobs to electric-powered microprocessors (see *Spare Rib* 83),* and fail to get the new skilled or security jobs in nuclear power plants, could at least measure out their happiness in electric coffee spoons. It is in the industry's interests—not ours—to get us as major consumers hooked on electricity.

For domestic heating, electricity is an expensive and inefficient form of energy. Moreover, nuclear power produces electricity which can't be switched on and off according to need. But people *use* electricity most when they come home from work and in the winter. So unless—or until—they can persuade us to cook in the middle of the night, nuclear power will never be able to replace coal or oil even in

*["Women and Chips," *Spare Rib* 83 (June 1979):19-22.—eds., *Alternative Papers*.]

producing electricity, because these will have to continue to be used for peak times. And, contrary to what the industry says, there are detailed proposals for alternative, safe, cheap energy sources that could more than meet even capitalism's industrial "needs". For a start, power stations that produce both electricity and hot water for heating could save us up to half the coal dug in Britain each year.

The Cost of Nuclear Power

The pro-nuclear lobby claims that the disadvantages of nuclear power (such as death) are outweighed by the cheaper electricity they say it produces. But in their analysis of its price they conveniently forget to include many of the costs. Delays and inflation have contributed to soaring costs in the construction of stations. In 1964, five AGR nuclear power stations were planned for Britain at an estimated £600 million. Only two of these are as yet producing any power and already they have cost £900 million above the estimate. The price of the uranium fuel has tripled, and can only continue to get ever more expensive. It's a *non-renewable* resource that costs more to mine as they have to dig it out of more inaccessible and poorer sites, the easy and richer sites being used up. The costs of maintaining security guards, and of 'decommissioning' a nuclear station after its maximum useful life of 30 years— because it's far too radioactive just to be switched off and abandoned—have not been taken into account. And, unbelievably, the industry has not added in the costs of transporting and disposing of nuclear wastes—perhaps because so far they have not worked out what they *will* do with the wastes.

Accidents like that at Three Mile Island, Harrisburg—when, on March 28, 1979, the nuclear reaction went out of control—are paid for by increases in the electricity bills, £16 million a month, in that case. At Hunterson in Scotland sea water was accidentally let into the new AGR, and the estimated costs of repair and alternative generation of electricity have run to over £50 million. This will go on to the Scottish bills. According to the "experts", accidents are only meant to happen every so many thousands of years. In the first quarter of 1979 there were 17 separate "incidents"— that's the industry's term for problems—in Britain alone, and from December 1976 to December 1978 there were no fewer than 75 incidents at Windscale. There have been explosions at nuclear power stations, and some spectacular near-misses—see, for instance, *We Almost Lost Detroit* by John Fuller. In short, they have lied.

It'll Cost the Earth

Money, however, is not the only cost. Operation of nuclear reactors produces large quantities of radioactive wastes (see technical box).* No solution has been found over the past 30 years of research for disposing of this waste, nor for completely isolating it from the environment. Yet the waste poses an enormous health hazard. In the meantime, it is being produced and stored "temporarily" in tanks that are leaking and stretched to overcapacity.

The used reactor fuels are the "hottest" and most dangerous waste. If a used fuel rod was lying without its shielding and you went past at 90 mph on a motorbike, you'd still die of radiation—in this case not through cancer, but from the direct effects of radiation poisoning: your body literally falls apart in a few days. These used fuel rods are transported from the power stations all round Britain to Windscale, Cumbria, for reprocessing, usually in goods trains and regularly through the middle of cities. After reprocessing, which separates out the plutonium and unused uranium, the remaining radioactive waste is stored as a liquid porridge in double-walled steel tanks. These have to be kept refrigerated in case they boil and explode—on no account can there be a power failure. These tanks corrode and eventually leak. Leakage into the ground—or worse, into the underground water supplies—eventually gets into our food and drink.

Even *less* attention has been paid to the management of those wastes innocuously termed "low level", but the concentration of plutonium in them may be even higher than in the "high level" wastes. 4000 tons of low level waste has been dumped by Britain in concrete drums in the Atlantic. Some have come back up, some have leaked, and some have been hauled in by fishing boats. The industry maintains that low level releases are diluted to "insignificant" levels in the sea. Apart from the question of whether any amount can be called insignificant, because the evidence shows that any level—including background cosmic radiation—is likely to cause some fraction of the population to get cancer or give birth to deformed babies, radioactivity becomes *concentrated* rather than diluted

*["How Nuclear Power Works," *Spare Rib* 90 (February 1980): 8. This box is not reprinted in *Alternative Papers.*—eds., *Alternative Papers.*]

Bonnie Acker/Syracuse Peace Council/LNS

when it gets caught up in the food chain. Plankton, the first link of the chain in the sea concentrate radioactive substances between 500 and 200,000 times, depending on the substance. Eskimos nowhere near atomic tests or reactors were found to have high body radiation levels, because the fallout from nuclear tests got into the lichens, caribou ate the lichens, and Eskimos ate the caribou. Someone eating half a pound of fish a day from the Irish Sea—the most radioactive sea in the world—could be getting a third of the current "permitted" dose from that alone.

In the "normal" operation of nuclear power stations, nothing can be done with some of the radioactive gases produced, so they are released into the atmosphere. Windscale alone releases 15 million curies of Krypton[85] a year (the background level is 12 curies). It takes ten years to decay to half of its original radioactivity; it's heavier than air, so it sinks and builds up close to the ground and the growing plants. Radioactivity builds up most in the outer, nutritionally rich parts of grain, so that wholemeal bread and brown rice, for example, are more affected than refined foods. Leakage from nuclear power stations is monitored by testing the milk from local cows, in which radioactive strontium[90] builds up—you see, the authorities are actually quite aware that radioactivity concentrates in food. Back in 1957, an accident—oops, sorry *incident*—at Windscale released 20,000 curies of radioactive Iodine[131] into the air; and in an area 200 square miles downwind of the reactor, 450,000 gallons of milk had to be poured away.

The Stable Society—Social and Political Consequences

So who controls this costly and deadly form of power in Britain? All the electricity-producing establishments are owned by the Central Electricity Generation Board. It's a highly capital-intensive hierarchy in which a few men at the top make all the decisions—despite the fact that it's a nationalised industry, they're not going to ask us what we think. Of course, this is a reflection of how society is run—everyone to their niche in the hierarchy, and "naturally" it is predominantly men at the top and women at the bottom.

Nuclear power is just not possible on a small, local scale; even a tiny nuclear power station would cost hundreds of millions of pounds to build, and they are far too dangerous to be near centres of population. But feminism is about individual and local decisions. The will to have control over our own lives—and nobody else's—is fundamental to Women's Liberation. To us, this necessarily implies decentralisation of all forms of power, without orders from above—whether they come from capitalist or socialist men.

Increasingly, the establishment's solutions to the problems posed by nuclear power threaten freedom of speech, association, discussion and privacy. Because the transport, use, disposal of nuclear materials is so potentially dangerous, the security forces will be greatly reinforced, and in the name of "national security" all kinds of restrictions will be sanctioned. What the government presents as hazardous is not the chance of a serious accident through technical failure or human error—they seem to have convinced themselves that this won't happen—but that plutonium, the material of the bomb, will get into the "wrong" hands. (As though their hands could be trusted!)

Whatever form accidents take, the effects would be the same. Disastrous. Already, the "rigorous" accounting procedures have lost track of pounds of plutonium around the world and a whole boatload of uranium was stolen at sea . . . The more radioactive substances are transported around Britain, the greater the official paranoia. The threat of terrorist misuse of plutonium is used to ensure that nuclear establishments are well guarded.

The most frightening threat is not terrorist attack but the erosion of civil liberties. Fear of sabotage is and will be used by the government as an excuse to restrict political dissent. Under the Atomic Energy Act of 1946, authorised officials may enter any premises without a warrant and without giving notice to the occupier, if they suspect atomic energy work is proceeding there. The nuclear police force have the power to arrest on suspicion and are not directly accountable to *any* government minister. Because of all the money and prestige invested in the nuclear power programme, and its enormous risks, the industry wants to silence any criticism of it by whatever means—from calling any opposition ignorant or anti-"progress", to tapping their phones and opening their mail, to killing them. Union organiser Karen Silkwood was poisoned and then run off the road to prevent her handing over evidence about safety infringements at the plant in Oklahoma, USA, where she worked.

As nuclear power comes increasingly to be relied on, society will have to adapt to its demands. *Any* measure could become legitimate in the name of safety. As feminists we're attacking the stability of the system by challenging the power of a few men to hold all the money and power. We'll have to be silenced . . .

Co-operation or Conquest?

The technology of our male culture is based on the imposition of the technologist's skill on the material with which he is working, with no concern for whether that material is alive or inanimate. Those of us who live in inner cities are particularly struck by the extent to which this technology is out of harmony with the living world, and many of us are aware of how we reflect this noisy, dirty and brutalising environment in our relationships with each other. Nuclear power is the extreme manifestation of a technology that relies on subjugation and exploitation. Its historical beginnings lie in the search for a more powerful weapon; the nuclear fuel cycle starts with companies robbing Native Americans and Australian Aborigines of their land to mine uranium.

Far from being the answer to rapidly decreasing fuel reserves, stocks of uranium are only expected to last for slightly longer than those of oil. Throughout the process we are in constant danger of being blown up or contaminated with radioactivity, with no possibility of recycling or adaptation. We are left with grisly monuments, concrete-entombed, radioactive, disused power stations round our coastline, waiting for 20 odd years to cool down before they can be dismantled, and waste products that are totally outside the birth and death cycle of our ecology, many of them remaining deadly for thousands or hundreds of thousands of years.

In contrast, there are sources of energy that could be used which are renewable, do not pollute, are adapted to nature, to the locality and the people living there and SAFE for us and future generations to come—wind, sunlight, waves or dammed rivers, alcohol, methane gas, heat from within the earth. These could provide diversified forms of energy which would be small, decentralised and easily understood and controlled by everyone. Use of these sources together with better insulation of buildings and general conservation would also provide many more jobs than nuclear power can. This is in keeping with the way we as feminists are aiming to work: co-operatively, sensitively and without power structures.

Better Active Today than Radioactive Tomorrow

The accident at Three Mile Island discredited the "experts", showing them to be both scared and lying. It caused a major surge in the anti-nuclear movement. *The China Syndrome,* which prophetically came out in the States nine days before that "incident"—it even contains a line that a nuclear accident could devastate "an area the size of Pennsylvania"—has gone on mass distribution worldwide. As costs of maintaining the nuclear industry become ever more crippling; as safety measures are shown to be totally inadequate; as the realisation grows that there is no such thing as a safe dose of radiation, the industry is losing support from the public. These factors and the recent occupation by anti-nuclear activists of the proposed nuclear reactor site at Torness have made a significant swing in public opinion in the surrounding area, for example: a poll in the local paper showed that 90% were against the proposed reactor and more local people are now prepared to be active in opposing it.

Nuclear power is a threat to us all. If we allow it to develop it will affect our political structures, our civil liberties, our food, even the air we breathe. Stopping nuclear power will not automatically bring us control of our lives, our immediate environment, or our bodies but success in this is an essential step towards the future that we as feminists want to build. It is our energy against their power . . .

What you can do

- *CONTACT—Feminists Against Nuclear Power,* Sheryl Crown, 58 High Lane, Manchester 21 (061-881 1788), or Jola, 24 Rancliffe Rd, London E6 (01-471 5711).

- *Friends of the Earth,* who are holding a national demonstration in London on March 29 to 'celebrate' the first anniversary of the Three Mile Island accident, they have local branches in many towns, 9 Poland St, London W1 (01-434 168/437 6121).

- *World Information Service on Energy (WISE)* has a WISE women's project, collecting every thing that's written around the world by women on nuclear power. WISE, c/o 34 Cowley Rd, Oxford (0865 725354).

- *READ—Undercurrents* for regular news on the fight against nuclear power (27 Clerkenwell Close, London EC1—this is also the address for the new **Anti-Nuclear Campaign**); *SCRAM Energy Bulletin* (Scottish Campaign to Resist the Atomic Menace, 2a Ainslie Place, Edinburgh 3). Both available at alternative bookshops or from PDC, 27 Clerkenwell Close.

- *Nuclear Power* by Walter Patterson.

- *Nuclear Power for Beginners* by Stephen Croall and Kaianders Sempler.

And encourage all your friends and relatives to see the film *The China Syndrome.*

3 APPROPRIATE TECHNOLOGY

The hopeful side to energy questions is treated in this section. Writers argue that answers to the alleged shortage of energy do not lie in large-scale projects but rather in decentralized, locally based solutions. Economy of scale is not economy when it endangers. John Mohawk opens the section arguing a classic Native American position in *Akwesasne Notes,* calling for a return to traditional respect for the earth. He also articulates the basic radical premise that technology is neither a neutral force used by different interests nor an inherent force for progress, but the product of a society, and thus reflects the inequalities and oppression in that society. Similarly, the American obsession with the new and with progress is attacked in "Something Old, Something New," where Mickey Spencer points out the recentness of the American preoccupation and hopes that American consumerism can be replaced with a philosophy of conservation and preservation.

More specific proposals for living in an ecologically sound way are presented in "What Is Appropriate Technology?" Describing appropriate housing, appropriate waste treatment, and appropriate energy sources, T. Paul Robbins provides an alternative society for energy-wasting suburban America. While Christopher Nyerges horrifies us with the long-lived effects of litter, Dan Knapp and Steve Ames, in "Turning Waste into Wealth," give us an idea of the problems involved in trying to recycle and a good deal of advice on how to get around these problems and organize neighborhood- and community-supported ventures. Andrew Maier shows us how on a small scale we can free ourselves from the apparent necessity of electricity by using bicycle-powered power tools. And at the other end of the spectrum, Andy MacKillop proposes in "Third World Energy" a reapportionment of world energy resources between the underdeveloped world and the capitalist West. Finally the waste of land, left lying unused and deteriorating by uninterested owners, is described in "Wasting Away," and proposals for communal reclamation are outlined.

"Powergate!" and "Powerline Health and Safety" both deal with electrical powerlines and their effects on the health of nearby humans and animals. The profit-seeking plans of utility companies in both of these cases are being fought by popular local groups who object not only to the dangerous and largely unresearched medical effects of these plans but also to carrying the economic burden of the companies' schemes through higher rates. Rate hikes are one issue that is covered in the mass media. But, typically, mainline articles focus on the quantitative issues of rate increases, rather than examining the source of these hikes—the structure and motives of decision-making in a profit-oriented energy business. These articles offer two examples of how the alternative press emphasizes the connections between everyday reality and the larger structures of society.

To emphasize once again the international character of many radical movements, "Hugging Trees: The Growth of India's Ecology Movement" is included. But lest we feel too satisfied with our ecologically sound solutions and our proposals for natural lifestyles, "Pig Ignorant: Who Is Optimistic? Not the Man with the Hoe" finishes the section, puncturing our visions with the harsh realities of competition and survival in the agriculture of a capitalist world.

—ES

From *Akwesasne Notes* 11, no. 5 (Winter 1979): 19-21

Technology Is the Enemy

by John Mohawk

A number of years ago, a group of students was sightseeing with Thomas Banyacya, well-known Hopi Traditionalist interpreter and spokesman. The group was from SUNY at Buffalo, and the tour followed the Niagara Gorge to Niagara Falls, past the myriad of chemical plants near the now-famous Love Canal, and on toward the Robert E. Moses Power Project. Thomas had given a speech the night before as part of a program to bring Native consciousness to the American public. He had told of the prophesy of the Hopi, and to the extent that such a teaching could be received by a college audience the adventure was a success.

He was impressed by the sights of the day, as is everyone who first sees the gorge, the falls, the industrialization of the Niagara Strip. By late afternoon, we had left the Falls and were where the highway signs announce the approaches to the Robert E. Moses Power Project. Suddenly, Thomas told us to stop the car. We pulled over, and he got out. For a long time, in silent awe, he stood beside the road, a few hundred yards from the gorge. Before him stretched the power transport network— the endless maze of cables which transport electricity from the Niagara Fall's generating plant to points throughout Western New York. He got back in the car, and we rode for a few moments in silence, past the transformers and the cable towers which dominate the landscape. Finally, he spoke softly:

"In the Hopi teachings," he began, "we are told that toward the end of the world, Spider Woman will come back and she will weave her web across the landscape. Everywhere you will see her web. That's

how we will know that we are coming to the end of this world, when we see her web everywhere. I believe I have just seen her web."

He didn't mean that the Hopi world was coming to an end, and that the power lines signalled an end of Hopi culture. He meant that *the* world was coming to an end, that the history of humans as a species was coming to some crisis and that the crisis was connected in some way to the appearance of those power transmission lines.

The teachings of Hopi culture are not easily translated into a way of thinking which is accessible to Western Technological Man. The Hopi Cosmology is an oral history of the Hopi people and the human species which interweaves a complex set of symbols in such a way that it illuminates a set of moralities which the West has generally found to be both confusing and inappropriate. But the Hopi Cosmology should be interesting to the Western mind in at least one category—it contains as a central element a "history", of Technology. (I'm not going to apologize at this point because words like "history" don't accurately apply to the Hopi version of the past, the word "Cosmology" isn't an accurate description of their teachings either. The language is deficient, not the Hopi mind.)

Technology, which is extremely prominent in Hopi ways of thinking, is virtually invisible in Western Conventional Histories. Since Western Conventional Histories shape Western Conventional Wisdom, it is really useless to talk about Technology unless we can talk about history and unless we can expect the fact that all of us are products of what is called Conventional Wisdom—those things which we accept to be true because "everybody knows" those things are true. The culture we were born into nurtured each and every one of us to a belief in certain premises, and our socialization in that respect is surprisingly complete. We are each of us "prejudiced" to certain beliefs, certain ways of seeing the world, and certain ways of being in the world.

If technology occupies a prominent place in the Hopi version of the human

experience, the role of technology in shaping human events in the Western world is seriously downplayed. In fact, the historical force of technology is almost invisible in the West. If technologies have had an impact on molding Western history, then those versions of Western history upon which English-speaking people were all nurtured were woefully inadequate in explaining those forces. For a number of reasons that I don't want to talk about here, Western history has been written largely with an eye to expounding upon personalities and events in ways which leave the role of technologies, to say the least, secondary. In the following few pages, I am going to delve into a version of history which states that the evolution of technologies has been the major moving force in all of Western history, and that the vectors of that evolution give us some insights into where it all goes and what it means to the future of us all.

The beginnings of technologies can probably be traced to that period of time several million years ago when ancestors of our species climbed out of trees and began life walking erect on the ground. There isn't much that can be said about that period of time, so little is really known about that phase of evolution. It is certain that over long periods of time, our species evolved from arboreal creatures to erect creatures which eventually inhabited the semi-arid savannah country of present-day Africa.

At some point, and it is not entirely clear at what point, proto-humans evolved from creatures entirely dependent, as are most creatures, on the raw gifts of Nature and ventured from their Natural habitat into an increasingly alien habitat to which they had not physically evolved. Human evolution took some revolutionary turns in the history of the world's creatures, not the least of which involved the human evolution of the development of culture as a means of surviving in environments to which the species was not physically adapted. As proto-humans left their ancestral habitat, they evolved new ways of surviving which required that they learn to do the things which Nature had not provided them at birth. As they moved into colder climates, they had to learn to fashion clothing to take the place of fur coats that other species evolved biologically. They had to learn to devise shelters, to eat what was available, and to shape and mold the things of their new worlds to their needs.

From the very beginning of "human"

WE ARE TRYING TO REBUILD THE MOHAWK NATION TO BRING BACK A WAY OF LIFE THAT IS NATIVE TO NORTH AMERICA FOR FUTURE GENERATIONS. CHILDREN— THAT'S THE BINDING FORCE IN GANIENKEH TODAY, THAT GIVES US THE STRENGTH

OUR ROOTS ARE HERE. THEY DO NOT EXTEND ACROSS THE OCEAN. WE ARE NOT VANISHING. WE ARE AS STRONG AS EVER.

OUR PEOPLE ALWAYS KNEW THAT SOMEDAY WE WOULD RETURN

Native American Solidarity Committee/ & Amherst Cultural Workers Collective/LNS

time, all things are products of "technology." There must have been many revolutionary technologies which enabled human populations to spread from their places of origin to inhabit nearly all places of the world, from the hottest and most arid deserts to the polar ice caps. Those technologies must have included such things as learning to work leather and to sew clothing, and to fashion tools from wood and bone. It is not preposterous to imagine that an awl and a sewing needle were at one time revolutionary technological developments which enabled people to fashion clothing which in turn allowed people to venture to and live in climates which had previously been too hostile for human habitation. It must

have taken tens of thousands of years for some of these inventions to take place and to have an impact. Inventions which made it possible for humans, who do not possess the fierce claws or powerful jaws of most meateaters, to kill and eat large grass eating animals were powerful inventions. Those kinds of inventions shaped human history. For hundreds of thousands of years, that cultural evolution was going on, and human populations evolved into creatures capable of expanding into many areas of the world, able to trap and ambush animals many times the size of humans, able to devise shelters adequate to provide survival in increasingly hostile environments, and having invented languages, which made it possible to transmit from one generation to

the next the group's accumulated knowledge.

All of that was going on long before the end of the Pleistocene. In fact, we have a lot of evidence to indicate that the concept of religion, the idea of a cosmological order of things, was pretty universal among mankind some 70,000 years ago, and may be one of the developments which set modern man apart in some ways from truly ancient man, although even that isn't entirely clear. By the end of the old Stone Age, (at the end of the Pleistocene) Man's most complex and marvelous technological feat—language—had clearly evolved to fascinating proportions. The hunting and gathering culture had lasted through several ice ages and seemed to have survived the test of time. By that time, Man had evolved so far from his origins that for all practical purposes there was no place left on earth where he could survive without his devised method of evolution— culture. And the culture of man—even in our Archeology textbooks—was defined by his tools and the way he lived in the space he occupied.

It was about ten thousand years ago that technologies started to evolve in new ways. The inventions associated with the New Stone Age took root in several places under varying conditions, but it is useful to look at the evolution of the West especially because it is there that the kind of technologies we must concern ourselves with were nurtured. It is entirely possible that at least some of the early technologies were born out of some kind of necessity. The hunting culture of the Old Stone Age comes to an end with the appearance of agriculture and animal herding. Those things probably were accepted only very gradually. The first crops were probably gathered and replanted because people were experiencing some kind of adversity —famine or near-famine. Until people began sowing and cultivating plants, those plants were gathered, and it seems highly unlikely that people would have adopted the tedious and strenuous work associated with most agriculture unless Nature failed to provide the food they needed abundantly enough to meet their needs. Once agriculture took root, however, it probably seemed like a Godsend to people who were in need.

As new technologies are introduced, human societies change in order to incorporate those technologies into their world. The introduction of agriculture seems to alter hunting and gathering societies in some relatively predictable ways. A hunting society is primarily patrilocal, and the spirits which people look to for their health and safety are largely animal spirits. Agricultural societies tend to be more settled and women play a greater role in the society which often becomes matrilocal and which looks to the spirits of plants increasingly for the same purposes. In the beginning, agriculture was a woman-based technology, and the society reflected that. In Europe, we know of the existence into historical times of Mother Goddess religions which have their origins in prehistory.

Sometime after the introduction of agriculture, at least among Indo-European people inhabiting the area known as the present day Steppes of Russia, animal herding was introduced.

A society's religion seems to be intricately related to its technology. The herdsman truly revolutionized the way humans saw the world, because he is a human who manipulates the reproductive aspects of the animals he herds and upon which the society depends for its food and clothing and, in many cases, for shelter. But if agriculture had a primarily female bent, herding has a very male cast. Males became dominant in the herding culture, and to a considerable extent, the same technology which is employed in herding is readily applied to societal organization. Herding cultures tend to be patriarchal, with women playing an extremely secondary role. The religion of herding cultures tends toward male sky gods whose attention focuses largely on the affairs of men. Animals had previously been thought to be sacred at least to the extent that they possessed spirits which could assist or injure humans. In the herdsman's experience, the animals' spirit became less and less important.

Hunters and gatherers who become herdsmen tend to become more hierarchical than agriculturalists and in fact sometimes evolve into extremely patriarchical societies. Herding is not a technology which provides a more attractive way of life compared to hunting and gathering—it provides a more efficient way. The animal supply is under human control, easily found, and usually required less territory than hunting and gathering. Animal herding made it possible for human beings to live on the grasslands, which hunters and gatherers could not do. Agriculturalists who lived in semi-arid regions were probably the first to

extensively practice water-use technologies, and were the first to build settlements. It is extremely possible that the first irrigation ponds were dug by agriculturalists who were experiencing crop failure due to lack of rain and who invented irrigation as a way of resolving this problem. The early permanently settled villages could have grown up around the use of this technology, although it is also possible that villages in dry regions sometimes arise in places where water is available and where the availability of that water is so critical that groups of people really can't move around very much during long periods of the year. It is interesting to note that when towns appear we also begin to see the appearance of priest-classes which not only control the religious life of the community but which also seem to be in control of the technology. Civilization (from the Greek civos) arises out of these roots, and it will remain constant that people will fashion their society after a model dictated to them by the technologies that define their material economy.

The evolution of civilization—in this case Western Civilization—was a very complex process. The steps from settlements which arose because people needed a reliable water supply for crops to the population centers which we call cities was a slow process and technologies which reinforced that process were evolved all along the route. It seems not unreasonable, when looking at the history of ancient Anatolia and the Fertile Crescent, that a series of events took place in those early towns. The towns which produced crops, mainly grains, also invented ways to store and keep track of those grains. The culture seems to have invented writing for the purpose of keeping track of things like grains for the purpose of trade, and also seems to have developed increasingly sophisticated kilns to make pots in which to store the grains against pests.

Eventually kilns developed which could produce enough heat to melt metal, and townsmen became the early producers of both clay pots and metal products. Metal was also useful for making weapons, and the technology of metal work was a guarded military secret for a long time. Metal workers need raw materials and there were no copper or tin or iron ores in the towns or nearby. This development gave rise to a need to open trade routes to get these things, and the opening of trade routes meant a need for a military to protect the caravans. Since it is easier and

more certain to own your own mine than to trade with somebody else, it became quite profitable to go out and colonize other lands and peoples to get the raw materials.

All this metal working and pot making and mining and transportation required more and more supportive labor. As trade developed, towns became permanent marketplaces and the markets generated needs for increased production that required more people employed in making trinkets and tools. Those people had to have other people who would protect, feed, house and supply them. In addition, there were others who were employed at managing the affairs of the town, its economy, and at seeing to people's spiritual needs. Each step in this expansion of civilization required and motivated the evolution of technologies, a process which could be called technological dialectic. Technologies arose and became popular according to needs in every case. When the Natural World failed to provide (and the Natural World does not provide for civilized needs), some inventor came along and developed a substitute.

These technologies arose in response not to human needs, but to the needs of that peculiar form of human organization known as civilization. In the ancient world the kind of pot that spawned the kiln that eventually smelted metal was not invented for the purpose of keeping a small family's grain safe from pests. It was invented to produce big pots which stored grains in the royal grainery. Most of the technological innovations such as metal processing were invented for the benefit of the city's need for trade goods and weaponry, and were not invented for the good of some now distant abstract called Humanity. In time, civilizations would completely forget the distinctions, and they will use the word Man to refer to Civilized Man. The conventional wisdom has it that technologies, at least some technologies, benefit Mankind. The historical fact is that Technologies were invented to benefit civilization. There is a difference.

Civilizations (especially Western Civilization) had the potential from the very beginning of being destructive to the point of being self-destructive. It is in the process of civilization that a region is exploited without regard to its material (ecological) limits. When humans become "civilized" they cease being "citizens" of a region, and they become actors in a process which disregards the reality of regionality.

The conventional histories to which Western peoples are exposed propose that histories are composed of personalities, battles, and dates of events. Those histories would have been more enlightening had people been required to look at the rise and fall of civilizations in material terms. How did each produce food, develop water resources, or provide its people with clothing? What was the source of raw materials, and what were its sources of energy? What technologies characterized the various sectors of production? Did the technologies of these civilizations meet with crisis, did they ever cross over an "invisible line" at which technologies were doing more harm than good? Conventional histories never seem to concern themselves with these questions.

The conventional wisdom has it that great civilizations fell because of invasions of barbarians and the imprudent leadership of morally deficient kings and emperors. But the area which was once called the Fertile Crescent is today a desert caused by centuries of soil erosion and salinization which were the long-term effects of technological innovations which once made the same area bloom. The conventional wisdom seems woefully incomplete. Barbarism and poor leadership may have been factors which appear at the decline of civilizations, but the causes of the erosion can be found elsewhere. Long before the barbarians reached the city gates, the limitations of technology had been reached, and the contradictions inherent in certain technologies had begun to take their toll.

Technologies have always defined cultures, and cultures have always had at least some impact on environments. Western cultures and Western technologies have

been defined by the objective, inherent in the culture, of supporting overly large concentrations of population. The underlying driving technoforce of the West has been expansion for the purpose of providing for the needs of population concentration. Decentralization of population centers is seen as the most serious of sins, for it is anathema to the culture, and the culture's technologies, en masse, are not adapted to that purpose. It will become clear as this discourse continues that the concept of an 'invisible line' has to do with a given technology's purpose. All technologies serve a purpose. When that purpose is to support inappropriately large population centers, then that technology has "gone over the line," and the contradictions of the purpose of that technology become visible.

It is arguable that the economy of a civilization—the market system—is the motivating force of the modern technological dilemma. In the Modern World, technologies of agriculture, for example, are not in any way divorced from the market system. We are living in a time when the needs of Western economies have clearly stated priorities, even within the Western economy. Given a need for the agricultural land versus a need for electricity, the culture of the West has clear priorities in favor of the electricity. Food is merely a commodity in the marketplace and receives no priority consideration because of its role in sustaining human life. The land, and its life-supporting function, is expendable. Subsistence farmers, whose existence makes more sense in a regional, millenial and species-specific terms, are readily sacrificed to the needs of the urban

centers. Lands which are flooded for hydro-electric projects are considered regional or national 'sacrifice areas.'

Western culture experienced critical periods of change whch gave rise to these kinds of priorities during the First Millenia A.D. The so-called Dark Ages were a period of major technological change. The ancient world was powered almost entirely by direct sun energy. Beginning around the Fourth Century, power-driven machinery appeared as the result of the development of windmills and water wheels.

Such inventions enabled the introduction of power-driven bellows which enormously increased the potential for the production of iron. Iron production required huge amounts of charcoal which was produced from hardwood trees. Iron also provided a material for tools which could cut down the European forests. At this same period, the iron plow was introduced which was now pulled by horses which were made more efficient for this purpose by the invention of the harness. The axe-cleared forest could be plowed and cultivated through the use of this technology by far fewer people than had been required previously, and the increased efficiency of this mode of production made it possible that more people were freed for more functions in the system of feudal estates which this technology made not only possible but inevitable.

All of this was unfolding as the motivating force behind the spread of the Christian techno-revolution. Christianity is an ideology of technology because the Christian message is that the pagan gods and spirits of the forests, mountains, streams and so forth are false gods and that streams and rivers aren't really sacred. Christianity paved the way for the philosophy that there is nothing wrong with taking an axe and a plow to the forest and reducing it to so much charcoal and so many acres of cropland.

By the Fifteenth Century, feudalism had spread through Europe, its cities were established, and the people were suffering from the plagues which accompanied the incredible filth that characterized that period of history. The forests were largely eroded. The symbols of that period are a man and a tool, and the Four Horsemen of the Apocalypse. The by-products of Medieval technology were the pressures which led to the European settler expansion into the Americas, Africa and Australia.

The technologies of ship construction and navigation probably "saved" Euro-

Jim Turner/LNS

pean society as we know it. Those developments made possible the mass transport of populations from Europe to the rest of the world (and mass transport of food and materials from the rest of the world to Europe) and ushered in the Modern World. New technologies enabled that process to take place at an ever faster pace. The inherent crisis of urban techno-society was delayed for several centuries by the "discoveries" of new lands, resources, and the adaptable technologies of non-Western peoples.

The Nineteenth Century saw the development of fossil fuels which delayed the crisis which was developing when the hardwood forests were becoming depleted. The use of fossil fuels led to entirely new dimensions of population growth and concentration. It is hardly remarkable that technology became a kind of religion in the West.

People had long ago abandoned "faith" in God as a way of life. Christ's admonition to people to trust in God (read Nature) when he said that God provides for the birds and will provide for the faithful as well. That idea was entirely disregarded by the Christian world. It was considered, in a manner of speaking, advice "for the birds." In fact, the West has developed more food-storage technology than any other people to guard against the possibility that God might not provide for the future. The true religion in the West was better expressed by the sentiments that "God Helps Those Who Help Themselves," and the more ways people invent to help themselves, the better.

At each point in crisis in Western history, the invention of new technologies can indeed be said to have "saved" the culture. So much for Faith. Have faith in technology, it works. At least, it has always seemed to have worked because there has been some new resource to tap when the old resource was exhausted, and because the West conveniently forgets those historical periods when no resource could be found and technologies depleted peoples' resources and left them stranded.

In the Twentieth Century, we are viewing the continuation of the drama of Western Man in his quest to stay one step ahead of disaster. Until now, the West has continually adopted technologies with disastrous results, but for more than four centuries it has been possible, whenever things went wrong, to simply move on to new frontiers.

Ever since the West embarked on this

path, necessity has truly been the mother of invention. What has changed has been what was necessary.

Some years ago, a film comedy sequence circulated which depicted a man who had spilled ink on a rug. To remove the stain, he had to get some ink remover, but the bottle cap was stuck. To open the bottle, he got a pair of pliers, but those were rusted together. To fix the pliers, he had to get a can of oil, but the oil wouldn't flow out of the can so he need a pin to open the hole. And he couldn't find a pin.

Something similar to that has been happening to technology over the past two centuries or so. The Industrial Revolution set in motion some entirely new processes and brought forth some new problems. Industrial technologies which the conventional wisdom said benefited everybody also produced dangerous by-products. Paper mills produced a lot of paper but also produced a lot of effluence and the people of Minneapolis had to build 18 water purification plants to put the water into a condition that people could stomach it. The cheap technology was never developed that could remove all the chemicals, and if everybody's drinking water was filtered through activated charcoal filters or distilled, true water purification would cost more than the entire dollar benefits of the industries that polluted the rivers in the first place. The problem with most technologies since the Industrial Revolution is that they involve the production of some kind of toxic chemical—lead emissions from cars, sulphur acid compounds from steel mills, carbon oxides from just about everything that burns—and the scale of those toxic chemicals has reached cataclysmic proportions.

Civilization-supportive technologies have always been ecologically destructive. We are now reaching a crisis whereby modern technologies have made much larger cities possible and have speeded up the process of habitat decay which in Mesopotamia took millenia. In fact, the Industrial Age may last only a few

poisons of many types condemn all complex organisms in the Northern Hemispheres.

The technologies of the Twentieth Century need to be approached with the same kind of materialist critique as was applied to the economics of the Nineteenth Century by writers like Karl Marx. How much does a certain technology—say coal-generated electrical power—cost the society when all the costs are included, including the costs of acidified land and forests, fish life and fuel transportation costs, acid runoffs and stripmined land? Can we begin to evolve a methodology—a technology of social critique—which weighs things in terms of Hopi thought—i.e. biomass costs? If we take a simple "essential technology" of the 1980s world and we then apply a regional analysis of its cost in biomass terms, we may find that we are rapidly eroding something that may be termed the Life Supportive Index of that area. And if we analyze the present technologies and their impact on North America, we may find that they are uneconomical in the Life Supportive Index balance book, even if we apply a price tag to the resources in dollar terms. It seems inevitable that we will find that the kind of society that we find ourselves in today is in fact a physical impossibility over the long run (the centuries-long run) and that what will be possible will require, out of necessity, an entirely new approach to the purpose of technology.

Right now, we are looking at the possibility that this culture will designate all the Northern Hemisphere as a "national sacrifice area." The present technologies have the ability to destroy the life support potential of huge areas of North America to the point that no culture, as we know it, can survive in those regions affected.

The television images of the future that is being pumped into the head of America's children offers the vision of a future haulocaust with total or near total destruction of the Natural World. The survivors of that haulocaust, according to these TV writers, will be those techno-aristocrats

LUPA/LNS

centuries before acid rains and chemical who find some answers in the form of man-produced and man-controlled environments. Their scenario seems to be about half right. The haulocaust part seems logical, and the idea that different technologies will be employed by humans thereafter, but will that process (assuming human survival) produce the automatic-door controlled-environment city that we are presented in popular science fiction?

Highly complex technologies have tended to disappear with past civilizations. The Etruscans developed incredibly sophisticated ways of fusing tiny gold balls into decorative patterns more than two thousand years ago. Modern science has been able to duplicate the effect, but we're still not certain how they did it then. People built great pyramids in Egypt and in Mexico, but the technology of stone cutting and moving was lost for hundreds of generations. There are numerous other examples of lost technologies, but one must ask why techniques of doing things could become forgotten.

Perhaps it was because those techniques of doing things cost those societies more than they could afford to pay. We should consider those questions when we look at technology from the perspective of the Twentieth Century. Technologies which generate centralization and which support that centralization are the very ones which pose a danger to the Life Support Index of our environment, just as similar (and now antiquated) technologies for the same purpose destroyed the LSI of civilizations past.

When the West makes an error, it tends to compensate for that error by continuing to make the same mistake, only at an accelerated rate. Those TV writers are crazy. They are telling the children of North America that Super-civilization technology got us into this mess, and Super-Super-civilization technology will get us out. That's crazy.

The Hopis are right. The power lines are a symbol of the end of this world as we know it.

BROOMSTICK

A PERIODICAL BY, FOR, & ABOUT WOMEN OVER FORTY

From *Broomstick* 2, no. 8 (July 1980): 10

Something Old, Something New

by Mickey Spencer

I live near a park which for ten years was cared for by the people who use it. Now the city is taking it over and making it into a "real" park. I watched the bulldozers viciously biting into the soft grass, digging up helpless plants, and bruising stately trees in order to make everything fresh and new. The ancient raspberry bushes crawling up the old wall were hacked down and replaced by a shiny new cyclone fence. Meandering footpaths were replaced by straight new concrete walks.

This national passion for throwing out the old and starting out new and "fresh" seems to me to have a lot to do with how older people are treated in this society.

But this throw-away mentality is now coming into conflict with another passion: —ecology: save, reuse, preserve. A very enthusiastic young ecologist patiently explained to me the conservation methods she recommends. I told her that since I was born during the Depression and grew up during WWII, I learned to save paper bags, elastic bands, and aluminum foil many years ago. Until recently, young people considered me a bit odd for doing this.

I hope we midlife women can benefit from this reawakening of appreciation for what we already have. Among the Navajo, a person of any age who is especially wise is called *hosteen*, meaning wise. Witches were usually women who had survived long enough to have gained great wisdom. I think now is a good time to foster and encourage this reality about ourselves.

Reprinted from *Broomstick: A Periodical By, For, and About Women Over 40.* 3543-18th St., San Francisco, CA 94110.

HOT TIMES

From *Hot Times* 3, no. 1 (February 1980): 7

What Is Appropriate Technology?

by T. Paul Robbins

A 1950's building was once defined as "something you plug into an aircondi-tioner," says Wilson Clark, California energy advisor.

This is the nuclear house, the reason why the Austin anti-nuclear vote lost last April. The suburbs felt threatened and believed that nuclear power was the only way to maintain a high-energy lifestyle. They may be right. Can the suburban lifestyle coexist with an energy shortage?

Appropriate Housing

There are many types of building methods that can save 50-90% on heating and cooling requirements.

The Savell Passive Variant Home in California uses walls made of concrete with insulation on the outside. The walls draw heat up in the winter thru a deep-set foundation, and draw heat down into the earth in the summer. The earth has an average temperature of 50-60 degrees, so the massive walls can collect and store solar energy in the winter and draw it away in summer. The cost is competitive with

Reprinted with permission from *Hot Times*, Austin, Texas.

conventional homes, yet it saves almost all energy used to heat and cool the home, for a saving of 60% of total energy.

On another scale, the Center for Maximum Potential Building Systems in Austin is working on homes made from native-earth materials like caliche and clay found in the region. The main cost is the labor to make the brick. These homes are important because they don't require imported building materials, promoting self-sufficiency and local employment.

David Blevins, a local Austin contractor, has done phenomenal work with gunnite-spray concrete houses. The frame of a house is laid with steel rebar and road mesh, then concrete is sprayed in a dome-like shape. These houses cost *half* of what it costs to build conventional housing. They do not need air conditioning, and with some modifications would not need much heating.

Solar water heating, with minimal gas back-up, can supply 50-90% of hot water needs. The most expensive hot water heaters can cost $2000 and still pay their cost back in money saved in 7 years. Solar water heaters trap sunlight in a glass top box to heat copper or aluminum. Metal can increase efficiency, but also cost. The Center for Maximum Building Systems has designed a 50% efficient hot water heater for a cost of 20 dollars. It is made from used fluorescent light tubes mounted on a recycled waterheater and then placed on mounting boards covered with recycled printing plates to further intensify the sunlight. The temperature will reach 150 degrees in summer and 90 degrees in winter.

Grapevines can be planted on the roofs of houses to keep the inside temperature 20 degrees cooler than outside. These vines take only 3 years to reach full growth, and shade the house in summer, yet die back in winter to let in sunlight.

Appropriate Waste Treatment

Sewage could be mixed with solid garbage in a giant pond—the fats, oils and plastics skimmed off the top, the metals combed with magnets. The solid ceramics would fall to the bottom to be used in roadbeds, the remaining slurry could be treated for pathogens and applied to farmland or forest floor. The water could be purified by sinking toward the water table.

What cannot be re-used can be reduced in a device called the Wallace/Atkins Biomass Generator into oil, natural gas, and charcoal.

Cindy Fredrick/LNS

Other methods of on site disposal, such as gray-water filtering systems which purify wash water and self-composting toilets which reduce waste by natural deterioration into usable fertilizer have great advantages.

Appropriate Energy

Remaining power needs could be provided with safe, decentralized energy production such as the Schneider Lift Translator, an incredible design for windmills and hydroelectric turbines that works on velocity rather than the height of the dam or the size of a wind propeller. It uses foils, like the wind flaps on airplanes, to catch the velocity, and can produce electricity for only 3 cents a kilowatt hour. Austin's rate is currently 5.6 cents a kwh and New York City pays 12 cents a kwh.

Another worthy invention is the Solar Dynamics generator. Heat collected from a parabolic mirror is taken up a liquid sodium wick to a storage vessel of eutectic (storage) salts, which can store heat to run a turbine for 20 days. It can also be put near residences or buildings, with a potential cost of about 2 cents a kwh.

One type of solar cell made by Selectro-Thermo in Dracut, Mass. collects heat and generates electricity at about 11 cents a kwh, falling to 8 cents with mass production. This invention is cost effective *now* in the Northeast.

Appropriate Society

These appropriate technologies could lead to a resurgence of small businesses and neighborhood self-sufficiency, alleviating much of the need for gasoline. Appropriate technology provides us with sane use of technology, maintains a comfortable standard of living without a huge waste of energy, makes for a more socially equal and less competitive society . . . an alternative to the nuclear house.

It is quite possible that several types of alternate power may be cost effective with conventional power soon—some methods, like windmills, are competitive now; others, like solar panels, may be competitive by 1986.

CO-OP
MAGAZINE

From *CO-OP Magazine* 7, no. 3 (May/June 1980): 22-28, 38-41

Powergate!

by Martha Retallick

Reprinted with permission from *CO-OP Magazine.*

Most of us probably place high voltage powerlines in the same class as highway underpasses and tunnels: they all interfere with the car radio. Imagining life without these lines seems almost like imagining life without electricity itself. So we resign ourselves to that bit of static in the middle of our favorite songs as we drive under the wires.

But there is a growing number of people

who think powerlines are not the benign bearers of electrical energy we once thought they were. For the better part of the last five years, the farm fields and small towns of western Minnesota have been a battleground in the struggle against a powerline built by two rural electric cooperatives, the Cooperative Power Association (CPA) and the United Power Association (UPA). Opponents have vowed to fight this line for 50 years if they have to, claiming the power it transports isn't needed now or in the future. Many of the line's most vocal opponents are rural members of the cooperatives that built it; they argue the line was not built for them but for the fast-growing urban areas the co-ops also serve, and they are paying for city power with sharply increased rates. In some cases these rates have doubled over the past two years.

The line has not just hit the residents of western Minnesota in their pocketbooks; many farmers who own land under or near the route of the line claim the line has affected them and their livestock physically, and they say they have the headaches, skin rashes, infertile cattle, and aborted calves to prove it. In 1977, the state's Department of Health recommended that the line be built but cautioned that research on the biological effects of high voltage transmission lines is still in its infancy. The state warned public school systems not to allow school buses to load or unload beneath the line. Farmers were told not to refuel their tractors under it. Today, many Minnesotans say they are tired of being used as human guinea pigs. They want the line turned off so health effects can be studied in research laboratories rather than in their croplands and pastures.

Also fueling co-op member protests is the line's cost. Since the project was begun in the early seventies, the price tag for the line has risen from $600 million to over $1.2 billion, due to inflation, cost overruns, and protests against the line. Neither side agrees on how much each of these three problems has raised the price; antipowerline forces zero in on cost overruns due to mismanagement, while the co-ops focus on protester vandalism and inflation.

At the heart of the controversy is a ± 400 kilovolt (400,000 volts) direct current (DC) transmission line that traverses 440 miles of primarily rural land from a coal-fired generating plant near Underwood, North Dakota to Delano, Minnesota, where it branches off into two smaller 345 kilovolt alternating current (AC) lines. One of these branch lines is already operating; construction on the other has been delayed pending the outcome of an appeal to the Minnesota state supreme court by opponents contesting the legality of the entire project. So far, powerline opponents have lost every case they have brought against the project. But despite their dismal record in the courts, opponents feel they have no choice but to sue the co-ops to make them responsive to their members.

Why Rural Electrics?

In 1935, it is estimated that only one American farm in ten had electricity. On unelectrified farms, kerosene lamps lit the house and the barn, windmills and hand pumps drew the water, and ice cut from the farm pond kept the refrigerator cold. Few who lived this life would want to return to it.

The private utilities were not about to take up the task of rural electrification.

They saw little profit potential in serving small numbers of customers spread out over a wide area. Not that these utilities were run by dark or sinister characters who had conspired to keep electricity out of the country; centralized power generation and distribution simply lends itself more easily to areas with high population density. Fewer poles and wires needed to be strung in order to serve such areas as Manhattan, not to mention the smaller distance meter readers and other service personnel need to cover in making their rounds.

During the Great Depression, the United States government finally stepped in. In 1933, the Tennessee Valley Authority (TVA) gave preference to farmer cooperatives and other rural co-ops in determining who got the system's surplus power. Then in 1935, President Roosevelt proposed a federal agency, the Rural Electrification Administration (REA), to guarantee loans and provide aid to rural electric co-ops. At first, Roosevelt's proposal was greeted with suspicion in the cooperative community. James Peter Warbasse, then president of the Cooperative League of the USA, cautioned against cooperative alliances with the "political state," since that state might gain control and "give self-help enterprise a bad name." Other co-op leaders wondered how government loans and influence squared with the Rochdale Principles to which most modern cooperatives adhere. Many farmers refused to grant easements for rural electric co-ops and would not give the co-ops permission to cross their land.

But by 1936, the Rural Electrification Administration had won congressional approval. The REA's mission was to help farmers and other rural residents obtain cheap, reliable electricity with low interests, long term loans. This it did well; nine out of ten farms had electricity. Today, rural electric co-ops serve 75 percent of the U.S. land base and own and maintain 44 percent of America's electric transmission lines.

UPA and CPA

The central players in the present controversy, United Power Association and Cooperative Power Association, are both generation and transmission cooperatives; that is, they generate their own power or purchase it from other utilities. CPA, with headquarters in Edina, Minnesota, sends its power to 19 member distribution co-ops throughout southern and western Minnesota. UPA in Elk River, Minnesota serves 15 distribution co-ops throughout

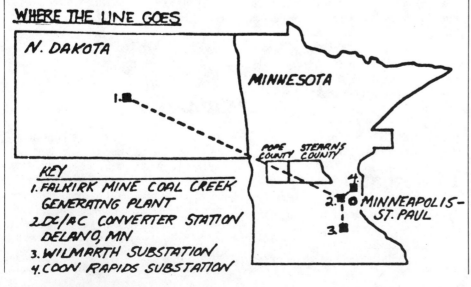

WHERE THE LINE GOES

N. DAKOTA

MINNESOTA

POPE COUNTY   STEARNS COUNTY

MINNEAPOLIS-ST. PAUL

KEY
1. FALKIRK MINE COAL CREEK GENERATING PLANT
2. DC/AC CONVERTER STATION DELANO, MN
3. WILMARTH SUBSTATION
4. COON RAPIDS SUBSTATION

northeast Minnesota and western Wisconsin. The electricity sold by both co-ops serves approximately one million people in Minnesota and Wisconsin.

Although most CPA and UPA members live in rural areas, the local distribution co-ops which have grown the most in the past few years are located around Minneapolis and St. Paul. In fact, recent figures show that about 20 percent of the co-ops' members live in the seven-county Twin Cities metropolitan area. As the Cities continue to expand out into rural areas, that figure is bound to grow; meanwhile, however, electric co-op membership in rural areas is declining. Opponents of the powerline say the future result will be a net decrease in electricity demand.

Despite the opposition's claims, UPA and CPA say their member demand is growing at seven to ten percent annually. The co-ops expect their future growth rates will be less, because of conservation and other factors, but they emphasize that demand will not decrease as protestors have predicted. "Historically," says literature put out by the co-ops, "the loads of rural electric cooperatives have increased at a faster rate than those of utilities nationally." Both UPA and CPA experience highest demand during the winter months; both say they have already reached the limits of their generating capacity and are running a deficit. With the line, they expect at first to have surplus generating capacity which could be sold to utilities outside their system. In two years, they say, their members will need this power.

Both co-ops saw these energy deficits coming as far back as 1972. That year, the co-ops say their power suppliers could no longer assure them that power would be available in the late seventies and early eighties. Even if this power were available, the co-ops predicted that the cost of purchasing it from other utilities would be more if they generated that power themselves. Unable to afford the costs of building two separate systems to meet rising member demand, CPA and UPA agreed to construct a jointly-owned power facility. The project would consist of a coal fired plant in North Dakota and a high voltage direct current powerline to carry the electricity to Minnesota. At Delano, Minnesota, a converter station would be built to convert the direct current electricity back into alternating current, the kind of electricity used in the home. From Delano, the power would be carried over two more lines, one heading north to UPA's service area, and the other heading south into CPA's area.

In 1973, the Minnesota legislature passed a law creating a state Environmental Quality Council, which required environmental impact statements for major projects such as the CPA/UPA line. The Minnesota Environmental Quality Council also had the power to choose the site for power plants and high voltage powerlines. A grandfather clause in the law exempted projects that began construction before July 1, 1974. By the end of 1973, the co-ops had applied for Rural Electrification Administration financing; the REA granted the co-ops an initial loan guarantee of $537 million in February 1974.

The following month, the state legislature passed a law that set up the Minnesota Energy Agency, which required that any major power generation or transmission facility built in Minnesota must first obtain a Certificate of Need. Rules and regulations for this new agency were not ready until November 1975. The co-ops did not obtain their Certificate of Need until 1976.

By July 1974, construction of the Delano converter station had already begun. This early start qualified the project for exemption from the siting law under the grandfather clause; CPA and UPA later voluntarily submitted their route for review and received approval from the MEQC. Also in July, the co-ops signed a contract with the North American Coal Corporation, the nation's largest independent coal company. Since REA loan rates were far below commercial rates, and since the coal company would save millions if the co-ops financed North American's Falkirk Mine and the proposed 1,000 megawatt generating station at the western terminus of the powerline near Underwood, North Dakota, the co-ops agreed to finance North American's part of the project. In return, the coal company agreed to supply the co-ops with six million tons of coal annually over the expected 35-year life of the Underwood facility. In November 1974, the REA approved an additional $96 million in loans to finance the coal mine and generating plant.

While up to this point UPA and CPA had done everything legally in the technical sense, the effect of their actions was not yet clear to their members or the public. When it became clear, the co-ops were hit with the public protest that still plagues them today, five years later. Early in the game, these protests went beyond public outcry. A co-op booklet says, "Some county planning commissions and county boards opposed a line routed through their counties and recommended the imposition of impossible or illegal conditions to permits with one county attempting to adopt new zoning regulations to exclude transmission lines.

The co-ops make a point of saying that such protests have been largely confined to Minnesota. "In fact," they say, "some 98 percent of North Dakota landowners chose to sign voluntary easements with CPA-UPA." But the co-ops fail to point out that the line crosses many unproductive stretches in North Dakota rather than areas such as the fertile small farms of western Minnesota. Minnesota has become the hotbed of protest because its people feel financially and physically threatened by this line.

Life Under the Line

Matt and Gloria Woida of Sauk Centre, Minnesota have opposed the powerline for

BUT SECRETARY SCHLESINGER, USING A NUCLEAR REACTOR TO BOIL STEAM FOR ELECTRICITY IS LIKE USING A BLOWTORCH TO

FOOSH

...WARM A BABY BOTTLE

SOUNDS REASONABLE

Jorgy/The Inkworks/Free for All/LNS

several years now. They are dairy farmers and have worked hard to make their land the productive place it is today. They are also members of the Stearns rural electric co-op, one of the 19 co-ops that comprise the Cooperative Power Association.

In years gone by, Gloria Woida was, by her own admission, "a middle class farmer's wife yelling about the boys who 'wouldn't go fight for their country' in Vietnam." No longer. For the past four years, this middle class farm wife has fought side by side with former antiwar activists from the Twin Cities in a very different battle. She has become one of the most articulate and outspoken members of the movement against the powerline, a movement which has also forged links with antinuclear groups and the American Indian Movement, and whose leadership has called the farmers "the new Indians."

"We first heard rumblings about the line in 1976," Woida says. By that time, protests were underway. When surveyors came to Stearns County, they had to be escorted by state troopers; they were greeted by angry farmers determined to hold them off with tractors, manure spreaders, baseball bats, even a couple of BB guns the troopers thought were high powered rifles.

In early 1977, the Woidas were notified that the powerline would cross their land and the co-ops were going to exercise their right of eminent domain in taking land needed for construction. By that summer, concrete bases for the steel towers had been installed on their farm. The day before the rest of the towers were to go up, the county sheriff came by their farm with a warrant for the arrest of the Woidas' 16-year-old son, Gerald. He was accused of pointing a shotgun at a powerline construction truck as it drove by. Although his parents were not home at the time, they do not believe Gerald did such a thing; Gerald also denies it. Nonetheless, he spent the night in jail and was to have a hearing early the next morning. However, Gerald's hearing was delayed until late in the day.

"They told us they were typing out the formal complaint, but when we finally saw it, it was only five or six sentences," Gloria Woida recalls.

Finally, the hearing was held and Gerald was released to the custody of his parents. As they drove up to their farm, Gloria Woida realized the reason for the delay: construction work on the towers had been finished that day while they were in court. Later, the Woidas received a letter telling them the charges against their son had been dropped. The Woidas demanded a formal apology from the Stearns County attorney; they never got it.

As the powerline towers marched closer and closer to the Twin Cities, the Woidas and their farmer colleagues gained new allies. The farmers had begun the protests, but soon found they had friends in the environmentalist and appropriate technology camps as well. The movement became not just a struggle against a powerline, but a struggle for safe, decentralized energy. Those who had once chanted "Hold that Line" had also begun chanting "No Nukes" and "Stop Big Oil." Like reports of Mark Twain's death, media reports of the death of the antipowerline movement in 1977 were greatly exaggerated. In October of 1978, a rally at the Delano substation billed as a "peaceful rally for justice" featured a march up to the gates by several demonstrators carrying a "condemned" sign. Police arrested them before they had a chance to attach that sign to the gate. The resulting court trial brought the protesters international attention.

The movement also gained clout in the political arena. Antipowerline activist Alice Tripp ran for governor of Minnesota in 1978. While she spent only $5,000, she received 100,000 votes in the primary—20 percent of the total.

The Unanswered Question

A key concern of the protesters has always been the effect that high voltage powerlines have upon animal and human health. Little scientific research has been done in this area, and the results have given ammunition to both sides. So far, the co-ops have not convinced the protesters that the line is completely safe, but the protesters have failed to convince the co-ops that the line—one of the most powerful ever built in the United States—should be shut down for good. Among the most vocal protesters are farmers who live with the line every day.

Ken Thurk, a dairy farmer from Villard, Minnesota, has been active in the struggle against the powerline. Like the Woidas, the Thurks farm is alongside the line. Ever since the line was energized two years ago, Thurk has noticed "a definite decrease" in his herd's milk production. The herd has also experienced two miscarriages and three premature calves were also deformed. One of his daughters developed a rash he attributes to the powerline.

Perhaps the crowning blow is what happened to the Thurks' electric bill. The longtime Runestone Electric Cooperative member notes that his rates have doubled since the line began operating. For several years, Runestone has had a running battle with CPA over the way the whole electric generation, transmission, and distribution system has been run. Runestone members believe they have been overcharged by CPA, and have voted several times to revoke their membership. They have recently been joined by five other CPA member co-ops wanting to do the same. So far, all have failed to gain the approval of the majority of the 19-member system needed to cancel their 35-year contract with CPA.

Despite the farmers' claims to the contrary, the co-ops maintain that their powerline is not harmful to man or beast. So far, says CPA's Robert Sheldon, there has been "no reliable evidence" produced that shows that powerlines such as this one are dangerous. He adds that the line traverses 16 counties in North Dakota and Minnesota, but so far complaints of ill health have only come from two counties in Minnesota: Pope and Stearns, both centers of protests against the line.

The Powerline Now

Today, the powerline operates, but sporadically. Periodically, insulators on the towers get blasted by shotguns—a case of the "insulator's disease," in movement parlance. Sometimes, one of the towers—which each cost at least $100,000 to replace—falls to the ground following attacks by the "bolt weevils," anonymous groups of irate humans wielding wrenches. These persistent weevils plagued the line long before it was finished; they most likely will continue to be a thorn in the system's side for years to come. The power co-ops have already tried posting guards along the entire length of the line; that didn't work. During the winter of 1977-78, the residents of Pope and Stearns Counties lived under martial law; that didn't stop the antipowerline movement either.

Antipowerline forces are now pinning their hopes on the outcome of a state supreme court appeal by the Southern Landowners Alliance of Minnesota (SLAM). SLAM was formed in 1979 to challenge the legality of the 345 kilovolt line that is slated to go from Delano substation to Mankato, 76 miles to the south. Members of SLAM contend they were not properly notified before their land was condemned through the co-ops' right of eminent domain. Should SLAM win, the movement will have gained its first victory following a long string of defeats

Are the Health Effects Being Suppressed?

When Virgil Fuchs chased some powerline surveyors off his farm in June 1976, he didn't know he was starting a protest movement against the line that would still be going today. The Belgrade, Minnesota dairy farmer belongs to the Stearns electric co-op, a part of CPA. He initially feared the line would cut up his land into separate pieces.

At first, Fuchs went through the proper legal channels, registering his discontent about the line along the way. He sat on two committees set up by the co-ops to evaluate the line route. In addition, he went to public hearings held by Minnesota Environmental Quality Board early in 1976. Later that year, the MEQB, by its own admission, destroyed some of the transcripts and tapes of testimony from those meetings. A corrected transcript from one of the hearings in which Fuchs participated had an estimated 150 gaps and unintelligible portions during testimony by farmers and expert witnesses on health effects, TV and radio interference, and powerline noise levels.

Two years after the missing tapes fiasco, CPA and UPA sponsored a two-day trip to the West Coast to see a powerline just like the one they were about to turn on. The co-op invited 93 people—both for and against the line—to come along. They visited the Bonneville Power Administration's ±400 KV DC line that goes from Dallas, Ore., to Los Angeles. One of those who went was Fuchs.

Along with other tour participants, Fuchs talked to landowners along the line, as well as experts from Bonneville. From his own inquiries, Fuchs estimated that the line was only operating at one third its normal capacity while the tour group was there.

Back from the tour, the co-ops said, "The question of health effects seemed to fade." Not for Fuchs. Today, Fuchs speaks bitterly about the line. It divides his land as he'd earlier feared it would. When he stood under the line in Oregon, at the estimated one-third capacity, he didn't feel a thing. Not this one. "It's like a vise on your head," Fuchs says.

But Fuchs and his family are not about to pull out their electrical cooperative in protest. Until they can generate all of their own electricity, they have no place else to go.

troopers. In 1978, both the Woidas and the Thurks were surrounded by a group of angry powerline workers after a series of incidents in which workers shouted obscenities at the Woidas as they drove past their farm. The farmers were outnumbered in this confrontation which easily could have erupted into violence; the Woidas feared for their lives that afternoon. They began sleeping with guns by their beds. For the Woidas, things will never go back to being the way they once were.

"I don't mind being called a radical," Gloria Woida now says. "I know we'll win in the end."

For more information on the UPA-CPA powerline, contact:

Cooperative Power Association (CPA)
3316 West 66th Street
Minneapolis, Minnesota 55435
(612) 925-4556

United Power Association
Elk River, Minnesota 55330
(612) 441-3121

Twin Cities Northern Sun Alliance
1513 East Franklin
Minneapolis, Minnesota 55404
(612) 874-1540

General Assembly to Stop the Powerline (GASP) publishes antipowerline newsletter
Hold That Line
Lowry Town Hall
Lowry, Minnesota 56349

Southern Landowners Alliance of Minnesota (SLAM)
c/o Timothy Hiniker
RR 1, Box 241
Kasota, Minnesota 56050

Martha Retallick is an assistant editor of CO-OP.

---

suffered in the courts. However, UPA and CPA feel confident they will defeat SLAM, and will be able to complete their $1.2 billion project by the end of the year.

But even if the co-ops win, the opposition believes the system will never operate successfully, and that it will only succeed in destroying UPA and CPA. They don't buy the co-ops' forecasts of an annual increase in electrical demand of seven to ten percent, and maintain that electrical demand has taken a permanent downturn because of conservation, a slowed economy, improved energy efficient, and the rising cost of electricity. One protest leaflet notes, "With electrical demand down, sales drop. Revenue will therefore be lower than anticipated, and to pay off the enormous debts incurred by their [powerline] project, they will have to raise their rates even higher. But this will drive demand even further down, necessitating higher rates, reducing demand, and continuing the vicious cycle into bankruptcy."

Whatever happens economically, the human side of the powerline debate has already brought major changes in the lives of Minnesota families like the Woidas and

the Thurks. Before the line came through, many of these people had never even received as much as a parking ticket. But last year, Jackie Thurk was arrested and convicted of assault after picketing at a powerline worksite. Her husband, Ken, has also been arrested and has photographs of himself being kneed in the back by state

Northern Sun News

From *Northern Sun News* 3, no. 3 (March 1980): 5, 9

Powerline Health and Safety

by Wendy Wibert

When Frances Slynn of Lowry walks beneath it while it's "crackling like sizzling

Reprinted with permission from *Northern Sun News*.

bacon," she says her artificial stainless steel knee buzzes and hurts. She also says her neighbor blames it for her recurring nosebleeds.

Ten sabotaged towers, 40 felonies, and over 100 misdemeanors later, the controversial 800-kilovolt direct current power line running through western Minnesota is finally transmitting juice. But the fight's not over—just stalemated for lack of evidence that the line is responsible for the recent epidemic of health problems in the area.

Many residents living along the line, which stretches from Delano to Underwood, N.D., claim they have suffered a host of inexplicable health problems since the power was first turned on. Common ailments include nosebleeds, fatigue, headaches, irritability, skin rashes and high blood pressure. At least two miscarriages have also been blamed on the powerline, although this has not been medically proved.

In fact, nothing has been proved, which is the root of the current problem.

The companies who built the line for over $1 billion, United Power Association of Elk River and the Cooperative Power Association of Edina, argue that researchers have been unable to adequately determine the effects of high-voltage DC electricity upon plants, animals and humans. Therefore, they conclude, the line must be safe.

The Minnesota Department of Health agrees with the power companies. "There isn't any evidence pointing to adverse health effects from DC power lines," said research scientist Larry Gust. He added, however, that more controlled research needs to be done on the issue.

Historically, man's curiosity with electricity began centuries ago, peaking in interest in the 1800s. Although many experiments were done on the nature of electric currents, nothing definitive came from them. The subject then was virtually abandoned until the military developed renewed interest in its effects on living organisms following World War II. Again, in spite of extensive research conducted by the Navy to determine behavioral changes in primates exposed to high-voltage fields, no solid answers were obtained.

They did discover, however, that ozone and air ions are also produced by electric currents. Later research has loosely linked these to respiratory problems and skin rashes, but in general, the subject of electricity-induced effects remains a mystery.

"I don't know what to think," said Dr. Vincent F. Garry of the University of Minnesota's Environmental Pathology Laboratory. "There is a tremendous need for research about electric fields and their effects on biological organisms, but studies already done are no help today and anything I could think of would cost millions and still be incomplete."

Reports given at the 1978 Pacific Northwest Laboratory's workshop on effects related to high-voltage DC transmission indicate that such fields can affect the immunological system, the nervous system, the cardiovascular system, behavior and exposed skin. A Veterans Hospital of Loma Linda, Calif., reported an increase of glaucoma, infertility and abnormal bone growth in exposed laboratory animals.

Critics are reluctant to accept such results readily, much less apply them to humans. "Much research on the hypothesis that high-voltage lines pose a serious health risk has been done on poorly-engineered exposure systems and was not validated by replication," concluded the Electrical Power Research Institute in their December, 1979, *Journal*.

But the people in Lowry don't care much about research—they want action right now. The strong citizen movement that has protested the line ever since the planning stage is spearheaded by the General Assembly to Stop the Powerline (GASP). Additional support has come from independent groups like Northern Sun Alliance.

Since most of the line passes over western Minnesota's rich farmland, a large number of farmers are involved in the protest. They say their families, like others in the area, have exhibited physical symptoms associated with electrical exposure. They also have witnessed a sharp increase in the number of aborted calves, a decrease in milk production, and general infertility among their livestock, according to Debbie Pick of GASP. And they blame it all on the powerline.

Farmers have also observed that birds change their flying patterns, wildlife flees, and cows and horses pastured near the line keep their distance while the line is transmitting, Pick said. "Animals have a high degree of sensitivity to electrical fields," she said, "and they evidently think it wise to stay away."

However, these observations are contradicted by Jack M. Lee of the Bonneville Power Administration in Vancouver, Wash., who studied the nation's only other DC line in Oregon. "Studies show that wildlife is basically unaffected by the line and in fact animals were observed grazing under the towers, using them for shade," he said. In fact, pictures taken during the study show eagles nesting in the power towers, although Pick argues that this is because the Oregon line is seldom used.

"Besides, if that is true," said Pick, "then

Bonnie Acker/LNS

I am worried that it is all part of an adaptation process where the animals are becoming 'electric junkies,' so to speak." She said some physicists have expressed concern that electrical fields interfere with natural fields in the body, creating a potentially habit-forming need for the interaction with external fields.

In any case, Pick is convinced that the people near the line are suffering real afflictions, not psychosomatic symptoms, as some pro-line people have charged.

Kate Randall of Northern Sun Alliance agrees. "No matter how much the line is hated, I refuse to believe that so many people would be exhibiting similar symptoms none have ever had before," she said.

Randall said the farmers' main complaint is that they "feel like guinea pigs."

"Their kids and livestock are sick and no one has any answers," she said. "All they want is for someone to shut it (the line) off until more is known."

Instead, the Health Department has opted for a feasibility study this spring to determine if a full investigation of the line is necessary, according to Gust. The study

would characterize the field, monitor the ion density during varying weather conditions, investigate the potential for shocks, and monitor farmers during the growing season when exposure is at a peak. "All of which would take between five and six years," Gust said.

In the meantime, the department has made no provisions for medical teams to study those who claim to be suffering from the undiagnosed symptoms, nor are they offering much immediate help. And the farmers feel more like guinea pigs than ever, according to Randall, because they are the ones being observed for effects this time, not laboratory animals.

"We've been playing footsie with the Health Department for a long time, and now they've dumped us in the lap of the Environmental Quality Board," said Pick. "Now GASP is entering negotiations with the EQB for action, not time-consuming research," she said. "They know very well what's going on, but they won't do anything about it—there's the controversy."

The present status of the controversy is

best summed by Tabershaw Occupational Medicine Associates in a recent report issued on high-voltage lines. "There is small doubt that the planned studies will turn up some field-induced effects. The questions about how serious these risks will be will continue to be debated in the regulatory and political arenas, and decision-makers will have to grapple with the issue of how one discriminates between a biological effect and a biological hazard."

WELL-BEING

From *Well-Being*, no. 55 (1980), p. 22

Litter: The Problem with a Throw-Away Society

by Christopher Nyerges

Wilderness. The very word suggests virgin land, pure and unadulterated, clear and fresh flowing water, tall majestic stands of trees, oxygen to fresh it hurts to breathe and as far as you can see, land unspoiled by the hand of man. All this, and more, was true "once upon a time . . . "

Due to a literal explosion in hiking, backpacking and outdoor sports, fragile

Reprinted with permission from *Well-Being: The Do-It-Yourself Journal for Healthy Living.* Christopher Nyerges is the author of "A Southern Californian's Guild to Wild Food" and "Urban Wilderness: A Guidebook to Resourceful City Living." He writes newspaper columns on hiking and biking, recycling, survival skills, and alternative energy.

environments are now being endangered and garbage is collecting on the trails. Backpackers and mountain climbers, who as little as ten years ago visited pristine mountain wildernesses, now report that many of these same areas are filled with the discarded items of campers. Many are shocked in their disbelief—others are both saddened and angered, knowing that once a wilderness area becomes so littered and damaged, it usually continues to degenerate and may never fully recover.

Someone who carelessly throws down a candy wrapper or empty bottle on a city street will likely do the same in the wilderness. This action may be justified by the deceptive thought of "Someone is paid to pick up my trash." But in the wilderness, miles from the bustling activities of the cities, the trash will normally just stay where it is tossed. And all of us do pay—not just in dollars—but with a deteriorating environment, lack of beauty, harm to wildlife, poisoned soil and water and countless other minute ecological changes that, added together, spell bad news not only for the health of the wilderness but for

all of us also. The work that is done to clean up the litter accomplishes only a "break-even" level of cleanliness at best—at a price tag of over a million dollars annually in only several national parks.

The Forest Service posts signs stating "Pack out what you pack in." But when the hiker loads his pack with weighty "essentials," many of these items are all too often discarded along the trail or in campsites as the work of the hike continues and becomes more strenuous. Many of these discarded items are going to be there for a long time, unless someone goes out of their way to pick them up.

Orange peels will usually decompose within a few months. Fecal matter will be decomposed within a month. Paper containers take up to five months to disintegrate beyond recognition. If you discard a worn wool sock along the trail, it'll be around for the next one to five years. Milk cartons and plastic containers will likewise be around for about five years. Polyurethane and plastic bags can take up to twenty years to fully decompose. Plastic film will be around for others to see for twenty to thirty years.

Nylon fabrics, such as pantyhose or ripstop, will take from 30 to 40 years to fully disintegrate. A leather shoe may take up to 50 years and a plastic Clorox-type container from 50 to 80 years to decompose. A

Vibram sole from a hiking boot will still be around for the next 50 to 80 years after you toss it. Polyester pants and clothes will take up to 30 or 40 years to decompose. All those convenient aluminum cans that are regularly discarded in wilderness areas will last from 80 to 100 years, and even longer if they are submerged in water.

Times of decomposition will vary depending on conditions. An item exposed to direct sunlight will decompose much quicker than one in a shady environment.

The shame of it is that those who do the littering may not even be aware of the consequences of their actions. Some litterbugs even look at themselves from a future vantage point looking back, and say, "Where would modern archaeologists be if the ancient Indian tribes did not litter?" I've heard this comment often enough to realize that some people actually believe and accept it, in spite of the fact that no real connection between modern litter and Indian artifacts exists.

But the modern litterbugs' "artifacts" do tell us something about the culture. Moderns seem to be bent on literally covering the entire surface of the earth with foolishly discarded bottles, cans, paper and plastic (much of which, by the way, could be recycled, thus conserving valuable resources and preserving the earth's beauty). Will we learn the hard way—consuming the earth's resources with such a voracious appetite that soon there is nothing left to consume as we sit in the great trashcan called Earth?

Each of us can take positive action by simply setting an example for others. The next time you are about to discard an object, ask yourself, "Do I *really* want to leave an object of my carelessness around for possibly decades?" And when you see others littering, speak up.

society garbage-people would occupy a most honored station.

For further information, you can contact Dan at OAT, P.O. Box 1525, Eugene, Oregon 97440.—Steven Ames

I. WHY IT ISN'T HAPPENING

Waste is the opposite of wealth; it is the residue left over after value has been extracted; it is nullity, a void . . . . Consume, waste, walk away, forget. This process is structured into our habits and our lives. It is The Way Things Are Done.

Anyone who has stood, as I have, through the long hours of a high-volume day at the dump, handing out informational leaflets, must conclude that it is a public spectacle, a massive ritual—dare I say it?—a deliberate flaunting on many levels of conspicuous wealth, real or imagined, temporary or permanent, paid for or not.

"Spotting loads" was a function we in Lane County's one-time Office of Appropriate Technology decided was necessary to maximize *Effective Recycling Behavior* in the early stages of our Metals Recovery Demonstration Project. One of our "spotters" would shepherd willing members of the public to separate desirable metals out of their mixed loads and drop them off at a metals recovery area. It worked! We made $2400 in hard cash—not free grant bucks—for the deficit-ridden county Solid Waste Division in our first (and only) ten weeks of operation, while segregating, sorting and marketing 30,000 pounds of high-grade elemental copper, brass, aluminum and steel at the Glenwood Solid Waste Center. In the process we doubled the volume of metals recycled through the county's metals operation.[1]

The success of this *highgrading* project, ironically, is also one of the reasons we were retired into involuntary unemployment by a county committed to the construction of a high-tech, failure-prone facility for centralized resource recovery. The highgrading project we designed is still going on—albeit in a crippled, inefficient form—but it now pays the salary of the former director of the Division of Solid Waste, who bailed out of the county's ill-fated experiment in garbage grinding before its final collapse, and into the arms of the largest private garbage-hauling contractor in the area. Casting a little light on such paradoxical behavior is one of the tasks of this article.

Journal of Appropriate Technology

RAIN

From *Rain* 5, no. 9 (July 1979): 10-14 and 5, no. 10 (August/September 1979): 4-7

Turning Waste Into Wealth

**by Dan Knapp
(and Steven Ames in Part II)**

A little homework will do wonders for Rain *readers before delving into this eye-opening exploration. That is—if you haven't done so already—go back and skim through "Mine the Trash Cans—Not the Land" in our November 1978 issue.* Written by the members of the Oregon Appropriate Technology consulting group, including Dan Knapp, it is easily our most requested back article. It is also a real revelation on how high-tech, mechanized resource recovery systems—like the dinosaur that lies idle*

*[Dan Knapp, Tom Brandt and Don Corson, "Mine the Trash Cans, Not the Land," *Rain* 5, no. 2 (November 1978): 4-8.—eds., *Alternative Papers.*]

in Lane County, Oregon—can be outperformed and outclassed by simple, labor-intensive hand-sorting systems that highgrade valuable metals out of the swelling solid waste stream. Turning Waste Into Wealth, *Part I, is Dan's broader indictment of this country's Waste Establishment—from the tunnelvision language it uses to create arbitrary divisions between liquid and solid wastes, forestalling the development of alternatives, to its anal compulsion to create totally new toxic waste problems out of the old ones it can't seem to solve. But just like the whole energy question, waste reality is changing very quickly. Many recycling microeconomies are already on line and working well—with even less subsidization than the solar alternative has enjoyed. It's entirely feasible that a larger recycling economy can pay its way. First, however, some barriers must come down. . . . In the* August/September Rain, *Part II of Dan's article, "How It Could Happen," will scope out some principles for organizing Effective Recycling Behavior in neighborhoods, successful examples and places to plug into for waste activism. It's been good working with Dan to pull this article together. I'm convinced that in an ecologically based*

Waste Knots

The spotter function was a real education in value. The thing that still haunts me the most is the occasional boxes I saw bearing assorted bottles of *biocides*—the kind you used to buy in the supermarket and now banned by the Environmental Protection Agency because they contained dioxins—all nearly full. The people who were dumping these boxes of liquid poisons thought they were doing a good thing: they were organic growers who had no use for pesticides and wanted to remove them from the homes they had moved into. And so these undesirables were intentionally consigned to the tender care of the Division of Solid Waste, not unlike the 30-gallon herbicide barrels someone tried to recycle through the metals recovery station one day, clearly labelled: DESTROY BY BURYING IN A SAFE PLACE.

What would happen next, I knew too well, was that some of the bottles would break after being thrown ten feet into the bottom of the pit, leaking their contents into the paper, food, wood, dirt and general disorder contained down there. The remainder would likely not survive the Terex tractor/compactor's inexorable push to the end of the pit, or the second drop down into the big White live-bottom transfer trucks that haul the well-mixed refuse to the county's new, experimental garbage mountain rising on the slopes of Short Mountain, whose collected waters—including small quantities of the *leachate* that has started squishing out of the rotten pile—drain down into Camas Swale, out into the south fork of the Willamette River, and back through Eugene on their way out to the Pacific Ocean. What do you think? Is Short Mountain a safe place for these biocides and their containers?

Salvage? Just Try To . . .

Here is another telling scene I witnessed from the catwalk at the end of the transfer pit at Glenwood: A woman was unloading two good, but old-fashioned, doors from her car. Next to her, a young man had just completed throwing his load into the pit, was straightening up, and saw those doors about to go over. Obviously, he wanted to ask her for them, but was indecisive. Chances are she would have given the doors to him, surprised that anyone would want them, but all the same glad to avoid the waste. But he didn't get the words out in time. The doors went down.

In fact, bound and determined to run its disposal operations efficiently, the Solid

Auth/Guardian/LNS

Waste Division can get downright mean when well-intentioned recyclers and other rule-breakers try to salvage valuable materials on their way to the pits. In a great many ways its purpose is to explicitly discourage salvage in favor of disposal. The designs invested in—like those at Glenwood Solid Waste Center and the rural sites, at Short Mountain and back through a succession of landfills—amount to an increasingly mechanized and centralized disposal system. This is what the fancy words Solid Waste Management reduce to in practice. Yet disposal is a myth. When you dispose of something, it still goes someplace. A wastebasket, a toilet, a drop box, a sewerline, a landfill, even an incinerator—these are places. Things disposed of continue to exist—and continue to matter.

Manic Disposal: End of the Landfill Era

Here are some national trend data on garbage, so you can see that our county is hardly alone in the mania for "disposal":

• The total volume of solid waste from mining, agricultural, municipal, industrial and sewage treatment activities is at least 2.8 billion tons a year and could be as much as 4 billion tons. This volume is increasing at a rate five times greater than the country's population.

• Municipal solid waste—the most difficult category of waste to manage—is the fourth-largest type by volume and increasing by 8 pecent annually.

• In urban areas where approximately 74 percent of the total population now lives, solid waste has doubled in volume in the last twenty years. While some 90 percent of the nation's waste is disposed of on the land, nearly half of all major cities will exhaust their landfill capacity within five years.

• Applying the current $27 per ton collection and disposal costs to our present waste volume, the annual national cost for solid waste management is about $7.8 billion, the third largest local expenditure funded from local revenues. If the 1985 projected costs of $50 per ton holds true, the fiscal impact of waste management on local government will be devastating.

• One great advantage of biological nutrient recycling over incineration schemes is that it can be done in smaller, more decentralized facilities located closer to the source of waste generation. This, inherently, is more efficient—especially when a high-quality end product and effective public education increase public acceptance and use of the humus and other forms of high-grade stored energy that are produced from the organic wastes.

• It is common practice to dispose of toxic materials at disposal sites not designed for hazardous waste disposal. Pits, ponds, and lagoons are often used for long-term storage or permanent disposal of liquid and hazardous wastes, and simple roadside disposal of hazardous wastes occurs as well. Although a large portion of buried solid waste is biodegradable, a small but significant portion of our waste volume—37 million tons—is extremely dangerous and capable of causing virtually permanent damage to our environment.[2]

Caught in the Act

Waste planners will tell you that nothing less than a system for disposing of the *total* volume of mixed waste is worthy of their attention. In sewage treatment circles, this is called the "baseline alternative," and it is the bottom line when it gets down to what the public's money is used to finance. Typically, all other smaller-scale methods, including recycling in its myriad forms, are rejected on the way to the Big Machine or the Big Burner. Either/Or, One-Best-Option at its best—the thought process is pure *reductio ad absurdum*. Here are some actual examples of waste planners in their act of exercising Either/Or, One-Best-Option logic to eliminate all small-scale, decentralized systems from consideration:

A personal favorite of mine is the set of working assumptions outlined by J. J. Troyan and D. P. Norris, engineers for the firm of Brown and Caldwell, in their cost-effectiveness study of "Alternatives for Small Wastewater Treatment Systems," paid for with a substantial grant and disseminated at public expense as a part of the EPA's Technology Transfer Seminar Program. Under the heading of *Problem Conditions*, Troyan and Norris recite the Catechism of sewage disposal:

> "To evaluate on-site sewage disposal systems and nonconventional community collection systems, three basic premises should be borne in mind:
> . . . if site conditions are suitable, the conventional septic/soil absorption system is the best type of on-site disposal system.
> . . . if costs are reasonable, a conventional gravity sewage-collection system is the best type of community system.
> . . . a conventional gravity collection system is the accepted standard for community sanitation against which all alternatives should be measured."

There you have it! While setting up their methodology for reviewing alternative sewage systems, authors Troyan and Norris manage to eliminate all waterless systems (primarily composting toilets), as well as most smaller, on-site biological water treatment systems, such as lagoons, greenhouse aqua-culture systems and recirculating sand filters from consideration! The rest of the book is an examination of the comparative economics of gravity versus pressure sewers, both of which usually assume conventional treatment. This citation has a special poignancy for me, as it has been utilized by Lane County's Water Pollution Control Division in by-passing serious consideration of on-site, small-scale nutrient recycling systems for local, small-town applications we have supported, and pushing ahead with standard sewer engineering. And what are the consequences?

A sewer system for water-borne wastes is the precise analogue of the open disposal pit for solid wastes—only it isn't open. It's a web of pipe underground and it has lots of small openings instead of one big one. Anybody can—and does—dump just about anything liquid into sewers. Everything gets mixed with everything else. Then chemicals along with mechanical and electric energy—all increasingly expensive—are used to separate the resulting goo into two fractions: a solid and a liquid. The solid is dried, aged and hauled by truck to various "disposal" sites. The liquid is doped with free elemental chlorine—a highly reactive element not found in concentrated elemental form in nature, at least on this planet—and piped into the local river, on its way out to the ocean. We are only beginning to understand the long-term effects of the presence of chlorine residuals in sewage effluents. The impact on aquatic ecosystems is frightening.[3]

Too Big, Too Small: Berkeley Gets Burnt

Sometimes, the Either/Or process can get pretty subtle: Berkeley, California, is facing the closure of its municipally-owned landfill (really a "bayfill" since it is several hundred feet out into the San Francisco Bay) by the early 1980's. So an engineering and architectural firm was hired as Prime Contractor to figure out what to do. Because there are strong recycling interests and widely-successful programs in Berkeley already, some recyclers were hired to do parts of the study. A good idea so far. A composting study was done, showing a small, but strong local market at a good price. A composition study was completed which revealed significant tonnages of recyclables were possible, given source separation. Meanwhile, in neighboring El Cerrito, the technical and social basis was being laid down for universal collection of source-separated recyclables. Perhaps reflecting these positive developments, the cover graphic for the three volumes of the Prime Contractor's report pictured a re-designed and upgraded version of a re-cycling center, including materials storage and a retail operation.

And yet, the Prime Contractor settled on a mechanized, centralized experimental garbage processing plant, including one or more incinerators to burn urban refuse. Since last year the whole thing has ballooned—from a single, experimental modular incinerator, to a 360-ton-per-day facility, to a projected 860-ton-per-day regional "burn plant," incinerating mixed wastes from the East Bay all the way down to San Leandro. The latest price tag is $10,000,000 set against a background of "potential" markets for the steam pro-

duced, a probable net energy loss when considering the complete process of burning refuse-derived fuel, unresolved, extraordinarily complex questions about toxic emissions, and a *still*-experimental and risky technology.[4]

To get a better sense of how this happened, consider the memorandum from a waste management engineer for the California State Solid Waste Management Board to the chief environmental engineer for the firm employed to coordinate the effort of providing "resource recovery" for Berkeley. Included in this memo are the conclusions drawn at a "screening of the alternatives" meeting between the various engineers involved, eliminating off-hand *all* biologically based recycling systems—including composting—in favor of the burn plant:

- Methanol, Ethanol, Ammonia and Hydrogen Synthesis were eliminated because several studies so far have shown that the economics of these processes require large systems of at least 1000 tons per day . . .
- Composting was conditionally eliminated. Although it is a demonstrated technology, there is not a demonstrated market for the compost in the quantities that would be produced by composting 200 tons per day . . .
- Biogasification should not be included. This technique is currently in a large-scale developmental process in Pompano Beach, Florida . . .
- Enzyme conversion of waste to protein is still in the early developmental stage; it is not ready for commercial operation, and therefore should not be included. The same can be said for using earthworms to convert waste.
- Fermenting waste to produce ethanol may be usable, but we have no information on any large-scale system using this process, except for a general description from Bolivia.
- Period.

So much for a consideration of alternatives. If I had to paraphrase this into a single statement, it would go something like this: "Biological processes were rejected because they are too big or too small, no single one is perfect, and we really don't know much about them anyway." Adding insult to injury, a subsequent document produced by yet another engineering consulting firm reveals that the planning has progressed to the point of *projecting the elimination of all recycling* at the Solid Waste Management Center, including materials storage and the retail operation, and even public access to the site—all as a part of the expansion to regional burn plant status.

Unfortunately, the "screening of alternatives" examples given above are all too typical of what is happening in waste planning circles as we near the end of the landfill era. In order to address this problem—and to make the people of Berkeley more aware that a labor-intensive materials recovery system would lead to remarkably different end results compared to any technology which indiscriminantly mixes and burns garbage—I was retained by local recyclers to critique the Plan as developed by their city's technical consultant. Here is part of my criticism concerning the decision not to put money or design time into anything but a burn plant.[5]

• Where did the 200 tons per day figure for composting come from? Even assuming 200 tons per day for the composting feedstock (a grossly inflated figure), there would still be less than 40 tons per day of finished humus to market or otherwise find uses for.

• What is a "demonstrated market," and why was this criterion not applied in the case of burning garbage as *fuel*, which not only lacks a "demonstrated market," but a "demonstrated technology" as well? (See *Rain*, Nov. '78).*

• What studies concluded that "economics of (alcohol) systems require large systems of at least 1000 tons per day capacity?" Did anyone look into the experience of China, which has built 4.3

_____

*Ibid.

Moviment Comunista de Catalunya/Organitzacio D'Esquerra Comunista/LNS

million small methane systems since the mid-1970s? Has anyone heard of the methane system being operated at the Washington State Prison designed by the Ecotope group? Did anyone contact Al Rutan of Minnesota, who has designed and helped to build several operating systems?

Trained Incapacity Is No Excuse

Evidently the engineers representing the city, the consultant group and the state were just ignorant of many of the systems they eliminated. While there are exceptions, it's generally true that engineers are rarely trained in biology or ecology, and are not made familiar with the experiences of "third world" countries, which have countless low-cost, operational, biologically based nutrient recycling systems. This built-in bias of the engineers often placed in charge of the planning phase of waste disposal needs to be exposed in light of the following:

• If, as seems undeniable, the problem of contamination of waste with toxic substances has been underestimated by engineers, then the commitment to rely on burning as the primary means of oxidizing and reducing the volume of organic matter will *increase* the quantity and quality of risks, while masking the effects. The pollutants will tend to travel faster through the airshed, and will be dispersed over a larger area. If air pollution of the type generated by the plant is deemed to be unacceptable, the community will have invested several years and a huge amount of paper credit for nothing—and more damage will have occurred in the meantime, making recovery more difficult.

• It can't be overemphasized that biological nutrient recycling systems do produce a usable end product—while incineration systems produce only a more concentrated and refined form of waste (e.g. ash, sludge or dust) or burden the environment.

• Nutrient recycling systems are themselves indicators of the quality of the inputs; if a worm-bed expires after being given a load of refuse-derived fuel to digest, it indicates that something is wrong with the refuse-derived fuel, and steps can be taken to adjust the infeed mixture, exclude toxics, etc. Such a "distant early warning system" is far more sensitive and timely than the lab analysis method, which had yet to devise tests for more than a fraction of the thousands of toxic and hazardous substances that have flooded our ecosystem in the twentieth century. It is also far less expensive.

The Threat to Biological Nutrient Recycling

More than ignorance, we are dealing with a distinct threat. Coming on the heels of a genuine flowering of labor-intensive recycling processes—all happening with little or no subsidy—the plan to usurp the largest share of available financing and credit to put incinerators and similar systems in place stands in direct contradiction to the major trends in effective resource recovery. Why should people be getting big money to talk and think about unproven garbage Supertech when labor-intensive recycling does it better *now* and could be expanded except for official stonewalling, harassment, lack of funding, lending capital and the like? Communities are being asked to transfer the pollution from the ground to the air, to put themselves at immediate risk, to accept welfare and "workfare" (the provision of a few high-paid jobs that often go to temporary, imported labor) in place of something useful, effective and productive to do. While Rome burns, we're all being asked to fiddle . . .

Research for this article was sponsored by the Lane Economic Development Council, P.O. Box 1473, Eugene, Oregon 97440.

_____

Notes:

1. *Metals Recovery Demonstration Project*, prepared by Don Corson, project design by Tom Brandt, Lane County Office of Appropriate Technology, 34 pp., 21 July 1978, out of print. (See *Rain*, Nov. '78.)*

2. William L. Kovacs and John F. Kluesik, "The New Federal Role in Solid Waste Management: The Resource Recovery and Conservation Act of 1976," *Columbia Journal of Environmental Law*, 3:205, 1977.

3. "Unnecessary and Harmful Levels of Sewage Chlorination Should Be Stopped," General Accounting Office, Report Number CED-77-108, 44 pp., August 30, 1977. This is a "study of studies" with a lengthy bibliography and further references and support literature. Excerpt: The National Academy of Sciences classify substances as "highly toxic" to aquatic life when 10,000 parts per billion will kill 50 percent of a test population within 96 hours. In the case of chlorine when tested, a 67% kill of brook trout was achieved within 96 hours with only 10 ppb. It has been acknowledged that early morning chlorine residuals from small wastewater plants may run as high as 22,000 ppb.

4. H. M. Freeman and R. A. Olexsey, "Energy From Waste: An Environmental Solution That Isn't Problem Free," in *News of Environmental Research in Cincinnati*, Industrial Environment Research Laboratory, USEPA, Cincinnati, 1977. "Very little has been published concerning the existence in refuse of potentially hazardous trace materials that might eventually

_____

*Ibid.

be found in off-gases and effluents." Significantly higher levels of heavy metals, ash and particulates, and chlorides are to be found in refuse-derived fuels than conventional fossil fuels, including coal.

5. *A Recycler Looks at Resource Recovery: The Berkeley Burn Plant Papers*, by Dan Knapp, 1979, $3.00 from Oregon Appropriate Technology, P.O. Box 1525, Eugene, Oregon 97440. An annotated commentary on proposals for garbage incineration strategies containing the critical analysis upon which much of the above article is based. Prepared under the auspices of the Community Conservation Centers of 2304 6th St., No. 2, Berkeley, California 94701.

PART II. HOW IT COULD HAPPEN

by Dan Knapp and Steven Ames

All the while, as our output of solid waste in this country multiplies and available landfills fill up, local communities are being encouraged by waste planners and equipment manufacturers to invest their credit in high-tech, high-capital "solutions" that promise to shred or burn solid waste out of existence. Some localities, compelled by the logic of doing more than simply burying waste, have taken such steps. Yet we're quickly learning that these centralized approaches to waste management often involve unproven technologies, questionable economics and unknown health risks. In treating waste so inflexibly, the high-tech people continue to draw community-based alternatives out of the equation—from sophisticated biological nutrient recycling systems, to practical source separation strategies, to the baseline possibilities for vastly reducing wastes generated in the home. Left only to the realm of experts, our communities, neighborhoods and individuals themselves may never find the chance to prove they can make the difference. It's *us* that is our own best hope.

Eugene Comes on Line

Looking at Eugene, Oregon, is a good case in point. I have been involved in this community's own unique responses to the waste imperative in the last few years, and have observed closely the experimentation and rapid development that has occurred in its various recycling systems—each evolving to fill a particular niche and every one changing with new conditions and possibilities. As awareness here continues to grow that the Reduce-Reuse-Recycle maxim is not only a matter of public ecology, but an energy-saving, job-producing alternative for turning waste into wealth and local self-reliance, it's probable

that newer recycling microeconomies will be brought on line, broadening this community's capacity to deal effectively with its waste. Here are some of the organizations now active in the area of solid waste that are starting to nudge Eugene towards sustainability:

● *BRING (Bring Recycling in Neighborhood Groups).* Still a good idea, BRING is the oldest of the post-Earth Day 1969 organizations which involves a drop-off collection system and processing center for handling recyclable post-consumer wastes. In 1979 BRING translates into a string of neighborhood locations—usually schools—which are visited by a truck (the BRING-mobile) on a scheduled basis to pick up bottles, flattened cans and cardboard and aluminum. BRING also receives recyclables at the Glenwood Solid Waste Center (site of Lane County's downed garbage grinder) which, with the help of the BRING-mobile, are further processed at the BRING headquarters and warehouse. BRING is a non-profit corporation partially subsidized by county monies and occasional CETA funds. It handles a large volume of recyclables but has also given rise to other recycling operations that have perceived new areas of need and new markets to be developed.

● *The Glass Station* is one of those operations: a non-profit corporation specializing in the retailing of reusable glass containers—those not covered by Oregon's Bottle Bill. It is amazing how good bottles look with their labels off and cleaned—by grouping them together attractive sets can be collected for any number of uses. A productive spin-off for the Glass Station has been to supply glass containers to co-ops and bulk food stores, which in turn resell the containers to customers as a convenience item. Such an operation illustrates perfectly the advantages of a *value-added* approach to re-use: the materials handled by the Glass Station are worth *minus* twenty dollars a ton if processed through the county disposal apparatus, *plus* twenty dollars a ton when recycled and sold as cullet, and an average of *five hundred dollars* a ton when sold as reusable glass containers! Started 2½ years ago by veteran recycler Alice Soderwall, the Glass Station utilizes a combination of paid and volunteer labor. With similar efforts it's certain that the value-added approach to reuse could be extended to any number of sectors—recycled dimension-cut lumber being a good example.

● *Garbagios,* not an outlet for Italian junk food, but a consumer-owned, worker-run garbage collection company is licensed with the city (Eugene has no municipal collection system) to pick up *source-separated* recyclables along with mixed garbage on a scheduled basis. The company charges the regulated fee for collection and sells the recyclables. Garbagios started as a very small project with two people, a small electric truck and forty customers, mainly environmentally-concerned people who wanted curb service as an alternative to drop-off recycling. Their recent promotional campaigns have been successful in generating rapid growth in customer demand for these services: only 1½ years since its inception, Garbagios has over 400 customers on five routes. A new addition this year is a larger truck with a custom-built bed having several built-in bins. Garbagios' experience is beginning to suggest that the economics is there for recycling-oriented companies to get into the hauling of commercial wastes as well.

● In addition to such new groups and new ideas are the more traditional approaches to reuse and recycling, *Goodwill, the Eugene Mission* and *St. Vincent de Paul,* all effective recycling organizations which have operated in Eugene for many years. Goodwill and St. Vincent specialize in reusable household goods, repairable appliances and clothing, while the Mission collects and markets an estimated 60 percent of the metro area's newsprint. All three use drop-off bins of varying design located in neighborhoods and shopping centers. Meanwhile, *Eagle Recycling*, a specialized paper recycling company, provides reorganized collection systems for recovery of high-grade office papers.

● With a diversified recycling economy growing, it's not surprising that recycling systems have started to mesh with public behavior and attitudes. Take the *Oregon Country Fair*, for example, a large, Eugene-based outdoor event which sponsors a varied marketplace lasting many days in a rural location. When its rapidly increasing volume of mixed wastes became a difficult collection and disposal problem, the fair staff reorganized its collection system—with the help of BRING—to provide for source-separation. Wastes were voluntarily separated by disposees into three categories: organics, bottles and cans, and mixed wastes (paper plates, utensils, etc.). Interestingly, the volume of mixed wastes generated dropped off drastically—a good reflection of Effective

Recycling Behavior as practiced by the public when given a rational collection system. In addition, materials handling by workers has been greatly simplified. It's a very popular system.

- As its experiences with local self-reliance increases, Eugene has also seen the creation of small consulting groups such as *Oregon Appropriate Technology*, which generally aim to further that transition. In addition to its other activities, OAT offers design services to communities and businesses wishing to initiate solid waste "highgrading" as a means of stimulating employment and generating large volumes of clean materials for reuse or resale. OAT also recently became involved in the design of collection systems that would feed into drop-off strategies such as those employed by BRING. Important back-up services for these alternatives are provided by groups like *Lane Economic Development Council* and *Blackberry Services*, which can advise on incorporation, business organization, capitalization, grants and so forth.

- And then there are the myriad repair shops sprinkled around the community, the free boxes, the quilters, stashers, composters, firewood cutters, house recyclers, junk artists, reuse dreamers—normal materialists with a different passion—people who get into the material before it gets into the solid waste stream, and as such do us all a great service. Theirs is the baseline of a larger recycling economy—behavior that needs to be encouraged.

Opportunities To Be Had

And there you have a feeling for one community's positive responses to our waste dilemma. Not the complete picture by any means, but a strong gauge of the capacity for people to start turning a crisis around in their favor with common sense and good work. What lies ahead will be conditioned by how quickly Effective Recycling Behavior becomes the conventional wisdom—including alternative demonstration systems on line—and how thoroughly the high-tech options are exposed for their inefficiency and inherent dangers. Somewhere in between, public officials and waste planners have a lot to learn—and to change.

Current arrangements are set up to frustrate and contain labor-intensive recycling. Mainstream plans, if implemented to completion, will lock up more and more capital and human energies into unprofitable, unworkable "resource recovery" machines that try to get a little electricity or steam hype from mixed wastes prior to "disposal." And don't forget the machines to clean up or compensate for the damages done by the primary processor units—the electro-static precipitators, sludge dryers, air and water filtration units. All drink lots of energy. Subsidies that allow garbage generators and collectors to make big profits off an energy and economic deficit sector should be ended in favor of source separation to permit recyclables to be marketed at a favorable price. This would defray rapidly rising collection costs and free budgets from the "albatross effect" of waste disposal subsidies going to garbage "interests." Small-scale recycling can thus be encouraged, capitalized, liberated.

It would help, too, if we would view action in this sector as a type of *production*. Materials saved are materials earned; that is, they are a potential feedstock for a potential production system. Direct sale for reuse is only one of the possibilities for marketing recovered materials. Materials may also be used directly in the production of entirely new goods, adding value and justifying a greater reward for imagination, creativity and *work*. As it stands, our system is organized to waste these materials and opportunities. But they *are* there to be had.

Comprehensive Neighborhood-Based Recycling: An Outline

It is such opportunities that myself and several others had in mind when we came together for a brainstorming session on neighborhood-based recycling systems not long ago. Our task was to plan a work program to get down to mobilizing Effective Recycling Behavior for an entire urban neighborhood, including the business and commercial sectors. People present represented the organizations with the "hands on" experience to know what they are talking about when it comes to the appropriate handling of waste materials. The neighborhood in mind was Whiteaker, Eugene's oldest neighborhood, the city's historic and cultural center, and recently the recipient of a one-of-a-kind grant from the National Center for Appropriate Technology to plan for maximum neighborhood self-reliance. The plan is not mine alone, but I have recorded it as it appears here; and while these are only objectives, they represent the shape of things to come—*if* we get behind and *push* to see that it happens. So don't be misled by its smallness, because it is capable of unfolding in all directions, as rapidly as we let it happen in our daily work. Now, here's what we'd like to do:

- Conduct a composition study and inventory, emphasizing waste audits for selected participating apartments, businesses or other large generators of wastes. This is a way of estimating the volumes and weights of recyclable "fractions" in the solid waste stream.

- Based on results, and keyed to the quantities and qualities recorded, locate or otherwise develop feasible marketing strategies or other exchange functions.

- Plan an educational and outreach campaign to increase public awareness and the practice of "source grouping" for recycling.

- Research and design efficient and cost-effective collection systems to make source grouping easier and more acceptable than "disposal." Aim for diversity rather than uniformity.

- Research and design materials transfer and storage systems appropriate to the quantity and quality of source-grouped materials recovered and discovered. An example, if using drop boxes, would be to construct liners or bins with handles which could be lifted out by a portable crane.

- Strengthen and work through existing local and labor-intensive recycling organizations.

- Include local young people by designing special attractions for them, including income opportunities. The same for older people, with the added proviso that their knowledge and skill be respected and encouraged. Let them be our teachers.

- Research and design central processing center(s) to facilitate a value-added approach to materials recovery. Include tool system.

- Identify and provide for segregation, cleaning, repair and marketing of reusable items.

- Stimulate secondary employment impacts by keeping materials organized and attractive, and by marketing in the neighborhood.

- Keep accurate records. Generate good working statistics.

- Develop strategic and necessary skills among project people: for example, lumber grading, metals cleaning and processing, marketing and bookkeeping.

- Encourage source reduction for undesirable, hard-to-recycle items. Encourage consumers to buy in bulk to eliminate excess packaging, etc.

- Provide information on program accomplishments to public decision-making bodies so that more effective decisions can be made on what to do with currently wasted resources.

• Think integratively and functionally, using the above goals to inform and direct daily actions. Planning, action, implementation and evaluation will happen continuously in each sector of involvement.

alternative sources of
energy

From *Alternative Sources of Energy,* no. 43 (May/June 1980), pp. 16-17

Muscle-Powered Conservation

by Andrew Maier

Yogurt-powered woodworking tools are the order of the day at an alternative high school in East Orange, New Jersey. Andrew Maier, shop teacher and anti-nuclear activist, is interested in the possibilities of muscle-powered machinery. To that end, he has built two treadle-powered woodworking tools, a lathe and a bandsaw, for use in the school's shop. The designer/ builder says that our lives have been "overpowered" through excessive use of electricity, and that wider use of "muscle power" is one way that Americans can wean themselves from the electric nipple. Andrew points out that after World War Two, cheap and readily available electricity spawned a host of wrongheaded appliances. Some are inefficient, like blow dryers and electric space heaters. Some things that worked just fine with muscle power were electrified (clocks and razors come to mind) with no resulting improvement in performance. And finally came uses for electricity that were just plain silly, like electric knives, tennis ball cannons, and finger nail polish buffers.

Goodbye to the On-Off Switch

Muscle-powered machines are a whole new way of looking at the work we do and the way we do it. Of course, doing with less electricity is not going to be an easy idea for many to accept. Some people who try out our bandsaw often treat the treadle as an on/off switch their first time around. They

take one step on it, feed in the wood, and then look surprised when the machine soon stops. Other people, brought up in this age of maximum consumption take one try at the machine and offer me some dubious "improvements" . . . "Hey, this is pretty cool—you could probably put a motor on it without much trouble!" That brilliant deduction was uttered by one of my own students. Like I said, getting unplugged is not going to be an easy task!

Our Freewheeling Tools

The mechanism itself is quite simple. A treadle pulls a bicycle chain over a five-speed bicycle freewheel. The ratchet action of the freewheel permits the machine to coast between strokes of the treadle, as a bike can coast without the pedals turning. The freewheel cluster and a Volkswagen flywheel are mounted on a 5/8 inch threaded shaft, powering a 14 inch pulley. The shaft turns in two automobile front wheel bearings whose races have been set into wooden blocks. The plain-looking machine tool uses standard size lumber throughout. Pieces are mortised and joined

with lag bolts to permit disassembly and modification. This same treadle module could be adapted to power a food grinder or mill, a jigsaw, sewing machine or tool grinder. An engaging "STEP HERE" sign graces the treadle board itself. With five gears to choose from, a steady rhythm on the treadle cuts wood several times faster than your arm will, and having two free hands on the wood assures control of the curved cuts that bandsaws do so well. The band saw was built from a kit sold by Gilliom Manufacturing Inc. of St. Charles, MO. A Sears, Rockwell, or nameless garage sale special will work just as well.

The freewheel is the heart of the lathe as well. Heavier construction is needed to dampen vibration when turning irregular pieces. More flywheel weight is used, on a 3/4 inch shaft through two pillow blocks. The apparatus, my fourth revision of the treadle lathe design, powers a standard Sears 12 inch wood lathe, bought cheap as a floor model.

Quieter than their electrified counterparts the tools are inherently safer, because they operate with less power and under greater control. Both were designed with accessibility in mind. Either one can be built, and hopefully improved upon, by people with moderate manual skills. Basic hand tools will do it. The only power tool I used was an electric drill. The basic treadle module measures 26 x 27 inches and is 29 inches tall. If all of the parts must be purchased, the cost will run about $80.00 but using scrap lumber can bring that figure down. The parts for either machine tool are available locally in most areas, and come from hardware, bicycle, and auto

whalen   Eileen Whalen/LNS

parts stores, with a trip to the junkyard for a flywheel or two.

As the cost of energy continues to rise, I'll be down in my shop designing and redesigning muscle-powered machinery. In the near future I will have plans for these tools available so that the idea of muscle-powered machinery can spread and be improved on by as many people as possible. If you're interested in plans or if you have some of your own ideas on the subject that you'd like to share, I can be reached at the high school: Changes Inc., 409 & 415 Prospect St., East Orange, N.J. 07017.

the magazine of radical science and peoples' technology

UNDERCURRENTS

From *Undercurrents*, no. 37 (December 1979/January 1980), pp. 9-11

Third World Energy

by Andy MacKillop

The supporting rationales and beliefs for the new wisdom are gaining more converts, at least in the West, by the hour. The usual arguments go like this: oil and gas supplies are depleting quite rapidly, but demand is still growing fast; the cost of these conventional energy sources is rising, to the point where *some* solar techniques are close to economic; and anyhow the great bulk of supplies are pre-empted by the West, and refined and distributed by Western oil companies. Producing, refining and distributing oil and gas requires complex, capital-intensive, large scale technologies. The fuels and the systems they depend on (like refining) cause pollution, and—usually the last argument marshalled to support the new wisdom—they are culturally 'inappropriate' to rural traditional peoples.

Each of these arguments contains truth, but not the whole truth, and has to be seen not solely through the Western world view. The process of economic social and cultural transformation going on in the LDCs has to date been based on fossil fuels (and hydro electricity), using entirely conventional 'Western' technology. These elements of the processes of change have been thoroughly assimilated—usually to a much greater extent than other Western imports, such as multi-party Westminster-style Government.

Short Supplies

The supply question is usually presented as the biggest and best argument for the new wisdom. There is just not enough oil and gas in the world to meet future demand. The LDCs, because of economic weakness, will get squeezed out of the picture first—so they *have* to go solar. The cause of this problem can simply and fairly be laid on the doorstep of the rich, Northern, developed nations. This group of people, the 20% of the global village who live in the smart part of town, are using 80% of world oil, and around 95% of world traded natural gas. Their political economies supposedly prevent any rational conceivability that they can use less, or different forms of energy. Over the past five years the North has responded, if that word can be used, to OPEC measures (price rises, production limits) to reduce demand by indulging in an orgy of inflation and unemployment. This has not gone unnoticed by the OPEC nations, who uniquely stand at the gap between both sides of the global village—they are ex-colonies of the West, but they hold the bulk of presently proven world oil and gas reserves, the resources that the West believes are its salvation. But they have no wish to extinguish their prime, and often only, export commodity. Neither do they wish the eras of direct colonial, and post colonial economic domination to linger on.

The OPEC countries are rapidly evolving a twofold political economic policy towards the users of their resources. They are getting *tough* with the rich industrial nations, and this is becoming much more evident because of the rising instability of the main oil payment currency, US dollars: and much *more flexible* with the LDCs. These nations, and particularly the newly-independent ex-colonies of the West, are seen by OPEC (most markedly by the Arab OPEC states) as urgently in need of real development support . . .

Ration the West and Help the Rest

Towards the West the OPEC nations have one simple, and bleak, policy: use less or face not only higher and higher prices, but actual physical rationing by quota or other mechanisms. The biggest reason for this is that oil production, and at a later stage gas production, must plateau off and begin to decline. As an immediate support to the LDCs several of the OPEC nations, in direct contrast to the West, have radically stepped up their aid. This can be called, cynically, charging people a new 'super high' price for something they cannot do without, and then giving them back a slice of the money that has been 'pirated' out of them. This is now a common response by Western energy and development experts when challenged on the *facts* of who gives how much aid. The Arab OPEC nations now give around 2.5% of their GNP, on average, to the LDCs— or *seven times* the average for the rich nation OECD club. It can easily be argued that the oil producers are, in fact, taxing the West and transferring some of the revenue to the LDCs, and actually helping the Third World by obtaining money they would not otherwise get from the West.

When we look at the current picture of where OPEC oil production goes, in relation to population size groups and political-economic affiliation, a massive asymmetry can be seen. The OECD group of rich nations are using at least 30 million barrels per day; a mere 10% cut in demand would free up sufficient oil to supply *all* the needs of the oil importing ASIAN nations, plus Pakistan, Taiwan, India and South Korea. That is, a population grouping of 800 million could have all their oil provided by a 10% cut in demand by the rich. We should not need to ask whether this is conceivable because many policy initiatives on energy growing in the West, most notably those following the Tokyo 1979 Summit, spoke of exactly this kind of cut being desirable and feasible. However it is much more plausible to argue that this kind of demand cut could only come through 'producer power', that is by OPEC deliberately restricting supplies.

It can also be argued that there is an *intrinsic* tendency for self-rationing of energy demand growing within the rich, or overdeveloped nations. This can be traced to the effects of economic processes such as business cycle recession; increasing structural unemployment; the growth of services and relatively low-energy activities (e.g. electronics). Each percentage reduction in growth of the Western economies leads to around a 1% cut in energy demand—appropriate energy management can ensure that this translates to a greater than 1% cut in oil (and imported gas), for example through upgrading the use of indigenous fuels, and conservation of energy. For the poor, or underdeveloped, nations the reverse is true—they *must* use more than 1% growth in energy demand to get a 1% growth of GNP, the reason being that as well as economic production they must achieve the growth of capital and therefore energy-rich, infrastructure and services. On equity grounds it is both rational and realistic to argue for faster growth in the poor nations. But without political admission of these facts it is convenient for the spokesmen of the rich nations, in all kinds of international forums, to say that the poor, as well as the rich, must be dragged down by high and rising energy prices. These same spokesmen can then argue, as they do, that yet more Western expertise and capital must be used to develop indigenous and usually high cost 'alternative fuels'. They do not go on to say that they hope this will cut demand for OPEC oil and gas, reduce prices and lenghten reserves, so that the rich nations do not *themselves* have to develop alternatives.

New Resources through New Co-operation

It is rapidly becoming clear that the world oil and gas resource picture is very

poorly known outside the established production zones—which for the 'free' World means N. America, parts of S. America, Europe and Middle East. A few figures show how little has been spent by the International Financial Institutions (IFIs), the World Bank and its affiliates, on finding more oil and gas, and developing it.

In the period 1974-76, and in relation to expenditure planned by the IFIs for 1977-81 a total of US $8.44 billion was planned to be spent on all energy developments in less developed countries. Of this some $8.367 billion was to be spent on electricity generation and distribution (much of this was oil-fired generation), and some $76 *million* was to be spent on all oil, gas and coal developments. That is the spending on electricity was planned at around 110 times that for oil, gas and coal supplies (World Bank Report 1588, 1977). The sheer inadequacy of this has been recognised, very late in the day, by the World Bank in its 'Programme to Accelerate Petroleum Production in the Developing Countries' (World Bank Jan. 1979). This makes the point that if nothing is done the LDCs will have an oil and gas import bill of around US $38.3 billion in 1985 compared with $14.3 billion in 1975. Recent price rises ensure that this figure is on the conservative side.

Based on the above figures the aficionados of alternative energy can claim that massive funds should be switched into the solar group of energy technologies. However this ignores at least two crucial points: the alternate fuels, apart from energy conservation (which is not a 'fuel') and *some* solar sources, are often *very* costly; and the likelihood of oil and gas finds, and

development of coal, in a very large number of LDCs is very good at the new international oil energy price. In regard to the costliness of alternate fuels it can be pointed out that Brazil, the country that has gone furthest and fastest with power alcohol fuels, needs a price of around *50 US cents* per litre for its sugar cane alcohol system to be economic. This is with probably the world's largest sugar industry, and the international sugar price down to historic lows—which means that alternate demand for sugar is very low. A price of US $150 per ton for refined oil products (i.e. over $20 per barrel) translates to only a basic price of around *12 US cents* per litre. Alternate fuels do not come cheap, and their development is only realistic when other economic, social and political factors play their part in making up the economic deficit they produce, compared with conventional oil supplies from the 'price gouging' OPEC countries. With many millions of workers in the sugar industry, and big landowners and corporations in a poor profit situation because of the low world sugar price, it was to Brazil's net benefit to develop sugar alcohol—there being an additional potential benefit that, if enough sugar went into fuel production, it might stimulate the world sugar price.

For most developing countries this is not the situation. Agriculture development should be tilted towards high value crops that can give good wages and fast rural development. But the rationale for accelerated oil and gas prospecting development in the LDCs is an even stronger argument against the 'alternate' fuels. The World Bank group, in its programme to accelerate petroleum production in LDCs made the point that exploration activities in some 38 countries out of 70 surveyed had completely inadequate accumulated data on which to make *any* conclusions regarding potential reserves; in another 22 exploration was 'moderate', i.e. very small scale in relation to that in the present oil production areas on the world. Of these 70 LDCs some 23 were judged to have High-Very High potentials for finding and developing commercial oil and gas, with the 'Very High' category meaning a good likelihood of finding oil fields able to produce 1.5 billion barrels or more (World Bank Jan. 1979). If this is then related to the total oil demand expected by the IFIs for the oil-importing LDCs in 1985, i.e. 7.2 million barrels a day, the possibility of making the entire group self-sufficient for 20 years or more was judged to be very good.

Nuez/Granma/LNS

Finding and then developing these sources remains the biggest problem, and it is, to say the least, complicated by the time factor—the rich nations show little inclination of limiting demand, and are becoming more brazen in their threats towards the OPEC nations. If they cannot control their warlike impulses, the kind of economic crash envisaged by Paul Erdman in 'The Crash of 79', due to attempts by the West to get oil by force, comes up as a real threat to the world.

The IFIs now acknowledge that there must be a massive increase in oil and gas exploration and development in the LDCs, and the January 1979 World Bank statement envisaged an increase in such effort to a level of around US $6.66 billion by 1985, compared to an estimate of some $13.3 billion being spent on oil search and development in rich nations at that time. While this is of course a welcome development it still only shifts world funding for such exploration and development to a situation where the oil-importing, majority LDCs have the *minority* of funds. Also, the IFIs of course envisage that the bulk of this work will be undertaken by Western companies using Western capital. Thus the long awaited advent of Technical Co-operation for Developing Countries (TCDC) provides *some* hope that this will not be the case.

Alternate Co-operation and Development

At present TCDC is in its infancy; however the concept now exists as a United Nations-level (affiliated to UNDP) organisation specifically for encouraging and organising the transfer of technical expertise and assistance *between* developing countries. Because the LDCs now include many oil producers, as diverse as Burma, Pakistan, Nigeria and Malaysia, it is reasonable to argue that at least a significant part of the technical expertise, as well as hardware, for the new World Bank plan for petroleum development in the LDCs can be obtained in and from other

The ITDG Power Project

One Appropriate Technologist who would not agree with Mackillop is Peter Fraenkel, Power Project Officer of the Intermediate Technology Development Group. For five years he has been developing wind and water mills and turbines suitable for local manufacture and maintenance in the Third World. Two are particularly promising: a run-of-stream river turbine and a microhydro electric turbine.

Run-of-Stream River Turbine

Traditionally, large undershot water-wheels were used in parts of the Middle East and the Sudan to tap small quantities of river current energy, but these are massive and material-intensive in relation to their power output, and are therefore uneconomic. With this in mind, the ITDG Power Project has developed a "low solidity" device which runs completely submerged in a river current and is therefore potentially quite efficient yet does not need much construction material. Initial work indicates that it can convert up to 40% of the energy flux, amounting to 720 W/m² (0.1 hp/ft²) from a 3 kt current.

This device is the same in principle as a Darrieus vertical-axis windmill or a Voigth-Schneider ship propeller. The initial prototype tested over the front of a motor boat on the river Thames is only 1 m in diameter by 0.5 m deep. It is planned to develop a larger version, to be suspended beneath a pontoon, for pumping irrigation water from rivers passing through arid regions (such as the Nile, Niger, Euphrates, Indus, etc). At the time of writing the Power Project is working on a design for a unit with a cross-sectional area of 3m² which could lift approximately 61 m³ (13500 UK gall) per hour against a 5 m (16 ft) head if submerged in a 3 kt (1.5 m/s) current. Large areas of fertile alluvial but arid soil that cannot at present be exploited economically for agriculture (due to the high cost of imported energy sources such as diesel or electric pumps) will become accessible to a device to this kind. We are hoping to test this prototype in Juba, Southern Sudan, in late 1979 or early 1980.

Later work will, it is hoped, result in a variant for electricity generation to

permit village electrification along well-developed rivers with adequate currents.

Microhydro Electricity

Most of the power projects have been preoccupied with lifting water, one of the most basic prerequisites for improved agricultural production in most parts of the world. However, rural electrification is another important need.

To this end, ITDG has supported work by an innovative hydro-power engineer in the West of England, Mr. Rupert Armstrong Evans, to develop further some promising small-scale hydro-electric equipment he has evolved. Some of this equipment is on the UK market and in use, but the Group and Mr. Evans have identified a need for low head turbines. Mr. Evans has also developed an electronic control system which eliminates many of the most expensive components in traditional turbines (e.g. no gates, spear valve, governor or mechanical linkage are needed) and which is more reliable and maintenance free with a quicker response than conventional hydro-mechanical control systems. For high and medium heads he has developed a family of Pelton Wheels which can also be electronically controlled.

As a result of identifying this need, ITDG has at its disposal a newly developed propeller turbine which can readily be machine-shop fabricated, economically in small quantities. Initial prototype testing gave an overall efficiency in the 65-70% range at a head of 4 m (12 ft), with a machine having an output of 6 kW. It is planned to test-manufacture and field-test prototypes overseas in the near future and several electronic controllers have already been sent by the Group to places such as Fiji, Nepal and Pakistan. At the time of writing about 30 are in regular use in UK installations.

For details of these systems refer to The Power Guide, *compiled by Peter Fraenkel and published by IT Publications (9 King Street, London WC2; 240 pp A4; £7.50 plus £1 p&p). This book lists a wide variety of internationally available small-scale power equipment and discusses the criteria for selecting an appropriate system for a special need; it is indeed "a mine of carefully assembled material".*

developing countries. When this new opportunity is linked with the recently-announced OAPEC and OPEC changes in aid and investment policy to improve and accelerate resource development in the LDCs, an altogether more hopeful approach can be taken towards the speedy development of new oil and gas supplies for the LDCs. It can be envisaged that TCDC, if able to freely use (i.e. without rigid tying) the increased funding available from the IFIs, can provide *much* more exploration and development effort, for the *same* costs, simply by using lower-cost non-Western expertise, plant and equipment. Greater provision of actual funds, from OPEC, can then be used to build a yet larger level of exploration and development. However it must be pointed out that TCDC has yet to prove itself in operation, and its earliest activities have concerned relatively small-scale rural development efforts in the main.

In many less developed countries the energy problem is just one of many problems that, by Western standards, are at crisis proportion. Taking the problem of wages, and the erosion of purchasing power through slowed economic growth, population growth, urbanisation and other factors of underdevelopment, a 1970 level of 100 for food and agriculture sector wages has shrunk to (in 1975) 69 in India, 61 in Philippines, and 57 in Bangladesh, while unemployment has risen an average of 50% in these and other nations of the UN ESCAP region. Many of such nations, despite nominal economic growth rates of 4% or so, have actual per capita GNP growth rates at around the zero to 1% per year level, while GNP per capita levels hover at not much above US $100-150 (UNESCAP 1979). To ask that such nations devote *hundreds of millions* of dollars to setting up high cost 'alternate' fuels, and use Western consultants, technology and capital—the most expensive there is—in order to do so, is both heartless and not practical.

For the rich nations the situation is entirely different: they have that rare combination of both duty *and* need, together with their own capital and expertise, to develop alternate energy sources. In doing so they can allow OPEC to keep up supplies to the LDCs while these nations develop *their own* petroleum sources. And in the next century, when these sources are themselves beginning to run out, the funds accumulated by the LDCs through exports of their own oil and gas, and though greatly

expanded economic activity based on secure and stable-priced energy, can be used to import the *Western* alternate energy systems. This does not, of course, mean that there should be no development of such energy systems in the LDCs—but it must be kept in proportion to likely reserves, be fully economic, and be approached without the hysteria that many Western spokesmen use to sell their new religion of 'energy independence'.

References

World Bank Report 1588. Minerals and Energy in the Developing Countries. World Bank, Washington, USA, May 4 1977.

World Bank Jan. 1979. A Programme to Accelerate Petroleum Production in the Developing Countries. World Bank, Washington, USA. January 1979.

UNESCAP 1979. Development Strategies in the 1980s for the ESCAP Region, UN Economic and Social Commission for Asia and Pacific. 1 August 1979.

the magazine of radical science and peoples technology
UNDERCURRENTS

From *Undercurrents*, no. 33 (April/May 1979), pp. 12-13

Wasting Away

by Timothy Cantell

Lord Strabolgi, giving the Government's views on the 'Strutt Report on Agriculture and the Countryside' last July, told the House of Lords that *'the steady increase in the amount of agricultural land taken for development is a cause of concern'*.

The soft-soap expression of caring seems rather mild when an average of 76,100 acres per *year* was transferred out of agriculture to other uses in the six years ending June 1975; and if that doesn't alarm you then remember that Bedfordshire covers 305,000 acres. So we are losing the equivalent of the entire county of Bedfordshire from farming every four years.

That paragon of established respectability, *Country Life*, has described the erosion of farmland as *'almost unbelievable collective national lunacy'*. Not only is our green and pleasant land being diminished but we are rendering ourselves more vulnerable to the uncertainties of European and world food supplies.

What is Lord Strabolgi doing about it? *'The policy of successive governments,'* he informed his fellow peers, *'has been to steer development away from higher quality land on to land of a lower quality whenever possible, and to prevent too much land being taken for any one development'*. In

Reprinted with permission from *Undercurrents,* the magazine of radical alternatives and community technology.

practice, the Government is protecting land in grades I and II while the remainder is largely expendable. But grades I and II add up to only 17% of agricultural land in England and Wales and even that fraction is far from inviolate.

There is certainly plenty of idle land available for development. The 'Centre for Agricultural Strategy' has estimated that up to 80% of urban land requirements in the next 25 years could be met from derelict and waste land. The *Urban Wasteland* report points out that the vacant land total for inner London (2,076) is only a little less than the area of Hatfield New Town (2,340) whose population is 26,000. Alice Coleman has found that the amount of dead and disturbed space in the London Borough of Tower Hamlets rose form 3 to 15% of the whole between 1964 and 1977 and she suggests that the 45 kilometres of corrugated iron erected must have cost at least £300,000.

The policy—albeit of successive governments—is inadequate as the statistics show. There will have to be a clampdown on the development of farmland of good and medium quality forcing developers to seek out the very poorest land and the huge acres of derelict and dormant land.

Wasteland has begun to appear on the political agenda. The Tories have promised a Domesday survey of publicly-owned land (they like to imagine there is no problem with *privately-owned* land) and the Labour Party's recent environment statement made several proposals including rating of empty land.

The Government however has done little apart from its inner city programmes and has not acknowledged that wasteland is a problem in medium as well as small towns.

Meanwhile some local groups are striking a symbolic blow for saner land use by cultivating land lying dormant. 'Friends of the Earth' groups in Leicester, Oxford, Redbridge, and many other places have been responsible for the successful tilling of idle land, and the FoE *Allotments Campaign Manual* is going into a second edition this year. Allotment associations themselves are taking on wasteland in places such as Reading and Cardiff. But vastly more could be done to bring together the 120,000 people on allotment waiting lists and the hundreds of thousands of acres of idle land.

The Civic Trust report, *Urban Wasteland*, called for a presumption against development on farmland, and suggested that anyone making a planning application to take land out of farming should have to state publicly:

• why the proposal was thought necessary;

• why it could not reasonably be located elsewhere, e.g. on vacant land in towns;

• and why it could not reasonably be located on farmland of lower quality than that proposed.

The local authority would refuse planning permission unless satisfied on all three points in the applicant's statement. So far the Government has shrunk from a move of this boldness, but the nettle will have to be grasped before long.

Despite current planning controls and Government policies, new development is mostly on virgin land on the edges of towns, while land becomes and remains idle within the towns. The evidence of corrugated-iron round wildernesses on the one hand, while builders' signs go up on green fields on the other, is there for all to see.

But Dr. Alice Coleman of the University of London is driving this point home with facts. From her surveys and resurveys of urban fringe areas, she is finding that the losses of farmland are accelerating, and that if present rates continue Surrey will have no farmland left in 130 years, a large area of South Essex and North Kent will have none in 87 years and Merseyside none in 39 years.

Manpower Services Commission labour could be used for the initial work of preparing the wasteland for use but only if a body is prepared to act as sponsor. In Bristol the 'Avon Youth Association' and the 'Youth Opportunity Centre' have converted a number of blighted or left-over sites to allotments using MSC manpower. Twenty-six plots have been created on British Rail land following extensive clearing, levelling, the provision of water supplies and the erection of huts and fences, and several further plots are planned including some in conjunction with the Windmill Hill City Farm Group. It is a good start but small in relation to the depletion of plots since the War. Bristol is not unusual in having lost half its allotments—from a peak of 13,500 in 1945 to just under 7,000 today.

With persuasion, local authorities, British Rail and other landowners may grant licenses to allow local groups to have temporary use of waste plots which may be needed one day by the owner. It would be nice to think that they might sell such land cheaply or donate it to community groups. Believe it or not this *is* happening in the USA where the Trust for Public Land acquires vacant lots and hands them over to locally-run neighbourhood land trusts. Apparently tax advantages sweeten the handing over of land in this way in the States.

From *WIN* 15, no. 30
(November 22, 1979): 8-15

Hugging Trees: The Growth of India's Ecology Movement

by David Albert

From newspaper and media accounts in the United States, it is easy to come to the conclusion that the gods do not look with favor upon the land of Gandhi. Cursed with poverty, disease, and over-population, India seems beset by a rising tide of natural disasters. Floods, droughts, typhoons, landslides, cyclones, tidal waves and famine return in a seemingly endless cycle of major and minor catastrophes.

But on closer examination we find that these disasters are not so "natural" after all. Changes brought about as a result of climatic and other natural conditions have been aggravated beyond proportion by the greed, quest for power, and downright carelessness of human agents. Tidal waves and cyclones have hit the east coast of India repeatedly, but the effects have been

Reprinted from *WIN: Peace & Freedom Through Nonviolent Action*, 326 Livingston St., Brooklyn, NY 11217.

distorted by the harvesting of trees close to the shoreline which had formerly acted as natural wind barriers and binders of the soil. The great Ukai Dam in Gujarat in western India displaced 180 villages. Since then the average rainfall in the area has dropped from 80 inches a year to less than 40 inches, changing the entire agricultural character of the region. Elsewnere, the lack of resistance of hybrid seeds to disease, shortages of chemical fertilizers and the lack of diversified agriculture have resulted in periodic famine. It is against this background of the subcontinent that the "Chipko" movement was born.

Uttar Pradesh, India s most populous state, is located in the north central part of the country. It shares a northern border with Nepal and China, and it shares something even grander—the Himalayas. The scenery in this region, known as Uttarakhand, is spectacular, filled with wooded slopes, sparkling streams, deep cataracts and mountain crests. It is a land of religious retreats, sacred shrines, and tourist outposts.

But like all of rural India, Uttarakhand is a land of great poverty. There is little cultivable land on the slopes and the population has increased beyond the ability of the land to support it. Those who are fortunate enough to get jobs usually work as lumberjacks, rock-breakers, or as porters for tourists. Workers generally receive from 1½ to 2½ rupees (19-31¢) a day.

The Uttarakhand area is geologically young and unstable, subject to periodic seismic shocks which cause the slopes to crumble. As population densities have increased, the forests have one after another been scoured for firewood at a rate much faster than the trees can grow back. This, combined with increased farming on marginal lands, has upset the ecosystem. The earth's surface can no longer retain its topsoil in the face of severe Himalayan weather conditions. Rain and wind, landslides and floods carry off precious soil nutrients, leaving patches of desert behind. The situation would have been very bad— even without additional political and economic factors.

Since gaining independence as a nation in 1948 and up until the fall of Indira Gandhi in 1977, India has followed essentially a single economic policy. Guided by the liberal Marxist thinking of Jahawarlal Nehru, the Indian economy was designed for the quickest growth of capital possible under a democratic form of government, and for the development of a new technologically oriented urban managerial class. This policy was (and is) consistently supported by the vast majority of India's Marxists who, like their compatriots in the Philippines supporting the Marcos regime, give first priority to the growth of an urban-industrial proletariat, even at the expense of human rights or the fate of the rural poor.

What has happened in the Uttarakhand region mirrors in embryo the economic direction of the larger society. The government forest department auctioned off trees at an increasing rate, starting in the early 60s. It made little or no attempt at creating local jobs or industry, but aimed rather at making it possible for industrial investors to amass capital and quick profits. Unsound practices in road-building, resin-tapping, dam-building, mining and quarrying, and the displacement of villages to virgin forest areas all contributed to the deterioration of the area.

As economic and "developmental" activity in the Uttarakhand region increased, unscrupulous labor contractors gained free reign over the area. In response, Chandi Prasad Bhatt, a young former bus company clerk, began to form labor cooperatives in 1962. For a time these cooperatives, with 700 temporary workers, began to threaten the monopoly of the construction contractors, who finally throttled them by

arranging the award of contracts to the co-ops at an assessed value lower than it would take to pay the workers to do the job.

Faced with losing contracts in construction, the cooperatives turned to the forests. Aiming to start cottage industries based on local natural resources, the Dashauli Gram Swarajya Sangh (Dashauli Village Self-Reliance Committee) was formed in 1964. They decided to bid on trees put up for auction by the forest department and hence try to create jobs for local people rather than make capital out of the trees. The community pooled resources in the Sangh. The success was short-lived, however, as the contractors bid forest lots beyond the financial reach of the Sangh and then made up their own losses through illegal tree-felling.

The Sangh then turned to medicinal herbs, a product which had afforded fantastic profits to traders who sold them to drug manufacturers. By pooling their stocks and sending Sangh workers to markets in Delhi, Punjab, and even Bombay, the villagers eliminate the intermediary traders and provide employment for more than a thousand people. With the profits they opened up several small factories for the manufacture of turpentine and resin from pine sap. They were convinced by now that forest resources held the key to their local economic survival.

The unusually heavy monsoon in the summer of 1970 flooded the entire region. Damage estimates ranged as high as $7.3 million (a huge figure in the northern Indian economy). The upper Ganges canal some 120 miles from the source became choked with silt and sand for more than 30 miles. The area was completely cut off.

The Dashauli Gram Swarajya Sangh prepared a report on the causes of the floods. They discovered that the deforested slopes had lost the capacity to retain water. As a result, massive landslides occurred. The river beds became filled with silt and rock debris, causing water to rise and flood over the banks. Although their analysis was ignored by the government, the cooperativists were never to forget their lesson in forest ecology.

The second problem which the cooperativists confronted was the avowedly socialist policies of the State government. In 1971, the government bought half the shares in a huge resin and turpentine factory. The small village cooperatives found themselves competing with the State

for raw materials provided by the forest department. As a result, the cooperatives brought raw resin at a price 30% higher than that paid by the factory co-owned by the State. While the State saw itself as socializing the means of production, the effect was to drain resources from the area, decrease local control, autonomy, and employment, and cement the State's alliance with the large shareholding capitalists.

The villagers began to hold demonstrations in October 1971 around three central demands: (1) an end to the contract labor system; (2) restoration of their traditional rights of securing fuel, fodder, and wood for home construction and agricultural implements from forests controlled by the forest department; and (3) an end to discrimination against smaller factories in the allotment and price of raw resin. But it would be two more long years before a movement was born.

The resin factories, lacking raw materials, closed for months in 1972. The Sangh found itself unable to pay wages and had to operate a common mess to prevent starvation. And then came the last straw which sparked the birth of the movement: tennis rackets!

American tennis buffs know that many of the best rackets made from light, durable ashwood come from India and Pakistan. For years, the Darshauli Gram Swarajya Sangh had requested and received a few ash trees to make agricultural implements—ox yokes and the like—for local use, as they had for generations. But in 1973 the forest department denied the supply, saying that instead they could use pine wood, which is heavy and weak. Meanwhile, the villagers at Gopeshwar, where the Sangh had its village headquarters, learned that the Simon Company of Allalabad, a manufacturer of sports equipment, had been allotted ten ash trees in the forest only six miles away.

When the agents of the company reached Gopeshwar with a permit for the trees they were to fell, local leaders of the four political parties in the area, village council representatives, several journalists and representatives of the cooperatives gathered to decide their course of action. Three protests had already been lodged with the State government. The State Forest Conservator was informed of the villagers' discontent. While official policy promised support to local industry, the government threw in its lot with the urban manufacturers. Tennis rackets are a lucrative export product.

Five suggestions were made at the agitated meeting of April 1, 1973: that the company agents and laborers be physically blocked from entering the forest; that the villagers lie down in front of the trucks coming to haul away the fallen trees; that the trees be cut down by the villagers before the company got there; or that they burn the trees as a symbol of their anger.

Chandi Prasad made his proposal. Since it wasn't their aim to destroy the trees but to save them, and since the future of the people in the region was wedded to the forests, he proposed that they *chipko* (embrace) the trees and let the axes fall on their own backs instead. The "Chipko" strategy was immediately adopted and word sent to magistrates and conservators throughout the area.

The State government promptly set up a new subcommittee to study the situation. Meanwhile, when the Simon Company agents showed up to collect the designated trees, they were startled by the size of the Chipko meeting at the edge of the forest. Unwilling to risk confrontation, the agents returned empty-handed.

The Government immediately tried to compromise by offering the local cooperatives one ash tree in return for the Simon Company's quota. The proposal was turned down and the Government increased its offer to three, five, and then ten trees. But the visions of the Chipko people had expanded beyond immediate needs— to the natural rights of the hill people to administer wealth, and the right of local cottage industries to priority in the use of forest resources.

It is likely that other forms of direct action might have been just as successful in preventing the cutting. But the "embracing" of the trees reduced to a socio-dramatic "picture" the inseparable relationship between the people and the survival of the forests. It made them recognize more fully that the forests had to be protected not only from unscrupulous contractors, but from their own unthinking wastefulness.

Fresh conciliatory efforts were made toward the Chipko movement as it gathered strength. The division forest officer informed Chandi Prasad that the Simon Company's permits for trees near Gopeshwar were being cancelled and the trees allotted to the Dashauli Gram Swarajya Sangh instead. The company would get its trees from Phata, 55 miles away.

And so the confrontation between the Simon Company and the Chipko movement was transferred to Phata at the request of the local people, with the same results. Word of the success of the movement spread, and the Government felt called upon to attack it. They were a government committed to the good of the people, and Chipko was a movement motivated by a narrow regionalism. The Himalayas were a national asset; they did not belong to a few villages. The forest resources benefitted the whole nation. Suppose people near a steel mill or electrical plant were to block distribution to the nation at large?

Nonetheless, the Government saw that its head-on collisions with the Chipko movement reinforced the movement's strength and speed by which it grew. Rather than do that, the Government abruptly lowered the price of raw resin to the cooperatives, hoping to take the wind out of the sails of a movement with much wider implications.

And it might have succeeded too, except for two factors. The first was "constructive program." The regional Gandhian "Sarvodaya" ("welfare of all") movement decided to join forces with Chipko's central thrust of forest preservation. One of the principles of Gandhian work in India is that it is impossible to prevent people from relying psychologically upon a central-state bureaucracy to meet needs unless the people themselves learn how to meet these same needs without it. The Gandhian movement thus began to teach people how to care for the forests without the oversight of the State Forest Department. Workers set out on long "padayatras" (consciousness-raising walks) to educate the villagers, just at a time when the movement would have otherwise been without a sharp focus.

The second factor was another set of flash floods following the monsoon in August 1973. Once again, the people had to face the fundamental reality that, regardless of government policy, there would be no life at all for them on the mountain slopes without the forest intact.

In the fall of that year, the Simon Company aggressively tried to swing public opinion. Agents went from village to village stressing that the company had fairly paid for the trees and had the necessary permits, and that opposing official orders would only land them in jail. They also spread rumors that Chipko leaders were only making trouble in order to be bought off by the Company.

In response, a larger meeting was called on December 22, 1973 in a village near the Indo-Tibet border, attended by village chiefs, regional committee members, and people from all the surrounding villages. The people demanded that the Government comply with their wishes, including the cancellation of the Simon Company's permits. The villagers had invited the Company's agents to present their side. But at the end of the meeting, the resolution to take Chipko action was unanimously passed.

As the people were dispersing, word spread that a documentary film was going to be shown that evening in a neighboring village by the Forest Department. The news spread and drew huge crowds who walked from as far away as six miles for the rare event. But no sign of a film or film van arrived, and the disappointed film-goers had to stay the night there and head back in the morning.

When the workers returned to the village of Rampur, they heard that some men had

Roger/Barricada/LNS

been going towards the forests with axes and saws. Seventy people set off in hot pursuit, to the accompaniment of drums, and were joined by others along the way. In the forest, the villagers discovered that five ash trees were already felled. They were appalled at the sight of the fallen trees, but consoled themselves with the fact that the Company had been unable to get the trees out of the forest. They resolved to stand guard over the trees around the clock, and organized rallies in village after village, drawing hundreds of people into the movement. The Company had been beaten; their permit expired on December 31, 1973, without having removed a single tree from the area.

When the list of Uttarakhand forests was prepared for auction, it included 2,451 trees already branded by the Forest Department in the Reni forest, high up on the Tibet border. The tribal peoples of the area were already aware of the ravages caused by deforestation. Many of the people in the area live on the upper slopes of the Himalayas, but move down to the river beds near the villages in winter. In 1970, hundreds of these temporary homes and fields had been washed away by floods. The people knew only too well that the clearing of the forests meant the crumbling of the slopes, thus threatening their very existence. The Reni people were ready for Chipko.

After pleading with forest officials to cancel the auction, the movement leaders decided to inform all bidders that they would face resistance from the people of the area. This had little effect, for after all, Chipko may have saved five or ten ash trees, but to stop tree-felling in a huge forest was another matter.

There were other problems. Clearly a mass movement of a much larger size and scope was needed. But it was also clear that political elements, ranging from the Communist to Congress parties, having witnessed the success of Chipko elsewhere, would attempt to use the issue for narrow political advantage. But Chandi Prasad had a clear perspective: As long as the common resolve remained intact—that the forest was to be saved by nonviolent means—the movement would prosper. The mobilization of the people would overcome the narrower sectarianism of the parties.

Several rallies took place in March of 1974. The Chief Minister of Uttar Pradesh again expressed his concern for the forests and its people but did nothing to stop the company which had made the highest bid from sending contract laborers to the borders of the forest in preparation for the harvest.

One night, later in the month, it was discovered that the lumbermen had gone into the forest to cut the trees. There were few men in the village at the time. Chandi Prasad was aghast and asked where all the men from the villages in the area were. The plot unfolded: They were all at the district headquarters at Chamoli to receive compensation for their lands. In 1962, lands had been expropriated by the Indian Army after the Chinese invasion in order to expand patrolling operations. Despite hundreds of petitions, no compensation from the central government had ever been paid, and the loss of fields and end of border trade between India and Tibet had reduced the villagers to extreme poverty. So when it was announced that compensation would be paid at Chamoli on March 26, the men rushed to be there. Central government, State government, and industry collaboration against the interests of the forest people was now crystal clear. Chandi Prasad set out for Chamoli, hoping to prevent a series of riots which would undo much of the public education which had built the movement.

The contractor had carefully plotted his operation. Laborers had been brought from far-off Himachal Pradesh, so that they would know nothing about the political situation surrounding their work. The buses stopped short of Reni village, and the felling party avoided the village by taking an alternative foot path to the forest.

But a small girl saw the procession of men with saws and axes and ran to the head of the local women's circle, who rushed out and collected 28 women and girls and began to climb up the forest trail. These women had never participated in political activity before—though they attended meetings, they almost never spoke but sat at the back of the hall and whispered.

The women quickly caught up with the laborers and begged them not to cut the trees, explaining that the mountain would fall on their village if the forest was thinned. They asked that the laborers return to the village and wait for the husbands to return from Chamoli in order to settle things.

Many of the contractor's men and forest department workers had been drinking. Some threatened to rape the women. Others shouted at them to stop obstructing their work. One drunk man armed with a gun staggered toward the women, who were frightened and with good reason. But one woman bared her breast and challenged him to fire, saying, "Shoot and you can cut down this forest. It is better you shoot me than destroy our mother."

The laborers were unnerved; most ashamedly walked down the trail. But even as the women were succeeding with one group of laborers, another group could be seen coming up the hill. The scene was repeated, this time with the women carrying the tools of those too drunk to manage.

Following the laborers down the hill, the women noticed that there was a narrow turning where a cement slab had been placed to fill a missing portion of the trail swept away in an earlier landslide. Seven women stopped there, while others continued down the trail. Using the laborers' tools, they pried the huge slab loose and it went crashing into the gorge. The road between the village and the forest was now severed.

The women remained all night at the end of the land, standing guard over the entrance to the forest. When the men from Chamoli returned with Chandi Prasad the next day, the women told the full story, carefully concealing the drunkenness of the laborers and the incident with the gun (which was only revealed much later). The women did not want the forest workers to lose their jobs; they were potential allies.

More rallies, marches, and petitions quickly spread through the region. Finally, after the movement rejected any bargain which would result in the felling of the Reni forest, the Government agreed to appoint a committee of scientific experts, government officials and Chipko leaders to evaluate the fears of the "illiterate villagers."

Even while the study was being conducted, the "save-the-tree" movement spread to encompass much of northern Uttar Pradesh. Time was clearly on Chipko's side. The constructive program, in which small teams of workers were assigned to plant, nurse, and defend small groves of young trees, resulted in more than 29,000 new trees being planted, without government aid. And as the villagers planted, the recognition and appreciation of the ecological and economic principles embodied in Chipko spread.

In mid-July 1977, the Government accepted the recommendations of the Reni Investigation Committee. The process of natural regeneration in the region was indeed very slow. The only "planned development" that would make sense in the area was aid to further nature's healing efforts. "Development" of Alaknanda and its tributaries would be totally banned for a minimum of ten years, and encompass an area of no less than 1200 kilometers.

Chipko can claim a major victory, for now. But economic stagnation, poverty and starvation, and the spectre of exploitation still threaten the Chipko people and their determination to create a humane and ecologically sound future.

David Albert is a nonviolent activist with Movement for a New Society in Philadelphia, and was North American representative to the Asian Seminar on Training for Nonviolent Direct Action held in India, December 1978.

From *CoEvolution Quarterly,* no. 22 (Summer 1979), pp. 24-26

Pig Ignorant: Who Is Optimistic? Not the Man with a Hoe

by Peter Laurie

As Pig taps out these unpretentious lines, he sits looking onto a grey scene. That scene is, or rather would be, if one could but see it, the Dorset countryside. Today, and for many days past, it has been wrapped in cloud. The contents of the cloud fall unceasingly on the earth beneath —often not bothering to unfreeze themselves, so that from time to time the wind throws a handful of deafening hail against the quaint diamond panes of my Victorian Gothick cottage. It has been the hardest winter for a century. In a country which has natural disasters properly under control, we were not pleased by the sea's determination to abolish a neighbouring village on the island of Portland. Twice sou-westerly gales hurled waves over the Chesil Bank, that twenty miles long, curving beach in the middle of England's south coast, and on the third occasion—a few weeks ago—in the middle of a calm evening, the sea gathered itself into a sixty-foot high hill, walked over the beach, over the sea wall, and demolished the entire place. There was no call for it. It was unnecessary.

It is a winter that makes Pig very glad that some years ago he was not seduced into reuniting his soul with the Land. For Dorset is full of people from London who are sick of the falsity and hypocrisy of city

streets and have come here to do something *real.* They are egged on by a very bad man called Seymour who makes a lot of money writing pretty books about self-sufficient farming. His books show you calm, wise, pastoral girls making withy baskets to hold the dozens of eggs their chickens yield. Grave but merry bearded men plough the land behind dear old Dobbin, confident that the earth will yield her increase in due season. Seymour tells them that a man and his family can live—and live well—on an acre and a half. Look at the vegetable garden! See the pretty cabbages! See the carrots, see the brussels sprouts! And all free, my children, save for a little healthful labour, a little dirtying of the hands with God's good earth.

Do not see the eelworm, the greenfly, the ringworm, the staggers, the botts, the lambs that are born rotten, the calves that live a miserable week scouring and stumbling, and die in convulsions. Do not ask why the crabbed arthritic little people from whom you bought your acre and a half for sums of money unprecedented in the history of British land prices, run off chortling and skipping, as fast as they can to London. They have spent a lifetime on this wet, acid, ungrateful land. They know that an acre and a half of it will not make you rich—no, nor a hundred acres and a half either.

To make a living from farming you need three hundred acres, which will set you back very near a million dollars. (British farms are very productive, and traditionally, people who make money in the city become gentlefolk by buying land. Hence these ridiculous prices.) If you have less land, you work it less efficiently, you are in competition with the big farmers, so you have to sell your products for less than they cost you to grow. Ah, say Seymour and the

self sufficients, we *don't* sell. We eat what we grow!

There are two snags to this: few farms raise good crops of: alcohol, salt, shoes, books, music, soap or toothpaste. If you are not to live like a medieval peasant you need money to buy these things. Secondly, you will raise calves and lambs—often feeding them by hand, struggling for their lives. They become your friends. If you are to eat meat you have to kill and devour them. It did not worry medieval peasants, but it will worry you.

I was lucky enough to experience these problems vicariously. I have two friends, one rich and the other poor, who went into small farms about ten years ago. The rich one bought a vertical bog—you don't believe me? Half his farm is so steep that you have to pull yourself up by clinging to trees. Yet water gushes out of the ground so copiously that you must wear fisherman's thigh boots. It grows tier after tier of wild orchid and scrubby pine. It grows very little that anyone but a woodpecker can eat. His animals get foot rot by standing all their lives in a marsh. Or else they fall down the hill and break their necks. But since he is rich, he can solve these problems by writing a cheque—and there are tax advantages still to being a farmer, so he is not altogether worse off. But you would have to describe him as 'Self Deficient.'

The poor one bought quite a good little farm from a man who had gone bankrupt and needed the money too desperately to wait for a better offer. He learnt how to farm well with no capital. He bred the local sheep, the Dorset Horn, an odd breed which will lamb in November to produce fat lambs for the market in April. Since ordinary sheep are just having their babies then, you get good money for young Horns. But—but, it means a winter of struggling with these little animals, trying to keep them warm and fed when all of nature intends the opposite. In the ten years my friend did this he aged thirty. He arrived gay, lithe, cheerful, handsome. When he finished he was stooped, lined, gray. For three years, while he was learning how to raise sheep, he and his wife and daughter never ate meat. Once I heard his wife—who had been a principal ballerina with the Rambert company in London— say, 'Oh John! You can't be hungry—you had an apple sandwich only yesterday!'

It was a thought provoking spectacle. As the winters rolled by, and all I had to do was sit in a nice warm room typing a few well-informed and witty sentences, I thought of John slithering on the icy mud with less envy. Even on golden summer evenings I learnt not to envy him. For he would look from his front door onto a golden ampitheatre of fields. I would, on the occasions I was there, see only beauty; he would see a field that needed draining at the cost of five thousand pounds, a ley of grass for hay that was not coming on fast enough, a hedge that needed fencing. With binoculars we would watch the mother fox teaching her cubs to hunt on the other side of the valley: for me it was an amazing privilege, for John a warning that they would be hunting his new lambs next winter at a cost of sixty pounds a bloody head.

It turned out all right in the end. Land prices had gone up so much in the time he was there that he was able to sell the farm for eighty thousand pounds that he had bought for twelve. He dyed his hair, bought some mascara, a purple scarf and a new Porsche, and went off to New York where he met Sid Vicious (alas, now deceased). His wife makes a fortune teaching ballet, a commodity much in demand in those parts.

And I take my afternoon constitutional past fields that someone else has to drain and plough and harrow. They must try and out-guess the bureaucratic bastards in Brussels who set European farm prices. They must worry about the foxes and the blight: owing to the political power of the French and German peasant, I can turn my typing into food at such an advantageous rate that I would be crazy to lay hand to harrow. I have even given up trying to talk

intelligently about it all. A few years ago I could tell ewe from hogg from wether. Now they just look like sheep—or are those animals called cows? More cassoulet anyone? Try this Montrachet—I think you'll like the bouquet.

Well, it is not really about money. It is about optimism, and the reason I have gone on at such length is that the land—which once seemed an inexhaustible source of optimism—has proved to be a false jade. Her service condemns one to a narrow, debilitating life. The 'nature' that obtains on farms—even on self-sufficient ones, which are clumsy reproductions of mid-nineteenth century agriculture—is about as natural as the hydrogen bomb. The great invention of agriculture, which eight thousand years ago freed man from the tyranny of finding every day's dinner on the hoof, at the expense of condemning ninety percent of the people to wizening labour, has now, in its turn, been vanquished. Hardly anyone needs to work on the land in the west: those that do, will only choose to because they cannot think of anything better. And that is what this piece is really meant to be about—though it got sidetracked. What can one do about which one can feel optimistic? Very little. My friends who consider themselves artists—either with brush or word—can only keep their spirits up by whistling in the dark. Those who went into industry, banking, commerce feel themselves on a slope as unstable as my rich friend's vertical marsh. Journalists report non-news about non-events to readers who care nothing about

either. Ecologists are staving off disaster.

Whom do I know who seems optimistic? There are not many. Archaeologists are, for they bury themselves in a past whose outcome is known—they are warm, comfortable, secure. Physicists are because the safe door which protects nature's secrets is beginning to cave in. They cluster about the vault, blasting the locks with psi meson beams, peeking inside with lasers, waiting eagerly for the moment when the whole universe will turn inside out like a glove. Molecular biologists are because they can feel the secret of life begin to stir under their hands. They will, they think, soon be as God, the giver of life. Computer people are because the gallop of their technology will soon put the whole of man's social life: his commerce, his business, his arts, his literature into their hands. And more: they will be able to encapsulate the seed of intelligence in their chips and release it from the inching of evolution. It took two hundred million years to get us here: in maybe a thousand more man will be done for, and the vital spark he nourishes so dimly will be on its way alone, unencumbered by the flesh.

As I said, it is a cold late Spring. Mid-April and there are no buds yet on the trees.

LNS

4 THIRD WORLD

This chapter is the longest in the book, and appropriately so, for the struggles of peoples of color in Africa, Asia, Latin America, and the United States, as well as the revolutionary situations in colonial and underdeveloped countries have nearly unanimous support from the world's radicals. The problems of southern Africa predominate in the consciousness of many activists, for it is in southern Africa that the power of colonialism, racism, and big business combine in the most obvious fashion. The importance of cultural resistance to imperialism, all too often ignored by radicals, as well as the media, is emphasized in an article on African music. The African section ends with a piece from *Undercurrents* that makes vivid the plight not only of African but of all Third World economies in which local food needs are sacrificed in order to produce cash crops for the world market.

The Middle East was a center of much struggle and controversy in 1979 and 1980 and two particularly pivotal areas of conflict, the Persian Gulf and Iran, are discussed in articles from *MERIP Reports*. Southeast Asia, too, has been in turmoil, with former allies attacking and invading each other. Many of the controversies there, however, are the direct results of the U.S. intervention in the 1960s and 1970s, and it makes sense therefore that the lone article representing Asia should be Torben Retboll's exposé of the dishonest reporting by *Reader's Digest* on Kampuchea.

A larger section on Latin America follows. Articles about El Salvador, Chile, and Colombia focus on ongoing revolutionary struggles against neocolonial regimes; rather than attributing these conflicts to random or senseless terrorism, these writers consider guerilla warfare as a legitimate tool in the fight against imperialism. The final two articles about Latin America focus on such a revolution that has succeeded—the Nicaraguan. Again, the authors take a sympathetic view quite different from the virulent anti-Communist attacks on the regime by the mass media.

Refugees have been an important topic in all media. Three articles on refugees suggest the wide range of political troubles created by the influx of both Cubans and Haitians to the U.S. Unlike the mass media, which focused on the number and race of the newcomers, stirring up patriotism and racism, the alternative media tried to examine the social, political, and economic factors that led to the flight from Haiti and Cuba and also to the problems faced by the newcomers in the U.S. Disillusionment on the part of the newcomers, tensions between them and other poor people, especially Blacks, and the political motivations behind the differential treatment of Haitians and Cubans by the U.S. government, all exacerbated by unemployment and falling standards of living in the U.S., are highlighted in this alternative analysis of the refugee "crisis."

Third World peoples, who build their own communities within Western bourgeois democracies, are perceived by the ruling class as a threat to the status quo and are oppressed economically, socially, and politically. Articles on Chicanos, Native Americans, and Black Americans end this section with issues affecting all national minorities in America—political repression, rebellion, betrayal, and racism, as well as struggles to maintain historical and cultural identity.

—ES

SOUTHERN AFRICA

From *Southern Africa* 13, no. 5 (June 1980): 2, 3

Four Years After Soweto: Resistance Escalates

by Andrew Marx

In the four years since 1976, a new annual ritual has emerged in South Africa. As the June 16 anniversary of the Soweto uprising approaches, South African blacks and their supporters around the world plan memorial rallies, while the apartheid regime braces for the possibility of a new wave of protests.

This year, though, the government hasn't had much time to worry about that possibility. Since early April it has been up to its neck in the reality of what the British weekly, the *Economist,* predicted could become "the most comprehensive racial confrontation it has yet experienced."

It all began innocuously enough back in February, when students at a single "colored" high school in Cape Town launched a campaign of protests against the "gutter education" offered in South Africa's separate and distinctly unequal black, "colored," and Indian school systems. By the time the Soweto anniversary neared, a school boycott had spread to every corner of the country, involving not only "coloreds" but African and Indian students, and not only high schools but every one of the country's non-white universities.

Estimates of the number of students who were boycotting classes to take part in all-day political meetings and demonstrations soared past 100,000. And even that didn't provide an adequate measure of the challenge posed by the months of mounting protests.

The student rebellion wasn't the only new wave of resistance to apartheid. It coincided with the largest and most militant surge of strikes by black workers

Reprinted with permission from *Southern Africa.*

since 1973. And in both schools and factories, renewed resistance struck a damaging blow at Prime Minister P. W. Botha's claims that apartheid reformed can mean apartheid preserved. For the high school and college students and urban factory workers who were marching and picketing represented precisely those sectors of the black population envisioned as a buffer against rebellion in Botha's "total strategy." . . .

Compounding the dilemma for Botha, the protests spread to several of the rural black "homelands," where the apartheid regime has dangled the promise of "independence" as an antidote to dissatisfaction with white supremacist rule.

Botha Policy Vacillating

Botha clearly recognizes a dilemma when he sees one. He proved it by vacillating. From one day to the next, Botha, Police Minister Louis le Grange and Minister of Colored Relations Marais Steyn bounced back and forth between conceding the existence of "justifiable grievances" and blaming the protests on "outside agitators." But neither threats that protesters were "going to get hurt" nor promises that grievances would be studied and redressed brought an end to the boycott.

For the most part, the police held their fire, leading the *Financial Mail* to remark with obvious satisfaction that "the lessons of 1976 have not been entirely lost."

"No bullets were used to quell the largely peaceful protests, though tear gas and batons were," South Africa's leading business magazine declared happily in its May 16 issue. Less than two weeks later, police opened fire with automatic weapons on a crowd of Cape Town teen-agers, killing two and seriously wounding three others. Still, the memory of the carnage in 1976 was apparent. Le Grange rushed to "express my regret that such an incident should have occurred and extend my condolences to all concerned."

Lessons from Soweto

While the government received praise for having learned certain lessons from the Soweto rebellion, the striking black

students and workers were demonstrating that they had learned more. Most of all, they showed their understanding of the decisive importance of unity.

From the start, student boycotters in Cape Town established a collective and clandestine leadership, known as the Committee of 61, which guaranteed both coordination of activities and a degree of protection against wholesale arrest of leaders. And from the start, statements and pamphlets issued by the Committee revealed a clear-sighted analysis of how, as one pamphlet explained, "short-term demands are linked up with the political and economic system of this country."

The students' "short-term demands" targeted "the general low standard and poor conditions surrounding colored education." They called for an end to discriminatory funding that allots white schools three times as much revenue per student as it does "colored" schools and ten times what it does for African schools. They insisted that pay for teachers in "colored" schools be raised to equal that in white schools, that "colored" students receive free text books as white students do, that the "war damage" of 1976 be repaired.

In these areas Botha and Steyn were prepared to concede "legitimate grievances." They were even prepared to cough up some extra funds to improve a school system described by an official committee just six months earlier as "a mess . . . headed for collapse."

But the students were not to be bought off with promises of extra funds and study commissions. Referring back to the Soweto rebellion, they vowed "not to be bluffed a second time."

"During 1976 the students revolted against an inferior education system," their representatives charged in a statement, "and similar promises—as are now being made by Mr. Steyn—were then also made that the situation would be rectified once order had been restored at the schools.

"After four years nothing has been done and the situation has deteriorated instead."

At the same time, the students made it clear that they saw their struggle as inextricably bound up with the broader struggle against "apartheid and the economic system it is maintaining." Rejecting an offer of negotiations from Steyn, the Committee of 61 explained. "We cannot negotiate our principles away. Our interests are opposed to the interests of those whom Mr. Steyn represents."

LNS

In keeping with the black consciousness philosophy that helped inspire Soweto, the "colored" students explicitly rejected their special status, identifying themselves as blacks, as workers, and as implacable foes of apartheid. Ominously for the government, most of their teachers have walked off the job in support of the boycott. In addition, the British *Financial Times* pointed out, "colored parents appear to be firmly behind their children. Parent support committees have been established in most major centers. In addition, the protest has spread to most Indian secondary schools and a handful of black schools, suggesting a growing identity of interest across ethnic lines."

Since that assessment was printed in early May, evidence of this "identity of interest" has grown rapidly. Increasing numbers of African students have joined the boycott, defying not only the government but several "homeland" leaders, including KwaZulu chief Gatsha Buthelezi.

The KwaZulu government and Buthelezi's Inkatha political party distributed thousands of pamphlets in black townships outside Durban in an attempt to end the boycott. But the effort was rejected by boycotting African students. "What we were waiting for was support not swear words," one student was quoted as saying in *The Post*, the paper read most widely by South African blacks. The story added that the student received "roars of approval" when he warned Buthelezi that "he must not prevent us. He must move."

Buthelezi aside, the students are not without friends in the clergy. More than fifty church leaders were arrested and jailed for a day during a demonstration in late May. They had marched in downtown Johannesburg to protest the arrest of a colleague who was accused of supporting the boycott. One of the jailed clergymen, Bishop Desmond Tutu, was accused by Prime Minister Botha of financing the student unrest. Despite Tutu's denial, such accusations, however groundless, often become the basis for detaining or banning irksome opponents under South Africa's awesome security laws.

Durban Strikes

The Durban area, known as a center of militant black union activity since a wave of strikes began there in 1973, is living up to its reputation once again. The Frametex textile mills, scene of one of the earliest 1973 strikes, recently fired 6,000 blacks who had gone out on strike. According to the *Economist*, "demonstrators have been stoning buses; armed police have been called in."

Other strikes have hit a Cape Town clothing factory and meat packing plants. And the strikers have won firm support from the surrounding communities and boycotting students. In townships outside Cape Town, even butcher shops have joined a consumer boycott against red meat. Boycotting "colored" students have raised funds for the strikers and have also invaded white suburban supermarkets, overturning meat coolers and jamming checkout counters with dozens of loaded shopping carts.

Meanwhile, as African National Congress militant Mavis Nhlapo pointed out in an interview published in *Southern Africa*'s Spring 1980 supplement on women, recent strikes have demonstrated a growing unity among black workers across racial lines.

"On one occasion," Nhlapo said, "the employers came and told the African workers to stand on one side and the 'colored' workers to stand on the other side. The workers replied, 'We are all workers. We cannot be divided. We know that we are all fighting for the same thing so you cannot tell us that "coloreds" have their union, Africans have theirs.'"

Much the same analysis has been offered by the boycotting students, both in their actions and in a series of pamphlets emphasizing the ties between their struggles and those of "our parents the workers."

"We must see how the fail/pass rate in schools are linked up with the labor supply for the capitalist system, how low quality school buildings are linked to the unequal allocation of funds to education for children of the oppressed and children of the oppressor, how inadequate library facilities are linked with the need to confine and limit the thoughts of the oppressed, how distorted history text books are linked with the need to obscure and propagandize against the proud history of resistance of the indigenous people against economic slavery, how, in fact, the whole educational system against which we are rebelling stems from the fact that we are denied basic political rights and thus political power."

Several weeks and more than 1200 arrests later, the students were still in the streets, demanding both better quality school buildings and basic political rights. And in spite of the widest sweep of detentions the government has attempted since its crackdown on Black Consciousness Movement organizations in October 1977, the wave of protests still appeared to be gathering, rather than losing, momentum.

SOUTHERN AFRICA

From *Southern Africa* 13, no. 4 (April/May 1980): 12, 13, 14, 24

Carrying the Burden of Apartheid

by Stephanie Urdang

Reprinted with permission from *Southern Africa*.

Almost twenty-five years ago, on August 8, 1956, the serene, manicured and very white capital of the South African regime found itself playing reluctant host to 20,000 women, mostly African, who had converged on Pretoria from every part of South Africa. Their protest was directed against the recent extension of the pass laws to include African women. Until then only men had been forced to carry the notorious pass book and suffer under the myriad of restrictions that came with it.

The march had been far from easy to organize. As preparations had gained momentum, police intimidation had mounted. Ignoring this, the women staged fundraising events, chartered buses, organized cars, and paid for train tickets.

In anticipation, the government banned all demonstrations in Pretoria that day. Undaunted, the women circumvented the law by marching in groups of two or three. Once assembled, they stood for thirty minutes in total silence in the wintry sun, before bursting forth to sing their national anthem.

The hurdles strewn across their path by the apartheid regime weren't the only resistance the women had to overcome. Some of their male allies in the liberation movement clearly felt threatened by the independence of the action. As the husband of one of the leaders of the march recalled wryly some fifteen years later, with a flash of lingering irritation: "We asked the women what we could do to help them and to protect them. They were taking on a potentially very dangerous task. You know what they answered? 'If you want to help us, you can stay at home and look after the children.'"

But while the march raised questions about the role of women, the women themselves made it clear that the apartheid regime was the main target of their struggle.

The Pretoria march was a high point in the 1950s—a decade marked by frequent militant demonstrations, by the increasing repression of the National Party government, and finally by the banning of the liberation movements. Throughout the decade, women played an important and active part, not only as supporters, but as initiators and organizers.

While the march could not change the laws, it showed a determination on the part of the women to continue their resistance against apartheid.

The effects of apartheid on women have been especially harsh. They had reason to protest.

Harsh Life in the Reserves

The apartheid regime has an insatiable need for cheap labor in order to fuel its economy and ensure continued high profits from its vast mineral resources, which are critical for both South Africa and the industrialized West.

Out of this need has come an intricate set of repressive laws designed to maintain and control all facets of the lives of the vast majority of the people. While African men provide most of this labor and receive unlivable wages, it is the women who bear the heaviest burden. This can be seen most starkly in the reserve areas.

In pre-colonial society, African women played a vital role in the economic life of the village, with greater responsibility for, and input into, subsistence production than the men. The advent of colonialism and development of apartheid have seriously eroded this role.

The apartheid policies and the critically reduced land area have diminished women's economic productivity, and with it their political and social role. This has increased women's dependence on their husbands, their fathers or their male guardians, thereby reinforcing the existing patriarchal system.

The premise lying behind the establishment of the so-called "bantustans" is that Africans may only be permitted into the prescribed "white" areas—the towns—in order to work. Once a man can no longer sell his labor, he is expected to return "home," regardless of how long he has lived in the urban areas.

The meager wages he receives for his labor barely cover his own basic needs, let alone those of his family left behind in the reserves. In theory, this family is presumed capable of providing for itself off the land, thus justifying the low wages paid migrant workers. In reality only a tiny fraction of families produce sufficient food for their own survival.

A depressing picture emerges. Much of the limited land made available for subsistence farming is not arable. It is simply impossible to survive without supplemental incomes from migrant workers. But women waiting at home find the flow of money from the men away at work both insufficient and unreliable. Very often the money does not arrive at all.

Yet to earn this pittance, the men have to

Selma Waldman/LNS

work on contract for years at a time, perhaps returning for a two-week period each year, often staying away from their families for several years at a stretch.

This disruption of family life is one of the cruelest manifestations of the apartheid laws. Besides economic hardship, it creates severe emotional stress. Wives do not have the same possibilities as their husbands for alleviating their loneliness, and must wait month after month, hoping for a letter, particularly hoping for one that contains some money.

In desperation women have left the reserves to find their husbands in the towns. This does not always end in a happy reunion.

One woman from the Tranksei, interviewed in 1978, described what happened to her. After failing to hear from her husband for months, and after agonizing over her hungry children, she borrowed money from friends and set off for Cape Town. When she finally tracked him down, he was embarrassed and angry. "He looks away but eventually tells me about this other woman. I can sense that it is this woman who has been eating the money that my husband should have been sending me and our children. She is now fat and attractive. I am starved and ugly in my husband's eyes. I have become a burden to my very own husband.

"Marriage is not worthwhile for us black women. It traps us. Men are having it all right in town with their girl friends and money, while we must keep home on empty pockets and empty promises. We feel lonely in that desolate place."

Little Better in Towns

Strict regulations prescribe the precise conditions under which a person may be permitted to remain in the urban areas. Given that women are not encouraged to be there, these laws affect them even more adversely than the men. The laws are so extensive and pervasive, so arbitrarily and indifferently carried out by government officials, that only a small proportion of women can actually consider themselves urban dwellers. The rest live constantly under the cloud of possible "endorsement out"—the rubber-stamped order that forces the bearer of the pass to return home.

To the woman who endorsed out, "home" can mean a barren area where no living relatives remain and where she has no contacts, or it can, and regularly does, mean a notorious resettlement camp unfit for human habitation.

In order to remain legally in the town, it is necessary to qualify in terms of the Bantu Laws Assessment Act, Section 10 (a), (b), (c) or (d). In essence, a woman has the right to remain in an urban area if she has lived there *continuously* since birth; or has worked continuously for the same employer for ten years or in the same area for fifteen; or is married to a man qualified under the previous two, on condition she entered the area legally in the first place; or if she has "special permission."

As bad as these regulations look on paper, they are nightmarish in practice. Many women will have spent disqualifying periods away at some point in their lives; perhaps as children they were sent to grandparents when their parents were working and unable to care for them, or left the city for the birth of their children.

Marriage does not legalize a woman's status, and may even have the opposite effect. Unless a woman qualifies in her own right (through birth for instance), she takes on the status of her husband. If he is not permitted to have his wife living with him in terms of *his* status, she will find herself endorsed out to his "home," regardless of the conditions she will have to endure there. Desertion, divorce or death by her husband can result in the same loss of qualifying status.

The essential feature of the life of most African women is its insecurity. In the rural areas, their very survival is at stake; in the urban areas, should their circumstances change or their illegality be discovered, they are uprooted from their community and from family life.

Women and Work

Despite the best efforts of the government to keep African women out of the wage labor market, the number of women workers has been growing. Driven off the land by its inability to provide sufficiently, women—like their men before them—have taken the route to the urban areas or onto white farms, more often than not illegally.

And so a point has been reached where one out of three African workers is a woman. There are two broad categories of employment in which African women are found in large numbers, and, not surprisingly, they are the least skilled: domestic workers and farm laborers.

The 1970 census (the latest available) showed that 91 percent of the female workforce was made up of service workers and agricultural workers, with the former predominating. Both these areas of work exclude unemployment benefits or other forms of social security, and are exempted from minimum wage guidelines—negligible though these social services are in the first place. In addition, the average woman worker earns a wage that is less than half that of the average male worker, and only eight percent of the white male's income. When they do the same work as men, they earn considerably less.

Most of the women working in the towns work as domestics in the luxurious homes of their white employers. Many work illegally, although this has become more difficult with the passage of a new regulation that imposes a heavy fine on the employer guilty of keeping any illegal workers.

If a domestic worker is living with her children in a township, she will have to leave them at a very early hour, only returning home late at night. After she has spent the day cleaning the large house of her "madam," cooking for the children, generally attending to their needs, she will return to her tiny, impoverished quarters, find food for her tired children, feed them out of her pathetic salary and fall asleep exhausted. Her energies are directed to the home and children of her employer. She has none left for her own.

If she is a "sleep-in" domestic, she will encounter more restrictions placed on her life. She will not be able to have her husband or lover stay in her room for even one night; neither can her children ever live with her. A woman who breaks these rules runs the risk of being caught in one of the regular police raids on domestic workers' quarters and jeopardizing her job.

Those who have not been able to make it to the towns or as domestic workers in the rural areas, turn to agricultural labor as the only other source of earnings. Farm workers are paid among the lowest wages of all categories of workers and even here women receive less than men. Men will seek other forms of employment if at all possible, but women seldom have this choice.

Since the 1960s there has been a growing need for seasonal workers, as white farms have become more mechanized and squatters and labor tenants have been forced to move off the land. Increasingly farmers are hiring migrants, thus avoiding the need to provide family housing for their workers. This has seriously cut back any of the benefits that might have come from working on a farm and increased the hardships women face in such employment.

The balance of the labor force is made up mainly of factory workers, although there are a fair number of nurses and teachers,

Lilian Ngoyi, 1911-1980

Lilian Ngoyi, whose exceptional talents as a leader and political activist won her wide respect both within and beyond the borders of South Africa, died in Johannesburg at the age of 68 on March 13.

She was already forty when she joined the African National Congress and, with her flair for public speaking and her strong personality, soon became one of its most active leaders.

She was elected president of the African National Congress Women's League, and a few years later became president of the Federation of South African Women. Founded in 1954, the federation was reported to have 230,000 members, mostly African. It had two major aims: to oppose apartheid and work for change, and to work for the rights and freedom of women.

Ngoyi was one of the many ANC active leaders. In 1956, she led 20,000 women in their march to Pretoria to protest the extension of the pass laws to include women.

It was not surprising that, in 1961, at the height of her effectiveness, she was placed under heavy banning orders. In 1973 these were lifted briefly, but were reimposed before too long, so that for sixteen years of her life she lived an isolated existence.

Despite the extreme hardships she endured, and the fact that she lived almost a third of her life as a "non-person," she was not broken. As she said in an interview:

"I must say I had a tough time, but my spirits have not been dampened. You can tell my friends all over the world that this girl is still her old self, if not more mature after all the experiences. I am looking forward to the day when my children will share the wealth of our lovely South Africa."

Although she did not live to see this day, she knew it would happen. Her contribution as an extraordinarily fine leader at a critical time in the history of resistance to apartheid had a vital impact on the course of events and will long be remembered.

relative to the number of African men in these professions.

Many of the laws, which have made the lives of African women so much harder, have been passed since that momentous march back in 1956. The extension of the pass laws initiated many other changes and the situation for both men and women has worsened year after year.

But this oppression has not been accepted passively.

Shortly before the twentieth anniversary of the Pretoria women's march, another important march took place in South Africa. This time it was Soweto students, marching to protest the system of "bantu education." Among them were the daughters and grandchildren of the Pretoria protesters, once again marching peacefully. The police responded with guns, and an uprising spread throughout the country. Over 1,000 students were killed before their resistance was subdued by the police.

The only possibility for real change in the society as a whole and for the end to the particular suffering of women lies in the total abolition of apartheid. That women have a special role in this process has been recognized by many women militants. As Winnie Mandela, who has been persecuted for her efforts, says:

"Black women not only have to face the repressive laws but also grave cultural difficulties. The struggle in this country, I believe, will be won by the women. I am fully convinced that the role of women in the struggle for my people is a major one and despite all the repressive laws they are faced with they have emerged as an outstanding group in fighting for the cause of black people in this country."

Stephanie Urdang, a long-time member of the Southern Africa collective is the author of a book on the role of women in Guinea-Bissau, Fighting Two Colonialisms. *She has recently worked on a study of women under apartheid for the United Nations.*

cursory, often skeptical, lines buried in the middle of an article. This preoccupation with official views and white reactions and interests dominated US reports from Zimbabwe throughout the election period.

Thus, although ZANU-PF and Patriotic Front (ZAPU), as ZANU and ZAPU were then known, complaints of serious intimidation and interference with campaigning by Rhodesian official and Muzorewa forces were confirmed by several international observers, including a US group, the major media preferred to rely on "official sources" for their views. John Burns' story of March 1 for the *New York Times* relied on a British official's interpretation of alleged voting fraud. On February 25, Peter Kent of NBC reported allegations of widespread intimidation by Mugabe forces. His only informants were Peter Gordon, a British election supervisor, and Bishop Muzorewa.

Robin Wright of CBS reported uncritically on February 28 that, "Because of mounting violence, the British Governor, Lord Soames, recently introduced laws that empower him to ban candidates, parties, and even voting in any district seriously disrupted by intimidation. There have been numerous grenade attacks on churches and political offices. Several candidates for Parliament have been abducted, injured or assassinated. And there have been more than 800 convictions for fighting among political opponents within the past two months." Wright included no interviews with either ZANU-PF or Patriotic Front (ZAPU) members, nor did she think it worth reporting the strong evidence that much of the violence emanated from Muzorewa's auxiliaries, and that at least one church bombing was the proven work of Selous Scouts acting as provocateurs.

The MacNeil/Lehrer Report of February 28 utilized film footage supplied by the BBC and commentary from two of the network's reporters. The sole guest for that evening's program was the British ambassador to the United States, Sir Nicholas Henderson.

Few reporters raised any questions about the way in which Lord Soames, in charge of the election proceeding, was collecting his information about violations and intimidation. Yet Michael Shuster, in Salisbury for *Southern Africa,* reported that "Most of the information that is reported about the continued fighting comes from the Rhodesians themselves. There is in fact no means of independently ascertaining the truth. Those members of the Commonwealth Monitoring Force

SOUTHERN AFRICA

From *Southern Africa* 13, no. 6 (July/August 1980): 2-4, 21

Telling It Like It Isn't: US Press Coverage of Zimbabwe

by Michael Beaubien

More than six hundred correspondents from two dozen countries (including correspondents from socialist countries granted entry for the first time) gathered in Salisbury for the recent election, in which Robert Mugabe became the first prime minister of an independent Zimbabwe. But Americans who had hoped that the ending of the tough censorship imposed by the Smith regime would result in an improvement in US media coverage were quickly disappointed. Reporting on the tense political situation prior to the election was

---

marked by the long familiar preoccupation with the status of whites, the same biased language, political outlook and reliance on Rhodesian officials for interpretation of events (see *Southern Africa,* January, 1980).*

Official Sources

Unbalanced reporting is an old problem in US media coverage of southern Africa. A study on coverage of Zimbabwe in major US newspapers, conducted by Howard University Professor Beverly Hawk, produced the startling statistic that in the three years from 1975 to 1978, quotes from white civilians outnumbered those from Black civilians by a ratio of two to one; Rhodesian officials were quoted almost four times as frequently as liberation movement leaders.

Hawk found that government versions of stories were given space and credence, while statements by liberation movement leaders were ignored or granted only some

---

*[Michael Beaubien, "Inadequate, Infrequent and Insufficient," *Southern Africa* 13, no. 1 (January 1980): 7-9, 26.—eds., *Alternative Papers.*]

assigned to security force bases have no way of knowing if the Rhodesian version of reported incidents is correct" (*Southern Africa,* March 1980).*

The Silent Majority

According to Professor Hawk, "Many correspondents seemed to share this idea that reporting disparity of white civilian opinion constituted balanced coverage . . . very few felt the resulting coverage was inadequate."

It is not surprising then, that with this combination of racism, reliance on Rhodesian and British spokespersons, and hostility, particularly to the ZANU forces, no one in the major US press corps came anywhere close to predicting Mugabe's landslide victory despite consistent ZANU-PF confidence in the outcome. Predictions all focused around possible combinations of seats won by Muzorewa and Nkomo forces, and the press people never bothered to check their forecasts with the voters who mattered—the African majority.

Even after the dramatic election result was announced, a momentous event in the African community, reporters went in search of white opinion for interpretation and explanation.

On March 3, David Brinkley of NBC began the Zimbabwe story: "In Rhodesia's election, it appears the Marxist candidate, Robert Mugabe, has won a landslide victory and will become Prime Minister. What this means for the country and for the white minority causes some nervousness and uncertainty among the whites. And some pessimism." Then came Peter Davis' report from Salisbury which detailed the feelings of Rhodesian whites.

John Burns, in his March 6 report for the *New York Times,* fared no better, his only allusion to Black opinion appeared in the following form: "Along Rhodes Avenue in the city center, a middle-aged Black mailman rode happily along on his bicycle, taking both hands off the handlebars to flap his elbows like a rooster, crowing like a cock [ZANU-PF symbol, editor] as he passed sidewalks packed with whites." The remainder of the article was devoted to Mugabe's election victory speech.

When Gregory Jaynes of the *New York Times* made his first attempt to solicit Black opinion, it was about the weather. On February 29, he wrote: "'The rain is an assistance,' said Andrew Muchabaiwa,

*[Mike Shustet, "Britain Undermines Free Elections," *Southern Africa* 13, no. 3 (March 1980): 5-8.—eds. *Alternative Papers.*]

who voted here today. 'Rain is a good sign to the African. The rain will give us a good poll.'" Yet, further along in this article Gregory Jaynes gave an indication of the problems he faced in soliciting Black opinion. He wrote, "The voters will not talk. An occasional bellicose drunk will shout something unintelligible, but for the most part the people in the lines outside the polling stations nod shyly when approached by questioners, even official Commonwealth election observers."

Gregory Jaynes' comment would seem to suggest that one way to overcome the Africans' natural hesitance to talk freely with Europeans would involve a greater use of African stringers or the employment of more Afro-Americans as correspondents in southern Africa. Earl Caldwell of the New York *Daily News* produced some of the finest reporting of any American journalist in Zimbabwe. (See his March 1 column for description of life in the free trustland with ZANU-PF).

Yet even accepting that there was some reluctance to talk to reporters, it seems clear that any serious effort could and did produce a response, especially from educated Africans in the urban centers.

Thus, on March 5, Caryle Murphy of the *Washington Post* interviewed several Zimbabweans in Salisbury providing the only reportage of Black feelings, concerns and expectations in the major media. Murphy spoke with Reeds Masango, a student in the Black town of Highfield, who told her, "Now we are getting the country in the right way." Providing some indication of Black expectations, Lillian Murombedzi told Murphy, "We want our salaries increased, better accommodation and better education." Reeds Masango also provided the reporter with an insight into Bishop Muzorewa's downfall. "When he got into power he did nothing for the people," said Masango. "He intensified the military call-up instead of increasing the wages."

In addition to the reluctance of most American correspondents to seek out Black opinion, most journalists seem to have made very little effort to get out of Salisbury. As a result American readers were never introduced to any members of either ZANU-PF or Patriotic Front (ZAPU), other than the leaders who were candidates for prime minister. There were no stories profiling the candidates for parliament. These included a number of Black women and a wide variety of people who had played many roles in the freedom struggles.

American readers were similarly never informed about the status of the thousands of refugees caused by the seven-year war. No American correspondents from the major media felt compelled to visit the refugee camps in Mozambique or Zambia, or report on conditions at any of the major border crossings.

Biased Language

American journalists have in the past been notorious for their biased language in characterizing members of the Patriotic Front. Throughout the war, members of the Patriotic Front were always labeled by American journalists as "terrorists" in an effort to discredit them. During the election period, American correspondents continued to rely upon emotionally-charged and politically-biased terms.

By the time of the Lancaster House accords, members of the Patriotic Front had evolved from "terrorists" to "guerrillas," but never freedom fighters. Ironically, members of the major media never reported on the language used by African and white Rhodesian soldiers, which referred to liberation fighters as "gooks." Perhaps this omission was due to concern about any parallels Americans might draw to Vietnam . . . some observers believe the term was imported along with US mercenaries.

The use of biased and emotive language was particularly evident in characterizations of Robert Mugabe, general-secretary of ZANU-PF. For Jay Ross of the *Washington Post,* he was the "guerrilla leader Mugabe (2/28)." Robin Wright of CBS found Mugabe to be "a hardline Marxist (2/18)." Peter Kent of NBC described members of ZANU-PF as "those who favor the Marxist policies of guerrilla leader Robert Mugabe (2/29)," while Jay Ross of the *Washington Post* saw them simply as members of "Mugabe's Marxist-oriented party (2/29)."

Such language appeals to knee-jerk anticommunism, relying on stereotypes, and avoiding any reference to background which might generate a less hostile response.

By contrast, other Black leaders were depicted in much cooler language, with references to Bishop Muzorewa, the Reverend Ndabaningi Sithole, and Nkomo, the veteran Black Nationalist.

Robert Mugabe

Interestingly, the characterizations of Mugabe underwent some transformation immediately following his electoral victory. For Peter Jennings at ABC, Mugabe became the "Nationalist guerrilla leader (3/4)." Mark Coogan informed his audience that "despite Mugabe's label of Marxist, African observers don't expect a communist state."

In a profile of Mugabe, Gregory Jaynes of the *New York Times* wrote, "Most white Rhodesians despise him. . . . Whites see Mr. Mugabe as a murderer and a communist. His base has been socialist Mozambique and his expressed ideology is linked to the views of Marx and Lenin. . . . Mr. Mugabe also sought to dispel concerns about him by presenting himself as a cultured, well-dressed political figure. There has been no suggestion of guerrilla connections. His well-tailored suits, mainly tan, have been set off by expensive shirts and shoes. . . . His talk reflects the five degrees he earned, three of them during eleven years as a detainee of the former white-minority government (3/5)."

Jay Ross added a comment on Mugabe's religious outlook for readers of the *Washington Post*. He wrote: "For a man seen as the devil incarnate by most white Rhodesians and even some Blacks, Robert Mugabe hardly seems to fit the image. . . . With his trace of a goatee, horned-rim glasses and natty suits often from London's stylish West End, he hardly looks like a man who spent ten years in Rhodesian prisons. . . . Although he makes no bones about his Marxist leanings, he has toned down that image in the last year, talking more about socialist principles in the manner of a European social democrat. . . . Mugabe is somewhat an anomaly since he was raised a devout Catholic and is now an avowed Marxist even though there is much evidence that he still practices his religion. . . . At one time, Mugabe called his political-economic philosophy by the ill-defined name Christian Socialism."

But not everyone was prepared to accept the view of Mugabe as a "Christian Socialist." On March 3, Robin Wright of CBS cautioned, "Although Mugabe has toned down his Marxist rhetoric since he returned to Rhodesia last month, Comrade President, as he refers to himself, is certain to mean major changes for Rhodesia and perhaps for all of southern Africa."

Ask No Questions

In general, American correspondents demonstrated their preference for Muzorewa by restricting their scrutiny of his campaign. To his credit, Gregory Jaynes of

the *New York Times* did report that "Money in great quantities distinguishes Bishop Abel T. Muzorewa's campaign for the leadership of this country (2/21)."

On February 25, Jaynes reported: "Blocked by Rhodesia's High Court from raffling off six new Peugeot automobiles to supporters, the bishop nonetheless concluded a four-day rally on the outskirts of Salisbury by supplying voters with bottles of syrupy orange drinks and leaden loaves of bread." What, no fishes?

Certain peculiarities in Muzorewa's campaign didn't altogether escape the attention of the writers for the *Washington Post*. On February 26, Jay Ross observed, "Muzorewa's virtually unlimited financial backing, apparently from South Africa, has given him a distinct disadvantage in the campaign. He has the use of four helicopters and a prop-jet plane, all of which create an image of power with his African constituency."

No one, however, bothered to tell American readers that Mugabe and Nkomo had no aircraft at their disposal or that the Rhodesians had ever confiscated some of their vehicles.

When pressed by Jaynes as to the source of his funding, Muzorewa stated, "We have said it does not matter where we get our funds, as long as it is not from communists." But that was the extent of any investigative reporting that took place in Zimbabwe during the election.

Soames: High Praise

If the press was hostile to Mugabe, and cautious with Muzorewa, it tended to be very generous to the major British actors in the electoral drama. On June 24, John Burns suggested that Lord Carrington was "a credible candidate for a Nobel Peace Prize," adding that "the governor's [Lord Soames] accomplishments have been considerable." On June 26, Burns reported that the governor was "enjoying himself." Soames is quoted as having said, "Of course I'm having a splendid time. I can't imagine anything for a politician that would be more fascinating, can you?" The governor went on to compare his performance to a magician. "It's all done with mirrors," he said. "I have an endless supply of rabbits. Didn't you know?"

A *New York Times* editorial on March 5 stated, ". . . praise is due the interim British Governor, Lord Soames, whose exemplary bluffmanship kept all the candidates off guard so that none could convincingly cry 'Foul!'"

Yet there was another, more serious view

SOUTH AFRICA PLAYS ITS BISHOP

Michael Scurato/Southern Africa/LNS

of the Soames role. American readers were given only a glimmer of this perspective in one op-ed column in the *New York Times* of February 24. In a detailed criticism of the British role in overseeing the transition to majority rule, Randall Robinson, director of TransAfrica (a Black American lobby for Africa and the Caribbean) wrote, "Lord Soames, the British Governor in Rhodesia, has favored the whites and their conservative candidate, Bishop Abel T. Muzorewa, while penalizing the Patriotic Front, particularly the Zimbabwe African National Union (ZANU)."

Among the criticisms of Lord Soames's maneuvers cited by Robinson:

• Permitting the Rhodesian Security Forces to return to full operational footing
• Deployment of over 25,000 armed "auxiliaries" loyal to Abel Muzorewa
• Allowing an estimated six thousand South African troops to remain in Rhodesia
• Failure to pursue investigations of terrorism and assassination attempts directed against the Patriotic Front
• Promulgation of a decree giving Soames the power to disenfranchise voters and prevent elections in certain districts
• Banning of ranking ZANU officials and election candidates
• Permitting the Rhodesian Army and Air Force to engage in political activities on behalf of Bishop Muzorewa, and
• Obstruction of the return of an estimated 200,000 refugees from outside the country.

Charges of British manipulation were so widespread that the Organization of African Unity called for a special meeting of the UN Security Council, and at a meeting in February a resolution was passed 14-0 which called on Britain to stop violating the London Agreement. Yet very little of this was deemed worthy of attention by American correspondents in Rhodesia.

American observers somewhat more open to the liberation movement's viewpoint, who were in Zimbabwe to monitor the election, got a cool reception from the media. In one passing reference John Burns reported, "Mr. Mugabe's criticisms have received some backing from international observer groups here to monitor the election, including a coalition of private American bodies with an interest in Africa that issued a statement today endorsing the guerrilla leader's complaints."

Dan Rather of CBS provided the only television coverage about the activities of the American observers. On March 3, he stated, "American observers who monitored the Rhodesian elections reported today that government Security Forces intimidated many voters, but, on the whole, they said, the election went much better than might have been expected and overall, did reflect the will of the people."

No Change for the Better

Traditionally, southern Africa is not news in the US. But the reporting on the Zimbabwe election shows that even when there is considerable coverage, its quality is poor. American reporters demonstrate a

preoccupation with the status of whites, a preference for interviews with white government officials and strong political biases. In Zimbabwe, these problems led journalists to ignore two of the most explosive aspects of the story—the presence of South African troops, and American mercenaries in the Rhodesian Army.

The continuing failure of the US media to present accurate and balanced reporting on southern Africa suggests the need for a return to what Herbert Matthews, one of America's foremost foreign correspondents, once called "partisan reporting." This was the method employed by the *New York Times* to cover the Spanish Civil War during the 1930's.

In the case of Zimbabwe, the media should have stationed correspondents in Mozambique and Zambia as well as Salisbury during the war. They should have been correspondents who enjoyed the confidence of the Patriotic Front leadership, and correspondents to whom Africans would talk. For if there is one prominent lesson to be learned from this study, it is that the failure to explore the experiences, feelings, and hopes of Black Zimbabweans led inevitably to a failure to anticipate the electoral victory of the Patriotic Front.

From *Caribbe'* 1, no. 1 (August 1979): 3

Fela's Afrobeat
Zombie

by Randall Grass

His music was banned from the airwaves. The police burned down his house, brutalized his women and arrested his followers. Repeated arrests for possession of marijuana failed to lead to convictions. Seems like a lot of harassment for a mere musician, but Nigeria's Fela Anikulapo-Kuti is not merely a musician. He uses his Afrobeat Sound to call African peoples all over the world back to their roots.

Reprinted with permission from *Caribbe'*.

Afrobeat, a prime get-down sound that cuts most disco-boogie, raises body heat *and* cultural consciousness. American radio stations and discos have played cuts from *Zombie,* his first American release. Fela's blend of jazz, funk and heavy African rhythms usually comes in fifteen-minute chunks designed for all-night partying—which doesn't fit into the three-minute hit format of A.M. radio. So Afrobeat is creeping up on America through grass-roots, word-of-mouth in the Black community.

They say James Brown once accused Fela of ripping off his sound. The rhythm-guitar riffs in Afrobeat do sound similar to the guitar riffs in J.B.'s classic funk. The resemblance ends there. From the ground up, Afrobeat mixes steady-state pulsations of several percussionists with intermittent electric bass, chunky guitar riffs and

moody electric piano. This bottom forms a foundation for jazz-inflected saxophone sounds of Fela backed by the insistent chants of a horn section and chorus of girl singers.

"I no be gentleman at all. I be Africa man, original," sings Fela in a sneering put-down of African bureaucrats who follow Western ways. Coming on Fela in mid-performance is like coming into the middle of a revival meeting. You may be singled out as the next target of his preaching. Fela's shows pull everyone back to the time when African music was a community event, not merely entertainment.

The sea of undulating bodies at the Shrine, Fela's personal club until it was closed by the Nigerian government, seemed part of a worshipful congregation responding to every nuance in the music, as Fela stalked the stage and preached into a microphone:

> "My friend just come from prison
> Him de look for work
> Waka waka (walk around) day and
>   night
> Police man stop him for road
> Him say, Mister,
> I charge you for wandering."
>   (lyrics from "Trouble Sleep")

A red light bathed the crowd with an eerie glow that lit flags of every African nation ringing the walls. Fela preaches pan-African unity. The sweet smell of hemp (pot) hung in the air and young girls climbed up on raised platforms to shake for their idol. A young boy would rush up on stage with a saxophone, handing it to Fela, who then began to blow jagged lines filled with anger, humor and a defiant declaration of badness. The band would push the dancers with an hour of continuous Afrobeat until *that* song ended. Nobody left the dance floor though. The next hour-long number kept the party from losing any momentum.

"Don't gag me," Fela wrote in a column for Africa's *Drum* magazine. In spite of the attacks and arrests, no one has. The Nigerian government didn't take kindly to his open mocking of soldiers (he called them "Zombies"), his scathing criticism of governmental services ("Upsidown") and his championing of the poor ("No bread!" he said). Fela's militance stems from his trip to America in 1969 where some American brothers and sisters helped him see that the fight for self-determination in America and the battle for African development were both part of the same struggle of African people everywhere for justice.

That message is in the music, not merely the lyrics. Afrobeat stands as Fela's answer to the slickified, discofied sounds marketed in Africa by American and British record companies. It also challenges Afro-Americans to check out their musical roots. The rhythm flows more subtly than the thump-thump of disco or the chunka-chunk of funk. Dancing to Afrobeat makes new demands, but, like the man said, "Free your mind and your ass will follow."

Behind the media image of black anger, Fela has consistently been a dedicated musician and community-oriented man proud of his family. Coming from one of the most illustrious families in Nigeria (his father a renowned educator and his mother an influential political activist), Fela studied music at the London School of Music. His wife and children stay in the background but he saw fit to include a picture of them on one of his LP's with the caption: "Fela's beautiful children."

Fela does like the ladies and his communal headquarters (before the fateful burning) were filled with bevies of pretty young beauties who gave him worshipful affection. Pictures of bare-breasted members of his harem often grace his album covers. In the lyrics of one of his songs, "Lady," he praises African womanhood:

"African woman she go dance fire dance
She know the man is master
She go cook for him
She do anything he say."
(lyrics from "Lady")

Anyone in America who plans to ignore Fela may find it impossible to do so. He is coming back.

"When I come back to America," he has said, "it will be as the king of African music."

Maybe he will find a post-Roots America ready for his message.

the magazine of radical science and peoples' technology

UNDERCURRENTS

From *Undercurrents*, no. 32 (February/March 1979), pp. 24-25

The Political Economy of the Peanut

by Simon Watt

During the centuries of the Atlantic slave trade about 250,000 Africans were taken in fettered batches through the seafacing door of Goree Island's slave house to the waiting boats and the infamous middle passage. This slave house or 'barracoon' as it was called, is of no mean construction with its courtyard and twin staircases curving up to the palatial merchant's rooms above the slave cells. It stands inconspicuously and unashamedly in a street of other 17th century merchants' houses—slaves were considered a legitimate trading 'good' like any other. Fought over by the French,

Reprinted with permission from *Undercurrents*, the magazine of radical alternatives and community technology.

English and the Dutch navies, Goree Island—a natural fort to defend the port of Dakar, Senegal's capital city—finished in French hands as the stronghold and administrate centre of their West African Empire.

Slavery was a fact of life for millenia before our fossil fuel era, and slaves were owned by Churchmen, gentry, and estate owners alike—although it was condemned towards the end by Adam Smith who considered it inefficient. The Atlantic traffic began in earnest after 1660 as a replacement for the indentured English servants and convicts whose labour value grew apace with the developing factory capitalism in England. With over 300 capital offences per year during the turbulent years of 1640-1740 and judicial corruption that made even hanging Judge Jeffries blush, the English poor—offered the noose or transportation—had provided a ready source of labour. The sugar plantation owners turned to West Africa for labour, making slavery with its moral and intellectual degradation the essential economic institution for the sugar plantations which provided much of the early

capital for Britain's Industrial Revolution. At home the planters lobbied for monopolies and created the rotten political boroughs whilst their trade rotted teeth. Slavery was abolished by the English in 1807 after a lengthy and emotional campaign by leaders whose hypocrisy has been devastatingly exposed by Eric Williams. The mercantilist policies which protected the sugar planters and their economy based on slave labour was pushed aside by the growing tide of more profitable factory capitalism with its philosophy of free trade and freedom of imports. The abolitionists were successful not on humanitarian grounds but because the West Indian sugar plantations were farmed out and had exhausted their soil.

Goree Island's slave house is now a museum with the costs, suffering, cynicism and humiliation of the trade soaked into the very stone work. Notices with descriptions and quotations on the past evils are pinned to the walls; written on note paper with a black felt tip pen as wet as blood, these notices are replaced each time it rains and their information is fresh and shocking. Whilst I was reading about the exchange rate of slaves and barrels of rum, and feeling absolutely ashamed of being white, a well-heeled Senegalese lady—the wife of an army officer—told me that white people would never be forgotten for the slave trade. But she added that the slaves were sold to the Europeans by African chiefs and entrepreneurs who had raided them from neighbouring tribes. The present leaders of Senegal are not true nationalists, she added, they have merely taken over where the French left off in 1960.

But the Government of Senegal, like those of many 3rd World countries, inherited an independence, an economy and a society whose culture had been seriously distorted by colonialism. One third of Senegal's 4.5 million people live in Dakar (which is growing at over 7% per year), a city built to administer the French West African empire of over 35 million people. Senegal has been left with an expensive city-bound bureaucracy. Industrial development around Dakar—started by the French for their empire to produce goods needing cheap labour (shoes, textiles etc) and those with geographical protection (cement, beer etc)—has suffered from the past. Independence has meant balkanisation of West Africa and the loss of wider markets. The multi-national companies that are attracted to the duty-free

Ollie Harrington/Daily World/LNS

Nuez/Guardian/LNS

Peg Averill/Syracuse Peace Council (from the 1980 Peoples Energy Calendar)/LNS

industrial zone for the cheap labour encourage an international division of labour; few African workers achieved skilled or supervisory grades; and 80% of national development funds come from overseas. But it is the peanut economy, Senegal's major export earner foisted last century to provide cheap vegetable oil for the French market, that provides strongest evidence of structural underdevelopment.

The Growth of the Peanut Economy

Europeans for several hundred years stayed in fortified camps on the coasts of West Africa, trading manufactured goods for slaves and tropical produce. With the slow abolition of slavery, African farmers, responding to market opportunity, turned to trading peanuts for imports. This caused severe dislocation and political reversals amongst the African leaders whose wealth was based on slave trading their fellows. With months of 'forced leisure', the farmers began to develop a cash crop as well as grow staple foods for home consumption. Exchange was by barter, the terms and benefits of which were largely set by African middlemen. The period before the mad scramble for Africa by England and France after 1880 during which evolution was said to have taken place at the pace of the Black has been seen as almost a golden era for Africans.

The brutal military thrusts and boundary carving, opening the colonies to more profitable exploitation, ended all this and dragged Senegal's economy into the French and world markets. Exports of primary produce, in this case peanuts were expected to pay for the colonial economy which itself was controlled and directed by and for European interests. With the banks following criteria of profitability imposed from outside, there was little early industrial development, such as the processing of the peanuts into oil. 'Petits blanc' traders from protected and inefficient French companies controlled buying and selling, stunting the growth of a local bourgeoisie who are only just appearing now at a time when there are few profits left in the marketing network.

French colonial public funds and near-slave labour financed the construction of railroads in Senegal, opening up large areas for further peanut growing and encouraging the internal migration of 'navetanes', seasonal workers who were provided with seed and who farmed as sharecroppers. Transport prices fell by 60 to 80% between 1890 and 1965, and peanut production grew from 45,000 tons to over one million tons in the same period, although now it is less than half this. But the transport subsidies encouraged the inefficient French monopoly traders and the colonial tariffs stifled competition.

The terms of trade for peanuts have declined, like other tropical primary products, by a factor of 7 in the last century. This means that the Senegalese farmers now have to do seven times as much work for an equivalent 'basket' of imported manufactured goods compared with a century ago. Peanut growing was totally unmechanised and was carried out by farmers using traditional agricultural techniques extended over unused land. Many farmers have since been forced by debts into wage labour on larger farms and mechanisation has hastened the drift to Dakar.

A large scale agricultural extension scheme was initiated for the sandy soils of Senegal's ground nut basin in 1964. Run by a French company, it covered 24,000 square miles with an agricultural population of a million. Its objective was to increase peanut production by 25%. The scheme, using intermediate technologies, introduced animal traction, ploughing, weeding and harvesting tools, fertiliser and improved seed with a glorious management structure from foreign exports in Dakar to district supervisors in each of the 45 districts containing 20 villages. The scheme was a flop, however. Devised to increase peanut production to cover the 25% expected reduction in export price when peanuts lost privileged entry to the French market in 1968 (demanded by the EEC), it caused farmers to grow more staple food such as millet and fewer peanuts. The Senegalese farmers were behaving economically in a perfectly rational way, having experienced the vicissitudes of the market for peanuts for several generations. They are not, like one colonial economist's savages, 'under the domination of custom and impulse, never forecasting the distant future, governed by the fancy of the moment, fitful in spite of their servitude to custom' etc! Between 1963 and 1968 the price of peanuts fell by a quarter, but the price of rice—bought by farmers from the cash sales of peanuts—increased by 35%. The returns to the farmers after mechanising and allowing for the extra work, are poor in most parts unless spare land is available, even under the best conditions, the increase in earnings for the working day are less than 20-25%—and the extra financial risk has to be carried.

Despite the fall in peanut product revenue in Senegal, or the increased sale by farmers of nuts and crudely processed oil moonlighted over the border into Gambia, there is still intensive effort by the world bank and other bodies to push peanuts and encourage mechanisation.

Last year with less than half its normal rainfall, Senegal lost half its peanut crop, which in turn weakened demand for locally produced goods as farmers' incomes fell causing widespread unemployment in the industrial sector. 200,000 tons of rice and 120,000 tons of wheat had to be imported on a commercial basis; bread is a French introduction, of course.

Senegal economist Samir Amin points out that the historical specialisation in peanuts has been a bad mistake. The farmers would be better off rearing beef cattle on their savannah lands, he claims, and Senegal's main agricultural potential lies elsewhere with irrigation in the developed Senegal Valley, growing early vegetables and sugar, or rice cultivation on the Guinea-Bissau border.

Amin suggests that Senegal should develop steel production to make railway lines and boats. These at least would add value to exports by refining Africa's wealth of exported minerals. It is also important to develop the neglected fisheries and high technology industry—the latter to allow West Africa a fairer share of the international division of labour and wealth, as well as the education that makes this possible. He also points to the waste in oil cake, animal products and skins, and the need to recycle scarce materials such as timber and fish wastes. (AT enthusiasts please note).

The Senegalese Government nationalised the peanut marketing network but at a time when there were no longer huge surpluses to be had. It is trying to finance its development programmes from a resource base whose international market price has been steadily falling. Despite being nominally socialist, the Senegalese government is forced to invite foreign capital and firms to invest on terms that are increasingly harmful to the Senegal economy. Agricultural development land for irrigation is nationalised but severe social divisions on the ground, a legacy of the slaving era of the past, inhibit and discourage the mass of the farmers from taking advantage of it. Having exhausted the possibilities of substituting imports with home-made products and with little access to modern technologies, it is difficult to see how the Senegalese can progress. Their main chance in the short term is to organise and strengthen themselves in a protected African economic community. What chance the New International Economic Order?

References:

Capitalism & Slavery, Eric Williams, Andre Deutsch 1964.
Neo-Colonialism in West Africa, Samir Amin, Penguin African Library 1973.
Operation Groundnuts, Lessons from an Agricultural Extension Scheme, Elizabeth Hopkins, 1971 from IDS Sussex.
An Economic History of West Africa, A. G. Hopkins, Longman 1973.
 (Never mentions Samir Amin.)

MERIP REPORTS
Middle East Research & Information Project

From *MERIP Reports,* no. 85 (February 1980), pp. 3-5

US Targets Persian Gulf for Intervention

by Joe Stork

US Secretary of Defense Harold Brown, at the end of 1978, confided to a reporter that in the years ahead the US would "have a very difficult time avoiding the choice" between armed intervention in the Third World and "severe damage to our national interests and resources." "You say how could it be worse than Vietnam?" he asked rhetorically. "I guess what I'm saying is that our vital interests are more likely to be involved. . . ."[1]

It was another month before Brown and other Administration policymakers got specific about which part of the world they were most concerned about, a month that saw the overthrow of the Shah in Iran, a border war between the two Yemens, and the conspicuous dispatch of warplanes, military advisors and arms to Saudi Arabia. The wraps came off such neutral terminology as "non-NATO conflict contingencies." President Carter's National Security Advisor, Zbigniew Brzezinski, requested that the Pentagon firm up contingency plans for a Rapid Deployment Force, with the Persian Gulf as the main target.

The 1,000 miles or so of oil reserves and producing complexes that stretch across the Gulf from Saudi Arabia's eastern province through the small shaikhdoms,

Kuwait, southern Iraq and into Iran's Khuzestan Province is the source of 34 percent of US petroleum imports, 61 percent of Western European imports, and 72 percent of Japanese imports,[2] and the site of more than half of the world's proven oil reserves. The growing dependence of the US and its major industrial allies on petroleum imports from the Gulf intersects with the increasing political instability of the region that Fred Halliday surveys in this issue.*

The latest events in Iran and Afghanistan have tipped the balance within the Carter Administration towards the proponents of possible armed intervention. Brzezinski has been emboldened to

*[Fred Halliday, "The Gulf Between Two Revolutions: 1958-1979," *MERIP Reports* 85 (February 1980): 6-15.—eds., *Alternative Papers.*]

announce that "Rapid Deployment Forces will give us the capability to respond quickly, effectively and *perhaps even preemptively* in those parts of the world where our vital interests might be engaged. . . ."[3] The concept of rapid deployment finds its pedigree in the weapons development programs of the McNamara-Kennedy years. Much of the planning and production of ingredients such as the giant C-5A transport aircraft, Landing Helicopter Assault Ships, and "bare bases" originated in the 1960s as a consequence of US intervention in Vietnam and the Dominican Republic.[4] This doctrine came to take a back seat in the late '60s and early '70s to the so-called Nixon Doctrine, the mercenary strategy that placed primary responsibility for counter-insurgency combat on regional allies. Iran was the undisputed "pillar" of this policy in the Middle East, as exemplified by its intervention against the revolution in Oman. The main test of rapid deployment was a very partial one: the massive airlift of weapons and munitions to Israel during the October War of 1973.

The rapid deployment concept surfaced within the Carter Administration in August 1977, in Presidential Review Memorandum 10, which considered it an essential component of the 'one and a half wars' doctrine.[5] Yet it took until December 1979 before an officer was designated responsible for implementing what has so far remained a paper-pushing exercise. Behind the inaction lie inter-service rivalries, some dubiousness even within the military establishment of the utility of such a force, and unwillingness to commit funds that

Peg Averill/LNS

otherwise could be thrown at multi-billion dollar aircraft carriers, strategic missiles and the like.[6] Recent developments in the Middle East have strengthened the hand of proponents of this force, but the chief factor has been Carter's commitment of up to $10 billion to the force over the next five years, allowing the services to have their cakes and eat them too. A jurisdictional struggle between the Army and the Marine Corps has apparently been resolved with the appointment of Marine Corps General Paul X. Kelley to head the force, thus insuring that the Marine Corps will not become extinct for lack of missions. Kelley's approach is gung-ho: before his appointment he remarked that "in looking at the 1980s, it becomes obvious that we need a sharper focus for the Third World. The US would do well to sharpen that focus before we let it slip through our fingers."[7]

The Corps has been practicing Middle East-type landings for some five years now, but lacks the means of getting there fast. The immediate budget commitment for fiscal 1981 is $220 million for the first two of a fleet of "floating bases," and $80 million towards developing a successor to the C-5A transport planes. The big bills will come over the next five years: the development of airlift capabilities is expected to cost $6 billion, and the "floating bases" another $3 billion, before the cost over-runs for which the Pentagon is famous. As a Library of Congress study observed, the Gulf "is more remote from the US than any other source of petroleum imports"—7,000 nautical miles by air, and much further by sea.[8] The Army's 82nd Airborne based in Fort Benning, Ga., has been the primary unit designated for Third World interventions, with a third of its 15,200 men on continuous alert. But the buildup of heavy weaponry in the Gulf region over the last decade makes the lightly-equipped 82nd ill-prepared for armed intervention in that region. A former Army staff officer with Strike Command, as Rapid Deployment Forces was known in the early 1960s, is skeptical about the latest flush of activity. "There's nothing new about it," he said. "Now, they're publicizing something out of deep standby and giving it a sexy title. If the [RDF] was committed anywhere, we'd be uncovered in eight other places."[9]

Other less-publicized elements of what could emerge as the Carter Doctrine are integral to any potential US armed intervention. US naval presence in the region has increased throughout 1979 with the addition of two destroyers to the three-ship Middle East Task Force ported in Bahrain, and carrier task forces now appear regularly in the Indian Ocean waters off the Gulf.[10] The Indian Ocean base at Diego Garcia will be "enhanced," and several Pentagon teams have visited the region recently to coordinate base usage in Oman, Saudi Arabia and Somalia. The Saudis have pushed the US to look to Somalia for permanent basing rights at the Soviet-built facility of Berbera, and turned down the offer of a permanent US base presence in Arabia itself.

This is a mere formality. The US military presence in Saudi Arabia is already quite large, in the form of training teams, technicians, and "white-collar mercenaries" who come in the employ of the large arms manufacturers. A high-level US "planning and command structure" team spent the spring of 1979 in Saudi Arabia supervising the reorganization of the Saudi Ministry of Defense and establishing a planning unit within it. The head of the team was Maj. Gen. Richard Lawrence, who also participated in joint US-Israeli-Egyptian military talks in Washington before taking up his Saudi assignment. Lawrence is regarded as a strong candidate to head up a proposed Middle East command, if that responsibility is shifted from US military headquarters in Europe.[11]

A RAND Corporation report for the Pentagon in December 1978 recommended that US planning "assign a more prominent role to the performance by US forces of certain key *noncombatant* functions, such as airlift, logistic support, communications and intelligence . . . to facilitate more effective military collaboration among friendly countries of the region. . . ."[12] Brown obviously subscribes to this approach. As recently as December he said, "I don't believe that American bases as such in that area are the right way to go. A number of countries in the area can maintain bases which, in an emergency in which they asked our help, we could then come in and use."[13] Certainly the huge Saudi military complexes being constructed by US firms—Al-Baten, Tabuk

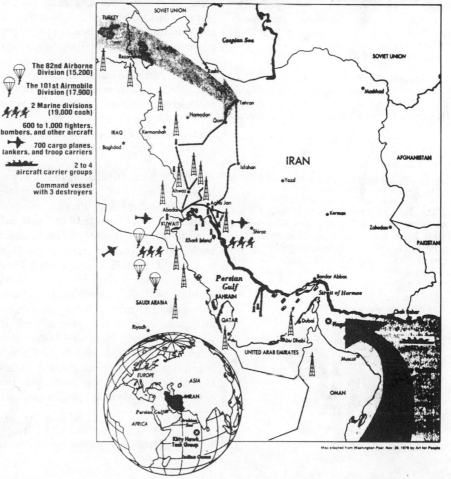

U.S. Forces Available for the Middle East

The 82nd Airborne Division (15,200)

The 101st Airmobile Division (17,900)

2 Marine divisions (19,000 each)

600 to 1,000 fighters, bombers, and other aircraft

700 cargo planes, tankers, and troop carriers

2 to 4 aircraft carrier groups

Command vessel with 3 destroyers

Map adapted from *Washington Post*, Nov. 25, 1979 by Art for People and Khemis Misheyt—as well as the former US base at Dhahran, would serve this purpose. Base facilities have also been offered by Morocco, Egypt and Israel, as well as Oman and Somalia.[14]

While publicly eschewing a formal military alliance with the US, the Saudi regime has, behind the scenes, used the rush of military equipment and advisors around the Yemen crisis in February 1979 to increase the US military presence in Saudi Arabia itself. *The Economist* of London, not usually given to exaggeration in such matters, wrote in October: "We believe . . . that there is a two-squadron revolving flight of American combat aircraft using Saudi airfields and serviced there by American personnel. We also believe that there are about 1,000 American servicemen, including army engineers, stationed in Saudi Arabia."[15]

Notes

1. *Washington Post,* Jan. 2, 1979.
2. John Collins and Clyde Mark, "Petroleum Imports from the Persian Gulf: Use of US Armed Forces to Ensure Supplies," Library of Congress, Congressional Research Service Issue Brief #B79046 (May 1979), p. 2.
3. *Washington Post,* Dec. 20, 1979. Emphasis added.
4. See Mike Klare, *War Without End: American Planning for the Next Vietnams* (New York, 1970), especially chapter six, "Strategies Mobility and Intervention—the Doctrine of Rapid Deployment."
5. *Washington Post,* Aug. 27, 1977.
6. *New York Times,* March 24, 1978; see also Col. James B. Agnew (Ret.), "'Unilateral Corps': Is the US Turning a New Strategic Corner?" *Army* (Sept. 1979).
7. *Washington Post,* Dec. 6, 1979.
8. Collins and mark, *op. cit.*
9. *Aviation Week and Space Technology,* Oct. 8, 1979, p. 13.
10. *New York Times,* Jan. 5, 1980.
11. *Washington Post,* June 3, 1979.
12. Malcolm Kerr, *et al.,* "Inter-Arab Conflict Contingencies and the Gap Between the Arab Rich and Poor," report prepared for Director of Net Assessment, Office of the Secretary of Defense, R-2371-NA. Emphasis in original.
13. *Washington Post,* Dec. 18, 1979.
14. Ibid.
15. *The Economist,* Oct. 13, 1979.

MERIP REPORTS
Middle East Research & Information Project

From *MERIP Reports,* no. 87 (May 1980), pp. 14-20

Revolutionary Iran and Its Tribal Peoples

by Lois Beck

Less than half of the total Iranian population of 35 million speaks Persian as a first language. Except for religion in the case of the four percent of the population which is non-Muslim, language is used by Iranians as the main distinguishing feature of population groups. As the revolutionary process continues in Iran, distinctions between the Persian and the non-Persian populations, including tribal peoples, will undoubtedly have increasing political significance. Persians dominate all urban areas of central Iran and most of the plateau. Most high-level religious figures are Persians. National wealth and power are concentrated in Persian hands; the largest segment of the upper class is Persian. Persians fill most government positions, are the most highly educated and professionally trained, and are the most subject to Western influence. In addition, Persian language and culture, having been propagated from the center, dominate the nation.

Iran's regional, tribally-organized populations, almost all of whom speak languages other than Persian as first languages, are regarded as national minorities. Many are located in strategic border, gulf, and oilfield regions; others are in often inaccessible mountains. They include, in approximate order of size: Kurds, Baluch, Bakhtiyaris, Lurs, Qashqa'i, Turkmen, Shahsevan, Arabs, and many other smaller groups, such as Afshars, Basseri, Hazaras, Tajiks, and Timuris. Iran's largest non-Persian population, the Turkic-speaking Azeris (Azerbayjanis), along with the majority of the nation's Arab-speaking population, are

not tribally organized. A "tribe" is a sociopolitical response to state pressure and, as such, is often territorially based. Tribal membership is defined primarily by political affiliation to leaders. Tribal members often claim to share kinship bonds and common ancestors, and notions of cultural distinctiveness are also a factor. Prior to the twentieth century, Iran's tribes had economies based primarily on nomadic pastoralism. Now most tribal populations are settled in villages and towns, have mixed agricultural and pastoral economies, and have become increasingly dependent on wage labor.*

Regional, tribally-organized populations played peripheral roles in the national effort to rid Iran of the Shah. The revolution was originally an urban phenomenon, and one that primarily involved Tehran. Tribal populations are not generally integrated into the urban religious institutions and the student and leftist organizations that were integral to the revolution; few demonstrations or other revolutionary activities took place in rural areas before the end of 1978. Tribal people working in the oil industry, as well as those who had migrated to Tehran and

*Discussion of the use of the term "tribal" is beyond the scope of this short essay. Four points though are worth noting here: (1) the sociopolitical units referred to here as "tribal" exhibit great variation across the Iranian landscape; (2) all named tribal groups, such as the Kurds and Lurs, consist of many sociopolitical units; (3) political participation and ethnic identification within tribal populations vary; and (4) "tribal" does not mean "traditional" (or "primitive") but rather refers to sociopolitical formations and responses which have occurred in both historical and contemporary times. The term "national minority" is in many contexts much perferable to "tribal group." However, this essay does not discuss all of Iran's national minorities, and, of the national minorities, the tribal ones have characteristics that the nontribal ones do not, such as certain political organizations, leadership systems, kinship structures, and relationships with other political formations.

Names of specific tribal groups and leaders are often intentionally omitted in the following discussion because of the rapidly changing political environment in Iran and the region. It is not clear what future is in store for Iran's tribal groups and leaders, especially in the event of the establishment of strong central government or in the case of foreign intervention.

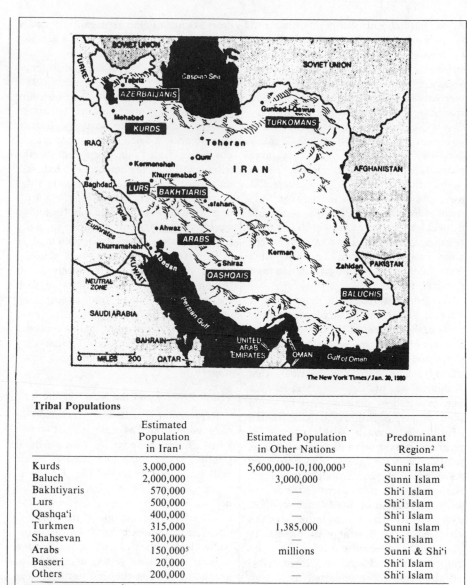

The New York Times / Jan. 20, 1980

Tribal Populations

	Estimated Population in Iran[1]	Estimated Population in Other Nations	Predominant Region[2]
Kurds	3,000,000	5,600,000-10,100,000[3]	Sunni Islam[4]
Baluch	2,000,000	3,000,000	Sunni Islam
Bakhtiyaris	570,000	—	Shi'i Islam
Lurs	500,000	—	Shi'i Islam
Qashqa'i	400,000	—	Shi'i Islam
Turkmen	315,000	1,385,000	Sunni Islam
Shahsevan	300,000	—	Shi'i Islam
Arabs	150,000[5]	millions	Sunni & Shi'i
Basseri	20,000	—	Shi'i Islam
Others	200,000	—	Shi'i Islam

1. Accurate statistics on Iran's tribal populations do not exist. Richard Weekes' *Muslim Peoples: A World Ethnographic Survey* (Westport, CT, 1978) contains essays, written primarily by anthropologists, on these and other ethnic groups in Iran. The population estimates derive partly from this source.
2. An estimated six percent of Iran's Muslims are Sunni.
3. The higher figure is that of Martin van Bruinessen, *Agha, Shaikh and State: On the Social and Political Organization of Kurdistan* (Utrecht, 1978), p. 22.
4. There are a significant number of Shi'i Kurds, and many Kurds belong to Sufi orders.
5. The estimated total Arab population in Iran is 615,000. For lack of statistical information, it is extremely difficult to determine the proportion of tribal to non-tribal peoples among Iran's Arab population. The best estimate is that Iranian Arabs are about evenly divided between Sunni and Shi'i Islam.

other cities for wage labor and education, participated in revolutionary activities along with worker and student groups, not as tribal representatives. These demonstrations were almost exclusively male, with exceptions in some cities in Kurdistan and in Shiraz, where young women in a tribal school demonstrated together in the streets, in tribal dress, with Turkic and Luri slogans.

Tribal People and the Pahlavi Regime

Tribal populations had as much reason to detest the Shah and the Pahlavi regime as the more revolutionary urban Iranians. Their political and economic structures had been debilitatingly undermined by both the Shah and his father. Since the 1920s tribal leaders had been subjected by the state to execution, imprisonment, exile, and property confiscation. Through history, tribal leaders had mediated between tribe and state; in this century, state action against tribal leadership was often the first and most important step toward political domination of the population. Under Reza Shah, nomadic pastoralists were forcibly settled. Mohammad Reza Shah provided no assistance to either migratory groups or those desiring to settle, and instead placed them under military control and restricted their movements and land use. Tribal populations, as well as many fellow citizens, were victims of incompetent and often corrupt government officials under both shahs, and political activities were restricted, most effectively after the creation of SAVAK in 1957. Those of tribal affiliation were not usually represented in government, except for some tribal elites, most of whom did not represent tribal concerns but rather their own class and personal interests.

Rural and tribal populations were subject to economic hardships in the 1960s and 1970s due to loss of land and work through pasture nationalization and national land reforms, increased capitalist penetration, and high inflation. Much agricultural and pastoral production became unprofitable; the state increasingly relied on imported food, which it brought in under cheap tariffs and sold at subsidized prices. It became cheaper for many Iranians to buy imported food than to produce it themselves. Tribal peoples were among the nation's most impoverished citizens. As residents of the state's most isolated, marginal areas, they received scant benefits from rapidly increasing oil revenues. National services such as education, health care, water control, and transportation were poorly developed.

In this context, the heavily-financed efforts of the Queen to glorify tribal and ethnic culture through arts festivals and handicraft production—both of which were oriented toward tourist and elite consumption—were worse than misplaced. Tribal populations, as well as all ethnic minorities in Iran, were denied many national rights under the Pahlavis and were victims of Persian chauvinism. National education, in which all students were required to read and write in Persian and in which Persian culture and civilization were stressed to the almost complete neglect of the contributions of other population segments, was culturally destructive. For tribal children who were offered formal education, most school teachers were urban Persians, as were almost all government officials in tribal areas. One exception was an innovative program in Fars province which did provide tribal teachers for many of the region's nomadic children.

The Revolutionary Process

The nation's tribal populations joined the revolutionary process as significant forces only with the decline and then virtual end of central authority in late 1978 and early 1979. At this time many acts against the central government occurred in and around tribal areas; these were not directed toward the revolutionary aims proclaimed by the Ayatollah Khomeini and other insurgent forces as much as they were responses to weakening central control and to the change in the balance of power in provincial areas. Except at times in Kurdistan and Baluchistan, they were not generally organized through local religious leaders. Anti-government disturbances occurred at government offices, gendarme posts, army depots, and customs stations. Often caches of arms and ammunition were the incentives. As the gendarmerie and army became ineffective, tribal groups attacked government officials and their local patrons and supporters. For one tribal group previously known for its state-threatening powers, the only reported "revolutionary" acts were attacks on two virtually deserted gendarme posts and the seizure of supplies abandoned by the French at an isolated mining camp on the day of the deposed Shah's departure from Iran.

The Khomeini regime has attempted to reinstate central authority in many areas through two new institutions which are under the aegis of the Revolutionary Council: Revolutionary Committees (komitehs) and Revolutionary Guards (pasdaran). In contrast to many lower-middle and lower-class urban areas, where the two units often represent the class interests and cultural identities of the people for whom they are responsible, this is not the case in many provincial and tribal areas, and some populations have resisted their presence. Only in regions where settled tribal groups are in the majority, as in much of Kurdistan and Baluchistan, are some komitehs comprised of fellow tribal members and supporters and are not the threatening, exploitative forces they can be elsewhere. Activist clerics (and their supporters) who are closely allied with Khomeini and other clergy in Qum are at the core of most komitehs. Komitehs tend to represent existing wealth and power structures, which in provincial and tribal areas are dominated by large landowners, merchants, and capitalist farmers and stockraisers. Along with the Revolutionary Guards, komitehs have taken over many governmental functions, including many gendarmerie functions. For that large proportion of Iranian tribespeople who are Sunni Muslims (see table), involvement in local affairs by a Shi'i state through Shi'i revolutionary forces presents additional difficulties. As is the case with Iran's non-Muslim minorities, they express concern about what citizenship in an expressly Shi'i state will mean for their own religious (and political) freedoms.

Kurdish resistance to the imposition of Persian, Shi'i revolutionary forces in their areas in the summer of 1979 brought about a state military response. The resulting death and destruction helped to convince many Iranians—tribal and nontribal—that Khomeini was not the kind of leader they had expected or desired. That he could send Iranian Muslims to kill Iranian Muslims so soon after his triumphant return from exile was a turning point in his relations with the national minorities, and resistance to him and his associates spread. Some tribesfolk had boycotted the March 1979 referendum on the Islamic republic, and boycotts increased with the summer's election of the Assembly of Experts to draw up the constitution and with the fall's constitutional referendum. Some tribal groups reportedly supported local gendarmes against Revolutionary Guards sent from Tehran. Revolutionary Guards and Committees were driven out of some towns in tribal areas, and insistence that they be removed from others was commonly expressed by many tribal groups. Various high-ranking state officials and clerics were sent from Tehran and Qum to negotiate settlements. In order to prevent bloodshed in several towns in Fars province, tribal leaders and local clerics agreed independently—without government involvement—that tribal members would not brandish arms while visiting town if Revolutionary Guards would stay totally out of the countryside (and hence out of local tribal affairs).

In August 1979, the government produced and distributed wall posters which depicted Khomeini as the benevolent patriarch of the nation's tribes, represented by men and women in a diversity of tribal dress. Other attempts to gain or restore loyalty were also evident. Khomeini offered support for tribal groups (along with condemnation of Kurdish dissidents) in his speeches. But on September 5, 1979, in a televised speech in which he officially greeted a delegation of Turkmen tribesmen who had walked from northeast Iran to Qum to present demands, he stated that all groups in Iran (and he named specific tribes) had suffered under the Shah and that none could expect immediate solutions to problems. Except for the Kurds, who were allocated a large sum for public works, those tribal groups formally requesting state assistance in such matters as land reclamation, roads, wells, schools, clinics, and cooperatives received no response, and their early exhilaration with the revolution turned into a deepening resentment. Some tribal leaders have become quite nationalistic in their attitudes toward Iran in the face of what they jokingly say is "the second Arab invasion."*

Tribal Peoples and the New Regime

Representatives of some tribal and ethnic groups, as well as some opposition and leftist groups, propose for Iran a federal political system with autonomous ethnic and provincial regions. The Khomeini regime has to date strongly rejected this notion, and there is no provision in the newly-adopted constitution for regional autonomy. Some tribal populations, especially those which extend across Iranian borders into other states, demand local autonomy and self-rule and have formally presented their cases to central authorities. Others, particularly those whose leaders had been systematically removed by the Pahlavi regimes, have not effectively articulated a set of demands. Few if any tribal groups demand total independence or secession from the Iranian state; most express the desire to contribute to and benefit from Iranian citizenship, including expected access to oil income.

The Kurds, who are the most organized in this regard, formulated the slogan "the self-determination of Kurdistan and democracy for Iran" at various sessions of the Conference on the Self-Determination of Kurdistan held in Sanandaj in the summer of 1979. Demands which they wanted

---

*They see the emergence of the Islamic Republic as a second sweep of Islam into Iran, and Khomeini as someone more concerned about Muslims beyond Iran's borders—the Palestinians, for example—than about Iranians.

legislated in the constitution included: Kurdish officials for the autonomous region, local police forces under local control, restrictions on the placement and activity of state army forces, constitutional safeguards for the customs and traditions of all national minorities, teaching in the Kurdish language at all levels, a Kurdish university, economic development, improved facilities such as medical services, and freedom of the press. Demands issued by some Baluch in the new Islamic Unity Party included: regional autonomy, appointment of Baluch to positions in the provincial administration, teaching in the Baluch language, and the right of free contact with Pakistani Baluchistan.

The establishment of productive links between minority populations and the government is currently impeded. Especially until the resignation of the Bazargan government in November 1979, a system of parallel governments existed in which the directives and understandings of officials from Tehran and Qum often differed. Both Prime Minister Bazargan and the Ayatollah Taleqani had agreements with Kurdish leaders about regional autonomy which were later ignored by Khomeini and the supporting clergy. In addition, revolutionary forces and self-styled vigilantes often act independently of either Tehran or Qum. Finally, political polarization within minority populations, especially between traditional leaders and young leftists, inhibits efforts to link populations with the center.

Linkages among Iran's national minorities, which might facilitate common efforts, are also weak. In the spring of 1979, Naser Khan Qashqa'i* proposed plans for a federation of southern tribes, and in January 1980 he spoke of a union of Iranian tribes, but to date no concrete steps in these directions have been taken. Effective political organization and capable leadership within single national minority populations could serve as a catalyst for broader movements. The Kurds and the Baluch, however, are the only tribal populations currently possessing formal political parties. The Kurdish Democratic Party was outlawed by Khomeini in the summer of 1979, and its leaders were sought by his revolutionary judge, the Ayatollah Khalkhali. Two other

*Naser Khan Qashqa'i, paramount Qashqa'i leader, had been in exile under the deposed Shah for 25 years. He returned to Iran in January 1979 and has been active in national, regional, and tribal affairs since then.

Kurdish political groups are the Marxist-Leninist *Komala* and *Fedayi Khalq*. In 1979 a Baluch group formed the Islamic Unity Party, and the activities of political parties in Pakistani Baluchistan are increasingly having an impact on Iran's Baluch.

Results of the Revolution

For Iran's rural and tribal folk, the major results of the revolution so far are the decline in central authority and certain local economic benefits. The revolution did not transform the nation's socioeconomic structure. New power figures tend to support the existing class system, although wealth and power are shifting from the control of the secular westernized upper class—much of which has left Iran along with its money—to the allied forces of the clerics and the bazaar bourgeoisie. For some rural and tribal folk, decline in government authority has allowed acts of resistance to established structures. Those populations politically organized and well armed are the most active in this regard. The resurgence of tribalism, rather than being the "survival" of an archaic form of organization, is instead a very contemporary response to current conditions of central weakness and to the center's attempts to establish political domination.

Nomadic pastoralists are seizing pasturelands taken from them in the 1960s and 1970s, and expelling such non-tribal occupants as capitalist herdowners. Many who had been forced out of nomadic pastoralism have now abandoned their villages or urban jobs to resume migration. Many pastoralists and agriculturalists regard the deposed Shah's land reforms as illegal and illegitimate. There is competition among landowners—large and small, tribal and non-tribal—over land, as well as peasant revolts and general resistance to landlords, many of whom are out of Iran or afraid to visit their lands. Individuals and groups desiring to retain or seize land often seek tribal support for their actions. Some peasants take by force the land they sharecropped, rented, or ought to have received under a genuine land reform, sometimes by simply harvesting standing

LNS

crops or planting their own. There is also some resistance to and action against tribal leaders who attempt to retain or regain former privileges. Some tribal leaders under land reform were entitled to keep, as private property, formerly communal tribal land. Certain tribal groups are now demanding these lands for themselves, and some are successful. Small groups of leftists in some tribal areas are attempting to coordinate these actions, while Revolutionary Guards are acting to preserve the status quo.

One issue on which Revolutionary Committees and Guards have supported rural and tribal peoples against existing exploitative relations is in moneylending and commerce. Until early 1979, many moneylenders and merchants charged from 50 to 100 percent yearly interest on loans and goods taken on credit; this was a primary cause of much rural poverty. With the establishment of the Islamic Republic, taking interest for profit was declared prohibited, and clerics and committees ordered that debts be recalculated to represent the actual amount of loans and purchases. Some of those who refused were publicly flogged or imprisoned.

Another local benefit of revolutionary conditions is greater economic productivity for many of the nation's tribal people. Soon after Khomeini's return to Iran, imported frozen meat was proclaimed unclean and ordered destroyed. Foreign suppliers are now said to be following proper Islamic procedures in animal slaughter, but meat imports are still reportedly much below that of prerevolutionary times. Demand for meat and dairy products is high and the nation's pastoralists—many of whom are tribal—are able to find a good market. Many former nomads have resumed pastoralism, often on land that had been taken from them or others under the Shah. Flock redistributions within some tribal groups have allowed the impoverished to become economically productive. Raiding seems not to be prevalent. Many who were wage laborers or heavily indebted before the revolution are now able to assume greater economic independence.

But for Iran's agriculturalists (tribal and non-tribal) whose links with the land had been weakened or broken because of the economic disruptions of the 1960s and 1970s, return to production is more difficult. Many irrigation works are ruined, land abandoned and no longer cultivable, land tenure systems disrupted, and kin-based relations of production undermined and altered by urban wage migration and the penetration of capitalist relations of production into rural economies. Agriculture demands a much higher capital investment than pastoralism, and many rural and urban Iranians are unable or reluctant to make the necessary financial commitment in these unstable times. The Khomeini regime's plans for an "Islamic" land reform have not resulted in action to date.

The State, the Tribes and the Left

Throughout much of Iran's history, the state has played a direct role in tribal leadership by such practices as providing tribal leaders with resources and responsibilities (local law and order, tax collection, army formation) and attempting to install or replace tribal leaders. Part of this pattern continues in revolutionary Iran for a reason found also in history: the state's inability to control and administer its regional, politically organized, armed populations. In some areas the state entrusts local—and not just tribal—affairs to tribal leaders. On at least several occasions in the summer of 1979, Khomeini publicly attributed peaceful conditions in Fars province to Qashqa'i leaders. State authorities, in particular secular officials and army gendarme officers whose forces are now weak, utilize tribal leaders as surrogate state officials and as mediators. One tribe's leaders are used to solve another tribe's disputes; the state has even transported leaders by helicopter to dispute locations.

Such use of tribal leaders can enhance and legitimize their regional and national position, inhibit local or leftist efforts to establish more egalitarian structures, and further undercut state authority and control. In September 1979 the prime minister issued an order demanding that the citizens of Fars province who were carrying arms submit them to state authorities within three days. The order was, however, first issued to a local tribal leader, who was expected to implement it. Nothing came of the order, other than an advancement of this leader's status. In another incident, gendarmes who were unable to end a fight between two tribal sections over pastureland stopped a tribal leader who happened to be driving to another location on other business and asked him to mediate the dispute. He agreed to the task but was unable to fulfill the mission; one of the disputants killed him on the spot. Another tribal leader, long in exile during the Pahlavi regime, boldly claimed that he could, within 10 days, end Khomeini's difficulties with the Kurds if Khomeini ordered him to take one thousand tribal warriors to Kurdistan. After he was condemned by fellow tribal leaders, he withdrew the offer.

Especially since the state's military involvement in Kurdistan last summer, Khomeini has attempted to blame tribal and other national minority unrest on leftist and foreign agitation. This draws attention away from minority group demands, increases tension between the state and its minorities, and increases the zeal with which Revolutionary Guards attempt to "restore order." An indication of the apparent ease by which the Western press accepts the Khomeini regime's explanations of provincial unrest is in the conflicting wire service reports on disturbances in the Gulf port of Bandar Langeh on January 5-7, 1980. The disturbances were first attributed to the presence of Qashqa'i and Khamseh tribesmen, then to disputes between resident Persians and Arabs, and finally to differences between Shi'is and Sunnis.

The extent to which national minorities and leftist groups are allied is not yet clear. Small leftist groups are found in most politically organized and active tribes, but they are having variable degrees of success in attracting support and developing common goals. Leftists who lack tribal origins have great difficulty in establishing rapport; this is especially the case for young, urban, Persian leftists. Where leftist groups have international affiliations, some tribal members express concern that their tribes will be used opportunistically—primarily as military forces to aid a leftist regime's establishment—and that they would be denied national minority rights once the new regime was in power. The example of the fate of Muslim and tribal minorities in the Soviet Union is frequently cited, and the developing situation in Afghanistan between the Soviet-backed government and insurgent tribesmen is closely followed by (conflicting) shortwave radio broadcasts in Persian from many sources including Afghanistan, Great Britain, Soviet Union, Voice of America, Israel, Romania, and Iraq.

Leftist sentiments and activities within tribal populations are found among the young generation, especially those who are formally educated and professionally trained. Some tribesmen who were military officers under the Shah in Dhofar (Oman) and Kurdistan—and who were radicalized by this experience—also have leftist inclinations. In southwest Iran it is especially teachers connected with a tribal education program originally sponsored by the United States who are leftist. The leftist core of some tribal groups consists partly of sons and daughters of former or established tribal leaders. They are usually Western educated, were active in leftist groups abroad, and have contacts with leftist movements within and outside Iran. As is true of many Iranian families whose members had different levels of revolutionary participation and who have different political affiliations, some tribal elite families are also politically split. In one case, the father meets regularly with Khomeini in Qum, the son quietly seeks out opposition leaders who are underground in Iran or abroad, and the daughter engages in grassroots activity in an urban shantytown where she provides health services and classes in literacy and Islamic law to formerly nomadic, now settled and impoverished, tribal women and children.

At the time of this writing (early January 1980), it is increasingly apparent that the Khomeini regime's hostility to the demands of tribal and other national minorities and its charge of foreign and leftist intervention are distracting attention from the regime's stated goal: the transformation of Iran from a secular, dependent capitalist, Western-oriented, monarchical dictatorship into a popularly-supported, economically viable, non-aligned, Islamic republic. In refusing to grant Iran's many national minorities basic democratic rights, the regime creates further difficulties and postpones coming to grips with other tasks at hand. Disturbances in tribal and provincial areas are largely the result of the center's continued intolerance of local desires for self-rule and its refusal to alter the Pahlavi policies of chauvinistic domination of the political, economic, religious, and cultural life of the countryside.

BULLETIN
OF CONCERNED ASIAN SCHOLARS

From *Bulletin of Concerned Asian Scholars* 11, no. 3 (July-September 1979): 22-27

Kampuchea and *The Reader's Digest*

by Torben Retboll

Events in Asia regularly outpace our slow review and production schedule. So it has been with this essay by Torben Retboll, based on a talk given before the Vietnamese invasion of Kampuchea. The crucial issue on Kampuchea is the nature of the Pol Pot regime. Battles between socialist states and revelations about executions within Kampuchea during the period when Pol Pot was leader also are important issues. We encourage the submission of analyses of those issues. But Retboll's purpose is a different one. He reminds us to be scrupulous, and he exposes certain "experts" who have been unscrupulous and deceitful.

In the summer of 1977, two journalists, John Barron and Anthony Paul, published a book which in the United States was entitled *Murder of a Gentle Land* and in Britain *Peace with Horror*. In both cases the subtitle was *The Untold Story of Communist Genocide in Cambodia.* The authors are both working at the institution, *The Reader's Digest,* which publishes a monthly appearing in 32 countries in 13 languages. In February 1977 *The Reader's Digest* published a summary of their book which thus became available to more than 30 million readers all over the world.[1]

As the title indicates, this is a strong attack on the Communist Party of Kampuchea (Cambodia) which came to power (headed by Pol Pot) in April 1975 after five years of civil war and which is accused by Barron and Paul of conducting a systematic and coldblooded genocide behind almost totally closed frontiers.

This is one in a series of essays with differing points of view on the intercommunist conflicts of Southeast Asia that have been published in the *Bulletin of Concerned Asian Scholars,* Box R, Berthoud, CO 80513. Reprinted with permission.

The Evacuation of Phnom Penh

On the face of it, the book appears to be a well-documented account with careful references for every single paragraph in the text. Actually their scholarship collapses under the barest scrutiny. On the evacuation of Phnom Penh, for instance, after saying that some people saw executions, they state that "although not everybody personally witnessed such summary executions, virtually everybody saw the consequences of them in the forms of corpses of men, women and children, rapidly bloating and rotting in the hot sun. The bodies, sometimes grotesquely contorted in agony, yielded a nauseating, pervasive stench, and they had a transfiguring effect on the hundreds of thousands of people being exiled."[2]

As evidence of this claim, so expressively described, they refer to three different sources: (1) interviews with a number of Cambodian refugees; (2) an article in the *Sunday Times* of May 8, 1975, and (3) a report from Associated Press, dated Bangkok May 8, 1975, and supposedly published in the London *Daily Mirror* on the following day.[3]

We are unable to check the refugee accounts, but we will return to the question of their reliability later on. The two published accounts, however, can readily be checked. Turning to the first of these, we discover that there is no *Sunday Times* of May 8, 1975, but on May 11 the paper carried a long article on the evacuation written by John Swain. Presumably this is the one they have in mind. Swain, however, has not seen any "summary executions" let alone "the consequences of them"—or at least he does not mention any in his article. Turning to the second of the published sources, we discover that there is no AP dispatch in the *Daily Mirror* of May 9, 1975. Instead there is a short item on the evacuation written by an anonymous *Mirror* correspondent who writes that the evacuated foreigners "heard reports of wholesale executions of Cambodians. But they never saw any themselves."

There is, in fact, an AP dispatch dated Bangkok May 8, 1975. It is written by two French journalists, Claude Juvenal and Jean-Jacques Cazaux. It appeared in the *Washington Post* on the following day, but

they too state that "not a single corpse was seen along our evacuation route." In other words, all the evidence which can be verified gives no support whatsoever to Barron and Paul's claim—certainly a remarkable fact which is not very likely to increase our confidence in those parts of their account which cannot be checked. When the fact that this claim was undocumented was pointed out to the authors shortly after the publication of the book, they simply denied having made any mistakes.[4]

On the other hand there are many eye-witnesses to the evacuation who are never quoted or cited in the book. In the first place we may mention Richard Boyle of Pacific News Service who explicitly denied the accusations that the evacuation was a "death march."[5] Secondly, the French reporter Patrice de Beer who wrote that "it is surprising that the people who have taken highways no. 1, 4 or 5—the principal roads of the evacuation—have seen only a few bodies, and often of soldiers. Nor did we see anything on our three and a half day journey from Phnom Penh to the [Thai] frontier. We are far from the thousands of corpses rotting in the sun at the gates of the city about which some people have spoken, which no one has seen with his own eyes, but about which they have heard an interpreter or a friend speak. . . . Strange as it may seem, no one has witnessed an execution. And as for the foreigners, no one has been hurt."[6] Thirdly, there is Father Jacques Engelmann, a priest with nearly two decades of experience in Cambodia, who reported that the evacuated priests "were not witness to any cruelties" and that there were deaths but "not thousands as certain newspapers have written."[7] And finally, the German reporter Christoph Maria Fröhder, who explained that "we too heard about the rumours. I drove to the place of an alleged execution twice, but found neither witnesses nor traces."[8]

The omission of these and several other sources along the same lines is not incidental; it is deliberate. When Barron and Paul collected material, they had—according to their own statement—all the international offices of *The Reader's Digest* at their disposal, and this meant they they were able to monitor almost every newspaper, magazine or book appearing in the main languages. The omissions are not a matter of inadvertence but rather a conscious attempt to suppress evidence which might disprove or modify their own conclusions.

Ponchaud and Lacouture

Barron and Paul also quote a communist official in the Mongkol Borei district who supposedly declared on January 26, 1976, that "to rebuild our new Cambodia, one million men is enough."[9] This statement—in several different versions—has been widely reported in the press as an official admission that a systematic slaughter of the Kampuchean population is taking place. But this contention does not seem to be reliable, either. In the summer of 1976, the Swedish magazine *Vietnam Bulletinen* published an interview with Jan Lundvik, an official in the Swedish State Department who had accompanied the Swedish Ambassador to China, Kaj Björk, on his visit to Kampuchea a few months earlier. Lundvik explains that "when the Cambodians say that they can make do with one million people, they mean that they can solve any task, no matter how few they are, and not that they are in the process of exterminating the remainder."[10] On the face of it, this interpretation—which has been totally ignored by the media—appears to be quite plausible. And its credibility becomes even greater if we take a closer look at the fate of this "quote."

It appeared first in an article in the French paper *Le Monde* of February 18, 1976, written by François Ponchaud, a French priest who lived in Cambodia from 1965 to May 1975 and who speaks the Cambodian language, Khmer. However, one year later, in March 1977, when he published his book, *Cambodge annee zero,* Ponchaud no longer used this telling statement from the communist official in the Mongkol Borei district, because here—with no explanation whatsoever—it has been changed into an anonymous communist slogan, a "horrible joke" he says, according to which "it is enough with one or two million young people to rebuild Kampuchea."[11] This inconsistency between two of Ponchaud's own quotes was pointed out by Noam Chomsky and Edward Herman in an extensive review-article in *The Nation* of June 25, 1977. As a result of their comments (and a further discussion in private letters) Ponchaud has now completely eliminated the passage in question from the American edition of his book—*Cambodia Year Zero*—published in June 1978. Yet it remains unchanged in the British edition of the book, published simultaneously, but not for sale in the United States because of a trade agreement between these two countries.[12]

This omission is not incidental, either. In fact, it turns out that several passages about which Chomsky and Herman had raised doubts have been rewritten or modified in the American version, whereas they stand unaltered in the British copy. None of these changes are marked or in any way explained by Ponchaud. The prefaces to the two editions are not identical, either, although they are both dated on the same day, September 20, 1977 (which is obviously false, since the American preface contains a reference to a letter from Chomsky, dated October 19, 1977). The American text opens with lavish praise of "the responsible attitude and precision of thought that is so characteristic of . . . Noam Chomsky. . . ." But in the British edition, this passage has been replaced by a strong attack on Chomsky; and furthermore an attack which is based on a series of crude and—necessarily—deliberate falsifications. All this is quite remarkable, especially in view of Ponchaud's repeated declarations of his own honesty and integrity. The petty deceit which he practices here and which is very easily exposed is not very likely to increase our confidence in those parts of his account which we are unable to verify.

The quote, however, lives on—notwithstanding Ponchaud's own (partial) retraction of it. In October 1978, Jean Lacouture—a French journalist whose 1977 review of Ponchaud's book was widely quoted in the press even though it was later revealed that it contained serious errors and gross distortions—published a book entitled *Survive le peuple cambodgien!* which is a strong denunciation of the "genocide" taking place in Kampuchea. But apart from a short survey of a number of articles and books, he hardly offers any hard evidence for this charge; and one of the few sources which he does mention is precisely this communist slogan which, incidentally, he even misquotes: "It is enough with one and a half or two million Cambodians to rebuild the country."[13]

'Famiglia Cristiana'

The most well-known passage in the Barron-Paul book is, however, their rendition of an interview that the Italian journalist Paola Brianti is said to have made with the Kampuchean former president Khieu Samphan during the August 1976 conference of non-aligned nations in Colombo, capital of Sri Lanka.[14] In this interview, which appeared in the Italian weekly *Famiglia Cristiana* on September 26, 1976. Khieu Samphan declares that "more than one million Cambodians perished during five years of war" and that "the present population of Cambodia is five million." Then the interviewer goes on to say that before the war in 1970, the number was seven million and asks what has happened to the remaining million. To which Khieu Samphan replies: "It is incredible how concerned you Westerners are about war criminals!" Via Barron and Paul, this statement has been widely quoted in the press as an official admission that one million people have been massacred by the communists. But in this case too, there is reason to be careful.

A check of the Italian original reveals, for instance, that the Barron-Paul rendition of the interview is inaccurate: They have "improved" the text by changing the sequence of the sentences and by transforming a part of the interviewer's question into a part of the president's answer. Furthermore, it turns out that Khieu Samphan never actually *admits* to the death of one million people; only the context seems to imply this. Indeed, in another passage—not quoted by Barron and Paul—he insists that "the stories of massacres that are being published by sections of the Western press at regular intervals are a disgraceful slander spread by traitors who had fled Democratic Kampuchea."

More importantly, the whole interview is presumably a fabrication. In the first place, the *Famiglia Cristiana* is a rather unknown religious magazine that is rarely cited in international politics, and it does not seem very likely that Khieu Samphan should have decided to give an exclusive interview to their reporter. Secondly, it is also extremely doubtful that Khieu Samphan should have placed the population of Kampuchea at five million—if only because the government just six months earlier had announced an official figure of 7,735,279. Finally, in a letter to Chomsky dated August 17, 1977, Ponchaud has stated that "I know for certain that the Italian journalist writing in that journal never interviewed Khieu Samphan: She was in the company of French journalists and never left them." And considering the fact that Ponchaud is known as a strong opponent of the present regime, his words must, in this case, carry much weight.[15]

However, in spite of repeated requests from Chomsky, Ponchaud has denied to expose the interview in public, and it continues to crop up in the media, such as in *Time* magazine and the *Boston Globe*. But whereas the *Globe* accepted a short response explaining the doubts, *Time* refused to print a similar letter.[16] Actually, this latter case is even more dishonest. It turns out that in preparation for this article *Time* contacted Noam Chomsky hoping to elicit from him a quote that there had been no atrocities which they could use. "But instead of giving them what they wanted, Chomsky explains, "I ran through a list of fabrications in which *Time* and its colleagues were involved. Specifically, I went through the whole *Famiglia Cristiana* story. Therefore their use of the fabricated interview was not a matter of inadvertence but rather conscious lying."[17]

Refugees

Barron and Paul knew perfectly well that the interview may be a fraud because Ponchaud has told them so in a letter of June 30, 1978, but they have no wish to deny the story, either. Instead they have continued their criticism of Kampuchea in a new article in *The Reader's Digest* of August 1978. Just like the book, this new article is primarily based on interviews with refugees in Thailand and—partially—France and the United States. Refugee accounts are often extremely unreliable; they must be taken seriously but with care and caution. Barron and Paul report accounts of hunger, terror and bloody massacres, about exhausting forced labor under the gun of guards and about summary executions of everyone who dares to voice the slightest complaint over the situation. As already mentioned, we are unable to check these interviews since they are not available in print. Even so, there is no doubt that their selection is strongly one-sided.

One Western specialist, Michael Vickery, who speaks Khmer and who visited camps in Thailand in 1976, was told by the refugees that the camp directors singled out witnesses who had brutal stories to tell for the benefit of Western visitors.[18] This fact is indirectly confirmed by Barron and Paul themselves when they explain, in the preface to their book, that they "approached the camp leader elected by the Cambodians, and from his knowledge of his people compiled a list of refugees who seemed to be promising subjects." And Vickery's skepticism is directly confirmed by the West German reporter Hans Ulrich Luther who, after having visited camps in the beginning of 1977, stated that "for a few dollars they will tell you anything."[19]

On the other hand there are many refugee accounts—readily available—that are never quoted or cited by Barron and Paul. In the first place we may mention a former medical student interviewed by the West German reporter Christel Pilz at the end of 1975. On the evacuation of Phnom Penh, this witness said that "we too were ordered by the Khmer Rouge [i.e. the communists] to move out into the countryside. We refused and said that we had to take care of the wounded. They realized that. They left us in peace, and even brought us some food. . . . In the middle of June the Khmer Rouge told us that we now had to leave Phnom Penh." And on his journey through the country, he explained that "in several places the people spoke about wholesale executions of soldiers from the defeated government. But this was not so everywhere."[20]

Secondly, the first wave of refugees arriving in Thailand in the summer of 1975 reported that they had been well treated by the communists and that they had neither been subject to nor seen signs of brutality.[21]

Thirdly, there are Peang Sophi and Khoun Sakhon who were interviewed respectively in Australia (1976) and the United States (1977) and who both denied the stories about systematic terror and massacres.[22] Finally, one should consider the Vietnamese refugee who explained in the beginning of 1978 that he had wandered from Vietnam through Kampuchea in 1976 without seeing or hearing about any executions or wholesale massacres.[23]

Barron and Paul are unable to refute accounts such as these because they can hardly accuse the refugees of being sympathetic to the Kampuchean government. Instead they simply decide to suppress them, creating the illusion that refugee accounts are consistent and that refugees always tell of communist atrocities.

Further Distortions

Several other points in the new article which can be verified also prove to be doubtful. For instance, they say that "the capital Phnom Penh, which previously had three million inhabitants, now has no more than 15,000." It is true that at the end of the war in April 1975 Phnom Penh held around three million people but at that time the city had been swollen by about 2.5 million refugees from the countryside. Barron and Paul do not explain that it was the U.S. bombing that these people were fleeing; nor do they explain anything about the catastrophic conditions of sanitation, health and nutrition under which most townspeople were living and which might be one of the motives for evacuating the city.[24] Naturally, this point may be considered less essential since no one denies that the city was evacuated or that the present number of inhabitants is not very great (officially 200,000). Still, the example seems to be relevant because it illustrates the way in which Barron and Paul manipulate the facts in order to give the darkest possible picture of the situation *after* April 1975.

Another important point is their description of the so-called massacre of January 28. They state that "on January 28, 1977, Cambodian forces crossed the Thai border and slaughtered the inhabitants of three villages" and add that "as evidence . . . the Thai government produced photographs of slashed and mutilated corpses" thereby creating the illusion that their claim is proved beyond doubt. It is not. In the *Far Eastern Economic Review* of February 11, 1977, Norman Peagam raised serious doubts about the Thai government's version of the events and showed that important evidence suggests that the massacre was, in fact, committed by the Khmer Serei, an anti-communist Cambodian organization, who knew that the episode would be blamed on the communists. This point of view has been further explored by Larry Palmer in the Australian journal *News from Kampuchea* of October 1977. But all of this is ignored by Barron and Paul.

In his speech at the International Cambodia Hearing held in Oslo in April 1978, Barron also presented the Thai government's version. He was criticized by Ponchaud who argued that the question had better be left open. Ponchaud repeated this point in his letter to Barron referred to above. But this too was ignored by Barron and Paul: obviously, facts are unnecessary and refutations of falsehoods irrelevant.

At the end of their article, Barron and Paul mention the visit to Kampuchea in January 1978 by three Scandinavian diplomats. They quote the Danish Ambas-

Ross Beecher/LNS

sador to China, Kjeld Mortensen, as saying that "we all . . . agreed that this must be the most radical upheaval in world history of a society in any country . . . " and they add the observation made by his Finnish colleague Penti Suomela that "it was like an absurd film, a nightmare." Both of these rather inane remarks are correctly quoted from the Danish paper *Jyllands-Posten* of January 23 and 24, 1978, but on the other hand Barron and Paul fail to report the quite significant statement from the diplomats that in their view there is no hunger in Kampuchea any longer.[25] Nor do they mention the four Yugoslavian journalists who visited the country two months later and who corroborated this latter view.[26] Thus, we are once again dealing with a deliberately one-sided selection and use of the evidence.

Conclusion

Naturally, one may ask why we should take two reporters from a journal such as *The Reader's Digest* seriously enough to examine their claims and conclusions. The answer (which is already partially given) is that Barron and Paul have had considerable influence on the media reports on Kampuchea. Several distinguished journalists and scholars have reviewed the book very positively, praising its "impeccable documentation." The book has already been translated into French and Norwegian. The media in many countries —including the Vietnamese—have quoted it repeatedly (the most well-known case being the interview with Khieu Samphan, already discussed). And at the International Cambodia Hearing in Oslo, two of the five "experts" invited were Barron and Paul. Therefore it would appear to be relevant to reveal that their account is unreliable and that they are consistently using falsified or dubious sources, crude suppressions and serious distortions in their attempt to "prove" the evils of communism.

If we return to where we started, it is now obvious that the subtitle of the book—the untold story of communist genocide in Cambodia—is an outright lie, because ever since April 1975 the Western press has produced article upon article condemning the "genocide" that allegedly took place. Nor is it true that before the communist "take-over" Kampuchea was a "gentle land" as the American title would have us believe. Underneath the smiling surface there were profound social and economic contradictions about which Barron and Paul fail to inform us. We are left, then,

with the allegation of "genocide" that hardly has been proved by Barron and Paul. And their hypocrisy becomes complete when it turns out that the undeniable destruction and mass murder caused by the American war machine in the years from 1970 to 1975 are never referred to—let alone criticized—by the authors of this book.

This is not to say that there were no atrocities in Kampuchea after April 1975 or that the refugee accounts are always false or even grossly distorted. Those relatively few persons who have cared about the facts and who quite unjustly have been branded as apologists of the new Kampuchea—such as, for instance, the late Malcolm Caldwell, Noam Chomsky and Ben Kiernan—have all stressed that refugee accounts *should* be taken seriously and that there has been considerable suffering for the population. But they have also insisted that Kampuchea's isolation from the outside world is no excuse for believing everything, and that information about this country therefore should be treated with the utmost skepticism. Nor is the purpose of this paper to defend any government in Phnom Penh but solely to investigate the credibility of the Barron-Paul accounts.

The conclusion of this investigation should now be obvious and it can aptly be drawn by a witness that hardly can be accused of being sympathetic to the communists, namely the former helicopter pilot, Lim Pech Kuon, who escaped to Thailand in the summer of 1976. Lim participated in the Cambodia Hearing in Oslo. Having listened to Anthony Paul's speech about the innumerable communist atrocities against the population he asked for the floor and then stated that "it is obvious that Paul does not know anything at all about Cambodia. Therefore it is not up to him to judge this country." It is hardly necessary to add that this poignant evaluation of the qualifications of the *Reader's Digest* editor is not mentioned by Barron and Paul.

Notes

A lengthier version of this essay will be included in my book, *Kampuchea and the Western Press, 1975-1978*, to be published in Denmark.

I would like to thank the late Malcolm Caldwell, Noam Chomsky (M.I.T.) and Ben Kiernan (Monash Univ., Australia) for their invaluable assistance and continuous inspiration.

1. *Murder of a Gentle Land*, (New York: The Reader's Digest Press, 1977); *Peace with*

Horror, (London: Hodder & Stoughton, 1977). The British edition contains a foreword by Jon Swain, a foreign correspondent of the *Sunday Times*, who witnessed the fall of Phnom Penh in April 1975.

2. *Peace with Horror*, p. 28.

3. Op. cit., p. 215.

4. Barron, letter, *Economist*, November 4, 1977 (reply to my letter of October 15). Paul, letter, *Far Eastern Economic Review*, December 9, 1977 (reply to my letter of October 28).

5. *Guardian*, New York, May 28, 1975. *Nation Review*, Melbourne, May 30, 1975, Pacific News Service dispatch, San Francisco, June 30, 1975.

6. *Le Monde*, May 10, 1975.

7. Appendix to Paul Dreyfus, . . . *et Saigon tomba*, (Paris: Arthaud, 1975), pp. 346-55.

8. *Der Spiegel*, May 12, 1975. Quoted by Oskar Weggel, "Zwei Jahre 'Demokratisches Kambodscha,'" *Aus Politik und Zeit Geschichte*, Bonn, July 2, 1977, pp. 3-20. For further reports in a similar vein—and similarly neglected by Barron and Paul—see Francois Schlosser, *Le Nouvel Observateur*, May 26, 1975; Jerome & Jocelyne Steinbach, *Phnom Penh libérée*, (Paris: Editions Sociales, 1976); Shane Tarr & Chou Meng Tarr, *The Peoples Voice*, July 13, 1975; and *Nexus*, July 1975, later expanded in *News from Kampuchea*, April & June 1977.

9. *Peace with Horror*, p. 197.

10. *Vietnam Bulletinen*, Stockholm, no. 2, 1976. A German translation of this appears in *Befreiung*, West Berlin, no. 7, June 1976.

11. *Cambodge année zéro*, (Paris: Juillard, 1977), p. 97. Actually, Ponchaud has given still another version of this quote in *Echange France-Asie*, Paris, dossier no. 13, January 1976, p. 17, where he states that "a Khmer Rouge confirmed: 'If only 20,000 young people will be left in Cambodia, then we will rebuild the new Cambodia with these 20,000 young people.'" But it was his versions in *Le Monde* and the book that were read and that then entered the press.

12. *Cambodia Year Zero*, (New York: Holt Rinehart & Winston, 1978), p. 71. *Cambodia Year Zero*, (London: Penguin, 1978), p. 92.

13. *Survive le peuple combodgien!* (Paris: Editions du Seuil, 1978), book list, pp. 78-80, quote, p. 91. A long excerpt of this book appears in *Le Nouvel Observateur* of October 2, 1978.

14. *Peace with Horror*, p. 202.

15. The authenticity of the interview was first challenged in the Australian journal *News from Kampuchea* in December 1977, next by Lewis Simons in the *Washington Post* of February 19, 1978 and then by William Shawcross in the *New York Review of Books* of April 6, 1978, using some or all of the arguments advanced here.

16. *Time* magazine, July 31, 1978; letter sent August 10. On August 21, *Time* printed five other letters in response to this article, none of which questioned the evidence presented there. Edward Giarusso, letter, *Boston Globe*, October 4, 1978; response printed on October 23.

17. Noam Chomsky, personal communication, August 29, 1978.

18. Michael Vickery, personal communication to Noam Chomsky, cited by Chomsky in an interview with Lewis Simons in the *Washington Post*, February 9, 1978.

19. *Frankfurter Rundschau*, May 6, 1977.

20. *Frankfurter Allgemeine Zeitung*, December 19, 1975.

21. *New York Times,* June 13, 1975.

22. David P. Chandler and others, *The Early Phases of Liberation in North Western Cambodia: Conversations with Peang Sophi,* (Clayton, Australia: Monash University, 1976); George Hildebrand, *Guardian,* New York, March 30, 1977.

23. London *Times,* January 30, 1978. The article has incorrectly been attributed to the *Financial Times* of the same date; see, e.g., *News from Kampuchea,* May 1978.

24. Evidence of this can be found in G. Hildebrand and G. Porter, *Cambodia: Starvation & Revolution,* (New York: Monthly Review Press, 1976). Ignored by the media, and not cited by Barron and Paul.

25. NTB report in *Arbeiderbladet,* Oslo, January 28, 1978. Also the *New York Times,* January 23, 1978.

26. Excerpts of their report appear in *Seven Days,* May 19, 1978. The full report in *Weekendavisen,* Copenhagen, June 2 & 9, 1978. See also the *Washington Post,* March 23, 1978.

nacla
report on the americas

From *NACLA Report on the Americas* 14, no. 4 (July/August 1980): 2-6

The Writing on the Wall

by Robert Armstrong and Janet Shenk

Tiny El Salvador caught the world's attention in 1977, when two priests were assassinated and the entire Jesuit order was threatened with extinction by right-wing death squads. The Carter Administration, a few weeks in office, saw in El Salvador the opportunity to demonstrate its alleged commitment to human rights.

El Salvador posed no threat to vital security interests. It was considered a safe place to push for overdue reforms. So the United States attacked the Romero regime for its abuse of human rights and encouraged an alliance between "enlightened" business sectors and the Christian Democratic Party, to prepare for a changing of the guard.

The United States could afford to be self-righteous until July, 1979—the victory of the Sandinista Liberation Front in Nicaragua. A link had fallen out of the chain. Central America—the backyard—was no longer a place to grandstand about human rights. From that time on, the primary goal of U.S. foreign policy in the region would be to avoid "another Nicaragua."

This article is part of a larger study, "El Salvador—A Revolution Brews," printed in Vol. 14, no. 4 (July-August 1980) of the *NACLA Report on the Americas* and available for $2.50 plus .50 postage. Reprinted with permission.

Today, three inter-agency task forces exist within the Carter Administration to monitor crisis situations 24 hours a day. Iran and Afghanistan are the obvious two. El Salvador—ignored by the media, unknown to the public— is now the third.

The crisis should have come as no surprise. As early as 1932, Salvadorean peasants, artisans and workers, armed with only machetes and stones, rebelled against their misery and joined an uprising led by the Communist Party. Within a month of the rebellion, 30,000 had been killed.

After the massacre, El Salvador's "Fourteen Families" returned to their ledgers, leaving generals and colonels to rule on their behalf for the next 50 years. More and more peasants were pushed off the land to make room for coffee, cane and cotton. Farmworker unions were prohibited by law, but the rural proletariat was growing into a latent social force. By 1973, they would be earning only $1.10 per day. By 1975, they would be organized into militant, extra-legal unions and mass organizations. They would be demanding more than higher wages.

By the 1950s, a sector of the ruling class had branched out from agriculture into marketing and finance. Now they were pushing for industrialization, but recognized that certain structural changes had to occur. Wealth, generated and concentrated in the agrarian sector, had to be more evenly distributed to create a market for industrial goods. Taxes had to be levied to finance the required infrastructure. Political unrest had to be quelled by superficial reforms.

A small schism developed within the ruling class. The more "enlightened," modernizing elements managed to gain control of the state (behind a military curtain, of course), but were powerless to carry out reforms that would affect even minimally the interests of more traditional sectors. A compromise was struck: industrialization would proceed, with support from the U.S. government and foreign investors. But nothing would be done to affect the basic distribution of resources and wealth: 60% of the land would stay in the hands of 2% of the population. If Salvadoreans could not afford to buy the products of their own labor, markets would be found abroad.

El Salvador did industrialize in the 1960s and 70s, first within the framework of the Central American Common Market and, after its collapse, by seducing foreign capital with tax incentives, free-trade zones and cheap labor. The average wage in the manufacturing and service sectors, in 1973, was $1.64 per day.

Economic expansion, and the growth of a state bureaucracy, created its own contradictions. Migrants from the countryside swelled the slum communities, or *tugurios,* that circled the capital city. The urban working class, growing in size and organization, tasted the repression that guaranteed stability to investors. And a new middle class, caught between the poles of poverty and wealth, was demanding a political voice and economic reforms.

In the early 1960s, professionals, bureaucrats and small businessmen formed the Christian Democratic Party (PDC), supporting a platform of moderate reforms. Intellectuals and middle sectors formed a social democratic party, the National Revolutionary Movement (MNR). And more radical sectors sought to forge a mass party of the left in alliance with the industrial working class.

By 1972, this electoral opposition was ready to challenge 40 years of military rule. Christian Democrats, social democrats and the Nationalist Democratic Union (UDN), the legal arm of the outlawed Communist Party, formed a united front, the National Opposition Union (UNO, meaning one).

Most observers agree that the UNO candidate for president, Napoleon Duarte, won the 1972 elections by a clear margin. But El Salvator's elite, like its counterparts throughout Latin America, refused to accept the people's verdict. The ballot-box was intended to legitimize military rule, not to end it. So the ballot-box was stuffed overnight, and by morning the victory had vanished.

Still, the ruling class refused to acknowledge its own vulnerability. The new Molina government tried to add a small dose of reform to the standard formula of heavy repression. It proposed a timid "Agrarian Transformation" that was supported by a small, more visionary sector of the ruling class, and applauded by the United States.

The old agrarian interests immediately cried "treason!" and mobilized to halt the reform and take control of the state. In 1977, General Carlos Romero, representing the most retrograde sectors of the bourgeoisie, became president by fraud and ruled by terror alone.

End of the Electoral Road

After 1972, the electoral opposition, with many of its leaders in exile, began to disintegrate. Serious questions were raised about the viability of an electoral strategy. What would ensure a different outcome the next time around, if votes were not enough? An obvious answer was arms. A split in the Communist Party led to the formation of the Popular Liberation Forces—Farabundo Marti (FPL), named after the leader of the 1932 rebellion. A dissident group within the Christian Democrats, joined by other leftists, formed the People's Revolutionary Army (ERP). (See political map.)

These groups took a two-sided approach to their work—focused primarily on the countryside where 60% of the people reside. One side was military: small scattered actions against the security forces, retaliation against government spies and torturers, and kidnappings for ransom. But the FPL in particular sought to avoid the fate of guerrilla groups in Latin America in the 1960s—their isolation from the masses and ultimate destruction. So it began a slow process of building roots among peasants and farmworkers—slow because the rural population was still traumatized by the massacre of 1932.

Organizers helped peasants build wells and roads to inaccessible villages. Their work coincided with the efforts of progressive clergy—imbued with the message of Medellin[1]—to organize rural cooperatives and teach that injustice was sin. Similar forms of work began in the cities—among students, slum dwellers and factory workers.

Between 1975 and 1977, three new organizations emerged, linked to the underground groups but carrying out open, mass work among all the oppressed sectors of the society. These were the People's Revolutionary Bloc (BPR), the Front for United Popular Action (FAPU)

and the People's Leagues (LP-28). Each represented a broad spectrum of constituencies, united in a non-electoral coalition.

These popular organizations became the main vehicle of expression for those whom the ballot-box had failed. Using civil disobedience and massive demonstrations in the streets, they pressed the demands of each constituency as a common project. Textile workers marched with peasants, demanding lower prices for seed and fertilizer; and vice versa, demanding an end to speed-up in the factories and starvation wages.

In rural areas, peasant and farmworker unions were organized despite the official ban. In the cities, trade unions were dominated by the government, aided by the AFL-CIO, or the Communist Party. The popular organizations urged militant disregard of the elaborate web of laws designed to stifle the workers' movement.

They said to hell with the procedures and organized *de facto* strikes and sit-ins. Very soon, existing locals were in the hands of BPR and FAPU workers. New unions were being formed by the BPR. And in the fall of 1979, FAPU won control of one of the largest federations, including unions controlling electrical power, water supplies and railroads.

Political education was an integral part of the experience. Each action was analyzed: why it won or lost, why victory did not solve the basic problem, and why revolutionary struggle continued to be a necessity. The popular organizations focused on demands that were rooted in the daily lives of the people. But organizers never hid their ultimate goal—socialism— and never ceased to draw the connections between poverty and dependent capitalism.

Government troops accelerated the education process. Demonstrators were

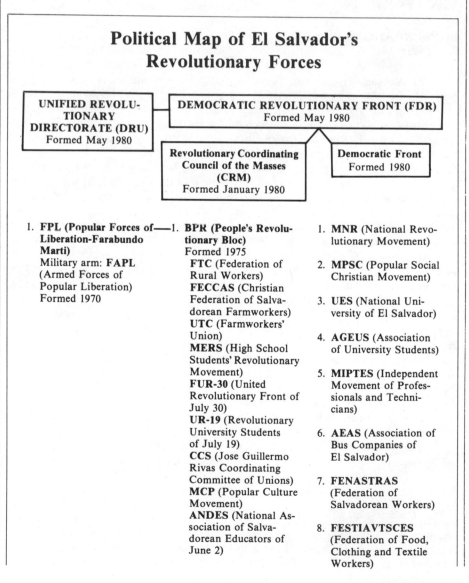

Political Map of El Salvador's Revolutionary Forces

UNIFIED REVOLUTIONARY DIRECTORATE (DRU)
Formed May 1980

DEMOCRATIC REVOLUTIONARY FRONT (FDR)
Formed May 1980

Revolutionary Coordinating Council of the Masses (CRM)
Formed January 1980

Democratic Front
Formed 1980

1. **FPL** (Popular Forces of Liberation-Farabundo Marti)
Military arm: **FAPL** (Armed Forces of Popular Liberation)
Formed 1970

1. **BPR** (People's Revolutionary Bloc)
Formed 1975
FTC (Federation of Rural Workers)
FECCAS (Christian Federation of Salvadorean Farmworkers)
UTC (Farmworkers' Union)
MERS (High School Students' Revolutionary Movement)
FUR-30 (United Revolutionary Front of July 30)
UR-19 (Revolutionary University Students of July 19)
CCS (Jose Guillermo Rivas Coordinating Committee of Unions)
MCP (Popular Culture Movement)
ANDES (National Association of Salvadorean Educators of June 2)

1. **MNR** (National Revolutionary Movement)

2. **MPSC** (Popular Social Christian Movement)

3. **UES** (National University of El Salvador)

4. **AGEUS** (Association of University Students)

5. **MIPTES** (Independent Movement of Professionals and Technicians)

6. **AEAS** (Association of Bus Companies of El Salvador)

7. **FENASTRAS** (Federation of Salvadorean Workers)

8. **FESTIAVTSCES** (Federation of Food, Clothing and Textile Workers)

2. **RN (National Resistance)**——2.
Military arm: **FARN**
(Armed Forces of
National Resistance)
Formed 1975

2. **FAPU (Unified Popular Action Front)**
Formed 1974
   MRC (Revolutionary Campesino Movement)
   FUERSA (United Front of Revolutionary Students, Salvador Allende)
   ARDES (Revolutionary Association of High School Students)
   VP (Proletariat Vanguard)
   OMR (Organization of Revolutionary Teaching)

3. **PRS (The Party of the**——3.
Salvadorean Revolution)
Military arm: **ERP**
(Revolutionary Army of
the People)
Formed 1971

3. **LP-28 (People's Leagues —28th of February)**
Formed 1977
   LPC (People's Campesino Leagues, Heroes of October 29)
   LPS (People's Leagues of High Schools, Edwin Arnoldo Contreras)
   LPO (People's Leagues of Workers, Marco Antonio Solis)
   LPU (People's Leagues of University Students, Mario Nelson Alfaro)
   ASUTRAMES (Association of Market Workers of El Salvador, Maristela Serrano)
   CB-LP-28 (Barrio Committee, Victor Orlando Quintanilla)

4. **PCS (Communist Party**——4.
of El Salvador)
Formed 1930

4. **UDN (Nationalist Democratic Union)**
Formed 1969
   AES (Association of High School Students)
   FAU (University Action Front)
   ATACES (Association of Farmworkers)
   CUT (Workers' Central)

5. **MLP (Movement for Popular Liberation)**
Formed 1979
   BTC (Brigade of Farmworkers)
   CBO (Workers' Bases Committee)
   BRES (Revolutionary Brigade of High School Students)
   LL (Leagues for Liberation)

9. **FSR** (Revolutionary Federation of Unions)

10. **FUSS** (United Federation of Unions of El Salvador)

11. **STISS** (Union of Social Security Workers)

12. **STIUSA** (Union of Workers of United Industries)

Observers:
1. **FENAPES** (National Federation of Small Business)

2. **UCA** (Catholic University "Jose Simeon Canas")

Source: Institute for Policy Studies.

machine-gunned by the Molina and Romero regimes, while para-military squads, the largest being ORDEN, roamed the countryside. But the political-military organizations of the left—FPL, ERP and the RN[2]—struck back, eliminating an ORDEN member, kidnapping a factory owner who used goons against striking workers, harassing the National Guard. Through kidnappings and bank expropriations, the revolutionary forces were able to finance the revolution without involving outside interests. At the beginning of 1980, they were thought to have a war chest of $70 million.

By 1979, the popular organizations had eclipsed the electoral opposition; had mobilized tens of thousands of people, including new sectors such as market vendors, public employees and white collar workers; had brought the brutality of the Romero regime to international attention. They did so by achieving a set of goals that had proved elusive to the Latin American left since the 1960s:

1. The insularity of each oppressed sector was broken down to achieve a basic alliance between peasants and workers, and a broader alliance with marginal and middle class sectors.

2. The isolation of the left was dissolved by developing a firm base within the working class and peasantry, through long years of steady organizing and political education.

3. Immediate economic demands, relevant to the daily lives of the masses, were pressed, within the context of struggling for fundamental change in the political and economic spheres.

4. Open mass work—vulnerable to extreme repression—was combined with military actions that served to demonstrate the vulnerability of the oppressors themselves, to deter potential collaborators with the regime, and to prepare for the larger battle ahead.

5. While maintaining different analyses and conceptions of the struggle, the popular organizations were able to complement each other's efforts and move consistently toward greater unity.

6. The building of large, popular organizations, that permeated every sector of the oppressed and encouraged their active participation in decisions, planted the political and organizational seeds for a system of popular democracy—before and after the victory.

Notes

1. The Conference of Latin American Bishops, held in Medellin, Colombia in 1968, urged the Catholic Church actively to take up the struggle of the poor against the social and political systems which oppress them.

2. The National Resistance (RN), one of the political-military organizations, was formed after a split in the ERP in 1975 (See "El Salvador," Part 1).*

*["El Salvador: Why Revolution?" *NACLA Report on the Americas* 14, no. 2 (March/April 1980): 3-35.—eds., *Alternative Papers.*]

From *The Guardian* 32, no. 25 (March 26, 1980): 16 and 32, no. 26 (April 2, 1980): 18

Chilean Cultural Resistance Rising

by Judy Butler (in two parts)

Sooner than later
when the sun has come out
and the rain of eternal love has showered us;
when those who have left
and those who have remained
are a liberated people;
you will feel deep within you
the justice of a people
who demand that the guilty be punished.

The above is a refrain from "La Vigilia," a musical homage to disappeared prisoners in Chile. Written in 1979, it has been presented in a variety of cultural events.

It is just one example of a flowering of political culture in Chile in recent years as the resistance against the dictatorship develops varied methods to rebuild a movement shattered by the brutal 1973 coup.

The Chile of 1980 is not the Chile of 1973 or even 1975. The junta's repression, for example, is more sophisticated. Tanks no longer patrol the streets, there is no longer a strict 8 pm curfew.

The resistance, likewise, has changed and developed. Activists talk of three forms—legal, semilegal and clandestine. All have their own forms of organization, their own purpose.

Today, cultural/political presentations are becoming common in urban areas of Chile. Established "penas" (political coffee-house type presentations) play to capacity crowds despite sporadic harassment by the authorities. In the poor neighborhoods, barely an evening passes without a poetry reading, theatrical presentation or musical performance by a local singer or group.

'Little by Little'

A Chilean trade unionist recently in the

Reprinted with permission from *The Guardian: Independent Radical Newsweekly* (New York).

U.S. called such cultural presentations the clearest manifestation of the reemergence of the mass movement. In a more poetic reference, one of the postcard-size publications designed to be passed from hand to hand in Chile said, "Little by little and all over the country, small lights are being lit. . . ."

It is perhaps difficult to appreciate the significance of these developments. But as example follows example, one realizes that these events offer for Chileans a chance to rekindle the spirit and the politics of collective resistance.

At the simplest level they are a defiant affirmation of the strong popular culture that by the early 1970s had sparked a new song movement throughout Latin America. Within the first weeks after the 1973 military coup, authors and performers of this music were hunted down as much as political party leaders. Not only were such symbols as singer Victor Jara killed, but in that first terror-filled year, the discovery of one of his records during the house-to-house police searches could be as incriminating as possession of revolutionary literature.

It becomes an act of political significance then to play the traditional indigenous instruments banned after the coup. (The ban was never lifted; it was finally ignored by the military as unenforceable and internationally embarrassing.)

At another level, both audience and performers use thinly veiled political themes—often historic figures who fought for Chile's independence from Spain—to express their personal protest in a forum that allows it to be experienced collectively.

The most impressive example of this collective expression took place two years ago in celebration of International Women's Day. It is viewed by many as a turning point in resistance consciousness. Mostly word of mouth had brought 5000 people to Caupolican Theater, a favorite site for political rallies before the dictatorship. A letter smuggled out of Chile at the time described the palpable militancy of the audience as they regained a sense of their collective strength, chanting and clapping for the speakers as they hadn't dared do in years. A high point came as Matilde Urrutia, widow of poet Pablo Neruda, was introduced.

The shouting and applause were tumultuous as the entire audience arose to pay homage. As the letter says, "It was as if in this one woman, wife of one of the only two permissible symbols of the left today (the other is Violeta Parra), all the nostalgia and hopes of a people were concentrated."

Caught off guard that night, the government forbade any more such massive events. But the military's spell of terror had lost some of its power. Two months later, on May 1—International Workers' Day—hundreds of people took to the streets in the first large public demonstration since the coup. Over 60 people were arrested, but it has not deterred the growth of public demonstrations. On International Women's Day this year, large street demonstrations were carried out in both Santiago and Valparaiso, resulting in the arrest of 130 men and women.

With the banning of large public events, gatherings are now simply smaller, more scattered, more frequent. As a Chilean wrote, "Penas have sprung up like mushrooms after the rain." Professional musicians who can't even support themselves in the more commercial penas sing for free alongside neighborhood performers at local ones. Writing about such a performance of some nearly forgotten campesino songs, the Chilean said: "The mixture of country people with professional musicians is more honest and greater than under the UP [Popular Unity], more alive than ever."

Finally, as a consequence of their decentralization into neighborhoods, the cultural events have often become more overtly political. One held last summer in a Santiago neighborhood was organized by the local "bolsa de cesantes"—group of unemployed workers. ("Bolsa" in military lexicon also means pocket of resistance.) Its theme was support for the Nicaraguan people's struggle against the Somoza dictatorship. The price of admission was one can of food—destined for Nicaragua. Said the moderator: "After all we can't just receive. We also have to give to help other struggles."

Repression Today

The growth of these cultural forms are, in part, the result of certain changes in the junta's approach to repression.

Today the repressive apparatus functions with greater sophistication and selectivity. Tanks on the street have been replaced by occasional groups of soldiers. People picked up for public resistance activity are usually conditionally released

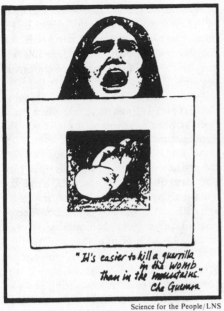

"It's easier to kill a guerrilla in the womb than in the mountains." Che Guevara

Science for the People/LNS

within the 5-day period mandated by the Supreme Court. While torture is still a feature of information-gathering and general repression, it less often ends in unrecorded death. The curfew has been changed to 2 am, and now informers are sent by the secret police to infiltrate the groups and keep an eye on them rather than immediately denounce any individual who dares express opposition to the military. Harassment too is more sporadic, though it still includes house searches and death threats.

There have been at least two reasons given for this. The junta says the need for wholesale brutality has passed, that the task of "rooting out all vestiges of Marxism" is virtually accomplished. According to leaders of the international solidarity movement, however, the junta's iron fist has been fettered by external pressure from governments and Chile solidarity groups.

Both are at least partly true. The junta has certainly done its best to destroy the momentum toward a socialist solution to Chile's economic and social problems. Some 50,000 of the most experienced political people were killed in the first few years, several hundred thousand leftists and progressives imprisoned and tortured, over a million voluntarily or involuntarily exiled, and untold numbers intimidated or rendered jobless—this out of a population of 10 million.

The left parties and left-affiliated unions were immediately declared illegal, including the powerful Central Workers' Federation (CUT). Even the bourgeois Christian Democratic Party was officially banned a

few years later when its leader, Eduardo Frei, awoke to the fact that he would not be heir to the military's "restoration of order" and began voicing opposition to the dictatorship.

Resistance Groups

International censure too has had its effect, though not as much as one would hope. "World public opinion," as expressed through bilateral and intergovernmental organizations, has forced the Pinochet regime to moderate some of its activities. It has also led the government to clothe the dictatorship in veils of legitimacy—frequently referred to as the "institutionalization process."

None of the dictatorship's maneuvers to undercut its bad press are aimed at improving the real economic or political conditions of the masses. After all, starvation wages, minimal state spending on public services and stifled political opposition are the cornerstones of the junta's claims of an "economic miracle." Nonetheless, some of the maneuvers have inadvertently provided a modicum of political space. And with each new opportunity the resistance movement fills that space and pushes against its limits.

Forms of resistance run the gamut from isolated, spontaneous expressions such as the frequent penciled scribbling of the resistance symbol—an encircled R—on walls and bus windows to complex strata of organization. When speaking of resistance organizations per se, as early as mid-1974 the left characterized them as legal, semilegal and illegal or clandestine.

Legal forms are seen as any organization that has been given legal status by the government, including most trade unions, church and social clubs, sports organizations and so forth. Particularly in the early years, when the state of siege prevented groups of any size from meeting in any other context, these organizations formed the only opportunity to engage in even the most cautious conversations.

Semilegal, or as they are sometimes referred to, "de facto" organizations are those which operate visibly and with a certain amount of government tolerance but have no legal standing. They include the "bolsas de cesantes"; neighborhood committees for housing, food sharing, etc.; various groups demanding information and reparation resulting from repression—relatives of the disappeared, of political prisoners, of those killed; the Committee for the Defense of Human and Trade Union Rights (CODEHS), and others.

These groups, which usually operate on a local or neighborhood level, are most often responsible for organizing the cultural events. They struggle for immediate democratic and economic rights, constantly advancing the recognition that dramatic changes in the system must precede real gains.

The motor force of the resistance movement comes from the clandestine resistance committees which began forming as tiny isolated cells within the year after the coup. They are organized within workplaces and communities, schools, parishes, rural areas and military bases, i.e., by constituency. They are made up of a handful of very carefully selected members, and function virtually without contact with other such committees, except through the head of each group. Their objective is the overthrow of the dictatorship, Their task currently is to weaken the dictatorship and strengthen the resistance movement.

PART II

To a foreigner visiting Chile, it would appear that resistance to the dictatorship is minimal.

But that is only true on the surface. A closer look, particularly at the poor neighborhoods and squatter camps, reveals a bustle of activity. People are becoming organized. And although their parties are banned, left militants pack their nonworking hours with meetings.

Most of the organizing is on a small scale—a neighborhood housing group, a youth group with classes and sports activities, a daycare center for children of disappeared prisoners. The groups don't always have a political content, but in many cases organizers view them as a means for drawing people out of their paralysis to take part in a collective response to conditions imposed by the dictatorship.

Meetings Banned

In the first years after the coup, meetings were severely proscribed. The few organizations that remained legal—student associations, sports clubs, mothers' centers, some trade unions—had their leadership replaced by supporters of the dictatorship. Despite obvious limitations, these legal forms were a focus of resistance work. Left organizers slowly and cautiously made inroads.

Today, six-and-a-half years later, these organizations have elected new leaders; candidates known as leftists have run and won.

In the largest and most important legal structure, the trade unions, the military regime has been most determined to maintain control. When the junta introduced its Labor Plan last August, it was openly and immediately rejected as a Bosses' Plan by even the most collaborationist labor leaders.

Some urged a boycott of the plan; others saw in its limited strike and collective bargaining provisions an opening for internal debate and action in which to develop more political forces. Still others saw the strikes as a means of gaining public and official attention. Among the more conscious workers, however, there was no illusion that the plan in itself would bring any real gains.

A leader of one strike effort explained its opportunities for building political consciousness and unity: "The strike isn't to just hang around waiting for the days to pass. We have to organize ourselves to pressure the company and demand improvements. . . . Everyday we eat from 'olla comun.' [Common pots—local soup kitchens contributed to according to one's capabilities and shared among all.] We go make our problems known to other unions. We seek solidarity."

To carry out a strike at all requires cooperation from other sectors—church and neighborhood organizations and rank-and-file worker groups—since neither unions nor workers have any financial reserves. The Labor Plan makes it expressly illegal to aid a striking union. In a recent strike, a group of workers was held five days by police after they were picked up on their way to appeal for monetary help in a Santiago neighborhood.

Since last August there have been hundreds of strikes. Although only a handful of them won even the most minor economic demands, unity was developed at the base level and new links were forged with other sectors.

There are many people who were devastated by events of the last six years. They lost jobs, homes and in numerous cases, one or more members of their family through imprisonment, disappearance, exile or death.

Gradually overcoming their fear, these people have gravitated together to press their particular demands. Such groups operate at what is called the semilegal level. They operate visibly and with governmental tolerance, but have no legal standing.

Though their political space is clearly limited, most of the groups have moved beyond the context of their original demands. The "bolsas de cesantes"—groups of unemployed—began at the local level organizing "common pots" for their neighborhood. Now they function across Santiago and the country through regional coordinating councils, even organizing soup kitchens for striking workers.

The relatives' groups (of the disappeared, of political prisoners, of those killed, of exiles who can't return legally) have also developed regional and national networks since their founding several years ago. Groups such as Committee for the Defense of Human and Trade Union Rights attempt to span such groupings to provide greater links. The immediate tasks of those groups are to pressure for economic and democratic demands. But they have learned that their demands will not be met as long as the dictatorship prevails.

Most of the cultural events described in the first part of this article take place in the "poblaciones" organized by one of the semilegal groups. Because the events are small and the audience is not likely to include any strangers, the events often turn into cautious political forums. And the dictatorship appears to be getting more agitated about the reorganization occurring in those poor communities, traditionally hotbeds of militancy.

Under the guise of a benevolent-seeming plan called "Operation Brotherhood," the government has been evacuating some of the squalid "campamentos" (squatter camps). Dispersing the residents to new government housing, the junta is thus breaking up organized communities.

The dislocated families are asked to sign titles of ownership for the new housing without knowing the provisions—one of which is that they must make payments. When they are evicted for nonpayment, as these unemployed families inevitably are, they are either shipped to another campamento, or on their own return to their old neighborhood to find their former homes leveled.

Eviction Fought

The latest campamento to be hit with an evacuation notice was Nuevo Amanecer. Organized as a result of land seizure in the late 1960s led by the Movement of the Revolutionary Left (MIR) this campamento was known before the coup as Nueva Havana (New Havana). The 340 families affected have publicly announced that they will resist eviction to the end. It is believed that this harassment corresponds, at least in part, to the all-out search for Andres Pascal Allende, secretary general of the MIR, who slipped back into Chile last summer.

The motor force of the growing resistance movement comes from the clandestine resistance committees which began forming as tiny isolated cells within the year after the coup. For obvious reasons they have been less able to coordinate their activities than more open groupings. Organized mainly by constituency, their membership often crosses party lines. Thus it is within these committees that debate about strategy and exchange of documents most often takes place.

THIS SPECIAL PROGRAM ON OUR NATIONAL INDEPENDENCE DAY IS BROUGHT TO YOU BY FORD MOTOR COMPANY, MOBIL OIL, GENERAL FOODS AND THE .

Rius/LNS

Their members function at all levels of society and in all types of activities—unions, poblaciones, schools and universities, business, presumably even in some levels of government. It is in this form that direction, insofar as possible, is given to more public expressions of resistance and that illegal actions are carried out. A large support demonstration for striking Goodyear workers last fall, for example, was organized by a resistance committee within the unions.

Illegal actions have included wall painting and the dissemination of political flyers and pamphlets—both of which are carried out at the risk of one's life. In recent years the character of such acts, referred to as armed propaganda, has escalated to include isolated bombings of selected symbolic targets, money expropriations, temporary takeovers of public transportation, etc.

Increasingly, people are outraged rather than cowed by repression. Most illustrative of this was the popular response to the junta's surprise acknowledgement last summer that Federico Alvares, a teacher, had died under torture shortly after being arrested.

More than 1000 people attended the funeral in a demonstration quickly called by word of mouth. Though the funeral was clearly infiltrated by police agents, the people's anger was openly expressed.

The condition of the left is almost unanimously admitted to be an obstacle in the generally positive trend of growing resistance and organization. In addition to violent repression, which keeps the parties relatively atomized and low in profile, the left is also characterized by contemporary versions of the same sharp political disagreements that existed during the time of the Popular Unity government. Even those parties that are more clearly identified as part of the revolutionary left have been unable to agree on a clear alternative to the political programs of the dictatorship—or for that matter of the bourgeois opposition.

For the most part, revolutionary left debates center on tactical questions, i.e., what is an appropriate timetable and what are the steps necessary to prepare for an inevitable period of armed struggle. But there is still a large tendency within the left, particularly strong in the pro-Moscow Communist Party and large sectors of the Socialist Party, that sees a necessary strategic alliance with the bourgeois opposition—in essence the Christian Democrats—for the overthrow of the dictator-

ship and the reinstatement of a bourgeois democracy.

This disunity at the level of party leadership arises out of more than theoretical differences over the anti-dictatorial struggle. It is also a result of isolation from grassroots sentiment. Because of security problems, people are reluctant to express their more fundamental political views, leaving much room for conjecture about the state of popular consciousness.

According to one Chilean who functions in several semilegal groups and who has worked within the trade union movement for decades, a majority within the popular sectors no longer has any faith in either an electoral strategy to end the dictatorship or a 2-stage road to socialism. They have seen within their own country and from numerous examples in Latin America that no climate exists for this.

Alternative Needed

"The people are ready and waiting for an alternative that will point the way toward socialism," he said. "The bourgeois opposition is not rejected, it's ignored. It is clear that the main enemy is the dictatorship, not the bourgeois opposition, but the popular sectors understand that a return to 'democracy' would be very limited. It won't take them where they want to go."

Others are less certain that such clarity prevails: "It seems that most people are operating in a more schizophrenic fashion—keeping all available options open and working in whatever ways are accessible to them to struggle against the conditions which, for the popular sectors, continue to worsen." This was the opinion of a progressive North American working for the past few years in a poblacion.

The debate at the party leadership level, both within and outside Chile, is apparently less divisive at the base level in Chile, where militants of several parties often work together in unions, semilegal groups and resistance committees. Their unity has been built step by step—just as it has in the other base level organizations—by planning events, strikes and illegal actions; by carrying them out jointly; and most importantly, by evaluating the results together. Not surprisingly, they have come to similar conclusions at this level of practice. What is lacking then, is a higher level of strategic leadership, a programmatic overview that can guide the work they are already carrying out.

In sum, the process is slow and strewn with obstacles. But the inexorable emergence of a mass resistance movement is proof that the junta has ultimately been unable to destroy decades of class-based political consciousness and aspirations.

From *Seven Days* 3, no. 10 (August 14, 1979): 18-19, 35

Time Bomb Ticks Under a Firm Hand

by Rosemary Galli and Gil Gonzalez

Eastern Antioquia, Colombia. Their fields are steeply sloped and the economic struggle is uphill for the Posada family on their three-acre farm 9,000 feet up in the lush, green Andes. A 12-year-old son works the hand pump. Maria drapes the laundry on hedges, stones, and the portico of their two-room, mud-floored house. Her

husband, Don Jose, works the alternating rows of potatoes, corn, and beans, intermingled with patches of cabbage and onions.

The beans will provide all the cash income, about $250, which will permit the family of seven to squeeze by another year. The potatoes the children are harvesting might have supplied a little extra income, but this year the crop was good all over the region, and prices have dropped so low that it isn't worth bringing them to market.

The Posada family is among the privileged, the 40,000 out of one million Colombian peasant households that have benefited from a government project established with the aid of the World Bank and other agencies. To keep the peasants on the land and unmoved by the exhortations of the area's Communist guerrillas, these programs have poured hundreds of millions of dollars into villages which until recently had hardly known the government was anything other than a police force. For the first time, the Posada's village has a school, a health clinic, and running water.

Despite such improvements, the Posadas and other peasants of Eastern Antioquia, one of the country's most fertile regions, are fighting a losing battle against creeping urbanization: Their neighbors are fleeing the burden of absentee landlords, creditors, and marketers to become the cheap industrial labor of the mushrooming, squalid urban slums. In 1975, the latest year for which statistics are available, unemployment was officially 14 percent, while underemployment was calculated at 19 percent in agriculture, 18 percent in industry, and 17 percent in services. Real wages have actually declined since 1970, as employers take advantage of the hundreds of competitors for each job opening.

The paradox is that low wages have limited the market for consumer goods. Like many Third World countries, Colombia's industrialization looks rapid on paper, but it is concentrated in relatively capital-intensive, often American-owned, export-oriented industries, and provides few products and little employment for the rapidly growing Colombian population of 27 million.

Once this lopsided economy is in place, windfalls like the 1975-77 coffee boom, when rising world prices brought additional billions of dollars for Colombia's leading exports, only exacerbate economic strains. Instead of investing their huge profits in productive industry, the Federation of Coffee Growers put it into U.S. Treasury bonds, banks, and speculative investments such as real estate. Easy money from the fabulously profitable cocaine and marijuana smuggling operations is laundered through the same channels. While the property owners and merchants have been caught up in this frenzy of rising profits, workers and peasants and the salaried middle class have seen their real incomes melt as a result of the 35 to 40 percent annual inflation.

The result is an explosive paralysis. Under the pact forged in 1957 to end a decade of civil strife between them, the Liberals and Conservatives share state power. Like his predecessors, President Julio Cesar Turbay Ayala, elected last year when only 35 percent of the adult population bothered to go to the polls,

represents a change without a difference: Control remains in the pockets of the same oligarchy of exporters—U.S. corporations; local industrial magnates; coffee, sugar, and marijuana growers; cocaine processers; and the big cattle ranchers. Their smuggling is often winked at, their taxes are minimal and often evaded. Someone has to pay, and the combination of wealth at the top and increasing misery at the bottom shows who.

The government's response to growing popular discontent has been some social welfare, and more repression. When bus fares were raised for the second time in one month in May 1978, the military responded to violent demonstrations by occupying the cities. Workers called a one-day national strike and high-school and university students joined the protest. Street battles were common; two students who had been tortured and murdered were found in a ditch.

Unrest continued through the summer. In September, President Turbay Ayala instituted a security statute which allows military arrests for ten days without charges and substitutes military courts for civilian in matters of "public safety." When 103 lawyers bravely issued a public protest, they were suspended from practicing. This "permanent institutionalization of a state of siege," as former president Carlos Lleras Restrepo termed it, has extended military control over matters formerly the province of judges, mayors, and even the police.

The Colombian army's skills in counterinsurgency and administration were first obtained in the countryside during the early 1960s when President Kennedy sent military and CIA advisers. Intelligence and police forces organized with the help of U.S. aid were subsequently placed under the armed forces, increasing their efficiency and effectiveness. With two decades of experience, they were ready to extend their reign to the cities as well.

On January 2, 1979, the generals got their excuse for full occupation when an urban guerrilla group known as Movimiento-19 seized over 5,000 weapons from a Bogotá arsenal. The army moved into action. Thousands of the usual suspects—workers, peasants, Indian leaders, and leftists—were arrested, but in addition doctors, lawyers, priests, internationally known artists, even ex-military officers, were rounded up. Both the liberal daily El Espectador and the radical weekly Alternativa, whose editors include the novelist Gabriel Garcia Marquez, carried firsthand

accounts of the torture meted out to detainees.

President Turbay Ayala has rejected all criticism of the army's actions. Despite a 20-year state of emergency, he recently boasted, it is only under his administration that Colombians have begun to feel secure from violence. "We do have martial law," he admitted to the French newspaper Le Monde, "but it operates legally." When asked about the charges of torture, which have received widespread publicity in Europe if not in the U.S., the president replied, "Detainees have been found with detailed manuals explaining how they should pretend they were tortured. The object is to arouse international intervention. I don't say that prisoners are given champagne and caviar, but prisoners are not tortured. I have asked the minister of justice and the attorney general a thousand times to be vigilant on this issue. We even have cases of detainees who have mutilated themselves so they can say they were tortured."

Part of this disagreement stems from a difference of opinion as to what constitutes torture. Commented Daniel Samper, a columnist for El Espectador, "I do not agree with the thesis that a bit of pressure is all right. Pressure in this case means lack of food and forced insomnia. It also means blindfolding people, making them stand up for four consecutive days, forcing people's heads into tubs of water, etc. This can kill."

Arrests have continued, and the government is now preparing a mass courtmartial of several hundred people accused of belonging to M-19; the military high command will provide both the prosecutor and the judges. Although the government claims that M-19 has been smashed and all the stolen weapons recovered, its guerrillas have continued to mount bold actions, including the seizure of a major newspaper plant in order to print 10,000 copies of their paper.

Legal leftist groups have also attempted, with mixed success, to show that they will not be crippled by arrests. In February, the Movement of Independent Workers and Revolutionaries (MOIR) and the Communist Party forgot their intermittent feuding to join with other groups in sponsoring a mass movement against the security statute. In March, under the initiative of Gabriel Garcia Marquez, bishops, liberals, and professionals came together with workers, peasants, and leftists for the first time in a forum to protest government repression.

"I don't fear a military takeover because Colombia isn't Uruguay, the conditions are very different," declared former president Lleras at the forum, "but I fear the possibility of a change in Colombian democratic rule. I fear the spread of corruption among some officials. . . . In any case, the army is not prepared to assume the tasks which it now has."

More radical critics are less satisfied with "Colombian democracy," even as it functioned under Lleras, and at the same time less sanguine about the likelihood of avoiding brutal military rule, which now burdens most Latin Americans.

A major problem for the left has been the sharp divisions between its two major parties, MOIR and the Communists, on many issues. Although the editors of the radical weekly *Alternativa* and others have complained that they are more interested in Peking and Moscow than in Colombia, disputes between MOIR and the CP actually reflect fundamental disagreements on the type of revolution needed and the methods necessary to carry it out.

MOIR now favors nonalignment on international issues in the interests of left unity, but the Communist Party insists that support for Cuban foreign policy is essential. MOIR will work only with unions independent of government control, while the CP believes in building alliances with unions tied to the Liberal and Conservative parties.

Disputes came to the fore once again this March, when the Communists joined radicals and representatives of the Conservative and Liberal parties in a two-day forum on government use of force and torture against the oppotition. MOIR sharply criticized the events on the grounds that the Liberal and Conservative participants, including former president Lleras, were sponsors of identical policies when they held high positions in previous governments.

In spite of these differences and state repression, labor, students, and the left have continued to expand their activities. Unions representing steel, oil, communications, public health, education, textiles, and shipping workers all went out on strike during the first half of this year. Several dozen independent labor unions with a combined membership of about 300,000 have formed a loose confederation whose aims include combating the security statute and fighting for Colombia's independence from U.S. domination.

There is no middle ground in Colombia.

What passes for democracy there cannot effectively maintain the grip of the Colombian oligarchy and U.S. interests; the state governs through naked force, and the only countervailing power is the people—workers, peasants, students, and intellectuals.

Rosemary Galli teaches at the University of Redlands in California and Gil Gonzalez at the University of California, Irvine.

From *third world*, 1980, no. 4, pp. 52-55

Colombia: 20 Years of Guerilla Warfare

Tracing the background of M-19, whose February feat in Bogotá hit the world's front pages. With characteristics all its own, the armed struggle in this country survives and grows but sees no quick victory.

With various groups active in city and country, long experience and great capacity to survive, Colombia's organized guerrillas have roots and characteristics differing from all others in Latin America. Beginning almost immediately after the "Caribbean crisis" of 1962, the movement was defeated but very soon replaced by new organizations that have operated uninterruptedly till today. Yet the movement of the 60s (students influenced by the Cuban revolution) already had precedents in the previous decade—campesinos resisting the terror that the government launched against them.

Unlike the typical armed revolutionary movement in Latin America, Colombia's has long continued to coexist with a regime that "tolerates" political opposition. In other countries where guerrillas went into action against regimes with a modicum of liberal legality, one of three outcomes soon resulted: the guerrillas were smashed (showing that the moment was inopportune), or the regime suppressed all liberal legislation (as in Uruguay in 1972), or a terrorist military dictatorship took over (as in Argentina). In Colombia none of

Reprinted with permission from *third world*. Based in Mexico City, *third world* is the English edition of a magazine on the Third World made by Third World journalists. Also published in Spanish and Portuguese.

these has so far occurred, yet the guerrilla movement's prolonged vitality shows that it is no "passing phenomenon" nor mere "adventurism" by students or urban petty bourgeoisie.

Another unique characteristic is its slowness in gathering influence among the masses, despite its demonstration of staying power over nearly two decades. It took less time for Cuba's 26th of July movement to be born, grow and triumph, for the Vietnamese to prevail over the world's greatest military power, for the Nicaraguans to oust the Somoza dynasty. Of course such movements do not follow any fixed rules, but the comparison reveals the peculiar "tempo" of the Colombian guerrillas' evolution, often a source of confusion to the foreign observer who tends to the hasty judgment that they have either been destroyed or are on the eve of taking power.

'Here Comes M-19'

In the second week of April 1974 a series of teaser ads appeared on page one of the Bogotá daily *El Tiempo*, chief organ of the liberal oligarchy. The first, in white letters on black: "Here comes M-19"; the second, "Wait for M-19"; and similar texts followed, as if to arouse curiosity about some new commercial product. The last of the series, with the key to the puzzle, never reached *El Tiempo*'s advertising department.

Instead, an item came to the paper's news desk around noon on April 19 which explained the enigma: a guerrilla commando had seized the Casa de Bolívar (the liberator's old home, now a museum), removed one of the illustrious former tenant's swords and painted on the walls: "With the people, with arms, to power, M-19." The new organization disseminated copies of its first proclamation to the Colombian people, explaining that Bolívar's sword had been grasped again to "fight for the second and final independence of Colombia."

The public-relations flair of M-19, and the keen political instinct shown in its first operation, hit the public imagination. At the same time it filled the high army command and dominant political circles with apprehension. For the military, after nearly a decade of vain efforts to wipe out rural guerrillas, it meant new complications in the task of repression: confronting the "irregular" war on new terrain—Bogotá, the capital city with its 5 million inhabitants, its vast slums, and the constantly renewed disgust of most of its people with the oligarchic regime. For the politicos it had a different but equally threatening aspect: claiming for itself the role of "armed fist of the ANAPO people," M-19 was announcing its intention of intruding into the heart of the country's great political problems.

Political Gimmickry

The ANAPO (National People's Alliance) to which M-19 proclaimed its adherence was a populist-type movement organized in the 60s by Gen. Gustavo Rojas Pinilla with a basically anti-oligarchic program that won rapid support from the urban masses, especially the very poor. Rojas Pinilla ran for President in 1970 and got more votes than the rival candidate backed by the Liberal and Conservative parties. He was swindled out of his victory by the President in office (a Liberal) who barred journalists' access to the vote tabulations, declared martial law, put Rojas Pinilla and ANAPO's less submissive candidates under house arrest, and announced the victory of the official candidate, a Conservative.

This frustration deepened the prevailing skepticism about a formally liberal system which was really an authoritarian instrument for the dominant bloc and which, thanks to a constitutional reform dating from 1957, established for Colombia the famous "alternation" policy: a legal gimmick under which Liberals and Conservatives have for 20 years alternated in power with total disregard for other parties or political groups and for the election results.

In face of this, M-19's proposal was both simple and disquieting. Noting that the April 1970 events showed the impossibility of legally displacing the oligarchy from power, it invited the ANAPO masses to support the armed struggle as the only viable means of securing a popular government. But the response was less swift and massive than M-19 leaders hoped and the

traditional ruling class feared. With Rojas Pinilla's death, the movement passed to the leaderhip of his daughter Maria Eugenia and her husband, Sen. Samuel Moreno Diaz, both of rightist tendencies, who took to harassing the ANAPO left and seeking a break with revolutionary positions. Furthermore the movement went into progressive decline, deserted by the masses who after the 1970 electoral blow seemed to lose all confidence in it.

First Kidnappings

M-19 responded with a more and more independent line of action. It commandeered supermarket trucks and distributed their contents in slum areas, intercepted factory transports and showered their occupants with revolutionary leaflets, and carried out a series of politically motivated kidnappings of which those of José Raquel Mercado and Benicio Ferreyra were most famous. Mercado was president of the Colombian Workers Central, one of the country's four union groups, and a model of sellout labor bureaucracy and its gangster methods. M-19 kept him for some months in a "people's prison," tried and sentenced him for "treason to the working class and the people," and executed him on the chilly morning of April 19, 1977.

Ferreyra, boss of the agribusiness firm Indupalme, was kidnapped when the firm's 6,000 African palm plantation workers struck for a raise and other elementary rights. In exchange for him, M-19 asked satisfaction of union demands and respect for the strike leaders. After a period of uncertainty the firm yielded and Ferreyra went free.

The most audacious M-19 action was its raid on Bogotá's Cantón Norte arsenal, accomplished through a tunnel on the night of Dec. 31, 1978, and yielding booty of some 5,000 rifles and other light weapons. The reaction of government, and military was tough. Protected by the recently promulgated suspension of constitutional guarantees, they launched a massive campaign of arrests and torture

aimed to wipe M-19 off the map. Resulting from this, 260 persons are still behind bars under a "war council's" charges of belonging to an armed organization.

FARC & the Communists

The Revolutionary Armed Forces of Colombia (FARC), with different politico-ideological tendencies and theatre of operations, is the other big guerrilla organization and the only one tracing a direct line back to the undeclared civil war of the 50s. In that time of official violence the campesinos had to organize in guerrilla groups of Liberal orientation (most of their members were Liberals); despite their lack of unified command and other painful deficiencies, they were the chief protagonists in popular resistance to the dictatorship of those days, but not the only ones. Hunted by the regime as ferociously as were the Liberals, the communists had to take refuge in the mountains and form armed units—never very numerous and of small military importance, but disciplined and moved by socioeconomic aspirations while the Liberal guerrillas were limited to purely political perspectives. Thus wherever communist guerrillas operated the masses were encouraged to be self-governing, to form militias and to some extent divide up the land.

The communist units also had a different attitude toward making peace. Liberal guerrillas accepted almost unreservedly the agreement for an end to the bloody struggle with the Conservatives for political power, and laid down their arms almost without a throught. How overtrusting they were, the experience of ensuing years would show. Peace returned to Colombia at the price of putting the old oligarchy back in power and of a regime dominated neither by Liberals nor Conservatives, but by the monopolies.

Anarchy, Terror, etc.

The communists were more wary. They suspended their armed activities without removing themselves from the current

Rius/LNS

created by the bipartisan peace agreement, and in rural areas under their influence succeeded in rooting their gains and preserving the organs of autonomous power, including the militias.This provoked the rightists into opening a Senate debate in 1964—in open connivance with the US embassy—against what Conservative leader Alvaro Gómez Hurtado called "independent republics" (actually the campesino communities of Marquetalia, El Fato, Guayabero and Riochiquito). The press simultaneously mounted a campaign to "prove" that anarchy and terror reigned in those areas, and rifles, guns and napalm followed the debate.

On May 18, 1964, the Colombian army began operations against the insubordinate rural areas, with over 16,000 soldiers of combined air-ground units. Overwhelmed by such superior numbers and firepower, the campesinos once again abandoned their plots and homes and took to the forested heights of the Colombian Andes, where they formed three guerrilla units under the command of Manuel Marulanda Vélez, Ciro Castaño and Oscar Reyes. Marulanda Vélez was to become through the years a legendary guerrillero, known as "Tirofijo" for his deadly aim with a gun.

Joint Resistance

Meeting for the Second Guerrilla Conference of the Southern Bloc in April 1966, the three above-mentioned groups agreed to join forces as the FARC. Its program included agrarian reform, land titles for campesinos, industrialization of rural areas, a broad credit system and remunerative prices for farm products. It also demanded protection for indigenous communities and the return of their lands usurped by big farming outfits.

FARC's growth over 14 years has been slow but steady. Militarily, its operations are directed against army patrols in the countryside. It has diversified its theatre of operation, incorporating into the primitive southern "front" neighboring areas along the Magdalena (geographically the heart of the country), Caquetá and Meta (to the east) rivers and the Urabá region on the Caribbean coast gulf of that name, near the Panamanian border.

Most of these districts are colonization zones, points on the interior agricultural frontier where social conflicts are substantially sharpening: areas, for the most part, into which landless campesinos move only to meet soon with challenges to their right to their plot from merchants to whom they become indebted, or from the landlord who arrives behind the first colonists—forcing the owner to sell. There is little of the orthodox about these transactions: the authorities do nothing or take the side of the big farmers, and all too often violence erupts. In this situation the guerrillas become the colonist's or day laborer's sole protection against the abuses of landlords and the crimes of their armed agents.

ELN & Camilo

Of all the revolutionary groups, the National Liberation Army (ELN) came nearest in the 60s to emulating the Cuban example. It was founded in 1964 under direct impact of the Cuban revolution, and began military operations on Jan. 7, 1965, occupying Simacota, a small town in Santander province. It quickly won university students' sympathies: leaders of the National University Federation, now defunct, joined its ranks and many more students followed suit. Its complexion changed when the priest Camilo Torres Restrepo joined it at the end of 1965. With a big mass following at the time, Camilo's departure from leadership of the United Front (which he had organized) to join the armed struggle in the mountains shook the country and gave ELN unexpected national importance. Camilo was killed soon afterwards in a military action, and his influence over the masses could not be absorbed by the guerrilla group. Nevertheless ELN put down roots in some campesino and worker communities (especially oil workers) while establishing links with some Christian mass movements.

The Priest Who Took Up a Gun

In an ELN ambush of a Colombian army patrol on Feb. 15, 1966, Camilo Torres was hit by two rifle bullets and died almost immediately. His compañeros were unable to rescue his body and had to withdraw into the forest. The soldiers kicked the body, photographed it, took fingerprints and buried it in a place still known only to the military.

Moved by the news, Colombians discovered overnight the depth of revolutionary commitment of a priest who, by family origins and ties to the power structure, could have led an idle and privileged life. Even when Camilo was about to join the guerrillas in clandestinity, the political oligarchs could not credit the genuineness of his political convictions and tried again to bribe him. In this they were as far off the mark as in so many other judgments of their countrymen.

Camilo's family expected him to become a lawyer or doctor; his entry into a seminary was his first act of rebellion, followed by others of more significance to his country's destiny. In 1962, as chaplain of the National University in Bogotá, he celebrated at the students' request a mass for the fallen, victims of the regime's bullets. "Some of these students may not have been Catholics," he said in his sermon, "but they have lived and died true to their beliefs and may have saved themselves." The words earned him a campaign of press calumnies and a solemn warning from the Cardinal.

Two years later he dedicated himself to the formation of a farm school in Yopal for training campesino leaders. Local landlords fumed that he was "training guerrillas" there. In the same year, as a director of the Colombian Agrarian Reform Institute, he opposed a nakedly pro-latifundist decision by the Institute and was angrily challenged by Conservative Party leader Alvaro Gomez Hurtado. Then he joined with a number of progressive intellectuals in an effort to halt "Operation Marquetalia," a 16,000-man war of extermination against the campesinos' agrarian movement in southern Tolima and Huila.

Finally, breaking the historic compromise between the Church hierarchy and the oligarchy, Camilo promoted the formation of a political movement, the People's United Front, which in short order united opposition groups and parties and mobilized popular discontent. The call won torrential response: the movement's paper sold 50,000 copies a week, its meetings and demonstrations drew crowds in every city, and trade unions entered into a dialogue with the revolutionary priest about the United Front program. It was in this feverish climate that Camilo joined the guerrillas in 1965. On Jan. 7, 1966, first anniversary of the founding of ELN, he set forth his reasons for taking up arms in a "Proclamation from the Mountains."

He died in his first armed action, but his example resounds increasingly through his country and all Latin America.

Between 1965 and 1972, ELN mainly operated in the Magdalena Medio region; in 1973 it decided to broaden out and create a second front in the northeastern forest zone between the last spurs of the central mountains and the Caribbean coastal plains. It threw heavy resources into this ambitious project which ended in decisive military defeat, with the loss of two of the Vásquez brothers (members of the leadership) and many fighters. The defeat seriously affected the organization's unity and produced an internal crisis, with Fabio Vásquez's retirement as top commander as one of its consequences. ELN is now in the process of complete reorganization.

Audacious MAO

The Workers' Self-Defense Movement (MAO) is in a sense the *enfant terrible* of Colombian guerrillas—the most recently formed organization (1978), probably the smallest, with purely urban field of action.

Its first big public action was the execution of the ex-interior minister Rafael Pardo Buelvas. Of all the armed actions in recent years, this was the most badly received by the left and by large segments of public opinion, who deemed it inopportune. Yet MAO has managed to establish itself by bold and imaginative strikes. Its top leader fell into police hands in 1979 and was jailed in Bogotá's Model Prison along with other MAO activists. One sunny Sunday morning his compañeros on the outside dynamited one of the prison's walls and whisked him and five others away.

More recently, one MAO activist jailed in Bogotá was taken to the Military Hospital for health reasons, and never arrived: the ambulance was intercepted enroute by a MAO commando which dealt with the escort and freed him. The audacity of both actions is underlined by the fact that they are the first of their kind successfully carried out in Colombia.

Somoza wrought among his own people.

The scenes were almost indescribably euphoric. People rushed into the streets waving red-and-black Sandinista flags and ran alongside the car caravan. They shouted greetings and slogans and applauded the commanders, who flashed victory signs and reached down thousands of times to shake outstretched hands.

'Thank God They Killed That Wretch'

The multitude paused in front of the Eastern Cemetery, where many of Somoza's victims are buried. An old woman expressed the common sentiment: "Thank God they killed that wretch who murdered our children."

As they passed the offices of the Managua daily *El Nuevo Diario*, Commander Tomás Borge paused to embrace the paper's editor, Xavier Chamorro, brother of Pedro Joaquín Chamorro, the victim of a Somoza-organized assassination in January 1978.

The Council of State, upon receiving word of Somoza's end, voted to declare September 17 the "Day of National Jubilation." Fiestas and parties were held in homes throughout the country. The Sandinista Defense Committees organized

Intercontinental Press
combined with **Inprecor**

From *Intercontinental Press* 18, no. 36 (September 29, 1980): 988-89

'National Jubilation' Sweeps Nicaragua

by Lorraine Thiebaud

Managua. The only regret in Nicaragua on September 17 was that bloody ex-dictator Anastasio Somoza Debayle was not brought to justice here.

As word spread of the bazooka blast in Asunción, Paraguay, that permanently deposited Somoza in the garbage can of history, Nicaragua exploded in a nationwide outpouring of joy.

All commercial activity ground to a halt as people huddled around their radios. When the news was confirmed by the FSLN National Directorate, people began hugging each other, patting each other on the back, shaking hands with total strangers. They raised their fists and shouted, "The buzzard is dead!" All Nicaragua seemed to be smiling.

Reprinted with permission from *Intercontinental Press.*

Arms linked and standing beneath a photo of Rigoberto López Pérez, the national hero who shot and killed Somoza's father in 1956, the nine FSLN Commanders of the Revolution issued a statement to the people of Nicaragua:

"Having confirmed that the genocidal tyrant Anastasio Somoza Debayle has been brought to justice, the National Directorate of the FSLN joins the people of Sandino in national rejoicing. We feel ourselves fulfilled in this heroic deed, achieving our rights and our desire for justice and vindication against the one who massacred thousands of Nicaraguans and plunged our country into misery and ignorance."

The FSLN statement hailed the "combative, self-sacrificing, valiant, and heroic" commandos who carried out the attack on Somoza. They embodied, the FSLN said, "the implacable will of Rigoberto López Pérez."

Joining the popular celebrations, the revolutionary commanders led a demonstration through the streets of the capital in open jeeps. They drove through streets of poor and working-class neighborhoods where the bombed-out remains of buildings are mute testimony to the hatred

Oswaldo Sagastegui/Informacion Sistematica/LNS

Goyo/The Call/LNS

burnings of Somoza's effigy, while women read his official death sentence.

Late into the night, bonfires lit up the streets, and the sound of firecrackers and marimba music was heard.

The most popular song was Julio Iglesias's *Paraguayan Night:* "Wherever you go, I will follow you . . ."

Heavy boots did not keep the young men and women of the Sandinista People's Army from dancing among the throngs that gathered in the Plaza of the Revolution in central Managua. Defense Minister Humberto Ortega had issued orders authorizing those who had risked their lives to unseat Somoza to join in the celebrations.

News reaching here from other countries of the reaction to Somoza's demise fell into two categories—those who shared the happiness at the elimination of the ex-dictator, and those like Ronald Reagan who said that it was "a sad loss." The 5,000 ex-National Guardsmen camped in Honduras were reported greatly demoralized at the loss of their commander-in-chief. David Hall of the U.S. State Department said only, "This is a problem of the Paraguayan authorities." Pinochet of Chile refused to comment.

On the other hand, Rafael Menjívar, executive director of the Revolutionary Democratic Front (FDR) of El Salvador, called the bringing to justice of Somoza "an example and a precedent for all other tyrants."

Anastasio Somoza Debayle, fifty-four years old, had been spending his exile in Paraguay since August 1979. He lived in a replica of his Managuan "bunker" in an elegant section of the capital, Asunción. He was protected by thirty well-paid bodyguards, as well as by the repressive apparatus put at his disposal by dictator Alfredo Stroessner.

On September 17, during one of his rare excursions away from his small fortress, Somoza's Mercedes-Benz was trapped by two cars. The occupants of one of the cars began firing machine guns. An exchange of bullets between the commandos and Somoza's bodyguards was cut short by a bazooka blast from the second-story window of a nearby house. Somoza's car exploded. Killed instantly along with Somoza were financial adviser Joseph Peittner and chauffeur César Gallardo.

Dinorah Sampson, Somoza's mistress for the past eighteen years, identified his remains. His body had twenty-five bullet holes.

Paraguayan authorities blamed the attack on two Argentines, allegedly members of the People's Revolutionary Army (ERP), Hugo Alfredo Yrurzun and Silvia Mercedes Hodgers. The Paraguayan police claim to have killed Yrurzun in a two-hour shoot-out in Asunción the night of September 18.

While Nicaraguans rejoiced, they also took time to recall September 21, 1956. On that night a young poet, Rigoberto López Pérez, shot the founder of the Somoza dynasty, Anastasio Somoza Garciá, father of Somoza Debayle. Nicaraguans were undoubtedly happy then also. But they had to suppress their emotions during the wave of repression that followed the assassination. National Guard commander Anastasio Somoza Debayle and his brother Luis sought revenge against the people of Nicaragua and their political opponents. Thousands were imprisoned, 3,000 in Managua alone—among them Carlos Fonseca Amador, who was to found the FSLN six years later. One hundred peasants were summarily executed, and children were tortured in front of their mothers.

U.S. imperialism provided the dynasty with technical assistance. A top CIA agent named Van Wyncle was sent to establish the National Security Office (OSN) shortly after López Pérez's deed. Washington also sent medical specialists to try to save the life of the tyrant, who died in a U.S. Army hospital in the Panama Canal Zone.

Today, repression like that of twenty-four years ago is being suffered in Paraguay. Dictator Stroessner asked for and received the aid of the Argentine dictatorship, which immediately sent marines to stop and harass small fishing boats and passengers in transit in the Paraná River. Stroessner sent troops to occupy the Asunción airport and sealed the borders. He offered a reward of 4 million *guaranís* (US $30,000) for information on those who brought Somoza to justice.

Somoza's son, Anastasio Somoza Portocarrero flew from New York to Paraguay to accompany his father's remains to Miami. The funeral was to take place in an elegant chapel owned by a Cuban counter-revolutionary. Members of Assault Brigade 2506, who were trained in Nicaragua in 1961 before invading Cuba at the Bay of Pigs, along with ex-members of the U.S.-created National Guard of Nicaragua, were to form an honor guard at the ceremonies.

Somoza was killed soon after he had declared to a West German magazine that "I feel full of strength and ready to fight." The interview was published the day of his death, 412 days after he fled the victorious Sandinista insurrection.

Gay Community News

THE WEEKLY FOR LESBIANS AND GAY MALES

From *Gay Community News* 7, no. 34 (March 22, 1980): 8-9

Gays Support the Revolution in Nicaragua

by John Kyper

On July 19, 1979, victorious guerillas poured into the capital city of Managua, Nicaragua, finally ending one of the most repressive dictatorships in twentieth century Latin America. For nearly half a century the Somoza family—Tacho and his sons Luis and Anastasio—had run this Central American country of two million like it was their own private enterprise, brutally suppressing all opposition and accumulating a vast personal fortune in the process.

As a result of the Somoza regime, 60% of the people remained illiterate and in extreme poverty, without running water, electricity or medical care. Of the children who survived until the age of four, 50% suffered from malnutrition. Under Somoza, the country had the highest per capita military expenditure in Central America—and the lowest in education and health. International aid money that poured into the country after the 1972 earthquake was siphoned off by Anastasio Somoza to finance his own businesses.

The United States has intervened in the internal affairs of the country since the middle of the 19th century. Nicaragua has been called America's first Vietnam because of repeated invasions by the U.S. Marines. The first Somoza in power, Tacho, who was assassinated in 1956, had been trained at West Point. He was made head of the Nicaraguan National Guard by the Americans and seized power in 1936, a few years after the American withdrawal. With American support he built up the Guard, which operated as the Somoza family personal army. Our tax dollars at work.

Opposition to Anastasio Somoza ran deep

through every sector of the Nicaraguan population, from *campesinos(as)* (peasants) to the bourgeoisie. This opposition was led by the Sandinista National Liberation Front, FSLN, named after Augusto Sandino, who led nationalist rebels against the Marines and then against Somoza until his assassination in 1936. The combined forces of the FSLN made Somoza's final overthrow inevitable, despite substantial U.S. military aid. Young Nicaraguan women and men, armed only with machetes, machine guns and Molotov cocktails fought for years against the well-armed and equipped National Guard, providing a painful image of American support of dictatorships.

Since July, a transitional government has been formed to aid in reconstruction and redevelopment of this war-torn country. Foreign visitors report that the spirit of cooperation and hope is inspiring and uplifting. At the same time, the problems faced by the government of reconstruction headed by five leaders are enormous. Not only do they have to deal with the effects of Somoza's exploitation, but they are saddled with a foreign debt—most of it to American banks—that is greater than all of the country's annual export earnings.

The current plan is to mix state-owned enterprises with private investment to get the economy functioning again. All of the country's secondary schools and universities will be closed on March 24, 1980, to enable students to participate in a giant literacy campaign. The Nicaraguan people are on the move toward a new future, and if they can balance the internal problems and contradictions without alienating the United States, they stand their first chance of real self-determination.

San Francisco is the home of the largest Nicaraguan community outside Managua. The tremendous excitement in the Latin community about the Nicaraguan revolution has spilled over into other communities of the city, including the gay community. In July, 1979, a gay educational event about Nicaragua sparked the formation of Gay People for the Nicaraguan Revolution, to work within the gay community to raise support for the reconstruction process. The group works with Casa

Nicaragua, a local community center and representative of the FSLN, which is leading reconstruction support work in California.

The connections are there to be made. "It has become clear that right-wingers who back anti-gay campaigns in this country are the same people who are attempting to destroy the revolution in Nicaragua," argues a pamphlet produced by the group. Somoza was a darling of the New Right, those folks whose profession is hate. U.S. Rep. Larry McDonald (D-GA), who has introduced anti-gay legislation into Congress, visited Somoza before he was overthrown and has lobbied to deny all aid to the new government.

Roberto is a gay Nicaraguan who helped found Gay People for the Nicaraguan Revolution. The following interview with Roberto and Linda, another member, took place on January 3, 1980, two days before Roberto left San Francisco to work in the reconstruction of his country:

John: How did Gay People for the Nicaraguan Revolution start?
Roberto: It was started back in June. There was a group of gay people who felt that there was a lot of gay energy for Nicaragua that was not being channeled properly; there was not a group aimed at progressive gays who were interested in doing political work for Nicaragua. And so four or five of us got together and put on an educational event. I was the only Nicaraguan, the rest were Americans.
J: What activities have you been doing?

FRENTE SANDINISTA DE LIBERACION NACIONAL

Helioflores/Informacion Sistematica/LNS

R: We have had quite a few fund-raisers. We have raised around $6000 for the Nicaraguan revolution. We have done a great deal of educational outreach work to the gay and lesbian community. We also have been doing some educational work, indirectly, with the Nicaraguan political groups here in San Francisco.

J: How large is the group?

Linda: We have about ten hardcore people, and we have about 20 others who are willing to work. Every event that we've had has been packed. We just had a [San Francisco] Mime Troupe benefit and we had standing room only. It seems like there's a tremendous amount of support, at least in the local gay community, for the work that we're doing. We've been getting very, very positive feedback on it, consistently.

R: Especially from the lesbian community.

J: How large is the Nicaraguan exile community?

R: It has been estimated around 40,000 people in San Francisco. Other exile communities are not as large. There is a large Nicaraguan community in Miami, which is made up of Somozista exiles and there are ones in New York, in Los Angeles, and in San Jose, Costa Rica.

J: How many of the people here, do you estimate, are returning to Nicaragua, now that the Somoza regime has been overthrown?

R: A very small percentage. I wouldn't think it would be over one thousand people.

J: Why do you think that is true?

R: The ones who were born in Nicaragua and moved here, now they feel they are too old to go back. These are people who came here in the '40s and '50s, so they are people now who are in their 50s and early 60s. They feel they have their lives already organized here. There also are people who don't particularly have a revolutionary spirit, a spirit to forego comfort. They are afraid of going to Nicaragua because it will mean that their standard of living is going to go down. Then the young ones, the ones who were born here, they don't feel so close to Nicaragua.

J: You've been here seven years. You could have been one of the people who are staying. Why are you going back?

R: I cannot use my case as the typical example of the Nicaraguan immigrants here. My family never emigrated out of Nicaragua, I was just a student. I always went back to Nicaragua on holidays, so I kept close emotional ties to my land, and I never felt like I was an American. I lived

here and I lived in Europe, too. Another reason why I want to go back is because I identify with what is going on politically in Nicaragua.

J: I was at a demonstration in July, just after Somoza had been forced to flee. I marched in your contingent. I felt a lot of support from the Nicaraguans there, generally. How have the relations been between the Gay People for the Nicaraguan Revolution and the local Nicaraguan community?

L: For the most part they've been very good. We have been given quite a bit of support. Our group, as well as the Gay and Latino Alliance and *Mujers En Lucha: Lesbianas Latinas*, all marched on Mission Street on July 14, and recently marched supporting the struggles in El Salvador. For the most part we have had tremendous support from Casa Nicaragua and from the Nicaraguan consul in San Francisco for what we're doing. We have been warmly welcomed, as has every other solidarity group.

J: Do you have any contacts with the gay community in Nicaragua? Did you come out there or did you come out when you were abroad?

R: I first came out when I was abroad, but I had a second coming out four years ago in Nicaragua, as well. I have contact with some gay people there—only with a couple of them—not with any gay organizations, because there are none. There has never been a gay organization in Nicaragua. But I know of some political gays in Nicaragua who are doing active political work, not as members of any gay organization but as individuals.

J: One of the things that a lot of people are very wary of are the possible parallels to Cuba, where, after the revolution, they imprisoned homosexuals in camps. You seem to feel that there's not that danger there?

R: I just don't see any reason why the Nicaraguan revolution is suddenly going to be using the gays as a scapegoat, because the issue of gayness in Cuba was not the same as it is in Nicaragua. First of all, Cuba had a real large American tourist trade. A lot of gay American tourist trade that came to Cuba to live it up. So there was a lot of male prostitution, of gay people very much into the commercialization of vices such as drugs, cocaine and the casinos. There was an element of capitalistic decadence inside the gay community of Cuba. That probably was what generated the hysteria against gays in Cuba. In Nicaragua the gays have never played a major role in any aspect of Nicaraguan life. I don't parti-

cularly foresee any witchhunt for gays—there's no reason for it.

J: What direction do you think the Nicaraguan revolution will take?

R: It's already on the path to a Nicaraguan version of socialism. It's going to be a very pragmatic version of socialism, going very fast in certain aspects, not so fast in others—according to our realities. I see it as definitely going to be a system in which the oppressed and the underprivileged classes are the ones who are going to benefit the most, at the expense of those who had everything before.

J: What can people in the United States do to support you?

R: They can certainly help a lot by doing fundraising and doing political education on the Nicaraguan revolution among the American public. With the money we will be getting the means and the tools to rebuild Nicaragua. Through the political education on Nicaragua, we are insuring that we will not have another North American military intervention in our country, which is still a possibility, especially if the right wing elements in the United States acquire executive power again.

L: How many American interventions have there been in Nicaragua?

R: We have had three in this century.

J: What contacts do you have with gay movements in other Latin American countries, and what connections do you have with local groups like the Gay and Latino Alliance (GALA)?

R: At this moment we don't have too many contacts, but before I go to Nicaragua, I'm stopping over in Mexico City to establish contact with people from FHAR [Frente Homosexual de Accion Revolucionaria—see *GNC*, Vol. 7, no. 8].* As far as the Third World gay groups in San Francisco, we have had some contact with them. GALA organized a benefit for Nicaragua in August, and we hope to work with them in the future.

J: Is there anything you want to add?

R: I would like to talk to the gay people who are interested in the revolutionary process of Nicaragua: It's not to be so demanding with the recognition of the gay issue because, first of all, we in Nicaragua, as gays, have never suffered an official witchhunt. We have not been put down, officially, by the government, ever. There's really no need for us for this strong

---

*[See John Kyper, "Organizing in Mexico," in Section 8, "Lesbians and Gay Men," below.— eds., *Alternative Papers*.]

recognition now of the gay movement from the authorities of Nicaragua. The kind of oppression we have felt has been social oppression, and that's very hard to eradicate. You don't eradicate that kind of oppression with laws and with statements. The only way you change society's attitudes is by working inside the society, by integrating inside that society. I feel that the direction for the gay movement to follow in Nicaragua at this point is not one of confrontation. I feel it's more [important] for gay people to integrate themselves into the reconstruction work in Nicaragua, to start coming out slowly to their friends and acquaintances, to show themselves as gay individuals who are productive inside the Nicaraguan revolution. Later on, once we have created a whole group of gay people who are very progressive, we can start banding together as a revolutionary organization, but not now.

L: Gay people who are interested could get in touch with our group, specifically, around helping us channel money in the name of gay people. Checks can be made out to Gays for Nicaragua, and we can send you a brochure. Any donation or letter can be addressed to P.O. Box 23984, Oakland, CA 94623.

HELP REBUILD NICARAGUA

Steve Karian/LNS

WIN

PEACE & FREEDOM THROUGH NONVIOLENT ACTION

From *WIN* 16, no. 6 (October 1, 1980): 17-21

Inopportune Landing in the Land of Opportunity

by The Popular Economics Research Group

Julio Soto and Carlos Martinez Perez want to play major league baseball. Each day at Campo Libertad, the tent city at the Eglin Air Force Base in Fort Walton Beach, Florida, that serves as a processing center for 10,000 of the recent Cuban refugees, Soto, Perez and others talk and play baseball. Their chances of making it to the big leagues are slim. Two scouts from the Cincinnati Reds visited the players in mid-May and left unimpressed. But even if their own talents were no impediment the two would still have problems. Bowie Kuhn, the commissioner of Major League Baseball, has temporarily forbidden the recruiting and signing of any of the 114,000 Cuban refugees. Like many of the incoming Cubans, Soto and Martinez. Perez are finding that the land of plenty that they anticipated may not live up to their

expectations. Instead, they have been greeted by the second worst recession in post-World War II US history and a pervasive lack of understanding of their flight.

Why the Exodus?

On April Fools' Day 1980, 25 Cubans hijacked a city bus and rammed it through the gates of the Peruvian embassy in Havana. In the process, one Cuban soldier was killed. The Cuban government quickly demanded that the Peruvians surrender the 25. The Peruvian government refused and granted the busjackers political asylum. In response the Cubans removed all protection from the embassy and people began entering the embassy grounds immediately. When the crowd grew to 750, Cuban officials announced that anyone who wanted to leave Cuba would be granted an exit visa provided that other countries would grant them entry visas. (Indeed, the Cuban government insisted, Cubans have always been free to leave the country. The problem, they contend, has been the restrictive immigration policies of receiving countries.) In four days, the crowd swelled to 10,000. The Cuban government sent in food and water and, amidst rumors of rape and food-hoarding on the embassy grounds, issued safe-conduct passes so that those inside the embassy could leave and return later.

Negotiations began with countries willing to receive the world-be exiles. Peru, Spain, Costa Rica and the United States made firm commitments to receive refugees, with the US volunteering to take 3500. After three days of airlifts to San Jose, Costa Rica, the flights were stopped. The Cubans then opened the port of Mariel, announcing that anyone who wished to leave Cuba could. According to Fidel Castro, "the building of socialism, the work of the revolution, [is] the task for free men and women." With Mariel open, any Key West skipper hardy enough to make the trip from Florida to Cuba and back could carry refugees away. The exodus began and has ended only recently after 114,000 Cubans have taken part in what the US press gaily termed the "Freedom Flotilla."

The reasons behind the decision to leave Cuba are varied and have been misunderstood and poorly explained in the United States. American officials and correspondents have pointed to some final failure of socialism or, at least of its Cuban version. Victor H. Palmeri, the US coordinator for Refugee Affairs, said, "Castro is really up against the wall now. For the first time I think his regime is shaky. He's in a frenzy about his problems." The regime hardly seemed shaky, however, when on May 1, a million and a half people gathered in Havana to support the government in a demonstration organized by the local "Committees in Defense of the Revolution." Most analysts agree that the socialist character of Cuba's society enjoys wide popular support. For instance, conspicuously under-represented among the refugees are black Cubans who have little incentive to leave a society where institutional racism has been largely eliminated and come to the US, where over 25% of blacks live below the official poverty level and white supremacist organizations such as the Ku Klux Klan are currently enjoying a resurgence. Clearly the motivations for the refugees range far beyond what President Carter identified as simple "freedom loving."

On the other hand, the Cuban government has labeled the refugees "escoria," or scum, and has explained their desire to leave Cuba as part of the petty delinquency of "lumpen" elements in the society. This explanation has been politically useful in Cuba, and it is in some part true—one Havana defense attorney discovered that his caseload had dropped by over one-third after the boatlift began. However, it too does not allow us to fully understand the situation. Privately, both Cuban officials and the Cuban people admit that the exodus has occured as a result of three factors—the petty delinquency the Cuban government emphasizes, Cuba's ailing economy and family ties to Cubans living in the United States.

Economic reasons, one recent visitor to Cuba noted, seem to be propelling at least 40% of the refugees. The Cuban economy, despite tremendous strides in the provision of housing, medical care and foodstuffs, has been unable to generate either a wide variety of consumer goods or sustained economic growth. These failures have been, in large part, due to the US economic blockade against Cuba which has deprived Cuba of a "natural" trading partner and spare parts for its pre-revolution capital equipment. In addition, US military provocation—the Bay of Pigs, spy flights, the base at Guantanamo—has forced Cuba to spend an excessive amount on improving its defense capability. Finally, the high costs of switching over to the Soviet Union and the socialist bloc as the major trading partners and Cuba's own initial problems with economic organization have contributed to the economic malaise. By the early 70s, Cuba had begun to adapt to the hardships of the blockade and had dealt with many organizational difficulties. Annual growth rates were approaching 10%— a fantastic level.

In recent years, however, those growth rates have not been sustained and, in particular, this year the Cuban economy has also been met by natural disasters which have severely disrupted production. The sugar crop, Cuba's main export, has been hurt by a disease called sugarcane smut. African swine fever has damaged the production of pork. Worst of all has been blue mold, a tobacco virus, which has ruined 90% of Cuba's tobacco crop. There has been speculation, in view of the fact that in 1969 the Pentagon engaged in weather-modification warfare against Cuba's sugar crop, that these disasters may not be so natural.

In addition to the difficulties of simultaneous crop failures and swine fever has been the strain placed on Cuba's economy by its assistance to governments and revolutionary movements in Africa and Latin America. A full 50,000 Cubans, both civilians and military personnel are extended across 35 countries. Non-military assistance has been burdensome; the 1500 Cubans aiding Nicaragua's literacy campaign are 1500 people not actively contributing to Cuban economic development. Particularly costly, however, have been the military actions in Angola and Ethiopia. While both have been overwhelmingly popular with the Cuban people, they have required significant economic sacrifice and the loss of some of Cuba's most capable and ideologically committed young people.

The Reaction of the Cuban People

While the vast majority of people committed to staying and continuing their efforts to develop the Cuban economy and its socialist character, some have chosen to leave. Despite free medical care, fixed rents, etc., the refugees believe that the economic grass is greener on this side of the straits of Florida. The belief that the United States is the haven of material progress was aggravated last year by visits to Cuba of over 100,000 Cuban exiles now living in the United States. As one Cuban commented, "These exiles, this scum left Cuba. I stayed. Now they come back. They are fat, they wear fine clothes, they can spend dollars to eat in restaurants I can't eat in, to drink in bars I cannot go."

Dissatisfaction has also been expressed by some Cubans over the costs of Cuba's international actions. A recent visitor talked to several Cubans who quietly complained about the constant sacrifices the Cuban people have to make in order to support "the boys in Angola," sacrifices an underdeveloped economy like Cuba's can ill afford. The combination of illusions about US wealth, smouldering resentment at sacrifices and general underdevelopment caused by US imperialism and aggravated by the economic blockade, begins to provide an understanding of the factors motivating many who left.

The Cubans think approximately 30% of the refugees wanted to leave because they have family in the United States, and this is reluctantly accepted by most of the Cubans who have stayed. Also leaving in this exodus have been a large number of lesbians and gay men, comprising as much as 20% of the refugee population. While there seems to have been an increase in official tolerance of homosexuality (e.g., Cuban textbooks on sexuality no longer group homosexuals with "sexual deviants" and the Union of Writers and Artists has defended the rights of gay artists), popular feeling against gays is strong. The lack of acceptance of an open gay culture has surely motivated many gay Cubans to join the refugee flight.

Cubans are glad to see the exit of "escoria" or scum, petty delinquents who have been unable to get along in Cuban society (in this number are small-time drug dealers, prostitutes, etc.). What angers them, however, is those who are leaving after they have received the best the revolution could offer—after their fellow workers sacrificed so they could go to school or join a micro-brigade to build their own housing. And what worries the Cuban people is the number of professionals and other prominent people who have left. A Havana neurologist, for example, was among those clambering aboard the boats at Mariel. He left, it is rumored, because he was denied the opportunity to be a surgeon and forced into neurology because of the "needs of the revolution." This sort of case is causing Cubans to raise questions about the possible excesses of the society they have constructed. Perhaps the sort of self-evaluation that in the 1970s led to Cuba's "Popular Power" democratic governmental structure will once again occur.

One hundred fourteen thousand Cubans, however, will not be participating in this evaluation; they have left. And for the original 25 who commandeered a city bus and started it all, the "Freedom Flotilla" has not become a reality. They remain in the Peruvian embassy, as the Cuban government will not allow exit to those who violate an embassy with force.

The US Reception

The Cubans have been welcomed in the United States by Carter's "open arms," a worsening recession and long waits for relocation from crowded refugee camps. They have been met too by unemployed US workers' anxieties that the incoming Cubans cannot be supported by an economy that fails to provide enough jobs for even American workers. At Fort Chaffee, Arkansas, Lazaro and Ofelia Melendez and their nine-year-old daughter, veterans of the Peruvian embassy over-running, were greeted by a picket of unemployed workers outside the gates. A sign held by an unemployed mother epitomized the pickets' emotions: "What are they gonna do now— relocate us Americans?" There have been similar demonstrations and pickets at almost all the refugee processing centers.

The refugee camps are overcrowded and processing of the Cubans into new homes in the US has been proceding slowly, mainly due to the inability to find US sponsors for the immigrants. These conditions have caused Cuban-American groups to criticize the federal government's handling of the refugees and have led to disturbances such as the outbreaks of violence at Fort Chaffee and Eglin Air

Force Base. These incidents have fueled the charges that the refugees' numbers include a large quantity of "common criminals" and mentally retarded or disturbed people and that the Cuban government took advantage of the boatlift to empty their jails and hospitals. Actually, federal immigration officers report that only one percent of the Cuban arrivals are suspected to be convicted felons or psychiatric patients. It seems that the wild assertions about the number of hardened criminals or mental "defectives" are part of the racist welcome the US traditionally provides for immigrant groups.

The Cuban refugees are in a real sense victims, victims of their own delusions about the good life in North America and victims of the US's unprepared but "open" arms. The Cuban exodus to the US was described by federal immigration officers as a "propaganda coup." Indeed, it is. With Soviet-US tensions rising, the US government finds itself able to proclaim the "failure of socialism" in the only socialist country in the Western Hemisphere. This ties in neatly with the general ideological and material preparation for US military action evidenced by the revival of the draft and the approval of massive spending increases for the Pentagon.

With the country in the midst of a recession that has been aggravated by military spending, a handy scapegoat has been found again. The unemployed workers outside the Fort Chaffee gates blame the Cuban arrivals for their troubles and not the economy that fails to provide enough work for those who need and want it. The Cuban refugees have ever been blamed for the racial divisions that plague their new country. In its usual display of factual reporting and logical analysis, *Time* magazine said about the Miami riots: "[Blacks] have won little redress—or even attention—because of the increasing Latinization of Miami (the Latin immigrants now represent 37.5%). And though the new violence was not directly connected with the recent influx of Cuban refugees, that influx threatened to put additional pressure on the blacks."

Black activists have validly pointed out the inconsistency between the federal government's handling of the Cubans and its early refusals to allow the Haitian refugees to enter the country. They have decried the hypocrisy of a government that extends "freedom" to those leaving Cuba and ignores widespread black unemployment in the cities of the US. Unlike *Time* and others in the US media, black leaders

have not sought to drum up antagonisms between US minority groups and thus sidestep the racism that oppresses black Americans or the police brutality and injustice which gave rise to the events in Miami. As one Cuban refugee, Gaspar Fernandez, said of the cause of the recent racial unrest, "It seems like a class difference."

A spokesperson for the Antonio Maceo Brigade, a leftist organization composed of the sons and daughters of Cubans who left in the 60s, said about the refugees, "They'll find it's not so easy to get rich in the US. There's plenty of discrimination against Cubans here."

That reality has already been made apparent to many Cubans. A nurse in Boston reports: "There's a new cleaning woman who's one of the refugees. When she first started, she was enthusiastic and worked hard. No one talked to her, though, none of us speaks much Spanish. People just ordered her around. As the weeks have passed, she looks more tired and kind of beaten."

According to a CBS News-New York Times poll, 48% of the American people say that the Cuban refugees would not be welcome in their communities. Federal immigration officials say that almost a third of those relocated from the refugee camps to new homes have returned to the camps, rejected by their families or those who agreed to put them up. One group of refugees, seven women, returned after their sponsor, a convicted murderer, allegedly asked them to dance topless and become prostitutes. And in recent weeks a number of airplanes have been hijacked to Cuba allegedly by refugees seeking to return to their homeland. A new refugee crisis has begun; not the logistical problem of moving 114,000 Cubans in order to produce a "propaganda coup," but the more serious problem of what will be done for them and what they themselves will do now that they are here.

The Popular Economics Research Group is a group of socialist economists and journalists from Amherst, Massachusetts.

From *In These Times* 4, no. 1 (November 7-13, 1979): 11, 13

These Political Refugees Are from the Wrong Place

by Patrick Lacefield

New York. Monica's day begins early. At 6 a.m. the 28-year-old Haitian immigrant leaves her room in a crumbling single-room-occupancy hotel on Manhattan's West Side to work eight hours in a garment district sweatshop. She takes home a little less than $80 a week, but every Friday manages to put away a few dollars, hoping to save enough to bring her six-year-old daughter to New York.

"I don't know how I will survive this winter," she says, in broken English with a thick Creole accent. "My heat is always off and on, mostly off."

Monica is *in* the United States but not *of*

Reprinted with permission from *In These Times: The Independent Socialist Newspaper.*

it. She is one of the several hundred thousand Haitians who fled their homeland for these shores, with 250,000 living in the New York area. Fully half, like Monica, are undocumented workers, here illegally.

For these refugees from a brutal tyranny in Haiti the words of Emma Lazarus engraved on the Statue of Liberty—"Send me your tired, your poor, your huddled masses yearning to be free"—ring with hypocrisy. They are refugees of political and economic difference at home and refugees of political, economic and social indifference here.

At the root of many of the Haitian immigrants' ills is the U.S. policy concerning immigration from Haiti. The State Department insists that Haitians are "economic refugees" and are ineligible for asylum or legal status. Indeed, under U.S. immigration laws, only those fleeing communist or socialist lands are recognized as "political refugees," a policy reflected in the difficulties encountered by Chilean Popular Unity supporters after the fall of Allende in 1973 when they attempted to apply for asylum in the U.S. The Immigration and Naturalization Service (INS) began last year to deport hundreds of Haitians, many of whom had washed up on the shores of Florida or the American base at Guantanamo Bay, Cuba, after a 700-mile voyage across a tempestuous Caribbean. Many of these Haitian "boat people," of course, never completed the voyage and were lost at sea. Many of those deported were subjected to official persecution upon their return to Haiti.

Ask Haitian activists in the U.S. about the purported difference between "economic" and "political" refugees and the most common refrain is disgust at the duplicity of the State Department. "Let me laugh," says Father Antoine Adrien, a member of the Haitian Fathers, a catholic order expelled from Haiti 10 years ago that set up shop in the Bedford-Stuyvesant neighborhood of Brooklyn to minister to the needs of Haitians.

"Do you think that half a million Cuban refugees were all 'political'? Nobody's asking that question of Cubans or Vietnamese or Hungarians because they come from left-wing dictatorships."

"The government of the United States is the father of the government of Haiti and you can't even put a hand between father and son," explains Jean Dupuy, director of the Haitian Neighborhood Center, three rooms in a crowded and shabby second floor walkup on Manhattan's upper West Side. He points to a lawsuit recently filed by the National Council of Churches Haitian Refugee Project, the Haitian Fathers, and the Haitian Refugee Project in Miami which charges the INS with conspiring to insure "the swift removal of the Haitians." The action, brought on behalf of 7,000 Haitian boat people, claims that the INS allows only 10 days for Haitian refugees to file asylum requests and has processed as many as 150 claims per day instead of its usual 10. There are an inadequate number of English/Creole interpreters and the INS regularly rejects asylum requests with form letters after only the briefest of deliberations. "They [the INS] have been blocked by the courts from further deportations," says Adrien, "but for how long? Even when it is a clear political case, according to their own terms, the State Department delays in granting asylum. I actually saw a letter from the State Department to a Haitian New Yorker who defected from the Haitian army. The letter assured him he could return without fear. Are they kidding?"

The current wave of Haitian immigra-

tion into the U.S. is far from the first. Black Haitians fought with courage and valor in several major operations against the British in the Carolinas during the American Revolution. And in 1790, after the fall of Port-au-Prince to the armies of independence leader Toussaint L'Ouverture, more than 130 ships carrying 5,000 French and their servants glided into Baltimore Harbor to a warm and sympathetic welcome from the American people. Within two days the citizens of Baltimore raised $11,000 in relief and Congress authorized President Washington to disburse $15,000 to meet the needs of these white teachers, lawyers, merchants and bankers. Americans, New Jersey Representative Elias Boudinot, opined at the time, were "bound by every moral obligation to relieve people at present our allies." The statement "our allies" made clear U.S. animosity and its fear of a free black republic in the Caribbean while slavery still occupied a prominent place in American life.

In 1957 François Duvalier—better known by friends and foes alike as "Papa Doc"—took control of the Haitian government and proclaimed himself President-for-Life. He unleashed his dreaded Toutons Macoute, a private police force known for its brutality, against political opponents and ruled Haiti with an iron hand. And he enjoyed the patronage and support of the American government in the form of military and economic aid, much of which was frittered away by a corrupt government infrastructure.

Suddenly, a new flood of Haitian refugees reached our shores. But these exiles were black, and no grand welcomes by citizens' committees or congressional appropriations awaited them. Frank La-Raque, a professor in the Black Studies Department at City College in New York, remembers. Twenty-two years ago he was forced into exile when he and other junior army officers sought—unsuccessfully—to thwart Duvalier's rise to power and uphold the Haitian constitution.

"The lie in the artificial distinction between 'economic' and 'political' is the immigration quotas," LaRaque asserts. "Before 1957 there was poverty but we [Haitians] didn't even fill our immigration quotas. After Duvalier and the start of political oppression it was different.

"There were three opposition candidates," LaRaque recalls. "One was kidnapped and exiled, a second was killed, and a third sought sanctuary in the Mexican embassy." Destruction of the free press,

unions, political parties, and the right of assembly followed.

The first wave of refugees was largely exiles such as LaRaque and middle-class professionals who sent money back to their families in Haiti. Later poor Haitians began fleeing their homeland as the Toutons Macoute seized land, houses, and businesses and ousted civil servants from the bureaucracy. Fields once productive of rich harvest of coffee, rice, and bananas lay fallow and this triggered increased unemployment and malnutrition. Poor Haitians—unable to secure tourist visas, used by their middle class fellow citizens to leave the country—turned to oftimes unscrupulous operators who smuggled them out of the country—for a price.

Patrick Lemoine, a Haitian who lives in Queens, spent six years in the much-feared Fort Dimanche prison. Nearly half the 200 prisoners interred with him at the start of his incarceration were boat people nabbed while trying to escape. When LeMoine was released in 1977, just prior to a visit to Haiti by Andrew Young, only six of the 200 were still alive.

Along with such grim tales, one hears stories dashed with an irony and humor that seem to have leapt from the pages of Graham Greene's *The Comedians*. Adrien and his Catholic order, for example, were expelled after refusing orders by a government functionary to turn out parochial students at St. Marcel's College to pro-Duvalier demonstrations. "I told him 'You ask me not to be involved in politics. I ask you not to involve me,'" he remembers. "A little later my entire order was expelled for being a 'rightist group with leftist tendencies.'"

To most Haitian émigrés, however, politics is a subject to be spoken of with caution. Reprisals against family members for criticism of the Duvalier regime here is common practice. Many Haitians also hope to return to their homeland someday and thus keep silent about political matters.

After "Papa Doc" Duvalier's death in 1971, the affairs of state fell to his 19-year-old, semi-literate son Jean-Claude. Jean-Claude, well-known for his penchant for conspicuous consumption, women, and widespread corruption, was inaugurated under the protection of U.S. gunboats, which cruised the coastal waters to fend off any efforts by exiles to thwart the junior Duvalier's ascension to power.

"My father made the political revolution," Jean-Claude is fond of saying, "and I will make the economic one."

Unfortunately the disparities between the rich and the poor have widened since 1971, private investment remains subject to expropriation at the whim of a corrupt officialdom and nearly half Haiti's budget is outside public accountability.

Haiti has come under increasing pressure from the United States, the World Bank and other lenders to place its financial affairs in some semblance of order—or else. Such an ultimatum would never have been presented to "Papa Doc."

Even if such problems as the land tenure system, the 80 percent illiteracy rate and the widening economic and social chasm between the capital and the countryside were too fundamental to expect the younger Duvalier to move against, the American government did harbor hopes for improvement in the "human rights" situation. And Jean-Claude Duvalier did announce a "liberalization." He allowed some Haitian exiles to return and placed some distance between himself and the Toutons Macoute. The controlled press cautiously began to criticize government officials, though not Duvalier or the system and three new political parties sprang up to contest for power.

On Aug. 31, however, two days after the New York Times hailed the "freer climate," the heads of the two Christian Democratic parties were arrested, charged with subversion, and have disappeared from sight. Earlier, on July 29, Duvalier reimposed total press censorship and asked the Toutons Macoute to demonstrate their support for him. "They proceeded to go on a spree of 'loyalty,'" explains LaRaque, "seizing property, harassing and killing opponents and much more. The Western powers do not like this. They would prefer that he say something and do something different."

In May, the State Department sent a study team to Haiti to investigate charges of ill treatment by the government of returnees. Though the team spoke to only 86 or 600 recently deported Haitians, it concluded that incidents of abuse were few and far between. But Haitian exiles differ with these findings. "It is very difficult to find addresses in Haiti, particularly in the countryside," asserts LaRaque, "and the Duvaliers have misled inspection teams by resorting to substitution or intimidation." Jean Dupuy of the Haitian Neighborhood Center, an exile who holed up in the Colombia Embassy in Port-au-Prince for five years before he was allowed to leave, agrees. "What of the 514 the team did not

speak to?" he asks. "How can one expect a person to speak freely with the prospect of retribution hanging heavily over his head?"

Though the Carter Administration has considered proposals to grant amnesty to all undocumented workers, Haitian activists rate Carter as inferior even to Presidents Nixon and Ford in his sensitivity toward the Haitian émigrés and the cause of human rights in their homeland.

"Now they want us to help count Haitians in the census and promise there'll be no reprisals if people come forward," remarks Adrien. "Yet we remember that in Florida they granted temporary work permits to Haitians only to cancel them two weeks later and use the data to hunt people down." Jean Dupuy waves his hand at eight battered file cabinets in his office. "We have more information here than immigration," he said. "If there ever is an amnesty, we'll be a primary source."

Haitian-Americans truly stand astride their homeland and the U.S. They desperately want the relative political freedom and economic opportunity that this coun-

try offers, but yearn viscerally for their native land. Most would return if they could. "I would return tomorrow," exclaims Adrien. Another Haitian, an actor-director in New York is less certain. "A friend of mine who lived in the States returned for a visit last year and the peasants called him 'white man.' 'You don't walk like a Haitian,' they told him."

"I could return now, if I wanted to," says LaRaque, "but to do so I'd have to tell the consulate that I'd changed, that I supported Duvalier." When LaRaque's mother died several years ago, he was unable to attend her funeral. "When I return it will be on my feet to a free Haiti, not on my knees accepting Duvalier," he proclaims. "Are we so different from the Vietnamese in deserving deliverance from oppression? Will you welcome all who come in search of freedom and opportunity or send us back to meet our fate?"

To hundreds of thousands of Haitians, strangers in a strange land, their hope for a future rests with our government's answer to that question.

From *Somos* 2, no. 7
(October/November 1979): 7-11

Judithe Hernandez and a Glimpse at the Chicana Artist

by Howard Kim

Artist Judithe Hernandez is not cynical about art. She just rejects the notion that artists are special people.

To her there is nothing especially important about their work.

"I really don't believe in the sanctity of art," she says, "If all my stuff catches fire or rots away, I really don't care. . . . It shouldn't last forever."

Her attitude is not surprising, considering who and what Judithe is.

At the moment she is one of a particular group of young, emerging artists who are

Reprinted with permission from *Somos*.

staunchly rebelling against tradition and, yet, shaping their own aesthetics from it.

Judithe happens to be Mexican-American, and that makes her work expressive of the Chicano point of view. If there is such a thing as Chicano art, she and her fellow artists are producing it.

She comments that "art should be as transcendental as life is."

There is something quaint and, yet, metaphysical in the remark. Her latest paintings and drawings tend to express the same balance between simplicity and profoundness like a subtle balance between different elements.

Her material echoes her Indian-Spanish heritage offset by years of traditional art training and some values she said she does not fully accept. The mingling of the old and the new mirrors the same attempt at assimilation that has challenged and produced the Chicano culture. Judithe seems keenly aware of this.

As an artist, she rejects many traditional Western beliefs about art. They go against her personal philosophy, a philosophy that is intimately tied to her cultural values and identity.

Among her contemporaries, she has been noted as being one of the best. Though her art is typical of the current direction they are taking, she breaks away by bringing to her work a profound sense of the past and a tentative judgment about the present. Her work stands out because of that tension.

Chicano art is most effective as social commentary. Its very existence is a kind of editorial about Chicanismo and its beauty, strengths and foibles.

Much of it is protest material that falls into a class of street art Judithe evolved from and has since surpassed.

Describing her early work as "off-the-wall stuff," she says with an amused smile, "I used to do giant death heads wearing pope's mitres with dollar signs in its eyes." The years were the 1960's, and there was heavy protest in the air.

Up to now she has made it a point to work mostly on paper and avoids canvas. It is her protest against the sanctity of art, she says, and a symbol of her minority status.

Her present work seems to reflect more thinking and careful study about her role as a well-schooled artist and a Mexican in American society.

The well-schooled artist was born at the prestigious Otis Art Institute in Los Angeles. She was one of few Chicano art students who studied there and received a Master's degree in fine arts in 1974.

Judithe implies that she learned enough about Western art to reject many of its idiosyncracies. By contrast, she tends to embrace what she terms "Third World art" for several reasons.

One of them is the people.

"It's a very Western idea," she states, "the idea of the individual as the most important entity in the universe."

In her work she avoids the individual, preferring the masses or a symbol of them. The art of Latin America, China and Africa tends to depict groups or movements of people. Mexican art before and after the Spanish influence [follows] the same pattern. It is a departure from Europe, where the portrait painter had a tradition of his own.

Rejecting the notion of "art for art's sake," Judithe believes that the Third World has historically approached its creations more sensibly.

Touching on the ancient cultures, she says, "The things they made that we consider art now and stick in museums were utilitarian objects for them. They simply made it in the best way they could . . . because that improved their function."

Art pieces played a practical part in the daily lives of ancient people. They served in households or were part of religious practices. Third World art has retained that kind of functional importance except that in many cases today it has become a form of political expression.

And what about Western art?

"Basically, art in the Western culture has always been for a very privileged class of people . . . . It is still reaching for a very exclusive kind of audience," she says.

Judithe discards the idea that art works are objects to be worshipped in museums and cherished for ages. She criticizes Western culture for surrounding art with a sanctity that is pointless.

The last series of paintings she exhibited in San Pedro and Santa Barbara earlier this year contained an almost insistent suggestion of death. But, she insists, its presence is not to be taken as morbid.

"Death to the people of Mexico has never been viewed with the same kind of horror that it is by people in North America," she observes, "I think that in the Third World that side of life is a constant along with disease and revolution."

In North America, "those sides of life that are inevitable and have a certain amount of terror aren't openly dealt with. There is so much money that you can cover it up. You can hide poverty, disease and mental illness," she adds.

Her own art is aimed at doing the reverse.

"I basically want to make people uneasy," she says. "I want them to stop and reflect about things they generally take for granted or don't even want to think about."

A soft-spoken, sensitive woman, she isn't easily excited by many things and maintains an air of personable grace in whatever she does.

As a rule, she lives austerely, shunning the social rewards most artists aspire to. Success is not important enough to her to make her sacrifice her way of life. If it comes she will welcome it; if not, there is no loss. That is her attitude.

While Judithe has taught at several colleges, including Occidental and Cal State, Long Beach, the lure of a full-time teaching job does not interest her. There is too much politics in it, she implies, to make it worthwhile.

Instead, she teaches art at Plaza de La Raza, a community center in L.A. while doing part-time college teaching. But her time really is devoted to work.

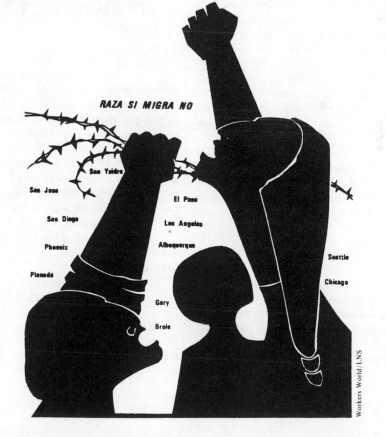

RAZA SI MIGRA NO

Most of it has been done in a large, second-story studio she shares with other artists in L.A. The huge studio is cluttered with canvas, drawings and art paraphernalia. Each artist works in the collective spirit of cooperation and respect that has kept the studio going. There she becomes absorbed in her work, paying meticulous, almost loving attention to her projects.

Judithe's modesty would deny any such claim. She seems to dislike overpraising anything—even art. She shuns dishonesty and makes a point of living as closely to her truths as possible.

The Mexican-American in her was born 31 years ago in L.A. Education was important in her home. Her mother had had some college experience and made certain that the children were led the same way. Judithe's brother studied law. But Judithe took to art from an early age. It was something, she says, she just wanted to do.

Since 1968 she has worked as an artist, designer or consultant on several art projects, including the *Aztlan International Journal of Chicano Research* at UCLA and the L.A. Citywide Murals Project.

Her murals and graphic projects have been displayed and become permanent works in a variety of locations in California. She also was cover illustrator for a number of publications, including *The Chicano Experience in the United States*, a social science quarterly published by the University of Texas.

In 1970, she took part in an exhibition at the Palacio de Bellas Artes in Mexico City followed by several other shows in Oakland, San Francisco, Pasadena and Sacramento.

Her work deals primarily with the Chicano experience in modern society. Many of her recent paintings focus specifically on women. While she remains an ardent supporter of the Chicano movement, her interest in the feminist wave is not as great.

She explains why. "I really don't feel a part of it. I find it basically an upper middle class, white woman's movement."

Though she is convinced that feminism has made significant strides for women, she argues that it addresses issues that are not relevant to the barrio.

"They're talking about equal pay when I think the biggest issue for women in the ghettos is a job, period; whether it's equal pay or not," she says.

If anything, Judithe's work will raise public consciousness about the complex, not often apparent, and generally enigmatic personality that makes up the Chicano. Her projects have depicted the drama of the old struggling with the new in a manner that avoids moral judgments but suggests that change is a synonym for time. Her murals like "El Mundo de Barrio Sotel" and "La Chicana de Aztlan" address issues facing the ghetto. Her paintings illuminate the mystery of her ancient culture like a tapestry revealing an arcane ritual play.

Consciousness-raising is a big social responsibility that most artists feel obliged in doing. But Judithe cannot see that role for herself. She tends to view her work as being no different from the job of most manual craftsmen. Yet her paintings say that she has taken on the responsibility and tried to achieve the closest point to perfection her ability can attain. She will someday have to work out her own view of herself and her duty as an artist but for the present she is committed to perfection.

"One of our biggest responsibilities," she ends, "and I feel very strongly about this, is that my responsibility as a Chicana and as an artist is to contribute to the growth and betterment of my community by doing a product that's good.

"If I turn out a mediocre product, that's the equivalent of shitting on the whole race, as far as I'm concerned, by not taking myself seriously and making myself better every time out."

From *The San Francisco Bay Guardian* 14, no. 43 (September 11-18, 1980): 1, 3, BG/TV D

Chicanos: The Rebellion Next Time?

by Reese Erlich

With the embers barely cool from the urban rebellions in Miami and Chattanooga, grassroots Chicano leaders say conditions exist for similar upheavals among the nation's second largest minority. There are an estimated 12 million Mexican-Americans and Mexican immigrants in the United States, mostly concentrated in Southwest and California. There has already been one major uprising, in the Moody Park district of Houston in 1978, as young Chicanos took to the streets to protest the police slaying of a young Mexican worker.

Just as nationally known black leaders were unable to quiet the youth of Miami, so today's young Chicano *vatos* have little in common with established Chicano figures. Many local leaders charge that the established Chicano lobbying and political organizations are out of touch with the new

militancy erupting in the barrios, on the campuses and in the farmlands of the Southwest.

The threads of this new Chicano militancy came together in Los Angeles Aug. 30 for the tenth anniversary of the Chicano Moratorium. Ten years ago, 20,000 Chicanos marched in East Los Angeles to protest the draft, the Vietnam War and the lack of Chicano rights. It was the largest political demonstration of Chicanos in U.S. history. When the 1970 demonstration erupted in violence, Los Angeles Times columnist Ruben Salazar, Brown Beret Lynn Ward and Angel Robles lost their lives.

Ten years hasn't changed much for Chicanos. Chicano youth face an unemployment rate of 19.9%. Forty percent of Hispanics drop out of high school. In 1980, the median income of a Chicano family is a full 30% less than that of whites. In many cities it is still dangerous to be Chicano and walk the streets at night. In the Bay Area, Barlow Benavides was shot and killed in 1976 while being searched by an Oakland policeman. The death was ruled "accidental." There have been numerous charges of police brutality against Chicanos since then, but few are reported in the media and few have resulted in indictments.

East Los Angeles hasn't changed much either since 1970. It still has the largest concentration of Mexicans outside of Mexico City. When ordering a donut at Winchell's, you're still more likely to be addressed in Spanish than in English. The billboards proclaim "Budweiser—es para usted." The strains of Mexican *corridos* from home record players compete with rock 'n' roll blaring from street radios. The barrio youth still wear sleeveless undershirts and khaki pants and sport mustaches more akin to Emiliano Zapata than Ceasar Romero.

The *vatos* were there Aug. 30 this year, along with their parents, students, workers and many others. An estimated 5,000 people from throughout the Southwest gathered in Los Angeles in the largest Chicano protest march since 1970. The demonstration was well organized and peaceful. But under the surface, there lay a boiling anger.

In seeking to take the emotional pulse of young Chicanos, the Guardian talked with four local leaders of the Chicano communities in California and the Southwest. They are not widely known nationally, but they are typical of the activists who will help shape the Chicano protests of the 1980s.

'It Could Break Loose'

In many ways, Raul Ruiz is a father-figure for today's Chicano college students. At 38 he is an associate professor in the Chicano Studies Department at California State University at Northridge in Los Angeles. He was one of the organizers of the 1970 Moratorium and testified at the coroner's inquest into the death of Ruben Salazar. A little heavier 10 years later and with his hair thinning, he still speaks with conviction.

Asked about future uprisings like Miami, Ruiz says, "I wouldn't be surprised. It could break loose in the future." He notes that issues troubling Chicanos are much the same as in 1970. "Police brutality, unemployment are still very much there. Now they're even worse. This demonstration is very, very good . . . and might serve as a catalyst for the future."

Ruiz noted the lack of interest in the demonstration by the Mexican American Legal Defense and Education Fund (MALDEF) and the League of United Latin American Citizens, two established groups. "As you can see, this group is very young. I don't think this is necessarily the constituency of a lot of the more traditional groups. These other groups might be doing good work or not. But I think this is an element that has traditionally been ignored

and they're making their presence known."

Sarah Campos, a media coordinator of the Mexican-American Legal Defense Fund in San Francisco, didn't attend the Aug. 30 event. Nor does she think that urban rebellions are likely to occur, although she says they "are not out of the question." "We want to work through the system—we want to contain the violence," she told the *Guardian*.

Ralph Hurtado, also of MALDEF, responded to criticisms that his organization is not responsive enough to the concerns of Chicano youth. "We're open to that kind of criticism," he told the *Guardian*. "Part of the problem is that we only take precedent-setting civil rights cases. It's hard to get government and foundation money for current problems. It took four years to get funding for immigration cases. We're a law firm—and that has its limits."

Guillermo Flores has a different perspective. He is the 32-year-old coordinator of a mental health clinic in the Chicano barrio of San Jose. A participant in the 1970 Moratorium, Flores was Northern California coordinator for this year's August 29 Chicano Moratorium Committee.

Flores works with Chicano youth seeking to end barrio warfare. "You never see any big-time politicians in the barrio trying to actually solve the people's problems," he observes. "The Chicano community doesn't want to rely on the system's leaders or institutions. There has historically been a struggle to establish institutions that meet the needs of the community. Today 90% of the patients at our clinic, for example, are Chicanos and Mexicans, are are 80% of the staff. We provide basic medical services for the community. The mental health clinic provides family counseling, as well as community activities like a *teatro*—a theater group."

Flores is also a member of the League of Revolutionary Struggle (Marxist-Leninist) (LRS), a nationwide communist organization with a multinational membership. The LRS was one of the major organizers of the Aug. 30 Moratorium this year. Flores is representative of a growing sentiment among some Chicanos that partial reforms are not enough—the whole system has to go.

"The demonstration's theme of land, liberty and unity—self-determination for the Chicano people," Flores says, "shows the growth of radical sentiment among Chicanos. It was a really popular theme. It recognized that Chicanos are an oppressed people. We have lived in the Southwest for

400 years and are actually a nation much like Quebec or Puerto Rico. Ultimately to win our rights we will unite with all oppressed people in this country to make a revolution."

That sense of nationhood and national identity as a people runs strongly throughout the modern Chicano movement, whether or not individuals consider revolution a real alternative. Herman Baca of the San Diego-based Committee for Chicano Rights (CCR) says, "We are a colonized people. That is a historical fact. Outside of the American Indians, we are the only national group covered by international treaty. We are a different type of people—our language, our history, our culture. Our communities are controlled by outside forces."

At 37, Baca is developing a national reputation for his work around U.S. immigration policies. Baca charges that the Border Patrol, rather than protecting the people of the United States from hoards of "illegal aliens," in fact helps protect "certain vested economic and political interests." Agribusinessmen and factory owners who need unskilled labor, charges Baca, utilize the Border Patrol to intimidate their workers and prevent unionization.

The CCR has received many complaints of Border Patrol mistreatment of immigrants. "Lately," says Baca, "we've been especially involved with the issue of children of undocumented parents being incarcerated in the federal prison system where they are being held as material witnesses."

In the past, Border Patrol agents made their arrests with a minimum of violence. Today they are encountering increased resistance. In several incidents last year in El Paso, crowds on the Mexican side of the border began hurling rocks and bottles at U.S. Border Patrol officers trying to make arrests. Are similar incidents and larger rebellions in the cities likely to erupt in the 1980s?

Baca answers yes. "Unless solutions are worked out, unless people are given the opportunity to participate, to define their own destinies, you'll see those kinds of manifestations. Desperate people do desperate things."

Far from the crowded streets of East Los Angeles or San Diego, Ray Otero is leading another kind of battle. Otero took off time from his job as a full-time organizer for the Land Rights Council of Chama, Colorado to speak at the L.A. Moratorium. Chama is a town of only 400 people, situated in the foothills of southern Colorado. It also lies within the Sangre de Cristo land grant, a one-million-acre grant given by the Mexican government to the people of that area in 1844.

"The people used that land communally for 113 years," says Otero. Carrying on the traditions of Mexico, the small farmers of Chama had used the land for common grazing, hunting and gathering wood. In 1960 the Mountain Tract—77,000 acres of the grant—was bought up and fenced off by lumber interests.

Formed in 1978, the Land Rights Council maintains the land grant is still valid and cannot be sold off to outside corporate interests. Working in both the legal and political arenas, the council has the support of the Catholic Church-sponsored Campaign for Human Development, which has given the council $177,000 in funding.

Although rarely publicized outside their local areas, there are hundreds of similar land grant battles going on throughout the Southwest. Many, like the one in Chama, are inspired by peasant movements in Mexico and Latin America.

"The struggle for land is international," says Otero. He told the *Guardian* the council supports everyone who is "poor and fighting for control of their land. We have good relations with Tierra y Libertad." (Tierra y Libertad leads a peasant movement in Mexico, using tactics including mass peasant marches and land seizures.) "We're 100% behind their struggles and they support ours."

For the people of Chama, the land is more than just something to farm. "We must gain control of our land," explains Otero. "For from the land comes the ability to do what you want, to think what you want." Otero doesn't predict major uprisings like the one that developed in 1967 when the New Mexico National Guard sent out tanks to stop the land grant movement led by Reies Tijerina.

"I do see our people fighting for self-defense," says Otero. And in words reminiscent of an earlier generation of Mexican revolutionaries, Otero says, "We do advocate that people should prepare themselves. We have no hang-ups about any work that people want to do—be it politically or with weapons in their hands."

From the villages of the Southwest to the urban barrios of California, there is a new mood of militancy among Chicanos. It is a mood born of frustration and anger, but also of national identity and pride. At the moment, that militancy is not organized into a cohesive force. Established politicians will certainly try to channel the anger back to the system, to prove the system works while advancing their own interests.

But there are also those in the Chicano movement who are convinced that the economic and political system of the United States cannot work, and that Chicanos must seek a more radical alternative, by whatever means necessary. Who proves to be right in the long run will largely depend on who can learn the lessons of the Aug. 29 Chicano Moratorium.

From *third world*, 1980, no. 5, pp. 61-65

In the Belly of the Monster

by Mark Fried

"To us, the wide open plains, the beautiful hills and meandering waters were not 'wild.' It was the white man who found Nature wild. Only for him was the earth infested with wild animals and 'savage hordes.' For us the earth was sweet and our lives were full with the blessings of the Great Mystery. The earth became hostile with the arrival of the white man who came from the east to oppress us and our families whom we love so much, with senseless and brutal injustices. It was when the animals of the forests began to flee as the white man approached that, for us, the 'Wild West' began."—Chief Luther Standing Bear, Oglala Sioux

Few people are aware of the fact that the Vietnamese people were not the first to bring the US Army to its knees. One hundred years prior to the Tet offensive, the Great Sioux Nation, under the leadership of Red Cloud, soundly defeated the US government's attempt at armed conquest. In the Treaty of 1868 the US acceded to each and every one of the Sioux demands, including permanent Sioux sovereignty over the territory which now encompasses most of the states of North

Reprinted with permission from *third world*. Based in Mexico City, *third world* is the English edition of a magazine on the Third World made by Third World journalists. Also published in Spanish and Portuguese.

and South Dakota, Montana and Wyoming (an area of about half a million square kilometers in the geographic center of the North American continent).

As observers of US imperialism today might guess, the 1868 Treaty was never honored. Several years after its signing Red Cloud was murdered and white settlers resumed their encroachment on Indian lands under the protection of the US cavalry. Little by little, the Sioux's land base was reduced to where today the Sioux Nation is spread over five "reservations" (as Indian territory is termed under US law), encompassing only one-tenth of the territory specified in the treaty.

Invasion, conquest and colonization have forged the recent history of most of the Indian tribes of North America. There are about a million Native Americans in the US today. Most of them live on the 300 reservations which cover one-fifth of the total land surface of the nation, counting Alaska where some 40 per cent of reservation land is located. Although the tribes' situation bears much in common with that of the colonies and former colonies of Asia, Africa and Latin America, underdevelopment on the reservation has not been the story of exploitation of cheap labor and raw materials, as has been the case in much of the Third World. Rather it traces the history of land "transactions" with the US government, for land was the tribes' only valuable resource.

Extermination through War . . . or Peace

The Red Cloud War was one of many fought by North America's native peoples against the white invaders during the 18th and 19th centuries. By the time of the American Revolution of 1776, white settlers, mostly British, occupied the entire eastern coast of the continent, having driven the native population several hundred miles inland. Although there were instances of peaceful coexistence and intermarriage (notably in the case of the Quakers in Pennsylvania), colonial leaders on the whole distinguished themselves by their ferocity to destroy the heathen. Gifts of blankets infected with smallpox were a favorite tactic, as were the liquor trade and outright slaughter.

It was under the Revolutionary American Government that westward expansion became a cornerstone of official policy. The bankrupt revolutionary state nationalized Indian lands, then sold them to wealthy speculators (including Washington, Jefferson, Franklin, Hamilton and other political leaders of the time), a policy which gained not only operating revenue, but the favor of the incipient bourgeoisie. These farsighted leaders of the new state (Thomas Jefferson in particular) felt that the economic development and future strength of the US depended on the exploitation of the natural resources at their disposal. European immigrants to work western lands abounded; wealthy speculators provided the credit mechanisms to facilitate the transfer of lands; What they lacked was public confidence in the safety of a move westward. Less than a year after the signing of the peace with Britain in 1794, General "Mad" Anthony Wayne resolved this problem by carrying out wholesale massacres of native people in Tennessee, beginning the genocide intended to remove any real or imagined human obstacles to westward expansion.

Wars of extermination against Indian peoples continued throughout the 19th century, at the end of which white people controlled almost every region of the country. Federal Indian policy—upon which Hitler claimed to have based his resolution of the "Jewish question"—

MARCH 29, 1864: UNITED STATES BEGINS A GENOCIDAL WAR AGAINST THE COLORADO CHEYENNE.

reduced the population from an estimated 25 million at the time of the first European contact at the beginning of the 17th century, to less than 250,000 by 1900, and effectively pushed the survivors into corners of no economic use to the United States.

Useless Treaties

The US government signed peace treaties with most tribes. Like the armistices between independent nations, they provided a legal settlement to their disputes. But in most cases military superiority enabled the US government to impose its own terms on Indian nations, defining their borders as well as their rights as "independent" entities. However, as in the case of the Sioux and the 1868 Treaty, even military defeat did not prevent the US government from systematically violating the terms of peace treaties when its interests so dictated.

The Original Peoples of North America

According to the US Bureau of the Census, officially there were 793,000 Indians or "Native Americans" in 1970, of which almost half a million live in rural areas and 300,000 in urban communities. Nevertheless, there are about two and a half million US citizens who claim to be descendants of the original inhabitants.

When white colonization began in the 17th century, many peoples lived in the territory now known as the United States of America. In the southwestern deserts lived the Apache, the Navajo, the Hopi, the Pima, the Havasupai and the Yuma. Kickapoos, Quapaws, Osages and Miamis roamed the central plains. Arapaho, Cheyenne, Pawnee, Crow, Kansa, Sioux and Ponca lived in the north, while Wichita, Comanche and Kiowa lived in the south. The west was inhabited by the Washo, the Paiute, the Ute and the Shoshone, and the Gulf coast by the Natchez, the Calusa, the Tonkawa and the Arawak. Chickasaw, Choctaw, Cherokee, Creek, Tuscanora and Shawnee lived in the southeastern forests, and in the northeastern forests lived the Mohegan, the Ottawa, the Cayuga, the Onandaga, the Wyandotte, the Narragansett, the Wampanoag, the Mohawk, the Delaware, the Seneca and the Oneida among others.

After the signing of a treaty the US cavalry would confiscate guns and horses. Then US government administrators would establish a hierarchical political structure—where none existed before—under chiefs appointed by them. The native religion would be banned and a host of Catholic and Protestant missionaries brought in to convert the population. Later, federal schools would be set up where only English could be spoken and where the history of the Indians was rewritten to favor the "Americanization" of native people.

Treaty-making came to an end in 1871 when the President of the US became the authority on reservation boundaries and could change them by executive order. In 1887 the US Congress passed the Allotment Act under which each Indian was given a plot of 10 to 640 acres of reservation land. After a small payment to each tribe, all leftover land was then opened to white ownership. The law also allowed individual Indians to sell their allotted land. During the following forty years much Indian territory—90 million of the 150 million acres that are inalienable according to the treaties—came under white control and the standard of living of Native Americans dropped precipitously.

The Indian Reorganization Act of 1934 halted the allotment of tribal lands, organizing the tribal governments which administer the tribes today under the authority and control of the Federal Bureau of Indian Affairs (BIA).

Corporate Offensive

In recent years Indian land has again come to the forefront of US strategic planning. As Third World countries have become increasingly assertive regarding their own natural resources, corporate planners have begun to seek their sustenance in mineral reserves located within US borders. It has been estimated that 90 per cent of the untapped energy sources in the US—including oil, coal, natural gas and uranium—lie on Indian land.

Partially in response to corporate desires, the BIA launched its Termination and Relocation policies during the 50s. The former instituted mechanisms to dissolve reservations and tribes as legal entities by removing their special status, while the latter was a one-way bus ticket to the nearest urban slum. Although certain reservations "disappeared" under these policies, the majority have managed to conserve their legal status. Yet a seasonal flow of

Indians between the reservation and the city did become common and most of the mineral wealth came under corporate control.

Reservations, Underdeveloped Enclaves

Reservations are pockets of underdevelopment within the world's most developed country. In various respects they have more in common with the Third World than with the rest of the U.S. Statistics regarding income and health indicate that Native Americans are by far the country's poorest citizens. Their income is about one-third of the national average, while life expectancy is 64 years or 10 per cent less than the average. Infant mortality is about 24 percent higher than the average for the rest of the country and unemployment on reservations is officially 40 per cent, although Indian leaders say that the real rate is somewhere between 70 and 90 per cent. The land is often too dry to be workable without heavy capital investments which neither the tribes nor individual Indians can afford. Small scale industry only exists on a few reservations.

How do people survive in this situation? The answer to this question is a simple one. In it lies the key to the functioning of the reservation economy and its particular form of colonialist underdevelopment.

What guns and Bibles could not do, the welfare system seems to have accomplished. The native people of North America are as dependent on the federal government as is a baby on its mother. People live in federal housing, they eat federal surplus food or food bought with federal food stamps, and they receive a federal welfare check every month with which they buy what little else they can afford.

Generations have grown up watching their parents being treated like children, and the effects have been devastating. Work as a fulfilling human activity has lost its meaning. Self-respect, hope, any sense of real community have been destroyed by cutting people off not only from the means of production but from the objective need to produce. The very fabric of society which binds one human being to another has been subtly torn to shreds by a "benevolent" institutional power. This situation has led to enormously high rates of alcoholism and violence as individuals seek an escape from the wholesale destruction of their culture. Nevertheless, any attempt to destroy a people, even with such powerful weapons as welfare, drugs and

forced removal, generates its own contradictions.

Organized Opposition

The past ten years have seen a marked increase in political awareness and activity on reservations. Many young people who

---

Mount Rushmore: The Ultimate Insult

The Black Hills of South Dakota are sacred territory for the Sioux people. These beautiful mountains, dotted with lakes and pine forests, traditionally were considered so sacred that no one lived there. For hundreds of years people came only to perform religious ceremonies.

Today the Black Hills are visited by literally millions of tourists every year. The sacrosanct land is now strewn with highways lined with neon signs and gift shops. The major attraction: Mount Rushmore National Monument, where the gigantic faces of four US presidents have been carved out of the side of the mountain. Truly it is an imposing spectacle to see the fifty-foot-high faces of Washington, Jefferson, Lincoln and Teddy Roosevelt filling half the sky. These four symbolic faces are reproduced in thousands of souvenirs for the vacationers who flock to this altar of patriotism.

Washington and Jefferson made personal fortunes speculating in stolen Indian lands; Roosevelt transformed Sioux territory into "national parks"; and Lincoln, noble Lincoln, who on the very same day he signed the Emancipation Proclamation to free the slaves ordered the public hanging of 39 Sioux in Minneapolis for the crime of rebellion. What does it mean for the Indian to see the faces of these white leaders carved in the sacred stone of the Black Hills?

Perhaps it is a testament to the tenacious resistance of the Sioux people: that genocidal wars and armed occupation were not enough; outlawing their religion and language was not enough; exterminating the buffalo—the basis of their economy—was not enough; confining them to isolated, barren reservations was not enough to subdue them. The white people—"greedy ones" in the Sioux's Lakota language—had to go the limit in intimidation.

---

were brought up in the city, as a result of the relocation policy, became radicalized along with other poor minorities during the 60s through their participation in the civil rights movement and the popular movement against the Vietnam War. They have since returned to their reservations as part of the American Indian Movement (AIM) to organize against corporate and government infringement on Indian rights. The AIM, founded in 1968, is a decentralized organization of progressive Native Americans which favors independence and a return to traditional ways.

Certain tribes have also initiated lawsuits against the federal government to regain their sovereignty over reservation resources as specified in the treaties. Several have achieved remarkable success on this score in both US courts and international tribunals. Nevertheless, corporate pressure for access to Indian mineral reserves marks a serious limitation to the legal struggle, as it is only too easy for the US government to change the rules of the game.

The legacy of colonization, with the added dimension implied by welfare, has made grassroots organizing on the reservations extremely difficult. The AIM has been obliged to concentrate much of its efforts on legal battles and solidarity work in cities and college campuses. Still, the AIM has merited fierce repression by the FBI. Many leaders have been killed, and more are in jail on trumped-up charges. That the FBI director considers it to be one of the most dangerous subversive organizations in the country is perhaps an indication of the importance the government places on corporate access to Indian mineral wealth. Given the current campaign to whip up patriotic Cold War hysteria, it is likely that the persecution of AIM will increase in the near future.

Since clearly the corporations and the US government have an overwhelming political and economic advantage, it remains to be seen whether the Native American people will be able to prevent indiscriminate corporate mining on their land. Their struggle to gain control over their natural resources is intimately tied up with the difficult internal struggle against underdevelopment and its bitter social fruits: corruption, apathy and disorganization. For, as has been shown time and time again in Asia, Africa and Latin America, only a conscious and mobilized people can stop imperialism in its tracks and set out on a path towards self-reliant development.

From *Akwesasne Notes* 11, no. 5
(Winter 1979): 9-10

Ogwahowaykah Henodeystah: 'A Place of Common Interest'

On November 20, 1979, Akwesasne Notes interviewed nine parents who have children attending Ogwahonwaykah Henodeystah, which translates roughly into "Indian Way School," on the Cattaraugus Indian Reservation in Western New York. The parents who participated in the interview were: Mrs. Wheeler, Mr. & Mrs. R. John, Mr. & Mrs. White, Mr. & Mrs. D. John, Mrs. Henderson, and Mr. & Mrs. L. Hemlock. One student, Mr. L. Hemlock, was also present. At some point or another, just about all of the parents responded to questions during the course of the interview, and their responses reflected a distinct consensus of opinion on the topics discussed. Because of this, we have omitted identification of the responses in terms of personalities, and have presented the interview as a group interview, which it was. What follows is the discussion at that interview.

Akwesasne Notes: What motivated you to start this project?

Parent: We did it because our children weren't learning in the public school. In our family we wanted to get more into the [Seneca] culture and the religion. It wasn't hard for us because for five or six years now we have been living by the Gaiwiio. It took the pressure off us when we took our children out of the public school.

AN: Before you developed this alternative to the public school, did those schools hassle you when you took your children out to attend the ceremonies?

Parent: We would ask for assignments a couple of weeks ahead of time, and they said that they don't plan their lessons that

---

Reprinted with permission from *Akwesasne Notes.*

far ahead of time. So the children would get behind. Now, since we have started this project, when something goes on at the Longhouse everything stops here and everybody goes there. It's like a different world.

AN: You say that the reason that you took the children out of the public school was that you had religious objectives. What were the things you were thinking about in terms of religion? Was it that you were concerned with ceremonies, or was it a desire to conform with the code of Handsome Lake that more or less instructs people to be wary of sending their children to the white man's school.

Parent: We have a family and we follow the Handsome Lake Code. It was hard for our children. They would come back to us from the public school and we were trying to keep our Indian ways alive. Then they would go back to school and have to adjust to that way and then come back again.

AN: I notice in one day at the school that language is a heavy part of the activity. None of the children speak the Seneca language, is that right?

Parent: Very little.

AN: So it's a real fear, a real worry, that unless some young people come along in the next few years that can speak the language and who know enough about how to carry on the ceremonies, that the culture will be lost.

Parent: Right. That was one of the reasons. But right now the young people aren't learning and we should start them while they are young. There are parents in the group who believe . . . that we can learn [Seneca language] right along with the children. That was very important.

AN: So the parents and the children are both going to the same classes, especially the culture classes, and are picking up the language together. How's that working out?

Parent: Well, it's been an adjustment. People have had to make adjustments . . .

AN: You started this school with no money. How many students did you have in the beginning?

Parent: Only seven. . . . We started out with seven, then people started asking

about the school and it went up to eleven.

AN: You taught classes by going house to house each day. It was a kind of travelling school . . . .

Parent: You could say we were on the move.

AN: What does it mean to have a school which is dedicated to conserving culture?

Parent: The thing people misinterpret is the activity between the language classes. We try to keep our thinking straight on that because it's a Family Day. We used to call it culture day for lack of a better word. Now we call it Family Day so that the parents do both come. We have two parents who speak the language. The entire family comes because we don't stop at kindergarten, we go down to preschool and toddlers so they're here too and if any of the workers of the family are free, they come too.

AN: People are going to criticize this effort because the children aren't going to receive diplomas and they won't be able to go someplace and get a job. How do people respond to that criticism?

Parent: That question comes up every time you turn around. The fact is that you have to function in the outside world, it's a reality. The children are learning the harder subjects as they would in public school, but they don't have nine subjects to carry every day. You know—music, art, industrial arts, and so forth. But they have basics, the very basics that they would offer in public school. Children advance in the school. The teachers should talk more about individual instruction. Everyone I run into—I try to tell them that public school is not working. It is obvious that it is not working and that people are dissatisfied with public school because it is just built on money. They don't care if the children learn to read or learn math in second grade. They may be way below their reading level and public school doesn't really care. But in a school like this you do care because it's your child and that's what it's all about—a family-oriented situation. It's hard to call us a school when you really sit down and talk to someone individually because we're trying to make it a way of life as much as we can. That's how I try to answer that question. The children advance here, you know. If someone doesn't like something they have the opportunity to bring it up immediately. If they see something wrong it's their family obligation to correct the situation.

AN: What motivated the peculiar nature of this school? What is there about the

Seneca culture that attracts people so strongly so that you go through all the sacrifice, the inconvenience, to teach this to your children?

Parent: It's really got to do with spirit. That's the reason I took Sheri out of the public school. I haven't had her in Gowanda but a couple of weeks. She went to kindergarten in the public schools. She's gone to three public schools so far. But I went to Gowanda and who knows better than me about Gowanda? Anyway, Sheri has a really good spirit and I want her to develop it.

AN: Let me reorganize the question. Many other "Indian Way" or "Survival" schools concentrate on a kind of generic "Indian Way." But there is really no such thing as "Indian" culture in a specific sense. There are specific cultures and languages—Lakota, Navajo, and so forth. This school concentrates on the Seneca Way, and that means that there is a specific Way of Life which can be taught in rather exacting detail. That means to me that the concept of culture isn't something that is idealized, that it is real and that children are exposed to the specifics of that reality. What is there about Seneca culture that is so attractive when its study is first-hand, when it is not idealized, when it is real?

Parent: The Way of Life. See, we don't gather in a school per se. Each family here participates whether they have children in the school or not. They are still part of a family. The bases are the families. The idea is to get children to understand that they are going to be participants in the culture. They are going to go to the Longhouse and help with the work, because that is what is supposed to be done when we have our doings. That's how things have always been. That's the Way of Life. When we're trying to teach the children the Way of Life they have to know their language first, and that's our priority. Everybody—the whole family should try to learn the language. . . . We've devoted ourselves to getting that language whether it's in the classroom situation, Section IV federal funding, or if it's in a home. Or in a school like this or a meeting place, however we can get it. We concentrate on getting that Way of Life across to the children, and everybody participates through the family. That's what builds the spirit because all these families come together here and practice that understanding of the Way of Life.

They go home and do the best they can do in the home to practice that Way of Life.

AN: Then it's not a school, as defined commonly as a place for children to go to be taught some theoretical or practical skill. This is a real effort to be with the children and redefine strength in their families. It's what learning would be if we didn't have schools. It would be like this with parents and children and everybody. . . .

Parent: . . . School also has another definition—that it's a place of common interest. I think that's a term that stuck in my mind because all of us here have a common interest. We are not relating to the kind of school they do out there. This is the term that's different—we all have a common interest. I decided to take my children out of the public school because of the attitudinal changes that they brought back from Gowanda. The fighting, the teasing, the calling down and that what I taught in my home was not being reinforced. When they come down here [to this school] there's a closeness—I guess it could be termed a social law. They don't tease like they had in Gowanda. They have respect for each other, which you can't find out there. They are getting back to a closeness, a brotherhood again that has been lost where everybody goes their own certain way, not caring about how your neighbor feels or anything.

AN: People are satisfied that there's a visible kind of progress being made towards those goals?

Parent: Sure, I can see it in my own children. It took a kind of adjustment because they had my oldest son for five years. But he's coming around. I ask the parents, well, is he changing? And it does show at home too because of the reinforcement that they get down here and through the reinforcement that he gets at home. We're not in conflict.

AN: Is it safe to say that the children are getting the basics of an education?

Parent: It's even better than public school because they aren't being pushed. We don't have to say "Hurry up and get this done." We say, work on it until it gets done and done well. In Gowanda, they are pushing through graduates that can read on a sixth grade level. What good is their diploma if they can't read and write well?

Parent: The basics aren't as important as all of those other things. The spirit of the Way of Life is more important and the basics are tossed in there. But they are not even [the same importance]. They are

important, but not in the way they are over in the public school where those skills are the end all and the be all.

Parent: There's a balance—we try to bring in a balance. A balance of the Way of Life and still develop their skills because we know, eventually they have to have those skills. So we try to provide them with not just survival skills, but to produce people who can read and write and express themselves and survive in an outside situation.

Parent: We're stereotyped. [Others] believe that we're keeping our children inside the reservation. Our children go to Buffalo, they travel more miles than the average Gowanda student. And they are in the public library a lot sooner than a Gowanda student would be there, developing skills in how to utilize the library or a public facility. If they can use those facilities when they are ten or twelve, even seven or eight, they are not going to be failures when they are twenty and in the city looking for a job.

Parent: We want our children to utilize basic skills.

Parent: We worry about basic skills on Monday and Thursdays. The other days we don't worry about that stuff.

AN: What people have articulated is that first, people have decided to take action because they wanted to strenghten their family life, and secondly what they look to as that strengthener of family is this Seneca culture or Way of Life. What they did was come together with their families to learn that process and also to interact with one another on a whole new basis, getting a whole new spirit of interaction. What is emerging out of that is that the children are learning, that people are satisfied that their behavior, their socialization, is moving along very well. By the way, that's the first time that I've ever heard that articulated— goals that were not goals for the children but for the family, which I think is a very important point to make. I don't know of anywhere where the family has taken it upon themselves to become stronger by making learning a family activity. In most places, schools are designed to replace that function of the family.

Parent: This is the first opportunity that I've ever had to have a say in the children's education, and to be right there. You can be there everyday if you want to, and this is one of the reasons I quit my job. I realized that I wanted to be with my children and it's a really important time. I got to thinking about their lives, what kind of lives they had. I always had a babysitter

when they got home. But that's not the same thing as being there when they get off the school bus. It's a real important time for the parents to be there, one of them at least. When I started coming here to school with my children there was a change. They said. "Gee it's nice having you around Ma." A lot of times we get on each other's nerves, but that's only natural. I can see them growing. It's a really, really good feeling. . . . I think the best thing that has come out of this for all of us is the peacefullness. We don't look at the clocks anymore. Some things you have to do on time. . . . The ladies in the Longhouse tell me that someday you're not going to think about a clock. You just know when things have to be done and you do them and that's it.

AN: When you *restart* something, it's different from simply starting. If everyone spoke Seneca and went to the Longhouse, if they grew up in it all their lives and as they got older they learned songs and how to do the ceremonies, they really wouldn't have to put much effort into it. That's really different from someone who didn't grow up in it and really has to strive, to struggle to find a way to learn. The teachings of Handsome Lake are probably the most strict of any surviving body of codes or teachings in all the world, not just the Native world. It doesn't leave a lot to the imagination, and it's almost totally different from "Indian Movement things." Gaiwiio involves specific rules of behavior, and requires an accountability to the Creator. In a way, your effort is going to be a test. Whether things that happen here work will be graded, in a sense, by the test of time. Whether this project continues on and grows will be determined by how well it meets people's needs. You've been here for two years, and you've just begun. What you're aparently talking about here is revitalization of a whole Way of Life. That will require teaching a whole group of people to put through the ceremonies of the Longhouse and that has to take at least ten years—it could take forty. What are your personal goals behind that kind of activity? What will you expect to come out of all this, besides all the work involved?

Parent: Satisfaction of serving the Creator. It's taken us a long time to really come to that point. It took me 17 years and now I can see we are totally into Gaiwiio. It just gives you a real satisfaction to live that life. It's a completely different Way of Life. There are so many things now that don't matter. Our children are happy. For the

first time this year, Lance sang Adonwhe. Leslie knows the Moon Ceremony songs. She amazes me all the things her little brain has picked up, things that she knows that we have to learn—she already knows. Her idol is Mrs. Green and she is learning so much. She's picking things up. Something has come to her from going to the Longhouse. She went to the Longhouse even when Lee and I didn't. She and Lance were always over there for all the ceremonies. The children went there and they have picked up a Way of Life and I know that they are going to do their darndest to make sure it goes on. This is a complete Way of Life to us.

AN: What is there in people's belief about the instructions of the Creator that impels you to this course of action? Why is this the right thing to do?

Parent: Because of the Life. The Life of the Seneca. That was one of the first things the students learned last year. How to pronounce it, what it meant, and all the things that are in that instruction. But not to just do it to get it done, but to do it because you believe in the Spirit of the Strawberries. I tell my daughter not to go to the Longhouse unless she feels good about doing it. If she doesn't feel good about doing it, she should either stay home or sit on the bench. If she doesn't feel the thanksgiving for the strawberries. . . . That's one of the signs in the teachings, that it's coming close that this earth is not going to carry on. It's not healthy and we're not taking care of it. To me, one of the reasons

that I wanted to start a school from my family point of view is because I felt that there was so much to learn and we don't have the time because the children are in school and we are at work.

A lot of times we talk in school about how they should not be bored picking wild onions because we picked them last year, and the year before. It shouldn't be a boring thing, but a refreshing thing that they are still here. We should give thanks for the harvest. There's just so much to learn from one yearly cycle. Learn basic things the first time around and the next year learn a bit more. It may take forty years. I think it will take until the day you go to your grave. Another reason this school was started is because it was clear that the old people are passing away. We don't have much more time to be worrying about reading, writing and arithmetic, you know. There's a couple of people in the School—maybe more than a couple, I can't speak for others—that if reading, writing and arithmetic were eliminated it wouldn't be a loss. If they're going to survive, someone will help them survive, they're not going to be illiterate, they won't be ignorant. When Lance did Adonweh, Edie and I just took the sweat off our brows because no one else down there knew how. And he didn't have any practice, he just did it. So that's what our school's about. We did it. We're doing it. We didn't sit around for two or three years planning, trying to get funding, trying to get a director who could direct us and figure out what is proper or improper. We just did it. And we felt that if we didn't do it, we would lose one more year. One more year would go by and our children would be cheerleaders or something like that that just didn't have anything to do with our Ways.

AN: It's clear to me now that the answers to the question I was going to ask about how this school will survive and how you're going to fund it is—however. You don't have a plan, don't need one. It'll survive somehow.

Parent: You want to buy a raffle ticket?
Parent: How about a dinner ticket?
Parent: I think that we were just meant to be because somehow people openly supported the school. We sell spaghetti dinners, *Akwesasne Notes* Calendars. Whatever we decided to do people said, well, yeah, I'll buy one or we'll give you a social, we'll raise some money for you. Sure, we want to write proposals for funding, but it's secondary to keeping this school moving and breathing.

AN: Have people thought about the possibility that these young people could grow up wanting to change the world they are living in in some very specific ways? Already I can hear you parents saying that we changed our values when we realized we were chasing things that weren't important. Now here you've got a family operation and these young people are going to see change, only they should be much more familiar with the realities of this culture much earlier than you were. They should know by the time they are fifteen or sixteen what you found out when you were a dozen years older than that.

Parent: Well, we're trying to live by the Gaiwiio in the school as much as we possibly can. I know a lot of people must think I'm crazy, because I don't speak the language. But the Gaiwiio has so many specifics about how you treat your children, how you treat each other, and I think that is integrated in this school.

Parent: But that's not what he was asking. He was asking what will Pete and Lance and Leslie do when they are twenty-four years old. They've got all this learning. Are they going to use it? I wonder if this teaching will hang on and teach them not only to teach their children, but to develop a community of the Haudenosaunee.

Parent: An expansion of our community, an expansion of our family.
Parent: Yes, we're thinking about that.

The Indian Way School at Cattaraugus has been supported entirely from community fund-raising activities, and they haven't developed a proposal and gone out into the world seeking funding. What is needed is money for a building to house the school, and to meet operating expenses on a day-by-day basis. Donations to their effort can be sent to:

Ogwahowaykah Henodeystah
P.O. Box 197
Brant, New York 14027

Letters of support and offers of any kind of materials (paper, school supplies) would also be gratefully received.

A REVIEW OF CONTEMPORARY CINEMA

From *Jump Cut*, no. 21 (November 1979), pp. 4-5

Blacks Britannica: Racism in Public TV

by Joel Dreyfuss

There is a significant if unflattering lesson about the state of American public television in the fact that it is more often criticized for what it excludes than for what it does. The recent controversy about BLACKS BRITANNICA, a one-hour documentary filmed for the weekly series, WORLD, once again exposes some of the failures of public television. The incident is also useful in examining the problems of race and perspective that plague much of the media in this country.

BLACKS BRITANNICA is a relentless and engrossing indictment of racism toward black immigrants to England, told from an obvious Marxist perspective. The film argues that discrimination in England

---

Reprinted with permission from *Jump Cut: A Review of Contemporary Cinema.*

is based on economics and fueled by opportunists across the entire spectrum of British politics. Told through the eyes and words of a cross-section of blacks, David Koff's film uses interviews, stock footage, and scenes of street life and violence to show how blacks in England are trapped at the bottom of an economic and political system which shows little compassion or concern about their fate. Rapid editing, overlapping dialogue and cinema verite all build to an emotional and violent climax whose conclusion is underscored by a reggae band's call for revolution. As Koff puts it, the film "reflects the increasingly militant response within the black community to the continuing attacks upon it, both by the fascist elements on the street and by the state itself." An official of the British Information Service in Washington called the film "dangerous" and asked for equal time. *New York Times* critic John O'Connor said the film not only documents the growing militancy, "but, quite clearly, the structure and tone endorse it."

The program was originally scheduled to air on July 13, 1978, but the showing was postponed so that WORLD's executive producer David Fanning could make some changes. "I never had any dispute with the central premise of the film or with its contents," Fanning said at the time. He argued that the changes were intended to make it more understandable to the American public. But later, Fanning told *Newsweek*: "I was concerned with the film's endorsement of a Marxist viewpoint."

Koff insists that two separate films now exist: his version and Fanning's. Fanning rearranged some of the sequences in the original version and removed about three minutes of footage including a sequence where British cops used black figures in target practice. The Koff film opened with an interview with black sociologist Colin Prescod that became the matrix of the documentary: "If one weren't wary of talking about conspiracy, because in all parts of this country . . . it's clear that at top national level, and certainly at local level, the state has moved to manipulate blacks in any way it wanted to." Koff's version goes on to show how urban renewal has been used to destroy black communities, and how black groups have fought against these measures, organized their own schools and groups. Old British newsreels, in condescending tone, record the arrival of blacks in large numbers during the 1950s. Prescod analyzes the newsreels and points out how immigration was used as a political issue in Britain before we see footage of a broad spectrum of politicians denouncing immigrants and their impact on the country.

Fanning used the newsreel shots to open the film, losing in the process the political irony of the commentator's statements. The comments of the British politicians are then heard, framing the film, as Koff argues, before we hear the blacks' analysis of the issues.

The two endings provide another example of subtle yet important differences. Koff has Prescod on camera summing up: "Britain, 'mother of the empire,' has had to welcome her children and allow them to settle. Because of racism they have not been allowed to settle in a dignified manner. And because blacks have refused to accept indignity and victimage, Britain is stuck with a rebellious black presence in its center. And there is no way that Britain can get out of this situation. And what the blacks who've been born here are saying is that they intend to obtain their rights, as dignified citizens, here."

There is a cutaway to street scenes as the voice continues: "We cannot get what we want in capitalist Britain. I'm not one for saying that because we can't get it in capitalist Britain, we go somewhere where we believe there is some 'socialism' or something. Anywhere, any place, any time we can't get it under capitalism, well then, capitalism has to go." There is a long shot of street fighting between police and a crowd of black youths that ends with the crowd surging around an official car. The car tries to back up, is trapped by the crowd, and the windshield is smashed to the reggae music of Steel Pulse's "Handsworth Revolution." The film ends abruptly, leaving the audience in suspense about the fate of the car's occupant.

The Fanning version moved the violent scene up to an earlier section, effectively reducing its emotional impact on viewers. The edited version is preceded by a statement that "while the film does not include the views of those who disagree with it, we feel it is valuable to hear these voices." This statement, and many of the cuts, help create absence of distance between the film and its subject and Fanning's version ends with Prescod's statement that . . . "they intend to obtain their rights, as dignified citizens, here," another subtle shift that now makes these words a plea for civil rights.

In watching both versions of BLACKS BRITANNICA, the viewer cannot help experiencing a strong sense of deja-vu. The complaints of blacks in Britain, the confrontations with police, the arbitrary application of the "sus" law which allows the arrest of people suspected of being about to commit a crime, and the rising tide of black militancy recall the 1960s in the United States, when the racial apocalypse seemed inevitable.

There were small numbers of blacks in Britain as far back as the mid-16th century; massive numbers passed through British ports during the slave trade but only a few remained in England to serve as laborers, servants, artisans and courtiers. Because the numbers were so small, there was no substantial racial friction between blacks and whites until World War I. Blacks came in large numbers from the West Indies to fight, but after the end of hostilities depressed economic conditions resulted in pitched battles between black and white seamen. Between the two World Wars, the first laws were passed to restrict black immigrants. Once again, blacks contributed to the British struggle against the Nazis despite numerous discriminatory actions.

In the 1950s, the flow of black and Asian immigrants became a flood. Seeking better opportunities, escaping the turmoil of nationalism and independence, thousands used the British citizenship granted them by the empire to enter England. As economic pressures grew, the developments were strikingly similar to those in the United States. There was discrimination in housing and employment, violent outbreaks, a disappearance of previous "tolerance."

There have been arguments that WGBH, the most active production center in the public television system, was concerned about offending the corporations which underwrite so many of its programs. I would suggest that the unease of Fanning and others is much less conscious, and at the same time, much more serious than that. BLACKS BRITANNICA helps put into focus some aspects of our own racial issues that have been blurred by the fog of neo-conservatism now sweeping the country.

In 1979, discussions of racial progress are made within the strict parameters of statistical information. Advocates of more stringent affirmative action point out the fact that blacks, as a group, earn less than whites; that whites with less education earn more than blacks, and that in fields which guarantee financial security—engineering, medicine and other professions—minorities are underrepresented. White neoconservatives, who have taken over the mainstream of American political thinking, use the numbers to point out changes for the better: the growth of the black middle class, the numbers of minorities in higher education, etc.

In a sense this struggle over definitions of progress reflects a more profound struggle for the *power* to define issues. The abandonment of the civil rights struggle by white liberals in the late 1960s took place at the very moment that blacks were raising the issue of power. In the 1970s, there is no question that blacks have acquired some material comforts denied them in the past. But the power to influence policy, to participate in intellectual debate and essentially to play a role in the shaping of America still eludes them.

The relationship of public television (or the film industry) to blacks reflects the phenomenon of powerlessness. The vision of public television as a source of alternative programming has never quite become reality—particularly for the minority groups which have so long been savaged by commercial television. Black demands for representation (during the Black Power era) led to BLACK JOURNAL and SOUL on the PBS system. But lack of funds and absence of institutional commitment led to their demise. At this point only BLACK PERSPECTIVE ON THE NEWS, a low-budget "talking head" show, provides a black input to the public television system.

Arguments have been made that blacks as well as whites benefit from MASTER-PIECE THEATER, British imports and classical music programs. No doubt they do, but the full range of the black cultural experience is not seen on commercial television. Since jazz is rarely seen on the networks, it is natural to assume that public television should fill that gap, but it doesn't. The minority view of America is an intriguing, enlightening and necessary perspective, but it isn't on television, commercial or public. The film industry decided a few years ago that "blaxploitation was dead" and a burgeoning industry was stopped cold. Blacks have been conspicuously absent from our most recent box-office blockbusters. In fact, this could be the first time in our history where our fantasies, as expressed in film, are more segregated than our reality.

BLACKS BRITANNICA reminds us that issues of black and white—in the U.S.A., in England, or in southern Africa—are essentially issues of power. The WGBH definition of "objectivity" is as invalid as Ian Smith's definition of majority rule—not because there cannot be some standard definition, but because those most affected are often excluded from the processes that lead to the definition or rule.

In the wake of the American Black Power movement, attempts to develop a systematic analysis of race relations were discounted. It was no longer fashionable to talk about "the system" or the impact of "institutions." Yet, we cannot talk intelligently about the treatment of blacks by Hollywood or PBS without examining "the system."

Noam Chomsky, in his latest book, *Language and Responsibility*, points out how our media is as essentially one-sided as the Soviet press. There is not a single socialist or radical columnist on a major American newspaper or magazine today. We are as bound by "state capitalism" today as Soviet readers are fettered by "state socialism." It is often argued that radicalism failed in America because workers were too well off. Actually, the full power of the state has worked to assure the failure of radicalism. What this has done is leave American political debate in a very crowded and windowless room. More and more, our "state capitalism" leaves us unable to understand what is going on in the rest of the world.

BLACKS BRITANNICA is a reminder that there are other ways to see the world, to analyze events and to place them in a context that enlightens and informs us even as we are aware of its political bias. What made the film less palatable for officials at WGBH was that BLACKS BRITAN-

NICA analyzed a subject much too close to home. It did not fit in with the official discussions of income, education and middle-class status that are comfortable for the majority of Americans.

In a memo announcing the inception of WORLD, producer David Fanning said: "We hope to use film and television to help Americans take off their special American glasses and look at the world through the eyes of others . . . we would tend to be interested in a film which proposes to explore an international situation in terms of the perceptions of some human beings that we would come to know. Standing in their shoes we would begin to see the world as they see it." Despite these lofty ideals, David Koff's BLACKS BRITANNICA became an affront to Fanning and WGBH. The station's lawyers have gone to court in this country and in England to block showings of Koff's version. This raises issues of artistic integrity, of the ability of independent filmmakers to gain access to the airwaves and many other legal and moral questions. But most of all the controversy should make us all aware of how power is distributed. There is no guarantee for blacks in Britain, or for powerless groups anywhere, to have their views expressed without modification or censorship in our highly touted system of Western democracy.

BLACK · SOLIDARITY · DAY · NOV. 5

Cindy Fredrick/LNS

From *Seven Days* 3, no. 6 (May 18, 1979): 6-10.

The Myth of Black Progress: 'Racism Is Dead, Long Live Racism'

by Michael Beaubien

Martin Luther King, Jr. once said in a speech honoring W. E. B. DuBois, "One idea he insistently taught was that Black people have been kept in deprivation by a poisonous fog of lies that depicted them as

inferior, born deficient, and deservedly doomed to servitude into the grave."

Recently in America it seems a new fog is riding in, bringing with it a glorified, yet equally invidious picture of Black life in America. The grinning "Step'n Fetchit," watermelon-chomping stereotype of the past has been shunted aside; in its place the media have inserted the sleek, slick image of the new Black middle class. Once again, the stereotype is an image of Blacks as white America would like them to be, this time free from the angry confrontations of the past, victors in the struggle for equality. And Blacks, in effect, are being asked to take the advice Senator Aiken of Vermont once offered the American government during the Vietnam war: "Declare you've won and go home." The problem is, American Blacks are home and they know where they stand. Nevertheless, the power of the media is such they can still convince many people that expectations have become reality: A recent Harris poll found that, in contrast to 1970, when three out of four whites believed that Blacks still experienced discrimination, in 1977 only one out of three still thought this to be true.

The sad reality, evident to anyone who has been to Watts, Detroit, or Harlem, is that Blacks have been slipping inexorably back to the economic position from which the civil-rights movement temporarily elevated them. The Urban League's 1979 report on the state of Black America, written by its research director, Dr. Robert Hill, presents a more realistic picture than the media myth: "Not only is the actual jobless rate for all Blacks still at depression levels, but the gap between the unemployment rates of Blacks and whites is the widest it has ever been." Hill concludes, "Black family income has fallen behind in both absolute and relative terms."

The centerpiece of the media effort to push the myth of Black progress is the increase in professional, managerial, and skilled blue-collar jobs held by Blacks. There are, in fact, more Blacks in these positions than ever before, but they make up only 3 percent of all the workers in these fields. The proportion of Black professionals and technicians has increased by only one percentage point since 1969, hardly the growth all the media hype would lead one to suspect. "Tokenism, rather than genuine compliance with affirmative action and equal employment opportunity requirements remains the rule, rather than the exception," says sociologist Dr. Kenneth B. Clark. And, as longtime civil-rights

activist Jack O'Dell points out, along with slight gains in the ranks of professionals, "there has also been growth in the number of permanently unemployed workers and growth in the number of underemployed."

Despite talk of the alleged growth of upper-middle and middle-income Black families, the Urban League report shows that between 1972 and 1976 the proportion of middle-income Black families (those earning $17,106 a year and above) wobbled downward for a while, then rose to just where it had been before—26 percent of all Black families. The proportion of upper-

income Black families (those earning $25,000 and up) has dropped recently.

Where, then, do all the figures on the improved status of Blacks come from? How can the media claim, with vehemence sometimes bordering on resentment, that more Blacks have made it to the top than ever before? Part of the answer can be found in the numbers game: by playing fast and loose with the figures, one can claim almost anything, all the while ignoring the real people whose lives are shifting along with the statistics. One source the media have adopted with relish is a Rand

Ross Beecher & Ron Richardson/LNS

No system is perfect.

REVEREND HERB DAUGHTRY, pastor of the House of the Lord Pentecostal Church in Brooklyn and an organizer of New York's Black United Front: Something has happened in America, something which always happens, that has limited the economic impact of the civil-rights movement: The power elite has become entrenched, and they've changed the rules of the game just as things were getting moving. They've become more elusive. This country is tightening up as the battle gets hot for the world's resources, as groups in other parts of the world claim what is theirs.

One of the tactics used to defuse the current anger of Blacks is to show middle-class families in the media: "Look at them! Surely things can't be as bad as they seem," proclaim the ads and articles. But that so-called middle class has no roots. A white middle class is insulated; it has some degree of political strength, some ties to the populace around it. The Black middle class has no protection. It is always on the edge of being eliminated.

Some of the tactics that were applied in the civil-rights struggle could still be effective. The combined income of

American Blacks—$80 billion, according to a recent book—makes them the ninth-richest nation in the world. If we withdrew as consumers, it would be terribly devastating to American industry and the economy.

I don't get worked up over the response of the Ku Klux Klan to the current economic boycotts in the South. The enemy is more elusive than the KKK. I'm more concerned with corporate America and the distribution of wealth. I'm also more concerned with what is being planned for Blacks in New York City. Is there really going to be planned shrinkage—eliminating Blacks from the city? And the police behavior in New York City far outdistances the KKK: they kill and maim, and they're called New York's "finest."

As a partial solution to some of these problems, we'd like to be able to form cooperatives, or help small businesses grow and produce the things we need—and still hold them accountable. We may bring values to this that will speak to people and not just to profit. But no matter what, you've got to eat, and you've got to have a place to live, and you've got to work: I see too much material need among my people.

David Omar White/Black American/LNS

MINORITY CONTRACT

Corporation study which makes much of the closing of the earnings gap between Black and white workers. The study has found, for instance, that the earnings gap between Black and white women workers has disappeared—meaning that all women now earn a skimpy 60 percent of white men's incomes. However, a careful reading of the report reveals that the increase in Black women's earnings had nothing to do with affirmative action; it represents a shift by women in the South from domestic work to light industry.

Although the median earnings of all Black individuals did rise from 62 percent of white earnings in 1969 to 75 percent of white income in 1975 as the report indicates, the ratio has been dropping ever since. The median income of Black families increased by 3.5 percent in one 12-month period (1976 to 1977), but the median income of white families grew more than twice as fast that same year, opening up the widest gap of the decade between the two groups.

It is by describing these very minimal gains out of context with the larger society, that the white establishment has been attempting to convince Americans that the emperor does indeed have new clothes, not luxurious perhaps, but of modest and

CHUCK TURNER, director of the Fannie Lou Hamer Housing Memorial Foundation in Boston—a subsidiary of the Third World Jobs Clearing House: Traditionally, the American system has pushed "trickle down and trickle up" theory: You create a middle class among the newer ethnic groups arriving here, and this seems to promise that everyone can benefit from the luck of some people. But a middle class doesn't mean anything. The vast majority of the wealth in this country is in very few hands. Worse, the theory still hasn't worked for most of the Irish or Italians or Poles in Boston; if it can't work for white groups, it won't work for Blacks. The American economy doesn't have the strength to create a Black middle class, if it wanted to: It can't maintain the middle class it has now.

I don't think we've made much progress since the civil-rights movement. There's a leadership group that's learning skills. But will they put those skills to the use of their people? And there's been no economic improvement. If there was any failure in the movement it was the failure of the national leadership to pay more attention to the vision that King had at the time of his assassination—his sense of a political and social and economic movement that would transcend the narrower framework of the civil-rights movement, to get a share of the resources that are here. After King's death, the leadership retrenched, in favor of a more "All-American" stance.

Flo Kennedy's Abridged ABC's of Racism

Florynce Kennedy is a lawyer and feminist activist

A is for assault: No mayor in any city has ever rushed to canonize a Black assaulted by a police officer or a woman beaten by her husband.

B is for bail: Bail frees corporate delinquents to walk the streets; it puts poor Black people inside jails to await trial.

C is for the criminal justice system: It's criminal.

D is for delinquency: the real delinquents raise the rent and utility bills, accuse labor unions of causing inflation, then tell you the delinquent is the kid who steals grandma's bag.

E is for the electoral process: More than 100 Black mayors have been elected in this country. If some of them are a disappointment, it's because . . .

F is for followers: As followers, we must understand that it was disruption that got us Black mayors. Pioneers can only cut down the trees; they can't necessarily build a four-lane highway.

G is for the good people: They're the key to oppression. Good Black people have always been afraid of angry Black people with guns.

J is for the jockocracy: Tall, Black young men on television, shooting balls, worshipped by millions. Muhammed Ali should run for president. He wouldn't win, but it would get a core of Black votes that could be bargained with.

M is for minorities: It doesn't matter if you call people minority or majority. Bank depositors outnumber bankers; tenants outnumber landlords; Blacks in South Africa outnumber whites. Numbers do not determine who's in charge.

M is also for the media and N is for the news: The media keep the real news from Black people, helping to make them patient in the face of injustice.

N is also for niggerization and O is for oppression: Oppressed people have the right to fight niggerization. The oppressed are niggerized because they're poor and they can't defend themselves. Being religious, they're inclined to take a lot of shit.

U is for unity: The white establishment, the banks, the KKK, would rather see 6,000 unified mice than one lion. We can't afford the luxury of arguing over unity—but we can form coalitions.

V is for victory and the right to violence: The right to violence is like the right to pee. You don't have to exercise it all the time.

W is for women. Black women are much more united than the media ever admits.

'He shouldn't need this anymore—racism ended in the 1960s!'

Konopacki/Rothco Guardian/LNS

sturdy cloth. But for anyone who chooses to look, the continued poverty and degradation this particular emperor has been forced to live in is all too evident.

In 1977 the number of white families living below the poverty line ($6,157 a year for a family of four) declined by 20,000 from the previous year, while the number of poor Black families increased by 20,000. Since the 1975 recession the number of poor Black families has increased by 124,000 and the number of poor white families has fallen by 298,000. Here again, transitions in the lives of Black women account for much of the havoc: The number of Black women heading families increased to 1,162,000 in 1977, and as with most female-headed households, their poverty deepened. The current figures work out to 4 out of 10 Black women heading families right now. A decade ago, it was only 2.5 out of 10; for white women the ratio has stayed relatively stable throughout the period.

The statistics on welfare are even more disturbing, showing that only half the Black families living below the poverty line receive any type of public assistance. Of the families that do receive welfare—25 percent of all Black families—nearly three-quarters need it not because they can't find work, but because their wages are so low a family cannot survive on them. In a sense, this is welfare for corporate America: the government is subsidizing low-wage industry·by supplementing wages below the survival level. "Since World War II no significant change has occurred in the employment probabilities of Black and whites," says Lester Thurow, an economist at the Massachusetts Institute of Technology. "At all points in time—good or bad—Black unemployment rates are approximately twice as high as those of whites."

At least half of all Black teen-agers are currently unemployed, and many of them have already been relegated to the status of

---

RITA SMITH, a worker in a prerelease program for women prisoners and director of the Harlem Self-Help Cooperative project: As a Black woman in this society, I realize the limitations that exist. They exist for the man I may love or the children I may bear. How can I be successful under such restraints?

I have borne seven children into the world and poverty is a part of the struggle. When some of them were growing up, we didn't have a table to eat off; we put newspapers down on the floor. But I am able to feed them with love for themselves and for life. I have given them the key to survival.

I am slowly changing the environment I live in. The tenants in my building in Harlem—I was born and raised in the building—bought it from the city. Everyone else is leaving the block. The city told me I might as well leave too, when I was on welfare. But I'm not going to be run off. I have educated myself and I am pursuing the profession of my choice. I have set up a meaningful value system that allows me to stay in my community and not run now that I've "made it." Now I can give and not just take. I can love life and not just live it. I am paying a price to maintain my dignity, and I am buying freedom for my children.

ZITA ALLEN, a graduate dance-history student at New York University and a dance critic: The Black middle class always gets a lot of play when there's static in the air. Magazines publish articles on who's who and guides to what's what in the Black "establishment"; road maps through the thicket of what is often an alien culture to alien writers. A recent article in a trendy local magazine listing New York's Black establishment, chronicling its powerlessness and lack of business development, belongs to this established journalistic tradition. And like its predecessors, the piece comes at a peculiarly unsettled time.

It comes at a time when the NAACP, which is listed as a group with clout, is so financially befuddled it can't afford to file an amicus curiae brief in the court battle threatening to destroy affirmative action in New York State. It comes when the KKK feels safe enough to secure the right for its members to hold jobs as prison guards. It comes when colleges, using the Bakke decision as justification, are axing financial aid for Black students. It comes when Black artists are suffering severe cutbacks in state and federal funding.

The media proclaims the existence of an "established" and "powerful" Black middle class. There is no need to chronicle the turbulent '60s and the pain and suffering that created the job and college openings which made this class possible. What we need to do is examine and ferret out the motivation behind the focus on this group. I'm reminded of statements from the South African and Rhodesian governments identifying tribal chiefs who are "safe," who can "share the power."

This is not to imply the Black middle class does not exist. I grew up in its clutches and, for a long time, took it for granted. There I was in Austin, Texas, with a father who was a political-science professor toting unquestionable academic credentials, including a degree from Columbia University, received at a time when that Ivy League school stated unblushingly that Blacks and Jews were admitted on a quota basis. My mother had a master's from the University of Texas—of all places—and belonged to one of the biggest Black landowning families in the state. My grandparents had all gone to college, and my family was wall-to-wall doctors, lawyers, real-estate brokers and concert musicians. It didn't seem strange or unusual to have a debutante ball (though it seems ludicrous now) or to join the sorority my mother and grandmother had.

But there's more to it. My father tells the story about how a Southern cop once stopped him on some dinky, out-of-the-way road in Florida. The cop claimed he was speeding, but it was obvious this policeman was only looking for some fun by hassling a Black motorist. Well, the cop saw on my father's identification that he was a professor at one of the well-known, Southern Black colleges. The cracker grinned and dropped the charges, saying, "Oh, you're one of our boys."

That's what these recent articles remind me of. Someone is saying, "These are our boys," What else? The article on New York admits that "power" as such is virtually nonexistent. It mentions complaints by Black politicians that New York City Mayor Koch is insensitive to the needs of their community. It admits that a 1977 study of minority-owned businesses shows "a slight setback for Blacks."

The article lists the "powerful," but hints at the reality that their power is an illusion. And yet the article also helps to perpetuate the myth of power.

The questions and problems surrounding the Black middle class and its relationship to the larger community of working class and unemployed Blacks is multifaceted and must be dealt with. But first one simply must ask just why, at this incredibly troubled time, does someone want to create the illusion of "power" and publicize a middle class which is actually only a buffer zone between the truly powerful and the rest of us.

hopelessly "unemployable." In the words of the *Wall Street Journal,* "they neither work not seek work," which would seem not too surprising in a society which cannot provide jobs for them. These teenagers on the streets are fast being joined by a substantial proportion of their parents. A decade ago 20 percent of Blacks and an equal proportion of whites formed this *lumpen* class, totally outside the labor force. The figures for whites have stayed the same, while the Black statistics have risen to 30 percent.

Unemployment has also lowered the number of Black families with more than one wage earner by about 2 percent over the last three years, while the percentage of white families with additional workers has remained about the same. In the "good old days" when a wife who didn't "have to work" was a status symbol, Blacks had the extra wage earners, often "colored girls" cleaning houses, while their children shined shoes on street corners.

The statistics seem to imply that white women and Blacks are competing for the same few jobs in a declining economy, but in the area where most women are segregated—clerical and service work—jobs are increasing at a pace fast enough to absorb most of the women, Black or white, seeking work. But in the area of unskilled labor where most Black men are clustered, jobs are disappearing due to increased com-petition from abroad and runaway shops.

The effects of unemployment, poverty, and racism are reflected both physically and mentally in the ghettos of America. A government report on health differences between Blacks and whites has found that Blacks live five years less on the average, have higher infant and maternal mortality rates, and die more frequently from hypertension, heart disease, diabetes, kidney disease, tuberculosis, and influenza. Representative John Conyers has said that Blacks are seven times more likely than whites to be the victims of homicide and that the 26 percent of gun-related killings among Black males between 1968 and 1975 coincided with the doubling of the unemployment rate in that period.

The stark truth is, Blacks are not making it, no matter how many Black professionals add gloss to the magazine pages featuring sterile analyses of the Black power structure. "Black Power" has become little more than a camp slogan to some, for Blacks remain powerless, while their potential strength is profound. The task remains to translate the formal rights won in the past into cold economic facts. And there are plenty of people out there, ready for the task, despite efforts to quiet them.

Michael Beaubien is a free-lance journalist and a staff member at New York's Schomburg Center for Research in Black Culture.

THE ORGANIZER

publication of the National Alliance Against Racist and Political Repression

From *The Organizer* 6, no. 3 (September 1979): 1

George Merritt: How Many More Trials? How Many More Years?

". . . On each of three occasions when I was tried, the prosecution presented the theory of a conspiratorial act for which somebody must be found responsible. The

---

Reprinted with permission from *The Organizer,* a publication of the National Alliance Against Racist and Political Repression, 27 Union Square West, Room 306, New York, NY 10003.

case was treated by public and press as a premeditated and planned assault upon the guardians of law and order. This was how the case was investigated and presented and tried. It was my misfortune to be one of those swept up in that hysteria, not as a participant but as a victim."

*George Merritt Jr., a National Alliance Executive Board member who participated in the founding of the NAARPR, is a political prisoner.** He is in jail only because the State of New Jersey is determined to make someone pay for the death of Patrolman John V. Gleason.

Merritt has been incarcerated for more than 9 of the past 12 years as the result of a

---

*[National Alliance Against Racist and Political Repression.—eds., *Alternative Papers.*]

racist conspiracy between police agencies and the prosecution. He has been tried three times on charges that he participated in the killing of a Plainfield, N.J. police officer on July 16, 1967, during an uprising in the Black community. The prosecution's lack of evidence is so great that two convictions were unanimously overturned on appeal, and those reversals were upheld by the state's highest court.

Oppressive living conditions that prevail in nearly every Black community triggered the uprising in Plainfield on Friday, July 14, 1967. On Sunday, July 16, Patrolman Gleason left his post to go into the Black community—which had been cordoned off—in pursuit of a Black youth who was alleged to have threatened a group of young whites. Gleason confronted and shot Bobbie Lee Williams, the unarmed young man he had followed, and a crowd of men and women beat Gleason to death, believing he had killed the young man.

The police terrorized the Black community: more than 100 homes were raided and scores of arrests were made. George Merritt was among 12 young people indicted; 11 were brought to trial for Gleason's death. On December 23, 1968, Merritt and Gail Madden, a young Black mother, were convicted by a jury of 11 whites and one Black and sentenced to life.

Of the 36 jurors who participated in Merritt's three trials, 34 were white. *It makes one wonder what the U.S. Constitution and its amendments mean when they purport to guarantee the accused's right to trial by a jury of peers.*

Prosecutors at Merritt's three trials routinely used their preemptory challenges to remove Black potential jurors. Molding for themselves juries that would be favorable to the state, the prosecutors at each trial were able to sway those juries with direct appeals to racist predispositions.

"Eleven years after the incident in Plainfield, the racism and lack of equality which characterized Merritt's first trial is still evident. Two innocent people remain in prison, still suffering as victims of crimes actually committed by society. George Merritt, despite three trials in which convictions were overturned twice, is now appealing to the Federal District Court. He and his codefendant, Gail Madden, face life terms because of the continued racism in the court system and the inflammatory and deadly attitude of the N.J. Policemen's Benevolent Association, which continually harassed Merritt when he was briefly out on bail. *We must demand, after all these years, an end to this racism, the restoration*

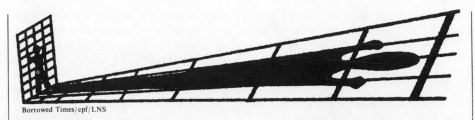
Borrowed Times/cpf/LNS

concerned in moving this struggle ahead. Reaching out to our friends, co-workers and community leaders, she stated, is of utmost importance in insuring that Gov. Byrne is flooded with protests. Ms. Davis ended by stating that we must force Byrne to respond to our call for justice and free Gail and George immediately.

of human rights in the State of New Jersey and the freedom of political prisoners George Merritt and Gail Madden."

More than 100 major religious denominations, trade union locals and community organizations and leaders petitioned Gov. Byrne for clemency on behalf of Merritt; Byrne refused the petition pending court decisions. *We ask how many more trials must George Merritt endure?* An international team of jurists visited Merritt in prison in August, investigating the charge of human rights abuses in the U.S. presented in the Petition to the United Nations brought in December, 1978. (See related story in this issue of *The Organizer* for a report on their findings.)* They concluded Merritt is the victim of a frame-up. *We ask how many more years must an innocent man spend behind bars?*

500 people enthusiastically responded to our Alliance's call for the emergency demonstration to Free George Merritt and Gail Madden on September 29 in Newark, N.J. Branches from Washington, D.C., Philadelphia, New York and throughout New Jersey brought members to the rally and march; but clearly the overwhelming majority of those present were from Newark and clearly they were demanding an answer from Byrne to the question of how long innocent people must suffer in New Jersey jails.

Essex County Alliance co-chair Jean Rubinstein brought the rally to its feet with her forceful demands for justice. A taped message from George Merritt was played to the gathering, calling to unity and an end to the racism that pervades our society. The demonstrators were outraged at the racism which has stolen 11 years from the lives of Gail and George.

Angela Davis, NAARPR co-chairperson addressed a cheering, energetic rally. She called for a stepped-up letter writing campaign aimed at Gov. Byrne demanding that George and Gail be returned to our community. Sister Davis emphasized that attending a rally can not be the last step but must be a beginning step for those

*["Jurists Conclude Human Rights Violations in U.S. Devastating," *The Organizer* 6, no. 3 (September 1979): Insert.—eds., *Alternative Papers*.]

Northwest Passage

From *Northwest Passage* 20, no. 11 (July 8, 1980): 10-11

Seattle Mirrors Miami: White Justice, White Guns

by Elizabeth Swain

Fifteen people died in Miami on May 17 and 18 in an outburst of violence and frustration. Racism is the central issue in the rioting that caused these deaths.

The acquittals of four police officers accused of the fatal beating of Arthur McDuffie, a black Miami man, set off the rioting. Miami blacks however, have been angry for a long time, having seen several charges of police brutality against blacks go unanswered.

In February of 1979, Nathaniel LaFleur, a black Miami school teacher, and his son were beaten and their home was torn apart by five police officers before the officers realized they had the wrong house. Subsequent investigations determined that no laws had been broken and charges could not be filed due to insufficient evidence.

Later in 1979, an 11 year old black girl was sexually assaulted by a white highway patrol trooper after he picked her up as she walked home from school. He resigned with three years probation. After undergoing four months of psychiatric treatment, authorities deemed it no longer necessary. In September a young black man was shot and killed by an off-duty police officer for no apparent reason. The shooting was found to be negligent but not criminal.

In contrast, the criminal justice system has been efficient in punishing blacks

Reprinted with permission from *Northwest Passage.*

accused of wrongdoings. Two well known black leaders in Miami have recently been charged and prosecuted in separate cases that involved operating an illegal gambling business and accepting kickbacks.

Arthur McDuffie, a 33-year-old black insurance executive, took a ride on a friend's motorcycle early on the morning of December 17, 1979. He died in a Miami hospital four days later. The state charged four Dade County police officers with beating McDuffie to death with flashlights and nightsticks, then wrecking his motorcycle to make his death look accidental. Medical authorities testified that McDuffie's injuries were so extensive that they could not possibly have been caused by an accident. A fifth officer was not charged because he turned state's evidence.

The trial of the charged was moved to Tampa by circuit judge Lenore Nesbitt due to the explosive nature of the case and the media coverage it had received. On May 16, a white jury acquitted the four officers after two hours and forty minutes of deliberation. By the following day, rioting had broken out in several black areas of Miami. On Monday May 19, the Justice Department announced intentions to seek indictments against the four men, charging them with violating McDuffie's civil rights. In the meantime two of the men have decided to return to the Dade County police force.

"The riot has little to do with McDuffie. It's about what's happening period," Richard A. Brown, Director of Community Organizing at Seattle's Central Area Motivation Program (CAMP), told the *Passage* recently. "Black people are mad as hell. We're tired of the double standard in America. The level of frustration is so high that black people in Miami took on the Secret Service police, the Dade County Sheriff's Department, Miami cops, several

SWAT teams, and thousands of National Guard."

It is important to recognize that the Miami riot was not just "McDuffie's revenge," as the media has dubbed it. The acquittals of the four Dade County police officers by a white jury should not be seen as a Southern-style verdict. This is a comfortable and over-used reason by non-Southerners to explain the overt injustice in this case. In 1978 Seattle police officer Dennis Falk shot and killed John Rodney, a black Seattle man. An unarmed trespassing suspect, Rodney was shot in the back as he fled. Officer Falk was exonerated of any wrongdoing and remains on the Seattle police force. In the fall of 1978, a police gun control initiative was turned down by Seattle voters. Seattle's failure to impose stricter control on police use of deadly force condoned the circumstances that allowed Rodney's death.

On October 23, 1979, Curtis Gilven, a 24-year-old black Tacoma man, was killed on a Kent street by Kent police officer John Fletcher. An inquest jury found the shooting an "accidental homicide" on November 30. The circumstances of the shooting remain confusing.

Curtis Gilven was driving a car with two companions early on the morning of October 23. Gilven, Christa Sandoval, and Donnell Hadley were seen by officer Fletcher at a restaurant in Kent twenty minutes before the shooting. Sandoval was attempting to collect money owed her by a restaurant employee. After a discussion, the three left the restaurant and got into their car, with Gilven driving. The police checked the license of the car and discovered that it was a stolen vehicle. (The car belonged to the family of a friend of Gilven's.) At this point, Officer Fletcher decided to stop the car. At no time did any of the occupants of the car behave in a threatening or disorderly manner. The only weapons present were those of the police. Within minutes after the car was stopped, Curtis Gilven had a fatal bullet wound in his chest fired from Fletcher's .357 magnum. The bullet entered his body from behind after travelling through the seat.

Fletcher's defense relied solely on the contention that his weapon had accidentally fired as he drew it from the holster. (It is standard police procedure for an officer to draw a weapon on a felony suspect.) The jury's finding of Fletcher's innocence was based on the lack of intention involved. There remains significant controversy over the possibility of a .357 magnum misfiring.

The weapon was examined and no defect was found. After a tearful plea to the jury, Fletcher was exonerated of any wrongdoing and is now back on duty. Fletcher has been on the Kent police force for nine years.

"I didn't intentionally fire. To me, it was unreal. If I didn't feel it [the gun firing], I would have thought someone else did it," said Fletcher during the inquest. Norm Maleng, King County Prosecutor, described Fletcher's behavior as "an over-reaction to a stress situation," though he conceded that the level of stress involved in the situation was low. Fletcher was approaching an unarmed and passive suspect. Six police cars had converged on the scene, with an undisclosed number of weapons drawn on Gilven.

Christa Sandoval, who was riding in the passenger seat of the car, testified that an officer was holding a gun "at no more than 10 inches" from Gilven's head. In addition, she testified that she heard more than one shot, but did not see the weapon fire. The other passenger, Donnell Hadley, was riding in the back seat. He testified that he had heard a shot fired from the rear of the car.

Bill Gilven, the victim's father and Deputy Director of the Tacoma Housing Authority, has criticized the investigation for its lack of depth. "The prosecuting attorney did not examine [Fletcher's] previous behavior as an officer. They should have delved more into his past conduct, whether he's used excessive force in the past."

The Gilven family has filed a $2 million suit in U.S. District Court in Tacoma. The suit charges Fletcher with acting "negligently and/or intentionally with callous disregard to the decedent's safety." No trial date has yet been set.

"What happened in Kent could happen in Seattle, Tacoma, and New York City," Gilven told the *Passage*. "The criminal justice system takes care of their own very well. With no outside review, there is little chance of justice." Gilven feels that a review board outside of the police department could have changed the circumstances that allowed his son's death. He stated that this kind of tragedy was inevitable given the excessive police presence and force in the situation. "There should be a dialogue between the criminal justice system and the community it serves. If dialogue is ongoing then at least some barriers are broken down."

In an incident related to the issues here,

Juan Salgado, a 36-year-old Mexicano, died of eight bullet wounds during a confrontation with two Seattle police officers on May 20. The officers are Duane Brown and Thomas Helms. The inquest held on June 23 found the shooting "justifiable homicide." "I thought the guy was going to kill me," said Helms during the inquest, "I thought he was going to shoot me. He kept coming at me. I didn't know it was a knife he had until he was on the ground." Salgado spoke only Spanish and had pulled a six inch blade from his belt after one officer approached him and grabbed him by the collar. The officers testified that they believed the knife to be a gun. Salgado had reportedly been behaving strangely in a bar he had just left.

The inquest upheld the officers' conduct on the basis that they were protecting themselves from possible harm. Little issue was raised of the excessive number of shots fired. The verdict was reached in less than a half an hour. The King County Prosecuting Attorney will determine whether criminal charges should be filed against the officers.

One night this June, three off-duty Seattle police officers were firing their weapons on East Madison between 20th and 22nd in the black community. Seattle Police Chief Patrick Fitzsimons has stated that he wants the three officers to leave the force. Controversy over Fitzsimons' statement has been created by the Police Guild's request for leniency. The Guild, a largely white group of officers within the Police Department, wants the officers suspended for thirty days without pay and fined $50 to $100.

"A separate set of morals exists for police in their private lives than for the rest of us," Brown says. The black community is angry that behavior of this type is allowed to happen in their community. As one black woman told the *Passage*, "It is significant that the police call themselves a 'force,' when in fact what the community needs is a police service. The good things that the police *could* accomplish are far outweighed by those things the police *are* applauded for."

Understanding racism is central to understanding the events described here. The racism implicit in high unemployment, scarce resources, and police brutality in minority communities is linked to capitalism in the U.S. One cannot survive without the other.

Unemployment in black communities across the country is at least twice that of

Daily World/LNS

the white population, close to 25%. The rate is 50% for urban black youth. Black children must face the reality that they may never work as they watch older family members and friends struggle with an unjust economic system. "Jimmy Carter was elected on 93% of the black vote and ran on a campaign of putting America back to work. Now his administration is fighting inflation through unemployment," says Jesse Jackson, head of Operation PUSH.

Legislation and affirmative action pro-grams that grew out of the civil rights movement have left the structure of racism basically unchanged. People are out of work and hungry. The federal food stamp program has been cut back. Food banks in Seattle and nationwide are reporting an inability to keep up with demand. CETA funding has been cut in half for the coming year, severely hindering an already inadequate program that is designed to provide jobs and opportunities for poor minority communities. A government that supports an $18 billion defense budget hike, subsidizes private corporations, and places little priority on the quality of human life has no committment to challenging racism.

Police disregard for the black community and the failure of the criminal justice system in prosecuting those guilty of brutality against the community head the list of complaints in Miami and elsewhere. "Ironically, it always seems to be minorities, and especially blacks, that are the victims of 'accidental' or 'justifiable' homicide at the hands of the police," says Brown. The police protect capitalist interests by enforcing the status quo on the streets. Because the police approach the black community with the same racism that exists in the rest of the society, and are either rewarded or unpunished for this, laws are selectively enforced on the streets. Discriminatory law enforcement means that many more minorities than whites die or are injured in confrontations with the police. Jails and prisons in the United States are full of minority prisoners.

There has been a tendency by the media, the creator and shaper of American experience, to characterize recent actions taken by minority people as "sixties style." A large perceptual gap exists in the white American psyche, one that only recognizes explosive action as the real thing. People must be killing each other, preferably on video tape, for the issue to gain credibility.

Racism exists in America, and has existed long before the mass media validated its presence with coverage of the civil rights movement or urban explosions of the '60's. Conditions continue to thrive that will create more Miamis and more killings by the police that are poorly investigated and prosecuted. The Ku Klux Klan, with its new college educated, white collar look, is still advocating white supremacy and genocide on the streets and in the workplaces of Seattle and across the country. The Equal Opportunity Program at the University of Washington, a program that has supported poor and minority students during the '70's in their struggle for equal access to education, has slammed the door shut. In a recent ruling by the federal Community Services Administration, Active Mexiconos, a Seattle community resource agency for Hispanics, has lost its appeal to regain federal funding. There's so much more that Seattle should be talking about than the volcano, but then no one can lay *that* one on you, can they, Seattle?

5 CORPORATE CONNECTIONS

Calvin Coolidge, in the rosy light of the pre-Depression era, noted that "the business of government is business." That maxim is still appropriate. In this section, the press investigates the relationships between corporations and social and economic problems, and it questions the validity of proposed solutions.

The section opens with a critical examination by Ben Bedell of the Chrysler bailout, while *Fifth Estate* spoofs Chrysler President Lee Iaccoca's "Open Letters to the American People." From *The Militant,* Harry Ring looks at the plight of New York City's straphangers and wonders why business is getting a free ride.

Freedom of the press is also treated here, as it is in several other sections, and the corporate connections to PBS—the Petroleum or, rather, the Public Broadcasting System—are analyzed by Pat Aufderheide from *In These Times.* She reports on the curious stance of the president of PBS, which gladly accepts corporate monies but refuses that of unions. Deborah Baldwin argues that corporate influence is even more insidious in the long anti-environmental ads of the big energy companies in the mass media. She dissects the assumptions behind these slick persuaders and suggests some home remedies.

Multinationals spend tremendous amounts of their profits on persuasion. The media feed themselves almost exclusively on this diet and cannot be relied on to criticize their sponsors. Nowhere is the corporation more obviously a brutalizing force than in the Third World, and it is in South Africa that the public relations effort is strongest, as Gail Morlan points out. An article from *Anti-Apartheid News* also makes it clear that the reality is much different from the picture painted by corporate propaganda.

The strength of the energy industry is also noted in this section. *Science for the People* analyzes the motives behind the construction of a nuclear reactor in an active volcano area in the Philippines, while *WIN* reports on pension funds and nuclear investments. Anna DeCormis examines the behind-the-scenes scramble to gain control of "alternative" sources of energy, while *Undercurrents* wonders at the Silkwood "victory"—with reason, as the recent court decision to revoke the rewarding of punitive damages indicates. And *Midwest Energy Times* and *Northern Sun News* examine the planned exploitation of energy-rich Native American land in the Black Hills.

But the energy industry isn't the only source of influence, as *Seven Days* and *Environmental Action* point out in reports on the petrochemical industry's "life itself" counterattack to regulation and on the link between political donations and environmental voting records. In *Science for the People,* Paul Barnett questions the objectivity of farm advisers in light of their close financial ties to chemical manufacturers and Don Hancock in *The Workbook* wonders at the impact on genetic uniformity of the concentration of seed patents in the hands of a few large corporations.

Finally, *Dollars and Sense* reports on modernization and monetization on the farm and the role of agribusiness, while *Hot Times* sees the shadow of corporate banking behind national security decisions.

—LD & ES

From *The Guardian* 32, no. 14 (January 9, 1980): 8

Chrysler Bailout: Workers Foot the Bill

by Ben Bedell

The average Chrysler worker will have to kick back $4000 over the next three years to keep his or her job.

On Dec. 23 Congress passed the $1.5 billion Chrysler federal loan guarantee. As part of the package, Chrysler workers must contribute $462 million to the corporation's recovery—or $4000 per worker. That is more than double the wage concession the United Auto Workers (UAW) made in contract negotiations with the ailing firm last year.

In considering the loan guarantee, Congress' main demand was the wage concessions by Chrysler's 110,000 workers. House and Senate hardliners wanted a complete wage freeze over three years, but settled for the $462 million figure. Even so, the workers' wage increases over three years will be cut from 33% to less than 20%. With inflation rising at more than 12% a year Chrysler workers can expect to have about 15% less real income at the end of the contract.

But many workers will accept the deal nonetheless. It is being presented by Chrysler—and the UAW leadership—as a choice between belt-tightening and unemployment.

The union is now set to reopen contract negotiations with Chrysler in early January. It says it will try to hold onto the cost of living escalator, pension and health benefits, but will probably trade away wages and benefits like supplemental unemployment insurance and a prepaid legal services plan. The UAW's Chrysler workers must ratify the final contract.

Sentiment in the plants seems to favor further reductions, as most workers are resigned to the tradeoff in order to save jobs.

"Right now," says Lois Sasser, a 30-year-old assembler at Detroit's Dodge Truck plant, "I go along with the deal. But I think Chrysler should give us something in the future for this." Her sentiment was echoed by Clarence Taylor, a 54-year-old worker who says that "if Chrysler is looking for us to give up something, then we should get something in return."

Some workers, however, are opposed to further givebacks. "I don't want to lose anymore," says Ronald Mazon, a 37-year-old skilled worker. "I'm supporting seven people now. I can't give up more. I should be getting more."

At a number of locals, Chrysler workers have expressed a willingness toward further cuts if they are guaranteed jobs for the life of the contract. "Chrysler comes to us saying 'We're all in the same boat, we all sink or swim,'" says Robin Comerly at Chrysler's Lynch Road plant. "I say fine, to me that means no layoffs, unless the company goes completely bankrupt."

The UAW's bargainers haven't said anything about demanding a no-layoff clause during the new negotiations. All UAW president Douglas Fraser has said is that he will not accept a total wage freeze.

Chrysler said it was "delighted" with the congressional package. But its survival is far from assured. It must still get over $500 million in immediate short-term loans from its bankers and another $1 billion in long-term private financing.

That task, however, is much easier now, given the federal contribution of a separate $1.5 billion loan guarantee. And Congress specified that should the company go bankrupt, it is the private bank loans, not the taxpayer loan, that will be repaid first.

"That removed a substantial obstacle from the bankers' point of view," one Treasury Department official told the *Wall Street Journal*.

Memories of the Past

The banks are still hesitant to extend the money, however, because they may lose some of it. "Additional funding wouldn't be on a prudent banking basis," one banker told the *Wall Street Journal* last week. Rather, he said, "it would be a political decision based on political considerations" of a possible Chrysler bankruptcy.

The "political considerations" were made obvious in a General Accounting Office (GAO) report to Congress on the issue. It concluded that a Chrysler shutdown would "throw the economy of southern Michigan into a downward spiral" resulting in over a million layoffs. Bank and government officials are well aware of the social turmoil such a spiral might precipitate. With the memory of the 1968 Detroit rebellion in the background, the GAO report mentions that "Chrysler is the largest employer in Detroit (74,000 people) and about 80% of them are Black."

Detroit Mayor Coleman Young explicitly referred to this problem in his comments before a House subcommittee considering the Chrysler bailout. "If you let Chrysler go down," he said, "the whole political framework of Detroit could go with it." Young has pledged to kick in $190 million in public funds as part of the rescue effort.

Ross Beecher & Ron Richardson/LNS

In an emotional last-minute plea to the House to pass the loan guarantee, Speaker Tip O'Neil (D-Mass.) also warned that failure to rescue the company could politically "put us in a hole we wouldn't be able to dig ourselves out of for 10 years."

Congress is offering one consolation to Chrysler workers. Some 40% of Chrysler stock to be given to them in return for wage concessions. The plan is also designed to "increase their stake in the company," according to a Senate sponsor of the bailout bill. But the stock is only worth $300 million at its current depressed prices. Shortly, it may be worth even less.

From *Fifth Estate* 14, no. 4 (October 22, 1979): 16

Would America Be Better Off Without Chrysler?

It's a fair question.

You've heard it from the pundits, the malcontents, the radicals, even the competition.

Now we'd like to set the record straight.

We've made our share of mistakes. We've squandered more than our share of corporate dollars that go down the tubes each year. We've produced shabby products and covered up information about their poor quality that would hurt us in the market. We've overworked our employees in outmoded plants on dangerous, obsolete machinery and broken their walkout strikes when they got fed up with their conditions. And we're willing to accept responsibility.

But what if we went under, what would happen to the more than 140,000 employees in 52 communities across the nation? No one has bothered to ask this very simple question. If we were to close up shop, they'd all be collecting unemployment benefits and welfare. They might start demonstrating; there might be bread riots. They might start thinking of better ways to spend their time than on production lines putting a washer on a bolt 3600 times a day. Then there would be real trouble. The very fabric of society would be threatened. Let's keep our workers on the line, America. Social stability needs Chrysler.

Would America be better off with a Big 2 instead of a Big 3?

Reprinted from *Fifth Estate*.

When it comes to competition, more is better than less.

With three companies you have more choices than with two. Let us say you are buying a luxury car and you find on the lot a Lincoln, a Cadillac, and a Chrysler New Yorker. Now, take away the New Yorker, and what have you got? One less choice!

Let us put it another way: three less two equals one, but one plus two equals three. What if Chrysler fails, and later Ford gets into trouble? Three less two equals: one big communist monopoly! You'll all be driving Slotne 600's! Then come to me and complain. (I'll probably have retired to Brazil by then.)

What is Chrysler asking for—a handout?

In all candor, I can only answer—yes! And why not? At stake is our capitalist system and our way of life. Because when you reduce things to the bottom line, our modern world is nothing without auto production. Anyone who wants our life as it is currently constituted to continue has a similar interest in the continuation of our Company.

Has Chrysler done everything it can to help itself?

Of course we have, but in a way this is beside the point. We can't just "help ourselves"; this is the late 20th Century, not 1880. Those ideas of a corporation independent of the state are ones from a bygone epoch.

Now, we need the government to enforce a strict wage freeze for all of our workers. We want our military to buy more of our vehicles (and perhaps use them, like for a little invasion of Saudi Arabia). We need the help of the UAW to not squawk when we increase the speed of the production line, and union help in starting to control the rabblerousers and saboteurs in our plants. We want the union to cooperate with use in getting rid of slackers and troublemakers, too.

That's not too much to ask, is it?

Does Chrysler have a future?

You can bet on it.

In fact, with the odds and all, it would be a lucrative bet.

We're a long shot, but we're going to come in.

As long as workers need money and cars to get back and forth to work, and as long as they are willing to keep going back in there and doing what we tell them to do, and as long as the costs of sabotage and rebellion don't become too prohibitive and interfere with the productive processes of this society, Chrysler will be around for a long, long time to come.

We're not bailing out!

You can bet on it. Just get good odds.

Lee A. Iacocca
Lee A. Iacocca
Chairman, Chrysler Corporation

THE MILITANT

A SOCIALIST NEWSWEEKLY/PUBLISHED IN THE INTERESTS OF THE WORKING PEOPLE

From *The Militant* 44, no. 13 (April 11, 1980): 5

Public Transit: Who Should Pay?

By Harry Ring

Reprinted with permission from *The Militant: A Socialist Newsweekly,* 14 Charles Lane, New York, NY 10014.

New York. In the legendary days of the great train robberies, the bandits would swoop down without warning.

But not the bandits who control the New York transit system.

They're already publicizing the new, higher priced subway token. The only thing left to be announced is the extent of the ripoff. Will the fare go from fifty cents to sixty? Or will it be seventy-five?

Why the new fare hike? Obvious, says

'Keep it up, kid—there's more where that came from!'

Mayor Koch. The workers are striking for more money.

But the minimum projected fare increase will be 20 percent, and the seventy-five cent fare would mean a 50 percent boost. Is that what they're offering the workers? And weren't they already planning to raise fares long before the strike?

Well, the subways and buses are losing money anyway, argues the Transit Authority.

For New York's strap-hangers, the subway system is a loser for sure. Millions of working people—particularly the lowest paid—are totally dependent on public transit.

The city has us by the throat. The fare is expensive. The trains and buses are unsafe, overcrowded, noisy, dirty outrages against human health and dignity.

But not everyone's a loser.

Like, for instance, the bankers who organized the sale of the BMT and IRT subways to the city forty years ago. For the first decades of this century, private owners had made a fortune from the subways. But they began to lose money.

So the banks obligingly loaned the city $310 million—a lot of bucks in those days—to buy the subways.

We'll reportedly be making the final payment this June. With forty years of steady interest we've paid those original bonds several times over.

Over the years the banks obligingly made more loans at higher interest rates so the old ones could be repaid. And as fares went up, service declined, and much-needed maintenance was ignored, the banks and bondholders have gotten their interest payments as regular as clockwork. It still runs more than $11 million a year,

according to the Transit Authority. In earlier years it was even more.

But that's only a relatively small part of the con game. The real swindle goes under the name of "self-sufficiency." That is, the argument that those who ride the subways should pay for them.

Why? The public school system isn't "self-sufficient." Neither are the city parks, or the libraries, or the fire department. Why the transit system?

True, there are people who never set foot on a subway. But it's their life line.

For instance, take the sweatshop operators in the garment district. Their profits depend on the labor of tens of thousands of workers who live in all five boroughs. Without the transit system the industry would fold.

The same goes for virtually all the other big employers in the city.

Not to speak of the restaurant industry, the department stores, Wall Street firms, and lots more.

Yet the owners of these corporations, whose profits are so dependent on the transit system, don't pay a dime. Unless, perish the thought, it's the chauffeur's day off and they can't get a cab.

Put an end to that incredible tax evasion and the transit system will stop "losing money" overnight.

Clock the people coming out of the subways at Herald Square headed for Macy's. Do a census of the people spilling out into the garment district, or down on Wall Street. Then tax the profits of all the business beneficiaries of the transit system.

With that kind of a fiscal approach, you could—as the Transport Workers Union recommends—abolish the subway fare.

Sounds utopian? It probably is—so long as the Democrats and Republicans are in city hall. They're direct accomplices in the great train robbery, and all the other crimes perpetrated against the working people of this city by big business.

But let powerful unions like the Transport Workers and others join in building a labor party. They could drive the bandits out of city hall.

A labor administration could run the city in the interests of the great majority, not the tiny clique of bankers, business executives, and slumlords.

A labor party in New York could lead a national fight to end the waste of billions of tax dollars on Washington's arms budget and get those funds used to rebuild and improve mass transit and all social services.

A labor administration could see to it that the people who run and ride the subways and buses controlled the Transit Authority.

With that kind of management, it could be a pleasure to ride the transit system. You could even learn to love the Big Apple.

From *In These Times* 4, no. 15 (March 5-18, 1980): 13

Public Television

by Pat Aufderheide

PBS is the poor sister of TV networks,

Reprinted with permission from *In These Times: The Independent Socialist Newspaper.*

constantly in search of handouts to supplement its meager federal budget, constantly dunning its viewers for small change in exchange for trinkets.

But there are exceptions to the "beggars can't be choosers" charity policy. PBS has decided that labor unions, at least in one instance, are unacceptable public TV sponsors. The instance is a planned TV series on labor history called *Made in U.S.A.*

For six years independent producer Elsa Rassbach has been planning an incredibly ambitious project—ten feature TV films on the history of American working people. The series spans the period 1830-1945, and dramatically documents the formation of an industrial, urban work force. Themes for several features are the work life of young women textile mill workers in Lowell, Mass., in the 1830s; the Homestead steel strike of 1892; and the migration of blacks into Chicago and their work and organizing in the meatpacking industry.

She has received, over the years, around $450,000, some $50,000 of which came from labor unions. The project is now at the point of production, with scripts in hand and a production link with Boston public TV station WGBH.

WGBH producer Peter McGhee and Rassbach applied to the National Endowment for the Humanities for part of the $12-$15 million needed for the entire series. NEH funding typically requires the recipient to match the grant with independently-raised funds. That was the point at which PBS president Larry Grossman told WGBH that labor union funds were unacceptable as matching money for the project.

Unacceptable?

Yes, union sponsorship of a labor history series was a violation of PBS' underwriting principles, which say that program sponsors cannot have a specific, direct interest in the product or subject of the program.

WGBH and Rassbach then petitioned PBS to reconsider, and to allow a maximum of 25 percent of the necessary funds to come from unions. PBS endorsed the idea of the project. Grossman wrote WGBH head Henry Becton, "PBS does recognize the public interest in a series of this nature and strongly supports the *Made in U.S.A.* project, particularly in light of public TV's need for labor-related programming." But while reluctant to rule out formally the possibility of such funding within a larger package, PBS has refused to reconsider until a total funding package is ready.

Discrimination

Rassbach supports the principle behind the underwriting rule. And the issue could be academic—right now the project is a long series of "ifs."

"The rules aren't necessarily bad ones," she said to *ITT*. "The key question is whether those rules are evenhandedly applied."

Nicholas Johnson, chair of the National Citizens' Communication Lobby and ex-commissioner of the FCC, put that key question more strongly.

"The devilish thing about this is that in some ways PBS is right. If they were set up to be noncommercial, if they had not accepted corporate money, if they had applied strict conflict-of-interest standards from the beginning, then one could conceivably support them now. But they violate their standards when it applies to corporations.

"In Madison, the technology series *Fast Forward* is made possible by a grant from a local computer store. That's no conflict of interest. Safeway can underwrite *Julia Child,* but that's not a conflict of interest. Martin Marietta can underwrite *Wall St. Week in Review* and benefit from an increase in stock market prices.

"And most outrageous of all is that program *Free to Choose* by Milton Friedman. *That's* not viewed as conflict of interest!"

Free to Choose is the conservative series on economics hosted by one of the architects of Chile's austerity economy, and purveying the ideas of laissez-faire. Its ideology was part of the sales pitch to sponsors. Eventually General Motors, General Mills, W.R. Grace, Pepsico, Readers Digest and 11 other sources put up $2.4 million for the program.

Labor unions too protest PBS' prohibition because it is discriminatory. Tom Thompson of the Amalgamated Clothing Workers told *ITT*, "Corporate funds are accepted with the idea that there's no ideological problem in doing so, but labor contributors are by definition tainted. I don't understand why corporate funding is not considered to include potential bias."

All Thompson wants is the right to play the same image game that the corporations are doing, even though, he says, "the resources of labor unions don't begin to match those of large corporations.

"We've been trying to analyze why unions have such a tarnished image even among liberals. We're reassessing our image and thinking of how we can show the things we can do and have done.

"We're not looking for propaganda pieces. We just want the story to be told."

Walter Davis, education director of the AFL-CIO, also charged, "They've got a double standard, and it ought to be explored."

That double standard applies as well to tax benefits for donations. "When corporations put money into programming they get a tax write-off. We don't. There's an indirect federal subsidy for corporations, and that affects taxpayers, and that's us.

"We're not interested in TV or films as such, but in correcting the image of the role of labor in this society."

The unions have a general interest in seeing working people's history on TV, and *Made in U.S.A.* deals with the formation of a work force rather than focusing on specific unions. Historians on the advisory board were incensed by the PBS implication that unions would influence content; in a press statement they commented, "At no point in the [five year] development of the project has any union ever asked us to tailor the approach of a series to its political outlook."

More than demonstrating a "conflict of interest," the issue challenges the rule of thumb at PBS that says corporate interest is general interest. Labor's demand for the right to donate raises again the issue that makes PBS officials squirm and PBS spokespeople babble—just who is the public, anyway, and what does it want? Does it really want a diet of wildlife documentaries, cooking shows and 19th century dramas? And who decides what "it" wants?

Mirrors and Skyhooks

PBS' arguments against labor union funding ultimately expose the trick mirrors and skyhooks used to pretend that corporate interest is not a special interest.

Elizabeth Shriver, general counsel for PBS, told *In These Times,* "We can't possibly accept money that is in such direct relation to the content. The best, in terms of the public's perception of the integrity of the program, would be if they didn't have any funding from labor unions."

Unfortunately for the legal mind, labor history is a subject on which anyone with money will have a strong opinion, because of the essential role of labor in getting that money. Asked about PBS' suggestion, Rassbach asked in return what the integrity of the program would look like if a series on working people's history were funded by major corporations. Or better, what the integrity would be of a program on big business funded by labor unions.

But for PBS, business is not always business—sometimes it's a sponsor. Corporate money does not stink. Several PBS spokespeople pointed to the commendable "variety" among their *Free to Choose* funders, nearly all huge corporations or corporate foundations. No one wanted to entertain the idea of 16 different labor unions supplying funds for *Made in U.S.A.*

PBS' associate director of underwriting, Peggy Hubble, who worked for two years on underwriting guidelines, justified the anti-union decision this way:

"Business is much broader than labor. Corporations put their profits into a wide variety of things. Labor unions are only going to put money into something in which they have a vested interest."

So the labor unions are looking for PR, while the corporations are merely investing in good will. Labor unions can only invest in something that *interests* labor union members. But corporations can invest in anything that *doesn't violate the interest* of stockholders, especially if it's conveniently close to the leisure interests of a stockholding class.

Hubble explained further about the difference between general and specific interest, in terms of *Free to Choose*. "*Free to Choose* is about free enterprise and against government interference. General Motors has a general interest in that kind of thing, but if that program had the auto industry as a subject it would not be appropriate." Since *Made in U.S.A.*'s subject matter is workers' history, and not even specifically union history, the same argument should be applicable to it.

Hubble pointed out some "judgement calls" made on the sticky issue of specific interest. A gas company was rejected as a sponsor for Julia Child's program because she cooks with gas. A large bank was an unacceptable funder for a series on small business, one part of which was concerned with loans. Eastman Kodak could not fund a series on the history of photography.

The underwriting department stays focused carefully on things, when they think of corporations. Gas. Cars. Loans. The focus is equally concrete when it comes to programming: Food. Bookkeeping. Photographs. The fiction is elegant—GM makes cars, not money. Programs don't present perspective, just facts.

To the underwriters, workers' history, in all its complexity, must be the object that unions retail. It's the private concern of labor unions, the special interest of a special interest.

Policy

PBS decision makers have to work hard to suggest they are being responsible to the public by taking this position. Consider Larry Grossman's fears: "We get nervous when the first money in is money from labor unions. People will look at the long list of unions in the underwriters' credits and accuse us of selling out."

Selling out? This from the "public" network that gives us Milton Friedman on economics courtesy of Lilly, Olin, Firestone and many more; *American Enterprise,* backed up by Merrill Lynch; conservative political commentary by Benn Wattenberg brought to us by LTV, Dow, Conoco and others?

From *Environmental Action* 12, no. 3 (September 1980): 21-25

The Ads You Love to Hate

by Deborah Baldwin

Every Sunday morning, in homes across the nation, thousands of otherwise peace loving environmentalists pick up *Parade* magazine and grit their teeth.

Try as hard as they might, it's nearly impossible to ignore those maddening advertisements called "Observations," brought to you, as so many things are these days, by Mobil.

Aimed at thoughtful Americans who haven't quite made up their minds to hate the oil industry, the weekly columns use a lavish blend of rhetoric, cajolery and offbeat humor merely, it seems, to plead for a little love and understanding. The ads typically cast Mobil's opponents as ne'er do well bureaucrats, klutzy Nader's Raiders and unwashed environmentalists. Only because of its great patience and forbearance, the ads imply, can Mobil cope at all.

Mobil's persecution complex may be extreme, but other giant corporations also suffer from what might be called media paranoia—fear of the press misconstruing a company's true intentions. In increasing numbers, these companies are bypassing the traditional journalistic gatekeepers— no, competing with them—by buying up editorial space or sponsoring commercials on radio and TV. The feeling seems to be that if you really want to get your message across to the thinking public, you have to

Reprinted with permission from *Environmental Action,* the monthly publication of Environmental Action, Inc., 1346 Connecticut Ave., Washington, DC 20036.

pay good money and do it right.

The implications are obvious. "Pretty soon," sighs one reporter who has covered the oil industry, "Mobil will take control of the *whole* editorial page of *The New York Times*—not just part of it."

Robert Caughlan of the nonprofit Roanoke Co., an ad agency that does work for public interest groups, views the trend less philosophically. Asked about the potential impact of corporate advocacy advertising, he remarks, "This is more important than people know. We should be glad most companies are only interested in selling Twinkies and toilet paper."

In their race to compete in the marketplace of ideas, companies like Mobil are finetuning some of the same Madison Avenue techniques that brought us Ultrabrite, Nestle's Quik and Prell shampoo. The intriguing question, though, is this: do opinion ads like Mobil's work?

And it's a hard question to answer conclusively. To a large extent, the answer depends on whom you ask and how you interpret Mobil's ultimate goals.

As far as most environmentalists are concerned, for example, Mobil's ads only confirm their worst expectations—hence the teeth gritting syndrome, which is apparently a regular side effect of advocacy advertising. Indeed, the experts say there is an identifiable audience that reads opinion ads simply because they express views some people love to hate. At the other extreme are the Mobil devotees, who read the copy because it expounds opinions they love to love.

The target audience, however, is somewhere in between.

They are the people who, well, gee . . . don't know . . . Mobil does seem to be getting a lot of grief lately . . . but, well . . . aren't their profits *awfully* high?

Mobil probably doesn't expect that after reading a few "Observations" columns, the

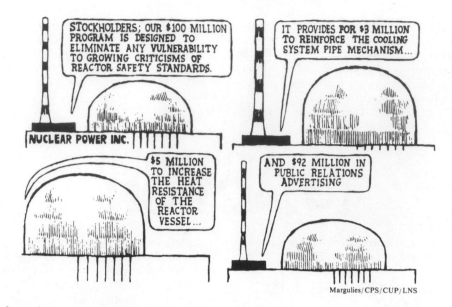

STOCKHOLDERS; OUR $100 MILLION PROGRAM IS DESIGNED TO ELIMINATE ANY VULNERABILITY TO GROWING CRITICISMS OF REACTOR SAFETY STANDARDS.

NUCLEAR POWER INC.

$5 MILLION TO INCREASE THE HEAT RESISTANCE OF THE REACTOR VESSEL...

IT PROVIDES FOR $3 MILLION TO REINFORCE THE COOLING SYSTEM PIPE MECHANISM...

AND $92 MILLION IN PUBLIC RELATIONS ADVERTISING

Margulies/CPS/CUP/LNS

fence sitters are going to leap to the defense of the oil industry every time obscene profits come up in cocktail party conversations. But there is always the hope that criticism of the industry will soften, that an appeal for understanding will smooth a few feathers, maybe even inspire some sympathy.

It's hard for a typical teeth gritter to believe Mobil's peculiar blend of plodding logic and abrasive rhetoric can sway Joe Public to any extent. The regular Thursday *New York Times* op-ed pieces, ground out each week by Mobil vice president Herb Schmertz, are often peevish and simpering. The "Observations" columns are generally pretentious, in that annoying, fake meek, Mobil way.

But it's Mobil's attempts to break into big time TV, perhaps, that seem the most outlandish. After an unsuccessful campaign to get the networks to change their rules on advocacy advertising—generally, such advertising is refused because it can lead to requests for free time from those with opposing views—Mobil decided to develop its own programming and to give it to independent stations willing to accept advocacy ads. (In the meantime, Mobil's print ads carried blow by blow descriptions of the oppressive networks and their haughty attitude toward the poor oil company. If the networks were so cheap they couldn't afford to give free time to environmentalists, Herb Schmertz allowed magnanimously, then Mobil would foot the bill for them. None of the networks took him up on his offer.) Soon shows like "Edward and Mrs. Simpson" began to appear on independent TV, sandwiched between Mobil's contemporary

"fables"—Aesop brought up to date a la Schmertz.

One of the spots, for example, features a troupe of professional dancers dressed up as squirrels, complete with furry tails pinned to their leotards. As the story develops, the selfish, shortsighted squirrel community drives away its chief nut gatherer when he dares to raise his prices. The moral: "So let the energy producers do their job. Don't drive *them* up a tree."

Then there's the one about the overworked, unappreciated, jumbo elephant who brings the rest of the lazy jungle animals their precious rations of water. *He* beats a hasty retreat when the pint size ingrates criticize him for eating too much on the job.

Then there's the one about the rabbits—but you get the picture.

Unlike Mobil's print ads, the TV spots spring up right in the middle of a show and can't be ignored by simply turning the page. They demand a response.

For years, the response among public interest groups to advocacy advertising has been generally low key. *Environmental Action* regularly used to dissect various Mobil claims in its "Debunking Madison Avenue" column, but in time Mobil debunkings became old hat. During the mid 70s, several groups pushed the Federal Trade Commission (FTC) to crack down on misleading issue ads—ads saying things like, "Thanks to us folks at U.S. Cement, pollution is no longer a problem"—but the FTC, for a number of reasons, decided to stay out of that controversy. Some public interest groups went on the offense in ad campaigns focusing on specific issues, bills

or referenda, but most found that too expensive.

Now there's something of a revival of interest in advocacy advertising, partly because so much of it is issuing forth from the *Fortune* 500 these days, and partly because some groups are experimenting with TV and radio spots for the first time.

The Washington based Citizen/Labor Energy Coalition (sneeringly referred to in one Mobil ad as "a letterhead group") recently joined forces with Energy Action and the Public Interest Video Network (*EA*, May)* to produce a rebuttal of the Mobil fables, and a number of stations have agreed to put the spot on the air.

(Broadcasters are theoretically required to offer free time under the so called fairness doctrine. The specific requirements of the fairness doctrine are hard to pin down, though. A station can decide to donate air time at 2 a.m. on Sunday, for example, or can claim that opposing views were already covered in regular news programming. And the fairness doctrine works both ways; much to the consternation of environmentalists, the nuclear industry is attempting to pressure stations to put *pro*nuclear advertising on the air as a way of balancing reporters' environmental biases. There is, of course, no equivalent of the fairness doctrine governing the print media.)

"We're trying to do two things," explains Energy Action's Ed Rothschild, "to let Mobil know they can't get away with this sort of thing, and to let the stations know they will have to deal with efforts [like ours], so they'll be less willing to accept [advocacy] ads in the future."

Similarly, a number of antinuclear groups in Washington, including Environmental Action Foundation and Nader's Critical Mass, got together recently under the banner of the Safe Energy Communications Campaign (SECC) to rebut an aggressive new media campaign by the nuclear industry. A similar coalition has been launched in Alaska to encourage fair coverage of local environmental issues.

Amid all the point, counterpoint debate, many citizens groups feel frustrated not only by a lack of resources, but also by a lack of knowledge about what makes advertising effective. Aside from making some media entrepreneurs rich, just what do advocacy ads accomplish? Does Mobil

*[Deborah Baldwin, "Coming Attractions," *Environmental Action* 11, no. 11 (May 1980): 26-29.—eds., *Alternative Papers*.]

indeed win friends and influence voters by nattering on and on about rabbits and squirrels? Beyond that, if Mobil and the rest of the corporate world are going to pollute reading materials and TV programming with messages that range from the silly and obscure to the downright misleading, should public interest groups be doing the same thing—of course, one hastens to add, in a much more responsible manner?

The experts disagree about which ads work and why. Some believe strongly that groups like Environmental Action must work within the system, learning to compete in the message marketplace, even if it means paying to do it. Others say don't bother—among them a public relations employee of one oil company that doesn't sponsor issue advertising, who snarls, "It'd be a waste of your damn money."

To gauge the effectiveness of a campaign, experts claim, it is important to first identify the campaign's goals and audience (see box). Many corporate ads, for example, may not be aimed at the general public, but at a particular class of opinion leaders—reporters, business officials, politicians or even prospective shareholders. "The ads also can reinforce employees' attitudes," points out Ron Vickers, who works for Needham, Harper and Steers, one of Washington's top ad agencies.

He ought to know. His firm recently attacked regulations affecting the auto industry in a heavy handed ad in *The Washington Post* sponsored by a letterhead group called the Automobility Foundation, an affiliate of the National Automobile Dealers Association. According to one industry insider who spoke to *EA,* more than anything else the ad probably made beleaguered auto dealers and their sales staffs feel better.

Advocacy advertising goes hand in hand with so called image advertising, which has played a role in corporate public relations since 1906, when the first institutional ad campaign was launched by the Mutual Life Insurance Co. *The New Yorker's* Michael Arlen, who has written a book at AT&T's current efforts in this area, reports that Ma Bell started doing image ads when an early corporate president decided that "advertising should be considered an instrument not merely of the company's attempts to sell its service, but also of its attempts to 'relate to' (or deal politically) with the public."

And Now, a Word for New Sponsors

A foundation created by ARCO is coming to the rescue of *Harper's.* A publishing concern partly owned by an oil conglomerate considers buying up United Press International. In 1977 Mobil alone spent $10.9 million on image and advocacy advertising—$2.5 million of it just on "Observations."

So how can environmentalists expect to compete?

Not easily, say the experts, several of whom offer the following bits of advice for would-be good guy sponsors.

• Don't spend a penny until you know exactly what you hope to accomplish and how. Only the rich and the foolish can afford to spend money just to hear themselves talk.

• Unless you've been made an offer you can't refuse—i.e., free time and free production assistance—forget TV. TV ads are expensive to make and expensive to air. And they are only effective if they are repeated. And repeated. And repeated. (This is called the Ultrabrite principle.) That costs money. Radio spots, in contrast, can be done for as little as $1,000 and radio time is far cheaper than TV time. Print ads, if they are done professionally and timed correctly, can also be an effective adjunct to a political campaign.

• Leave the fussing and fuming to Herb Schmertz. "Often tough ads are only morale builders," explains PR expert Peter Sandman. "There's still a case for them—reporters read them, for example—but my own guess is that soft sell ads work better."

So, let's say some crumby developer wants to build a shopping center in the local wildlife refuge. Don't climb on a soapbox to smear the profit hungry real estate industry. Instead Sandman recommends a low key radio spot describing how lovely the refuge is at this time of year and suggesting that bird lovers get out there and enjoy it. That is, before it's too late.

• Search for common demoninators. "Half the time [environmentalists] are attacking the audience," says Sandman, "when the key concept in persuasion is to find where you've got similarities and to stress that—not the differences."

Often public interest ads reinforce the already converted while scaring away potential sympathizers. One citizens group lobbying for a state oil tax, for example, produced a colorful TV spot featuring noisy pigs jostling for positions around a messy trough. (Get it? Pig Oil.) Unfortunately, the Mobil like metaphor may have made some viewers feel sorry for the poor animals—the oil tax was soundly defeated.

• Be professional. "There is a constituency that hates slickness," Sandman notes dryly, "but it's almost disappeared," adding, "The country we inhabit has enormous respect for power and professionalism." In other words, amateurish ads that describe your group as representing the impoverished minority aren't likely to attract support —except, of course, from those who already identify with your cause.

• Exploit pocketbook issues. If the neighborhood dam enthusiasts are pushing some wasteful boondoggle, talk to the public about cheaper (and, incidentally, more environmentally benign) alternatives. As a general rule, says Robert Caughlan of the Roanoke Co., a do gooder ad agency, "I wouldn't do any of the handwringing environmental stuff—I'd go right to the economics."

• Tell the story as completely as possible. "The message should be clear, and simple and attractive," says former ad executive Jerry Mander, "without using techniques that are imitations of corporate behavior. You have an obligation to tell the story as completely as possible in a print ad, which can stay alive, which people can read and study."

• Be realistic. One shoestring campaign isn't going to change the world. Keep in mind this awesome statistic: 83 percent of all network TV time is controlled by a mere 100 corporations. The majority of all Americans, of course, depend overwhelmingly on TV for information and news.

Over the years, various public relations experts have suggested that changed behavior—not glossy ads—are the true source of a company's social image. Be that as it may, most companies with sizable advertising budgets engage from time to time in image and issue advertising, a trend that really caught on during the 1960s, when many firms, caught off guard by burgeoning government regulations and an angry public, began to fight back. According to the magazine *Working Papers,* nonproduct advertising jumped from $230 million in 1971 to over $474 million six years later.

Because it's so hard to define "advocacy" in print advertising (and the FTC has given up trying), many of the ads you see in magazines like the *Columbia Journalism Review* and on the op-ed pages of major newspapers make political statements, but do so in somewhat veiled terms. This allows the sponsors to deduct the costs of such advertising from their income taxes as a business expense, which all save Mobil regularly do. Many involve pointless preaching, while others refer indirectly to controversial issues; polite attacks on big government are popular. There are ads which are designed to demonstrate how caring an impersonal conglomerate can be ("The best ideas are the ideas that help people," intones ITT), or which merely address some abstraction the company finds appealing. The Container Corporation of America, for example, runs an ad in *The New Yorker* featuring a royal blue, tent shaped compugraph, against which is photographed what appears to be a dead insect perched on a thorny green onion. In tremulous pink script alongside, the artist has written some impenetrable comments on evolution. As a philosopher, one is tempted to say, the Mobil subsidiary makes good throwaway containers.

As inane as many ads' claims may be, some of the tougher ones do provide the already converted with rhetorical ammunition. "The ads strengthen convictions and give people information to support their opinions," says Harvey Shulman, the one time director of the public interest Media Access Project (MAP). "They serve to reinforce the attitudes of those who already agree with them."

Mobil's internal studies of the effectiveness of its advocacy campaigns—something that is reportedly an issue among Mobil bigwigs—are, of course, not publicly available, and attempts to reach Herb

Schmertz were unsuccessful. But one high ranking executive of the Louis Harris polling firm, which did a study for Mobil, told *EA,* "Our data has tended to indicate that Mobil's advertising is counterproductive among certain leadership groups."

Similarly, a former congressional aide who has seen Mobil's own studies of its ad campaigns' effectiveness also hints that many of Herb Schmertz's efforts may be in vain. With a note of cynicism, he adds, "They have the money, and it would look bad to their supporters not to spend it. . . . They feel better because they're out there fighting." He points out that the push to promote the industry's views on the energy crisis began around the time of the oil embargo, when product advertising would have been pointless, but profits were up, and an existing advertising bureaucracy was lusting for a new outlet. "There's a lot of controversy within the industry about the effectiveness of Mobil's ads," he concludes.

An unimpressed spokesperson from a Mobil competitor echoes some of this by complaining, "Mobil's PR department is headed up by a lawyer, and the lawyer's mentality can only advocate or defend—they feel that's all they can do." He pooh poohs Schmertz's fulminations on the *Times* op-ed page, but hastily (and perhaps revealingly) adds that if a campaign like Mobil's didn't exist, the industry would have to create one.

That's probably because at the very least, ads like Mobil's provide a language and a context for industry's broader lobbying efforts. A recent opinion survey by the prestigious firm of Yankelovich, Skelly and White reveals that Americans are

generally more skeptical of corporate integrity and more supportive of major regulatory laws than ever before. At the same time, however, today's Congress is overwhelmingly sympathetic to cries for regulatory relief, evidence, some observers believe, that advocacy campaigns and other corporate PR efforts are reaching if not the public, at least the public's representatives in Washington.

"The ads do a lot of things," insists Larry Zacharias, an attorney who previously worked with the FTC's now defunct project on corporate advocacy advertising. "They tell politicians to go ahead and be conservative—we can always change the minds of the rabble." Not incidentally, he theorizes, the ads also serve to intimidate the opposition, because they imply that no matter how apparent the need for social reforms is made in general news coverage, corporations can always counter by buying still more space to outshout their opponents.

Peter Sandman, who teaches courses in environmental communications at Rutgers University, sees a more insidious side effect of corporate issue advertising. The unstated goal of companies like Mobil, he notes, "is inaction. It's much harder to get people to do something." A public interest group is likely to use what little advertising space it has to ask its supporters to lobby Congress, to write letters, to send money— *to do something*—while big business demands nothing more than total apathy. One doesn't have to read too closely between Mobil's lines to get the message that if we citizens would just leave the oil companies in peace, they'd find a way out of the energy crisis on their own.

Jerry Mander, a former ad executive who did work for the Sierra Club and other good guy groups and author of a book called *Four Arguments for the Elimination of Television,* says with a note of resignation, "Where there is saturation advertising, people tune out, and that's a win for the corporations. People give up." Television accelerates this phenomenon, he believes, because it serves as the primary source of information for most Americans. "Americans aren't dumb," he says. "They're deprived."

Few corporations promoting ideas engage in the kind of mind numbing saturation advertising that made products like Ultrabrite famous, but Mander and others believe the day when that will happen is not far off. Recent Supreme Court rulings have strengthened the rights of corporations to freedom of speech, something Mander, for one, finds disturbing. "It's political speech," he fumes. "It ought to be outlawed. Human beings should be making those statements—not corporations." Corporate freedom of speech, of course, is not only reflected in increased advocacy advertising, but also in floods of "educational" materials, special reports to shareholders, mailings to political figures, background papers designed for journalists and utility bill inserts.

Most media reformers would stop short of gagging corporations altogether. Andrew Schwartzman, current director of the Media Access Project, believes the key is to improve the fairness doctrine and to attempt to apply it to other media. (Utility companies could be required, for example, to provide space for antinuclear propaganda in their bill inserts.) While Jerry Mander, in his words, "despairs of reform," Schwartzman responds, "I share the cynicism about regulatory measures,

but we have made some measurable gains. We've spent 10 years trying to improve the system, and we've made substantial progress. That's why we're subject now to so much attack."

Interestingly, while Mobil's ads have not necessarily made Americans fall in love with the oil industry, there is some circumstantial evidence linking Mobil's PR efforts with its rising share of the gasoline market. Faced with having to choose between that company with the mean looking Xs in the middle of its name and the clean, intent looking Mobil typeface, the average automobile driver apparently opts for the latter. There may well be more to this than Mobil's generous public relations expenditures, but perhaps consumers do believe Mobil deserves credit for trying—almost endearingly—to communicate with the public. Not to mention providing us with all those great shows on public TV.

the role of US corporations in South Africa.

The uprisings threatened the stability of the apartheid state and demonstrated both the demands of the blacks for fundamental change and the brutal power of the Pretoria regime.

They provoked university students in the US to call for divestment of stock in companies doing business in South Africa. Many churches, unions, and members of the black community joined in demanding an end to bank loans and corporate investment by US firms.

Faced with this situation, the companies moved to justify their continued presence in South Africa. They could no longer remain silent as they had in 1970 when the Polaroid Corporation, itself under pressure from black US employees because of its South Africa activities, had urged in vain other US firms to join it in a program of South African workplace reforms.

Within a few months of the announcement of the principles in early 1977, 120 corporations had signed them, hailing them as a great step forward.

What had changed in the intervening years was not the nature of apartheid nor the nature of the corporations, but the nature of black resistance to apartheid.

The Sullivan principles provided precisely what the companies were looking for: a guaranteed public relations success which promised maximum credit for minimum change. The principles sound impressive. They mandate nothing, and there is no way they can be effectively enforced.

SOUTHERN AFRICA

From *Southern Africa* 12, no. 7 (September 1979): 14-15

Sullivan Code— Cleaning Up the Corporate Image

by Gail Morlan

Despite the Reverend Leon Sullivan's claims that his principles of labor reform can be "a tremendous force for change and a vital factor in ending apartheid," the principles serve in fact as part of a strategy to perpetuate the corporate status quo in South Africa. Well over 100 U.S. companies doing business there have endorsed the principles. But they have endorsed them not to end apartheid, but to justify their continued operation under apartheid. The Sullivan principles are, fundamentally, a sophisticated public relations effort.

Black Militancy Provokes Corporate Response

This public relations effort was made necessary by a new militancy among black opponents to the South African system. According to Sullivan, the principles which bear his name grew out of an overnight 1975 visit to Johannesburg during which he was urged by black and white leaders to make US companies agents of change in South Africa. Returning to the US, Sullivan, a General Motors board member, spent many months meeting with corporate executives and finally emerged with the six principles and 12 leading US corporation signatories.

In the months during which the code was being developed, South Africa was shaken by powerful black protest which started with an uprising led by young Soweto students in 1976 and eventually left an estimated 1,000 Africans dead. Pictures of defiant black children facing armed white police shattered US public indifference to events in South Africa, and helped destroy public complacency about

No Challenge to Apartheid

Apartheid is not the product of some outmoded race-discrimination which simply makes it difficult for blacks to move up the job ladder.

Apartheid is a tightly meshed system of total dispossession that deprives blacks of their citizenship, freedom of movement, land ownership, organizing rights, and education. The whole purpose of the system is to maintain the black population as a vast reservoir of powerless, cheap labor, to be used when and where the bosses decide.

The black demand for change in South Africa involves real political power, the destruction of the entire apartheid system, and the achievement of the right to make laws, to shape the economic future of the country, and to be free of the pass laws and security police. None of these things

Statement of Principles of U.S. Firms with Affiliates in the Republic of South Africa

Each of the firms endorsing the Statement of Principles have affiliates in the Republic of South Africa and support the following operating principles:

1. *Non-segregation of the races in all eating, comfort and work facilities.*
2. *Equal and fair employment practices for all employees.*
3. *Equal pay for all employees doing equal or comparable work for the same period of time.*
4. *Initiation of and development of training programs that will prepare, in substantial numbers, Blacks and other non-whites for supervisory, administrative, clerical and technical jobs.*
5. *Increasing the number of Blacks and other non-whites in management and supervisory positions.*
6. *Improving the quality of employees' lives outside the work environment in such areas as housing, transportation, schooling, recreation and health facilities.*

We agree to further implement these principles. Where implementation requires a modification of existing South African working conditions, we will seek such modification through appropriate channels.

We believe that the implementation of the foregoing principles is consistent with respect for human dignity and will contribute greatly to the general economic welfare of all people of the Republic of South Africa.

---

are affected by the Sullivan principles.

There is a fundamental contradiction between the demands of South African blacks and the needs of US corporations, a contradiction that the Sullivan principles attempt to obscure.

US corporations have been attracted to South Africa because it has a highly controlled labor force. The Sullivan principles do not change this fact. Sophisticated companies are quite willing to make work place alterations and even recognize company unions. But they are not prepared to allow militant unions with the power to represent the real needs of the workers. They will argue with the government over the right to use more blacks as skilled workers, but they will not confront the government over apartheid.

The Bantustan Policy

Perhaps the most damaging effect of the Sullivan principles is the impression they give that reform is possible in South Africa, and that US corporations have the will and the power to improve the condition of South Africa's black majority. Quite the contrary is true. As US involvement has expanded, conditions for blacks have grown worse. US corporate investment in South Africa has nearly tripled in the last ten years now approaching $2 billion—one-fifth of all foreign investment there. US bank loans now account for about one-quarter of all South Africa's foreign loans.

US presence provides jobs for about 100,000 people or 1 percent of the official work force, including 70,000 Africans, "coloureds," and Asians.

While US corporate investment has grown so has the systematic dispossession of some 20 million Africans who make up over 70 percent of the population. The cornerstone of this dispossession is the bantustan policy. Under this system, 13 percent of the land area is allocated to the 80 percent, divided among eight "tribal groups." Every African is assigned to one of these groups, and it is with this group, located on a fragmented, isolated, and often desolate bantustan, that each individual is supposed to identify. There are no African South Africans left, only Zulus, or Xhosa, or Tswana, whose country is some "independent homelands" undergoing "separate development."

The ultimate in black dispossession, the bantustan policy is a strategy guaranteed to supply the economy with the one resource that cannot be taken from the blacks: their labor power.

US corporations, with or without the Sullivan principles, are unwilling and unable to abolish the bantustan system. In fact, the principles could be thoroughly discussed without even mentioning the bantustans, which is to say that they could be implemented fully within a system that maintains forever white power and black subjugation.

Workplace Reform and the Myth of Monitoring

Even at the level of in-plant reform, the principles leave gaping holes. US companies have always avoided close critical inspection of their operations, both in the US and abroad. The independent information gradually assembled on US corporate operations in South Africa has revealed a record of acceptance of apartheid norms, and close and friendly relations with powerful South African institutions.

Now change is promised—but how will such change be monitored? Minority groups in the US know that even with the weight of federal equal opportunity legislation on their side they have often been unable to force company compliance. Workers have never found corporations eager to see the development of strong trade unions.

Why should things be different in South Africa? There custom and the law are on the other side—and indeed new laws such as the Protection of Business Act specifically shield businesses by making it illegal to provide information on corporate operations without consent of the minister of economic affairs.

An Obstacle to Change

Since the Sullivan principles are basically a public relations effort, it might be argued that although they can't do any fundamental good, they also do no particular harm.

But the principles are not neutral and innocuous, because by justifying a continued US corporate presence in South Africa, they are being used to defeat attempts to end US economic support for apartheid.

The fact is that a continuing flow of foreign capital is vital for the growth, even the survival, of today's South African economy. Giant projects such as the new nuclear power stations aided by Westinghouse, and the gas-from-coal plants involving Fluor and Babcock and Wilcox —both will strengthen the apartheid state's ability to resist change—all need huge infusions of foreign capital and know-how. The Sullivan principles allow the dollars to keep pouring in.

In addition US corporations in South Africa produce a range of products necessary to keep the wheels of an industrialized economy turning. Some corporations, such as General Motors and Ford, give direct strategic assistance to the South African government by supplying trucks and other vehicles to the police and military.

Yet Fluor, GM, and Ford have all signed the Sullivan principles. So, too, has Control Data, whose chairman commented in 1979 that "the little bit of repression that is added by the computer in South Africa is hardly significant" compared with the good the company feels it is doing. Other signatories include Mobil and Caltex, which refine almost half of all oil used in South Africa and continue to sell petroleum to the government and the military.

Blacks Demand Withdrawal

Only the dismantling of the bantustan system and the destruction of apartheid can meet black needs in South Africa. This is no job for the corporations; they want reforms to improve and preserve the system, not a revolution which will destroy it.

Throughout South Africa black voices have been calling on the foreign corporations to get out, to stop supporting the apartheid state. The African National Congress and the Pan Africanist Congress call for withdrawal.

It is time to recognize the Sullivan principles for what they are: a part of the strategy to enable US corporations to reap high profits while remaining in South Africa. They are an obstacle to black liberation.

Gail Morlan was for many years a member of the Southern Africa *magazine collective; she is now writing a novel.*

Anti-Apartheid News

The Newspaper of the Anti-Apartheid Movement

From *Anti-Apartheid News*, May 1980, p. 10

The Golden Windfall

Whites, especially those in the upper income brackets, will be in the main beneficiaries of the South African government's budget, announced at the end of March. And the military/police apparatus of the state gets a large financial shot-in-the-arm.

These two key features of the 1980-81 budget expose the claims of the Botha regime to be seeking peaceful and just solutions to the country's problems as sheer windowdressing.

Finance Minister Horwood had a veritable golden opportunity to put the government's money where its mouth is, into substantial reforms in the fields of black housing, transport, education, health and rural development. Not that this would have satisfied the basic political aspirations of the black majority. But it would have given substance to the image Botha has been cultivating of a leadership bent on major change and on defusing the racial tensions which have now been heightened

Reprinted with permission from *Anti-Apartheid News* (newspaper of the British anti-apartheid movement).

by the victory of the liberation movement in Zimbabwe.

The opening was provided by last year's astronomical increase in the price of gold. The windfall resulting from this gave an unprecedented boost not only to the mining companies' profits, but also to government revenues. The Exchequer ended the year with an unforeseen surplus of almost R300 million. Few governments in recent times can have had such a handsome gift dumped in their hands.

The way Pretoria has used its undeserved good fortune shows how it is beholden to the white electorate and to the owners of corporate wealth in particular. It is determined to defend the system of racial exploitation to the death, despite the clear lesson of Zimbabwe which showed once again the ultimate futility of all such racist ambitions.

The budget abolished the loan levy system of tax for both companies and individuals, making concessions on individual income tax worth £335 million. As an example of how this benefits the already super-privileged white managerial and professional elite, a married man with two children earning £11,173 a year will pay 23 per cent *less* income tax this year.

Social security benefits, another area where the regime's real intentions can be readily revealed, show the same discrimi-

nation in favour of the dominant white group. Most whites fall within the pension system while most blacks fall outside it, and pensions, like everything else, are graded according to race. This differentiation was increased by the budget, which raised white pensions by R12, more than double the increase given to African pensioners (R5.50).

The poor, and especially the unemployed, saw their position immediately worsened by the removal of a subsidy on bread which led to an 18 per cent increase in the price of a white loaf and a 23 per cent rise for the cheaper brown loaf.

With other consumer prices rising rapidly, and rent increases of 60 per cent or more already in the pipeline for Soweto and other black townships, the prospects for black working people are grim.

Last year's big wave of bus boycotts in Natal showed how explosive is the transport problem for black commuters, who find themselves having to live further and further from the 'white' cities and industrial-commercial centres, and to pay more for their daily pilgrimage to work. Yet the government maintains the Black Transport Services Account at the ludicrously low level of R12.5 million—a mere half a million rand up on the previous year.

Defending the system, not ameliorating it, was once again the top priority. The basic allocation for defence was R1,890 million (just over one billion pounds), 17 per cent up on the previous year. However, this does not include a separate Special Defence Account and various other funds.

All told, the South African Defence Force will have R2,074 million to spend in the current year (1980-81), with authorisation to commit a further R272 million if necessary.

This makes Pretoria far and away the biggest military spender in Africa—bigger even than Nigeria, whose military budget in 1979 was £112 million smaller than South Africa's, and which this year reduced its defence spending. Of the Exchequer's gold-derived surplus from last year, over half was transferred directly to the Special Defence Account, which finances arms purchases. Its massive R1,161 million share of the military spending reveals how determined the regime is to buy the best that modern technology can supply and to assemble a huge stockpile of arms. This underlines the importance of the international arms embargo as a key means to frustrate Pretoria's designs.

With the police vote up by 26 per cent to R309.8 million and the prisons vote up by 11 per cent to R110.6 million, few blacks are liable to mistake the much-vaunted increase in the vote for black education (up by 32 per cent to R240.3 million) as a change of heart by the Botha regime. At best it represents a long overdue and woefully inadequate first step towards bringing the deliberately stunted Bantu Education system more into line with the needs of the apartheid economy, which can no longer look to blacks solely as a source of cheap unskilled labour.

The mounting discontent in black schools has, in fact, prompted a number of warnings that the eruptions of 1976-77 may be preparing to repeat themselves again.

From *Multinational Monitor* 1, no. 1 (February 1980): 13-14

Multinationals and Third World Development

by Richard Barnet

Increasingly, global resource systems are being managed by multinational corporations. The mining, melting, refining, and mixing of animal, vegetable, mineral and human resources into products for sale is an integrated operation on a planetary scale. Viewed from space, the Global Factory suggests a human organism. The brain is housed in steel and glass slabs located in or near a few crowded cities: New York, London, Frankfurt, Zurich, and Tokyo. The blood is capital, and it is pumped through the system by global banks assisted by a few governments. The financial centers, New York, London, Frankfurt, Tokyo and their fictional extensions in such tax havens as Panama and the Bahamas function as the heart. The hands are steadily moving to the outer rim of civilization. More and more goods are now made in the poor countries of the southern periphery under direction from the headquarters in the north, and most are destined to be consumed in the industrial countries.

Global corporations exploit their superior bargaining power in weak, disorganized societies to carry out a series of activities which can offer exceptionally high profits for the worldwide enterprise but which often promote economic and social back-

This article is reprinted with permission from *Multinational Monitor.*

wardness in poor countries. The manipulation of transfer prices (administered prices for transactions between foreign subsidiaries and the headquarters of a multinational corporation) rob the countries of foreign exchange and reasonable earnings from exports. The technology transferred by multinationals, which is usually designed for the home market in a developed society, is inappropriate to the needs of poor countries. It often displaces jobs and is overpriced. The products manufactured in poor countries are beyond the reach of a majority of the people who lack the money to buy them. Such products—automobiles, household appliances, expensive packaged foods—are consumed by local elites in enclaves of affluence or they are exported. The export-led model of development of which the multinational corporation has been the principal engine has meant crippling debt and increasing dependence upon the rich countries, their private banks and the international lending agencies which they control. Because of their superior control over capital, technology, and marketing, global corporations can dominate local economies and preempt the power to plan for the society.

The development model that emerges by default when the global corporation assumes control of the commanding heights of the economy is a highly inequitable one: The gap between the rich and poor increases and the bottom 20 percent of the society appears to be worse off in terms of having its basic needs met than before the development process began. Multinational corporations exert political influence in favor of rightist regimes which are committed to social and economic relationships that preserve inequalities. The political power of multinational corporations is firmly committed against redistributive experiments as in Salvador Allende's Chile or in Michael Manley's Jamaica. This power is now exercised principally through banks and international lending agencies. The huge debt owed by Third World countries to public and private banks provides effective leverage to discourage redistributive strategies that, from the viewpoint of the multinationals, threaten financial or political stability.

Multinationals thus bring their own model of development with them. This model conflicts with a strategy to meet the basic needs of the poor majority. A basic needs strategy involves shifting resources to people without money, to clean the water in rural areas where it is a necessity of life but not a commodity. Such investments are not in the economic interest of multinational corporations. From the point of view of the corporation, the priority public investments are roads, harbors, subsidies for high technology, and other expenditures to develop the infrastructure to support profitable private investment. Money should be spent on the productive enclaves of the society and not wasted on the rest. Spending money on those who do not produce, according to most economic theory, is a recipe for ruinous inflation.

The multinational corporations are of course interested in Third World markets, but even for relatively low-cost items, the market is limited. The corporations have no interest on producing goods suitable for the consumer or use of the poorest 60 percent of the population. They are not in the business of producing low-cost housing, cheap and nutritious food, or village medical care. The technology they transfer to Third World economies, such as nuclear power plants, computers and gas-guzzling harvesters—tends to be inappropriate. Like any other profit-making institution, the multinational operates under a narrow

Peg Averill/CALC Report/LNS

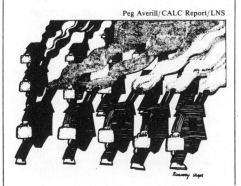

set of goals—profit maximization, long-term stability, and growth. Its purpose is obviously not productive to meet the basic needs for which there is no immediate, high-profit market.

The process of industrialization in the Third World is taking place almost automatically. The pace differs greatly from country to country, but the basic social effects are much the same. The subsistence economy in which money was rarely used—small peasants bartered their cotton for a little wheat, or some rice for the rare luxury of a pair of shoes from the village cobbler—is being sucked into the international money market. By the magic of modern fertilizer, miserable grazing land suddenly becomes valuable. The high-technology agriculture of the "Green Revolution" has driven hundreds of thousands of peasants off the land. When agribusiness moves in, their labor is no longer needed.

The industrialization of the Third World via the multinational has destroyed jobs in the countryside without creating anything approaching equivalent opportunities inside the factory. The pressures on the corporations are to extend the useful life of capital-intensive technology developed in their home countries and to keep their Third World payrolls down.

In an industrializing world in which the principle activity is getting and spending, more and more people are thus becoming irrelevant to the productive process, either as producers or consumers. More than a billion people cannot find enough work at wages adequate to provide food for their families. Every sign suggests that the number will increase dramatically. It is the monumental social problem of the planet, the cause of mass starvation, repression, and crime, petty and cosmic.

Richard Barnet, a founder of the Institute for Policy Studies, is co-author, with Ronald Muller, of Global Reach: The Power of the Multinational Corporations. *His latest book.* The Lean Years: Politics in the Age of Scarcity, *will be published by Simon and Schuster in May.*

From *Science for the People* 12, no. 1 (January/February 1980): 23-26

Blueprint for Disaster: Westinghouse Brings Nukes to the Philippines

by E. San Juan, Jr.

Sensational chic? Or plain and simple truth?

Consider the following facts: Westinghouse Electric Corporation has sold a nuclear reactor costing $1.1 billion to the Marcos dictatorship in the Philippines. This 620 megawatt reactor is being constructed in Morong, Bataan, on the slope of an active volcano, Mt. Natib. There are three other live volcanoes within a twenty-mile radius. In addition, the plant

---

sits astride a major earthquake fault and is on the Bataan peninsula which is subject to frequent tidal waves from the South China sea. Morong, Bataan, is 45 miles west of the commercial and cultural center of the Philippines, metropolitan Manila, with a population of at least seven million people.

The Union of Concerned Scientists in the United States has reviewed the plant design and found over 200 major engineering defects.[1] In a secret study, recently leaked out, the International Atomic Energy Agency concluded that the volcano on which the reactor is sited could explode anytime.

Although President Carter has issued a decree making reactor exports subject to the requirements of the Environmental Protection Agency (EPA), the US Nuclear Regulatory Commission (NRC) which is the chief environmental agency concerned in this case has still not established definite and tested standards for evaluating overseas reactor orders. Like most Third World nations, the Philippines has no nuclear regulation, multiplying the chances of accidents, including a meltdown disaster.

What is more revealing is that the NRC itself has admitted that the Philippine plant design has not been rigorously tested for safety, especially for earthquake and volcanic dangers. It admitted that no adequate Environmental Impact Statement (EIS), required for licensing domestic reactors, has been made for the Philippine project. Certainly after the Harrisburg incident, this plant could never be built in the US. But it is being built in a country where the US has investments of over $7 billion (with a $1 investment yielding from $6 to $10)[2] and has about 20 military installations, chief of which are Clark Air Force Base and Subic Naval Base.

Since 1972, the Philippine government has ruled by marital law and has abolished civil rights and democratic freedoms, such as free speech, the right to strike and the right of assembly.[3] Over 70,000 political dissenters, by Marcos's own admission, have suffered imprisonment. Amnesty International, the International Commission of Jurists, the US National Council of Churches, and even the US State Department, have identified the Marcos government as repressive, as a consistent and systematic violator of its citizens' human rights.

Since 1972, with the US debacle in Indochina, worldwide and domestic public opinion have become sensitized to overt forms of US intervention in the Third World. Ironically, the Carter administration has increased its military aid to Marcos by 138 percent, from $31.8 to $75.5 million.[4] These public monies will be used to pay for the tanks, planes, bombs, howitzers and ammunition that Marcos badly needs to maintain himself in power and enrich his family and friends. At the same time these weapons will be used to brutalize 45 million Filipinos (of which 5 million are Filipino Muslims or Moros waging fierce armed struggle in the southern Philippines)—all in the name of a presumably anti-communist "New Society" blessed by the International Monetary Fund and the transnational corporations. It is in this context that we should appraise the issues and problems presented by the Westinghouse adventure.

Construction of the plant began in 1977. To negotiate and win the contract over its competitor General Electric, Westinghouse is reported to have paid as much as $40 million to Herminio Disini, an in-law and business associate of Marcos.[5] This kickback, or more euphemistically, "commission fee," is now being investigated by the Department of Justice. It is generally understood that no license can be granted for reactor export while this investigation into corporate bribery is being conducted.

Immediately after the construction began, about 100 families were driven from their homes. Over 11,000 residents in the vicinity of the plant, mostly poor farmers and fishermen, mounted a protest when they realized that the project would jeopardize their lives. Already their lives have been severely disrupted with the destruction of their farmlands, grazing fields, orchards, fishponds, and other means of livelihood. One of the townspeople wrote recently:

> This nuclear plant alarms us because we are already experiencing the effects of the project on our livelihood and on our health. Many of us have no more land to till. The lands where we used to get our food and livelihood from are either bought at low price or confiscated because they are needed by the plant. Before, the fishermen used to fish near the shore. Now, the National Power Corporation has driven the fish away because earth fillings are washed directly into the sea. Parts of the mountains abundant in fruit trees and other crops are already levelled off.

With their homes wrecked and their livelihoods at stake, peasants and workers alike have continued to resist the project despite harassment and arrests. Fifty thousand Filipinos have already risked imprisonment by signing a petition opposing the construction of the plant. Marcos in turn has responded by severely suppressing any organized dissent. One construction worker engaged in organizing workers, Ernest Nazareno, was arrested and brutally tortured by Marcos security forces. In June 1978 he disappeared and is now presumed to have been secretly executed, the first murder victim of the reactor.

Earlier, one Methodist pastor was threatened with arrest merely for asking questions about the possibility of nuclear accidents, airborne pollution, and so forth.

Steve Karian/LNS

Since the people militantly reject the reactor, Marcos has permanently stationed two companies of the Philippine Constabulary to guard the area, thus offering Westinghouse a "favorable investment climate."

In addition to these transnational corporations, the other prime beneficiaries will be two huge US military bases, Clark Field (home of the 13th Air Force) and Subic Naval Base (main repair facility and ordinance depot for the Pacific Seventh Fleet). These two outposts constitute the key strategic springboards for continued US intervention in Asia, Africa and the Middle East. Over 16,000 US troops, excluding civilian personnel and families, are now stationed in the Philippines: they will be serviced, and at the same time endangered, by the nuclear plant.

Various studies have shown that the electricity generated by the reactor will benefit primarily transnational corporations which have factories operating in the adjacent Bataan Export Processing Zone.

Nukes and Native Peoples

Besides the starkly real presence of unacceptable health and safety hazards due to siting, design and the lack of any viable plan for disposal of lethal waste (the vast Pacific has been proposed as the most accessible dumping ground), the Westinghouse reactor is also a genocidal threat to indigenous peoples. In August 1978, the Philippine Energy Ministry and Australia signed an agreement binding Australia to provide a regular supply of unprocessed uranium to the Philippine plant. (Canada is the other prospective supplier.) What this implies is the further eviction of indigenous peoples of Australia from their ancestral lands where uranium is being mined, with the rest of the land contaminated by radioactive debris. This disaster is occurring right now in Native American communities, whose lands account for 25% of US uranium production.

The Uranium Moratorium Movement in Australia has condemned this blatant sacrifice of human lives for profit, exposing how the US, with its highly sophisticated enrichment know-how, depends on raw uranium furnished by Australia and other nations to maintain uninterrupted profitable sales of enriched uranium—a necessary ingredient for nuclear plants.

Inside this Zone, US and other foreign corporations run their tax-free factories employing a Filipino labor force (mostly women) which is prohibited from strikes and union organizing and is paid roughly $1.00 per day.[6] ($6 is considered by the government the average cost of living per day.) In the final analysis, it is the super-exploited Filipino workers and farmers who will pay for the reactor and subsidize the forces that continue to extract the value of their labor power: the US-based conglomerates like Ford, Exxon, Mobil, and smaller corporations.

Given the historic collusion between the state and business in a "free enterprise system," it should come as no surprise that US taxpayers are financing the sale of this reactor, which is now on record as the most expensive reactor ever sold. "It's one reactor for the price of two," commented one Filipino high official in the Marcos cabinet.

The most questionable aspect of this deal is the role played by the Export-Import Bank. Supported by people's taxes, the Ex-Im Bank is subsidizing the Westinghouse reactor with $644 million in loans and guarantees, the largest loan package ever to a developing nation.[7] This financial support, which is half the cost of the reactor, appears to be in violation of the Human Rights Amendment to the Foreign Assistance Act of 1977, which forbids aid to oppressive governments.

With the accelerating impetus of the anti-nuclear movement in the US and Europe, the nuclear industry has now turned to developing or underdeveloped countries to make profits. Of the many reactors operating throughout the world, most have been built or licensed by US transnational corporations.[8]

Domestically, the industry had a shocking *zero net sales* from 1975 to 1978. But in that same period it sold five reactors worth over $2 billion to Third World clients, most of them under repressive, authoritarian regimes. With public consciousness sensitized and mobilized by the Three Mile Island near-catastrophe and the controversy surrounding it, there are bound to be more cancellations, freezes and shutdowns.

But of course Westinghouse, like other transnational corporations, recognizes neither territorial boundaries nor human rights. How could it be embarrassed by its "standard operating procedure" when the US government itself, which supposedly should set the example, persists in doling out millions of tax dollars to subsidize reactionary despots in South Korea, Taiwan, Chile, Brazil and other countries where 23 of the Third World's 32 reactors are planned.[9]

Within the wider perspective of political economy, the Westinghouse deal represents a desperate corporate drive to recoup losses incurred in a declining domestic market where sales are paralyzed due to public disapproval. The trick is to dump nuclear technology in the Third World where a ferocious trade war between US, French and German corporations rages.[10]

There is at least one profoundly instructive lesson to be gained from analyzing the Westinghouse-Marcos connection. It exposes in quite undisguised fashion the conjuncture of various socio-economic factors illustrating how nuclear energy as presently controlled by profit-making corporations dovetails with the global planning imposed by such bodies as the US Agency for International Development (AID), World Bank, IMF, etc. on the Third World.

It is a matter of public record that AID and other monetary agencies endorse, sometimes insist on, capital-intensive projects designed to service only foreign corporations with the technical know-how. The "trickle-down effect" will benefit only the local junior partners of these multinationals, a handful of urban-based merchants and bureaucrats. For their part, the technocratic, right-wing elites of the developing societies recognize that the centralized form of nuclear technology affords them powerful mechanisms for controlling the lives of their subjects. What is at stake are national sovereignty and genuine popular democracy. For if Westinghouse will control the installation and repair of the reactor, and the US government licenses its export and use, then the Philippines will be dependent technically, economically and politically on the US. Philippine society will continue to be dominated by a privileged minority of technocrats, businessmen and generals. Other energy sources (like geothermal and water) are available in the Philippines, but they will not yield profit bonanzas for Marcos and his patrons.

In the Philippines 70 percent of the labor force functions largely as landless tenants and subsistence farmers, who will consume only 2.3 percent of the electricity produced. Widespread poverty plagues 99 percent of the people, the inflation rate is 14.5 percent

CONSIDERING THE AMOUNT OF RADIATION YOUR COMPANY'S NUKE HAS RELEASED, WHAT OF VITAL IMPORTANCE WILL BE MOST AFFECTED BY THIS DISASTER?

OUR PROFITS.

Michael Scurato/LNS

and unemployment/underemployment totals 40 percent. Eighty percent of Filipino children under the age of six are malnourished. Diseases due to poor water supply and inadequate sanitation cause the highest number of deaths. Confronted with these fundamental problems and immediate needs of the majority, the Marcos regime betrays its real essence as an inhumane, bankrupt, irrational system. With a staggering debt of $8 billion, it has committed $1.1 billion for the Westinghouse reactor—a massive drain on national resources—chiefly in order to benefit foreign corporations and the subservient elite, about 1 percent of the population.[11]

Practically all the substantial issues concerning energy being debated today converge in this campaign to halt nuclear export to the Philippines.

What is being targeted here is not just the biological and ecological impact of nuclear technology, but also the function of government and institutions (for example, the role of the Ex-Im Bank in underwriting virtually all reactor exports), corporate bribery, Washington's material and political support for dictatorships, and last but not least the wanton violation of human rights and subversion of the democratic and libertarian aspirations of peoples. In sum, what is at issue is the comparative merit of different social and political systems, contradictory ideologies, and contradictory world-outlooks. The manifold linkages are being explored and publicized by the Campaign for a Nuclear-Free Philippines, a loose coalition, founded in April 1978, of environmental, anti-nuclear, and anti-martial law groups, including Friends of the Earth, Nautilus Alliance, Mobilization for Survival,

Friends of the Filipino People, and others.

In July 1979, when Marcos, in deference to heavy international criticism, was forced to postpone the project, an international review board was formed to assess the health and safety impact of the plant. This is the first time in history that nuclear export has been challenged either politically or legally. This campaign to urge NRC denial of an export license to Westinghouse, together with a demand to halt all funds allocated by Ex-Im Bank, is bound to establish a precedent-setting case. If successful, it will mean a defeat for corporate interests and a victory for the people.

As Westinghouse presses the NRC to expedite the granting of a license, the Campaign for a Nuclear-Free Philippines and two environmental groups based in Washington (the Center for Development Policy and the Natural Resources Council) have filed a petition for the federal courts to intervene in the reactor export. On September 28, 1979, the State Department recommended the granting of an export licence to Westinghouse for this project. Immediately, various organizations spearheaded by the Friends of the Filipino People demanded that the NRC hold hearings before making the final decision. So powerful has been the popular response against this project that Marcos himself ordered a halt to the construction, allowing Westinghouse to make "fundamental changes in the design."[12] Marcos and Westinghouse itself are sensitive to public pressure, hence their concession for modifications in design. However, the location still remains the same. And even if honest and conscientious changes are made, would this solve the real and potentially disastrous impact of this reactor on the lives of millions of Filipinos, as well as 27,300 US citizens living in the vicinity of the plant (at Clark Air Base and Subic Naval Base)?

References

1. Letter of Daniel Ford of the Union of Concerned Scientists to President Marcos, dated Feb. 13, 1978. Quoted in Walden Bello, Peter Hayes and Lyuba Zarsky, "500 Mile Island: The Philippine Nuclear Reactor Deal," in *Pacific Research*, First Quarter 1979, p. 2. See also *Philippine Liberation Courier* (March 10, 1978), p. 2.

2. In pre-martial law days, the business editor of the *Manila Times* (March 4, 1971) stated that in 1969, "some $7.08 were remitted for every dollar that was brought into the country. In 1970 it was $7.079." Quoted in Alejandro Lichauco, *The Lichauco Paper: US Imperialism in the Philippines* (New York: Monthly Review, 1973), p. 26. See also Corporate Information Center, National Council of Churches of U.S., "The Philippines: American Corporations, Martial Law, and Underdevelopment," *IDOC* 57 (Nov. 1973), pp. 11-13; "U.S. Imperialism in the Philippines," *Philippine Liberation Courier* (Dec. 15, 1978), p. 5; Guy Whitehead, "Philippine-American Economic Relations," *Pacific Research* (Jan.-Feb. 1973), p. 6.

3. See Dept. of State, *Report on Human Rights Practices in Countries Receiving U.S. Aid,* Feb. 8, 1979, entry on the Philippines: Amnesty International, *Report of AI Mission to the Philippines* (London, 1976), pp. 5-6; International Commission of Jurists. *The Decline of Democracy in the Philippines* (Geneva, 1977), pp. 46-49; Association of Major Religious Superiors, Philippines, *Political Detainees of the Philippines Book 3* (1978), pp. 1-8.

4. See Charito Planas et al., *On the Withdrawal of U.S. Bases from the Philippines* (Washington, DC, 1979), p. 5.

5. See *New York Times,* Jan. 14 and 18, 1978; *Asia Finance,* June 15, 1977, p. 80.

6. The best detailed studies of present-day wages and living conditions of the majority of Filipinos are Enrico Paglaban, "Philippines: Workers in the Export Industry," *Pacific Research* (March-June 1978) and Ohara Ken, "Bataan Export Processing Zone: Its Development and Social Implications," *AMPO* X (1978), pp. 93-119. For an update on socioeconomic data, consult Friends of the Filipino People, *Conditions of the Filipino People Under Martial Law* (1979), and Bernard Wideman, "The Philippines: Five Years of Martial Law," *AMPO* IX (1977), pp. 62-70.

7. On the nature of the Export-Import Bank and its subsidy to the nuclear industry, see Bello, *op. cit.,* pp. 7-13 and Jim Morrell, "Aid to the Philippines: Who Benefits?" *International Policy Report* (October 1979), pp. 10-11. On the Ex-Im Bank's support to the Marcos dictatorship, see Walden Bello and Severina Rivera, *The Logistics of Repression* (Washington, DC, 1977), pp. 57-58.

8. See *Business Week,* Dec. 26, 1978, p. 54; *Nucleonic Week,* Nov. 24, 1977; Norman Gall, "Nuclear Setbacks," *Forbes* (Nov. 27, 1978), p. 104.

9. See *Nuclear News,* August 21, 1978, pp. 67-85.

10. For the fierce challenge posed by France's Framatome and West Germany's KWU (both nuclear conglomerates) to U.S. counterparts in Third World countries like Brazil and Iran, see Norman Gall, "Atoms for Brazil, Dangers for All," *The Bulletin of the Atomic Scientists* (June 1976), pp. 5-6; and *Business Week,* Nov. 27, 1978, p. 44.

11. On the distortion of Philippine socioeconomic development by this reactor, see James Drew, *Brief of Intervenor/Petitioner* (Friends of the Filipino People) submitted to the U.S. Nuclear Regulatory Commission, Nov. 2, 1979, pp. 15-17; and especially the affidavit (included in the brief, pp. 21-38) of William L. Cummings, an American who worked for several years on the proposed plant. On the question of why nuclear power is generally inimical to Third World socioeconomic progress, see Bello, Hayes, Zrasky, *op. cit.,* pp. 14-29; *Nuclear Export Monitor,* Vol. 1, #1 and #2.

12. *Philippine Times,* Nov. 26, 1979.

PEACE & FREEDOM THROUGH NONVIOLENT ACTION

From *WIN* 16, no. 2 (February 15, 1980): 12-13

Pension Funds Prop Up Nuke Industry

by J. A. Savage

A week before the Manhattan Project focused national attention on the landlords of the nuclear industry at Wall Street, a small university town in northern California found out that its money had been used to help purchase a worthless piece of radioactive real estate known as Three Mile Island #2. The City Council was not pleased. That week the City of Arcata took a stand on keeping its money out of nuclear investments.

Arcata, like many other cities across the nation, has money invested in utilities which use the funds for the construction of nuclear power plants. Public employees have a portion of their paychecks deferred to support their eventual retirement. These "pension funds" take wing from the worker's pocketbook and land at the state capital, where the money is then invested through the Public Employees Retirement System (PERS) or another large pension system.

In California, the three largest retirement funds, PERS, State Teachers Retirement System and the University of California Retirement Fund are heavily committed to nuclear power. These funds in this state alone have combined assets of $18 billion, of which $2 billion or 11% is invested in nuclear operating utilities.

Reprinted with permission from *WIN: Peace & Freedom Through Nonviolent Action,* 326 Livingston St., Brooklyn, NY 11217.

These public investment institutions are among the few large investors that still throw money at nuclear reactors. Utilities used to be a "safe" investment. Brokers would tell little old ladies and gentlemen to invest in power companies because they turned over solid returns over a long period of time. This is obviously no longer true. If the utilities that own the partially-melted Three Mile Island reactor fold because of the enormous cost of clean up and decommissioning, California public employees' $20 million investment in Jersey Central Power and Light will amount to nothing more than a piece of land that will be worthless for 250,000 years.

Public pension funds most often buy the first mortgage bonds of utilities, secured by whatever property they represent. In the case of a coal company, if the company folded the bondholders would get the coal plant. In the case of a bankrupt nuclear utility, the bondholders would get the reactor shaft.

Even the entrenched financial community balks at the economy of splitting atoms to boil water. Bank of America, the nation's largest commercial bank, called for a suspension of loans to the nuclear industry, although the bank now loans money for nuclear fuel. A spokesperson stated, "It wouldn't be following the 'prudent man' rule to be making loans for construction of nuclear projects or facilities while this massive review of the industry takes place."

(Investment institutions are required to invest in accordance with the "prudent man" rule. A court ruling during the Depression stated that pension funds must be invested the way an individual of "prudence and reason" would invest. If an investment is lost on something that everyone else is investing in, then there is no legal penalty. But if the pensions are invested in something that other institutions won't touch, then it is illegal.)

The Bank of America has a paltry $220 million in loans to the nuclear industry worldwide. Yet the public pensions in California have more than $434 million sunk into Babcock and Wilcox reactors alone.

One reason the financial community is pulling out of nuclear investments is because any large scale accident will be a total loss. Although taxpayers bear the cost of individual lawsuits because of the Price-Anderson Act, the investors could be stuck with the balance of the construction debt and the cost of decommissioning the plant.

Shutdowns also affect the profitability of a nuclear investment. The construction debt must be paid even if the plant isn't delivering electricity. The utility must meet electrical demand so it purchases power from elsewhere on the grid. In the case of Three Mile Island, it costs $24 million a day for replacement power.

While many big-money institutions tremble at nuclear's financial fallout, they love to get their claws on public pension funds. When they do, you can bet that they invest the money in their interest and not in the interest of the employees. Claims on pension fund money are so important that a corporation's bond ratings sometimes depends on whether a pension fund (notably California's) will invest in the company's bonds.

Pension funds are the largest pool of capital in the United States. They hover now at a sum above the entire United States gross national product for 1978. This money belongs to working people and it is terribly abused.

Two brief tales of pension fund abuse come from the East.

US Steel-Carnegie pension fund accused Citibank of New York of a $3 million scam in 1974. They sued Citibank for propping up Topper Corporation with employee money when Citibank knew the corporation was in financial trouble. Citibank

bought $3 million worth of Topper's bonds 80 days before it went bankrupt using Carnegie's pension funds. The proceeds from the sales of these bonds went to pay off Topper's debt to the bank. The $3 million was lost.

A more incredible tale involves the Amalgamated Clothing and Textile Workers Union (ACTWU) and J. P. Stevens. The union called a boycott on Stevens' products in 1976 to protest its union-busting activities. Through pension funds, ACTWU has ended up controlling 25% of the outstanding stock in the nefarious J. P. Stevens Corporation. ACTWU has billions of dollars of funds in Manufacturers Hanover, Irving Trust and New York Life Insurance Company. They have loans of over $147 million out to J. P. Stevens.

Back in our small town in northern California, the City Council is more powerless than the eastern unions. The Council has little control over the City's investments and the public employees have even less control over where this portion of their earnings is spent. Clerks, maintenance people and other staff know the Humboldt Bay Nuclear Power Plant looms in their backyard. Many of them don't like it and yet their money is being used to build its newest brother at Diablo Canyon. The workers never see the part of their paycheck used for retirement—until they retire. The money is transferred to the state where one man, who speaks with the clarity of Elmer Fudd, invests it. In California, one man invests $10 million of the public money every day.

Public employees can vote for representatives to an investment board but voter

turnouts are miniscule. It is somewhat akin to getting a card in the mail with your insurance bill asking for a proxy vote. Elections are largely ignored and in California, the employee-elected members tend to be the most conservative.

The City of Arcata, or any other local government that has a contract with PERS, can pull out of the system, though this concept gives the City Manager headaches. Once an entity pulls out of PERS, it can't get back in. Most institutions are afraid to make investments on their own, although putting money in a local savings and loan at six per cent interest would beat the return on most PERS investments. And at least it would funnel retirement money into the local economy. California's money buys into Three Mile Island in Pennsylvania and General Motors tanks in South Africa—it could be used to help public employees and others buy houses at an affordable interest rate. And the workers would still get a better return for their retirement than what the man in the state capital gets for them.

Pension funds are one of the few places nuclear utilities can still go for construction money. You can find out where your city, county, union or company's pension funds are invested. Ask for their investment "portfolio." For more detailed information, send for the California Public Policy Center's new study, "Financial Fallout: Pension Funds and Nuclear Power," $5, from 304 S. Broadway #224, Los Angeles, CA 90013.

J. J. Savage is a freelance writer and activist with California Campaign for Economic Democracy and the Redwood (anti-nuclear) Alliance.

Cindy Fredrick/LNS

Nukes: Which side are you on?

the independent radical newsweekly
Guardian

From *The Guardian* 31, no. 31 (May 9, 1979): 6

Basic Political Maxim: Know Your Enemy

Oil Firms Dominate Nuke Industry

by Anna DeCormis

Reprinted with permission from *The Guardian: Independent Radical Newsweekly* (New York).

So you're antinuke? And you want to ban nuclear power?

Perhaps your major focus has been your local utility company, connected with a nuclear plant in your area. But behind the utilities looms the nuclear industry—the corporations that produce the fuel and equipment to make nuclear power and weapons. (And working in collusion with them is the federal government and the Pentagon—but that's a different story.)

One basic political maxim is: know what you're up against. And who is behind nuclear power in this country?

The major oil companies dominate the nuclear industry. In the 1960's they saw the limits of the world's oil reserves—and the end of their corporate lives if they stuck exclusively to oil.

So they set out to gain comparable control over other energy resources, uranium and coal. And for the same reason, they are now acquiring the technologies for harnessing geothermal and solar energy. Clearly, the problem is more than a question of safe and unsafe technology.

As a result of their buying binge, 10 of the largest oil companies now hold half the nation's uranium reserves. They also own 40% of the industry's milling capacity, which is used to process ore into yellowcake powder. The reserves and the mills are the foundation on which the entire nuclear power and weapons pyramid is built.

The 10 oil companies, led by Kerr-McGee (see table), include Exxon, Mobil and Gulf, three of the infamous "Seven Sisters" which make up the international oil marketing cartel. This is the cartel that is giving the U.S. its second phony oil "shortage" in five years.

And Gulf, second biggest holder of reserves, was also part of the international uranium cartel. That cartel succeeded in more than quadrupling the price of uranium in the early 1970s.

Commenting on the dominance of the big energy companies, the head of the Tennessee Valley Authority (TVA) warned last month: "The lifeblood of the country is in the hands of a few people who have more power than the government."

TVA chairman David Freeman should know. The giant government utility is the nation's biggest buyer of uranium, as well as the owner of large reserves of ore. Its own operations serve as a yardstick with which to measure the prices and profits of the private companies in the field.

And TVA records, updated at the end of February in "The Structure of the Energy Markets," point to the highly inflationary effect that concentration of nuclear resources has had on uranium prices and utility rates.

The table on this page demonstrates that fewer than 50 companies account for all the major nuclear operations. (Manufacturers of components and the big construction firms, like Bechtel Corp., which build the power stations, have been omitted.)

A few names crop up repeatedly at various stages of the industry and will presumably turn out to be of particular interest to the antinuclear movement.

These companies include Kerr-McGee, Exxon, General Electric, Union Carbide, Allied Chemical and duPont.

Kerr-McGee is already well-established as a primary target, thanks to Karen Silkwood. The company's plutonium fuel fabrication plant in Oklahoma, where Silkwood worked before her alleged murder by company agents, has been shut down.

But Kerr-McGee remains No. 1 in both uranium reserves and milling capacity. Further, the company holds a key position as one of the two processing companies engaged in conversion. (Conversion involves processing before and after enrichment. Yellowcake is transformed into a fluid, and enriched gaseous uranium is solidified in preparation for fabrication into fuel.)

Who Owns What in Nuke Field

1. MINING
Uranium Reserves
Top 20 hold 72%
Kerr-McGee
Gulf Oil
United Nuclear
Exxon
TVA (US)
Phelps Dodge
Atlantic Richfield
Mobil Oil
Continental Oil
General Electric
Getty Oil
Union Oil
Pioneer Nuclear
Phillips Petroleum
Union Pacific-Mono Power
Internat'l Minerals & Chem.
Westinghouse
Union Carbide
Cleveland Cliffs Iron
Commonwealth Edison, Chicago

2. MILLING
Yellowcake
15 own 100% of capacity
Kerr-McGee
United Nuclear-Homestake Mining
Atlantic Richfield
General Electric
Exxon
Continental Oil-Pioneer Electric
Union Carbide
Phelps Dodge
Standard Oil (Ohio)-Reserve Oil & Minerals
Atlas
Union Pacific-Mono Power
Federal Resources-American Nuclear
Rio Tinto Zinc
Commonwealth Edison, Chicago
Newmont Mining

3. CONVERSION
Uranium hexafluoride (UF6)
Uranium dioxide
2 own 100%
Kerr-McGee
Allied Chemical

4. ENRICHMENT
3% uranium for utilities
2 operate 100%
Union Carbide-Oak Ridge, Tenn.

Goodyear Tire & Rubber—Paducah, Ky.
90% uranium for weapons
1 operates 100%
Goodyear Tire & Rubber—Portsmouth, Ky.

5. FABRICATION
Fuel rods, etc.
8 produce 100% of major elements
Uranium
Westinghouse
General Electric
Babcock & Wilcox
Combustion Engineering
Exxon
Gulf Oil-Royal Dutch/Shell
W.R. Grace-Davison Chemicals
Plutonium
Babcock & Wilcox
General Electric
Rockwell International
Shut down:
Kerr-McGee
Gulf Oil-Royal Dutch/Shell
W.R. Grace-Davison Chemicals

6. REACTORS
Elec. generating equip.
5 produce 100%
Westinghouse
General Electric
J. Ray McDermott (Babcock & Wilcox)
Combustion Engineering
General Atomic (Gulf Oil-Royal Dutch/Shell)

7. REPROCESSING
Recovery of plutonium, etc.
Govt. plants
2 companies operate 100%
duPont—Barnwell, S.C.
Allied Chemical—National Reactor Testing, Idaho
Shut down
Getty Oil, West Valley, N.Y.

8. WASTE STORAGE
Temporary facilities
Mostly at sites of 72 operative reactors

High-level waste
Allied Chemical-Gulf Oil-Royal
   Dutch/Shell—Barnwell, S.C.
General Electric, Morris, Ill.
Low-level waste
Allied Chemical-Gulf Oil-Royal
   Dutch/Shell—Barnwell, S.C.
General Electric, Morris, Ill.
Low-level waste
Chem Nuclear—Barnwell, S.C.
Nuclear Engineering
TriState Nuclear
and others

9. WEAPONS
   Govt. plants
   Nuclear materials:
   3 companies make 100%
   Warheads: 7 companies make 100%
   Enrichment

90% uranium
Goodyear Tire & Rubber—Paducah, Ky.
**Reactor materials—
plutonium, tritium, etc.**
duPont—Barnwell, S.C.
United Nuclear—Hanford, Wash.
Components
Rockwell International—Rocky Flats,
   Colo.
Bendix—Kansas City, Mo.
Monsanto—Miamisburg, O.
Union Carbide—Oak Ridge, Tenn.
duPont—Barnwell, S.C.
General Electric—Clearwater, Fla.
Assembly
Mason & Hanger—Silas Mason Co.—
   Amarillo, Tex.

Sources: Tennessee Valley Authority: The Structure of the Energy Markets, 1979 Update, Dept. of Energy; American Nuclear Society.

Exxon's interest in nuclear energy is pervasive. The biggest oil company in the world is also fourth in U.S. uranium reserves, sixth in milling capacity and one of eight fabricators of fuel rods.

Exxon continues to explore for uranium. Last year a Canadian subsidiary made a major discovery and the company is seeking Australian government permission to participate in the development of a large deposit there.

Exxon's fabricating operation (which it says loses money) provides fuel to 10 generating plants in the U.S. and five abroad and has orders for 20 more, according to the 1978 annual report.

A Guide to the Nuclear Bomb Industry

It all began with the bomb. And there'll be no stopping the exploding danger of radiation unless both nuclear power reactors and the weapons program are shut down. (And then there will still be the problem of wastes.)

The production process that results in bombs and missile warheads comes under the jurisdiction of the Department of Energy (DOE), not the Pentagon, as might be expected.

The nuke weapons process starts at the uranium mines in the West, and for part of the way involves the same procedure and the same corporations as nuclear fuel for the utilities.

Then at the enrichment level weapons production develops into a specialty.

As it turns out, the horror of U.S. nuclear weaponry is the domain of only 10 companies. And the pinnacle company—the sole assembler of warheads according to DOE—is an outfit that few people have heard of: Mason & Hanger-Silas Mason Co., a privately owned construction firm based in Lexington, Ky.

For DOE, Mason & Hanger operates the Pantex assembly plant in Amarillo, Tex., under a 1979 contract worth $76 million.

Six Companies

The six companies that supply Mason & Hanger with components are all well known: General Electric, duPont, Union Carbide, Monsanto, Bendix and Rockwell International, which produces triggers at Rocky Flats, Colo.

Further back in the production process, Goodyear Tire & Rubber, duPont and the independent company, United Nuclear, produce the enormously potent materials, such as plutonium, that are packaged into the warheads.

Mason & Hanger, established in 1827, is a heavy construction and engineering firm, historically closely linked with the Army. It is owned by about 75 of its 3800 employees, a company spokesperson told the Guardian. Employees who demonstrate sufficient dedication to the company are allowed to buy stock.

The Pantex plant was originally used to load atomic bombs. Mason & Hanger has been operating it since 1956, currently with 1800 workers. The company spokesperson described it with enthusiasm as "a very good operation."

Further, in partnership with Avco Corp. (finances, aerospace), Exxon is developing a method of uranium enrichment. And it designs storage racks for the pools where utilities temporarily stash their spent fuel rods.

However, General Electric is perhaps more significantly integrated through various levels of the industry. It is ninth in mining reserves, fourth in milling, one of eight fuel fabricators, one of the two leading builders of reactors, a reluctant storer of high-level nuclear wastes (a use found for its inoperable Morris, Ill., reprocessing plant). And it is also one of the half-dozen producers of components for nuclear weapons.

Union Carbide, a conglomerate with a wide variety of interests mostly relating to minerals and metals, operates the famous gaseous diffusion plant at Oak Ridge, Tenn., built during World War 2 to enrich uranium for the bomb. (It was powered, and still is, by TVA electricity.) The company also owns uranium reserves, milling capacity and produces components for weapons.

Allied Chemical, Goodyear Tire & Rubber and E.I. duPont de Nemours merit attention for they, like Union Carbide, seem to have a near-monopoly of certain nuclear technology. Allied, for instance, is one of the two currently operating reprocessing plants (which recover plutonium and other materials from reactor waste).

Goodyear Tire operates one of the two government enrichment plants and is the sole producer of weapons grade uranium.

And duPont, the biggest U.S. chemical company and a historic producer of conventional explosives, has moved with the times. It operates a reprocessing plant and produces reactor materials and components for weapons all at the government installation at Barnwell, S.C.

The strategic position of these corporations in the nuclear industry is only a hint of their power. They are also among the largest industrial companies in the country. Exxon ranks No. 2, Mobil 4, Gulf Oil 7, General Electric 8, duPont 16, Union Carbide 21, Goodyear 22, Allied Chemical 84 and Kerr-McGee 142—on the Fortune 500 Largest list.

But even their massive size is not the whole story. A Senate study of directorates made last year looked into both direct interlocks (where a director sits on two corporate boards) and indirect interlocks (where two corporate directors meet on a third board).

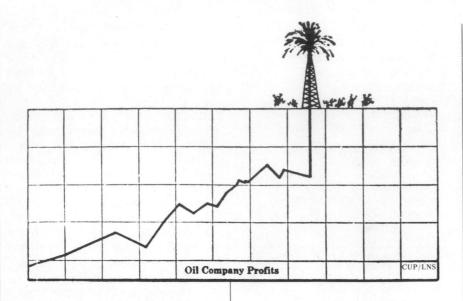

Oil Company Profits

CUP/LNS

The study showed that Exxon, for instance, interlocked indirectly with its supposed competitor Mobil Oil six times and with Atlantic Richfield (see list) four times.

Exxon also had one direct and eight indirect interlocks with American Tel. & Tel., 15 with General Motors and, among many others, direct interlocks with Citicorp, Chase Manhattan, Prudential Life, Metropolitan Life, in addition to six indirect locks with J.P. Morgan.

In short, the nuclear industry is embedded in the heart of U.S. capitalism. If you want to be effective, you can't attack one without attacking the other.

the magazine of radical science and peoples' technology

UNDERCURRENTS

From *Undercurrents*, no. 37 (December 1979/January 1980), pp. 32-33

Silkwood and After

by Jim Garrison and Clair Ryle

When Karen Silkwood was run off the road and killed on Nov. 13, 1974, she was carrying documentation that she said would prove conclusively that the Kerr-McGee (KM) Nuclear Corporation was guilty not only of gross violations of worker health and safety standards but of quality control regulations as well. She worked at the KM plutonium facility in Oklahoma as a lab technician; she was also a union representative with a special responsibility for the area of worker health and safety. As a union representative for this area, she had interviewed all the KM

Reprinted with permission from *Undercurrents,* the magazine of radical alternatives and community technology.

workers who had ever reported management violations of the health and safety rules; she had memorized the Atomic Energy Commission (AEC) regulations promulgated to safeguard the health of the workers; and she had conducted her own health and safety inspections of the plant during her free time, compiling a list of over forty serious violations. Her concerns were primarily because of the fact that workers were put on the plutonium production lines without any training in many cases; because of radioactive spills that were so large that dozens of workers were getting irradiated at a time; and because the KM management, in order to meet production quotas, ordered the workers to stand in the contaminated areas and *continue working* while clean-up crews attempted to clean up the mess around them.

Magic Marker

The most serious violation Karen discovered, however, involved the fact that KM officials were knowingly 'doctoring' with *magic marker*, the safety inspection

X-rays which, by AEC regulations, had to be taken of each plutonium fuel rod to insure that it was not leaking radiation through faulty welding. The AEC demanded perfectly welded fuel rods because, if defective, they could cause a serious accident in the plutonium fired liquid metal fast breeder reactor they were designed for. On Nov. 1 just 12 days before she was killed, Karen finally secured copies of two separate 'magic-marker doctored' fuel rod safety inspection X-rays, doctored by one Scott Dotter, the special laboratory technician who the KM management had specifically assigned to conduct the final safety inspection X-raying of the fuel rods. Silkwood discovered that not only was he doctoring up the X-rays indicating faulty welds but that the mere *number* of the fuel rods he 'cleared' each week was *itself* a direct violation of AEC regulations requiring that no one inspector be allowed to give the final clearance on over a certain percentage of the fuel rods leaving the plant.

On the night of Nov. 13, Silkwood was carrying the above information to Steve Wodka, a union official, and Dave Burnham, an investigative reporter for the *New York Times*. She never got to the meeting. As mentioned, she was hit in the rear, forced off the road, and killed. Her car was towed away, and the documents she had with her disappeared.

Callous

Over four years later, in the Spring of 1979, a federal court case brought against KM by Karen's parents has proven that what she was asserting concerning KM was in fact true. One of the witnesses, Dr. Karl Morgan, often referred to as the 'father of health physics' for his role in the setting of standards for radiation releases in nuclear

karen silkwood... willing to go ahead when other people were afraid

Win/LNS

facilities, testified that the KM plant where Karen had worked was the 'filthiest' nuclear facility he had ever seen in his thirty years in the industry besides the reprocessing plant in New York. He further stated that KM showed a 'callous' attitude towards the safety of its workers, pointing out that the KM training manuals made no mention of the fact that one could contract cancer from radiation exposure.

Paper Geigers

Former plant workers stated under oath that their training had been so deficient that teenage workers, not even aware that plutonium was toxic, often played at who could get 'the hottest the fastest'. Workers said that plutonium spills were often painted over instead of cleaned up if they kept happening in the same place often enough, workers left the plant contaminated, and plant supervisors were warned ahead of time of upcoming 'surprise' AEC inspections. There was also testimony stating that workers used uranium for paper weights, threw it around the rooms at each other, and even took uranium home to give to the children to take to school for 'show and tell'. One of the four plant supervisors, Jim Smith, branded the KM Nuclear Facility a 'pigpen', testifying that security was so lax, workers could have thrown plutonium over the back fence or simply taken it past the guards by telling them it was to be thrown out as waste.

As to the question of the faulty fuel rods, workers testified that there were defects in both the stainless steel tubes that form the outside of the rods *and* in the fuel pellets put into the stainless steel tubes. One worker, Ron Hammock, testified that 'even though we rejected them, we would go ahead and ship them because we were too far behind in production.' He said workers under orders from their KM supervisors would simply sand down the welds which seemed defective, which weakened them even further.

Guilty

After hearing these facts, the six person jury found KM guilty and decided to award $10 million in punitive damages to deter KM from continuing negligent corporate practices that endanger the lives of employees. The jury also awarded $550,000 for personal injury damages, making KM responsible for the plutonium planted in Silkwood's apartment a week before her death and for the internal bodily contamination she suffered as a result.

The Silkwood victory is still not complete, however, for the faulty fuel rods she died trying to reveal the facts about are slated to be *used* in the plutonium Fast Flux Test Facility (FFTF) before the end of the year. Loading of the fuel pins is expected to start in November, 1979, and the reactor is scheduled to 'go critical' in the Spring or Summer of 1980.

Owned by the Westinghouse Hanford Company, the FFTF is located near Richland, Washington, and is considered the current centerpiece of the long and so far unsuccessful campaign by the government and the nuclear industry to commercialise the liquid metal fast breeder reactor (LMFBR).

Dream Cycle

LMFBR's are the nuclear industry's dream of the future and the answer to the industry's most critical question: where to get enough fuel to keep their plutonium economy running. Nuclear power plants are now fueled with uranium but less than one percent of natural uranium is the fissionable isotope U-235 which the reactors need to operate. When uranium is mined, therefore, it must go through an extremely capital and energy intensive process to 'enrich' it to the desired level of U-235—generally between 3 and 4%. The inherent inefficiency of this process, however coupled with skyrocketing prices for both the uranium itself and the energy used to mine, mill, enrich, fabricate, and transport it, is threatening the entire industry with economic bankruptcy.

The answer given to this problem is not the obvious one: that the nuclear fuel cycle be shut down and recycled into alternative energy schemes. Rather, government and the nuclear industry assert that what must be done is to build huge breeder reactors which will produce or 'breed' new plutonium fuel even as it burns the fuel in its core. This is accomplished when atoms of abundant but otherwise useless Uranium-238 absorb neutrons which are produced in the fissioning of the plutonium. The breeder thus turns into fuel part of the 99% of the natural uranium which ordinary reactors do not use.

Failure Point

Various designs have been proposed for breeders, but the one which has been selected for development is the LMFBR—so called because it uses liquid sodium metal as a coolant, and because it relies on fast moving neutrons for breeding.

The Westinghouse FFTF has been designed as a testing facility for future breeders. It is not designed to generate electricity; instead, the 400 megawatts of power it generates—an enormous amount for a 'test' facility—will be dumped into the desert air of eastern Washington. Nor will the FFTF breed any plutonium, as this is unnecessary for its experimental purposes. In every other way, however, it will operate exactly like a LMFBR.

The Department of Energy, who contracted the Westinghouse Corporation for the facility, plans to push some fuel rods to their failure point. It also plans to place in test positions fuel that is known to be defective. Although the 'experts' insist that there is no danger in this, they base these assertions on 'mathematical modelling' and computer predictions. They expect the FFTF to 'verify' these predictions. But what if their predictions are wrong? If they are, the people living near the facility will be the real experimental guinea pigs.

Supercritical

Nor is this all. The 9,000 fuel rods that the KM plutonium plant produced are to be used as the 'driver' fuel which will power the reactor. Faulty fuel rods here are acknowledged even by the government to be potentially catastrophic, for a faulty fuel rod can casue a disturbance in the flow of the sodium coolant. If this is done, then the liquid sodium might not reach a portion of the fuel it is meant to cool. This blockage can lead to what the 'experts' euphemistically call a 'core disruptive accident'. In plain English this means a nuclear explosion. Unlike normal reactors which, if there is a meltdown release larger amounts of radioactivity in the form of a cloud, breeders, because they work off plutonium, can go supercritical and explode like nuclear bombs.

As early as January of 1975, the Westinghouse Corp. receiving the KM fuel rods stated that 57 of one particular shipment were not 'free of all visible oxide, scale, splits, laps, cracks, seams, inclusions

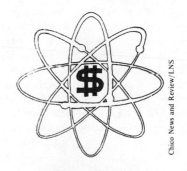

Chico News and Review/LNS

and other defects.' Thirty-eight of these were eventually accepted by the Department of Energy, however, because it 'determined that the defects were minor', according to Leroi Rice, a quality control official at the project. A May 1975 report from Westinghouse indicates that a quality assurance supervisor was using scotch brite on fuel pins listed as having clad inclusions. Although the inspector was told that these pins would not be shipped, they were shipped the following month.

Appeasement

KM engaged in a production speed-up around June 1974 as well which according to worker testimony in the Silkwood trial led to a situation where even inspection of the fuel rods ceased. When the speed-up was announced, they no longer examined all the sides of the fuel rods, only the side visible to them. A later report by the Energy Research Development Agency (ERDA) confirmed this testimony, although KM replied that the regulations did not require a complete examination. The workers also pointed out that visual examination could not reveal defects on hidden surfaces. To appease the public and fulfill their regulatory responsibilities, ERDA did eventually evaluate some fuel rods from one particular lot and had two of the rods examined through cross sectioning. ERDA's findings were that the rods examined were acceptable. A report by Battelle laboratories in Hanford three months later, however, asserted that one of the fuel rods ERDA had examined contained a large defect that had not been detected in previous examinations.

Protest Now!

A Government Accounting Office (GAO) investigator finally stated the obvious by recommending that each and every fuel rod be checked. The Department of Energy, however, has resisted this recommendation and has refused to even let an independent investigative panel undertake a study of the fuel rods. The official reason for this refusal is that any such study would be 'prohibitively expensive'. When the plant was proposed in the late 1960's, it was expected to cost $87.5 million. Now that construction is complete, costs have risen to over $647 million. Inserting the fuel rods and firing up the reactor will bring total costs to over $1 thousand million. With the lives of people all over the northwest part of the United States at stake, we must ask the Department of Energy whether this is the time to start cutting costs.

Time is short. The fuel rods are scheduled to be fixed into the core this month but they have not yet actually started to do this. *Local anti-nuclear organisers around Richland, Washington have asked for national and international support.* They have asked that letters be sent to certain key senators who have expressed interest in holding hearings on the matter. If hearings are held, the current schedule of fuel rod insertion will be postponed indefinitely. The two Senators are Sen. Hart and Sen. Hatfield. Any letters sent to Sen. Hart should ask specifically that he call for indepth hearings on the FFTF through reviewing the material. The letter to Hatfield should encourage him to continue the inquiries into the Nuclear Regulatory Commission recommendations to the Department of Energy on the safety issue concerning the FFTF. He had stated that if he is not satisfied with the Department of Energy's response he will ask the GAO to hold hearings. At this time the GAO appears to be the only branch of the US government that is capable of holding objective hearings.

ADDRESSES:
Senator Gary Hart
254 Russell
Senate Office Building
Washington, D.C. 20510

Senator Hatfield
1401 Dirksen
Senate Office Building
Washington, D.C. 20510

LOCAL CONTACT PERSON:
Creg Darby
Hanford Conversion Project
P.O. Box 524
Pasco, WA 99301

FOR MORE INFORMATION:
Claire Ryle, Jim Garrison
RADIATION & HEALTH INFORMA—
TION SERVICE,
9 Marion Close
Cambridge CB3 OHN
0223-350917.

MIDWEST ENERGY TIMES

Serving The Safe Energy Network

From *Midwest Energy Times*, April 6, 1979, p. 3

Multi-Nationals Call Black Hills 'National Sacrifice Area' in Bid for Coal and Uranium Mines

Uranium mining is about to begin in the Black Hills of western South Dakota. This region has been slated as a "national sacrifice area" as part of the federal government's Energy Independence Program. Over 700,000 acres of the Black Hills are now being explored by multi-national corporations. These include Kerr-McGee, Tennessee Valley Authority (T.V.A.),

Reprinted with permission from *Midwest Energy Times*, Madison, Wisconsin.

Union Carbide, Mobil, Gulf Oil, Westinghouse, and Exxon. There are already over 100,000 claims staked. The uranium deposits lie in a cresent shaped formation which circles around the eastern edge of the hills from the Edgemont in the south and as far as the northwestern corner of South Dakota.

In the early 1950's uranium was discovered in the area around Edgemont. Several corporations including Union Carbide and the T.V.A. explored the area and ran mining operations until 1972, when it became financially unprofitable. According to Bruce Ellison, an attorney for the Black Hills Alliance: "That mining operation has already produced radioactivity in Edgemont's water supply far above the 'safe' limits. Run-off from the blowing dust of the old mill tailings has radioactively contaminated the streams and surrounding land. Renewed uranium development in this area can only produce worse damage, irreparable damage." Open pit mines, strip mines, solution mines, new railroad systems, and the influx of hundreds of thousands of boom-town workers are some of the visible effects that can be expected if these corporations are allowed to mine.

Uranium mining—the front end of the nuclear fuel cycle—is a highly toxic undertaking. It produces radioactive by-products which will contaminate the water tables and poison the air. Officials in the United Mine Workers Union estimate that 80-90% of uranium miners can expect to die of lung cancer. By 1975, 25 of the 100 Navajo miners who worked in the Mesa Mine in the Four Corners region, were already dead of lung cancer. In the area around Edgemont (Fall River County) where uranium was mined in the 1950's, the cancer rate is twice that of any other county in South Dakota. Uranium mill tailings—about 3 million pounds of them—were left in the open 100 yards from the Cheyenne River. Blowing dust and the leaching from rain into the water tables and surrounding areas have contaminated the whole town.

Uranium is only one of many major areas of energy development. All mining in South Dakota has been made more feasible due to U.S. District Court Judge Bogue's recent decision that companies do not need to file an Environmental Impact Statement to get a patent for their mining operations. Beyond the mining of uranium, several large companies also plan to strip-mine the Black Hills for coal. They will take 2.6 million acre-feet of water per year and they estimate they will run out of water before they run out of coal.

AMERIKA - YOU ARE LIVING ON THE BLOOD OF THE INDIAN NATION

Rachel Burger/LNS

The plan that the T.V.A. has put forth calls for five major pit mines, three of which will need water diverted from the Cheyenne River and pumped back in. How the T.V.A. plans to decontaminate that water is something that has yet to be explained. Extensive dewatering plans and the probability of radioactive runoff revealed by the T.V.A.'s Draft Environmental Statement have caused much consternation among local residents. T.V.A. had originally promised to make up for any lost water by installing pumps or hauling water themselves; area ranchers and farmers now report that corporations refused to enter into any such agreements.

The key to all the exploration activities is water. Near-droughts in the area and conflicting estimates as to actual amounts of water present and replenishable have created concern among many. So has the lack of consultation with and consideration of Native tribes regarding the usurpation of their water rights.

The circle of nuclear energy begins and ends with water, as it begins and ends with people's rights (particularly Native people's). As massive amounts of precious water are used for all anticipated energy "development," and as construction of uranium mines, mills and nuclear power plants creates contaminated drinking supplies, this area faces the real possibility of becoming a radioactive desert. The Black Hills becomes a prime target for disposal of this country's thirty-year accumulation of nuclear waste: A "National Sacrifice Area."

It is important to recognize that the politics of nuclear power are intricately bound with Native American sovereignty. Over two-thirds of the uranium reserves in the United States are found on Indian land. In 1974 100% of the uranium produced in this country came from Native American land. Indian peoples are subjected to severe repression by three stages of the nuclear fuel cycle: (1) mining, (2) milling and processing uranium, and (3) the disposal of radioactive waste. Exxon corporation has a 400,000 acre lease in the Navajo nation, a lease that could not be approved until the Secretary of the Interior had waived 13 regulations. Exxon is planning to dispose of radioactive waste on these leased lands. The Navajo and Spokane Nations are the major suppliers of uranium. The Bureau of Indian Affairs approves the leases for the mining of Indian land.

The Black Hills are historically the

sacred, ancestral lands of the Lakota people—a place where over the centuries the Lakotas have gathered in prayer and ceremony. Throughout the hills there are many formations, artifacts, and wall paintings which have a special spiritual significance to the people. In 1868 the Fort Laramie Treaty between the U.S. government and the Lakotas insured rights of sovereignty and self-determination in the Black Hills region for "as long as the grass shall grow, and the rivers run." This is still a valid legal document.

Native Peoples are demanding a right to their own sovereignty, self-determination, and to a radiation-free future for their children. The Black Hills Alliance and friends, actively support Native struggles and urge others to do so too.

Nuclear technology is a violent technology. It is violent at all stages of the nuclear fuel cycle. Harrisburg sits on a foundation of death and destruction. It was not an accident, not a fluke, but the logical and end-product of such a technology. The Black Hills have been labeled a "national sacrifice" area. In truth we have all been sacrificed to the multi-national corporate structure. We have been sacrificed to greed and profit. Before we can insure a world free of technologies of death, we must actively confront the corporate state. Only then will we be free from the omnipresent threat of nuclear power.

Akwesasne Notes/LNS

Northern Sun News

From *Northern Sun News* 2, no. 3 (March 1979): 2-3

Exploiting Indians' Lands for the Hard Energy Path

by Merle Greene

Indian nations have been in the Western Hemisphere for a long, long time. The U.S. government, by comparison just new-born, has systematically exploited the Indian lands and resources and the native people.

Historical experience is a tragic precedent: copper and iron from the Chippewa, gold from the Black Hills—sacred to the Lakota, and oil from Oklahoma.

Today there are new frontiers. Mobil Oil, Kerr-McGee, Exxon, Gulf and Continental Oil, and Anaconda, to name a few, are leasing large areas of Indian land for mining uranium and coal. In 1975 Indians received 60¢ a pound for uranium valued at $30 a pound on the market.

Yet Indian people continue to live in poverty and dependence (the annual per capita income of the Navaho people is $900 a year), while multi-national energy corporations thrive. The issue is multi-faceted: Riding in the balance are questions of

- contaminated water
- polluted air and land
- diseased inhabitants in areas with high levels of radioactivity
- exploitation of Indian land through govt. and corporate collaboration
- cultural and physical genocide of Indian peoples. (K)

The Bureau of Indian Affairs (BIA)

Lands of the Indian nations are in trust with the federal government. This means that the Bureau of Indian Affairs, a part of the Dept. of the Interior, acts on behalf of the govt. to regulate Indian affairs.

The rationale for leasing Indian land was, undoubtedly, to generate revenue. For whom?—is the question. Indians make a pittance off the leases, while national and multinational corporations get cheap labor and cheap minerals.

There seems to be, however, a conflict of interest since the Dept. of Interior—which is finally responsible for BIA decisions—also administers the Bureau of Reclamation and the Bureau of Mines. Many of the leases negotiated for use of Indian land are for durations 15 times that of average public land leases. (B)

Federal officials have always had a hard time distinguishing Indian resources from public resources. This explains, in part, their rationale for leasing. Public land is usually leased for royalties in dollars per unit as opposed to a percentage of production value. So the BIA tends to follow the same policies in regard to Indian land, and offer leases with the same clear conscience.

In addition, the BIA has no independent statistics on the number, quality, value or market of natural resources on the land it is expected to administrate. And, unlike private corporations, the BIA has no real incentive to maximize Indian revenues. "The government is the trustee of the Indians and coordinator of the national energy policy. That has to be a conflict of interest." (C)

Many corporations are sitting on the coal land they are leasing while the land value rises. "Lease speculation is rampant," reports the Council of Economic Priorities of New York, a non-profit, public-interest organization. "Over 25% of all federal leases have changed hands since 1973 and 1/3 of all state leases have been assigned at least once" (meaning they have changed ownership).

Only a very small number of the leases are now in production. A law was passed in 1975 to require corporations to begin production within 10 years of purchase or forfeit the lease, but this does not apply to prior leases. (H)

Uranium Mining in South Dakota

Fifty-five percent of the U.S. uranium supply is on Native American land. Most of that is concentrated on the Navajo and Laguna Pueblo reservations and in the Black Hills areas of South Dakota, the Paha Sapa.

Uranium mining and milling is to begin in the Paha Sapa by 1979-81. Over 99,000 acres of uranium claims have already been laid by the energy corporations through the U.S. government. Large blocks of uranium claims have been filed on land near Edgemont in the Black Hills National Forest and in the Nemo Canyon between Rapid City and Deadwood and in the Custer National Forest.

Uranium mining in the Black Hills is highly undesirable for several reasons:

1) Local land is owned and controlled by outside corporations. The Tennessee Valley Authority (TVA), Union Carbide and Yoming Minerals (Westinghouse) have large claims in the southern Black Hills. Because TVA is a federal agency, local and state residents and governments have little control over it.

"If land has been purchased or leased by someone from the state and mineral exploration or mining permits are granted to developers, the mineral permit-holder has prior rights over the surface landowner or leasee. They can drill, build, or mine and the surface operator can only ask for damages." (I)

2) Large quantities of water are needed by uranium developers. Extracting uranium from sandstone, for example, involves a process of pumping chemicals into an aquafir. In the past, aquifers have been contaminated.

3) Air and soil are polluted by radioactive gas and dust, especially when uraniferous coal (coal containing uranium) is burned. Due to TVA's mining in the 50's and 60's, Edgemont's water is radioactive above safe limits. The run-off and blowing dust from old mill tailings and tailings ponds has created contamination of streams and surrounding lands. Fall River County, in which Edgemont is located, has twice the cancer rate of any county in South Dakota. (I)

Uranium Mining on Navaho Lands

The Southwest is the second focus for uranium mining:

- The world's largest uranium stripmine is located near the eastern border of the Navaho reservation.
- Exxon is now mining and milling on 400,000 acres in the Four Corners area of the Navajo Nation.
- Gulf Oil is sinking the world's deepest mine shaft into Mt. Taylor, one of the four sacred mountains of the Navaho people. (K)

Past experience allows little optimism for the future. In 1969 Kerr-McGee's uranium mines were exhausted after 16 years. During that time, Indians earned as little as $1.60/hr. for working the mines. By

June 1977, 18 of the 100 Navaho miners were dead and 21 more were feared dying. (Figures were much higher in other sources.) Kerr-McGee refused responsibility for their illness and would not pay medical expenses. It spokesman pointed out that Kerr-McGee had interests all over the country and couldn't be expected to keep up with a few mines in Arizona. (E)

Families near Red Rock had never been informed of the radioactive nature of the tailings and actually used them to construct their homes. A study by the Environmental Protection Agency in 1975 found serious radioactive contamination of the drinking water supply, as well, near the mines and mills of Grants, a boom town.

The first demonstration of Indian (and non-Indian) people against the nuclear industry took place at the same time as the Seabrook rally last June. The National Indian Youth Council (NIYC) and Citizens Against Nuclear Threats called for a moratorium on all new mining until the problems of untreated radioactive tailings and the stabilization and seepage into ground water are solved. (K)

Thus far, one major concession has been won in the courts. Until recently, the Navaho people received a small lease fee plus 13¢ per ton of coal (2% its market value), according to a 1960's agreement. (Note that there is a discrepancy between these statistics and those cited in the introduction of this article.) The coal companies then paid taxes to both state and federal governments.

The Navajos have since filed suit and won. The Copple Decision forces five corporations which operate a $600 million generating plant in Page, Arizona to pay taxes to the Indians. This could significantly affect the Cheyenne and Crow Indians, who are now studying the decision.

Coal Mining on Navaho Lands

The NIYC and 13 residents from the

Nichols/N.L.G./LNS

Navajo community of Burnham, New Mexico, have filed suit to stop the proposed coal stripmining on the Navaho reservation.

The defendants include the Sec. of the Interior, the Commissioner of the Bureau of Reclamation, the Director of the U.S. Geological Survey and the Director of the Natl. Park Service. The suit charged that the leasing and consequent exploitation of the Navajo land will result in irreparable damage to the Navajo lifestyle, land, air and water.

The proposed coal stripmine will force 200 Navajo people from their homes. They now live by raising livestock and dry farming. Many Navajo people, relocated as a result of similar energy projects, have been forced to move into nearby cities—a transition that makes practice of their lifestyle and culture difficult.

Navaho culture will be adversely affected in other ways. The land in question contains many burial sites and areas of religious importance. It also sustains native herbs used in healing ceremonies.

Much of the Four Corners area was occupied from 900-1300 A.D. by a pre-pueblo Indian culture. These peoples developed sophisticated agricultural systems and transportation routes. Remnants of their culture will be destroyed unless there is a full inventory of the area before mining begins.

The land is also rich with paleontological treasures. There are only three other places in the world with as rich a geological formation as that found in northwestern New Mexico. Yet the Environmental Impact Statement neglected to consider any of this.

A final concern, which summarizes most of the above, is that the reclamation promised by the Consolidated Coal Company and El Paso Natural Gas Company (CONPASO) will be inadequate. Because of the harsh, unpredictable weather, and lack of water, the Navahos claim that full reclamation of the land would be next to impossible. (D)

Coal and the Northern Cheyenne

There are 5 billion tons of coal under the North Cheyenne reservation—about 90% of all surface strippable coal in the U.S. It is particularly valuable because the coal has a low-sulphur content and can more easily meet air quality control standards.

The North Central Power Study—consisting of a number of corporations—wants to invest in mining and electric

utilities in the area. Their effort was supported by the government even though many of the 40+ coal-fired generating plants were on 1868 Treaty lands and some on or near reservations.

The reservation land is already leased or optioned for stripmining although actual mining has started only off the reservation. Impact on neighboring reservations was not considered. The Indians' concerns (similar to those of their white neighbors in Wyoming near Douglas and Red Desert) are as follows:

● the effect on residents' lifestyle: not allowing time to prepare for impact of mines and mills. (B)

● use of Indian labor only for unskilled jobs.

● influx of non-Indian labor for skilled work.

● creation of an "instant city" with all its social problems.

● insufficient water to meet both mining needs and needs of the land, plant and wild life and people. It is feared that river and drainage system will breakdown with industrial use. (B)

Because of ambiguous language in different sources, it is unclear whether AMAX, Chevron, Consolidated and Peabody Coal Companies and NSP have from 1966-73 mined on the Northern Cheyenne land through some kind of permit or lease—or whether the "agreements" are still tentative. There is a consensus among the sources, however, that 56% of the Northern Cheyenne reservation was or will be victimized by corporate mining. (A)

In 1973 the Northern Cheyenne Research Project was organized. Its purpose is to get information on the effect of off-reservation developments. Inventories of gas and oil on the reservation will also be made, since the BIA has none. (C)

The Northern Cheyenne Council has accused, the BIA of a breach of trust for advising—against the interest of the tribe—to accept "unconscionably low economic terms" and has directed it to terminate all coal permits and leases. (B)

The violations were so flagrant that the Dept. of Interior responded to the Tribe's petition by virtually stopping all coal work. The Cheyenne then filed for a new air quality status for their lands—Class One ("pristine")—and won! The Montana Power Company was, therefore, denied construction permits for coal mines Colstrips 3 and 4.

A new court decision (North Cheyenne

v. Hollowbreast, 1976) allows the tribe to function as a unit in negotiating land and mineral rights, rather than as a loose affiliation of individuals (with whom companies prefer to bargain).

Perhaps most important, tribes have come to realize that the best way to insure sovereignty over their lands is to exercise it. Private interests have been immensely successful in gaining access to reservation resources because the tribes themselves had never passed "legislation" (isn't it ironic?) to the contrary. Now the newly-created Environmental Protection Commission will adopt its own regulatory legislation.

The People's Grand Jury, Washington, D.C., however, reports the future less optimistically. It was generally felt that such moves won't stop the strippers, only slow them down. AMAX, in their 1974 annual report, describes it in terms of "delay and increased costs." (A)

Rhode Island Powerline

The Narragansett Indians of Rhode Island are engaged in a struggle similar to that of the farmers in South Central Minnesota. The New England Power Co. (NEPCO) wants to construct a powerline through tribal land. So far, construction has been delayed: first, a cooling system plan was rejected; later, the General Services Administration, which was contracting with NEPCO, neglected to file an environmental impact statement.

Apparently an alternative route is planned. But if a nuclear plant is built nearby, the same problem will surface again. At best, all lines will be routed around the claim and the two reactors will be only a few miles away.

Here's the good news: since 1974 the nuclear plant has fallen four years behind schedule and its cost has risen enough to make financiers nervous. (J)

We all are (or will soon be) threatened by the effects of nuclear energy—whether in the mining of uranium, the production process, the disposal of its wastes, or in the threat to civil liberties resulting from a fear of nuclear sabotage.

But, if any one people is immediately affected by uranium and coal mining, and their after-effects, it is the American Indian. What they have at stake is not only their land, air and water, but their survival as a people. Encroachment on their land challenges their way of life as well as their sovereignty over what little land they have left.

Bibliography

An attempt has been made to document this information as carefully as possible. Since small bits of info were drawn from diverse sources, it is hard to be exact without elaborate footnotes.

The capital letters in parenthesis cite the source(s) for most of the preceding paragraphs.

(A) *The AMAX War Against Humanity* by the People's Grand Jury, Washington, D.C.

(B) *The Third Internatl. Indian Treaty Conference*, Standing Rock Sioux Reservation, Wakpala, S.D., June 1977.

(C) *Akwesasne Notes*, Autumn 1978.

(D) *Americans Before Columbus*, May 1978, "NIYC and Navajos Sue to Stop Stripmining."

(E) Native American Solidarity Committee. March 1978.

(G) *Akwesasne Notes.* Late Spring 1978, "Now This is Planned" by Russell Means.

(H) *Mpls. Tribune*, Nov. 13, 1978. "Coal Leasing Seen as Giveaway of Resources."

(I) *S.D. Uranium Development Fact Sheet:* 'Do You Know?' by S.D. Representative Friends of the Earth, Alpena, S.D.

(J) *Progressive*, Aug. 1978. "Indians and Nuclear 'Progress'" by Bill Solomon.

(K) *WIN*, July 20, 1978, "Native People Oppose Uranium Mining in New Mexico."

From *Seven Days* 3, no. 7 (June 5, 1979): 23-26, 34

The Chemistry of Risk: Synthesizing the Corporate Ideology of the 1980s

by David F. Noble

You don't need a conspiracy—tho there was on a baser or street level, i.e., murders, bribery, beatings, trickery, payoffs to military, etc.—but you do have a movement—as if oil had a Voice—of "right-minded" men thoughtful, conservative, well fed, and well paid, all dependent on petro-chemical culture—exquisite executives and exquisite academicians—all with clean hands. . . . And the Government thru foundations was supporting a whole

field of "scholars of war" who took as an assumption that the culture of the West was rightly built on petrochemical scientism.

"T.S. Eliot Entered my Dreams,"
Allan Ginsberg

You can't turn on the tube or turn the page of a newspaper or magazine these days without being assured that chemistry is life itself or that risk taking is nature's way. Ironically, these messages are being brought to us by Monsanto, Union Carbide, and the other giants of the petrochemical industry, an industry that specializes in producing nonbiodegradable synthetic chemicals unknown to nature—chemicals whose use involves risks essential to life only as it must be lived in modern corporate capitalist society. Propaganda like this could give nature a bad name. Why are the petrochemical companies spreading it now, and what does it all mean?

Remember how in *The Graduate* Dustin Hoffman's uncle advised him to go into "plastics"? He was right. Since World War II, the modern petrochemical industry—makers of detergents, films, synthetic fibers, pesticides, etc., as well as plastics—

has been among the most successful in the U.S. in terms both of growth rate and profitability.

But during the past decade, the industry has been under increasing attack as a result of the adverse environmental and health effects of its synthetic chemical products—in particular, DDT, PCB, Kepone, fluorocarbons, vinyl chloride, acrylonitrile, benzene, and saccharin. For the industry, this attack has meant skyrocketing product-liability insurance premiums and costly court settlements, such as the $13 million in damages charged to Allied Chemical in lawsuits over a recent incident involving the dumping of the toxic pesticide Kepone in Virginia's James River. Most important, the attack has come from new-style governmental regulatory agencies such as the Environmental Protection Agency (EPA), the Occupational Health and Safety Administration (OSHA), and the Consumer Products Safety Commission (CPSC). The laws under which these agencies operate make them capable of doing more than hurting the public image of corporate giants. They can hurt profit margins as well. For example, the Toxic Substances Control Act (TSCA), passed in late 1976, empowers the EPA administrator to regulate the manufacture and distribution of chemical substances—such as DuPont and Monsanto's acrylonitrile and Hooker Chemical Company's PCB—judged to "present an unreasonable risk of injury to health or the environment." Also particularly damaging to the industry has been the Delaney Amendment to the Food, Drug and Cosmetic Act which requires that the Food and Drug Administration ban all food additives—such as saccharin—known to cause cancer in humans or laboratory animals.

Having failed to prevent the enactment of the regulatory legislation in the first place, the chemical companies are now embarking upon a sweeping counterattack, designed to deprive regulatory agencies of popular support, undermine their effectiveness from within, and generate public confusion about the issues. It's a tall order, but they have ample unnatural resources at their disposal. Working independently and collectively, the chemical companies are pushing a four-pronged attack against regulation: (1) a propaganda campaign; (2) political efforts—the so-called regulation-reform movement; (3) methodological efforts—the legitimation of "risk-accounting"; and (4) ideological efforts.

1. The Propaganda Attack

Mobil Oil, knighted by *Fortune* last year as the "champ of advocacy advertisers," spent $3.2 million on "grass-roots lobbying." Everyone is familiar with the Mobil ads by now—and their message that regulation is a threat to free enterprise. Such "issue advertising," as it is called, has become a common form of influencing public opinion, and the petrochemical industry is a leader in the field.

Monsanto's theme is: "Without chemicals, life itself would be impossible"; but the chemical their ads focus on is "ordinary table salt," not acrylonitrile or PCB or DDT. The ads suggest again and again and again that chemicals are natural, benign, and essential to life as we know it. No mention of synthetics or carcinogens, only the repeated whines: Where would we be without chemicals? Where would we be without the white-coated wonders of science? Where would we be without Monsanto?

Union Carbide is relatively new to the mass propaganda business but has been coming up to speed quickly over the past year. A corporate giant with over $7 billion in sales in 1977, Union Carbide produces such well-known consumer products as Everready batteries, Glad bags, and Prestone antifreeze as well as a great number of industrial products. In the early 1970s, the management stonewalled public and governmental efforts to make the company clean up plants that were polluting the air over large areas of West Virginia: *Fortune* observed that "the imbroglio had earned the company the reputation of a reactionary ogre obsessed with profits and disdainful of the environment."

In 1976 Union Carbide responded by pulling all its public-relations activities together under one roof—the Communications Department—and giving it orders to "engage in public policy dialogue on issues that affect our business." Union Carbide's Communications Department identifies key issues—which range from energy policy to international trade to environmental safety—and then sets up the multi-million-dollar strategies for dealing with them. Propaganda efforts include speeches, tapes, canned editorials, and educational films for public schools, disseminated from a central Washington office and "public-affairs centers" in twenty states. Some two hundred Union Carbide managers are currently busy giving speeches, lobbying, writing articles for newspapers and magazines, and otherwise spreading the prepackaged company line.

Jackson Browning, corporate director of health, safety and environmental affairs for Union Carbide admits, "We are well aware that the public is suspicious of the chemical industry as a whole." In their attempt to counteract this well-founded distrust of the industry, Browning and his associates have

Bülbül/LNS

adopted a dignified, "Come let us reason together," style intended to give the appearance of putting the question of risk "in a reasonable perspective" and eliminate emotional nearsightedness. Their propaganda is paradoxical, appealing to people's emotional need to view themselves as rational. After all, everyone would like to think that they are behaving in a sober, reasonable manner even when dealing with "hot" issues such as cancer, which arouse genuine fear, suspicion and hostility.

There is little doubt that the firms are cooperating in their propaganda effort. Just as they worked together with the Business Roundtable (an association of the largest American corporations) to defeat the labor-law reforms last summer, so Monsanto, Union Carbide, Allied Chemical, Dow, and DuPont are coordinating their antiregulatory campaign, under the auspices of such chemical-industrial groups as the Manufacturing Chemists Association (MCA), the American Industrial Health Council in Scarsdale, New York, and, most recently, the Chemical Industry Institute of Toxicology, the trade-association laboratory in North Carolina. (The oil companies are coordinating their activities through the American Petroleum Institute.)

2. The Political Attack

The propaganda campaign of the petrochemical companies is an indirect "winning-the-hearts-and-minds" approach; the political campaign for "regulatory reform" is more direct. Their efforts take several forms. The most traditional is billed as a fight against government interference in free enterprise: Giant companies like Mobil pose as embattled freedom fighters, holding the line for democracy against the encroachments of authoritarian socialism. It is never mentioned that these firms attained their present size and monopolistic power through a century of industry-sponsored government regulations to restrict competition, stabilize prices and production, subsidize innovation, and protect capital. Despite the blatant absurdity of monopoly firms rushing to defend free competition, the appeal seems to work—especially when it is tied to individualism, democracy, and progress. Union Carbide's Browning can rail against government regulation and then point to an opinion poll (done for his company) showing that "66 percent of the public favored

individual risk/benefit decisions."

If freedom, individualism, and democracy are at stake in this battle against regulation, so too, we are told, is progress itself. "Already innovation has been stifled," complains Manufacturing Chemists Association president, Robert Roland. Chairman Connor of Allied Chemical threatens that, if regulation continues, "business will become increasingly reluctant to develop products that offer important benefits but carry with them certain risks that are not completely avoidable."

For all their concern about the fate of free enterprise, democracy, and progress, the chemical companies have focused most of their attention on the *economic* consequences of regulation. In the early 1970s, for example, chemical manufacturers announced that a proposed federal standard for vinyl chloride, a known carcinogen, would cost two million jobs and $65 billion. Their trade association declared that "the standard is simply beyond compliance capability of the industry." The standard was adopted and the industry continued to flourish, without job losses and at 5 percent of the industry's estimated cost. In 1975, during the debates over the Toxic Substances Control Act, the industry hired the Foster D. Snell consulting firm to investigate the costs of the proposed legislation. Again, the findings showed that the costs were prohibitive. But when members of Congress requested the raw data, they were told that it had been destroyed according to a prior agreement among the participating firms.

Since the enactment of the TSCA in 1976, the chemical industry has redoubled its regulation-reform efforts, demanding even more stridently than before that "economic impact statements" (or "inflation impact statements") be required for all regulations—a not-too-subtle inversion of the intent of the original "environmental impact statements" required by EPA and other agencies. Major studies of the costs of regulation are now being conducted by the Business Roundtable and the Manufacturing Chemists Association (with representatives of DuPont, Dow, Monsanto, Shell Oil, and Allied Chemical). In 1974, President Ford acceded to the industry by issuing an executive order requiring "inflation impact statements" for all proposed regulations. In 1976, before he left office, Ford renewed his directive, this time calling for "economic impact statements." President Carter joined the cam-

paign at the end of March with his own executive order requiring so-called regulatory analyses not only of proposed regulations but also of those already on the books. Indeed, regulation reform seems destined to become a central strategy in the Carter administration's "war" on inflation.

Defenders of the regulatory agencies have begun to mount a counteroffensive, arguing that the social and economic costs of regulating are less than the costs of not regulating. Nicholas Ashford, chairman of the National Advisory Committee on Occupational Safety and Health has argued in the *New York Times* that "the costs of not regulating in the past are coming to light today; the costs of not regulating in the present would be a disgraceful legacy to workers, consumers, and industry in the future." Similarly, Mark Green, director of Public Citizens Congress Watch, has pointed out that "the abolition of slavery or child-labor laws certainly would never have passed a cost/benefit test."

3. The Methodological Attack

In the past when regulators identified a chemical as carcinogenic, that charge alone was enough to alarm the public, rally support behind the regulation, and put the chemical industry on the defensive. The offending company was compelled to trot out its own toxicologist to dispute the

IS YOUR JOB MAKING YOU SICK?

Headaches, dizziness, stomach trouble, problems with your ears, eyes, lungs, or skin may be caused by materials you work with or by conditions on the job.

charge. Today, corporations like Union Carbide have begun to shift the very nature of the debate. They now readily concede that their products are carcinogenic, but blandly insist that the acknowledge risk of cancer be put in "perspective," that it be compared with other risks and traded off against product benefits. Life, after all, is risky.

The growing industry demand for some "perspective" on risks, is generating a new engineering methodology, a new "calculus" for the measurement and assessment of risks. The measurements are done in several ways. For example, the probabilities of risk involved are calculated and compared to the risks of natural occurrences such as tornados. Norman Rasmussen of the Nuclear Engineering Department at the Massachusetts Institute of Technology trivialized the risk of nuclear accident in his now infamous "Reactor-Safety Study," by comparing it to the risk of being hit by a meteorite. This is called "comparative risk analysis." Other forms of measurement include traditional "cost/benefit analysis" and "risk/benefit" analysis, in which both risks and benefits are calculated—say, the risk of an airplane crash and the benefits of getting from New York to Boston in less than an hour, the jobs created by the aircraft industry, etc.

All of these risk-measurement techniques tell us only about estimated costs or risks or benefits, not what they mean. Measurement procedures are always suspect (Why has this been measured and not that? How do you put a value on human life? How do you compare apples and tumors?) but the assessment procedure is the most slippery part of the analysis. The most common technique is to reduce everything to dollars and cents: The policy that costs least with the same benefits or risk-probability wins. Another method is known as the "acceptability" technique. What kind of risks do people normally accept? Dams burst, yet people voluntarily build houses downstream from them. Airplanes crash, yet people voluntarily fly in them. Thousands die each year in automobile accidents, yet they continue to buy cars and drive them. The probability of accidents for each of these and similar activities or events is calculated, and these become the standards of acceptability. Risks to health presented by a particular chemical or industrial process are measured; if found to be less than "standard acceptable risk" they are judged worth

running. (Horrified by the consequences of carcinogenic pollutants? You take a greater risk driving to work every day. So what's all the fuss?)

Such "risk-accounting" methods, according to Herbert Inhaber of the Canadian Atomic Energy Control Board, often yield "surprising results . . . substantially different from that expected on the basis of intuition. [Yet] without this knowledge we cannot make a fully informed judgment." For example, in his exhaustive study of the "relative risks" of different energy technologies Inhaber found that supposedly benign sources of energy, such as solar, wind, and water, are actually more dangerous than nuclear! Similarly, computer-aided risk researchers at Stanford used a "multiple-criteria approach" to measure "risk/benefit trade-offs," "minimum reducible health risks," "maximum acceptable cost," and "implicit value of human life." Their conclusion: The use of alternatives to asbestos, a known carcinogen, cannot justify their social and economic costs.

Such analytical approaches are not without their critics. Mark Green points out that human-life values vary considerably from study to study (the University of Rochester puts the figure at $350,000, the American Enterprise Institute at $2.5 million and Cornell University at $1.5 million) and that industry defines and controls all the raw information about costs that must be used in the studies. "Given the current state of economic art," he argues, "mathematical cost/benefit analyses are about as neutral as voter-literacy tests in the Old South." A House of Representatives oversight and investigations subcommittee has suggested that "the limitations on the usefulness of benefit/cost analysis in the context of health, safety, and environmental regulatory decisions are so severe that they militate against its use altogether." And a Library of Congress review concluded that such studies "tend to support the vested interests of the sponsors of the estimate or to fit the hypothesis of the individual making the estimate." One M.I.T. mechanical engineering professor, who has himself done many such assessments—of the risks and benefits of LNG (Liquified Natural Gas) transport—has come to the conclusion that the whole approach is best described as "scientific pornography." It is less colorfully described as a sophisticated political tactic in the fight against regulation.

But to the business community, pseudo-scientific "risk-accounting" has the status of what *Science* magazine calls a "new religion." Robert A. Roland, president of the Manufacturing Chemists Association has recently argued that "whether government understands, accepts, and applies risk/benefit analysis to regulation will be the most consequential question facing the chemical industry in the 1980s." The new religion is preached through the sermons of Browning of Union Carbide. "The less grandstanding and inflammatory rhetoric used by all sides, the better," Browning exhorted the members of the Florida Audubon Society recently. There is a need, he urged, to get beyond "adversary relationships" toward "reasoned, productive and positive," "moderate" and "responsible" discussion. There must be "bridge-building" and, for that "more research" in order to attain a "balanced policy" through a "reasoned measuring of both the risks and the benefits."

But petrochemical-industry leaders understand that they do not have the public credibility to provide such "reasoned" measurement themselves, so they have begun to call for what Jackson terms an "independent, nonpolitical panel of top-flight scientists." The obvious site for such disinterested drudgery is the university, the supposedly neutral turf of serious scholarship.

4. The Ideological Attack

The science-based chemical industry is no stranger to the campus. During the great wave of expansion of American universities in the 1920s usually the first new building to be constructed was the chemistry building, built at private industry's expense. University-based industrial research is an old story, whether done in

college laboratories or affiliated research institutes like Batelle or Mellon. So are fellowship and recruitment programs and extensive faculty consulting. Now the industry is taking advantage of this long-time relationship to forge new kinds of ties. Essentially their purpose is twofold.

First, industry is seeking scientific credibility for their studies of the adverse effects of regulation. For this they need two types of expertise, that provided by chemists and chemical engineers and toxicologists and that provided by the new breed of policy analysts, experts in the gamesmanship of "risk accounting." These "experts" are found in chemistry, chemical engineering, and toxicology departments (all with ties to the industry) and in the political science and economics departments and the new policy institutes that increasingly dot the campuses. These sectors of the university will provide the expert testimony, the reams of data, the scientific publications, and, perhaps most important, the new generations of advisors and experts—unsuspecting students whose nimble minds will be occupied by never-ending exercises in complex risk analysis.

Second, the chemical industry is attempting to purchase ideological legitimation for their propaganda campaign, to foster a "serious" debate about the question of risk: How do societies "cope with risk"? What determines the social and individual "acceptability of risk"? The site for such discussions will be the new interdisciplinary centers for the study of "technology and society," "science and the humanities," "science, technology, and society," and the like, established on campuses throughout the country in recent years. These centers are monuments to the "selfless" largesse of the Mellon Foundation, the Exxon Foundation, the Sloan Foundation, and other private and public "money boys." Before long, we will have lecture courses and symposia, special issues of scholarly journals, and theses and term papers, and fellowships and special professorial chairs—all devoted to hiding the real issues of power and control in a verbal haze of obscurantist prose, driving home the industry's message: Things are much more complicated than we thought.

On this ideological front, the chemical companies are just now beginning to marshal their forces: not surprisingly, the best indication of what is to come is provided by the recent experience at America's premier corporate service centers, M.I.T. and Harvard.

Currently in the throes of a major corporate fund-raising drive, the M.I.T. leadership has begun negotiations to establish a chemical-industry-funded risk institute. Plans call for the establishment of a "Program on the Environmental Effects of Chemicals." With the initiative and funds coming from DuPont, Monsanto, and the Manufacturing Chemists Association, the program will focus on both the scientific and policy issues of the chemical regulation question and will bring together chemists, chemical engineers, toxicologists, nutritritionists, political scientists, economists, and "policy experts" from both M.I.T. and neighboring Harvard.

Meanwhile, at Harvard, which received a whopping gift from Monsanto two years ago, a new interdisciplinary program has been established at the School of Public Health. Directed by a director of the Upjohn Corporation, the program focuses on "issues of both science and public policy related to chemicals in the environment," it emphasizes new "methodologies for quantitative risk assessment" and "policy decisions and regulation: their scientific basis and their social, economic, and political consequences." In return for the Harvard and M.I.T. imprimaturs, the industry will provide funds for search, staff, fellowships

and facilities. While these new programs will lend the industry campaign against regulation some scientific legitimacy, other more humanistically oriented courses will carry on the serious yet safe discussions for which academia is known.

With the public numbered by the multi-million-dollar multimedia propaganda barrage, regulatory agency staffs bogged down in niggling debates over numbers, experts enlisted in the cause for a "balanced" approach to risk and would-be social critics overwhelmed by the perplexity of it all, the chemical industry campaign against regulation is proceeding full speed ahead. Out of sight are the propagandists themselves and out of mind are the political questions that underlie regulation: the contradiction between production for social need and health and production for profit; the issue over who decides what will be produced and how it will be produced; the debates about private property and public control. The new corporate ideology for the 1980s once again tables these long-standing items on the American agenda.

David F. Noble is a historian and author of America by Design: Science, Technology and the Rise of Corporate Capitalism (*Knopf*).

From *Environmental Action* 11, no. 10 (April 1980): 9-14

And Here's the Filthy Five: Environmental Action's New Campaign to Clean Up Congress

by April Moore

Months of research by Environmental Action have revealed a pattern of political donations by some of the nation's biggest polluters. Dubbed the Filthy Five, these companies and their top officials gave a

total of $714,131 to congressional campaigns and candidates in 1978. The corporations—Dow Chemical, International Paper, Republic Steel, Occidental Petroleum and Amoco Oil—are polluting our democratic system of government as well as the nation's air and water.

The corporations are the target of Environmental Action's 1980 campaign to clean up government.

EA's research into corporate giving records and congressional voting proves that industry gets a return on its largesse. Today's Congress is overwhelmingly receptive to corporate claims that we don't have to strengthen cleanup programs. When an environmental regulation does ensnare one of the Filthy Five, often the company is wealthy enough to divert the government with a lengthy legal battle or simply to pay a fine which can be easily passed on to the consumer.

The companies are generous to many but certainly prefer some members of Congress over others. They particularly like to give to representatives or senators from districts where they own plants. For instance, while International Paper (IP) made contributions of $500 or less to fewer than a third of the New York State delegation, the company reserved its big gift of $2,500 for Rep. Gerald Solomon (R), who represents the 29th district. That district just happens to be the site of IP's Corinth plant, a consistent violator of Occupational Safety and Health Administration regulations.

Most congressmembers, of course, accept some contributions from corporate political action committees (PACs). But when a representative or senator gets money from a large number of polluting companies, he or she is probably giving the companies something in return. In 1978, Senate minority leader Howard Baker of Tennessee, for one, received contributions totalling $15,300 from all five of the Filthy Five. According to the League of Conservation Voters (LCV), which rates congressmembers on their environmental voting records, in 1978, Baker voted against the environment 68 percent of the time.

Sen. Bennett Johnston (D-La.), who LCV says voted against the environment 78 percent of the time, also received money from all the Filthy Five. Their contributions to Johnston's 1978 reelection campaign totalled $8,640. Johnston has supported several measures aimed at gutting the Clean Air Act, including amendments to weaken auto emission standards for nitrogen oxide and to weaken the act's ban on construction of new power plants and manufacturing complexes near areas of pristine air quality such as national parks.

Environmental Actions's Filthy Five Campaign is a national drive to make Congress more receptive to citizens by cutting the strings between a handful of giant corporations and their clients in Congress. From now until the November election, EA will keep close track of all money Senate and House candidates and incumbents receive from the Filthy Five. The names of the people who accept Filthy Five money will be announced and the candidate or congressmember urged to give the money back.

The Filthy Five Campaign replaces the Dirty Dozen, an earlier Environmental Action bid to get pollution out of Congress. That campaign, conducted every two years since 1970, targeted for defeat 12 of the environment's worst enemies in Congress and helped end the political careers of a full two-thirds of those targeted. But despite this, Congress is as hostile to environmental issues today as it was 10 years ago.

So EA has decided to focus on those who really wield the power—the corporations. EA staff members and volunteers began work on the Filthy Five 10 months ago, first identifying the 100 corporations with the most affluent political action committees. The list was narrowed down to the 40 who wreaked the most havoc with the environment, and then EA researchers combed Federal Election Commission files to find out who received campaign contributions from the 40 firms. Recipients' voting records were analyzed to determine the 10 corporations with the greatest clout and those 10, in turn, were studied for violations of the Clean Air and Clean Water Acts, Occupational Safety and Health Administration (OSHA) regulations and other environmental laws. EA looked at the contributions of the 10 companies' PACs, their board members and their top level executives. From those 10 come the Filthy Five—the corporations with the dirtiest pollution practices and the most success in getting Congress to vote against the environment.

Now, through the Filthy Five Campaign, voters, workers and neighbors of polluting facilities can fight back.

"Money from the Filthy Five is just too dirty to accept," says Peter Harnik, campaign coordinator. "EA is calling on every candidate, regardless of party or persuasion, to reject all future financial support from these persistent lawbreakers. We are also urging candidates who have already received money from the Filthy Five to return the contributions."

To begin with, let's meet the companies in question.

Dow Chemical

Dow Chemical brought mustard gas to the trenches of World War I, napalm to Vietnam and the herbicide 2, 4, 5-T to American forests and roadsides. It has also brought money to Congress. Through its nine PACs and donations from company officials, Dow gave $179,080 to approximately 175 congressmembers and candidates in 1978.

Until last year, seven million pounds of the defoliant 2,4,5-T were used annually in the United States. But in March 1979, the government responded to reports of an abnormal number of spontaneous abortions among women in the Alsea, Ore. timbering region where 2,4,5-T and another Dow product, 2,4-D, had been used extensively (see related story, page 3).* The Environmental Protection Agency (EPA) ordered an emergency suspension of 2,4,5-T use in forests, along roadways, around homes and in watersheds and recreation areas.

Dow, manufacturer of 50 to 60 percent of the nation's supply of the potent poison, is fighting EPA even though the herbicide accounts for only two-tenths of 1 percent of Dow's annual sales of $6 billion. Dow claims money is not the issue. What is important, the company says, is to stop environmentalists and public health advocates from using what Dow says are untrue, imprudent scientific assertions to restrict the production and use of chemical products.

And, Dow says, any problems which might arise from 2,4,5-T use are not its fault. Thousands of Vietnam veterans who were exposed to Agent Orange, a defoliant made with 2,4,5-T, have suffered from problems such as cancer, loss of sex drive, lowered sperm count and children with birth defects. More than 300 have joined in a $10 million class action suit against Dow. Dow's reaction has been to sue the government, claiming Uncle Sam should reimburse the company for any claims awarded against Dow in the veterans' suit.

Vietnam veterans are also suing Dow and another Filthy Five company, Occidental Petroleum, along with eight other companies, seeking an end to the sale of all chemicals contaminated with dioxin, which is found in 2,4,5-T.

The deadly dioxin causes problems even before it contaminates final products. A byproduct of chemical processes at Dow's Midland, Mich. plant, dioxin is now turning up in fish caught in the nearby Tittabawassee River. "Don't eat the fish caught downstream from Dow," the Michigan Public Health Service cautions. But Dow has claimed the dioxin in fish near Midland comes from "natural" causes. Oddly enough, the company has failed to explain why those natural causes did not affect fish caught upstream.

The Midland plant is an historic polluter of the air as well. EPA has declared the plant out of compliance with the Clean

---

*[Deborah Baldwin, "The War Comes Home," *Environmental Action* 11, no., 10 (April 1980): 3-8, 31-32.—eds., *Alternative Papers*.]

Air Act, but no schedule has been set for making the facility comply. The agency is now suing Dow, asking $20 million in fines for years of air pollution violations.

Dow's record in Michigan didn't prevent a number of the state's politicians from taking money from the chemical company. For example, Dow gave former Rep. Elford Cederberg (R), whose district included the Midland plant, $7,300 for his 1978 reelection bid. The company gave a little more—$10,500—to the state's Republican senator, Robert Griffin, for his 1978 reelection campaign. But Dow's money didn't quite do the trick; both Griffin and Cederberg were defeated.

Another of Dow's polluting plants is located in Freeport, Texas. In the 1978 race to represent the Freeport area in the House of Representatives, Dow decided to play both sides of the fence. The company gave $1,000 to Republican candidate Ron Paul and $2,200 to Democratic incumbent Bob Gammage. (Paul won.)

Problems also exist at Dow's Plaquemine, La. plant, where a cloud of poisonous chlorine gas leaked from the plant two years ago. The Plaquemine site is also a regular violator of its water discharge permit.

Dow is as irresponsible to its employees as it is to the environment. "Why should we have a no risk workplace?" Dow's chief executive Paul Oreffice once asked at a press conference. Despite the company's extensive research into chromosome damage resulting from workplace exposure to toxic chemicals, Dow has not done anything about the problem, according to geneticist Dante Picciano, formerly with Dow. Dow failed to release Picciano's study showing elevated rates of chromosome breakage in workers exposed to the carcinogen benzene. Claiming the data was difficult to evaluate, Dow did not tell the exposed employees "for fear of alarming them prematurely."

Despite Dow's run-ins with the public and the law, the corporation's 1979 earnings shot up 36 percent over 1978.

International Paper

The world's second largest paper making company, International Paper (IP) reports soaring profits and sales. Owning 7.2 million acres of land, IP is reportedly second only to the federal government in terms of U.S. land holdings. Congress shares in the company's prosperity. In 1978, IP's PAC—Voluntary Contributors for Better Government—gave $173,442 to 177 congressional members and candidates.

But IP's plants manufacturing paper, health care products and other goods are among the more notorious violators of the Clean Air and Clean Water Acts. The company's Ticonderoga, N.Y. plant has angered citizens groups for years and the state of Vermont successfully sued IP for dumping hazardous paper products in Lake Champlain. The company was fined $500,000 and ordered to limit the mill's discharges and to install an advanced treatment system to filter wastes before dumping. IP then built a new mill which, it claimed, was a model facility.

But not everyone agrees. "The three feet of brown foam on the water marks the spot where the mill dumps its wastes," says Thad Bronson, a lifelong resident of the nearby community of Cornwall, Vt. Phosphates and suspended solids are still so concentrated, he says, that parts of the lake never freeze, even during the area's frigid winters.

Citizens near the mill filed a class action suit against the company two years ago for its polluting practices, but the U.S. Supreme Court refused to hear the case, stating that each of the plaintiffs had not suffered $10,000 or more worth of damages. Another class action suit, asking $282 million in compensation and punitive damages, is pending in U.S. District Court.

IP's Mobile, Ala. plant has "lots of spills and overflows," according to an EPA official. Just two months ago, the plant contaminated Mobile Bay with 41 million gallons of acidic effluent. IP was fined $47,750 last summer when a major wastewater spill resulted from the company's failure to shut down for necessary repairs. Air pollution standards, EA has learned, are also ignored at the Mobile plant. The company burns a polluting mixture of bark and oil without adequate controls, and EPA is expected to take enforcement action against IP soon.

The Jay, Maine IP plant has been fined three times in the last year and a half for bypassing the wastewater system and discharging effluent directly into the Androscoggin River. But that hasn't kept Maine politicians from taking IP money. Rep. Olympia Snowe (R), whose district includes Jay, received $2,040 from IP in 1978 when she ran successfully for Congress. Sen. William Cohen (R), who used to be the congressmember from the district now represented by Snowe, received $5,000 from IP that year for his successful bid to move up to the Senate.

Three more of International Paper's chronic polluters and OSHA violators are located in Arkansas' fifth district. In 1978, the representative from that district, Beryl Anthony, received $2,250.

Republic Steel

A major producer of steel, aircraft and building materials, Republic Steel and its top officials gave out $76,875 to 82 representatives, senators and candidates in 1978. The politicians accepted the money although Republic is a longtime violator of pollution and occupational health and safety regulations.

What Is a PAC?

Political Action Committees (PACs) can be established by corporations, unions and other political groups. Most corporations use their PACs to funnel money to sympathetic members of Congress and candidates. A PAC may legally contribute up to $5,000 to a candidate in any one primary or election race. Federal election laws stipulate that the money must come from employees and not the company itself, but the corporation can finance PAC staff and office expenses.

While federal election law specifies that no firm may coerce employees to contribute to the company PAC, some companies report an astonishingly high level of giving more than 70 percent for high level executives in some firms. A number of companies offer their employees a payroll deduction plan to make employee giving to the company PAC as simple as possible.

Over the past three years, Republic's Cleveland, Ohio plant has been cited repeatedly for violations of the city's air pollution code. Last summer, Republic finally agreed to clean up, but the company's promises proved empty. By October, Republic had still not changed its ways and the city filed a criminal citation against the company. If convicted, Republic Steel could be fined up to $1,000 a day for each day it continues to violate the code.

Meanwhile, Republic, which has plants in other Ohio cities as well, gives out lots of money to the Buckeye State's congressional delegation. The company's 1978 gifts to 11 of the state's 23 representatives totalled $3,700.

A Republic subsidiary, Reserve Mining Co., has been accused of discharging 67,000 tons a day of taconite tailings from its Silver Bay, Minn. iron ore plant into Lake Superior. The asbestos like tailings showed up in the drinking water of all three states bordering the lake. Reserve Mining was fined more than $1 million for polluting the lake and violating air emission standards, but managed to talk EPA out of a $3.1 million fine by promising to build cleaner, more efficient facilities.

Rep. James Oberstar (D), whose district includes Silver Bay, received a $500 contribution from Republic in 1978. In that same year, Republicans Rudy Boschwitz and David Durenberger each received $2,000 from the steel company for their successful 1978 Senate bids.

Republic's Gadsden, Ala. steel plant has been repeatedly criticized by the state's Air Pollution Control Commission, which last fall sought a permanent injunction against Republic. EPA is seeking $10,000 a day for each day of continuing violation and is also filing for $10,000 a day in fines against Republic for failure to comply with the Clean Water Act. Two years ago, the Alabama attorney general took Republic to court, charging the plant's excessive dumping of cyanide had caused a fish kill in the Coosa River.

All these violations in Alabama, though, did not deter four of the state's seven representatives from each taking contributions from Republic, which also gave to both candidates in the Walter Flowers-Howell Heflin Senate race (Heflin won).

Repeated violations of New York State's plan to implement environmental safeguards prompted EPA to seek an injunction to halt Republic's Buffalo, N.Y. plant's air polluting activities. The agency is also seeking a $25,000 a day fine.

EPA isn't the only federal agency offended by Republic's flagrant disregard for the law. OSHA officials have levied an astounding $210,241 worth of fines against the company since 1973.

Occidental Petroleum

Occidental Petroleum is the only corporation that has been formally investigated by the Securities and Exchange Commission (SEC) four times in the last decade. Oxy, as the company calls itself, also scores high in terms of profits. The oil, gas and coal firm reported 1979 revenues of $9.6 billion, up $3.3 billion from 1978, causing profits to soar.

While shareholders may be delighted with the company's progress, EA and other citizens groups charge that Oxy's subsidiaries, including Hooker Chemical, Oxy-Chem and Island Creek Coal, are perhaps doing more to decimate environmental quality and human health than any other group of firms. This doesn't faze a lot of politicians, though. In 1978, the company's PAC and its officials gave $108,225 to 89 representatives, senators and candidates.

Who Got What

Senators, representatives and candidates who received contributions from four or more of the Filthy Five's officials and/or PACs in 1978.

Name, party, district	Won or lost	LCV 1978*	Total
M. Allen, D-Sen, Ala.	L	24	$ 3,500
Flowers, D-Sen, Ala.	L	44	1,900
Dickinson, R-2, Ala.	W	2	1,450
D. Young, R-1, Ark.	W	8	3,750
Armstrong, R-Sen, Colo.	W	27	15,800
Scott, R-2, Colo.	L	—	2,800
McClure, R-Sen, Idaho	W	16	5,500
Jepson, R-Sen, Iowa	W	—	4,000
D. Crane, R-22, Ill.	W	—	2,750
Porter, R-10, Ill.	L†	—	13,750
Kassebaum, R-Sen, Kan.	W	—	7,500
Jeffries, R-2, Kan.	W	—	3,200
Hopkins, R-6, Ky.	W	—	3,650
Johnston, D-Sen, La.	W	26	8,640
Livingston, R-1, La.	W	3	5,039
Cohen, R-Sen, Maine	W	79	8,200
Griffin, R-Sen, Mich.	L	19	33,650
G. Brown, R-3, Mich.	L	48	7,300
Vander Jagt, R-9, Mich.	W	23	2,950
Durenberger, R-Sen, Minn.	W	—	11,300
Boschwitz, R-Sen, Minn.	W	—	10,000
Cochran, R-Sen, Miss.	W	21	7,900
Helms, R-Sen, N.C.	W	18	3,600
Martin, R-9, N.C.	W	27	4,100
Aronoff, R-2, Ohio	L	—	3,700
C. Brown, R-7, Ohio	W	19	1,500
Devine, R-12, Ohio	W	13	1,750
Edwards, R-5, Okla.	W	13	1,500
Schulze, R-5, Penn.	W	27	1,250
Clinger, R-23, Penn.	W	—	2,750
Pressler, R-Sen, S.D.	W	40	2,250
Baker, R-Sen, Tenn.	W	32	15,300
Duncan, R-2, Tenn.	W	27	1,750
Beard, R-6, Tenn.	W	19	1,850
Tower, R-Sen, Texas	W	0	6,725
Krueger, D-Sen, Texas	L	25	6,200
Archer, R-7, Texas	W	17	5,450
Wolf, R-10, Va.	L	—	3,800
Roth, R-8, Wisc.	W	—	2,500
Cheney, R-1, Wyo.	W	—	3,400

*League of Conservation Voters rating in 1978, if applicable.
†Lost election, but was later appointed to seat.

Hooker shocked the nation when reports of Love Canal hit the press two years ago. The Oxy subsidiary dumped tons of toxic chemical waste in the area near Niagara Falls some 30 years ago. The chemicals leaked from the Love Canal landfills, contaminating drinking water, playground areas and some nearby homes, forcing scores of residents to evacuate. When sections of the community turned into ghost towns, Hooker president Donald Baeder said the company was innocent. "Not a single person has been injured by the company's practices at any of these former waste disposal sites," he told an incredulous public.

EPA is suing Hooker for $124 million — $117 million to clean up Love Canal and five other dump sites around Niagara Falls and $7 million to reimburse the federal government for its emergency cleanup and evacuation measures.

Hooker has also been sued by New York State, which is seeking $515,000 from the company for its misuse of three Long Island landfills. The 420 violations include dumping 1.6 million pounds of toxic chemicals in the Bethpage municipal landfill.

In Michigan, Hooker was told to spend at least $15 million to clean up its 880 acre dump in Montague, which had been in use for more than 25 years and which contains several deadly compounds, including carcinogens used in pesticide manufacture.

None of this apparently bothers Rep. Guy Vander Jagt (R), whose congressional district includes the Montague facility. While accepting smaller contributions from the rest of the Filthy Five, Vander Jagt took $1,000 from Oxy.

Meanwhile, the SEC is investigating Hooker to determine whether the company knowingly omitted information about its

Bülbül/LNS

dump sites from the quarterly reports required by the agency. The *New York Times* reports that the company knew as early as 1968 that the Montague site was contaminating groundwater.

Another Oxy subsidiary, OxyChem, dumped tons of DBCP and other hazardous chemicals into waste ponds around the company's Lathrop, Calif. factory. Production of the pesticide DBCP has been banned in California because it is believed to cause male sterility. Meanwhile, the congressmember who represents Lathrop, Norman Shumway (R), accepted an $800 contribution from Occidental in 1978.

OxyChem has its share of air quality violations too. The company's White Springs, Fla. sulfuric acid manufacturing plant has refused to comply with federal and state regulations regarding acid mist emissions. But Rep. Don Fuqua (D), whose district includes White Springs, accepted a $500 contribution from Occidental in 1978.

Occidental Petroleum's coal operation is another unrelenting violator of environmental standards. The Island Creek Coal Co., whose $200,000 a year president is former Tennessee Sen. Albert Gore, has been cited for assorted stripmine violations. The list includes failure to dispose of toxic wastes properly and conducting blasting within 500 feet of a gas line. Island Creek has agreed to pay only about one-third of the $105,110 in fines levied against it.

As of October 1979, Oxy was subject to 31 proceedings by EPA, the Coast Guard, the Interior Department and state and local governments. OSHA has also found numerous violations, levying $77,730 in fines against the company since 1972.

Amoco

The Filthy Five list would not be complete without oil giant Amoco. Amoco's disregard for the health and safety of its employees is legendary, and a number of its facilities are illegally polluting air and water. But some members of Congress like Amoco. In 1978, the company PAC and officials contributed $162,650 to 176 members of Congress and candidates.

Between 1961 and 1972, workers in Amoco Chemical Corp.'s New Castle, Del. facility were exposed to asbestos in the production of polypropylene plastic. After a lengthy battle, Amoco finally agreed to demands from the Oil, Chemical and Atomic Workers Union (OCAW) that employees be examined for asbestosis. Amoco said the tests showed no evidence of the debilitating lung disease, but two years later, when the medical records of 12 employees were reviewed at Mt. Sinai Medical Center in New York, 11 were found to show signs of asbestosis, according to OCAW.

OSHA has cited Amoco for failing to record "illnesses arising from occupational exposure to asbestos" and for requiring an employee with a serious health problem to work under conditions that could cause "death or serious physical harm." A ruling is expected shortly on the two citations.

"Amoco has the worst environmental record on the Gulf Coast," says Sharon Stewart, a citizen activist who lives near

	Dow Chemical Company	International Paper Company	Republic Steel Corporation	Occidental Petroleum Corporation	Standard Oil Company of Indiana (Amoco)
Headquarters:	Midland, Michigan	New York, New York	Cleveland, Ohio	Los Angeles, California	Chicago, Illinois
Sales (1977):	$6.2 billion	$3.7 billion	$2.9 billion	$6 billion	$13 billion
Corporate rank:	25th largest U.S. corp. 3rd largest U.S. chemical company	57th largest U.S. corp. 2nd largest U.S. paper company (1st in assets)	84th largest U.S. corp. 5th largest U.S. steel company	27th largest U.S. corp. 1st largest U.S. mining and crude oil production corp.	12th largest U.S. corp. 6th largest U.S. oil company
Chief executive officer:	Paul F. Oreffice	J. Stanford Smith	William J. Delancy	Armand Hammer	John E. Swearingen
Principal products:	chemicals; metals; plastics and packaging; pesticides; medicines; coatings	paper and pulp; oil and gas; packaging, wood and wood products	steel and steel products	industrial, specialty and agricultural chemicals; plastics; crude oil; gas; coal; phosphate	refined oil products; crude oil; natural gas; chemical products; fertilizers
Notable subsidiaries or affiliates:	Dow Corning Corp. (50% owned)	Canadian International Paper Co.	Reserve Mining Co. (50% owned)	Hooker Chemical and Plastics Corp., Island Creek Coal Co., both wholly owned	
Amount of money contributed to candidates (1978):	$179,080	$173,442	$76,875	$108,225	$162,650
Number of candidates receiving money:	189	177	82	89	176

Amoco's Texas City, Texas plant. The plant was fined in 1977 and 1978 for Clean Air Act violations, but air pollution problems persist. Frequent carbon monoxide releases are the result of plant damage caused by an explosion last year, according to local OCAW safety officer Bob Galloway. Frequent equipment failure also produces sulfur dioxide emissions, says Galloway, who claims the Texas Air Quality Board has failed to respond to repeated union complaints.

Meanwhile, Amoco has been very generous to the Texas congressional delegation. In 1978, the oil company gave a total of $9,500 to 16 congressional incumbents and candidates. One recipient was Robert Krueger, the Democrat who ran unsuccessfully for John Tower's Senate seat.

A number of Amoco facilities are violators of water pollution standards. Amoco's Jackson County, Mo. plant, for example, did not comply with federal water pollution standards in 1978 or 1979. EPA is expected to file suit.

Amoco's Wood River, Ill. plant, which discharges cyanide and ammonia into the Mississippi River, violated its EPA discharge permit for 20 of the 24 months ending December 1979. Meanwhile, Amoco has been helping out one of Illinois' senators, Charles Percy (R). Percy received the largest legal contribution from the oil company—$5,000—in 1978.

Meanwhile, Amoco is handing out money to congressmembers from states where the company hopes to develop synthetic fuels. Amoco gave $5,000 to William Armstrong (R-Colo.) in 1978 to help him in his successful Senate race. Politicians from Wyoming also raked in the goodies. Amoco gave Sen. Alan Simpson (D) $4,000 for his successful campaign and gave $1,000 to the state's new at large representative Richard Cheney (R).

The record is clear. Politicians are eagerly accepting money from corporate outlaws. Rather than being shunned for polluting the air and water and endangering the health and well-being of all of us, officials of these corporations are welcomed enthusiastically in many House and Senate offices. Their money funds campaigns and, in return, the companies win friends on the Hill.

"The economic interests that poison the environment are polluting government as well. At stake is our democratic way of life," says Harnik. "We must develop a more balanced system of government where lawmakers are responsible to those who elect them, not those who buy them."

The 1980 Filthy Five Campaign is an effort to induce that kind of responsibility. It also coincides with Big Business Day— April 17. The campaign marks the first stage of a drive by environmentalists to zero in on the powerful forces that influence Congress.

"We know now that it is not just a matter of which individuals hold congressional seats, because the influence of corporate giving is often overpowering," says Harnik. "Only by controlling those who control Congress can we make our Congress a democratic institution in which environmental concerns are given a fair hearing.

"We'll consider this campaign a success if we can get even a fraction of the Filthy Five's money out of Congress. Ultimately it's the only way citizens groups will ever get a fair and honest hearing from our elected representatives."

What to do: The Filthy Five will continue to dump money into campaigns, and politicians will continue to take all contributions offered them—unless people like you demand a change.

• Write, call or make an appointment to visit your representative and ask him or her to sign the "Pledge of Independence," renouncing any campaign contributions from the Filthy Five.

Official "pledges" are available from Environmental Action, or make up your own using the text in the accompanying box.

THE CANDIDATE'S PLEDGE OF INDEPENDENCE
"I pledge my independence from polluting companies and as a symbol of this commitment refuse to accept contributions from the following corporations— Amoco, Dow Chemical, International Paper, Occidental Petroleum and Republic Steel— so that I may always represent my constituents in clear conscience."

• Write a letter to your local newspaper, pointing out the political impact of Filthy Five contributions. Ask your newspaper to make monthly reports on the most recent contributions of the Filthy Five companies and who received them in your state.

• Write a letter to your Senate and House candidates informing them that your voting decision will be influenced by whether they accept campaign funds from the Filthy Five companies.

SCIENCE FOR THE PEOPLE

From *Science for the People* 12, no. 4 (July/August 1980): 8-10, 29-35

The Pesticide Connection: Science for Sale

by Paul Barnett

Rancher George Neary, who raises cattle in California's Central Valley, is unhappy with what he calls "chemical huckstering" by the land-grant college in his area, the University of California (U.C.). "The University farm advisors came through here with a traveling road show telling all the ranchers that they ought to dip their cows in Toxaphene," he says, adding that the treatment is both unnecessary and

---

This article is reprinted with permission from *Science for the People*, copyright 1980.

---

dangerous. Last winter, state officials ordered Neary's herd dipped, and he lost 500 aborted calves and 100 poisoned cows. He has filed an $11 million lawsuit that names not only the state officials who dipped his cattle, but also the University of California veterinarians who investigated the incident and placed the blame for the cattle deaths on Neary and his hired help.

Federally funded Farm Advisors work in every farm area in the United States. They are backed by the $750 million a year research effort conducted by professors at land-grant colleges. Land-grant college extension and research is regarded by most farmers as a neutral, unbiased source of information.

Farmers like George Neary feel that the objectivity of these scientists is being compromised by the close financial ties to chemical manufacturers. The allegation is backed by some scientists within the land-grant establishment. "Chemical companies are brazenly buying University goodwill," said the late Robert van den Bosch, a world renowned entomologist at the University of California at Berkeley. "This to me is corruption."

Gift from chemical companies help support the university scientists' work. Companies that manufacture pesticides gave 420 gifts worth some $689,000 to the University of California Division of Agriculture in fiscal year 1978-79.[1] These gifts went to support the work of both farm advisors and research personnel.

Other victims of pesticide misuse have also charged that scientists at the University of California have minimized and even suppressed information about the hazards of pesticides. The Oil, Chemical and Atomic Workers Union has filed suit on behalf of 20 workers sterilized by DBCP against Dr. Charles Hine of the University of California at San Francisco. DBCP is a soil fumigant used to kill nematodes, microscopic worms which feed on crop roots. The action claims the workers were harmed because Hine suppressed evidence that the chemical damaged the testicles of experimental rats.[2] Named as co-defendant in the suit is the Shell Chemical Company, a DBCP manufacturer which gave Hine $400,000 in research grants and employs him as a private consultant.

Northern California residents concerned about the health hazards associated with sprays of 2,4,5-T on timberlands found formidable opposition from U.C. scientists. "Commercial preparations of 2,4,5-T are about as poisonous as diesel oil, paint, or nail polish remover," testified plant physiologist Boysie Day before the California Senate.[3]

"Day was very impressive with his University credentials and all," says Ruth Ann Cecil, a leader in the community movement which sought to stop the spraying. "But he only talks about the immediate effect of ingesting some herbicide—the acute toxicity," she says, "He ignores the whole question of the long term effects."

"In terms of safety and public health effects, the University of California does relatively little research,' says Dr. Ephraim Kahn, who recently retired from his position in the State Department of Health Services, where he was in charge of pesticide safety. "The question of chronic, delayed, or longterm effects, such as cancer, are just not known." Kahn says that although certain mixtures of pesticides are far more toxic than would be predicted by adding their toxicities, no one has really looked into this effect, called potentiation.

Kahn says that the University of California does far more research work on evaluating pesticide effectiveness. Chemical company grants, he feels, have oriented the University in this direction.

James Kendrick, head of the U.C. Division of Agriculture, disputes the allegation that the gifts might interfere with scientific objectivity. "The accusation is that money leads the faculty around by the nose—which I strongly resist, because the faculty isn't that easily lead around by the nose," says Kendrick.[4]

Chemical companies usually specify which University scientist is to receive their gift. The Auditor General of the California State Legislature studied the gift system and reported that "the University regularly performs research on proprietary (brand name) agricultural chemicals and pharmaceutical products as a result of donations from manufacturers of the products involved." Gift documents sometimes specify the methodology and delivery dates of research, the auditors found.[5]

Support from the private sector does influence research programs at the University of California, according to Charles Hess, Dean of the College of Agriculture at the Davis campus. "But all of this is a healthy relationship rather than an unholy alliance," the Dean maintains.[6] The support from the private sector is seen as "a valuable means of exchanging information, and keeping academic research relevant to real life needs."

There is some indication, however, that research grants influence University priorities. The chairmen of the 25 departments in the College of Agriculture on the Davis campus answered a survey on the factors which can influence choice of research topics. Their most popular response was "money can influence' (or dictate) what research gets done."[7]

Most of the costs of University of California research, including the cost of the scientists' salaries, laboratories and offices, are paid by the taxpayer. For each dollar of mini-grant support that they give, pesticide manufacturers can obtain $5-10 worth of research on their products. The mini-grants are treated as tax-deductible donations to a charitable institution, so, in effect, the tax-payer subsidizes the mini-grant as well.

"The mini-grants are a cheap buy for the chemical companies," says U.C. entomologist Andy Gutierrez. "If the University didn't do the studies, then they would have to do the research themselves, and of course their results would be more suspect than those of the University. They get a lot for their $2,000 grant—the researcher's time, University facilities, equipment, vehicles, and a whole lot of other things wrapped up into a little package that says the University tested this, therefore it's o.k. But it costs more than $2,000 to do the tests, and the University subsidizes the rest of the work."

Where the University scientists' participation in regulatory decisions is a matter of public record, it can be seen that they frequently lobby on behalf of products of their mini-grant benefactors. U.C. Davis entomologist Harry Lange, for example, supported an emergency exemption from registration requirements for Mesurol, a product of Chemagro, a pesticide company that has given Lange 18 gifts worth $17,975. Farm advisor Norm McCalley received $12,800 in 13 grants from companies that sell Benlate and Captan, products which he asked to be granted a special local needs registration.

The chemical companies also make direct gifts. Farm advisors Hodge Black and Marvin Schneider, for example, took a deep sea fishing vacation to Cabo San Lucas Mexico, at the expense of the Stauffer Chemical Company. FMC-Niagra reportedly chartered a fishing boat to take a group of U.C. scientists salmon fishing off the coast near San Francisco. Scientists freely admit receiving travel expenses, meals, and lodging from chemical companies. Farm advisor Norm McCalley received $2,000 from pesticide manufacturer ICI Americas, Inc., to pay for his expenses while he was on leave from the University.

Dan Hubig/PNS/LNS

U.C. Berkeley entomologist Andy Gutierrez reports, "University scientists get travel expenses from chemical companies to go to national meetings. The various pesticide companies have hospitality suites which are overflowing with University scientists, who are getting drunk on free liquor."

It is a sort of pesticide payola, purveyed to generate good will. There are few rules which regulate it. Peers tolerate and even expect it. To some it looks like science for sale.

II.

Scientists at the University of California have had a crucial role in developing the state's pest control system. Professors research the effectiveness and the hazards of new chemicals. Farm advisors from the University Cooperative Extension Service recommend to growers which of the more than 10,000 available products they ought to use. University graduates become chemical salesmen, government officials, and farmers. Pest control is a billion-dollar-a-year, chemical intensive business in California. Pesticide use has soared above 300 million lbs. a year, and represents 20 percent of the total U.S. use.

A damning appraisal of the pesticide intensive status quo comes from the University of California's own Division of Biological Control. Scientists from the Division studied the state's 25 most serious pest insect species and found 17 had developed resistance to insecticides. Because chemicals also kill beneficial insects, eliminating natural control mechanisms, pesticide use often causes new pest outbreaks. The U.C. scientists found that 24 of the 25 have become more serious pests because of this pesticide side-effect. "The evidence clearly suggests that intensive insecticide use has not reduced or ameliorated insect problems," they conclude, "rather it has intensified them."[8]

The Biological Control scientists advocate a multifaceted pest control approach, called Integrated Pest Management (IPM). IPM uses resistant crops, predatory insects, and other non-chemical controls, along with a trained consultant who monitors the insect populations so that pesticides are applied only when they are absolutely necessary. Despite the expense of hiring this consultant, cotton growers who use IPM have reduced their pesticide use by as much as two-thirds, cutting average pest control costs by $7.19 an acre and maintaining good yields.[9]

An Integrated Pest Management program has also been developed for California pear orchards.[10] "The pear growers who have switched to Integrated Pest Management have cut their pesticide use by 30 percent," says Pat Weddel, an advisor who has worked with the pear program from the beginning. The program has saved growers money, while protecting the crop.

Despite these promising beginnings, few farmers use IPM and California remains the world's most intensive user of pesticides. Though pesticide use has doubled in the last eight years, the cost of insect caused crop damage is increasing rapidly. California farmers are caught on a treadmill of increasing pesticide use. As they spray more, they create new pest problems, and once again increase their chemical use. If the successes of IPM in the cotton and pear industries are representative, then farmers are being overcharged by as much as $500 million a year for unnecessary chemicals. The increased chemical load is also creating new public health and environmental problems.

But even in the crops where the IPM system has been developed, relatively few growers have yet improved their pest control practices. "There's no guarantee that anything we develop is going to be implemented," says biological control scientist Dick Garcia. The crucial link between researcher and farmer is the farm advisor—the University of California Cooperative Extension Service.

Pest control recommendations made by the University are heavily weighted towards chemicals. An evaluation by the Cooperative Extension Service of its 4,300 published pest control recommendations found that 93 percent were for chemical control. Only 7 percent described biological, microbial, or cultural control methods.[11]

One problem is that information on non-chemical pest control discoveries does not necessarily reach the farm advisor. Though U.C. has 20 pest control specialists to act as a link between researcher and farm advisors, there is no pest control specialist for the Division of Biological Control. Leon Tichinin, former director of the farm advisor's office in Santa Clara County, says "Chemical company representatives were a good source of information. University researchers were slow to get information to the Extension Agents, while the people from the chemical companies were always there with the most current information."

Another explanation for the extension agents' predeliction for pesticides is the hundreds of mini-grants that they receive each year from pesticide manufacturers. The University of California Extension Service received $161,450 in chemical company gifts in fiscal year 1977-78. The funds came as 139 grants to 31 different farm advisors. Usually amounting to no more than $500 to $2,000, the grants are earmarked for use by a specific farm advisor. The gifts are used for research on pesticide effectiveness. Mini-grants have evidently deflected farm advisors from giving pest control advice to merely evaluating chemical products.

Curiously enough, the Smith-Lever Act, enacted by Congress in 1914 to create the nationwide extension service, specifies that the principal function of the farm advisor is to educate farmers about the research of professors in the Land Grant Colleges. In California, the extension service does quite a bit of research on its own. J. Vernon Patterson of U.C. Extension reported that the farm advisors were conducting about 75 percent of the University's testing of pesticides for vegetable crops.[12]

Many of the farm advisors' recommendations are for specific brand names of pesticides. Farm advisors frequently recommend the brand names of products manufactured by their mini-grant supporters. Pesticide Extension specialist Michael Stimman says that growers want University publications to cite brand names and not the generic ones because millions of dollars of chemical company advertising have taught them only these brand names. Farm Advisor recommendations are not necessarily based on University tests, according to Stimman. Manufacturers' claims are considered to be a reliable source of information. "In most situations though, the researcher has had hands-on experience with the chemical," says Stimman, who adds that "there is a difference between having experience with a pesticide and conducting a controlled scientific experiment."

Richard Doutt, a retired research entomologist from U.C. Berkeley, studied the effectiveness of the insecticide Sevin and found that it was reducing grape growers' yields. Doutt says he had "excellent proof" that Sevin was causing crop loss by interfering with berry set, and asked the Farm Advisors to remove it from their list of recommendations. They refused to strike it from the list, a move that Doutt says "was due to the power of the chemical companies over Co-operative Extension." He adds, "Chemical company grants can't help but influence University scientists."

Win Hart, a professor of nematology at U.C. Davis, recently testified at a federal hearing that some mini-grant sponsored research into the effectiveness of new pesticide products is reported on a confidential basis to the manufacturer. Hart testified that he and other scientists have reported to the chemical manufacturer that a new product does not work, but that the company has gone ahead and marketed the pesticide anyway.

U.C. Extension entomology specialist Clancy Davis says that the Farm Advisors have encountered a "research gap" that has impeded the development of IPM in other crops. Not enough basic research has been done. The biological control scientists blame the research gap on a shortage of funds, and an unsympathetic University administration. "Obviously there are no chemical companies that come down here to give us money," says Don Dahlsten of the Division of Biological Control. "We spend all our time chasing after little grants."

"The budget for biological control, in terms of real dollars, is shrinking at a phenomenal rate," says Andy Gutierrez. "It's going down the tubes fast. I doubt that we have 10 percent of the operating budget in terms of effective dollars that we had in 1968." Recognizing the financial squeeze, Gutierrez went to the University administration in 1972 to ask it to submit a bill to the state legislature for a special appropriation for IPM research. "The thing never got off the ground," he says.

In 1975, the administration launched an effort to eliminate the Division of Biological Control by merging it with the more chemically oriented Division of Entomology. The eight biological control scientists would lose their autonomy and become part of a 35 member department. Robert van den Bosch would be stripped of his position as Chair of the Division of Biological Control. "You could write a scenario of agribusiness putting pressure on University officials—get these people off our back," says Dahlsten, who joined his fellow scientists in fighting the consolidation tooth and nail. After an outpouring of support from scientists throughout the world, the U.C. administration abandoned its plan.

The new pest control approach was given a big boost when the National Science Foundation (NSF) and the En-

vironmental Protection Agency (EPA) jointly funded a six-year nationwide program to develop IPM for five crops and the pine beetle. Headed by Carl Huffaker at the Division of Biological Control, the program developed a short season cotton cropping system that increased the profits of Texas farmers by $150 an acre. It also introduced a wasp into Florida citrus groves that has parasitized scale insects, saving growers $10 million a year in reduced insecticide costs.[13]

Finally, after seven years of lobbying and numerous study committees, the persistance of Andy Gutierrez and his fellow scientists paid off. The state legislature has granted the University's $1.1 million request for funds to do Integrated Pest Management research and extension. The funds are to be used for research grants, a computer to process research data, pest control manuals on IPM practices for several crops, and to hire 5 IPM Farm Advisors. The first year of the program has been spent appointing advisory committees, planning, and writing and reviewing grants proposals.

III.

Alfred Boyce, former Dean of the College of Agriculture at U.C. Riverside, said that University researchers have come to regard close cooperation with the chemical industry as part of their job. "I can remember a time when it was not considered ethical by some Federal and

State (Experiment Station) workers to associate with representatives of industry, either professionally or socially," said Boyce. "That attitude began to disappear in the mid 1930s, and I think had completely disappeared by the end of the war." In place of an adversary relationship, he said, a cooperative effort has developed, where University researchers help generate the data that chemical companies need for convincing government agencies that their products are safe and effective. Public research agencies, he added, invest about as much money in doing this research as the chemical manufacturer does.[14]

The scientific expertise on particular products is often developed by research projects that have been supported by a manufacturer's grant. The professors who become "expert witnesses" at government regulatory proceedings are frequently subject to a conflict of interest. They may feel obligated to their research sponsor for past assistance, and they are concerned about future grants.

Don Crosby, an environmental toxicologist from U.C. Davis, has supported continued use of 2,4,5-T before both the state and federal government.[15,16] The herbicide was a component of Agent Orange, the jungle defoliant used in the Vietnam War. More recently, seven million lbs. per year have been used in the U.S. to treat forests, rice fields and grazing land.

The controversy over 2,4,5-T centers around its minute but inevitable contami-

Dave Hereth/LNS

"WELL IT STARTED OUT AS A DEODORANT, BUT WHEN WE HAD IT TESTED ON RATS IT GAVE THEM CANCER... —SO NOW WE'RE MARKETING IT AS **RAT POISON!**"

nation by a by-product of the manufacturing process, the dioxin TCDD. TCDD is one of the most toxic molecules ever discovered. It is able to cause birth defects and miscarriage in animals, at extremely low concentrations. Crosby's research showed that when TCDD is spread on a dish and set in the sun, it is broken down into harmless products[17] With the authority of the prestigous University of California, his study became a key argument in the defense of 2,4,5-T. Crosby has received $24,900 in gifts from the manufacturer, the Dow Chemical Co.

Crosby's studies did not, however, include actual measurements taken in areas where 2,4,5-T has been used. As he himself wrote, "no actual measurements of dioxin dissipation from herbicide treated forests appear to have been reported.[18]

To bridge this research gap, the state asked Crosby to help with additional tests. "What we did was to put plastic panels out where a spraying operation was going on, and collect these panels after different periods of time, measuring the amount of dioxin that was present," he says. The expense and difficulty of measuring minute quantities of dioxin prohibited him from monitoring dioxin levels in soil, trees, or water courses.

U.C. plant physiologist Boysie Day has also been active in the defense of the herbicide, testifying before hearings of the state legislature and department of agriculture. He is so firmly convinced that the chemical is safe that he ate some of it for a television news program filmed in his Berkeley laboratory. "I was demonstrating that 2,4,5-T is not acutely toxic," says Day, the former director of U.C. agricultural research.

Boysie Day and Don Crosby were appointed to a scientific task force that recommended continued use of 2,4,5-T, saying, "The evidence indicates that the TCDD contaminant in 2,4,5-T is well below levels hazardous to humans and other organisms.[19]

"Our participation in the committee," says Day, "came with the support of the Council on Agricultural Science and Technology (CAST)." Based at Iowa State University, CAST calls itself a "consortium of scientists" who provide key information to government decision makers. The organization receives tens of thousands of dollars of support from at least 36 different chemical manufacturers, including the Dow Chemical Co.

In April 1978, eight women from Alsea,

Oregon petitioned the Environmental Protection Agency, asking it to ban 2,4,5-T. Among them they had suffered 11 miscarriages between 1973 and 1977, which they felt were caused by the herbicide. "We are not trying to make rash, unsubstantiated claims," they wrote, "but we are interested in seeing if there is a cause-effect relationship. Some of us do know that large acreages near our homes and in our water drainages were sprayed within a month before our miscarriages."

When a study of Oregon hospital records showed the miscarriage rate in Alsea to be significantly higher than the rate in a control area, the EPA issued restrictions on the use of the herbicide. "The Alsea study has all the dignity of a rumor," says Boysie Day. "It was a political decision by the EPA, plain and simple. There is no danger to people from 2,4,5-T use," he maintains.

The University of California has a program to provide information on pesticides that are suspected of being a threat to public health or the environment, to the Environmental Protection Agency. The objective of the program is to submit both risks and benefits data," says Harold Alford, U.C. Pesticide Impact Co-ordinator and director of the program. A committee is formed to provide the EPA with information on the suspect pesticide. The committee includes University professors, state officials, and representatives of the manufacturer of the pesticide, or lobbyists from pesticide industry associations. Scientists from the University school of medicine have never participated in a committee. Nor has the program invited labor unions, state OSHA officials, or environmental groups. Many of the University scientists appointed to these committees received mini-grants from the manufacturer of the pesticide.

"We are gathering largely benefits data," acknowledges Alford. "Sometimes we rebut the risk, but in most cases we don't. As a rule, we spell out the need for a chemical in California, how important it is, and why we need to keep it." He adds, "If we came by information showing a greater risk than EPA knew about, then we'd send it to them. We haven't done that though, because we don't get that type of information."

Outside of this program, however, information that the University scientists discover on the safety and effectiveness of chemicals is not usually reported directly to the government agencies that register

pesticides. Since chemical companies are responsible for submitting the data, they have the option of turning over only those studies which put their products in the most favorable light. Government agencies consider this registration data a "trade secret" and none of it, not even the University studies, is open to the public.

By some estimates, pesticide-induced illness makes agricultural work one of the most dangerous occupations in California.[20] Virtually every year there are dramatic episodes of workers falling ill, involving as many as 100 people working in a single orchard or vineyard. "Occupational injury from pesticides is a subject of great concern from the public health standpoint," said state Health Director Dr. Louis Saylor in releasing the results of a 1969 survey of more than 1,000 farm workers. The public health study found that 25 percent of those surveyed had sought medical treatment for pesticide poisoning in the previous year.[21] "A large percentage of pesticide-related injuries involve serious, disabling illness," said Saylor.

On the job poisonings have been largely attributed to organophosphates, potent insecticides which harm both insects and humans by interfering with the nerve enzyme cholinesterase (a strong nerve stimulator). Many organophosphates degrade into even more toxic compounds which may be absorbed through the skin by touching treated crops or foliage. Residues are also toxic when inhaled. Symptoms of this kind of poisoning include nausea, tremors, vomiting, headache, cramps, weakness, and impaired breathing.

Pesticide safety became a key issue delaying the resolution of the California table grape boycott. Negotiation over safety provisions caused an extra one year of delay before contracts were finally signed between the United Farmworkers Union and 28 Delano grape growers in 1970. That year, the Health Department investigated four more mass poisonings involving 175 workers in San Joaquin Valley citrus groves. Occupational Health Chief Thomas Milby headed up a task force which was appointed to help resolve the worker safety problem.

Out of Milby's group came "worker reentry intervals," state regulations ordering workers to stay out of orchards for a specified time after spraying. FMC-Niagra Chemical Co. protested the new regulations arguing that the 30-day waiting period required for its organophosphate product Ethion could be shortened to seven days.

A safety trial was set for an orchard near Lindsay, California. J. Blair Bailey, the pesticide safety specialist in the University of California Co-operative Extension, helped with the test. "We set up the orchard, did the application," says Bailey. "It was a co-operative study with FMC." FMC-Niagra supplied the doctor who took blood samples from workers, and analyzed the cholinesterase level.

The Agribusiness Accountability Project, a public interest group, charged that the chemical company used "human guinea pigs" to test dangerous chemicals in violation of the new re-entry standards.[22,23] Field researcher Al Krebs said the subjects were not volunteers, and were not informed of the experiment's dangers. The test included a 24-year-old man under treatment for chronic headaches, a 44-year-old man with diabetes, a 15-year-old girl with a recent skull fracture, and a 38-year-old woman suffering from anemia.

"Some people accused us of using these people as guinea pigs, but we weren't," says Bailey. "I was working right alongside them, and didn't subject them to anything I wasn't subjected to."

After several trials with different chemicals. Bailey reported that workers could re-enter orchards sooner than the new state regulations allowed. He recommended that the state Dept. of Food and Agriculture shorten the reentry time for parathion, an organophosphate that is the most common cause of the mass poisoning of field crews.[24] A later University study, by Robert Spear of the U.C. School of Public Health, showed Bailey's recommendation to have been ill-advised, and that the re-entry period was actually too short.[25,26]

A group of scientists headed by Wendell Kilgore at U.C. Davis studied the health of workers who entered a peach orchard recently sprayed with the insecticide Guthion.[27] While the study was in progress, one worker refused to give any additional blood samples. He was fired from the picking crew, and complained to state officials. The grievance eventually reached the Director of Health, Dr. Jerome Lackner, who was so angered by the coercive nature of the tests that he successfully obtained a directive forbidding the use of farm workers in future experiments. Lackner suggested that the University scientists should seek ranch managers, professors or

University regents to be the subjects of future tests.

When the U.C. Davis Guthion study was complete, the chemical's manufacturer, Chemagro, used it to petition the state to relax the reentry standard. Dr. Keith Maddy, head of the Worker Safety Unit of the Dept. of Food and Agriculture, said this was not done, because while the orchard may be safe after 48 hours, in a week or so, a poisonous breakdown product makes the orchard hazardous again. "The U.C. Davis people came out with data that at 48 hours there was not significant cholinesterase depression, but our position is that if you wait another week, you'll be up to your eyebrows in trouble," says Maddy, adding, "to my knowledge, the University didn't go back and study what happens in a week."

Chemical manufacturer Rhodia, Inc., approached U.C. public health scientist Robert Spear about a study on the safety of its product Zolone. "What they wanted was to get the re-entry time down from 21 days to seven, for some market advantage I'm not clear on," says Spear. He proposed a methodology, which was revised by the chemical company. While the company's influence was balanced by the input of state health officials, its grant did determine which product was studied. Rhodia gave $74,000 to support the study. Spear says he decided to accept the grant and undertake the project because it would allow him to extend his methods to a new pesticide and a new crop.[28] As a result of the study, the state shortened the reentry interval on Zolone to 14 days.

Several U.C. scientists have been active in opposing the ban on the pesticide DBCP, a soil fumigant used to kill nematodes, microscopic worms which feed on crop roots. "We're unhappy with the loss of DBCP because at present there is no suitable replacement," says Winfield Hart, a nematologist with the University of California at Davis. He estimates that the ban may cause the loss of $1 billion worth of fruit trees and grapevines. Both Hart and Armand Maggenti, another U.C. scientist who opposed the ban, have received grants from DBCP manufacturers or formulators.

The first suspicion that DBCP was harming human health came from workers who mixed and canned the pesticide at the Occidental Chemical Company plant in Lathrop, California. They wondered why

so many men working in the plant's pesticide division had not fathered children. "It was a theory among the guys for at least four or five years," says Ted Bricker. A medical check showed Bricker's sperm count to be down, and he encouraged his co-workers to get themselves checked as well.

Though the state Dept. of Health and two University health scientists had been notified of the workers' concerns, it was a pair of filmmakers making a documentary on dangerous jobs who put up the $100 it took to have a local medical clinic run the first fertility checks. Fourteen of the Lathrop workers were found to be sterile; 34 had reduced fertility.[29] DBCP workers in Arkansas and Alabama were also discovered to be sterile. One man developed testicular cancer.

Trials to prove that DBCP can be safely used to kill nematodes in orchard soils were conducted by U.C. farm advisor Doug Johnson. He was assisted by a representative of Amvac Chemical Corp., a DBCP supplier. During the trial, they handled DBCP during loading and unloading without protective clothing, gloves, or respirators, and spilled some chemical twice. Johnson picked up a handful of dirt from one of the spills and sniffed it to see if it contained DBCP, which it did. State health inspectors observed the trial and criticized "the cavalier attitude and utter disdain for minimizing exposure to a known carcinogen."

Johnson told a *Los Angeles Times* reporter that he and the Amvac representative were "only doing what we've done for 20 years. We don't feel the material is hazardous."[30] In the last three years Johnson received $29,750 in gifts from pesticide companies, including DBCP manufacturer Dow Chemical Co. "Chemical company mini-grants have allowed us, and me in particular, to acquire equipment that we normally wouldn't have been able to acquire," he says. Johnson recently resigned from the University to accept a job with a pesticide company.

In the last two years DBCP has become nothing less than a public health disaster. The film about the Occidental workers was named "The Song of the Canary," because as the canary warns the coal miner of dangerous air, the chemical worker is testing the safety of toxic chemicals for society. It was a prophetic title. High levels of DBCP residues were found in food. California health officials discovered that

155,000 people had been drinking water contaminated by hazardous levels of the pesticide, and ordered more than 40 municipal wells shut down. Lois Rossi, a biostatistician at the EPA, calculates that 10 ppb (parts per billion) of DBCP consumed in drinking water over a lifetime would cause 2,000 new cases of cancer per million population.[31]

In October of 1977 the state Department of Industrial Relations held hearings to investigate why such a potent poison had been overlooked and allowed into the workplace.[32] Among the witnesses was Dr. Charles Hine, who did research showing DBCP damages the testicles of experimental rats in his lab at the U.C. School of Medicine in San Francisco. Although he was employed by the University, and was working in its laboratory, said Hine, his research was supported by a grant from the Shell Chemical Corporation, and was reported on a confidential basis to Shell.[33]

Hine recommended to Shell that exposure to 1 ppm (part per million) would be a "no-effect" level for chemical workers, though he had no experimental data to prove it. He suggested further studies to the vice-president of Shell's Agricultural Chemical Division, but dropped the subject when the Shell executive said they would not be necessary. "I think we should have gone to a no-effect level, and I admit the error in this thing," he testified. He agreed with hearing officer Don Vial's assessment that his research priorities were set by a "market place concept," that they are a matter of "who is going to come up with the money to do what you've considered objective research."

Hine was also asked about his financial ties to Shell. Since he joined the University faculty in 1947, Shell contributed approximately $400,000 to his University research projects. Also since 1947, Hine has been receiving consulting fees from Shell. His private San Francisco laboratory has a contract to supply health data to the Agricultural Chemical Division of Shell.

Charles Hine was not the only U.C. scientist to ignore the hazards of DBCP. Chemists, nematologists, toxicologists and occupational health specialists, more than a dozen scientists in all, ran studies on the compound. Their research showed that it could be applied to the soil to kill pest nematodes, that it was relatively safe, and that little residue appeared in treated crops.

Though the scientists were on the public payroll, their research was supported by 30 Shell grants worth $47,800. Most of these funds were used in research projects to demonstrate the usefulness of Shell products, including its brand of DBCP, Nemagon.

"Facts developed are to be used in support of label registration and the development of sound recommendations, where justified," wrote Shell executive W.E. McCauley in a letter that accompanied one of the gifts.[34] "More specifically, we are interested in the development of data to support the use of Nemagon Soil Fumigant," said his letter, which added that the actual activities "should be discussed in greater detail with our local representative."

Bert Lear, a nematologist at the Davis campus, reported to the University administration in 1965 that "Studies in greenhouse and laboratory showed that tomato seedlings absorb DBCP through the roots and translocate it upwards.[35] The result was never published, Lear says today, because "That wasn't our purpose. We were just testing DBCP movement in soil." Unaware of the studies, the Food and Drug Administration incorrectly assumed that since DBCP is applied to the soil and not the plant, then no residues would appear on produce.

Though their research showed DBCP is highly soluble in water[36] and that it has a low affinity for soil,[37] Lear and Doug Johnson, a graduate student who helped him with his research, did not test to see how deeply the chemical would leach. "We only checked what happened to DBCP after one irrigation," says Johnson. It was a tremendous oversight. After 20 years of use, DBCP has evidently leached down hundreds of feet to contaminate ground water supplies.

While most University research was focused on testing of chemicals to control nematodes, at least one scientist is studying non-chemical alternatives. "It has been long believed that decaying vegetable matter, manure, and similar soil amendments can restrict some nematode populations in the soil," reported U.C. Riverside nematologist Ron Mankau. "Such materials may favor the development of fungi and other organisms that attack nematodes.[38] Last year Mankau and two other Riverside nematologists reported success in cultivating a fungus which can parasitize the eggs of the root knot nematode. They

used it to reduce nematode populations in peach orchards.[39]

Though most farm groups oppose the DBCP ban, one grower wrote the Dept. of Food and Agriculture urging it to keep the ban. He claimed that there would be no nematode problem if farmers used cover crops and manure to build up organic matter in the soil.

In response to the discovery of DBCP induced sterility of chemical workers, the California legislature appropriated $2 million to establish an Occupational Health Center at the University of California. The goal of the center is to train occupational health scientists and improve job safety in California.

Quite ironically, the man who has been criticized as part of the problem has been put in charge of the reform. The University has named Dr. Charles Hine as co-director of the residency program of the new center, where he will supervise the training of physicians.

"We oppose Hine's appointment not just because of this involvement in suppressing his DBCP research, but also because he has done studies minimizing the hazards of working in the lead industry," says Ellen Shaffer, President of the U.C. Medical Center Employees Union (AFSCME). Her local has joined with environmental groups and locals of the Teamsters, longshoremen's and chemical workers' unions in forming the Coalition for a Responsible Occupational Health Center. "To meet the needs of working people, the center must have a component for direct worker education, and an advisory board with firm labor support," she says.

IV.

A critical question for the future success of controlling agricultural pests in California, is whether University scientists will act independently of the marketing concerns of the chemical industry. As the system now operates, pesticide manufacturers influence what pest control strategies get studied. Their gifts go to those professors who are developing uses for specific pesticide products.

In order to get a more balanced research effort, attorney Ralph Lightstone of California Rural Legal Assistance suggests that a pesticide research fund be created. "The state could increase the tax on pesticides, and just take the money the industry is already willing to give," says Lightstone. The advantage of such a system, he points out, would be in cutting the strings tied to chemical company gifts. "The funds could be allocated according to the academic excellence of the scientists, and not by the marketing priorities of pesticide manufacturers," he says.

Reform minded faculty like U.C. Berkeley physicist Charles Schwartz have asked the Fair Political Practices Commission (FPPC) to adopt a conflict of interest code that would require faculty to disclose consulting arrangements and gifts from private industry. The Commission enforces California's political reform act, a post-Watergate ballot initiative that requires government decision makers to disclose their income and investments. It also makes it illegal for a government official to influence a decision when personal economic interests are at stake, and sets penalties for officials who use their office for financial gain.

The FPPC has decided, however, that the University conflict of interest code need not apply to professors. The reason for this exemption was given by chairman Daniel Lowenstein, who said, "The basic concern is academic freedom. There is a very strong concern built into the state Constitution that those who teach and do research should be free from outside control and outside supervision of those acts."

The irony of the FPPC decision is that those closest to the pest control controversy claim that outside influences are already at work. As Robert van den Bosch said, "I believe that the agri-chemical industry is taking advantage of its carefully nurtured ties with people in the University to promote its own version and self-definition of Integrated Pest Management, to the detriment of the sound pest control system which many of us have been striving so long to develop."[40]

References

1. "Donations for Agricultural Research—July 1, 1978-June 30, 1979," *California Agriculture*, Vol. 34, No. 2, pp. 18-20, February, 1980.

2. Labor Occupational Health Program, "DBCP Warning Ignored: State Hearings," *Monitor*, Vol. 4, No. 8, November-December 1977.

3. *Agrichemical Age*, "In Defense of 2,4,5-T," p. 14, June 1978.

4. Sward, Susan, "An Ironic Touch to the Ag Pesticide Research Story," Associated Press, *Woodland-Davis Daily Democrat*, March 10, 1978.

5. California Auditor General, "The University of California System: Private Support Program." *Report to the California Legislature*

715.5, Calif. Joint Legislative Audit Committee, June, 1978, Sacramento.

6. Univ. of Calif., Davis, Office of Public Affairs, "UCD Research Ties Termed 'Healthy' —not 'Unholy,' "Press Release 792699, December 12, 1979.

7. Fujimoto, Isao and Emmett Fiske, "What Research Gets Done at a Land Grant College: Internal Factors at Work." Presented at the 1975 Rural Sociological Society Meeting, San Francisco.

8. Luck, Robert F., R. van den Bosch, and R. Garcia, "Chemical Insect Control—A Troubled Pest Management Strategy," *Bioscience*, Vol. 27, No. 9, pp. 606-611, September, 1977.

9. Hall, Darwin C., "The Profitability of Integrated Pest Management: Case Studies for Cotton and Citrus in the San Joaquin Valley," *ESA Bulletin*, Vol. 23, No. 4, pp. 267-74, 1977.

10. Barnett, William W., C. S. Davis, and G. A. Rowe, "Minimizing Pear Pest Control Costs Through Integrated Pest Management," *California Agriculture*, Vol. 32, No. 2, pp. 12-13, February, 1978.

11. Stimman, J. and J. Swift, "Analysis of University of California Pest Control Recommendations, Appendix I," in Univ. of Calif. Response to Calif. Dept. of Food and Agriculture Hearing on Environment Defense Fund Petition Pertaining to Licensed Pest Control Advisors, 1977.

12. University of Calif. Co-operative Extension Service, "Minutes of Administrative Staff Meeting," October 31, November 1-3, 1972.

13. Marx, Jean L., "Applied Ecology: Showing the Way to Better Insect Control," *Science*, Vol. 195, pp. 860-862, March 4, 1977.

14. University of Calif. at Davis, *Conference on the Use of Agricultural Chemicals in California*, Proceedings, January 15, 1964.

15. Rominger, R. E., "Report of the Director on Phenoxy Herbicides," Calif. Dept. of Food and Agriculture, April 6, 1978, Sacramento.

16. "California's Response to the EPA's Rebuttable Presumption Against Registration of 2,4,5-T" Compiled by the University of California.

17. Crosby, D. G. and A. S. Wong, "Environment Degradation of 2,3,7,8 tetrachlorodibenzo-p-dioxin (TCDD)," *Science*, Vol. 195, p. 1337 (1977).

18. Crosby, D. G., "Conquering the Monster—The Photochemical Destruction of Chlorodioxins," American Chemical Society Symposium Series No. 73, Disposal and Decontamination of Pesticides, 1978.

19. Council for Agricultural Science and Technology, *The Phenoxy Herbicides*, Second Edition, August 1978, Ames, Iowa.

20. Swartz, Joel. "Poisoning Farmworkers," *Environment*. Vol. 17, No. 4, June, 1975, pp. 26-33.

21. Calif. Dept. of Public Health, "Calfornia Community Studies on Pesticides: Morbidity and Mortality of Poisoning," Report to Office of Pesticides, Bureau of State Services (EH), US Public Health Service, January 15, 1970.

22. Mintz, Morton, "Farm Group Says People Were Used to Test Pesticides," *Washington Post*, February 11, 1971.

23. Walters, Robert, "Pesticide Tests: Human Guinea Pigs Used?" *The Evening Star*, February 10, 1971, Washington, D.C.

24. University of California, "Ag Specialist

Describes Test Results," *University Bulletin*, Vol. 21, No. 6, September 25, 1972.

25. Spear, Robert C., et al, "Worker Poisonings Due to Paroxon Residues," *Journal of Occupational Medicine*, Vol. 19, No. 6, June, 1977, pp. 411-414.

26. Spear, Robert C., et al., "Fieldworkers' Response to Weathered Residues of Parathion," *Journal of Occupational Medicine*, Vol. 19, No. 6, June, 1977, pp. 406-410.

27. Kraus, J., et al., "Physiological Response to Organophosphate Residues in Field Workers," *Archives of Environmental Contamination and Toxicology*, Vol. 5, pp. 471-485, 1977.

28. Poppendorf, W. J., R. C. Spear, J. T. Leffingwell, and J. Yager, E. Kahn, "Harvester Exposure to Zolone (Phosolone) Residues in Peach Orchards," *Journal of Occupational Medicine*, Vol. 21, No. 3, March 1979, pp. 189-94.

29. Wharton, Donald, T. H. Milby, R. M. Krauss, and H. A. Stubbs, "Testicular Function in DBCP Exposed Pesticide Workers," *Journal of Occupational Medicine*, Vol. 21, No. 3, pp. 161-166, March, 1979.

30. Taylor, Ronald B., "DBCP Still Used Despite Danger," *Los Angeles Times*, p. I, part I, June 28, 1979.

31. Rossi, Lois, "Risk Calculation Utilizing Recent Data on DBCP Levels in Drinking Water," U.S. Environmental Protection Agency, Washington, D.C., June, 1979.

32. Calif. Dept. of Industrial Relations, "Occupational Safety and Health—Dibromochloropropane Inquiry," Day III, October 18, 1977, Henderscheid and Associates, Shorthand Reporters, San Francisco.

33. Anderson, H. H., C. H. Hine, J. K. Kodama, and J. S. Wellington, "An Evaluation of the Degree of Toxicity of 1,2-Dibromo-3-Chloropropane. I. Chronic Feeding Experiments in Rodents," U.C. Report No. 228, Confidential Report to Shell Development Co., Dept. of Pharmacology and Experimental Medicine, U.C. School of Medicine, 1958, San Francisco.

34. McCauley, W. E., Letter to M. W. Allen, Chairman of the Dept. of Nematology, U.C. Davis, March 15, 1966, From Pesticide Development Dept., Shell Chemical Co., New York.

35. Lear, Bert, "Project No. H-1626—Annual Summary of Progress for Year," U.C. Agricultural Experiment Station, Years 1964-1966.

36. Johnson, D.E. and Bert Lear, "The Effect of Temperature on the Dispersion of 1,2-Dibromo-3-Chloropropane in Soil," *Journal of Nematology*, Vol. 1, No. 2, pp. 116-121, 1969.

37. Johnson, D. E. and Bert Lear. "Evaluating the Movement of 1,2-Dibromo-3-Chloropropane Through Soil," *Soil Science*, Vol. 105, pp. 31-35, 1968.

38. Mankau, R., "Natural Enemies of Nematodes," *California Agriculture*, p. 24, September, 1959.

39. Stirling, Graham R., M. V. McHenry, and Ron Mankau, "Biological Control of Root Knot Nematode in Peach," *California Agriculture*, pp. 6-7, September 1978.

40. Van den Bosch, Robert, "Memo on the University's Co-sponsoring with WACA and CAPCA of Pest Management Seminars at Bakersfield on May 10, 1977 and Fresno on May 11, 1977," Letter to U.C. Vice-President J. B. Kendrick, May 6, 1977.

SCIENCE for PEOPLE

From *Science for People*, nos. 43/44 (1980), pp. 27-30

Plant Breeding Under Capitalism

by Jonathan Jones

What is plant breeding? Is it ideological? Would it be very different in a socialist society? What does looking at plant breeding and its associated scientific work tell us about the relationship between science and capitalism, and about appropriate responses to capitalist science? These are difficult questions but there is much in the history of agriculture that is instructive.

What lessons one learns reflect one's habits of interpretation, and I want to make mine clear by briefly talking about science and ideology. Science is a social process integral to the economy and mentality of industrialised Western societies. Part of the reason for this is that it is based on a powerful methodology for finding things out that are new, surprising, and offer the possibility of manipulating Nature for personal or corporate gain. Ideas are tested, and those found wanting are dumped. Those not found wanting are circulated in journals and conferences, and perused thoughtfully by amongst others, the captains of industry. This is hardly surprising, but other aspects of the class partisanship of science are more subtle, and so we have to talk about ideology of or in science. For example, certain avenues of research may never have been opened up, because at a crucial early stage in the development of the field, it became clear that there was no money in it. So any given set of facts that seem perfectly reasonable and true, are only what they are because of hidden choices. Clear misapprehensions may exist about the context of the research: for example to get a research grant in the USA to work on plants it is almost obligatory to say something about the possible applications of research in easing the 'world's' food problem, at a time when

Reprinted with permission from *Science for People,* magazine of the British Society for Social Responsibility in Science.

the USA can't get rid of all the food it produces. And many workers in this area actually believe they are doing something useful. Another aspect of science is that the scientific elites reproduce and support the power relations in society as a whole, both in the scientific hierarchies and in the scientists' roles as experts. But this ideological aspect of science does not *preclude* the validity of its observations, though a point of view that is manifestly absurd can be quite informative about the lack of objectivity of its proponent.

Plant breeding is a technology, not a science. It is concerned with producing varieties of crops which can be registered and earn royalties via plant breeders' rights legislation. Farmers buy these new varieties if they increase the profitability of their agriculture. Their production is based on genetics: take two varieties, make a cross, and select in the second and subsequent generations for desirable products of the recombination in the first generation. The criteria of selection are cultural as well as agricultural. So if certain agricultures were socialist rather than capitalist, then one would have to talk about plants bred for different societies, and of capitalist genotypes and socialist genotypes. Most plant breeding is designed around the agriculture of the richest farmers, and it is important to put it this way rather than suggesting that plant breeding is *causing* changes in agriculture.

A few examples should illustrate this. The classic one is that of the Green Revolution.[1] It purported to be the technological fix to end all food shortages, but the reality is more complicated. The technology involved the breeding of high yielding varieties (HYVs) which could thrive on large quantities of fertiliser without falling over, and could, under appropriate conditions of pesticide application and irrigation, double or treble existing yields. The catch for most farmers, lay in the amount of money required to purchase the technology to provide these appropriate conditions. Other effects were less obvious; for example the price of grain fell in some areas which meant that thousands of peasant farmers earned less money in those rare good years when they produced a surplus. Also, by putting more carbohydrate into the grain, the protein

concentration actually fell. And of course, a new market was created for US petrochemical firms (such as Esso, owned by Rockefeller, whose money paid for the original Mexican work which led to the Green Revolution). The steam was taken out of pressure for land reform, and for the breakup of large, underused privately owned estates—why do anything politically rash when technology can solve your problems?—and so US foreign policy was reassured. And the science concentrated on researching into production by highly capital intensive systems with a few crops, to the neglect of working on varieties of local species and peasant production systems. The rich got richer and peasants were dispossessed and moved to the cities in droves. Food production, malnutrition, and social divisions all increased. The lot of the rural poor in many areas actually deteriorated. This account is somewhat oversimplified but it does reflect what happened in many areas of Asia and Latin America. Apologists would argue that to bring the peasantry into the mainstream of economic life, temporary uncomfortable changes are inevitable, and that this discomfort is more than compensated for by the increases in food production. The only reason for their acuteness is that these changes are happening in decades instead of the 300 years they took for European agriculture. But there is no inevitability about new technology impoverishing thousands and lining the pockets of a few, except in a free market economic system where wide disparities in wealth already exist. In the Green Revolution choices were made which affected the species which were varietally developed, the criteria by which they were selected and the agricultural systems for which they were designed. These choices favoured local elites, US foreign policy, and multinational agrochemical firms at the expense of those most in need of help, the rural poor.

Some examples are closer to home. An unusual law suit has been filed in California, against its university at Davis.[2] It is remarkable for the fact that it is suing science because science is not neutral. The plaintiffs (California Rural Legal Assistance) demand that the university cease all research on any agricultural mechanisation process which conveys 'a special economic benefit to narrow private agribusiness interests at the expense of farmworkers, small family farms, consumers, taxpayers and the quality of rural life.' University of California, Los Angeles, Davis (UCLA

Davis) reply that 'the basic mission of the university is research and the creation of new knowledge, and that acceptance of the plaintiffs' proposition would require the elimination of all research of any potential practical application'. These are big stakes in the USA. UCLA Davis' work, state financed to the tune of $150,000 a year, has been to mechanise agriculture: among their achievements has been the development of automatic tomato pickers and sorters, and the breeding of a thick skinned square tomato which can withstand their attentions. As a consequence, summer-time employment for thousands of migratory workers has substantially declined. The United Farmworkers Union has found its bargaining power reduced. One tomato grower, the target of an unsuccessful UFW campaign, brought a $200,000 tomato picker and harvester and cut his labour force from 100 to 28, and at the same time got rid of his 'troublemakers'. At UCLA Davis, they say 'the machine won't strike, it will work when the owners want it to work'. Is this a neutral technology? Do all taxpayers benefit equally from the support of the UCLA Davis programme? It looks more as if the major beneficiaries are the large corporate and private farms in the area, which grow a large proportion of all the tomatoes grown in the USA, and that the losers are their workers, small growers (who can't compete in the market), and consumers who pay taxes for the research grant, and for the unemployment benefit for those made unemployed, and get tasteless tomatoes at high prices into the bargain.

At this point it is worth looking again at some of the arguments advanced by the establishment. 'The universities' responsibility is to create new knowledge or information, to develop new ways to produce food as efficiently as possible, and to be aware of new developments and so forth. But in terms of the conflict of social goals, that's not only our job but the job of society, of the legislature', said Professor Charles Hess of UCLA Davis in a recent interview. But whose efficiency is at stake? Not the efficiency of earning enough to support the lives of migrant workers and their kin. And Hugh Bunting, professor of agricultural development overseas at the University of Reading says that[3] 'societies use technical advances in accordance with their existing mores and social arrangements, which it is the business of politics rather than agricultural science and technology to alter.' While this latter point

is true, agricultural science cannot plead neutrality if it is at the same time being designed around the enriching of the already rich. The content of agricultural science is a result of politics, not a challenge to it. Another quote from Bunting is revealing—'the job of technology is to provide the cake, and the job of politics is to distribute it'. Ironically, it is as if he assumes that a socialist millenium has arrived, and the means of production belongs to 'society'. But instead of being socially owned, the cake machines are privately owned, and the more efficient they are made, the more they serve the interests of the owners rather than the employees. The criteria around which new technologies are developed are political as well as technical criteria.

So what about Britain? The biggest plant breeding organisation in this country is probably the Plant Breeding Institute (P.B.I.) in Cambridge, grant aided by the Agricultural Research Council (ARC). It works on a range of crops, but in the words of one worker there 'compared to wheat, everything else is peanuts'(!). Its major competitor in cereal breeding is a private company called Rothwell Plant Breeders (of which more later). The general atmosphere is staid and self-congratulatory. The wheat breeders have good reason to be pleased with themselves because they certainly achieve their own aims, which are mainly to create HYVs for animal feed, which is what most British wheat ends up as. The PBI has won two Queen's Awards for Industry for services to exports. Recently, more effort has been put into creating HYVs of good baking quality. There are frequent visits from industry— ICI, Unilever, Fisons, Ciba Geigy and even Rothwells, its competitor. And of course all the botanical journals arrive in the library: *New Phytologist*, *Plant Physiology*, *Planta* etc. You can't tell where the science stops and the economics start.

But the economic context is bizarre. In the EEC there is a huge dried milk mountain. Where does it come from? Cattle. And where do they come from? Animal feed. There is no shortage of animal feed, yet extensive research is put into producing more. Wheat is generally grown on the best agricultural land, where there are more large farms and a higher level of mechanisation; for example the 'animal feed baskets' of East Anglia and Lincolnshire. To those that have shall be given—it's the same old story. Compared to expenditure on wheat research, expendi-

ture on wheat research, expenditure on hill farming or improving health and safety for farm workers is derisory. The real priority in increasing the efficiency of food production is to compete more effectively in the EEC market with our 'partners'. And the CAP which guarantees farm prices and so generates overproduction is a defence against an aggressive food exporting policy in the USA.

What of the future? There are certain developments at the present time which could well be very significant. Probably the most important has been the growing trend for large petrochemical companies to buy up plant breeders and seed merchants; the purchase of Rothwell Plant Breeders and Nickerson's seeds by Royal Dutch Shell, and of Pioneer Hi Bred International by Ciba Geigy are conspicuous examples of this. Agrochemicals have long been one of the growth points in sales of chemicals, and it is hard to resist the temptation to think that these companies are basically out to protect their markets. After all, after investing £10M in developing a new pesticide one does not want a plant breeder producing a resistant variety, and eliminating the market. Many companies are entering the field, with ICI in Britain and Monsanto in the USA working on producing varieties which respond well to synthetic growth hormones, or which are resistant to weedkillers. The Monsanto example is particularly interesting, because they are working on tissue cultures of alfalfa, enabling the screening process for herbicide resistance to be speeded up. It turns out that the basis of the resistance lies in a hundredfold amplification of the gene coding for an enzyme which inefficiently degrades the chemical. In the absence of selection for this amplification (i.e. in the absence of the herbicide), the copy number of the gene reverts back to wild type, so that even in the absence of weeds the herbicide must still be applied to a crop to maintain resistance. Invest in Monsanto, kids, their markets are assured! This tissue culture work is indicative of a growing preoccupation of these companies with biotechnology. It is surprising that they have not got into it sooner. As oil prices continue to rise, chemical feedstocks derived from contemporary rather than past photosynthesis will become more attractive. Brazil is using a gasohol for vehicles, containing 20% ethanol obtained from fermentation of sugar cane derived sucrose. Photosynthesis, possibly in huge vats, could provide large quantities of single molecules, or of more complex ones, such as alkaloids and steroids of commercial significance. A slow start on this work at ICI has been blamed on the fact that the older generation there are all chemists who are reluctant to move into areas outside their expertise. Other companies have been quicker off the mark: Ciba Geigy, for example, fund one of the best equipped tissue culture labs in Europe at their research centre in Basle. The central threat is that these companies are in a position to extend into agriculture their ability to define the mode of production and the relations of production in the chemical industry. Nickersons seeds (I mean Royal Dutch Shell) own a subsidiary called Universal Plant Breeders International with branches in over twenty countries including many in the Third World. They are in a position to influence the kind of agriculture that develops, and the consolidation of the power of local elites, and the markets that are opened up for foreign business, without having to do any farming at all. And this takes place in the USA despite antitrust laws which are supposed to prevent this kind of vertical integration. A new era of genetic imperialism is beginning.

Another aspect to this genetic imperialism is the response to recent alarm expressed about the erosion of the 'world's' genetic resources. UN/FAO sponsored collecting expeditions journeying to obscure parts of various Third World countries, especially in the Middle East, to collect wild species or local cultivars which are related to present day crops. The idea is that by screening this seed for disease resistance or protein quality, and then storing it in seed stores, the advance of the HYVs through the grain growing areas of these countries will not permanently eliminate all the natural variation that exists for these characters, and there will always be a broad range of genotypes to select from in a breeding programme. What happens to this seed? It is stored in duplicate in genetic banks in Europe and America. In some countries private firms are actually able to bid for promising accessions, but in most cases samples of accessions are supplied free to private and public breeding organisations who are interested. Useful characters can be bred into new varieties which can then be marketed abroad as HYVs. So a favourable genotype, in an ancient cultivar in a country such as Turkey, can be effectively ripped off by the FAO, acquired by a seed firm, bred into a HYV, and returned (at a price) to the country of origin. Other 'world' resources (such as oil) don't seem to get this treatment. A price is paid for the processing, but the resource (and many Third World countries have few enough resources as it is) should also be paid for. One of the reasons why it isn't in the case of crop plant genetic resources is that food is presented in the media as being above market forces, and as a resource with which altruism should be exercised. In fact it is very big business. Any idea that 'food is for sharing' (God I hate those badges) only serves to mystify that fact.

Can capitalism be shown to have actually retarded breeding strategy in any case? This is hard to prove, but the example of F1 Hybrid seed is interesting here. The scientific basis is in the phenomenon of hybrid vigour. All of the major maize varieties in the USA are F1 hybrids. Different crops display hybrid vigour to differing extents and wheat shows it to a much lesser extent than maize. However, an enormous amount of research effort has gone into looking for it in wheat. One of the obvious attractions of hybrid seed for a seed firm is that the farmer *has* to buy new seed each year, and the possibility of farm saved seed is eliminated. This would considerably increase the cereal seed market. And Richard Lewontin is reported to have argued that the F1 hybrid breeding strategy in maize has been counterproductive, because the short term interest of hybrid seed has been pursued at the expense of the long term need to pursue a programme of recurrent selection in an outbreeding population of maize cultivars in order to broaden the genetic base for selection. As a result this base is extremely narrow and quite vulnerable to a new race of disease. One doesn't need to be convinced of the counterproductivity of emphasis on hybrid seed to see that the direction of research work has been influenced by commercial imperatives.

So what do these examples tell us about science, ideology and truth? Is applied science any more ideological than pure science? What are the most appropriate political responses to capitalist plant science?

My view is that, except for sciences which directly affect human beings' perception of themselves and their societies (such as psychology) the most politically important ideologies lie in the choice of questions to ask, rather than in what the results are or how they are interpreted. People tend to forget that science involves doing experiments and that this does confer a considerable degree of open-mindedness on scientific thought (though only within certain limits, of course). It is this openmindedness which leads to those new discoveries so dear to the hearts of company directors, and of course some discoveries that aren't, as well. In molecular biology no one is very interested in a new idea unless experiments can be designed to test it out. If you don't believe someone else's experiments you can repeat them yourself. Doing experiments to test an idea can provide information about previously unimagined processes or structures. The recent discovery of split genes is an example of this. This discovery has generated a whole series of new experiments and data which derive from questions that no one would ever have asked if there had never been any evidence for split genes.

Is this an example of partial autonomy of science from ideology? Could ideology really be constitutive at this branch point in science? I would say that it could be, but not at a level which leads to much political struggle. One can indeed argue that Francis Bacon's[4] vision of science involved in a very capitalist division of labour in the production of knowledge, and that in a sense every aspect of scientific activity is imbued with certain characteristics of this vision and those which succeeded it. For example, reductionism and the analytic process are preoccupied with the structures of components rather than with understanding the whole system or process. Lewontin and Levins[5] have expressed very clearly the ways in which Marxism could enrich our understanding of Nature, and of the history of science. They would not deny, however, that the discovery of unsuspected aspects of the structure of genes in higher organisms must inform and expand our ideas about how these genes are expressed in the life of the organism. It is not that reductionism does not work, it is just that reductionism on its own is not enough, and that reductionism on its own is symptomatic of a manipulative attitude to life.

But anyway we do not object to capitalism because it impedes or distorts the development of scientific ideas, though we can see that an over-reductionist science is not out of place in a society which spawned the production line, the IQ test and the Vietnam War. And we certainly would not want Marxist perspective to advance science and make it more efficient at maintaining the power of the ruling class.

So if the politically significant ideologies of science lie in a class bias in the choice of the problems for study, and in the myths surrounding their significance for, say, solving the world's food problem then the applied sciences are more ideological than the pure sciences. On the other hand, if the aspects of the behavioural sciences exemplified by the work of Jensen & Eysenck on racial difference in IQs is symptomatic of the whole of science, then all science is equally ideological. Even if this is true, I am convinced that it can only lead to political struggle within the human sciences. Who would ever wear a badge saying 'Fight emphasis on structure rather than process in molecular biology!'? I don't wish to suggest that all there is to politics is wearing badges, even badges which say 'wearing badges is not enough', but any sort of a political struggle on those lines looks a non-starter.

So what is the appropriate response to capitalist science and in particular, capitalist plant breeding? It really is very difficult. I agree with Bob Young that it would be desirable to intervene at the point of organisation of new technologies, and it seems to me that the UCLA Davis law suit is an example of an attempt to do just that. The history of the struggle is instructive. It came about because there was a clear relationship between the new technology and the increase in power of employers over the workforce. In most cases the relationship is nothing like as clear. So what really needs to be done is to look at the history of agricultural science in political terms, interpreting the material in the light of the fact that choices of technological and scientific problems are political choices as well as technical ones, and the related fact that those who try to perpetuate the idea that the choices are apolitical have something to hide. It is only worth the effort if it materially assists the struggles of farmworkers and others in the food industry against deskilling, diseasing, disemploying or plain degrading technology. One of the most difficult parts of the project is the imagination needed to see what other choices might have been made, and why they weren't. A political problem with this is that it is hard to avoid invoking the hoary old use/abuse model. I think this is a pseudo-problem. There seems to me to be nothing wrong in talking about ways in which existing technology could be or could have been used to ask different questions or make different products, both with a view to historical analysis and imagining a socialist future. A challenge to

a technology at its point of origination cannot however be realistically made by a few highly motivated workers in a research institute. Only when the labour movement is prepared to challenge new technology at its origin can any progress be made. And there is a real role for BSSRS in analysing the histories of different technologies, in agriculture and elsewhere, to provide the information on which political challenges can be built. Several of us in the Agricapital Group are interested in pursuing this in agriculture, and if anyone is interested in

getting involved with this, they should contact the Agricapital Group via the BSSRS office.

Ref. (1) The Green Revolution in "How the Other Half Dies", Susan George, (Penguin).
Ref. (2) Nature 278 768 26 April 1979.
Ref. (3) In an article in New Scientist 29 March 1979, p. 1043.
Ref. (4) David Dickson, Radical Science Journal 8, 1979.
Ref. (5) Lewontin & Levins in The Radicalization of Science, Rose & Rose (Eds.), Macmillan 1976.

THE WORKBOOK

From *The Workbook* 5, no. 6 (November/December 1980): 213-18

Seed Patenting: An Invitation to Famine

by Don Hancock

Introduction

The great Irish potato famine of the last century, large corporations of today and patenting of life forms in the future seemingly have little to do with each other. However, just as millions of Irish people starved and were displaced 140 years ago because their imported, genetically similar potatoes could not withstand disease, patenting of seeds in Europe and the United States is resulting in increasing and dangerous genetic uniformity in many food plants. The implications of this uniformity are sobering for this country and the rest of the world. A growing concentration of seed patents in the hands of a few large corporations, many of which also exert significant control over fertilizers and pesticides, indicates that seed prices will almost certainly rise rapidly. Many (supposedly uneconomic) varieties will be lost because of corporate marketing which promotes their patented seeds rather than traditional varieties. Small farmers, already fighting for survival all around the

Reprinted with permission from *The Workbook*.

world, will have even less control over the seeds that they must use. Thus, it is not unreasonable to predict that blights will occur and that starvation will increase, especially in poor nations.

Genetic Uniformity and Corporate Control

The concern about genetic uniformity has grown markedly since the enactment of the 1970 Plant Variety Protection Act (Public Law 91-577, 7 U.S.C. 2321). The stated purpose of the Act was "to encourage the development of novel varieties of sexually reproduced plants and to make them available to the public, providing protection available to those who breed, develop or discover them, and thereby promoting progress in agriculture in the public interest."[1]

While in theory seed patenting should protect diversity by protecting the small breeder's invention from being stolen or misused, in fact patenting has produced *less* diversity and more corporate control over the seed industry. As a practical matter, universities and large corporations have the resources to spend years developing new plant varieties. Thus, as of December 1979, a few corporations had effectively gained control over many plant varieties:

3 corporations hold 80% of patents on beans
4 corporations hold 45% of patents on cotton
4 corporations hold 60% of patents on lettuce
4 corporations hold 62% of patents on peas
4 corporations hold 48% of patents on soybeans
4 corporations hold 36% of patents on wheat

Crops with less patenting activity show

even higher levels of concentration. For example:

4 corporations hold 69% of patents on barley
2 corporations hold 100% of patents on cauliflower
1 corporation holds 100% of patents on China Aster
1 corporation holds 100% of patents on eggplant
2 corporations hold 100% of patents on sweet peas
3 corporations hold 100% of patents on tobacco[2]

While some would say that there is no potential for famine since more hybrid seeds producing ever higher yields are being created (and patented) each year, there are disturbing indications that a disaster could happen even here. In 1970 nearly 15% of the U.S. corn crop (non-resistant hybrids) was blighted. The resulting study of the situation by the National Academy of Sciences found that "most crops are impressively uniform genetically and impressively vulnerable."[3] Furthermore, since there are few efforts to maintain traditional, genetically diverse plants that have evolved over centuries, these are rapidly becoming extinct.

Moreover, as with many other areas of agriculture (not to mention most other industries), a few large corporations are gaining increased control over seed development and marketing. "Recently some 50 seed companies have been bought out—principally by large petrochemical and drug companies. . . . Increased profits from plant patenting have probably contributed to this trend, yet Department of Agriculture proponents refuse to authorize a study of this situation, preferring instead to push for immediate passage of more patenting laws."[4] Since the initial legislation in 1970, plant patenting was not substantively discussed in Congress until 1979 when the pending amendments were introduced.

Current Legislation

HR 999, reported by the House Agriculture Committee on June 20, 1980, and S 23 are the current legislative proposals to expand plant patenting to cover six vegetables excluded from the original act—okra, celery, peppers, tomatoes, carrots and cucumbers. Unlike ten years ago, there is now considerable controversy about plant patenting. Led by the National Share-croppers Fund, a number of organizations, including the National Farmers Union, Family Farm Coalition, National Center for Appropriate Technology, the Environ-

mental Defense Fund, Sierra Club and the Consumers Federation of America, among many others, oppose the amendments and are raising serious questions about the necessity and appropriateness of plant patenting until much more definitive information is available.

On the other hand, proponents of expanding plant patenting maintain that corporate research has increased since 1970 and that "the number of new varieties has increased from 94 to 227 (141 percent) for soybeans, from 139 to 231 (66 percent) for wheat, and from 64 to 96 (50 percent) for cotton." Furthermore, proponents maintain that *small* companies not large ones receive most patents. About 80% of the applications over the past 10 years have been from private breeders, with over 75 percent of these applicants being "received from small (less than 500 employees) U.S. companies. Only slightly more than 20 percent of the certificates issued went to large companies, meaning almost 80 percent of the varieties now protected by the Act are in the province of small private breeders, experiment stations and foreign breeders."[5]

The obvious differences in figures cited by proponents and opponents is explained by the fact that small companies which have been acquired by large companies are counted as being large companies only by the opponents, while USDA ignores this fact. Including subsidiaries, five companies held 30% of *all* patents granted as of March 1979.[6]

Europe and the International Union for the Protection of New Plant Varieties (UPOV)

Plant patenting did not originate in the U.S. but began in Europe in the early 1960s. Consequently, plant patenting is most extensively practiced in the European Common Market countries where many vegetables are now classified as "legal" or "illegal" in a "Common Catalog." People, therefore, cannot even plant backyard traditional (and illegal) varieties without risking heavy fines. "Dr. Erna Bennett of the Crop Ecology and Genetic Resources Unit of the United Nations Food and Agriculture Organization in Rome estimates that *by 1991, fully three-quarters of all the vegetable varieties now grown in Europe will be extinct due to the attempt to enforce plant patenting laws.* Dr. J.G. Hawkes, professor at the University of Birmingham [U.K.] and president of Europe's Association of Plant Breeders, confirms this dire prediction."[7]

The International Union for the Protection of New Plant Varieties (UPOV) includes mainly the European nations and encourages plant patenting. UPOV is based in Geneva, Switzerland and was formed on December 2, 1961 by European nations to protect plant breeders' titles to their hybrid plant varieties. Members are nations, usually represented by their Agriculture Departments. Presently, UPOV is making efforts to greatly increase its membership and is trying to include a number of Third World nations. While the

WATCH THIS ... BIG BUCKS

R. Diggs/CUP/LNS

Genetic Uniformity

Extent to which Small Numbers of Varieties Dominate Crop Acreage in the U.S.

CROP	MAJOR VARI-ETIES	% OF ACREAGE DEVOTED TO THESE VARIETIES
Bean, dry	2	60
Bean, snap	3	76
Cotton	3	53
Corn	6	71
Millet	3	100
Peanut	9	95
Peas	2	96
Potato	4	72
Rice	4	65
Soybean	6	56
Sugar beet	2	42
Sweet potato	1	69
Wheat	9	50

SOURCE: The National Academy of Sciences. *Genetic Vulnerability of Major Crops*, 1972

U.S. is presently not a member of UPOV, many seed companies would like the U.S. to join, a move which the Agriculture Department is currently considering. Though the decision to participate or not to participate is not dependent upon the current congressional bills, the bills include amendments to extend the period of the patent protection from 17 to 18 years to be in conformity with UPOV's requirement of a minimum of 18 years' protection for woody plants, including vines, fruit, forest and ornamental trees.[8]

While it could be argued that traditional, non-patentable plants only have to be as good as patented plants, that is not the logic that is used by the seed companies. "Good" to the seed industry means high-yielding and profitable, with no consideration for maintaining genetic diversity or the long term health of the crops in question. Furthermore, why should a company with a patent on a variety of wheat or corn, for example, not promote it much more than a traditional variety upon which they would not have a monopoly? Europe shows that seed corporations follow only the "logic of profit." "In West Germany, only 5% of the varieties offered for sale are *not* patented. All cereal varieties in the United Kingdom are patented."[9]

The Impact of Corporate Control

The move toward increased control of various aspects of agriculture by large multinational corporations is certainly not limited to seeds. And there is little question that, if successful, this control will have devastating impacts on small farmers in the U.S. and in the Third World.

Generally, corporate hybrid seeds are high-yielding because they are bred to utilize large amounts of fertilizers and water. Difficult as it already is for small farmers to compete with large corporations in marketing, storage and transportation capabilities, if seeds are not available or are only available at a very high price, the small farmer will be further squeezed. If many of the currently-used, traditional seeds are deleted from company inventories and seed catalogs, plant patenting could also pose a threat to the growing interest in and development of organic farming.

An indication of the future for seed costs if patenting increases is the fact that an unpublished National Science Foundation study, using Department of Agriculture statistics, shows that seed prices have been increasing more than any other farm input since the passage of the Plant Variety Protection Act in 1970.[10]

While the above mentioned factors are affecting small farmers in Third World nations, they may try to maintain current practices if they can survive market pressures exerted by corporations. But as seed companies are bought out by large corporations, there will be a greater emphasis on international marketing. And as with other items ranging from soft drinks to television shows, the advertising and marketing power exercised by large corporations will be used to dominate the seed market in poor nations. Thus, these traditional farmers, unable to afford the expensive hybrid seeds and attendant levels of water and fertilizers, will increasingly be pushed out of farming and

New Owner	Seed Company	New Owner	Seed Company
*Amfac, Inc.	Field Seed and Nursery	NAPB (Olin & Royal	Agripro, Inc.
Anderson Clayton (ACCO)	Paymaster Farms	Dutch Shell)	Tekseed Hybrid
	Tomco-Genetic Giant	Occidental Petroleum	Ring Around Products
Atlantic Richfield (ARCO)	Dessert Seed Co.	Pioneer Hi-bred	Lankhart
Cargill	Dorman Seeds		Lockett
	Kroeker Seeds		Peterson
	PAG		Arnold Thomas Seed Co.
Celanese	Cepril Inc.	Pfizer	Clemens Seed Farms
	Joseph Harris Seed Co.		Jordon Wholesale Co.
	Moran Seeds		Trojan Seed Co.
Central Soya	O's Gold Seed Co.		Warwick Seeds
Ciba-Geigy	Funk Seeds Int'l	Purex	Advanced Seeds
	Louisiana Seed Co.		Ferry-Morse
	Stewart Seeds		Hulting Hybrids
DeLalb	Ramsey Seed	Rorer-Amchem	Jacques Seed Co.
FMC Corp.	Seed Research Assoc.	Sandoz	National-NK
Garden Products	Gurney Seeds		Northrup-King
Grassland Resources	Taylor-Evans		Rogers Brothers
Hilleshoeg/Cardo	Int'l Forest Seeds Co.	Southwide, Inc.	Delta & Pine Land
Int'l Multifoods	Baird Inc.		Greenfield Seed
	Lynk Bros.	Tate & Lyle	Berger & Plate
ITT	Burpee/O.M. Scott	Tejon Ranch Co.	Waterman-Loomis Co.
Kent Food Co.	L. Teweles Seed Co.	Union Carbide	Keystone Seed Co.
Kleinwanzieberer		Upjohn	Asgrow Seeds
Swatzucht AG	Coker's Pedigreed Seed		Associated Seeds

*The largest sugar company is acquiring the nation's second largest wholesale seed nursery pending completion of final negotiations.
—Source: National Sharecroppers Fund

will migrate to cities where they will remain unemployed.

Moreover, if there are no efforts made to maintain and preserve the traditional seeds that have been used for food production in the Third World nations and have served as the historic base for crops in food growing areas throughout the world, they will be irretrievably lost. When the inevitable blights come, the Third World and to a lesser extent the U.S. and Europe, will not be able to fall back on these traditional seeds; food production will drop sharply—with resulting increases in starvation.

What Can Be Done?

Actions can yet be taken to reverse these ominous trends, including conservation of existing plants, collective action to create market alternatives, protective legislation, and monitoring of corporate activities.

1) Conservation of plants can be achieved by increasing funding for both collection and storage of plant genetic resources (seed banks), similar to the existing facility at Fort Collins, Colorado and the United Nations International Board for Plant Genetic Resources. "Plant preserves" could also be developed to keep food crops growing and protected, in the same way that wildlife refuges and wilderness areas protect other natural and animal resources.

2) Alternatives can be created by farmers banding together to buy traditional seeds, educate the public of their value, and thereby develop stronger local markets. Local people can help establish small "plant preserves" and support small farmers using traditional seeds.

3) Legislation is needed to improve marketing incentives for small farmers using traditional varieties (governments subsidize plant experimentation, so why not also protect and encourage traditional varieties?). To make this effective, legislation must also either eliminate or limit patenting or require that traditional varieties be protected. Provisions for limiting corporate control (including vertical integration) in agriculture should also be considered.

4) Corporate expansion should be monitored internationally as well as by individual countries. The concept of environmental impact statements could be extended to apply especially to exportation of seeds to Third World countries. "If old varieties will be replaced, the company should be responsible for seeing that they do not become extinct. If a company will not make this guarantee, it should be prohibited from marketing in a given area."[11]

Conclusions

While the seeds used to produce the food we consume are seldom considered by the average consumer, they are absolutely critical to life. Patenting seeds, just like patenting chemical life forms, raises vital concerns. At risk is not only the maintenance of genetic sources that have developed over thousands of years, but the long term viability of our agricultural system. The public should be educated to and involved in decisions that will so obviously have a profound effect on their future. Seeds must *not* be allowed to become the province of a few large companies, rather we must all be interested and insist upon genetic diversity and real competition in this country and throughout the world.

Resources

Frank Porter Graham Demonstration Farm and Training Center
National Sharecroppers Fund
Route 3, Box 95
Wadesboro, NC 28170
(704) 851-9346
(The best United States source for information on Seed Patenting.)

Graham Center Seed Directory, by Cary Fowler. $1.00. 1979. From Graham Center (above address). Includes seed distributors from around the nation and an excellent essay on seed patenting.
Rural Advance, published at the Graham Center. Subscriptions: free, published quarterly. Updates the work of the National Sharecroppers Fund, small farmer issues and seed patenting.
Acres, U.S.A.: A Voice for Eco-Agriculture regularly covers seed patenting as well as many other agricultural issues. Subscription: $8.00 per year (12 issues). From: Acres U.S.A., PO Box 9547, Paytown, MO 64133.
H.R. 999—From your Representative, U.S. House of Representatives, Washington, DC 20515. The House seed patenting bill. Also ask for Report 96-1115.
S. 23—From your Senator, U.S. Senate, Washington, DC 20510.
The Senate seed patenting bill.
National Academy of Sciences. *Genetic Vulnerability of Major Crops*, 1972, 307 pp. *Conservation of Germplasm Resources: An Imperative*, 1978, 118 pp.

End Notes

1. *Congressional Record*, October 2, 1970, p. 34676.
2. Testimony of Cary Fowler before the Senate Agriculture Committee on Agricultural Research and General Legislation on S. 23, June 17, 1980, p. 9.
3. National Academy of Sciences, *Genetic Vulnerability of Major Crops*, 1972, cited in Cary Fowler, *Graham Center Seed Directory*, Frank Porter Graham Center, Wadesboro, NC, 1979, p. 12.
4. "Seed Patenting Legislation," A Special Update in *Rural Advance*, Spring/Summer 1980, published by the National Sharecroppers Fund.
5. Committee on Agriculture, *Plant Variety Protection Act Amendments*, House Report 96-1115, June 20, 1980, pp. 4-5.
6. Cary Fowler, "How Multinationals Gobble Up the Seed Companies," *Acres U.S.A.*, Vol. 10, No. 10, October 1980, p. 6.
7. Testimony by Cary Fowler before the House Agriculture Subcommittee on Department Investigations, Oversight and Research on HR 999, July 19, 1979, p. 6.
8. Committee on Agriculture, p. 6.
9. Testimony by Cary Fowler before the Senate Agriculture Committee, p. 4.
10. "How Multinationals Gobble Up the Seed Companies."
11. *Graham Center Seed Directory*, 1979, p. 16.

From *Dollars & Sense*, no. 56 (April 1980), pp. 14-16

The World Bank Down on the Farm

"*Perhaps more than any other institution in the world, the World Bank is* helping large numbers of people move out of absolute poverty toward a more decent life."

—World Bank President, Robert S. McNamara

Reprinted with permission from *Dollars & Sense*, a monthly magazine which offers a critical view of the U.S. economy in nontechnical language.

A former president of the Ford Motor Co., and a chief architect of the Vietnam War, as Secretary of Defense under John Kennedy and Lyndon Johnson, Robert McNamara has spent the last twelve years as head of the vastly influential World Bank.

As such, he is fond of eloquently describing the miseries of the world's poor and asserting that the Bank is leading the assault on world poverty. With $10 billion worth of loans in 1979 and its finger in almost every rural development pie, there's no doubt that the Bank is leading the assault. But just who and what is it assaulting? The following article examines rural poverty in the Third World, how the World Bank explains this poverty and what it is doing about it.

Rural poverty in the Third World is severe. Millions of men and women farm tiny parcels of poor or exhausted soils inadequate to support them at a decent level. Millions more work as tenants, paying a large portion of their produce to non-working landowners, or as laborers, who have no land of their own and must sell their labor for a pittance on a daily or seasonal basis. Still more millions have been driven to seek a precarious existence in city slums because they find no possibility of supporting themselves in the countryside.

In the World Bank's view, these people are poor, not because they have been crowded off the best lands in their country or deprived of land altogether by rich local elites and foreign agribusiness. They are poor because "throughout the developing world the rural poor have neither shared adequately in their country's progress nor have themselves been able to contribute significantly to it. Their destitution has in

effect ruled them out of the entire development process."

The Bank's solution to the poor having been left behind by development is *modernization*—large doses of fertilizers, pesticides, earth moving equipment, construction materials, and expensive consultants, all designed to bring poor subsistence farmers into the commercial economy and to increase the amount they produce. This must happen, however, within each country's existing social structure. McNamara states clearly that the Bank's agricultural program "will put primary emphasis not on the redistribution of income and wealth—necessary as they might be in many of our member countries—but rather on increasing the productivity of the poor, thereby providing for a more equitable sharing of the benefits of growth."

The Landless Don't Count

But when the World Bank says "the poor," they don't mean the poorest. One group the Bank does very little to help are those who don't own any land. Even in the Bank's own conservative estimates, the landless make up 40% to 60% of the population in many Third World countries. The Bank's rural development policy is based on the notion that benefits from the increased output made possible by projects such as irrigation systems will eventually trickle down to the landless poor—by generating more farm employment. But agricultural researchers Betsy Hartmann and James Boyce, who have studied World Bank projects at first hand, doubt that the

poor are really helped by this. They ask, "Is giving aid to the rich so they can hire more poor at subsistence wages really the best way to help the poor?"

Only regular, decently paid employment can be a solution to the poverty of the landless, but while the Bank has announced a few token employment creating projects, it has more typically exerted its influence to keep wage levels low in order to encourage foreign investment and to keep export prices "competitive" on the world market. More often than not, these agricultural exports are grown on large farms where the landless provide the necessary—and cheap—labor.

One rare World Bank project actually provided farmland to be worked cooperatively by landless residents of a Bangladesh village. However, the co-op excluded two-thirds of the village's landless, and the loan made available only $4000, a pond for cultivating fish, and three acres of government land. (There was more government land in the village, but it was usurped by well-off villagers and not included for co-op use.) The workers' income was still such that they also had to work for the village landowners to survive.

The Biggest Still Benefit

The Bank prefers to aid those poor "with some tangible assets, however meager (a small farm, a cottage industry, or a small scale commercial operation in the urban centers)." But the Bank's definition of "small" allows it to "target" a wide variety of people. In Guatemala, for instance, the Bank defined "small farmers" as anyone with less than 110 acres of land—a category that encompasses 97% of all Guatemalan farmers. Half of the Bank's funds went to "small farmers" thus defined, while the other half went to "medium and larger" farmers in the top 3%.

Bangladesh is a country with a large number of what the World Bank calls the "absolute poor," (those people with a per capita income of less than $100 a year). One Bank project loaned the country the money to buy 3000 deep tubewells providing the irrigation necessary for an extra crop of rice during the dry winter season. According to a Bank press release, each well was to serve between 25 and 50 farmers joined together in a cooperative irrigation group.

But Hartmann and Boyce, who lived for nine months in one of the villages covered by the project, discovered that the tubewell in their area had wound up the property of one man, the richest landlord in the village.

What Is The World Bank?

The International Bank for Reconstruction and Development—more commonly known as the World Bank—was formed, along with the International Monetary Fund (IMF), near the end of World War II. The Bank was intended by the advanced capitalist countries to organize the handling of loans for reconstruction of war torn economies and development of poorer ones.

Membership in the IMF is a prerequisite for membership in the World Bank and eligibility for its loans. The headquarters of the two sit side-by-side in Washington DC, joined by corridors at several levels. Control over decision-making is not on a one-country, one-vote basis. Rather, each country has voting power in proportion to the size of its contributions, with the U.S. holding the largest voting bloc, 23%.

While agricultural and rural development projects received 25% of the $10 billion World Bank loan total in 1979, they are far from all that Bank funds. Other major loan categories include transportation (19%), industry and finance (16%), and electrical power (14%), with smaller amounts going for tourism, urban development, education, population control, and other projects.

Though the World Bank is a powerful institution in and of itself, its power is multiplied by its central position among international development institutions. By persuading other funding agencies, such as the UN, to contribute their money to projects endorsed by the Bank, it substantially increases its leverage over development policy.

AGRIBUSINESS

Peg Averill/LNS

And the cooperative irrigation group amounted to a few signatures he had collected on a scrap of paper. The landlord got his $12,000 tubewell by spending about $300 on bribes to local officials and had it installed in the middle of his own 30 acre tract. This is only half the area that the tubewell is capable of serving, but the price the landlord charged neighboring small farmers for the water was so high that the well has never been used to its full capacity.

Hartmann and Boyce asked a foreign expert working on the Bank project if their village was atypical. He told them: "I no longer ask who is getting the well. I know what the answer will be and I don't want to hear it. One hundred percent of these wells are going to the 'big boys.' First priority goes to those with the most power and influence: the judges, the magistrates, the members of Parliament, the union chairmen. If any tubewells are left over, the local authorities auction them off. The big landlords compete and whoever offers the biggest bribe gets the tubewell."

World Bank planners are far from surprised by such turns of events. Whatever happens, they do not intend to rock the local boat. In a 1975 "Sector Policy Paper" on rural development, the World Bank stated: "In many countries, avoiding opposition from powerful and influential sections of the rural community is essential if the program is not to be subverted from within."

The policy paper adds, "It is notable that rural development schemes usually do not aim to provide benefits exclusively to the rural poor. . . . Often the rural development objective is subordinate to the objective of increasing . . . marketed output."

A Bank Like Any Other

When you get down to it, increased production is what the World Bank seeks to encourage more than anything else—and for a very clear reason. The World Bank is, in fact, a *bank*. Though countries receiving Bank loans are expected to contribute to the projects themselves, those loans have to be repaid—with interest—just like any other loans.

But hungry people who grow food so that they can eat better do not generate much money for repaying loans. Only if they grow enough to *sell*, that is, a "marketable surplus," will loans get repaid. The World Bank itself notes that "Lending only to those with investment opportunities sufficient to produce significant marketable surplus is perhaps the best way to reduce the level of default."

At first glance this may seem to contradict the Bank's stated aim of targeting the poor directly so as to meet their "basic needs." But the Bank's policy statements make clear that it favors the destruction of what is left of subsistence production and the integration of all agricultural lands into the commercial sector. How? By producing a surplus of cash crops, for the domestic market or for export.

"Rural development," states the Bank's Sector Policy Paper with that name, "is concerned with the modernization and monetization of rural society and with its transition from traditional isolation to integration with the national economy."

Certainly subsistence farming should not be idealized. But these farmers are not totally isolated from the market—they may have to sell part of their crop to pay taxes and rent, and to buy the few other goods which they need but can't produce themselves. In a poor country, a subsistence farmer with an annual cash income of only $100 may well be better off than the farmer who must go into debt to buy fertilizers, pesticides, farm equipment, and whatever else is deemed essential for modern cultivation and surpluses.

Commercial farming also brings additional risks beyond the natural environmental ones: market prices can fluctuate according to events in other parts of the world; farmers' costs may surpass what they are able to make, even with increased output; a crop's vulnerability to pests may increase when uniform genetic stock is used. But the World Bank says only that farmers must accept "the risk associated with increasing their output."

Besides the risks, commercial farming also means diversifying into non-food crops. Since crops like rubber and cotton can't possibly be eaten by those who grow them, farmers must produce for the market. In 1978, the World Bank's annual report listed $258.5 million in loans for tea, tobacco, jute and rubber crops. And loans focused on food crops such as vegetables, sugar and cashews, explicitly designated as going for export promotion, amounted to another $221 million.

"Agricultural exports aren't necessarily bad, but they tend to strengthen the mechanisms that cause hunger," write Frances Moore Lappe and Joseph Collins in *Food First*. "To weigh their impact one has to ask: who is in control of the return from those export earnings? Does the decision to focus on exports represent a choice of the rural people themselves?"

Who is in control of these export earnings? The answer involves the important fact that the World Bank's rural development policies also benefit a whole other economic segment that could hardly be called poor—U.S. and other foreign agribusiness corporations. A future article will examine their role, the Carter Administration's "Human Rights Campaign" and its effect on World Bank policy, and peasant resistance to World Bank projects.

Sources: Lappe & Collins, *Food First;* Cheryl Payer, "The World Bank and the Small Farmer"; *NY Times* 4/2/78, 2/3/80.

HOT TIMES

From *Hot Times,* October 1980, p. 3

Diplomacy Means Never Having to Say You're Sorry

Reprinted with permission from *Hot Times,* Austin, Texas.

While the network anchors measure the first year of the decade in terms of how many days American hostages have been held in Iran, the White House is doing its best to keep the issue clouded. While a parade of Iranian leaders issue multiple demands from the U.S. the one that sticks most in the American craw is the apology. Iran would like the U.S. to apologize for having the CIA bring the shah to power, for training his secret police, and for arming his police state regime. Carter has, thus far, refused. When Khomeini recently issued demands without an apology included, Reagan suggested the U.S. accept, indicating that the *Apology* was the big issue.

But the emphasis on the apology is a convenient way of ignoring the truth. Carter knows that American pride has been stirred to patriotic militarism over the hostages, and as long as it stays there the real issues can be played down.

Those issues are the financial demands. If Carter unfreezes Iranian assets in U.S. banks and returns the six billion that the shah ripped off from Iran, the American banking establishment would be in severe trouble. Loss of those holdings would cripple Chase Manhattan, Citibank, and the Morgan Trust. What the president won't admit is that he has sold the hostages to protect the banks and so he needs the apology demand to keep the issue clouded. If they return the hostages the banks won't have a good excuse to keep the money.

—Todd Samusson and Sammie Ritter

6 REPRESSION

The word repression calls to mind images of goosestepping stormtroopers, barbwired detention camps, thought police, slaves' shackles, the bonds of a foreign land ruled by an inhuman, law-slandering dictator. But repression can take more subtle forms. And what distinguishes the forms addressed here is not that they take place in the absence of order and legitimacy but that they occur in and are sanctioned by a law-abiding society, by the keepers of the law.

The section opens with the hostage crisis in Iran. The *Fifth Estate* sees the danger, not in the holding of the hostages, but in the nationalistic outcry that action caused. John McIntosh laments the hostages and victims of repression throughout the world, and *MERIP Reports,* examining "moderate" Jordan, wonders if it could be the next Iran.

The Central Intelligence Agency has been the subject of numerous exposés by both the alternative and the mass media. The *Covert Action Information Bulletin* has been one of the major sources of information on United States intelligence agents working under cover. Of special note is their "Naming Names" column, which culls from public information documents the names of agents working under light cover. Articles from *Covert Action* also report on the CIA's activities in attempting to recruit black professionals to work in African nations, on propaganda techniques of CIA-connected wire services in Jamaica, and on the, until recently, overlooked terrorist actions by a network of Cuban extremists. *CounterSpy* features an open letter questioning the past CIA connections of Gloria Steinem and the reaction of the feminist community to that disclosure.

Public Eye and *Organizing Notes* scrutinize the levels of police control around the country, noting incidents of police spying, surveillance, and excessive violence, while William Kunstler, a longtime counselor to the American Left, looks at loopholes in the "contract between the FBI and the American people."

The strategies for rehabilitation behind prison walls are analyzed by a number of publications. The issues of prisoners' rights and resistance, privacy in prison, and the Clockwork Orange effects of behavior modification are discussed in terms of the overcrowding, program cuts, and increasing violence behind the walls.

Finally, *The Guardian* and *WIN* look at the increasingly strident activities of the Ku Klux Klan and the Nazi Party. Lynora Williams looks back at the investigation into the November 1979 slaying of Communist Workers Party members, while Chip Berlet offers a first-person account of a Nazi rally and wonders whether the frenzy over such gatherings overlooks the real issue of racism.

—LD

From *Fifth Estate* 14, no. 5 (December 4, 1979): 1

Crisis in Iran—None for Me, Thanks

THE U.S.—THE RETURN OF PATRIOTISM

Just as the Ayatollah Khomeini succeeded in consolidating his crumbling support among the Iranian masses by diverting attention from his own crises onto the U.S. Embassy and the Shah, the U.S. government and the politicians have been able to generate support and undermine growing political disaffection by whipping up an hysterical campaign around the issue of the embassy hostages in Tehran. Hence, the pervasive cynicism about politics in general and the government in particular, combined with the frustration and rage underlying life in every sphere of contemporary life, has given way to sporadic outbreaks of anger and violence against "Foreigners." Now everyone suddenly figures out what has been wrong all along about their lives and about the deteriorating social terrain: Iranians, anti-Americans, foreigners, etc.,—just as certain sectors of the German population were to come to the conclusion that "Jews and communists" were responsible for their problems in Weimar Germany.

It is probably safe to say, however, that most Americans have remained unimpressed with the protests of a vocal minority of superpatriots. The burning of Iranian flags and similar displays of xenophobia have been limited to numbers in the low thousands and made up of student lunch-hour affairs, VFW/American Legion beer busts and the like.

This is not to say that public support for any sort of military adventure aimed at Iran or pogrom against Iranians in this country could not be mobilized as long as the majority of people refuse to see the U.S, as anything but a "benign giant" being victimized by religious fanatics; but at this point, neither Carter nor the media is interested in carrying on a "Remember the

Maine" wardrum campaign. What is particularly discouraging is the public anger and self-organized demonstrations over the freedom of a group of hostages whose sole function is to carry out the foreign policy of the U.S. generals and oil corporations, when this same public is faced with a thousand abuses every single day under this system with never a peep.

Despite our horror at seeing a revolution against the vicious police state of the Shah succumb to the inertia of Islamic totalitarianism, what unavoidably concerns us in a more direct way is the tense atmosphere created in the U.S. by bloodthirsty, jingoist militancy. Such an atmosphere, formed against a backdrop of mass passivity, makes criticism of and opposition to the government as well as opposition to the patriotic, warmongering posturing and hysteria a dangerous, even provocative act. "Don't break step," snarl the patriots when confronted by even the suggestion that the U.S. government is in the wrong or that the aspirations of the Iranian students may have a shred of legitimacy. Beat up the foreigners and anyone else who spits on the flag. We'll all march together once more—the goosestep.

Of course this could not have happened at a better time for U.S. capital, which is falling apart economically and which has seen its support inside the U.S. and out eroding at a steady pace since the Vietnam War. Even sociologists are publishing reports describing how the "Iranian crisis" has managed to "unite" Americans around the flag, making it possible to forget much more pressing problems at home. Nationalism and militarism, long since discredited since the Vietnam debacle, are being revived.

If the American people allow the climate of hysteria and mob mentality to grow, then they may soon see themselves herded into a war to defend oil company profits in the Middle East. They will see the draft reinstituted, see their children sent off in waves to die. Opponents and critics of the government could find themselves jailed or attacked by right-wing mobs. Any group demonstrating, say, against the construction of a nuclear plant, will face the possibility of having to defend itself from patriotic bullies who accuse anti-nuclear

activists of putting the United States at the mercy of the sheiks and mullahs. Ultimately, the spectre of nuclear confrontation with the Soviet Union should be remembered, as well as the grim possibility of seeing racist riots and the detention of Arabs and other Middle Eastern people in the U.S. in concentration camps, just as Japanese and Japanese-Americans were victimized during the Second World War.

We say no to the hysteria and the patriotism generated around this pseudo-crisis of diplomacy! If the American people allow themselves to be suckered into a war against the people of Iran, then they will end by paying in blood. And if anyone comes out ahead, it will certainly not be the Iranian people, or the American people, but the politicians, the military, the banks, and the oil companies. Turn the guns around! We have enough grievances of our own! No to war! No to patriotism! No to the capitalists and the state! We spit on the American flag and the Iranian flag, on all flags. We have no use for flag wavers. We have an entire world to recover. Let us begin by refusing to become pawns in the designs of leaders and politicians. Let us begin by taking control of our own lives.

IRAN—THE AYATOLLAH CAPTURES THE REVOLUTION

The confrontation between Iran and the United States over the seizure of the U.S. Embassy in Tehran Nov. 4 and taking of 63 hostages (later reduced to 50) by Islamic student militants has brought to the fore the worst features of this epoch. The grotesque spectacle of a million Iranians marching in lockstep, chanting praises of a decrepit mullah and a reactionary religion is matched in this country by a sudden upsurge of patriotism one would have thought impossible just a few weeks ago.

As in all modern crises, the institutions of domination—the political state, capital, and in this case, religion—stand illuminated in such a manner as to make their social function obvious to all who are willing to drop the mystifications of this society. However, for those willing to continue behind the definitions of social reality and the crisis as posed by the leaders of nations, they are condemned to simply act out the age-old patterns of rulers and ruled.

While the clique of rulers in each country manipulates the real grievances or fears of the people for their own purposes, nothing should be allowed to obscure the righteousness of the anger of the Iranian people toward the U.S. government for the role it has played there. The U.S. Embassy in Tehran was, and is, a "nest of spies" that did indeed decide policy for its client state, allowing it no more independence than the worst "banana republic" of Central America. It was the same gunboat diplomacy which installed the Shah Reza Pahlavi in power after the 1953 CIA-directed coup and which operated the Embassy as the Middle East office of the National Security Agency. It was a spy station par excellence—necessitated by the rich oil fields of Iran and its proximity to the Soviet Union's southern flank—as well as dumping ground for sophisticated U.S. technology and weaponry geared toward maintaining American dominance in the region both economically and politically. So sensitive was Iran and the Embassy that no less than two ambassadors to that country later surfaced as directors of the CIA—Richard Helms and William Sullivan. All of the Shah's brutal, repressive police force and military received training in the U.S. as did the torturers of the hated SAVAK.

To be frank, it is beyond our capacity to extend sympathy for the American hostages or to share any indignation about the seizure of the Embassy. Empty phrases like "violation of international law" or the "sanctity of diplomatic immunity" have meaning only to those who cherish the world as it is and have been made a mockery too many times before every nation-state for us to show any concern.

Further, to suggest that one ought to be concerned with the rules governing the conduct of politics between segments of international capital is a bit much to swallow. We care nought what the vultures or their functionaries heap upon one another and when the hostages turn out to be imperialist diplomats, professional spies and career marines—sorry, but no sympathy. We have too many other hostages and prisoners being held in this country and around the world to shed tears over those who are part of the mechanism keeping our comrades imprisoned.

Still, none of this should be taken in any way as support for the Moslem fanatics parading in anti-hill fashion through the streets of Tehran, pledging their loyalty to Islam while whipping themselves with scourges. Rather, the seizure of the Embassy has to be seen as part of the skillful maneuvering of a consummate politician, the Ayatollah Khomeini, to recapture the political support he had lost in the days prior to the crisis.

As in any revolutionary situation, the events of the last year in Iran have proceeded at a whirlwind pace. The overthrow of the Shah's bloody regime unleashed a torrent of popular revolutionary activity which extended well beyond the desires of the mullahs, who intended to capture all of the outpouring behind a reactionary 12th century concept of an "Islamic Republic." Instead, again as in every Revolutionary situation, all things became possible. Iranian women discarded their symbol of submission, the *chador* (veil); thousands of oil workers, teachers and those in other industries formed workers' councils, putting forth demands that had nothing to do with the Ayatollah Khomeini's religious fanaticism.

The main props of the bourgeois state began to disintegrate: the military and the government apparatus collapsed, with as

Michael Scurato/LNS

much as 50% of the Shah's army deserting and bureaucrats giving orders with no one paying any attention. Each day saw new demonstrations of workers demanding control of industry or women demanding equality. Publications of every political stripe began demanding a carrying through of the revolution that had only been begun with the toppling of the Shah. Unemployment reached almost 50%, leaving thousands free and undisciplined in the streets to demonstrate or to discuss the events of the day.

At the same time the forces of reaction led by the Ayatollah and the priesthood caste of mullahs began moving in an opposite direction: their idea of the overthrow of the Shah was to resubject Iran to a different tyranny—that of Islam. In Khomeini's Islamic Republic everyone would submit to the iron laws of the Koran; women would appear in public fully veiled, employees would submit to their employers; movies, alcohol, extra-marital sex, homosexuality and other features of the "decadent" West would be ruthlessly removed. To enforce his vision of the future (based on the past) the Ayatollah's Islamic Guard began executions and public floggings of not only SAVAK police torturers (upon whom we shower no sympathy), but also those who violated the Ayatollah's moral preachments. The anti-semitic bent of the religious regime became apparent as several unfortunate Jews met the firing squad as a result of charges of being part of a "Zionist conspiracy."

All of this did not go unresisted by those segments of Iranian society who would suffer the most cruelly at the hands of the

proposed theocratic state. Opposition to the rule of mullahs had grown almost to the proportions of civil war during the summer. On August 12, 50,000 leftists and liberals marched in Tehran chanting "Death to this fascist government" and were set upon by 5,000 armed Islamic goons brought to the scene by Khomeini's trucks. Similarly, a march of women who refused to cover their bodies was also set upon by mobs of religious fanatics with iron bars and clubs.

Oil workers began strikes against the Ayatollah's harsh labor policies and in the capital of the province of Gilan, workers marched in the streets chanting "Death to Khomeini." Shortly before, fishermen in an adjoining region battled police after they had liberated a government fishing vessel and distributed its catch to a local village. Resistance to the mullahs also came from ethnic Arabs and other minority nationality and religious groups as well as among the separatist Kurds, who the new government attacked with a ferocity matching that of the Shah's 25-year campaign against them.

Seeing the opposition grow, the Ayatollah grasped desperately for a way of uniting the country around him. His seemingly senseless resumption of the Shah's war against the Kurds was in part an attempt to reassemble the Army which had disintegrated and partly an attempt to mobilize Persian nationalism against this minority to create a unity that was growing ever more dim.

The action of the students in seizing the hostages was, if you will, a godsend for the Ayatollah. The justifiable hatred of Iranian people for the U.S. government galvanized public support around Khomeini and re-established him as the symbol of the Iranian revolution as he was in the first days of the Shah's overthrow. It's not that opposition to Islamic reaction has diminished as much as it is almost impossible to air the grievances that had convulsed Khomeini's rule during this last summer when Iran is locked in combat with the behemoth of North America. Two weeks after the occupation began, tens of thousands of Marxist-Leninist Fedayee guerrillas marched in Tehran and several thousand unemployed occupied a government office demanding jobs, but these were heavily over-shadowed by events at the Embassy.

The crisis has also reinvigorated the Khomeini-instigated Assembly of Experts which had been preparing a theocratic constitution for Iran embodying the most reactionary aspects of Islam giving the Ayatollah the legal authority to rule. All of Iran's politicians, realizing they were being outflanked by the mullahs, opposed the Assembly, as did large sections of the populations. But with the Embassy seizure it was suddenly the duty of all of those faithful to Islam to support the constitution, and on December 2 and 3, the faithful dutifully trooped out to vote the priests the authority they sought.

The change in the people from a mood of opposition to one of compliance is rooted in the mass character structure produced by state society, which leaves its members feeling secure only when subjected. It creates the cannonfodder for the giant marches chanting pledges of fealty to Islam which culminated in the sickening spectacle of flagellants during the recent religious holidays. This is humanity reduced to its most grotesque, barely worthy of the name, a transformed species from that which we were in the wild.

The final piece in the puzzle of Iran comes together with the others when one looks behind the religious fanaticism to view the emergence of Islam in the modern world in contention with Marxism as the leading counter-revolutionary ideology. From Khomeini in Iran to Khadafy in Libya to Zia in Pakistan and throughout the Arab world, while presenting the face of religious fundamentalism separate from the political economy of their nations, the star and crescent is used as the ideology within which capital is developed in the Mideast and Asia. The Shah, for all of his much vaunted "modernizations," was like the Russian Czar acting as a fetter on the development of a truly modern economy. The Shah's systematic looting of the Persian economy to the tune of billions of dollars sucked from oil production condemned the country to an existence which supported only the limited expansion of capital. Just as modern capital was constructed in the USSR and China under the aegis of state socialism, in England under Puritanism and protestantism and in France under the scientific Enlightenment, in this epoch Islam has moved to the fore to organize national capital in Third World countries where Marxism is not a meaningful force. Islam contains the mass psychological elements necessary to mobilize large segments of the population around a program of self-sacrifice and submission necessary to exploit labor for the creation of a national capital that does not see its fruits flee the country to foreign hands.

Khomeini, however, must be seen as only a moment in the development of events in Iran. The Ayatollah has support among the bazaar merchants and elements of the unemployed but eventually, when the current crisis has passed, the mullahs will be forced to confront the real crisis facing Khomeini's regime; the disintegration of the state apparatus, the massive unemployment and the total collapse of investment capital. Khomeini will have to be replaced by a force that can at once assume the mantle of religion and mobilize capital and the people in a coherent manner.

To deflect the trajectory of Iranian capital necessitates the throwing off of not only the mysticism of religion, but eventually confronting the fake opposition of the left in that country and take up the project begun in the first days of the revolution when all things were possible. Only at that time can a real transformation of human society occur.

Northern Sun News

From *Northern Sun News* 6, no. 7 (July/August 1980): 16

Hostages

by John McIntosh

Free the Hostages.

in Iran

the leftists in Chile
the crowded in Walla Walla prison, Washington
the workers, Blacks & punks in Brixton gaol, U.K.
Liberate phony Democracy Wall, Peking
the victims of apartheid in South Africa
Stop the forced sterilization of poor women.

Rescue the Hostages!

of authority, power-trip, behavior
  modification
in senior citizen ghettoes
of fat boy capitalist thieves
Release the anarchists in Spanish jails
democrats in Cuban prisons
Radicals & lawyers in Social-
  Democratic, perfect
police state, West German cages.

Untie the Hostages!

the Palestinians in Israel
the Jews, Ukrainians, Latvians, union
  organizers
in "U.S.S.R."
the dopers in Turkish jails
the "disappearing" in fascist Argentina
the drafted in army(s)
Stop the forced drugging of mental
  patients.

Unshackle the Hostages!

of violent, sexist, macho advertising
of future poison 3 Mile Island(s)
from radio-TV half-truths
from C.I.A.-K.G.B. terrorists
from work ethic fanatics
from Anita Bryant, fundamentalist
  prudes.

Pardon the Hostages!

the bored schoolchildren
the unemployed in Watts, L.A.
the young junky in Bed.-Stuy., Brooklyn
the Sioux at Pine Ridge, South Dakota
Stop the deportation of Mexican &
  Haitian workers.

Liberate the Hostages!

in Timor, Euzkadi, Ireland, Zimbabwe,
Kurdestan, Quebec, Puerto Rico
the majority Indians in Bolivia
the famished in Cambodia
the Rastas in St. Vincent.

Emancipate the Hostages!

of Big Oil
of kings & shahs
commissars
cops
gurus
Moonies
K.K.K.-Nazi creeps
bigot, patriot, war-hawks
of ayatollahs
popes
politicians
bureaucrats
missiles
borders &
a million deceptions.

FREE THE HOSTAGES!

MERIP REPORTS
Middle East Research & Information Project

From *MERIP Reports*, no. 84
(January 1980), pp. 23-24

Letter from Jordan: External, Internal Forces Make Regime Vulnerable

by a Special Correspondent

Last July, the Union of Jordanian Engineers held a forum in Amman on the "Economic and Technical Consequences

of the Egyptian-Israeli Peace Accord." The participants expressed the fragile hope that the meeting would lead to similar activities in the future, for Amman is a city bare, not only of green grass, but also of political discussion and activity.

When Palestinian students at Jordan University, for example, attempted to organize an art exhibition on Land Day, March 31st, to show solidarity with their brothers and sisters under Israeli occupation, they were assaulted by intelligence agents. During these protests, the university was closed. In one incident, a large number of students were forced to lie on their stomachs and were beaten by the police. Some of those arrested still wait behind prison bars. Next year does not

promise relief. In his commencement address, which drew little applause, King Hussein delivered stern warnings against "extremism" and "sabotage" (*al-takhrib*), the same term used by Israel to describe the Palestinian resistance.

The media is extremely restricted. Newspapers can publish complaints about water shortages, a real problem especially in summer, or they can carry articles criticizing the developmental policies of the Arab world. They cannot, however, criticize, even by allusion, the "rational course" set by His Majesty, nor can they include any other material which the censor would classify as "insinuation," like demands for freedom of speech, free election, or the return of the guerillas to Jordan. The Camp David Accords, and its principals—Carter, Begin and Sadat—provide the main expressive outlet for cartoonists and editorialists. Otherwise, writers remain silent or risk being jailed or emigrate to London or Paris, where a series of Arab publications have sprung up recently as a result of the inflow of exiled Arab journalists.

The portrayal of King Hussein as a "moderate" in the American Press only masks these brutal realities. Regimes must be assessed on the basis of their relation with their own people, not with Israel and the United States. Political repression is the "stick" with which the monarch props up his regime.

The "carrot" is an economic one. Remittances from over a half a million Jordanians working abroad are coupled with aid from the governments which have a stake in maintaining the status quo in Jordan. The Hashemite dynasty, installed by the British as an integral part of its imperial dominion of Palestine and the Arab east, continues to serve as a loyal client of the leading western power, and is in turn bolstered by it. Britain was replaced in that role by the United States after World War II. Israel counts on Hussein to preserve peace on its eastern border and never ceases to make clear its readiness to intervene on the King's behalf should the throne be endangered. The kingdoms and sheikhdoms of the Arabian peninsula, themselves western clients, have an intrinsic interest in a stable monarchy in Jordan.

More recently, Syria has joined the list of the King's backers. Since Assad took over in 1971 and began to orient Syria more towards the West, he has forged a logical alliance with Jordan, no doubt with some ambitions for a "greater Syria." Iraq has also been drifting in that direction. In a period of increasing economic ties with Western Europe and Japan and virulent anti-communist campaigns inside the country, Iraq has been subtly moving away from its "rejectionist" line on the Palestinian question, in practice if not in rhetoric. The Iranian revolution and the Egyptian-Israeli treaty, signed under American auspices, compelled the ruling Ba'thist parties in Syria and Iraq to shelve their seemingly irreconcilable differences at least temporarily. As a corollary to these developments, Iraq sought to improve its relations with Jordan.

For Jordan, these political approaches have economic equivalents. At the Baghdad Summit conference of Arab states and the PLO opposing the Sadat-Begin pact, the Jordanian government was promised an annual check of $1.25 billion for the next ten years, an increase of $.5 billion over previous years, ostensibly to strengthen the country's military posture against Israel. Arab aid accounted for over one half of the government's 1979 budget. If we consider U.S. financial aid, UNRWA expenditures, and remittances from Jordanian emigrants, the dependence of Jordan on foreign capital becomes almost total.*

This foreign capital has engendered palpable changes in the country's social structure. The middle class of small property owners, civil servants and professionals has expanded rapidly. Although, characteristically, no official figures are available on income distribution, this class can be discerned in the sprouting concrete houses on the hills and valleys of Amman and other major cities, despite astronomical land prices.† In the highly laissez-faire economy of Jordan, the big bourgeoisie and the middle class have expended their revenues chiefly on imports and real estate. Jordan's imports ($1400 million) exceeded its exports ($200 million) in 1979 by seven to one. Only lately have some investment allocations begun to find their way to productive, medium-size industry. Apart from military spending, the government itself augments the imports bill by opting for "prestigous" projects—Ameri-

can-style highways, ultra-modern telecommunications centers—which are of little value to the majority of the people but can be built only by foreign contractors and with imported equipment. Thus Jordan, itself producing no petroleum, exhibits economic phenomena similar to many oil-producing countries: meager production, massive consumption and imports, and high inflation rates.

The shops, cafeterias and streets of Amman and other major cities abound with imported consumer goods: German automobiles, Japanese tape recorders and television sets, Chilean apples, American television programs. Foreign products bring culture with them. Along with political repression, they have stifled the growth of indigenous-culture. Violent American, sentimental Indian, and sterile Egyptian films are what the movie theaters and television show. A book worth reading is likely to have been printed outside the country. While the West Bank is witnessing attempts to revitalize national culture in the form of theater, music, poetry and painting, despite the obstacles raised by Israeli military occupation, Jordan silences all these forms of cultural expression because they inevitably evoke "nationalist" sentiments anathema to the monarchy. This "cultural alienation" may help explain why religious organizations, which otherwise do not seem to have made any serious headway, find recruits mainly among the youth of the middle class.

There is an uncertainty about the future political course in the area, which in turn affects the inflow of foreign capital. The lack of a productive base and rampant inflation place the middle class in a precarious position. At this point, the Palestinian segment of this class does not appear willing to jeopardize its material gains by confronting the regime over its "Palestinian" policy despite its long-standing hostility to the Hashemite monarch. Should its economic position deteriorate, or should the King decide to join Sadat's caravan, the middle class might assume an active role in opposition to the regime.

The absence of a significant industrial base and the fact that more than 28 percent of Jordan's workers have migrated to the Gulf and elsewhere renders the working class a fragmented force. Urban workers have won some advances, like overtime and severance pay, but wages for unskilled and semi-skilled workers are held down by the influx of Egyptian and Syrian labor, especially in the construction sector.

Spencer Levy/Win/LNS

Physically, the Jordanian section of the class is sparsely distributed across the country. Its Palestinian counterpart is amassed in the refugee camps, crowded slums which endure as a cradle of militant Palestinian nationalism. In the face of a powerful repressive apparatus, the army in particular, the refugee camps would find it extremely costly to challenge the regime on their own. They must be joined by effective parts of the Jordanian and Palestinian working and middle classes.

In the countryside, which harbors about one third of the population and a similar fraction of the total labor force, foreign aid has benefited the big landowners and the rich peasants.* These classes control the rural cooperatives and can secure government loans to pay the climbing costs of modern machinery, fertilizers and seeds. Poor peasants, having no access to credit, fall into debt and are finally driven to the urban centers. By nurturing the middle-rich farmers and making them dependent on it, the government has been successful in establishing a loyal social base in the countryside, something leftist parties have not generally been inclined to do.

The combination of external and domestic forces has situated the Jordanian regime in a vital yet vulnerable position. None of the parties in the Middle East conflict seem able to afford alienating the Hashemite throne, but neither does the throne seem able to afford alienating any of them. The regime recognizes the Palestinian Liberation Organization as the legitimate representative of the Palestinian people and holds protracted negotiations with its leadership, but has not permitted even the publications of the PLO to be distributed in Jordan. The King receives Yasser Arafat on the border but does not allow him to visit the camps. Jordan has not taken part in the tripartite talks on "self-rule" for the West Bank and Gaza, yet retains its "good neighbor" policy with

---

*US aid to Jordan has been running over $200 million per year, with the largest share for military expenditures. UNRWA expenditures in Jordan are approximately one-third of the total UNRWA budget of $143 million. Remittances from Jordanians working abroad were estimated at $500 million in 1977—*Eds*.

†A *dunum* (1 acre=4.05 dunums) in a residential area can sell for over $60,000.

---

*Rich peasants own 200 to 1000 *dunums*.

Israel. Jordan's free-wheeling client capitalism does not preclude plans for economic integration with "socialist" Syria. While Crown Prince Hassan, the chief amateur planner of Jordan's development, visits the Soviet Union for a week and signs trade deals, the royal family remains an incorrigible satellite of the West.

CovertAction
INFORMATION BULLETIN

CovertAction Information Bulletin, no. 4 (April/May 1979), pp. 14-17

CIA Recruitment for Africa: The Case of Howard University, Washington, D.C.

Kemba Maish, 33, is a professor of psychology at Howard University in Washington, D.C., the preeminent black university in the United States. She teaches clinical and community psychology. She is a member of the Association of Black Psychologists, and has been very active in black organizations since the '60s. Her doctoral dissertation was on Black Power and Pan-Africanism.

Imagine her surprise, then, some months ago, when she returned a phone message she had received at Howard and heard the operator answer, "Personnel, CIA."

This was the beginning of uncovering a pervasive and sinister CIA recruitment program for Africa, aimed at black professionals at Howard and elsewhere. Kemba Maish debated whether to say anything to anyone; simply being contacted by the CIA can raise questions with friends and colleagues. But she realized that not speaking out would be falling into the CIA's trap. It was more important that the community be aware of what the CIA was doing. She taped an interview with WHUR, the Howard University radio station. The night her interview was to air, between the 5:15 news summary and the 6:00 news program, the tape of the interview disappeared.

The CovertAction Information Bulletin *contacted Ms. Maish, and she agreed to tell, once more, her story—alerting black students, teachers and professionals to this menace threatening the black community in America and, ultimately, African people wherever they are in the world. The interview was conducted recently by the Washington staff of the* Bulletin. *The text follows:*

CAIB: Tell us what happened, how you first had contact with the CIA, and when you realized what was happening.

KM: Approximately April of last year—I had been at Howard almost a semester at that time—I received a call from someone named Roy Savoy, I was out at the time and he had left several messages.

CAIB: Did you know the name, or who he was?

KM: I had never heard of him. Naturally, I tried to get back to him. The first time I called, the person who answered said, "Personnel, CIA." I was very curious as to why Personnel, CIA, was trying to get in touch with me. When I finally talked with him, of course I was still upset, but I decided to sit back and relax and hear what he had to say. I wanted to hear his whole program. He said that he was black, which was very clear from our conversation, and that he was the director of some section of the CIA which was recruiting black people, specifically black psychologists, to go to Africa and develop profiles on foreign nationals. I asked him what he meant by foreign nationals, did he mean develop profiles on African people. He said no, that I would just be developing profiles on communists that were in Africa so I wouldn't have to worry about spying on my own people. He went on to talk about paying me a fantastic salary, paying my way to Africa, all kinds of very enticing programs.

CAIB: Did he talk about under what guise you would do this, what you would say you were doing, your cover?

KM: No, not at that point.

CAIB: Did he mention sums when he talked about money?

KM: No, he really didn't, but he implied that it was much more than I would be getting at Howard. That would be something we could negotiate, the salary. Then he went on to tell me how he got my name, without my asking. I was wondering, but I was going to wait. He said he had gotten my name from the University of Maryland, that first he had gone to the director of one of the black programs at Maryland.

CAIB: Did you know who that was?

KM: Yes, somebody who was outspoken on the Maryland campus and generally concerned about black people.

CAIB: Did Savoy say that he had obtained your name from him?

KM: No, this was just the first step. He got the names of professors in the psychology department from that director.

CAIB: Could you tell from the way that Savoy explained it whether the director knew that he was giving names of professors to the CIA?

KM: Yes, I got the impression that he knew. Savoy told me that he had received the names of professors from him, but that Oscar Barbarin in the psychology department gave him my name.

CAIB: Had he been a professor of yours?

KM: Yes, I had worked with him very closely; he was on my thesis and dissertation committees. Both my Master's thesis and my dissertation involved looking at the relationship between political activism, political orientation, and positive mental health in black people. Barbarin had worked with me for two or three years, so he knew my interest in issues related to the liberation struggles of all African people.

CAIB: So Barbarin knew that you were not a conservative?

KM: Oh yes, he knew everything about me and my political activities. After Savoy told me that Barbarin had given him my name, I was still sitting back, not saying anything. When he finally finished, I told him he was a traitor to the African people. I went through the whole thing, about the connection between the FBI and the CIA, about what the FBI had done with the Black Panthers, Fred Hampton, Mark Clark; and Malcolm X, Martin Luther King, within this country. Then I mentioned how in Africa the CIA had organized a *coup* against Kwame Nkrumah, and had actually murdered Patrice Lumumba. I went on down the line. I said, how could you possibly do this? Then he said he was sorry he'd called me if he had upset me. I said I was glad he had called, I was glad that I had the opportunity to say what I wanted to say to him, and he just said he was sorry, that he wouldn't bother me again.

After the call, I started to be concerned about being contacted. I began to wonder why, with my background, the CIA would contact me. In a way I was personally incensed, how dare they? I tried to figure out what it was. Either they hadn't done their homework, which I doubt very seriously, or they thought that if they could get me, a black psychologist who knows African history, African politics, and who had been involved in political organizations for some time, they would have a perfect person.

I had been assuming they would think I couldn't be bought, but why should they think that? They've obviously bought other people, this was just one more person. Obviously I wanted to go to Africa; maybe they could make me think I was doing some service to the African people. So after I thought about it, it began to make a little sense. I thought they would think, well, even if she says no, she wouldn't go public because of all the paranoia. But my feeling was that it is better to be in the open about it. I felt I had to let African people know what is happening, so that they can protect themselves. That is more important than personal considerations.

That was when I arranged for the interview with WHUR. I figured that if they were beginning to seek out black professionals in the psychology department, if they were already getting names, this was a very destructive sequence of events. I didn't know where it would stop. So I talked to the people at WHUR, and did an interview with them, several weeks after it happened, explaining what had happened and what implications it had for the black community, because Howard is the foremost black institution in the U.S. The fact that they are recruiting and using Howard as a training ground was extremely important for black people to know, to be aware of. The interview was taped, and a small part of it was played on the 5:15 news summary, a summary of what is coming later. Then, about 45 minutes later, at the time for the regular airing, the tape was mysteriously missing.

As far as I know, WHUR never found out what happened to the tape.

CAIB: What did you do then?

KM: I decided to go back to Maryland to talk to both people who were involved in giving names. I did just that. I went back and talked first with the director. I asked him how he could give out names to the CIA, and first he said, well, he didn't give out my name. I told him that it did not matter, that he was still acting as a CIA agent whether he realized it or not. He became quite angry that I had come to him because he hadn't given anyone my name. He said that they come to him for all sorts of information. I should add here that Roy Savoy was a student at the University of Maryland. He had just graduated in the last year or so, and he came to the director as an ex-student now working for the CIA and interested in having some names of people to do whatever. Perhaps that made it a little more palatable to him.

CAIB: How did he justify this with his political beliefs?

KM: I asked him that. I said, with all that you've done, how could you give names to the CIA? You know what the CIA has done to our people. He repeated that he didn't give the names of any students. He was really upset, and at first I don't think he realized the implications of what he had done. He asked if I was questioning his commitment, and I said that I was; it wasn't the words that mattered, it was the actions.

His rationale for what he had done was that they could have gotten the names anyway, so he didn't feel that he was giving away anything they couldn't find out themselves. I explained that by giving them certain names from the Department he was giving them information, he was telling them which professors would be the most likely to have information about black students. He saved them from having to go through the Department Chair, who might not have had the knowledge of the black students and professors that the director of a black program did.

We eventually talked for a long while, and finally he said he had learned a lot from our discussion and would never do that again. He just hadn't realized the implications of what he was doing. He is a serious person, and I never thought he would do what he had done purposely. So he was another of those unwitting agents.

Then I went to see Oscar Barbarin, who had actually given my name. Barbarin at that time had been at the University of Maryland about three years. We are both members of the Association of Black

Psychologists. I've known him since about 1973, and he knows my political persuasion and the many activities I've been involved in.

CAIB: Had he been supportive of it?

KM: Certainly. He was concerned about black people, and I don't think he would ever consciously do anything against black people. I went to see him, and I was furious. He knew what it was about; he was physically upset; he knew why I was there. I don't know whether the director had called him, or he just knew that in a matter of time I'd be there. I asked him how he could do it, how he could give the CIA my name? He said that a number of government agencies come to him for names and information; he saw the CIA as just another government agency. I was shocked that he would even say that. I told him that he was supposed to be politically aware, that he had to know what the CIA has been doing, not only in Africa but also around the world. And he said he never stopped to think about it. He said that after he gave them my name he realized maybe he shouldn't have done it but then it was too late.

CAIB: Did he say what they asked him for, what sort of criteria they had when they were asking for names?

KM: He said that they were looking for black people who wanted to go to work in Africa. Barbarin knew that I knew a lot about African history, African politics, as well as having been politically active. He said he didn't think I would be interested but I might give them the names of people who would be interested. I told him that was even worse. Not only was he acting as an agent for the CIA, but he was assuming that I would also act as one. I told him that he had no idea what he was doing, that he could get me killed, just by having my name on a list. He said he was really sorry, and he didn't realize the implications of what he had done, and he was very upset that I would call him a CIA agent. But I told him that was the role he was playing, whether he realized it or not. That's the key point to me; a lot of people don't realize what they are doing and they are getting a lot of other people involved in something they have no idea about. Or they are closing their eyes to it; they don't want to face the fact that if they turn down the CIA, they might jeopardize some funding or grants. Perhaps they want to cooperate so it won't interfere with the development of their careers.

Right after this, I called the Association of Black Psychologists, and I told them the

CIA is recruiting black psychologists to go to Africa. Savoy had already contacted them and they knew his name. We discussed how dangerous it was for African people all over the world. The CIA knows that wherever African people are, we could fit in—in Africa, the Caribbean, South America—all they have to do is train us, teach us the language, teach us the particular customs, and we'll fit right in. They've already used black people from this country to infiltrate liberation movements and progressive groups both in Africa and in the Caribbean, basically using one group of African people against another.

We started to talk about the conference in St. Louis we had coming up in August. They told me that Roy Savoy had already inquired about the conference which was to take place, and wanted to set up a booth. I asked them to call the people in St. Louis and alert them.

When I went to St. Louis, I found out that Roy Savoy was there, had his name tag on, had set up a room, and was already recruiting. The communications were really bad, and somehow he got in through the St. Louis people.

I managed to get the executive committee to allow me a few minutes to explain my experience with Roy Savoy, and to point out that he was already at their convention. A lot of them were shocked. He had registered openly as CIA, and I tried to explain the implications of this to them as an organization. They proceeded to get rid of him then, but by that time he had already contacted a number of students and professionals. I began to speak with people there and realized that a number of professionals around the country had been contacted. Not only professors at Maryland, but also professors at Howard, and elsewhere, had given names.

What I'm saying is that it is not just me as an individual; many students and professionals are being contacted. Just the other day a student at Howard told me he'd been contacted by the CIA, and he was angry too.

CAIB: It sounds from all the evidence that the are doing blanket recruiting, that they will contact a large number of people, and be turned down by so many percent, and so many percent will agree. If you said no, well, you were just one. What they didn't count on is your going public, and we should talk a bit about that, about why you feel it is important to go public.

KM: I guess it's most important for African people to understand the impli-

cations of all this—what these people have done in the past, who they are, what their connections are. The major corporations are tied up with the police and the intelligence network, as well as the military. And a lot of people look at the spy programs on TV and think there's nothing wrong with being a spy, all these people have exciting lives and are doing a service to their country. People must understand that they are not doing a service to us in America, they're doing a service to the large corporations and to the American government, and to maintain profits—but in terms of our lives, all the FBI and CIA have done for us as a people is to kill us and our leaders and to destroy our organizations, not only here but around the world. They're doing it through our institutions, through our black organizations—they're recruiting us and we think we're doing a service to our people when actually we're helping to destroy our people.

It's important that people understand this and begin to work against it, to expose it every time it happens. I know of about ten people at Howard and other places who had been contacted, and not one of them had said a word. Yet, when I spoke up, they began to say, you know, they contacted me too. But they just kept it to themselves and were angry about it. You have to expose this, to let people know you've been contacted, and it's easier to do that once we all do it. Then there isn't as much paranoia and suspicion, and we have each other's support against retaliation.

CAIB: What kind of rap were these students given?

KM: Basically the same kind of thing, that they would be helping the African people and they would be working against communism. That's been played up so much both in Africa and here that a lot of people think they would be doing a service. Also a lot of black psychologists have gone to Africa, and a lot more want to go. There is a big push toward African psychology, and if you want to know anything about it, well you have to go to Africa, and this is a way to go to Africa. Sometimes they do this very indirectly, and people don't know under whose auspices they're going. They're just getting the money to go.

I should mention that all of this applies to foreign students too. The CIA has a program where they recruit "nationals"—people born in a particular country—to go back to that country as a CIA agent. We should talk about the dangers here. These students need to be alerted, need to understand whose agents they are if they

work with the CIA. They will not be working in the interests of their people, but working against them.

CAIB: How would you sum this all up for our readers?

KM: I want to make the point of how organized this recruiting effort really is, and how dangerous it can be, not just to African people, but also to all people of the "Third World." At this point in time, in the "Third World" in general, and the African countries (Africa and the Caribbean) in particular, the masses of people are rising up against the old order characterized by centuries of colonialism and neo-colonialism. The CIA has had a long history of interfering in the internal affairs of other countries. By putting down the rebellions of the people, destabilizing governments, destroying organizations, planning and financing *coups*, and murdering leaders, the CIA has attempted to change the course of history in places like the Dominican Republic, Guyana, Jamaica, Cuba, Chile, Iran, the Congo, Ghana and Angola, just to name a few.

In the African world they have found it much easier to infiltrate by using black agents rather than white. In fact, it was black CIA agents, born in America, who were instrumental in the overthrow of Kwame Nkrumah in Ghana in 1966 and in the invasion of Guinea in 1970.

This use of black against black is also reflected in the position Andy Young occupies as U.S. Ambassador to the United Nations. In that capacity he travels throughout the African world, seeking to make American imperialist policy more digestible simply because it comes in black hands rather than white. African leaders aware of this ploy have told him it won't work. The revolution of the African world is not the civil rights struggle of the 60s. The people will not be placated, they will not be bought off.

This new consciousness not only informs the people of past transgressions but also brings with it new vigilance which alerts them to potential CIA agents. Based on the recent overthrow of the U.S.-supported oppressive and exploitative government of Eric Gairy in Grenada, one might expect the CIA to attempt to overthrow or intervene in the affairs of the New Revolutionary Government of Grenada. But the people are organized against such interference. The CIA reign around the world is coming to an end.

We must not become the enemies of our people. We must organize against all CIA activity. We must fight the CIA.

CovertAction
INFORMATION BULLETIN

From *CovertAction Information Bulletin*, no. 9 (June 1980), pp. 29-34

Naming Names

This column will continue to be a regular feature of the *CovertAction Information Bulletin*; we do not believe that it can be constitutionally suppressed by the government. If any of the proposed laws designed to censor this column out of existence are passed, we can assure our readers that we will fight them in the courts.

With this issue, in any event, we present forty CIA officers and one Pentagon intelligence chief. They comprise thirteen Chiefs of Station, eight Deputy Chiefs of Station, and nineteen senior case officers, from, in all, thirty-one countries.

Algeria

We have located **Norman H. Descoteaux** at the Algiers, **Algeria** Embassy, where he is undoubtedly the Chief of Station. Descoteaux, whose biography appears in "Dirty Work: The CIA in Western Europe,"* was the Chief of Station in Kingston, Jamaica, exposed by Philip Agee in his 1976 tour of that island. Descoteaux, born June 15, 1936 in Maine, first served under military cover as a "political analyst" with the Department of the Army from 1962 to 1965, when he assumed his first post under diplomatic cover, as a political assistant at the Guayaquil, Ecuador Consulate General. In 1967 he was transferred to Buenos Aires, Argentina, as a political officer, and in 1970 he resumed military cover as a "program coordination officer" with the Department of the Army. In 1973 he was back again in Ecuador as a political officer in Guayaquil. He returned briefly to Headquarters in

*[The following are cited as sources throughout the article: Philip Agee and Lois Wolf, *Dirty Work: The CIA in Western Europe* (Secaucus, N.J.: Lyle Stuart, 1978), 734 pp.; Ellen Ray . . . et al), *Dirty Work 2: The CIA in Africa* (Secaucus, N.J.: Lyle Stuart, 1978) 523 pp.; Philip Agee, *Inside the Company: CIA Diary*, (New York: Stonehill, 1975), 639 pp.; and back issues of *CovertAction Information Bulletin* (Washington, D.C., 1978-).—eds., *Alternative Papers*.]

1975, and late that year assumed his post as Chief of Station in Kingston, where he played a major role in the unsuccessful destabilization campaign against the Michael Manley government. He left Jamaica, being replaced there by Dean J. Almy, Jr. (as noted in *CAIB* Number 1), sometime in 1978, and, as of January 1980, our sources note his presence at the Algiers Embassy.

Another case officer in Algiers is **Claude Patrick Connelly**, born September 26, 1943. Connelly served in the Calcutta, India Consulate General from 1972 to 1975 as an economic-commercial officer, before being transferred to the Colombo, Sri Lanka Embassy. While we are not certain how long he remained in Colombo, our sources indicate that as of at least November 1979 he was stationed at the Algiers Embassy.

Argentina

The CIA officer who is the Deputy Chief of Station in **Argentina** (under Joseph A. DiStefano, reported in *CAIB* Number 2), is **Conrad C. Schubert**, born July 28, 1927 in New Jersey. Schubert entered the CIA under military cover, working for the Department of the Army from 1952 to 1960, at which time he switched to Air Force cover until 1965. That year he commenced diplomatic cover as Attache and political officer at the Santiago, Chile Embassy. In 1966 he was transferred to Buenos Aires, Argentina, still as a political officer. In 1970 he was back at Headquarters until at least 1975, from which time there are no records regarding his whereabouts. However, our sources have indicated to us that at least as of January 1980 he was posted once again to the political section of the Buenos Aires Embassy, probably to become the CIA Chief of Station upon the departure of DiStefano.

Austria

The Chief of Station in Vienna, **Austria** is veteran CIA officer **David Warner Forden,** born September 11, 1930 in New York. Forden also first served with the Agency under military cover, as a plans officer with the Department of the Army from 1956 to 1962. State Department records note that from 1962 to 1964 he was

in "private experience" as a "consultant" for a "management consulting firm." This was obviously further CIA work in "deep cover" with some private firm, perhaps an Agency proprietary. It would of course be of considerable interest if any *CAIB* reader should come across any reference to the company which employed Mr. Forden. In 1965, after Polish language training, he was posted, now under State Department cover, as Attache and political officer in the Warsaw, Poland Embassy. Later that year he became Second Secretary, and remained in Poland until 1967, when he returned to headquarters. In 1970 he was posted overseas again, this time to the Mexico City, Mexico Embassy, now Deputy Chief of Station. As of late 1973 he was back again at Headquarters; no records relating to his whereabouts have been located until he appears on the October 1979 Vienna Diplomatic List, which states that he arrived in Austria to take up the cover post of Attache in August 1978. As far as *CAIB* can ascertain, Forden is still there, and the Chief of Station.

Forden's Deputy Chief of Station appears to be **Arthur H. Stimson,** born January 5, 1927. Stimson served as CIA Chief of Base in the Munich, Federal Republic of Germany Consulate General, under cover as a political officer, from 1972 to 1976. The next record uncovered relating to his whereabouts is the same Vienna Diplomatic List of October 1979, which indicates that he assumed his post there in April 1979.

Bolivia

A senior case officer serving since late 1978 in La Paz, **Bolivia**, is **Walter C. D'Andrade,** born October 21, 1940 in Massachusetts. D'Andrade's diplomatic covers have included economic officer in the Recife, Brazil Consulate General from 1964 to 1967; political officer at the Lisbon, Portugal Embassy from 1968 to 1970; and political officer at the Rio De Janeiro, Brazil Consulate General from 1972 to 1975. During the intervals he appears to have been stationed back at Headquarters in Langley. In September 1978, after another stint at Headquarters, he appeared in the political section of the La Paz Embassy.

Burundi

As of at least September 1979, the new Chief of Station in Bujumbura, **Burundi** is **David M. Ransom**, whose biography is found in "Dirty Work 2: The CIA in Africa." Ransom, born August 26, 1944, served in Abidjan, Ivory Coast from 1972 to 1974; in Dakar, Senegal from 1974 to 1975; and in Nouakchott, Mauritania from 1975 to 1977, when he returned to Headquarters for a respite from his African CIA career. As of September 1979 our sources indicate that he has been at the Bujumbura Embassy, undoubtedly as Chief of Station, Ransom replaces George H. Hazelrigg, the Chief of Station noted in *CAIB* Number 2.

Canada

In September 1978, *CAIB* editors, speaking in Toronto, informed the audience that the Chief of Station in Ottawa was the notorious Stacy B. Hulse, Jr., the former Chief of Station in Greece, who had unsuccessfully attempted to thwart the overthrow of the junta (and who was Richard Welch's immediate predecessor—and the original target of the group which assassinated Welch). Newspaper reporters who attempted to reach Hulse were informed by the Embassy that he had, coincidentally, just left Canada. Hulse had, indeed, reached acceptable retirement age, whether his rapid departure was coincidental or not. *CAIB* has now learned that his successor, and still Chief of Station at the Ottawa, **Canada** Embassy is **John Kenneth Knaus**, born May 30, 1923 in Iowa. U.S. government records show that Knaus, after receiving his BA, MA, and PhD at Stanford University served in an "unspecified government service" from 1951 to 1956, indicating that he has been with the Agency for nearly 30 years. In 1956 he appeared as a "foreign affairs officer" with the U.S. Information Agency, now the International Communication Agency, and on occasion a cooperative CIA cover agency, where he served until 1958. From 1958 to 1972 there are no entries regarding him in the Department of State records. Then, in May 1972 he surfaced as a political officer at the Tokyo, Japan Embassy where he served until late 1974, when he returned to Headquarters for at least two years. The records are silent from 1976 to 1978; then, in the November 1978 and June 1979 Ottawa Diplomatic Lists he is found as an Attache at the Ottawa Embassy—clearly Stacy Hulse's successor as Chief of Station.

Colombia

A senior case officer now in the Bogota, **Colombia** Embassy is **Charles Stephen Smith**, born November 22, 1936 in Missouri. Smith, whose full biography appears in "Dirty Work," served from 1964

to 1966 in the tell-tale cover position of "program analyst" for the Department of the Army, when he moved to the Agency for International Development as "assistant program officer" and "community analyst" in Vientiane, Laos, until mid-1969. From 1969 to 1974 he does not appear in State Department records. Then he resurfaced as a political liaison officer at the Madrid, Spain Embassy. In January 1978 he returned to Headquarters, and, in May of that year, he was posted to Bogota where, we are informed by our source in Bogota, he is found in the Consular section.

Ecuador

Our sources indicate that the new Chief of Station in Quito, **Ecuador** is **Robert Clayton Brown**, born October 9, 1924 in Illinois. Brown has been with the Agency since at least 1957, and possibly ever since he graduated from Syracuse University in 1950. In 1957 he was posted to Munich, Federal Republic of Germany, as a "geographic analyst" for the Department of the Army. In 1965 he moved to another form of cover, this time AID, as an assistant program officer in Bogota, Colombia, where he served until 1967, when he returned to Headquarters. In 1970 he was back under diplomatic cover as a political officer at the San Jose, Costa Rica Embassy—in fact Deputy Chief of Station; in 1973 he was transferred, in the same capacity, to Buenos Aires, Argentina, where he served until at least 1976, becoming, in 1974, Chief of Station. Records for the next two years do not mention him; as of December 1978, however, he was posted to the political section in Quito, again as Chief of Station.

Finland

We have located a case officer in the Helsinki, **Finland** Embassy, serving under the new Chief of Station, Robert T. Dumaine, uncovered in *CAIB* Number 6. He is **John David Stranford**. Stranford's State Department records are scant, indicating that he was an economic-commercial officer at the Rio De Janeiro, Brazil Consulate General from 1974 to 1977, and that, as of at least September 1979 he was Third Secretary at the Helsinki Embassy. However, information available to *CAIB* confirms that he is, in fact, a CIA case officer.

France

Significant changes have been uncovered by our sources regarding the Paris,

France CIA station. For one thing, Eugen Burgstaller, the long-time Chief of Station has left (and, testified last month before Congress, admitting his CIA employment); for another, Francis John Jeton, the CIA's Paris-based chief of Africa operations has also left. Our sources have indicated that Burgstaller was replaced by **James M. Potts** and Jeton was replaced by **Serge Taube**. However, as their biographies, outlined below, indicate, it is logical to assume that Potts has taken over Jeton's job, and Taube is now Deputy to **Edwin Franklin Atkins**, who, as noted in *CAIB* Number 3, was transferred to Paris in late 1978, and is now filling the ailing Burgstaller's position. (Burgstaller's and Atkins's biographies appear in "Dirty Work"; Jeton's is found in "Dirty Work 2.")

James M. Potts, born September 9, 1921 in Louisiana, has been with the CIA since at least 1951, when he commenced ten years undercover as an "analyst" with the Department of the Army. From 1960 to 1964 and from 1968 to 1972 he served in Athens, Greece, first as Deputy Chief of Station, and then, after a tour at Headquarters, as Chief of Station. In 1972 he returned to Langley as Deputy Chief of the Africa Division, moving up, in 1974 to Chief of the Division, where, for the next two years he spent his most notorious period as the director of CIA Angola operations. His role has been fully described by John Stockwell in "In Search of Enemies." He was also intimately involved in the Space Research Corporation scandal involving the illegal shipment of arms to South Africa. His whereabouts from 1976, after the conclusion of the Angola fiasco, until September 1979, is not known to us. However, extremely reliable sources relate that at that time he was posted to the Paris Embassy. Although, as noted, his arrival did not exactly coincide with Jeton's departure, his background demonstrates that he must be filling the crucially important role of chief of Africa operations. The role of Paris as the center of western operations aimed at Africa is well-documented. The French, of course, play a major role in Africa in their own right, and for a long time it has also been the center of U.S. activity.

Serge Taube, born December 2, 1931 in New York has been with the Agency since 1956, and he commenced work under diplomatic cover in late 1957 as a political assistant at the Jakarta, Indonesia Embassy. In 1960 he returned to Headquarters, and in late 1962 was posted to Vientiane, Laos, as a political officer. Three years later he moved to the Rangoon, Burma Embassy, as an economic officer, returned to Headquarters in 1967, and, in 1969, was posted to Moscow, U.S.S.R. In 1971 he returned again to Headquarters, where he remained until 1973. There are no entries relating to him in State Department records from 1973 to 1977, when he appeared briefly at Headquarters before posting, again, to Jakarta, by this time as Chief of Station. Then, according to our sources, he was transferred, as of at least January 1980, to Paris.

Guatemala

Our sources both in Washington and in Guatemala have enabled us to uncover the Chief of Station, the Deputy Chief of Station, and two senior case officers, in this strategically important Latin American nation. The Chief of Station at the Guatemala City, **Guatemala** Embassy is **V. Harwood Blocker, III,** born October 19, 1936 in France (of American parents). Blocker has been with the Agency since at least 1963, when he first appeared in State Department records, while briefly at CIA Headquarters in Langley before his first posting, in early 1964, to the Santo Domingo. Dominican Republic Embassy as a political officer. From 1966 to 1968 he was back at Headquarters, and then posted to the Rio De Janeiro, Brazil Embassy. In 1970 he moved to the Recife, Brazil Consulate General, and in late 1973 was back at Headquarters. We have found no State Department entries covering 1974 and early 1975, but by May 1975 he was posted to the Lima, Peru Embassy as a political officer, serving, in fact, as CIA Deputy Chief of Station. In October 1977 he was transferred to Guatemala City, now Chief of Station, and was still there at least as of a month ago. He speaks fluent Portuguese.

Blocker's Deputy Chief of Station is **Peggy M. Maggard.** While we do not possess Ms. Maggard's date of birth, one of our sources, who has met her, informed *CAIB* that she is at least 50 years of age. This would suggest that upon the departure of Blocker she might assume the Chief of Station position. Maggard first appears in State Department records in April 1964, at Headquarters. In 1965 she was posted to Mexico City, Mexico, ostensibly as a clerk-stenographer. (If this was truly her job, it indicates the remarkable opportunities for advancement in the CIA.)

In 1968 she was posted to the Caracas, Venezuela Embassy, now as a political assistant, and remained there until at least 1970. No entries have been found in State Department records for the period from 1970 to 1979, during which she clearly advanced in the ranks. According to our sources, she arrived in Guatemala City at least as of October 1979, as the Deputy Chief of Station.

Joel H. Beyer is one of the CIA case officers exposed in Kingston, Jamaica by Philip Agee in 1976. Prior thereto, Beyer, born April 13, 1934, had served in La Paz, Bolivia from 1970 to 1972, and in Santo Domingo, Dominican Republic from 1972 till mid-1975, when he was posted to Jamaica. In February 1977, a few months after his exposure, he was back at Headquarters. Our sources indicate that as of October 1977 he had been transferred to the Guatemala City Embassy as a political officer, in fact, a senior CIA case officer.

Finally, our sources have noted the presence in Guatemala City, since December 1978, of **Michael J. Dubbs,** born August 28, 1943, another case officer. Dubbs served as a political officer at the Sao Paulo, Brazil Consulate General from 1969 to 1973, when he returned to Headquarters. The next reference noted places him at the Rio De Janeiro, Brazil Consulate General from 1975 to 1978, when, as noted, he was transferred to Guatemala City.

Guyana

Several sources have led *CAIB* to conclude that the new Deputy Chief of Station in Georgetown, **Guyana** is **James Lee Adkins,** born March 22, 1935. Adkins was under cover as a political officer at the Santo Domingo, Dominican Republic Embassy from 1971 to 1974. The next record found indicates that from 1976 to 1979 he served at the Santiago, Chile Embassy, in the economic section, before being transferred, in January 1979, to Georgetown.

Haiti

The Chief of Station in Port-au-Prince, **Haiti,** who appears on the January 1980 Port-au-Prince Diplomatic List, is **William C. Wagner, Jr.** Wagner served from 1970 to 1973, in the Santiago, Chile Embassy, and from 1973 to 1975 at the Montevideo, Uruguay Embassy, both times under cover as a Consular officer. We have no information for the period from 1976 to 1978, when, after a brief stop at Headquarters, he was transferred to Haiti,

becoming, certainly by this year, Chief of Station. Wagner's biography indicates that he must be a specialist in dealing with the extreme right wing.

A case officer serving under Wagner is **David M. Buss.** The Diplomatic List indicates he arrived in Haiti in August, 1979.

India

An experienced case officer, the Deputy Chief of Station in New Delhi, **India**, is **William Wood Douglass,** born October 31, 1933 in Tennessee. Records indicate that he joined the CIA in 1955. Douglass first appears as a consular assistant in the Damascus, Syria Embassy, from 1959 till 1963, when he returned to Headquarters. In 1964 he was transferred to Beirut, Lebanon as an Attache and an Arabic language trainee. In 1966 he was posted to Jidda, Saudi Arabia, and in 1969 was again back at Headquarters. In 1971 he was back in Beirut, this time as an economic-commercial officer, and in 1973 returned home again. No entries have been found covering 1976 to 1979, but our New Delhi sources confirm that as of at least September 1979 he was at the New Delhi Embassy in the political section, in fact, the CIA Deputy Chief of Station.

Another case officer stationed in New Delhi is **Waldimir Skotzko,** born November 6, 1941 in Washington, D.C. Records indicate that Skotzko served under military cover from 1965 to 1970 in the uncommon guise of "editorial assistant." In 1970 he transferred to Department of State cover, and in 1971 was posted to Zagreb, Yugoslavia, after language training in Serbo-Croatian. In 1973 he was back for more language training, and was sent the next year to the Tehran, Iran Embassy. In 1978 he was transferred to Kathmandu, Nepal, returned late that year to Headquarters, and, as of December 1979 was posted to the political section in the New Delhi Embassy.

Japan

A senior case officer in the Tokyo, **Japan** Embassy is **Juan F. Noriega,** born March 1, 1933 in New Jersey. Records state that Noriega served privately from 1964 to 1966 as an "advisor" to an unspecified country, quite unusual cover. Our sources confirm that the country was, in fact, Nicaragua, and Noriega's job was the training of Somoza's bodyguards. From 1966 to 1969 he was stationed under State Department cover as a political officer at the Montevideo, Uruguay Embassy, a position noted by Philip Agee in "Inside the Company." He was back at Headquarters from 1969 to 1971, when he was transferred to Mexico City, Mexico, still as a political officer. No entries have been found for the period from late 1972 until late 1979, when, in October, he was transferred to the Tokyo Embassy.

Jerusalem

Reliable sources confirm that the Chief of Base for the CIA in **Jerusalem** is **Stephen Elroy Montgomery**, born October 29, 1936 in Kentucky. Montgomery first appears under State Department cover in 1966, as a linguistics intern. However, that same year he assumed the giveaway cover of "political analyst" for the Department of the Air Force (indicating that he was recruited from the State Department by the CIA), until 1968, when he went back under diplomatic cover, posted to the Calcutta, India Consulate General as a political assistant. In 1969 he moved to the Madras, India Consulate General as an economic-commercial officer, and in 1971 was transferred to Colombo, Ceylon (now Sri Lanka), as a political-economic officer. In 1975 he was back at Headquarters, and, although no entries have been found for 1976 and most of 1977, as of October 1977 he was posted to the Jerusalem Consulate General, and is listed on the Jerusalem Consular List of February 1980. He is clearly the Chief of Base in this politically and historically critical city.

Libya

CAIB's sources have uncovered a case officer at the Tripoli, **Libya** Embassy, **Kenneth Mitchell Sapp**. Sapp was posted to the Bombay, India Consulate General in 1978, serving ostensibly as Vice-Consul, and, as of at least November 1979 was transferred to Tripoli.

Mali

The new Chief of Station in Bamako, **Mali** is **Danny M. Loftin**, born March 8, 1943. Loftin, whose biography appears in "Dirty Work," was undercover from 1968 to 1972 as a "research analyst" for an unspecified government agency, and in 1972 was posted to the U.S. Mission to the United Nations. In 1973 he was briefly back at Headquarters before posting to the Leningrad, U.S.S.R. Consulate General. In 1976 he was at the Geneva, Switzerland Mission, and, according to our sources, he was at Bamako at least as of December 1979. In an interesting example of creative research, a *CAIB* reader noticed, as set

forth in "Dirty Work," that State Department records indicate Loftin received a Master's Degree from the University of Kentucky in 1967. The records of that institution, however, show no master's thesis under the name of Loftin ever filed. Mali may have been shortchanged!

Nepal

We have uncovered a case officer assigned to the Kathmandu, **Nepal** Embassy, **James M. Senner**, born October 2, 1942 in Wisconsin. After signing up with the CIA in 1968, he entered upon State Department cover in 1969, with Farsi language training, and was posted in 1970 to the Kabul, Afghanistan Embassy as a political officer, and shortly thereafter, as a consular officer. In 1974 he was moved to the Madras, India Consulate General as a political officer. As of at least December 1979 he was at the Kathmandu Embassy.

Nigeria

Several sources have confirmed to *CAIB* that a case officer in Lagos, **Nigeria** is **Paul Fisher Bradley**, Bradley served under diplomatic cover at the La Paz, Bolivia Embassy from 1977 to 1979. Our sources indicate that as of at least October 1979 Bradley was transferred to the Lagos Embassy.

Norway

The Deputy Chief of Station at the Oslo, **Norway** Embassy is, according to our sources there, **Robert A. Dooling**, born September 26, 1933 in Kentucky. Records indicate that Dooling served as an "analyst" with an unspecified government agency from 1962 to 1963. The next entry states that as of late 1966 he was under cover as a foreign affairs officer in the Europe Department of the State Department. There are no entries for the period 1974 to 1978. Then, as of at least January 1979 he appears as an Attache at the Oslo Embassy, according to the October 1979 Oslo Diplomatic List. He is serving under Chief of Station William E. Camp, noted in *CAIB* Number 6.

Pakistan

A senior case officer in the Islamabad, **Pakistan** Embassy is **David Edward Thurman**, born November 30, 1937 in Missouri. State Department records indicate unspecified government experience from 1960 to 1962 and from 1965 to 1966 with Kansas State College in between. In 1967 Thurman was posted to the Colombo, Ceylon (now Sri Lanka) Embassy as a

political officer. In 1972 he was back at Headquarters, and in 1973 he was posted to the Karachi, Pakistan Consulate General as a consular officer. He is not listed in State Department records from 1976 to 1978. Then, as of at least January 1979, he is found at the Islamabad Embassy.

Singapore

Mentioned on the August 1979 **Singapore** Diplomatic List is a senior case officer, **Edward Robert McGivern**. McGivern, born April 19, 1936 in Montana, was an "editor" for the Department of the Army in 1964, and then spent the next two years "on loan" to AID as a province officer in Vietnam, before returning to his interesting cover as an editor in 1968. This suggests that McGivern was a part of the CIA Vietnam operations in the heyday of Operation Phoenix, the Agency's massive assassination program. In late 1968 he commenced diplomatic cover, at the Taichung. Taiwan Foreign Service Institute language school. In 1969 he was posted to the then Embassy at Taipei, Taiwan as a political officer. In 1973 he was posted to the Rangoon, Burma Embassy, as a political-economic officer. In 1976 he returned to Headquarters though we have found no information covering 1977 to 1978. Then, as of November 1978 he was at the Singapore Embassy, as Second Secretary.

Sri Lanka

In *CAIB* Number 6 we reported the presence of a senior case officer at the Colombo, **Sri Lanka** Embassy, **Richard W. Rauh**. Our sources, both in Washington and in Sri Lanka, indicate that Rauh is now definitely the Chief of Station, having filled the post formerly held by Jack S. Ogino, who, as noted in *CAIB* Number 8, left Colombo around September 1979 to become Chief of Station in Beirut, Lebanon.

Sudan

Robert Ervin McCall, III, a case officer whose biography appears in "Dirty Work 2" and in *CAIB* Number 4, has been transferred, according to our source, to the Khartoum, **Sudan** Embassy, as of October 1979. Since 1977, McCall had been at the Addis Ababa, Ethiopa Embassy in the consular section.

Swaziland

Wilfred J. A. Charette, whose biography appears in "Dirty Work 2," has left his post as Deputy Chief of Station in Accra,

Ghana and moved to the Chief of Station slot at the Mbabane, **Swaziland** Embassy, as of February 1980, according to sources there. Prior to this service in Ghana, Charette had served as Attache in Addis Ababa, Ethiopia.

Tunisia

We have located a case officer in the Tunis, **Tunisia** Embassy, **William Baker Carleton.** Carleton served from 1973 to 1975 at the Rabat, Morocco Embassy, first as a clerk in the political section and then as a political officer. There are no entries on him in State Department records from 1975 to 1978, when he appeared at the Tehran, Iran Embassy. As of at least September 1979 he was transferred to Tunis, in the economic section.

United Kingdom

We have located a senior case officer in the London, **United Kingdom** Embassy. He is **Thomas Edward Carroll,** born September 17, 1936 in New York. Carroll was serving as a political assistant in the Rio De Janeiro, Brazil Embassy from 1963 to 1965, when he was transferred to the Sao Paulo, Brazil Consulate General, as a political officer. In 1968 he was back at Headquarters. The next record entries indicate that he was at the Santiago, Chile Embassy from July 1973 until at least August 1975, indicating that he was part of the CIA team which worked with, and supported, the bloody Pinochet *coup* of

September 1973. Record entries are again lacking from 1975 to 1979, when, as the London Diplomatic Lists indicate, he surfaced, in April 1979, as an administrative attache at the London Embassy.

Zaire

CAIB's sources have confirmed that **Dwight Spaulding Burgess,** whose biography is given in "Dirty Work 2," and who is there located at the Lubumbashi, **Zaire** Consulate, is, in fact, the Chief of Base for the CIA in this critical African ally of the United States.

Zambia

Robert K. Simpson, a senior case officer whose biography appears in "Dirty Work," is located, as of at least November 1979, in the Lusaka, **Zambia** Embassy, in the economic section. From 1971 to 1976 Simpson, born December 1, 1940 in Rhode Island, was a political officer at the Helsinki, Finland Embassy. In 1976 he was transferred to the Madrid, Spain Embassy, where he served until at least late 1978. Our sources confirm that he has been in Lusaka since at least November 1979.

The Pentagon

Military sources have noted that Major General **James Arthur Williams,** born March 29, 1932 in New Jersey, a 1954 West Point Graduate, was appointed in March 1980 the Deputy Assistant Chief of Staff for Intelligence of the United States Army.

American Press Association, described herein, is a case study of present day CIA covert propaganda. Indeed, the methodology employed is strikingly similar to the CIA's use of *El Mercurio* against Chilean President Salvador Allende.

The story is complicated, and intertwined, but revolves around IAPA and its General Manager, James B. Canel. In what follows, we try to unravel the many threads of this story.

Prizes

In October 1979 the *Daily Gleaner* received the Maria Moors Cabot citation in recognition of its services in defense of "press freedom in Latin America." Serving on the Board which awards the Cabot citations is James B. Canel, General Manager of the Miami-based IAPA. Although the prize is administered by the Columbia University School of Journalism in New York City, the Board is totally independent of the University, and is, reportedly, a creature of IAPA. Canel, in fact, is part of a select group which has been giving awards to each other for some time. In 1960, Canel himself received the Cabot award. In 1972, Canel gave the IAPA "Freedom of the Press" award to Arturo Fontaine of *El Mercurio.* Simultaneously the American Legion gave its "Freedom of the Press" award to *El Mercurio* owner, Agustin Edwards, a multi-millionaire who owned vast resources in Chile. At the ceremony honoring Edwards were the past four IAPA presidents.

It was not until December 1975 that the Senate Select Committee report "Covert Action in Chile: 1964-1974" revealed that the day after a September 14, 1970 meeting between Edwards and CIA Director Richard Helms, the now famous meeting between Richard Nixon, Henry Kissinger and Helms occurred in the Oval Office, at which time they sanctioned the destabilization of the Allende government, and in February 1979 with the use of classified documents, *Inquiry* magazine revealed that both Fontaine and Edwards were CIA agents. In fact, Edwards is known to have been a CIA agent since 1958, running other agents, laundering CIA money, and the like. Edwards, a long-time crony of Nixon, and whose cousin is married to David Rockefeller, is at present well placed as the vice-president of Pepsi-Cola's international division. Edwards was president of IAPA in 1969, and both he and another CIA operative from *El Mercurio,* Rene Silva Espejo, are still on the IAPA board. In 1968 Edwards had been

CovertAction
INFORMATION BULLETIN

From *CovertAction Information Bulletin,* no. 7 (December 1979/ January 1980), pp. 10-12

The CIA and the Media: IAPA and the Jamaica *Daily Gleaner*

by Fred Landis

Fred Landis is the author of Psychological Warfare and Media Operations in Chile,

1970-1973, *and a former researcher for the Senate Select Committee to Study Governmental Operations With Respect to Intelligence Activities (the Church Committee). He is at present a journalist in Santa Barbara, California.*

In its efforts to influence, and perhaps topple, the government of Prime Minister Michael Manley of Jamaica, the CIA has used proprietary wire services, agents, assets, a major international press organization, and stock propaganda themes. These efforts have been on a hemisphere-wide basis, but are currently most evident in the local anti-Manley newspaper, the *Daily Gleaner.* The close partnership between the *Gleaner* and the Inter chairman of IAPA's Freedom of the Press Committee, which during the past decade has given its awards to the wire services discussed below, who, of course, reciprocate.

Wire Services

The major CIA-connected wire services reaching Latin America and the Caribbean are Agencia Orbe Latino-americano, Copley News Service, Forum World Features, and LATIN. (Two other wire services reaching the Caribbean, Reuters-CANA and World Features Services, are reputed to have ties to British intelligence—but that is not within the scope of this article.) The *Daily Gleaner* has subscribed to, and run stories from, both English-language services. In addition, since the exposures of many of the services, the *Gleaner* has taken to running wire service articles, often datelined Washington, with no source attribution at all.

Agencia Orbe Latinoamericano was identified by Philip Agee in "Inside the Company: CIA Diary" as a feature news service serving most of Latin America, financed and controlled by the CIA through the Santiago, Chile station.

Copley News Service was identified in the August 1977 *Penthouse* in an article by investigative reporters Joe Trento and Dave Roman as "the only [media] organization that the CIA had 'full cooperation with' for nearly three decades," and was later confirmed by the *New York Times* as "the CIA's eyes and ears in Latin America."

Forum World Features, incorporated in Delaware but based in London, produced six articles a week plus photographs for 150 newspapers in some 50 countries around the world, including the United States. It was exposed as a CIA proprietary in the summer of 1975 by the London magazine *Time Out*, and later in the London *Guardian*, the *Irish Times,* the *Washington Post,* and *More* magazine. In the May 1978 *More,* freelance author Russell Warren Howe, who worked for a number of years for the FWF—unaware of its Agency relationship—described it as "the principal CIA media effort in the world."

LATIN was identified in 1975 by the *New York Times* as a CIA wire service, eliciting a sharp rebuttal from former CIA Director Richard Helms. LATIN was not, technically a proprietary, but CIA agents and CIA funds played a crucial role in its development. Fraudulently proclaiming itself as the first Third World news service, LATIN was started and owned by two former IAPA presidents to offset the influence of Cuba's Prensa Latina. According to a former LATIN executive, it developed out of the practice of Agustin Edwards calling Julio de Mesquita Neto, publisher of the Brazilian newspaper *O Estado de Sao Paulo*, and yet another IAPA president, every Thursday afternoon to exchange information. By July 1971 LATIN had been consolidated into a hemisphere-wide wire service owned by *El Mercurio* and four Brazilian newspapers. In 1974 the governments of Mexico, Venezuela and Costa Rica attempted, through indirect means, to purchase LATIN. These efforts were thwarted by Edwards who personally laid out a cool $400,000 to do so. Despite denials by both Helms and Edwards, the January 16, 1976 *Washington Post* identified LATIN as a CIA wire service.

The Hub

The Inter American Press Association, with its own wire service reaching some 1000 newspapers, is the hub of the entire Latin American media operation. Its past presidents and board members read almost like a roster of key CIA agents in the Latin American media. The late James S. Copley, founder of Copley News Service, whose CIA ties date back to before 1953, was president of IAPA in 1970. Two other CIA agents still at Copley are current IAPA board members. Agustin Edwards was president of IAPA in 1969, as noted, and Neto was president in 1972. One of Edwards' CIA operatives from *El Mercurio* is also on the present IAPA board. IAPA, in short is the intersection of the CIA's propaganda operations in Latin America.

In the Senate report discussed earlier it states that, as part of its war against Allende, "the CIA, through its covert action resources, orchestrated a protest statement from an international press association and world press coverage of the association's protest." In its classified version the report identified the association as IAPA. The individual whom the CIA contacted in September 1970, and who issued the protest, was James B. Canel.

The History of IAPA

The IAPA began in 1926 as the first Pan American Congress of Journalists, at the instigation of the U.S. State Department acting through the American Society of Newspaper Editors. During World War II, it devoted itself to counteracting pro-Axis propaganda in Latin America. After the war, though, the Pan American Congress of Journalists was not as willing to follow the lead of the State Department as it had been. Instead of viewing this as a natural consequence of the lack of a common enemy to rally against, the State Department attributed the change in mood to national chauvinism and communist sympathies among the Latin American delegates.

Thus, in 1950, the CIA orchestrated a *coup*. The annual congress was to be held in the United States that year, and the CIA had the State Department refuse a visa for any member which the CIA considered suspect. The approved delegates then met and voted to reorganize the association in such a manner that only publishers, proprietors, and editors could vote. Some journalists could remain, but only with associate, non-voting status. This CIA *coup* was followed in 1953 by the expulsion from IAPA of members with "pro-communist" tendencies. One of the chief inquisitors was James B. Canel.

IAPA's stock theme is to warn that "freedom of the press" is threatened in whichever corner of the world U.S. influence is on the decline. Concurrently, IAPA elevates to its board of directors the publisher of whatever CIA media outlets exist in any "threatened" country. James B. Canel began his journalism career as editor of the *Havana Post*. In his view, there was plenty of freedom of the press in Cuba under the Machado and Batista dictatorships. But in 1959 Canel was already an IAPA executive and spent the following year telling the world that Fidel Castro was a threat to freedom of the press.

Similarly, as the crisis over Chile loomed, four *El Mercurio* executives were elevated to the IAPA board—Agustin Edwards, Hernan Cubillos, Rene Silva Espejo, and Fernando Leniz. Edwards, as

noted above, had been a CIA agent since 1958. Cubillos was identified in the October 23, 1978 *Los Angeles Times* as "one of the CIA's principal agents." Cubillos, who was Edwards' attorney as well as assistant, is now Foreign Minister of Chile; after the *coup*, many *El Mercurio* executives entered the junta government. This information had been leaked from the trial of former ITT official Robert Berrellez, who, with Harold Hendrix, another ITT official, was being prosecuted for perjury before the Church Committee during its investigation of the role of ITT and the CIA in Chile. (The government's indictment admitted that Berrellez and Hendrix were in frequent contact with CIA officer Jonathan Hanke in attempts to thwart the Senate hearings; and according to an October 23, 1978 *Washington Post* article, there were hints that numerous other CIA officers, career men like William Broe, Henry Hecksher, Ted Shackley, Tom Polgar and Jacob Esterline, may also have been involved in those attempts.)

After the trial commenced, both Berrellez and Hendrix then appeared on the staff of the *Miami Herald.* The CIA apparently justifies its domestic media activities such as those at the *Miami Herald* and with the Copley papers in San Diego, California, because both cities are used as bases for Agency operations in Latin America and the Caribbean.

After the death of James Copley in 1973, CIA representation in the Copley organization and in his IAPA slot was maintained by William B. Giandoni and Victor H. Krulak. Giandoni was identified as a CIA media asset in the Trento and Roman expose mentioned above. He was Copley's Latin America editor, and is now the general manager. He received the IAPA "Freedom of the Press" award in 1975 while a member of the IAPA Freedom of the Press Committee and its board of directors. "Butch" Krulak was until 1976 vice-president and director of Copley and an IAPA board member. Previously he had served as a Marine Lieutenant-General in Vietnam. Other Copley staff who have worked directly for the CIA or under the direction of CIA media executives include Ed Christopherson and John Philip Sousa.

Christopherson was identified as a CIA operative by the *New York Times* on December 27, 1977, and was intimately connected with the Agency's operations in Chile after the fascist *coup.* Sousa, grandson of the composer of military marches, writes whatever patriotic themes

Giandoni tells him to. In 1976 Congressmen Harkins, Miller and Moffett went to Chile to investigate human rights conditions. In anticipation of a critical report, Copley News Service sent Sousa to Santiago to produce pro-junta articles. His first piece was reprinted in the February 4, 1976 *Times of the Americas,* in the February American-Chilean Council Bulletin, and was introduced into the March 31 *Congressional Record* by Larry McDonald, right-wing activist and Congressman from Georgia.

Other CIA agents at *El Mercurio* with IAPA connections include Thomas P. McHale, a member of the IAPA Freedom of the Press Committee, and Enrique Campos Menendez, a former IAPA board member. Both are Chileans.

The *Daily Gleaner* and IAPA

The marriage between the *Daily Gleaner* and IAPA extends back at least to 1968. In the ensuing decade, IAPA bestowed scholarships upon a large number of *Gleaner* staff people for study in the U.S., many at Columbia University School of Journalism, which also administers the Cabot prize. Consistent with the pattern of CIA-inspired destabilization efforts against the Jamaican government, especially beginning in late 1975, Oliver Clarke, *Daily Gleaner* chairman and managing director, was duly promoted in 1976 to IAPA Executive Committee membership. The scale of anti-Manley propaganda in the *Gleaner*'s pages escalated sharply.

In September 1970 the CIA, in the person of Agustin Edwards, prepared a 24-page background brief for *Time* magazine to use in its coverage on Allende's election victory and, according to the CIA, "the basic thrust and timing [of the *Time* story] were changed as a result of the briefing." (Church Committee report, "Covert Action." April 1976, p. 14.)* The main themes were repeated in the IAPA newsletter over the next four years!

In September 1970 the specific theme which the CIA had James Canel push through IAPA was "the threat to the free press in Chile." The principal themes, in order of frequency, were: Allende's threat to *El Mercurio*; Chile's links to Cuba; and economic failure and collapse in Chile, as in Cuba.

It is not difficult for anyone following the *Gleaner*'s pages over the past few years to see the striking, direct parallels. The same themes are still being used; the Manley government's threat to freedom of the press (as personified by the *Gleaner*, of course), the links between Manley and Cuba, and the economic difficulties of the Jamaican economy. The analogies are sobering, given the brutal fascism which has held sway in Chile the past six years.

---

*[Similar text available in U.S. Congress, Senate, Select Committee to Study Governmental Operations with Respect to Intelligence Activities, *Covert Action in Chile, 1963-1973: Staff Report,* 94th Congress, 1st sess., Committee print (Washington, D.C.: Government Printing Office, 1975), p. 25.—eds, *Alternative Papers.*]

From *CounterSpy* 4, no. 1 (October 1979): 6-7

September 6, 1979, Statement

We feel that we must respond to the latest in a series of attempts to suppress inquiry into the details and nature of Gloria Steinem's association with the Central Intelligence Agency. We are alarmed that the most visible commentary on these

---

As published in *CounterSpy: The Magazine for People Who Need to Know.*

events has come from several well-known figures in the feminist movement who not only condone but endorse this suppression. Because feminism's appeal and impact spring from a fundamental intellectual honesty, it is particularly distressing that the suppression of dissent may be seen as some kind of official feminist position.

In 1975, after *Redstockings* researched Gloria Steinem's affiliations and raised questions about her political past, Steinem published a "Statement" in connection with her activities on behalf of the Independent Research Service, a CIA-funded group. Many feminists found this document neither entirely credible nor to the point, and they have persisted in seeking more enlightening answers.

Because of the consciously counter-revolutionary role the CIA has played at home and abroad over the years, it makes sense to expect a participant in the women's movement—especially one who has come to symbolize it—to fully discuss her past relationship with the CIA. We are still waiting to hear Steinem's opinion of the Agency; the last one she gave characterized the CIA as "liberal" and "farsighted" (The *New York Times,* February 21, 1967).

The events that prompted us to send out this letter include:

1. Gloria Steinem, Clay Felker (most recently publisher of *Esquire*), and Ford Foundation president Franklin Thomas were among those who threatened to sue for libel if Random House allowed the CIA chapters to be published in the Random edition of *Redstockings' Feminist Revolution.* At the same time, *Newsweek/Washington Post* publisher Katharine Graham and Warner Communications—a major *Ms.* stockholder—also complained. The offending chapters were deleted. Thus, Steinem and her powerful supporters successfully used the threat of litigation to exercise prior restraint over publication.

2. When Steinem learned that the *Village Voice* had assigned journalist Nancy Borman to prepare an article on the censorship of *Feminist Revolution,* her attorneys, Greenbaum, Wolff & Ernst, threatened suit against the *Voice* if any mention of Steinem's CIA association appeared in the article. After some delay to allow the *Voice*'s legal counsel to review the material, the *Voice* published the article (May 21, 1979), and in subsequent issues several letter-writers responded with attacks on Borman and the *Voice.*

3. In May 1979, when *Heights & Valley News,* a New York City neighborhood paper published by the Columbia Tenants Union, began a series on the material deleted from *Feminist Revolution,* Steinem's attorneys again threatened suit. But instead of threatening the Columbia Tenants Union corporation—as they had the Random House and Village Voice corporations—they sent a letter to each of CTU's 32 board members. Board members cannot be individually sued for a corporation's acts, except in a few instances not relevant here (many non-lawyers may not know this); but Steinem's attorneys stated in their letter to the board members

that publication of the material "could subject [them] to individual liability." *Heights & Valley News* stood up to this attempt at intimidation and is continuing the series.

All this legal harassment was in response not to any actual instance of false, malicious defamation, but to the potential raising of embarrassing questions about some feminists' relations with the power elite.

We think that Steinem and her associates have not made a convincing case for cutting off discussion. At question is not just the right to debate one woman's past associations, although this is often important. There is an urgent need for wide-ranging debate in the feminist movement on such questions as:

● Do feminists think there are special topics on which it is defensible to stifle discussion? Why do we put up with bad-faith appeals to "sisterhood"?

● How far should feminists go in making compromises? Which kinds of compromises help us reach our goals? Which hurt?

● Is there a conflict of interest problem that our movement needs to solve—as other movements have tried to solve it—when movement representatives accept positions on the government or corporate side of the bargaining table?

● Are "right-wingers" the only reason for growing number of setbacks for women? Or is the feminist movement failing to discuss its own serious mistakes?

● Does dependence on government and corporate funding and foundation grants increase or decrease the effectiveness of feminist groups? Does it distort their politics and activities?

● What is to be done about government and corporate spying and intervention in the feminist movement?

These questions are not personal but political. They are at the heart of our survival as a movement. We will not be silenced.

Note: *Copies of the two articles reviewing Steinem's CIA associations, which were in the original edition of* Feminist Revolution, *are available for $1.00 from* Redstockings, *P.O. Box 1284, New York, NY 10009:* Redstockings' *information packet on the censorship of the book's Random edition is $1.00. Copies of the Sept. 6, 1975,* Majority Report, *containing Steinem's statement and annotations to it, are $.75 each from Majority Report, 49 Perry St.,*

New York, NY 10014. Copies of the Voice *article and letters of response are $.50, cash or stamps, from the Statement Group, c/o Nancy S. Erickson, 619 Carroll Street, Brooklyn, NY 11215.*

Gilda Abramowitz, New York City
Dee Alpert, NYC
R. L. Annchild, NYC
Marilyn Banzhaf, Washington, DC
Bea Baron, Bronx, NY
Jane Barry, Philadelphia
Pat Barry, Philadelphia
Rosalyn Baxandall, NYC
Frances M. Beal, Brooklyn, NY
Harriet Bernstein, Philadelphia
Louise Billotte, San Francisco
Nancy Borman, NYC
Gayle M. Brauner, LaGrande, Ore.
Lynne Carlo, NYC
Eileen Casey, Brooklyn
Susan P. Chizeck, Princeton, NJ
Cindy Cisler, NYC
Heather Cottin, Bayville, NY
Coca Crystal, NYC
Agnes Cunningham, NYC
Ann C. Davidson, Philadelphia
Charlotte Dennett, NYC
Carole DeSaram, NYC
Hodee W. Edwards, Oakland, Calif.
Dorothy Engleman, NYC
Nancy S. Erickson, Brooklyn
Lisa Forman, Warrington, Pa.
Harriet Fraad, New Haven, Conn.
Carol Giardina Freeman, Jacksonville, Fla.
Elizabeth Griggs, NYC
Sara Grusky, Washington, DC
Stephanie Haftel, Rochester, NY
Carol Hanisch, New Paltz, NY
Carole Heath, Rochester
Judith Lewis Herman, Cambridge, Mass.
Nellie Hester, NYC
Jan Hillegas, Jackson, Miss.
Susan-Leigh Jeanchild, West Palm Beach, Fla.
Patricia Korbet, NYC
Janet Kruzik, Jackson Heights, NY
Lavonne Lela, Rochester
Barbara Leon, Gardiner, NY
Sherry Lipsky, Philadelphia
Pamela Lloyd, NYC
Rita Loughlin, NYC
Kathleen Maynard, Gainesville, Fla.
Charlotte J. McEwen, Ottawa
Aurora Levins Morales, Berkeley, Calif.
Janet Mulkeen, NYC
Amina Muñoz, NYC
Donna O'Sullivan, Prince Albert, Sask.
Marge Piercy, Wellfleet, Mass.
Sharon Presley, Astoria, NY
Colette Price, NYC
Lynne Randall, Atlanta
Bethany R. Redlin, Lambert, Mont.
Judy Reichler, Callicoon Center, NY
Vickie Richman, Brooklyn
Marlene Rupp, Gainesville
Susan B. Sands, NYC
Kathie Sarachild, NYC
Kathryn Scarbrough, Rochester
Gay Schierholz, Carson City, Nev.
Victoria Schultz, NYC
Judy Seigel, NYC
Ingrid Shaw, Gainesville
Marilyn Skerbeck, Washington, DC

Deborah Smith, Bronx
Susan J. Smith, Washington, DC
Mindi B. Snoparsky, Houston
Deborah Thomas, San Francisco
Page Thompson, San Francisco
Tish Webster, NYC
Nancy A. Whitacre, Lancaster, Pa.

Nancy Wolf, Prince Albert, Sask.
Ellen L. Wooters, Philadelphia
Jean Yanarella, Beacon, NY

Distributed by the Statement Group, c/o Nancy S. Erickson, 619 Carroll Street, Brooklyn, NY 11215, October 1979.

the Public Eye

From *The Public Eye* 2, nos. 3/4 (1980): 27-31

Police Terror: An Example and a Context

by Patti Hirota

In Miami, nine white cops brutally beat a Black businessman to death; the cops are acquitted by an all-white jury, sparking a rebellion by angry Blacks in that city. In Detroit, police are being sued for using cattle prods on suspects. In Oceanside, California, the police stand by while the Ku Klux Klan marches in full riot gear without a permit, and then brutally attacks local residents with clubs, chains and dogs. In response to these and many, many other incidents of police terror, cries of protest are being heard around the country.

People across the U.S. are organizing to demand an end to police terror. But in this struggle, many people are confused about what should be done and what role the police have historically played in our society. In Oakland, California, a wave of police killings has prompted numerous citizens to call for restraints against police brutality, but different solutions being offered reflect different political perspectives. This article will examine the case of Oakland, California, specifically the police shooting of Charles Briscoe; but it will also delve into the causes—economic, societal, and historic—of police terror, from which we can learn the proper solutions.

Oakland Police Spark Protests

In Oakland, California today, com-

plaints of excessive police force are higher than in the late 1960's, when the Black Panther Party was organizing for self-defense against police attacks on the Black community. These new attacks resulted in four unwarranted shooting deaths in 1979:

• March 17: Melvin Black, a 15-year-old Black youth was shot in the back 13 times by three officers, two of whom were in plainclothes. Black was shot while fleeing *unarmed*. He did not even match the police description of the sniper they allegedly were pursuing. City inspector Burr found no evidence to support the conclusion that Melvin Black was or was not a reported sniper. His report merely charged the police with using faulty judgment. U.S. Attorney Hunter's federal grand jury report found "no evidence" to prosecute the police.

• Charles Briscoe, a 37-year-old International Association of Machinists (IAM) steward at the Naval Airwork Facility, was shot by police ten times at a range of 15 feet—four times with double-odd buckshot and six times with a .357 magnum. Police came to the scene in response to a call that three shots had been fired outside an Oakland restaurant, and that a man was lying on the ground. According to one police report, an Officer Robert Fredericks arrived at the scene, and asked Briscoe, who was getting into his van, to hold it, Briscoe took off, Fredericks followed on a high speed chase. Briscoe pulled into a closed gas station, and got out of the van, and aimed a rifle at Fredericks. Fredericks fired 4 shots from his 12-gauge shotgun at Briscoe. Briscoe, apparently *not wounded*, ran into the van and reached under the seat. Fredericks then fired 6 shots from his revolver, a .357 magnum. Briscoe's rifle never fired.

The coroner's report said that both of Briscoe's legs had been broken by the shotgun blasts, making it highly questionable that he could run to his van. No

reports by the police, district attorney or U.S. Attorney have been released. According to the local newspaper, Robert Fredericks, the police officer implicated in the Briscoe shooting, has been involved in six shootings, four resulting in death. One of the victims was young Black Panther Bobby Hutton, who was killed in 1968. Fredericks has never been prosecuted.

• November 18: Talmadge Curtis, a twenty-one-year-old Black man was killed by Officer Tomek, who was one of two plainclothes policemen involved in the Melvin Black shooting. Curtis was shot in the head as he was fleeing unarmed from a stalled car. Police claimed Curtis was in a car that seemed to match the police description of a car connected to a store robbery. Roberts, Curtis's friend, was booked for Curtis's murder, under a California state law that says if one is involved in a felony which results in murder, he can be charged whether he did it or not.

• December 21: Francis John, a Black male, was stopped for double parking in East Oakland. Police claimed John engaged in hand combat with police and the police revolver "went off" twice—in John's chest.

In early January 1980, another Black man was shot and killed by Oakland police after a quarrel with his wife. This is the fifth controversial killing of a Black male in the last 10 months. Still the city has taken no action. Reports, special investigations have led nowhere. Not a single policeman has been put in jail or even suspected for these killings.

Response to Police Shootings

After Melvin Black's death, the Oakland City Council set up a special task force on citizen complaints. The task force did not take any real action. After Briscoe's death, workers and friends packed City Hall twice to demand a special investigation and the

NLG/LNS

release of police reports. In response to this pressure, the City Council activated the Task Force on Citizen Complaints, which eventually proposed a five-member police review board limited strictly to fact-finding. The purpose of the review board was to bring the community and the police closer together. The NAACP originally pressed for a police review board with powers to review police policy and make recommendations. They have since compromised and supported the more limited fact-finding body, but with an enlarged membership.

Various political trends have begun to emerge: the city government, the police and law and order groups, reformists such as the NAACP, and the newer anti-fascist organizations such as the Charles Briscoe Committee for Justice. Each differs on what the exact problem is and how to deal with it.

The City Council and the Mayor are primarily concerned with serving the interests of big business, like the Port of Oakland, the Raiders Football team, and real estate investors. To maintain a relatively stable community, the city has assumed the guise of mediator—giving in to the *most limited* of demands around police review in hopes of pacifying citizen anger and preventing an explosive situation. They have not acted in any way to restrict the powers of the police or to prosecute them, and it is not likely that they will. The police that kill and the city government that covers up those killings both serve those in power.

The Police Department (OPD) and local law and order groups are calling for greater power and autonomy for the police. The OPD and the press claim that police hands are being tied by the anti-police climate. The Oakland Police Officers Association held a 450-person march to City Hall protesting the Mayor's "anti-police" stand, and community demands for a police review board. They called for an investigation of all organizations advocating a police review board.

Many groups, including the IAM 739, the NAACP, OCCUR (Oakland Citizens on Urban Renewal), and Black ministers pressed for a police review board. From their perspective, the review board would restore *confidence* in the police and encourage greater *cooperation* between police and the community. Traditional leaders of the Black community, largely professionals, small businessmen and clergy leaders, are urging a *strong* mayor form of city government, rather than a non-elected city manager form. The mayor is now Black; the city manager is white. An increase in power for the mayor will "go a long way towards answering some of our problems," they argue. They see the problem as being one solely of race, rather than one of class *and* national oppression. They also think that Black police would help solve the problem. This denies the fact that the basic role of the police, whatever nationality, is repression. It poses the problem as being one of *individual* cops, instead of the function of the police as a whole. In fact, the last nine shootings of Blacks in Oakland were done by white, Black, Asian, and Latino police officers.

These solutions for legislative change only, are therefore no solutions. They simply channel our anger into reforms. They foster the illusions that the current economic system can indeed serve all classes, all the people—we just need better people in those positions. History reaffirms that legislative change benefits a small handful, while the majority are left in the same basic condition. What's more, Police Review Boards have been around for over 25 years but they generally have not worked because they have been emasculated of their power (and potential power), or had their funding cut after they showed they could have some impact.

The Why and the Wherefore

It will be impossible for community groups to develop effective plans for protesting against police brutality without an understanding of why police terror is once again on the rise, and the historical role played by the police in our economic system.

Police violence of the sort currently being experienced throughout the country is caused by the periodic economic crisis of the system we call capitalism, which is once again hitting the U.S. working class very hard. The poverty programs and federal aid of the early 1970s, which acted as a partial buffer to the recession of 1973-74, are being cut back, putting the burden of the faltering economy on the backs of the working class, especially the national minorities. Proposition 13, the Bakke decision, anti-school busing laws, cuts in unemployment insurance are a few examples. Runaway inflation, wage cuts, loss of cost of living allowance clauses, massive layoffs in the auto and steel industries, all mean greater hardship for the working people of this country.

Already an economically depressed area, Oakland particularly feels the crunch from loss of industry and jobs. East Oakland has one of the highest infant mortality rates in the country (next to Harlem), rents have risen 50% in the last seven years, and whites have been fleeing to the suburbs, leaving Oakland with a 54% national minority (largely Black) population.

Anger, discontent and frustration have grown. To protect the class rule of the bourgeoisie, the state must use increased force and intimidation to squash attempts to organize and prevent organized resistance against the police, when the community is attacked. The repressive apparatus of the state as a whole, in particular the police and para-military fascist organizations such as the KKK, is being strengthened and directed at Blacks and other national minorities. It is precisely to maintain this particular oppression, and to keep the working class *divided* and under *control*, that the ruling class utilizes the police. They are used to help maintain the system of capitalist exploitation. In the name of controlling crime, they attack the victims of the system of inequality that produces poverty and crime. This is no recent development.

History of U.S. Police

Some of the earliest organized police forces with wide jurisdiction were the southern slave patrols in the 1700s. Their job was to catch runaway slaves and to prevent and suppress slave insurrections. Although poor whites were sometimes used by the plantation owners in the patrols, they were also terrorized by these early police when they challenged the rulers of this slave society.

In the North and West, settlers in isolated farming communities often armed and organized themselves into their own militias. But the growth of the police as an organized, large-scale force, a standing capitalist army, paralleled the development of large-scale industry. As large-scale capitalist industry grew in the U.S., so too did the proletariat as an organized class. The capitalist owners of the large factories directly initiated and controlled the modern-day police force, which today numbers tens of thousands in a single city.

The growth of resistance by the working class to capitalist exploitation and the efforts to unionize were met by the capitalists' efforts to bust unions, pit worker against worker, white against Black, immigrant against third and fourth generation worker. The strikes and demonstrations of the workers in this period were met by some of the most brutal repression the world had seen to that date. The beatings and murders, strikebreaking and assassinations were carried out by the police, organized as bands of thugs, or in agencies like Pinkerton's.

The police were directed in their day to day activities by the capitalists. Businessmen were appointed as Police Commissioners or Superintendents. Anything that threatened private property rights and the state rule of the capitalists was defined as "criminal." Thus all strikes, demonstrations, meetings or protests by workers were illegal and subject to attack. Early American labor history is filled with examples of meetings disrupted, labor leaders arrested, picket lines fired upon, workers beaten, strikers' wives and children murdered by the police.

The police also served to enforce national oppression. In the South, municipal police replaced the roving slave patrols in the job of suppressing Blacks and poor white workers and farmers. In the Southwest, the infamous Texas Rangers was organized to steal land and property from Mexicans and Native Indians, and to hand it over to the new Anglo capitalist landlords. Their rule was "Shoot first, ask questions later," and to this day the rule hasn't changed.

History has shown that the police have never been around to "serve and protect" the working class. They have protected and served the capitalist class by suppressing the organization and revolutionary struggles of the working class and national minorities.

As capitalism has developed in the U.S., the police have also developed. Though some of its forms have changed, the function it serves remains the same.

The New Image

Today, the police are part of an immense state repressive intelligence network still aimed at suppressing the working masses. These repressive agencies include the CIA, FBI, National Guard, local "Red Squads" and state troopers, all the way to local police departments. The incredible gathering of information on tens of thousands of citizens by these agencies is only one aspect of their repressive activities. This vast intelligence network has been involved in everything from political assassination of people like Fred Hampton to the routine infiltration and disruption of every progressive political movement in the country.

With the rise of popular outrage over the magnitude and character of activity of these agencies, sparked especially by the disruption of the Civil Rights and anti-war movements and the murder of various political leaders in the Black revolutionary movement, the idea of "community relations" developed. This new approach stressed the need for the police to develop "ties" with the community. Policemen were put back on the beat, and departments were expected to maintain "friendly relations" with their communities. By using terms like "ties, interaction and community relations," the police seek to hide their real role as a repressive agency of the capitalist class. They seek to pose as neutral in the class struggle.

Many citizen review boards or complaint boards were set up in the last fifteen years. They are based on the concept of increasing public confidence in the police. Although the police departments put up a fight against these boards, they also realize that they can be useful, even necessary, in terms of maintaining order and hiding the fact that police killings and repression continue. These boards try to present the state as a mediator of conflict between classes, rather than as an instrument of the ruling capitalist class.

The police "review" boards, "community relations," special use of women or national minority police are programs aimed at making the problem appear to be a few "bad cops," a few crazy individuals.

In reality, these tactics to pacify the masses, to make the police more acceptable, to promote the view that police are neutral, that they "serve and protect" all classes of society. These are tactics designed to maintain the practices of police terror and murder against working and oppressed people in the U.S.

Any attempts to combat police brutality and wrongful shootings must take these realities into account or they are doomed to failure.

One Effort

Groups such as the Charles Briscoe Committee for Justice (CBCJ) formed in Oakland in September, 1979 are beginning to organize resistance to the growing police terror. The CBCJ is an organization of working people of all nationalities which has marched, picketed, leafletted and fundraised to demand that police who murder must be brought to trial and jailed. They demand an end to police terror. While they support genuine legislative reforms, they see the main push must be for organizing and relying on the masses, not on government institutions. To make civilian review of police meaningful, they have proposed a police disciplinary board (an *elected* body to discipline police officers and recommend civil or criminal charges). The CBCJ has also initiated a petition campaign demanding that the governor and attorney general of California pressure to bring officer Fredericks to trial. They have targeted Briscoe's death as part of the overall rise in police and fascist terror. The committee describes itself as follows:

"The goals of the CBCJ originally were to get policeman Fredericks off of the police force, to bring Fredericks to trial for murder, to get an independent investigation of the killing, and to get masses of people behind these demands.

"CBCJ members and other workers at Briscoe's workplace, the National Air Rework Facility, and also various community people began to attend Oakland City Council meetings to have their demands complied with. The City Council ignored these demands, and procrastinated in doing anything to get justice for Briscoe or stop repression in the community. After four months no official reports have been released!

"On November 3, 1979, CBCJ held a rally and march in downtown Oakland to demand an end to police terror in the community. Numerous speakers talked of the need to get a speedy trial for Fredericks, to release the police reports on the killing and to stop police terror in the community. Since that time, 3 more Blacks have been killed by the Oakland police. One was Talmadge Curtis, another Francis John, and the other was James Bell. Curtis and Bell were both shot down in cold blood. None of these men were criminals, but were working people with families. This shows further that the police are not representing our interests. CBCJ feels that the police are here only to protect property and not to protect lives. It does not matter what nationality or race the police are. The police do not punish the real criminals. Since these further killings the CBCJ has taken the position that it wants to fight against fascist terror and police attacks on working people and minorities.

"On December 11, CBCJ held an informational picket in front of City Hall during the City Council meeting. It also puts out literature and demanded at the meeting that the murderers of Briscoe and Curtis be brought to swift trial, and to establish a civilian disciplinary board which had the power to fire and suspend officers from the force."

The Solution?

In the immediate period, we must continue to demand an end to the vicious and brutal police killings and terror around the country. We must build organizations that fight police and fascist attacks against all working people and nationalities, and see this as part of the effort to build multinational unity in the struggle against our common enemies—the rich owners and those who protect them. We must raise the demand that police and fascists who commit crimes must be brought to trial, and tried by juries reflecting the multinational composition of the working class.

It is only through the forging of such unity, and the understanding of the source of our problems that we will someday build a society where parents will not be afraid to let their children out on the streets alone, and where we will not have to keep wondering—who will be next?

Patty Hirota is active in the Charles Briscoe Committee for Justice and a representative of the Communist Party USA/Marxist Leninist (CPUSA/ML); San Francisco Bay Area District. For more information about the work of the Committee, and to send contributions, write c/o UNITE! newspaper, P.O. Box 6206, Chicago, Illinois 60680.

may be sure that they were inadvertent and not the result of purposeful insensitivity or lack of respect for the tenants."

Suit to Be Filed

Attorneys with the New York Civil Liberties Union and the National Conference of Black Lawyers are currently preparing a multi-million dollar lawsuit on behalf of some of the tenants. The suit will charge that the FBI violated the First, Fourth and Fifth Amendment rights of the tenants. **Contact:** Richard Emery, NY CLU, 84 Fifth Avenue, New York, New York, 10011 (212) 924-7800.

Organizing Notes

From *Organizing Notes* 4, no. 5 (July/August 1980): 7-10

Organizing Around the Country

FBI STAGES EARLY MORNING RAID IN HARLEM

Early in the morning on April 19, over 50 FBI agents rushed through an apartment building at 92 Morningside Avenue in West Harlem on a "tip" that Assata Shakur (Joanne Chesimard) was in the building. (Shakur escaped from a New Jersey jail last November.) Armed with shotguns, machine guns, and a fugitive warrant, the FBI agents proceeded to break down doors, forced tenants out of bed and out of their apartments, and then rummaged through closets, drawers, and other personal possessions. Several women were forced to expose their thighs to the agents because Shakur is reported to have a tattoo on her thigh.

The apartment of Ebun Adelona was singled out for special inspection. The night before the raid, Adelona had held a baby shower, which was attended by a former defense attorney for Shakur. According to friends, Adelona's only other link to Shakur was that she had helped raise funds for Shakur five years ago.

Reprinted with permission from *Organizing Notes.*

Agents Return

Six black FBI agents returned to the Morningside Avenue apartment building on April 24. The agents, assigned to the Office of Professional Responsibility, were all dressed in atypical FBI attire—jeans and current "punk" fashions. Some tenants spoke at length with the agents before the agents identified themselves as FBI-affiliated.

Tenants Send Letters of Protest

William Shield, chairman of the tenants association—who attributes his heart attack just after the raid to the FBI's action—contacted the FBI by letter on April 30: "It is impossible to understand why your agents, without the requisite search warrant mandated by law . . . physically and in many cases at gun point, threatened, searched, harassed, abused and detained innocent persons." Noting that the conduct of the investigators from the Office of Professional Responsibility was just as unacceptable as that of those participating in the raid, Shield demanded a written apology and a copy of the internal FBI investigation.

Webster replied on May 5, saying that he was unaware of any misconduct by FBI agents, and that the FBI would pay for any property damages resulting from the search. He said that the Bureau would provide a copy of the investigative report if the tenant group filed an FOIA request. Webster continued, "I ask your understanding . . . If mistakes were made, and that is what we seek to understand, you

PHILADELPHIA POLICE DESTROY INTELLIGENCE FILES

On July 8, Police Commissioner Morton B. Solomon announced that virtually all the police intelligence files had been destroyed and that the department had changed its policy regarding investigations into legitimate political activities. The documents which were destroyed included information on anti-war organizations, the Black Panthers, and the July 4th (1976) Coalition. At one point under former Mayor Rizzo, the files were believed to have totalled 18,000.

The file destruction follows pressure for reform by community groups. In February 1980, local activists met with representatives of Mayor William Green, shortly after the mayor took office, to discuss the status of the files and the possible development of an ordinance or internal guidelines on police intelligence activities (See *Organizing Notes*, Vol. 4, No. 2).* The group, including representatives of ACLU and NLG chapters,

*[Back issues of *Organizing Notes* (Washington, D.C.: Campaign to Stop Government Spying, 1977-) are cited as sources throughout the article.—eds., *Alternative Papers*.]

CPF/LNS

requested that persons named in the files be given an opportunity to see the documents and that the documents later be destroyed, perhaps at the end of one year. Administration officials requested that a written proposal be submitted for the disposal of the files; when the two parties next met in late June, the police officials informed the activists of the files' destruction.

According to Spencer Coxe, of the ACLU, "We were surprised at the speed with which this was done and we are gratified they are destroyed. We would have preferred that the subjects of the files would have had a chance to see them first."

Commissioner Solomon also announced that the police will monitor and maintain records on individuals and groups only when there is a "potential for violence": and that photographs and other records will be destroyed following a demonstration or investigation if no violent or criminal activity takes place. The Commissioner admitted that the police had photographed and later destroyed pictures of recent peaceful demonstrations held by the Puerto Rican Alliance and by police and file department employees who are concerned about personnel cutbacks in their departments. Contact: Jayma Abdoo, 1425 Walnut Street, Philadelphia, PA 19102 (215) 563-8312.

CALIFORNIA

Los Angeles On June 4, Mayor Tom Bradley made his first public comment on the growing controversy about spying and infiltration by the city's police department. In a letter to the Police Commission, he said he would not tolerate further police spying and urged the Commissioners to develop guidelines to prevent future abuses.

Bradley's stance was taken several days after the Citizens Commission on Police Repression (CCOPR) released 45 additional police intelligence documents received in the spying lawsuit, *CAPA v. Gates.* The documents included detailed reports prepared from 1975-1977 by police officers, Connie Millazzo, Jon Dial and Eddie Solomon, who had infiltrated several lawful groups. (See *Organizing Notes,* Vol. 3, No. 4.) Citing other abuses, the LA *Herald Examiner* on June 16 revealed that the Police Department Intelligence Division (PDID) had also spied on national figures such as Jesse Jackson, Martin Luther King, and Dick Gregory while they were in Los Angeles. Other charges of recent harassment have

been made by the Campaign for a Citizens Police Review Board, a coalition of groups concerned about police spying and brutality issues. At a June 5 press conference the campaign charged that the police harassed at least 8 people while they were collecting signatures to place a proposal creating an independent Police Review Board on the November ballot.

In the June issue of its newsletter, *Rap Sheet,* the CCOPR announced three goals for the coming months: 1) enact a Freedom of Information Act that would permit release of PDID's intelligence files; 2) Abolish the PDID and 3) pass an ordinance outlawing police spying in Los Angeles. Charging that the PDID is "beyond reform" (as proposed in guidelines covering intelligence investigations presented by the Police Commission (see *Organizing Notes,* Vol. 4, No. 2) the CCOPR has called for a boycott of the upcoming hearings on the Commission's proposed guidelines. CCOPR members believe that participation in the guidelines process would drain energies from their legislative goals and break the tremendous momentum that now exists for action to stop police spying activities. Contact: Linda Valentino or Jeff Cohen CCOPR, 633 S. Shatto Place, Los Angeles, CA 90005 (213) 387-3937.

Los Angeles On April 22, Revolutionary Communist Party member Damian Garcia was killed and another RCP member was seriously wounded in a scuffle which erupted as they attempted to sell the party's newspaper in a housing project. No suspect in the murder has been found. The RCP has since charged that Garcia was "deliberately singled out" for the "police-hit-job" because of his participation in an RCP demonstration a month earlier at the historic Alamo site in Texas. RCP also claims that the LAPD deliberately stalled in getting to the housing project so that the assailants were able to leave the area and avoid arrest. An LAPD officer stated later that the killing resulted when local people took "umbrage at the Communists (for) being on their turf." For more information write: National May Day Committee, PO Box 12039, Detroit, MI 48212.

San Francisco On June 6, Jane Margolis, a member of the Communications Workers of America, received a letter of apology from Deputy Director of the U.S. Secret Service, Myron I. Weinstein, in which he regretted her arrest at a CWA convention last summer. (After the militant CWA

member urged the union to prevent President Carter from speaking at its meeting, she was pulled from the convention floor by a local police officer and Secret Service agents and detained until after Carter's speech was completed. Shortly thereafter she filed suit against the Secret Service charging harassment. (See *Organizing Notes,* Vol. 4, No. 3.)

Weinstein's letter stated that the Secret Service agent's action was "based upon a misunderstanding" and that while he regretted the incident, the Secret Service "cannot be absolutely certain that other misunderstandings will never occur."

The letter and a $3500 check constituted a settlement in the suit between Margolis and the Secret Service. Contact: Union Committee Against Secret Service Harassment, PO Box 12324, San Francisco, CA 94112 (213) 483-6892.

DISTRICT OF COLUMBIA

DC On May 21, the Coalition for a Non-Nuclear World filed an FOIA request for any documents on the Coalition held by the FBI, DOE, NRC, Department of Defense, CIA and the US Secret Service. The requests were made by Donna Warnock, a Coalition Secretariat member, following a series of disruptions throughout a week of Coalition events, held from April 25 through 28.

Among the disruptions was a burglary on April 24 at the home of two Coalition staff members, which resulted in the theft of the Coalition check book and a list of funders. One staff person awoke to discover a man rifling Coalition files in her bedroom.

On March 28, Robert Klotz of the DC Police Department advised Tina Hobson of the U.S. Department of Energy that photographing demonstrators was a "standard practice" used when "there is a potential for arrests." (See *Organizing Notes,* Vol. 4, No. 1.) Responding to a request for information about a previous photographing incident made by Hobson and Coalition staff member John Miller, Klotz said that he expected that the Police Department would also photograph the Coalition's April 28 civil disobedience demonstration at the Pentagon.

Note: A number of FOIA requests for files from the FBI, DOE, NRC and other federal agencies have been made by anti-nuclear activists since the last issue of *Organizing Notes. If you are interested in making a request on behalf of your organization or as an individual, if you* would like to know which local anti-nuclear groups have filed requests thus far or if your group has made a request already—please contact the Campaign!

ILLINOIS

Chicago On June 27, the Spanish Action Committee of Chicago, a Puerto Rican Community group, filed court papers to amend the ongoing police spying lawsuit, *Alliance to End Repression et al. vs. City of Chicago et al.* to include charges that, in 1966, the Chicago Police Department's Red Squad: infiltrated SACC; identified a couple who was leaving SACC and encouraged them to publicly charge that the SACC was communist influenced; and later assisted the couple in creating a competing group, the American Spanish Speaking Peoples Association.

At the time of the infiltration, SACC was rapidly gaining support for its organizing activities in Chicago's growing Hispanic community. Following the Red Squad's counterintelligence activities, its membership declined because of the loss of key leaders. The organization regrouped several years later with different goals. (Documentation of the Red Squad's actions was obtained through discovery in the *Alliance* case.)

The Alliance case is consolidated for discovery purposes with *ACLU et al. vs. City of Chicago et al.* and *Chicago Lawyers Committee for Civil Rights under Law vs. City of Chicago et al.* In response to a motion filed by *Alliance* plaintiffs, the Judge has ordered all parties to be ready for trial by August 28, 1980. **Contact:** Richard Gutman, Chicago Political Surveillance Litigation and Education Project, 407 S. Dearborn Street, #690, Chicago IL 60605 (312) 922-5413.

MICHIGAN

Flint On June 6, *The Flint Voice,* a small Michigan newspaper which is known for its investigations of local political corruption, was refused a temporary restraining order to prevent local police from conducting further searches of the paper's offices for evidence relating to the allegedly premature release of the city ombudsman's report that criticized Mayor James Rutherford. In refusing the restraining order, Circuit Court Judge Phillip Elliott ruled, however, that the police must go to him or a justice of the state of Michigan to request a search warrant for any additional searches.

At issue is a Flint city charter provision that makes it a misdemeanor for a city official to release a report by the ombudsman that is critical of a city official before the official has had four days in which to respond. Police deny that the searches are aimed at discovering the paper's source in obtaining the report, but the *Voice* editor disagrees, saying that the investigation is "politically motivated" and is aimed at discovering who blew the whistle on the mayor. Attorneys for the *Flint Voice* are currently preparing a lawsuit that they hope will raise questions beyond those raised in the *Stanford Daily* case. (See *Organizing Notes,* Vol. 4, No. 4.) **Contact:** Michael Moore, *The Flint Voice,* 5005 Lapeer Road, Flint, MI 48509 (313) 742-1230.

NEW HAMPSHIRE

Concord Three gubernatorial candidates are debating whether any future demonstrations at the Seabrook nuclear site should be permitted. Over the past several years, taxpayers, conservatives and pro-nuclear residents have protested the use of state money to pay for expenses resulting from the demonstrations.

As part of his campaign, former Governor Meldrim Thompson is calling for higher penalties for demonstrators; Executive Councillor Louis D'Allesandro would ban all protests. Current Governor Hugh Gallen says existing laws are sufficient and that laws suggested by the other two candidates would be unconstitutional.

On May 29, the New Hampshire Senate passed a resolution opposing the anti-nuclear demonstrations and agreed to consider legislation to create a felony charge should persons or groups "advocate and conduct unlawful, violent demonstrations." **Contact:** Robin Read, New Hampshire Research Project, Box 383, Portsmouth, NH 03282.

Seabrook In a letter dated May 27, PBS affiliate Channel 11 protested the misrepresentation of two State Police officers as Channel eleven employees. During the Coalition for Direct Action's attempted occupation of the Seabrook plant on the weekend of May 24, the two officers, dressed in street clothes, carried Channel 11 press credentials and a videocamera with the station's logo. News Producer Chip Neal filed a complaint with the State Attorney General's office, characterizing the police action as "deceptive, unethical and dishonest." Press Secretary to the Governor, Dayton Duncan, whose office controlled press credentialing during the demonstration, replied on June 3, saying "the incident is regrettable and the result of errors in judgment." He assured Neal that the use of television credentials "will not happen again."

WASHINGTON

Seattle On July 7, David Hoff was approved by the City Council for the position of Special Auditor to review police intelligence files. Hoff is the former president of the Washington State Bar Association; he was appointed by the Mayor in June, and had the support of the Seattle Coalition on Governing Spying.

Under the Seattle Intelligence Ordinance passed in July, 1979, the auditor position was created to provide an independent review of the intelligence files. **Contact:** Kathleen Taylor and Tom Parsons, Seattle Coalition on Governing Spying, 2101 Smith Tower, Seattle, WA 98104 (206) 624-2180.

CovertAction
INFORMATION BULLETIN

From *CovertAction Information Bulletin,* no. 6 (October 1979), pp. 8-9

Cuban Exile Terrorists on Rampage

"Fidel Castro will speak at the opening session of the United Nations. . . . There are those pledged not to let him leave the United States alive. Frankly his presence in New York is an affront to thousands of Cuban exiles who ought not passively accept it, no matter how much sacrifice is necessary, no matter how many may have to fall, no matter how many may be blown up."
—*Ultima Hora,* September 9, 1979.

This chilling and provocative public call for terrorism in the gossip column of a Cuban exile newspaper is only the latest outrage perpetrated by a small but deadly group, created and nurtured by the CIA over the past twenty years, and now, according to some, berserk and beyond the control of its former masters.

For two decades, Cuban exile extremists have been at or near the center of nearly every sensational terrorist action in the Western Hemisphere and several in Europe and Africa as well. Police sources believe that the elite of this group number less than 100, spread out within the exile communities in New York, New Jersey, Miami and Puerto Rico. But they are men who have known each other for twenty years, they are very hard to infiltrate, and with only a single exception they have with impunity bombed, maimed and killed on four continents.

Their latest campaign—blatant threats on the life of Fidel Castro who is scheduled to visit the United States sometime in October, coupled with leaflets calling for demonstrations at and around the United Nations—is a logical outgrowth of their hatred for the government of their homeland, a hatred inflamed and fostered over the years by the CIA.

Throughout the 1960s, and well into the 1970s, this Cuban exile network worked for the CIA and its associates not only in innumerable raids against Cuba, most notably the Bay of Pigs fiasco, but as mercenaries in the Congo and in Vietnam, as the footsoldiers of Watergate, and as hired guns for the DINA of Chile and other such secret services—all of them at one time or another creations and pawns of the CIA.

But even the CIA and the FBI are beginning to realize that they have created a Frankenstein monster. The U.S. government, quick to condemn terrorism abroad, is hosting one of the most vicious terrorist organizations on earth. The footsoldiers are dangerous, professional criminals, hitmen and drug dealers. They threaten not only Cuba, which is in fact quite secure, but also the vast majority of the Cuban community in the United States, who want no part of them, as well as U.S. and foreign citizens who may have business with Cuba.

From the early 1960s these terrorists perfected their skills under Agency tutelage—the use and handling of explosives, demolition and bomb construction, and, through the Agency's and their own Mafia connections, the arts of kidnapping and assassination. They have assassinated diplomats in Washington, Argentina, Italy and elsewhere. They have blown a Cubana airliner out of the skies in Barbados, killing everyone aboard. And in recent months they have launched a frontal attack against any contact with Cuba. They have bombed the Cuban United Nations Mission in New York and the Cuban Interests Section in Washington; they have bombed travel agencies for the same reason; they have bombed newspapers for sympathetic statements about Cuba; they have even bombed a pharmacy in New Jersey to protest the shipment of medicine to Cuba.

Their only real mistake was the brazen belief that they could kill with impunity in Washington—traditionally a safe haven for diplomats. The September 1976 murder of Orlando Letelier and his associate Ronni Moffitt in downtown Washington forced the Justice Department to move with some vigor against this network. The Cuban terrorists had demonstrated that the U.S. government no longer had any control over the monster it had created. Four underlings were caught and convicted; the U.S.-born organizer who planted the explosives, whose ties to the CIA were well established, got off with a few years imprisonment.

Except for the Letelier/Moffitt investigation, however, there has been little movement against this network. Weapons and drugs charges are routinely dismissed or only perfunctorily prosecuted. Perhaps, like so many of the people involved in Watergate, many of the leaders of this network know too much. Yet it would seem that too much is at stake for the United States. These terrorists are a threat to many diplomats at the United Nations and in Washington. They add fuel to the arguments of those who want the United Nations to move from violence-torn New York City and the United States in general.

The authorities have not moved against this network, even though more and more is known about them. Their line has become more public—and more frenzied—with the commencement late last year of a dialogue between the Cuban exile community and the government of Cuba. Despite the condemnation of this dialogue by the terrorists, it has resulted in the release of more than 3,000 prisoners, the granting of exit visas to all of them and many others, and blanket permission to Cubans outside the country to return to visit their relatives. The terrorists have been brutal; at a rally recently in Miami, one of the leaders of the Bay of Pigs Veterans openly threatened thousands of people in the audience. "We're not going to kill you people who visit Cuba," he said,

Talk—an inexpensive commodity, i.e., Talk is cheap.

HUMAN RIGHTS

Peg Averill/LNS

"we're just going to make life painful for you."

In a recent article in *New York Magazine,* free-lance investigative reporter Jeff Stein has taken a close look at the terrorists, particularly the northern New Jersey community. On a side street in Union City, New Jersey is found the public headquarters of the Cuban Nationalist Movement, a group with such illustrious alumni as Guillermo Novo Sampol, who, in 1964 fired a bazooka from Queens, New York across the East River to the United Nations, and through a window when Che Guevara was visiting. Members of the organization have been linked to major drug dealing, and to almost all unsolved Cuban terrorist actions over the past several years. Although credit for most of those actions has been claimed by two groups, Omega Seven and Commando Zero, authorities are quite certain that both are merely different names for the Cuban Nationalist Movement. Indeed, Stein documents the overlapping identities quite well, and quotes both federal and local officials who agree.

With all this information at hand, why have the authorities not moved more forcefully? Is it really true that with so many longstanding contacts in the Cuban exile community the government cannot infiltrate these bands of terrorists? How can they chat publicly in their newspapers and leaflets about trying to kill Fidel Castro when he visits the U.N.? If it were any other group, if it were the Pope, or President Carter who was being so threatened, do we seriously think that arrests would not be immediately forthcoming?

At the Sixth Summit of Non-Aligned Nations, Fidel Castro said: "It is all too well known, and has been admitted officially in the United States, that the authorities of that country spent years organizing and methodically plotting to assassinate the leaders of the Cuban Revolution, using the most sophisticated means of conspiracy and crime. In spite of the fact that these deeds were investigated and publicized by the United States Senate, the U.S. government has not deigned to give any kind of apology for those vituperative and uncivilized actions."

Perhaps the U.S. government has ceased its attempts to assassinate the leaders of the Cuban Revolution; they have not stopped those who publicly announce they are continuing that campaign. Since the U.S. government, most notably the CIA, organized and trained those people, one would think that its obligation to capture and destroy the Frankenstein monster is clear. It should not be left to the angry village mob.

CUP/LNS

Although Mr. Bell referred to the Charter as "a contract between the FBI and the American people," a close look at its provisions reveals quite the opposite. For example, even though the Bureau's powers are expressly limited to the investigation of "criminal conduct," the latter term includes "terrorist activity" (a non-federal crime) which is defined as behavior seeking to influence governmental policy through a "violent act that is dangerous to human life or risks serious bodily harm or that involves aggravated property destruction. . . ." In effect, such an authorization would permit the FBI to investigate political groups even without the commission of a predicate crime.

Furthermore, the agency is expressly empowered to investigate the activities of individuals or groups when it comes to the unilateral conclusion that there is a "reasonable indication" that they "will" engage in criminal conduct. Such vague and undefined language virtually sanctifies the FBI's past illegalities and opens the way to their chronic repetition on an awesome scale. During then Director Clarence M. Kelley's testimony before the Church Committee (12/10/75, Hearings, Vol. 6, pp. 283-4),* he made it quite clear that the Bureau could "be expected to depart from its traditional role . . . and take effective steps which are needed to meet an imminent threat to human life or property," a comment that led the Committee to

---

From *Quash* 4, no. 4 (September/October 1979): 3

Proposed FBI Charter: Legalization of Illegality

by William M. Kunstler

The stated purpose of the proposed FBI Charter, which is now pending in Congress, is to provide legislative protection against repetitions of the agency's demonstrable past criminal conduct. Paradoxically, the public impact of the revelations

This article first appeared in *Quash: Newsletter of the Grand Jury Project,* published by the Grand Jury Project, New York, NY.

of the Bureau's massive illegal and unconstitutional activities by the Senate Select Committee to Study Governmental Operations with reference to Intelligence Activities (Church Committee) has generated a document which would, in effect, institutionalize and legalize many of the very excesses it was purportedly designed to prevent. Unfortunately, when the Charter was unveiled by Director William H. Webster at a news conference on July 31, 1979, he was joined by Senators Edward M. Kennedy and Strom Thurmond, the chairperson and ranking minority member of the Senate Judiciary Committee respectively. Rep. Peter Rodino, the chairperson of the House Judiciary Committee, former Attorney General Griffin B. Bell and his successor, Benjamin R. Civiletti, in urging its swift passage in both the House and the Senate.

---

*[U. S. Congress, Senate, Select Committee to Study Governmental Operations with Respect to Intelligence Activities, *Intelligence Activities: Hearings Before the Select Committee to Study Governmental Operations on U.S. Intelligence Agencies and Activities,* 94th Congress, 1st sess., Senate resolution 21 (Washington, D.C.: Government Printing Office, 1975), Vol. 6: *Federal Bureau of Investigation,* pp. 283-284.—eds., *Alternative Papers.*]

...We, your elected representatives, will defend and protect American freedom even if we have to dismantle the Constitution to do it... a free America is a SECURE America...everybody in bed and lights out by 9:30...

Peg Averill/Peoples Alliance/LNS

order: (1) to obtain information or evidence necessary "for paramount prosecution purposes" (2) to establish and maintain "credibility or cover . . ."; or (3) to prevent or avoid "death or serious bodily injury or danger thereof to themselves or another." The granting of such carte blanche to FBI personnel is to insure the continuation of most of the abuses uncovered by the Church Committee, and to fly directly in the face of many of the latter's recommendations.

Another particularly frightening aspect of the Charter is what is termed a "civil investigative demand." The FBI by the service of a mere request, will be able to compel "third parties," such as banking, telephone, credit and insurance companies, to turn over the records of persons or organizations under investigation. Additionally, the Bureau will be permitted to destroy its records ten years after the completion of an investigation, regardless

observe that the principle of illegal covert activities "has not been rejected." The proposed Charter uses almost the identical language employed by Kelley to prove that point.

Indeed, the current draft not only does not prohibit the use of the investigative techniques condemned by Senator Church as "intolerable in a democratic society," but authorizes many of them without any external review. Moreover, informants are still to be used to infiltrate organizations and, with Bureau approval, may participate in criminal activities when deemed necessary "to obtain information or evidence . . . or prevent or avoid death or serious bodily injury. . . ." These informants, whose identities would be protected from disclosure under the Freedom of Information Act, can now be recruited from the ranks of attorneys, physicians, clergy, and members of the news media, despite their "obligation or legal privilege of confidentiality," as well as from more traditional sources. Whatever the nature of their recruitment, informants are not encouraged to refrain from urging or provoking criminal conduct as well as furnishing the tools and knowledge required to entrap others into committing illegal acts.

Undercover agents, who may also be used to infiltrate "a group under investigation", are given more leeway than informants insofar as the commission of criminal acts are concerned. They are expressly authorized to break the law in

On July 31, 1979, the FBI presented its proposed Charter at a press conference in Washington. The composition of the press conference accurately reflected the nature and purpose of the Charter much as a guest list reflects the nature and purpose of a social gathering. In attendance were FBI Director Webster, Attorneys General Bell and Civiletti, Congressional sponsors Kennedy and Rodino, *and 350 FBI* agents as invited guests. No one who had been "targets" of the illegal activities the Charter is declared to outlaw was invited. The families of Martin Luther King, Jr., Viola Liuzzo, Fred Hampton, Mark Clark, and the many other individuals and groups harassed, abused, disrupted, and destroyed by the FBI were not among the invited guests. Nor was a single public interest group devoted to the struggle to preserve, protect and expand civil rights and civil liberties invited to be present to represent these uninvited "targets."

A reading of the Charter makes sense of that press conference. S-1612 is not aimed at eradicating the vestiges of a political police from public life. S-1612 *does not control or limit, much less abolish* the illegal and unconstitutional practices which the Ervin and Church Committees revealed the FBI has engaged in since its inception. In fact, S-1612 makes it legal for the FBI to use those very techniques—electronic and

physical surveillance, mail and trash covers, infiltration, informers and the rest—and makes it legal for the FBI to "investigate" lawful, peaceful activities of all kinds including demonstrations. What the FBI did illegally to persons and groups active for social change (unions, civil rights groups, churches, peace and women's groups) in the 1960's and before, it would now be able to do legally—if S-1612 were adopted.

In the aftermath of Watergate and the Church Committee hearings, the public and Congress demanded that the abuses of power by the FBI and other "intelligence" agencies be curbed. The Charter is the administration's response to that demand. It has the endorsement and support of the head of the FBI, two "reform" Attorneys-General, the President and two liberal Congresspersons (Kennedy and Rodino) who contend that what they are offering is the best balance between constitutional rights and the needs of the FBI. As we examine the serious deficiencies and frightening empowerments of the Charter, it is clear that this administration and this Congress are not likely to give the American people a charter which will control the FBI.

An analysis of the major provisions of S-1612/HR5030 reveals that they will seriously restrict the exercise of civil liberties and the activities of individuals and groups working for social, political and economic change.

—*Prepared by FOIA, Inc., 36 West 44th St., New York, N. Y.*

of whether any subject mentioned in them has had the opportunity to obtain or examine them.

The Charter specifically states that breaches of its provisions will not create "a civil cause of action against the United States . . . or against any officer, agent, or employee or former officer, agent, or employee of the United States Government." Other than internal disciplinary action the only other penalty provided for the punishment of those who violate its provisions is "a civil penalty up to $5000" to be imposed, when considered justified by the Director. However, such a penalty can only be exacted when there has been a finding that the offender "intentionally use[d] any of the sensitive investigative techniques" prohibited by the Charter.

When President Carter sent the FBI Charter Act of 1979 to the Congress, he stated that "this Charter strikes the proper balance between assuring both that the civil rights and liberties guaranteed to Americans by our Constitution are protected and that the FBI can fully pursue its appropriate functions." While Mr. Carter may fully subscribe to this wholly desirable thesis, the legislation he has so forcefully endorsed is, in essence, a codification of what the Bureau has been doing for decades—and continues to do today— namely, the taking of the law into its own hands for what it considers to be the 'greater good' of the country. The Charter does nothing more than to legitimize what the Church Committee referred to as 'a sophisticated vigilante operation aimed squarely at preventing the exercise of First Amendment rights of speech and association, on the theory that preventing the growth of dangerous groups and the propagation of dangerous ideas would protect the national security and deter violence."

"to create resentment in the mainland against Puerto Ricans." He warned that such a conclusion would be erroneous. "There is no anti-American feeling in Puerto Rico. We're Americans ourselves. We don't 'anti' ourselves." Resident Commissioner Baltasar Corrada del Rio furthered the claim that the assailants were foreign *independentista* radicals. FBI spokespersons asserted that the assault was committed by independence oriented terrorists from the U.S., not by island Puerto Ricans.

In the first few days, responsibility for the investigation was given to the Commonwealth police force. Superintendent of Police Cartagena took personal direction of a "massive manhunt." Special undercover agents were assigned to help in "tracking down suspects and interviewing witnesses." Cartagena admitted that the leads were slim and that the testimony received from the eyewitnesses was not good. Nevertheless, he charged that "leftist political leaders who incite young people with rhetoric are dangerous people."

The FBI Takes Charge

A little over a week after Sabana Seca, a front page headline with three inch letters in El Nuevo Dia announced "FBI IN PUERTO RICO." The FBI had taken over. Hundreds of extra agents were sent to Puerto Rico. They farmed out across the island. Agents went to Vieques and interrogated leaders of the Fishermen's Association and the Crusade to Save Vieques. On the mainland they invaded

From *Puerto Rico Libre!* 5, no. 6 (May/June 1980): 5-6, 24

Intimidation and Entrapment: FBI & Grand Jury in Puerto Rico

by Ellen Chapnick

On March 13, 1980, a federal grand jury met in San Juan to consider evidence regarding the assault on a Navy bus in Sabana Seca, Puerto Rico last December. Although the only legitimate function of a grand jury is to review evidence and decide whether it is sufficient to support an indictment, the Sabana Seca grand jury has not charged anybody. The federal grand jury clearly was the latest attempt by the U.S. and the pro-statehood Commonwealth governments to exploit Sabana Seca in order to investigate, discredit, and

Reprinted with permission from *Puerto Rico Libre!*

dismantle the Puerto Rican independence and progressive movements.

The Beginnings

Sabana Seca was transformed from the name of a small community 15 miles west of San Juan to an "incident" at dawn on December 3, 1979, when a school bus transporting 18 U.S. sailors from their base to their posts at a U.S. naval communications installation was waylaid and ambushed. Two sailors died and others suffered injuries. Three Puerto Rican organizations—the Volunteers of the Puerto Rican Revolution, the Boricua Popular Army (Macheteros) and the Armed Forces of the Popular Resistance— issued a joint communique claiming responsibility for the attack. They proclaimed that they committed the ambush to avenge the murder of Angel Rodriguez Cristobal in his jail cell in Tallahassee, Florida, and the assassinations at Cerro Maravilla of two young *independentistas*, Carlos Soto Arrivi and Arnaldo Dario Rosado.

Governor Romero Barcelo immediately attributed a different goal to the ambush. He announced that its "main purpose" was

Cindy Fredrick/LNS

homes and offices of independence groups and leaders and of persons working to get the Navy out of Vieques. If rebuffed, they waited in the street or talked with the family, neighbors, and friends. Some were chosen for special treatment—their homes were searched while they were out, they were followed daily, phones were obviously tapped and agents returned repeatedly to obtain "cooperation."

The FBI and police did not restrict their investigation to Sabana Seca. Activists were questioned about the structure, membership, purposes and politics of their organizations. Relatives and neighbors were asked whether they knew if a certain person was a "subversive" or might be a terrorist. On December 21, 1979, several independence groups responded. They held a joint press conference to inform the Puerto Rican people that a group of militants are being persecuted by the FBI and the police. "There is interrogation without basis" and attempts "to discredit them in their communities." The group predicted that the government would use the federal grand jury as an excuse for further abuse.

The FBI was able to prepare a better story for the next day's newspapers. They explained that agents were "visiting residential sectors of the Island to learn about the daily activities of certain persons identified with the independence cause" because Sabana Seca had been "linked to militants in the struggle for Vieques and for Socialism." Moreover, the FBI had an idea of who the "brain of the group" is. It was doubtful that arrests would be made before the end of the year.

A new tactic appeared one week later. All of the Island's daily newspapers featured sketches of 14 men. The drawings, which were accompanied by detailed descriptions, had been released by the FBI. Persons recognizing any of the men depicted were urged to call a special confidential number immediately.

Since the FBI alleged that only four men were involved in Sabana Seca, they explained that some of the drawings were of eyewitnesses and possible members of the same clandestine group of assailants. The FBI also announced that it had interviewed four hundred persons in Puerto Rico, San Francisco, Los Angeles, New York, Chicago, Philadelphia and Miami. It was convinced that the terrorists were still in Puerto Rico and that they had relations with the U.S. independence groups, particularly the FALN. There was

no explanation of why the FBI would release photo-like drawings of "terrorists" they were planning to arrest.

Nevertheless, one week later, the FBI declared that they had a lot of information on the suspects and were "preparing to arrest them at any moment." Slightly contradictory was the assertion that charges would be filed "as soon as we have the necessary evidence." The more conservative statement proved true. No arrests were forthcoming. Progress reports to the press ceased. Surveillance, interrogation and intimidation efforts against the independence and pro-Vieques forces continued.

Countermeasures

Meanwhile, the independence and pro-Vieques forces mobilized to resist the FBI invasion and the expected grand jury. An ad hoc committee composed of representatives of independence and pro-Vieques groups was formed in early January. The committee realized that activists, as well as the periphery, were unprepared for such an intense assault. Leaflets that warned: "The FBI is in Puerto Rico—Don't talk" and "Stop the Grand Jury" were distributed. Seminars were given on the repressive purposes and tactics of the FBI and grand jury and on the political and legal defenses available in confronting them.

Nelson W. Canals, spokesperson for CUCRE stated that documents obtained from the FBI unit working on Sabana Seca "evidenced the persecution and hostility to which leaders and activists for independence in Puerto Rico have been

submitted." He noted that the list of principal suspects includes "persons known for their struggle and compact with the independence of Puerto Rico, some of whom have been victims of hostility, persecution and even fabricated cases in the past."

FBI Bureau Chief Bernardo "Matt" Perez identified the list of suspects as an official FBI document that was robbed, but not from the San Juan FBI office. He said that the release of the documents could be a crime and that there would be an investigation that might culminate in a federal grand jury. Canals retorted that he was aware of the risk and had no intention of cooperating with the investigation or the grand jury.

The Grand Jury

One week later, the first subpoenas to appear before the federal grand jury were served. By March 8, 1980, four persons had been subpoenaed to appear before the grand jury on March 13, 1980. One was one of the "unknowns" on the suspects list, Carlos Rosario Pantojas of Vega Baja, Puerto Rico. Jose Angel Rosario, also of Vega Baja but no relation, was ordered to bring his car registration with him. The two others were an aunt and uncle of Alberto de Jesus, who is listed as a principal suspect.

A team of lawyers filed numerous motions on the day set for the appearance. A Motion for a Continuance, so that they would have adequate time to prepare, was summarily denied. Judge Perez-Gimenez neither heard oral argument nor ruled on the witness' motion that the subpoenas be

Peg Averill/LNS

voided because the grand jury was unlawfully using the subpoena on its own and because the federal grand jury lacked jurisdiction. Similarly, he neither heard nor ruled on the witness' request that the government disclose any unlawful electronic or other surveillance prior to their appearance.

In a highly irregular procedure, Special Prosecutor Brian Murtaugh, who had come from Washington D.C., insisted that the four appear even though the judge had not decided the motions. After efforts to obtain a hearing were unsuccessful, the witnesses appeared one-by-one. First to be called was Carlos Rosario Pantojas who was asked three questions including whether he would agree to furnish hair samples, handwriting samples, fingerprints and a photo. He refused to answer any questions and was excused but told he could be recalled at any time. The other three were called in rapid succession; they were asked only their names and excused subject to future recall.

Witnesses and lawyers were standing in a park across the street from the courthouse preparing to go home when four U.S. Marshals marched towards them and served them with the U.S. Attorney's petition asking for a court order requiring Rosario to produce the samples requested by the Grand Jury. The Attorneys were casually informed that the judge would hear oral arguments on the motion in five minutes. An extension was granted until 8:30 the following morning. Without listening to any argument by Rosario's lawyers, Judge Perez Gimenez ordered him to produce the exemplars by 2:30 that afternoon. Rosario decided to comply with the order.

None of the four witnesses have been recalled and no new subpoenas are known to have been issued. However, it has been learned that other persons did appear and testify on March 13. Grand Jury proceedings are secret so their identities and the questions they were asked and information they provided is unknown.

The Future

We have not heard the last of the grand jury. The FBI and the U.S. and Commonwealth governments need it too badly. The Grand Jury has broad subpoena powers that neither the FBI nor the U.S. attorney has, and they need to use it to further their investigation of Sabana Seca and the independence and pro-Vieques movements in Puerto Rico. Moreover, many independentistas and progressives have decided that they will not cooperate with the grand jury. The right to refuse to answer any questions is extremely limited and a position of non-collaboration usually results in incarceration for contempt. Thus, the Grand Jury can be used to jail, selectively, leaders and other activists without ever filing criminal charges or going through a trial. Finally, after so much fanfare and bragging about being close to an arrest, the FBI and Special Prosecutor will have to convince the Grand Jury to indict somebody.

The countermeasures were effective in slowing the FBI-Grand Jury process. The educational campaign against talking to the FBI has been effective. The release of the FBI's secret documents was an important psychological victory. FBI agents have admitted that the government was surprised by witnesses so well versed in their rights and represented by trained and vigorous lawyers. These efforts will continue. A united and strong independence and pro-Vieques opposition to the government's attempts to use Sabana Seca against them is being forged. It will be an important struggle for PRSC to watch and to support it in the next period.

Quash/LNS

QUASH newsletter of the GRAND JURY PROJECT, INC.

From *Quash* 5, no. 2 (April 1980): 3

Black Farming Cooperatives Threatened

For the past ten weeks, over ten file cabinet drawers of documents all belonging to the Federation of Southern Cooperatives (FSC) have been in the possession of a Federal Grand Jury in Birmingham, Alabama. The documents were turned over on February 7 after efforts to quash a subpoena calling for, among other things, "any and all books, records, reports, papers, memoranda, applications and proposals" submitted by FSC or its affiliated cooperatives for federal funding from 1976–1979, failed.

The Federal grand jury investigation into FSC follows a wave of similar investigations into community-based groups throughout the country. (See *Quash*, Volume 4, Number 4 for accounts of ones in New Jersey)* Now, FSC, an important resource and service association for Black people in the rural South, is also being threatened by a grand jury investigation.

During the 1960s, harassment, mechanization of farming and increased eviction from their land all were used to eliminate jobs for Black people in the South who were beginning to wield some political power as a result of the successes of the civil rights movement. Many were forced to sell their land and leave the region in search of jobs and a place to live elsewhere. In response to this situation, some of those determined to stay began forming co-ops and it was out of this movement that FSC developed. Though the primary focus of FSC continues to be cooperative economic development it has widened its scope in recent years to address other needs such as housing, health, women's job opportunities and skill training. One of its most recent projects is

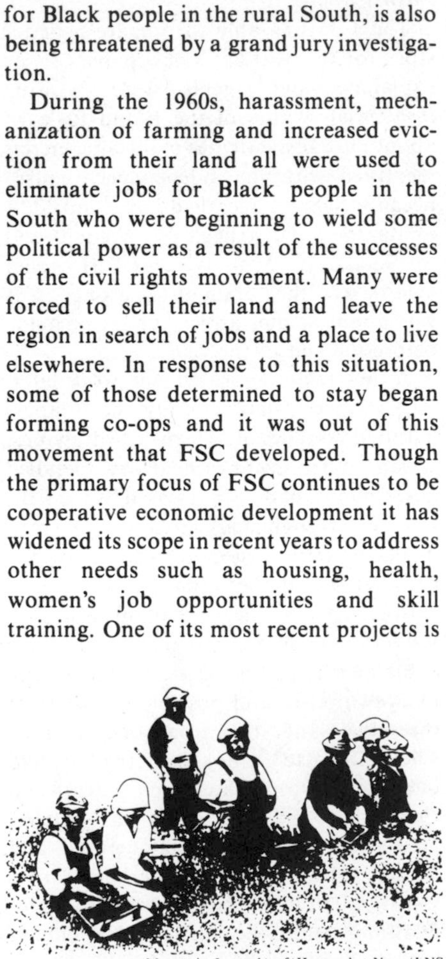

Mountain Journal/cpf/Haymarket News/LNS

*["Grand Juries Sweep New Jersey: Target Community Action Programs," *Quash* 4, no. 4 (September/October 1979): 6, 2.—eds., *Alternative Papers.*]

This article first appeared in *Quash: Newsletter of the Grand Jury Project,* published by the Grand Jury Project, New York, NY.

the "Forty Acres and A Mule Endowment Fund," a name taken from a demand raised during Reconstruction. Since its founding, FSC has gone from an initial membership of 22 to 100 co-ops in 12 states.

Not surprisingly, FSC has not been told exactly who is making the charges against it or what the nature of the charges are. A month before the current grand jury investigation, in fact, FSC received a letter from the General Accounting Office indicating that it had conducted a preliminary audit of FSC but found no basis or need to conduct a full scale audit. That inquiry came about as a result of a complaint filed by the newly elected white Congressperson for Sumter County, Alabama, where FSC has an office, Richard Shelby, who received a letter charging FSC with use of federal funds for political purposes from four other white officials in Sumter. And although FSC is not exactly sure about the reasons behind the current investigations, their feeling is that the white officials of Sumter were so outraged by school boycotts led by Black people there last year, which brought national attention to the county, that they now want to destroy FSC.

"We in the Federation have nothing to hide," Executive Director Charles Prejean stated in a recent issue of *Monthly Bulletin*, the newsletter of FSC. "We have done nothing wrong. We have handled and administered over $15 million in Federal and private funds since 1967. We can and have accounted for every penny. Every penny has been utilized to support and assist the development of cooperative self-held economic activities among low-income people in the rural South."

But while noting that FSC was "willing to cooperate with the federal and state government in any legitimate investigation" Prejean stated that FSC would not "stand idly by and allow racist politicians to destroy our organization, that took many years of painstaking work by thousands of people to build."

"We are very concerned that local racist politicians have the power and influence to bring the full force of the Federal judicial system in Alabama against a community based, minority directed and operated effort. . . . The Federation has never before in its history confronted a challenge of this magnitude and significance to its survival and existence as an organization. We feel the FBI is retrogressing back to the tactics of the 1960s and succumbing to pressure from the Ku Klux Klan to harass and intimidate innocent groups like the Federation and our members because we are trying to change the fundamental economic conditions and correct the exploitative relationships in our society."

FSC Attorney Howard Moore noted at a meeting of FSC staff with supporters in New York City that the Federation should not be diverted from its objectives by the current investigation but also stressed that they should be on guard. "If you're looking for a needle in a haystack," Moore said of the current investigation, "you may not find the needle; but if you find a nail, that will do."

"One objective of the federal authorities is to tie up the organization," Moore commented in the *Monthly Bulletin*, "and cause it to spend so much time on legal defense that it loses sight of its real purpose. This case also points up the many abuses and misuses of the grand jury system. The grand jury in this instance is being used to conduct a fishing expedition through FSC's records in hopes of finding a case against them. We oppose the use of the grand jury and police power of the state against poor people's organizations."

The Federation has written and sent out a letter and fact sheet to over 2,000 individuals and organizations around the country. And over 300 letters of support for FSC have been written to federal officials in Washington.

From *Outlaw* 8, no. 1 (Spring 1979): 2

Behavior Modification on Big Scale in California

by John Irwin

The California Department of Corrections is converting several of its big prisons into large behavior modification programs. For instance, San Quentin and Soledad are divided up into "units" which are partially or totally segregated and which have very different levels of freedom, privilege, and deprivation.

At the top in San Quentin is West Block Honor Unit in which prisoners have free run of the block until 10:00 p.m. (or 12:00 a.m. for citizens row); electrical outlets and permission to have any appliance they can obtain in their cells; license to decorate their cells; and their own canteen.

At the other end is SHU (Segregated Housing Unit) with the prisoners locked down for at least 20 hours a day (they are supposed to have four hours of exercise each day, but this is often denied them), two meals in their cells, visits through glass and telephones, and no frills in their cells.

In between are a variety of levels of privilege and deprivation.

According to the plan, a prisoner starts somewhere in the middle, such as in East Block in San Quentin, and then with good behavior, rises up to the top and with bad, descends down to the bottom. Supposedly, it is all a matter of behaving oneself.

The CDC is following this plan as a response to the fantastic control problems it has faced in the last decade. We must note that this strategy of control is the latest step in a long series of attempts to keep California prisoners under control by keeping them divided. This strategy started with the administration's intense reaction to the prisoners' moves toward unity in the late 1960s and early 1970s. The prisoners had temporarily suppressed their hostilities, formed bridges across factions, and often acted in unity. They constructed revealing and profound criticisms of the unjust and brutal practices in the prisons which they sent to the outside society and organized many demonstrations to draw attention to their struggle.

Though most of the activities were very non-violent and non-destructive, the CDC responded with an intensity which crushed the unity. They abolished organizations suspected of being involved in the "political" activities and, through segregation, transfer, or parole, removed prisoners suspected of being leaders of the "prisoner movement." This left the prison open to gangs and cliques.

Then prisoner to prisoner violence reached such heights that no prisoner could ignore it. One had to affiliate with some clique or gang, or get out of the way. The violence between cliques and gangs escalated. Since then, the administration has been trying without success to get control over the new violence.

Let's look at what the new strategy is producing and is likely to produce in the future. First, take its most positive aspect, the "honor prisoner," the resident of West Block, who has finally worked his way up to the top. He has his T.V., his stereo, maybe a rug, and a nice chest of drawers (even a simulated fireplace). He gets to roam around the cell block, buy his goodies at a special canteen, and stays away from the melee out there in the other cell blocks. Life is pretty soft, but precarious. One slip and he is out. The man has him by the institutional short hair. He has made him into a nice boy who knows his place.

Then what happens to him when he gets out? Things are different on the outside. There are no nice cells and simple routines to which to conform. Outside you have to struggle. The honor system, in an insidious way, has encouraged a type of conforming adjustment which only works in a few locations—e.g., plantations, prisons, totalitarian regimes, and the service.

However, this is not the most serious problem. At the other end, those who tumble to the bottom and cannot climb back out of the pit, continue to give the administration fits. Now, take note that it

Free for All/LNS

is not hard to tumble into and remain in the pit. Pettiness, arbitrariness, prejudice, and suspicion all operate in the classification processes which place and keep men in SHU or whatever they call the hole. These are not impartial proceedings with due process and remedies to correct injustices, but totally autonomous, authoritarian systems with strong tendencies toward arbitrariness and prejudice.

Once in the prison's pit, all men do not, because of the "maximum security" and the constant surveillance, finally conform as the naive may expect. Some people held in these situations for long periods of time, believing that they have been treated extremely unjustly, become embittered, enraged, and totally inured to threats. So, behavior modification systems, with levels of stratified privilege and deprivation, inevitably end with an embittered residue of prisoners who are not deterred by threats of violence or more punishment and who will strike back at every opportunity. Many of them are convinced that they will never get out of prison or segregation alive and believe that they have nothing to lose but their self-respect.

Now, this obviously does not set well with the rehabilitative goals of behavior modification. The intention is to produce rule followers who can make out in the outside world. (We have already shed doubt on the outside prospects of the model conformer produced by behavior mod.) In addition, the control problems are near impossible. What occurs is an ongoing war between prisoners in segregation units and between the prisoners and guards. Nothing stops it. What next? Place them in separate boxes and pump food and air to them through pipes? How else are you going to learn 'em? And learn 'em what?

Why Behavior Modification Is Used In Prison

Behavior modification has been widely used in American prisons to attempt to break the wills of those who rebel against oppressive conditions or who cause the authorities trouble.

The practice received national attention because of program START (Special Treatment and Rehabilitative Training) used in the Medical Center for Federal Prisoners at Springfield, Missouri.

START involved complete isolation under brutal conditions which included beatings, chaining prisoners to their beds, and administering mind altering drugs, with a gradual easing of the terror as

"behavior" improved. Those who would not cooperate were threatened with permanent isolation.

The courageous resistance of half a dozen START victims, along with public pressure and legal action, led to the program's termination May 1974. Several months later federal Judge John W. Oliver ruled that all future mandatory prison behavior modification programs which lacked minimal due process procedures constituted a violation of a prisoner's constitutional rights. Nevertheless, such programs continue in the federal prison at Marion, Illinois and in numerous state institutions.

Leonard Peltier, leader of the American Indian Movement, says of Marion Federal Penitentiary, Behavior Modification Unit H: "No matter where you go you are never out of the sight of your captors; T.V. cameras and two-way microphones are everywhere that pick up almost every word whispered in the hallways. A very weird thing to get used to. *A Clockwork Orange.* Complete control."

The fundamental purpose of Management Control Units and all other similar behavior modification units is to break the will of prisoners, especially political prisoners. These units are the modern day slave breaking camps. The method used is to continually subject the prisoner to a constant dose of mental and physical harrassment, aggravation, provocation, brutality and possibility of assassination. The majority of the prisoners in these units are locked down because of their "ideas," their "thoughts," their "influence," and because of what they represent to others.

Behavior modification is a weapon used against rebellious prisoners. It is just as violent and dangerous as traditional forms of repression like clubs and chains. Techniques in the arsenal of prison administrators include total isolation and sensory deprivation; intentional harassment to push prisoners into disciplinary infractions; the forced use of drugs; aversion therapy using shock treatments; and forms of neurosurgery like lobotomies.

Confrontation therapy teaches people to accept oppression and how to oppress others. Inmates are made to think they are socially sick individuals and are pushed to take their anger against the authorities out on one another.

John Irwin is a member of the board of directors of the Prisoners Union.

From: *Big Mama Rag* 8, no. 7
(1980): 6

Why the Prison System Doesn't Work

by Marianne Hricko Stewart

Prisons are relics of the Middle Ages. They are modern day debtor's prisons—for the rich can buy their way out with lawyers, bailbonds, appeal bonds, judges, political and Presidential pardons. Slavery is still with us, for the poor are still the slaves of the plutocracy in America—but legally—in prison. Racism is still strong when the prisons overflow with high percentages of minorities, the poor and weak have always been slaves, economically and sociologically. Prisons should not exist. One of the best things we could do for our society—and for our modern world—would be to destroy every existing prison at dawn, and to add another Amendment to the United States Constitution illegalizing and abolishing prisons forever.

Each year—as the crime rate increases legislators make it their duty to announce that "prison is to be rehabilitative" or "prison is not to be rehabilitative, but punitive. It is to be a method of punishment because 'rehabilitation' doesn't seem to be working." (Legislators perceive these things, I believe, not by statistics, but by letters from the P.T.A., the Jaycees, and comments dropped at cocktail parties and banquets given by Congressmen, for Congressmen, governors, the elite, etc. Forsooth, in their expensive cars, high-rise offices, luxurious houses in secluded and electronically guarded neighborhoods, they are too isolated and insulated from reality to realize anything but where their next campaign contributions are coming from.)

Since "rehabilitation" consists of making license plates, cutting threads in

"industry," making milkshakes and sandwiches at the police snackbar, opening boxes at the "canteen" and warehouse, and clerical work (at which prisoners can make minimum wage in the "free world"), it is not too surprising prisoners do not spend their prime time on this upon release. Also, there is not an enormous demand for cosmetologists or LPN's who spent most of their time in yard work, scullery, maintenance or buffing floors; the minimum wage *still* prevails, if one is lucky enough to land a position in any of these captivating positions. Even getting work is often difficult for an ex-prisoner—because he or she has a "record" and society believes someone with a "record" to be less trustworthy than someone who bought their way out of prison with an expensive lawyer or campaign contribution. Added to the prisoner's lack of education in the "free world," inadequate or non-existent education in prison, and undesirable past ("record"), the prisoner must go back to the streets and get work immediately (at slave wages, in most cases) or face returning to prison. In this desperate situation, any work will be taken—unsatisfactory as it may be—usually robbing the ex-inmate of self-esteem which he or she lacks already. This is, of course, the spring-board to the refreshing, deep waters of crime. Almost invariably, or inevitably, the ex-prisoner gets caught and is no longer ex. Recidivism continues to be "a problem" whenever

penologists speak at DAR meetings or editors devote a week to "crime in the streets." Instead of trying to cure cancer with a band-aid, society should begin at the beginning, and take a logical look at the reasons people are in prison in the first place.

Many of the women at C.I.W. are here on 187's (murder), or reduced counts (second degree, manslaughter, accessory, etc.). Many other women are here on petty larceny with priors (if jailed two or three times for shoplifting a dress, smoking grass, or putting a needle in their arms and supporting the habit by prostitution, and *again convicted* of shoplifting etc., they are imprisoned for years). A few have broken probation by "being suicidal." Some are here for robbery, burglary, check-cashing, forgery, and drug possession or sales. A good look at all crimes (aside from murder and reduced counts) will now be taken. We will call these monetary crimes.

Anatole France once said, "The law, in its majestic equality, forbids all men to sleep under bridges, to beg in the streets, and to steal bread—the rich as well as the poor." Laws have been passed which seem "Just" but are instead directed only against the poor because only the poor need to be, for survival, in the situations outlawed. These laws, such as prostitution laws, seem "Just," but outlawing prostitution is comparable to discriminating against the crippled by outlawing wheelchairs; the law is "for everyone," but only the crippled are hurt, precisely because they need wheelchairs so much. Obviously, people who steal money need it. (For the few who took it without needing it, we will classify them with the 187's.) Poor people, nearly all of them without decent education, will never receive decent salaries which will support a family. This is a fact.

NEXT.

JUDGE

For the People/LNS

Even with both parents working, the financial problems and pressures are overwhelming, and this is a major reason why poverty usually leads to broken homes. It is so much easier for the head of the household to deal drugs to support his or her family well—since drugs are prevalent in poor neighborhoods where the "Syndicate/Mafia" distribute drugs profusely. (As someone once said, speaking of alcohol, "When you're poor, you juice it." And I will add, "When you're poor, you lean on crutches," more so than most middle-class people.) After dealing awhile, the dealer usually is overcome with curiosity about heroin, cocaine, etc., develops a habit, and finds the habit expensive. This is where robberies, burglaries, forgeries, check-cashing, larger drug sales, and prostitution come in.

Now we not only have a poor person (all proceeds go to organized crime after awhile), but a sick person, and a "crime problem." Do we put this person in a cage?

Does this solve his or her economic problems?

Does this solve this person's educational problems?

Does an incarcerated person acquire ethics and principles this way?

Does even a child treated in a punitive manner in every way, every day, grow to become a mentally well-adjusted, well-socialized pillar of society?

And as far as sickness goes, our penologists are comparable to witch-doctors attempting to cure a social disease by shaking fingers and sticks at the victim.

In fact, this is how most prisoners relate to the symbols of society (judges, prison officials and police), and society as a whole upon release. Ex-prisoners still have their situation and sickness (the psychological need for crutches), and it will most likely get worse. More crimes will be committed.

When any society treats part of itself as less than human, not entitled to the rights, privileges and equality of the rest, victims become criminals, and criminals victims.

The *answer* to the waste of money spent on prisons each year (penologists call it money spent on prisoners—$12,000+ spent on each woman, $18,000+ spent on each man, and $28,000+ spent on each juvenile), and the waste of humanity, *is very simple*: employment and hospitals.

Hundreds of thousands of jobs, perhaps even an infinite number, are available and are going begging—only because they are volunteer positions. There are openings everywhere: children's hospitals (such as Children's Village, USA, in Beaumont,

CA), geriatric hospitals, psychiatric hospitals, and homes for the multiply-handicapped. Tutors are needed in the barrios and inner city, in schools, and in community centers. Free clinic staff, apartment and house-finders, runaway and drug counselors, and free-clothing store workers, are all needed. Carpenters, electricians, plumbers, carpet layers, masons, wreckers, etc., are needed to teach others: journeymen and apprentices could practice repairing and renovating old houses, or demolishing slums to clear the way for other apprentices who are draftsmen or in the construction industry. Farmers and food-co-op workers are needed. Volunteers are needed to fix refrigerators, television sets and other appliances which are near-necessities. Painters, dial-a-ride drivers, mail carriers, librarians, musicians, gym teachers, and coaches and youth counselors are all needed to teach and help others. The list goes on and on.

And what is done is: Pay each person who would otherwise go to prison a salary of $12,000 per year to fill a position in whichever areas their interests lie.

Not only do we help society, but also would-be prisoners. Even those who have no interest in humanity will agree that much money will be saved—not only in the absence of prisons, but also in a much smaller police force.*

In Canada, one of the band members of the Rolling Stones was arrested for possession of drugs. His sentence was to give a concert in which all proceeds would go to the blind. This is just one example of what an enlightened society, an evolved civilization, would do to impress a lawbreaker that he or she must follow its rules or pay penalties. Yet, this is a positive act, not a negative one. It is from the mind of the future rather than the past.

Now, we ask, what about those people who keep getting into trouble, committing "criminal" or anti-social acts, those who've been given chances time and time again? And what do we do about those who are dangerous to others as well as themselves?

_____

*I should add right here that society, in order to help itself and "fight crime," must put fewer restrictions on people, realizing each person's right to do with his life what he will as long as he does not infringe on others' rights. An example would be doing away with senseless ideals like "vice" and "vice-squads." Victimless "crimes"—such as prostitution, after-hours drinking, and gambling—are only "crimes" because there are laws which outlaw them. Such laws are illogical and give "vice-squads" untold millions in salaries of wasted tax-dollars each year.

What do we do with those who have committed murder, manslaughter, arson, mayhem, assault and battery, rape, and other crimes of violence? Since there is an incredibly low recidivism rate among convicted murderers, clearly the 25 and 15 year determinate sentence law just passed does nothing but give the public a false sense of security.

Rehabilitation hospitals are the answer. Most psychiatric hospitals have units or buildings expressly for the treatment of penal code patients—that is, those who have broken laws and pleaded insanity, or have been judged insane or mentally deficient by prison administrators and sent to the hospital. I propose well-funded psychiatric hospitals—better known as *rehabilitation hospitals*—where patients are treated on a one-to-one basis with psychiatrists, social workers, group counselors familiar with psycho-drama and

Peg Averill/Win/LNS

interpersonal communication. Perhaps most important are facilities for frequent Family-Living-Unit visits (for at least one week) where the patients may be observed interacting with their families; often, one or more members in a family have a detrimental effect on the patient, and these adverse circumstances must be solved in the context of the entire family group. Psychiatric technicians and nurses would see that patients were treated with respect, concern and a positive attitude. These staff could also lose their jobs, by majority vote of the patients.

Improving economic, social and psychological situations in families is the greatest step in improving society. We will need, probably, two of these hospitals in each state— to alternate programs, discerning which are most beneficial and discarding those which are not. Those with histories of assault and battery and other smaller-scale crimes of violence should be sent to rehabilitation hospitals *before* they appear in court charged with murder or manslaughter.

If real concern *with economic backing* is shown the outcast in society, crime would be nearly non-existent. Someone once said, "walls and bars do not a prison make. . . ." Discrimination, red-lining, Prop. 13 cutbacks against social programs, poor and illogical social programs, high housing costs, lack of good schools— especially in poor areas—because of tax distribution, unemployment, and drug addiction are all forms of invisible prisons; they are the invisible violences of society. They are the real cause of "crime and violence." And the Criminal Justice System (and it is "criminal" as it exists today) makes as much sense, is as rational, as Kafka's book *The Trial* or "In the Penal Colony"—where "Be Just" becomes the ultimate hypocrisy and rationalization for sadism.

Very important, extremely important, is the pervasive idea that victimless crimes should not be considered "crimes." Drugs should be gradually decriminalized as people are given something to live for in society; there is too much legislation of morals by those who care only about surface appearances and statistics.

We could begin implementing many of the previously mentioned programs tomorrow, taking money in California's savings account *and reducing the prison budget* because of a reduction of prisoners. We could begin giving those prisoners overcrowding the prisons today early release dates *and* good jobs funded by CETA (the

salaries, of course, being increased to their pre-proposition 13 states) and other federally funded as well as state-funded jobs.

Cruel and unusual punishment not only results from overcrowded prisons, but from the existence of prisons. We cannot, none of us, attain the stars while one man or woman still remains in the Dark Ages; this is true for those in prisons, and also for those who put them there.

PRISONERS UNION JOURNAL

From *Prisoners Union Journal* 9, no. 6 (November 1980): 4-5

Privacy in Prison: Where to Draw the Line

by Ken Kelly

We are all guaranteed a certain amount of privacy according to the U.S. Constitution. This privacy should be afforded to prisoners and their families with only reasonable limitations for security purposes. The problem lies in the fact that every administrator and every guard has a completely different concept of what may or may not constitute privacy for a prisoner and his or her family. In addition, the vast majority of decisions by CDC personnel are blatantly unreasonable and arbitrary.

Penal Code 2600 defines the extent (or, more correctly, limits) of a prisoner's rights while incarcerated: "A person sentenced to imprisonment in a state prison may, during any such period of confinement, be deprived of such rights, and *only* such rights, as is necessary in order to provide for the *reasonable* security of the institution in which he is confined and for the reasonable protection of the public [emphasis added]."

To most people, including myself, this section of the penal code seems to be a reasonable and effective statement by the legislature. Reading that paragraph, any reasonable person might conclude that the intent of the lawmakers was to insure that prisoners do not harm themselves or anyone else, and that they do not escape from the institution where they are confined.

Unfortunately, our legislatures, for all their good intentions and hard work, are

not blessed with having capable, reasonable, intelligent agents to carry out their wishes. As a result we have arbitrary and often idiotic interpretations by administrators and guards within the CDC as to the intent of our lawmakers. This often leads to expensive litigation, harassment and sometimes even violence.

Since there are so many different areas that are affected by penal code 2600, I will attempt to confine my remarks to the area of privacy during confinement.

Employees in Control

The working concept of CDC employees is that a prisoner is a number, object, thing, etc., and as such has absolutely no right to privacy at any time. The amount of privacy granted a prisoner depends solely upon the whims of the employee who happens to have direct control of the prisoner at any given moment.

Obviously it would not be unreasonable for a guard to conduct a private strip-search of a prisoner if he or she had good reason to believe that the prisoner was concealing drugs or a weapon. However, more often than not guards will conduct strip-searches in crowded hallways or other open areas as a simple, routine method of harassment. If for some reason the "goon squad" (search and investigation team) of an institution decides that they don't like a particular prisoner, they make it even more unbearable by ordering the prisoner's family and friends to submit to strip-searches before being allowed to visit. This serves absolutely no purpose other than to humiliate and harass the visitors, since each inmate is routinely strip-searched after each visit anyway. Moreover, it is generally the attitude of guards that prisoners' visitors are somehow second class citizens by virtue of being associated with the prisoner.

There is also generally some form of harassment by guards during visiting periods and at times it is absolutely outrageous. I have seen guards tell a prisoner's wife that she could not sit on her husband's lap because it might lead to sexual excitability. I've seen other guards tell prisoners they could not kiss their wives for longer than 20 seconds at a time for the same reason. At all prisons there is constant supervision throughout the entire visiting period that borders on being maniacal. At any given moment there are several guards walking around the visiting room glaring at people or harassing them in some manner. They have two-way mirrors at certain spots for undetectable monitoring and some prisons even have very sophisticated closed-circuit T.V. monitoring of prisoners' cells as well as the visiting room.

When I was at Vacaville it always seemed incredible to me that they would have 10 or 12 guards walking around peeping through windows from various vantage points, as well as two or three members of the goon squad, for the sole purpose of trying to catch the sight of some prisoner feeling his wife's leg or breast. At the same time they're crying loud and long to anyone who will listen about how understaffed and overworked they are.

Neither Rain, Snow, or . . . ?

Another common practice is for the guards on the graveyard shift to censor the outgoing mail from prisoners. These guards sit around a table with the prisoners' "private" letters to their loved ones and read them aloud to each other, sometimes within the hearing of other prisoners. Imagine your most private, innermost thoughts to your wife or lover being broadcast and laughed at by some big-mouthed pervert who is really getting paid to look for contraband, escape plans, threats, etc. What very unprofessional conduct indeed, and this practice is the rule rather than the exception.

I have also seen instances where guards would take photographs of a prisoner's wife or lover from a letter and pass them around making lewd and obscene remarks. There have been many cases where guards have even gone so far as to make contact with a prisoner's wife or girlfriend and promise to grant special favors to the prisoner if the woman would grant sexual favors to the guard.

I must say in all fairness that this type of behavior by guards is very definitely frowned upon by administrators in California, but it still happens much too frequently and mostly goes undetected by the administration. Even when it is detected it is almost always impossible to

prove because the prisoner's wife or girlfriend is afraid of the other guards retaliating against her husband or lover and will not testify against the guard. Privacy then is not even possible for the friends and family of a prisoner under the present system.

I have yet to read anywhere in the California Penal Code, or any other penal code for that matter, where it says that part of a prisoner's punishment is to have his or her right to reasonable privacy trampled on day after day by a bunch of self-righteous, depraved goons who dare to call themselves professionals.

In reality what has happened is that since the legislature has decreed that the purpose of prison is punishment, without setting down specific guidelines to follow, it has opened up the door for every director to force his or her own idea of morality upon the people they are charged with keeping confined. Then what happens is that each Superintendent or Warden interprets those rules and makes his own rules for posting in his institution. Finally, the rank and file guards interpret and enforce these rules as they see fit according to their own morality. In the final analysis it is always the guards on the line who run each institution as they want and these are the people who control the amount of privacy that a prisoner may or may not enjoy.

Most prisons have sections that they set aside for "model" prisoners in which they allow a greater degree of privacy. This privacy can range from curtains on the cells to private rooms for which prisoners are allowed to carry their own keys, depending on the type of institution. Many prisoners will actually compromise some or all of their ideals or ethics to gain this privacy; others will go to even greater extremes, such as informing on other prisoners. Of course the majority of prisoners will not go to this latter extreme, but enough of them do to ensure that those in control will continue to trample on people's privacy.

The Importance of Privacy

One of the psychologists at Vacaville a few years ago who realized how much privacy affected a person's mental well being, designed a program to help control the prisoners in her unit. If a prisoner obeyed all of the rules she set down during the week (which usually included taking all psychotropic drugs that were prescribed by some incompetent physician), the prisoner could earn a certain number of points. When enough points were accumulated by the prisoner he would get to spend some time alone in a room that she had fixed up rather nicely for this purpose. I'm not attempting here to argue behavior modification techniques, I am merely pointing out how important a role privacy plays in the human psyche.

A really ridiculous example occurred while I was in prison in Arizona a number of years ago, and was housed in a dormitory with about 80 or 90 other prisoners. After the lights were turned out at 10:00 p.m. the guards would monitor what was going on in the dorm by peeping through the windows from outside. One of the guards working this shift (called Jerkoff Joe by the cons) had managed to struggle through reading the rule book and stumbled upon the paragraph pertaining to "unnatural sex acts." Well, Joe must have asked other guards what this meant and was told that it meant masturbation, which delighted Joe to no end since he knew that those perverted convicts were doing that every night.

For the following few weeks Joe would peep through the windows of our dorm and wait for the telltale sign of blankets moving, whereupon he would come crashing through the door to arrest the guilty party, handcuff him and take him off to the hole. The highlight of Joe's career came when he caught some guy fornicating with a ripe cantaloupe. After awhile though, Joe's reports became too embarrassing to the administration and they transferred him to the day shift. This was because the rules at that time required that

N.C. Anvil/LNS

any prisoner who was busted for an unnatural sex act must have his family notified by the administration of the exact nature of the offense.

Now I admit that administrators cannot allow total privacy within the institution because it would invite rapes, stabbings, escapes, etc. However, I see no reason not to allow prisoners to be alone with their visitors if they wish, unmolested by the leering gaze of guards. Visitors must pass through metal detectors before visiting and prisoners must undergo a strip-search after each visit, so why not allow privacy during the visit? I suppose it's because prison administrators and guards have somehow decided that intimacy with loved ones is a privilege and not a right of birth for U.S. citizens.

There are punishment advocates who will maintain that we should strip prisoners of all rights, including privacy . . . that punishment is the only solution in spite of the fact that even capital punishment has proved time and time again not to be a deterrent. I suppose this is a valid argument if you happen to believe in vengeance rather than prevention. Given the fact that about 99% of all convicted felons return to our communities at some point, I would prefer to have any tax money go into programs to resocialize people rather than to wreak vengeance upon them.

Learning to love and be intimate with another human being is one of the fundamental processes necessary in any society for a healthy adjustment by individuals within that society. By stripping prisoners of the right to this fundamental process we only reinforce the negative conditioning they presently hold to be true, that people are "things" or "objects" to be ripped off at will. It seems totally unreasonable to me to expect prisoners or anyone else to love and respect the society around them if all they are ever shown is hatred, apathy and degradation.

One of the ways to accomplish this end, from my own personal experience, is to develop programs that will encourage prisoners and their families to learn intimacy and the other feelings and emotions that go into forming responsible human relationships. We cannot, with any degree of success, continue to treat people as animals and expect them to learn humanity.

You can take the kindest, gentlest old dog in the world and make him mean and vicious by putting him in a cage and poking sticks at him for a few years.

From *WIN* 16, no. 4 (September 1, 1980): 9-12

Resistance Behind the Walls

by Scott Myers

If we could open the files of all the jails and prisons in the US, we would see that the 1970s ended and the 1980s began with a wave of prison strikes. Prisoners' resistance movements are escalating in the face of an all-out assault on prisoners' rights—many of which were only gained in the last 10 or 15 years.

It's hard to say where and when all the strikes have occurred, how long they lasted, or what the outcome was, but enough reports of protests have filtered beyond the walls to give us a sizable list: Marion, Illinois Federal Prison (two-day strike of 400 in early January, three-week strike of 400 in late March-early April); Missouri State Penitentiary (several days' strike of 150 in March); Angola, Louisiana State Prison (one-to-two-week hunger strike in August 1979); Walla Walla, Washington State Prison (numerous strikes during the past year); New Mexico State Prison (a well supported hunger strike two-to-three weeks after the deadly riot); Tennessee State Prison for Women (one-day protest in February); Rikers' Island, New York City (90 prisoners boycotted court proceedings for several days). In addition there have been other group protests and acts of resistance in the St. Louis City Workhouse, the Indiana State Penitentiary in Michigan City, Indiana, and undoubtedly many other prisons and jails.

Some common threads run through all these protests, and similar problems are exploding in hundreds of prisons and jails across the country. Overcrowding, for example, is epidemic. In 1978, according to the National Council on Crime and Delinquency, the prison population in the US was "rising dramatically at the rate of

Reprinted with permission from *WIN: Peace & Freedom Through Nonviolent Action,* 326 Livingston St., Brooklyn, NY 11217.

1000 per week." In just the past five years, 200,000 new prisoners have been crammed into the system.

At the same time that US prisons and jails are bursting at the seams, deep cuts are being made in rehabilitation programs, inmate services, probation, parole services and even basic necessities such as food allotments for meals. The Institute for Southern Studies, which publishes *Southern Exposure,* offered these rehabilitation figures in a special issue on southern prisons in 1978: Louisiana—42 of 6731 prisoners in work release programs, Tennessee—2% of corrections budget for "rehabilitation services," Texas—$47,000 out of a $67 million budget for work release, Kentucky—4% of budget for "career development," Georgia—800 of nearly 12,000 prisoners in rehabilitation programs.*

To add to these problems, incidents of beatings are increasing; longer sentences are being imposed; and behavior control programs are spreading. Such practices are turning our prisons into tombs for more people every day. The re-institution of road gangs in Georgia and the large prison farms systems like Louisiana's, Arkansas' and the Texas Department of Corrections' (TDC) signal an attempt to take back victories won as far back as the 1930s when chain gangs were abolished. The return to punishment and retribution as the prison's main purpose has turned back the clock behind the walls.

While this attack on prisoners' rights is being mounted inside, economic and social forces beyond the walls are operating to fill the jails and prisons to the brim. Unemployment; reduced wages, salaries and benefits; welfare cutbacks and child-care cuts do not only destroy poor and working people's ability to buy food, transportation or heat. Their ability to pay for justice is destroyed too. A fair trial, something most blacks, Latinos and Native Americans rarely receive, has too high a price tag for more and more people.

The greater weight of this injustice still falls on youth, minorities and poor white

*[Marc Miller, "The Numbers Game," *Southern Exposure* 6, no. 4 (Winter 1978): 25-26.—eds., *Alternative Papers.*]

RESISTANCE

cpf/LNS

men. But other groups—women and Vietnam veterans for example—are now being incarcerated in greater numbers than ever before. An astounding 25% of state and federal prisoners are Vietnam War-era veterans. With plant shutdowns and permanent layoffs spreading, we will continue to see more working people in our jails and prisons. The age of Jean Valjean has returned, American style.

To make matters worse, the conditions in these jails and prisons have been deteriorating rapidly in recent years. At the Missouri State Penitentiary for example, a 1978 court hearing revealed that dilapidated cell blocks left inmates shivering in 40 and 50-degree temperatures in the winter. In many of the older prisons, mice, cockroaches and rats are quite common, particularly in the prison kitchens.

Medical care is woefully inadequate. Some prison "doctors" aren't even doctors as a Tennessee state judge discovered during a 1978 court case. After investigating every prison in the state, the judge discovered that there wasn't a single licensed full-time physician in the entire system. He reported that he found "completely untrained personnel delivering medical care, inadequate physical plant, pharmaceutical procedures and record keeping."

In other cases, doctors are simply ill-trained and ill-informed in certain areas of medicine. The American Civil Liberties Union of Virginia won a major victory in such a case. A prison doctor and staff psychiatrist were prescribing the powerful behavior-modifying drug Prolixin to inmates without knowing the proper dosages, intended purposes, or possible harmful side effects which include irreversible stiffening of the extremities, tremors and immobility. A prisoner whose health was permanently destroyed won several

hundred thousand dollars in damages in the case.

Disease is rampant in many prisons. Illnesses such as tuberculosis are becoming more widespread. Common sicknesses such as the flu or even the common cold spread quickly from inmate to inmate in overcrowded, poorly ventilated dormitories. Prisoners are also being exposed to toxic chemicals. Women inmates at the Alderson, West Virginia Federal Prison report that the dangerous chemical 2,4-D is being used as a herbicide on the prison's compound. 2,4-D is one of the key toxic elements in Agent Orange—a defoliant used in Vietnam which has permanently injured many Vietnam veterans (see "Agent Orange: Vietnam's Deadly Legacy," WIN, 5/15/80.).*

Inmate wages, already pitifully low in most prisons, are being held down. In the sugarcane and cotton fields of Angola's plantation/penal colony in Louisiana, prisoners have their labor, their health and their lives drained out of them in return for *two cents an hour*. Angola is no southern aberration either; in 1979 it held over 4000 prisoners, making it a contender for the largest prison in the Western world. Super profits can be obtained from 4000 prisoners working for two cents an hour. Great enough profits can be obtained from prisoners working for 60 or 80 cents an hour as many federal prisoners do. Furthermore, such low wages put many of the items that "free" people buy—education, food, toiletries, paper, stamps, books, clothing, etc.—increasingly out of prisoners' reach.

You can bet that Lane Kirkland, the AFL-CIO union leader who sits on the Federal Prison Industries Board isn't very concerned about inmate wages. Nor are he or any of the corporate leaders on the Industries Board shedding any tears over the increased use of inmate labor on road gangs in Georgia, Texas, Louisiana, Mississippi and Illinois. With little support

*[Tod Ensign, "Agent Orange: Vietnam's Deadly Legacy," *WIN: Peace & Freedom Through Nonviolent Action* 16, no. 8 (May 15, 1980): 4–7.—eds., *Alternative Papers*.]

from traditional sources, prisoners have been increasingly making use of the strike as a means of protest.

Strike and Administration Response

The January 1980 strike at Marion was a short one. It happened spontaneously. At dinner one night in the prison's general population, a prisoner suddenly stepped up on a table and announced that prisoners in 1-Unit, the "hole" at Marion, were being kept under intolerable conditions. For the next two days the prisoners simply stayed in their cells when the work call was made. No formal negotiations were established. After two days everyone returned to work as though nothing had happened. The administration knew something had happened, but was clearly thrown off balance by a tactic they couldn't respond to in their usual efficient, violent fashion.

But on too many occasions, the prison administrations respond to a strike with vicious repression. Harsh reprisals are often visited upon the striking prisoners. Some prisoners at Marion were severely beaten, on the bottoms of their feet even, for their participation in the March-April 1980 strike. One of the beaten prisoners, Donald Richardson, gave an affidavit that said, "Four or five guards hit me repeatedly with nightsticks all over my body, telling me all during the beating, 'Say "Please, Sir." Say "Sir." Say "I'm sorry, sir." ' In addition, new charges will often be brought against striking prisoners, adding years to his or her sentence. Cruel punishment is also sometimes inflicted as after the hunger strike in Angola last year when those who still refused to eat were put in "the hole" indefinitely. A mother whose son was punished this way wrote *Southern Exposure* saying, "I've heard my son's cries, and I've heard his pleas, and I can't seem to do anything to help him."

Without public support, it is difficult, if not impossible for prisoners to win these strikes. The prison administration has too much power. They put the most political prisoners in segregation, sometimes even on the eve of a strike if they have received prior warning from a "snitch." The news media is forbidden access, which means the

Upstream/LNS

prisoners cannot bring their case directly to the public. The administration usually refuses to negotiate with any representative group of prisoners, then attempts to coerce prisoners individually into returning to work. All kinds of threats can be made and carried out against individuals who have no rights.

The ultimate threat, though, is confinement in control units, administrative segregation units, control centers or other units with various names but the same purpose—to break the inmate resister. Indefinite solitary confinement is the rule in these units. Guards are instructed to log the so-called "behavior pattens and attitudes" of prisoners who are put in these sealed tombs. Surveillance is intense. In Marquette, Michigan's control center, loudspeakers are equipped with microphones that can pick up inmates' conversations. Prisoners are more vulnerable to the use of physical force and even tear gas in these units because the units are small, separated from the rest of the prison, and prisoners are never allowed to congregate. In this way, the inmate protester is easily isolated and punished.

In spite of these reprisals and the slim chances of an actual strike victory, the prison strike is still the most potent political weapon that prisoners possess. The very fact that it is a political weapon makes it potent and therefore a threat to any prison regime. A strike compels the public to see the prisoners in a new light; it is a forceful, consciousness-raising action. Suddenly the public is presented with an obvious political act that has absolutely no "criminal overtones," and thus serves to break through anti-prisoner stereotypes. As a result prisoners win support—the one development no prison regime can stand. They want, they need, and they are used to total control. When the community becomes sympathetic to the prisoners cause, that control begins to slip.

The Attica Tradition

The Attica Rebellion of 1971 set in motion the movement that is still alive today by inspiring the support and sympathy of a large, international community. It was for this political act that they were brutally slaughtered in Attica's occupied D-Yard.

Attica, which we shouted ". . . is all of us!" is now literally everywhere—in nearly every prison in the US. Fortunately, the spirit of the Attica Rebellion has never been completely destroyed. Unified politi-

cal action, mostly nonviolent, almost always interracial, is still common in many jails and prisons. As Victor Bono, former Marion Brother and name plaintiff in a class action suit to close Marion's control unit, said, "We are human beings, men who live and die, and we do not want these conditions to continue—to be warehoused and be somebody's experiment as the government is doing to us. Surely you workers and students would not condone this cruel and unusual treatment, and yet it goes on without your knowledge. Now you know. It is a reality. We are its victims, and it is happening here in America, and only you the people can stop it with your support of us."

People and organizations struggling to build this prisoner rights movement have a clear-cut task: to bring poor and unemployed people, students, minorities, working people and others to see the prisoners' cause as their own. Educating the public about prisons is thus a top priority for prisoner rights organizations. They need to lobby the legislatures and challenge the prisons in the courts. But they need to do even more. Ultimately they need to build a movement that can bring hundreds and thousands of people into the streets and public squares just as the anti-war, civil rights, labor and women's movements have done.

Let's start supporting the prisoners when

they strike! Let's start supporting them when they reach beyond the walls! One way we can do this in the coming weeks is by supporting and participating in the September 2-13 "Walk With the Marion Brothers," starting in East St. Louis, Illinois, and ending in a mass rally at Marion. Speakers at the rally will include Reverend Ben Chavis, Daniel Berrigan, Larry Gara, Raphael Cancel Miranda and Reverend Leon White. A broad-based group of civil rights, peace, church, Native American and prisoner rights organizations are mobilizing for the walk and rally. Participating groups include the War Resisters League, National Lawyers Guild, Commission for Racial Justice of the United Church of Christ, Fellowship of Reconciliation, National Alliance Against Racist and Political Repression, National Committee to Support the Marion Brothers, Leonard Peltier Defense Committees, Jonah House and others.

It should be noted too that the rally date, Saturday, September 13, is also the ninth anniversary of the Attica Rebellion. What better way to celebrate the memory of the prisoners who died there and rededicate ourselves to the prisoner rights struggles of today!

Scott Myers is codirector of the National Committee to Support the Marion Brothers.

From: *The Guardian* 32, no. 13 (January 2, 1980): 3

Greensboro: Long History of Struggle

by Lynora Williams

The streets of Greensboro on a weekday morning are so empty that they are deceptively quiet.

Deceptive because the silence makes it hard for a visitor to believe that five people were gunned down here by racists Nov. 3 as

Reprinted with permission from *The Guardian: Independent Radical Newsweekly* (New York).

they demonstrated against the Ku Klux Klan (KKK).

Deceptive because in the city's southeast section, the quietness gives no indication of the depths of the anger and potential militancy of the area's Black residents, who have a long history of fighting racist injustice.

Deceptive because the city's ruling class uses the stillness as the warp on which it is attempting to weave a startlingly bold white-wash. This cover-up attempt, however, is already under attack.

"Now they're trying to tell us we can't believe our own eyes," exclaims 26-year-old Black resident Michelle Lee. "The story around here is that [the KKK] fired in self-defense."

Five leading members of the Communist

Workers Party (CWP) were slain here six weeks ago in the Morningside Homes housing project in the Black community. The five—Jim Waller, Mike Nathan, Bill Sampson, Sandy Smith and Cesar Cauce—were all long-time activists. One, Smith, was a Black woman, the others were white men. Nine other people were wounded by gunfire.

Throughout the city, a major textile center in the region, Black people readily spoke about their response to the KKK/Nazi murders. Almost uniformly they condemned the Klan despite mixed feelings about CWP.

Downtown, Woolworth's seems to be the early afternoon center of activity, and it is here one can begin to get a pulse on Black reaction. Significantly, it was here that four Black students from a local Black preparatory school launched the historic sit-in movement of the early 1960s. On Feb. 1, 1960, they riveted themselves to the counter stools; when they refused to move, a new era began in Black history in this country.

Waiting at the counter for his take-out lunch, James Ingram muses about the killings. "I was in the vicinity when it happened," he said. "First I didn't know what was going on. I thought it was caps or something. When I found out, it was a mess. I ran inside. If I'd had my piece I would have shot me a couple of Klansmen."

Ingram, 23, like many other Black residents of Greensboro, was angry at the killings and even angrier at the treatment of the KKK by city officials. "I can't believe they let them out on bond after killing five people and shooting a whole mess of others," he says. "If I'd shot even one person I'd still be in jail."

In the Morningside neighborhood, many residents expressed continued disbelief about the shootings. Malley Robinson thoughtfully folded his clothes in the laundromat, where picture windows open out onto the murder scene. "If me and a few dudes of my color had been running around with guns, we'd have been in jail," he said. "It sounds like a set-up. They saw everything and they didn't do anything. What does that sound like?"

Sixteen-year-old Terry Apple, playing pinball in the Morningside Homes recreation center, tried to put on a bravado as he described what he saw when he ran out and saw the slain demonstrators on Everitt Street. But he couldn't suppress the shiver that ran through his body. Bitterly he

argued, "They should ban the Klan. The courts should do something about them."

Student Response

Students at the predominantly Black North Carolina Agricultural and Technical University (A&T) here have in general been severely jolted by the killings. They were "shocking for our generation," said David Caldwell, 20. "It surprised us that this could happen. They [the killers] just went on shooting, just like they used to do in the last century when they all got on trains shooting at the buffalo so the Indians couldn't have them."

School officials, however—bolstered by government and media reports—have attempted to undercut organized student response. The day before a funeral march Nov. 11 for those killed by the Klan, for example, the entire school was shut down. With ruling-class rumors of a potential "riot" spreading throughout the city, riot-equipped police and undercover cops swarmed over the campus while helicopters swooped overhead. And to a limited degree, the campaign worked; some students now express fears of "violence" if protests take place.

The A&T administration took its action knowing the consequences if student discontent were not channeled; in the early 1970s Greensboro was a key center of activity for the nationally organized Youth Organization for Black Unity (YOBU), and many residents still remember the days when student Willie Grimes was killed during 1969 community/campus rebellions. No one was ever indicted for his death, but it is widely believed that it was a cop who shot Grimes in the head.

Because of this and other remembrances of struggles past, the Black community is not convinced by the current campaign to white-wash police involvement in the CWP members' death. The city's Black weekly for example, the *Carolina Peacemaker*, headlined its article on a police department probe of the killings: "Morningside report whitewashes police."

Rewriting History

The internal investigation is the centerpiece to a sophisticated ruling-class attempt to rewrite the events of the massacre. In the 100-page report, the police department concluded that it had done its best under the circumstances—although community members note that the cops were conveniently absent from the scene of the killings even though they were well

aware of the potential for Klan violence.

"It is concluded," the report said, "that the police officers assigned to the march performed their duty in a professional and reasonable manner and there is no evidence to indicate that any officer hindered or interfered with the march."

The Ku Klux Klan, in turn, has used the police report to bolster its own claims that they shot in "self-defense"—accounts the local press dutifully printed on page one.

Unfortunately, there are those who have gone along with the scheme, limiting the historic significance of the events to a shootout between two equally guilty forces. Local NAACP leader George Simkins, for example, has said about the Nov. 3 killings: "I don't see what happened as anything racial. I don't see it doing any damage to race relations." Simkins was described by one community member as "worse than most NAACP leaders."

Businessmen have also rallied behind the police version. Chamber of Commerce head John Parramore explained, "In our dealings with people from outside Greensboro, we are trying to emphasize our city was an unfortunate victim of outsiders and that Greensboro rallied together after this incident."

The report reveals many questions about police conduct. The most striking is that although the cops knew that there were up to 40 armed Klan members and supporters en route to the demonstration, they did essentially nothing to prevent them from proceeding since "there was insufficient probable cause to stop and/or arrest the members of the caravan."

And though the report contains several CWP documents, it doesn't have one piece of information on the KKK's political beliefs or strategy and tactics.

The report also shows that police knew the Klan was interested in the march. The same day the CWP announced the rally, according to the report, "a man came to the police department and requested a copy of the parade permit. . . . Upon questions by officers, the man said he was a member of the Klan and his name was Dawson." The police gave Dawson a copy of the permit—yet he was never subsequently arrested for questioning in the shootings. Community members are asking, Why not?

Among other highlights of the report:

• Police knew there was a good possibility of a confrontation, although a Detective Cooper thought "that if any confrontation occurred it would probably be at the ending point of the parade," it says. Cops also knew that the Klansmen were armed, although the antiracist demonstrators were instructed to come without weapons.

● When a caravan of KKK members and sympathizers was reported to be moving toward the demonstration site, which is not easily accessible, one officer reported that he and his squadron were not in position "because most had stopped to get a sandwich."

● When shooting broke out at Morningside Homes and was reported by Cooper, the policeman on the scene, Lieut. P. W. Spoon ordered: "Don't all come to the area, I'll advise further when I arrive on the scene." Spoon instead ordered police units to go to the Windsor Community Center about seven blocks from the shootings. Although some demonstrators had gathered there, the designated starting point of the action—as indicated on the permit and as the cop on the scene knew well—was at Morningside Homes. CWP members maintain they publicized the community center as the starting point in hopes of avoiding a confrontation.

● At only one point did a cop suggest that some of the nine cars in the KKK caravan be stopped. Just one vehicle, a van, was halted near the scene. To date, only one of the other vehicles has been found, although the report claims that Cooper, a detective, took a picture of the caravan before it reached Morningside Homes.

● The police place the onus of the Nov. 3 events on the CWP for its "belligerence." "After careful review," the report says, "it appears certain factors which either inadvertently occurred or were deliberately created caused a conflict of information regarding the starting time and place of the march."

If one probes the history of Greensboro, it is understandable why the police would feel compelled to cover-up the real nature of the events of last November. For Greensboro has a long and militant history of Black struggle—and it is a struggle that could erupt anew at any moment.

First, there were the lunch counter sit-ins of the early 1960s, when the name Greensboro became synonymous with a new movement. And in 1969, when Grimes was gunned down, officials virtually turned the Black community into an occupied area, with National Guard taking up station on streetcorners throughout the city.

One community resident recalled the occupation, stating: "I've been trying to convince my mother that we ain't safe. We can't bury our heads in the sand. I remember when troops made formation on her front yard. How easily we forget."

But there is also the brutality of everyday racism, which continues to this day despite the myth of the "new South." In fact, points out Southern Conference Education Fund member Lynn Wells, "Greensboro is Jimmy Carter's 'new South.' People should look at Greensboro and ask, 'Is this any kind of place to live?'"

And the Black community—now estimated at 33% of the 155,000 people here—is saying "no" to that question. It continues to fight for quality education and employment, and against police brutality and a racist judicial system.

Last year alone, the city's Human Relations Commission received 1350 complaints of racism. For several years, a key struggle has been to get the city to adopt district elections instead of citywide elections that allow the 7-member city council to have only one Black.

This is the backdrop for the brutal murders here Nov. 3. And this is why the attempted cover-up, despite initial successes, will not work in the long run.

Criticism of CWP

But while residents of the Black community are primarily angry at the police department, the mayor, the KKK and the Nazis, they are also critical of CWP's role in the community. These criticisms have been fanned by distorted reports in the local media, but there is no doubt that they originated in the Black community.

Many stress, for instance, that the CWP did not adequately notify residents of the project that there would be such a demonstration in their neighborhood. CWP has repeatedly denied these charges, saying that it did tenant organizing in Morningside Homes and that 20 families had given prior permission to CWP members to use their homes during the protest.

Others feel the CWP's language inflamed the KKK and did not take into account the political realities of North Carolina. In an open letter to two Klan leaders, for example, the CWP wrote, "We are very clear on what you are doing and that you and the KKK are a bunch of 2-bit cowards. . . . We challenge you to say in public where and when you hold your

rallies so that the people can organize to chase you off the face of the earth."

Bob Smith, a member of the recently formed Concerned Citizens Against the Klan, in particular criticized the CWP characterization of the KKK as a small group of cowards easily crushed by armed skirmishes. This attitude, Smith and others have charged, ignores the larger question of the racism which feeds organizations such as the Klan and which cannot be eradicated until capitalism is overturned.

A number of community members are even more critical of CWP's posturing since the killings. Although the organization has stressed that it wants unity with other groups, in practice, critics say, this has not been so.

"You are having a kind of loggerjam right now," said Cleveland Sellers, a local Black activist. "A broad section of the Black community wanted to put into focus what the real issues are, giving some kind of historical analysis of the Klan and the fact that the violence took place in the Black community. But the community is having a difficult time expressing itself due to a lot of innuendos, misconceptions and adventurist activities that have occurred since the Nov. 3 incident. These things have forced the Black community to not respond in the way they are capable."

Sellers, a 7-year Greensboro resident, has been closely associated over the years with Student Nonviolent Coordinating Committee, YOBU and its predecessor Student Organization for Black Unity, and the All-African Peoples Revolutionary Party.

Because of these difficulties, local activists are worried about organizing for a scheduled Feb. 2 demonstration here called by the National Anti-Klan Network. "In a lot of ways, we are back at square one," Sellers commented. "At this time there is no [community] support for any activity where there is no clear separation from the CWP. I don't think this should be mistaken for antileft sentiment. That's not what it is. It has to do with the tactics employed in this city by the CWP and others who have shown no respect for the wishes and level of consciousness of the Black community."

The future, Smith says, "must include the political reorganization of the Black community in response to these attacks. We must have a coalition from the left to the center. We must reject the things that divide us . . . and fight for the liberation of our people, or we face a very dangerous situation."

PEACE & FREEDOM THROUGH NONVIOLENT ACTION

From *WIN* 15, no. 36 (November 1, 1979): 4-9

Confronting Neo-Nazis in Chicago

by Chip Berlet

The signs appeared in our neighborhood overnight. "White Power Rally" said the red type in inch-high letters. "Time: 2:00, Sunday, Sept. 30th [1979]—Place: Gage Park, 55th & Western."

Gage Park is the southwest Chicago community where I live; and the park itself is just two blocks away. Gage Park High School was the scene of violent race riots several years ago, and Western Avenue, which bisects the park, also separates blacks from whites. A white power rally had the potential for turning ugly, especially with the recent ultimatum by the Department of Health, Education and Welfare ordering widespread busing to desegregate Chicago's schools.

The poster was obviously keyed to the busing order with a paragraph of text reading: "Is it fair to bus white kids far from their homes into black schools, where they are physically abused—all in the name of 'integration'? How can blacks live in luxury on welfare without working, while white workers can bearly (sic) make ends meet? Do powerful jewish (sic) organizations control what you see on television and read in the newspapers? Is the 'gas crisis' a phony stunt by the federal government to raise profits for the businessmen who bank-roll politicians?"

Frank Collin and the Neo-Nazis

The rally was scheduled by the National Socialist Party of America which is headquartered just south of Gage Park near Marquette Park. Last year the NSPA and its leader Frank Collin staged a massive White Power rally at Marquette Park that drew thousands of people. Collin

garnered national headlines at that time by threatening to march his stormtroopers through the predominantly Jewish Chicago suburb of Skokie. He has not been as successful in capturing public attention this year, but neither has he been inactive.

Collin was arrested in late June near Cleveland after a battle with members of the Jewish Defense League who disrupted a Nazi meeting at a Howard Johnson's Motor Lodge.

Collin was in Ohio to speak at a neo-Nazi rally in Parma, as part of his efforts to unify the many small neo-Nazi cells throughout the country under the banner of his National Socialist Party. The older National Socialist White Peoples Party, based in Arlington, Virginia, has long been unsuccessful in uniting American neo-Nazis, especially since the assassination of its founder, George Lincoln Rockwell.

Collin has been able to forge a coalition with at least six neo-Nazi groups in the Midwest, South and West, and works closely with Gerhard Lauck, who edits *The New Order* which serves as the Party's official newspaper. Lauck works out of Lincoln, Nebraska and supplies neo-Nazi material to the growing fascist clubs in Germany where, technically, Nazi and neo-Nazi material is banned.

Neo-Nazi organizing is on the rise. Last year a NSPA leader in North Carolina registered as a Republican for a state senate seat and campaigned openly as a Nazi. One third of the voters cast ballots for the stormtrooper. In Canada some 13,000 voters in Ontario signed petitions seeking official recognition for the neo-Nazi Nationalist Party of Canada. Red and black posters bearing swastikas have begun appearing at bus stops and train platforms in Latino and black communities throughout the southwest side of Chicago. There have been several small Nazi rallies in Chicago suburbs, and a rash of anti-Semitic activities has plagued Chicago's north side where one synagogue was vandalized, its wall defaced with swastikas, and a Torah burned.

This activity is not limited to Chicago. Since the first of the year, at least 36 incidents of racially-motivated vandalism have been reported in one county of Long Island, New York, including swastika-

emblem fires, cross burnings and other attacks. Following the announcement of the September re-running of the television mini-series "Holocaust," the network and local stations were deluged with mail and phone calls protesting what was termed the "myth" of the murder of six million Jews. On the days the program was aired, pickets appeared outside the television studios in several cities.

Still, the number of actual members of the various neo-Nazi formations remains small.

A Real Threat

There are those who say the Nazis in Chicago are not a real threat. If you count only the handful of uniformed stormtroopers in Collin's National Socialist Party of America, this is true; but add on the pack of loud-mouthed lumpen louts who patrol Marquette Park in their "White Power" T-shirts, and the threat begins to grow.

Then include the frustrated and frightened white working class home-owners who bitterly blame their struggles to make ends meet on the blacks just across Western Avenue. They don't like the Nazis in their tree-lined neighborhood, but they nod in agreement when the stormtroopers tell them what will happen to property values and their daughters if they let blacks into the community.

To these people add the right-wing politicians who pander to the racial fear inflamed by Collin and his followers; and then include the real estate agents who reap windfall profits through their blockbusting made so much easier by the Nazis' propaganda.

Shake/LNS

This is the real threat of the Nazi movement in Chicago. The Nazis' highly-publicized activities incite racial hatred, and not only pave the way for more substantial and better-organized right-wing political movements, but also mask the activities of the blockbusters, segregationists, redlining bankers and insurance agents, busing opponents, conservative politicians, and others who carry on their daily racist assaults with little publicity; all while Collin captures the headlines.

Blacks are unable to purchase a home in the Marquette Park area. Some who have tried have been firebombed. Blacks cannot walk through the park itself without fear of serious physical injury, even though a large black community is just walking distance away. Racism is the real issue in Marquette Park, not Nazis; but as long as Collin continues to spew out his genocidal schemes of racial hatred, the real issues involved will never be adequately publicized. This is the conundrum of Marquette Park: Collin and his Nazis are few in number and pose no real threat to democracy. Collin, as a highly-publicized racist, creates a smokescreen that masks the real threat. Is Collin therefore a real threat?

Roots

The Marquette Park area, like many Chicago neighborhoods, is an ethnic enclave. The area is composed of Lithuanians, Poles, Czechs, Slavs, and other Europeans, many of whom are refugees from countries now under the Soviet sphere of influence. Marquette Park also has one of the highest concentrations of city employees, especially police and firefighters, in Chicago.

On the east, the neighborhood is bordered by Western Avenue, a broad and busy street which now serves as a demilitarized zone between the white Marquette Park area, and the Black neighborhoods that have been pushing west at the rate of several blocks per year. Blockbusters, using a technique based on racial fear and threat of disastrous property value losses, have been unable to crack the Marquette Park area, and have turned their efforts north and south.

It is in this tense neighborhood that in 1970 Frank Collin, a young former follower of George Lincoln Rockwell, established the National Socialist Party of America. He figured he would receive widespread support. He was wrong. To this day Collin can muster no more than 30 uniformed brownshirts at a rally, and many of these neo-Nazis are not from the Chicago area.

Collin is a rabble rouser in the truest sense of the word; his only constituency outside party members are several dozen street punks who hang out in Marquette Park. Even their loyalty is doubtful. "We hate the Nazis, they're assholes," said one hefty dude in a "White Power" T-shirt. "But we hate the niggers more. We like to beat up the niggers, see, and the Nazis bring the commies and the niggers to the park for us to beat up, see. But, you know, if there wasn't anyone else around, we would beat up the Nazis."

Collin's demonstrations in the Marquette Park area generally ended up in confrontations with police during the years from 1970 to 1976, and the Chicago Park District ordered Collin to post an insurance bond ranging from $100,000 to $350,000 before they would grant him any more park permits.

Meanwhile, various civil rights groups made several attempts to demonstrate against discrimination in Marquette Park, and virtually every attempt ended in violence, even when the Nazis stayed inside their headquarters near the park. The Nazis do not have a lot of support—but racism does.

The Skokie Hysteria

In the summer of 1976, Collin was arrested on disorderly conduct charges for staging a park demonstration without a permit. Collin enlisted the aid of the American Civil Liberties Union in getting a park demonstration permit without the massive insurance bond. The city and the park district refused to waive the insurance requirement and in March of 1977 Collin announced he would stage a rally in Skokie, a Northern Chicago suburb with a large Jewish population including many survivors of Nazi concentration camps.

Collin candidly admitted the Skokie demonstration was a stunt to force the Chicago Park District to allow him access to Marquette Park. A protracted legal battle that eventually reached the Supreme Court pushed Collin into the headlines. Tension increased exponentially after a July 23, 1977 civil rights march to Marquette Park ended up in a race riot.

Collin and his party members were threatened with arrest if they set foot on the street during the civil rights march, but a crowd of 1,000 mostly young whites gathered in the park anyway. The police stopped the civil rights march of 20 demonstrators almost a mile from the park, but the pent-up emotion of the racist crowd in the park burst forth in a running street battle. Rocks and bottles were hurled at passing black motorists, at least two cars were overturned and demolished, and several blacks were roughed up before police forced the white teenagers back into the park where they eventually dispersed.

With the aid of the ACLU, Collin continued his Skokie march plans, but he agreed to wait until the legal battle was over before staging a demonstration. There were two lawsuits: one over the proposed Skokie march and various legal maneuvers to prevent it, and the original suit against the insurance bond requirements that prevented Collin from marching in Marquette Park.

As the legal battles bounced from District Court to Federal District Court to the Court of Appeals to the Supreme Court and back, the hysteria over the proposed Skokie march grew to feverish proportions. Several groups threatened that blood would flow if the Nazis marched in Skokie. Collin finally hinted that he would trade Skokie for Marquette Park, but that offer became moot when a federal judge ruled the insurance requirement unconstitutional.

Protecting Rights Selectively

Collin celebrated his victory by staging a demonstration in downtown Chicago on Saturday, June 24, 1978. Several thousand counterdemonstrators waited for his appearance, many of them with the intent of physically attacking the Nazis.

Police reinforcements were brought in before Collin was led out of the federal building with 25 uniformed brownshirts at his side. His speech was drowned out by the roar of the crowd. Eggs and tomatoes rained down on the Nazis, as well as the unfortunate journalists who had been herded together in front of the brownshirts. Soon rocks and bottles were thrown and the Nazis scurried back into the federal building as police began to disperse the crowd of counterdemonstrators. There were one dozen arrests. The counterdemonstrators were photographed and videotaped by police agents standing in the second floor window of another federal building across the street from the plaza. Although some of the counterdemonstrators were members of the Jewish Defense League, most of the protesters were progressives from civil rights, pacifist, radical, socialist and communist groups representing almost the entire spectrum of leftist organizations. This fact was generally ignored by the press which focused on the helmeted JDL.

A few weeks later, on July 9, 1978, Frank Collin finally staged his Marquette Park rally.

Marquette Park—July 9, 1978

It was a bright, clear, hot and altogether typical Chicago summer day, as hundreds of counterdemonstrators gathered in a quiet black neighborhood east of Marquette Park. After several false starts, the group moved through the black community calling for the residents to join in the march to confront the Nazis. The demonstration swelled to over 1,500, but as the chanting crowd turned west to head for Marquette Park, they were stopped by police who formed a human wall three deep at a railroad underpass some ten blocks east of the park. The anti-Nazi protesters were told they would not be allowed any further. Police barricades blocked off every side street leading toward the park from Western Avenue. A 100 block area was cordoned off. People entering the area from any street near the black neighborhoods off of Western Avenue were asked for identification and proof of residency.

In Marquette Park, some 2,000 people gathered to hear Collin make his familiar speech of racial hatred. Collin stood behind rank after rank of helmeted police. A few counterdemonstrators made it into

Workers World/LNS

SMASH THE KLAN!

the park and several scuffles ensued. Dozens of plainclothes police descended upon each confrontation and led the participants out of the park. Seventy-two arrests were made.

After the rally was over, roving bands of white youth started attacking the counterdemonstrators.

"Get the nigger," came the cry after the mob finished forcing a Jewish anti-Nazi demonstrator to swim across a small pond to escape injury.

"Kill that nigger! Stomp him!" a young white punk yelled as the terrified black youth realized he had pressed his luck too far by staying in Marquette Park after the rally by the neo-Nazis ended.

He ran well, dodging fists, but a leg snaked out and caught him in the shins and he fell. Face down in the grass of the lovely pond-dotted park in Chicago's southwest side, he only had a moment to consider his plight before the first boot smashed into his ribs.

"Kill the nigger, kill the nigger," chanted the crowd feeling the excitement of bringing the quarry to bay—reverting to the gruesome primitivism captured in *Lord of the Flies*. More boots, then fists, and as the black youth struggled, his shirt was reduced to shreds. Blood trickled down from his nose, and the corner of his mouth was split as another fist found its mark.

A balding, middle-aged man rushed into the midst of the crowd of taunting teenagers and grabbed the black youth in a protective huddle. He too, became the target of attack; but other defenders joined him and a tight knot of bodies, with the dazed black youth at its core, pushed its way through the screaming crowd towards a line of police who had been watching the incident with indifference from several hundred feet away.

When the bleeding youth reached the police they grabbed him and pushed him into a squad car. The car sped off towards Western Avenue, the border between black and white neighborhoods in this working class community.

A few moments later the unruly crowd surrounded a small group of protesters from a neighborhood synagogue.

"Go back to Skokie, Jew bitch," yelled one white youth at a young woman. "Do you sleep with the niggers?" Why don't you go back to Africa with them?"

"Jews go home, Jews go home," the crowd chanted. "We don't want you here you nigger-lover," shouted a teenager in a "White Power" T-shirt. The police moved in and took the small band of Jews into a

waiting paddy wagon to get them out of the park.

"Get the gas," shouted a young kid; and young and old alike laughed heartily at the sight of the Jews being led into the paddy wagon. "Six million wasn't enough," someone yelled.

The Conundrum

There are those who say Frank Collin and the Nazis aren't a real threat. They are a symbolic threat, however, and they must be confronted wherever they appear. Their actions and ideologies breed racial hatred and lead people to accept authoritarian solutions to society's problems. They cannot be ignored. Their statements cannot go unchallenged.

A conundrum is a riddle—and its answer is a play on words. If Frank Collin and his neo-Nazis are a symbolic but not a real threat to democracy, who can state what the real threat is? Perhaps the answer is: The real threat is the State, which defends the rights of Nazis while ignoring illegal racist activities, and refuses to allow anti-Nazi and civil rights demonstrators to freely exercise their rights.

Thousands of police protected Frank Collin on a Sunday afternoon in Marquette Park; but let a black youth try to walk unmolested through the park any other day of the year—where are the police then?

One Response

With the track record of Frank Collin fresh in our minds, we met with several neighbors the day of the scheduled rally and made signs saying "Gage Park Residents Say No to Nazis" and other slogans. At the appointed hour we arrived at Gage Park and were joined by another group of counterdemonstrators from the Liberation League, which is active in fighting the Nazis and the Klan in several cities.

Small groups of residents stood in clumps across the street from the park waiting to see what would happen. In the park itself there were some 10 anti-Nazi demonstrators, four pro-Nazi residents, three plainclothes police, and two photographers. According to police, Frank Collin cruised by the park with a carful of Nazis and decided to bag the rally. Without a gigantic media hoopla, Collin it seems is a paper tiger.

Finally a rival group of Nazis (from a group based in Cicero, Illinois) walked into the park followed by a crowd of young teenage boys, some on bicycles. The streetclothed Nazis walked up to the counterdemonstrators and a brisk argument ensued. Carloads of police materialized from sidestreets but despite several threats of violence by the Nazis, the anti-Nazi demonstrators kept their cool. The police let the debate continue for awhile and then announced the rally permit had expired. The Nazis left the park chanting "White Power! White Power!" accompanied by most of the teenagers.

Some of the local youth remained behind to talk with the anti-Nazi residents and protesters, however, and afterwards we all agreed the response to the rally had been a success.

With increasing frequency, Nazis are being met with persistent protests wherever they appear across the country. Whether it is an organized group or a handful of residents, counterdemonstrators have been successful in challenging the Nazi message of hate. It is a small step, and the greater issues of racial hatred, authoritarianism, and exploitation remain to be solved; but even a small response is better than no response—and perhaps can become a starting point for educating those people who mistakenly believe the Nazis have solutions to the problems which face them and their families.

7 WOMEN

All issues are women's issues. Racism, union busting, militarism, all the grievances aired and all the solutions proposed in this volume affect the quality of women's lives. Women's issues, women's contributions, women's writings, and women's publications, therefore, appear as a matter of course throughout the volume.

We chose, however, to bring together in this section those articles that not only contain distinctly feminist perspectives but that relate directly to the evolution of feminism in the United States. They constitute an indictment of a society that devalues characteristics and work traditionally associated with the female (passivity, dependence, nurturing), binds women into restrictive social and economic roles, and encourages violence against women. The section begins with fear, with violence, with pain, as Gail Groves reminds us that women in our society are expected to live in perpetual fear, to lock themselves in, to depend on men for protection. Del Martin draws the feminist conclusion that rape is an integral part of our social structure, a means of social control.

But the women writing in these pages are not content to be victims; they are strong, resolved, uppity. As they defy social taboos, they share their experiences of rape, battering, and harassment; they plan for self-defense, work toward eliminating sex role typing, develop theory, and organize. These women are writing, struggling for control of body and soul. Sue Gould and G. C. Guard describe how they prepare women physically and emotionally for self-defense at Chimera, Inc. Jill Lippitt introduces the strategy behind the feminist movement against pornography—a strategy to use, not limit, first amendment rights. Violent pornography is everywhere. Tacie Dejanikus confronts it in a Hollywood film and in film reviews in the *Los Angeles Times* and the *New Yorker*. *Ms.,* owned by Warner Communications, seems unwilling to refuse advertising that both blatantly and subtly displays degrading images of women.

Articles on economic realities for women follow. They shatter the myths of the success of affirmative action and of unlimited opportunities for women in the workplace. Natalie Sokoloff reminds us that women make only fifty-nine cents to the dollar a man makes. Phyllis Eckhaus shows us that little has changed in our educational systems and that girls are still being prepared for low-paying, non-decision-making jobs.

These women are not only developing an awareness of the ties that bind; they are building a new set of support services to meet their needs and a culture to inspire their growth. Susan Bell writes about women from feminist health centers working with medical school students to produce more responsive medical care. Marilynn Norinsky describes the fight to save midwifery and preserve the right to deliver a child at home. Thelma Norris reflects on the history and state of the art of women's music. Z. Budapest argues for rediscovering goddess-centered religion. Barbara Smith condemns racism in the women's movement as incompatible with feminist principles and challenges white women to confront it.

Unlike the Women's Section in your daily newspaper, this section begins with violence and ends with a recipe, one which provides the basic ingredients for feminist research, analysis, renewal.

—PJC

WOMANSPIRIT

From *WomanSpirit* 6, no. 22 (December 1979): 52

Take Back the Night

by Gail Groves

Beautiful black night
Swirls in through my opened window
I long to embrace her
And I remember
My daughter out walking alone
On the beach
My sister
Running bare-headed
Through the streets
My mother, grandmother
Walking to a bus-stop,
A car,
Taking a short-cut through a vacant lot,
A wooded lane
My lover
Me

And I remember fear
And why we have not done
All those things.

Take Back the Night!
Let her lie within our arms
Let her shelter our warm bodies
Let her feel us through her passing
Let us creep up her backbone unafraid.

At midnight
last Wednesday on the west side
a woman was raped
on the path from her car to her house

At 4:00 am
a woman watering her garden
by the beach before sunrise
was attacked

At 6:00 am
a woman was accosted in the
two blocks between her home
and the factory

At 8:00 am
I heard a woman scream outside my door.

It has been decided that every woman
who lives

Reprinted with permission from *WomanSpirit.*

for a whole average lifetime
will be raped twice.

We know that the day
is twenty-four hours
and that of that
twelve will be darkness.

Rape—any act which (attempts to) invalidate woman as person, as subject, denies her autonomy, robs her of power to control her own body. Commonly accepted attitudes toward women around the subject have implied that women are accomplices to their own brutalization. We hear this on television, we see it in movies, we read of "victims" (rather than successful self-defenders) in the daily papers. Our mothers tell us to do the "right things" or we will get hurt.

We are taught to fear the night. We learn to be afraid of darkness, of what might lurk there. We are taught that there is danger in nature, in the outdoors, in every bush and tree that might hide our attackers from us. We are told that even the full moon offers us no protection, that streetlights will allow our attackers to see us better, that even in daylight a woman can be raped.

As women who have grown to fear the darkness, we have a need for rituals to exorcise these fears. The men who lurk can feel our fear, like dogs can, emanating as we scurry from house to car to bus-stop to taxi-stand to house. We need strong rituals to purify our bodies, to drive the fear from its hiding place, to acknowledge it, then banish it from us.

We are less afraid if we are two or three women traversing the night. If we combine our strength to take back the night, we might be thousands, be millions of women with our torches, our candles, our bright lights, our loud shouts of triumph echoing, silence and darkness falling before our voices and our light.

In this Take Back the Night ritual, we validate that we are persons, women, united, strong and fearless. We reclaim the night as our sister, the earth in darkness our mother, the moon our shield. We say we are rich in the darkness, not ready to be robbed. We say that we will drive back the fear in our souls, that we will reach out with our arms wide and touch no assailants, they will have fled before us.

Once the night was ours. So she shall be again. What will the night of the fearless woman, or two or two thousand, do to the man who might want to hurt a woman on the streets at night? Will he think, once or twice? Will the men stay home? Will they join us, marching? Will the women stay home? Will they join us? Marching? How will I as a woman feel, after this? When I choose to walk down a street at night, will I feel the thousand silent sisters walking with me? Will I hold my head up high? Will I be able to forget the slow sure progress of four thousand women shouting in a Mardi Gras parade of color and sound?

I had forgotten how it felt to walk unafraid in the darkness. As a child I knew it. The bushes and trees were my friends. I could dart into an alleyway or take a secret short-cut. I knew a thousand ways to get from my house to school without anyone ever seeing me. I could hide and prowl and see everyone, everything. The earth was my home, I could feel her protect me. I could climb a tree as fast as a squirrel and scream like a jaybird in the clear night. I could hear every whisper, and see every moment. Not the most silent Indian could get within fifty feet or I would sense her. I could hold myself completely motionless or tear like the wind through the trees and home. We played Hide and Go Seek in the dark! That was our training. Do you remember? Running and screeching toward "home" we filled the night with sound, we were filled with night.

Do you remember? Remember with me that we once had the night within us, we were the night. Be the night with me once more, my thousand sisters. We shall not forget again.

From *Big Mama Rag* 7, no. 10 (November 1979): 9, 25

Del Martin on Violence Against Women

transcribed and edited by Constance Perenyi

Founder of the Daughters of Bilitis, an international lesbian organization started in 1955, Del Martin has long been known as an activist involved with feminist issues. Since 1975, she has worked as a coordinator for the National Organization of Women's National Task Force on Battered Women and Household Violence. Currently self-employed as a freelance writer, Martin is the author of Battered Wives *(Glide Publications, 1976), and, along with Phyllis Lyon, she co-authored* Lesbian Woman *(Glide Publications).*

The following address was presented as part of a panel discussion at the first National Conference on Violence Against Women.

I've long had a fantasy that we would move all the women who live in unratified states—move them out until the ERA was ratified. And now I know where to move them—to Washington, D.C. For two years we have tried to get domestic violence bills passed in the House and Senate. We've done that organizing. We have done our lobbying. But they do not pay attention. What is more important is building up a defense plan. What is more important is drawing on radical thinking.

And I am disturbed by legislators who come to our conferences and say their thing and then leave, and do not listen to what is going on here. [Editor's note: this is in reference to a "campaign appearance" by Rep. Tim Wirth that disrupted the panel discussion at which Del Martin gave this address.]

Perspective

Writing my book *Battered Wives* helped me put the women's movement into focus, into a perspective of the whole. And I found that every issue we have ever addressed in the women's movement applies to battered women. That what we are dealing with is woman hatred, that the patriarchal, social and economic system depends on the control and subservience of women. And that the ultimate means of this control, when all else fails is the use of physical force. To be born female is to be subjected to continuing acts of violence, physical and psychological, against one's being. In today's so-called "enlightened" society, a girl-baby is not apt to be drowned at birth, nor are a young female's feet bound; but she will be nonetheless punished for disappointing her father who must have sons to prove his manhood, to carry on his name, and to give him immortality. Wife-beating dates back to the beginnings of monogamous pairing marriages. In earlier, primitive societies, women were highly esteemed among the clan. But with the advent of the monogamous marriage, the mother right was replaced by the father right, and wives were held in tight control in order to protect the husband's honor and his identity as father.

A woman was obligated to marry and to obey her husband or suffer the consequences.

Christianity embraced the hierarchal family structure and made marriage sacred and gave the husband permission to castigate his wife and beat her. According to early English Common Law, the very being, the legal existence of the woman, is suspended during marriage or at least is incorporated into and dominated by that of the husband. In marriage, the woman loses her personhood. She is identified in terms of her husband. Legally, he is head of the household, responsible for supporting the family. She is subordinate and responsible for housework and childcare. With few exceptions, she takes her husband's name, his domicile, and becomes his legal dependent. Her labor is a duty to be performed without value or compensation. In many states, the husband has exclusive authority over what we call community property, including all the wife's earnings, and can dissipate the family assets without the wife's prior knowledge or consent.

Jean Baker Miller in her book, *Towards A New Psychology of Women,* says that the dominant groups usually define acceptable roles for subordinates, which typically involves providing functions that no dominant group would want to perform. Functions that a dominant group prefers to perform are carefully guarded and closed to subordinates on the basis that the subordinate is unable to perform them because of innate defects or deficiencies of mind or body, and therefore is incapable of change or development.

Steve Karian/LNS

She also points out that if subordinates adopt the characteristics assigned to them, that they are considered well-adjusted. This is a means by which development of a group legitimizes an unequal relationship, incorporates it into the cultural values, moralities, and social structures, and thereby obscures the true nature of the relationship—that is, the existence of inequality. In patriarchal society, men assume roles of dominance and assign women roles of subservience. To be masculine is to be strong, active, rational, aggressive and authoritarian. To be feminine is to be submissive, passive, dependent, weak and masochistic. And normal adult behavior, sex unspecified, is equated with male characteristics. Men thus experience no dichotomy between adulthood and manhood because society says the two are identical. But the woman who tries to be a healthy adult does so at the expense of being feminine. The woman who adjusts to her so-called normal role does so at the expense of being an adult. Society, then, has constructed a no-win situation for women. Femininity is held out as the carrot for women, but to be feminine is to play victim.

Media

I want to talk about media, media in the way of advertising of products, and what effect it has on women as victims. There's the billboard for the Rolling Stones' album, "Black and Blue," showing a bound woman with the caption, "I'm black and blue from the Rolling Stones and I love it." There's the advertisement for a pants company in Los Angeles called "Cheek," and they show a man spanking a woman's cheeks. When the advertising agency was confronted by some outraged women, they were told, "We wanted to come up with something men could really identify with. We really wanted to give it to them." And then there's the billboard in the national campaign of the Bowling Association that says in big, huge letters, "BEAT YOUR WIFE" and in small letters, "Go bowling tonight." When the executives of the Association were confronted, they said, "We meant beat in the competitive sense. We meant take your wife out and show her who is boss."

Images in the media and pornography teach us that women are victims in the same existential sense that grass is green; that women like to be victims, that women expect to be victimized, that women are easy targets for brutal behavior, that victimized women are entertaining and amusing to contemplate, that the normal male is sexually aggressive and brutal. And moreover the frequency with which the media portrays woman as victim, and especially their routine association with humor, trivializes the entirely serious phenomenon of violent crimes against women.

The violence against abortion clinics, the bombings, burnings, raids, and vandalizing which occurred while patients were being treated and the death threats against employees and warnings that their children would be kidnapped or murdered should not have surprised us. Those who claim to be pro-life are also for the death penalty and against gun control. The right-to-life catch phrase is a cover-up for patriarchal forces who would deny women control of their own bodies, their own lives. Again, violence is the ultimate weapon against uppity women.

And of course, the victims were to blame. If these women did not advocate reproductive freedom for women, they would not have provoked attack. In patriarchal society, all violent crimes are regarded as victim precipitated. A woman is raped because of the clothes she wears, because she travels the streets alone, because she is or is not a virgin, because she is weak and vulnerable. A wife is battered by her husband because she did not obey him, because she could not read his mind and failed to fulfill his every whim or desire, because she asked for it, because she got pregnant, because she talked to another man. A girl-child is a victim of incest because of her seductive behavior, because of her desire for parental attention and affection. Women are killed because they dared to fight back, because they were unfaithful to their husbands, because they were lesbians, because they were too beautiful. Men, on the other hand, who are the perpetrators of the violence, are commonly excused for their violent acts. The man's family was under stress, he lost his job, drank too much, his mother had an extramarital affair. No matter how horrible his crime, the man is somehow vindicated by such rationalizations.

Our society has set up women as victims. To try to break out of that victimization is to be further victimized. The never-married woman who is looked at with pity and scorn as a reject, the woman who strives for economic independence and tries to further her education is subject to sexual harassment by her supervisors on the job or her professors; and the lesbian who dares to build a personal life irrespective of men is a pariah. By her very being, she rejects women's assigned roles; she dares to be independent. By society's terms that means she is branded as illegal, immoral and sick. In patriarchal society, which depends on the control and subservience of women, being a lesbian is a capital offense. Society has many ways of forcing lesbians into conformity. They are beaten and raped— "All a lesbian ever needed was a good man." Lesbians are also threatened with murder, subjected to shock treatment, driven to suicide, disowned by their families, fired from their jobs, blackmailed, purged from government services, and deprived of their children.

Fair Game

Since the advent of Anita Bryant's religious crusade against lesbians and gay men, there has been a marked increase of violence by youth gangs and by police who regard them as fair game. Sexual Trauma

Bülbül/LNS

Services in San Francisco reports an increase of rapes against open lesbians and women who are considered suspect. Cases of police harassment and brutality in and around lesbian bars has been reported in various parts of the country. And recently, at a hearing before the U.S. Commission on Civil Rights in Houston, representatives of the Gay Political Caucus entered into the public record documentation of over 100 individual cases to show that Houston police officers have used perjured testimony, physical and verbal abuse, selective enforcement of the law, and an alleged cover-up of a murder all to conspire against homosexuals.

The worst part of being a lesbian is to have to keep it secret; being privy to the daily knowledge that what you are is so awful that it cannot be revealed. The years, sometimes decades of soul-searching, untold agonies of self-doubt, guilt, painful inner conflict and isolation can be personally devastating. To remain silent is tantamount to being party to the annihilation of women's selves. To accept herself for who she is, a person of worth and dignity, is a lesbian's greatest challenge. And the worst crime of violence to me is that perpetrated by women against women —when so-called feminists who are supposed to be about the business of liberating women reject lesbians as the albatross of the women's movement.

The different kinds of violence against women cannot be separated from ourselves. We talk in terms of "us" and "them" at our peril. As women, we have all been sexually harassed or raped or battered— think about that. Have you ever had an argument with a man in which you backed down because you were intimidated? Did you think that if you took that argument a step further he might just strike out at you? Did you ever stay in a relationship longer than you should have? Did you stay because you felt responsible for the other person? Did you stay because of the children? Were you afraid of loneliness? Did you have doubts as to whether you could live by yourself and support the children on your own? Did you ever have intercourse with a man even though you did not really want to have sex with him then? Have you ever faked orgasm? Have you ever felt humiliated or degraded by sexual remarks made by the men you work with? Has one ever made a pass at you? Did your boss ever try to seduce you? Were you ever called a lesbian or a whore because you rejected a man's advances? Or because you have become an advocate for women?

Get in touch with those experiences and your feelings about them. Then you will know that you are no different than the battered woman, the rape victim. It is only when we understand our collective victimization that we begin to redefine ourselves as women and change the structure of our world.

Magazine on Ending Violence Against Women

From *Aegis,* March/April 1979, pp. 5-6.

Rape and Virginity Among Puerto Rican Women

by Mercedes Rodríguez-Alvarado

Rape is an act of violence against the physical and emotional integrity of a human being. It's a critical experience in the life of any woman and tends to be more critical when the victim of the assault is a virgin. Virginity is one of the most traditional and respected values in Puerto Rico. Preservation of the value of virginity is prevalent among our women themselves as well as among our families in general. From our experience at the Puerto Rico Rape Crisis Center in Rio Piedras we have observed that one of the main problems stated by victims and their relatives is their concern with the conflict followed by the loss of virginity.

The loss of virginity, as a fact, could be a traumatic event in the life of many women, no matter how positive or natural are the circumstances surrounding the experience. The Puerto Rican woman learns, from a very early age, that in her virginity are represented her dignity, honor, respect and femaleness. At the same time, when a woman is dishonored, the family as a collective suffers the public humiliation, shame and disgrace. Certainly, one of the most painful and intimidating ways of losing one's virginity is being a victim of rape.

The sexual assault, as an unexpected and violent act against a woman, generates real fears and stress usually present after those events which threatened the victim's life and personal security. This is more evident when one can feel close in your flesh and soul, the brutality of someone who appreciates very little and disregards too much the integrity of your self. That's why rape, even as an isolated incident in a woman's life, is almost always followed by a sequence of psycho-social reactions that deals with the unique experience of the affected woman with herself, with her peers, with other reference groups and with her immediate community. If it's true that women are not responsible for the aggression, where they are regarded only as objects, from our particular reality it is also true that society justifies rape from a male oriented perspective and punishes women for the act itself and its consequences.

Unfortunately, we are facing a crime that so many times stays unpunished and, after all, we charge the woman for the social expenses. Besides the usual exposure to fear, anxiety, pain, anger and indignation experienced by victims of rape, women also have to face the feelings of humiliation, shame and guilt associated with the loss of virginity. This shame is present, not only within the privacy of the woman, but grows quickly because of the attitudes of those who are close to her, in the form of pity, rejection and gossip.

Gossiping is an ordinary activity among our people and rape cases provide infinite possibilities for this purpose. What is very interesting from a sociological perspective is not only the content of the stories and the process of spreading the gossip, but the impact of this underground communication in the victim's life.

Gossips have the power of changing or conditioning behavior. What people say about what had happened or could happen to a rape victim has a real impact on the way she views her reality. It is almost impossible not to care what people say about you. In this sense, you are not only what you feel or think you are, but what the others feel and think about you.

The social response to the physical

"damage" of the rape victim makes extremely difficult the reconciliation of the feelings related with the loss of virginity in the woman. Objectively, if a woman is a virgin and is raped, after the sexual assault she will continue to be a woman and a virgin. Nevertheless, it is a pity that socially, virginity is more valuable in its physical component than in its spiritual and moral qualities. Vaginal lacerations or a scar in the hymen in no way can change a woman's reputation, integrity, purity or honesty. The only thing that could change in a woman after a forcible rape is her consciousness about her vulnerability to masculine domination and her approach to violence as a social phenomenon. The sexual assault should not diminish the woman's options and possibilities that are already restricted because of being female.

Our society needs to think more deeply and seriously about the experience of rape among our women. We must identify the cultural, religious and social bias that makes it so difficult to express solidarity and fairness towards the rape victim. We can no longer blame the victim for the violent acts that we should all claim as our responsibility. The rape victim deserves no more shame, for that shame should be for all who make possible and feasible the task of a rapist.

Mercedes Rodríguez-Alvarado is the Executive Director of the Commission for the Improvement of Women's Rights, P.O. Box 11382, Fernández Juncos Station, Santurce, Puerto Rico 00910.

Magazine on Ending Violence Against Women

From *Aegis*, May/June 1979, pp. 29-31

Six Black Women: Why Did They Die?

prepared by the Combahee River Collective

The following material is reprinted from a pamphlet prepared by the Combahee River Collective, a Boston Black feminist organization. The pamphlet was written as part of the organizing done around the murders of six Black women. Since the pamphlet was written, five other women have been stabbed to death. Along with a resource list of all the Boston area groups and organizations who either provide services to women who have been victimized or are holding meetings to organize against the murders, the pamphlet contains self protection information. Copies of the pamphlet are available for $.50 each from the Combahee River Collective, c/o AASC, PO Box 1, Cambridge, MA 02139. Bulk prices available upon request.

Recently 6 young Black women have been murdered in Roxbury, Dorchester

and the South End of Boston. The entire Black community continues to mourn their cruel and brutal deaths. In the face of police indifference and media lies and despite our grief and anger, we have begun to organize ourselves in order to figure out ways to protect ourselves and our sisters, to make the streets safe for women.

We are writing this pamphlet because as Black feminist activists we think it is essential to understand the social and political causes behind these sisters' deaths. We also want to share information about safety measures every woman can take and list groups who are working on the issue of violence against women.

In the Black community the murders have often been talked about as solely racial or racist crimes. It's true that the police and media response has been typically racist. It's true that the victims were all Black and that Black people have always been targets of racist violence in this society, but they were also *all women*. Our sisters died *because* they were women just as surely as they died because they were Black. If the murders were only racial, young teen-age boys and older Black men might also have been the unfortunate victims. They might now be petrified to walk the streets as women have always been.

When we look at the statistics and hard facts about daily, socially acceptable violence against women, it's clear it's no "bizarre series of coincidences" that all six victims were female.* In the U.S.A. 1 out of 3 women will be raped in their lifetimes or 1/3 of *all* women in this country; at least 1 woman is beaten by her husband or boyfriend every 18 seconds; 1 out of every 4 women experiences some form of sexual abuse *before* she reaches the age of 18 (child molesting, rape, incest—75% of the time by someone they know and 38% of the time by a family member); 9 out of 10 women in a recent survey had received unwanted sexual advances and harassment at their jobs.† Another way to think about these figures is that while you have been reading this pamphlet a woman somewhere in this country has been beaten, raped and even murdered.

These statistics apply to all women: Black, white, Hispanic, Asian, Native American, old, young, rich, poor and in between. We've got to understand that violence against us as women cuts across all racial, ethnic and class lines. This doesn't mean that violence against Third World women does not have a racial as well as sexual cause. Both our race and sex lead to violence against us.

One reason that attacks on women are so widespread is that to keep us down, to keep us oppressed we have to be made afraid. Violence makes us feel powerless and also like we're second best.

The society also constantly encourages the violence through the media: movies, pornography, *Playboy, Players, Hustler, JET,* record covers, advertisements and disco songs ("Put Love's Chains Back On Me"). Boys and men get the message every day that it's all right, even fun, to hurt women. What has happened in Boston's Black community is a thread in the fabric of violence against women.

Another idea that has been put out in this crisis is that women should stay in the house until the murderer(s) are found. In other words Black women should be under house arrest. However, Daryal Hargett, the fifth woman killed, was found dead in her own apartment. If and when they catch the murderers we still won't be safe to leave our houses, because it has never been safe to be a woman alone in the street. Staying in the house punishes the innocent and

Boston Globe, April 1, 1979, p. 16.
†Statistics from the paper "Grass Roots Services for Battered Women: A Model for Long Term Change" by Lisa Leghorn. Available from the U.S. Commission on Civil Rights, Washington, D.C.

protects the guilty. It also doesn't take into account real life, that we must go to work, get food, pick up the kids at school, do the wash, do errands and visit friends. Women should be able to walk outside whenever they please, with whoever they please and for whatever reason.

WE WILL ONLY HAVE THIS RIGHT WHEN WOMEN JOIN TOGETHER TO DEMAND OUR RIGHTS AS HUMAN BEINGS TO BE FREE OF PHYSICAL ABUSE, TO BE FREE OF FEAR.

The last idea we want to respond to is that it's men's job to protect women. At first glance this may seem to make sense, but look at the assumptions behind it. Needing to be protected assumes that we are weak, helpless and dependent, that we are victims who need men to protect us from other men. As women in this society we are definitely at risk as far as violence is concerned but WE HAVE TO LEARN TO PROTECT OURSELVES. There are many ways to do this: learning and following common

LNS

sense safety measures, learning self-defense, setting up phone chains and neighborhood safe-houses, joining and working in groups that are organizing against violence against women are all ways to do this.

The idea of men protecting us isn't very realistic because many of us don't have a man to depend upon for this—young girls, teen-agers, single women, separated and divorced women, lesbians, widowed women and elderly women. And even if we do have a man he cannot be our shadow 24 hours a day.

What men can do to "protect" us is to check out the ways in which they put down and intimidate women in the streets and at home, to stop being verbally and physically abusive to us and to tell men they know who mistreat women to stop it and stop it quick. Men who are committed to stopping violence against women should start *seriously* discussing this issue with other men and organizing in supportive ways.

We decided to write this pamphlet because of our outrage at what has happened to 6 Black women and to thousands and thousands of women whose names we don't even know. As Black women who are feminists we are struggling against all racist, sexist, heterosexist and class oppression. We know that we have no hopes of ending this particular crisis and violence against women in our community until we identify *all* of its causes, including sexual oppression.

misleading impression, we don't wear martial arts uniforms in self-defense classes. We find that women are more able to identify with us, are more open and less afraid to question us because of this policy.

Chimera doesn't offer classes in one set location; our instructors travel to classes throughout the state. This often puts us in touch with women who have not been exposed to a feminist perspective regarding self-defense. Unlike our feminist students who are psychologically prepared to fight back and just want to know *how*, these women also want to know *why*. They don't think they'd be able to defend themselves, and they really don't feel they have the *right* to fight back. Both do equally well learning the physical skills, but some are hampered psychologically because they believe the following myths about self-defense:

Self-Defense Myths

"I can just talk my way out of an attack."
Experts who suggest that women are magically able to come up with just the right words to discourage a potential rapist are also the first to tell her she's too inept even to consider fighting. They say if talking doesn't work, she is free to "try anything," but trying anything when you know nothing is not a viable option.

The underlying message is that a woman should talk her way out of an attack because the rapist is probably really a nice guy who was led on by something she said or did, and she should find a way to put him off nicely. Fortunately, more women are becoming unwilling to use so-called "feminine wiles"—passivity, flattery, trickery and deceit—as their only means of defense.

"I couldn't bring myself to hurt someone."
Women may be worried that their only option in fighting back is to cause permanent damage or to kill, or they may be squeamish about a particular technique such as gouging eyes. Self-defense is not limited to maiming and killing techniques and there is a whole range of less harmful responses that women can use. For instance, they can thrust the heel of their hand into the attacker's nose instead of gouging his eyes; or stomping on his instep and kick his shins, instead of kicking to the knee. Generally the attacker would prefer to leave with a minor injury rather than to stick around and risk a more serious one.

When women say they don't want to hurt someone, they are often thinking about a specific individual such as an ex-boyfriend

Magazine on Ending Violence Against Women

From *Aegis*, Winter/Spring 1980, pp. 19-24

Chimera: Self Defense for Women

by Sue Gould and G. C. Guard

This issue, Kuchi-Waza News is happy to welcome Chimera. Chimera is a group in Chicago, Il. organized in response to the needs of women for self-empowering self-defense. Chimera has grown; there are now

"Chimera's" located in cities in several other states.

Chimera, Inc., Self-Defense for Women was founded in 1976 by Andra Medea, co-author of *Against Rape*. Its purpose is to develop a standardized self-defense curriculum and to train feminist self-defense teachers. We teach a twelve-hour basic course and a twelve-hour advanced course, and we have teachers in Illinois, Indiana, Arizona, Minnesota, Texas and Kentucky.

We encourage students to take up one of the martial arts after our course, and all of our instructors are required to be proficient in one or more of the martial arts. But because we don't want to create a or their boss, and for these men they might feel badly resorting to the more disagreeable blows. However, we ask them to think of a truly brutal rapist, such as the man who chopped off a 15-year-old girl's arms when visualizing the use of more destructive tactics.

Often a woman can avoid an attack altogether, just by taking the standard precautions of making sure she's not being followed and checking her car before getting in. She can discourage many a would-be attacker by her confident, alert manner and assertive behavior.

"I'm not strong enough to defend myself against a really strong man."

Women sometimes visualize a rapist as a man of incredible size and strength, with a bodybuilder's physique. However, most men who attack women are of normal size and proportions. They look like the neighbor across the hall, your boss, or your ex-boyfriend because they are. But even a small woman attacked by a large, powerful man has the option of fighting, because self-defense is not a matter of strength; it relies on speed, timing and accuracy.

Men have more muscle in their upper body than women, but all that really means is that men are bigger, and more weight equals more force. No matter how hard he tries, a man cannot make his eyes, throat, nose, knees or testicles big and strong, and almost every woman has enough strength to strike to these areas.

Newswoman Mary Laney has just finished her report on self-defense featuring a Chimera class. The anchormen smile indulgently and ask her if she could break some man's knees. They look like they're expecting her to say, "Oh, no, *I* couldn't do *that*!" and to smile, but instead she stares at them evenly and says, "Yes I could, if provoked."

"I'd be caught by surprise and would freeze and forget everything."

Women who freeze and forget everything probably didn't know any defense in the first place. It is unreasonable to expect an untrained woman in an attack situation to do something she has never learned and never practiced. Women who go to the trouble of taking a self-defense course want to learn and remember the techniques, and they do. Women who have thought about how they would respond in an attack are better prepared to defend themselves than

women who have never thought about it at all.

Most attacks are not surprise attacks; they are planned, and usually something leads up to or precedes the attack. Every woman we know who has been attacked has told us that a warning signal went off in her head beforehand. She may not have known what to do or even what exactly was wrong, but she knew that something was out of place; something was wrong with the situation and she felt incredibly uncomfortable and uneasy.

"If I struggle, he'll only hurt me worse."

There is a fundamental and distinct difference between struggling and fighting. Ineffectual flailing, hitting and pleading will not harm him and will feed into his sense of power (the typical media stereotype of the helpless woman beating on his chest). Actual fighting techniques such as breaking the kneecap and jabbing the windpipe will leave him disabled and in pain, not angry.

No man is invulnerable to pain. Even if he is high on drugs or alcohol and temporarily immune to pain, he will not be able to walk away with a dislocated kneecap; he will not be able to see if *his* eyes have been gouged.

The counterpart to "he'll-only-hurt-me-worse" is usually heard in this form from the police: "He was *only* going to rape (rob) her, she screamed (hit him) and made him angry. She *forced* him to hurt her." Surely a woman with the power to control her attacker's response would be able to get him to leave her alone in the first place. Women who are told to worry about what he *might* do, need to be able to deal with what he *is* doing.

"I was expecting a man to teach the class!"

In some of our classes, we've been greeted with "You're the teacher? But you're a woman!" Many women automatically assume that the course will be taught by a man and even some of the women who know a woman will be

---

We are outside. One woman has stayed to punch and kick the bag before we put it in the car (the dummy has a heart, arms and legs). She is energetically and correctly striking as a passing male stops to observe. He draws the only conclusion possible: "Gee, you sure must hate men."

---

teaching the course expect us to at least look and act like a man and be large, musclebound and authoritarian.

Perhaps the theory is that men would have more insights into the motivations of rapists, or would know the best way to defend against a man, but this isn't true. Currently, most men who teach self-defense to women have no real insights, typically view rapists as deranged psychotics (certainly not like someone similar in attitude to themselves), and ignore or belittle women's concerns with the jeers, whistles, grabs and other sexual harassment that women face daily.

Besides the fact that men never experience the sexual harassment that women do, most men have no concept of what it's like to be a smaller, weaker person, and many of their defenses rely on physical strength. Men also tend to go for a flashy technique where a simple one would suffice. Because all our instructors are of fairly average build, women find it easy to identify with us; they know that if a technique works for us, it will probably work for them.

Consciousness-Raising Techniques

Before we teach the physical skills, we start by telling women they still have the option of giving up and submitting. We're not taking that option away or saying that because you have taken our self-defense course, you must fight to the death (but if you do, make sure it's his). What we want them to do is add the option of fighting. Some women don't expect to learn physical defenses from our course: they assume that we will give them the standard "defenses": don't go out after dark, don't go out alone, don't use public transportation.

Women develop their own survival skills and strategies, but they may not recognize them as such. One woman has always looked at reflections in windows to make sure she isn't being followed. Another woman once screamed at a man who was harassing her but then felt guilty about it. In class, these women's reactions were supported, and they discovered they weren't being paranoid or overreacting, as they had believed.

Women role-play the part of a male harasser with uncanny accuracy. They surprise themselves with how well they all know the come-ons and lines. They spontaneously applaud each other's efforts and give encouragement to the progress made by their sisters. We celebrate small as well as large victories: the quiet student

WORKIN' WOMEN

CRAP INC BOSS — DO WHAT *I* TELL YOU!

CRAP INC BOSS — THIS JOB IS A DRAG I NEED ROMANCE! SLAM!

YOU'RE MY WOMAN SO DO WHAT... *I* TELL YOU!

Bülbül/LNS

who makes her first real yell, a 75-year-old woman who successfully breaks out of a wrist grab, and the woman who reports that she no longer lets her boss paw her. For many women, the Chimera class is their first consciousness-raising experience with a womens' group.

To prepare themselves mentally, we ask women to do the following:

We ask women to deal with the "little rapes." Women who may not have ever been the victim of an attack may find role-playing more difficult than someone who has. However, all women have been bothered by come-ons at work and whistles and cat-calls on the street. If they can take control in these situations, they will have a better chance of fighting off a more aggressive attack.

We ask women to confront their fears. By physically or mentally acting out a fearful situation, each woman can experiment with a whole range of tactics in a safe environment. One group of women in a college dormitory was concerned that an attacker could hide behind the washers in their laundry room. By acting out the situation, they found it was far too difficult to fit behind the machines, and impossible for someone to jump out and catch them by surprise.

We ask women to think of themselves first. Women paralyzed by fear ask themselves questions with no answers: "What will my boyfriend do? What will my parents think? Why is he doing this? Why is this happening to me?" Since hers are the only actions she does have control over, a short, assertive formula—"How do *I* feel? What do *I* want?"—can help her decide what to do.

We ask women to replace destructive

stereotypes. Women on TV and in the movies almost never defend themselves competently. We ask women to mentally rewrite the fate of the helpless woman, and develop a scenario where the woman acts competently to protect herself. We ask them to put themselves in the same role and see themselves reacting correctly.

We demand that women be positive about themselves. Women who say "I can't kick!" after only two attempts are not being fair with themselves. Women who have practiced a kick forty times never tell us they can't do it. Practice always works, and improvement comes with repetition. They may not be able to kick powerfully or to their own satisfaction, but they can kick. We ask them to say instead, "I didn't do *that* kick well." or "My kick isn't very strong *yet*." or "I didn't get this the *last time* I tried it."

Physical Techniques

We use a variety of physical exercises to let women test their abilities. We don't use all of these in every class, but these are the ones that have proven to be most effective to show women what they've learned.

Yelling. Yelling scares the attacker, alerts other people to your predicament, starts your adrenalin going, and makes your strikes and kicks more powerful. A loud *"Kia"* (yell) will tighten the abdominal muscles and take a lot of the pain away from a blow to the stomach. Some women are just not comfortable with yelling and need practice. Many women are physically unable to give a good yell because they are breathing too shallowly and don't have enough air in their lungs to begin with. Taking several deep breaths rushes oxygen to the brain, so a woman can think more

clearly and have the necessary air to expel a commanding yell.

We have women yell when they are grabbed so they can see the startling effect this can have on an attacker. We also sometimes have the women playing the attackers yell as they grab, so that women learn not to be intimidated just because someone raises his voice to them.

Creative hold-breaking. After we've demonstrated how to get out of the standard grabs and holds (chokes from behind, bear hugs, wrist grabs, etc.), we sometimes have women in the class who still think there might be some way they can be grabbed that they don't know about—a position in which they would be totally helpless. We invite them to try. The defender must let herself be grabbed, and the attacker can be as outrageous and inventive as she wishes. The defender's first reaction may be an unproductive maneuver, but she quickly finds a workable solution. And if she doesn't the attacker—who is uncomfortably aware of how vulnerable *she* is—can help her out.

Unless they've already tried it, we can have each woman grab her partner in a bear hug and lift her off the ground. Women who have done well defending themselves when their feet were on the ground are sometimes at a loss when they are up in the air. They soon find, though, that even if they must change the angle of a blow or kick, the attacker remains as vulnerable as before—sometimes even more so.

Blind attacks. This exercise helps to convince women that they won't be totally helpless if they are grabbed in the dark, have their glasses knocked off, or are taken completely by surprise. The defender stands in a defensive position, hands up to block, in a front stance ready to kick. The attacker circles her, quickly and lightly touching her at random while keeping up a running flow of conversation (preferably something to put the defender in the mood to kick: "Hey honey, how about a little kiss?" or "You're so cute when you're mad!"). The defender pivots to always face the attacker and can block and kick at will, but she must do all of this *with her eyes closed.* It is the attacker's responsibility to avoid being kicked.

Unbendable arm. In this aikido* exercise, a woman resists having her arm bent first by tensing and using physical force and then by relaxing and using her inner strength. Many women delightedly try this

---

*A particular martial arts style.

on their male friends who refuse to believe that relaxing the muscles can be more effective than tensing them.

Breaking boards. It takes a high degree of skill in the martial arts to be able to break several boards at once, from any position and with any part of the body. But any woman has the ability to break a single board with a front snap kick. And any woman who can break a 1″ thick, 12″

A middle-aged woman stares in disbelief at the board she has just broken easily with a kick. "My husband told me I couldn't do it," she says. "I told him we were going to break a board in this class and he said 'Well *you'll* never do it.' (pause) I can't believe I did it."

square pine board could also easily break a kneecap.

Fear of rape prevents women from fully participating in society. Women are not free to live, work, attend school or conduct their social lives when and where they choose. Chimera believes that self-defense is a way for women to take control of their own lives.

You can write to Chimera at 37 S. Wabash, Chicago, IL 60603.

"The name Chimera (ki-mere-a) is that of an awesome female mythical beast whose name has come to be associated with an imaginary fear. While women's fears of attack are far from imaginary, the fear that they are helpless to defend their own security is one which Chimera is dedicated to defeat."

racist and elitist state would do with the expanded powers of suppression which we feminists might give to them.

By asking that violent pornography be made illegal through government legislation, we end up with a strategy that pits us against the very people who by rights should be our allies. Civil libertarians, political progressives and many people of color have had long histories of fighting against government repression, and while often the First Amendment did little to protect them, still, they oppose any expansion of the state's power to suppress ideas. Not only would we be fighting our potential friends, but ironically, we would most likely be supported by the reactionary Right. The Right doubtless would support banning pornography, as it has supported banning obscenity, banning dissemination of abortion information, banning sex education, and banning open advocacy of lesbian/gay rights. The Right is all for banning ideas. Does anyone really believe that we could safely stop at violent pornography once we let the government start banning?

Our power is better spent by directing it against the pornographers in our own communities. We should use our own First Amendment freedoms to speak out, organize, picket, demonstrate, and demand that merchants not sell violent pornography, that theatre owners not show woman-hating films, and that men not purchase such materials or patronize such events.

By working at the grassroots level to expose and eliminate the woman-hatred within our culture, we can build a strong feminist movement which may one day eliminate sexism from our society.

From *Newspage* 4, no. 5 (May 1980): 4

Choosing a Strategy to Fight Pornography

by Jill Lippitt

The First Amendment prevents the government from suppressing ideas. While we as individuals have a Constitutional right to picket a pornographic theatre and attempt to close it down, the First Amendment prevents the government from taking sides. Any legislation against violent pornography constitutes state action to suppress the woman-hating ideas within it. Since the First Amendment clearly prohibits this kind of government action, the only way to get around it legally is to argue that violent pornography should be seen as a special exception which is not lawfully entitled to protection from government interference by the First Amendment.

A great deal of impressive work has been done by feminist legal scholars who are interested in developing just such a legal exception, or theory, which would allow the government to ban violent pornography. To me this begs the basic strategic

question of whether or not it is in our real long-term interest to legitimate an expansion of the state's power to suppress unpopular ideas. If we work to erode the historically broad protections of the First Amendment, are we prepared for the consequences as other interest groups argue, for example: that since abortion advocacy is inherently dangerous to the lives of the unborn, abortion pamphlets should be banned as an exception to the First Amendment, as well. While I am firmly convinced of the righteousness of our arguments against pornography, I simply do not trust what the patriarchal,

From *off our backs* 10, no. 10 (November 1980): 3-4

'Dressed to Kill' Protested in Six Cities

by Tacie Dejanikus

The first day the ad in the *Pittsburgh Press* for the movie "Dressed to Kill" said: "What happens to Kate in the shower is the latest fashion in murder." The second day the ad read: "What happens to Liz in the elevator is the latest fashion in murder." On the third day it said: "What happens to Bobbi in the apartment is the latest fashion in murder." Next, as reported in their newsletter, members of the Pittsburgh Women Against Sexist Violence in Pornography and Media tried to place an ad that read: "Bomb scares are the latest fashion in theaters showing violence against women." The *Press* refused the ad on the grounds it might lead to an increase in bomb scares and that then someone might get hurt.

In Rochester, N.Y., members of the independent Women Against Violence Against Women (WAVAW) held a "die-in" at two suburban theaters showing the film. Several women, dressed in torn clothes and covered with slash marks made with red grease pens and black eyeliner would scream and lie down as other members threw a blood-like rose water and red dye mixture over them. At least ten men, during four weeks of protest beginning October 1, told the women, 'That's right, I am a rapist,' Maria Scipione, of WAVAW, told *off our backs*.

In San Francisco, Los Angeles, New York City, and Boston, feminists coordinated for the first time a national picket against the $6.5 million-budget "Dressed to Kill." Women Against Violence Against Women (WAVAW) in Los Angeles, Women Against Violence in Pornography and Media (WAVPM), and Women Against Pornography (WAP) in New York City arranged to hold simultaneous pickets on August 28. The Los Angeles protest was held August 16th because the movie was scheduled to leave and the Boston demonstration occurred the week of August 18th.

Feminists chose to protest "Dressed to Kill" "because we wanted to get across a feminist viewpoint," Dorchen Leidholdt, of WAP said in an interview with *off our backs*. The three groups are opposed to censorship, respect First Amendment strictures against the imposition of prior restraint on any form of speech, and are opposed to general prohibitions of the production, distribution, and display of pornographic materials. Feminists condemned the movie's making violence against women appear erotic, the extensive sexist advertising that affected non-movie goers as well, and the enthusiastic response by respectable critics.

Feminists also protested the movie, Bridget Wynne of WAVPM told *off our backs,* "because some of the rapes and murders are portrayed as women's fantasies, the film shows a member of a sexual minority (a transvestite) as the murderer, and because the film takes situations in which women are genuinely frightened such as deserted subways and makes this

fear look glamorous." This is the third time recently that a movie showed a murderer as other than the usual assailant, a heterosexual male. In "Cruising" the killer was a gay male and in "Windows," a lesbian.

The racism in the film was also objected to. The WAP flyer pointed out that "black men are presented as sociopathic rapists and cops who are in collusion with rapists."

The WAP flyer describes the opening scene of the movie, written and directed by Brian De Palma and produced by Filmways, Inc. This scene "shows a naked Kate Miller played by Angie Dickinson, photographed in a steamy shower, suddenly hoisted up by her crotch, a hand slapped across her mouth, her face twisted in anguish, screaming as she is raped by a stranger from behind. Vincent Canby, the movie critic of the *New York Times,* called this "the sexy, comic opening sequence." (See review on this page.)* As it turns out, this scene is the woman's fantasy. De Palma ("Sisters," "The Fury," "Carrie") said that "This movie is basically about a woman's erotic fantasy life and it's got to be shocking on some levels and the fantasy I'm dealing with—being forcibly attacked by a faceless stranger is very prevalent, not something I dreamed up." On the contrary, "The film is a gigantic male sexual fantasy, not about women's eroticism," Leidholdt said.

Many critics agreed with De Palma about the film's erotic qualities. Gary Arnold in the *Washington Post* called it "a

---

*[Dorchen Leidholdt, "Review: A Closer Look at 'Dressed to Kill,'" *off our backs* 10, no. 10 (November 1980): 3.—eds., *Alternative Papers.*]

triumph of seductively prolonged suspense and tantalizing, glamorous pictorial invention . . . [the director's] elaborate, sensuous orchestration doesn't deny the audience sensational payoffs." David Denby in *New York* magazine called it "the first great American movie of the eighties . . . violent, erotic, and wickedly funny . . . the violence of this movie . . . leaves one exhilarated rather than shaken." Sheila Benson, in the *Los Angeles Times,* wrote glowingly, of this "sustained work of terror—elegant, sensual, erotic, bloody, a directorial tour de force . . . it is even better the second time." Andrew Sarris of the *Village Voice* initially wrote a review criticizing the film for being too derivative of Alfred Hitchcock's "Psycho." After the New York City demonstration, he wrote a second review saying "women have every right to hate 'Dressed to Kill' if they can take it seriously enough." San Francisco reviews labelled the violence in the movie as glamorous and erotic.

According to a critical but non-feminist article by Robert Moss in the October issue of *Saturday Review,* De Palma is the most popular of four contemporary U.S. film directors who form a "new breed of brutalist directors." The other three are Martin Scorsese ("Taxi Driver," "Mean Streets"), Paul Schrader ("Blue Collar," "Hardcore," and "American Gigolo"), and Walter Hill ("The Warriors"). These directors view the city as a "pit of vice, grimly polluted and inhabited by the worst kinds of predators and human refuse: rapists, murderers, muggers, junkies, weirdos" and see violence "as an inherent part of the urban rhythm." Scorsese, De

I'M TIRED OF HEARING HOW MEN ARE THREATENED.

Palma, and Schrader have had close professional contacts, and Schrader and Hill are friends.

Pauline Kael, the *New Yorker's* highly esteemed movie reviewer, is one of this group's most feverent supporters. She has hailed De Palma as a "master sadist," celebrating his "persistent adolescent kinkiness," "his delight in trashiness," and "his blissfully dirty mind." Not only are women critics doing men's dirty work for them, but also the actress, Angie Dickinson, representing a totally male-identified view of women, perpetuates men's lies. Talking about the exclusion of two graphic throat cuttings and some below-the-waist nudity in order to get the film an R- rather than an X-rating, Dickinson says, "I would love to have seen my character, Kate Miller, get it in the throat. Kate was *such* a bore." The X-rated version was shown to New York City critics, is reported to be making the rounds of Beverly Hills private screening rooms and will be shown abroad.

While De Palma's "Dressed to Kill" can be seen as part of this "brutalist school," it is also part of a trend in recent horror movies made by lesser known and less "technically brilliant" directors. According to the movie critic for the *Chicago Tribune*, Gene Siskel, these types of films, linked by their brutal attacks on women, have been increasing. The women in these films are "either sexually repressed or liberated and the more liberated, the more intense are the rape scenes," Andrena Zawinski, of the Pittsburgh Women Against Sexist Violence In Pornography and Media, told *off our backs*. One of the first in this trend was the 1973 "The Last House on the Left" which grossed tens of millions of dollars and tells the story of two teen-age girls who hitchhike to a rock concert against their parent's warning and are soon attacked by slobbering rapists. The next film, "Halloween," was even more succesful. "Halloween" is about a killer who attacks three young and often lightly-clad baby sitters. The killer is a sexually frustrated young man, who initially "went crazy" after seeing his promiscuous sister making love to her boyfriend. Many similar movies followed this hit: "Friday the 13th," "Prom Night," "He Knows You're Alone" (a thriller about a maniac who spurned by his bride-to-be stabs other brides-to-be to death), "I Spit on Your Grave" (the victim who is repeatedly raped by three men is an independent young woman who leaves her Park Avenue apartment for a summer of writing in a New England cottage. She is

attacked after we see her sunbathing in a bikini). According to Robert Court, vice-president of Twentieth Century Fox, 45% of the audience for these typically R-rated films are 12-to-17 year-olds.

What "Dressed to Kill" and some of these other films do is "assert that women crave physical abuse, that humiliation, pain and brutality are essential to our sexuality," as stated in the WAP flyer, but some people think these are just bad movies.

off our backs

From *off our backs* 10, no. 7 (July 1980): 10

Sexist Ads in Ms.

by Tacie Dejanikus

New York. *Ms.* magazine received over 800 complaints in response to an ad in its June issue for Club Cocktails. The ad shows the close up of a young middle-aged woman's face with a tense smile and a come-hither sparkle in her eyes. The caption, in quotes, read "HIT ME WITH A CLUB."

Many of the protest letters included a copy of the ad to go into *Ms.*'s No-Comment section, reserved for sexist advertising from other sources. Courtney Dillon, a sales representative in *Ms.*'s advertising department, said that the ad came very late and didn't go through the usual process before it was sent to the printer. It would have been rejected if *Ms.* had discussed the ad first, she said. In the July issue of *Ms.*, Gloria Steinem, editor, wrote an editorial note about the ad.

Dillon said that *Ms.* does reject some ads such as a Maidenform bra ad that the agency wouldn't change. *Ms.* also rejected an ad for stockings that said "Gentlemen Prefer Hains." Another time *Ms.* told a jewelry advertiser that an ad with the word "girl" would lead to complaints from readers if it weren't changed. The ad stayed as it was and there were complaints.

While the Club ad involved a double entendre with a message of violence against women (although Courtney Dillon believed it was intended as a double entendre from card playing), other ads in the *Ms.* June 1980 issue were also sexist. In a letter sent to *Ms.* and *off our backs*, Monique

Koller complained about an ad on pg. 43 that is for a drink called "Zombie." The headlines are "He made me a Zombie." Koller also mentioned an ad for "Alba '77," a low calorie drink, on pg. 66, that shows a slender woman in very short red shorts with her leg up. Her crotch is near the center of the picture and her head is completely hidden by a glass of the chocolate drink. On pg. 22 a Wolfschmidt Vodka ad shows a woman with a dress falling off her breasts leaning against the Czar?, a man, the copy tells us, "who stood like a giant among men . . . who could bend an iron bar on his bare knee. Crush a silver ruble with his fist. He had a thirst for life like no other man alive." On pg. 41 an ad for diet 7-up has a man tell a woman to "Just smile, Lynda, I'll do the talking." She has made a statement about the drink and asked the man for confirmation, a common male-female interaction.

Courtney Dillon said that *Ms.* has received letters complaining of sexist advertising before, including a criticism of a Leggs ad for stockings. The ad said "Nothing beats a great pair of Leggs." Dillon didn't think that was sexist. "It depends on who is saying it and what it's about," she said. "There are no men in the ad saying that and it's a product that can make you feel better, not sexy."

She is upset when women put their energy into protesting *Ms.*'s advertising when they could put some energy into "the major issues discussed in *Ms.* articles." She also mentioned that *Ms.* has been a leader in getting ads that are not considered women's products, like cameras and cars, when companies and ad agencies initially strongly resisted. "Ads pay for publishing the magazine," she added.

When asked how often *Ms.* refuses ads or asks agencies to change ads, Dillon said that most people just won't give us advertising that is sexist. "It's a slow process of educating assholes."

Because *Ms.* is perceived as a feminist publication, it has a special obligation to pay as careful attention to its ads as to its articles. We all know the powerful but often subtle impact of ads. Much of the advertising in the June and earlier issues of *Ms.* uses images and messages that have kept women oppressed for centuries. Women as sex objects, women as crazy, women as less than men. The ads often contradict the message of *Ms.*'s articles. There were ads in the June issue that weren't inherently sexist (without discussing the usefulness of certain products, prices, etc.), but one sexist ad in a feminist magazine is inexcusable. *Ms.* must make sure that its employees understand the many nuances of sexism so that they can more vigorously reject sexist advertising and educate advertisers. However, it would be naive to assume that the editorial staff doesn't recognize the "soft" sexism of much of *Ms.*'s advertising and that they don't knowingly make serious compromises.

system of profit which benefits the few and the system of male domination which benefits men (though it benefits men of different classes in different ways) if we hope to unknot these bonds on women in both the home and market.

In order to get a better understanding of how the ideologies of patriarchy and capitalism reinforce each other, let us look at the following diagram.

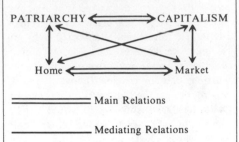

———— Main Relations

———— Mediating Relations

From *Women* 6, no. 3
(April 1979): 64-66

How Patriarchy & Capitalism Affect Women's Work

by Natalie Sokoloff, Baltimore

The "working woman" is the symbol of the 1970's. Well over one-half (59%) of all women in the U.S. between the ages of 18 and 64 were employed in 1978. This is in sharp contrast to the expected employment patterns of women in other periods of our history.

But while the number of women in paid work has increased dramatically, women have continued to be employed in typically "female" or sex segregated jobs—lower status and lower paying. Add to this the fact that the GAP between women's and men's wages has steadily INCREASED over the last three decades (from 64¢ in 1955 to 59¢ in 1975 earned by a woman employed full-time, year-round compared to a dollar earned by a man so employed) and it becomes evident that the "progress" of the "working woman" is nothing to write home about.

How can we reconcile woman's rising employment rate with her increasingly disadvantaged position in the labor market? Dr. Elizabeth Koontz in her recent speech to the Southeast Regional Conference on the National Commission on Working Women suggested two possible

reasons for the continued poor position of women:

• First, an "invisible shield" of sex role stereotypes and myths about women, which women have internalized; and

• second, the "brick wall" of sex discrimination.

Located immediately behind the "invisible shield" of sexist ideology and its debilitating images of women is a "not-so-invisible brick wall called sex discrimination." By sex discrimination, Koontz means the system of sex-segregated jobs and lower-paid job classifications reserved for women.

Behind both the shield and the brick wall, I would add, is a larger, even more recalcitrant structure which keeps women in their place, a system built of the interrelated forces of patriarchy and capitalism which reinforce each other in both home and market. These are the economic ties which bind women so tightly. It is necessary to change both the

Women Working Full-time and Year-round Earn Less than Men and the Gap between Men and Women is Increasing

Annual Median Income

	Women	Men	Women's income as a percentage of men's
1955	$2,719	$ 4,252	63.9%
1960	3,293	5,417	60.8
1965	3,823	6,375	60.0
1970	5,403	9,104	59.4
1975	7,504	12,758	58.8

(Source: Adapted from U.S. Department of Labor, Bureau of Labor Statistics: *U.S. Working Women: A Databook*, 1977.)

The idea that patriarchal attitudes, which keep women in the home dutifully performing "women's work," benefit capitalism is not a new one. But having women primarily responsible for the production and reproduction of housework and childcare services in the home is profitable not only to capital but also to the individual men who are their husbands. In the former instance, capital gets women's labor in the home free when it pays wages to the women's husbands; then it gets a woman's labor cheap when she herself enters the work place. Capitalism is therefore provided with a "safety valve," whereby men, angered and alienated by what happens to them on the job, take out their feelings on women and children in individual homes, rather than on capital itself. In this way, worker discontent is dissipated and worker stability ensured. But the fact remains that individual men are vouchsafed an arena—the home—to assert their privilege and domination, as well as to have someone take care of their needs. In our society, every worker needs a housewife, but only male workers get them.

The capitalist class benefits most from this system—through the super profits they make from women's exploited labor and the divisiveness created between men and women in a sex-segregated market. On the other hand, individual working class and middle class men also benefit from the higher wages and better jobs they gain because women do the low waged, less desirable work on the job; men don't really have to compete with women for status and achievement, and their jobs usually give them power over women. Thus the very structure of the job market serves to create

EVER NOTICE WHEN THE ECONOMY COOLS DOWN ... WE GET THE FREEZE OUT!

Bülbül/LNS

greater patriarchal privilege for men on the job as well as strengthen the sexist attitudes which such privilege engenders. This inferior position helps to tie women to their traditional roles and self concepts both on the job and at home.

This continued wage inequity acts as another force to strengthen the patriarchal leverage that men have over women in the home. Maintaining women as "secondary workers" (even when they are the head of household) keeps them in unstable, marginal, low-paid employment and insures their continued financial dependence on their men. Thus, while it has been correctly argued that encouraging women to work in waged labor is potentially liberating, the miserably low wage is not sufficient to give the economic security and independence necessary to cut the knot of domination at home; it only recreates patriarchal benefits on the job and reinforces patriarchal control in the home.

Motherwork

Aside from this general pattern of mutual reinforcement between capitalism and patriarchy, there are a number of specific ways in which these two forces interact. One of these is in the area of "motherwork."

The limitations placed on women by their biological and social role as mothers has perhaps been the most widely accepted reason for women's disadvantaged job position. It is not simply the fact that women "mother" that is the problem, however; women have always "mothered." The main problem is the form and nature of mothering that was created for modern industrial society. The ideology and organization of motherhood in our society is very much a product of the relations between patriarchy and capitalism as they

have developed since the mid-to late-1900s in this country.

The definition of women as full-time wives/mothers/homemakers emerged among the wives and daughters of entrepreneurs and merchant capitalists in the northeastern U.S. during the twentieth century. Prior to this time, all members of the pre-industrial family worked at home, either in agriculture or in some form of domestic production. To be sure, men's and women's work in the home was divided upon sex lines. But it was only when the personal world of the home was separated off from the social, more powerful world of "paid work" for men that the institution of motherhood as we understand it today emerged.

A mass production society (developing in the monopoly capitalist period between 1890-1920) required a method to ensure mass consumption. Full-time housewives became an integral part of that process. Children were no longer producers, as they had been in pre-industrial, agricultural times. Moreover, while children had been employed along with adult men and women in the very early stages of the industrial revolution, this increased pool of workers had lowered men's wages. This situation led to efforts by owners of industry and unions in the 19th and 20th centuries to make market work "men's" work and home work "women's" work, efforts which resulted in protective legislation, child labor laws, intensified sex segregation of the labor force, and the creation of the family wage.

The exclusion of children from the workplace resulted in new difficulties in training and supervising them. Someone was needed to inculcate into children the discipline and ideology required of society's next generation of workers by the hierarchical social relations of the developing industrial society. Both men and capital chose women to do this work: women would work in the home without any direct financial remuneration; women would be economically dependent on the wages of their husbands for their own and for their children's economic survival. This set-up was to be made possible through the establishment of the "family wage"—a wage sufficient to allow the women to stay home, raise children and maintain the family, rather than having all members of the family out at work" (Zaretsky, 1978).

It was most of all, then, women's socially designated role as child*rearer* that allowed her to be put and kept in the home. The

elements of this new ideology, all too familiar to us by now, asserted as "natural fact" that

- children required full-time, undivided adult attention
- women were particularly endowed by nature to provide this care
- retirement to the home would not only shield women from the evils of the outside world, but would also bring them certain rewards.

This comparatively new definition of women's work is crucial in determining what happens to women in the labor market today. Before we can explore this idea in more detail, however, we need a clearer understanding of the work that is mothering. Jessie Bernard (1974) has coined the word "motherwork" to describe the hard, difficult, joyful, tiring, boring, exciting, UNPAID WORK women do in their social roles as mothers. In addition to the total emotional and physical care of children and husbands, "motherwork" includes the teaching of attitudes and values to the next generation of home and market workers. It can be said to consist of several different and interconnected features. Bernard specifically identifies these as (1) *mothering*—which consists of the emotional and physical care of infants and children: touching, rocking, soothing, smiling, feeding, teaching, playing, disciplining, etc.; and (2) *added housework*—the extra cooking, cleaning, laundering, shopping, sewing, driving, etc. necessitated by care for children. (It has been estimated that housework with no children consists of 1000 hours of work per year. With a child over six, this figure increases to 1500 hours per year; with a child under six, hours increase to 2000. There are only 8736 hours in a year.)

It is as an extension of this "motherwork" that women enter the job market; when they go into waged labor, they go as MOTHERS. This may be understood in at least the following ways:

1. Most importantly, women are motivated to enter the labor market in order to fulfill their duty as mothers in the home—to secure money to purchase goods and services no longer produced in the home;

2. Once in the labor market, women—all women—are treated as mothers—former, actual, or potential;

3. As paid market workers, women continue to do "mothering" on the job.

Let us explore each of these in turn.

Cindy Fredrick/LNS

On the "Spot"

Women enter the labor market to buy the goods and services they need in their role as mothers. Bernard argues, "Labor force participation is mainly a different kind of motherwork; it provides college for grown sons and daughters and even help in establishing themselves." Just as industrial capitalism pushed out of the home goods that had once been produced there by women, monopoly capitalism has now pushed services out also. Education, healthcare, nursing, psychotherapy, baby-sitting, food preparation, clothing, shoes, laundering—all now have to be purchased in the market with wages. Women must now sell their labor power to fulfill their responsibility as mothers.

A second major consequence of this new construction of mothering is that when women enter the labor market they are treated as mothers—past, actual, or potential. This phenomena is attested to by the increasing literature treating employed women as "working mothers" rather than as "female employees." The old rationalization for not advancing women still holds: if the woman is single or newly married and without children, she will not be given a responsible job with high wages since, it is said, she will probably leave when she has a chance to marry and have children. This *apologia* persists despite the fact that male turnover and absenteeism rates are similar to women's, the crucial difference being that women leave the market for lack of child care or other family services, while men leave a particular job for personal advancement. Men's reasons for leaving are always more acceptable, for men are understood as workers; women, on the other hand, are understood as mothers.

More recently, the charge of women's "instability and unreliability" as workers has abated as it has become economically worthwhile for a company to exploit women as part-time workers. According to a vice-president of the Prudential Insurance Company, which employs 1,000 part-timers in its Newark headquarters:

The thing I've always liked about them (housewives who work part-time) is their stability and conscientiousness toward the work. They really make an effort. The housewives appreciate our efforts to tailor work to their schedules. The advantage is that they are on call, in and out. (Quoted in Jerry Flint, "Growing Part-Time Work Force Has Major Impact on the Economy," The *New York Times,* April 12, 1977.)

Mothers are still cheap labor, but at least mothers of school age children have become reliable.

Secondly, because women are "mothers first" and because men are paid a "family wage," women are always classified as "secondary workers" in the family. This assumption holds true whether the woman is single, a grandmother, married, divorced, or whatever. Being viewed as a mother in a nuclear family rationalizes the low wages of all women all during their life cycle.

As we all know, "motherwork" does not end at home. Women perform such mothering tasks on the job as nurturing, soothing, healing, teaching, and giving sexual comfort and ego support. Even unmarried women with no children of their own must mother men at work. These mothering tasks are sometimes paid for—as nurses, teachers, social workers, etc.—and sometimes expropriated—boosting the bosses ego, making coffee, getting his reports into final shape before typing them, doing housecleaning tasks to help present the boss to the public, etc.

To conclude, the ties that hold women back are the social relations of patriarchy and capitalism and their supporting ideologies, as they operate both at home and on the job. But as smoothly as they seem to mesh, their linkage *can* be broken. For by bringing us into the workplace to exploit us, capitalism and patriarchy expose us to the insights, skills, and relationships by which we may learn to free ourselves. But we must understand the strength and effect of patriarchal ideology and structure as they restrict women not just in the home but on the job as well. Otherwise, we will only be untying one set of knots.

the
second wave

From *The Second Wave* 5, no. 3 (Summer/Fall 1979): 23-30

Towards a Feminist Economics: A Global View

by Kathy Parker and Lisa Leghorn

Throughout the world, there is great variation in the amount of control women exercise over their lives. The political and economic categories which traditional

First printed in *The Second Wave: A Magazine of Ongoing Feminism,* Box 344, Cambridge A, Cambridge, MA 02139. Reprinted with permission. The authors' ideas are expanded in a book which will be published by Routledge and Kegan Paul, London.

theorists broadly define as industrialized, non-socialist Third World, and socialist countries tell us almost nothing about the treatment of women by the major economic and social institutions within each system. These categories, defined by men, refer to the division and organization of resources and power between men. They are inclusive of women only when our work falls under men's spheres.

Such categories are inadequate. They fail to describe female experience of the economies. The active role women have played outside the home in revolutionary China differs strongly from the reabsorption of women into the home in revolutionary China differs strongly from the reabsorption of women into the home in revolutionary Algeria. The anti-sexist legislation in Sweden stands in marked contrast to the strict divisions between men and women in Japanese society, though both are Westernized industrial countries.

Women in the Economy

Analysis of women's work is especially lacking at the international level. Invariably, it begins with abstract generalities which are applied to our lives only insofar as they match biased expectations. "Development" efforts all around the world reflect this bias: access to education, agricultural training and resources are usually made available only to men, even though it is often women who have traditionally done the work involved. This process changes women's roles, as it did in the chrysanthemum-growing areas of Kenya. When agricultural programs designed after a British model paid only for the work performed, the women, who had traditionally done all the cultivating, had to stop.[1]

Each economic system has made certain assumptions on the basis of sex, as well as on sexual preference, race, class, religion, and relative values put on work or time, to determine the distribution of the wealth created. These assumptions may mean that certain people obtain a life of leisure at the cost of others, or that surplus is distributed equally among members of the community. The assumptions about women determine what we are worth economically, and what percentage of social wealth must be allocated to us to maximize production relative to our consumption.

To understand our collective part in the production and consumption of the goods and services that maintain human existence, and to attempt to take control of that process, we must begin with the life experience of women. The consciousness-raising process (which has taken different forms in different societies) allows us to define for ourselves what constitutes work, power, and control, both from personal experiences and the experiences of other women. Through continual comparison with women's experience historically and cross-culturally, feminist theory can incorporate the components that will enable us to act on our analysis.

From this perspective we can see that women receive less remuneration than men for their work in terms of money goods, and leisure time. Universally male appropriation of women's work denies women economic power.

The form this takes differs from society to society. It would be dangerous to compare statistics from different countries on access to abortion or childcare, for example, without also examining their history. We are assuming, though, that a set of institutions within one society can be compared to a set within another, for the purposes of learning under what conditions women can obtain more power over our lives. The valuation of women's fertility, women's access to resources, or the extent of their networks might be examined within the context of each different culture.

We need ways of looking at societies which reflect a woman-centered view of the economy. This would involve categorizing societies according to the degree of power women have within them. We have devised three classifications along a continuum:

1. Societies where women have *minimal power*. They are dominated by men in all areas of life, with no support for women by economic or social institutions in word or deed, and few opportunities for women to share their experiences. We include Japan, Peru, Ethiopia and Algeria here.
2. Societies in which women have *token power*; varying amounts of paid work and access to resources, but little substantial power to affect those institutions in which they participate. The USA, USSR and Cuba fall into this category.
3. Societies where women have some control over their lives, and are supported by institutions within the dominant culture, for example, China, Sweden, or the Ewe of West Africa. We call this *negotiating power*.

In the first category, minimal power, the lack of economic resources available to women combines with powerlessness in the community and the lack of control over their reproductive functions to create barriers in every direction that a woman might turn.

Nowhere is this more clearly exemplified than in Ethiopia, where women enjoy no support. By puberty, every woman has been given a clitoridectomy, and sometimes infibulated (an operation which involves scraping away the outer genitalia, sewing the outer lips of the labia together, leaving only a tiny hole for blood and urine to pass through.) A woman is assigned a husband by her family, often at birth, or kidnapped into marriage if she leaves the family compound alone. The product of her work in the fields, along with that of her co-wives, goes to the hands of her husband and his landlord. Women can earn money carrying water or firewood long distances, but this money buys food or other necessities for their children. Men and male children are fed first, and often enjoy nutritionally superior diets. Women's opportunities to speak to other women are severely limited by the social codes. Men's power over their wives is sustained through the religious and social mores, woman's economic dependence, wife-beating, enforced isolation, repeated pregnancies and malnutrition.[2]

Countries in which token power is given to women may encourage female participation in the labor force, or allow alternative institutions to provide services for women, but such benefits are dependent on the temporal generosity of the male-dominated institutions. Concessions may be given to women to reduce militancy or to make them *think* they are benefitting equally or almost equally in order to gain the full benefit of their productivity. In these societies women still do not have a place within mainstream where they can demand that their needs be met. The recent firing of Bella Abzug as co-chair of the National Advisory Committee for Women graphically illustrated the "prerogative" of those in power to ignore women's demands.

Cuban women were strongly encouraged to take on jobs in fields or factories to aid in the national development process. Cuban ideology changed drastically in order to define this outside work as a desirable woman's role. Many women accepted this new definition, though institutional supports developed slowly. In 1973 only 16% of children with working mothers could be accommodated in spite of expanded family networks and "guerilla day care" organized by rural women. The burden of domestic work still fell squarely on women's shoulders. When it became apparent that they frequently missed work and eventually left their jobs, women's "second shift" was "discovered." Only at this point was a new Family Code enacted, calling for equal participation and responsibility in the home. As one woman put it, "If they're going to incorporate us into the workforce, they're going to have to incorporate themselves into the home, and that's all there is to it."[3] This history serves as a clear example of how women's needs are neglected in a male-dominated society, unless they coincide with men's needs or unless we build a separate power base from which to present our demands.

In no contemporary society do women enjoy equal economic authority or social prerogative with men. However, some cultures, by virtue of unique histories or revolutionary changes in which women actively participated, have developed institutions which afford women some resources of their own, or support mechanisms, including women's networks. These resources help women to survive emotionally and physically, and provide a base from which to fight for further changes.

In traditional Ewe society in West Africa, women were given their own fields when they married, and always had an independent income. Each village had a queen mother who represented the women's interests and participated in the council of elders (otherwise all male). Her role involved everything from helping women with marital problems to organizing a strike of women in the market to achieve particular demands. Today most Ewe women still have independent incomes: 90% of the distribution of wholesale and retail goods in Togo is controlled by women. But though women still look to the queen mother as a source of help, she is decreasingly recognized as a part of the political structure by neo-colonialist regimes.

Development

Within the guidelines of male supremacy, women's status and specifics of life change with the needs of the dominant group (though these may be influenced to a varying extent by the women's needs and demands). Processes such as imperialism and development affect women differently than men, changing the balance of power between them.

In token societies it is especially noticeable that new activity is frequently demanded of women during war and industrial expansion. Then as the needs of the dominant male group change again, the new roles quickly become "unwomanly." In the U.S., popular images such as that of "Rosie the Riveter" were cultivated to encourage women's participation in production during World War II. When the war ended some women never left their skilled jobs, but economic and social pressures slowly forced most back into the home.

Until 1968, there was a childless tax in the U.S.S.R., and abortions and divorces were difficult to obtain. Hero mothers, receiving stars for numbers of children, influenced women's images of themselves as good Soviets. In Sweden many reforms were brought about to break down sex

roles, and provide supportive services to women—at a time when there was a critical male labor shortage.

By contrast, in Moslem-dominated North Africa "development" brought some positive changes for women. These included technological aids, admission to schools, infibulation in hospitals rather than on dirt floors with razor blades and broken bottles, and new family laws. But changes in women's roles have still been limited to those adapted to men's needs.

What Do We Produce and Who Benefits?

When a woman tries to direct her own life, her lack of economic power often makes it nearly impossible for her to act. No matter how skilled her work, or how prestigious her social position, a full-time housewife has little or no money which she can use to escape a battering husband. Economic power alone cannot give women control over their lives, but their lack of economic power can undermine them in other areas.

Women have traditionally been responsible for full-time childcare and domestic maintenance. This work has been considered part of "female nature," totally outside the realm of the economy. This is a 24-hour-a-day job for which a woman is not paid, and so her time goes unrecognized and all her work is devalued. She may carry water and firewood, process food (cleaning, chopping, pounding, drying, canning), cook, make household tools, clean house, shop or trade, sew, wash, etc. When there are fewer conveniences the work is backbreaking; when there are more, the work is expanded by demands of

J. Peterson/LNS

male living standards, including such "necessities" as ironing, house decoration and spotlessness. Women's duty to love, cherish and obey the men to whom they are attached is part of a contract for which they are ostensibly supported financially, or reimbursed with an exchange of services, but in most societies they have little recourse when men don't fulfill their part of the bargain.

Leisure time for others is one of the by-products of housework. At noon in an agricultural commune in China, a woman spends her two hours "off" picking up and returning the children to daycare, and preparing, serving and cleaning up after lunch. Her husband enjoys leisure time that is made possible at his wife's expense. A working woman in Japan prepares dinner for her husband while he is out drinking with his friends. In both cases, the leisure time women create for men enables the men to return to their jobs somewhat refreshed, a benefit accruing to their employers. In much of Africa colonialism exacerbated the existing inequities between men and women so that men have greater material benefits in addition to greater leisure. Taxes demanded by the Europeans necessitated cash, which could be acquired only by jobs made accessible to men. Many men were forced to leave their villages to work in far-away mines and factories. They sent back little of their income because urban living costs were high, and they often paid for wifely services in the form of meals, prostitutes, etc. A study in Zambia found that in 1940, 79% of the men had spent 2/3 of their adult lives away from the villages where 3/4 of the women lived, yet had sent back only 10% of their wages to their families.[4] The village women were required to take on men's work as well as their own, and additional paid work to support their families. When men were sick or unemployed they returned to the village to be supported by the women's economy. In this case women's work makes possible a higher material standard of living for the family, and even higher for the husband in particular.

Women's and men's work both usually sustain the biologically defined minimum standard of living, while women's work makes possible (often for men only) a higher culturally defined minimum. It is not uncommon throughout Africa to see men bicycling or driving past women walking 5 to 10 miles to market with as much as 50 pounds of produce on their heads. In Kenya, taxes coming out of peasant women's crops go to build schools and provide services for men in urban areas, services that these women and their daughters will never use.[5] In the U.S.A. the monetary value of women's unpaid labor has been estimated at several trillion dollars annually.[6]*

The division of time, money and power between men and women is similar to the division that has existed between Western industrial and Third World countries. The Third World countries provide cheap labor and raw materials which the industrialized countries use to produce manufactured goods and technology. Third World countries receive very little compensation for their work, although it is essential to the world's economy and the industrialized nations' survival, while the West receives all the profits in the form of cash, global resources, and leisure time.

Many theorists state that women have a role "complementary" to men's role, whether women and men both do the same general kinds of work, or work within their "own spheres." ("Complementary" means that men dominate the human ecological niche and women share the leftovers.) Peasant women may own land in Peru only if they are widows or single mothers without living male relatives, and even then their roles in community government are restricted.[7] In the U.S. women are segregated into the lowest paying job categories more today than 20 years ago.[8]

Women's paid work of all types is usually an extension of our work in the home. In many Third World countries women's subsistence agriculture sustains the entire family. However, since they don't produce crops for export, or to market, they are not counted in the statistics of agricultural workers. Value is only attributed to goods which are exchanged outside families. In China, work points are allotted on the basis of productivity. The Chinese woman mentioned above is not given any workpoints for her noontime childcare and food preparation. When her

*Cross-culturally most men seem to give an equivalent percentage of their resources to their families, whether in time or money. Middle-class Western men or Third World men in well-paid positions sometimes give more money or purchased goods, but very little in the form of time spent on childcare or work around the house. Poor men are able to give little money but sometimes give time to the household. Except in very wealthy families where servants do domestic work, the work of sustenance falls on women.

longer workday results in lower agricultural productivity, she is penalized a second time with fewer work points.

When employed outside the family network women usually receive the lowest pay for the menial repetitive work, as at home, whether in factories, agriculture, or in offices. In many Asian and Latin American countries, women have done as much as one-fourth of the work in the mines. In Malaya and pre-revolutionary Viet Nam, they have done most of the heavy unskilled construction work, for which they have been paid far less than the men.[9] In 1972, women working at "better paying jobs" in Japan earned 47.5% of what men earned, and the same year women in Britain earned 59.3% of what men earned.[10] It is estimated that 23% of manufacturing company profits in the U.S.A. were made by paying women less than men ($5.4 billion less in 1950 alone).[11] And of course none of these figures include unpaid work in the home.

Violence Against Women

When women begin to organize independently or act or think as individuals, physical violence, such as rape, wife abuse, sexual and non-sexual abuse of children, the burning of "witches," etc., has served historically to keep women in line. The Mundurucu men of Western Brazil utilize gang rape as an institution to punish any woman who is considered too aggressive or independent.[12] In Peru a man can beat his wife severely for asking another man to help her with work. Physical violence serves the function of keeping women tied to the men they live with, or terrified of exercising alternatives. In some societies food deprivation is used as a means of disciplining wives, as well as routine nutritional discrimination.

The clitoridectomies and infibulation noted above are one example of violent control of our sexuality, prevalent in Africa, Asia and South America. Men's control over our reproductive lives keeps us "barefoot and pregnant," and consequently tied to husbands. If we are poor or Third World women, less direct violence in the form of sterilization abuse can prevent us from having children when we want them. 20% of married black American women, 35% of Puerto Rican women, and over one million women in Brazil, among others, have been sterilized.[14] Organized opposition to abortion, and birth control methods which are dangerous to women have resulted in millions of deaths and

illnesses from illegal abortions and infections.

Along with physical violence, women are subject to many forms of coercion which may be termed psychic violence. Concepts of "bad women" and "good women" operate to insure that women fulfill social expectations. In the West, if a woman acts too freely, she will be called a prostitute, lesbian, women's libber or bitch. In regions of Peru if a woman asks something of her husband in public he will be called a *saco largo* (henpecked husband) by other men. She will probably get an extra beating as well as a reputation as a poor wife.[15] The "bad woman" threat separates women from each other so that they hate and fear women who respond differently to male expectations, just as the housewife and prostitute often have contempt for each other.

Myths which are fed to women make them fear that alternatives to submissiveness will make things worse (for them). They produce more goods and services in the attempt to be accepted, and hate themselves because they can't meet the "good women" standards. The distinction between cultural ideals and actual norms is important to recognize as a means of social control. Women are often trapped in the middle, investing a great deal of time and energy in trying to meet the socially ascribed ideal.

Women living in neo-colonialist countries spend huge portions of their annual earnings on baby formulas, responding to campaigns teaching them that babies who are bottle fed are healthier than breast-fed babies. The result is that village women spend their scant resources on bottle formulas while living in poverty and have even less ability to accumulate capital for their own needs. Babies are often severely protein deficient, because the expensive formula is usually diluted, and the necessary sterile conditions are very difficult to maintain. The infants become susceptible to a wide variety of diseases that their mothers' milk would have protected them against. In Chile, the mortality rate for bottle-fed babies (80% of 2-month-old babies) is three times that of breast-fed babies.[16]

In all cultures, prestige serves to reinforce social ideals. For women this is usually acquired through our support of men and male-defined institutions. In some countries, the most prestigious women are those who produce many children insuring future workers. In others the importance of male pleasing appearance is emphasized. Bengali women belonging to the middle class must treat their hair and skin, Western women have "voluntarily" worn girdles and platform shoes, and women in Viet Nam used silicone and plastic surgery to fulfill American males' expectations. Even when not physically damaging, this effects our self-image, and creates great profits for cosmetic industries.

Strategies for Change

Historically, women throughout the world have attempted to make changes in their lives and the lives of future women. Their struggles take the form of individual acts of incredible courage, and in some cases the struggle is a collective one. Women in a village get together to share work, to make demands, to go on strike, and women working outside the home organize at their workplaces, create childcare cooperatives, etc. The particular form that women's struggles take depends in large part on whether they live in a culture where they have minimal, token or negotiating power.

Minimal Power Strategies

In societies where women only have minimal power, their energies have usually gone into survival. Women struggle with unwanted marriages, malnutrition, and many work-related diseases. Many decide that their only option in crisis situations is suicide.

Women's collective action in these societies attempts to consolidate their long hours of work, and protect their survival mechanisms. In Kenya, village women are forming roofing collectives. The maintenance of the thatch roofs in their compounds, a time-consuming and difficult job, is "women's work." None of the women could afford to replace the thatch with tin roofs alone, but together they pool their savings and buy one roof at a time.[17] In Italy women are the backbone of the community movements to reduce prices. In Turin alone 600 families moved into empty apartment complexes because of a housing shortage and high rents, organizing collective daycare in some buildings.[18] In Japan women are organizing for better daycare facilities so that they may work when and where they want, without worrying about their children's safety.[19] Other Japanese women are campaigning to have more women's work-related illnesses accepted as occupational hazards. Typing, keypunching, and childcare jobs are being held increasingly responsible for the "inflammation of the tendon sheath and cervical syndrome." More employers are held responsible for the woman's health care, job security during treatment, and for improving working conditions.[20]

In several countries women are focusing directly on the protection of their lives and health. In Italy, where women have traditionally had very few rights, they have recently won the right to abortions through their collective action.

The most important aspect of these strategies is that they have been developed by women to meet their own needs, not the needs of their society. Working together they are developing their own sense of self worth separate from male definitions. Each action brings women's lives more under their own control. Women in Italy now have some opportunity to use their time for themselves, that would otherwise have been claimed by illness and more child-raising.

Where women hold minimal power, male reaction to these attempts to change tends to take place on a very individual level. All the traditional types of violence against women are used to control women and their economic situation. It can be drastic as the killing of women who disobey their husbands, or the ostracization of women that do not fit the norm. Under minimal power women are usually in a more vulnerable position because they have to deal with these counter-attacks individually.

Token Power Strategies

Women with token power usually have some of the basic rights that women with minimal power are fighting for. With survival more assured, they make attempts to consolidate reforms into undeniable rights for women, to increase opportunities in every area of life so that women are segregated less into the least rewarding areas. In some countries women organize services that were not formerly provided to protect and improve the quality of women's lives. Others encourage open discussion of women's status to discover the inequalities that exist. Women's caucuses may exist to elect sympathetic officials.

In Iceland 99% of women in the capital and 99% of women in the villages went on strike on October 24, 1975 and attended public meetings to discuss their status. The display of unity successfully demonstrated the inability of the economy to function without their work.[21] Their demands for higher pay, equal employment, better representation in the Farmers' and Trade Unions, daycare, and financial recognition of their work in the home must now be seriously dealt with by the government.

A group of women in Quebec have written and produced a play which describes several women striking for wages for their housework. A judge eventually grants them an increase in family allowances of five dollars a month. Because the women have changed through the process of arguing their case, they begin to expect help from their families, and plan future action together.[22] The processes of political change are illustrated, and the lively discussions afterward let women share their experiences as houseworkers.

There was a national strike of women cleaners in Sweden. These women were traditionally isolated from one another, ignored by the unions and by job legislation, and paid very poorly.[23] Their recent success had to come from building networks among themselves and acting on their experience, outside male definitions of labor organizations.

Groups of women in the U.S., from Puerto Rican women in Boston to women in Appalachia, are teaching themselves to drive against the wishes of their husbands and fathers. They wish to increase their mobility, and so their opportunities for jobs, and to save time and money for themselves.

Wherever women have token power, they are building networks of services including rape crisis centers, refuges for women in crisis and medical centers. These services represent a base of operations outside the male professions. Though they can be destroyed by the male economy, while they exist they help many women. Women's experience of self-determination in these areas also increases their ability to act independently in the future.

In token power societies many of the forms of individual punishment are used that are used against women with minimal power, including battering, rape, etc. However, backlash on a social level has happened in staggering proportions. Men have attempted to close British refuges for battered women by taking them to court for overcrowding. In the U.S., the Ku Klux Klan sent threatening notices to women who participated in the International Women's Year Conference in Houston, and cooperated with other right wing

Eileen Whalen/LNS

groups to attempt to keep women from attending the conference.

It is no historical anomaly that these repressive movements, supported by the wealthy, male-dominated right wing, are taking place as women begin to make concrete first steps toward changing society. Backlash is also taking place internationally in informal situations where groups of men harass known lesbians. Vandalism and bombings of many abortion clinics across the U.S. have occurred.

Negotiating Power Strategies

In the few contemporary cultures in which women have negotiating power, women's struggles have taken two forms: working towards greater equality with men, and fighting externally imposed changes which negatively affect women's status.

Today in areas of West Africa where women have been active in trading, there are associations of market women who have come together to lobby in their own interests. Periodically there are strikes in the town and village markets, sometimes initiated with the help of the queen mother.

Women's struggle for freedom has had a history of well over 100 years in China, but women were not able to make fundamental changes until the 1949 revolution. Women then formed Women's Associations to air their grievances and confront their husbands' privileges and abuses of power with the support of the revolutionary government. In the past the women might have been punished rather than the men.

However, the Associations have been increasingly absorbed into the government since the revolution. When the government had consolidated in the mid-1950's, stability and a "harmonious" family life were stressed. Throughout, the Associations have been working with the government, accepting and promoting *its* priorities.

Until now women in China have usually been supported when they made demands for change. In 1976, women began to demand that men share the housework, and as long as women remained strong and vocal, the party supported them and men began to change their habits.[24] As long as women in China maintain their independent visions and the revolution is seen as an ongoing process of social transformation, they will be able to make more fundamental changes. Otherwise, their efforts will be utilized by a male-dominated government to its own ends, inevitably different from those that women envisioned.

For women to be able to consolidate their gains as well as to continue making new ones, they must have independent sources of power from which to stand strong against resistance, punishment and backlash. An encouraging development has been the growing dialogue and linkages between women from different countries on an individual and collective level. The international feminist support that was rallied several years ago aided the case of the Three Marias in Portugal. In March, 1976, women held an International Tribunal on Crimes Against Women in Brussels, sharing information and experiences and documenting the herstory.[25] Wellesley College sponsored a "Women in Development" conference in 1976, which a great many women attended. Unfortunately the conference was dominated by white North American academic women in form, structure, and content, negatively affecting the possibility for real interchange.[26] This experience highlighted the need for western women to confront their own racial and cultural biases to make the dream of international feminism a viable one.

For true equality to exist between women and men in any culture, the very basis of domination and exploitation will have to be eradicated, including all the patriarchal norms and assumptions which are sustained by women's oppression. Patriarchy must be completely transformed from its very roots, including the extent to which women have internalized white male values and assumptions. The creation of matriarchal economies and cultures throughout the world means just such a transformation, not a reversal of power, but a whole new way of looking at and structuring power.

Footnotes

1. R. Apthorpe, ed., *Land Settlement and Rural Development in Eastern Africa*, Rampala, Nkanga Editions, Transition Books, cited by Achola Pala and Ann Seidman, unpublished paper

2. Alemnesh Bulti, Interview, October, 1976

3. Carollee Benglesdorf and Alice Hageman, "Women and Work," *Cuba Review*, Vol. iv, no. 2, Women in Transition, NY 1974

4. G. Wilson and M. Wilson, *Analysis of Social Change*, 1945, cited by Pala and Seidman, *op. cit.*

5. Zarina Patel, talk given at Goddard-Cambridge, 3/3/77

6. Leghorn and Warrior, *Houseworker's Handbook*, Cambridge, MA, 1974

7. Sue Bourque and Kay Warren, talk given at Goddard-Cambridge, 4/14/77

8. William Mandel, *Soviet Women*, Anchor Books, Garden City, NY, 1975, pp. 107, 125-126

9. Ester Boserup, *Women's Role in Economic Development*, St. Martin's Press, 1970

10. ILO, Yearbook of Labor Statistics, 1973, in Equality of Opportunity, Report VIII, Geneva, 1975, cited by Cordell and McHale, *Women in World Terms*, Binghamton, NY, 1975

11. Joan Jordan, *The Place of American Women*, Vol. 1, no. 3, Revolutionary Age, 1968

12. Yolanda and Robert Murphy, *Women of the Forest*, Columbia University Press

13. Kay Warren and Sue Bourque, talk given at Goddard-Cambridge, 4/14/77, *op. cit.*

14. *Boston CESA Newsletter*, 1976, "Population Control," article distributed by Boston CESA

15. Kay Warren and Sue Bourque, talk given at Goddard-Cambridge, 4/14/77, *op. cit.*

16. Anthony Astracham, "Milking the Third World," *The Progressive*, July 1976

17. Zarina Patel, *op. cit.*

18. *Power of Women Journal*, Vol. 1, no. 3, Henley on Thames, January, 1975, p. 3

19. Azuma Hidemi, "A Child's Dream—The Beginning of Struggle for Daycare," Information Packet on Women in Japan compiled by Fabienne Melchior, unpublished, p. 68

20. Nojiri Yoriko, "Women's Occupational Diseases," *op. cit.*, Information Packet, pp. 14-16

21. "When Women Stop Everything Stops," *Power of Women Journal*, Vol. 1, no. 5, London, 1976, pp. 18-19

22. Le Theatre des Cuisines, *Moman Travaille Pas, A Trop D'ouvrate!*, Les Editions du Remue-Menage, Montreal, 1976

23. Monica Sjoo, "Sweden, Now We Are 'Equal,'" *Power of Women*, Vol. 1, no. 4, London, 1975, pp. 12-13

24. Joan Hinton, "Politics and Marriage," *New China*, June 1976, pp. 32-34

25. Diana Russell, *Crimes Against Women: the Proceedings of the International Tribunal*, Les Femmes, Millbrae, CA, 1976

26. Eleanor Leacock, "Reflections on the Conference on Women and Development: III," Vina Mazumdar, "Reflections . . . IV," *Signs*, Vol. 3, no. 1, Autumn 1977, pp. 322-324

WOMANEWS

From *Womanews* 1, no. 9 (September 1980): 1, 5

Preparation for Poverty: Girls and the New York City Vocational Education System

by Phyllis Eckhaus

That the schools track white kids into college and black and Hispanic kids into the streets is a familiar story. Less familiar, but equally insidious, is how the schools manage to track girls into "women's work," those service and clerical jobs in which women have long been exploited, while boys continue to reap the benefits of vocational training in the skilled trades.

In the New York City schools, there are virtually no girls being trained in those fields most likely to lead to gainful employment in the 1980's. Take, for example, the enrollment figures for the several trade schools specializing in electronics and engineering:

School*	Girls' Register	Boys' Register
Chelsea Vocational	0	1190
Alexander Hamilton	111	1021

*Register as of 10/31/79. New York City Board of Education, Office of Educational Statistics. See also the accompanying course enrollment chart.

Reprinted with permission from *Womanews: N.Y.C. Feminist Newspaper and Calendar of Events.*

School	Register	Number
William Grady	27	1978
Thomas Edison	41	2432

However, the schools do boast almost 8000 girls (and 300 boys) taking steno. According to Department of Labor projections through 1985, the supply of secretaries will exceed jobs available, while the demand for people to fill high paying craft and industry jobs will continue to grow. Though prospects for boys in New York City job programs are rosy, girls are being trained for a future of poor pay and unemployment.

Tracy Huling, of Full Access and Rights to Education (FARE), describes the Board of Education's attitude towards affirmative action: "They think if they've opened the door, they've done enough. In fact, if no one walks through that door, they haven't done shit."

Huling's account of the Board's pathetic attempts to promote "sex equity" in vocational education suggests that in practice, the door to equal education is left ajar. The malign neglect of affirmative action for girls in school vocational programs is symbolized by the city's 1980 comprehensive program plan for occupational education, submitted to Albany in fulfillment of funding requirements. Though improving job training for girls was a major focus of the legislation that provided the funds in the first place, the city found it sufficient to address that issue in a seven page appendix to the 300 page document. In disregard of state law, the Board held no public hearings on the plan.

The city's vocational schools are under the direction of George Quarles, head of the Center for Career and Occupational Education. He has consistently shown himself indifferent to affirmative action for girls. While funds received by his division mandated the employment of a full-time staffperson to promote "sex equity," for over six months the position has been empty and the money allocated elsewhere. When confronted with this misuse of funds, Quarles responded "Don't worry, the money's not being wasted."

Quarles' attitude is typical of the Board of Education, where priorities are determined according to which outside groups scream the loudest—1980 has been the year of the handicapped and the bilingual, who had to bring the Board to court in order to receive redress. Women have not been vocal, and consequently, the consciousness of Board officials remains fixed at subterranean levels.

Nowhere is this sexist ignorance more evident than in the Board's famed drop-out report, issued last fall. Written to call attention to the overwhelming numbers of drop-outs from New York City high schools, the report makes little effort to identify who drops out or why. In fact, the drop-out report does not once break down the 45% drop-out figure by sex, nor does it

Enrollments in Occupational Education Courses Traditionally Dominated by Single Sex

Day High Schools 1979-80					
Courses	**Boys**	**Girls**	**Courses**	**Boys**	**Girls**
Automotive	2708	18	Food Trades	467	776
Aviation	1929	24	Machine & Metal Trades	710	40
Construction Trades	1559	58	Printing Trades	66	437
Computer Technician	479	30	Dental Office Assisting	17	315
Dental Laboratory	96	38	Practical Nursing	3	460
Drafting Trades	313	29	Medical Technician	287	540
Electrical Trades	1429	23	Data Processing	1285	1293
Environmental Trades	421	0			
Electro-Mechanical Trades	2003	17			

*Figures provided by the Center for Career and Occupational Education, New York City Board of Education

acknowledge the severe attendance problems faced by high school girls who are pregnant or have children.

This is no small omission. The New York State Department of Health estimates the number of pregnancies among New York City girls aged 17 or younger at 15,000 a year. About a third of these pregnancies result in live births. Recently introduced programs to reduce the drop-out rate do little to alleviate the daycare problems of these thousands of teenage mothers.

Judith Layzer, of the Board of Education's Advisory Council on Occupational Education, sees the absence of a statistical breakdown by sex as evidence that the drop-out rate is viewed solely as a male problem. "The drop-out rate gets such attention because people are afraid male drop-outs will turn to violent crime." Musing on the absence of girls from the report, Layzer notes that "pregnant girls don't riot in the streets."

Tracy Huling estimates that about half the girls in New York City schools drop out, and that three-quarters of these girls are pregnant or already have children. In her work as a child advocate, she has found that schools actually encourage pregnant teenagers to drop out.

"They're treated like lepers," she says. "Principals see pregnant girls and they have visions of kids fucking in the hallways." Huling reports that tactics in the administrative war against pregnant students include denying them elevator passes or time off for medical care, and requiring that they take gym class. Once the girls give birth, they are urged to leave school and devote themselves to fulltime motherhood.

Daycare funds for vocational education students were available from the state, but the Board did not choose to apply for them. George Quarles explained this decision by claiming that there are already too many daycare centers in New York City and that he knew this because of the large number of girls he places in the centers to receive job training. "He kind of stuck both his feet in his mouth in one sentence," Huling observes.

In fact, according to the Human Resources Administration, there are only eight publicly funded daycare centers in the city which accept children under the age of three years. They scarcely meet the city-wide need. Five of the centers are in Brooklyn; other boroughs offer almost no assistance to mothers with infants.

Once girls leave school, the training available to them becomes even more limited. CETA programs in New York City severely underrepresent women and minorities. Though women make up three-fifths of the city's CETA-eligible population, they receive only two-fifths of CETA jobs, and these are mostly clerical. According to the Committee for Women in Non-Traditional Jobs, women represent less than 5% of the trainees in the city CETA programs in the blue collar trades.

Again, the training situation is worst for women with children. "It's easier to get an education if you're a male mugger than a teenage mother," says Jane Kelley of Women in the Trades. She explains that the CETA-sponsored Youth Employment Training Program requires trainees to put in an eight-hour day, without adequate provisions for childcare. This results in young mothers postponing job training until their children are old enough for school or regular daycare; by this time, the women themselves are past the maximum age-limit for apprenticeship programs allowing entry into the skilled trades. Several groups, including the New York City-based Women in Apprenticeship Project, have recently brought suit in federal court charging that age discrimination is *de facto* sex discrimination.

It is one of the ironies of affirmative action programs that once having targeted disadvantaged groups, they then fail to provide the support services (such as bilingual training or childcare) that would enable members of these groups to take advantage of the programs offered. This failure to provide support services ends in the programs excluding the people who need them most. Judith Layzer notes that were the city to contract with "community-based" women's groups to design and administer job programs, support services would automatically receive greater emphasis.

Layzer argues that, as currently administered, CETA programs turn away those least prepared to survive in the job market. When her Committee for Women in Non-Traditional Jobs succeeded in obtaining CETA statistics from the Department of Labor, they discovered that 75% of the Hispanic women in city CETA programs had at least a high school diploma. "Why can't they find the women without high school diplomas?" Layzer asks. She protests, "They're creaming the crop."

In addressing the problems of "sex equity," the city has acted as if women are essentially the same as middle-class white men. Until those in charge of affirmative action for women realize the gross absurdity of this position and begin to acknowledge the entire complex of social and economic factors that make for the oppression of our sex, the door they open to equal education will continue to be marked "Men Only."

From *Women* 6, no. 2 (March 1979): 5-9

Generations: Conflict and the Ethnic Experience

by Nancy Jelkunas, Baltimore

Several years ago I took my son to visit the museum in our local historical society. And as I was wandering among the various exhibits celebrating America's past, I

suddenly realized: *this is not my history.* The finely stitched size 3 silk dresses, the ornately carved silver serving sets, the formal portraits of the state's first families—none of this had anything to do with my own personal history. My immigrant grandmothers were stout. They wore long wool skirts and men's sweaters, and cotton stockings rolled below their knees; their husbands, when I knew them, sat at the kitchen table in their long underwear and drank coffee out of white dime store cups. Most of the pictures I have of my ancestors are photographs taken on very special occasions.

Something in me was triggered by that experience in the museum. I began to investigate my own past, and find the history and culture belonging to me. I wanted to know who I was in relation to where I'd come from, and I wanted to try and resolve some of the conflicts I was experiencing as the granddaughter of immigrants who was also a middle class high school teacher and graduate wife.

Justina Dobrylas and Clementina Miskitas, my maternal and paternal grandmothers, were two of the millions of immigrants who came to America in the early years of the twentieth century. Justina came from Poland and settled in Brockton, Massachusetts; Clementina was from Lithuania and came to live with an uncle in Scranton, Pennsylvania. Their experiences in this country were similar to that of many immigrant women. Within a few years of arrival, they married men of their own immigrant group. Justina married Ignacy Katkowski in 1904; Clementina wed Joseph Jelkunas in 1909. Joseph remained a semi-skilled factory worker all his life. Ignacy worked in various factories during his early years in America and gradually became a self-employed carpenter. He was, apparently, an energetic, aggressive, wiry man who was very intelligent and greatly frustrated. Factory work in the 20's for both my grandfathers, as for so many, was dangerous, degrading and boring, so they changed jobs periodically looking for different or better work. Unhappy with their jobs and with what they had (or didn't have), both men took their frustrations out on their wives: through occasionally uncontrolled brutality in the early years, by sullenness and constant complaining throughout their lives. Both marriages endured rather than flourished.

Central to each of my grandmother's life was her children and her home. Life seemed to be an endless effort to keep the home functioning as smoothly as economic circumstances allowed, for neither husband had steady work, there were too many children, and something was always breaking down, falling apart, wearing out. When things got too bad financially, both women worked outside their homes as piece workers, domestic help and farm laborers. "Good managers" is how I've heard people describe women like my grandmothers.

Yet the lives of my immigrant grandparents were not completely circumscribed by poverty and hard work. Each family was rooted in a supportive network of relatives and friends from the old country.

Regularly they would all get together, including the children, for parties and picnics, where there would be food and drink, music and dancing, pleasant talk and laughter. Often on Saturdays after work they would push the furniture in somebody's house against the wall and dance and eat and talk; my family has many stories of who was found drunk in the bathtub and who was flirting with whom at these events. There were special occasions too, like the autumn potato roast, when a whole group of friends and relatives would get together, roast potatoes in the ground and then have a feast.

The Catholic Church was also extremely important, for my mother's family in particular. It gave structure to their lives and it was a place to get together with other Polish immigrants. It was also, for my grandmother especially, a source of strength and meaning.

What conflicts my grandparents endured as they pursued their lives in America are mostly lost to me; they had all died before I had the sense to talk with them in any complete way about their experiences. But there were, certainly, conflicts. On the one hand, life in America was in certain ways objectively better for them than life in the Old Country had been: they didn't die in religious or political conflicts like many of their countrymen did, they didn't wind up in Displaced Persons camps, they did have enough food and adequate shelter. And most of all here in America they had expectations, expectations that if not they, then their children and grandchildren might achieve material security, might even, if they worked hard enough, "get a little ahead." Nor were these expectations totally unfounded. At the end of their lives, my grandparents all had modest savings accounts. One set owned a few acres and a home; they lived on the 2nd floor, a relative lived on the third, and a Polish refugee family rented the first floor. All four grandparents saw their sons and daughters moving into the white collar world and their grandchildren going to college, becoming professionals.

Yet there were conflicts with the larger American society: experiences of discrimination and prejudice against "Pollacks" and "Lits"; conflicts with those in authority—teachers, bosses, priests. My mother's father and a group of Polish men actually left their church in the 1920's, because they felt the pastor was too dogmatic and authoritarian, and formed

their own parish. And my grandparents had difficulties in coping with the urban industrial world they had moved into, in adjusting to the regimen of factory work, to a house or apartment with no land around it, to a society that looked down on them as foreigners, to working too hard for too little. It was hard for them, I think, to figure out how to survive in America.

In 1908, angry and dissatisfied with not enough money, no steady job, a difficult marriage and poor living conditions, my mother's parents decided to return to Poland. My grandfather rigged a leather harness to carry my grandmother's heavy sewing machine on his back, so she could earn money sewing, and they went back to my grandmother's village to live. After a few years, however, to avoid being drafted into the Russian army, my grandfather came back to the United States and stayed with his brother, leaving his wife and 3 children with her father. My grandmother eventually—and somewhat reluctantly—joined him in the U.S. Only after World War II did they realize that going back to Poland was impossible. They bought several acres of land and built a house there, my 50-year-old grandmother carrying huge stones for the foundation in a wheelbarrow. Building that house was an acknowledgement that they were going to stay, I think, but they never became citizens.

Expectations, the promise of mobility, and the conflicts of that promise and the psychic cost have been my grandparents' legacy to their children and grandchildren. Both my grandfathers "drank too much" as we say in the family. And according to my mother, her mother used to comfort herself in bad times with the saying, "If you live in hell long enough you'll get used to it." What frustrated expectations, what lifetime of pain and conflict does all this suggest? These are the questions I must answer if I am to understand that I am the granddaughter of Justina and Ignacy Katkowski and Clementina and Joseph Jelkunas.

By the 1920's, the Katkowski and Jelkunas families had moved to Bridgeport, Connecticut. There were relatives there and jobs in the local factories. In the 1930's, two children from these families, Mary Katkowski and John Jelkunas, met at a dance. Mary had been working as a maid for a wealthy family since she was 14; John worked in a factory, but as a high school graduate, he had hopes of a desk job, "a clean job." In 1941 the two married, a marriage postponed for years because of the Depression and then almost immediately disrupted when John was drafted in service during World War II. Finally in 1945, they began an orderly domestic life, living first in an upstairs apartment in the house where Mary worked, and then in a duplex dome in a WW II federal housing project. I was born there, in that same year, and we lived in that house until I was 9.

Such are the facts, the external arrangements of my parents' lives. But what conflicts, what choices made or not made, underlie these facts? It's very difficult to write about one's own parents: there is the tendency to blame, to get out old hurts; and there is the possibility that one's love for them can blind one to certain contradictions.

It seems to me that the central conflict in my parents' lives has been to reconcile their immigrant background with their desire to move into mainstream America. Neither immigrants nor "100% Americans," they had a disorientation similar to my grandparents: Where do I fit? How do I carve a place out for myself in the world? And these questions were complicated by the dilemma experienced by so many children of immigrants: What is one's ethnic and class identity when you're upwardly mobile?

My parents, unlike some others of their generation, changed neither their name nor their religion in the effort to integrate into the middle class. And perhaps more important, they retained certain cultural values from their background. Family connections were of primary importance. Throughout my childhood, we visited grandma nearly every Sunday afternoon. And my mother doesn't have "friends"; her social relations are all with her family. She and her three sisters live in the same town and are in contact several times a week. They totally rely on each other for both material and emotional support. When two of my aunts were widowed in their 40's and left with young children, my mother simply "took over." She had only one child and besides, she could drive, so my mother took them to the grocery store, to church, to a movie, everywhere; she became like a second mother to one of my aunt's four children. The expectation has always been that each of the sisters would be there for the others because they are family. That is simply the way families are. To this day, the four women are a

powerful, amazing combination who dominate the scene whenever the family gets together.

Other cultural values my parents retained are the importance of working hard, saving and "taking care of things." My mother still has the furniture she bought when she got married and she waxes it regularly. When I was growing up, she cleaned, cleaned, cleaned. If you dirtied a dish, she washed (and dried) it immediately. To save a few cents, she soaked uncancelled stamps off envelopes and reused them, cut buttons off worn-out clothes for future use, made pillow cases out of old sheets, bought a year's supply of toothpaste, toilet paper, soap and shampoo "on special." My father, too, worked hard. In over 40 years of work, he has probably never had more than a week's vacation at a time. And for several years, he held down two jobs.

It was precisely the value placed on hard work and thrift learned from their own immigrant parents that allowed my parents to move into the lower echelons of the middle class, "to get a little ahead." In 1954, when I was 9, they bought a 3 bedroom ranch house on a quarter acre of land in one of Bridgeport's burgeoning suburbs. And (as my mother often reminded me) they were able to provide me with certain "advantages," notably a private high school and college education.

But the effort to adopt a mainstream American way of life led to certain cultural tensions within my family. My mother's efforts to add middle class "decorator touches" to the house included a sunburst clock over the mantle and plastic flowers on the dining room table. Her desire to import "culture" led her to purchase grocery store encyclopedias and record sets and *The Reader's Digest*. Although it has been extremely important for both my parents to move out of the ethnic enclaves they grew up in, they are to this day ill at ease with middle class American forms of social life. Neither of them has joined religious or civic groups. Almost never, when I was young, did we have guests other than family members in our home. And I can remember how, when I was about to be married, my mother fussed and fretted for weeks before my upper middle class in-laws came to visit, and how over-solicitous, how over-hospitable she was with them. She always says, "The people I have the most fun with are the old timers, the people I grew up with."

My parents' disorientation in a world

they thought they wanted spilled over into the day-to-day social relationships within my family. My parents took few risks—material or emotional—for unexpected behavior could easily have disrupted their careful, orderly conserving of resources so necessary to "get a little ahead." There was little spontaneity, little enthusiasm for pleasure of any kind in my family as I was growing up. Our family life was characterized by routine, order and a boring sameness.

My father withdrew frequently into a moody kind of privacy. He was away at work a lot and when he was home he slept, read the newspaper, did crossword puzzles and hardly ever talked. My mother was, above all else, always home. As she explains it, she never worked outside the home because my father "wouldn't let her." I'm sure that's partially true; my father's background taught him that women worked only when men's salaries were too meagre to support the family. But I also suspect that she stayed home because she felt inadequate to face the world, unsure of her place in it, scared to deal with different kinds of people. To work in a factory would have been humiliating; to work in an office might mean she'd have to engage with people who were more educated, more middle class than she was. So, she stayed home.

However, my mother found herself in an increasingly empty role as technology simplified the tasks of housework. She did perform certain necessary functions like cooking meals and washing clothes and her thrifty ways provided a "profit margin" for our family's economy. But her life was not like her mother's; all this did not fill her time. So she dealt with her frustrations by busying herself with the minutiae of housekeeping and by *taking care of me*, an only child. She read to me daily from the time I was less than a year old, she made my clothes, she embroidered them, she ironed them fastidiously; she ordered, regulated, controlled, and also loved me very much.

Not only did I fill up my mother's time, but I also served as the focal point of that legacy of expectations which my parents inherited from their parents. They looked to me to get even more ahead, to have even nicer things. They made valiant efforts to teach me "manners," to give me "advantages" like dancing and piano lessons. And they actively discouraged any early romantic attachments that might have tied me down at age 20 with a local boy and a couple of children. Instead they made sure I went away to college.

So where do I find myself now? In conflict, like my grandparents, like my parents, between the familiar values I grew up with and the circumstances I find myself in now. Is this, I wonder, the basic ethnic experience in America? I have accepted the old value of family in my life, and I think the solidness of my marriage is grounded in a real internalized expectation that a family hangs together and works things out. I don't expect a marriage to be gloriously happy all the time, so I've stuck through some things that other people who don't have this value so engrained in them might not have. I've also accepted the value of hard work. From the day I turned 16, I've worked at jobs ranging from sales clerk to college instructor. I've always been a joiner and had numerous projects going at once. In fact, it seems as though there's been something I've "had to do" almost every hour of my adult life. And I'm always telling my son not to "waste time," to "find something interesting to do."

Yet even though I have more education and more money than my parents, I don't think I've simply bought a mindless drive to "get ahead." My parents and grandparents were upwardly mobile to the extent that they were because they worked incredibly hard. I've seen that, and I, too, presently teaching and working on a Ph.D., expect to work hard throughout my life.

Of course, like my parents, I've paid a price for my choices. I'm tenser than I'd like to be, anxious about doing a good job. Like them I find it hard to be spontaneous, to take risks, simply to have a good time and enjoy life.

But in other ways there are enormous differences between who I am now and the values I grew up with. Despite my parents' best intentions, from the age of puberty it was obvious I'd never make it as a middle class lady: I was (still am) clumsy and near-sighted; my size 12, 36C body hardly conforms to the WASP ideal; clothes, make up and "doing" my hair have always been impenetrable mysteries to me. Although my family life might seem typically middle class—I live in a nuclear family of a husband-wife-and-one-child in a mort-gaged single family home—its internal realities are decidedly not. I have little interest in spending great amounts of time or energy—or money—creating "a nice home." I just do what is necessary as simply

and quickly as possible. The same is true for my responsibilities as a mother. I don't protect my son physically (my mother freaked out when I took him outside when he was three weeks old; she thought he would get sick and die or something), I don't read to him a lot, make his clothes or fuss over him. And unlike my parents, I enjoy important friendships and activities totally outside the realm of my family.

And yet, like my parents and grand-parents I too feel a sense of "dislocation"; I too am not comfortable in an upwardly mobile society. At work, I just don't know the rules of how you're supposed to act. I tend to spill over my desk; I take up lots of space and like to carry on running conversations, even from across the hall. But other people just seem to sit quietly and do their work. I feel socially disoriented, too. I find it difficult to invite people over for dinner (my mother found it impossible) the way middle class people are supposed to. I can't figure out how to move gracefully between the dining room and the kitchen, and I don't know how to carry on polite conversation. In fact, the pieces of my background make me feel alienated everywhere: with ethnics and the working class, and with middle class academics and "professionals."

Because I feel like I don't fit anywhere, I've had to face the ambiguous legacy of my family. And I've begun to see—through the conflicts that I, my parents and my grandparents have had—how destructive social life in America is for ethnics. America has provided some real economic advantages and freedom from religious and political persecution for some people.

But the illusion that there's no price to pay for this makes America ruthlessly cruel. Mobility disorients people; my family may have improved its lot materially over the years, but the cultural and psychic cost has been high. My grandparents and parents learned that, I think, and I have had to learn it too.

I have tried to resolve some of my conflicts by working in such fields as oral history, family history and women's history, by trying to recover the historical experiences of "ordinary people," and by encouraging others to view their own lives in their cultural and historical contexts. My left political views and my feminism have also helped make the contradictions in my life bearable and sometimes even beautiful.

Left politics and feminism were hardly part of my parents' expectations for me. But perhaps they weren't so unexpected either. Despite my parents' awkward efforts to move into the middle class, their love for their families and their inability to forget "where they came from" generalized itself into a real respect for ordinary, hard-working people. And like most such people, they had a gut-level understanding that larger social and economic forces controlled much of their lives. It was too much of a risk for them to act on that knowledge, but they did communicate it to me.

And at a recent family wedding when I saw, as I'd seen many times before, my mother and her sisters dancing the polka together with great joy, I realized that maybe I'd learned something of feminism from her, too.

∫INI∫TER WI∫DOM

From *Sinister Wisdom*, no. 10 (Summer 1979), pp. 29-30

Notes on Age, Rage & Language

by Robin Ruth Linden

Age: the mark of time, temporal context for discrete fragments of constancy and

First published in *Sinister Wisdom,* Box 660, Amherst, MA 01004. Reprinted with permission.

change. How do we learn to hear simultaneous and independent voices inside our Selves, as a fugue, sometimes as answers to questions we're afraid to ask, pointing directionality, possibility, purpose, meaning?

I am 22. I want to say this with pride. Rather, I feel pangs of shame, inclined to apologize for not being 40, with the experience, grace and wisdom I imagine that implies. How I am still locked into their chronology, their static measure of time.

** * **

"Act your age." To remind us we are

deviant, violating lines of control. To return us to their control.

I've often wondered why I cannot remember so much of my childhood. Fifteen years of images and feelings are shrouded in darkness, like being depressed or sleeping without dreaming. Yet, as a child I felt unspeakably deep rage that was neither confirmed in nor translatable to their language.

Even now I can scarcely begin to speak of it.

** * **

Being out of control, though, involves a shift in center or locus of control, from Other to Self. It *is* being in control, although it may *feel* chaotic—or even torpid.

Rage: pre-verbal and unutterable, even to our Selves and also, mutual and articulate and therefore, political and directed, is caused by and the result of being outside their control: in a natural state of wildness.

** * **

Semantic equivalents to "act your age":

"Why are you being so stubborn?" Meaning: nothing you are—or could be— concerned with is as important as you think it is. You should be dispassionately occupied with dolls or boys—things Other than your Self.

"You're much too young to take life so seriously—you're just too sensitive." Meaning: feeling deeply is inappropriate to your age.

** * **

Thus, age is a bludgeon for restoring children to the control of adults.

** * **

Adults exercise physical as well as psychic and symbolic coercion. Violence against children is so pervasive and normative that most of us scarcely notice when a mother slaps her child in the supermarket or when a father threatens his adolescent son with his fist. For years, I thought that all parents "spanked" their children and thus, that my father's occasional beatings weren't so bad.

And yet, how consistently fearful I was of his demonstrating upon my flesh the power—and simultaneously the powerlessness—he felt over me. From whom did I learn that I was responsible for and deserving of his violent humiliations, that I was the cause of his rage? What about those remarkable "exceptions"—my friends'

parents for whom such acts were unthinkable? In their example I came to understand that my father's violence was chosen and deliberate, not precipitated by me.

As an adult, I retain vivid memory traces of my father's violence: his power and his rage. Still, I feel sometimes terrorized that my own rage will "cause" the violence for which, as a child, I was made to feel responsible.

** * **

Power: the first arena of struggle between children and adults. How early we are taught to deny our deepest intuitions, our intensity: not to trust our Selves. As children we become complaisant, feeling as our own adults' contempt and fear for our deepest feelings, our sense of justice.

Adults deny the consequences of the power they wield over children, concealing their choices and beliefs as inevitable, ineluctable facts. Adults deny the struggle for power between children and themselves. Yet each of us must see the world unmediated—through our own eyes.

** * **

Women have begun speaking of the conditions which shaped our earliest years: incest, battery, rape, infinite gradations of psychic and physical abuse. In the face of such violence we are speechless, disenfranchised from language, utterly without means to translate our nerves' truth.

Without language there is no imagination, no possibility.

Our silence was not participation in adults' coercion, though: we knew our own truths. We resisted, we felt and we survived.

To insist on the truth in our feelings, the clarity in our perceptions against all odds—this is what it means to survive. This struggle we choose: to render into language yet unnamed knowledge, the sense dwelling deep in our cells as instinct.

** * **

Until the essential condition of childhood changes, we can expect that this violence will continue to escalate.

** * **

As women, we have the common experience of childhoods imbued with violence. As lesbians, violence remains for us an ordinary reality. Our lives can never be free of violence until male presence and control, as we presently know them, cease. It is a matter of survival that we encourage each other and our Selves to alchemize our ancient rage and the silence swelling inside it.

Lynda Koolish has deeply encouraged this writing, patiently hearing me forth from silence. Leigh Star's wisdom and understanding constantly urge me to make real what I can yet imagine. Her loving friendship is profoundly enspiriting. Adrienne Rich's Women and Honor: Some Notes on Lying *has inspired much of my thinking and feeling in this piece.*

WOMANEWS

From *Womanews* 1, no. 5 (April 1980): 3

Something New in Contraception

by Dana Shilling

On February 16, at Feminist Healthworks, Lynn Kramer and Julie McCartney held a program about contraceptive methods. Unfortunately, they had no dramatic news to report: no startling new contraceptive that is perfectly safe and completely

effective has been found. But they did describe the most harmful, most invasive methods of birth control and what alternatives are available. Kramer and McCartney began by discussing the dangers of birth control pills, the IUD, the "morning after" pill (DES) and the monthly Depo-Provera shot (a massive dose of progesterone).

Kramer and McCartney displayed the cervical cap, a small rubber object which looks like the top of a baby bottle, that has not undergone the intensive testing needed for FDA approval. How effective the cervical cap is over many years of use is unknown. Though the cap has been used for almost a century in Europe, and anecdotal reports are very favorable, statistics from controlled studies are not available. The cervical cap's advantage over the diaphragm is that the cap is much smaller and fits very closely over the cervix—so it is less noticeable in use and less likely to be displaced.

After discussing intrusive chemical and mechanical contraceptives and barrier contraceptives, Kramer and McCartney explained three "natural" birth control methods. (They mentioned in passing that Dr. Bronner, of peppermint soap fame, is testing an organic spermicide, containing citric and acetic acid in a neutral base.)

Body Temperature/Cervical Mucus methods (described in Margaret Nofziger's book *A Cooperative Method of Natural Birth Control*) require a woman to observe and chart her basal body temperature and/or the condition of her cervical mucus, then add the rhythm method to these calculations to find her "safe" period. This method calls for heterosexual abstinence or alternative birth control methods during a woman's fertile period, which must be exactly calculated. A woman's body temperature spikes right after she ovulates and on fertile days, the cervical mucus is thin and stretchy (like egg white) while on infertile days, the cervix is dry or has a little bit of pasty, sticky mucus.

To use the body temperature and/or cervical mucus method, a woman must keep a chart for several months and find her own patterns of ovulation. If a woman's cycle is very regular, she may be able to use this method successfully; otherwise, she may face unwanted pregnancy or long periods without heterosexual intercourse. Another caution is that viable sperm (those not weakened or killed by spermicides) can live up to five days. If an egg (which can only live for eight hours) is released any time during the five days after intercourse, it may be fertilized. An "ovutimer," a machine that registers the viscosity of the cervical mucus and therefore potential fertility, is still being tested, so don't bother looking in the corner drugstore yet.

Lunaception, developed by Louise Lacey, is another natural method, based on the theory that women normally ovulate on the full moon and menstruate at the new moon, but that modern lighting conditions have disrupted the biological clock. Lacey's system calls for women to sleep in a room with all light blocked out all month, except for three days midcycle, when a small light bulb is supposed to trigger ovulation. Whatever the scientific validity

of this theory, its inconveniences are obvious.

Herbal medicine is another ancient discipline that is being re-studied. Many herbs can cause the uterine muscles to contract, either bringing on a delayed period or causing a very early abortion (typically, not later than ten days after the missed period). Feminist Health Works publishes a book, *Herbal Remedies for Women* ($2.50), and also has 44 fact sheets about women's health in English and five in Spanish. McCartney and Kramer warned that, although some herbs can be used safely, pennyroyal oil is a very potent and dangerous drug and should *not* be used as

an herbal abortifacient. Sometimes massage of the reflexology and acupuncture points for the uterus (on the inside of the ankle and the heel) can be used to bring on a delayed period, according to the panelists.

In short, the age-old problem of safe and effective birth control is still a problem—perhaps because birth control technologies have been developed to control women rather than give women control over their own bodies. Maybe the biggest advantage of natural birth control methods is the way they encourage women to know their own bodies and take responsibility for themselves.

August 1980 • Vol. 12, No. 8

NEWSLETTER

National Abortion Rights Action League

From: *National Abortion Rights Action League Newsletter* 12, no. 8 (August 1980): 1,4

High Court Upholds 'Hyde'

"There is another world 'out there,' the existence of which the Court . . . either chooses to ignore or fears to recognize."
—Justice Blackmun in his dissent to *Harris* v *McRae* ruling

On June 30, 1980 the U.S. Supreme Court ruled in *Harris* v *McRae* that versions of the so-called "Hyde" Amendment which severely restrict the use of federal funds for Medicaid abortions do not violate the Constitution. The 5-4 decision was delivered by Justice Stewart, who was joined in the majority opinion by Justices Burger, White, Powell, and Rehnquist. Empassioned dissents were filed separately by Justices Marshall, Blackmun, Stevens, and Brennan.

Harris v *McRae* was appealed to the Supreme Court by the U.S. Solicitor General after federal district court Judge John F. Dooling ruled it unconstitutional to deny funding for medically necessary Medicaid abortions.

For a number of us sitting in the

courtroom on June 30, the Supreme Court decision was a shock and a severe disappointment—bringing with it the certainty that poor women will be further victimized by unresponsive legislators and their own unfortunate circumstances.

Immediately after the Court's decision was announced, Justice Stevens began to speak. Noting that the Court only allows one dissent to be read aloud **each year**, he firmly and eloquently read his dissent to the Court's ruling on *Harris* v *McRae*. He said: "[B]ecause a denial of benefits for medically necessary abortions inevitably causes serious harm to the excluded women, it is tantamount to severe punishment. In my judgment, that denial cannot be justified unless Government may, in effect, punish women who want abortions."

Justice Marshall, in a separate dissent, wrote: "The Court's decision today . . . represents a cruel blow to the most powerless members of our society. . . . The Court's opinion studiously avoids recognizing the undeniable fact that for women eligible for Medicaid—poor women—the denial of a Medicaid-funded abortion, is equivalent to denial of legal abortion altogether. If abortion is medically necessary and a funded abortion is unavailable, they must resort to back-alley butchers."

It is extremely important to understand that the Court did not prohibit the use of Medicaid funds for abortions. It only ruled that Congress has a right to limit Medicaid

"DADDY?"

Bob Englehart/Civil Liberties Reporter/LNS

The Spokeswoman/LNS

WE CAN'T ALLOW A WOMAN, RIGHTS OVER HER OWN BODY

WE MUST PROTECT THE FETAL TISSUE

LIFE IS SACRED

NEXT WEEKS SERMON WE NEED THE DEATH PENALTY

"THIS WEEKS" SERMON NO ABORTION

Bülbül/LNS

These women may be forced to bear unwanted children.

ANS/LNS

RAPE VICTIMS

YOUNG GIRLS

OLDER WOMEN

POOR WOMEN

funds for abortions if it so chooses. By the same token, Congress can also restore full funding.

The High Court also did not say that the denial of funding for medically necessary abortions is either just, responsible, or sound social policy.

It is not the mission of this Court or any other to decide whether the balance of competing interests reflected in the Hyde Amendment is wise social policy. If that were our mission, not every Justice who has subscribed to the judgment of the Court today could have done so. But we cannot, in the name of the Constitution, overturn enacted statutes simply "because they may be unwise, improvident, or out of harmony with a particular school of thought." Rather, "when an issue involves policy choices as sensitive as those implicated here . . . the appropriate forum for their resolution in a democracy is the legislature." (*Harris* v *McRae*)

The following is a summary of the *Harris* v *McRae* decision:

• The Court held that Title XIX of the Social Security Act (Medicaid) does not require a participating state to pay for those medically necessary abortions for which federal reimbursement is denied under the Hyde Amendment. (The current "Hyde Amendment" only allows federal reimbursement in cases of life endangerment, rape, or incest.)

• *Roe* v *Wade*, the 1973 landmark Supreme Court decision, established the freedom of a woman to decide whether to terminate a pregnancy as a constitutional right (part of the right to privacy). According to Justice Stewart, funding restrictions of the Hyde Amendment do not impinge on this right because "a woman's freedom of choice does not carry with it an entitlement to . . . financial resources. . ." In his dissent, Justice Brennan strongly disagreed with this conclusion, stating that "by thus injecting coercive financial incentives favoring childbirth . . . the Hyde Amendment deprives the indigent women of her freedom to choose abortion over maternity."

• According to the High Court, funding restrictions do not violate the equal protection component of the Fifth Amendment because encouraging childbirth, except in the most urgent circumstances, is rationally related to the legitimate governmental objective of protecting potential life—even when the protection of potential life damages the health of the woman.

Justice Marshall, in his dissent, said that the decision would mean an increase in the number of poor women who will die as a result of the denial of abortion funding. He reiterated his stand that "the state interest in protecting potential life cannot justify jeopardizing the life or health of the mother."

• The Court did not rule on the constitutional issue of whether it is a violation of a woman's religious freedom to be denied public payment for an abortion that she seeks for religious reasons.

The Supreme Court *Harris* v *McRae* decision is a tragedy for hundreds of thousands of low-income women who will be denied access to safe, legal, Medicaid-funded abortions while Medicaid will continue to fund all costs of prenatal care and childbirth. It is clearly evident that elected Members of Congress and state legislators will make the final decisions regarding an eventual restoration of funding and the legality of abortion altogether. This is hopeful, because we know that if enough of the pro-choice majority gets involved in the election campaigns of pro-choice candidates—and if this pro-choice majority votes—we will keep abortion legal and we will someday have Medicaid funding again.

SCIENCE FOR THE PEOPLE

From *Science for the People* 11, no. 5 (September/October 1979): 8-14

Political Gynecology: Gynecological Imperialism and the Politics of Self-Help

by Susan Bell

Introduction

How do health activists institute change in the medical system? A problem commonly faced by them is whether to work to improve a basically sexist and oppressive medical care system or to create their own structures. Does it make sense to institute short range reforms or to struggle for long term radical change? By "improving" the health care system it may be possible to generate more humane health care but at the cost of strengthening an already oppressive system.

Change in the medical system can be instituted in a number of spheres: at the level of federal or state policy making, in private and public funding, in the area of services or scientific research, and in education. In this article is a discussion of these issues in light of the experiences of a group of feminists involved in a program to teach pelvic examinations to medical students in 1975-76 in Boston. Hence, the focus of this article is on change in the medical system at the level of physician education.

There have been numerous analyses of medicine as an institution of social control and of the particular ways in which medicine oppresses women[1]: Women consume the largest proportion of health services (for themselves and their children), take more prescription drugs than men, and are admitted to hospitals more often than men. Most physicians are white men. Whether women seek private gynecological care, clinical or hospital services, most of them encounter practitioners who have learned how to perform pelvic examinations in the organized medical structure which is part and parcel of the larger racist and sexist society.[2]

Medical students traditionally learn incorrect and/or distorted information about women in textbooks and lectures.[3] They are taught to act as if the pelvic examination is as matter-of-fact as any routine examination, while at the same time learning to use unnecessary and uncomfortable examining techniques.[4] They are told to use stirrups and drapes routinely: both of these techniques are usually unnecessary and often uncomfortable for routine examinations. Traditionally they have practiced pelvic examinations on prostitutes, plastic "gynny" models, clinic "patients"* and anesthetized women. The women are often not asked for consent to furnish their bodies for teaching material.

It has been acknowledged by some educators, critics of medical education, and dissatisfied students that this way of teaching is unsatisfactory. To remedy the situation, some educators have altered the information taught to students and the way in which they learn practical skills. One such improvement, introduced in the 1960s, has been the use of "Simulated Patients" (also called "Programmed Patients") instead of real "patients."[5] "Simulated Patients" are people who have been taught to exhibit historical, physical, and psychological manifestations of an illness when examined by students. They have been employed in a variety of settings to teach cognitive, interpersonal, and technical skills.[6] Prostitutes, friends of medical students, and community women have been recruited to serve as "Simulated Patients" to teach pelvic examinations and patient management skills to medical students. Depending on the emphasis of a program, women might be chosen because they are healthy or because they have specific ailments.

Students, physician-instructors, and "patients" benefit by the use of "Simulated Patients." Students try out practical techniques on them, thereby decreasing their own anxiety and embarrassment about examining people, and increasing their ability to discuss the examination openly in front of the "Simulated Patients." They learned to perform examinations in a realistic way and physician-instructors are able to evaluate students' performances in a standardized way. Hospital and clinic "patients" are saved from repetitive, inept examinations, and

*The term "patient" will be used in quotes to remind the reader of the debates over the definition of health and illness in society and over the power relations between provider and consumer of medical care.

ultimately receive care from better-trained physicians.

The Pelvic Teaching Program

In mid-1975, women medical students at Harvard Medical School approached a member of the Boston Women's Health Book Collective to discuss the possibility of finding women to serve as paid "pelvic models." The women medical students were displeased with current teaching practices. They specifically wanted feminists since they thought that the use of feminists as "pelvic models" would greatly improve the learning process and would provide a counterbalance to institutionalized attitudes toward women as passive recipients of medical care. The book collective contacted women at Women's Community Health Center (WCHC) in Cambridge who agreed to a limited number of "modelling" sessions for second year Harvard medical students at local hospitals.[7]

The members of WCHC, a self-help women's health center, saw themselves as part of the movement for radical social change, committed to the eradication of sexism, racism, capitalism, and imperialism. In practical terms, this means basic changes in the medical system as part of changing the overall structure of society: for instance, a breakdown of hierarchical relations among provider and consumer in which the provider has a monopoly over skills and information, women providing health care for women, and an end to "for-profit" medical services.[8]

Implementing a program to teach medical students was a focus of controversy in the WCHC from its inception. Some health center women saw it as a low priority issue in the sense that it would entail putting energy into professional medical education and detract from other health center programs which were directed towards implementing long-term changes. In addition, some women expressed concern that the program would serve to strengthen the medical system by teaching physicians how to "manage" their "patients" (by changing their behaviors without changing their power in doctor/patient encounters). Other members of the collective thought that teaching medical students would be a way to improve existing services for women and therefore that it would be a useful interim reform. They also thought that it would be a way to direct money from the medical schools to part of the women's health movement and

a way of gaining access to the medical educational system. This controversy influenced the process of setting up the Pelvic Teaching Program (PTP) and of evaluating and changing it over time and was never completely resolved at the Women's Community Health Center.

In late 1975, the WCHC expanded this program by recruiting women who were not members of the collective. They also formalized the program by creating an ongoing group called the Pelvic Teaching Program. The PTP was a semi-autonomous program of the Women's Community Health Center. It was also the first attempt in which collective members worked along with women who were not members of the collective. This led in part to difficulties in communication and questions about power and decision-making among group members and also between the group and WCHC. For instance, to what extent could the Pelvic Teaching Program devise and implement its own structure and to what extent was it accountable to WCHC? Were WCHC members in the PTP more powerful than the others in the group? Could WCHC direct the PTP? The course of the PTP can be traced in stages, each marked by a new protocol.

The First Protocol

In the first sessions changes in standard teaching methods were relatively superficial: "pelvic models" were each paid $25 for each teaching session. In each teaching session, four or five medical students did a bimanual pelvic examination* on a consenting, knowledgeable woman, while taught by a physician-instructor. Sessions focused on attitudes and the manner in which students learned to perform a pelvic examination. They left intact the role of physician-instructor. Meanwhile, the femi-

*A person conducts a bimanual pelvic examination by inserting two fingers into a woman's vagina and feeling her cervix (tip of the womb or uterus, which extends into the vagina), and with the other hand presses down on her abdomen. In this way, the person doing the bimanual pelvic examination can feel the size, shape and position of a woman's uterus and cervix. A bimanual pelvic examination also includes checking a woman's external genitals.

A speculum is an instrument that is used to separate the walls of a woman's vagina to be able to visualize her vagina and cervix. By use of a mirror and light a woman can see her own vagina and cervix.

For complete information about what a good gynecological or pelvic examination should include, see *Our Bodies, Ourselves*, by the Boston Women's Health Book Collective.

nists did research to find out what had been taught at Harvard and what the professors and students were interested in implementing. The feminists met to evaluate this limited program and then met with the professors and medical students to draw up a protocol. The physician-instructors and medical students were pleased by this limited program. It facilitated more efficient, comfortable teaching sessions. The feminists were dissatisfied. In a retrospective analysis they wrote that "although we gave active feedback as the exam was being performed, the physicians were the major instructors and the students looked to them to handle the tough problems and to field questions regarding pathology. We had very little control over the teaching sessions."[9] The success of these limited sessions was disquieting: the women realized that while they were ensuring more humane and better exams for women, they were also solidifying physicians' power over women by participating in training sessions in which students learned how to instill trust in themselves by making women more comfortable and informed about pelvic examinations. They saw that this accommodation to the current medical system was a way to strengthen the medical system rather than to change it. They thus proposed a new protocol, which was accepted and implemented.[10]

A Second Protocol

The second protocol included changes both in the teaching group and in the teaching sessions. The feminists created a formal group, called the Pelvic Teaching Program, and recruited community women to become members. Community women were selected using the following criteria: prior enrollment in a self-help group (this would ensure their familiarity with the concepts and practice of the self-help movement and WCHC familiarity with them): a willingness to share skills with medical students; a commitment to delineate and to critique the underlying goals of the current medical system in their teaching sessions; and a commitment to interrupt sexist, professionalistic, or otherwise offensive behaviors during the sessions. WCHC members were included on the basis of their willingness to put energy into teaching medical students and to participate in a controversial new program.

In teaching sessions, they implemented the following: two feminist instructors from the PTP met with four or five

students, at least one of whom had to be a woman. Members of the PTP instructed students, and physicians, if present at all, assumed the role of silent observers. The feminists required a written contract and were paid $50 for each session instead of $25 for each "model" to emphasize their altered status. Each session was focused on a well-woman approach to medical care, describing the wide range of normal conditions. They demonstrated how women can examine their own genitals using a plastic speculum, light, and mirror. Each teaching institution agreed to reproduce and distribute to the medical students "How to Do A Pelvic Examination," written by the feminists from WCHC.

Part of their proposal was not accepted by Harvard. This included purchase of an information packet written by feminists for each student as well as a separate second session to give information about women's health concerns in more detail to the students.

The Pelvic Teaching Program, now consisting of five WCHC members and six affiliated women, began to meet in an ongoing self-help group amongst themselves, to share criticisms, and perspectives about the program, as well as to devote energy to practical training, information, and skill sharing on a personal and political level. They used the group as a way to cope with embarrassing or offensive encounters and to devise strategies to avoid them in future sessions. They also used the group as a way to share their feelings about their dual roles as "models" and instructors.

They shared information about their program through meetings with other women, in reports to WCHC, and through the health center newsletters. At times, women in the PTP felt misunderstood or unsupported by WCHC. One of the ways in which the PTP and WCHC addressed this issue was by requesting that WCHC members who were not in the PTP observe teaching sessions to understand through first-hand observation what the instructors experienced. Within WCHC and the PTP individually, as well as in dialogues between the two, they addressed the controversial questions about the usefulness of an interim reform in physician education compared with other long term changes; they looked at power relations and communications between the PTP and WCHC.

The PTP wrote to *Health Right,* a newsletter published by women's health

activists, outlining their new protocol, and pointing out why specific changes were made. They requested that any women thinking of teaching pelvic examinations to medical students contact them. They thought that this would be a way of empowering themselves and other women, realizing how isolated they had been when their own program began. As a result of their own experiences they strongly suggested that any women who were going to teach pelvic examinations be involved in a group, so that they could share skills and support for each other.

The report in *Health Right* generated criticism as well as excitement within the women's health community. Although some thought it was a victory to find members of the women's health movement being asked to teach medical professionals, others felt that training doctors was simply a cooptation of long-term strategies.

Up to this point, the PTP was similar to parts of other "Simulated Patient" programs. Responses to the PTP by students and physicians were similar to those enumerated in accounts of "Simulated Patient" programs that I surveyed: student response was favorable, with a few exceptions. Physicians who observed sessions reported that the teaching was excellent. Generally students felt more at ease, learned technical skills more thoroughly, and were better equipped to perform examinations on patients. Some of the negative responses of the students reflect the difference in the PTP from the "Simulated Patient" programs: some were distressed by the "women's libbers" stance of the feminists.

In the Spring of 1976, the members of the PTP analyzed the program and began to assert their unique political perspective. It happened in three ways:

1. Through the political development of the group itself.

2. By means of the issues that the feminists, as part of the women's health movement, wanted to address through the PTP.

3. In the institutional response of the medical schools to the Third Protocol.

The second protocol left basic contradictions unresolved. As nonprofessionals, they taught professionals techniques that only professionals could use legally; men learned how to practice medical care for women; fragmented medical care was encouraged by the program since the feminists met only once with students, thereby offering limited and isolated information; heirarchical power relationships between provider and receiver and amongst providers were not confronted.

After their analysis of the second protocol and its implementation, the members of the PTP met as a group to write the *Position Paper* to evaluate their experiences as a group and as individuals, and to devise a new protocol that would meet their needs and serve their political purposes. The *Position Paper* outlined their self-criticism and their suggestions for questions to be raised by other women before beginning to teach pelvic examinations. They circulated this in Boston women's publications, in *Health Right,* and in *Women and Health,* and sent out copies of it to any people who had inquired about the PTP over the past year. By this time, members of the medical profession had heard about the PTP as well, and wanted information about the program and copies of the manual written by the feminists as a sourcebook for their own programs.[11]

In discussions leading up to the formulation of the third protocol, the women in both the PTP and the WCHC addressed the ongoing issue of reform versus radical change. In their analysis of events, they concluded that as a reform within the medical system the PTP had been successful, but that it had failed to institute long term change.

In order to emphasize their self-help politics, a third protocol was devised which would make explicit the differences between their point of view and the point of view exhibited by creators of the "Simulated Patient" programs. They devised a program which would be acceptable to them and nearby, they expected, not acceptable to the medical schools. Rather than presenting a critique, they proposed a new program, thereby requiring that the medical school officials respond.

The Third Protocol

The third protocol included the following changes: first, teaching would be limited to women. The PTP as part of the self-help/women's health movement was committed to reciprocal sharing, and learning through reciprocity is not only different from, but more meaningful than, one-way learning. The PTP could only have integrity as a self-help experience if there was reciprocal sharing. This would entail being examined as well as examining. By definition, then, the teaching of pelvic examinations would be limited to women. By limiting the teaching to women, they wanted to force all the medical students to address the question: should men be providing gynecological care for women?

The feminists had also found that despite their efforts to the contrary, they had felt embarrassed and exploited by some of the male students—and they wished to avoid focusing attention on this part of the training. By teaching only women, they thought that it would be a more positive experience for themselves and rid them of sexual exploitation during the sessions.

Second, each teaching group of four or five women would include not only medical students, but also other hospital personnel and consumers, taught by two women from the PTP. By doing this, the feminists would address the issues of hierarchy and elitism among medical care providers and between providers and consumers, which encourage physicians to maintain a monopoly of skills and information. Instructors would exchange roles with others in the teaching group, emphasizing the need for a breakdown of the rigid hierarchy among physicians, nurses and other health workers as well as that between powerful physicians and passive "patients." They would also promote identification and recognition of similarities between provider and consumer rather than objectification and distance. This would help to demystify and defuse the physician's power and be a way of stimulating discussion about these issues.

Third, the new protocol called for three or four sessions with the same individuals to allow time for analysis of the politics of medical care, to share health information of special relevance to women, to discuss what a good examination should include, and to perform self-examination. This would challenge the teaching of medical care as fragmented and episodic. By placing the technical skills and information within the general context of the politics of medical care, they would stimulate discussion about commonly held assumptions about what students are learning and why.

Fourth, the PTP raised their fees, in recognition of their value as instructors, and of the ability and common practice of the medical schools to pay higher consultant fees. Fees were raised to $750 for the four sessions.

The issues addressed in the third protocol were hierarchy, sexism, fragmentation of learning skills, profit, and division between provider and consumer. By this time, the PTP had been approached by the other area medical schools, Tufts and Boston University. As had been predicted by the PTP, no medical schools wanted to implement this program. Reasons varied: it was too expensive; it discriminated against men. As long as the PTP fell within the acceptable range of innovations, exemplified by the "Simulated Patient" programs, it remained an acceptable program. When it confronted basic power relations and current assumptions about the goals of medical education, the PTP became unacceptable to current teaching programs. At this stage, in the summer of 1976, the PTP ended: women received inquiries and sent out the third protocol after that date, but have no longer taught sessions.

Discussion

What can we learn from the experience of the PTP? One way to evaluate it is to see in what respects the women successfully implemented a reform in physician education. The PTP demonstrated that a group of nonprofessionals could devise and implement a program. By example, then, the women demonstrated within the medical community that "consumers" can educate themselves and become active members in the medical community. The PTP established themselves as credible teachers to both medical students and physicians. By identifying themselves as feminists, the PTP openly brought political awareness and political issues into a teaching situation and confronted sexist attitudes and practices as they emerged in the teaching sessions. In addition, by emphasizing use of common language to describe medical procedures, and by demonstrating how a woman can participate in the examination, they focused on the distinction between provider and consumer and suggested ways that the consumer could gain more power in the encounter through knowledge and skills. They self-consciously went about channeling money into the women's health movement and got a good first-hand look at medical education. They created a need for feminists to teach pelvic examinations to medical students. They accomplished this both by their success in the first two phases, and also by their visibility in the women's health movement by doing this: medical students and health activists read about their success and the way that they went about teaching and meeting as an ongoing group, and saw by their example that it was possible.

The feminists wrote and circulated a manual for teaching pelvic examinations which is still in demand. The PTP gained considerable attention not only in the local medical and women's communities, but also nationally, through publications and networks. They continue to receive requests for protocols, for copies of their manual, and in general for information about how to implement pelvic teaching programs.[12]

However, in their own analysis, the PTP concluded that these successes were insufficient to outweigh the time and energy necessitated by the program. Their decision can be better understood if we turn to three issues: first, the PTP lacked a complete understanding of the history of "Simulated Patients" programs; second, the PTP evolved as a semi-autonomous group out of the WCHC, raising the issues of power and communication within a group of collective members and affiliated women, and between the PTP and the WCHC; and third, they carried on an ongoing dialogue about the advisability of instituting an interim reform.

In some respects, the task of the PTP had been made more arduous by their lack of complete knowledge and analysis of other programs. As we have seen, the development of the PTP occurred through its own experiences rather than being shaped by a vision of the eventual outcome.

When the feminists designed the protocols, it was without a historical analysis of the use of "Simulated Patients" and without a complete overview of contemporaneous programs (having only looked at what had been taught at Harvard previously and screened one videotape of a program in which a physician performed a pelvic examination on a "Simulated Patient"). If they had begun with a complete overview of precedents already set by other innovative "Simulated Patient" programs, they might have chosen other strategies with which to confront Harvard with an educated overview. The first two protocols followed essentially the same lines as "Simulated Patient" programs. What seemed to the feminists, at times, as risky and dangerous at Harvard, had already become institutionalized in other medical schools.

It was with the third protocol that the women were not only devising a better program, but were also explicitly challenging commonly held assumptions about

medical care and explicitly stating some of their own political goals: to eradicate hierarchy and professionalism; to have women provide women's health care; to redefine the distinction between provider and consumer and to empower the consumer vis-a-vis the provider; and finally to challenge the monopoly over money and resources that medical schools have.

As a new program of the WCHC, the PTP was the focus of an evolving mechanism for implementing similar WCHC programs in the future. This process entailed working out problems and concerns raised during the course of the group about ways to facilitate communication and decisionmaking in a semiautonomous program; at times this process was frustrating and stressful.

In addition, the PTP was never wholeheartedly supported by members of WCHC. Not only were the women in the PTP constantly re-examining their goals and strategies, but they were shaped by the ongoing controversy in WCHC about whether to teach medical students. This contributed to a sense of frustration and exhaustion when the PTP evaluated the first and second protocols and drew up the third.

Finally, the task of initiating reforms in physician-training necessitates constant confrontation of the educational structures and individuals serving to oppress women. On the one hand, the struggle faced by the women to implement even the first protocol at Harvard demonstrates the threat they posed as feminist nonprofessionals entering the confines of medical providers. On the other hand, the ability of educational institutions to absorb and co-opt innovations is striking: teaching medical students ways to improve the pelvic examination for women was taken by them as a technique of managing their "patients" in sessions taught according to the first and second protocols. This ability was taken seriously by the feminists in their evaluations of the success or failure of the PTP, and must be recognized by others considering similar programs. What might appear to be positive reforms in theory might prove to be cooptations in practice, and hence not positive in the long run. Because the feminists paid close attention to the impact of their program during the process of setting it up and implementing it, they were able to evaluate it realistically.

In retrospect, we can see that the PTP was successful in some important ways and provides a thoughtful and politically

responsible example of the ways in which health activists might institute change in the medical system. The experiences of the PTP also underline the necessity of an ongoing reassessment of the long range implications of short term reforms, not only in theory but in their practical application.

References

1. For example, see the following: Kotelchuck, David, ed., *Prognosis Negative*. New York. Vintage Books, 1976; Dreifus, Claudia, ed., *Seizing Our Bodies*. New York, Vintage Books, 1978; Boston Women's Health Book Collective, *Our Bodies, Ourselves*, New York, Simon and Schuster, 1976.

2. Nurses, nurse practitioners and physician assistants also perform pelvic examinations. It is beyond the scope of this article to look at the differences among these professionals and between them and physicians.

3. Bart, P., Scully, D., "A Funny Thing Happened on the Way to the Orifice: Women in Gynecology Textbooks," *Am. J. Soc.* 78:1045-1050, 1973; Howell, M., "What Medical Schools Teach About Women," *N. Engl. J. Med.* 291-304-307, 1974.

4. Emerson, J., "Behavior in Private Places," in H. P. Dreitzel, ed., *Recent Sociology No. 2: Patterns of Communicative Behavior.* New York, The MacMillan Company, 1970, pp. 74-95; Shaw, N. S., *Forced Labor,* New York, Pergamon Press, Inc., 1974.

5. Teaching hospitals and clinics associated with medical schools provide services and are also training institutions. Hence "patients" receive care and provide teaching material.

6. See the following for discussions of these programs: "Announcement: Using Nonphysicians to Teach Pelvic Examinations," *Contemporary Ob/Gyn.* 11:173, 1978; Billings, J. A., Stoeckle, J. D., "Pelvic Examination Instruction and the Doctor-Patient Relationship," *J. Med. Educ.* 52:834-839, 1977; Godkins, T. R., Duffy, D., Greenwood, J., Stanhope, W. D., "Utilization of Simulated Patients to Teach the 'Routine' Pelvic Examination," *J. Med. Educ.* 49:1174-1178, 1974; Holzman, G. B., Singleton, D., Holmes, T. F., Maatsch, J. L., "Initial Pelvic Examination Instruction: The Effectiveness of Three Contemporary Approaches," *Am. J. Obstet. Gyn.* 129:2, 124-129, 1977; Johnson, G. H., Brown, T. C., Stenchever, M. A., Gabert, H. A., Poulson, A. M., Warenski, J. C., "Teaching Pelvic Examination to Second-Year Medical Students Using Programmed Patients," *Am. J. Obstet. Gyn.* 121:5, 714-717, 1975; Kretzschmar, R. M., "Evolution of the Gynecology Teaching Associate: An Education Specialist," *Am. J. Obstet. Gyn.* 131:4, 367-373, 1978; Schneidman, B., "An Approach to Obtaining Patients to Participate in Pelvic Examination Instruction," *J. Med. Educ.* 52:70-71, 1977.

7. Information about the Women's Community Health Center (WCHC) and the Pelvic Teaching Program have been gathered from the following sources: Women's Community Health Center, Inc. "Experiences of a Pelvic Teaching Group," *Women and Health* 1:4, 19-20, 1976 (this is a reprint of the *Position Paper*, June,

1976, available from WCHC, 639 Massachusetts Avenue, room 210, Cambridge, Massachusetts 02139); WCHC, Third Annual Report, Cambridge, Mass., 1977; WCHC, "Letter to the Editor," *Health Right*, 2:3, 2, 1976 (The address for *Health Right* is 41 Union Square, Room 206-9, New York, NY 10003); WCHC, "Announcement" *Women and Health*, 1:1, 17, 1976; WCHC, "How to Do a Pelvic Examination," 1976; WCHC, "Proposals to Teach Pelvic Examinations to Medical Students," 1975 and 1976; Norsigian, J. "Training the Docs," *Health-Right*, 2:2, 6, 1975-76; Other sources have been informal and formal discussions with the PTP and the WCHC. As a member of both the PTP and the WCHC, I have drawn from my own experiences as well as from the above sources.

8. The development of the PTP could be analyzed from the point of view of the medical institutions as well as from its self-concept. This article will concentrate on the PTP from the feminist perspective.

9. The quote is from the *Position Paper*.

10. Through various networks, other women's health groups and publications heard about these sessions, *Health Right, Women and*

Health, and *Liberation News Service* published information about the program.

11. The PTP has refused to supply copies of their manual to any members of the medical profession out of context.

12. For discussions of the PTP written by members of the medical profession, see the Billings and Stoeckle article and the Announcement, listed in Note #6 above.

This article is a revised version of a presentation given at the fall conference of the Massachusetts Sociological Association on November 4, 1978. I would like to thank members of the Pelvic Teaching Program, the Women's Community Health Center, and the Science for the People Editorial Collective for their help and support in writing this article. Charlotte Weissberg provided sisterly criticisms.

Susan Bell is a founding member of the Pelvic Teaching Program and worked at the Women's Community Health Center in Cambridge, Mass. for two and one-half years. She is currently completing her doctoral dissertation, which is a critical history of diethylstilbestrol (DES), a synthetic estrogen.

HEALTH/PAC BULLETIN

Health Policy Advisory Center

From *Health/PAC Bulletin* 11, no. 4 (March/April 1980): 19-20

Women: Birth of a Struggle

by Marilynn Norinsky

Marianne Doshi, Elizabeth Leggett, Carolle Baya, and Rosalie Tarpening are just four of the most recent victims of the struggle for humane, safe childbirth. As birth rates declined during the 1960s the practice of obstetric medicine became less profitable, simply because there were fewer patients to receive this care. And as existing standard obstetric practice has come under fire from a number of different fronts, because of its dehumanizing obsession with technology, its high costs, and its less than laudable infant mortality statistics, more and more women turn to the only real alternative: homebirth. And as the popularity of homebirth increases, the medical community becomes more threatened— and more vicious.

California legislators introduced legisla-

tion in 1977 to legalize lay midwifery and give it autonomy from the medical profession (see "Lay Midwifery: The Old Becomes the New?" *Health/PAC Bulletin*, no. 79, November/December 1977). By September 1978, when the bill became law, there was no mention of midwives at all. The bill had become an authorization for any government agency to apply to sponsor a pilot project for "training innovative health care personnel." The change in emphasis is attributed to the California Medical Association's (CMA) strong opposition. This organized opposition to midwifery extended to the delivery of medical care itself, as clearly evidenced by the case of Marianne Doshi, a lay midwife from San Luis Obispo, charged with second degree murder and practicing medicine without a license.

After an apparently uneventful labor, the baby of a couple Doshi attended at a home delivery exhibited breathing difficulties at birth. Doshi administered mouth-to-mouth resuscitation until the local firemen arrived and mechanically induced breathing. The infant and her mother were taken to Sierra Vista Hospital, where the mother was refused admission because she had no attending obstetrician. Numerous sources report that this was the result of an

agreement among local county obstetricians to refuse prenatal consultation and care for women planning to deliver at home. The baby was subsequently flown 200 miles to Mt. Zion Hospital in San Francisco, where she died five days later. The parents filed no charges against Doshi. Doshi was arrested and charged, however, by the County of San Luis Obispo.

Doshi was cleared of both charges on October 20, 1978, by San Luis Obispo Superior Court Judge Richard Kirkpatrick. In his ruling Kirkpatrick defended the right of parents to deliver children at home and called for better communication between the medical community, the educational community, midwives and parents seeking alternative childbirths. John N. Miller, Chairman of the California chapter of the American College of Obstetricians and Gynecologists, commented after the hearing, "The difficulty I find with the judge's decision is that these people are totally unlicensed. They are just a group of people, some with no qualifications, whose only experience in some cases is having watched five or six people give birth. They have no comprehension of the complications that can arise in childbirth." Yet the very bill which would have established licensure criteria (education, apprenticeship, etc.) was the very bill decimated by the CMA, Miller himself and numerous other medical groups and individuals.

Midwifery itself is not the issue. Midwifery is a growing specialization in the nursing profession. What is at issue is *who* becomes a midwife, where the midwife attends births, and how much autonomy the midwife has.

The nursing profession has recognized both the criticisms of modern obstetric practice and the demands of women to have more wholistic, supportive prenatal and delivery care, and created a midwifery specialty, certified by the American College of Nurse Midwives. Certified nurse midwives do much to alleviate a number of the recent criticisms, but they have not been able to solve all of them. By state regulation, and professional choice, most nurse midwives confine their practice to hospitals or birthing centers. Thus the demand for home birth attendants is largely ignored by the obstetrical profession and certified nurse midwives. Nurse midwives bring with them a medical bias towards birth, at least more so than lay midwives. Nurse midwives are trained to see themselves as "apprentices" of obstetricians, having the same relation to them that physician assistants have to family practitioners.

In Tennessee, where The Farm is known for its safety record of midwife-attended out-of-hospital deliveries, Elizabeth Leggett, RN, had her nursing license revoked by the Tennessee Board of Nursing for practicing midwifery without certification. Tennessee has no laws regulating lay midwives, and lay midwifery is specifically exempt from the state's medical practice act. The charges? "Unprofessional conduct, performing functions she is not prepared to handle, and being unfit or incompetent to handle forseeable consequences." At issue here was the fact that Leggett was an RN, since, "If she weren't a nurse, the board would have no case, because Tennessee law does not regulate midwives," according to Elizabeth Hocker, RN, executive director of the Tennessee Board of Nursing.

Doctors in Tennessee are no more receptive to homebirths than are doctors in California. The Childbirth Information Association has "been looking for over three years for a doctor to help us set up a safe home delivery service for women who want it." One such doctor was found, but was allegedly threatened with loss of hospital privileges until he withdrew his assistance. President of the Tennessee Medical Association, John B. Dorian, feels that anything is better than the home for delivery. "The specialty of gynecology actually got its start from the repair of home deliveries," commented Dr. Terry DeWitt, a "local obstetrician" who refuses prenatal care to any woman anticipating home delivery.

The attacks keep coming. In St. Augustine, Florida, Carolle Baya, a birth attendant and home birth educator, was charged with practicing midwifery and medicine without a license. Although there had been no bad outcomes or parent complaints concerning Baya's birth attendances, the charges were initiated by Dr. Anthony Mussalem, one of the two practicing obstetricians in her community. Dr. Mussalem's complaints led to Baya's termination as a Lamaze instructor for the County School Board and to the (aforementioned) charges from the State Attorney's Office, as well as an attempted injunction to "temporarily and permanently enjoin Baya from attending home childbirth" until she was granted a midwifery license. The attempted injunction would have been the ultimate catch-

22—licensure is contingent upon attendance of a specified number of births! Baya had been pursuing licensure as a midwife for over a year prior to the levying of charges against her.

Florida's 1931 statutes regarding midwifery were declared unconstitutional by Judge Richard O. Watson in a six page opinion, October 10, 1979. The opinion applies only to the Baya case, unless, after appeal by the State and the Department of Health and Rehabilitation Services (HRS), the decision is upheld in the Florida Supreme Court. As of December 1979, no appeal had been filed.

HRS, however, proposed new regulations for midwives while the decision was being awaited. Among other provisions, the legislation would require a physician to "certify" a patient as suitable for lay midwife delivery and to forbid lay midwives to attend a woman having her first baby. It is expected that this legislation will be introduced in 1980.

The most recent case to come to our attention, and the most serious known charge to date, is that of Rosalie Tarpening. Tarpening is a licensed physical therapist who first assisted at a friend's home delivery some 10 years ago in Madera (Monterey County), California. Since then, Tarpening assisted over 350 home births, with an infant mortality rate of 2.7/1,000 live births. The rates for the

county were so high (23.9/1,000), that a trial program recruiting nurse midwives was initiated, lowering the rates to 10.2/1000. Tarpening's rates compare most favorably with the county statistics cited above. Until November 28, 1979, Tarpening had no problems in any of her assistances. On that date, Tarpening assisted in what was to become a still birth. Although the family had no complaints, the District Attorney, after learning of Tarpening's presence at the home, charged her with *first degree murder* and practicing medicine without a license. The preliminary hearing is scheduled for February 28, 1980.

The struggles for the legitimization of lay midwifery cited here are part of a much larger struggle in obstetrics, and health care in general, today. Financial factors lend credibility to the cries of women for nonhospital-based deliveries, since the latter are obviously less costly. Traditionally, childbirth has been woman's domain. The development of forceps and anesthetic technology allowed the male medical profession to dominate childbirth here in the United States. As the women's health movement grows stronger, this dominance is challenged. The cases cited here are just the beginning of a long, protracted struggle for the control of a human birth experience—and for the control by women of their own bodies.

PAID MY DUES
A Quarterly Journal of Women in Music

From *Paid My Dues* 4, no. 1 (1980): 7-8

Women's Music: Where Are We Going?

by Thelma Norris

We at PMD *are particularly concerned, as women's music enters its second decade, with the future challenges and directions of our movement. We hope to explore this fully, and from many viewpoints, in our next issue, and are inviting all of you to*

Reprinted with permission from *Paid My Dues.*

participate. To start off the dialogue, we have asked Thelma Norris of Women in Music/Chicago, to give her views on some aspects of the development of women's music up to this time and to explain what she sees as some of the challenges to be faced in the coming few years.

Women's music had perhaps its most visible beginning in late spring, 1972, at the First National Women's Music Festival in Champaign, Illinois. The festival and the movement itself began as a reaction against the music industry's stereotyping of women performers, through both the material they sang and their "packaging." The first national festival promised its audience stars from the music industry, but when the stars did not appear, musicians such as

Where Are We Going?

What do you see as the future of the women's music movement? In what direction would you like to see it going? How best can it get there? What do you see as the most difficult problems facing the movement? What are your ideas for meeting those problems?

We are inviting you to think about and write about one or more of these questions. Then, in our next issue, we plan to print some of your thoughts and ours. In order to insure consideration for publication, we need to hear from you by July 31.

Margie Adam, Meg Christian, and Cris Williamson came together, discovering their common interests and ideals. Returning home, supported by wildly enthusiastic audiences they found at the festival, the participants eventually became a foundation for the women's music movement. Today this movement has developed into a network which includes musicians and their support staffs, women's recording companies, studio engineers, record distributors and promoters, concert and coffeehouse producers, sound and light technicians, and festival organizers—to name a few!

Women's music has always been conceived of as an alternative structure to the music industry and the major labels. This structure is based on the mutually recognized politics of its members, the least common denominator of which is joyfully acknowledging the strength and potential of women. Not all that much has changed at the major labels in the past eight years that women's music has existed as an alternative structure. Glance at the record covers,

Jaqueline Peterson/LNS

or listen to the music produced "on schedule" by very creative women musicians on the major labels. Look at the list of women musicians dropped by the record companies when their sales fall. All this attests to the fact that mass-marketing a woman musician is still mass-marketing a stereotype in the minds of many record and artist management companies. Women's record labels give their musicians more autonomy over their recorded material, the recording process, album covers, and touring. WILD (Women's Independent Label Distribution Network), a two-year-old organization of record labels and distributors, is working not only on how to promote and distribute music in this highly competitive and pressurized field, but also on ways to do that job in a non-oppressive environment. And while I don't suggest that the women of WILD are always successful, the process of trying to create that environment is a constant reminder that the alternative focus of women's music is imperative to its staying firmly rooted in the developing women's consciousness.

Today, while remaining close to these roots, women's music is reaching out in many directions, and taking its cue from many sources. Some artists are concentrating more intensely on women-only audiences in women's community settings, while others are looking to clubs, film, "above-ground" concert halls, and national music press for additional audiences and settings. Will Cris Williamson or Alive! succeed the seventeen-piece all-women swing band, Maiden Voyage, onto the Johnny Carson show? Will they then receive offers for film and recording contracts from over-ground sources? Will they, or other musicians, be attracted to working outside the women's music network?

On the other hand, while performers such as Cris Williamson and Holly Near drew consistently large audiences on recent national tours, concert attendance for other artists seems to be declining. Likewise, some new records released by established artists are selling well, while records by new artists are selling more slowly than expected or receiving exposure to only tiny audiences. And other troubling signs are in evidence: performers in one club had their date disrupted because the audience didn't like another featured woman performer. In two other instances, artists have been hit by objects thrown from the audience—once with a paper cup, another time with fruit—because they

performed with a male musician. What do all these events and trends mean for the future of women's music?

For one thing, it seems practically important during this period that audiences be willing to follow musicians into different performance spaces or be willing to allow them to play to other audiences there. While perhaps a musician will not give the same performance in a more public space than when she "comes home" to perform for the women's community audience, we must appreciate that a performance in a more public space can be challenging and exciting, both to the musician and audience. If "women's music audience" comes to mean an intolerant, possessive audience, attentive to relatively few performers, musicians will be forced out of the network and will be absorbed by other music or entertainment cultures.

I think it is vital that women's music remain an alternative structure, but also a structure that is flexible enough to respond to artists' changing needs. When musicians can perform both in mainstream clubs and in community concerts, when new musicians can tour reasonably and develop audiences, then the alternative of women's music will not only survive but will be the healthy catalyst for the forward movement of women that it was always conceived to be.

The network must continue to try to work creatively and cooperatively with each other, and to develop financial frameworks to ensure the survival of everyone involved in the work. It also becomes crucial that musical environments continue to improve, that productions and record albums be well-conceived and achieved, and that a supportive yet challenging environment exist in which artists can concentrate on musical skills. This will mean more years of musical creativity for the artists, the audience, and the network. But it must come—it can only come—with patience, commitment to excellence, more highly charged creativity and promotion activities, and better cooperation and trust.

I hope this article has opened up questions that will be responded to by musicians, audiences, record companies, and everyone identifying personally and professionally with women's music. The dialogue, in itself, can be a foundation to future growth.

Thelma Norris of Women in Music/Chicago has been a concert producer and record distributor for the past five years.

From *WomanSpirit* 6, no. 24 (Summer 1980): 26-27

Christian Feminist vs. Goddess Movement

by Z. Budapest

The "inheritance" of Christianity for women is pain. The "inheritance" of witches from the Christian ideology is mass murders. The silver lining in that black cloud is the surviving Christianity and the leaving and rejecting Christianity.

Recently I have been reading *Christianity and Crisis,* and I came across Rosemary Ruether's article, "A Religion for Women: Sources and Strategies."* This is a challenge to the Goddess Movement (which she calls Feminist Wicca) and because of the mention of my name in it alongside of friends like Carol Christ and Naomi Goldenberg, both who tried to have a dialog with Rosemary in vain, I take up this challenge and answer her questions. I too don't expect Ms. Ruether to come over to the Goddess' side, but I would expect her not to ask the same questions over and over again after so many of us already responded to it. Most of all I respond because Rosemary Ruether became lately an avid writer about witchcraft, which I find with great alarm since nothing good ever came of Christians focusing on our religion historically. She has given speeches against the Goddess religion, and has not deepened her knowledge about the Goddess movement in many years of debate with women of her caliber.

1. What is the basis of our total rejection of biblical religion for feminists?

I posed this to my students and as usual in the Goddess culture I got a variety of answers: Why not? Why not reject a body of thought forms that was a single force

*[Rosemary Ruether, "A Religion for Women: Sources and Strategies," *Christianity and Crisis* 39 (December 10, 1979): 307-311. Reprinted in *WomanSpirit* 6, no. 24 (Summer 1980): 22-25.—eds., *Alternative Papers.*]

Reprinted with permission from *WomanSpirit,* Box 263, Wolf Creek, OR 97497.

and still is in our oppression as women? Another answer was, "I don't believe that we should foster a 'One Book fetish' any longer." Others said, "I think we can write better books, and have."

For my own part, I say: Biblical religion created patriarchy. I don't care how wonderful some chapters are that Rosemary finds, or that she finds solace in those lines, I judge a body of thoughts by what happened after many societies accepted it and practised it. Deeds are what I look at, not their particular "big black book." Societies that are Christian today afford low status for women and created rape of the earth. That's what counts. Two thousand years is enough to see if any idea won't work for humanity. (It might work in privileged seminaries where Rosemary teaches, or cloisters, but for women it's a bummer. The Bible is boring, which is always an earmark of lacking inspiration, lacking life. We can pump up a corpse, we can paint its cheeks, we can deck it out in fancy places with flowers, it will still remain a corpse.)

2. How helpful is the specific religion we choose as alternative as means to achieve changes which we desire, and . . . other feminists who find some things helpful in the Bible, also desire?

I also posed this challenge to my students. Here are some answers:

I have found self love and self realization through the Goddess.

Goddess religion gives me ecstasy while in life.

Taught me how to create my own reality; how to control my life, my body and my soul.

Goddess religion makes "sense" to me because it's a study of nature.

There is no greater god than mother nature.

Goddess religion works! I don't question why? Do you question why butter melts in the sun?

Again for my part, I must say inner changes are all we can do for now. From inner changes, from the realized divine-woman-soul will flow the dictates of a gentler society where violence is not glorified as it is in the Bible. From a generation of Goddess women will come

the divine leadership that saves the planet earth. From women only will come the necessary step by step program. We hold no guarantees. All we say is that the society that the Goddess created in the past was life affirming, and we can guarantee that. We cannot pass our great promises to Christian ladies who feel betrayed by their own tradition and are looking over to the witches' side, where it is traditionally not safe to look. We cannot woo the Christian lady who finds herself discounted by her brothers and excluded from priesthood. We can only say, help us create the future. To begin, you must let go. To see ahead you must go step by step. The vision is now being self created and divinely created. Trust that. You trusted less. You trusted god the man. (Say bye-bye.)

But these questions are but the top of the iceberg of Ruether's attitudes about women's religion. I sensed a hostility in her article which I would also like to respond to.

Ms. Ruether repeatedly sees the Goddess Religion as a "cult" while her tradition is "religion." She also states time after time (after many of us told her how we believe, and after all we are authorities in our own beliefs), that the Craft is based on dualities. Christianity is a duality. Goddess of the Ten Thousand Names and Guises is to say the least a Trinity (another steal into Catholicism), and then She is multi-aspected! So how can she say this again and again unless she is fixated to spread duality herself? Ms. Ruether's further ignorance about the Goddess comes out when she states (and it is damaging since she is seen as a religious authority) that it is a religion of the Goddess and the King. She said men made up this concept so as to make themselves kings in earlier patriarchal times.

While I agree that in early patriarchal times the Goddess religion still survived and was evidenced, it by no means started then. The stone age, not the bronze age, is where the Craft comes from. I expected from a scholar deeper understanding than insisting that men made up the Goddess religion. She only needs to read Merlin Stone, a scholar of the Goddess, to get her facts, but the Christian lady didn't.

To correct it, the Craft is the religion of the Mother and her Child. Those kings who became consorts to queens didn't live past six months, so what men would try to invent such a preposterous career for other men?

The thrust of her hostility comes down

on me in particular since I have influenced the Craft and Goddess movement through my ten years of ministry. She accuses us that we set up a pathological pattern for men because we revere the Goddess more than the god. First of all, in my tradition I have no god to revere, thank heaven! Second, the Mother is more revered than her Child. Is that pathological thought form? I don't think so! The fear of the female supremacy is on the other hand a pathological fear. It's men who kill, maim, rape the earth. Women have not needed violence to dominate. I suggest Rosemary is male-identified. She finds herself alone in this, since no man in Christianity worried about the "pathological thought forms" concerning women, as she does for men. Too bad.

Decadence and separation from the main stream of women is reflected in her next attack, warning us to be careful lest we import into the male-female dualism (!) a 19th century romanticism which was foreign to the Craft.

Rosemary, who has time to worry about romanticism today? We worry about eating and breathing, and drinking clear water. We worry about nukes, smog, etc., so let me assure you the Craft will not have time to fulfill your fears about the 19th century romanticism.

Next, she thinks that the role of men in the Craft as sons and lovers is not good enough. It is a reversal, she thinks. To me, this reflects a glaring lack of self love. Why would a woman believe that to be lovers with women is a raw deal? Sex objects are not lovers, Rosemary. To be lovers with women is an honor. Women have not created a porno industry where the concept of sex object comes from. Women did not need sado-masochistic pictures to stimulate their sex lives. Women have not needed men except for lovers, and always had them for sons. This isn't a reversal, it's an elevation of men to be serving, stimulating, having fun with women. Women who are lovers with women don't think they have a raw deal. I was lovers with men, and believe me, I would not change for the world. Being a woman's lover is nurturance, affection, good sex and great times.

Rosemary is jealous about genetic witches. She claims that nobody passed down the Craft to anybody. (Obviously, if she isn't in on it, it doesn't exist.) This insults the generations of women who risked their lives remembering and passing down to daughters what they knew. My dear mother (rest her soul) would laugh long and hard hearing this. My aunt Titi who mixes potions according to old recipes, would talk back to Ms. Ruether in sharp corrections. I, who am a genetic witch, can only conclude, Wake up, Rosemary, get off your high horse. Stop insulting me and mine.

In the symbolic reversal, she again attacks the Goddess Movement, saying we just reversed what was there to begin with. Instead of the all-father, we have an all-mother. The problem is that the reversal happened when Christianity was in diapers. It was the men who did it, not us, taking the Source of life out and instituting a man instead. The self created male is a lie.

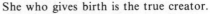

She who gives birth is the true creator.

Lastly, I resent Ms. Ruether's implication that while we work on women's liberation, she is ever so cleverly into human liberation. Excuse me, but women are humanity. Women create the human race. Women's product is Humanity. This is at the heart of it all, I feel. Whatever happens to women will happen to their children. There are only two kinds of people in this world: there are the mothers and there are their children. There is no race, no status, or no other division when a woman looks at the world. The status of women is the status of the people. That's all we've got. The rest is variety.

Well, so much for the challenge. Now for some challenge back. What can we expect in line of contribution from Christian feminists? I see them in a kind of purgatory, between the worlds. They are neither here nor there. Did they use their power to fight visibly—for example, porno-violence? Did they speak out against the Pope? Did they stage pray-ins, sit-ins, fight-ins in their respective denominations? Are they just criticizing their non-Christian sisters because they are spectators of the changes they desire, no longer the inventors of it? The social and spiritual changes. Are they taking back the knowledge they got from the men to women's communities? Are they going to fade away as a phase? Who pays their bills? What risks have they taken?

I want Rosemary on the Goddess' side, but I am not prepared to take a beating from her to accept her. If the Christian ladies want to come over where the cultural changes are happening, they must approach us with gifts and fresh ideas. I am not content with Ms. Ruether continuing her assault against us for years as a form of positive critique. It doesn't lead anywhere. Christianity has not given us anything in the last decade to make it even worth considering as a heritage. The critique has all been done. So what's new?

The Goddess Movement influenced the general Women's Movement, inspired writers to write new books, artists to create Goddess shows, films, altars of beauty and magnitude, temples of vision. Magazines, classes, institutions, religious services, dances, libraries, transformed attitudes about religion within the Movement, influenced mainstream feminism in the last decade. Obviously, this rich path is worth spending your life on. No excommunications, fear not rejection. But, Rosemary, leave your Big (beloved) Black Book at home. It's time.

From *WomanSpirit* 6, no. 24 (Summer 1980): 27-29

Another Response to a Religion for Women

by Carol P. Christ

Before responding to Rosemary Ruether's "A Religion for Women: Sources and Strategies," let me correct two errors of fact which appear in the article.* Judith Plaskow and I are co-editors of *WomanSpirit Rising: A Feminist Reader on Religion* (Harper & Row, 1979), and the statements made about reformists and revolutionaries in feminist religion in that book are the product of our work together. Second, while I am very proud of the conference "The Great Goddess Re-Emerging" (not the Return of the Goddess) held in Santa Cruz in 1978 (and by the way open to men as well as all women), I do not take full credit for it. The conference was the inspiration of Carolyn Shaffer, and she along with Hallie Iglehart, Charlene Spretnak, and myself worked as a collective to organize it.

Also let me remark that in reading Ruether's article, I was not always certain which statements were meant to apply to my work, since her article focused on Naomi Goldenberg's *Changing of the Gods,* and mentioned me occasionally along with others as someone whose work was similar "to some extent." I must also say that some of the blanket statements Rosemary Ruether makes about the work of feminists who reject Biblical religion as the basis of their feminist theology/spirituality strike me as precisely the kind of "hostile caricature" (to use her own phrase) Ruether finds offensive.

Ruether states that "I don't expect her

*[Rosemary Ruether, "A Religion for Women: Sources and Strategies," *Christianity and Crisis* 39 (December 10, 1979):307-311. Reprinted in *WomanSpirit* 6, no. 24 (Summer 1980):22-25.—eds., *Alternative Papers.*]

Reprinted with permission from *WomanSpirit,* Box 263, Wolf Creek, OR 97497. Part II of this response by Carol P. Christ appeared in *WomanSpirit* 7, no. 25 (Fall 1980): 11-14.

(Goldenberg) to get excited about the Bible because I am, any more than I am going to get excited about Freud because she does. What I do expect from *feminist thinkers* [my italics] is respect for the integrity of the quest in different cultural contexts." I have enormous respect for Rosemary Ruether's brave and pioneering work in religion, as I have made clear in the introduction to my new book *Divine Deep and Surfacing: Women Writers on Spiritual Quest* (Beacon, 1980) and elsewhere. I will always be in her debt. Furthermore, it was Judith Plaskow's and my intention to respect "the integrity of the (feminist spiritual) quest in different cultural contexts" in our book *Womanspirit Rising.* More than half of the articles in the book are written by women who are working within the Jewish and Christian traditions. Moreover, in the introduction Judith and I specifically state that, "We believe that the diversity within feminist theology and spirituality is its strength. Each of these feminist's positions has a contribution to make to the transformation of patriarchal culture. The fundamental commitment that feminists in religion share to end male ascendency in society and religion is more important than their differences" (p. 15). I would not have co-edited a book with so many articles by women working within the Biblical traditions if I could do no more than "speak of Biblical ideas in an extremely simplistic way that makes one think they had never studied the document at all . . . [presenting it] through a screen of hostile caricature that ignores almost all of its actual content."

This leads me to believe that the real problem Ruether finds in my work is that I do not make Biblical ideas the basis of my feminist work in religion, and that while I respect many of the feminists who work within the Biblical traditions, I find much of the work of those working outside the Biblical traditions more exciting and significant.

Ruether hypothesizes that anger or "hostile feelings" have made the Bible a "closed book" to the feminist thinkers who do not use Biblical tradition as the basis for their work. I find it odd that Rosemary Ruether (who once stated in a Harvard theology class that "anger" was one of the new "theological virtues" replacing "faith,

hope, and charity") would allege that anger had blinded the intellect of other feminist thinkers. I would not deny that I am angry at the sexism within the Biblical tradition which is expressed in traditional ethical teachings about marriage, sexuality, birth control, and abortion, in traditional patterns of male leadership, and in traditional references to God in male generic language. Nonetheless, anger is not the reason I fail to use the Biblical tradition as the basis for my theology. I believe that anger at tradition and even God can be expressed within the circle of faith and tradition. My Ph.D. thesis on Elie Wiesel's Jewish theology after the holocaust (Yale, 1974, unpublished) discusses the relationship between anger and faith in considerable detail. If anger were the basis of my quarrel with Jewish and Christian traditions I would advocate the expression of anger in theology and liturgy. My article "Expressing Anger at God" (*Anima* 5, 1, Fall, 1978), written from a reformist perspective, discusses how this could be done.

The reason I do not use the Biblical tradition for my feminist vision is an *argument* about the effect of the *core symbolism* of Biblical tradition on Jews and Christians. This argument was stated clearly by Mary Daly in "After the Death of God the Father" in 1971 (an article reprinted in *Womanspirit Rising*). Daly argues that the core symbolism of Biblical tradition is the male God, God as "Lord," "King," "Son," etc., and that the use of this symbolism enforces the notion that males ought to have authority in religion, family, and society. Stated this simply, the argument may strike some as "extremely simplistic" or as "hostile caricature" (both phrases are Ruether's). Yet anyone who reads Daly's work carefully knows that her argument is not simplistic. She acknowledges that the theologians have always asserted that God is beyond sexuality, and she is aware that there are some passages in Bible and tradition which indicate that some thinkers have seen beyond the image of God/Jesus as male. Ruether herself admits that Goldenberg's view (which is a restatement and refinement of Daly's) that Yahweh and Christ "were shaped by males principally to deify themselves and to sanctify the power of men over women in patriarchal societies" is one which Ruether "would be disposed to take very seriously. Although I (Ruether) don't think it is the whole truth about these figures, it is much more deeply true about the way they have actually functioned culturally than most feminists, as well as traditional theologians, have been willing to grant." On this point I believe Goldenberg, Daly, Ruether, and I are in agreement. And I am very eager to underscore the places where we agree, because I firmly believe that feminists working within and without tradition share a great deal.

But though Rosemary Ruether agrees with the feminist criticism of God language stated above, there remain important differences between her thought and that of Daly, Goldenberg, and myself, Ruether acknowledges that she herself thinks of God as the "great Matrix (which) is neither male nor female" and prefers to think of "Her as She in personal prayer," though she would "not dogmatize that preference as a universal." But attention to God/dess language has not been a prominent theme in Ruether's work to date. This suggests to me that Ruether may not acknowledge the depth of the damage that had been done to female and male psyches by the symbol of God as male. For Daly, Goldenberg, and myself, as well as for Starhawk and Z. Budapest, who are also mentioned by Ruether, the predominant references to God in masculine language in the Biblical traditions are *the most significant* fact about these traditions from a feminist perspective. For these thinkers and for me the specific sexism within the traditions based on the Bible are the logical (according to the logic of symbols) outcome of the core symbolism. That there are elements within the Bible and the traditions based on it which are critical of, or counterpoints to, the core symbolism is interesting, but does not fundamentally alter the effect of the core symbolism on the vast majority of those who adhere to these traditions. For these thinkers (myself included) the most important task of feminist theology is to unloose the hold of God-He on the psyches and behaviors of men and women. Or to put it another way, it is to enable women to learn to trust their own experience—spiritual and otherwise —and to reject the notion that all of their experience must be filtered through the lens of male authorities and male-centered traditions in order to be legitimate.

Rosemary Ruether believes that there is a "critical or liberating" tradition in the Bible which can be useful for women despite the predominant male symbolism and language for God in the Bible. Ruether calls this tradition the "prophetic-messianic" tradition. Of it she writes, "Unlike most of Christian theology, the Bible for the most part, is not written from the standpoint of world power, but from the standpoint of people who take the side of the disadvantaged; the rural population against the landowners and urban rich; the small colonized nations against the mighty empires. In the New Testament, this is continued . . . This inclines the Bible to a view of God as One who does not take the side of the powerful but who comes to vindicate the oppressed." While the field is not Biblical scholarship, I will hazard a critique of the tradition Ruether wishes us to take as the basis for feminist theology.

Though it indeed appears that some of the prophets were from rural as opposed to urban backgrounds, and as such were representatives of the dispossessed, much of the Bible was written and/or edited by a relatively comfortable, urban (and it should be added misogynist) priestly class. Many of the priestly writings are concerned with excluding women from the central roles in the cult. Thus I cannot agree with Ruether's statement that "the Bible *for the most part* [my italics] is not written from the standpoint of world power." Though I too find some of the ethical injunctions of the prophets inspiring, I find them embedded in a patriarchal "Yahweh alone" theology which I find repulsive. For every prophetic injunction against those who "sell the righteous for silver, the needy for a pair of shoes" (Amos 2:6), there is a threat against those who worship "on every high hill and under every green tree" (Hosea 4:13). Surely many of the people who worshipped Gods and Goddesses in these rites were following ancient traditions of their peoples, and I have no doubt that many of them were from the rural poor group which Ruether idealizes. I also speculate that many women as well as men from all classes found the notion of a Goddess who was connected to nature comforting. While not desiring to idealize the non-Yahwists, I also cannot wholeheartedly embrace the prophetic tradition of the Hebrew Bible which is so vindictive against those who worship in other traditions. It seems to me that this prophetic tradition is also one of the key roots of religious intolerance in the West. Moreover, the fact that Goddess religions in which women play key roles were among the religions in which women play key roles were among the religions condemned by the prophets certainly has contributed to the antipathy toward female leadership and female God/dess symbolism in Judaism and Christianity. Even apart from these considerations, however, the fact that the judgment on the rich in favor of the poor in the prophetic tradition is delivered by a male God makes me question the validity of the "critical and liberating" potential of this tradition for women. For one of the messages conveyed to women by this tradition is that they must be judged, punished, and forgiven by a male authority figure (Yahweh and his representative, the male prophet) in order to be saved. This latter point applies to what Ruether defines as the liberating potential for women of the New Testament as well. For however much Jesus included women and the dispossessed in his community, the fact remains that the New Testament clearly portrays it

Let the Faithful know the JOYS of Poverty

Bülbül/LNS

as *his* community, and the message conveyed to women is that they must turn to a male savior figure in order to find salvation. Ruether also alludes briefly and positively to the God of Exodus who "drowns the horsemen of the Pharoah." As I read Exodus, the God who, I agree, took the side of the oppressed Hebrew slaves, is modeled on the holy warrior ideal. God proves himself the most powerful holy warrier by drowning Pharaoh's horsemen with their horses. This is certainly not the God I seek.

Ruether argues that this liberating prophetic-messianic tradition "can only be recovered by a thoroughgoing criticism of the way Christianity has generally functioned." I would argue that the traditions Ruether cites as liberating are not themselves adequate models for feminist theology and spirituality.

Though there are many other points in Ruether's article I would like to dispute at another time, there is only one point I will address here. In her discussion of Naomi Goldenberg's interpretation of Freud, Rosemary Ruether argues that the feminist principle of interpretation must be two-sided: first to unmask sexism, and second to name and redeem those insights found in patriarchal philosophies and visions which can be useful for feminist reconstruction of culture. I find that principle unexceptionable. However, I find it more difficult to apply to the Christian worldview than to the work of a secular thinker. For the Biblical vision has never been understood to be one vision among others from which one can—on the basis of human judgment —select that which is useful and liberating and reject that which is not. The Bible has always been understood as *the* vision which is the source and norm for all authentic vision. Thus when Ruether and others insist that feminist spiritual vision ought to be grounded in the prophetic-messianic tradition of the Bible, it sounds to me like she is saying in yet another way that the source and norm of spiritual vision must be found in the writings of Biblical tradition, not in one's (women's) own spiritual experience and thinking. It is possible that Ruether is suggesting something more radical—that the Biblical vision has no more or less claim on anyone than the writings of Freud or other secular thinkers. But if this is so, I don't understand why Ruether is so upset that some feminist thinkers have not made the Biblical vision a constitutive element in their spiritual vision.

WOMANSPIRIT

From *WomanSpirit* 6, no. 24 (Summer 1980): 29

The Second Time Around

by Katherine A. Anderson

Eve was a second attempt.
First there was Lilith,
who didn't quite work out
for various unexplained reasons
having something to do perhaps
with being made not of rib
but equally of earth.
Chucked out of the garden she was
but not so peacefully,
oh, no, she compensated for
feelings of rejection
by stealing and killing babies,

Reprinted with permission from *WomanSpirit*, Box 263, Wolf Creek, OR 97497.

bewitching men and animals and
generally raising a ruckus
and behaving inappropriately
from a place outside the walls,
her own place where
She ruled.

Back to the old drawing board: Eve
with her mild-as-milk curiosity
that other behind the snake-eyes;
no-one to blame really,
tempted as she was, she did eat
and old Adam out to lunch,
what can you expect from a woman?
I think I'll keep her, Adam said.
1) What's done is done etc. etc.
2) Her new blushes excite me.
3) Even now, especially now,
facing God knows what out there,
she's a better risk than Lilith.
That crazy bitch I could not abide.
Reminded me entirely too much of
my Mother.

FRONTIERS
a journal of women studies

From *Frontiers* 5, no. 1 (Spring 1980): 48-49

Racism and Women's Studies

by Barbara Smith

Although my proposed topic is black women's studies, I have decided to focus my remarks in a different way. Given that this is a gathering of predominantly white women and given what has occurred during this conference, it makes much more sense to discuss the issue of racism: racism in women's studies and racism in the women's movement generally.

"Oh no," I can hear some of you groaning inwardly. "Not that again. That's all we've talked about since we got here."

Reprinted with permission from *Frontiers: A Journal of Women's Studies.* Special issue: Selected Conference Proceedings from the National Women's Studies Association, 1979.

This of course is not true. If it had been all *we* had all talked about since we got here, we might be at a point of radical transformation on the last day of this Conference that we clearly are not. For those of you who are tired of hearing about racism, imagine how much more tired we are of constantly experiencing it, second by literal second, how much more exhausted we are to see it constantly in your eyes. The degree to which it is hard or uncomfortable for you to have the issue raised is the degree to which you know inside of yourselves that you aren't dealing with the issue, the degree to which you are hiding from the oppression that undermines Third World women's lives. I want to say right here that this is not a "guilt trip." It's a fact trip. The assessment of what's actually going on.

Why is racism being viewed and taken up as a pressing feminist issue at this time and why is it being talked about in the context of women's studies? As usual the impetus comes from the grassroots, activist women's movement. In my six years of being an avowed black feminist I have seen much change in how white women take responsibility for their racism, particularly within the last year. The formation of C.R. groups* to deal solely with this issue, study groups, community meetings and workshops, articles in our publications, letters in newspapers, and the beginning of real and equal coalitions between Third World and white women are all phenomena that have begun to really happen and I feel confident that there will be no turning back.

The reason racism is a feminist issue is easily explained by the inherent definition of feminism. Feminism is the political theory and practice that struggles to free *all* women: women of color, working-class women, poor women, disabled women, lesbians, old women, as well as white, economically privileged heterosexual women. Anything less than this vision of total freedom is not feminism, but merely female self-aggrandizement.

Let me make it quite clear at this point before going any further something you must understand: white women don't work on racism to do a favor for someone else, to solely benefit Third World women. You have got to comprehend how racism distorts and lessens your lives as white women, that racism affects your chances for survival too and that it is very definitely your issue. Until you understand this no fundamental change will come about.

Racism is being talked about in the context of women's studies because of it being raised in the women's movement generally, but also because women's studies is a context in which white and Third World women actually come together, a context that should be about studying and learning about all of our lives. I feel at this point it's not only about getting Third World women's materials into the curriculum, although this must be done. This has been happening and it's clear that racism still thrives, just as the inclusion of women's materials in a college curriculum does not prevent sexism from thriving. The stage we're at now is having to decide to change fundamental attitudes and behavior, the way people treat each other. In other words, we're at a stage of having to take some frightening risks.

I'm sure that many women here are telling themselves they aren't racist because

they are capable of being civil to black women, having been raised by their parents to be anything but. It's not about merely being polite: "I'm not racist because I do not snarl and snap at black people." It's much more subtle than that. It is not white women's fault that they have been raised for the most part not knowing how to talk to black women, not knowing how to look us in the eye and laugh *with* us. Racism and racist behavior is our white patriarchal legacy. What is your fault is making no serious effort to change old patterns of contempt. To look at how you still believe yourselves to be superior to Third World women and how you communicate these attitudes in blatant and subtle ways.

A major roadblock for women involved in women's studies to changing their individual racism and challenging it institutionally is the pernicious ideology of professionalism. That word "professionalism" covers such a multitude of sins. I always cringe when I hear *anyone* describe themselves as "professional," because what usually follows is an excuse for inaction, an excuse for ethical irresponsibility. It's a word and concept we don't need because it is ultimately a way of dividing ourselves from others and escaping from reality. I think the way to be "successful" is to do work with integrity and work that is good. Not to play cut-throat tricks and insist on being called "Doctor." When I got involved in women's studies six years ago and particularly during my three and a half years as the first Third World woman on the Modern Language Association Commission on the Status of Women, I quickly began to recognize what I call women's studies or academic feminists. Women who teach, research, and publish about women, but who are not involved in any way in making radical social and political change, women who are not involved in making the lives of living breathing women more viable. The grassroots/community women's movement has given women's studies its life. How do we relate to it? How do we bring our gifts and our educational privilege back to it? Do we realize also how very much there is to learn in doing this essential work? Ask yourself what the women's movement is working on in your town or city. Are you a part of it? Ask yourself what women are living in the worst conditions in your town and how does your work positively affect and directly touch their lives? If it doesn't, why not?

The question has been raised here

whether this should be an activist association or an academic one. In many ways this is an immoral question, an immoral and false dichotomy. The answer lies in which emphasis and what kinds of work will lift oppression off of not only women, but all oppressed people: poor and working class people, people of color in this country and in the colonized Third World. If lifting this oppression is not a priority to you then it's problematic whether you are a part of the actual feminist movement.

There are two other roadblocks to our making feminism real which I'll mention briefly. First, there is Third World women's anti-feminism which I sometimes sense often gets mixed up with opposition to white women's racism and is fueled by a history of justified distrust. To me racist white women cannot be said to be actually feminist, at least not in the way I think and feel about the word. Feminism in and of itself would be fine. The problems arise with the mortals who practice it. As Third World women we must define a responsible and radical feminism for ourselves and not assume that bourgeois female self-aggrandizement is all that feminism is and therefore attacks feminism wholesale.

The other roadblock is homophobia, that is anti-lesbianism, an issue that both white and Third World women still have to deal with. Need I explicate in 1979 how enforced heterosexuality is the extreme manifestation of male domination and patriarchal rule and that women must not collude in the oppression of women who have chosen each other, that is,

Cindy Fredrick/LNS

---

*[Consciousness-raising groups.—eds., *Alternative Papers*.]

lesbians. I also wish I had time here to speak about the connections between the lesbian-feminist movement, being woman identified and the effective anti-racist work that is being done by many, though not all lesbians.

In conclusion, I'll say that I don't consider my talk today to be in anyway conclusive or exhaustive. It has merely scratched the surface. I don't know exactly what's going on in your schools or in your lives. I can only talk about those qualities and skills that will help you to bring about change: integrity, awareness, courage, and redefining your own success.

I also feel that the women's movement will deal with racism in a way that it has not been dealt with before in any other movement—fundamentally, organically, and nonrhetorically. White women have a materially different relationship to the system of racism than white men. They get less out of it and often function as its pawns whether they recognize this or not. It is something that living under white male rule has imposed on us and overthrowing racism is the inherent work of feminism and by extension feminist studies.

Barbara Smith is a black feminist writer and activist who lives in Roxbury, Massachusetts. She has been a member of the Combahee River Collective, a Boston black feminist organization, since 1974. The Collective began doing workshops on racism in the women's movement in 1977 which she feels provided the experience necessary to conceptualize this talk. Smith recently co-edited "The Black Women's Issue" of Conditions, *a magazine of writing by women with an emphasis on writing by lesbians. She currently teaches for the Women's Studies Program at the University of Massachusetts, Boston.*

This paper was given as one of the closing Sessions at the NWSA Conference.†

---

†[National Women's Studies Association.— eds., *Alternative Papers*.]

QUEST
a feminist quarterly

From *Quest* 5, no. 1 (Summer 1979): 20-26

Women Do Theory

by Jane Flax

Editor's Note: This article is an edited version of a presentation delivered at the Feminist Theory Workshop sponsored by the DC Area Feminist Alliance, May 6-7, 1978.

I begin with an overview of feminist theory and a discussion of the activity of theorizing. I then present a theoretical framework that I've developed after trying various theories and finding none of them sufficient to explain the range of things I think a feminist theorist needs to explain.

Let me say a little about how I ended up doing feminist theory. I have been interested in philosophy and political theory for a long time. I am also interested in psychoanalysis, and have practiced

as a feminist therapist. So, partly, I've been trying to put together more traditional ideas of theory with those I've learned as a therapist, especially from psychoanalysis.

Very early I began to connect theory with political activity. I chose political science because I thought there I would learn about politics—which was a mistake. Some political scientists seem to consider theory to be something done 3,000 years ago by Aristotle and Plato, unrelated to the present world. And yet, one of my attractions to theory was that through it, I could learn to systematize my experience. Political science was not much help.

Over time, however, I have found traditional theory to be very helpful in recognizing other people's mental processes as they try to understand the structure of the world systematically. That is, much traditional theory is a kind of internal discourse among thinkers—like a 3,000-year conversation in which people take up each others' ideas and reapply them. I'm interested in many parts of that discourse: what can politics do; what is the ideal political system; what are just relationships; what does "equality" mean?

These issues have been dealt with in the women's movement, but not always in the context of theory. For instance, what it would mean to have a really liberated society is a question of equality and justice that has been debated since the first political theory was attempted. But feminists don't often think of our questions as part of that ongoing political discourse.

In traditional political theory, however, the relationships between men and women, and the status of women, are rarely discussed. They are certainly not generally seen as problems. Some traditional political theorists talk about the family and the role it plays for the state of course; and some have argued for the liberation of women. Plato, for instance, argued that women *could* be philosopher kings since these should be chosen on merit and no inherent proof existed that women were any less intellectually capable than men.* Other political theorists, however, have argued that woman cannot think abstractly and has a less developed moral sense. Thus, part of the problem feminist theorists face is taking the general "grammar" and concepts of traditional theory and applying them to women and the issues that affect us.

This brings me to the questions, "what is feminist theory?" and, more generally, "what is theory?" The most important characteristic of theory is that it is a *systematic, analytic* approach to everyday experience. This everybody does unconsciously. To theorize, then, is to bring this unconscious process to a conscious level so it can be developed and refined. All of us operate on theories, though most of them are implicit. We screen out certain things; we allow others to affect us; we make choices and we don't always understand why. Theory, in other words, makes those choices conscious, and enables us to use them more efficiently.

For example, implicit in my choices about the work I could do is an understanding of where power lies, what I'm likely to be able to do, where I'm likely to meet the most frustration, and when I'm likely to be most effective. I might not think through those things consciously, but I make choices on these bases. If you push that explanation, you'll find a series of assumptions about the way the world works, what's available (to me), and what

---

*An interesting sidelight is that the head of Plato's academy was a woman who was stoned by the Christians—one of the first of the Christians' many acts against women playing an intellectual, active role.

isn't. That's implicit theorymaking. The problem is to make it explicit.

Blocks to Explicit Theory

One of the problems with theory is that women aren't supposed to be able to do it; women aren't supposed to be able to think abstractly. So when you say to a woman, "Okay, now let's read theory," she's likely to panic.

In addition, theoretical writing is often so full of jargon that it seems divorced from ordinary experience. Unfortunately, many theorists have an entrepreneurial interest, a territorial mentality, and they encourage everyone else to believe that their work is impossibly complex. This discourages women—and men—from engaging in theory because it seems hostile and unintelligible. I don't think that the issues *are* inherently so difficult or so far removed from ordinary understanding. I think theorists build turfs and *make* it difficult for others to understand that turf—just like any other professional.

Feminist Theory

Feminist theory is based on a series of assumptions. First, it assumes that men and women have different experiences; that the world is not the same for men and women. Some women think the experiences of women should be identical to the experiences of men. Others would like to transform the world so that there are no such dichotomous experiences. Proponents of both views, however, assume that women's experiences differ from men's, and that one task of feminist theory is to explain that difference.

Secondly, feminist theory assumes that women's oppression is not a subset of some other social relationship. Some argue that if the class system were destroyed, then women would not be oppressed—I don't classify that as feminist theory. Feminist theory assumes that women's oppression is a unique constellation of social problems and has to be understood in itself, and not as a subset of class or any other structure.

It also assumes that women's oppression is not merely a case of what the Chinese call "bad attitudes." I have problems with the word "sexism," because the term implies that women's oppression will disappear when men become more enlightened. On the contrary, I think feminist theory assumes that the oppression of women is part of the way the structure of the world is organized, and that one task of feminist

theory is to explain how and why this structure evolved.

Feminist theory names this structure "patriarchy," and assumes that it is an historical force that has a material and psychological base. What I mean by "patriarchy" is the system in which men have more power than women, and have more access to whatever society esteems. What society esteems obviously varies from culture to culture; but if you look at the spheres of power, you'll find that all who have it are male. This is a long-term historical fact rooted in real things. It's not a question of bad attitudes; it's not an historical accident—there are real advantages to men in retaining control over women. Feminist theorists want to explain why that's so.

Patriarchy works backwards as well. It affects the way men and women feel about themselves, and is so deeply internalized that we can't imagine a world without gender. As much as we talk about androgyny, or some situation in which gender isn't so significant, I don't think any of us could imagine a world in which gender would not bring with it many special meanings. *We* may still want to attach special meanings to gender, but a feminist theory would argue that the power attached to gender should disappear; it should not determine whether a person is excluded or included in whatever is esteemed by society.

Goals of Feminist Theory

Feminist theory has several purposes. The first is to understand the power differential between men and women. How did it come into being? Why does it exist now? What maintains it? How do the power relations between men and women affect other power relations—for instance, race and class—and how does patriarchy reinforce other oppressive power structures?

Secondly, the purpose is to understand women's oppression—how it evolved, how it changes over time, how it's related to other forms of oppression, and finally, how to change our oppression.

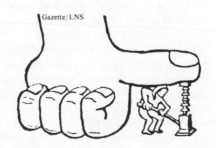

Gazette/LNS

In feminist theory, one issue that emerges consistently is the necessity to understand the family, because it is one of the central mediating structures between all other structures of oppression. The family is where we're internally formed, where we learn about gender, where we experience class and race systems in personal and intimate ways. Therefore, understanding the functions of the family should be one of the crucial goals of feminist theory; yet it remains an area that is particularly undeveloped.

A third purpose of feminist theory is to overcome oppression. Feminist theory is the foundation of action and there is no pretense that theory can be neutral. Within feminist theory is a commitment to change oppressive structures and to connect abstract ideas with concrete problems for political action. It is senseless to study the situation of women without a concomitant commitment to do something about it. The theorist has to draw out the consequences of the theory and use life experience as a part of her basis for understanding, for feeding into the development of theory.

Traditional political theory has always been attached to action. Plato wrote *The Republic* partly because he thought that Athenian democracy was degenerating and he wanted to understand why, and how. It's only contemporary social science theory that claims to be objective, neutral, value-free. I don't think any form of knowledge is neutral, but certainly feminist theory cannot claim neutrality. I think that's one of the problems of women's studies programs. They are too often developed as though they are mere intellectual exercises; some may be, but the study of women is not.

The Evolving Theoretical Framework

I assume that feminist theory must point to a clear and real base for the oppression of women—feminist theory has to be rooted in human experience. I also assume that there are three basic realms of human activity.

The first is production—we need to produce food, clothing and shelter for our survival. (Obviously, different cultures will produce in different ways. Even people who live on tropical islands have to organize the gathering and preparation of coconuts.) Marx called this the material substructure of human life, and I call it the realm of production.

People also need to reproduce. Not only must we produce the next generation biologically, but we also need to reproduce good citizens for the society. We need to inculcate the values, attitudes, and beliefs appropriate to that culture. A good American citizen will have ideas and expectations very different from a good Mesopotamian citizen living 3,000 years ago. But no matter which society, somehow the unformed person must be trained in its values. In our society, acculturation is conducted by a variety of organizations, including the family and later the school, and the state is involved in setting out certain policies which translate into procedures for acculturating individuals.

The third realm of human activity is the individual's internal life. This is what Freud called "the unconscious," and what I call "psychodynamics." The psychodynamic sphere is where our biological and our mental lives meet, and must be organized. One of the most important aspects of this sphere is sexuality. One of the questions feminists must ask is how a basically "polymorphous species"* ends up, in most cultures, a genitally-oriented, heterosexual and monogamous species. Though all cultures allow varying degrees and varieties of sexual pleasure, every civilization channels its citizens' eroticism into practices acceptable to the society.

When we talk about the situation of women, we must examine how all three spheres cooperate to produce our oppression. The elimination of an oppressive structure in one sphere only is inadequate because the other spheres will re-emerge as even more oppressive.

For instance, in the Soviet Union, where the class system is supposedly abolished, men *still* retain the power. The upper structure of the Communist Party is almost entirely male. And while women may move into occupations (as in the United States), those occupations lose their prestige when they do.†

Why didn't the oppression of women disappear? For one thing, the structure of the family was not altered—no efforts were made to change the reproductive spheres‡

---

*Seventy-five percent of physicians in the Soviet Union are women, but a physician there is like a social worker here.

†It's not permissible to be a homosexual, or to engage in sexual relations with many different persons of either gender in the Soviet Union, China or Cuba.

‡Polymorphous means that we can derive erotic pleasure from a wide variety of experiences; not only from experiences between ourselves and other persons, but also between ourselves and all sorts of physical objects.

So, even though one structure of oppression may have been dealt with, the other two remain intact. Hence, we cannot expect women to be fully participating persons, nor that the full range of women's experience will be expressed in social values. This is a material view of women in that it locates oppression within our material lives. And yet it also teaches us to look at each of the three spheres of human activity, to see how each one particularly impinges upon women.

The Intersection of Spheres

One of the most important characteristics of the family is that all three spheres intersect here. In our society, the family is the structure in which we learn to repress and channel our sexuality—where homosexuality is forbidden and where heterosexuality is promoted. It's also the place in which, obviously, external authority is transmitted by and translated in our parents' teachings. It's in the family that the standards of acceptable social behavior are first taught.

Even though most production is no longer done within the family, this is still the structure in which we are taught behaviors appropriate to our class. Lillian Rubin, in *Worlds of Pain,* shows that working-class people become acculturated in the proper expectations of their class and that these expectations are perpetuated from generation to generation. So, the class system impinges upon the family, not only in the obvious ways (such as the kinds of housing or childcare you can afford), but also in more subtle ways.

Other structures influence and are perpetuated by these three spheres. The state, for example, structures and benefits from the ways reproduction and psychodynamics interact in class divisions and modes of production. It also benefits from the lingering effects of the psychodynamic sphere on political and personal action.

Reproduction is obviously segregated on the basis of sex. Women are nurturers, men are authority figures—a very important distinction in terms of the developing person. This means that both acculturation and reproduction are sex-segregated.

Thus, as feminism teaches us, the class system is not the same for men and women. It's a mistake to take traditional class analysis and impose it upon the experience of women when it is clear that women's work is sex-segregated and class-segregated (80% of women work in jobs where

more than half the jobs are held by women).

And finally, the psychodynamic sphere so thoroughly remembers that we're either a *male* or a *female* person, that gender becomes part of who we are. Thus, though we succeed in developing an analysis of patriarchy and capitalism, we still find ourselves repeating old, self-defeating patterns. We can't explain how this happens. Rationally, we've got it all worked out, and yet something refuses to change. That's partly because a great deal happens unconsciously, as we act out old patterns that are accessible neither to reason nor to control since the psychodynamic sphere *is* unconscious. It's the realm of dreams and associations. It's the world of sexuality; it's your internal life. But also it's hard for us to grasp because feminists haven't done much work on it.

Conclusion

My assumptions are, then, that these three spheres of life are crucial for everybody, that they're experienced differently by men and women, and that both the experience and the oppression of women are rooted in all three. I believe we must examine each sphere to see how women's and men's experience are different, and how it contributes to that difference. If we would end the oppression of women, we must transform all three spheres; change in one sphere alone will not liberate women.

The psychodynamic sphere can be changed by completely transforming the rearing of children. Dorothy Dinnerstein's book, *The Mermaid and the Minotaur,* is a good reference on the transformation of childrearing. Dinnerstein maintains that both males and females have to be present in the child's life from infancy. It's important that children not be raised by one female person, or a group of female persons. The child also needs peers. In fact, it makes day care and childrearing not something that enables women to work, but locates both right in the center of feminist demands. A feminist revolution must deal with the way children are reared. To create liberated persons requires a transformation in childrearing.

It also means that homosexuality is not just a nicety we support to appease our lesbian sisters. We must recognize that heterosexuality is also part of the structure of the oppression of women. Sexual repression is one of the ways in which women are oppressed and one of the ways in which patriarchy is maintained. On another level, restraining sexuality is a very powerful way of controlling people—as Wilhelm Reich understood in his analysis of the Nazis. Therefore, to fight for a variety of expressions of sexuality has to be part of feminism. It shouldn't be incorporated because lesbians insist, "What about us?" It's absolutely central to feminism. These are two concrete conclusions which grow out of an analysis of the psychodynamic sphere.

Jane Flax is a professor of political theory at Howard University.

8 Lesbians and Gay Men

The lesbians and gay men writing in this section challenge the attitudes, laws, and social mores that condemn homosexuality. They have chosen to work through gay organizations and presses to break the silence and confront the persecution and physical and emotional abuse imposed on them because of their sexual preferences. Through these publications gay people who have been written out of history are rediscovered, issues of importance to the gay community are reported, and androgynous people have a forum for the exchange of experiences and insights. Typical of this exchange are the first two articles in the section by Tommi Avicolli and Ran Hall, exhibiting the strength and sensitivity they have gained while struggling for their sexual identities. Their visibility is a political as well as a personal act; their right to love, to live free of restrictive stereotypes is at issue.

Carl Wittman and Eleanor Cooper provide a history of the gay movement from its origins in the New Left movements. Wittman traces the gay male movement back to the Stonewall rebellion in 1969 and Cooper tells the history of the lesbian movement—at times one with the gay movement, at other times one with the feminist movement, and often a movement unto itself. JR Roberts explores lesbian history and culture while researching the etymology of the word dyke. M. Adams interprets the commonly misunderstood concept of lesbian separatism.

Harold Pickett introduces the International Gay Association, which attempts to coordinate the efforts of lesbian and gay organizations in securing gay rights and contributing to gay culture and community. Scott Tucker, Leo Casey, and Gary Kinsman survey the damage done to the gay community by the movie *Cruising*. John Kyper and Michiyo Cornell describe organizing efforts in Mexico and the United States, respectively.

In feminist, lesbian, and gay organizations—the three are rarely distinct—individuals often move beyond single-issue politics and conscientiously respond to other social ills and prejudices. Here Jil Clark and Cindy Stein confront racism and Gerald Hannon alerts us to the concerns of gay people who are physically disabled.

Many lesbians have children, whether by previous heterosexual relationships or artificial insemination. Lois outlines the social pressures on lesbian mothers and praises their abilities.

Sue Cartlege and Susan Hemmings close the section musing over questions few heterosexual people are ever asked and few homosexual people can avoid.

—PJC

Gay Community News
THE WEEKLY FOR LESBIANS AND GAY MALES

From *Gay Community News* 6, no. 33
(March 17, 1979): 8

The Masculine Mystique: 'Got to Be a Macho Man'

by Tommi Avicolli

I can remember my father yelling at me for running like a girl. He tried to teach me how a boy is supposed to run. I could never understand the difference.

I was always an effeminate child—I played with dolls, was close to my sister, and avoided sports. I was everything an all-American father loathed in a son, the kind of a boy the other fathers thanked god they didn't have, the kind they warned their "little men" to stay away from, lest it rub off on them. My uncle once went on a crusade to "reform" me and whenever he would see me, he'd lecture me on how a boy was supposed to behave.

Boys, I observed, not only played sports, but fought and bullied each other and girls. They mocked females for their emotionality, their vulnerability (while boasting of their own invulnerability), and for not understanding their crass ways. I didn't want to be like them—I preferred to remain alone rather than play with them. That's how I survived the fifties—I avoided everyone and spent a lot of time by myself.

At first, the sixties were, for me, a joy. Finally someone else was saying what I had been thinking and yet was unable to articulate—that the macho male was an abnormality, a charlatan, a savage, totally passé in a civilized world. The hippies became my idols—harbingers of a new world where men could dance and paint and love. Even love. But I was mistaken, misled, deceived. I had read the signs wrong. No one was saying it was all right for men to love each other in a sexual way. Men could "love" each other in a figurative sense, like brothers—dig? I had been deceived by Donovan's robes and beads and gentle lyrics. I thought that Jim Morrison's invitation to free love was

meant for me, too. In reality, he was only inviting straight men to ball more "chicks." I thought Dylan meant to set up a new order of things.

But the new order was a reflection of the old. The sex roles were the same—men were in the studios recording the anti-war songs, or on the streets battling the "pigs," while earth-mother, hippie women remained at home making babies and bread. Gays were, according to the correct political line, products of the capitalist decadence that gave us Nixon and Mitchell. In fact, left-wing spoofs on the administration loved to picture them as homosexuals—complete with Nixon in bra, lipstick and panty hose. The utopian sixties came crashing down around me, leaving me despondent and desolate.

When the seventies and the Gay Liberation Front at Temple University came along, I emerged with a new vision of the gay male as a forerunner of a liberated species of males. And for a time, we almost made it happen.

In the beginning (1971) we wore our hair long and carried copies of Millett's *Sexual Politics* (our bible) into classrooms around the campus. We were a fiery, defiant bunch—struggling for alliances with wo-

men and blacks, and confronting each other in rugged C-R sessions* in the hopes of developing ideologies untainted by the masculine ethic. We abhorred the masculine mystique and all of its manifestations; we hated the jock, the upwardly mobile (at the expense of his humanity) business major, the cool college dude looking for a wife. We declared ourselves sissies, faggots, effeminates, and queens, boasting of our contempt for the standard masculine images we had been told to emulate. We despised Clint Eastwood, James Bond, John Wayne, and Archie Bunker. Instead, we foolishly idolized David Bowie (an androgyne, a forerunner of the ambisexual beings to come, we thought), the New York Dolls, the Cockettes, and others who profited on being freakish. All too late, we discovered that Bowie, Alice Cooper, and the other products of the musical ennui of the early '70s were college jocks in drag. When the makeup washed off, so did the high consciousness. When all was said and done, much had been said and nothing at all done. Bowie went disco, and Cooper became the darling of the talk show circuit, charming the very people who recoiled in disgust at his bizarre appearance a few years before.

But still we continued digging into ourselves, looking for answers on how to start a revolution among men—to spark in

*[Consciousness-raising sessions.—eds., *Alternative Papers.*]

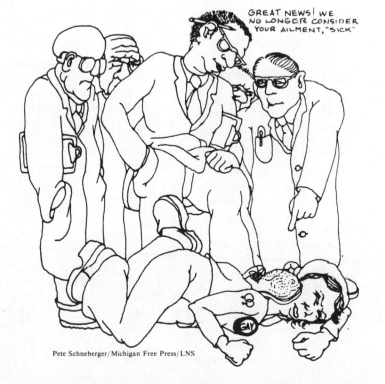

GREAT NEWS! WE NO LONGER CONSIDER YOUR AILMENT "SICK"

Pete Schneberger/Michigan Free Press/LNS

them the desire to throw off the macho image and give birth again to their humanity. We talked to Male Liberation classes; we ran a man for homecoming queen at Temple; we mingled with the "chic" glitter rock crowds in an attempt to recruit their support. But their main interest was not to fight against the male role—they actually enjoyed it. When the glitter phenomena died out, they returned to their denim and their swagger, abandoning bisexuality, gay friends, and androgyny. Most of them married and are now working on their second kid.

With the death of the androgynous glitter rock, the fifties came back into vogue. Hair got shorter, clothes more gender-identified and lyrics more mundane. The few of us who had started the C-R groups on effeminacy drifted away from the gay political groups. I resigned as president of GAA in 1976 and retired to three years of writing novels, plays and newspaper articles. In those three years something happened to the gay male community—something akin to what happened to black men in the midst of their struggle for civil rights. The Village People sum it up well when they sing, "I got to be a macho man."

Macho is in. It's evident from the way men in general are dressing. TV understands this—that's why programs like "Brothers and Sisters," "Happy Days," and "Making It" are so popular. The '50s greaser has been reborn as—surprise—the seventies greaser! And nothing's changed but his hair cream.

Gay men have not gone unaffected by this trend. We—who have been deprived of our manhood, who have been called sissies and queens, and who have never been thought of as men—are striking back in the worst way possible: by asserting our masculinity. See, we're saying, we can be as masculine as you are. We can dress, act, and think just like you. Blacks went through it—trying to emulate the macho white man. Now it's our turn as gay men.

We have skin magazines which glorify traditional masculine-identified bodies; S-M porno which condones rape; contests for a Mr. Such-and-Such which brings out muscles and masculinity (while in the opposite direction we have Miss Gay America contests which glorify the feminine stereotype). Harmless fun?

As Warren Farrell points out, the U.S. Surgeon General has concluded in studies that TV does affect the behavior of those who watch it. Images—whether they be on TV, in the movies, or just prevalent ones in a community, do give us a message, even if it is only a mental one. Images can become the man. It happens in South Philadelphia (or South Boston, or the Bronx) all the time.

I hope "macho" is just another trend in the gay male community—one that will pass away in time the way glitter rock did, or the way certain expressions do. I hope somewhere along the line the way we—as gay men—can once more return to the important question of how to incite a revolution which will return to us our right to love, feel, and live in peace with our fellow creatures. Machismo is a disease, something to be vaccinated against, a parasite to loathe and guard against, a scum that destroys everything around it.

SINISTER WISDOM

From *Sinister Wisdom*, no. 13 (Spring 1980), pp. 39-40

Views: Publishers, Readers, Writers, Editors

by Ran Hall

The first lesbian book I ever read was *Patience and Sarah*. I was married at the time and had just had my second child. I was also in love with a woman who was engaged to be married. We called our love friendship. It was a deeply emotional and an extremely painful relationship because we could not recognize what we felt. Lesbian literature was hard to find on the library bookshelves. It was five years before I read *Rubyfruit Jungle*. I had moved to Florida, leaving behind that relationship which had been destroying us both.

I read *Rubyfruit* to my husband who enjoyed Rita Mae Brown's humor almost as much as I; but while he was laughing, I was slowly absorbing what Rita Mae was saying: "It's O.K., in fact, it's great!" Now *that* was a whole new thought for me! She used a word that I heard and knew the meaning of but had never thought of in relation to myself or what I felt—lesbian. She made me question my choice of mate and regret that I had not followed my desires five years earlier.

Two more wasted years passed and then the phone rang. With her first word it all came back, the pain and the fear and the love that I had tried so hard to forget. After a couple of months and ridiculous phone bills, she came for a visit. The years had taught both what we wanted. My search for

words became serious as did my awareness of myself as a woman. Robin Morgan's *Sisterhood Is Powerful* gave me places to look for answers. One step led to another and slowly the hidden world of women revealed itself—lesbian centers, bookstores, resorts, bars and other women's books, magazines and newspapers. The discovery that I was not alone made me high for months. I remember the first time that I went to a lesbian center. I called on the phone, and they said they had a bookstore. I was terrified, but I had to go. I do not know what I was afraid of, maybe of being thought of as a lesbian, or maybe of the women themselves. Whatever it was, I knew I had to get those books. I went and bought as many as I could carry. On the way home I was filled with a curious new feeling of pride. With my husband in the other room, I opened my treasures. Hungry for knowledge and understanding, desperate to touch this new world ahead of me, I read every word and wanted more.

The next year was one of doubt and certainty, confusion and discovery as my woman lover and I sorted out our lives and ourselves to finally "be together." I read *Sinister Wisdom* in the bathtub; I have read it while riding in the car at night by the passing street lights, on supermarket lines, and in bed with my morning tea. I have re-read every issue and every word. I read *The Notebooks That Emma Gave Me* while I waited four hours in line at the driver's license torture chambers, and I have read it while walking to the store. I have read like a starving person eats. The words gave life to my reality and block out this imaginary place where my body resides.

For years I read words that were not written for me, that ignored my very existence, blatantly and without apology; words that referred to all beings as *he*, to all thought as *his*, to all people as *man* and to spirit and soul as *man's*. The effort to translate is beyond me at this point; I am deaf to their words as they are to mine.

I look at my bookshelf and see Sarah Aldridge, Rita Mae Brown, Barbara Grier, Coletta Reid, Andrea Dworkin, Mary Daly, Jane Rule, and Adrienne Rich. I read and with every word I feel a deepening gratitude for the women who have the courage, strength, and love to write these words for me. Their gift has given me the strength to think and feel and love as a woman, as a lesbian, and as a writer. Every time I read the words of a lesbian I say a silent thank you.

Gay Community News
THE WEEKLY FOR LESBIANS AND GAY MALES

From *Gay Community News* 6, no. 47 (June 23, 1979): 11

San Francisco, 1969

by Carl Wittman

The events around the Stonewall riots in New York ten years ago will go down in gay chronicles—and even in straight history books—as The Beginning of The Gay Revolution. Occasionally a voice from an older generation will point to events before 1969; impressive as they were for their times, they remained isolated, lost to those of us who thumbed through the H's of psychology book indices, trying to cope with being queer in the '50s and '60s.

In contrast, the events in 1969 began a decade of remarkable change in gay consciousness, and "Stonewall" is the symbol of that beginning. An occasional rancorous voice from the West Coast will try to point out that they had actually started gay liberation before "Stonewall." It is a bit like arguing about whether Christ was actually born in February. Symbols are . . . well, symbols.

But the spring months in San Francisco were full of ferment. The simultaneous development of liberation consciousness in gay centers across the continent is an indication of the depth and strength of the wave which was about to crest and crash down. This account of those pre-Stonewall months in San Francisco may help to make sense of what was happening.

Gay liberation at its inception was not a liberal, middle class "all we want is our rightful share of the pie" movement. "Stonewall" has come to mean, especially since Anita Bryant and Briggs, gay rights. Gay culture has come to mean "The

Advocate Experience," electing officials, look-alike masculinity, and making money in real-estate. But the attitudes of those involved in the events of 1969 in San Francisco (and elsewhere?) were not liberal. Large numbers of disenchanted young people were "dropping out," quite different from "wanting in." And many of the hippies were gay. No longer having jobs, respectability, or propriety, it was only a matter of time before we would begin to call America on how it was treating us.

I moved to San Francisco from New Jersey in 1967: It was the hippie summer of 1967, but I was considerably more interested in the open and friendly cruising on buses, city streets, and in parks. I was intoxicated by how different it all was from the bleakness and covertness of the Newark train station or Columbia library johns. Dolores Park was a few blocks from where I was staying, and during the sunny afternoons there were lots of pretty men sunbathing. I went home with one of them, and after sex he told me about SIR*—this gay group to which he belonged. He was part of a skit at a social event there that weekend.

Well . . . back east I had heard about a student Mattchine group at Yale or Columbia, but it seemed very unreal, distant, definitely unerotic. The notion of bridging my social and sexual worlds or even, god forbid, my social and sexual and political worlds . . . I was fascinated. I went to the SIR meeting that week, but left quickly. The place was filled with very bourgeois people—by which I mean I felt uncomfortable in my jeans. I didn't have or want the job that they all seemed to have and value, and talk about the civil rights movement or the war or feminism would have been out of place. I wrote to a friend that it was like being a Black Panther when

the only organization for you was the NAACP.

The next year was filled with militant activities on other issues: mass draft resistance at the Oakland Induction Center, the "mutiny" at the Presidio Army Base, a teachers' strike at San Francisco State College. In the SIR magazine, *Vector*, there was an article by a striking teacher proposing that gay people organize and fight for their rights. I hurried over to meet him at his apartment, and we exchanged ideas, but neither of us knew others who felt the same way.

I was doing draft counseling, and after one weekend retreat for draft resisters, I remember coming home feeling very crazy. I felt like the only queer in the world who cared about ending the war. I sought out one gay friend who kindly listened to my impatience.

So in the early spring, when I got a phone call saying "Gayle was fired from his job for being gay. There's going to be a picket line downtown this afternoon," it wasn't as if I were a blank slate. But I was bowled over by the idea: US PICKET? Stand out there right in cold daylight, with people watching? It is hard now, after ten years of being "out" to remember what was so shocking about the idea. Subconsciously, perhaps, I thought *I* didn't need to get organized—that would be an admission of personal failure. I was brought up to involve myself in organizing for *other* people—"those people"—but certainly not for myself. It was jarring somehow to see myself as one of "them."

But only for a minute. "*Yes*, I'll be there. Where? When? My mind raced through all the picket lines I'd been on: for blacks, for Cuba, for the Vietnamese, for women—and it occurred to me that the alienation I'd always felt about politics might change now. This one was for me.

I couldn't wait to share it. I ran out of my apartment and crashed into Sally, who was a "hippie lady" living next door. I told her about it, and asked her to come—she smiled and said yes. She thought it was a neat idea, like a new drug—it might widen your consciousness.

An hour later I got off my little motorcycle and chained it to a tree, a half block away from the picket line. It was in the financial district, at the offices of a steamship company, which had fired a man because his picture had appeared in a Berkeley "underground" paper with his lover. Ostensibly that's what we were protesting. But in fact, most of us could care less about employment at a Mont-

Reprinted with permission from *Gay Community News: The Weekly for Lesbians and Gay Men*, 22 Bromfield St., Boston, MA 02108.

*[Society for Individual Liberty.—*eds., Alternative Papers.*]

gomery Street business. We were homosexuals, who had hidden ourselves forever, who were there to "come out" right there on the street, chanting and marching. People stared strangely. Gay men on their lunch hours crossed the street hoping not to be noticed. Two dozen of us circled around, Sally and baby too.

The most intense feeling I had was joy that *there were other people like me.* I struck up a conversation with a friendly, long-haired man, who had been thrown out of the Air Force for being gay. After the picket, I offered him a ride home on my motorcycle. Halfway up steep California Street, the front wheel of the bike lifted off the ground and we barely kept from falling—we were too heavy, sitting too far back. We collapsed in laughter, and I felt like I had known him all my life, the brother I'd always wanted, who was queer too.

That evening we crowded into an apartment living room, over sixty people—brothers and sisters everywhere. Yesterday I knew only two gay people who were "aware of social issues—here were thirty times that many. I don't remember anything else that night, other than the excitement, which apparently everyone else felt too. In one day the curtain had been drawn back, and we could see each other.

Those next six months—from April to October 1969—were a whirlwind of change. The sun still rose in the morning in the east, but just about everything else altered, or so it seemed. We were making up for lost time. At one time we were trying to define a new gay way of living, and correct the world's injustices—all as soon as possible. There was a massive demonstration at the Hearst newspaper office, which turned into a bloody police riot. A friend used his welfare check to start *Gay Sunshine.* We started a gay street theatre group, and I was part of a gay consciousness-raising group. Gay communes sprung up. People who'd never have met (and wouldn't today) were partying together. The man on the back of my motorcycle became a close friend, and at the theatre group I met the man who would be my first "lover."

And somewhere in the midst of all that, we heard the news about a bunch of street queens in Greenwich Village staging a full scale riot against the police. We were, of course, delighted—it confirmed our notion that the gay revolution was accelerating. Queens, freaks, we'd turn the whole world on its side.

Looking back, our naiveté was con-siderable. We considered ourselves feminists, but had only the barest inklings of why lesbians didn't rush into our arms. We didn't reckon on a resurgence of Christian fundamentalist bigotry. Class differences among gays seemed insignificant at the time. We never dreamed of the commercialization of a gay market. And the ascendency of respectable, middle class gay rights advocates like NGTF* and David Goodstein would have been an idle thought.

In the intervening years, the connotation of hippie has become more negative: my friends say things like "when we used to be hippies." But it was the confluence of hippie and queer which erupted into the events of 1969, at least in San Francisco. Certain thoughts were thinkable, certain actions possible, when one dropped out of

*[National Gay Task Force.—eds., *Alternative Papers.*]

gainful employment or education, when one's family was thousands of miles away, when the dream of everything being free and everyone being lovers was seriously entertained. In 1979 we can't pretend we're back in the '60s, but those thoughts, actions, dreams are the gay movement, right from the beginning.

Last fall I met a 17-year-old Harvard freshman who said: "You must be a leftover of the '60s. I have great respect for those days." He was "out" to his dorm, and perhaps his courage to do that was based in the same spirit as our picket line 10 years ago. I would like it better if there were less interest in becoming "accepted"—gay cops, gay schoolteachers, gay soldiers, all certified by the city council and the state legislature, and more interest in the part queers might play in creating something better. I find it hard to say that to the Harvard freshman and not feel like a leftover. Maybe he'll read this.

The Lesbian Feminist

From *The Lesbian Feminist*, June 1979, p. 3

Lesbian Pride: Ten Years and Beyond: A Personal and Political Perspective

by Eleanor Cooper

Many of us have come in contact with the Lesbian feminist movement since it began and many have experienced the effects of Lesbian pride much as I did when I walked into the Wooster Street firehouse in 1972 where the Lesbian Liberation Committee of GAA met. For the first time I met proud Lesbians; a weight was lifted from my shoulders, and I felt free for the first time in years. It was the beginning of a continuing change in my life and identity. As soon as I experienced Lesbian pride, I realized that I could fight back, and I began to focus my newfound energy on changing the society

Reprinted with permission from *The Lesbian Feminist.*

that had misinformed and oppressed me.

In late June, 1969, the Stonewall rebellion exploded on Christopher Street. I listened to the reportage on WBAI and read the accounts in the underground press, the same way I learned about all the other movements and rebellions of the '60s. I heard about all of the excitement, but I was only a bystander then.

One year later there was a march of 10,000 in N.Y.C. to commemorate the first anniversary of the Stonewall. This was the first Christopher Street Liberation Day. There was a movement underway and Lesbians were part of it. Lesbian poet Fran Winant was there and was immortalized along with other exhilarated Lesbians and Gay men from the Gay Liberation Front in one of the first gay liberation posters. This poster was the image of gay liberation as was Fran's poem, "Christopher Street Liberation Day, June 28, 1970." "We cover the Sheep Meadow, shouting, lifting our arms. We are marching into ourselves like a body gathering its cells, creating itself in the sunlight. We turn to look back at the thousands behind us. It seems that we will converge until we explode. Sisters with sisters, brothers with brothers, together."

By late 1970 these same GLF women had written a paper called "Leaving the Gay Men Behind." They had formed Radicalesbians who wrote "The Woman Identified Woman." This analysis of Lesbian oppression and Lesbian pride is the most basic statement of Lesbian feminism and has been read by many thousands of women. "Only women can give to each other a new sense of self. . . . This consciousness is the revolutionary force from which all else will follow, for ours is an organic revolution."

Also in 1970 some of the Radicalesbians had participated in the Lavender Menace zap of the Second Congress To Unite Women, an historic confrontation of the anti-Lesbian attitudes which had permitted the exclusion of the Lesbian issue from the conference agenda. One of the women who was there was Ginny Vida, now the media director of the National Gay Task Force. She says that this was the first message of pride in loving women that she had heard. She described it as deeply moving and similar to a religious experience when the Lavender Menaces gave their personal experiences, debunked the stereotypes and asked women to come forward to support the right of Lesbians to speak out.

We have seen Lesbian Feminism as the fusion of our love of women as lovers and the valuing of the female principle and of the interests of all women. These essential principles are embodied in our Lesbian feminist organizations that have grown up all over the country since the early '70's. A major part of this development has come about because we have been in the forefront of the fight for women's issues. At the same time we have had our own separate groups which have focused on the needs and issues of Lesbians and brought our issues to the women's movement.

In May of 1973 Lesbian Feminist Liberation was formed after breaking away from the Gay Activists Alliance, much as Radicalesbians had split from GLF. From the beginning we were dedicated to the goals of Lesbian visibility, positive Lesbian identity and the confrontation of sexism and heterosexism in the society. We began

Knoxville Gazette/LNS

with Lesbian Pride Week. Then, on August 26th, Women's Suffrage Day, we zapped the Museum of Natural History with a huge lavender dinosaur. The museum was targetted for its failure to represent the role of women as significant in the culture of the world, because of the sexist labeling of their exhibits, and also because they totally ignored Lesbians. *Lesbian Tide*, an L.A. publication, ran a color picture of the sapphasaurus on their cover. We got some media coverage, and thanks to diligent work by feminist anthropologists the museum has made some changes.

Political actions and public education have made some recognizable inroads on people's attitudes towards Lesbians. It would have been impossible 10 years ago to mention the word *Lesbian* and expect that other women would feel solidarity with us. Even five years ago we would not have expected the tremendous support for Lesbian rights that we saw at the International Women's Year Conference in Houston, 1977. The participation of Lesbians in the state conferences had brought the issue to the national conference.

Jean O'Leary, who was the only Lesbian IWY commissioner and who had prepared the resolution on sexual preference, read it before the delegates and a sea of women stood up in support of us. Balloons were released and an incredible snake dance wound through the cheering, screaming women. It was a brilliant promise for the future of unity with a broad spectrum of individual women and women's groups.

Today we can take for granted that there will be at least *some* brief glimpses of our lives in the media. We also have massdistributed books that tell the truth about Lesbians. We have our own records, magazines, newspapers and books available in our own bookstores. We have cultural events for Lesbian feminists and we have a community identity. In New York we even have a Lesbian Herstory Archives that is preserving aspects of our lives and ideas for future generations of Lesbians. *We* are responsible for the greatly increased availability of information about ourselves and the reality of Lesbian experiences. We have Lesbian hotlines and discussion, rap, and support groups as well as all types of counseling. These are all essential links to the Lesbian community that help women to find their Lesbian identity and pride instead of living in isolation.

There are all sorts of political, social, and cultural outlets for Lesbians in our organizations and groups. We also have the opportunity to participate in large conferences, gigantic music festivals, and other events where we can be with hundreds and even thousands of Lesbians in one place and at one time. This could never have happened in the past and it is a very positive promise of our future. Lesbian pride has sustained our efforts to transform our lives and it is the essence of the Lesbian feminist future.

ƧINIƧTER WIƧDOM

From *Sinister Wisdom*, no. 9 (Spring 1979), pp. 2-11

In America They Call Us Dykes: Notes on the Etymology and Usage of 'Dyke'

by JR Roberts

The women-loving women in America were called dykes

First published in *Sinister Wisdom*, Box 660, Amherst, MA 01004. Reprinted with permission.

*and some liked it
and some did not . . .*

Judy Grahn, from
"A History of Lesbianism"

In *Sinister Wisdom* 6, five Lesbians spoke intensely and articulately concerning the silences in our lives and how patriarchal language has been used against us, how the fears of vulnerability and censure check our tongues, rendering us powerless, isolated, and invisible. How the power to name is the power to be. Lesbians have long been the object of vicious "namecalling" designed to shut us up, make us shrivel and slink away. *Dyke* is one of the words that has been negatively and violently flung at us for more than a half century. In the Lesbian/Feminist 1970s, we broke the silence on this tabooed word, reclaiming it for ourselves, assigning to it positive, political values. The reclamation of *dyke* has also necessarily involved an historical/etymological search for its origins. Our generation of Lesbians has been stymied, mystified, and intensely curious as to how and why we have come to call ourselves *dykes*.

The term appears to have originated in the United States. Although *dyke* is used in England, the terms *lesbian, Sapphist,* and *butch* have been traditional there (Partridge 1968). In the United States, *dyke* is a cross-cultural term found in both Anglo-American and African-American slang. In African-American slang, *dyke*, as it stands alone, does not seem to have been in widespread use as of 1970, but more commonly appeared in combination with *bull* to form *bull-dyke*, signifying an "aggressive female homosexual," *bull-dagger, boon-dagger,* and *bull-diker* being variations. *Bull* was/is used in Black culture to indicate Lesbian (Major 1970; Berry 1972).*

The earliest known references using *dyke* or *dike* (an earlier? spelling no longer in wide usage today) to describe "masculine" Lesbians, or Lesbians generally, date to circa 1920s-1930s, indicating at least a half century of usage.† Partridge indicates that *dike* denotes a "female homosexual" and that the term comes from the combination *bull-dike* (Partridge 1968), which was used among Black people as early as circa 1920s-1930s (*AC/DC Blues* 1977). Godfrey Irwin, a compiler of tramp and underworld slang, likewise supports this definition of *bull-dike* in a letter to Partridge dated September 18, 1937. During the thirties, *bull-dike* was also being used among prison inmates at Sing Sing to indicate a woman who practiced oral sex on men (Hargan 1935, as quoted by Partridge 1968). It is interesting that the homosexual *bull-dike* and the heterosexual *bull-dike* were both associated with so-called "unnatural" and socially unapproved sexual behaviors. This is one of many connections existing between homosexual slang, heterosexual

---

Bull was a tabooed word circa early twentieth century, not to be used in mixed company, signifying "the male of the species." Less offensive terms like "top cow" were often substituted. *Bull bitch* was a rural term applied to "masculine" women (Wentworth 1944; Wentworth and Flexner 1975).

†Earlier, at the turn of the century, *dyke* was one of many slang terms denoting the vulva (Farmer and Henley 1890-1904:338).

slang, and woman-hating slang.* By the 1940s we find *dike* or *dyke* listed in slang dictionaries to indicate "masculine woman," being synonymous with other words signifying "Lesbian" (Berry & Van den Bark 1942, 1947).

In the pre-Liberation forties, fifties, and sixties, "Lesbian slang" was often role-related. *Dyke/dike* and *butch* were used to signify "masculine" Lesbians who wore "men's clothing" (Stanley, June 24, 1977; Aldrich 1955:54). "Feminine" Lesbians were *femmes* or *fluffs* (*Vice Versa* 1:6, November 1947). Among Midwest Black Lesbians the words *stud* and *fish* were used respectively (Sawyer 1965). Special terms indicating varying degrees of "mannishness" were formed by adding prefixes, for example: *bull-dyke, diesel dyke, stompin' diesel dyke.* As Lesbian linguist Julia Stanley indicates, *dykes* in our own time, the Lesbian/Feminist seventies, has undergone a change in meaning from a once pejorative term to a politically charged definition. This has occurred within the liberation movements of Lesbians and gays. "To be a dyke or a faggot," writes Julia, "refers to one's political identity as a gay activist . . . but redefining old terms that have been pejoratives for so long is not an easy process, nor is it something that takes place overnight. Among women, new definitions are being made among usages of old terms. As we redefine the old pejorative labels making them our own, what we choose to call ourselves also takes on political meaning, defining one's political position" (Stanley 1974:390-391).

The personal is political. The personal is also historical. On many levels we Lesbians today have experienced historical/political transformations. Sometimes it is possible to recall an exact time and place where transformations occurred. Although I don't ever recall having used the word *dyke* in the old pejorative sense, I do remember when I first began using *dyke* in a liberated sense. It was late 1973; I had just "come out" via the Lesbian/Feminist Movement. During a conversation with an older Lesbian friend who had come out years earlier without the aid of a movement, I referred to the two of us as *dykes*. Her reaction was equivalent to "Hey, wait a minute! Watch yer mouth!" as if I had

---

*See "Sexist Slang and the Gay Community: Are You One, Too?" by Julia Stanley and Susan W. Robbins. Available from J. Stanley, Department of English, University of Nebraska-Lincoln, Lincoln, Nebraska 68588.

uttered some terrible obscenity. She then proceeded to enlighten me as to the older, negative meaning. But, I said, I don't see it that way at all. To me *dyke* is positive; it means a strong, independent Lesbian who can take care of herself. As I continued with the movement, *dyke* took on even stronger political implications than "activist." It signified woman-identified culture, identity, pride and strength—women, alone and together, who live consciously and deliberately autonomous lives, no longer seeking definitions or approvals according to male values. Soon my older friend also began identifying positively with the word *dyke*.

Exercising this new power of self-definition, we now have a variety of names and definitions with which to describe our many political selves. Our Lesbian lifestyle is very diverse, and our use of language and choice of names and definitions reflect our many cultural, racial, ethnic, class, regional, and political backgrounds, as well as our generational perspectives. Today the straight world continues to use *dyke* in the old pejorative sense. There are a number of Lesbians who do also, and are repulsed by it. These Lesbians may not have been exposed to the current movement, or, being concerned with their status and survival in the straight world, they may reject the term as harmful. There is also a segment of the Lesbian population which grew up, came out, and participated in the earlier Lesbian culture before 1970 who retain the negative definition they have always known. So the definition of *dyke* has changed only for *some* Lesbians, not for all.

There are some questions to be wondered about. If *dyke* has different definitions today, is it possible that there were different definitions in earlier times? Did all Lesbians before the 1970s generally define *dyke* negatively? Was it such a distasteful term, or were there those Lesbians who felt a sense of pride at being labeled *dyke*? What did it mean to them? Where did the American tradition of the "mannish" Lesbian as *dike/dyke* come from?

The term *dike* or *dyke* had probably been around to some extent before the 1930s-1940s when it first began to be documented in slang dictionaries. Slang terms often originate among special groups, some of which are "outcasts" of mainstream society whose members feel alienated from the values of the dominant culture. Such groupings may be based on age, race, ethnic, or class background. Among such groups have been the younger generation, Blacks, hoboes, criminals, street people, artists and writers, gays and Lesbians. The creation of new words and new definitions for old words serves a social and political purpose: it may constitute an act of power and rebellion for those who feel and are powerless; or it may provide a sense of validation and identity denied by the dominant culture, eventually becoming "Standard English," or they may fall into disuse or remain the linguistic property of the special group. Slang terms may be collected and listed in published lexicons, dictionaries, and the sauri. Definitions may change with time. These are slow, complicated evolutions influenced by social, economic, political, and intellectual ideas and events in the dominant culture and among those outcast groups.

Currently, there are several theories concerning the etymology of *dyke* or *dike*, which are threaded together by the androgynous concept of the "manly-woman." Several have to do with ancient Greek legends. Poet Elsa Gidlow raises the possibility that the word *dyke* may have had its origins in the Greek word *dike*, that is Athene, the "manly-woman" who is the principle of total order (Stanley, June 24, 1977). There is also the related Flexner and Wentworth (1975) hypothesis that *dike* probably came from *hermaphrodite,* the *-dite* being "clipped" off and later evolving into *dike,* due to a regional (Coney Island??) mispronunciation. Cordova adds support to this hypothesis when she reports conversations with older Lesbians who indicate the folk belief that the root word of *dyke* was once *hermaphrodite,* with its origins in the Greek myth of Hermes and Aphrodite who join to create the androgynous creature (Cordova 1974:22). Of the *-dite* to *dike* theory, Julia Stanley comments: "For reasons of my own, I've never bought the *-dite* to *dike* explanation, primarily because /t/ hardly ever becomes /k/ in natural languages. I'm not saying it's impossible, especially in an unstressed syllable, where an alveolar *might* be heard as a velar, just that it's unlikely" (Stanley, June 24, 1977).

My own recent research has turned up an interesting, but never before cited, usage of *dike* dating from late nineteenth and early twentieth century America, representing another possible, and perhaps more viable, origin, based in the social customs of the people rather than in classical allusion. Both Schele de Vere (1872) and Clapin

(1902) in their compilations of Americanisms indicate *dike* as denoting a man in full dress, or merely the set of male clothing itself. Schele de Vere says this is a "peculiar American cant term, as yet unexplained." Clapin, however, indicates that *dike* likely resulted from the corruption of the Old English *dight* (Anglo-Saxon origin). *Dight* meant to dress, clothe; to adorn, deck oneself (Johnson, 2nd ed., 1827). In listing *dike,* Mathews (1951) indicates a possible connection between *dight* and the English dialect *dick,* both of which meant "to deck or adorn." By 1856 *dight* was cited by Hall as being nearly obsolete in the United States, while *diked* and *diked out* were in use. The word *dike* probably came to America with the English at the time of colonization, but once in America other usages may have developed. Both Clapin and Schele de Vere indicate that *dike* was not only used as a verb, but also as a noun to describe a person of either sex who was all dressed up. However, *dike* as a person or as a set of clothing most often referred to the male sex.

There is growing evidence that during this same time period a number of women in both the United States and Europe were adopting male attire, both permanently and on occasion. Katz has called some of these women "Passing Women" (Katz 1976: Ch. 3). These women dressed, lived, voted, worked—literally "passed"—as men in the mainstream culture. Some were of the middle and upper classes, or were artists. Others were independent, working class women who took on the guise of men in order to survive in a world where women had few options. As "men," these women, some of whom were Lesbians, married other women and raised families. They could live and enjoy their lives with women and still participate in the greater opportunities and privileges awarded to men. This choice was often based in explicit or covert feminism. When discovered, however, these women were often punished by society—arrested, fined, imprisoned, exposed, and forbidden to wear male clothing. Sometimes the contemporary media picked up on the appearances of these "she-men," and a number of rather sensational articles appeared, accompanied by photographs and drawings. Some of these graphics which are reproduced in Katz indicate women dressed in a "full set of male clothing"—from hat to suit, to cane or umbrella, watch fobs and chains, to vests and shoes. Lesbians and other radical women—such as the feminist Mary C.

Walker, Harriet Hosmer, and Edmonia Lewis, the Black/Native American sculptor—were also dressing in much the same manner in the United States and Europe, not especially for the purpose of "passing" as *men,* but for the real and implied emotional, political, and social freedoms inherent in the male costume. This radical expression of emancipation (which has centuries of tradition behind it) continued well into the twentieth century and included both women of color and white women.

It seems possible that in the American culture where the term *dike* denoted "the full set of male clothing" or "a man in full dress," this term could also have been applied to *women* who dressed in such clothing. Possibly these early radical women, dressing and passing in male clothing, both permanently and on occasion, were in fact our first *dike* sisters in America.

Again, Julia Stanley, who feels that the above etymology for *dyke* is the most viable she has heard, comments: "Your proposed etymology doesn't exclude the possibility that Wentworth and Flexner were correct in their hypothesis. That is, you may have come up with the 'missing link' in the semantic development of the word *dyke,* since it is stretching it a bit to relate it to the Germanic *ditch*" (Stanley, June 24, 1977).

If my hypothesis is correct, it could further be proposed that the meaning of *dike* was changing during the time period from the late nineteenth century of circa 1930s-1940s, that *dike* had begun passing from a predominantly positive male and/or neutral meaning to a derogatory female slang term. Linguistically, it may have gone through a process called "degeneration of meaning." By the 1930s *dike,* preceded by the equally tabooed *bull,* had been assigned sexual and derogatory meanings which could be applied both to Lesbians and to heterosexual women practicing tabooed sexual behaviors. By the 1940s-1950s-1960s the pejorative term *dike/dyke* was almost exclusively applied to "masculine" Lesbians, with other meanings becoming more obscure, though not yet obsolete. Linguists have found that this "process of degeneration" is a pattern often occurring to words which make such a male to female transition.

For this same period of possible linguistic change, there is growing evidence indicating a general altering of attitudes toward women's relationships with each other.* Increasingly, more negative aspects were being assigned to such relationships in the twentieth century than had been assigned them in the nineteenth century. Medical and psychiatric science was labeling such relationships "unnatural," "degenerate," and "sick." All manner of "masculine" characteristics of both a biological and psychological nature were attached to Lesbian women, as well as to other women who "deviated" from traditional, "god-given" (male-defined) "female roles." Speculating once again—since words and their meanings are used to reinforce the values of a given society, it may be that the linguistic change described above was related to the social/political change concerning definitions of Lesbianism and female sex roles. If a concept is assigned negative values, then the language used to describe that concept will also assume negative meaning. The language becomes a vehicle by which the value is perpetuated. Thus *dike*, once used to describe a well-dressed male, becomes a vulgar and hateful epithet to be hurled at women who rebel against confining roles and dress styles.

It is interesting to note how our "new" radical definitions echo the "old" radical traditions as signified by the term *dike/dyke*. Betty Birdfish, a friend in Chicago, wrote to me about a Lesbian dance to be held there, and how "wimmin are talking about 'dyking themselves up' for it." In my next letter, I asked Betty exactly what that meant—"dyking ourselves up." She responded:

About 'dyking ourselves up': I think it can mean a whole lot of things. In general, dressing up so one feels most beautiful, most proud of herself. I've seen that take many forms in the dyke community, at events. For example, Allison with her hair in corn rows and beads, wearing African garb. Or Jogie with a tuxedo and panama hat. Or Beverly looking like a gypsy with loose-flowing clothes, jewelry scarves and wearing scented oil. Or wimmin with tailored blazers and slacks and vests. Or even wimmin with long-flowing ankle length skirts or dresses. Many interpretations. Many expressions. For me 'dyking myself up' has been getting more definite in its expression lately. For the dance I

wore a pair of high-waisted black slacks, a white shirt with tie and pin, and a black satin, double-breasted, padded-shouldered, very tailored, old jacket. I felt very strong and beautiful in it. Before the dance, I had 'practiced' dyking myself up in a more radical way: I put on a different long sleeve shirt with collar and a silk tie that has wimmin together painted on it. I put my hair up in a bun, very close to my head so that it looked short, and put on a 'mannish' (I wish I had another word) straw hat. I looked like old-timey photos of Lesbians who you know had longer hair, who put it up, dyked up in suits, waistcoats, or tuxedos. I liked the way I looked, but wasn't ready to go 'out' yet in full dyke array. So I modified it for the dance. For me, 'dyking up' means the tailored suit: elegant, comfortable and strong. I guess I don't see this wear as just a 'masculine' privilege—but clothing that wimmin/dykes can wear to feel good in. I think I'm no longer as afraid of feeling 'butchy': to work on my body, to develop muscles and strength, to be more active physically (sports, karate, etc.), to move with more force, strength, confidence. I'm realizing how stifled I've been by society which condemns this development in wimmin. And I realize how our own dyke community continues to condemn it by labelling it 'butchy' and therefore 'male-identified' and therefore wrong. I don't care anymore (in my head—but not yet in my gut) about all those condemnations—I want to grow in ways I know I've always wanted to. (Betty Birdfish, August 4, 1977)

For the Lesbian of yesteryear, getting "diked up" may have had the same exhilarating, liberating, and fearful effects it has for contemporary Lesbians, but even more so since few women at that time wore pants. To wear "male clothing" before the advent of trousers for women and the so-called "unisex" fashions of today, was indeed radical and revolutionary. It signified a rebellion against male-defined roles for women, which "women's clothing" symbolized and perpetuated by rendering women passive, dependent, confined, and vulnerable. Yet this autonomous act of rebellion also made women vulnerable to punishment, ridicule, and ostracism.*

*It should be noted that these vulnerabilities were not experienced by women *only* in the nineteenth and early twentieth centuries. As late as 1968, Lesbians were being arrested in Dallas and Houston, Texas for wearing "men's clothing." See: "Special Release to the Ladder," *The Ladder* 13:1/2 (October/November 1968): 40-41; "Who Can Tell Boys from Girls," *The Ladder* 13:1/2 (October/November 1968): 41-42.

*See Carroll Smith Rosenberg, "The Female World of Love and Ritual: Relations Between Women in Nineteenth Century America," *Signs* 1:1 (Autumn 1975): 1-29; Alice Echols, "The Demise of Female Intimacy in the Nineteenth Century or 'There Wasn't a Dyke in the Land,'" unpublished paper, n.d., 34 pp.

Dike/dyke need not remain a vulgar epithet of self-hate, shame, and negativism, a term signifying "masculine." This is the definition which a heterosexist, dyke-hating society has formulated and which many Lesbians past and present have unquestioningly accepted. By defining some of us as "men" and some of us as "women," society has sought to divide us, to create inequality based on heterosexual roles, thereby defusing the political power of *women loving women*, reducing it to a pseudo-heterosexuality which, according to their thinking, is both artificial and inferior to the "real thing." *Dike/dyke* still remains a word hidden in history. But this new etymology suggests the possibility of some quite radical origins. Rather than wincing at the word *dyke*, we might better remember and commemorate those early Lesbians and feminists who refused "women's clothing" and "women's roles." They may have been our first dyke sisters.

Sources

AC/DC Blues: Gay Jazz Reissues, Vol. 1. St-106, Stash Records, Mattituck, New York, 1977.

Aldrich, Ann. *We Walk Alone*, New York; Fawcett, 1955.

Berrey, Lester V. and Van den Bark, Melvin. *American Thesaurus of Slang.* New York: Thomas Y. Crowell, 1942, 1947.

Berry, Leonard J. *Prison.* N.p.: Subsistence Press, 1972.

Birdfish (Alwin), Betty. Letter to JR Roberts. Chicago, Illinois (August 4, 1977). Collection of JR Roberts.

Clapin, Sylva. *A New Dictionary of Americanisms.* New York: Louis Weiss, 1902.

Cordova, Jeanne. "What's in a Name?" *Lesbian Tide* (June 1974):21-22.

Farmer, J.S. and Henley, W.E. *Slang and Its Analogues* (1890-1904). Reprinted ed., New York: Arno Press, 1970.

Hall, Benjamin H. *A Collection of College Words and Customs.* 2nd ed. Cambridge: John Bartlett, 1856 (1851). Reprinted ed., Detroit: Gale Research, 1968.

Hargan, James. "The Psychology of Prison Language." *Journal of Abnormal and Social Psychology* 30 (1935):359-365. (Note: the "more unprintable expressions" such as *bull-dike* were omitted from the published list, but were available upon request to those who were "especially interested in the subject.")

Johnson, Samuel. *A Dictionary of the English Language.* 3 vols. 2nd ed. London: Longman, Rees, Orne, Brown, Green et al., 1827.

Katz, Jonathan. *Gay American History: Lesbians and Gay Men in the U.S.A.* New York: Thomas Y. Crowell, 1976. Pb., Avon, 1978.

Major, Clarence. *Dictionary of Afro-American Slang.* New York: International Publishers, 1970.

Mathews, Mitford. *A Dictionary of Americanisms on Historical Principles.* 2 vols. Chicago: University of Chicago Press, 1951.

Partridge, Eric. *A Dictionary of Slang and Unconventional English,* 7th ed. 1967); Supplement 1970, New York: MacMillan, 1970.

Partridge, Eric. *A Dictionary of the Underworld.* 3rd ed. London: Routledge and Kegan Paul Ltd., 1968.

Sawyer, Ethel. "Study of a Public Lesbian Community." Masters Thesis, Washington University. St. Louis, Missouri, 1965.

Schele de Vere, Maximillian. *Americanisms: The English of the New World.* New York: Charles Scribner and Co., 1872.

Stanley, Julia P. Letter to JR Roberts. Lincoln, Nebraska (June 24, 1977). Collection of JR Roberts.

Stanley, Julia P. "When We Say 'Out of the Closets!'" *College English* (November 1974): 385-391.

Vice Versa 1:6 (November 1947). (Includes discussion of role-related slang; examined by Elizabeth Bouvier at the Homosexual Information Center Library, Hollywood, Calif.)

Wentworth, Harold. *American Dialect Dictionary.* New York: Thomas Y. Crowell, 1944.

Wentworth, Harold and Flexner, Stuart B. *Dictionary of American Slang.* New York: Thomas Y. Crowell, 1975.

THE LEAPing LESBiAN

From *The Leaping Lesbian* 3, no. 2 (1979): 3-5

Thoughts on Separatism and Lesbian Identity

by M. Adams

There are contradictions inherent in the breed of lesbian feminism we declare to the world today. I know you've heard the slogans: Woman Identified Woman, women who love women, etc., as if we have pledged undying allegiance and love for all women. It is implied that lesbians plead the cause of women as a sex. I am suspicious of these sentiments. It is uncomfortable to love all women when the vast majority of them prefer men; worse, it is a setup for rejection. It is painful to identify with women as a class, our history of oppression, when the lot of women has been and I believe primarily continues to be a morass of misery and suffocation. And my pride prevents me from identifying with the multitudes of women who remain pathetic victims in their lives. I believe too strongly that it is necessary to take responsibility for one's life, breaking whatever rules it is necessary to break in the process, and orient oneself towards survival in the fullest sense of the word.

I am a feminist not for the battered wives and rape victims, but primarily for myself. I am a lesbian because it allows for the fullest emotional and sexual expression of

my being. I am not trying to blaze a trail for the women who have failed me to follow: my mother, whose self-hatred was contagious; my first lover, who was so thirsty for male approval she could give me nothing; and all those who have given in to cowardice. I am not waiting for these women, I am leaving them.

Most lesbians, I feel, harbor confused and ambivalent feelings towards straight women. We feel to be "good feminists" we ought to be supportive of another woman's choice of lifestyle, criticism is somehow unkind and certainly not polite, and above all we are afraid of being too alienating. We reject thoroughly their way of life, yet in our relations with them this is rarely, if ever, confronted. This is a fundamental dishonesty, in ourselves as well as our relationships with straight women, and relationships contaminated with dishonesty must be dominated by fear.

A Basic Fear

This fear is a basic one. One source is simply that in a society dominated by men who harass, abuse, humiliate and otherwise oppress women all the time, most women still give primary loyalty and love to men. This is a force we grow up with, and it must undermine our trust in the strength of our connection to other women. Recovering this trust is a healing process in which some degree of lesbian separatism can play a vital role. As lesbians we are on the fringe, alienated from an overwhelmingly sexist and heterosexual culture, and we are the only members of society who choose to love and support women first. This fact makes us threatening to both straight men and women, but also gives us the potential we have for strong bonds within our community.

I don't see this potential being realized; rather, I perceive a great deal of insecurity, conformity, and fear of confrontation. One trivial example of this is a friend of mine I know who likes to dress up, but whenever I see her at a lesbian party she is wearing jeans and suspenders, and a blue jean shirt. Another example is the categories "politically correct" and "politically incorrect" which, frankly, I despise. They inhibit dialogue; in fact, because they are intimidating, they encourage silence, discouraging political confrontation and discussion that we need. This conformity and these fears can only come from a basic lack of trust, a fear of community judgment that inhibits individuals from exploring and expressing themselves. Conformity is accepted, not enforced, yet discontent and resentment simmer beneath the surface, and complaints about the community are expressed privately to friends.

A Basic Lack of Trust

We must develop as individuals for the community to be strong. We must test our bonds, through confrontation and self-assertion, to know their strength. The fact that the community is narrow is the responsibility of those who have conformed, who have not asserted their discontent (I include myself). I want to develop as the generally deviant personality I am within a community of lesbians, but in order to do so I must recognize that I have to make my own space. The notion that supportive sisters will provide one is a myth.

In the community of strong individuals that I envision, lesbian separatism is a necessary ingredient. But before I continue I want to make one thing perfectly clear: I am not implying that one should only relate to lesbians, that other friendships are "politically incorrect." Lesbian separatism needn't be a total lifestyle in order that a separate lesbian space have an important and respected place in one's life, a place where certain vital work is done that can't be done anywhere else. We don't prioritize our needs *as lesbians* and that deprives us of strength.

It is vital work for us as women to come to trust our bonds to other women enough so that we feel we can be ourselves without fearing rejection. A lesbian's strongest bonds are with women, and the strongest bonds that straight women have are with men. This implies prioritizing relating to lesbians, for lesbians are most worthy of the trust we are trying to develop. We have been betrayed by women throughout our lives: it was mother who first socialized us to be oppressed, to be straight, who feared for us and therefore taught us to fear for ourselves. Self-acceptance is so difficult to attain because our mothers and fore-mothers didn't possess it, and therefore couldn't extend acceptance to us. Emotional deprivation creates insecurity, fear that we will not be accepted for ourselves, that many of us carry from the straight world and our families into our lives as lesbians. Hidden fears like this contaminate the community. Though not justified, to be dispelled they must be personally confronted.

The above I consider to be the more intimately personal reasons why developing a separate lesbian identity is important and healthy. Separating ourselves makes the process of strengthening ourselves, despite a weakening culture, easier. As a community we also need a separate lesbian space so that we can explore who we are without defensiveness. There have been many political lesbians in this town over the past nine years who have put great political energy into many causes, but have hardly even explored their own. I believe these women have exaggerated our strength while overlooking our weakness. Like every other minority group we need a place to gather to assert and explore our identity in the face of a hostile culture. If anything we need this more than other minorities for lesbians have been so scattered, hidden and isolated, and none of us have grown up within a lesbian community; rather, we have to search out other lesbians as adults. A basic issue is how to assert and explore our identity as lesbians in the face of patriarchal culture and history in ways that are most liberating for ourselves. I think it is important to ask ourselves why these issues have not been a priority; perhaps it indicates a lack of self-respect.

Developing an identity as lesbians, as a separate minority group, is low priority in part because we fear losing what little legitimacy we possess if we assert our separateness from straight women. The Michigan Women's Music Festival is obviously a lesbian music festival—to call it a women's music festival is a failure of nerve. Many events that are overwhelmingly lesbian we don't dare label as such, for fear of alienating women. We are so afraid of being deserted by straight women

that we will shut up in order not to alienate them. This evasion of our own identity is called supporting other women's choices. I am definitely not against women's events—they have a vital part to play—but that's all

there is, and I don't think it's enough. As lesbians we have no legitimacy in the eyes of society, and rather than strike out on our own and find it for ourselves, we continue to cling to the past.

Gay Community News
THE WEEKLY FOR LESBIANS AND GAY MALES

From *Gay Community News* 7, no. 26 (January 26, 1980): 8-9

Making Our Movement International

by Harold Pickett

On November 26, 1979, the International Gay Association (IGA) opened an American Liaison Office in Washington, D.C. Edmund Lynch, IGA's General Secretary, travelled from Dublin, Ireland, to preside over the opening celebration at the new office.

The IGA, which represents lesbian and gay organizations in more than 20 countries, stated that the purpose of the Liaison Office is "to inform Americans about conditions of lesbians and gay men in other countries" and to "issue alerts when the Secretariat calls for coordinated international action to emergency situations."

The IGA was formed in Coventry, England, on August 26, 1978. The aims of the Association, stated in its Foundation Document, are:

to apply concerted political pressure on governments and international bodies in the pursuit of gay rights; to maximize the effectiveness of gay organizations by coordinating political actions on an international level; to promote the unity of gay people throughout the world by the collection and distribution of information on gay oppression and liberation; to work for the liberation of gay people.

Twelve gay organizations founding the IGA represented people from North America, Europe, and Australia. Today, there are 35 member organizations and 60 associate members throughout the world. While only gay men attended IGA's

Reprinted with permission from *Gay Community News: The Weekly for Lesbians and Gay Men*, 22 Bromfield St., Boston, MA 02108.

founding conference in Coventry, lesbians have begun organizing their participation in the Association. There will be a "women's section" at the April, 1980 IGA conference in Barcelona and lesbian participation is expected to result in the group's change of name to ILGA—International Lesbian and Gay Association.

An August 1979, statement by lesbians in the IGA said, in part, "We decided to try to have one organization together with gay men, because we think that one organization can be more powerful. Also, gay men and lesbians have experiences of oppression of homosexuality in common. Both gay men and lesbians have to fight against *forced heterosexuality*. But at the same time we know that the situation of gay men and lesbians is different. In many countries, gay men still have to fight oppression laws, while lesbians are very often ignored as homosexuals *and* women."

Important topics for lesbians were noted as: "custody; the right to have children by means of AID (artificial insemination), adoption or otherwise; work; violence against women; education and health; and discrimination within the gay community."

Early in December 1979, General Secretary, Edmund Lynch and Clint Hockenberry, IGA's American liaison, visited New York City. During the brief visit, they discussed the Association with *GCN*.

Asked to describe the background of the present IGA, Lynch said "Back in 1974 in Edinburgh when the first Congress of Gay People [was called], they decided it would be a good idea to set up an [international] organization. [The delegates] decided to call a meeting in Puerto Rico the following year, but it fell through."

The main reason the proposed 1975 meeting fell through was because "the Dutch people who are pretty much the leaders in gay rights, felt the time wasn't right yet."

"Then, out of the blue, someone suggested in early 1978, that we should get together" for another meeting. "Position papers were drawn up by the Irish, the Dutch, and the Italians." This time, "we all went along to meet each other and we all thought the time was right."

"We were able to get rid of issues" which weren't popular with all the groups and just concentrate on "the most important thing that we had in common, which was, that we were gay."

The group was organized somewhat along the lines of the United Nations in terms of assisting member groups. For example, if a country or national group wants help on a certain project because it would cause them political problems in their own country if they worked on it themselves, they can turn to the Association for assistance. Again, a group may not be able to work on a certain project because of that group's constitutional or specified aims. Sometimes a group simply doesn't have anyone able to work on a given project. In these instances, the IGA offers valuable support.

The politics of the group is "to fight against any oppression against gay men and lesbians. It's as broad as that," said Lynch. "Within the grouping, there are people who are to the left of politics, to the right, and people in the center." Gay atheists, Christians, and Jews, and people of all races are members.

Lynch said, "I think this is the first opportunity that gay organizations around the world have had to organize themselves on a professional level. We haven't the money, but money isn't everything. Our approach is: if you want to play against government, you've got to play at their own game and beat them.

"Gay people are everywhere, like the way the Communists have cells in all parts of the government. It means that we have gay people in every area of government. We would never have known, for example, about Cyrus Vance's cable, an internal memo, that gay people are to be stopped in their own countries before coming here, unless some gay person or supporter of gay rights within the State Department gave it to us. That's the important thing.

"In the same way, European gay people were able to stop the introduction of new anti-gay legislation last year in Greece. [Gay groups] approached Parliamentarians in Holland to sign a letter, which went to the Greek government, saying that they would not support Greece's entry into the European economic community 'if the anti-gay laws were passed.'

"The Greek government responded by announcing the day before our demonstrations that the bill was being withdrawn, that it was put in by mistake as part of the Greek military junta [bills]." This excuse was, of course, a face-saving attempt, but "They knew that they needed the European economic community."

Clint Hockenberry pointed out that "sometimes it's important for a small, weak, isolated group, such as the Greeks, to realise there are other gay people out there who are supporting them. We, here in the United States, remember very well what happened in Dade County and how the Dutch took out an entire full-page ad in a local newspaper during the referendum. It gives people a sense of optimism and hope.

"The local Greek group responded to the IGA thanking all the organizations which had put pressure the Greek government. They said, 'We were a tiny, isolated group who could never have defeated the Greek government alone. But with the help of an international lesbian and gay community, we were able to beat the Greek government.' They promised, out of gratitude for this kind of international pressure, that once their group was strong enough, they in turn would help other groups in other countries who are weak and being oppressed in the same situation that they were under.

"It's this kind of international aid among the lesbian and gay community that can have some important effects," Hockenberry added.

Lynch stated, "Gay people around the world, when they organize themselves can be most disruptive."

He described a situation where Finland was prohibiting distribution of information about homosexuality, unless it was negative. They wouldn't even allow publicizing of the American Psychiatric Association's change in its classification of homosexuality. Gay groups brought this issue to the Chair of the United Nations' Committee on Press Freedom. The Committee was necessarily forced to support the gay position, not because it was a gay issue or a matter of supporting gay rights, but because it was an issue of freedom of the press. The Finnish government received protests from around the world and Lynch said they are now rethinking their attitudes.

"Without this flow of international scientific information from Sweden or from other countries into Finland," Hock-enberry said, "the values of Finnish society would never change. It would [remain] very homophobic in its orientation." The Finnish government "put a great deal of restraint on the development of the Finnish gay movement by denying people, for example, the information from the American Psychiatric Association. This international focus can embarrass a country and cause changes where the individual group wouldn't have that much pressure."

Continuing to stress the necessity for national groups to assist one another, Lynch said, "In Europe, we took gay liberation from the Stonewall riots in 1969. The American people have so much to offer the Europeans, but then we have so much to offer the American people as well. In the same way with the other countries, it's a two-way process. The time is right now. We can all help each other. We have to put away our differences. It's important that we all work together and forget about the people we may not like on a social level or whose politics we may not like. Every organization has something to offer, whether that organization has all the resources at its finger-tips or whether the only resource an organization has is one person who can staple things together. Everyone has to work at something."

Hockenberry commented, "We're not just talking about politics, either. We're talking about cultural exchanges, too. Gay people are not just (specifically) political, though sometimes their art is political. We are multi-dimensional. There's a lot to celebrate in the gay experience, the humor, the art, the joy."

Still, the necessary, immediate focus of the IGA is on political assistance to local gay groups and on international organizations which affect the rights and dignity of gay people.

Individuals around the world are writing IGA and Lynch said, "We're hoping some of them will form organizations" in their own countries. For example, Hong Kong

Workers World/LNS

would be IGA's first member organization in Asia if the local group develops there. There are contacts with people in Central America. Lynch also said, "We're in touch with people behind the Iron Curtain. We have problems there that we're overcoming. We're able to get a lot of our [material] into the East European countries by diplomatic courier."

The Dublin Information Centre and Secretariat generally coordinates the IGA offices, while Amsterdam is the Financial Centre and also "looks after Eastern Europe." Dublin, though, "never does anything in isolation without consulting Amsterdam" and other concerned offices. A "rather active" office in New Zealand attends for Asia "for the moment" and Spain "looks after North Africa."

"We have made sure," Lynch said, "that we always have phone numbers of individuals in different organizations so that we can keep in touch.

"If there's a political situation that needs quick action, an organization immediately phones Dublin or Amsterdam. We then put into operation our snowball telephone system where we're responsible for calling another country and getting a reply from that country's contact people." Then they, too, make calls of their own.

Lynch said by using such a system "we were able to get 2,000 Danish people on the streets in 24 hours to demonstrate against the Iranian arrests" of homosexuals.

"It's very important to use modern methods of communication," he said.

The "life-line" is one important IGA project which involves an international effort to save individual lives in local situations.

Hockenberry said, "Gay refugees are a new phenomenon which is becoming more recognised now, whereas before, it was something that occurred, but no one was able to document it."

Lynch explained the purpose of Life-line as being to rescue people who may be in danger of losing their lives. Many such people become gay refugees.

For example, in November 1979, IGA offered to work with gay and lesbian Iranians in the United States who face deportation, stating that they "*may* be able to use their homosexuality as a defense to remain the United States. Because of the executions of gay men in Teheran [early in 1979], openly gay students may assert they would be in danger by returning to Iran because of their sexual orientation. Anything that can

establish political refugee status may be successful to delay or defeat deportation under these circumstances." IGA stated that U.S. deportation hearings examiners "have stayed deportation of homosexual aliens in the past where political refugee status was determined."

If a student found it impossible to raise the issue of personal homosexuality during a public hearing, IGA said it would "attempt to locate, through its European member organizations, another host country" for that person.

Lynch said that if Iranians "admit their homosexuality in a public hearing, should they ever return to Iran after the political climate has changed, the social values that condemn homosexuality will nonetheless remain the same. They will, on record, be identifiably homosexual. That's why they're between the devil and the deep blue sea.

"On the one hand, people can use their homosexuality as evidence in a case . . . and as part of the defense [to stay in the country]. But what Iranian wants to come right out in the open and say that? It's a very different situation for that person.

"In the alternative, a person who is homosexual and Iranian may be able, very quietly, to slip into a friendly country and, therefore, will not have that public image of being homosexual. So we're trying to balance it off, giving leeway for lesbian and gay Iranians to remain quiet about their homosexuality.

"Next year, it could be Chilean students or it could be anyone. But if needed, the groundwork is done," Lynch said.

Another Life-line incident occurred around the time of the executions of the twelve gay men in Iran and concerning a leading Italian activist. ("The Italians are great activists, but they never tell you about anything and suddenly they find themselves up to their necks in trouble!")

The Dublin office received an unexpected phone call from the Italian group saying, "We need action!"

"On what?" they were asked.

A leading activist was in Teheran—"He's about to be shot by the Iranians!"

"What's he doing in Iran?"

"He's there on behalf of the Italian organization doing a protest—and also on behalf of the International Gay Association."

"Why weren't we told about this beforehand? We're supposed to know!"

"We thought it was too important to tell anyone and we must get him out. He's going to be killed tomorrow at 12 noon!

He's going to make a speech in front of the main prison, where he might be invited in, and we might never see him again!"

Dublin was able to get in touch with the European Broadcasting Corporation simply because an IGA leader worked for the National Broadcasting Service. A morning conference was set up by telephone and Telex: "There is a good story, we think, in Teheran and we would like it. Do we have any film crews there?"

A French film crew happened to be available and they went out to the prison to shoot (*with film*) the Italian delivering his speech.

He was invited into the prison, but the Iranians knew the press was outside. So they released him an hour later, drove him to the airport, kicked him on a plane, and sent him home.

The National Broadcasting Service (and the IGA) was notified that the film was on its way. They said "Thank you very much" but never used the film. There was never any intention of using it; it had served, though, as a solution to a very immediate Life-line problem.

Lynch said, describing yet another situation, "Two days before I came here by London, there was an Argentinian whose English visa had expired and he was being sent back to the Argentine. He didn't want to go back because they knew he was gay. He felt that he would simply disappear once he returned. A lot of gay people have 'disappeared' in that country. Through our British organization, we were able to arrange for two barristers to go to the Home Office, which is the equivalent of your Justice Department, to lobby for the person to be allowed to stay in England. It worked. Cases like that don't get much publicity."

Other major projects concentrate on such international organizations as the United Nations, the World Health Organization, and Amnesty International.

Hockenberry said, "We have obtained information on the procedures for applying for consultive status at the United Nations as a non-governmental organization. Over the next few months, we will be working on that as a high priority."

Certain specific requirements must be met before the application is presented to "thirteen countries which are part of this one committee for reviewing our status and our application. It's a year-and-a-half process we're talking about. So we have to do the work over the next few months and then get through the politicking that's behind it. The consultive status will give us privileges and the use of certain facilities at the U.N. and allow us to testify on issues of importance to lesbians and gay men."

A 1980's International Women's Conference is being planned and Hockenberry said "We're hoping some discussion of lesbian rights and concerns will be on the agenda. Lesbian issues never have been addressed in a world body. This seems like an appropriate forum."

Such a conference could help the situation at the U.N. Gay people, or people according to their sexual orientation, are not included in the list of those protected under the United Nations' Declaration of Human Rights. The list protects people according to language, nationality, ethnic background, race, religion and sex.

Hockenberry feels "it's going to be an uphill fight on an international level, similar to our fight here nationally" to get "sexual orientation" added to the list.

"It's going to be even more complicated once we begin the task of sensitizing the world body to the concerns of lesbians and gay men," Hockenberry said.

"Also," Lynch said, "at the same time that we are applying to the United Nations for consultive status, we are applying to the Council of Europe which deals with human rights issues. It also means that some of our member organizations will be applying to the European economic community for a grant to carry out projects on discrimination within Europe."

Lynch said one of IGA's on-going projects "is to get the classification of homosexuality as a disease eliminated from the World Health Organization [WHO]."

"What we have done is to establish a work project at the Liaison Office to correspond with the major project areas of the IGA as a whole," Hockenberry said. "We will have one person at the Liaison Office responsible for that project and working with other people. It's going to take several years to change the policies of the World Health Organization, whether we can go through a committee structure or whether we go before the full body.

"The National Gay Health Coalition and other organizations are going to cooperate with us in this specific area. We have to delete WHO's classification of homosexuality as a mental disorder."

The importance of obtaining such a change, Hockenberry said, occurs quite often because nations use the WHO classification as a basis for defining homo-

sexuals as "sick," or as "sexual deviants." "Canada, as a nation, will not take a stand until the World Health Organization changes its tune."

Sweden, another example mentioned by Hockenberry, maintained it had to uphold WHO's classification of homosexuality and couldn't change their "sickness" designation until WHO first changed its own classification.

Hockenberry said Swedish gays began to pressure the government until their actions finally culminated in what they called a "sick-in." Gays called their employers and said, "I'm sorry, but I can't come in to work today." The employers asked, "Are you ill?" "Yes," the employees answered, "I'm seriously ill—I'm seriously homosexual!"

"At that point," Hockenberry said, "the employer was bound to give sick leave from work on those grounds. The employee was covered. Thirty to forty people in the Stockholm area last August called their employers during the sick-in. In October, the Swedish government changed its classification.

"This was not [entirely] because of the sick-in. The sick-in was just one of the things that helped to advertise the fact.

"The Swedes will support the [WHO] change now, along with the American delegation."

IGA has been working to get Amnesty International, the human rights organization, to adopt homosexuals as a group as "prisoners of conscience" whenever homosexuals are found to be imprisoned because of their sexual orientation.

At Amnesty's 1979 Belgium International Council meeting, Lynch said, "They moved somewhat closer [to the adoption of homosexuals as 'prisoners of conscience'] in that they will take up the issue where people as *gay activists* are arrested and imprisoned because of gay activities in fighting for issues."

For the record, the U.S. Section of Amnesty International states it "had been instructed by its 1979 Annual Meeting to advocate the adoption as prisoners of conscience all those imprisoned solely for their sexual orientation," a position which "did not carry" at the International Council Meeting (ICM) in Belgium.

A letter from AI/USA clarifies the debate: "It is important, however, to stress that the debate was not on the question of whether or not the imprisonment of homosexuals is a violation of their human rights. As the resolution states, it clearly is. The issue debated was whether this partic-

ular human rights violation falls within Amnesty International's restricted mandate, and if not, whether the mandate, and consequently the workload, should be expanded."

Besides those "imprisoned for the advocacy of homosexual equality," the prisoner of conscience distinction can be applicable where homosexuality "can reasonably be assumed to be a pretext . . . for repressing any other advocacy" apart from violence or violent activities. Thus, a gay person imprisoned for homosexuality as an excuse to silence protest on any issue can be considered a prisoner of conscience.

Amnesty states it "already can, and does, work against the execution and torture of all prisoners, including those arrested on charges related to homosexuality."

In addition, the 1979 resolution recommends the International Executive Council "to ask one or more national sections jointly to prepare an overall study of the problems involved in the possible acknowledgement of persons imprisoned solely because of their sexual orientation or nature as prisoners of conscience and present that study to the ICM in 1981 or 1982."

Lynch said, "The work is not over yet. There's nothing stopping gay people who are not politically out-front from joining their local section of AI. Then, when others raise the issue of the adoption of gay prisoners, they [the closeted gays] will dutifully put up their hands in favor. This is the way people can act as 'sleepers.' They've done their political act, yet no one knows whether they're gay or not.

"The important thing is that we must prepare our information [carefully] for submission to get gay people adopted as prisoners. We must make sure that our facts are correct. We're in the best position to know about people who are imprisoned. Perhaps if people are imprisoned, because of the prison system, they are being abused as gay people. But we must do our homework. We must get involved."

"We can't achieve our aims in two years. It's an on-going process. We must show that we're concerned about *other* people who are imprisoned. We can't be one-sided about this. In other words, we've got to take our place within Amnesty and we've got to work with people who may not have worried about us before."

"Another problem," Lynch said, "is that the people who are preparing the information on prisoners for adoption have basically ignored gay people and have been discriminating in their presentation of information. It's up to us to see that it doesn't happen in the future."

Allies for the IGA vary, according to Hockenberry, "depending on where they need our support and from whom we can get support." Usually, the Northern European countries and the groups there are helpful. Sometimes a non-gay organization will serve as a mediator with a country that would be resistant to meeting with an identifiably lesbian and gay organization.

Some countries, especially the Nordic countries, and the United States, to some extent, can be approached directly. The Western developed countries are most accessible, Hockenberry said, "because their national movements are at least open and becoming stronger. Their national governments have to pay attention to them. They may not want to, but they realize this is becoming an increasingly powerful pressure group. Therefore, they at least have to talk to the group, whereas groups in the developing world are back where we were a decade ago. They don't have the organizations by-and-large. There are some just now beginning and that's an exciting thing to see happen."

Sometime in the future, Lynch said, he would like the IGA to hold a conference in North America. "It's unfair to ask North Americans always to come to Europe and that would give us the opportunity to come here.

"It would be interesting to test the Immigration Laws, whether we'd be banned from coming in. That's a political issue for American gay people because it won't affect us too much as tourists. There might be a lot of gay people here, though, who would want to bring over their gay lovers.

"The Dutch have changed their laws on immigration and now let gay persons bring in their lovers. There are certain conditions. For example, they must be in touch with each other for two years writing letters."

Of course, the American Liaison Office will be concerned with U.S. Immigration and Naturalization policies, along with other major IGA interest areas. The office will also work with the World Council of Churches and international labor organizations, pushing for their support for gay rights around the world.

Lynch also stressed he would like for gay people to have "old magazines, flyers, hand-outs, or any gay momentoes that

they're going to throw out" to, instead, put them in a package and mail it to the Liaison Office. "What you might think is of no use, the Liaison Office might want. It's very important that we protect our own culture and not let what has happened before happen again."

The IGA has designated the 28th of June as "International Gay Solidarity Day." Lynch said, "We tried to bring this as near to Stonewall (as possible), but everyone celebrates Stonewall at different times.

"On this one day, the idea is that every gay person wear a flower—a carnation. Not being nationalistic, of course, I suggested we all dye our carnations green, like Oscar Wilde who wore green. People would certainly see the visibility of gay people with their green flowers all around the world. It means that television would pick it up. At least the flower would stand out. It's a way of using symbols."

Hockenberry said, "Since this trip, we expect the number of American organizations (in the IGA) to increase dramatically. It brings up another problem on an organization level: nobody wants Americans to dominate it, including the Americans. It brings up: how can we have better representation and still remain an international body?"

Lynch felt the situation was "very healthy." He said, "We have to come up with some form of system that is equitable. Clint and I have drafted a document toward this which has to go around to all the other organizations. I think it will be carried. It's not to downgrade any one country or to make any one country stronger than the other."

Funding for the IGA comes from

member organizations. "Each member organization pays the equivalent of 100 Dutch guilders." Lynch added, "That's not enough money, there's no doubt about it. We need much more money. The way we're trying to raise it is by opening up associate membership to individuals. They will receive all our communications with the exception of confidential material, which, by its nature, has to remain so. Hopefully, people will also send in donations."

Individual membership is $15; $20 for a household; and $25 for a media or associate member organization. Individuals and groups interested in becoming IGA members should contact the Washington, D.C., Liaison Office.

Lynch remarked on his visit to the United States, saying, "One thing I've found interesting is how strong the gay community is becoming here is the States." He noted that political parties are sending representatives to fund-raising events. "That's a step in the right direction. The politicians, at least, are beginning to realize that gay people, especially in your society because of the vote system, often make the difference in their getting elected or not. I think that's quite clear with the Mayor of Washington, D.C. He seems to have lived up to all his promises. I think the American gay people should be very proud of this."

For further information about IGA, write:

International Gay Association,
Liaison Office
c/o Gay Community Center/DC
1469 Church Street NW
Washington, D.C. 20005, U.S.A.

The office telephone number is (202) 234-6268.

From *Body Politic,* no. 58 (November 1979), pp. 23-27

Sex, Death and Free Speech: The Fight to Stop Friedkin's *Cruising*

by Scott Tucker

Reprinted with permission from *The Body Politic,* Canada's gay liberation newsmagazine.

Having been censored out of history, do we want our history constructed by the censors? Having been made invisible, can we now appear only as corpses?

The Ramble, a bucolic thicket on the west side of Central Park, has been a cruising spot for as long as anyone can remember. Cole Porter celebrated it in song in 1935 ("Picture Central Park without a sailor . . . "), and it is still one of New York's most popular rendezvous, sun-dappled and casual by day, more intense at night.

And more dangerous. One night last summer a gang of toughs roamed through with baseball bats ("We went out to get the queers," one of them said later in his court testimony) and beat six men. Five were taken to hospital, seriously injured.

This morning, though, the place seems idyllic: gay men in cut-offs and swimsuits lie sunning, talking, now and then rising to go off into the woods. For a while I wander the twisted paths, picking my way through the dense growth, and finally sit down on a bench to read my book of essays by Rosa Luxemburg and eat fruit from my knapsack. Police barricades are still up nearby: the night before, William Friedkin had been shooting a castration killing scene here for his film, *Cruising*.

I am in New York for the protests against the film. On August 20, eight hundred of us had marched from a rally in Sheridan Square to a film site on West Street. We had shrilled our disco whistles like a swarm of angry locusts and had whooped Indian war cries—"The streets belong to the people!" On West Street the cops surrounded us. Somebody handed me an egg and I figured eggs can't beat clubs—I was saving it for Friedkin when a cop took it. "But it's for my breakfast," I said, and then added, "Sit on it."

Mounted police charged into a large group that had broken away to get closer to the filming. Nightsticks cracked on skulls and some of the protesters began to throw bottles. One man tried setting fire to a camera cable with a book of matches and was quickly circled by kicking, clubbing cops. A dozen of us broke through, grabbed the cable and began a tug of war with the police until they pummelled us back. For the first time in my life I called cops "pigs."

Interviewed in the *New York Times*, Friedkin called the protesters "a gang of unruly fanatics." *Soho Weekly News* columnist Allan Wolper warned that "The Constitution isn't stamped 'For Gays Only'. . . . The people leading the sit-downs and whistle blowing against the film will lose their war for equality if they manage to win their battle for censorship."

What constitutes censorship? What constitutes self-defence? The subtleties and ambiguities had been considered. The protesters themselves were acutely aware of them. Tugging on that cable—knowing I wanted to destroy that camera, stop the filming—I suddenly saw how it had

crystallized for me. I knew exactly what I was doing.

This morning in the Ramble, though, certain questions remain. Should we have been trying to stop *Cruising*? Was that possible or realistic—or desirable? Should we have simply said, not in *our* neighbourhood, not on *our* streets? Should we have waited until the film is shown at theatres and planned protests then?

Because *Cruising* burst like a bomb in the gay community, there wasn't always time for these and other questions to become clear. Key issues were hedged or obscured or not recognized by gay spokespeople, by the filmmakers and by the "free press" defending "free speech" without ever making connections with "free" enterprise.

Some questions can only be left open, but to others the protesters, the filmmakers and the film itself can provide answers.

Biting the Big Apple
Rough Times for Rough Trade

Toronto is such a small city that when Carole Pope and Kevan Staples of Rough Trade decided to do the soundtrack for Friedkin's *Cruising*, just *everyone* (south of Bloor) knew in a matter of hours.

A lot of people felt a sense of betrayal. Many of Rough Trade's most devoted fans are gay, the lyrical contents of Pope's songs are filled with gay imagery, and on stage she presents an alluring camp image of "tomorrow's dominant woman." Only a week before the word on Rough Trade and *Cruising* got out. *Village Voice* columnist Arthur Bell saw Rough Trade perform and was so astonished he didn't believe Pope was from Toronto or that she wrote her own lyrics.

If a criterion of genius is being ten years ahead of your time, Carole Pope and Kevan Staples deserve that accolade. They were new wave when they started out as The Bullwhip Brothers in Yorkville in the hippy days of 1968. But faced with a provincial Canadian attitude that if Toronto is good, New York must be better, and a branch plant record industry controlled by the American giants, they still don't have a record contract. (One album, recorded by a small Canadian company, has sold 32,000 copies world-wide since 1976.)

In the meantime, Pope and Staples have starved on the one hand, and won an Etrog for best film score of 1978 (for Allan King's *One Night Stand*) on the other. So when Carole Pope says *Cruising* is a break for them, you know where she's coming from.

When they were offered the chance to score *Cruising*, Pope and Staples flew off to New York to look at rushes. Since they'll be doing music for the bar scenes,

most of the clips they saw were shot in S&M bars; they also viewed footage of one of the murders, which Pope admits was "gruesome." However, she says, "There are some valid things about the film, too. First, Al Pacino, as a cop, goes through a great sexual identity crisis and ends up living with a rather ordinary gay man. Also, the film is about corruption in the police force.

"*Cruising* is about an aspect of gay life, and I don't see why people shouldn't see it. I don't think people will be taken in by the violence. As for the sex and S&M going on openly in the bars, well I believe in sexual freedom above all else, and it didn't offend me.

I'm glad we're doing it because I write satirical lyrics. You can be damned sure I'm going to make fun of what's happening. It's also going to be dance music—new wave R&B. Maybe the soundtrack album will help change music in gay bars and give us some relief from disco.

"We went into this with a lot of reservations. But it's our big chance."

Knowing the problems Canadian rock bands face when they compete with the American music industry, I can understand some of the frustration Pope and Staples have had to deal with. At a very basic political level they are victims of American cultural imperialism which exploits whatever Canadian art it can, and starves the rest.

I can't help feeling that sense of betrayal, and I wonder if their decision to score *Cruising* may not harm their careers more than it helps them.

But I am left empathizing with what is essentially, an indefensible position.

—Robin Hardy

'I'll Show You a Gay Corpse'

In 1969 William Friedkin directed the film version of Mart Crowley's play, *The Boys in the Band*. Earlier that year gays in Greenwich Village had fought back a police attack at the Stonewall Inn, and a new generation of activists—not just "politicos," but people from throughout the gay community—protested the film's depiction of gays as doomed queens.

Friedkin defended his film then by saying that "*The Boys in the Band* is not about gay life. It's about human problems. I hope there are happy homosexuals. They just don't happen to be in my films." "You show me a happy homosexual," says one character in the movie, "and I'll show you a gay corpse."

Cruising offers gay corpses in spades, and Friedkin is equally disingenuous in defending it. "This isn't a film about gay life," he told journalist Vito Russo. "It's a murder mystery with an aspect of the gay world as background."

Jerry Weintraub, the film's producer, told the *New York Daily News*, "The gay leaders keep asking me why I don't make a nice film about homosexuals. I don't know what that means."

Neither does the American public. The truth is that happy homosexuals "just don't happen to be" in *any* Hollywood films—unless they go straight. The more substantially a story deals with homosexuals, the more sad or sinister the film. *The Boys in the Band* was a sad gay melodrama with campy comic relief. *Cruising* is an utterly unrelieved gay horror film.

The script of *Cruising*, written by Friedkin, is based on a 1970 novel by Gerald Walker, an editor at the *New York Times*. At the time the novel appeared, gay activists asked Walker what he thought the book's social effects would be. "Ah, it's not my business," he replied. A police lieutenant in the book says of gays, "They think the straight world is the enemy, but it's themselves." All but spoken, this remains the key message in William Friedkin's film.

The Homosexorcist

A previous film by Friedkin, *The Exorcist*, portrays the gradual, gruesome possession of an amiable teenaged girl by Satan. After great struggle Satan is finally exorcised, but dark powers still lurk and loom in the world.

The script of *Cruising*, which the filmmakers kept so secret that *Village Voice* columnist Arthur Bell described it as more difficult to come by than knowledge of Skylab's crash sites," was leaked late in July by someone involved in the production. This third draft, dated June 1, shows that possession and exorcism are still dominant themes for Friedkin.

In the first scene, a tugboat captain discovers "a severed gangrenous Human Arm" floating in the polluted Hudson. Later in the city morgue "the camera stays hypnotically on the lifeless limb" while a detective asks questions and a medical examiner deciphers on the arm a tattoo reading "Pleasure." (A later scene, in which a fashion designer is knifed in a porno movie booth, juxtaposes the orgasm of a man getting whipped in the porn flick with the death agony of the designer. Moral: The wages of sin is death.)

Friedkin claims *Cruising* is a murder mystery, but his script contains no puzzle as to "whodunit"—"it" in this case is a series of dismemberings of gay men—only as to *why*. Early on we get to see the killer as he stabs a man in the back while fucking him; we aren't left guessing who it is that's going around cutting off cocks and stuffing them in his victims' mouths.

A straight cop, played by Al Pacino, is sent out as an undercover "gay" decoy to find the killer. "How far do I have to go?" Pacino's character asks his captain. "If we send out an undercover narc, he grows a beard and long hair but he doesn't have to become an addict." But during his immersion in the leather and S&M bars he becomes possessed. He breaks up with his girlfriend and becomes interested in an unsuccessful gay play-wright, with whose jealous lover he has a violent quarrel.

The killer is also portrayed as a failed artist, but a heterosexual, a narcissist fond of musicals. Whenever moving in for the kill, he speaks in "The Voice of Jack." The killer has a humiliating encounter with his father and we learn that the Voice of Jack is, in fact, his father's voice. This encounter turns out to be imaginary: dad is long dead, though son continues to write him letters begging for approval. Killing exorcises the

---

Cruising and the Constitution
The First Amendment: Sold to the Highest Bidder

As is common in battles concerning basic rights in the United States, people on both sides of the *Cruising* barricades harked back to the Constitution to justify their actions. Two constitutional amendments are directly relevant to the controversy roused by the film and the protests.

The First Amendment reads, "Congress shall make no law respecting an establishment of religion, or prohibiting the free exercise thereof; or abridging the freedom of speech or of the press; or the right of the people peaceably to assemble and to petition the government for the redress of grievances." This amendment, part of the US Bill of Rights adopted in 1791, codified many of the basic freedoms for which the former British subjects had fought a revolution more than a decade earlier.

(Canada, of course, did not join in that rebellion. In a recent article in *Saturday Night*, US social critic Edgar Friedenberg, a resident of Nova Scotia for the past ten years and author of the upcoming book, *Deference to Authority: The Case of Canada*, noted that the language in which each country frames its basic rights still shows the difference:

"Where the first five words of the US Bill of Rights are 'Congress shall make no law,' the Canadian document provides that: 'Every law of Canada shall, *unless it is expressly declared by an Act of the Parliament of Canada that it shall operate notwithstanding the Canadian Bill of Rights*, be so construed and applied so as not to abrogate, abridge or infringe . . . any of the rights or freedoms herein recognized.' "

The Canadian Bill of Rights, therefore, applies only when Parliament agrees it should. It is not part of the British North America Act, Canada's "constitution," and could be repealed by a simple act of Parliament. (It was, in fact, suspended for six months while the War Measures Act was in force following the 1970 "October Crisis.")

In practice, the rights afforded by the US First Amendment have never been as absolute as the language makes them seem. The individual *states* were not bound by it until 1868, when the Fourteenth Amendment was ratified. It reads, in part: "No state shall make or enforce any law which shall abridge the privilege or immunities of citizens of the

United States; nor shall any State deprive any person of life, liberty or property without due process of law; nor deny to any person within its jurisdiction the equal protection of the law."

Both these amendments have been instrumental in extending and maintaining civil rights and liberties in the US. The First has protected religious groups, dissidents and cranks of all kinds from government suppression—most of the time—and the Fourteenth has provided the basis for other amendments guaranteeing the vote to black men and later to women. It is also the basis for the Equal Rights Amendment women are now struggling for, and for the civil rights US gays seek.

Writing about *Cruising* in the *Village Voice*, Richard Goldstein noted, "If you look behind the First Amendment to the people who are raising it as a defense to slur, you see that for the most part these are white, male heterosexuals. The farther away you get from this nexus of authority, the less likely you are to find people who think freedom of speech means very much without the rest of the Constitution—especially the Fourteenth Amendment.

First Amendment rights were of little use to blacks or women before the Fourteenth (and later) amendments guaranteed that they, too, would be allowed to exercise them. The same is still true for those who don't have the money or the power to make their free speech *heard*.

The rights some Americans take for granted were not achieved without struggle. The First Amendment was born not only of the Revolution, but also of the vigilance of six of the thirteen original states, which refused to ratify the strongly centralist Constitution without a guarantee that a Bill of Rights would be included. The Fourteenth Amendment secured rights which were won only after four bloody years of civil war; even after that, passage of the Amendment generated riots across the defeated South in which upstart blacks were murdered by white mobs.

We can hope to moderate the social struggles that will inevitably accompany efforts to achieve economic democracy, but we don't dare delude ourselves as to what even moderate struggle may involve.

"Those who favour freedom and yet deprecate agitation," wrote black Abolitionist Frederick Douglass in 1857, "are people who want crops without plowing up the ground."

—Scott Tucker & Rick Bebout

punitive father and the killer's own suspected homosexuality—briefly.

The cop and the killer finally cruise each other one night in Central Park. The killer muses nihilistically on the cosmos and "black holes," and both then enter a dark tunnel (shades of Freud). They drop their pants. ("How big are you?" "Party size." "What are you into?" "I'll go anywhere." "Do me first." "Hips or lips?" "Go for it.") Both reach for their knives, but the cop "garrots" the killer first. As he dies he stares, unbelieving, at the cop "in whom he sees—his father—himself." The next script note adds that the cop is now "released. He's done his job, he's made a choice, and he's a civilized member of society." Granting that Friedkin intended irony here, it is the first sign of it in the script, and it occurs in a parenthetical note that the director may appreciate, but the public will not see.

The cop's own exorcism appears successful, but demons lurk again when a fresh gay corpse is found—the failed writer to whom the cop had been attached. The film ends with the cop's promotion to Detective and his return to his girlfriend.

Friedkin adds one touch to this story that may seem gratuitous but which in fact perfects the emasculation of a predator driven to castrate his prey. In a morgue scene a medical examiner informs the police lieutenant that one victim's anus was "dilated at the time of death" and that he found some semen. "Aspermia," he said. "No sperm. Your killer is shooting blanks." Friedkin does *not* have the killer dress up in the clothes of a long-dead mother; he may have refrained only because Hitchcock's *Psycho* beat his psycho to it.

In what may have been a concession to protests against *Cruising*, producer Jerry Weintraub once mentioned the possible inclusion of "a good, healthy gay relationship" in the film. In the context of the other characters in the script, this couple would look like vegetarians in a tribe of cannibals. The few gays with any character have but two roles: killer and victim, and not even all the victims are painted in more than two dimensions. *Cruising* doesn't explore the lives of gay people. It murders them in sequence and exploits their deaths.

'You Wouldn't Talk to Us . . .'

When gay activists first learned of plans to shoot *Cruising* in the Village, many pleaded with the filmmakers simply to *consult* with the gay community. In an open letter to Friedkin, journalist Doug Ireland wrote, "You didn't want to talk to anybody. Instead you went to the Mine Shaft . . . and hired its people as consultants. Now we know that the Mine Shaft is owned by two heterosexual ex-cops . . . Well, since you wouldn't talk to us, we decided to talk to you—in the streets."

By early June the film was in the second of eight weeks of on-location shooting. In his regular column in the *Village Voice*, Arthur Bell reported that the film promised to be "the most oppressive, ugly, bigoted look at homosexuality ever presented on the screen," and urged readers "to give Friedkin and his production crew a terrible time if you spot them in your neighborhood."

On July 23 more than 600 gay people packed Washington Square Methodist Church for an emergency Town Meeting, responding both to Bell's warning and to the meeting flyer which read, in part: "*Cruising* is a film which will encourage more violence against homosexuals. In the current climate to backlash against the gay rights movement, this movie is a genocidal act." Doug Ireland, who helped organize the meeting, later reported in the *Soho Weekly News* that the audience was asked how many of them had been targets of anti-gay violence within the last year, or had friends who had been. More than half raised their hands. Outside, meanwhile, a group of young toughs sharing anti-fag jokes with the cops harassed the 100 or so gays who couldn't cram into the church. The gang later got into their car and tried running people down on Christopher Street; one woman's hip was injured.

Ireland was asked at the meeting whether protests against the film might violate free speech rights. "We're not attacking Billy Friedkin's right to make this film," he responded. "We're just telling him we don't want it made off our backs. That's not censorship, that's self-defence."

The day after the July 23 Town Meeting, gay activist Ethan Geto led a group to meet with Mayor Ed Koch and ask him to withdraw Friedkin's film permit. Koch refused. "To do otherwise," he said, "would involve censorship. It is the business of this city's administration to encourage the return of filmmaking to New York City to whatever extent feasible with filmmakers." When Nancy Littlefield, the City's liaison with film companies, was asked by phone if she thought *Cruising* would be good for the city and its citizens, she replied, "Anything that brings this city seven million dollars is good," and hung up.

Koch was right: withdrawing the film permit *would* have been censorship. But Littlefield's point was lost on no one—the "principled" stand on free speech was also a very profitable one.

Good Citizens, Good Money

In an interview with Pete Hamill of New York's *Daily News*, Friedkin said, "I went to the Anvil and the Mine Shaft (two village leather bars) for three months. The guys in it seem to enjoy it; it's unique, unusual, and that's why I'm looking at it. I'm trying to capture the energy of it and the quality of ritual. I have no idea what it means to them, but it's a commitment."

Speaking of the undercover cop in *Cruising*, Friedkin says, "He's initially repulsed as many people might be. If you dropped a citizen of Grand Rapids into the Mine Shaft, he'd probably collapse."

Friedkin knows, of course, that good citizens will pay good money to collapse. There is a profit to be made from incomprehension and intolerance.

He takes pains to express his *own* tolerance: "There is no comment in this film that it is degrading or that it's wonderful—just here it is," he told Vito Russo in an interview. "These scenes could be run as documentary footage. I don't find what goes on in these bars particularly shocking. I find myself in opposition to the gay community people who find sex bars offensive and condemn them. There's no doubt in my mind that this film won't provoke violence against gays, but I think it might very well provoke more men into this kind of life."

A neutrality, a liberality, then, appropriate to a film on Eskimo domesticity or a flick on household plumbing—so Friedkin would have us believe. But what is "this kind of life" he portrays? Is it a kind of life we would care to see anyone provoked into? As one actor in the film, Paul Sorvino, put it: "It's dangerous to be gay." *Cruising* presents this danger as though it were the Nature of Things rather than examining *why* it is dangerous to be gay in this society at this time.

If Friedkin thinks he's directed a documentary, Jerry Weintraub thinks he's produced a morality play. "What if the film

A Cruising *Who's Who*
Billy and Jerry and Ed—and Arthur

Director **William Friedkin** is no stranger to the gay scene—at least not the parts he chooses to see. Before directing *The Boys in the Band* in 1969, he paid a visit to Fire Island's meat rack with author Mart Crowley. "It's a gigantic pit with 200 to 300 guys in a daisy chain batting each other in the ass," he recalls. "One guy got real close to me. He said, 'I think you're cute,' and I turned around and got out of there as quick as my legs would take me."

For *Cruising*, Friedkin decked himself out in leather and got friendly cops he met while filming *The French Connection* to take him out to what he calls "the gay underworld—that part of the gay world that is closely involved with sex and drugs." In his *New York Times* interview, he reports being fascinated by the S&M bar scene. "It seemed to me to be very exciting. And unusual. And outside my own experience."

Clearly. In his script for the film, Friedkin has tough S&M types cruising the Ramble in open-toed sandals (shades of *Boys in the Band*?), and a leather bar habitue who responds to an ambiguous comment with the oh-so-butch barb, "I beg your hard-on?"

Jerry Weintraub, the 44-year-old Brooklyner who is producing *Cruising* for Lorimar Productions, has mixed feelings about the protests against the film. "Before, I had to wonder how to sell it," he says, "but now, as a national hard news story, people are titillated. People in Des Moines will be running to see it."

But: "When they start messing with the First Amendment and my freedom to make a film, I'm against that. I respect their rights, I want them to respect mine."

Weintraub confided to Vito Russo that he had resigned from the American Civil Liberties Union when they defended the First Amendment right of Nazis "peaceably to assemble" in Skokie, a predominantly Jewish suburb of Chicago. "The Nazis are a clear danger," says Weintraub, "but my film is an unknown quantity. You haven't seen my film yet, right? So nobody knows yet."

The *New York Times* not only gave Friedkin an interview in which to defend his film, but also editorialized in support of his right to make it. Why is the *Times* so attentive to Friedkin's free speech rights when, during the week of the protests, it did not see "fit to print" that hundreds of demonstrators had been at film sites every night?

Just possibly because one of its editors, **Gerald Walker,** stands to profit from the film. He wrote the book on which it is based in 1970. Arthur Bell interviewed Walker when the book appeared. As Bell walked in the door, Walker pulled a switchblade from his pocket, said, "I want you to know I'm not anti-gay," and used the knife to clean his nails. Asked about this later, Walker says, "I was just trying to give the interview some colour."

During New York's 1977 mayoral campaign, **Ed Koch** responded to a whisper campaign hinting he was gay by holding hands with Bess Myerson. Thus reassured, the public elected him. He has since come out—in support of the death penalty and the closing of eight city hospitals, including three desperately needed by the black and Latin communities. During filming of *Cruising* he refused to halt City cooperation with the filmmakers.

Yet he had wooed—and got—gay votes, and issued an executive order banning anti-gay discrimination by City agencies as soon as he took office.

What has the proclamation meant in reality? Not much in a city whose Council annually turns back broader gay rights bills. In an interview with Vito Russo, gay officials in Koch's administration said they feel co-opted. "For all the clout they have," Russo concluded, "gays inside the system may as well be as dead as Harvey Milk. And now the gays on the street know it, too."

Articles in the *Times* and elsewhere have reduced the protests against *Cruising* to a personal vendetta against William Friedkin by *Village Voice* columnist **Arthur Bell,** who has been cast in such roles as the Fuehrer, Robespierre and the Ayatollah Khomeini.

Bell agrees that his *Voice* column

helped spur the protests, but he prefers other comparisons. "What the Declaration of Independence was to Jefferson," he says, "that column was to the gay community." Bell has also been accused of damning Friedkin for a sin he himself commits: exploiting violence against gays. Bell *has* written about such violence, but has always set it firmly in context. One of the stories he covered was the murder of Addison Verrill, a semi-closeted writer for *Variety*, who was killed by a man who had been an extra in Friedkin's *The Exorcist*.

Gay journalists besides Bell also have been active against *Cruising* both in print and on the streets. **Doug Ireland,** who did a *New York* magazine cover story on the beatings in the Ramble last year, wrote Friedkin an open letter in the *Soho Weekly News.* "You can make this film, as is your right," he told him, "but not with the imprimatur of our community." Ireland helped organize public actions against the film; at one point he was beaten by a bouncer for leafletting in a gay bar.

Richard Goldstein did a major piece on the protests in the August 13 issue of the *Village Voice.* Writing about the S&M bars *Cruising* exploits as backgrounds, he noted, "Illusion—not danger—is the point. The people who go to these bars know they are visiting a Luna Park of the libido; most of the people who patronize *Cruising* will think they are seeing ordinary life. Billy Friedkin wouldn't know ordinary gay life if it hit him in the face—which, apparently, it has."

Longtime gay activist **Vito Russo** interviewed Friedkin during filming and, in the resulting article in **New York,** let the director talk himself into the ground with assertions that *Cruising* is not anti-gay. But he gave the last word to the wife of a Lorimar Productions executive who, while reading the script, was asked "Aren't you afraid that the film shows all homosexuals as violent and sado-masochistic?" The woman leaned over and whispered, "I used to be a model in New York, They're *all* like that. I know."

—Scott Tucker and Rick Bebout

impose one's needs on some segment of the environment in the form of demands is aggression; submission is to permit some segment of the environment to impose its needs on oneself. . . . To call submission an act of will is correct, for the segment of the environment one manipulates is one's own body and one's own personality for the sake of what one judges to be one's own advantage. Actually, then, submission is really aggression. . . . "

In contrast to Peckham's elegance and erudition, John Rechy is passionate and polemical in his book, *The Sexual Outlaw.* "Explore the dynamics of gay S&M: Playing 'straight,' the 'S' humiliates and even tortures the 'M' for being 'queer'. . . ." He adds, "I believe in the necessity of exploring the real, not the rationalized world of S&M. I believe the energy produced by this hatred turned inward dissipates the revolutionary energy. Redirected, refunneled, that inward anger would be converted into creative rage against the real enemies from without. The conclusion is inescapable. The motivation of the 'M'—*as well as of the 'S'*—is self-hatred. There is no 'S' in such gay relationships. The whimpering 'masochist' and the 'tough' posturing 'sadist' are, in reality, only two masochists groveling in self-hatred. Gay S&M is the straight world's most despicable legacy."

Rechy and Peckham represent only two points on a spectrum of polemic and speculation about S&M, but both strive to comprehend their subject. *Cruising* exploits S&M crudely to mythologize our lives, to make them fit material for Horror. Friedkin not only reveals, but *strives for,* incomprehension.

Sado-Machismo

In his *New York Times* interview, Friedkin discussed his fascination with the leather bars. "Obsession—there was true obsession in those places. All the films I've made deal in one way or another with characters who are obsessed, driven, perhaps sexually confused, given over to a macho image, which is generally bluff, and living on the edge of danger."

During filming, Friedkin told Vito Russo that the killer in *Cruising* "is not gay" and the cop "doesn't kill anybody in the film." A crew member confided to Russo, however, that the cop *had* become a killer and *is* gay.

But suppose the killer isn't gay, just "sexually confused." If queerbashers and killers are false straights or latent queers, then true and tolerant straights are released

serves as a warning to a young guy who comes to New York looking for a thrill? What if it says to him, don't do this stuff; go and find a good relationship."

That young guy might like to take Uncle Jerry's advice, but *Cruising* gives no clue where to find such a relationship. It also makes S&M mythologically dangerous and evil, the medium for the message that homosexuality and homicide go together like Peggy Lee's "Love and Marriage."

"I don't pretend to understand places like the Mine Shaft," says Friedkin. "But they exist. They are part of the world. And yes, they're violent. While I was doing my research, there were two murders at the Anvil." What he fails to mention is that those two murders were in no way sexual. One involved a pickpocket, the other a rowdy drunk.

Since *Cruising* is really a horror film like *The Exorcist,* and since the Incomprehensible is crucial to Horror, Friedkin has no profitable motive in understanding the context and meaning of gay S&M. Gay people themselves have every reason to be more comprehending.

Gay S&M

When gay extras were being selected for *Cruising,* they were asked what kind of sex acts they'd perform and in what degree of nudity. They were also asked to provide their own leather gear, so almost all who were hired were, in fact, regular patrons of leather and S&M bars.

"I have friends in there who are extras, and I need the money just as much as they do," said one protester at a film location. "But it's a political act to be in this film, and those people are dead wrong." I was among those who called these extras traitors.

Did we feel betrayed by these gay men being in leather in the film?—or by them being in leather *at all?* That is, did we feel that gay S&M shouldn't be exposed, or that it shouldn't *exist*? Motives, like crowds, are always mixed. The extras who worked for Friedkin were indeed betraying the gay community, but the ambiguous impulses of those who called them traitors must be acknowledged.

In his book *Art and Pornography,* Morse Peckham writes, "It does not seem to me theoretically possible to cut more deeply into the very heart of human behaviour than does sado-masochism, for it reveals nakedly and with full intensity the adapting animal." After expressing some scepticism that loving kindness is "naturally" human, Peckham notes, "To from any complicity in crimes which *queers commit on queers*.

In reality, genuinely straight queer-bashers and killers do exist, and what they express is not only aberrant "homosexual panic." They express, in its most intolerant form, the average sado-machismo of the average straight man.

Sado-machismo is as pervasive as God and Kleenex, can be as invisible and seem as innocuous. *It* is as much the subject of *Cruising* as gay S&M is—if we can decipher it through the distortions produced by Friedkin's lens.

Sex itself is only one of the things that panic straight men about homosexuality. Beyond that panic is a deeper fear about the intimacy, the tenderness and the non-hierarchical relations such sexuality can engender between men. These are potentially subversive of the whole social hierarchy: sado-machismo cements each one of us into our "proper" place in the pyramid. It operates when dads jeer sons for sissiness, when husbands beat and rape wives, when straight punks bash queers, when fundamentalists attack feminists— *and when we submit*.

Patriarchy would not be such an abstraction if we talked more about how sado-machismo is actually passed from father to son. A straight young Baptist recently asked me, "Don't all gays hate their fathers? Our pastor says that's why all gays hate God the Father." Underlying such mythology is the fact that fathers do serve as the punitive arm of the patriarchy, having themselves been punished into loyalty. The dominant ideology about gay men is that we were punished into deviance: the penalties worked too well, producing anomalies contradictory to the rule of the fathers.

What makes the killer in *Cruising* tick? His father. Sons like the killer serve as a warning to all fathers: to punish sons *out* of deviance, *punish with care*. The terms of this warning are fictional and personal: the effect is personal and political.

Gays can be a threat to patriarchy if we are not crushed or co-opted by it, but a positive effect can't be explained by a negative cause. Homosexuality has its own positive social dynamic for persevering against penalties. In gay S&M interactions the "S" may signify either Sadist or Slave, the "M" either Masochist or Master. A reduction of S&M to the give and take of pain—or to murder, as in *Cruising*— ignores the permutations of power which it may involve. Masochists may be masterful and sadists slavish. Often S&M involves

rituals and fetishisms where there is no pain or even contact.

Cruising, however, simplifies and falsifies: gay S&M means dying and killing. The film "documents" at a glance realities which require contemplation. Gay S&M roles may be "acted out" quite seriously, but they are not immutable. Friedkin was not serious in his claim that he wished "to capture the quality of ritual" in gay S&M: he confuses its consensual and reversible roles with the coerced and inflexible roles sado-machismo imposes on us in the world at large. The masks of gay S&M may sometimes mold the face, the postures may sometimes mold the person, but only rarely does the act become fact: only rarely are the roles chosen in gay S&M truly injurious or fatal. The roles sado-machismo imposes on us are often so. In Philadelphia, where I live, a cop was recently acquitted after he blew the brains out of a black teenager who was handcuffed. Many of the extras in *Cruising* also wore handcuffs hanging from their hips, but while gay S&M may toy with that terror and may inevitably reflect the dominant context of sado-machismo, it is by no means equivalent to it.

Free Speech, Free Enterprise

During the protests, many gay men realized for the first time just what kind of struggle women are waging against media misogyny and abuse. Feminists at a recent conference on pornography watched a slide-show of media assaults, epitomized by a *Hustler* cover showing a woman being fed into a meat grinder. That kind of imagery is big business, and with its images of gay men dying with their cocks hacked off and stuffed in their mouths, so is *Cruising*.

When it came right down to the police barricades, *Cruising* had on its side Mayor Koch, mounted police and riot squads armed with guns and clubs, the film crew goons, the power of the "free press" (the *New York Times*, which barely noted the protests, saw fit to print a half-page of Friedkin defending the film), and, most crucially, the full power of "free enterprise." The film's budget was $17 million.

What did gay militance have on its side? A handful of gay journalists, a few informers from the crew, 20 extras who quit the production in disgust, 1,500 people at one protest, only five at another, weapons consisting of slogans, leaflets, whistles, and later eggs and bottles.

And next to no bucks. When gay bar owners exercised *their* free enterprise rights by covering their signs and refusing to

become part of the film's backdrop, producer Jerry Weintraub likened them to members of the Ku Klux Klan. If cops barricaded Harlem streets so that the real Klan could film a racist movie there (using either Uncle Toms or whites in black-face as extras), would it be Klannish of blacks to boycott businesses that collaborated with the filmmakers? Nonsense: this would be seen as community self-defence, the kind of defence gays use against a clan of straight bigots and profiteers invading *their* turf.

"Mass rallies and marches and sit-ins— that kind of civil disobedience is welcome, it's important," said Friedkin in the *New York Times*. "If that had been directed against *Cruising*, I might very well have— no, I *would* have been persuaded to stop filming." Having made aliens of some of us, Friedkin tried to divide us further by pitting his idea of "welcome" protests against the "unruly fanatics" who *did* rally and march and sit-in to stop his film. The great majority were moderate and became more militant only as the situation itself grew more provocative.

Who finally initiated the violence? I don't know and I doubt anyone does for sure. Some might say our puny power should never have been pitted against their great power, that doing that was in itself a delusion induced by sado-machismo, that such a confrontation could only lead to bad press, injured people, and defeat. I can't dismiss that argument: I don't accept it, either.

I was made sick by the heads bloodied on the night of August 20, and I wasn't thrilled to be clubbed myself. But our puny power was sufficient for Stonewall. Defeat followed that occasion in the sense that business-as-usual was restored. But, in fact, oppressive Law and Order were from then on increasingly challenged. Without such a "defeat" as Stonewall, how could we have gone on to other victories? Though we disrupted some scenes, Friedkin finished filming in the Village, and *Cruising* is scheduled for distribution in February. A defeat? Only for those who imagined they could fight this skirmish with free enterprise as though it were the whole campaign.

Years ago, Hannah Arendt roused a storm of protest when she wrote of "the banality of evil" embodied in a man like the Nazi criminal Eichmann. Gay people on both sides of the barricades were called Nazis, the protesters for their tactics, the S&M extras for their lives. If we are to know our enemies, we'd better *not* make a Nazi of Friedkin. But Arendt's insight is useful in understanding him: he's an extremely banal man. Nothing "alien" is human to him. He's not greatly evil himself; he's just one of those people who makes great evil possible.

Will the film directly provoke murders, as some claimed, or was this simply "rousing" rhetoric? Direct cause and effect is usually hard to prove, but films like *Cruising* can charge an already stormy atmosphere so that lightning finally strikes "at random." And the messages such a film carries help to keep us fearful and in our "proper" place in the hierarchy of power.

We have already recognized that industry cannot be allowed to pollute our environment "freely," and anti-nuclear activists have already moved from symbolic action to actual obstruction. The cultural environment is also full of ideological radiation. We have good grounds for viewing the film industry as an abused public utility, good grounds for demanding resources to make our own films. With a budget of $17 million going for *Cruising*, pulling a production cable was little more than a symbolic act. But it was one way to say we won't let free enterprise monopolize free speech.

Defend free speech? To be sure. But often you must *create* it first. The surest defence of such rights as now exist will come from those working for *economic* democracy. The right to say what one wants means little to those who haven't got the bucks—and the power that comes from those bucks—to make themselves heard. Free speech costs. So far, most people can't afford it.

The Political Is Personal

In one newspaper report a frustrated protester at a film site was quoted as saying, "There's only one way to stop *Cruising*, and that's to stop cruising."

If we stop cruising, then *Cruising* will have stopped *us*. Is there any good reason why the streets and parks should not be safe for simple gay sociability? Even for sex? Women have long feared to walk the streets at night, knowing the risk of rape, knowing how cops and courts blame the victims. But now women are marching en masse to demonstrate that they will "Take Back the Night." Certainly gay people should respond with equal courage.

I remember the first time I visited the Anvil bar. A young man was bound on stage and was getting fist-fucked by a burly man in a leather hood. The young man couldn't take it; he said so and the hooded man stopped, unbound him and took off

his hood. They smiled at each other and then kissed.

Where are the films that show *this* reality? Where are the films that would explore the ambivalence about sexual submission and domination? Where are the films that might present the positive aspects of the rough-and-ready communalism of back-room bars, beaches, parks, instead of "documenting" such sexuality merely to shock a public which is fanatical about the "private nature" of sex? Such shocks are calculated to bring profit, for they confirm rather than challenge foolish and resentful morality.

That day in the Ramble I met a beautiful blond dancer, a boy from Texas. We sucked and fucked and did not castrate or knife each other. Friedkin has made two films about gay men focusing on physical and

emotional wounds. He does not turn the camera on himself, on the weapons he wields against us. He doesn't care to show gay affirmation, gay resistance, the thousands of everyday acts by which we survive and love each other.

Of what *Cruising* shows, William Friedkin says, "It's there. It exists. It's the truth." But "It" is simply a pantheon of tired archetypes—doomed queens and sinister freaks. Such archetypes have shaped our lives. To recognize stereotypes is to demystify archetypes: it is to change our lives. If we must inevitably live by one mythology or another, let's at least have a choice in creating our own.

When we protested in the streets, that's what we were trying to say. We're here. We exist. We, too, are the truth.

From *Body Politic*, no. 63 (May 1980), p. 24

Whose Freedom and Whose Press?

by Leo Case and Gary Kinsman

Recent debates over the protests against the movie *Cruising* have once again revealed deep political divisions among gay and lesbian activists. In this column we will explore one of the central issues in these divisions—freedom of the press—by briefly examining the positions in these debates.

In the anti-*Cruising* controversy, two significant patterns appear. First, prominent members of the gay media—the editors of *Mandate, The Advocate, The Sentinel*, and a *Body Politic* columnist— were among the most visible critics of the anti-*Cruising* campaign. Secondly, the arguments marshalled by these individuals were remarkably homogeneous. The protests—or in the case of the columnist from this journal, most of the protests—against the film were repeatedly characterized as attempts at censorship and suppression, and as an attack on freedom of the media and press. By their line of reasoning the

Reprinted with permission from *The Body Politic,* Canada's gay liberation newsmagazine.

campaign would undermine the gay community's own struggle against censorship: gays will have little credibility, they argued, if we oppose censorship when it is directed against us, but still seek to use it against others.

Hidden within this argument is a series of important, but unspoken, assumptions. While the opponents of the anti-*Cruising* campaign claim to be defending free media and press, they use a particular and limited notion of freedom, a "free market" notion, to define those free media. This notion of freedom is given full expression in the view that those who own or control the press and media must be allowed to print or film what they wish. The content, and hence the social impact, of a movie or a news report must be left entirely to the discretion of the individuals who produce the movie or the journal; the sum total of their individual decisions will yield a pluralist world in which all views are freely expressed. To limit the discretion of these individuals is to "censor."

This "free market" notion of freedom is founded upon the idea of an individual's right to private property, a right which should not be restricted in any way or by anyone. The media are seen as the property of their corporate owners and their hired representatives, and the "common good" is served when they are free to use or dispose of their property as they see fit. The apparent exceptions to this unlimited freedom, such as the restrictions placed on the publication of libelous material, actually confirm the general rule; these exceptions concern the rights of other individual proprietors. Within this perspective all rights belong to property-bearing individuals.

Those who support this commonly held notion of freedom assume that this is the only meaning that can be given to a free press. But there is an alternative notion of freedom which has been used by some of us who organized against *Cruising*. This view does not base itself in an individual's unrestricted right to private property; rather, it roots itself in the needs of communities of people. It begins with the understanding that open media are the primary means for a community to acquire a *knowledge* of itself. It is such media that the various isolated parts of the community can find the tools of discussion and information.

From the perspective of this alternative view, the content and social impact of the media are a matter of vital concern to the community they serve. Accordingly, it maintains that those who produce the press should do so in trust for the community, allowing for the widest possible community input and control.

Proponents of both of these views oppose governmental censorship, especially of community organs such as *The Body Politic*. But agreement on opposition to governmental censorship should not be allowed to mask more fundamental points

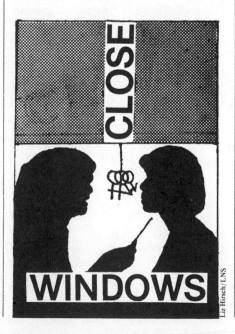

of difference. The two views diverge on the question of the media's relationship to the community they serve.

The first, orthodox view regards community input and control of the media as no different than governmental censorship: both restrict the property rights of the individual. It sees the community as a passive audience and it limits the prerogative of the community to the right to purchase in the marketplace. An audience can choose as individuals to consume or not to consume, but it has no right—by this definition—to interfere collectively in the actual production of the journal or the film. It is from this viewpoint that gays and lesbians protesting against *Cruising* are equated with a board of censors, even when they suggest tactics no stronger than an organized consumer boycott.

In contrast, the second or alternative view argues that it is not possible to have real freedom in the media without community input and control. It is, or should be, obvious that a passive individual consumer has no meaningful choice in deciding whether to see *Cruising, Windows,* or *Boys in the Band*. The privately owned and controlled media industries have not produced gay- or lesbian-positive images on their own initiative: the pluralist world—there is something for everyone—is a myth of "free market" ideology. Genuine pluralism exists only when oppressed groups develop the power to force access to the media. Yet, the power to determine the alternatives from which a consumer can choose lies in the hands of these industries, for this power is the power *to produce and distribute* the film or journal.

In a society such as ours this power rests almost exclusively in the hands of those who own the media: the fundamental issue is the identity of these owners. In the case of Hollywood film studios, this ownership is concentrated in multi-billion dollar conglomerates. The gay and lesbian communities, as well as other oppressed communities, can not gain access to media industries by buying out some of these massive multinational corporations, nor by starting an alternative corporation with sufficient capital to compete with them: such scenarios are utter foolishness that ignore the basic economic facts of life. Our political project is to transfer the power now concentrated in the corporate structures of the media to the communities they should be serving. And in our context, the

alternative view of a free press necessarily assumes the form of an anti-corporate, broadbased movement for social change that includes many oppressed communities. The campaigns against *Cruising* and *Windows,* and the campaign a few years back against *Snuff,* are a first step in that direction.

These, then, are the main dimensions of the debates over censorship and freedom around the anti-*Cruising* protests. In examining them, some clues can be found as to why this campaign has generated such an angry and charged debate within the gay movement. By raising the issue of the relationship of the major Hollywood film corporations to gays and lesbians, anti *Cruising* activists have implicitly called into question the relationship of all media to the community they serve. The anti-*Cruising* campaign has, in part, indirectly challenged the relationship of the gay press to the gay and lesbian communities. While all of the gay press expresses some degree of concern for the issues that affect the gay and lesbian communities, many of these journals treat us as passive audiences with no rights but that of a consumer "choice."

The response of these members of the gay media to the anti-*Cruising* protests is not, therefore, simply the advocacy of an abstract notion of freedom as the right to unrestricted private property. It is also the defence of their limited social power, a social power acquired through the ownership of media in a society of private property. To the extent that they persist in viewing themselves and our communities in these terms, they shall also continue to side with the major media and press in their confrontations with oppressed groups.

The analysis we have presented has many other implications which cannot be pursued in this space, but which are worth future exploration. For example: What political role do the gay media and gay leadership play when they define themselves and our communities in terms of "free market" feedom? What kind of knowledge, or theory, of our communities will they produce? How are these issues analyzed by those feminists who have been visible in opposing media misogyny and in critiquing the elitism of professions such as journalism? And how should we understand the open hostility of many critics of the anti-*Cruising* campaign to what they view as a homogeneous feminism?

Gay Community News
THE WEEKLY FOR LESBIANS AND GAY MALES

From *Gay Community News* 7, no. 8 (September 15, 1979): 10-11

Organizing in Mexico

by John Kyper

Only recently has gay liberation come into public consciousness in Mexico. The *Frente de Liberacion Homosexualle* (FLH) was formed in 1971 in response to the firing of several homosexual employees by the Sears store in Mexico City. But its members cancelled a planned picket because of fears they would be attacked. The memory of Tlatelolco was still fresh, when the army had machine-gunned a demonstration during the 1968 Olympic Games, killing 500 and wounding 2000, and invaded the University of Mexico, imprisoning thousands without trial. In June, 1971, police had allowed vigilantes to attack a leftist demonstration and kill 100 people.

Instead, FLH established several rap groups. The energy eventually dissipated, however, and after a couple of years the last rap group had disbanded. There followed for several years sporadic attempts to start gay organizations, with scant success.

Juan Jacobo Hernandez, a French teacher at the *Universidad Autonoma Metropolitana*, was one of the veterans of FLH who formed the *Frente Homosexual de Accion Revolucionaria* (FHAR— Homosexual Revolutionary Action Front) in April, 1978, in response to numerous anti-gay assaults and murders and police harassment in the Federal District. The group first protested a play by a group of Uruguayan exiles that portrayed soldiers of that country's dictatorship as homosexuals dancing the tango, and cast three effeminate young men as the high bourgeoisie. Jacobo wrote a letter of protest for the group, but only he was willing to sign it for publication, in *Unomasuno*, an influential, left-wing daily.

Like other countries under the Na-

Reprinted with permission from *Gay Community News: The Weekly for Lesbians and Gay Men,* 22 Bromfield St., Boston, MA 02108.

poleonic Code, homosexual activity per se is not illegal in Mexico, but the influence of the Catholic Church intensifies the prejudices of a culture so imbued with machismo. FHAR and most other progressive movements are consciously leftist; Mexico is a country with socialist pretensions (it never recognized Franco's Spain or broke relations with Cuba) and such extremes of poverty as are rarely seen in the United States. As the more conservative gays are closeted and totally uncooperative, there is no place yet for an organization like the National Gay Task Force, or a newspaper like the *Advocate*.

FHAR's first action was to participate as a contingent in last year's annual July 26th march commemorating the Cuban revolution. The march also marked the tenth anniversary of the beginning of the student movement that was crushed at Tlatelolco Square. Many of the prisoners taken after the massacre were still being held in 1978, and a demand of the march was their release—which the government later did.

The gay contingent was small, only 30 people, but it caused a sensation. As Jacobo put it, "We came out in every newspaper in Mexico. Nobody could believe it—not the Right, not the Left. We surprised everybody. Everyone wanted to know what we were doing." Some leftist publications, like *Unomasuno* and *Siempre*, a mass-circulation magazine, gave them sympathetic treatment. *Siempre* recently published an interview with Jacobo and other FHAR members.

Much of the bourgeois press, however was sensationalistic and violently anti-gay. Slurs like *"lilos colorados"* ("red lilies") were commonplace in their coverage of FHAR. *Alerta*, a rag combining the sewer journalism of the old *National Enquirer* with the homophobia of its present "respectable" incarnation, has been a particularly flagrant example of gay-baiting.

After July 26th police retaliated against gays by raiding the bars. In September four gay men were brutally tortured and murdered in a large apartment building. Gory press accounts falsely accused the four of having been in an "orgy." In a classic case of blaming the victim, police

again pulled raids, arresting 200. A week later FHAR filed suit against the police and demonstrated outside their headquarters. They were joined by members of *Oikabeth*, a lesbian group, and by other feminists and leftists. The last 25 arrestees were released. Harassment continues: in January seventeen "hustlers" were arrested on the streets of the capital and forced to pose for the press in humiliating poses.

FHAR is publishing introductory pamphlets about homosexuality and about legal rights. It has its own newspaper, *Nuestro Cuerpo (Our Body)*, and magazine, *Politica Sexual*, and also plans a hot line. Early in June 100 of its members participated in a massive march against the Somoza dictatorship in Nicaragua, and at the end of the month 1500 marched for Gay Pride Week.

A conservative backlash is beginning to emerge, however: the hitherto cooperative *Unomasuno* failed to publish one of FHAR's letters in July. After an inquiry it was learned that President Lopez Portillo, at a meeting with press representatives several days after the Gay Pride march, had expressed his "concern" that the widespread coverage given to homosexuality "could cause an impact on the Mexican family." Censorship is that subtle in a country that does not enjoy the same degree of press freedom that is taken for granted in the United States. FHAR must be careful that its own publications don't get shut down by the government.

Joint actions had been planned for August 14th to protest the attempt by the Immigration and Naturalization Service to bar two gay Mexicans from the United States, after they were detained and interrogated at San Francisco International Airport. Simultaneous demonstrations were to have been held at American Embassies in Mexico City and London, and outside the San Francisco office of the INS, where the two were to face a deportation hearing. The demonstrations were cancelled after the INS issued a nationwide directive halting attempts to ban gays from the country.

Jacobo visited San Francisco in January and August to obtain support from the American gay movement. He was interviewed in January by David Noel Hinojosa, a writer for the *Bay Area Reporter*. Also present were Pat Brown, a long-time gay liberationist of Berkeley, California, and Carlos Toimil, a compatriot in FHAR.

Noel: Tell me about the traditional gay places in Mexico. Are there bars and baths?

Jacobo: Gay life is class-oriented. People with no money go to the street. Those with a little money go to the movie houses, or to a steam bath—could be very pleasant or very unpleasant. The baths are dark, dank and smelly. You have few choices: if you're gay, you go to the street, a movie house or a steam bath. The last place is a bar—going to a bar costs you 150 pesos [about $7] just to get in. There are only seven gay bars in Mexico City, whose metropolitan population is now 18,000,000.

(Jacobo has subsequently discovered improvised dance halls in proletarian neighborhoods around Mexico City, where drag queens dance along with families and elderly people. Generally, working class people are much less anti-gay than members of the middle class.)

N: Of the highly visible gay people, do they fall into the upper, middle or lower classes?

J: Upper class gays are not visible. They go to Acapulco and New York. Middle and working class gays are highly visible, especially the working class. (Unemployment is high—almost 50% of the Mexican working class population can't get a job.)

N. Give us some of the background of the movement.

J: There were the raids in September, of gay places. If you're obviously gay and on the street by yourself at two in the morning, they accuse you not of homosexuality (not illegal) but of prostitution. When you get to the police station you have to pay a 5000 peso fine, which is the minimum working class wage for a month. If you don't have the money, you go to jail for 15 days. If you go to jail and you're a worker, you lose your job. So you give the police anything: your watch, your money, etc. If you don't have anything, they rape you or they make you set somebody else up. They may make you give them names of other people. They can take anything you have of value if you don't want to go to jail. These people went to jail, so we staged a march on the police station, which was very successful.

The penalties had been illegally high, and the protest resulted in their being reduced back to a 300 peso fine and 36 hours in jail.

N. How many people do you have?

J: There are approximately 300 in the different groups—FHAR, Oikabeth and Lambda [a more conservative group]—but only 25 are active and know enough to speak with any authority. FHAR's membership is almost entirely male.

N: Is the gay movement close to the feminist movement?

J: Yes, when we came out on July 26th, they marched with us. We participated in a demonstration at the Canadian Embassy to protest the kidnapping of an Algerian feminist in Canada. She was kidnapped by her brother after she announced she didn't want to return to her husband in Algeria. Disagreements between men and women in the movement are similar to those that have been encountered in the United States and Canada.

N: Are you in touch with other gay groups in Latin America?

J: Yes, we are: Costa Rica, Guatemala, Colombia, and Brazil. Gay liberation is very widespread in Brazil, but they suffer repression. Their newspaper *Lampiao* was in trouble recently, because of its leftist politics. In Colombia they're underground. In Costa Rica, kind of underground, but well organized. They had a good publication in Costa Rica called *Pa Fuera (Out)* [not to be confused with the Puerto Rican gay publication of the same name]. Argentina was liquidated after the 1976 coup and many of its members have disappeared. Some gays were tortured and killed; others who were members of leftist groups have gone underground.

N: What is the purpose of your trip?

J: We want to make American gays know we exist, to raise funds and make contacts. In August we contacted COHLA [*Comite de Homosexuals Latino-Americanos*] in New York. We've contacted many groups in San Francisco, including the Third World Gay Caucus and GALA [Gay and Latino Alliance]. We want to have an exhibition of Mexican gay art here, to raise money. I was talking with Don Jacobs of San Francisco Gay Rap, and he asked, if we can't help with money, how else can we help? I said, with books, with literature. If they send us books, that's money to us. American books are very expensive in Mexico. Send us newspapers, letters, anything.

N: What do you hope to achieve?

J: We want to make our presence known to gays outside Mexico. We want to be in the press to gain world opinion. We don't want oppression there to go unnoticed. That way people will be more careful how they treat gays in all countries.

It's a matter of *life and death* for the movement to receive outside support. Before we came out, no one knew about us. Now they are so shocked they cannot articulate a response. As soon as they can see our weaknesses they are going to let us have it. If there is more organized harassment and we have no outside aid, we are lost. If we are isolated, we are lost. We need support. I must stress this.

If we can keep this up, we will reach Mexican homosexuals, the intellectuals, the middle class—we have to reach them. We think that gay rights in our country are not enough because they can be easily won. There are no specific laws that attack us. We think that our condition in Mexico is not due to politics but to machismo. We will not be free until all are free.

People wishing to contact FHAR can write to Apartado Postal 13-320, Mexico 13, D.F., Mexico.

GAY INSURGENT

From *Gay Insurgent*, no. 6 (Summer 1980), p. 16

Living in Asian America

by Michiyo Cornell

An Asian American Lesbian's Address before the Washington Monument

Sisters and Brothers,

I am here to represent the Lesbian and Gay Asian Collective, which was formed at the first National Third World Lesbian and Gay Conference (Oct. 12-15, 1979) this weekend. I don't know if any non-Asian American lesbian and gay men know how important this moment is. This is the first time in the history of the American hemisphere that Asian American lesbians and gay men have joined to form a network of support of, by and for Asian American lesbians and gay men. I must interject a little comment here. I am being careful to use the phrase Asian American because we are not hyphenated Americans nor are we always foreign born women and men from Asia. We have been in this country for over 150 years! We live in *Asian America*. It is a statement of our experiences and a statement of racism in America.

I am in awe of this moment and what it can mean for Asian American lesbians and gay men. America has called us the "model minority" and has claimed we are 200% Americans. The truth is that because we are less the ½ of 1% of the population of this country and because of the lies that the American media perpetrates about us, we have difficulty in impacting even Third World lesbians and gay men. We are called the model minority, the quiet, passive, exotic erotics with the slanted cunt to match our "slanted" eyes or the small dick to match our small size. But we are not.

For years Asian Americans have organized against our oppression. We protested and were lynched, deported and put into concentration camps during World War II. We must not forget that the United States of America has bombed, napalmed and colonized Asian countries for decades. Thus it was possible for America to bomb Hiroshima and Nagasaki and to continue to economically colonize and rape Asian countries. It could rape and murder Vietnamese women, children and men then claim that "Asians don't value human life."

I am an Asian American woman, a mother and a lesbian. Because these things are difficult to put into a neat package, because I am genuinely different—I know that I live in the face of this country's determination to destroy me, to negate me, to render me invisible. And the reality is that non-Asian Americans are ignorant of our existence. We share the same problems that other Third World lesbians and gay men share. Because of fear of deportation, because of Asian American dependence on our families and Asian American communities for support, it is very difficult for us to be out of the closet. But we need to come out of the closet for not to do so would be living a lie, and the great lie, which is America, can use that weakness not only to destroy Asian American lesbians and gay men, but also our Third World lesbian and gay sisters and brothers.

We have a right to our sexuality, to our love and to our racial identities. This is something that sets us apart from and challenges white lesbians and gay men. We demand that you white lesbians and gay men begin to think of how you repress and oppress your Asian American lesbian and gay sisters and brothers. You share oppression from homophobia with us but unless you begin to address your white skin privilege and actively support Asian American lesbians and gay men, you will not have our support and you would lose out on a chance to build the kind of world we all need, to live decently and lead full productive lives.

We must realize the capitalist system uses not just sexual preference but race and class as well to divide us. To our Third World sisters and brothers, gay and straight, I would like to say we all share the same oppression as Third World people, and for that reason we must stand together or be hanged separately by what Audre Lorde calls the "noose of conformity."

To our closeted Asian American lesbians and gay men, I would like you to consider how we become accomplices to our own sexual and racial oppression when we fail to claim our true identities.

I have a three-year-old daughter and any risk that I must take to build a free future for myself and my daughter is worth it. It is as concrete and as abstract as that.

Gay Community News
THE WEEKLY FOR LESBIANS AND GAY MALES

From *Gay Community News* 7, no. 31 (March 1, 1980): 10, 11, 14

Lesbians Struggle with Racism

by Cindy Stein

Many events in 1978 and 1979 prompted work in the Boston women's community around the issue of racism. Last winter, as the numbers of black women murdered in the city grew, a racially mixed group of women, called the Bessie Smith Memorial Collective, organized a meeting at Amaranth, the women's restaurant, to discuss the problem of community racism. This initial meeting sparked two subsequent gatherings where workshops were held and various aspects of the problem were discussed. One such workshop was facilitated by a few women who had been meeting in a small group to recognize and confront their own racist attitudes and feelings. They urged others to begin their own groups.

The six women interviewed here have been meeting regularly, once a week, since last winter. Their own words illustrate what they do, how their process works, what they hope to accomplish and what their fears are in confronting the attitudes and feelings that they have about people of color.

In our discussions about this interview, one concern that surfaced was an appre-

hension that their responses to questions would be interpreted in a manner different from the way in which they were intended. I would, therefore, urge readers of this article to keep in mind that the issues being confronted are difficult ones which involve attitudes taught to us from the first day of our lives right up to the present. Questions like "What is racism?" are complex and have no ready-made answers. None of what is said is meant to pose definitive answers or is meant to show that these groups are *the way* to end racism. In addition, an attempt to grapple with these questions does not always produce clear and articulate responses, especially when an interviewer puts one unaccustomed to public speaking on the spot. What is shown is simply one method chosen by a group of lesbians that has helped them examine an ugly aspect of their socialization and has been instrumental in forming their vision of a saner society.

Cindy: How does the group work? What kind of process has developed over the last year that's helped things go smoothly?

Martha: We've been meeting as a group since about April and we meet once a week. There are several specific procedures that have evolved and that we've incorporated into our meeting time. One is that we always start out our meetings by saying one thing that's good for us in our lives. One of the reasons that we did this was because we knew that the work that we're doing is really hard and often painful work, so we thought that it was real important to start out with a positive frame of mind and something that was self-affirming. It can be something from any aspect of our lives that we'll go around and share. Also, it brought us as a group closer personally. It helped to develop trust.

After we finish that, we go around and each of us will say one thing that we have thought, done or somehow participated in during the past week that we consider racist. It took a lot of work for us to pare down all of the qualifications that go around whatever that experience was. It occurred to us that what we had to do was to just say it: specifically, outright, unqualified and direct. Sometimes that engenders discussion, sometimes we say it, acknowledge it and pass on. That varies a lot. Then, after that, we either carry on a discussion from one particular comment that someone has made or talk about something we've all read, or we share some kind of educational experience that we had during the week.

Sharron: Also, we've begun to have discussions about positive things we've been doing to fight racism. That is one thing that allows us to feel good about the things we do.

Martha: A couple of other things we've done together are cultural, political or educational. We went to Music for Peace which was a concert to promote racial peace at New England Conservatory. We went to the Art of Black Dance and Music. That was really terrific. We also went to a hearing on the closing of some Boston public schools which is very related to the issues of busing and desegregation. We're going to have a counselor come in to work with us for two or three hours specifically on racism. We'll be discussing our feelings and delving deeply with counseling skills that we feel can help us.

Cindy: Some people have seen an irony in the practice of forming racism groups that are all white. Yet many groups, like yours, are deliberately all white. Why?

Margie: A lot of issues came up about how, when white people try to "deal with their racism," we end up just sapping people of color of their energy and we dump on them. If, for instance, there was a black woman in the group, we would all even just physically look at her when we were talking about something and really load it all on her shoulders. Also, we wouldn't say probably three-quarters of the things we end up saying. It's really scary to say a lot of stuff and really own up to it because some of it's really racist. I think that if there was a black person in the room I would be totally inhibited.

Gail: They shouldn't have to hear it. I feel that white people are responsible for

dealing with our own racism and admitting it to ourselves. There's no need for people of color to listen to a lot of the shit that's inside us. Their role isn't to take care of us.

Sharron: We have more than enough material from our own lives, from our own guts to educate ourselves about what we need to do to change racism, starting with ourselves.

Martha: One other thing, too, is that part of our being white is to recognize that racism is a specific problem for us as white people to deal with in our lives. It is a problem *for us* and, therefore, we must confront it from our viewpoint as white people.

Gail: It's also very painful and dehumanizing for us as white people to be racist. It's not something we want to be. It hurts us as well.

Cindy: Why an all lesbian group?

Fredi: I feel that our shared lesbianism and feminism gives us a whole lot of support and strength in our own lives in many ways. It's recognizing our own oppression and instead of being bowled under by it, we have the guts and the will to fight it. I carry over the sense of feeling the weight of power in the world against me as a lesbian into my feeling that I need to fight and deal with any kind of power that's used against a group of people, as a group of people, by the political, economic and social systems. I recognize oppression when I see it because I myself have experienced it directly in my life. I need the support of other women to fight it, too.

Sharron: Initially, I wasn't opposed to being in a group with straight women. One thing that was important to me was that they had some consciousness around race and class issues. But I was not willing to expend any energy in the group educating someone who was straight about lesbianism. I know that there are straight women who don't need that education.

Cindy: What can lesbians and gay men take from our experiences as oppressed people to help us deal with racism in ourselves?

Carol: It has often turned out that when we have been trying to make some connection with how it feels to feel invisible or how it feels to be misunderstood, that's the place where we connect with it. It's by knowing the ways that that's happened to us as lesbians in a homophobic world. There's some shared emotional pain and anger.

Martha: One thing though that I always

feel is important to distinguish is that we, as lesbians, have the choice to be visible. (There are ways, though, that we are made invisible by the lack of acknowledgement that we exist in the same way that people of color or women are made invisible.) Yet as we walk down the street, we have that choice that we can make ourselves known or not as gay or lesbian people.

Cindy: What is racism?

Sharron: For me, for someone to be racist there has to be an implied sense or position of power. In other words, when people make comments about black people being racist toward whites, that isn't what the issue is. In order for anyone to be racist, they have to be in a position of power and privilege. Just as when women make statements that express prejudice against men, it's a totally different thing than a man expressing negative comments against women.

Gail: Racism is the systematic oppression of one group, blacks and other people of color, by another group, whites, specifically because of color or race.

Carol: Some of the stereotypes that we have of blacks and other people of color are not accidents. The stereotypes provide a way to say, "That person's where they are because they deserve to be there," which is exactly how the power works to keep us thinking that things are OK when in fact we are living in a society that systematically oppresses people of color.

Cindy: Do you have any boundaries in the group which you set when you discuss racism? What I mean is, do you talk solely about the oppression faced by blacks, or by all people of color?

Fredi: I work in a multi-cultural center with Spanish-speaking people who are of similar skin color to me, but who are distinguishable as a cultural and racial group. I realize that that affects my ways of dealing with Hispanic people and I've talked about that in the group.

Cindy: Why do you think it is important for white people to form small groups to discuss racism?

Sharron: I can remember when I first became a part of this group, I didn't even know what "racism" was. I was so terrified of any thought that I had about blacks. I thought it was going to be so unacceptable for me to admit the feelings that I had. And I think that everybody in this group shared that. And as a result of us being able to create a forum where we feel comfortable and open with each other, to explore some of those feelings, and then in fact find out what they are, we can move past them and grow.

Gail: For me, racism is a really ugly thing and a really painful thing to see inside of me, so it's been important to have the support of the group, to first of all be able to acknowledge that it's there. Second, to begin to be able to deal with it. To understand its origins and understand ways in which I can work to get rid of it in myself. And also to begin to feel that I can get rid of it myself and it doesn't have to be a permanent fixture inside me, where I don't want it.

Martha: It's absolutely imperative for oppressed groups to work together, to begin to understand and support each other's work. The Willie Sanders case is a clear example of racism and sexism working hand in hand to oppress black people and women and to enable crimes of intense violence against both groups to be committed. My understanding of racism will empower me to fight sexism as my understanding of sexism empowers me to fight racism.

(Willie Sanders is a black man who was arrested and tried for one of a series of rapes that occurred in a mostly white neighborhood of Brighton in the fall of 1978. Many feel Sanders was falsely charged with the crime by a police force desperate to dispel the fears of neighborhood women and to quiet complaints that they weren't doing anything to catch the rapist. A protest movement, initiated by the city's black community and joined by many whites, exposed a series of unconstitutional and exploitative methods used by the police to build a case against Sanders.)

Cindy: How do you handle the type of criticism which sees the work you're doing as pure "talk and no action." Is there a difference between talking and doing? When can the two come together, if at all?

Carol: Mainly what we do in the group is talk. The way that it becomes incorporated in "doing" is apparent to me in the difference between our discussions now and our discussions when we started. When we started, most of us were so afraid of being racist that we couldn't look at any of what we did. Now, we look at some of what we do and discover that we are beginning to make our positions known when we feel that something that is going on is racist. And so, the connection is, that by talking about racism and becoming clear about what it is, so that we're not so scared of it, we can begin to find ways to do things differently.

Gail: Another way in which the talking, the thinking and the reading has really helped in terms of my own personal life, is that I'm better able to interrupt something racist. I'm better able to actually see what's going on and understand what's going on. Whereas before, I may have been confused and felt bad and not have really been able to act in particular situations. So it's helping me in terms of my everyday life.

Martha: On a very specific level, my work involves me a lot with people of color and so on a daily basis I hold myself responsible for my actions in my work. So that it's imperative to me to be able to shed my fears, set aside my guilt and to be clear with the people I work with and to be able to see, identify and act on racism when it's there. Also, to distinguish things that are not racist. A lot of things that go on are occurring because of the people who are involved as personalities. To be able to make that distinction, I feel, is a real crucial aspect of understanding racism.

Margie: I think that something Martha said about guilt really struck home because a lot of what we were doing at the beginning was plowing through all the guilt that we were having, that was impeding us from doing anything. I think that really owning up to racist things that we were doing and saying and putting aside the guilt, helped us start working instead.

Sharron: One of the things that's been a real turning point in my life was that I made a conscious decision to move to an integrated neighborhood. The reason I did this was that I looked around at my world and realized that most of my neighborhood was white, most of where I worked was white. That was what my background had been, too. I can remember the first week or two, after I moved, I went to a nearby park and saw a huge group of black people, men, women, and children, riding horses. Just seeing blacks in a variety of different settings forced me to examine a lot of those deeper gut feelings that I grew up with and to move past them in a way that wasn't just "heady." In order for me to break down the stereotypes that I grew up with, it's necessary for me to throw myself into a situation where I'm going to come into contact with people of color and have positive individual relationships and work with people of color politically.

Cindy: How has the experience of this group helped you to deal better with people of color, and in particular, women of color?

Fredi: I think it's helped in two ways. In one sense, I've felt that I have a lot of racist feelings inside of me. For instance, when I see a white person doing something I dislike I see it as an individual doing something I don't like, yet when I see a black person doing something I don't like I see them for their color instead of for who they are. I didn't want to admit that I felt that way, so what I did was to back off from dealing with people of color. Now I admit it and try to deal with why I feel that way and change it. That leads into the second thing, which was that I felt so uncomfortable being around people who are different from me, that I just avoided it entirely and kept my world white. For example, if I knew that there was a multi-racial group of women working on a feminist issue, six months ago, I would have been terrified of working on that because I would have been afraid to make a mistake, a blunder, etc. Now I feel that I can do it. If I make a "mistake," I'll deal with it. So being in this group would enable me to work in that group, and I think, work well.

Sharron: One thing for me that's felt really positive is to be able to ask questions of people of color. For instance, black people learn to protect themselves from white people, and because of that they might not trust me in situations where we need to work together, but we need to get that out in the open. That's something that I've broken through and it's been really helpful for me.

Cindy: It sounds like some progress has been made. But what remains to be done? Where do you encounter problems and stumbling blocks in discussing and dealing with racism?

Carol: I think that's a big stumbling block for us, in the process of the group, is that we got to a position where we've started to realize what's racist in us. The first thing that happens is that we felt it was overwhelming. When you recognize that it's horrible, it's still there; it doesn't immediately go away. There are a lot of meetings that ended in frustration where we'd say, "OK, so here it is, I know where it is, how am I going to do anything different from it?" And that's still, personally, a stumbling block for me whenever I come up against something new or something that I hadn't realized.

Fredi: I know one of my fears is to feel like I'm not doing enough. To feel like I'm moving at a snail's pace and to get discouraged. And I have to realize that I learned racism for a long, long time and it's going to take me a lot of hard work to get rid of it and change it, and even to recognize it.

Gail: Another area that's been a real stumbling block is just the intense amount of guilt that gets in the way of recognizing racism in ourselves, in dealing with it. The guilt is just paralysing in a lot of ways.

Martha: I think it's crucial to realize that the work goes on forever. There's always more to do. Primarily, what I feel we're working on is to recognize how we've been socialized and to separate our present values that we each hold from the ones we learned growing up. Racism is a part of a whole system of oppression that must be fought.

Carol: One thing we've done with this group is to take very seriously the suggestions and the reaching out that come from women of color. That's there. It's not like it doesn't exist. We just have to pay attention to it and use it.

Cindy: What kinds of fear do you have about publicly discussing racism and your group's process?

Sharron: I think I'm afraid of judgements. I think that it's still hard for me to judge myself and so I'm still sensitive to the judgements of other white women and of women of color.

Gail: I think also we're all really aware that we're definitely not there yet and it's going to be a long struggle and it's hard to be honest about where you are when you know you're not where you want to be.

Cindy: I want to ask you to describe your backgrounds particularly as they relate to relationships with people of color or how they might have shaped your views toward people of color?

Martha: I realize in answering this that we haven't in this interview addressed the issue of class at all. I come from an upper middle class background, a very white, largely Protestant neighborhood. The schools that I went to were primarily white, very few people of color. My experience with people of color whose lives are significantly different from mine was limited until recently.

Fredi: I also came from an upper middle class background which meant I had a lot of choices in my life. I grew up in Newark, New Jersey, at a time when it was changing from a city with a white power structure to a city where blacks were struggling for and getting power within the city. It was also a time of white exodus to the suburbs. In high school I moved to the suburbs away from an all-black high school and ever since then have been out of touch with

black people . . . I'm Jewish. As a Jew, I was brought up with a sense that one needs to constantly fight against oppression and that there's real survival threats if you don't. I was also brought up within a community of activists and activism was presented to me as a way that people who were struggling together had the most power. I think that those are roots that I draw on now.

Margie: I grew up in a fairly homogeneous neighborhood of Jewish and Italian middle class people. That pretty much isolated me from any contact with black people until high school when black students were bused in. There was quite a division there. I think that was the beginning of my realization about racism. Another thing that helps me to focus on things in the group sometimes is that I am the child of immigrant parents who are still quite "foreign" when people meet them. That has helped me in dealing with people who are "different" because they speak differently or don't do everything the way American, white, middle class people do. That's given me a different outlook on things.

Gail: I come from a white middle class background as well. I didn't have much experience with people of color until I worked at the Massachusetts state prison in Framingham a few years ago. That's a prison for women.

Sharron: I grew up in the South and come from a white, middle class, heavy Irish-Catholic background. When I was twelve, I moved to Guam, an island in the Pacific, where I had a lot of exposure to people of color from Micronesian islands and from Japan.

Cindy: How can we as white women help to alleviate the anger and frustration that is often voiced and felt by women of color who try to work within the gay or lesbian movements? What can be done to eliminate tokenism and the exhausting of the energies of the same third world people again and again?

Carol: We must learn to be honest in our dealings with people of color. I know that when I encounter, for instance, a straight woman who's able to ask questions, who is able to say where ever she really is, and isn't scared, I can feel that difference.

Fredi: One of the things I've learned in this group is about seeing things through white eyes and thinking that that's the way that everybody sees things. One of the ways in which we can make more room for people of color to feel comfortable and to

feel effective in working with us is to make sure that we listen to what they have to say. We have to learn that this is everybody's struggle and that everybody's views are important. We don't just go ahead with what we think and what we see and assume that everybody else feels and perceives the same way.

Fredi: One more way that our racism really comes through is if we think that there are only a few black women who have thought about being women or that there are only a few black gay people in this world. Those are the racist thoughts that are behind tokenism.

Cindy: As lesbians, many of us have formed attitudes toward men as a class of oppressors. Our feelings are often expressed through fear, anger, or even hatred. How do those feelings toward all men fit into a discussion on racism, where racist attitudes we've learned are focused on *all* people of color, both female and male? Are men of color treated differently by you than white men are?

Carol: Sexism is no excuse for racism and racism is no excuse for sexism. In dealing with our feelings toward men of color, we've had to allow ourselves to feel angry about something that's sexist coming from, let's say, a black man, while not excusing the things that we can find in ourselves that are racist toward that same black man.

Gail: Also I've realized that it's real easy for us to respond to sexism from a black man with racism. We would like to not do that anymore.

Martha: There is a conflict because black men belong to the group which oppresses us and also belong to the group which we oppress. This causes a lot of confusion.

Cindy: What are the goals of the group? If it ever terminates at any time, what would you like to come away with?

Martha: One of the women in the group is going to be leaving it. Her reasons are very positive. She feels that she has found ways to integrate her political work against racism with her consciousness raising. We realize that that is one of the primary goals that each of us has—to find a place where action and thought and feelings merge, so that we can activate our lives in such a way to find that integration ourselves. In a sense, that could be the goal for each of us and yet we also know that we've established among the six of us a really wonderful, beautiful trust and a support for each other, so that years hence, we may not be meeting together but we do have a really common, solid foundation of support that we can always refer back to.

Sharron: We want to have a conference with other women in the city who are involved in groups similar to ours. I'm very curious to be in touch with those people and other people who may not be involved in groups but who really feel that struggling against racism is a political priority. It would be wonderful to come together to share those things.

Fredi: We want to be more effective in working with people of color, particularly women of color, against oppression.

Those who wish to respond directly to this group, other than through the Community Voices pages of GCN, or those who want more information about forming

racism groups, may write to these women c/o Cindy Stein, Gay Community News, 22 Bromfield Street, Boston, MA 02108. All letters will be forwarded.

Bibliography

"Face to Face, Day to Day, Racism C-R" by Tia Cross, Freada Klein, Barbara Smith and Beverly Smith, *Sojourner,* May, 1979.
"Disloyal to Civilization: Feminism, Racism, and Gynophobia" by Adrienne Rich, *Chrysalis,* #7.
Letter to *GCN* from Barbara Smith, *GCN* Vol. 7, No. 6.
Black Scholar, May-June, 1979.
"The Myth of Black Macho: A Response to Angry Black Feminists" by Robert Staples, *Black Scholar,* March-April, 1979.
Conditions: Five, Vol. 1, No. 2, Autumn, 1979.

Gay Community News
THE WEEKLY FOR LESBIANS AND GAY MALES

From *Gay Community News* 7, no. 14 (October 27, 1979): 1, 9

Third World Conference Meets

by Jil Clark

Washington, DC. "Welcome to *your* historic first National Third World Lesbian/Gay Conference—not *a* conference, not *the* conference, but *your* conference. . . . It will be as Latin, as Asian, as American Indian, as black, as third world as we each make it. If your needs are not being reflected—speak up. . . ."

"Divided we can only gripe about our oppression. United we can overcome our oppression."

These were the greetings given to approximately 600 participants in the workshops and ethnic caucuses of the first National Conference for Third World Lesbians and Gays on October 12 to 15. The purposes of the conference, as stated by its planners in the National Caucus of Black Gays (NCBG), were to establish a national political service organization that would reflect the concerns and needs of lesbians and gays who are part of a racial or ethnic minority in this country; to pass resolutions which reflected the goals or

Reprinted with permission from *Gay Community News: The Weekly for Lesbians and Gay Men,* 22 Bromfield St., Boston, MA 02108.

stated the demands of different ethnic or racial caucuses which convened during the weekend; to build a communications network of third world lesbian/gay organizations and individuals, closing "the gaps which currently separate the east from the west, the Asians from the American Indians, the women from the men." Conference planners also envisioned a weekend of "confronting the issues of racism, sexism, classism among, by and against racial/ethnic minorities."

How closely did the conference resemble the vision of NCGB? "I was totally impressed," was the enthusiastic response of Barbara Smith. "There were so many black and third world lesbian and gay people there. It was one of the few times I've been to an event where I didn't feel I was in the minority. That was really gratifying. . . . They [heterosexual third world people] can't tell the lie that we don't exist."

Smith, herself a black feminist, recalled being particularly moved by black feminist poet Audre Lorde, Saturday night's keynote speaker. "She said that it's really important that we don't use differences as a reason to put each other down. She said that we sometimes have a jugular vein psychology which [compels us] to kill and to annihilate the differences . . . that can actually be enriching and enlivening."

Asked by *GCN* whether she felt that the men at the conference had a better understanding of feminism than most third

world men, she replied, "I think black men have a lot to learn. . . . But I was not blown away by their sexism. I feel that if there are possibilities of lesbians and gay men working together, the possibilities are even better among black lesbians and black gay men because we do have quite a bit in common—particularly our being black."

Smith commented on the conference planners' emphasis on having resolutions drafted by the various caucuses (black, Latino, Asian, American Indian, Jewish, non-third world). "Having been in Houston [for the U.S. International Women's Year Convention in 1977] where a lot of resolutions got passed, [I've come to understand] that . . . writing something down on a piece of paper doesn't get us very far. All the resolutions we passed in Houston made us feel good, but the President and Congress could just throw them out the window. . . . I think that developing strategies for organizing around third world lesbian and gay issues might be more productive than passing resolutions that may or may not meet those needs. . . . For example, we could *create* something—like a newsletter for parents of third world lesbian and gay people—instead of making a resolution. Resolutions usually contain a 'should.' "

Armondo Gaitan praised the organizers of the conference as "a small group of people who pulled it [the conference] off beautifully." Gaitan, a Boston area facilitator for the conference, told *GCN* that "overall, I got a very positive feeling from every ethnic group there. At first they were a little irate that there wern't more Asians and American Indians there."

Gaitan was a panelist in a workshop called, "Examining Racism/Sexism/Ageism Among, By and Against Third World Lesbians and Gays," and a participant in the Latino Caucuses. *GCN* asked him what the participants in those workshops had said about sexism. "Men realized that men are the instigators of sexism," said Gaitan. "When men had their separate caucuses [sexism] is the first thing that came up. It's often avoided in the broader gay movement. I think that it was very significant that, in a third world conference, sexism was brought up because [third world gay men] are notorious for our sexism."

Gaitan said that over one-third of the people from the conference—about 200—marched down to the main march on Sunday and that he and four other conference participants took part in the national lobbying effort on Monday.

"We ended up having a long session with an aide to Senator [Edward] Kennedy. It was interesting that [non-third world lesbians and gays who were lobbying Kennedy's office] forgot all about us. I learned from this experience to be more vocal and not to be absorbed. If we don't provide the space for ourselves, there is a tendency for the larger movement to forget about us," he said.

The Combahee River Collective offered a workshop for women only entitled, "Lesbian Feminism and Third World Women." "Capitalism," a member of the black feminist collective told the sixty women present, "never did anything for black people—except divide us." A lot of the discussion centered on economics—the pressing need for black women to develop an economic analysis and realize that economics is not remote and abstract but rather is as concrete as what is—or isn't—available on the supermarket shelves. The women talked about the need for income sharing among black women and among white and black women in a culture whose creed, as one woman present expressed it, isn't "give and take," but rather "take and take."

Tia Cross, a non-third world participant in the conference, described its effect on her as "profound." She said, "It was exciting and moving to me to be with so many third world lesbians and gay men because most of my experience has been sharing with a *small* group of black lesbians. I, too, have been effected by the myth that there are not that many third world gay people.

"I found myself returning again and again to what it felt like to be in a small minority—white people—at this conference. I kept thinking about the fact that my black lesbian friends are usually in a minority and how different my experience of being in the minority is from theirs. For one thing, even though I was in a minority at the conference, as a white person I still have a lot of power in society. Secondly, the openness that white people extend to black people at predominantly white events is most often well-meaning but ignorant, whereas I was very aware that the black people at this conference who were open to me not only know what it's like to be in a minority at an event, but they also were not at all ignorant about my experience as a white person. Black people in this country *have* to know what white people are up to, how we act, and who we are, in order to survive. That's the difference."

The Salsa Soul Sisters from New York City conducted several workshops. At one, they talked about their evolution into a radical group for third world lesbians only. "We [in Salsa Soul] kick and scream at each other about our political differences, but the bottom line is unity for black and third world lesbians. It's good for us to have a place where we can fight our differences out. You can have different expectations and that's all right as long as you don't have the expectation that yours will always prevail."

Shortly after the workshop began, one of the sixty-or-so participants posed the question: "Would we deny the same type of support system to a white woman who said that she can't identify with white people?" A Salsa Soul sister explained that white women can come to meetings but can't belong because Salsa Soul is a third world organization. The woman then asked a second question: "Isn't that the same as what white people do to us?" (She later explained that she felt that the two situations were not the same, but she wanted to hear the differences clearly articulated.)

This question was met with a flurry of responses from around the room.

"She said she can't identify with being white? Well, what if I say I can't identify with being black? What good will that do me when I want to go somewhere?"

"New York is white organization city—take a look in our phone book! But there's only one organization for us [black lesbians]."

"I left Salsa Souls because of a white woman."

"As a black lesbian feminist, I'm disturbed by your questions. The reality is that I'm a nigger, you're a nigger and she [the hypothetical white woman] is not. If I choose to be color blind, I'm being suicidal."

"They [white women] have the power to *choose* to identify with us."

"Do you realize what you are asking me?—to leave my burning house and come take care of you. My first priority is black lesbians, because if they survive, I survive. If they don't survive, I don't survive. And I'm going to survive!"

From *Body Politic*, no. 60 (February 1980), pp. 19-22

No Sorrow, No Pity: A Report on the Gay Disabled

by Gerald Hannon

Richard was a premature baby. Fifty years earlier he might have died at birth. But this was 1953, and little baby Richard was placed lovingly in an incubator of reputable American make. No one would know for many, many months, but some of the machines did not work very well, and babies across North America were quietly

Reprinted with permission from *The Body Politic,* Canada's gay liberation newsmagazine.

breathing an oxygen mixture so rich that their retinal tissue slowly burned away. "I was one of the lucky ones," Richard told me. "Some grew up with really horrible brain damage. I just grew up blind." Richard is officially a handicapped human being. He is one of an estimated 200,000 disabled persons in Toronto alone—though numbers are hard to come by because nobody's counting. The conventional wisdom is that the handicapped represent 14% of the population—one in seven. But however many there are, the numbers, according to an article in *Physiotherapy Canada,* are growing. The "new paraplegics of Canadian society," it says, "are young people between the ages of 14 and 19"—smashed up in car accidents, snowmobile disasters, even run-ins between ten-speed bicycles.

For Richard, an excess of oxygen slowly

burned away his vision. For Scott McArthur, born in 1952, there were a few struggling minutes in the throes of birth when oxygen was cut off, and in those minutes brain cells died like lights going out in a panicked and desperate city. His intelligence was not affected, but Scott grew up with a condition known as cerebral palsy—CP. His days are spent in a wheelchair. His speech is distorted and laboured; anyone unused to it will find him very difficult to understand. His movements appear spastic and uncoordinated. If he is not careful, he will drool.

Like Richard, Scott McArthur is gay.

People like Richard and Scott have not been figures in our landscape. I know, I know that there are gay men and women everywhere—that they are single, that they are married, that they appear at every economic level and in every race and nationality, but. . . . Maybe it's our dogged insistence on our essential health as gay people, on our persistent view of ourselves in our own media as whole, active, healthy, bright and beautiful. Maybe that's it. But I feel that somehow, way at the back of our own closets we have built another one, and into it we have shoved our gay deaf and our gay blind and our gay wheelchair cases, and we've gone on with the already difficult enough problems of living as gay people.

If we've built that second closet, society has made it easy for us. We are not likely to meet the disabled in the workplace—of the employable blind, for example, 80% are unemployed. The general unemployment rate among the handicapped is usually given as 50%. And as for socializing—next time you're at your favourite gay spot, count the stairs.

The lives of many disabled gay people are passed in institutions. Scott McArthur lives in one—he asked me not to name it because he has to continue living there. When it was built, it was widely seen as a progressive and innovative institution. But when Scott moved in five years ago, residents were forbidden to shut their doors if they had a visitor of the opposite sex. That rule has changed, but even today there are no rooms that can accommodate couples, and it is generally expected that visitors will leave by midnight. No overnight guests are allowed.

Scott has known institutions most of his life, and this is not the worst of them. But in none of them has leading a sexual life been very easy.

"I can remember being interested in men since I was ten years old," he told me.

"When I got into my teens, I began paying other boys in the hospital for sex. My parents gave me spending money, and I spent it paying the other kids to jerk me off. A few years later I was spending close to $200 a year for sex. But I didn't call myself gay—I didn't know what it meant. But I knew I wanted men."

Scott was caught, of course—one thing almost no one has in any institution is privacy. He was told it was bad to have other boys jerk him off. He tried to talk to the staff psychologist about his mysteriously developing sexuality, but it didn't work. He went back to paying the other boys. Shortly after that his parents received a letter saying that Scott was ready to be discharged.

As Scott said, "It was a nice way of kicking me out."

He stayed in his parents' home in Nova Scotia for five years. Not very much happened. Once, with the conniving of a sympathetic housekeeper, he managed to order some porn from the States. Shortly thereafter a letter from Canada Customs arrived—his mother was the first to read it—informing him that copies of *Hot Rod* and *Circumcision: A Study in Pictures* had been seized as "immoral and indecent." Scott was handed the letter, told it was obviously some business of his, and there the matter lay.

We who are able-bodied remember what coming out was like. It was not easy, it required privacy, a chance to surreptitiously look things up in books and magazines, a chance to get out alone for a while and maybe "accidentally" wander by that place you'd heard "those" people went to. Maybe, if you were lucky, you found somebody sympathetic to talk to. All of the people I talked to for this article have spent part or all of their lives in institutions where privacy is almost non-existent, and where the administration, acutely aware of its dependence on "public money," has been quite frankly terrified of the topic of sexuality.

"Blind people don't fuck." That is Richard's summation of the attitudes of not only the School for the Blind in Brantford, but a lot of the gay people he runs into.

Richard went through grade 12 at the blind school. Every second Friday there was a very carefully chaperoned dance with the blind girls to which the blind boys dutifully went, and from which, before midnight, they were efficiently hustled back to their own residence. "I used to suck off one of my roommates," Richard said.

"And I used to hear a lot of other people's doors opening and closing after everyone was supposed to be in bed. We had no privacy though—anybody could come in or out because we weren't allowed to lock anything. We used to call the place 'The Zoo'—there'd always be people coming on tours to see the 'poor blind kids.' "

Nothing was ever said about sexuality. Blind people don't fuck. For Richard, the rationalization that he was sucking off his roommate because women were unavailable was beginning to wear a little thin. "Anyway," he said, "from as far back as I can remember I loved being with men. I used to have this great crush on my old man. I loved climbing in bed with him when I was still a kid and we both just had our underwear on."

Again, the institution. The Canadian National Institute for the Blind—the CNIB, "snib," as Richard calls it—is one of the powerful ones. Richard is not very happy with snib. "Having your life run by the CNIB is like having your life run by a church group," he says. "They're arbitrary, they provide 'services,' they have a custodial attitude." BOOST (Blind Organization of Ontario with Self-help Tactics), of which Richard is a member, says that fewer than a third of the people on CNIB's board are blind, and that they've insured, in fact, that the blind *can't* have control. Richard simply snorted when I asked him if the CNIB was a place for the blind to turn to for information on sexuality. I went to check.

I had to because the CNIB has basically cornered the market on information for the blind. Their braille and "talking book" library in Toronto is the blind person's national library. I spoke to the CNIB's Pat Trusty who, if she is nonplussed by my probing questions about the availability of adequate sex information for the gay blind, does not show it. She promises she will check their holdings. I ask about pornography; she promises she will check that too. In the meantime she lends me a great stack of catalogues giving a partial list of titles. Leafing through them, I discover they have *The Joy of Sex*—but not the gay male or lesbian versions.

Trusty, who is nothing if not co-operative, calls back in a week and says, yes, the library does have one title. It is *The Gay Theology*. I do not tell her it is a dreadful book. There are, however, eight more titles in the US that would be available on interlibrary loan, if requested. There are some good titles—*The Gay Mystique*, for example, or Churchill's

Homosexual Behaviour Among Males. There is nothing specifically about lesbians, and nothing published in the last five years. There are no gay liberation periodicals. There are, however, volumes by those twin quacks of psychoanalysis: Irving Bieber and Edmund Bergler. There is also the temptingly titled, *Homosexuality: Its Causes and Curses.* And no, there is no available pornography.

Trusty assures me, however, that a selection committee of the CNIB will consider any request for the conversion of printed material to braille or talking book. Fat chance. "Sighted" people may cruise a gay magazine for weeks before they dare pick it—even at the relative anonymity of a newsstand. It doesn't seem very likely to me that a gay blind person will put him- or herself on the line before an unknown quantity like a "selection committee"—no matter how badly the material may be wanted.

Richard, of course, had access to no information at all. Richard had to slowly stumble out of the closet. He called a gay counselling line a few times but got nervous and hung up. And because he couldn't see, and because he had no access to any written material on gayness, he developed some very peculiar ideas about what gay people were like. All he had to go on was voice—and for him, gayness became the stereotyped lisping, mannered male voice. *He* wasn't like that, but somehow he knew that he and those "queenly" voices were after the same thing, and somehow it was all wrapped up in a man who would be taller than he, and have a deep, resonant voice and a furry, muscular arm—something he could get to check, by the by, since it happens to be perfectly okay for a blind man to take another man's arm when walking.

He went looking for that man at The Barn, a Toronto gay bar. And there he ran into some of the same paternalistic attitudes that enraged him at "snib." "One man came up and asked if I knew what kind of bar this was. I said, sure, it's a gay bar. He said you mean you go home with people? And I said no, I simply stand around all night like a statue." Richard says he also got *very* tired of people saying "isn't that too bad." Or people yelling in his face because they feel he must be a little dim as well. Or people who want "to look after me." Now, he says, he gets a lot of the initial tension out of the way by introducing himself as "that weird blind person who may fall over you."

You get to say something like that, of course, only if you happen to have a pretty good self-image. That wasn't always the case for Richard, but it helped to discover he could pick up two or three people a week at The Barn during what he now terms his "whoring phase." Phase over now—he's involved in a relationship, has a job with BOOST, and plans to keep plugging away in the fight for disabled rights. "It means more to me than the gay struggle," he says. "I have more to gain for one thing—like a job somewhere other than BOOST, and independence."

Independence. Like most everyone else, the disabled want to control their own lives. And if they must live in institutions, they want to control those institutions and make them responsive to their real needs.

John Kellerman has been fighting that battle—until recently, a rather lonely one—for 12 years. When he tried to move back into a group home he'd left a year and a half earlier, he was told he couldn't because he "raised too much shit. And *I* thought I was doing everything I could to make it a better place by organizing the residents and so on."

Out of the Silent Closet

At a gathering of the deaf, hearing people are the disabled.

Early last month I attended a meeting of the York Rainbow Society for the Deaf, and after an exhausting four-hour session came away with some hint of what it must be like to spend most of your time unable to communicate. In a room with 15 other gay people, I was the only one who couldn't "talk." I sat helplessly by while issues were debated, while people chatted and joked, while tempers frayed, while a cake was brought in to celebrate president Bonnie Perry's 29th birthday—and unless one of the two speaking members took the time to translate, I was deaf to an articulate and expressive flurry of hands—sign language, the fifth largest language in the world, according to Raymond Barton.

Barton is 27, totally deaf, mute, one of three deaf children of two deaf parents, and the man who got the York Rainbow Society going. I met Raymond at Randy Vivian's apartment— Randy was my guide and translator. Partially deaf himself, an expert lipreader, apparently tireless and endlessly good natured, he translated questions, answers, threw in his own comments, told me his story and from time to time jumped up to make coffee. Which left me briefly alone with Raymond, which was awful. I was suddenly sitting alone in a room with an attractive, articulate, energetic man and all I could do was smile. I tried writing notes—and discovered that small talk looks *very* small when you have to write it out. So I smiled. He smiled. I became deeply interested in the decor. And, thank god, Randy came back with coffee.

"Communication," he said, "is the number one problem for the gay deaf." You're telling me.

The York Rainbow Society has become part of the solution to that problem. It began about three years ago when Barton came back from San Francisco determined to duplicate in Toronto what he'd found in SF—gay deaf meeting gay deaf in places other than the bars; working, as their national constitution put it, "to encourage and promote the educational, economical, and social welfare; to foster fellowship; to defend our rights and advance our interests. . . ." There was already a loose network of gay deaf in Toronto— I remember they were almost a fixture at the Parkside Tavern for a period. Always at the same tables, they signed vehemently all night, had a good time, left, and seemed impenetrable as a social group. Other people tried not to stare. Out of the bar crowd, out of the private parties that were held from time to time, Raymond and Randy and Bonnie Perry, chums from the not-so-good-old days at the school for the deaf in Belleville, managed to pull together enough out-of-the-closet gay people to get the York Rainbow Society off the ground.

Now the group meets monthly— mostly at members' homes, arranges regular socials, has started a newsletter, and will host, this coming June, the fourth international convention of Rainbow Societies. There are two Canadian groups (the other is in Montreal), 15 from the States, and the organizers are confident that more than 300 gay deaf will descend on the Westbury Hotel June 19 for the three-day conference.

Hearing gays, by the way, are

welcome both to join the organization and attend the conference—though anyone contemplating doing so without a grounding in sign language would be wasting his or her time.

There are only four lesbians in the group right now, which makes it a little lonely for Bonnie Perry, into a second term as president, but it's still preferable to being surrounded by hearing lesbians who might just turn away from you when they discover you're deaf. It's happened. I ask her if she's been to LOOT (The Lesbian Organization of Toronto). She says she means to, but is uncertain of her welcome, and shy. For the time being, even if she's made a bit uncomfortable by the raunchy humour which binds the men together, Bonnie Perry will be working, along with Raymond, along with Randy, along with the dozen other people in the group, to "build a good future for deaf gay people. We have to reach into their closets," she told me, "we have to bring them out."

Raymond too spoke to the group that afternoon about the gay deaf they hadn't reached yet, about the awesome,

silent closet it was their responsibility to empty. He is an intense, compact man and his signing is lean, eloquent, fluid. And fast—Randy kept up a halting translation as best he could, but it was a marvellous burst of eloquence and clearly a challenge. At the end, he said "we're deaf and gay. Love each other. Respect each other." They broke into wild applause—inaudible to him, audible to me, visible to both of us. More—because they stamped the floor, as deaf people do when they want to get your attention, and that stamping sent a trembling through the floor, up through all of our feet, into all of our heads so that we shared, briefly, something that didn't need a translation. Raymond had made us *feel* community.

And all of us knew that feeling.

If enough hearing people are interested in learning sign language, Raymond Barton is willing to begin classes. Write him c/o York Rainbow Society for the Deaf, 29 Granby St, Toronto, ON M5B 1H8.
Address of the Montreal group is Association des Bon Gens Sourds, CP 754, Succ R, Montreal, PQ H2S 3M4.

from the Hotel Toronto last September—nobody gave me any reason. I was just there in the lobby waiting for a friend."

The worst incident he remembers occurred when he left a friend at a street corner and hailed a cab. When he got in, the driver took a good look at him and refused to drive off. John refused to get out. The driver, in desperation, began offering money to passersby if they would take John off his hands. He was offering two dollars. John says it was the most humiliating experience of his life.

I think John would call that taxi driver a "normal" person, and he does not have a very high opinion of normality. "Normal persons are very frightened persons," he wrote in a short essay. "They are frightened of themselves, and of people who are different, or who have different ideas, so why should we as disabled people try and degrade ourselves even more by becoming normal? Why not change the world . . . ? Normal people need a purpose for living, and we need people to help us. They need people to look up to, we could be them?"

In those thoughts, John is beginning to reconceptualize the very categories into which our thoughts are strait-jacketed. Already we have come some way from the times when a Sunday afternoon's entertainment was a trip to Bedlam to watch the mad cavort. And I suppose even that was an improvement over Byzantium under Justinian, where those born deaf were deprived of their civic rights. (Justinian was the emperor, though, who thought homosexuality caused earthquakes. Not a very scientific regime, that one.)

But we are still some way from seeing that to be handicapped means simply to be human in a slightly different way. UNESCO has published a paper which outlines the stages through which public attitudes develop with reference to the handicapped. There is the philanthropic stage, the public welfare stage, the stage of fundamental rights, the stage of the right to equal opportunity, and finally, the stage of the right to integration. In that final stage, it is the very notion of norms and normality that is called into question. Suddenly one is faced with questioning whether there is very much difference between an individual with a baby carriage facing a staircase, and someone in a wheelchair facing a telephone booth. In both cases, the problem is not the "handicap." The problem is the telephone, or the stairs. "The difficulties of the disabled often reveal difficulties experienced by all," notes the UNESCO report, and cites an example

Like Scott, John Kellerman has CP. It hits people in many different ways, though, and John can walk (although very awkwardly) while Scott can't. But John's speech seems much more affected, and I find him more difficult to understand. He's patient enough to repeat everything five or six times if that's what it takes, and I'm persistent enough to keep asking, so we struggle through.

John defines himself as bisexual. He has fantasized about having sex with women, but remembers how he used to love to watch construction workers in the summer even when he was just a kid, how he was fascinated by their bodies. "I used to be afraid," he says, "of being condemmed by gay people for wanting both. But it hasn't really happened—mostly it's having been brought up in a society that says we have to love one or the other."

John says that he was so desperate for information on sexuality that he helped organize one of the earliest conferences on the topic just so he'd finally learn something. "I went to Queen's Park in 1974 and got $2,000 and we actually got something going. I felt ecstatic—I'd been so hung up about organizing and about sex generally. But the conference was great."

That hadn't been his first effort,

however. In the early 70s he helped found a group called ALPHA, Advancement League for the Physically Handicapped, and that group successfully lobbied the city for the grading of sidewalks and the initiation of Wheel-Trans, the transit commission's project for the physically disabled. More recently, he has organized a citizens' committee to plan activities for 1981—the International Year of the Disabled. "One thing that sort of frightens me," he said, "is that we'll be inundated with do-gooders. That scares the hell out of me."

John Kellerman is an activist, but every activist has a private life. Or tries to. "I'm very lonely," he says. "I want to develop a relationship with someone, but nothing much has happened with either men or women. I've often wanted to go to the baths, but I'm afraid to because I'm afraid they wouldn't let me in. I went to two in Winnipeg and they wouldn't let me past the door. I don't go to many bars because I have a real complex about going, though I haven't had any problems in the gay bars I've gone to here. It's been worse in straight bars and restaurants. Sometimes they ask me to leave. Sometimes they allow me to stay, but then I just sit there and nobody ever serves me. I was physically removed at an American university where "the abolition of architectural obstacles for six handicapped students made life better for all the students."

Every one of us begins life as disabled. We don't ordinarily think of infancy in quite that way, but it is a period during which we are entirely helpless and dependent. For many of us, old age has some of the same effects. And most everyone, at some point in his or her life, will be briefly bedridden, or have a limb in a cast, or need psychiatric help. That is certainly not the same as spending your life blind, or deaf or in a wheelchair, but it does indicate that we are talking about a spectrum here, not discrete and mutually exclusive groups. We are talking about ways of being fully human.

Sex is a fully human need. Sex that is masturbation, sex that's just a quickie with no names exchanged thank you very much, and sex that takes place as part of some broader relationship. Many disabled have known only masturbation. Not a few find even that impossible.

Scott McArthur works for the MCC as a referral person when that church gets calls from the gay disabled. "Someone called me last week," Scott told me. "He was desperate. He told me he couldn't even masturbate. Where could he go, he asked me, where could he go. I had to tell him there was nowhere he could go."

It's the big taboo. The disabled are supposed to have "more important" things to think about. A report from the Sex Information and Education Council of the United States notes that "in the name of benevolence and protection, many people still take the position that sex information would 'hurt' the disabled. Why should Pandora's box be opened to a person who is unable to use what is there? . . . After all, disabled people are fragile and not expected to take care of themselves." As one straight woman said at a sex and the disabled conference a few years ago, "I had come out of the rehab centre and after 22 months of hospitalization we had never discussed the word sex, except amongst us, as paraplegics and quadriplegics. We were taught repression. We were taught that if we couldn't have something, don't rock the boat."

Blind people don't fuck, as Richard would say. But if the disabled do, or want to try, or—god forbid—if they're disabled enough to need assistance, then most of our institutions would really rather not hear about it. The public—not to mention Mom and Dad—might not be quite ready to hear

Stair Trek: Nightlife by Wheelchair

A quick survey of Toronto gay spots indicates most establishments would rather admit to clubbing baby seals to a pulp than to closing their doors to the disabled. The one exception: the Quest Tavern at 665 Yonge Street. The manager, a Mr. Jackson, refused even to talk.

The most positive responses came, not surprisingly, from businesses where the manager or owner has had some kind of personal contact with the disabled. Roy LaRose, manager of Katrina's, says people in wheelchairs are "absolutely welcome" at his disco. "My brother has been disabled since he was 19," he said, "so I know all about the problems they can run into."

John Bannerman, manager of the Richmond Street Health Emporium (260 Richmond St E), has worked with the retarded, and emphasizes that the blind, the deaf or anyone in a wheelchair is welcome—though he notes that there a lot of stairs, and the washrooms are not designed to accommodate wheelchairs. "Someone with CP is already a customer," he says, "and though he can walk, he can't talk and communicates with a board and stick."

Pat Murphy, manager of the women's bar Fly-by-Night (212 Dundas St E), is a former social worker, and guarantees any woman a warm welcome. "Wheelchairs should try the back door," she says, "there's only one step."

Every other bar, bath and disco in town has also put out the welcome mat—up to and including guide dogs. (It is a criminal offence to refuse entry to a blind person because he or she is accompanied by a guide dog.) A few establishments said staff would be willing to help if there are problems. They are Dudes, at 10 Breadalbane; 18 East at 18 Eastern Ave; and the Roman Sauna at 742 Bay Street.

Most gay watering holes in this town *do* seem to have a lot of stairs, and none have washrooms adapted to wheelchairs, so a willingness to be friendly certainly doesn't solve all problems. It's also pretty easy to talk a good game to an inquiring reporter—both the St. Charles and Parkside taverns made welcoming sounds, but I'm told both have refused service to CPers in wheelchairs.

All gay community events organized by local groups extend a warm welcome to everyone. Most have provided help over the stairs when necessary, and at least one seminar has been signed for the deaf.

TBP is interested in hearing from you if you've had any problems at any bars, baths or discos in town. Give us a call at 863-6320.

that part of little Johnny's or Mary's physical therapy includes lessons on how to masturbate.

The topic, however, is finally beginning to surface among professionals at least. I spoke to Michael Barrett of the Sex Information and Education Council of Canada (SIECCAN). He has long been an advocate of sexual rights for the disabled—you're unlikely to find a seminar or conference on the topic which doesn't feature him either as an organizer, chair, or one of the speakers. I ask about sex and the gay disabled, and he admits that he has run into almost nothing on the topic. He is a very gay-supportive individual though, and makes sure the topic is raised whenever he gives a workshop or seminar. He sends me a package of materials to look through, and it is depressing. I think homosexuality was mentioned twice—once in passing, and once thus: "When the patient's sexual

activity is homosexual or otherwise variant, physician-patient communication is ordinarily further restricted." Indeed.

I did a bit of checking—again with institutions, because institutions are so frequently "home" for so many disabled. The general reaction might best be described as "cautious." And where gay sexuality is concerned, a kind of benign neglect seems to be the rule.

Mrs. Ann Pahl is the administrator of Participation House, a permanent residence in Markham for the multi-handicapped. There have been two marriages at Participation House. She says there is no problem with casual sexual encounters, but the individuals would probably have to ask the staff for assistance, at least out of their wheelchairs, and it would be given. There can be no overnight visitors though—if residents want that sort of thing they're expected to book into a motel. She was quite frank when I asked whether a gay couple could set up house: "I certainly wouldn't be shocked, but to protect myself I'd have to present it to the Board for approval. I'm afraid we couldn't take it lightly; we're dependent on the community and the government for volunteers and funds. We're all very conscious of our community image, and we're closely watched by Queen's Park. People might be critical of anything that isn't pretty mainstream."

I was pleasantly surprised, though, that Pahl was equally frank about how the needs of those who can't masturbate are met. "Staff will help if requested," she said. "Of course some staff are quite comfortable with this, others are not, and only those who can handle it get involved. We don't use mechanical sex aids yet, but that may come."

Ms. Margaret Graeb, the administrator at Bellwoods, a residential centre for handicapped adults, is rather more cautious. She is "not sure" whether any of the residents would be completely unable to masturbate, and on the topic of staff participation: "We're not ready for that yet. I'd be concerned about the kinds of relationships that might develop. I'd be worried about how other residents might feel. I guess I'm not prepared to see that happening yet."

Asked if homosexuality was part of general discussions of sexuality, she said she thought it was "touched on."

The situation isn't much better out there in the great wide world of the "gay ghetto." Everyone I talked to had a horror story to tell. Deaf men will have someone come into their room at the baths, begin to have sex with them, discover they're deaf—and get up and leave. Scott has been told to get out of the Parkside Tavern—or face the cops. Told he would not be allowed in Charlie's, a local disco, without an escort. At gay dances he *can* get to, the music is usually so loud that anyone unused to his speech problem will find him impossible to understand. Richard has heard people say, loudly enough for him to hear, "Why does *he* have to come to a place like this?"

As disabled activist Pat Israel said at a workshop on sexuality, "Everyone's handicapped, only some people's wheelchairs are on the inside, not on the outside where you can see them."

Then there's the emphasis on youth and beauty—an obsession that pervades the entire culture, and one the gay world certainly shares. "It's one that *I* share,"

Scott told me. "I want an attractive man."

None of this is very easy for anybody. Disabled people used to make me unbearably uncomfortable. If I saw a wheelchair coming my way, I would make some excuse to cross the street. I spoke about this to Tom Warner, a gay activist who's been involved with handicapped groups in the Coalition for Life Together. "I have two disabled relatives as well," he told me, "so I should be used to it. But one night I got picked up by a man in a car, and it was only after I got in that I noticed the wheelchair in the back. I went home with him and we went to bed and it didn't really work out. I think he was quite depressed. But his legs were so cold. I flinched every time they touched me and of course he sensed it. But I couldn't help it."

None of this is going to be easy. But change is coming—partly because the disabled themselves are pushing against every constraint society has managed to put in their way, and not a few of the people doing the pushing are our gay brothers and sisters.

"Talk to us," Scott says. "If you see somebody in a wheelchair, talk. If you can't think of anything to say, go over and say 'I've never talked to anybody in a wheelchair before and I don't know what to say.' Maybe it'll get something going."

"I want to see more co-operation between minorities," says John Kellerman. "We have to understand our commonalities and differences. We have to talk, we have to discuss problems and tactics."

"Solidarity," said André Malraux, "is the most intelligent form of egoism."

They do not want pity. They say listen, and understand. They do not want help. They say co-operate. To be handicapped is one way of being human. They say that they are all that men and women *can* be.

From *Women* 7, no. 2
(1980): 18-22

Lesbian Mothering

by Lois, Baltimore

"The normal family in this society is composed of a mother, father, 2.4 children, a dog and a cat" (National Lawyers Guild, 1978), and, although single parents who become so through death or divorce are considered normal in some contexts, the lesbian mother is a contradiction who is not supposed to exist. In fact, however, she does exist: it is estimated that there are well over 1.5 million lesbian mothers in this country.

Lesbians can be mothers for a variety of reasons. Authors of *Lesbian/Woman,* Del Martin and Phyllis Lyon maintain that:

mostly these are women who were unaware of their Lesbian tendencies until after they had married and had children. Or they are women who suppressed their Lesbian feelings, convinced, as most heterosexuals are, that these feelings merely represented a natural phase in their lives and would disappear after

they experienced marriage and motherhood. There are some women, too, who consciously rejected the gay life in favor of the more societally accepted and respected heterosexual relationship (Martin and Lyon, 1972).

Hunter and Polikoff add that the feminist movement has also been instrumental in producing lesbian mothers:

In the past few years, it has helped to bring women together both emotionally and sexually. Some women who previously had accepted their heterosexuality without question have begun to broaden their view of their own sexuality to include relationships with women. Some have decided to reject heterosexuality finding a total commitment to women to be more personally fulfilling and more politically positive. Some of these previous heterosexual women have children (Hunter and Polikoff, 1976).

Having established that there is a substantial number of lesbian mothers, is there a need for further discussion? Don't the children of these parents progress through developmental stages just like the children of heterosexual parents? Logic would assume that such is true; however, society is not yet comfortable with alternative lifestyles, and judges ruling in custody cases typify society's homophobic reaction to lesbian mothers. Lesbian mothers are judged not on the quality of their parenting but on the basis of their sexuality. Thus, most custody cases decided in open court are lost on the standard of the "best interests of the child."

In cases where custody is granted to the mother, rights may be dependent upon adherence to restrictions. For example, in one situation, the mother won custody but was limited to seeing her lover only when the children were in school or visiting their father. Harsh restrictions are given even to the lesbian mother who loses her children but is granted visitation rights. Announced one judge granting such rights:

> I may be prejudiced but I think homosexuality is an illness. I hope you're concerned enough about your kids not to kiss them on the lips, because everyone knows venereal disease is rampant among homosexuals. If the children ever find out that you are a lesbian and ask you about it, I want you to tell them that you are sick. If you refuse to do this, you can tell me now and you will never see them again (*Mom's Apple Pie,* 1978).

There are, undoubtedly, special issues involved in lesbian parenting—some challenges and some advantages.

Author, editor, and heterosexual mother Sidney Cornelia Callahan writes that a good parent basically protects and nurtures her child. Through providing this care, the parents enjoys, entices, and encourages the child into life. Simultaneously, the good parent withdraws and separates from the child so that it can become independent and grow (Callahan, 1973). To ease such transitions throughout childhood, perhaps all children should have lesbian mothers: researchers comparing lesbians and heterosexual women have found that lesbians were more independent, resilient, reserved, self-sufficient and composed (Hopkins, 1969) and that they rated higher in self-confidence (Thompson, McCandless, Strickland, 1971). One who is self-aware and self-assured would seem to be better able to nurture, care, and support while also letting go.

An apparent bonus of being raised by a gay parent is that the child, because her parent is not held by more traditional sex roles, may become a more androgynous individual. Dorothy Riddle reports that androgynous persons have been found to

be more socially competent, have received more honors, were more active, and had higher self-esteem and identity integration (Riddle, 1978). Two lesbian mothers living together with their children illustrate this integration of theory and practice:

> We are all sexual human beings. It is not who you love but how you love that is important. We hope our children will have a very strong sense of self and be able to love and trust themselves and others. It is important to live fully in the present. The ability to accept and love yourself and be able to deal with your present situation is what is most necessary in dealing with any future challenges, changes, and situations. The children know that we love each other and that we love them. This is what matters.
>
> People should be free to develop and explore their own sexuality in non-alienating and non-oppressive ways. Neither of us has ever gotten into role playing. We are two women who love each other and live together with our children. We are individuals and we want to raise our children to be free to be individuals. Neither an all female nor an all male role is desirable. To be fully human is to have a balance of masculine and feminine qualities within each person (*RT: Journal of Radical Therapy,* 1974).

In the day-by-day joys and woes of parenting many lesbian mothers believe that their childrearing problems are no different from those of heterosexual parents, particularly those who are divorced (Martin and Lyon, 1972). Bernice Goodman, a psychotherapist who has worked with lesbian mothers' groups concluded that similarities between heterosexual and gay parents are much greater than the differences. Additionally, she found the same range of personality types, expectations about child development, knowledge and ignorance of childrearing. The primary difference Goodman found was guilt experienced by some lesbian mothers who were uncertain about how their lifestyle might affect their child's development. Once this guilt was worked through the lesbian mothers were able to deal effectively with their children's fears and problems (Goodman, 1977).

As in all families with children, lesbian mothers "worry when their children are sick and make endless peanut butter sandwiches" (Mahaney, 1978). Social worker Bernice Augenbraun adds that she knows of no problems unique to the lesbian

mother except that she is constantly oppressed by the attitude of society (Augenbraun, 1977). This writer would venture to say that although lesbian mothering involves joys, sorrows, fears, worries, and limits similar to heterosexual mothering, some unique problems are created because of society's aversion to gay people in general and lesbian mothers in particular. From society's repressive attitude flows concern about whether children should be told of the lesbianism and about the reaction of children should the mother decide to live with her lover. Some mothers are further concerned about having male friends with whom their daughters and sons can identify (Martin and Lyon, 1972) and the further complications created by that identification.

This latter matter does not worry all lesbian mothers because they consider it undesirable that their sons should grow up like their fathers. They are adamantly in favor of the child learning to relate to women as people and equals. For these mothers, the worry is not providing a male image but rather attempting in some measure to counteract the bombardment of male-identified, stereotypic behavior learned from peers, television, and school. A Chicana mother who felt this way stated that it was unnecessary for her 14 year old

Johanna Vogelsang/off our backs/LNS

to be macho in order to know he is a man. "He doesn't have to role play in order to prove his manhood. He knows he is a man and is having no trouble with his identity. What he doesn't understand is what all the fuss is about, why his friends have to pretend to be something they are not" (Martin and Lyon, 1973).

Other mothers who do seek males with whom their children can interact are concerned particularly with sons, with bringing children up in a nonsexist way. This poses another problem because they find older, nonsexist male role models to be scarce or nonexistent (Hall, 1978).

Lesbian mothers also wonder about the manner in which they, as feminists angry at certain male characteristics and at the male's dominance in the culture, can let sons know their feelings without making them feel bad about themselves. As one lesbian mother asserts:

I don't want the kids to feel bad about themselves but I don't want them to turn into bad people either. I want to let them know what my values are. For instance, being insensitive to feelings is what I think of as most offensively male. And that's something I think I can help them with. It's not a matter of telling them not to be strong. It's more a matter of fairness—that you don't make rules for women that you don't have for men. That you're not going to grow up and get married and expect your wife to do all the shitwork (Sanford, 1978).

Whether to come out to their children and if so, the best time to do this is another worrisome consideration for lesbian parents. Should the knowing child speak to some disapproving outsider, the mother may face a custody suit. Conversely, if the child is told and simultaneously cautioned to keep her mother's lesbianism a secret from significant others such as the father or grandparents, a rather heavy burden is laid on the child.

Additionally, warning the child to be cautious can instill fear; this emotion was detected by one mother whose son inquired whether the police would arrest her if they knew she was gay (Sanford, 1978).

Family and marriage counselor Betty Berzon recommends disclosing one's sexual identity to children because "if there is secrecy and tension around the topic of sexuality in the home, the children may grow up believing that sex is something to be frightened of and to keep hidden." Berzon avers that disclosure by the mother is an act of faith in her children (Berzon, 1978). The voices of lesbian mothers must again give us clues:

I think for those of us who are lucky enough to be able to be out to our kids, there are great results. Because we make ourselves open to our kids in this one area, we are open to them in a lot of ways. This is something we dare to do to be different and sometimes it hurts to be different. That we share that with them creates a very special relationship. It also helps them understand prejudice. They begin to see that a kid who calls another kid some name about their religion or race is probably being as bigoted and narrow-minded and hateful as someone who calls their mother a dyke. They can make connections that many people are never able to make (Sanford, 1978).

And:

I came out to my ten-year-old son in the context of a relationship with someone he really cared about. And I kept wondering, is he really as cool about this as he seems? A few months later we were visiting my parents and he tried to intervene with them for me. He came out of the room throwing his hands up and saying, "I tried to talk with them, but they are totally unreasonable" (Sanford, 1978).

The final problems encountered by some lesbian mothers is maintaining family equilibrium when there is a new mate. Some mothers point out that they experience no greater stresses with this than would any heterosexual family gaining a stepparent (Martin and Lyon, 1973). It may well be that the degree of disruption depends, as it does in heterosexual families, on the extent to which family members feel, among other things, self-confident and loved.

Hall delineates one case in which the lesbian lover has recently become part of the family. In this instance, the new parent, perhaps because of her socialization as a woman, behaved as a "supermom." The new parent was subsequently rapidly deflated when she was not readily accepted by the child. This dismay gradually evolved into clashes between the biological and the new parent over discipline of the child (Hall, 1978). At this point, similarities between this family and its heterosexual counterpart are again apparent.

As the gay liberation movement becomes more active and gains more rights for its members, social agencies and the courts will need to become more knowledgeable about lesbian mothers and their families clinically and legally as mothers fight for custody rights.

Lesbian mothers and their children are currently threatened with being separated because of the sexual preference of the mother; it is in the interests of social agencies and courts to initiate studies concerning lesbian parenting and the physical, emotional, and psychological development of their children.

Research studies should assess the sexual identity and the adjustment or lack thereof of children raised by lesbians so that courts may realize the validity or falsity of their fears. Without such studies, our best resource may well be the children themselves:

My name is Lisa. I am 7 years old. Soon mommy has to go court cause my daddy wants my brother and me to live with him. He says it's because mommy's gay. That's stupid. Gay mommys are the same as any other one. Well my mommy is my best friend. We do every thing together. We talk, sing, play. Some of my friends mommy just cook and clean house. My mom really loves us and we don't want to live with daddy. We love him too but mommy is spesal to us. Some people are afraid of lesbians but other people are afraid of dentists too. It's silly. Mommy's friends are nice and happy and they make mommy happy too. If I have to live with daddy I will cry and run back to my mom. She will cry too I think. The end.

(*Mom's Apple Pie*, 1979)

A Selected Bibliography on Lesbian Mothering

Berzon, Betty. "Sharing Your Lesbian Identity With Your Children: A Case for Openness" in *Our Right to Love: A Lesbian Resource Book*, pp. 69-74. Edited by Ginny Vida. Englewood Cliffs, New Jersey: Prentice-Hall, Inc., 1978.

Callahan, Sidney Cornelia. *Parenting*. Garden City, New York: Doubleday and Company, Inc., 1973.

Goodman, Bernice. *The Lesbian: A Celebration of Difference*. Brooklyn, New York: Out and Out Books, 1977.

Martin, Del, and Lyon, Phyllis. *Lesbian/Woman*. New York: Bantam Books, 1972.

National Lawyers Guild. *A Gay Parent's Guide to Child Custody*. San Francisco: National Lawyers Guild, 1978.

Sanford, Wendy C. "Parents Who Are Gay," in *Ourselves and Our Children: A Book By and For Parents*, pp. 173-177. Edited by the Boston Women's Health Book Collective. New York: Random House, 1978.

Wyland, Francie. *Motherhood, Lesbianism and Child Custody*. Toronto, Canada: Wages Due Lesbians Toronto, 1977.

Journals

Green, Richard. "Sexuality Identity of 37 Children Raised by Homosexual or Transsexual Parents." *American Journal of Psychiatry* 135 (June 1978): 692-697.

Hall, Marny. "Lesbian Families: Cultural and Clinical Issues." *Social Work* 25 (September 1978): 380-385.

Hopkins, J. H. "The Lesbian Personality." *British Journal of Psychiatry* 115 (1969): 1433-1436.

Hunter, Nan D., and Polikoff, Nancy D. "Custody Rights of Lesbian Mothers: Legal Theory and Litigation Strategy." *Buffalo Law Review* 25 (Spring 1976): 691-733.

Klaich, Dolores. "Parents Who Are Gay." *New Times* 7 (July 1976): 34-42.

"Lesbian Mothers." *RT: Journal of Radical Therapy* 4 (December 1974): 18.

London, Jan. "Lesbian Mother." *Women: A Journal of Liberation* 4 (Winter 1974): 23.

Osman, Shelomo, "My Stepfather Is a She." *Family Process* II (June 1972): 209-218.

Riddle, Dorothy I. "Relating to Children: Gays as Role Models." *Journal of Social Issues* 34 (1978): 38-58.

Thompson, N. D., McCandless, B. R. and Strickland, B. R. "Personal Adjustment of Male and Female Homosexuals and Heterosexuals." *Journal of Abnormal Psychiatry* 78 (1971): 237-240.

Newsletters

"All About Me." *Mom's Apple Pie,* February 1979, p. 6.

"Local Mother Fights Back." *Mom's Apple Pie,* May 1978, p. 2.

Film

Augenbraun, Bernice. From the film "In the Best Interest of the Children: A Film About Lesbian Mothers and Child Custody." Los Angeles: Iris Films, 1977.

Gay Community News
THE WEEKLY FOR LESBIANS AND GAY MALES

From *Gay Community News* 7, no. 8 (September 15, 1979): 8-9, 13

Children of Lesbian Mothers Speak Out

by Betsy Smith

While listening to the children of lesbian mothers with whom I spoke during the following interviews I had many different reactions. These ranged from sadness to amusement, anger, pride and respect.

It was painful at times to hear so many children speak about their fear that their friends would find out about their mothers' lesbianism. I became furious, not at the children or their mothers, but at a homophobic world that creates such a hostile environment for gay parents and their children. This is yet another area where gay people and our children are victimized. This blatant oppression can be heard through the voices of these children.

I felt a tremendous amount of respect for all the parents and children I met. Most of these children, whether or not they are aware of it, have incredible insights into life and growing up. They have a strong and sophisticated sense of what is fair and what is unjust. John, who is 13 years old,

Reprinted with permission from *Gay Community News: The Weekly for Lesbians and Gay Men,* 22 Bromfield St., Boston, MA 02108.

was able to draw a parallel in the power dynamics in this society between gays and straights, and teenagers and adults. When I was John's age, I was making queer jokes without any awareness of what I was saying. These children all had a consciousness that many of us didn't begin to develop until much later.

This is obviously not a definitive article about the lives of children of lesbian mothers. Every child will have his or her own story to tell. I interviewed boys and girls of diverse ethnic and class backgrounds. Unfortunately, I was unable to contact any children who lived with their gay fathers to interview.

There have rarely been articles written about children of gay parents, and the articles that are published are not in the form of complete interviews. Instead, they contain many of the writers' biases. I have tried to refrain from interjecting my own biases, although sometimes that was impossible, and instead have transcribed almost everything the children said to me (omitting only what was incoherent on the tapes). I hope this will reflect the scope of the feelings different sons and daughters of lesbian mothers have.

Rockel is an eight-year-old girl who lives in Cambridge with her mother, Joan, and her mother's lover, Daphne.

B: How did you find out your mom was gay?

R: Well I knew a long time ago—but I didn't know exactly what gay meant.

B: What did you think it meant?

R: I knew that Joan was gay.

B: Do you remember talking to Joan about it?

R: Well, once I asked a friend of Joan's, "Is Joan gay?" and she said "Yes, do you know what that means?" I think gay means when a woman loves another woman or a man loves a man—the same kind of sex.

B: Do you think that's okay?

R: It doesn't matter to me. I wouldn't really care if she loved a man and a woman . . . because she's happy with what she's doing . . . with who she's loving.

B: So it doesn't matter to you if Joan is involved with a man or woman?

R: Well, if she weren't involved with Daphne it would be all right. But I won't be very happy when they break up . . . if they break up.

B: You feel pretty attached to Daphne?

R: Yeah.

B: Do you spend a lot of time with Daphne?

R: Yeah—when I spend time with Daphne I spend time with Joan.

B: Do you think your mother's relationship with Daphne is as good as your friend's parents?

R: Yeah . . . probably. I don't think mothers and fathers get along as well as wives and wives . . . or women and women. It's just that I've never heard of women getting married . . . I guess a priest marries them.

B: I think it's done but not very often. Rockel, do you ever see your father?

R: I'm going to see him real soon.

B: Do you see him often?

R: No . . . once a year. And now it's going to be even less because he's moving to the midwest. I wouldn't mind seeing him more often. If he were around here I would at least want to see him three times a year because it's weird not seeing him more often. Well, it's not really weird because I'm pretty used to it cause they broke up when they were two. I mean when I was two. Two years old is pretty young to get married.

B: Do you ever talk to your friends about your mother being a lesbian?

R: Are you crazy? Never in my whole life will I. Susie is the only one because her mother's gay. But she doesn't know what gay means, is, or what. Her mother just told her and her brother that she was gay and that's it and didn't really explain it.

B: What do you think of that?

R: I think that was sort of stupid because I asked Susie once in school, "Susie, is your mother gay?" and she said, "I don't know" . . . like I would but usually I say no when people ask me that in school. Like if a person is attacking someone around their waist or something someone will say, "Eww, you're gay."

B: Do you hear those comments often in school?

R: Yeah . . . but at summer camp where I am now there isn't enough time for kids to think about if someone's gay. I wonder why it's so stupid to a lot of people . . . that gay is stupid?

B: What do you think?

R: Probably they don't have any relatives who are gay who can see that they're fine, or they're married and they think that's fine and they wouldn't want it to be any other way . . . or their mother or father says, "those queers or gays" or something like that. A lot of times that's where a child gets things about gay people. I'm sort of on the verge of seeing what people would do if they knew my mom was gay and like I asked my friend, "What would you do if I said my mom was gay?" and she said, "I wouldn't be your friend anymore," and I thought I'll never tell her. Can you imagine a person doing that? But some of my friends are too close to me to not be my friends anymore.

B: Why do you think people have such strong reactions?

R: Maybe because she was brought up knowing that she was gonna get married and have a kid and everything. For some time now I've been saying to people that I might not ever have a husband and get married and have a baby.

B: You say that to your friends?

R: Yeah.

B: And what do they say?

R: I say I might adopt a baby.

B: Do they think that's a crazy idea?

R: No . . . 'cause my other friend is thinking of adopting. I mean just because you have eggs inside you don't have to make them babies.

B: Can you describe how it's different having a mother who's gay?

R: All of my friends . . . they believe their mothers and fathers. They believe that in every home there is a mother and a father and a sister and a brother and a baby . . . like if you're playing house everyone says that. And like in school when they send notes and it says, "Dear Parents" sometimes I cross out the "s" because Joan isn't a parents. Also girls call their parents moms and dads but Joan likes me to call her Joan.

B: Do you ever hear the word faggot at school?

R: Some but you more hear the word queer.

B: Did you go to Gay Pride Day?

R: I wanted to go but I was scared to take the risk of losing a friend.

B: Which friend?

R: Any one. Just in case. I went to the beach instead.

B: Had you ever been to a Gay Pride Demonstration before?

R: Probably when I was younger . . . like in my fours and fives. And no one cares if you're four or five.

B: Do you ever talk with your other friends about your mom being gay?

R: No . . . I don't really need to talk about it . . . as long as you're a friend it doesn't really matter if your mom is gay.

Ann and John are both 13 years old. They are friends and live in the suburbs of Boston.

B: What does it mean to you that your mother's gay?

J: It doesn't really bother me. Sometimes it can get in the way, like when my mother has a new lover. Once my friend came over and I said, "Ma, I want you to meet my friend." She was in the other room and I didn't really want us to walk in on them. You have to be more careful than you would if your mother was straight. Sometimes it's a little awkward. Like when your friends are talking about how people are fags or gay people are weird it can really bother you sometimes.

B: I was wondering if kids use those words a lot at school?

J: Well, I use them a lot too. I don't use them around my mother. If I do then she says, "John, I don't want you to use those words around me." And if my friends use them she really jumps on them. I would feel weird if a mother said that and if I didn't know they were gay and someone called their son a faggot and then the mother jumped on them. It would feel weird if I were the kid getting jumped on. Sometimes I say those words and sometimes I just ignore them.

B: What does the word faggot mean to these other kids?

J: Sometimes they just use it as a swear—they don't really mean it. A lot of times now kids are just saying "Aw, you're gay" and it's supposed to be an insult.

A: They also call people lezzies.

J: You probably hear that more than I do—girls would probably hear that more than boys.

B: Do you and your mother's lover get along, Ann?

A: Yeah. Sometimes if I have a friend over it's a little hard 'cause Heidi isn't very careful. And if I have a friend sleep over I just say "Let's go to Dunkin Donuts for breakfast" before they get up. I lie a lot to cover up. I say "My mother's having a friend over because they're making costumes for a party" or something like that. You sort of have to cover up your eyes.

B: Do you feel angry that you have to do that?

A: Yeah! Sometimes I take it out on my mother.

B: How do you take it out on her?

A: If she's having her lover over for dinner I'll start yelling at my mother and say, "Why does she always have to come over?"

B: . . . You mean when it's not as if you don't like her lover, but you're just angry about it . . .

A: Yeah.

J: Some of my good friends were gonna come on a long trip with us but my mother said she'd have to come out to them and I didn't really want to do that. One of them knew but the other friend would probably tell everybody and I didn't want that. And one time we were going out to a fancy restaurant and I said "Ma—no holding hands under the table." And she said "Why not?" and I said "It's kind of embarrassing. What if someone walks in that I know." We got into a big fight and I ended up not going.

B: Does it ever make you angry at society or the rest of the world or do you just get angry at your mother?

A: A lot of people are saying it's against the law to be lesbians or gay isn't it?

B: Well—there are certainly no laws that protect gay people, that's for sure.

A: I don't think that's fair. They shouldn't judge people like that . . . I mean if that's what they want to do they shouldn't hold it against them. They're not really doing anything wrong.

B: Do you agree with that, John?

J: Yeah. A lot of people say it's not normal but then you say, "Well, what is normal?" In the olden days like in Egypt there were a lot of gay men and women. It's been around for a long time . . . like pot . . . in a little while I'm sure it will be legal. It'll be like drinking—there'll be an age limit 'cause it's as bad as drinking. It's something like that. Maybe being gay will be like that but not with an age limit.

B: So you think things are changing?

J: A little but not as much . . .

B: Why do you think things are changing?

J: 'Cause more gay people are coming out and telling the world what they think about it. Just like drinking, but the law changed even though the young people didn't want it to. It's like the young people don't have as much power as grown ups, like gay people don't have as much power as straight people.

B: Do you agree with that, Ann?

A: Yeah.

B: Have either of you seen the film *In the Best Interest of the Children*?

A: No . . . I saw that film on TV about the lesbian mother who had a little boy and a big boy . . .

B: In Texas or something . . .

J: And the father came and took the boy away in the truck?

B: What did you think of that show?

J: It was pretty bad . . . Just because she was a lesbian. And the big boy didn't really want to stay . . . The father had all the money . . . but the little boy wanted to stay with the mother but the judge wouldn't let him. I think it should be up to the kids instead of the law.

B: You mean custody cases.

A: But then if the kids want to change their minds they can always change it I think. The parents might not want it but they should let them do what they want.

J: Unless they're little babies . . . then the parents should decide. I think it still should be the same . . . Like the mother should keep the child until they're old enough to decide.

A: Unless the mother doesn't want to.

J: That's also true. Like in court cases the mother has equal custody of the child unless the child wants to leave real bad.

B: Are there other things you can think of like that, where people should make their own decisions but the law makes it for them?

J: There's a lot of things I can think of but there are good reasons—like drinking and stuff . . . 'Cause teenagers do sometimes over-drink. And if you have a car—especially rich teenagers, who get nice cars and stuff and then go soup them up. If you drink you can have an accident.

B: John, do you get along with your mother's lover?

J: Yeah . . . the thing about my mother's new lover is I like her. She likes my kind of music and she's not that affectionate. My mother's sort of softened her up. She's not that affectionate in public. Before they used to pull the curtains when they would hug and kiss and now they don't as much and it really bothers me. We're on the first floor and people can see in pretty well and it's a busy street.

B: If people did find out, like the neighbors or kids at school . . .

A: Some did . . .

B: How?

A: I don't know—they didn't know for sure. Kids at school. I just said it wasn't true.

B: Were they friends of yours?

Feminist Communications/cpf/LNS

A: Not any more.

B: **What about your real friends?**

A: Two friends know.

J: Are their mothers gay?

A: Janet's mother is bisexual. Her mother and father still sleep together but her mother's also a lesbian.

J: How 'bout your other friend?

A: That's kind of a mystery.

J: Haven't you asked her?

A: Yeah, but she says no, but it kind of looks like it. It's hard to explain. They have lots of roommates. The girl next door knows my mother's gay.

B: **How does she feel about it?**

A: I don't know. I've never talked to her about it.

J: The only friends who know about my mother being gay are kids whose mothers are gay too. I know one of my teachers is gay. I found out by accident. I saw him down in Provincetown holding hands with a guy—and other kids have seen him down there too. My mother said that if he sees me next time and he gets all embarrassed I should just say, "That's all right—my mother's gay too."

B: **Did you hear about the Briggs Initiative in California—that law that they tried to pass which meant that gay people couldn't teach?**

J: I remember that. I don't think that's very fair. I mean they should keep their personal lives out of the job but it's hard. Like once when we got a new teacher everyone started asking him if he had a wife. And I mean it could be awkward for the teacher. Like if he brought his male friend to school he'd have to say it was a brother or friend or something. It's a little awkward. Then if the school board found out, he could get fired.

B: **Have you ever been to any demonstrations, like gay pride day?**

J: No but I went to a conference once. It was kinda awkward last year when I was talking to a friend and said I was going to the conference and I called it a mother's conference and my friend's mother said, "Oh, I'd like to come to that. It sounds interesting," and I had to say it was locked and no new could come. It was like a club . . . it's kinda uncomfortable—not all the time.

B: **How did you like the conference?**

A: It was all right.

B: **What did you like best about it?**

J: There was a big lake out there.

Danny is a 12-year-old boy who lives in the suburbs north of Boston with his mother and his 8-year-old brother.

Betsy: How do you feel about being interviewed? Does it feel weird to you?

Danny: Sort of. I've never been interviewed before. But when I become president of the United States I'll be interviewed a lot.

B: **Maybe I'll come interview you then, I was wondering whether you ever talk to kids at school about your mom being gay?**

D: No. I talk to my friends a lot but we don't talk about homosexual stuff.

B: **Do any of your friends know your mom is gay?**

D: No.

B: **I know the word faggot is used commonly with kids. I was wondering if you get offended by it?**

D: Once in a while but none of my friends use it. Kids who use it probably don't know what it means.

B: **Do you remember what the first things were that you heard about homosexuals?**

D: I don't really remember. I guess I never really thought about it.

B: **Do you have any other friends whose mother or father is gay?**

D: I don't know. I know some kids I know whose parents are divorced but I don't know if they're gay or not.

B: **Does your mother have any friends whose kids are your age?**

D: Yeah. In the Lesbian Mothers' group.

B: **Do the kids get together?**

D: Yeah. They were all going to go camping this week but I'm going away.

B: **Do you get together with that group?**

D: There's big outing every year and we all go camping.

B: **How many people go on these outings?**

D: Last year there were a lot more than the year before. There were about 20 or 30 . . . maybe 15 kids . . . 20 if you count the babies.

B: **Do you hang out with the kids all the time?**

D: Yeah . . . there's John and Joey . . . and I hang out with them.

B: **Do you and John talk about your mothers' being gay? Does it help to know there are other kids with mothers who are gay?**

D: Yeah. It's good to know . . . but I don't feel bad that my mother's a lesbian. We don't talk about it much. The first year when we went there was a rap session and they made sort of a movie about us talking and videotaped it.

B: **What did you rap about?**

D: Oh; I don't know. Two years ago we talked about what the meaning of the word faggot meant. And the different feelings we have about our mothers and our first reactions and if we told other kids . . . stuff like that.

B: **Do you remember more about what you talked about?**

D: I don't remember . . . we didn't do it much last year.

B: **Has it been helpful in some way?**

D: Yeah, just to know . . . sometimes you think you're the only kid whose mother is gay and it's nice to know that there's someone else like that.

B: **Are there things that you can talk about that you really like about your mother being gay?**

D: I don't know. I think my mother can't have a better life than she has now. It's better than most men and women. After she got divorced and was going out with men for a while they weren't as friendly. Judy is real friendly . . . so . . . that's one advantage. And I guess you could call Judy a second mother. She does a lot of stuff with me and my brother. She's real nice and she understands a lot of problems.

B: **Does Judy spend a lot of time with you?**

D: Last week she came out overnight and stayed and then went back. They either divide up the weekend so one night they stay here and then the next night at Judy's or else they spend the whole weekend here with us. Last weekend we all went to New Hampshire to an amusement park for Mother's Day.

B: **Are there ways in which your mother has been involved with Judy that have made you think more about sex roles? Do you know what I'm talking about?**

D: No.

B: **Well, I guess I think there are ways in which we are brought up to believe that boys will be with girls and girls will be with boys and that's what you're supposed to do . . .**

D: I think that it's because homosexuality was never brought out before. It's always been so secret . . . so . . . if you were a homosexual you'd never tell anybody before . . . you'd be totally secret so no one would ever have any way of finding out that boys *can* be with boys and girls can be with girls.

B: **Sounds like it's made you think about that stuff a lot more. Did you think about this a few years ago?**

D: No.

B: **Some people think that the reason**

kids shouldn't grow up with gay parents is that the parents will make them gay. What do you think of that?

D: I think that's a lot of shit.

B: You don't feel pressure from your mother to be gay?

D: No. None.

B: What's it like not having a father in the house?

D: It doesn't matter.

B: Do you think it's necessary that families have fathers?

D: No. Most of the time all fathers do is sit around and watch Monday night football.

B: Do you worry that your friends will find out that your mother's a lesbian?

D: No. It wouldn't bother me if they found out.

B: You're not concerned that they may be upset about it?

D: No.

B: Do you ever go with Judy and your mother to events like Gay Pride Day?

D: Occasionally I go to Lesbian Mothers' night.

B: Do you and your brother talk much about Judy and your mother?

D: No. I don't talk to him much about anything. I like to be as far away from him as possible.

Karl (11 years old) and Maria (12 years old) are brother and sister. Jeff is 10 years old. Charlie is nine years old. All of them live in working class sections of Boston.

B: Jeff's mom told me that some of you went to the Gay Pride Demonstration (1978). How'd you like it?

C: It was all right.

J: It was fun. We threw peanuts at people.

B: At who?

J: At people in the streets.

B: Did you ride on the float?

J: Yeah . . . that's where we threw the peanuts from.

B: Was that the first Gay Pride demonstration you went to?

J: No.

C: Yeah.

J: I been to all of them.

B: How'd you like it?

J: Sometimes it's boring.

C: It's boring when you have to walk all the time.

J: Eating all those peanuts . . . that was heaven.

B: Was it fun? Was it like a parade?

J: Yeah. It was better than a parade.

B: Were there a lot of other kids there?

All: No . . . not that many.

K: There were some little teeny babies . . . 2 months old . . . three months. There was a little baby like that.

B: That big huh? Just fit in your palm?

K: Yeah.

B: Did it feel like a celebration?

J: It felt corny. I felt a little embarrassed when the people on the street would watch you. And they see all these kids. But then you sort of end up feeling proud.

J: It's coming up again in a few weeks.

B: Are you all going to the one this year?

All: Yeah.

J: We can throw some more peanuts!

B: Were there balloons?

J: Yeah. All tied to the float. Lots of gay colors.

C: You mean pink?

B: Do you ever go to anything else that's related to your mother's being gay?

M: Yep. Like going to marches about Governor King or the president.

J: King stinks.

M: And a lot of gay people are there . . . and at the demonstrations for the women who were murdered.

B: Do you ever go to concerts with your mother?

C: Yeah, I do. I went to the Holly Near concert . . . and I went to a couple a long time ago.

B: Did you like them?

C: They were kinda boring but they were okay.

B: I was wondering how you all found out your mother was gay?

J: I don't know. I kept asking her and she never really told me. I just grew up knowing somehow. After you go to all the marches you figure out what it is.

B: Do you and your mother talk about it at all?

J & C: No.

C: I don't like talking about it.

J: Me either.

B: How come?

C: It gets boring.

K: Yeah, you say, "Hey ma, how'd you get gay?"

B: Do you feel okay that she's gay or disappointed?

C: Yeah, I feel good that she's gay because now I got all these friends together.

B: You mean the kids of the different friends of your mother?

C: Yeah.

M: It makes you not feel so alone.

B: Do you get along with your mother's lover?

C: We get along fine. We get along all the time.

B: How do the rest of you get along with your mothers' lovers?

M: I get along with her. She's crazy.

B: How do you mean?

M: Cause she likes to do fun things like go to carnivals and spend money. She likes to go places. Sometimes she tells my mother it's okay if I skip school to go somewhere with her.

C: Really?

K: How come she doesn't do that with us?

B: What else does she do with you besides take you to carnivals?

M: Out to eat and stuff. We play games . . . funny games.

B: Do you think she and your mother have a good relationship?

M: Yeah.

J: Not mine. They're separating right now. I still see Carol cause she lives near here. I feel sad about it but . . .

C: I see my father every summer.

J: I used to go with him but then they had a baby and the baby took my place.

B: Do you feel good that he lives in Maine or would you rather have him living around here?

C: I don't know. I'd rather live with both of them instead so I could see them all the time.

B: Do your other friends at school know your mother's gay?

All: No.

C: I'd get laughed at.

K: I'd be embarrassed.

M: I wouldn't.

K: You wouldn't be embarrassed?

M: No. I wouldn't be embarrassed. If they don't like it that's too bad. You can't change it.

C: And it's not your fault.

K: I would get embarrassed though. Just because they make fun of you.

J: But I bet lots of kids in the class—their mothers are lesbians if they ever brought it up. They probably wouldn't believe you if you told them your mother's gay.

B: Has anyone ever been mean to you because of it?

M: Yeah. Sometimes when you're walking in the march or something they look at you like you're crazy or something.

J: Yeah. And they stare and say, "Kids . . . how could kids do that!"

B: Do any kids use the word "faggot" or "queer" at school?

All: Yep.

J: They have fights and call each other faggots and stuff like that.

C: This kid called me a lezzie once.

B: What do you think she meant by that?

C: I bet she don't know what it means. She said, "Hey lezbo."

K: I use those words sometimes. It's just another word. Faggot to me means sissy.

B: Do you think that's a bad thing to be?
K: No.

C: I used to be a sissy.

B: Then why do you call people faggots?

K: Just to get rid of them . . . or make them chase you or something.

J: I use those words sometimes, but when I think about it after, I think I'm just making fun of my own parent. I use it but I know in my own head what I'm really saying.

B: Do you feel proud of your mother being a lesbian?

J: Yeah, in a way.

K: Yeah, kinda. When I found out that my mother was gay it just dawned on me— what is that? I didn't know what it is.

J: I thought it meant real happy.

K: Yeah. Me too. She said, "I'm gay" and I said, "I know you're happy."

B: Do you have adult men you're friends with?

All: Yeah.

C: Some of them are gay too.

B: Is it important to you to have them as friends?

All: No.

J: It doesn't really matter. It's just that you know there's someone around who cares for you. . . that knows your parents are gay and won't make fun of you or anything or laugh at you.

B: Some people would say that if your mother's a lesbian and has a son that . . .

J: They're supposed to be called a bastard if they do.

C: Yeah. I'm no bastard.

B: Well, I was thinking more that people think it's bad because a son should have a father . . . what do you think of that?

J: I think it's wrong, really. They can make it through their life without having a father all the time.

B: Some people also think that gay people shouldn't have kids because their kids might grow up thinking they should be gay.

J: I don't think it's true because a kid can grow up to be whatever he wants to be. He can be gay or straight.

K: I know. I could get married if I want.

J: I'm not going to be either one of them. I'm just gonna live by myself . . . me and my alligator. And I'm gonna get a St. Bernard and a monkey.

K: I'm gettin' me a BIG dog. I might have some kittens and a dog.

B: I was wondering if you knew who Anita Bryant is?

M: Yeah . . . I know a lot about her.

B: Like what?

M: She don't like gay people and all that stuff.

B: What do you think of people like Anita Bryant who thinks that gay people

---

shouldn't be allowed to do certain things . . . like be teachers for example?**

M: Well, if she wants to be against them that's all right but she shouldn't be like that.

B: Like what?

M: Like that. If she wants to be against gay people she should keep it to herself and not tell other people that stuff.

B: How would you feel if one of your teachers was gay?

M: I wouldn't mind. It wouldn't make any difference. They're probably the same as any other teacher.

---

spare **Rib**

From *Spare Rib*, no. 86 (September 1979), pp. 43-47

How Did We Get This Way?

by Sue Cartlege and Susan Hemmings

If you are a lesbian, chances are you've spent a lot of time wondering how you got that way. Heterosexuals rarely give their sexuality a second thought. They may worry about sex and all its complications but it won't usually have crossed their minds to ask themselves why they've grown up heterosexual. And very probably no-one has ever asked them to justify or explain it.

This one-sided state of affairs, where homosexuality is seen as deviating from what is 'natural', accounts for the kinds of questions we as lesbians ask ourselves about our sexuality, and the kinds of answers we can come up with. If you have to start by assuming you're the one who is different, even before you can ask yourself why and how, you will come up with different explanations than if you assume you're 'normal'. Heterosexual people could ask themselves all the questions raised here, but they don't. Not unless they're among the handful of feminists who are especially interested in the effect of social

pressures on the way we develop our sexual identity.

It's not only a climate of 'difference' in which lesbians have to define themselves but one of almost total *in*difference. It's not just, "Why am I like this?" but, "Do I really exist at all?" Even when people are *trying* to be helpful, lesbians constantly fail to get a mention: "We must recognise the fact that love, whether it be between a man and woman, or man and man, can achieve a pure and glorious relationship if it is expressed with restraint and discipline." (Bishop of Southwark, June 1979.)

Being able to assert that you're alive and well and lesbian often leads to becoming more interested in why it is that, despite all the counter pressures, and despite the conspiracy of silence on the subject, you've managed to end up that way. Here are some of the discussions we've had with each other and with friends about the origins of our lesbianism. We looked at the more frequently encountered theories— some of them seem to contain grains of truth, but none are totally satisfactory. They can't be, because they are inherited from a society which classifies us as unnatural and unhealthy.

*So, how did it start, how did it all begin? I'm trying, yes, I'm trying hard to find My lesbian . . . origin.**

---

*The poems which follow are verses from a song, 'Lesbian Origin', which Susan wrote for the Lesbian Left Revue Theatre Group, and the quotations are from conversations with Sue's friends.

Baby Bio:
The Genetic Explanation

Now what's the problem, sisters?
I'll tell you what I say—
It's quite straightforward, the reason why
I'm gay:
Way back in the embryo I was formed that
way.

"I knew I was different. I just wasn't interested in the things the other girls were into—boys, clothes, makeup, etc. I was a tomboy. My father kept saying: 'It's time you got out of those dungarees and into a skirt.' I played a lot of sport specially netball, because I was in love with the netball teacher. I just kept falling in love with women all the time—never with men. I was very isolated. I didn't have any images of lesbians, didn't really know what the word meant. I just knew I was different.

Many women, both heterosexual and lesbian, remember being strongly resistant to efforts to 'feminise' them when they were younger—and have memories of always being different in their choice of playthings, games or friends. Many had crushes on other girls and women. Lesbians often say that they were aware, as far back as they can remember, of being strongly attracted to girls and women. But the difference for those lesbians from heterosexual women with the same memories is that lesbians placed an important emotional significance on those experiences. We didn't 'outgrow' it or 'transfer' it onto boys. Lesbians who feel this is specially true of their history often say they were *born* lesbian.

This was the view of Radclyffe Hall, who told the publisher of her book, *The Well of Loneliness* (first printed in 1928), that homosexuals, "being from birth set apart in accordance with some hidden scheme of nature, need all the help that society can give them". It's an explanation which homosexuals themselves use, when they are putting their trust in the liberal tolerance of the great mass of heterosexuals.

The idea that homosexuality is an innate, inherited characteristic, a freak of the genes, has twin advantages. It reassures nervous heterosexuals that they can't catch it: after all, if it's genetic, it can't be infectious. And it allows us to say that it's not really our fault: after all, you can't punish us for a handicap. But there are serious and dangerous drawbacks to this explanation. It can, and has led to the views held by those who think we should be exterminated. Hitler had thousands of homosexuals slaughtered along with the Jews and other groups he considered less than human. Then there is the contemporary research featured in May of this year, on BBC's *Horizon*. In 'The Fight to Be Male' homosexuality was discussed in these terms: "Derner is now studying mothers in the fourth month of pregnancy, the time which he believes is the critical period . . . He is measuring the testosterone levels in their wombs . . . He follows the selected children growing up, to prove low testosterone in the womb leads to homosexuality . . . then the next step might be to inject (*into the womb*) more testosterone—and so prevent homosexuality" . . . and thus breed us off the planet, as if we were mutations.

At an entirely less objectionable, though still personally painful level, these genetic arguments lead to the commonly held belief that there are two kinds of homosexuals: those who were born like it, so can't help it, and those who were born 'normal'—but are just plain wilful. Mother of a lesbian: "You want all the fun, and none of the responsibility." Daughter of a lesbian: "You could at least *try* to find a man. After all, you must have done it at least once."

It's not surprising that under such pressures, many of us who do not really believe we were 'born' lesbian, often want to claim that we were, just to get the nagging world off our backs. Look, we say, lay off, we can't change just to suit you. But those of us who are feminists, as well as lesbians, have a deep suspicion of all genetic theorists, knowing how often they've used their research to 'prove' that women are born inferior to men, or blacks to whites.

For us, the major drawback of the total dependency of biology as an explanation is that it leaves no room for the possibility of changing sexuality, or sexual practice, or attitudes toward these. And it successfully lets heterosexuals off the hook from ever having to explain *their* sexual selves.

Psycho-Dyke:
Theories from Your Dark Past

"Please tell me expert therapist
Why've I grown up a freak?
I hate being gay
And I'm going up the creek."
"Your mummy was too dominant,
your daddy frail and weak.
But don't despair, for help is here:
your future's not too bleak.

That's ten pounds fifty please, and
I'll see you Tuesday week."

"When I was five, I can remember walking with my mother down a long, dark lane to our house. And I remember saying to her, 'Don't be frightened, Mum.' I always felt very protective towards her. My father was away a great deal, and I think that's why I'm a lesbian."

'Psychological' theories of the origins of homosexuality are perhaps even more popular now than biological ones. In some ways this is progress. At least psychological theories, through their examination of early relationships, pay some recognition to the idea that sexuality may not be 'natural' and God-given, but formed by the society we live in, and by our own particular backgrounds.

Many women have found that exploring the past, through consciousness raising or through feminist therapy, has been enormously liberating, shedding light on murky private fears and lifting the burden of guilt. It has given us the opportunity to make some sense of our personal history, by discovering how much of it is similar to other women's. So exploring our lives in this way has been very rewarding for many women, lesbian or otherwise.

But in the 'common-sense' world outside the radical influence of feminist theory, lesbianism is still seen as a deviation from the norm. Psychology doesn't tell us we are morally reprehensible, but the drift of the explanations it gives us is still negative: "immaturity" in failing to transfer the early love for the mother on to the father; "mother-fixation" resulting from a broken home or not enough love and affection in childhood. Psychology may claim to make no judgments. But lesbianism is still seen as a problem to be analysed, often an illness to be treated. In any case we can't win. Even those rare psychologists who don't start off by seeing us as freaks say that the pressures we have to live with will *make* us into freaks. Phyllis Chesler (*Women and Madness* 1972) describes this trap: "Most psychoanalytic theorists either sincerely misunderstand or severely condemn lesbianism. Some do both. The 'condition', they say, is biologically or hormonally based. No say others, it is really an environmental phenomenon. In any event all agree, it is maladaptive, regressive and infantile: even if it isn't it leads to undeniable suffering—and is therefore maladaptive, regressive and infantile."

Psychological explanations which are mainly rooted in our childhoods can sometimes mean endless agonising over 'coming out' to the family. This, rather than confronting the wider world's attitudes to us, comes to be seen as the crucial problem. Hard though it is to do, accepting that you'll have to go ahead in your life without your family's approval is something not reserved for homosexuals alone. Most people who hold radical political views, or live subversive lifestyles, have had to rid themselves of the 'parent in their heads', or at least shut a big door on some of their past lives.

As far as the media are concerned, psychology can be used to explain all female aberrations, not just lesbianism. Women terrorists are depicted as spoilt middle class malcontents longing to get back at their fathers. Violence among teenage girls is the result of reversed sex-roles, with women's liberation to blame. And psychology is used to predict the dire results of feminism—a generation of farmed-out, nursery-reared children with no sense of security. We are all sick, unless we conform to men's idea of femininity— pretty, passive and unchallenging.

The notion that those of us who haven't conformed are strong and healthy, rather than weak, sickly deviants, hasn't yet gained much popular appeal! Lots of people still believe that lesbians are women who, because they are too ugly to attract men, or because they've had bad experiences with men, turn to each other for comfort. A male Labour MP visiting a Sappho meeting exclaimed with genuine surprise, "But this room is full of attractive women!" It's true that many of us have given up the search for Mr Right. Is that a weakness? Why potter on with hope in your heart—for what might be a lifetime— looking for that non-sexist dream man? Psychologists have seen us as battle-scarred invalids who couldn't take any more in the rough and tumble of hetero-sexual competition, rather than as strong-minded realists with a positive preference for women. Lesbians have had to be tremendously strong to resist all the pressures which insist that women search out Mr Right. So it's hard to see why the image of us as 'invalids' has survived for so long.

Cupid's Dart:
The Romantic Conversion

Why do you want to make things so very black or white?
I'm not an actual lesbian, so don't label me, all right?

I just met my girlfriend at a party one night . . .
It's not her sex that matters. It just feels right.

"I think I'm a lesbian because I fell in love with a woman. I suppose I could have fallen in love with a man, and I'd be heterosexual. I don't know, because I've never felt that total emotional involvement with a man. But I didn't think of myself as a lesbian—not until my girlfriend called me a 'fucking lesbian'. The only images I had of lesbians were of pipes and tweeds, and I knew I wasn't like *that*."

So does love really conquer all—even the massive edifice of heterosexuality? Certainly most women become lesbian through powerful romantic feelings for another woman. And such feelings (stars crossing, bolts from the blue, chemistry at work . . .) often *seem* to enter our lives from outside, sweeping us off our feet. But it's unlikely that we just happen to fall in love. We create and nurture romantic feelings, consciously or otherwise, partly to give ourselves the chance to make emotional leaps, and to bring about drastic changes in our lives which we otherwise might not dare to make—such as straight to gay.

Heterosexual romance is highly valued but, as yet, gay romance has had a mixed response. In the sex-education kit recently published by the Campaign for Homo-sexual Equality, ideas about 'romance' are used to get the tolerance of the straight teenager. As prime targets for romance propaganda they will *surely* be under-standing of the gay teenager who's only asking for the same 'right' of someone to love? But even the romantic explanation has not so far, brought us society's indulgence. Maureen Colquhoun's rela-tionship with her lover was presented in that way in a *Woman's Own* article last year: 'It's Marvellous to be in Love Again'. "It simply didn't matter whether she was a man or a woman", ran the article. But it certainly did matter to Maureen's political colleagues, who campaigned locally and nationally for her to be removed from her job as MP.

Lesbians who use romance as the total explanation for their sexual preference sometimes cut themselves off from other lesbians, because they seem to be saying, "I might be one now but next time, who knows, it might be a man." No-one likes being straightjacketed. We all complain now and then about being labelled, stuck in a group we don't entirely identify with. But

lesbianism is a wider experience, a deeper commitment than can be contained within one individual and privatised passionate relationship. To represent lesbianism just in terms of one, or even a series, of intense romantic experiences would not account for the loving feelings which many lesbians have for women friends, and women in general. There are many celibate lesbians, who are not just waiting for the next big romance to show up. Heterosexuals do not 'lose' their sexuality when they are celibate. Nor is a lesbian less of one if she is not within a sexual relationship. Sexuality cannot be collapsed into sex, nor can love be contained just within romance.

The Sisterhood Theory

We came home from the meeting feeling utterly depressed.
Why can't Arthur Scargill see that women are oppressed?
Linda stayed all night: in the morning we caressed,
And I realised all the loving feelings I'd suppressed. . . .

"I began being attracted to other women as soon as I started going to women's liberation conferences. I suppose my life had become more and more involved with women, and they seemed far more interesting than my husband, or any men, more exciting, more glamorous. And I certainly saw lesbians as the elite of the movement—as well as being very nervous of them. Looking back now, I suppose I can trace elements of my earlier life which with hindsight could be pointers to lesbianism. I was always very competitive with boys when I was a kid. I never wanted to be like my mother, stuck for years staring across a pile of dirty dishes at the neighbours' side wall. But without the women's movement, I just don't know if I would ever have taken the step of becoming a lesbian. The only images I had before were of fat girls at school with spots who held hands in the back row when we had a film—I assumed they turned to each other because boys rejected them. As soon as I heard about gay liberation, and positive images of gayness, I changed my views."

This quotation isn't necessarily typical of all the hundreds of women who've become lesbians 'through the movement'. To many of us, lesbianism contained not so much a glamorous excitement, or a way of marriage, but rather an extension of the closeness that grows up between women working together politically, and depending on each other, as well as enjoying more relaxed times. A lot of us asked ourselves, "If I'm feeling all these things for women, why am I keeping my sexual feelings separate?" It began to seem like a false and unnecessary separation, forced on us by men. That is not to say that women who choose to remain heterosexual, or who tried lesbianism, but gave up, are behaving 'falsely'. Many such women have said they feel very 'oppressed' by lesbians in the movement who, they say, present their sexuality as more feminist. But all along the problem has been that it's lesbians who have had to explain themselves, not heterosexuals. So it must come as something of a painful shock to women who are sexually drawn to men, when they feel they have to justify it. They are experiencing what lesbians have always had to endure—having to explain themselves.

The history of the women's movement both here and in the States includes a period when feminists didn't want lesbians to be terribly vocal, in case it put other women off joining. And such attitudes still exist. In consciousness raising groups women exchange anxieties about lesbianism, and constantly have to deal with boyfriends and husbands taunting them on the topic. And when two women do decide to become lovers, enraged husbands and all the local papers scream 'Women's Lib Turned Her Into A Man Hater'. It's hardly surprising that women prefer to skate around the issue of sexual preference, except for a brief "Well, I don't know, I've just always needed a man in that kind of way". Lots of women feel they have cracked sexism in their personal lives, either by finding a nice man who isn't so hung up on conventional sex roles, or by training one not to be. Indeed, by doing so they have struggled to make painful and important changes in their lives. But sexism is not just about sex roles; and having the good luck to find your Mr Right won't change a sexist society. Nor, automatically, will finding Ms Right. But a lesbian relationship is far more threatening to the status quo than even the most radically reformed heterosexual one.

"When I first joined the women's movement, as a heterosexual feminist, my women's group spent most of the time talking about sexuality and relationships. We talked for hours about sex, problems with men, how we resented sex roles (like how come men have this inability to clean cookers), how we hated being whistled at in the street, how we had been shy teenagers,

how men had let us down—all those kinds of things. But we never wondered how we got to be heterosexual. The question just didn't arise. I suppose, like the rest of the world, we assumed that was the norm. So all our questioning about why a woman's role *within* heterosexuality was constructed in such and such a way, never once extended to questioning heterosexuality itself."

But even if you become a lesbian through your feminism—growing to love and trust other women, and choosing your sexuality—you still won't escape the sexologists. It is still biological freaks plus psychological cripples versus the rest. Recent American researchers call the (relatively) chosen homosexuality of women's movement lesbians *pseudo*homosexuality. According to them, if we weren't born this way, or if we didn't get this way because of inadequate parenting, we're just damn phoneys.

So What's the Answer

So, how did it start, how did it all begin?
We're trying, yes, we're trying hard to find
*   our lesbian origin.*
If only we could find it, it would be just
*   great—*
Then the straights could tell us how they
*   got so straight.*
So let's think about it sisters—but where
*   should we begin . . .*
Is it a sociological,
Biological,
Psychological,
Astrological, or . . .
Phenomenological
Lesbian origin?

We ourselves find it hard to choose any one particular theory about our lesbianism, especially because they are all far too close, except for the Sisterhood Theory, to the kinds of ideas foisted upon us all our lives by people who wish we'd grown up 'normal'. We certainly reject, as total explanations, all those which end up making us feel hopeless and powerless—like Born That Way, or Psychologically Disordered—because these only serve the purposes of those who would like us to shut up, and put up with our misfortune as invisibly as possible. Then again, we personally don't place too much trust in the theory, popular among some feminists, which places us at the forefront of all women, as utopian models of what all women could achieve, if only. . . . For one thing, we think it's extremely unlikely that there'll ever be a day when all women

are lesbian. And for another, being 'models' would be a pretty intolerable burden, given the reality of our messy everyday lives.

So we mainly go along with the idea that sexuality is constructed out of general social conditioning, which men control, and have done for centuries, saying what women may do and how. And within that warping culture, each of us has a particular and personal history. Like heterosexual feminists, we are clear in our minds that heterosexuality, as it is practised in our society, is a key part of the system which always benefits men. Romance, legalisation of pair-bonding, raising of children within the enclosed and privatised family, are all bound together in ways which oppress women. It is through heterosexuality that most people see this whole interlinking system as 'normal' and even 'natural', a perception which for most people is so fixed that they can't even question it.

There has been considerable pressure from some gay groups over the past few years to say to the straight world, look, we're just the same as you, we just want equal rights. This has been the main element in the campaigns of gay reformers. In many ways our lives *are* the same. And obviously we can't change everything, even where we'd like to. Yet we ourselves feel that we really are different. We want to take our difference, whatever its origin, and study so we can understand it *in our own terms*. We think it's up to us to say why our difference is important, and how we want to use it. It is not for heterosexuals to contain us within their oppressive and defensive definitions.

Among lesbian feminists there is no 'correct line' on how we came to be this way. Ultimately we do not want to spend too much time in the tunnel of research into our individual pasts—the possibility for changing things lies ahead, not behind. And we've all to some extent now come out of the tunnel with the ability to proclaim, against all odds, the potential of women to love other women, and to include our sexuality within that love. For us, "How did we get this way?" isn't a little cry of bewilderment in a hard world, but a challenge to everyone who still thinks that sexuality has nothing to do with politics, and that sexual preference is an inherited and unchangeable part of their nature.

We'd like to thank all the women who've helped us work out the ideas and to write this article.

9 WORK

The uneasy relationship between organized labor and movements for change has had a long history in this country. The labor movement itself grew from the radical idea that workers should unite to gain better working conditions, better pay, better chances at achieving common dreams. Yet big unions have become as much a pillar of established society as big corporations, and the apparent success of pure and simple unionism has made any radical philosophy anathema to their leadership. One notable exception was the Congress of Industrial Organizations in the 1930s. The recession of the 1970s and 1980s, however, has forced many who were satisfied with the gains in wages and benefits to reevaluate the union philosophy that is not saving their jobs, and the economy may yet provoke the same impulses as it did in the era of the Great Depression. This section takes a look at the various fronts on which the battle is being waged.

Not only economic pressures but pressures from management and government as well may radicalize union members. The mass media also plays its role, as is shown in the article from *The Militant*. American newspapers and magazines are supporting the struggle of the Polish workers to overthrow their oppressors, although they usually take the other side in domestic union questions. Their support is ironic, for they misconstrue the real intent of Solidarity as a return to capitalism, when it is in fact an attempt at worker control. It is further evidence of the blindness that comes with adherence to the status quo.

That even the seeming obsequiousness of American unions has not been enough for American business is clear as whole factories are abandoned in the search of cheaper, non-union, labor markets, and existing unions and organizing drives are harassed and crippled. The articles from *Northwest Passage* and *Dollars and Sense* tell of the "union free" strategy, while those from *Equal Times, Southern Struggle,* and *Changes* tell of the attempts of migrant laborers and millworkers to gain justice. Another part of management union-busting attempts, more subtle in approach, is the productivity myth, which Kim Moody and Thom Richardson explode as an attempt to pass the inflated buck. *Radical America*'s in-depth study of economic influences on the auto industry shows how precarious is the linchpin of the economy and how necessary is a vigorously radical union position.

Union members are fighting back: against management and, in more difficult situations, against their own conservative leaders. The Women's Alliance to Gain Equality gives tips on fighting union busting and sexual harassment on the job. Steve Dawson looks at worker-ownership plans, where employees move toward controlling the product of their labor, while John Darwin and Hilary Wainwright report on British workers and community members who are demanding more of a say in the decisions made on the line. The most touchy problem—trying to change the leadership inside the union without harming the union itself—is one that is being fought by the rank and file of many unions. *Convoy Dispatch* records the discontent of teamsters with their management-oriented leaders.

Women at work suffer these problems and many others. Working in newly opened positions, they are the vanguard who are fighting hard for equality. *Off Our Backs* and *Heresies* look at the blue-collar woman in Martha Tabor's interview with Linda Butcher, a woman doing a "man's" job, and Constance Pohl's story on women on the docks. *Big Mama Rag* looks apprehensively at the white-collar woman in a review of a book on the training techniques for the executive, professional woman. Kristin Lems gives us a song of the land and the women who farm it. And Leo Griffin shows us men in the nurturing role, the traditionally female work.

—LD & ES

A SOCIALIST NEWSWEEKLY/PUBLISHED IN THE INTERESTS OF THE WORKING PEOPLE

From *The Militant* 44, no. 32 (September 5, 1980): 23

How U.S. Gov't, Media View Polish Events

by Suzanne Haig

The capitalist press in this country has responded to the upsurge of Polish workers with expressions of sympathy. The *New York Times* in an August 19 editorial even called the workers' demands "exhilarating."

"The insurgent workers," they rejoiced, "are not talking about just food and wages. They are also demanding the unthinkable —political rights."

The U.S. government has been more cautious. With the elections in view, Carter has dropped gentle hints that he sympathizes with the Polish workers, but the government has carefully avoided any statements that might be viewed as encouraging the workers or criticizing the Polish government.

But are the U.S. rulers and their news media really as sympathetic to the Polish workers as they claim?

One thing should arouse immediate suspicion. Since when has the government or press given sympathy to workers' struggles in this country?

No major paper hailed the demands of striking oil workers earlier this year. And when the transit workers struck this spring in New York City not just for "food and wages," but also "demanding the unthinkable"—the political right to strike against the city government—the *Times* supported the imposition of heavy fines against them.

No. The media and the rulers of this country have not one drop of sympathy for the Polish workers. They have merely seized the opportunity to make some propaganda against socialism.

For example, the August 21 *Christian Science Monitor* wrote: "What is billed

Reprinted with permission from *The Militant: A Socialist Newsweekly,* 14 Charles Lane, New York, NY 10014.

as a Workers' Paradise is, in fact, a workers' prison in which the industrial workers are deprived of any say in the government."

Socialism means a low standard of living and the absence of political rights, they state, while capitalism, by implication, means the opposite.

But the Polish workers don't regret having overthrown capitalism and established a workers' state. They oppose only the bureaucrats who misrule that state.

They have no desire to go back to capitalism which brought nothing but poverty, hunger, illiteracy, disease, foreign rule, and fascism to Poland.

They don't want to turn the steel mills, shipyards, railroads, and mines over to individual capitalists. They are not fighting for *less* control over production and government, but *more* control. They want to advance toward socialism.

They believe they can better lead society than the narrow-minded corrupt bureaucrats who are only concerned with maintaining their privileges at the workers' expense.

The U.S. rulers are playing a double game. While they gush over the plight of the Polish workers, they support the austerity measures which the Polish government is taking against these workers.

They harp on the importance of the Polish government paying its $20 billion debt to capitalist banks in the United States, West Germany, Britain, and France.

Big business wants the debt—including the extortionist interest rates charged by the bankers—to be taken out of the workers' hides.

Thus the *Wall Street Journal* complained August 21 about the Polish government's policy of "buying off workers' discontent with various subsidies" which had kept the prices of meat and other necessities "artificially low relative to income." It sounds a lot like their complaints about the "excessive" wages and benefits of workers over here.

In the same vein, the August 22 *Christian Science Motor* praised the effort of the Polish government to "put its economic house in order."

"Raising meat prices—the issue which sparked the labor strikes—was a reasonable thing to do," they said.

And in words familiar to every American worker it added, "The workers need to appreciate the need for labor discipline and higher productivity."

Some support.

Much of the press coverage has been occupied with fears of possible Soviet troop intervention into Poland. Such claims are used to portray the workers' struggle as hopeless and to suggest that the workers better go back to work quietly lest they provoke Moscow.

The talk about Soviet troops is also used to try to line up the American people behind Washington's murderous foreign policy.

The spectre of Soviet action is a means of justifying reinstituting the draft, beefing up the nuclear arsenal, spending more on the military budget, at a time when the American people are opposed to such war moves.

Despite this propaganda, Washington's interests in Poland today lie with the Stalinist governments in Moscow and Warsaw—not with the workers.

This was indicated in an article in the *New York Times* by Bernard Gwertzman on August 25. "For the moment," Gwertzman noted, "there seems to be a convergence of interests in Washington and Moscow, with both capitals interested in seeing Poland's rulers and populace working out a suitable compromise that avoids disruptions that would threaten the stability of central Europe."

Since Washington cannot hope to foster a capitalist counterrevolution in Poland, it supports the Gierek government. They know this government will do nothing to inspire the masses at home or abroad to struggle for a socialist future.

The gains being won by the Polish workers terrify Washington and Wall Street.

The Polish workers are showing us, along with working people around the world, how to fight against attacks on our rights and standard of living.

They are demonstrating in action the tremendous power that workers can wield against their oppressors.

Further victories by the Polish workers could raise the possibility of a revolutionary workers' government emerging in Poland. Imagine a Cuba in the heart of industrialized Europe!

When push comes to shove Washington

would certainly prefer even an invasion by Soviet troops to that outcome.

The heroic fight of the Polish workers is directly in the interests of working people in this country. They deserve our full solidarity.

'Same Old Merchandise!'

ATTACKS ON DEMOCRACY

Northwest Passage

From *Northwest Passage* 20, no. 4 (January 29-February 18, 1980): 7

It May Be Slick, But It's Still Union Busting

by Louis Howe

Union busting for the 1980s may be taking on a new face, but don't be fooled. It might look benevolent, but it is still union busting. On January 10 and 11 the ANALOG Corporation in Seattle scalped business people $500 apiece for attending a management seminar called "MAKING UNIONS UNNECESSARY While Increasing Profits and Productivity." Months before ANALOG's president Steve Keely had sent out invitations to prospective companies.

"Good Morning!" begins the sales pitch. "Knowing what your people think, how they think, and why they act the way that they do is the basis for your ability to *increase profits and productivity* and enables you to remain union free."

Keely's attitudes towards unions and workers is naively candid. His use of the phrase "your people" to refer to workers is just as condescending as wealthy southerners used to be when they referred to "our negroes." But management often talks about workers that way, and it seems natural enough for a manager to regard unions as a threat to "profits and productivity." What is new here is the idea of manipulating workers' *psyches*. The question isn't whether or not a union is needed, but whether or not workers *think* a union is needed. Dr. Charles Hughs came all the way from Dallas to tell Keely's clients just how to keep workers thinking that they don't need unions.

It sounded like a good idea to over thirty companies. Companies like K2 Corporation, Universal Seafoods, and Boise

Reprinted with permission from *Northwest Passage*.

Cascade all sent people to the seminar to hear the Hughs message. It was a little paternalism mixed with deceit.

"This is not an anti-union seminar," Keely told the *Seattle Times*. "It is the same thing they (the unions) are talking about. We're interested in good management to the point where unions are irrelevant. The unions don't understand that."

What crap! "Good management" might fool some workers into believing they don't need their unions, but the only way to make unions truly irrelevant would be to create industries with no bosses. A seminar designed to do that might be called, MAKING MANAGERS UNNECESSARY WHILE DECREASING WORKER EXPLOITATION.

Keely's comments failed to reassure the union members picketing his seminar. The picketers were great. They were coordinated by Local 8 of the Hotel, Motel, Restaurant Employees and Bartenders Union, and they disrupted things to the point where the seminar had to move several times.

"We raised so much hell they had to move," said Jeanie Barr, picket coordinator. The seminar had to leave a hotel, then a marina, and finally wound up at the Tyee Yacht Club on Seattle's Lake Union.

The picketers were close behind. "We just followed them," said Barr, "we wondered where in the world they were going. They started going down all these little streets. I don't know how they ever found that place."

The Tyee is a private club. A man wearing a coat and tie and holding a two-way radio stood outside checking membership cards. The picketers couldn't get inside. It was raining and the seminar was almost over. Everybody decided to leave.

This was the second seminar of its type to be held in Seattle this winter. The first, Martin Jay Levitt's "Living Without Unions," was held in November. Union pickets were so vocal that Levitt canceled the second half of his presentation and left town. Two more anti-union seminars are scheduled for the spring, the next one in April. Local 8 of the Hotel, Motel, Restaurant Employees and Bartenders Union will be there. Anyone wishing to help out should call them at (206) 624-2326.

dollars & Sense

A Monthly Bulletin of Economic Affairs

From *Dollars & Sense*, no. 61 (November 1980), p. 18

Busting the Union-Busters

information from Charles Bagli

Reprinted with permission from *Dollars & Sense,* a monthly magazine which offers a critical view of the U.S. economy in non-technical language.

Skoler, Abbott and Hayes is a prospering law firm operating out of Springfield, Massachusetts. Their specialty is union busting, particularly in hospitals and related health care establishments. But after chalking up a string of successes at hospitals across New England, the law firm struck out at the Amherst Nursing Home in Amherst, Massachusetts.

The nursing home's 65 workers, mostly women with an average pay of $3.26 an hour, are represented by District 1199 Health Care Employee Union. Co-owners

Betty Kravetz and Louis Cohn hoped to rid the nursing home of the union and any ideas of improvement when the contract ran out last May. And three months more of negotiating only produced a measly 25 cents an hour wage increase.

Management's strategy was to force a strike, knowing that the workers, many of whom bring home $99 a week, could not afford to stay out long. Union organizers, recognizing the handiwork of Skoler, Abbott and Hayes, then went on the offensive. Before the strike, informational picket lines were held at the nursing home to publicize the issues: a living wage, better patient care, and union security. Leaflets explained that low wages meant high turnover (45 out of 65 workers in three months) which in turn led to inadequately trained staff.

Three days before the strike, the union organized a demonstration at Skoler, Abbott and Hayes' offices. The rally was held to highlight the central issue of union busting *before* management could dominate the media with claims of workers' indifference to proper health care.

The strike began on schedule and as it developed, so did broad community support. The area was inundated with leaflets. Students and faculty from the University of Massachusetts, a tenant group (Cohn also owns apartment complexes in the area), women's groups, university clerical staff (also negotiating with Skoler, Abbott and Hayes), and members of a nearby United Electrical Workers local walked the picket line and donated badly needed funds.

In the course of the strike fifteen people were arrested. The town manager, fearing escalating trouble, ordered police not to escort scabs into the nursing home as they had been doing. Scores of picketers continued to show up at 5:30 every morning. And on the day before management finally began to negotiate again, women workers from the nursing home led a spirited march of 300 through downtown Amherst. Town officials, in a panic to preserve the bucolic image of their college town, pressured management to "please settle," which they did, on the sixth day of the strike. The strikers won a wage increase, safety language and an agency shop.

The AFL-CIO estimates that there are now more than 300 firms specializing in the multi-million dollar practice of foiling union elections or breaking unions. But union activists facing firms like Skoler, Abbott and Hayes can win even at small establishments like the Amherst Nursing Home.

Men against women, white against black —that's the kind of "Industrial Relations" this Company likes to see!

Cindy Fredrick/LNS

UNION W.A.G.E.

From *Union W.A.G.E.*, no. 58 (March/April 1980), pp. 8-10

What Can You Do When the Union-Busters Come to *Your* Workplace?

by Tish Fabens

EDITOR'S NOTE: *3M, a union-busting firm active in more than 100 representation elections a year, works with industries with large numbers of women employees, including hospitals, insurance companies, universities, banks, and retail stores.*

Professional union-busting is a growing business these days. Companies of high-priced consultants are offering employers slick consulting services to make sure their employees never organize. The largest of these union-busting companies is known as 3M and has a "success" rate of 93%. Originally known as Melnick, Mickus, and

Reprinted with permission from *Union W.A.G.E.: A Working Women's Newspaper.*

McKeown, the firm is now called Modern Management Methods. 3M is located in Deerfield, Illinois, outside of Chicago, although the 50-60 consultants working for the firm have been found working all over the country. Paid up to $850 a day, the 3M consultants run a very sophisticated, behind-the-scenes anti-union campaign, using threats, intimidation, personal attacks, and firings if necessary. 3M is best known for its work in hospitals, but it has also worked with universities, manufacturing and retail businesses, and banks. The anti-union campaigns in each workplace are very similar. For this reason much can be learned about the strategy and tactics of 3M from workers who have been through such a campaign. Hospital workers in several Boston hospitals and the clerical and technical workers at Boston University have had experience with 3M during unionizing efforts over the past several years. Only District 65 at Boston University has been able to defeat 3M in Boston. The suggestions from these organizing groups of how to fight 3M were very similar and are presented here to help union activists who encounter anti-union consulting firms in their workplaces.

Divide and Conquer

First let's look at the strategy and tactics of the 3M anti-union campaign. Management usually contacts 3M when the first signs of serious unionizing activity appear. The consultants agree to work for the company only if their presence in the workplace is kept a secret *and* if they have total control over the decisions made during the anti-union campaign, such as disciplinings, firings, and grievances. Both administrators and supervisors are held accountable to the consultants, and anyone who breaks the rules of the "game" set up by the firm puts his/her job on the line.

The first thing 3M does when it comes into a workplace is to get a general picture of the departments that will be in the bargaining unit. The racial, sexual, and ethnic makeup of each department is noted, as well as where there has been organized discontent, what the general union sentiment is, and what the complaints are in particular departments. As the drive progresses, the consultants focus on specific departments and individuals in an effort to divide and conquer.

Racism is one of the most common tools 3M uses to divide workers—telling white workers that such-and-such a union is a "black union" and they wouldn't want to belong to it, or trying to convince workers of different departments that they have nothing in common and so shouldn't work together. Whatever tensions exist among people in a workplace will be noticed and inflamed by 3M in order to divide people and defeat the union.

A general strategy of 3M is to have anti-union workers work for them by providing information about coworkers, writing leaflets, or talking with people. They also try to isolate and slander pro-union people to reduce their influence with other workers. It is the large group of undecided workers that the 3M consultants and supervisors really focus on during the drive. 3M will use whatever means necessary with people to prevent a union from winning an election. One Boston hospital using 3M had 38 unfair labor practice charges issued against it by the NLRB in a four month period. 3M knows that they will outrage many people in the workplace with their unethical and often illegal tactics. Their strategy assumes, however, that more people will be intimidated into voting "no" than will become angry and vote "yes"; so they are willing to risk angering people.

The "front-line troops" for the anti-union campaign are the lower-level supervisors. They are told exactly what to say to everyone in their department. For example, 3M might tell a supervisor to "go back to your department and talk to everyone about strikes," or "tell them that if they vote for the union they will lose all their present benefits." The next day, or later the same day, the supervisors have to come back and tell the consultants what they found out—how people reacted, which anti-union arguments were effective, who could be pushed farther, etc. . . . One-to-one meetings between workers and supervisors are used most often. In that way there are no witnesses to any illegal statements that the supervisor might make, and so any possible unfair labor practice charges are hard to prove. Supervisors meet more and more often with the consultants as the drive progresses; daily meetings occur close to the time of the election.

During the whole drive, the "front-line supervisors" are under the constant threat of losing their jobs unless they produce information about specific people, convince people to vote "no," and do whatever else the consultants demand of them. The fact that supervisors are not protected by the National Labor Relations Act for unionizing activity adds fuel to 3M's pressure tactics. Several hospital workers spoke of cases where supervisors who were pro-union actively worked against the union in order to save their jobs.

At Boston University, however, a significant number of supervisors did not work against the union, and this had a big influence on winning the election. This happened partly because several of the supervisors were former members of the bargaining unit who had been promoted. But probably more important was the independence of the different academic departments in the university which made it easier for each supervisor to follow her or his own conscience. In hospitals and other more hierarchical workplaces, the pressure on supervisors is much greater, and few supervisors can withstand the pressure from the top.

3M's Anti-Union Propaganda

About three or four weeks before the actual election, 3M floods the workplace with letters explaining management's

Eileen Whalen/LNS

position on unions and outlining different anti-union arguments. Most of the letters signed by management are actually written by 3M itself; in fact, the same or similar letters have been found in different workplaces in different states. Supervisors are usually urged to hand-deliver these letters to people in their departments and are carefully coached on what each employee should be told. As always the response of each worker is noted so that 3M can know exactly how everyone will vote. 3M doesn't expect the flood of letters to convince people of their anti-union arguments, but it will at least confuse them. 3M realizes that they only have to plant a small seed of doubt in people's minds in order for them to choose what is familiar to them, and so vote against the union. It is this confusion and general tension throughout the workplace that is so hard and yet so important to counter in trying to defeat 3M. There are some suggestions here from other people's experiences for how to fight 3M's anti-union campaign.

Most people who have been through such a campaign say that the key to beating 3M is to have a very strong counter organization. The organizing committee should be large and representative of the bargaining unit by race, sex, job descriptions, and shifts. The one-to-one personal contact between workers and supervisors is what is most effective in scaring people and convincing them to vote against a union. With the immediate supervisors as the "front-line troops," 3M is able to have a ratio of about one supervisor to every ten workers and so is able to spread rumors and lies quickly. Any union drive must have at least as good a ratio of union activists to workers in the bargaining unit. In the same way a supervisor has an assignment from 3M to spread this rumor or tell that lie, so members of the organizing committee should each be responsible for updating and informing an equal number of people. 3M cannot be outpapered with union leaflets or newsletters, so being able to talk with every worker in person is vital to winning the election. The evaluation of whether a drive can actually beat 3M should be based on this type of assessment of how large and how representative the organizing committee is.

The organizing committee must also be clear and strong about what the major issues of the drive are, so that it does not get totally panicked and distracted by 3M's campaign. It is important not to get into a totally defensive position of always responding to 3M's attacks. The anti-union arguments from 3M are predictable and can be prepared for. The real issues of the drive (job security, benefits, cost of living adjustment, whatever) are what should be continually explained and emphasized to people. Good preparation for the campaign by a strong organizing committee will make it possible for this to happen.

Everyone in the drive should be thoroughly prepared for the anti-union campaign *before* it happens. It is useful to look at anti-union literature from other workplaces, and people can prepare their own answers in advance. Practicing talking with supervisors and anti-union workers during union meetings can give people the confidence to defend themselves in real situations. Exposing 3M's tactics to people early in the drive can take some of the wind out of their sails and even turn some of their arguments in your favor.

Know Your Legal Rights

People in the drive also need to be well-informed about the specific union they are working with and their legal rights to organize. This requires the union's showing any dirty laundry it has to those in the drive, so that no one will be surprised by what 3M brings up during the campaign. Everyone should know facts about union dues, how decisions are made in the union, etc. so that all slander of the union or union activists by 3M can be answered confidently with concrete information and facts.

Everyone should also be informed of their legal rights, so that when supervisors ask people what they think of the union, they can confidently say, "it is illegal for you to ask me my opinion about the union." People in the bargaining unit should realize that the *more* they know and the more they are involved in the drive, the *better* protected they are.

It is useful to expose 3M during the drive for management will continually deny such a firm exists while at the same time try to slander the union by calling it "outsiders." The organizing committee at Boston University found out that 3M was advising the university administration six months before the firm actually came to the campus. So the organizing committee was able to expose 3M's tactics early in the drive in the literature they wrote and the conversations they had with co-workers.

During an organizing drive of nurses in a Boston suburban hospital, members of the organizing committee found out that a third 3M consultant had joined the union-busting "team." They wrote an open letter to this new consultant, welcoming him to the hospital and detailing the role he had played in his last union-busting job. This was successful in exposing the existence of 3M at the hospital and undermining its credibility at the hospital.

Exposing 3M

Different hospitals have had varying degrees of success in convincing fellow workers that 3M actually exists. It is easiest

Michael Scurato/LNS

to expose them when there is concrete proof such as a cancelled check to the firm or actual phone lines and offices that can be located. Even without such proof, however, the existence of a union-busting firm at your workplace should be explained fully to everyone in the drive. Where good relationships with supervisors exist, it is good to continue them, but trying to organize supervisors to support the drive is usually not worth the time and energy it takes away from organizing those in the bargaining unit. At Boston University, the organizing committee had prepared information packets for those in the drive and sent them to supervisors also along with a specific letter explaining the union drive to them. Such efforts to keep lines of communication open are helpful, but should not be done at the expense of keeping those in the bargaining unit informed.

It is hard to imagine the state of tension and upheaval that develops during a 3M anti-union campaign until you actually experience it. There are, however, facts about 3M and possible tactics for defeating them that we can share with each other. It is important that we who are trying to unionize share such information with each other so that we can successfully counter this movement that is undermining the rights of workers to organize. Hopefully this exchange of information and suggested tactics will continue.

equal times
BOSTON'S NEWSPAPER FOR WORKING WOMEN

From *Equal Times* 5, no. 88 (May 12, 1980): 8

J. P. Stevens: A Matter of Social Justice

by Margaret Naville

J. P. Stevens is the second largest manufacturer in the United States with 81 plants across the country—most of them in the south. In 1978 Stevens sales amounted to $1.65 billion and the company declared assets of $955 million.

Over 43,400 people work for J. P. Stevens and the company claims that 24% are minority and 42% of them are women—97% of these work in blue-collar, unskilled or maintenance jobs.

Most of the textile workers are not covered by a union contract so as a result many of the working conditions and salaries are lower than the national average. The company claims that it pays workers an average hourly wage of $4.28. According to Bureau of Labor Statistics, the average hourly wage among other manufacturing workers in this country is $6.16.

The pension system at Stevens is no

better. It wasn't until 1976 that the company adopted a pension plan which replaced the one lump-sum-upon-retirement profit sharing system. This new plan gives the workers credit for only up to ten years of past service prior to 1976.

After each year a worker gets $4 a month. For example, if a worker retired in 1979 with 13 to 45 years of service, they would get a monthly pension of $32.00.

The battle waged by workers in the plants to increase salaries and improve working, safety and health conditions has been a long one—one that's not over yet.

Since 1963 J. P. Stevens has been involved in nearly 1000 violations of the law and in over 140 individual cases which have involved over 2000 employees.

WE CAN'T GIVE YOU A RAISE IT'S INFLATIONARY!

Most of these cases were tried in court together and have resulted in 22 separate National Labor Relations Board (NLRB) decisions against the company.

The violations include the company's unlawfully threatening workers with discharge, discrimination against women and minority workers, unwarranted firings, coercing, interrogating and conducting surveillance of people who are involved in union organizing. They have also been charged with blacklisting people who were fired and were union supporters.

The company has also been found guilty of "inciting racial discord and threatening plant closures." Many of these investigations are still pending or awaiting court decisions.

In 1976 The Amalgamated Clothing and Textile Workers Union decided that boycotting one third of J. P. Stevens products would be an effective weapon against the company. The boycott, the union organizers say, "Is a matter of social justice and a moral issue rather than a labor versus management action."

Through elections, bargaining, court decisions and the boycott, the union has won bargaining rights for approximately 6000 workers in at least 12 of the plants.

At one large Stevens plant located in Wallace, North Carolina, Stevens was ordered to recognize the ACTWU as the bargaining agent for some 1000 workers. They were also told to pay "all reasonable costs and expenses the union incurred during the organizing campaign leading to a February 1975 vote, and with interest."

In 1979, the NLRB ruled against the company saying that their expensive "pre-election misconduct interfered with the free choice of employees in Wallace." The union lost an election in 1975 but only after the company's "illicit campaign destroyed a free election atmosphere," the board said.

Gloria Jacobs is an ex-J. P. Stevens Textile Worker. Last week she was in Boston to talk about her experiences working for the company before she lost her job. She has spoken before the Los Angeles Board of Public Works and soon after her testimony the board voted unanimously to bar any municipal purchases of J. P. Stevens textile products.

Jacobs worked in the Stevens mill in Wallace, North Carolina for six years as a grader in the finishing department—a skilled job. In her last year at the company she had to work an eight hour day, six day week, with no lunch hour or breaks. She made about $8,000 a year.

While working in the plant, she contracted a lung "condition" and later she was fired for being "sick too much." Jacobs says she got no compensation for her medical problems which, she claims, are directly related to working in the high cotton fiber dust filled rooms.

She also says that the company refused to move her to a light dust area but told her she could stay home whenever she didn't feel well enough to work. She then became a strong union supporter.

Jacobs was fired in March, 1979 for "excessive absences." Four other workers at the Wallace plant were also fired that year for their union activities, they say. They all have complaints pending with the National Labor Relations Board.

Since her dismissal, Jacobs, who has two children, has not been able to find other textile work in the area—she's been blacklisted, she says—and has instead gone back to school in North Carolina to study law. Her husband works in another textile mill which is unionized. It's located 30 miles from their home.

Of the boycott, Jacobs says that things haven't changed much for the workers in the plants but the boycott has helped to make other people aware about the working conditions and that they do still exist. We talked to her recently about the struggle.

One Woman's View

Gloria, what's happening with the J. P. Stevens' boycott?

The main reason for the boycott was to ask other people to help out the workers at the J. P. Stevens plants. We need a contract in the mill in Wallace.

In 1975 we had an election and we were voted down by 48 votes. We took the case to a federal court judge and he said that under the circumstances there couldn't be fair elections at the plant. The court ruled that the company had to bargain in good faith.

So far the company has refused to bargain with us and the boycott is the only way we have to put pressure on them and get them to change and abide by the law.

Has the boycott had any effect on J. P. Stevens then?

In some ways it's had a tremendous effect. Now that the public knows what kind of company Stevens is (and the boycott has given them a bad reputation), and if it's as bad as people are beginning to believe it is, then they're not going to buy the products.

Many people who worked at the company and who have left, have gotten brown lung disease but the company still refuses to acknowledge that people are getting it from working in the factory. It's often hard to keep up with what the company's up to. They use so many names on their products and sometimes they even use numbers so that people who want to support the boycott have to ask the store manager if something they want to buy is made by Stevens. And that's had a powerful impact.

Have working conditions changed much since the boycott?

No, not really. But the company claims they have. Six weeks ago a young man, 19 years old, was crushed to death by a big bale of cloth. It weighed about a ton. He had just got in on the night shift and was walking through the mill on his way to his workplace.

Things are a little better since the union came in but many things have not been corrected. Many of the same safety violations still exist. People are still getting hurt and they still get no medical compensation, or the compensation that they do get may as well be nothing.

What about salaries and benefits at the mills? Has anything been done to improve them?

No, they really haven't. Usually when people work they expect that they are going to get a raise sometime—you know, the same as other mill workers.

But at Stevens there are no provisions for cost of living increases so things are basically the same. Since the union has come in, a few things have happened that have worked to the benefit of the workers.

In plants where people never got breaks they now can get a 20-minute lunch break and two ten-minute breaks. But we have to keep the pressure on. People who have feelings for other people are not going to buy products when they see people working in such bad conditions.

Gloria, are there some things that have gotten worse for workers in the Stevens plants?

Yes, they are still firing people for supporting the union. They are still discriminating against women and blacks. You see in Wallace, the company employed between 1000 to 1200 people and that's just about everybody in that town. The company actually supports the town, the town feeds the company. So it's easy to understand how a company as large as J. P. Stevens can put so much fear into its employees.

You mentioned sex discrimination and race discrimination. What is being done about them?

Nothing. As far as I know nothing has been done to change the discrimination that's going on in those plants. It's only been a year since I was fired. Before that I trained several men for jobs that I was highly qualified for. Then these men got the opportunity to be my supervisor. They

even got the company to send them on to school. They did it all the time and they still do it all the time. They will go out and hire a male when they've got women there on the job who can already do that job.

What kind of job did you do at the factory?

I worked from 1973 to 1979 as a grader, which meant that I had to inspect the material and which also meant that I had to lift 40 to 70 pound bales of cloth. The rolls would come off every minute and within that minute you had to load the material on a flat bed with wheels and complete all the inspection and paperwork that went along with that. That all had to be done before the next bale came off the roll.

I was making about $1.80 an hour when I started and always worked six days a week and eight hours a day without any breaks. For the last four weeks at the plant in Wallace, people have been working seven days a week. You see, once the company can get the warehouse stocked then they start laying people off. So they work the people all those hours in a shorter period of time and can afford to lay them off.

How many of the J. P. Stevens workers are women?

I'd say about 45% and they mostly work in unskilled jobs or blue collar jobs. And most of the women have husbands who also work in the company. I wouldn't say that more than 2% of the women who worked in the company held white collar jobs.

With all this going on and in spite of all the violations that the National Labor Relations Board has fined J. P. Stevens for, why don't the workers just strike?

The courts have said that J. P. Stevens has to bargain with the union and give the workers a contract. The company keeps appealing the court's decisions. If the workers don't have a contract, they are in no position to go out on strike. And they are also in a bind if they go out on strike

Steve Karian/LNS

because the company can just pack up and move out or they'll hire scabs to do the work. While you're out there waiting for the courts, someone else is in there doing your job and you're just left out.

Do you feel that the NLRB is effective?

Sure it's effective but their laws just aren't strong enough for a conglomerate company like J. P. Stevens. They have been called the biggest, the most notorious, recidivous labor law breaker in the United States. And the funny thing about it is that they just keep right on breaking the law. It's cheaper for them to go ahead and pay a

fine. In the last 15 years they've paid out close to 1.5 million dollars in fines. Now if they make 40 million a year in profits, what's 1.5 million? They are just too big for the law.

So what do you do?

What you have to do is ask the public to help you, as we are. The only thing that company understands is money and if people and the government stop supporting them financially, then things can change. The company finds it a lot cheaper to pay out the fines rather than get their act together.

Southern Struggle

FIGHTING TO BREAK THE CHAINS OF ALL OPPRESSION

From *Southern Struggle* 38, no. 3 (March 1980): 1

Brown Lung Stalks South

by Christine Lutz

Despite strong industry resistance, mill workers are beginning to make the cotton business pay for byssinosis—brown lung.

Byssinosis is a disease that turns a mill worker's lungs into a spiderweb of holes. The cotton dust in a factory's air destroys the alveoli, or air sacs, in the lungs.

So brown lung sufferers first find themselves coughing or short of breath when they return from a weekend off to the plant. After a little as a year (but, more often, after several years), the byssinosis is irreversible and deadly.

A victim cannot walk more than a few yards without stopping, cannot sweep a floor or climb a flight of stairs without resting. In the disease's advanced stage, only an artificial breathing mechanism keeps the millworker alive.

The Southern Poverty Law Center has filed the first class action suit from brown lung victims. The suit charges that mills deceive workers about the disease and defraud them on workmen's compensation when they become disabled. The case, against Burlington Industries in the Carolinas and West Point Pepperell of

Reprinted with permission from *Southern Struggle,* Southern Conference Educational Fund, Atlanta, GA.

Georgia, asks for $15 million in damages.

Brown lung is one of the targets of the National Lawyers Guild's 1980 summer projects, also. NLG lawyers will be working with the Carolina Brown Lung Association in Georgia and Virginia, by researching workmen's compensation laws, organizing BLA chapters and teaching paralegal skills to mill workers.

Fully one-quarter, and possibly more, of all cotton mill workers are stationed in areas with high enough dust levels to cause the disease. People who open and comb bales of cotton, spinners and weavers are the most susceptible.

In 1979, the federal government estimated that 100,000 mill workers suffered from byssinosis and that 30,000 people, including retirees, would never be cured.

The textile industry, however, refuses to spend money to cut down on the cotton dust levels or compensate brown lung sufferers.

For example, 18,000 Carolinians have byssinosis. Carolina textile companies have compensated *320* former workers, paying each an average $13,500.

WHO WORKS IN THE TEXTILE INDUSTRY?

in Georgia:	122,000	people
in Alabama:	50,000	people
in Virginia:	50,000	people
in Pennsylvania:	50,000	people
in North Carolina:	250,000	people
in South Carolina:	141,500	people

ONE OUT OF EVERY FOUR OF THESE WORKERS WILL CONTRACT BROWN LUNG, A DEADLY DISEASE.

If you believe that you have brown lung, or if you need help in filing a compensation claim, contact the Brown Lung Association. The office phone numbers are: Charlotte, 704-376-0426; Stanly County, 704-485-3112; Lincoln-Gaston, 701-922-8761; Greensboro, 919-273-2666; Eden, 919-623-2689; Roanoke Rapids, 919-537-1858; Durham, 919-688-0512; Erwin, 919-897-7443; Rockingham, 919-997-4788; Aiken, 803-593-3649; Columbia, 803-796-7763; Greenville, 803-269-8229; Spartansburg, 803-585-5303; and Anderson, 803-224-4067.

Cotton dust's effect was exposed in 1705 in Italy. But as late as 1969, *America's Textile Reporter* called byssinosis "a thing thought up by venal doctors who attended last year's [International Labor Organization] meeting in Africa, where inferior races are bound to be affected by new diseases more superior people defeated years ago."

W. O. Leonard, chairman of the N. C. Textile Manufacturers' safety and health committee, says "We recognize that there is a problem affecting some employees. We just feel like this thing has been blown out of proportion."

Half of the nation's textile workers live in the Carolinas. The federal government inspected 128 mills in South Carolina in 1974, and found 101 to have dust exceeding the danger limit. Three out of four mills inspected in North Carolina had three times the legal amount of dust in the air (which is 1 milligram per cubic meter of air over eight hours).

But what happens to these companies? The textile companies appeal the federal government's citations, and cases are still dragging on from the '74 inspection.

Cannon Mills provides a good example. In 1975, inspectors discovered that Cannon's Roberta Mill had deadly dust in its air, and did not provide respirators for the workers.

OSHA records, in fact, show that Cannon knew it was violating safety standards in 1973. But Cannon's only penalty was a $650 fine, which was revoked by Labor Commissioner Billy Creel. The Roberta Mill operated until 1978, and no safety measures were ever taken, except to give employees dust masks, which are mostly useless and always uncomfortable.

The Occupational Safety and Health Act was passed by Congress in 1970, leading to industry-wide cotton dust limits. Six years ago, the government ordered the mills to clean up or else.

But today, the cotton mill owners are still pleading poverty. "If we put in new equipment, we'll go broke!"

And within a few years, 165,875 mill workers will not walk a block without pain because the textile industry refuses to clean up the mills.

From *Union W.A.G.E.*, no. 61 (September/October 1980), pp. 2-3

Sexual Harassment Used to Keep Women in Their 'Place'

by Karen Povorney*

*[And the women of Women Organized Against Sexual Harassment.—eds., *Alternative Papers*.]

Reprinted with permission from *Union W.A.G.E.: A Working Women's Newspaper*.

"I leaned over to pour some coffee for a customer when I felt a hand on my leg. Instinctively, I jerked back and asked the customer what the hell he thought he was doing. He smiled and said, 'I was just giving you a little extra attention!' The manager, who had been standing across the room watching the entire incident, winked at me when I looked over at him."
—Waitress

"I was the only woman in a crew of thirty men doing carpentry work on a construction job. I was always asked to move the heaviest materials and laughed at when I couldn't lift them. The men would say, 'What's wrong, honey, just spread your legs and give a heave.'"
—Carpenter

The women in both of these examples have been sexually harassed. Sexual harassment occurs in many forms and degrees of subtlety. Whether we are whistled at in the streets or propositioned on the job. As women in a sexist society we are almost all recipients of unwanted sexual attention. In a *Redbook* survey of 9000 working women it was found that 90% had been sexually harassed. Although the phenomenon is widespread, it is only recently that the issue has come into the foreground for consideration. This is primarily because sexual harassment has in most cases been regarded as an acceptable (established) way of men relating to women, and unlike rape, it is a more subtle form of male tyranny and power abuse, and therefore harder to name and challenge.

Sexual harassment occurs when a supervisor or co-worker subjects a woman to unwanted sexual attention, coerces her into sexual relations, and/or punishes her for a refusal, thereby affecting her job or emotional well-being. Sexual harassment is manifested verbally (sexist remarks, propositions, innuendos, subtle pressure for sexual activity) and/or physically (touching, patting, pinching, brushing against a woman's body, subtle pressure for sexual activity, physical assault, rape). Sexual harassment can also pollute the work environment in the form of pin-up posters, sexist jokes, and remarks not specifically directed at any one woman. It is important to recognize that sexual harassment is a power relation as well as a sexual relation. It is an abuse of institutionalized power or authority by men. Sexual harassment is a form of sex discrimination that, in interaction with class, race and other forms of discrimination denies women the opportunity to live and work comfortably.

Sexual harassment is a means by which women are kept in their "place." The majority of women work in traditionally female jobs which include service and

Conference on Sexual Harassment
November 8, 1980   all day
    Place to be decided soon
Workshops:
    What to do if you're harassed
    Support groups
    Community Organizing
    Legal Information—more
Please contact Karen at 841-6277
or call Union WAGE, 282-6777.

clerical work. These jobs are low paying, offer few prospects for advancement, little job security, and are primarily non-unionized. Within a traditionally female job, sexual harassment is often an extension of women's domestic role. The boss treats his secretary as a surrogate "wife" who, in his view, will complete the task while catering to his personal and sexual needs. Within non-traditional jobs, sexual harassment is often the most direct means by which both male bosses and male employees terrorize women into performing below their capacities or leaving their jobs. Men resent women's entrance into these male preserves due to their traditional attitudes toward women's work. A woman who is competent at what has traditionally been viewed as a man's job represents a kind of independence that undermines male authority. A woman in the trades, for example, challenges sex role stereotypes and raises the possibility that she can and will act independently of men in other areas of her life. She may experience a sexual harassment like the one outlined in the second example.

In both traditional and non-traditional work, women experience devastating emotional, economic, and social effects from sexual harassment. The survey conducted by Working Women's Institute found that 63% of the women who had been sexually harassed evidenced physical symptoms of stress, often requiring medical and/or therapeutic relief. Women who have been sexually harassed struggle with self-blame and guilt as a result of having been taught that women are ultimately responsible for their objectification by men. Women find it hard to bring forward charges of sexual harassment because of this self-blame and lack of public support. A woman may deny the experience, telling herself that it was less horrifying and intimidating than it was. She may even view sexual harassment as flattery, given that women are taught to appreciate male interest particularly if it comes from a man who is of a higher class. This distortion of what she really knows to be true is often reinforced by the attitudes of coworkers and bosses. They may feel that she should expect such unwanted attention and be able to handle it, or, even worse, may believe that she led the man on.

While harassment is a common and shared experience for women, it does not affect all of our lives in the same way. A woman's job, her race, class background, age, sexual preference and political views all influence both the form of harassment

she receives and its impact. Men often choose particular groups of women to harass because of their economic, political and/or social vulnerability, all of which make it unlikely that these women will publicly resist or report the overtures. Among these groups are: women of color, working class women, older women, lesbians and feminists. Racism promotes sexual stereotypes of Third World women, encourages the trivialization of their experience, and may promote disunity among women workers because many white women have yet to confront their own racism. Working class women lack economic or social resources to protect them from sexual harassment. Ageism promotes the devaluation of older women relative to young "attractive" women and promotes the public denouncement of lesbians for their choice of lifestyle and the disavowal of support by straight women. Conservatism and fear encourage men to intimidate women who refuse to comply with role expectations or who resist male aggression. For all these women, sexual harassment is a survival issue. They often face two choices: that of enduring an intimidating and coercive experience while managing to hold onto the job, or that of confronting the harasser and thereby running the risk of losing the job and future employment credibility.

Sexual harassment is dealt with inadequately by employers and unions, and until only recently, by the courts. Most employers and unions have not taken a firm stand against sexual harassment in the form of a policy statement and an effective grievance procedure. In fact, there have been few open and supportive discussions of sexual harassment on the job and in union meetings. Women often experience personal and political isolation on the job, a situation that is fostered by employers who encourage competition, racism, homophobia, ageism and other means of dividing the workforce.

Steps to take if you've been sexually harassed:

• At the first sign of trouble, tell the harasser you aren't interested in his offer. Be firm but polite. Don't give him ammunition to use later.

• If he continues to harass you, complain to your union, a grievance committee or personnel department. It's in the companies' interests to rectify the problem. A lawsuit is costly for them, too.

• Keep a diary. Mark the time, date and

place of each incident. List witnesses. Note any physical or emotional stress you have related to the incidents. If you see a doctor due to stress, report that too.

• Look for support among your co-workers. Other women he has pressured may be willing to substantiate your charges, if not join the fight.

• Push your union, if you have one, to create a Safety Committee or a Sex Discrimination Committee. If a woman's caucus doesn't exist, create one. Work out a definition and policy statement regarding sexual harassment. This should include a grievance procedure which the union and employer can adopt.

• If you quit because the situation is intolerable, detail your charges in a letter to the head of personnel. That way, your complaint is on record should you file for unemployment benefits.

• If you are fired for turning down your boss's advances, talk to an attorney. You may have to prove your charges before you can collect unemployment benefits.

• File for Workers's Compensation and/or Disability Insurance if you believe you can establish that you suffered emotional damage from harassment. The testimony of a psychologist, friend and co-workers is needed.

• You can sue the company under Title VII of the 1964 Civil Rights Act (federal level) and get back wages and/or a grievance procedure under Compensatory and punitive damages. You must file within 180 days of the last incident or having been fired with the local Equal Employment Opportunities Commission (EEOC).

• You can sue in civil court for Intentional Infliction of Emotional Distress (DEFH), assault and battery, retaliation, etc.

• You can also sue through the Fair Employment Practices Commission (FEPC). You must file within one year of the last incident, or having been fired. There is a 90 day extension if you did not know the incident was sex discrimination. This Commission is more progressive than the EEOC, allowing you to collect for emotional distress as well as back wages and may process your case faster. (EEOC does not cover emotional distress.)

• In all cases of proof, you are not required to take a lie detector test.

Other options:

• Call California's Occupational Safety and Health Administration (Cal/OSHA) and request a "Special Order" (California

Labor Code, Section 6305[b]). Special Order covers unsafe conditions, devices, or places of employment which pose a threat to the health or safety of any employee and which cannot be made safe under existing standards.

• Contact the city licensing bureau and complain that a company that engages in sexual harassment should not be licensed or should be penalized.

This article was written by Women Organized Against Sexual Harassment (WOASH), a community based organization which services the bay area. We serve as an advisory and support group for women who have been sexually harassed in service, clerical and non-traditional fields. Our current caseload includes custodial workers, waitresses and secretaries. We are in the process of defining and solidifying WOASH and welcome any help and input. Presently we are planning an all day sexual harassment conference scheduled for November 8 in coalition with Union WAGE, BAYWAR, The Rape Prevention Center, and other feminist groups yet to be contacted. If there is any interest in joining this network, please contact Karen P. or Karen H. at 841-6277. Meetings are usually held on Thursday nights, presently in the east bay.

off our backs

From *off our backs* 9, no. 2 (February 1979): 14-15, 24

Linda Butcher: Striking While the Iron's Hot

by Martha Tabor

Linda Butcher, a 33-year-old welder, works with a shipfitter in the barge fabrication division of the DRAVO Corporation's Neville Island shipyard, just outside of Pittsburgh, Pennsylvania. Here she is one of 4 or 5 women in a workforce of about 500 men. Working first as a laborer on a United Mine Worker road construction project in 1974, she's done different kinds of blue-collar work for the last five years. She comes from a working-class family in Waynesburg, Pennsylvania, where she grew up and, until recently, lived most of her life. The first in her family to go to college, after teaching several years and doing graduate work in educational psychology, she switched at age 28 to blue-collar work. She is a lesbian and is open about this with her co-workers.

The following interview is part of a longer one taped in November, 1978. We talked in The Islander, a restaurant-bar near DRAVO, owned and run by Katherine, a woman who had done blue-collar

Reprinted with permission from *off our backs: a women's news journal*, 1724 20th St. NW, Washington, DC 20009.

work for fourteen months during World War II. "They didn't write books about us then." Someone should.

I felt Linda had a strong sense of personal humility and a lot of self-knowledge. It puts a large strain on a woman to decide to allow me to follow her around photographing for several days at her work place. The work at DRAVO is highly socialized (unlike that of a truck-driver for example) and plenty of stress is already on any woman in such a situation. The morning of the third day I spent inside DRAVO Linda mentioned that her stomach was in knots and she was having trouble sleeping—both due, we agreed, to the added stress my presence was causing. Linda has a thoughtful way of speaking— her words are turned over carefully and come from the core of herself, her experience.

Work & Work Relationships

Q: What's hard about this work?

A: The part I dislike about the work the most is when I'm not able to relate to the people I'm working with on some kind of a level. It's being unable to relate as a human being on an honest level with the guys I work with, not being able to communicate as friends, as equals, as human beings, that bothers me.

But there are high points too because there are often times when I'm able to relate to them. Like the most recent thing—I was working outside and it was raining. And before a person gets his or her 30 days in he or she doesn't take a pass (quit for the day because of weather). So I had my 30 days in and I said to my foreman John, "I'm going home." And he said, "Wellllllllll . . . you've changed a lot!" Insinuating that I wasn't staying there because I was a woman. Anyway, this guy, he let my foreman know right then that it wasn't because I was a woman that I was responding like that, but because I had my 30 days in.

That . . . that makes you feel great. To have a worker stand up for you like that and realize that this is a classist issue, not a sexist issue and that the boss is trying to segregate you and to cause all this derision and division between us on the basis of sex and color.

Q: What about racism?

A: Generally I go by vibes more than I do anything else and I get a lot more positive vibes from black men. They recognize that we're in the same boat. I walk past them and they give me a big smile, "Hi, how are you?" Every time. They recognize we're in it together. They can empathize with us in our oppression and vice-versa and that feels real good. There's still an amount of distrust and that's an individual matter as to how much there is . . . I see black women and black men, even black gay men, with mistrust because I'm white. But I think we're all actually trying and I feel that we're evolving in some sense socially. . . .

But there's a lot of racism at DRAVO. I hear it all the time.

I just tell the men that I like women and I tell them anything that will irritate them. (Laughs)

Bülbül/LNS

They think "There's no hope for her." I'm openly gay and they don't want to accept that fact because it's too threatening. They don't want to admit that I don't want them and don't need them. And so they say, "You know, if I were a woman working here, I'd say the same thing because I'd want all these guys to stay off my back. So I'd say that too." And I just look at them and smile because (laughing) you know—you can live with your belief and yet I can still say "I'm gay" and survive at DRAVO and if I can't then I'll do whatever I have to.

I can go out of DRAVO. But there are a lot of guys who can hardly get out other than go to a gas station and pump gas. They feel locked in—especially if they have families —a wife and children. It's something I have to contend with a year, a year and a half, but they may have to contend with it the rest of their lives.

In many ways they have the same problems here I do. They don't like the smoke, they don't like getting in the hold; they don't like all the noise in the barge shop; and they don't like being made to feel like idiots by the foremen. They have the same problems I have and they identify with me on that basis and just temporarily sometimes they'll overlook sex. It's about the only time in blue-collar work that I can get really close to men because we can identify with each other's sufferings—right there.

It's either—"You hand me that rope or I'm dead" or "I hand you the rope or you're dead." And we do it and we help each other as we pull each other up. So on that level I feel a lot closer to the men because I experience survival.

Getting into Blue-Collar Work

Q: How did you get into this work?

A: This other woman actually got me into it. I was teaching at the time but she and I frequented the same bars and she kept telling me: "Linda, I know they're discriminating against me. I know it and I can't get a job." She was trying to get a job on a United Mine Worker construction site building a 17 mile road from Kirby, Pennsylvania, to the Monogahela River to haul coal out on. She kept telling me, "They're really giving me a dirty deal."

I got irritated. They were running over a woman, discriminating against a woman. So I said, "Patty, I'll help you." Until then getting a construction job had never entered my mind. So I started talking to some of the guys who worked construction

there and they gave me the run-around too. I got angry. I tried to get on as a laborer and they wouldn't hire me. So I told Patty we'd file a discrimination complaint. But when it came down to it, she didn't have the nerve to do it. So I came into Pittsburgh myself and filed the complaint. The company found out that I'd got a docket number and was actually taking them to court so they bargained with me outside of court and being naive and ignorant, you know, about what I could have won, I said, "Ok, I'll take the job." I probably should have sued for back wages. So I stuck with it and I didn't go back to teaching. That's how I got into the work.

It's really unusual for a woman to be that tough and angry and fight like that. We're conditioned not to make waves. We're afraid of being disliked. I have a lot of respect for you going to bat like that for another woman and yourself.

A: Well, I thank you for that. I guess I'm sort of that way. In NOW 5 or 6 years ago a lot of women thought I was extremely radical and had a lot of courage, a lot of nerve, and I just couldn't understand their timidity . . . not that I don't have my own insecurities—I do. But I knew the law was on my side and NOW was pushing too. So I went through with it.

Family & Sexuality

I sort of feel that people will like me if I like myself. If I can't be proud of myself then . . . I guess it's because my mother loved me somewhere along the way. A lot of it's got to be accredited to her for loving me, giving me that confidence. She always told me that I was good. . . . I was good at this, I was good at that. I was a strong person. I should try and be free and be my own person—so I believed her.

My feminism and my involvement in blue-collar work is related to my sexuality and my relationship with my parents. You can't separate them. Having a strong mother made all the difference in the world. My mother waitresses and my father is an alcoholic and I went through some traumatic experiences with him seeing him beat my mother up. Things like that had some influence on my development in turning me against men, away from men, I'm sure they did although I think everybody's bisexual if they're raised normally . . . (laughing) that doesn't happen too often.

I was married for six years. I'd had no exposure to gay life. I lived in a small

community and it was the thing to do and although I realized I was gay, I figured . . . well, at least I'll try this thing and if it fails I will have tried it. My husband knew I was gay before I married him. I told him that I was attracted to women and fell in love with women even though I had no experiences with them until I was 31. It wasn't until after I got a divorce that I decided I might as well investigate gay life.

So I started coming to gay bars in Pittsburgh. And it was sort of frightening to go to a strange bar in a metropolitan area, because I wasn't familiar with cities. But that only lasted a night or two and I made friends and found out they were normal just like everybody else. I didn't feel uncomfortable long. Just initially.

I had tried to go society's way and there was no way I was going to be happy being untrue to myself and living with someone I wasn't that emotionally attached to. It wasn't fair to either myself or him. It was what I had to do.

I feel now if I don't say that I'm gay it's insinuating to myself at some level that I'm not proud of myself and of the feelings I have towards women and towards myself and I'm proud of myself.

I think that gay women often have a strength that straight women or even feminist women don't have. I know that in my early days in NOW—about 1970—they were arguing whether lesbians should be accepted into the organizations, should be recognized, and how that was going to split them, turn the public against them and I had to sit there and listen to that knowing all the while that it was gay women who led NOW. There's some kind of energy there . . . it has something. . . .

Blue-Collar Work Experiences

Q: Turning back to your involvement in blue-collar work, after you first got hired on the United Mine Worker construction site with the support of NOW, what work did you do?

A: Well, when I was first hired on, I started out as a laborer, but I also worked as a blaster, mechanic's helper, what else? Laid pipe, heavy equipment operator—I got a lot of skills working for them. It's different in the UMW, it's not as specialized and good as the trade unions. They don't have apprenticeship programs. The mine construction work is also different from mining. And I find the men different from those at DRAVO, worse.

I still can't figure out why they seemed worse to me, but I have the feeling that it's because this DRAVO is close to a metropolitan area and I think the men are more well educated, more up to date, on women's issues. There's a different consciousness here. It might be the time lapse from when I started in and of itself, but I don't think so.

Q: After you got on, what problems did you face?

A: I tried to get this woman friend of mine into the UMW one summer. She's a certified welder and they wouldn't take her. Well, finally I told her that she should try to get into this painting company and get on with them. And I saw the union grasp hands with the company to keep a woman out of a job.

One day I found out that they had brought guys down from Pittsburgh who didn't even have union cards to work for that painting company. I went straight to the union president and I said, "I know you're trying to keep her out and everything and that's one issue, but this issue is that I don't believe that these guys are in the UMW and I want to see their cards." They didn't have cards. They had to sit around from 10 o'clock in the morning on and wait for their rides home. They never came back again. They were trying to work these guys from Pittsburgh, who didn't even have employment applications over here.

Her application had seniority over—what's his name?—the son of the union officer. This guy got his son in and she had more seniority than he did. And he continued to work there all summer and there was nothing with the Human Relations Commission. She has a suit filed against the UMW with the Human Relations Commission. But that company, the painting company, was small and there isn't much women can do when they're dealing with small companies. That was pathetic. The UMW connived with this ABC Painting Company of Pittsburgh to keep her out.

Q: What was the reaction of the men when you did that?

A: I got all sorts of different reactions. Men didn't know how to handle that. In a way I felt I had some semblance of respect from them. Some fear . . . all kinds of things . . . but all in all they were so afraid of women and what I stood for that they were out to stop it. That's all.

To my knowledge, I'm the only woman who's ever been on UMW construction

sites in the State of Pennsylvania other than that other woman, Patty, who I helped get on. At least in Southwestern Pennsylvania. I tried to get other women on, but in the four years myself and Patty, who worked as a flag woman all the time, were there, we were the only women. I did everything I could to catch their little slip-ups. The coal mines were a different story. Underground work they seem to be recruiting women . . . but for construction work they try to keep women out.

They also tried to keep me from acquiring any skills at all. I applied for an iron-worker's job and they blocked me. I pushed hard and went to the union officials and read the contract and found they had to let me be an ironworker . . . but I lost two weeks work as an ironworker because they discriminated against me. You have to fight all the way.

That's not to say the men aren't discriminated against too. There's a lot of nepotism . . . but sexism is the sharpest point of discrimination. I have a suit filed against U.S. Steel too, on one of their jobs using UMW construction workers . . . I applied for a position as a mechanic's trainee and the men they hired had no experience . . . But other men were discriminated against too. They just didn't have the recourse I do. I want to get skills.

Feminist Futures

Q: I know you want to get into a craft union eventually. Where do you see that leading, after you finish the apprenticeship?

A: I want to learn and grow. I like the idea of being self-sufficient. I'd like to live on a farm and grow my own food and take care of the equipment. Live with other women—gay and straight, not necessarily barring men. I don't know if I can say what I want to be.

For a long time I searched for what I wanted and I've finally decided that I'll never know because once I get it, I don't want it. I just want to be as free as possible—learn, grow, be able to empathize with other people. The way I feel about myself comes first and then the way I feel about other people.

I was into education for quite a long time. I was the first in my family to go to college. I got out of high school and I didn't know what I wanted to do. I had decent SAT scores. And the guidance counsellor said, "You ought to go to college." And I decided I didn't want to be a waitress like my mother was because I could see where

that leads. I certainly didn't want anything to do with men who beat you up. So I thought I might as well go to college and I went. My parents seemed to want me to do that . . . and they'd be proud of me if I did.

So I taught high school and did graduate work and was into books for approximately half my life and now this. I miss the mental stimulation, yet I'm learning.

School was the thing that stifled me. Teaching became stifling. . . . The purpose of the educational system seems to be to support a socio-economic strata. As far as preparing people for employment is concerned, it's a crock of shit. When I was at West Virginia University I was introduced to some ideas like those of Christopher Jencks from Harvard. He compiled statistics and found that socio-economic status makes more difference than SAT scores or intelligence test scores or whatever and I believe that. Money makes more of a difference as far as everybody is concerned. One's growth. One's experience.

In the public high school where I taught, I saw upper class children get away with murder and lower class children get penalized for it. So I must say I'm as much of a classist as I am a feminist and sometimes I have conflicts deciding which is primary. But that's good because it has helped me to be more open-minded to men who I see starting to identify with women as union sisters and realizing that class is what it's all about. Like the incident with the rain pass I mentioned.

You asked how I think things will change and that's the question of the century. . . . I don't know. I don't have much hopes that people from the upper classes can empathize with the problems of the poor or of women or of blacks. . . . I don't know. I saw a lot of classism in NOW—conflict between upper-class women and working-class women too.

I tend to be sort of a separatist at heart. I mean separate from this society. . . . I mean we can hardly breathe the air. If you walk out the door here on Neville Island there are 54 industries. We're not going in the right direction and we're destroying ourselves. I'm not sure that women would do it differently, but I'm sure that change lies more with oppressed peoples than it does with those who are on top. I don't think those who are on top are willing to make changes because . . . after all they are being supported by the system right now.

Recently I've gotten involved with women who identify themselves as witches. . . . And I think that being a witch is being a very strong feminist and realizing the power that lies in developing our own mythologies and denying Christianity and male religion. It means realizing as someone said . . . I think it was Jung who talked about the collective unconscious—that if a revolution is to come about—that's where it's at.

You asked me what was going to bring change? And there's no doubt as Lenin and the Beatles said, "Revolution is in our minds." It takes consciousness, vibrations, energy, spirit. And that's got to come about and I see it happening . . . it's identifying on a subconscious level with women and getting this energy together. It's powerful. And I have a belief that that's where it's at as far as feminist revolution until that happens, until that energy comes out. But it is happening. . . . I've seen it happening between women, between sisters.

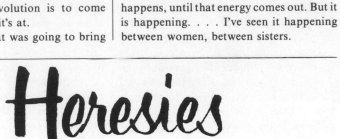

Rocking the Docks: Women on the Waterfront

From *Heresies* 2, no. 3 (Spring 1979): 73-75

by Constance Pohl

Two women, one black, one white, hold small hooks in both their gloved hands as they face each other over a 140-pound burlap bag of coffee. They bend down, spear the burlap with the hooks and, in a single rhythmic motion, swing the bag onto a pile of cargo.

Across the way, two other women knock over a 700-pound drum and roll it across the floor. "Don't let that heavy drum fall on your feet," advises a longshoreman behind them. "You'll snap your toes off. Remember, if you can't do something, ask for help. There's always somebody down in the hold. And don't do anything until you first see it done by someone else."

Women—black, white and Hispanic—are preparing to begin work on shipping docks in February. More than sixty of them have registered for work with the New York-New Jersey Waterfront Commission. For the first time, women have been accepted as dock workers in the area.

Why do these women want such strenuous work? "The money is fabulous," answers Gwen Wells, who has been a

Teamster and holds a college degree. "I need the dough," says Mary Baffi, who is divorced and has three children. A high school graduate, Mary had been making $2.90 an hour at the phone company. No special skills or education are required to be a longshoreman, a job that guarantees an annual income from $18,000 to $22,000. The sole requirement for a job as cargo checker, which pays $24,000 a year, is to be able to read, write and count well enough to record the amount of cargo that goes on and off ships. These are salaries few—if any—unskilled women ever hoped to earn.

"If they make it onto the docks, they should keep on meeting together," suggests Tom Webb, a black longshoreman who has been a shop steward for eight years. "Otherwise the women will be systematically weeded out. I know. They're doing it to the black longshoremen."

"Sticking together is what won these jobs in the first place," adds Mary Baffi. "Women from all walks of life are getting together so they can make a living."

This effort began when, for the first time in nine years, there were openings last spring for two hundred cargo checkers, and a group of women tried to apply for the jobs. Although shipping companies employ the cargo checkers, the New York-New Jersey Waterfront Commission, which acts as watchdog on the waterfront, must first approve the applicants. Filling out the Commission's registry papers is the essential first step to applying for a job. On August 15, 1978, six women applied for registry papers at the Commission's office in downtown Manhattan. Three of the women were black, one was Hispanic and

two were white. Accompanying the women applicants were three representatives of the National Organization for Women.

"We want to apply for the jobs of cargo checkers."

"There are no applications available for any jobs," said Al Miller, a clerk at the Waterfront Commission. "The only jobs open are pier guard and warehouseman, but you will need a letter from the companies that are going to hire you."

"We understand jobs for cargo checkers are going to be available."

"No. All they are doing is transferring longshoremen internally to the jobs of cargo checkers."

"What are the requirements for cargo checkers?" asked one of the women.

"You must be able to read and write and pass a proficiency exam," Miller answered.

"What companies are hiring pier guards and warehousemen?"

"I can't give you their names, but they're in Jersey."

As the women were leaving, a male employee called out, "Hey, Al, you should have asked one of them for a date!"

On leaving the Commission office, the group went directly to the Equal Employment Opportunities Commission and filed discrimination charges. "It was clear that the Commission was not interested in having women working on the docks in any capacity," explains Jane Silver, Job Developer for N.O.W., through whom the action originated. The Commission had effectively barred women from the docks by reserving the cargo checker jobs for longshoremen only, since zero percent of longshoremen are women and according to Executive Director of the Commission, Leonard Newman.

At day's end the women sat together over coffee discussing their situation: How could they win the jobs, and how could they deal with the problems that would arise once they were actually working on the docks? A lawsuit against the Waterfront Commission would have to be initiated, claiming civil rights violations. The women's lawyers would seek an injunction to prevent the Commission from assigning any more of these jobs. One hundred sixty-five longshoremen had already been transferred "internally" to cargo checker, and there were more than forty women who wanted to apply for the remaining thirty-five positions.

These women see themselves as a collective breaking into an all-male world;

Cindy Fredrick/LNS

they agree that they must support each other totally once they are on the docks, and they must let no excuse be used against them which might cost them those jobs. "That afternoon we talked with the other women about getting those jobs," recalls Debra Brown, who is presently working at N.O.W. as a legal assistant under a CETA (Comprehensive Employment and Training Act) project grant. "We know we're going to be harassed. We decided we are going to organize ourselves as a women's cargo-checking collective to guarantee our own protection."

"Say we should luck up and get these positions," adds Celeste Collier, who works under a CETA grant at N.O.W. as a community organizer. "We would be frightened. Most of us have children. We will have to work in fear because we know the men don't want us there. They will threaten you with physical harm."

"Still, I'm ready to take that job!" interrupts Debra.

"We know we're going to have to stick together and support each other," continues Celeste. "We need a cargo checkers' women's collective to guarantee that we're treated fairly on the job and not harassed and that we are treated with respect just as in any other workplace. Many of us will not be able to work in the same place. They are going to make it hard for us."

"I don't care, as long as they pay me," interjects Debra, who doesn't want anything to stop her from getting that job. "I'm not there to make friends; I'm there to make money."

Celeste agrees. "All I want is a decent day's pay for a decent day's work."

Jackie O'Shaughnessy, another of the women who has filed discrimination charges against the Waterfront Commission, counsels women working in or trying to get into the trades. She finds the spirit of the women applying for cargo-checking jobs similar to that shown by women in other nontraditional work. "There is a high level of women trying to support each other and help each other with their problems," she reports. "The unity of the women lies in trying to figure out approaches to the problems of harassment and discrimination and such."

The group first came together through Jane Silver of N.O.W., which receives federal funds for job development through CETA. "The purpose of the program," she explains, "is to assist women in obtaining entry-level blue-collar jobs which have been traditionally reserved for men." On first hearing about the openings for cargo checkers, Jane telephoned women who had previously come to the program in search of employment. Debra Brown was already working at the N.O.W. offices. Jackie O'Shaughnessy was a CETA worker on the "Blue-Collar Woman" project, sponsored by Women in the Trades. The other four original applicants for cargo checker jobs were on welfare and anxious to find work.

Since August 15, when the six women first applied, nearly one hundred women have joined the group. Many were brought in by N.O.W.'s public service announcements on radio, TV and in the press. "There has been a tremendous response from women interested in apprenticeships and jobs such as assembly line work, guarding property, repairing machines, unloading cargo at warehouses and other nontraditional work," says Jane Silver.

Many women who seek help from the Job Development Program have no clerical skills or degrees. The project was specifically designed for such women. "Since they are unable to obtain professional or clerical positions, the only remaining jobs for these women are in sales, waitressing or hospital work," explains Jane Silver. "Many of these jobs pay only the minimum wage. Only through blue-collar jobs do semiskilled or unskilled women have any hope of rising above the poverty level." One third of the women heard about the Job Development Program at welfare offices. Of the one hundred women hoping to become cargo checkers, thirty-five are on welfare, seventeen have a yearly family income under $5,000, and seventeen have a family income under $10,000.

"If women could get those jobs, there would be much less need for welfare assistance," points out Celeste Collier. "It's often said that we minority women are lazy and don't want jobs. Offer women jobs like this for $24,000 and they'll take them!"

"Ordinarily, women who are domestic workers have to hit four or five houses in a day," adds Debra Brown. "Why should women work for $4,000 a year and leave their children unsupervised? You can't pull yourself out of the hole like that."

Particularly significant is this group's composition. Black, white and Hispanic, the women work together and support each other. Jackie O'Shaughnessy, a white woman, is optimistic about the bonds among women of different races as they try to break into nontraditional jobs. "This effort provides an economic basis for black and white women to work together, which we have not seen in a whole lot of years."

Debra Brown, who is black, agrees. "This is the kind of opportunity that working-class women need to bring them together. There are a lot of obstacles that keep us apart, and the more things that bring us together, the more unified we will be. We all work, and we're all discriminated against as women. We must see that we're all women despite our color. Hey, we all want a better chance, and we're not going to get it any other way."

In November, pressured by the women's court action, the New York Shipping Association (representing the shipping companies) and the International Longshoremen's Association jointly distributed job applications. On one day's notice, one hundred nine women were mobilized by All-Craft and N.O.W.

After the women received the applications, they had to be registered by the Waterfront Commission and have a physical examination. On January 22, 1979, the Commission issued temporary registrations to women as longshore workers, and it was official. By early February, women would be loading and unloading cargo in the holds of the ships. Meanwhile, the suit concerning the cargo checkers is still in court. Will the International Longshoremen's Association have to change its name now? "That is the least of our problems," replies Jane Silver. These women worked together, and they won. At least the first round.

Northwest Passage

From *Northwest Passage* 21, no. 3 (September 30-October 20, 1980): 9

The Missing Male

by Leo Griffin

I have been working with children and doing childcare, in some capacity or another, for the past three years. I have worked staffing childcare rooms for political events and have helped take care of some children whose single parents needed some time out. About nine months ago I took a job as a preschool teacher and worked in a daycare center serving thirty kids. Since that time I have had the opportunity to think about what men experience working in daycare centers, what they enjoy and what is difficult for them.

It is very satisfying to work with children, they are so alive, so affectionate, curious and less restrained than us "adults." I have memories of laughing, running, intense questions, and lots of hugs. But I also remember being worn out from intervening fights, never getting enough one-on-one time with individual kids, and feeling sometimes as if I was saying the same things a million times. We had a staff of eight at our daycare; a cook, three childcare specialists, three aids and a director. Three of us were men—Michael who cooked, Larry who was the director, and myself. Though the children saw and worked with us all at various times, I was the only male "teacher" who was constantly "on the floor," as it's called, with the five other women who worked there. The staff increased after I left due to increased enrollment, but in spite of this, now fewer men work there and none are "on the floor." I know all of the children get high quality care, but I do wish they could get a chance to experience both women and men as nurturing.

Government figures report there are 1,442,000 childcare workers in the U.S. and that 95.2% are women. Although it is well known that men are not encouraged to go into this field (men are often urged to go

into elementary education rather than early childhood development), it's rarely pointed out what limits them from entering this field.

To begin with, men are afraid of being considered "weird" if they play with or hold children that aren't their own. Not surprisingly, we usually feel uncomfortable when we attempt to. Often the fear is well-founded. A male friend of mine summed it up this way: "People would ask me if one of the children were mine and when I said no they gave me a look like I was a pervert or something for wanting to work with children."

We are also scared or uncomfortable working with children because we never had that responsibility before. Men don't usually babysit when they are teenagers or have to take care of their younger brothers or sisters. It's distressing, the first time you hear someone say "I hate you" or have to fix food for them, or change their diapers. I was put back by the realness of these children who asked me questions I'd hoped they never would ask but did, and by laughter, uncontrolled and riotous. Aside from being scared one might be made fun at for liking kids—just like before when you wanted to play with dolls. Even if nothing is said by others or felt by yourself about liking to work with children, your other male friends are studying business, computers, law or maybe education. Few are wanting to work with young children—how unusual, considering that many are going to have or have had children of their own.

Men are also turned away from working with children by something women experience too. It is a low-paying and even worse, a low-prestige job. Being a daycare teacher is something that is a little hard to feel proud about. In a two-year survey of male daycare workers, 70% left the field within two years (compared to 50% of the women). Pay and standard of living, and the lack of opportunity for advancement were the two major reasons for leaving that men cited. Childcare aide wages are about the same as that of a restaurant worker and in our society you are judged by what you make. Most men are conditioned to compete, to be the breadwinner, so they find it difficult to respect themselves when

they have such an unimportant job and get paid so little. Consequently, the men that try teaching young children usually switch to another occupation. Men go on to other jobs, ones where they probably will make more money. In the survey already mentioned, 79% of the men who changed jobs went into human service work, a slightly higher paying, "more respectable" profession.

People convey their disrespect or surprise that men do daycare in different ways. When people asked what line of work I did, my response was usually greeted with a pause and followed by, "Oh that's interesting," which conveyed that it was somehow odd that I chose to work in a daycare center. It goes beyond being unmanly—one is typified as unsuccessful. Even my father, who is normally supportive of work I do asked, "You're not thinking of continuing in that kind of work are you?" This surprised me and when I inquired why, he replied, "Well, it's not a very good kind of work for a man to go into." Even though I realized it was a low-paying and low-prestige job, I still enjoyed it and still work as a substitute there every once in a while.

But I did quit working there. I stopped because of a mixture of reasons that usually stop men from working in daycare centers and I quit because I felt I couldn't do the work as well as the other women who worked there. I felt that I didn't have the stamina or the ability to care about children all the time: I wasn't "excellent" like it seemed the other staff were and it frustrated me that I wasn't getting better. I went back to school after I left the daycare and took a part-time job at a local community action agency. I eventually felt like a lot of the men in Bryan Robinson's survey who left the work but of whom 100% said they would recommend men go into childcare anyway.

Men and children both learn from each other by men working in daycare centers. Men learn to challenge themselves by doing things they don't normally do—like singing, comforting children, dancing with them, and reading to them—in order for most men to do this requires a good deal of loosening up. I remember having to dance with children for the first time, so embarrassed in the beginning that they were so much freer than I and then later starting to enjoy it. I painted, crayoned, made faces and all with sheer enjoyment for the first time. There is no one to compare myself against, no one to put me down, no one to compete with. Men learn to care for children. By tying shoes, cooking for children and just watching them play, men begin to experience what it means to be tender and supportive.

Children learn from men working in daycare centers, too, and for some children this is the first exposure they will have to men as many are the sons and daughters of single moms. These early exposures are crucial as children tend to identify with adults and model themselves after them. From what I have seen, many children experience men as taller, deep voiced and more threatening than women; it's important to subdue this impression and overcome the authoritarian mold in which they are sometimes cast. It is especially important that young boys overcome the feeling that men can't be supportive of each other. Men working in daycare centers begin to show that men can be sensitive and nurturing, and can at least be supportive of children.

In these and other ways, children learn about and get to see men in traditional and non-traditional roles. What lifestyles, vocations and feelings they have are broadened by characteristics that are usually seen as identified with one sex or the other. Many of the traditionally male stereotypes are valuable human qualities: being strong, articulate, organized; and some are not: being overcompetitive, argumentative, violent, etc. It is important that young people respect their good qualities so that they can have the potential to change themselves. It is also important that as young people they are exposed to both women and men. If more men worked in daycare centers, maybe these things would change.

Bibliography

Department of Labor. *Employment and Unemployment Trends During 1979.* Washington: Government Printing Office, 1980. Table A-23.

Robinson, Bryan E. "A Two-Year Follow-up Study of Male and Female Caregivers." *Childcare Quarterly* 8, no. 4 (1979): 279-294.

From *Big Mama Rag* 7, no. 2 (February/March 1979): 13

Games-man-ship Spells Defeat

by the Working Women's Action Group

The Women's Workforce Organizing Committee, a newly formed group in Denver, distributed a critical book review at a nursing conference held the first week of December.

Among the management-oriented books which are required reading for nursing students at Colorado General Hospital is one that outdoes all others in putting women down and in opposing efforts to better the conditions of work for the vast majority of women. The title of the book, written by Betty Lehan Harragan, is

Reprinted with permission from *Big Mama Rag: A Feminist Newsjournal.*

Games Mother Never Taught You: Corporate Gamesmanship for Women. It is being vigorously promoted in government "affirmative action" projects across the country, apparently in an effort to undermine union organizing. The book offers women the illusive promise of personal success instead of giving us the skills and vision necessary to assure improvement in the working conditions and opportunities of women in general.

In reviewing critically the contents of this book, the Committee hoped to alert women to the way feminist goals are being turned upside down by educators who attempt to further individual and corporate interests in the name of "women's liberation."

The first chapter of the book is titled "Working is a game women never learned to play"(!?). The idea is that being an executive is the only "work" worthy of the name. Women are warned not to get into unionized jobs even if they pay better than non-unionized ones, because if you are in a

job that is unionized you "have no place to go" careerwise. This holds for all skilled work, manual work, and service work, as well as staff positions in education, research, or other professional areas (like nursing, which is called a "narrow profession"). Only jobs having to do with management and promotion are worthy of our aspirations as women. In pursuing the "CEO" (Chief Engineering Position), "Many women will discover that they have a knack for the game; others will need more and longer practice sessions; some may decide they'll never be any good and drop out entirely. But even this last group will benefit from understanding the game because everyone who works for pay in American organizations is part of this national sport, if only a cheerleader or part of the clean-up force" (p. 35).

The author's thesis is an attack on affirmative action because her thrust is to describe the grim reality of "getting ahead" in terms which automatically exclude the majority of working people, and then to convince the losers that they just weren't persevering enough, clever enough, etc. It is an attack on women because we are made to feel "deficient" if we balk at getting into big-time managerial work (even if this means disregarding quality patient care, for instance, in the case of nurses). At the same time, we are given false promises that if we behave like men we'll be treated like men. Actually, we would probably be laughed off the stages as she suggests.

We are also promised by Ms. Harragan that if we play the game well, someday we may be in a position to change the rules. There is no evidence to support that—the only times institutions we work in have become less brutalizing is when many people, primarily workers, have organized to change the rules. The author has not an ounce of respect for people who actually do the work in our society, and even less for those who attempt to organize in their own interests or for the public in general who demand quality performance from us.

Public Interest

Besides attacking working people as losers, and depreciating those of us who would like to do "meaningful work" in the public interest instead of pursuing "careers," the author degrades us as human beings over and over again by discounting working peoples' struggles for better conditions. She declares that the drive for money is the *only* goal worthy of our energies. "Facing up to the brutal reality

Bulbul/LNS

that the unemotional accumulation of money is a prime indicator of female coming-of-age may be agonizingly hard for many women, but every teenager can tell you that growing up is a painful experience" (p. 230).

What about working peoples' struggles against harmful chemicals in the factories or fields, against unsafe machinery, bad lighting, intolerable noise levels, heat, cold, lack of childcare, and lack of sanitary facilities? What about struggles against speed-up, involuntary overtime, harassment and systematic discrimination? These are not mentioned at all in a book whose first chapter is titled "Working is a game women never learned to play!"

We are told that the quickest route to success is to cater to our immediate supervisors, even if this means crass manipulation to protect her/his ego at the expense of other women. We are told to eat lunch and socialize only with people on our own level or above, to learn the language and deceptive habits of men, while all the time "keeping your eye on the ball" (getting ahead). Whose interests are really served when nursing instructors separate themselves from students, when RN's separate themselves from LPN's, and when head nurses separate themselves from staff? Is this the kind of "liberation" we are looking for as women?

Frequent Changes

Ms. Harragan advises women to change jobs frequently and lay not stress on the development of expertise in the work we do. Men get ahead by defending their prerogatives and using their wits, she says, not by offering valuable services to the public. Women should do likewise. Such advice, besides dehumanizing us, discounts the very real obstacles women face as a group and the very real risks we run when we attempt to play it cool and rough. One false move and we could be out on the

street, or begging for a job of any kind, at minimum wage.

All this makes little difference to the author of *Games Mother Never Taught You* because it is evident to the reader by the time she has read through to the end that Ms. Harragan is not as interested in educating us as she is in entertaining us, and in serving the companies and institutional bureaucracies we work in by keeping us down and out, unorganized and powerless, and awestruck by the fact that a few women are being permitted to "rise above their station" and get into positions where they can push other people around for their own advantage. In short, her only interest is in *selling her book.*

We are not told what Ms. Harragan's own experience is in the "corporate game," but on the last page of her book we are informed: "Betty Lehan Harragan is a management consultant devoted to women's equal participation in the private enterprise system. She teaches a course on corporate gamesmanship at the Womanschool and lives in New York City." Working women can do without her and the teams of women living high off government grants, promoting books such

as hers in the name of "nursing leadership," "executive nursing," and the so-called "affirmative action" for women.

The Women's Workforce Organizing Committee suggests that readers look critically at other books assigned to CU nursing students, such as *Managerial Woman* and *The Executive Nurse,* both of which also attempt to draw nurses into corporate-style thinking. On the positive side, articles criticising this perspective can be found in *Women and Health,* a journal which can be found at the Denison Library, Colorado General, published by SUNY, College at Old Westbury, Old Westbury, N.Y., 11568, and *Science for the People* (especially March/April and May/June issues, 1978), published at 897 Main St., Cambridge, MA., 02139. These latter are predictably, not assigned to CU students.

Women interested in working with others to better conditions in nursing and other occupations can contact the Women's Workforce Organizing Committee, 722-3210 or 572-1440. The group meets at the Mennonite Church, 9th Avenue and Elati, the first Saturday of every month, 11:00 a.m. Childcare is provided in the same location.

SOCIALIST MONTHLY

CHANGES

magazine of the International Socialists

From *Changes* 2, no. 6 (July/August 1980): 8

Fight for Justice Hits Tomato Fields

by Neil Chacker

Reprinted with permission from *Changes: Socialist Monthly,* a magazine reflecting the views of the International Socialists.

It's a long way from the dusty grape fields of California to the muddy tomato fields of Ohio, but they have something in common. In both places a determined struggle is going on to improve the lives of some of the most oppressed people in America, the migrant farmworkers.

Most people are familiar with the work done by the UFW in California. Not as many have heard about the Farm Labor Organizing Committee, FLOC.

There is nothing good to be said about tomato picking. The work, stooped over all day, is back-breaking. Wages average about a penny per pound. The fields have to be gone over three times as the tomato ripens unevenly. Work availability is dependent on the unpredictable weather.

For FLOC to win improvements from the farmers would be hard enough. What makes it infinitely worse is the fact that the Ohio tomato farmers are completely dominated by the Campbell's and Libby's canneries. The union first struck and won contracts with Ohio tomato growers in 1968. But in response to pressure from the large canners—dominated by Campbell's—who refused to sign contracts with unionized growers, FLOC was pushed out of the fields.

Every winter, before the crop is even planted, the canneries sign a contract with each farmer stating how many tons of tomatoes will be bought at what price. The farmers claim that the prices dictated by the canneries leave no room for higher wages for the pickers.

According to Science for the People collective of Ann Arbor:

"If we statistically break down the gross receipts from the tomato industry by the proportion that goes to each group of recipients, a rather dramatic result emerges. Fully 83% of the gross receipts go to the cannery and retail outlets. The farmer gets 9%. The migrant laborer and the cannery worker each get 4%. In other words, the people who produce the tomatoes get 17% of the gross receipts, while those people who do not engage in production but merely own the production facilities get 83% of the receipts. It is clear that the canneries benefit the most from the tomato farm industry."

Not only do the canneries set prices, they also control the product. The canneries dictate what varieties of tomato will be planted, how they will be sprayed and fertilized, and when they will be harvested. In 1979, to bypass the farmworkers, Campbell's and Libby's announced that they would only buy from farmers that used mechanical harvesters.

Mechanization of the tomato fields requires the use of a tough, thick-skinned breed of tomato that is inferior in taste and nutritional qualities to previous varieties. The mechanical pickers only cover a field once, so that some of the tomatoes picked will be green or over-ripe. Only relatively large farms can afford to mechanize. Finally, the machines are useless when heavy rains turn the fields to mud, as happened in 1979. Between the rain and the strike, a big chunk of the 1979 tomato harvest was never picked.

FLOC's principal demand is for the right

to participate in negotiations between the growers and the canneries. Campbell's and Libby's have stubbornly refused to consider this demand. They maintain that since they do not employ farmworkers, they are not a party to the dispute. But because these corporations set the price per ton paid to the growers, decide what type of tomatoes will be grown and control the pace of mechanization, it is clear that it is the corporation and not the individual grower who has the power to bargain.

"Once the grower signs a contract in the winter or spring prior to planting time, Campbell's becomes the sole owner of that grower's tomatoes and the grower becomes more or less a field man for Campbell's" according to a letter from Baldemar Velazquez, FLOC President.

Modest Demands

The modesty of FLOC's contract demands is an illustration of just how bad conditions are for the farmworkers. They include:

1. 35¢ for each 33 pound basket of tomatoes picked or $3.25 an hour; which ever is greater.

2. 28 hours guaranteed wages every two weeks.

3. 15¢ per mile travel payment from the worker's home state.

4. Health coverage during work-time.

5. Cleaner and safer labor camps.

6. Representation as third-party during negotiations between the farmers and the canneries.

FLOC's activities fall into three areas: picketing struck fields in Ohio during the harvest, publicizing the strike in Texas and Florida (where most of the farmworkers come from), and building a nation-wide boycott of Campbell's and Libby's products.

The boycott has attracted widespread support, with boycott committees active in 46 cities. A number of schools have dropped out of the Campbell label redemption program, by which the company donates school equipment in exchange for labels collected by the students. Several unions and religious organizations have also endorsed the boycott.

In response to the boycott, and as a means of undercutting FLOC, Campbell's recently offered $250,000 to the Ohio Council of Churches for retraining and childcare for migrant farmworkers. The Council declined the offer, saying it would be more appropriate for Campbell to deal with the union.

This recent action of Campbell's indicates that the company has been forced to admit that it has some responsibility for the migrant workers. A FLOC statement said, "Campbell wants to be able to tell the public that they are meeting some of the FLOC demands without dealing with FLOC."

For information on how best to support the boycott contact FLOC, 714½ S. Saint Claire Street, Toledo OH 43609 (419) 243-3456.

BROADSIDE

From *Broadside*, no. 142 (July-December 1979), p. 9

Farmer

by Kristin Lems

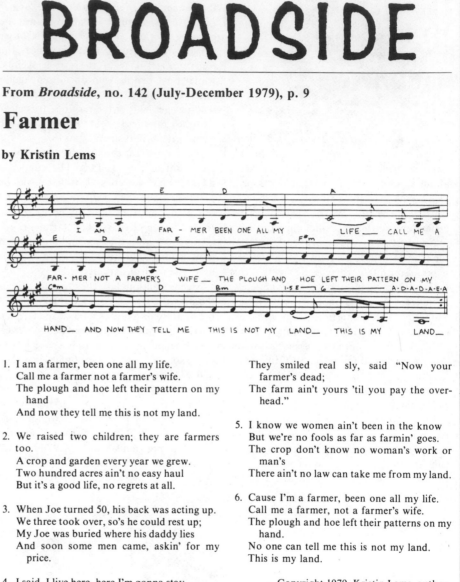

1. I am a farmer, been one all my life.
Call me a farmer not a farmer's wife.
The plough and hoe left their pattern on my hand
And now they tell me this is not my land.

2. We raised two children; they are farmers too.
A crop and garden every year we grew.
Two hundred acres ain't no easy haul
But it's a good life, no regrets at all.

3. When Joe turned 50, his back was acting up.
We three took over, so's he could rest up;
My Joe was buried where his daddy lies
And soon some men came, askin' for my price.

4. I said, I live here, here I'm gonna stay
What makes you think I wanna move away?

They smiled real sly, said "Now your farmer's dead;
The farm ain't yours 'til you pay the overhead."

5. I know we women ain't been in the know
But we're no fools as far as farmin' goes.
The crop don't know no woman's work or man's
There ain't no law can take me from my land.

6. Cause I'm a farmer, been one all my life.
Call me a farmer, not a farmer's wife.
The plough and hoe left their patterns on my hand.
No one can tell me this is not my land.
This is my land.

Copyright 1979, Kristin Lems, author.
Kleine Ding Music

Many farm states still have laws stating that a woman must pay a crippling inheritance tax to keep the farm if her husband dies. No such problem exists for the man should she die. If there were ever a true partnership of equals, it's in farming! Farm women in the Midwest have taught us all a great deal—this song is a tribute to them and their sometimes unconscious feminism, and to the ongoing urgency for the Equal Rights Amendment in the face of so many discriminatory laws!

This song is from the album *Oh Mama!* by Kristin Lems, Carolsdatter Productions, 908 W. California, Urbana, Illinois 61801.

Labor Education & Research Project

LABOR NOTES

From *Labor Notes*, no. 20 (September 25, 1980), p. 14

The Productivity Myth: Everyone in the World Works Harder Than You

by Kim Moody

How often have you heard an employer or a government official bemoan the "declining productivity of the American worker"? How often have you heard that the productivity of workers in other nations is surpassing that of American workers?

And how often have you heard both of these complaints from people who were asking you or some other worker to speed up your labor, make some concessions on your contract, or give back something in order to spruce up productivity?

Before you start believing what they say, consider a few facts:

• Productivity, meaning output per worker per hour, is meaningful only in relation to the output of physical goods. While management has tried to maximize profits by applying productivity measures to service, clerical, retail, teaching, and transportation jobs, these measures are not based on the output of items that are homogeneous or equivalent. An excellent discussion of this is to be found in the June issue of *Monthly Review*.

• Even in manufacturing, the measure of output per hour can be misleading because the content, complexity, and even nature of the product may change over the years. It is one thing to compare over a period of many years output per hour of steel or coal, and quite another of computers or even automobiles.

• Aggregate productivity figures are spurious on a number of grounds, but particularly because they lump together industries, or even operations within a single industry, that are growing with those that are declining.

• Even accepting these figures, however, it is evident that there is not a decline in the

Reprinted with permission from *Labor Notes*.

productivity of most manufacturing workers in the United States. The productivity figures continue to rise over the years. What is true is that they rise at a slower rate. This long term trend is not a function of workers' "laziness," "restrictive work rules," or much of anything attributable to the behavior of workers.

Long term improvements or declines in productivity or its rate of growth are a function of major technological advances or the lack of them. This is something experienced by all industrial nations at one time or another. The difference in productivity rates between the U.S. and Japan or Germany has to do with the timing of industrial development, not with alleged worker discipline, the singing of company anthems or any of the other, usually mythical, attributes of the workers in those countries.

• The actual declines in productivity that do occur, as in the first quarter of 1980, result almost entirely from the slowdown of the economy. In every recession, layoffs lag behind production cutbacks, resulting in the same number of workers producing fewer products. This has nothing to do with the speed of the workers or even the state of technology. It has everything to do with the business cycle inherent in the economic system and with the economic policies of the various administrations in Washington over the past several years.

• There is little doubt that U.S. labor productivity has grown more slowly in the past several years than that of a number of other industrial nations—largely because of the timing difference in industrial development and because American businessmen prefer to invest in mergers, speculation and other countries, thus letting U.S. plant and equipment become outmoded. However, as a study of seven leading industrial nations released in May by the Department of Labor shows, there is a little more to the question than that.

The long term rate of growth of productivity has slowed down for most industrial nations. Comparing the 1960s and the 1970s, the average annual rate in manufacturing for Japan fell from 10.5% to 4.7%, Germany from 5.7% to 5.4%, Britain from 4.2% to 1.8%, France from 6.1% to 5.0%, Italy from 7.1% to 4.6%,

Canada from 4.3% to 3.2%, and the U.S. from 3.0% to 2.2%. In the most recent couple of years the U.S. performed more poorly than others largely because several major U.S. industries—auto, steel, coal, tires—slumped before any of the effects of the recession hit Europe or Japan. The timing is different, but the trend world-wide is unmistakable.

In terms of the actual costs of labor (unit labor costs) in the 1970s, the U.S. turns out to have the lowest annual average rate of increase of any industrial nation except Germany. The U.S. rate was 6.3%, Germany's was 5.5% and Japan's 8.1%. Other major industrial nations were far above these levels.

This picture does change in the last couple of years, with the U.S. rate increasing and Japan's and Germany's slowing down. But again, this reflects the business cycle and not the behavior of U.S. workers.

Put in terms of U.S. dollars, U.S. unit labor cost increases are lower than anyone's, even Japan's, for the decade of the 1970s. While this is a reflection of the decline of the U.S. dollar in relation to most other currencies, it is in U.S. dollars that American employers must think.

The moral of this story: don't let yourself be bilked by flashy statistics showing that everybody in the world works faster and harder than you, demands lower wage increases, and allows more "flexible" working conditions. More than many government figures, productivity statistics are constructed on the subjective and self-interested views of management rather than by any scientific or objective criteria.

Northwest Passage

From *Northwest Passage* 20, no. 13
(August 19-September 9, 1980): 8-9

Propaganda on Productivity: You Aren't Working Hard Enough!

by Thom Richardson

Publications like the *Wall Street Journal, Fortune, Business Week* and others regularly complain about the problem of lagging labor productivity. Republican presidential candidate Ronald Reagan has made the attack on sluggish productivity growth a central tenet of his campaign. And Jimmy Carter is using it even now to justify his pro-business economic policy.

They say that falling labor productivity is causing inflation in particular, and America's economic decline in general. But that's nothing new. Conservatives have employed the falling productivity argument for some time. The only difficulty is that their argument is a sham.

Business and its friends in government like the declining productivity argument for two reasons. First, it enables them to justify lower wages. If productivity doesn't rise, they contend, then workers shouldn't be paid more. Second, it provides a handy excuse for inflation. The business press contends that inflation has to result if wages rise faster than productivity—that is, if the amount of money people have to spend increases faster than the amount of goods there are to spend it on.

Paul Volcker, Chairman of the Federal Reserve (the U.S. central bank), agrees: "Now if we fail to recognize that [productivity has declined] and people try to catch up with the existing standard of living or try to increase their standard of living, you get a process going that only feeds the inflation, because wages move ahead of prices and then push up costs further, and up goes the price level some more."

Labor productivity has actually increased during the Seventies, not decreased. At the same time, those exorbitant wage increases that the business press cites simply don't exist. On the average, weekly paychecks did increase in the Seventies—from $119.83 in 1970 to $219.91 in 1979. But these figures aren't "real," for they don't take inflation into account. *After adjusting for inflation,* earnings were *down* from $103.04 to $101.02! (These figures are in 1967 dollars.)

According to the Bureau of Labor Statistics (BLS), a dollar today is worth about one half of what it was ten years ago. A trip to the grocery store makes that clear. In effect, we now earn about what we did in 1965. The decrease hasn't been uniform; real earnings have risen in some years and fallen in others. But the trend is clearly downward; the $100 increase in our paychecks has simply vanished.

Worse, our prospects for the future don't look much better. Volcker thinks that "the standard of living of the average American has to decline." And President Carter set wage increase guidelines at 7½-8½% in January. Since inflation is still running much higher than that (18.1% in the first quarter of 1980), most companies will gladly try to hold wages within the President's guidelines. (They may not be so willing, however, to stay within his price guidelines!) Consequently, though paychecks will probably continue to rise in the forseeable future, *real* wages should continue to fall.

It certainly sounds fair; employees should be paid in proportion to how much they produce. If they produce more, they should be paid more. On the other hand, if they produce less, they should naturally be paid less. The business press claims that inflation has resulted because worker paychecks have risen while productivity has fallen.

Yet this, a key business explanation for inflation, collapses for the simple reason that its proponents neglect to take inflation into account when computing their statistics. Ironic, eh?

Economists usually define productivity as the quantity of output per input. In the case of worker productivity, it's output per labor-hour. So in the auto industry, for example, productivity is a measurement of the number of cars (holding quality constant) produced per hour worked. Since the figure refers to actual goods rather than prices, it doesn't need to be adjusted for inflation.

Contrary to what the business press implies, labor productivity has fallen during only two of the past thirty years. In every other it has risen, sometimes by more than 4%! What these conservatives are complaining about is merely a *slowing of the rate of increase*—not an actual decrease—in labor productivity.

During the past decade, labor productivity has increased at an annual rate of 1.4%, down from the 2.4% pace of the Fifties and Sixties. Still this amounts to an 18.5% increase for the decade. Yet according to the Bureau of Labor Statistics, weekly earnings (in constant dollars) actually fell by 2% in the same period. Real wages have thus fallen while productivity has increased. Yet when we are told over and over that our inflation is

PRODUCTIVITY AND REAL WAGE INCREASES

Year	Change in Real Weekly Earnings	Change in Labor Productivity	Difference
1970	−1.3%	0.7%	2.0%
1971	1.9%	3.3%	1.4%
1972	4.1%	3.5%	−0.6%
1973	0.0%	1.9%	1.9%
1974	−4.1%	−3.0%	1.1%
1975	−3.2%	2.1%	5.3%
1976	1.4%	3.5%	2.1%
1977	1.2%	1.9%	0.7%
1978	0.2%	0.5%	0.3%
1979	−3.1%	−0.9%	2.2%

(Source: Economic Report of the President, 1980)

WORKIN' WOMEN

caused by too many dollars chasing the available supply of goods and services, administration officials and business spokesmen omit the fact it's not the worker's dollars that are doing the chasing. In fact if prices followed wages, they would have dropped roughly 20% in the Seventies.

Still, productivity growth has undeniably slowed—and that leaves an important question. If slower productivity growth is a problem, then what's causing it?

The conservatives would have us believe that workers are fundamentally lazy or greedy, that their "attitude" is bad. This belief stems from the conservative desire to use productivity as a bargaining chip in the wage bargaining process. The argument is full of holes. Other explanations consider declining investment, research and development, and the changing composition of the job market.

Labor productivity traditionally drops right before a recession, and stays low until it's almost over. (See preceeding table, especially years 1970, 1973 and 1974.) Since we're now in an official recession, it only makes sense for productivity growth to have declined during the past two years.

Recessions affect productivity in the following way. Business inventories build up when consumer demand slows, prompting the firms to cut back on their purchases. Manufacturers see demand fall off, and decrease production. When they

do so, some workers aren't needed quite as much as they were before, but one can't fire ½ of a worker—at least now very well. Consequently, that worker's productivity (and the productivity of thousands like her) declines.

For example, custodial workers must maintain an auto factory whether it is running at 100% capacity or at 50% capacity. But when the plant is producing at only 50% capacity, the productivity of the custodial workers is only half of what it is during times of 100% production: since his/her wages now only cover the "custodial costs" of half as many cars as they did at 100% capacity.

There are longer-run factors that have worked to slow productivity growth, in addition to the short-run effects of recession. Among these, probably the most important is the declining rate of capital investment per employed person over the past 25 years. (Capital refers to plant and equipment, and it's plant and equipment that makes one productive.) Physical capital increased at an annual rate of about 2.5% between 1946 and 1966. It slowed slightly to about 2.1% from 1966 to 1973. During the next five years, however, the growth rate of physical capital in the U.S. dropped to one half of one percent (0.5%).

Slower growth of capital investment in the U.S. probably has a number of causes. Foremost is the higher cost of energy, since it makes machinery more expensive—and

less profitable—to run. Also, lower taxes and wages in underdeveloped autocracies are attracting the investment dollars of U.S. multinationals, contributing to the decline in U.S. domestic investment. Most huge American conglomerates now have some operations outside the U.S. Many, including Ford and Citicorp, make most of their profits on overseas production.

Research and development (R&D) results in better, more productive, plant and equipment. R&D expenditures also slowed during the Seventies. While high in the Sixties (averaging 5%, sometimes near 8% or 9%), increases in R&D spending have fallen to between zero and 4% during the past decade. The slowdown has coincided with the drying up of government funds. Washington paid for over 60% of total R&D in the Sixties (through tax breaks, grants, etc.). That rate had fallen to about 50% in the Seventies.

Furthermore, for the first time, fewer people are employed in manufacturing goods than are involved in providing services. Drawn by lower wages in the Third World, U.S. manufacturing has declined and left this country with proportionally more service jobs. This transformation of the job market has also had an effect on labor productivity overall. It's brought the growth rate down. Service sector jobs made up 48.9% of the job market in 1970; today that percentage has risen to 54.4%. These jobs are less amenable to productivity increases than are manufacturing jobs.

The services, like waiting tables or driving taxi, simply have outside limits beyond which they cannot become more productive. Although labor-saving new computer technology is making industries like banking and insurance more productive, such increases have limits, and are not the norm for the services as a whole.

Conservatives argue lagging productivity is responsible for inflation. This argument is not only wrong, it serves to cloud the real issue: *American labor has produced more and been paid less.* But then, the argument's purpose was to cloud the issue.

Conservatives employ their productivity argument for two reasons. They use it first to justify lowering wages and second to blame labor for inflation. In neither case are they correct. Business has no justification for lowering (even real) wages. And inflation is not caused by American labor's wage demands.

From *Radical America* 13, no. 1 (January/February 1979): 31-37

Auto in the Eighties: Uncars and Unworkers

by Al Fabar

What will the U.S. auto industry look like in the decade ahead? How will its development shape and be shaped by the level and forms of autoworker struggle? I will argue that three events external to U.S. auto itself—the 1973-74 oil embargo and price rise, government-imposed fuel economy standards, and the re-emergence of intense international auto market competition—are changing the face of the U.S. auto industry. Cars must be redesigned and made lighter, and the government's regulatory timetable enforces a rapid redesign schedule. As a result, the industry will have to increase its profit margin on small cars; this will intensify competition with the imports and will require a risky overhaul of pricing structures and qualitative improvements in production efficiency. These improvements will necessitate new systems and techniques of productive organization, which will fundamentally alter the status of auto workers. In the new social relations of production, openings for—and threats to—greater working class consciousness are likely. Part I treats the deep changes in the auto industry, and examines their causes. Part II explores the possible ramifications of those changes for working class politics in the industrial sector.

Changes in the Auto Industry

The year 1973 was something special for the auto industry. More U.S. cars were sold than in any model year before or since. The industry made record pre-tax profits of $6.7 billion, or approximately $7,400 per autoworker. Riding that performance, the entire U.S. economy soared to new heights: record incomes, record profits, and record employment.

But 1973 went out quite differently than it came in. When OPEC (the Organization of Petroleum Exporting Countries) hiked crude oil prices late in the year, the industry went into a tailspin. Not since 1929 had such a sudden and precipitous downturn hit auto. Not only that; the problems were much more complicated this time around. First, there was the exhaustion of the normal three-year cycle in auto sales: good years in 1971, 1972, and 1973 probably would have meant a bad year in 1974 and perhaps 1975 as well. Second, the OPEC price hike—quickly translated into sharply higher gasoline prices and, during the embargo, into reduced availability as well—affected the industry's model mix. Big cars weren't selling and the industry made very little profit on each small car it sold. For example, in 1978 General Motors earned an operating profit of $1,362 on each full-sized car it sold, compared to just $449 on each compact and a mere $147 on each subcompact. Third, sales of small, fuel-efficient imported cars were beginning to look serious: their share of the U.S. market grew from 0.8% in 1955 to 15.4% in 1973.

1974 was bad, and 1975 even worse. New car production tumbled 2 million units from 1973 to 1974, then by a million more in 1975. By early 1975, over 230,000 U.S. and Canadian autoworkers—about one-third of the total—were on layoff. Every company but General Motors was losing money. In addition to the cyclical industrial crisis, the seeds of a riskier future were being sown: specifically, Congress passed EPCA, the Energy Policy and Conservation Act of 1975. EPCA, strongly opposed by the auto companies but endorsed by the UAW in the belief that nothing else would make Detroit compete with small car imports, mandates a doubling of new car fuel economy from 1973 to 1985. Not only was Detroit losing money in 1974 and 1975 on its heretofore popular "gas guzzlers" but now it was going to have to come up with an extra $3 billion per year to retool for the production of smaller cars on which lower unit profits had always been the rule. This $3 billion amounts to an increase of about 40% over the industry's "business as usual" capital

spending program. Thus the companies must not only match, but far surpass, their historical per vehicle profit targets.

The financial risks associated with the transition to a greater production of smaller cars has been masked, largely because the 1976-1978 period has seen steady improvements in sales, productivity, and employment (though the 1973 employment record still stands). The risks of this transition will be clearer as auto sales drop in the next recession. Auto production rose 2 million units from 1975 to 1976, another million in 1977, and 300,000 more in 1978. In addition, light trucks are selling like wildfire, so that while 1978 new car sales did not quite match the 1973 record, total sales (cars, trucks and buses) broke the record with room to spare.

Everywhere but Detroit, reports of three years, each better than the one before, would be good news indeed. But as William Priebe of a major parts supplier, Dana Corporation, had put it in August, 1977, "I really hope 1978 will be a bummer. If not, we'll probably have a severe fallout in 1979." Following the sales cycle, with "good years" in 1976, 1977, and 1978, expectations are for a "bad year" in 1979 and a worse one in 1980. Bad years mean sagging profits, and sagging profits are just what the industry doesn't need at precisely the time that it needs *more* money—much more—in order to avoid fines for failure to comply with federal emissions and fuel economy laws and in order to weather unexpected events without substantial dividend reductions.

Whether or not auto sales adhere to their usual cycle, the basic contours of the industry's evolution in the 1980's are clear enough. Cars will become smaller, lighter and more expensive, partly because of a campaign to sell cars with lots of optional equipment. Smaller and lighter cars will satisfy the dual needs of compliance with FPCA and more resolute competition with the imports. More expensive cars will allow increased production of smaller models without disastrous implications for profitability. With rising costs of imports (because Japanese and German currencies are rising relative to the dollar) Detroit hopes to put Americans into the plush leather driver's seat of an AM/FM/digital . . . $6,000 Pinto. And while the latest data on optional equipment sales suggests that the strategy may work, its failure could cost billions.

The rising price of new cars, relative to other goods and services, will somewhat dampen the demand for new automobiles, though the level of dependence on autos for travel in the U.S. and Canada will probably keep demand from falling so far as to actually reduce industry revenues. Furthermore, a slower growth rate in new car sales will help to stave off the ultimate saturation of the North American market. A recent study by the Organization for Economic Cooperation and Development (OECD)[1] estimates saturation—defined as the point at and beyond which all new car demand becomes mere replacement demand—at a level of 600 cars per 1,000 population. The U.S. is at 520 today; using U.S. Census forecasts of population growth, and assuming a slightly decreased rate of growth in sales, one can infer that the "car density ceiling" of 600 will be reached in the mid-1990's at a vehicle (cars plus trucks plus buses) level of about 17 million units, or 15% above 1977 output. This amounts to *annual* output increases of about 0.8%. If auto industry productivity continues to rise at its 1957-77 trend rate of 3.5% per year, and if the annual hours of direct labor do not change, employment will decline 2.7% a year. In that event, instead of today's 700,000 hourly workers in the industry there will be fewer than 450,000. However, it is probable that UAW gains toward a shorter work year and work career will keep industry employment from falling as far as these figures suggest.

The Costs of Transition

If the industry's strategy of down-sizing and up-styling works sufficiently well to keep average profit per car from falling, total earnings will stay in the neighborhood of $7 billion. But $7 billion in annual profits will not mean what it once did, because federal mandates in the areas of emissions control and fuel economy will require capital spending that will devour much of that sum. Of Ford's planned capital spending of $20 billion from 1978 to 1985, for example, nearly half can be traced to the effects of government regulations. Of GM's $30 billion outlay for 1977-85, at least $12 billion is regulation-inspired. Understandably, the industry sees regulations as taxes, and like any industry wonders whether it will be able to pass them on to the public through higher prices without hurting sales volume.

Changing Forms of Work and Struggle in Auto

From the standpoint of autoworkers, the transition means major changes in the mix and content of jobs. Down-sizing means new tooling, reversing a trend of decreased demand for skilled labor. If lower sales result from higher relative new car prices, the number of production jobs will decline faster than it otherwise would. But most important, down-sizing and other aspects of car redesign give the companies an opportunity to revamp much of the production process. New plants, new machines, and new routines are being introduced at record rates. GM boss Pete Estes estimates that computers will control 90% of all new auto plant machines by 1988.[2] Greater use of robots, such as the Unimate welders at Lordstown, is inevitable, and with it will come faster line speeds—meaning even greater discipline built into the technology itself. Because the overhaul of industry technique has of necessity begun at the tooling level and filtered down to final assembly, the phenomenon of machines appearing to control the activity of people will spread out of assembly plants to become the rule elsewhere. Skilled autoworkers will, one would expect, come to see the production process more as unskilled and semi-skilled workers do now.

At one level, this is nothing more than the coming to fruition of the standard Marxian prediction of increasing proletarianization; but it is more than that as well. The new auto production technologies, based on advances in the semiconductor/microprocessor sector, allow increasingly precise monitoring of materials handling and production technique by management, uncovering long-established worker "short-cuts" and discovering previously undiscovered waste. The depth of drill holes, for example, can now be measured electronically (from the temperature of the bit), as can the rate of flow of paint in sprayers. As a result, drill bits will last longer, and less labor time will be allotted to drill press and paint spray jobs. These and similar changes certainly reduce auto workers' range for discretion and task-specific craftsmanship.

The most important result of this new technology is to make obsolete the *arbitrary* appearance of shop floor discipline. The pace of work will increasingly be controlled by machinery, not supervisors. Foremen, already a waning force in auto assembly plants where the line itself is the real enforcer, will likewise grow less relevant to work in non-assembly operations. Without human supervisory personnel to blame for the factory experience, the only viable target for anger will be the organization of work itself. The perpetrators of discipline will be largely invisible, locked away in corporate offices monitoring production on video screens and with computers. The problems of the shop floor, and the way it feels to many autoworkers, will tend to collapse into a *single sentiment of outrage at being in the position of worker.* For if it is true, as Marx argued, that the germ of higher social relations resides today in the most extreme nuances of the existing alienated relations, it is altogether possible that autoworkers are engaged not primarily in a struggle between the companies and themselves as workers, but between factory relations and a collectivity realized only through the *negation* of worker-ness.[3]

This is far from sure, of course. In the changing production system in auto, there resides the potential for several different, indeed conflicting, reactions on the part of politicized workers. First, growing opposition to automation and "robotization" may occur. Those auto workers who are older, more experienced, and whose self-definitions were formed in less mechanized times can be expected to tend toward this response, justifying their stance by appeals to job security.

Second, "cybernation" may provide greater opportunities for the left. If the UAW continues to lose control of the production process, monitoring of work pace and production standards, and if workers perceive the need for alternative forms of *organized* activity, then the best-organized left groups with plant contacts stand to assume crucial positions of leadership. On the other hand, the auto companies' ability to "source" (farm out) work to small supplier firms—and "double-source" (to two identical suppliers as a hedge against strikes at either one)—will tend to undermine the left's capacity to organize around single workplace issues.

Third, one can imagine an uneasy alliance between the anti-automation forces mentioned above and the "rational unionism" majority.[4] The former are too weak by themselves to have much effect, but the latter has no real job security

Pour/LNS

program. But together the two could convince the industry that a slower, more consultative—if no less inexorable—introduction of new technologies is the only way to move ahead without inviting an unpleasant surge in autoworker militancy. The GM-UAW "quality of worklife" committees could well be the mechanism for such consultation.

From the standpoint of left strategy much depends on which of these three reactions—anti-technology, consultation, or an alliance of the two—predominates. Those socialist groups that emphasize "shop floor struggle" will probably find some success among the anti-technology workers, and the fact that the UAW has not fought automation will help such groups distinguish themselves from the union. In the end this may hurt, however: in the UAW even the dissidents claim loyalty to the union. Perhaps, therefore, groups that seek merely to reform the union as a whole, rather than appealing only to the anti-technology forces, stand the best chance.

But many workers will not find much that is attractive about either 1930s style "class struggle unionism" or jointly managed monotony. They will not want their "old jobs" or their "old struggles" or even their new jobs. Among all these alternatives, they will want none of them, or more to the point, none of *it*. They will, in a word, not want to be "workers."[5]

It would not be wrong to characterize this last statement as a prediction of disgust with all models of struggle or collaboration currently offered by the union *and* the left. Certainly, it should not be read to be an endorsement of cynicism or resignation. Rather, it should stir a sense that new realities demand a qualitatively amended approach to political activity. Such disgust, after all, is one way that the "space" is created in which new commitments can arise. The autoworker who comes to reject both what exists *and* what is held out as the future is not necessarily rejecting all possible futures.

This is not the place to present another "future" and oppose it to other, more time-tested—and time-worn—proposals. But it can and should be said that what past and present offerings lack, and a key source of their failure to catch on, is an obstinate refusal to place workers as people, as intellects, as citizens at their center. The problem, after all, is not in how cars are made, but in the appropriation of the right to decide how (and how many, and

whether) to make cars and every other product and service.

This alternative future starts with the question of what needs people develop in their experience, including their experience of struggling to realize individual, sectoral, and even class interests. The conclusion is that the pursuit of interests by auto workers (slowing down automation, winning job security pledges, etc.) will produce fewer and fewer successes as it comes up against the inexorable restructuring of the industry. But because the socialization of production and the introduction of technology are intensifying, the needs that may surface should be easier to recognize than in the past. The need for non-private control over *industrial* decisions surfaces when *task* decisions become buried in the production "system" itself. The need for explicit planning makes itself felt as auto workers balance the social goal of fuel conservation against the private means of "efficiency drives." Finally, the increasing impoverishment of auto work shows the need for institutions which affirm that the collaboration among people who work does not end when the whistle signals the end of the shift.

Notes

I am grateful for the editorial assistance of Allen Hunter.

1. OECD, "Long-Term Perspectives of the World Car Industries," Paris, Feb. 1978.

2. Elliott M. Estes, President of General Motors, address to the Society of Manufacturing Engineers, Detroit, October 31, 1977, reported in Bureau of National Affairs, *Daily Executive Report*, November 1, 1977, p. M-2.

3. The distinction between struggle as workers and struggle against worker-ness parallels the distinction between *interests* and *needs*. See Jean Cohen's review of Agnes Heller, *The Theory of Need in Marx* (London, 1976) in *Telos* 33 (Fall 1977), pp.170-84.

4. This alliance might, for example, serve as a partial resolution of the post-war tension between skilled crafts-workers in the U.A.W. and the International. The former have tended to take a craft/protectionist stance in response to their dwindling numbers in the industry, while the International Union has insisted on a contractual policy of non-resistance to new labor-saving technologies—in return for a 3% annual "productivity factor" added onto wage rates.

5. John Lippert ("Shopfloor Politics at Fleetwood," *RA* Vol. 12 no. 4) has argued that hostility to "worker identity" is concentrated in a particular age group. At least one insider agrees; discussing a stratum of workers, "largely young . . . that is responsible for a disproportionate share of absenteeism, challenges to shop floor discipline, and wildcat activity," a Ford Motor Company vice-president goes on to note that "This is not just a shop phenomenon; rather, it is a manifestation in our shops of a trend we see all about us."—B.J. Widick, *Auto Work and Its Discontents* (Baltimore, 1976), pp. 10-11.

COMMUNITIES journal of cooperative living

From *Communities*, no. 39 (August/ September 1979), pp. 30-33

The Industrial Cooperative Association: Blending Theory and Practice in Workplace Democracy

by Steven Dawson

EDITOR'S NOTE: The Industrial Cooperative Association is a Boston-based nonprofit

Reprinted with permission from *Communities: Journal of Cooperative Living*, Box 426, Louisa, VA 23093.

organization that develops worker-owned and controlled businesses. The ICA has helped several New England cooperatives obtain financing, marketing, and technical assistance, and has specialized in the creation of a unique legal/financial model for worker cooperatives.

Worker-ownership is a rarely experienced, yet much heralded phenomenon in the United States. When four years ago, in the face of a threatened plant shutdown, Vermont Asbestos Group (VAG) became a worker-community owned mining company, progressives everywhere took heart: workers could indeed run a multimillion dollar business where a multi-national corporation had failed.

Worker-ownership supporters were again encouraged when three years ago employees and citizens of Herkimer, New

York successfully bought a furniture factory which its conglomerate owner had threatened to close on the grounds of "inadequate profits."

In both cases, jobs were saved and progressives felt proud; soon both companies increased their profitability, and supporters were fairly beaming.

Then something went wrong: both companies began to do "too well." In Vermont the VAG Board of Directors decided to invest profits in a new enterprise, despite major dissent from the "worker-owners." Over this and many other issues, workers threatened to strike (*"Their own company?" asked the dismayed progressives)* and individual workers thought seriously of cashing in their own valuable shares.

In Herkimer, the furniture company was so successful it developed the habit of buying other companies in other states (*"When we talked about 'community control of enterprises'" said disenchanted supporters, "we didn't mean the community of Herkimer, New York should control enterprises in the community of Vineland, New Jersey.")* Workers in the Herkimer plant complained that, after a brief honeymoon period, they again felt treated like "just employees."

Despite these disappointments, those supporting worker ownership should still keep the faith: important lessons can be learned from VAG and Herkimer. Most important: early beliefs that lack of *financing* and lack of *management/business* "know-how" are the factors limiting the spread of worker-ownership can now be laid to rest. Clearly, in the two companies described above, financing and business expertise were well organized and still worker-ownership failed to create a lasting, "progressive," institution.

Instead, closer examination suggests the true limiting factors seem to be an enormous lack of sophistication in the *legal, financial,* and *organizational struc-*

tures needed for a stable worker-cooperative, and in attention to the need for *cooperative education,* i.e., helping employees and managers adjust to their new roles as "co-owners."

The Industrial Cooperative Association (ICA) was created in early 1978 to develop a sophisticated approach to these two questions of structure and education. With help from the American Friends Service Committee (New England office), and support from the Mary Reynolds Babcock Foundation, the ICA helped finance and re-organize two industrial cooperatives, created in the wake of factory shut-downs (see box: "The severe effects of plant closings on communities").

The first to return to production as an industrial cooperative was the Colonial Cooperative Press of Clinton, Massachusetts. The old Colonial Press was one of the largest book manufacturing companies on the East coast, and was Clinton's largest employer.

Clinton was the site of President Carter's first "town meeting" engagement. Just as Carter's motorcade was leaving town, the Ohio-based conglomerate which owned Colonial Press announced its closing. Since that day, the elected leaders of the former employees have worked with the ICA to re-establish the Press as a cooperative. The employees organized $420,000 of private and public investments, and began operation in November of 1978, becoming the first industrial cooperative organized in the United States in the last twenty years.

The Severe Effects of Plant Closings on Communities

Interest in worker/community ownership has grown dramatically as the incidence of factory closings by out-of-state conglomerates has increased.

In the late 1960's, national and international corporations in the United States purchased large numbers of unrelated manufacturing firms. Present economic conditions are now forcing a significant amount of divestiture of these same firms.

The result has frequently been liquidation rather than sale; Massachusetts alone had over 780 major plant closings (companies with over 50 employees) between 1960 and 1978, with a resulting loss of over 160,000 jobs. Research has shown, moreover, that not all these closings are the result of simple market forces: corporate management has often been culpable in the closing of reasonably healthy plants.

Corporations will rid themselves of viable plants for a number of reasons. Corporate overhead of centralized companies, for example, typically requires a minimum of 16 to 22 percent profit, far above the profit level an independent firm needs to remain viable. Also, conglomerates cannot afford commitment to any one plant: they must concentrate on *over-all* profit, often resulting in an unwillingness to overcome obstacles at a particular plant. Finally, critical mismanagement has been discovered in

several case-studies of major closings by out-of-state owners.

When a conglomerate decides to unload, the strongest subsidiaries are usually sold; the weaker subsidiaries, however, are often used for tax shelter and cash flow until market competitiveness is totally destroyed, at which point the plants are simply shut down. Usually, only a few weeks notice is given the employees and community.

Of course the terminated employees experience the brunt of that distant decision. Lack of sustained employment particularly effects minority, blue-collar, and older workers; those who do find work must accept on average significant, permanent reductions in annual earnings. Terminated workers also tend to experience impaired physical and mental health, and show a reduction in community involvement.

As importantly, however, a shutdown affects the entire community. The decreased buying power of the unemployed workers in turn harms area merchants, resulting in loss of sales and further unemployment. Payroll, corporate, and real estate taxes are lost, just when the need for unemployment and welfare services for those same terminated workers must increase. If the plant was a significant part of an area's economy, a "bad business climate" can create a devastating cycle of disinvestment.

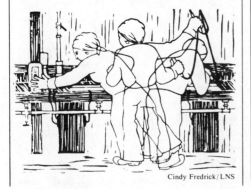

Cindy Fredrick/LNS

The second cooperative the ICA assisted was International Poultry of Willimantic, Connecticut. International Poultry was also formed in the wake of a plant closing by out-of-state owners: seventy-five workers, mostly minority women, lost their jobs when Menorah Kosher Poultry closed in late 1976. After more than two years of frustration and persistence, a "further processing" poultry operation opened in early May, 1979. The cooperative now employs 20 workers, mostly Hispanic and Black women.

Any attempt to answer the questions of cooperative structure and cooperative education must be firmly rooted in a philosophy. The philosophy of the ICA's work is based primarily on three central moral principles.

The first is the *fruits-of-their-labor* principle, which is the moral foundation for the decentralist system of private property. This means that a group of people, investing their skills, energy and time, have the right to the resulting profit of that enterprise. The concomitance of this right is, of course, that those people also have a *responsibility* to the rest of society to pay for the resources used up by that enterprise in the process of production.

The application of this principle to a worker cooperative means that profits are distributed *not* on the basis of how much money someone invests in the business, but rather on the basis of each person's skill, experience, and numbers of hours worked.

The second principle is of *self-government*, a central principle of democracy that states that the people who are to be governed by a government should be the sole electors of that government. While self-evident, this principle must be carefully transferred from the *geographical* setting of, say a municipality, to the *functional* setting of a business.

The application of this principle means that, in most *manufacturing* businesses, the people governed (i.e., affected by decisions) are the workers, both blue and white collar, and thus they should be the only people having voting control over the enterprise. Concern over effects of major consequence to the community (such as a polluting industry) can be mitigated by providing the community some regulatory powers designed, in effect, to place reasonable limits around decisions workers may make. Those limits can be placed by a municipality, or in a more progressive vision, a neighborhood-based organization with an economic development agenda.

For the application of this principle to *retail* businesses, such as a drugstore or department store which provides service directly to the community, a case can be made that the "affected population" extends beyond the workforce into the neighborhood. In such instances, the ownership and decision-making structure might extend to include direct neighborhood representation on the board of the enterprise.

For example, in inner-city Dorchester, Massachusetts the Finast food chain shut down a supermarket claiming it could not be made profitable. The supermarket was the only food store in a 1½ mile radius; its removal left elderly and low-income residents without any place to buy groceries.

The Codman Square Community Development Corporation (CSCDC, a neighborhood organization) decided to buy the building and re-start the store as a community controlled venture. Knowing the store could not possibly succeed without full commitment of the store's employees, the CSCDC publicly committed itself to some form of worker-ownership in the enterprise. The ICA was asked by the CSCDC to help in the initial financial structuring of this "Community/worker cooperative," and is now helping in the conversion to 50 percent worker, 50 percent neighborhood control.

The final principle is *equality of vote*. The application of this as an enterprise is a one person-one vote structure of voting for all workers, both blue and white collar. Thus

The Mondragon System of Industrial Cooperatives in Spain

The ICA has drawn a great deal of structural and educational information from a system of cooperatives in Spain called the "Mondragon complex." The Mondragon system, perhaps the most successful group of cooperatives in the Western World, was founded by a priest, Father Jose Maria Ariznendi.

After the Spanish Civil War, Don Jose Maria settled in the city of Mondragon in 1941 and began his work by reviving two moribund church associations. In 1956, the first industrial cooperative was founded at Mondragon. Today, the cooperatives have grown into a complex of 65 firms with over 14,000 members. The range of industrial products includes electronic equipment, machine tools, refrigerators, and stoves.

The cooperative complex is built on three community institutions:

1. The *Caja Laboral Popular* (Labor Bank) which functions as both a credit union with over 200,000 members and a community-based development organization with an entrepreneurial department of about 70 members who carry out a program of social and economic research and technical assistance in the development of new cooperatives;
2. The *Escuela Politécnica* which now includes a research and development unit and Alecoop, a cooperative factory staffed with work/study students; and
3. The *League for Education and Culture,* a broad association of parents, teachers, students, and community supporters that serves to link the educational system of the cooperative complex to the community in general.

The production firms in the Mondragon complex are organized as workers' cooperatives on a one-person/one-vote basis. Thirty percent of the surplus of "profit" of each cooperative is set aside; part for the social benefit of the whole community and part for a collective reserve fund. The remaining seventy percent goes to the members in proportion to the number of hours worked and the rate of pay received.

At the center of the Mondragon complex is the Labor Bank, which is the key to the dynamism of the cooperative complex. In American terms, the Labor Bank is both a Community Development Credit Union and a Community Development Corporation. In the twenty years of growth from one cooperative to sixty-five cooperatives, only one has ever failed. The Guipuzcoa province, which contains the city of Mondragon has one of the highest population densities of any comparable areas in Europe, and yet it now has essentially full employment.

no matter how much one gets paid in a cooperative, or how much one invests, one's vote remains equal with all other workers.

While this principle too may be self evident, it was ignored in both VAG and Herkimer where workers and citizens could buy as many voting shares as they wished. This allowed concentration of ownership, particularly among managers who had more money to invest, and led to distrust among the workers. The ignoring of the second principle of self-government in VAG and Herkimer allowed unaffected citizens to purchase shares, and led to an unorganized dispersion of voting control to investors outside the enterprise.

The ICA has taken these three principles and developed a financial/legal model for worker-owned enterprises that has been incorporated in a set of model by-laws. While much tinkering remains, there now exists a reasoned, pragmatic method of structuring a lasting worker-owned institution.

The three cooperative enterprises mentioned above which the ICA has assisted have been in operation for just a few months. A formal process of cooperative education has just begun in each, and much must still be earned by workers, managers, and the ICA itself.

For the ICA, education is a concept which includes much more than classroom discussions of "cooperation." It means the structuring of effective decision-making and planning processes, information systems, lines of authority, grievance procedures, and the important role of a union with a cooperative.

When devising such structures with blue and white collar workers in enterprises of 50 to 300 people, the experience of small, usually middle-class collectives is only of limited value. For helpful models the ICA must turn to the large, successful industrial cooperatives found almost exclusively outside the United States, for example the Mondragon system of cooperatives in Spain (see box).

What has already been learned about the broad concept of education, from experiences like VAG and Herkimer, is that worker-owners "do not have any expectations of downing tools and calling a meeting every time a decision has to be made, but they do expect to be kept informed, consulted, and to have a say in setting overall company policy" (Janet Johannesen, graduate researcher of VAG). Thus a pragmatic line must be drawn between, on the one hand, utopian visions of collec-

tive councils, and on the other, traditional attitudes of managers withholding information and making decisions "on behalf of" the workers.

The Industrial Cooperative Association will continue to assist the creation of manufacturing cooperatives in the U.S. The ICA is able to help organize cooperatives in the New England area, with a particular focus on Massachusetts. However, the ICA can also consult with people wishing to form cooperatives outside the New England area.

Anyone wishing more information can contact the ICA at: 2161 Massachusetts Avenue, Cambridge, Massachusetts 02140. Telephone: (617) 547-4245. The ICA is seeking Associate Members who will support the work of the ICA through their pro bono technical assistance and their financial support. ICA Associate Membership is $25.00 ($12.50 low-income and student), and Members receive the quarterly ICA Report and ICA publications free of charge.

Steven Dawson is the Project Coordinator for the ICA.

the magazine of radical science and peoples technology

UNDERCURRENTS

From *Undercurrents,* no. 32 (February/March 1979), pp. 20-21

Workers' Plans

**by John Darwin and
Hilary Wainwright**

In this extract from a paper presented to the recent CAITS conference in 'Alternatives to Unemployment' (see Eddies*)* John Darwin and Hilary Wainwright argue that co-ordinated Workers' Plans can be one way in which trade unionists and community activists can join together to challenge the power of the giant industrial—and governmental—empires.*

In the last few years, as the economic crisis has deepened and as capital's need for wage control has intensified, wage issues have become increasingly sharp. But fighting on the basis of wage demands alone, workers have been unarmed in the face of closure, competitive failure, and the imposition of productivity deals. As a result workers fighting wage restraint have been all too easily isolated and defeated.

Why does every strike in crisis-ridden companies like British Leyland become so easily isolated, and the workers involved so pressured by the threats of government and management? A major reason is that, by pressing claims solely concerned with wages, the impression is easily created that the strikers are cutting their own throats as far as jobs and prices are concerned.

*[A conference sponsored by the Center for Alternative Industrial Systems cited in the "What's When" section of the "Eddies" column in *Undercurrents* 30 (October/November 1978): 6.—eds., *Alternative Papers.*]

Reprinted with permission from *Undercurrents,* the magazine of radical alternatives and community technology.

In a certain sense they are; insofar as they are not *also* pressing for alternative plans to secure jobs and control prices. The core of the conventional 'economistic' approach is the idea that workers should merely press their wage claim, to such a point where the present economic system is clearly unable to meet the perfectly reasonable demands of the workforce. At this point the workforce, believing their demands should be met, realise the need to overthrow the system which cannot meet them. The fatal flaw in this approach is that, however reasonable people feel their demands are, if they cannot see how their demands *could* be met if things were organised differently, then they are very unlikely to take the risk of jeopardising their futures within the existing system. And so they back down. The importance of workers' plans (including demands on employers to keep prices down) in wage struggles is that they show practically that there *is* an alternative to production for an unpredictable market whose fluctuations are determined by the restless search for profit. The alternative they hold out is production for *use,* funded from profits directly or through government subsidies and fought for by workers throughout the economy. At British Leyland's Speke plant they began to think of invalid cars, road rail vehicles and so on. But they were too late.

Workers Plans against the Cuts

If workplace campaigns have in the past suffered from their failure to take account of the end-product, the problem has been even more marked on the other side. Community campaigns have suffered through their failure to take account of the production process, and this has been most obvious in the campaigns against public spending cuts. In the years when the welfare state was growing, community groups were able to take for granted that there was money available for the improvements they demanded. When the pot of gold vanished so did many of the campaigns. Local Councils replied to demands for better facilities by saying that they had no money to pay for them, and activists had no practical answer.

For example, the Tyneside Action Committee Against the Cuts (TACAC) drew up a list of 'Constructive Alternatives' covering housing, education, public transport, health and social services. These ranged from specific demands, such as a better housing repairs service, to very general demands, such as nationalisation of the construction industry and the drugs companies. What they did not do adequately was to show how these different demands were related to each other, and what they meant in terms of practical campaigns. If the local Council, for example, tells you that they cannot improve the repairs service for your housing estate because they have to pay interest on their capital loans, how do you react?

The link with production needs to be made in two ways; first, by developing campaigns concerned with the immediate finance needed to improve services; and second, developing campaigns on the longer term issues of what should be produced.

Red Bologna

An example of the first type of campaign took place in Bologna in 1974. The Unions drew up a programme which demanded a direct contribution to social services from private employers. They focussed on two issues: free public transport and an adequate nursery service to allow women to work. The costs were to be met by a 'social deduction from the highest incomes and from profits'. The contribution required from an employer was to be negotiated by the Unions as part of work contracts.

The second, and wider, question, concerns the type of production presently occurring in an area, and its relation (or lack of relation) to the needs expressed by community groups. We are not suggesting an exact link—a 'seige economy plan' for each area—but instead a long term process of linking (a) on the productive side, resources which are blatantly wasted (the unemployed, empty factories, idle capa-

city) and resources which are blatantly misused (producing armaments), and (b) on the consumer side, existing campaigns for socially useful products—such as campaigns for better public services, for a more economical heating system, for greater provision for the elderly, for cycleways.

The problem with our present campaigns is that they frequently lack credibility—they are fragmentary and unrelated, or they are overgeneralised, and therefore divorced from the immediate problems. Many people, as a result, prefer the rough comfort of what they know and have to the vague promises of socialism.

One recent attempt to get beyond this impasse has been the production of the 'Red Paper on Housing' by a group of socialist housing activists. This is an attempt to bring together the three key elements which usually appear only in separate form:

1. An analysis of the present housing system, showing that a serious crisis remains, and that there can be no adequate solution under a system geared toward profit. This part shows the relationship of housing problems to the present production, finance and use of houses.

2. A demonstration—though only, of course, in outline form—that a socialist alternative to the present system is realistic, can work, and will provide solutions. This is not presented as a 'blueprint'—the intention is simply to give some real substance to socialist claims; to show, for example, that there are ways to attain an adequate house building programme, and there are ways to eliminate all the 'exchange professionals' who make a rich living from the buying and selling of owner-occupied houses.

3. An account of what this means for housing campaigns *now*. The point made here is that the general and far-reaching nature of the changes required does not make immediate campaigns futile, and that such campaigns can provide the basis for more general campaigns.

Confronting the Real Centres of Capitalist Power

One of the greatest dangers in the move towards workers plans is that instead of seeing them as the basis of a direct challenge to the present system, we see them instead as the basis of small scale alternatives to that system, but which nevertheless are designed to fit comfortably into the system. The mounting

enthusiasm for small scale producer co-operatives illustrates these problems. We are now in a situation where unemployment stands at one and a half million, and will get much higher. The true situation is already masked by a welter of job creation programmes which are reducing, on a temporary basis, the number of unemployed.

This strategy holds real dangers of diversion from the central problem. It might be argued that small firms which are producer cooperatives can overcome the normal problems which occur in the small business sector—the 'scab sector' as it has been accurately named. But even if they do so in their *internal* relations, there remains the problem that they must co-exist with a capitalist system based on production for profit.

A study of Japanese industry recently cited as a major competitive advantage the fact that the large Japanese industrial groups usually have behind them a hierarchy of suppliers and sub-suppliers, with varying levels of trade union protection, wage levels and job security.

10,000 small firms supply services or components to British Leyland and Chrysler. The intervention of the Government in rescuing these firms has so far prevented many of those 10,000 from collapse (though for how long). This interdependence, and this vulnerability, remains unavoidable for the great majority of small firms, including Producer Co-operatives. One of the major intentions in the development of workers' plans is to challenge the power and prerogatives of private capital. We need to be aware that concentrating our energy and resources on small scale job creation is a total abandonment of that challenge. The top 100 companies in Britain already account for some half of manufacturing output, assets and employment. The workers they require will diminish in the future, but their 'dominance of the commanding heights of the economy' will continue and grow. As the conclusion of the recently published report on Tyneside's 'Permanent Unemployment' (Benwell CDP) puts it:

'What we can expect in the future, unless a serious challenge is made to this whole system, is that the multi-nationals will continue to build up capital intensive industrial bases, aided by massive subsidy from national governments who are competing to get new sites into their own countries. At the same time official reports and policies will encourage the development of the 'informal sector' in inner city areas. Here local authorities will play the major role of providing incentives: and again competition will be fierce, as each council makes use of their new powers to fight each other for a few more jobs'.

The Role of Trades Councils

If bargaining for the implementation of alternative plans drawn up from below is to be a realistic alternative to waiting/pressing for planning agreements; and if we are to guard against the reactionary separation of the struggle within the big corporations from the struggle in the community and small firm sector; then we need to think more critically of how workers plans should be developed beyond combine committees like those at Lucas Aerospace and Vickers.

Too much faith in the possibility of government support has perhaps tended to inhibit thought in this direction. Building up general political pressure to back the proposals of combine committees seemed enough. However once the limits of political pressure are understood, a very important distinction becomes clear. Taking support for the Lucas plan as an example, it is the distinction between demanding that the government force Lucas to implement the plan and, on the other hand, turning your own union branch, tenants group, trades council etc. into an embryo planning body itself. For example members of NUPE* could demand, either nationally or in particular hospitals, that orders for more kidney machines (or other medical equipment proposed in the Lucas plan) be taken up as part of the unions wage bargaining.

Similar initiatives are possible in the NUR† and T&GWU‡ with the road rail vehicle, and among car workers with the power pack etc.

Trades Councils could be an important part of such an alliance. Their role has always been to bring together workers in all industries and sectors, to be a focal point for community campaigns wanting trade union support and to represent the Labour movement in various local institutions. The form of unity they have achieved has normally been on a very defensive basis, although they have taken a lead recently in co-ordinating many of the campaigns

---

*[National Union of Public Employees.—eds., *Alternative Papers*.]

†[National Union of Railwaymen.—eds., *Alternative Papers*.]

‡[Transport and General Workers' Union.—eds., *Alternative Papers*.]

---

against government policy. In most areas they tend to unite mainly public sector workers: a disproportionately small number of trade unionists in the private manufacturing sector take them seriously. In the past trade unionists have in the private corporate sector felt confident in their strength to go it alone, extending their organisation only across the company and rarely across the locality. In a sense it seemed that anything more was unnecessary; jobs could be defended, wage claims won, without links with public sector workers and community organisations. And the fight for more public expenditure could be left to the Labour party.

Faced with the crisis and the impasse of a

---

sectional approach to fighting its effects, the conditions for unity are fundamentally more favourable. But firstly a sense of demoralisation in the face of all this has to be overcome. Unity won't come simply through calls for it. It requires policies which show a way out of the impasse; which show alternatives to the apparently immutable constraints behind the crisis— the market, government's spending priorities, the private appropriation of wealth. If Trades Councils, working with combine committees, were to take steps to draw up alternative plans which started from needs already fought for, and human capacities cast aside as redundant, they would be beginning to provide such policies.

CONVOY DISPATCH
Voice of the Teamster Rank and File Since 1975

From *Convoy Dispatch*, no. 7 (June/July 1980), pp. 6-7

Where Your Dues Dollar Goes

by Douglas Allan

No real union man or woman should object to paying dues. Our union needs funds to be strong. To have a strike fund, to operate our halls, and to organize new members.

At the same time, no union officer should have the right to bleed our union treasury for personal enrichment.

Yet personal enrichment, to the point of becoming millionaires, is at an all time high in our union. This year a *record* number of Teamster officials made salaries in six figures. In most International unions, *no officer* is allowed to make this kind of money.

Our jobs, wages, and conditions are under attack. But our officers' wages and conditions are doing fine. Even better than fine; they live like, and think like, top management. How can a person who gets a giant salary, luxury cars, jet planes, unlimited expenses, vast and multiple pensions, how can such a person feel the problems of the working Teamsters? How can they fight on our behalf? They cannot.

Reprinted with permission from *Convoy Dispatch.*

What They Do for Their Money: Members of the $100,000 Club Convicted of Felonies

While a list of the IBT* officials convicted of criminal activities to the detriment of the rank and file could go on for page after page, it is notable how several of the top paid IBT officials have been invoked with Criminal convictions.

William Presser ($173,422) was convicted in 1971 of taking payoffs from employers.

Rudy Tham (just shy of the $100,000 mark at $98,323) was convicted this Spring of embezzling the members' funds while entertaining mob-tied figures.

Anthony "Tony Pro" Provenzano (family income from IBT payroll: $297,778). His murder conviction was just reinstated by New York's highest court on May 29.

George Snyder ($185,000), former secretary-treasurer of Local 806, Hempstead, Long Island. Snyder was convicted in May for embezzling over $1.4 million from the Local's pension and health and welfare funds. His excuse: he was only taking an "advance" on money he would receive some day anyway!

Officers' "Blue Chip" Pensions

TDU research reveals that IBT officers, in addition to helping themselves to lavish

---

*[International Brotherhood of Teamsters.—eds., *Alternative Papers*.]

The Top of the Heap

Name	Local Union	City	Number of Jobs	Total
Frank Fitzsimmons[1]	299	Detroit & Washington	2	$296,853
Donald Peters	743	Chicago	2	245,590
Jackie Presser[2]	507	Cleveland	6	231,676
William D. Joyce	710	Chicago	2	228,881
Roy Lee Williams	41	Kansas City	7	174,008
Joseph Kelahan	710	Chicago	1	173,422
William Presser[2]	507	Cleveland	3	163,821
Louis Peick	705	Chicago	4	157,168
M. E. "Andy" Anderson	986	Burlingame, Calif.	4	156,828
Joseph Morgan	769	Hallandale, Fla.	5	155,838
Harold Friedman[2,3]	507	Cleveland	2	145,308
Arnie Weinmeister[2]	117	Seattle	5	144,731
Robert Holmes[2]	337	Detroit	5	138,661
Ray Schoessling	744	Chicago	2	138,893
Bernard Adelstein[4]	813 & 1034	New York	3	137,146
James E. Coli[2]	727	Chicago	2	121,271
Frank Matula[2]	396	Los Angeles	2	120,859
Joseph Bernstein	781	Chicago	2	118,659
Edward Lawson[5]	213	Vancouver, B.C.	3	118,065
Weldon Mathis[2]	728	Atlanta	4	113,336
Joseph Trerotola	803	New York	6	109,405
Vincent Trerotola	803	New York	4	109,183
Salvatore Provenzano[2]	560	Union City, N.J.	5	106,847
Rocco DePerno[2]	182	Utica, N.Y.	4	103,751
Jesse Carr[2]	959	Anchorage, Alaska	2	100,266
Rudi Tham	856	San Francisco	3	98,323
William McCarthy[2]	25	Boston	5	86,005
John Cleveland[2]	730	Washington	5	79,193
John Felice Jr.[2]	293	Cleveland	4	76,193

[1] *Includes $124,589 for legal fees to defend Fitz against PROD charges of corruption and sweetheart agreements.*
[2] *Based in part on 1978 reports.*
[3] *Also President of Bakers and Confectioners Local 19: $231,025.*
[4] *Also got paid for pension trusteeship: $9,670 not included in above total.*
[5] *Incomplete.*

multiple salaries, also enjoy multiple pensions. While the complete picture may never be known, it is clear that several IBT officers are planning on collecting *at least six pensions* when they retire. Included in this select club are Jackie Presser and Harold Friedman of Cleveland and Bernard Adelstein of Chicago.

Other top Teamsters are hardly candidates for poverty upon retirement, with eligibility for at least five pensions or four pensions hardly uncommon. William Presser, Donald Peters, Bobby Holmes, Frank Fitzsimmons, Louis Peick, Ray Schoessling, and Salvatore Provenzano are all in this bracket.

How much does it all add up to? Take an "average" top Teamster. One of the men on our chart who makes more than $150,000 per year (there are 10). Assume they are employed by the union for about 30 years and retire at about age 60. Then, taking only two most common officers pension plans into account—the "Family Protection" Plan and the "Affiliates Plan"—such an officer would be able to draw $180,000 per year. ($30,000 from the Affiliates Plan; $150,000 from the "Family Protection" plan.) If we can assume that this "average" officer receives *more* than two pensions, then his total could easily go over *$200,000 per year.*

And while these same officers have turned the members' pensions to the mob as a source of cheap and easily defrauded loans, their own pensions are invested in only blue chip stocks and bonds. There is no chance *their* funds won't be solvent when its time to collect that little $200,000 per year nest egg.

Ed Lawson: International Vice President. Director of the Canadian Conference. Pres. of Local 213. 1979 compensation: $118,065.

"Local union meetings? What are those?" That's what best summarizes the attitude of "Senator" Ed Lawson, who has not attended a meeting of Local 213 since Nov. 1977. (He also has the worst attendance record of anyone in the Senate.)

Lawson is notorious among the rank and file for endorsing wage guidelines of 4% while raising his own salary well above that figure. He is also infamous for having signed the 1977 National Pipeline Agreement *before* the members had an opportunity to vote on it. He is the highest paid labor official in Canada—but owes his allegiance and most of his salaries to one man in Washington.

Roy Williams: International Vice President. Director Central Conference. President, Local 41, Kansas City. 1979 compensation: $174,008.

Williams' mammoth salary comes from his vast web of positions centered in the Central Conference. Williams has been indicted on occasion for such things as embezzling union funds, but his associates have been convicted while he got off. When his friend Floyd Hayes decided to turn states evidence, he was murdered in 1964, with no arrest ever made. A 1971 Labor Department internal report states that Williams was "under the complete domination of Nick Civella," the reported head of the syndicate in Kansas City. Williams appointed Civella's nephew to be "Health and Safety Director" for the Central Conference.

What We Can Do!

TDU believes that no officer should be making more per year than the highest salary paid to members working in the Industry.

Can It Be Changed? The answer is yes. But it will not be easy.

Article III, Section 9(a) of the IBT Constitution states, in part: "Thirty days prior to each convention, Local Unions, Local Union officers, *members* in good

Robert Holmes, Sr.: International Vice President. Pres., Local 337. 1979 compensation: $138,661.

Holmes gets four separate pensions. Local 337 members who worked 40 years at Kroger's Detroit bakery got none. He presided over the rip-off of all Central States pensions until the government forced his resignation as trustee. Under his leadership, Teamsters in the grocery industry have been hit with mileage pay, productivity quotas, and substandard new hire wages.

Jackie Presser: International Vice President. Vice President of the Ohio Conference and Joint Council 41. Sec-Treas. of Local 507, Cleveland. 1979 compensation: at least $231,676 (based in part on lower 1978 reports).

His giant salary is only the tip of the iceberg. He is a millionaire who has never worked a day in his life in any Teamster industry. He inherited the "family business" (our union) from his father, who was convicted of labor extortion and destroying union records.

Jackie also defaulted on a million dollar pension fund loan, but later was appointed a Fund trustee. Presser makes much of his money in business deals, such as being a partner with an officer of Leaseway, one of the largest trucking companies in the U.S.

standing, or General officers, shall have the right to send to the General President proposed amendments or additions to the Constitution, or resolutions which shall be submitted to the Constitution Committee when it meets."

Corruption Starts at Home

Teamster	Relative	Total
Bernard Adelstein	Alan (son)	$ 72,838
	Martin (son)	79,916
Joseph Bernstein	Joseph (son)	112,876
	Robert (son)	101,005
Rocco DePerno	Rocco A. (son)	23,119
John Felice Jr.	John Sr. (father)	35,273
Frank Fitzsimmons	Richard Francis (son)	79,174
	Donald (son)	57,947
Harold Friedman	Patricia	16,200
	Allen	53,000
Robert Holmes	Robert (son)	63,255
Weldon Mathis	Wilbur (brother)	36,956
Donald Peters	Harry (brother)	69,447
Salvatore Provenzano	Anthony (brother)	51,952
	Josephine (niece)	41,674
	Nuncio (brother)	54,093
	T. Reynolds (brother-in-law)	43,212
Ray Schoessling	James (son)	48,604
Rudy Tham	Evelyn	25,418
Joseph Trerotola	Vincent	101,183

What would happen to the amendments that you or I might send in, as *individuals*, aiming to limit the salaries of our International officers? You guessed it—they would end up in the waste basket.

But we have other rights that will work much better and that right is to present motions at our local membership meetings. If 20 or more Locals passed a motion at their Local membership meeting that the Delegates from that Local speak and vote at the IBT Convention on an amendment limiting the International officers salaries, then we could make some impact on the issue.

Remember: our officers will only do that which we, the Rank and File, insist they do.

10 ORGANIZING

Alternative press publications are at once products of, vehicles for, and mirrors to social, economic, political, cultural, and personal activism. They are not easily distinguishable from the purposes, methods, and processes of the vanguard organizations and individuals that produce them. They serve as organizing tools, often incorporating calls for action, specifics of what needs to be done and how, and lists of people and organizations to contact in articles and running calendars of community and activist events. Organizing efforts, strategies, and actions are often reported and critiqued here as well.

In this section people are organizing to reclaim control over their lives, their communities, their society. Bimbo Rivas, Linda Cohen, Brent Sharman, Josie Rolon, Miquel Algarin, Susan Friedman, and Fred Good invite you to witness the miracle of sweat equity homesteading in New York. John Brouder and Carol Greenwald describe the aftermath of Black Monday, November 27, 1979, when the Board of Directors at U.S. Steel ordered the closing of two steel mills in Youngstown, Ohio. Jan Bervoets introduces the squatters' movement in Amsterdam.

Articles focusing on the movement to stop nuclear power follow. Of special note are John Breitbart's comments on the structure of organizations in this movement that rely on consensus in decision-making and nonviolent direct action and that have been purposefully kept local and non-hierarchical.

Boycotts brought economic and social pressures to bear on large corporations in 1979 and 1980. The status of the ongoing boycott of the Nestlé Corporation to force an end to their allegedly manipulative promotion of infant formula in Third World countries is reported in *HealthRight*. The success of a Women Against Violence Against Women boycott against Elecktra Records is announced in an article from the *Women Against Violence in Pornography & Media Newspage*.

John Judis, David Moberg, and John McClaughry take a critical look at the new Citizens Party. Sarah Young and Sherrie Mentzer describe their efforts in organizing a Take Back the Night march, held to begin to reclaim the right of women to come and go as they wish free of fear and insinuation. Rape and other displays of dominance and violence detract from the quality of men's lives as well as women's. Thomas Levine analyzes the trauma suffered by men who are raped.

Legislation proposing reinstatement of mandatory draft registration appeared in 1979 and was signed into law in July 1980. Allan MacRobert and B. J. Norman document the spontaneous reactions from individuals and organizations to what was perceived as a first step toward war. For a time women were being considered for inclusion in the draft. Janis Kelly makes it quite clear that feminism and materialism are incompatible and that the liberation of women presupposes fundamental changes in existing institutions, not merely integration of women into established roles. Robert Ellsberg and Dave Dellinger make strident arguments for working for peace and resisting the draft. And in the midst of it, Joe Bangert, Sheila Morfield, and Annie Vercker remind us of a war that is continuing tragedy, as veterans of the Vietnam War who were exposed to Agent Orange continue to be denied requisite medical care.

—PJC

PEACE & FREEDOM THROUGH NONVIOLENT ACTION

From *WIN* 15, no. 43
(December 20, 1979): 6-11, 18-19

[Loisaida: Three Articles]

LOISAIDA: THE REALITY STAGE

by Bimbo Rivas

Bimbo Rivas is a poet, builder and administrator at the community Townhouse in Loisaida.

"In Loisaida there is Fertility roaming the caverns of the brains," begins a poem by a citizen of that place. Loisaida, like Dulcinea, the heroine of Don Miguel de Cervantes's *Don Quijote*, is an entity that dwells in the minds of its creators and its lovers. Romantic?

Some people of Loisaida are an explosion transcending what humans know about how to struggle. They are breaking the barriers that have blinded and kept us from seeing and thinking. The magnetism created by these human beings attracts— is positive—and belongs to every living organism on this planet. Romantic?

The flowers growing in the East 4th St. anfiteatro and pocket community garden can give testimony without speaking. The solar energy panels on 523 East 5th St. nourish and warm with their collective heat the bodies of its dwellers. Romantic? Positive? The very sun, provider of the energy necessary to sustain nature, has become Loisaida's ally. Romantic?

Water tanks, built by children of Loisaida, adorn once murky basements with swimming organisms (fish) that will provide food and fun for generations to come. The same children sweep with tender love and care the perimeter of "La Plaza Cultural" where proud edifices once stood built by immigrants of yesteryear who have passed on; immigrants whose children used the very same stones to climb away from the Lower East Side and into the voids of

America the Dream. They are proud of "La Plaza."

They are proud of their immediate heritage—Chino Garcia, Alfredo Hernandez, Grupo Cemi, Peter Acevedo, Tato Laviera, Lolita Lebron, Hazel and Mambo, the Crosstown Committee, Roberto Badillo, Dona Carmen Pabon, Jorge Brandon, Luis Guzman, Luis and Jose Ortiz, El Committee, Tu Casa Studio, Charas Incorporated, Carmen Carnales, El Teatro Ambulante, the 6th St. Block Association, Max Olivas, El Perro, El Gallo, El Machete, Pupa, Pastor Juan Hernandez of the Pentecostal Church, Josie Rolon, Edgard Rivera, Juvenal Calderon, Father Bradley and all the other miracles and silent heroes who touch their everyday existence. They are proud of the dream promised to them and believe no other. Romantic? Positive? Cervantes should see it now. Incredible . . .

In Don Quijote's mind, there is no room for reality. He does not believe Sancho Panza's pleading attempts to manifest to Don Quijote the fact that the woman whom he thinks is a beautiful princess bewitched by a powerful sorcerer is really an ordinary farm girl whose charge is to feed the pigs. Don Quijote refuses to accept that reality and sets out to rescue the beautiful Dulcinea.

Don Quijote clearly identifies the evil doers who have imprisoned his love. And with the purest motivation in his own conviction embarks upon a series of adventures all leading toward the rescue and liberation of his princess.

Loisaida is plagued with the highest incidence of early death, the worst housing facilities, the most chronic unemployment, the highest percentage of fatherless families, the greatest number of drug addicts, the highest prices, the lowest number of cultural and educational institutions, and the worst sanitation, medical, recreational, nutritional and economic development facilities. Nevertheless, some of its citizens talk about the days when there will truly be a hometown with all the mechanisms and institutions, civic centers, educational and political virtues promised to the children. Those who have promised are anxious to

serve the town of Loisaida and have made the lifelong commitment to heal the cancer and make out of it the model that will insure the happy existence of all its citizens forever. Romantic?

Coming back from a state of death brought on by abandonment, greed, irresponsibility, bureaucratic, democratic-technocratic government, hate, prejudice, intolerance, egotism, bigotry, and dishonesty is not going to be an ordinary effort. It will require something these citizens call "The miracle of Loisaida." They even identify such miracles. They go to those places or individuals that have been certified as miracles because of the impact that a particular action or activity has had toward making the dream a closer reality. Romantic? Boy, oh boy!

The milagros ritual takes place during Christmas time. The citizens march together from miracle place to miracle place putting homemade banners in front of those buildings that house a miracle. A miracle could be an institution or an individual. The banners read "I am a miracle of Loisaida." They stay up until they are destroyed by the wind, snow, heat or rain. What's happening here? On Labor Day, while every other group is out of town celebrating, these human beings take to the streets with brooms and plastic bags and sweep all the garbage from the streets. Then they all meet in Tompkins Square Park and have a festival where music, poetry, dance, puppets, plays, artistic exhibitions, food, drink and merriment abound. This is done without any fanfare and is considered a day to celebrate work.

Traditional cultural events that have not been celebrated by the Puerto Rican citizens of Loisaida in New York City since the early days of the great migrations of the late 40s and early 50s are being revived. Among these are "La Fiesta de Cruz," a religious spring welcoming fiesta dedicated to the cross that Jesus carried on his way to Calvary, and the "Fiesta de Reyes," held in January celebrating the Epiphany or the Adoration of the Magi. In the last five years Loisaida citizens have added other fiestas such as the birthday of Don Pedro Albizu Campos who is considered to be the great patriot of the revolutionary movement to free Puerto Rico from the dominion of the United States government. This fiesta is becoming a High Holy Day in Loisaida.

During the 1979 celebration of Don Pedro's birthday, one of the poets reciting remarked to the hundreds of spectators at

La Plaza Cultural, "If anyone should ask you where the spiritual guidance comes from to the people of Loisaida, you can answer immediately. Don Pedro Albizu Campos!" The response was a thunderous "Viva Puerto Rico Libre! Viva Loisaida Libre! Viva Don Pedro Albizu Campos!" (Don Pedro died some years ago after a prolonged incarceration in United States federal prisons where he was held because of his activities to launch an armed revolutionary struggle in Puerto Rico to end the island's colonial status. This status derives from 1898 when, at the eve of the Spanish-American War, the United States military forces, led by General Miles, invaded Puerto Rico and overthrew the autonomous constitutional government that the people had won from Spain after a long, arduous struggle.)

Another festival which has found a place in the Loisaida calendar is "La Fiesta de Loisa" where the traditional dances of bomba and plena are manifested in a pageantry of dance and chorus reflecting the ancestral heritage the Loisaida citizens received from the African slaves that were brought to Puerto Rico by the Spanish. Loisaida also participates in the Puerto Rican Day Parade on 5th Avenue and in the "Fiesta Folklorica" held in Central Park in August. Romantic? You bet.

In the "Loisaida movement," as some observers call it, there is not a visible identifiable organized central leadership. The ingredients that make up the "movement" are elusive, sporadic, germinating and in flux. . . .

The movement has begun, there is no turning back. These people of Loisaida intend to reach their goals, transforming whomever they touch with the virtues imbedded in their souls, in their everyday interaction with each other as well as with the transient visitors that come by.

Loisaida is still in the "Reality Stage." The stench of putrefaction sometimes feeds the summer air because the pest control

Eileen Whalen/LNS

forces are not enough to clear the mountains of garbage that develop in many of the abandoned buildings, in the streets and in the sidewalks. Empty lots become garbage depositories, and junkies looking for a high cannibalize the citizens with their bad habits of mugging and burglarizing.

Too many Loisaida children are in jail. The economics of the town is not enough to compete with the returns that cocaine and heroin, amphetamines and methadone bring. Young men and women earnestly seeking a decent future are destroyed by the lack of outlets, places to develop and activities to heal their anxieties. Funding for programs that can provide some jobs is for the most part given to those established bureaucratic, non-relevant programs which produce institutions that spend their time giving advice but doing nothing for Loisaida or its citizens.

Recruitment into the most productive groups of Loisaida is achieved by a self-selective process. Therefore, converts are very rare. The number that become lifetimers in making the dream a reality is uncannily small. One organization had a party to celebrate the addition of two more members with lifetime commitment in a year's time. That was considered such a great accomplishment that they created a holiday for themselves celebrating that day from then on. For the most part there are no salaries yet; for the lifetimers committed to the movement survival becomes a hobby.

The colonial dependency state of mind is one of Loisaida's greatest enemies. The will to be self-sufficient is a foreign entity. It is not readily understood.

The welfare check is the main income. Minds become sleepy and work, hard work, is not associated with progress. The dependency syndrome infuriates the organizers who are trying to motivate these people to do something for themselves, to be self-starters.

The environment tends to further decay some Loisaida human beings into passiveness. The lifetimers are furiously trying to develop the open spaces with gardens, plazas and playgrounds in order to compete with watching TV, getting high, and hanging out.

The lifetimers are multi-skilled, multi-artistic, but there are not enough of them to make a dent in the general state of laziness and dependency that cripples the town.

The road to a healthy community is

going to be a long one. Important sub-movements such as the housing movement have too many contradictions, and internal bickering between these organizations is appalling.

The main organizations that could accelerate the rate of growth work too far apart from each other to be effective. There is too much waste and too much overlapping, with no central communication network to serve the town.

The cultural movement is at its fetal stage and chronically undernourished. The main artists are starving. Too many people from outside the community hold positions of power and direction. This has to be turned around. As a result of this reality artists and citizens don't trust the organizations. No faith in leadership has evolved. Apathy and lack of action is instead their way. The self-selected citizens of Loisaida have vowed to change these things, to overcome all obstacles.

When Sancho Panza told Don Quijote that the windmills were not dragons, he did so without intimidation. He told Don Quijote exactly what he saw. Don Quijote told Sancho that he was crazy. By the end of the book, Don Quijote finally accepts Sancho's view of the world as his mind returns to sanity. Don Quijote dies and Sancho and his family are well provided for in Don Quijote's will.

The lifetimers in Loisaida believe that their sacrifice is not in vain. They believe that if they develop and take care of their community that the community will eventually take care of them. Romantic?

These people see themselves as the modern renaissance of goodness. They have reactivated the values of honor, respect, morality, integrity, tolerance, peace of mind, belief in God and Jesus Christ, and helping one's neighborhood help itself—and they have made these qualities and beliefs an integral part of their characters and their existence.

They have searched into their history and found strengths and values that parallel those of the greatest civilizations that have ever existed. They have identified their cultural heritage and the nobility of their blood lines. They have reactivated the dormant juices of spiritualism and are motivated by love for a community, for a fatherland, for a motherland. Romantic?

They are artistic, prolific, intelligent, humane, understanding, healthy in mind and body, proud, hardworking and family-loving. They call themselves brothers and sisters. They want to reassess humanity and build the foundations for the dignity and well-being of a happy and peaceful future for all people in a safe environment. Romantic?

Don Quijote would have no complaints should he ever stop by Loisaida.

REBUILDING A COMMUNITY

by Linda Cohen and Brent Sharman

Linda Cohen is a planner and Brent Sharman is an organizer with Adopt-A-Building. Both have been working in the community for several years.

Loisaida, in New York City's Lower East Side, consists of 30 blocks of six-story residential buildings. Built around 1900, these tenements were intended to house thousands of immigrant families who slaved for low wages in New York's then-thriving industrial economy.

Many families were forced to live in cramped quarters with little light or air and often doubled up or did piecework in the small rooms. The population here was once the densest in the world next to Calcutta, India.

Today's residents of Loisaida inhabit the same apartments. Years of intense use, landlord neglect, and minimum maintenance have led to the present extremely deteriorated conditions. Adopt-A-Building was organized to remedy this situation.

The rationale given for the lack of services, public and private, in our area, is that poor people and their ghettos are not economically viable and they are no longer needed as a source of cheap labor in Manhattan. As neighborhood housing is destroyed, developers bid for the large, valuable tracts of land. They will make their profit by building and developing housing that will be too expensive for the current community people to live in. Our people will have to move to other low-income or lower-middle-class neighborhoods. Bankers refuse home improvement loans and mortgages in these areas also, and the cycle goes on. This process of displacement is now moving poor and working people out of the cities in the Northeast, and building up the suburbs and the Southwest. Areas with the greatest

services will be reserved for the managerial class.

New York City government also plays into this process because its goal is the maintenance of current civil service jobs on the payroll. Recently, for example, there was a public service contract to build sewers in part of our neighborhood. Non-residents did the work and spent their salaries outside the community. The work was not completed, and residents were left with a muddy street and broken sidewalks. The city also has increased already high real estate taxes, an act which hastens the deterioration cycle in our area. Banks became more powerful through the Emergency Financial Control Board, which must approve all city expenditures.

We must struggle against the combined force of banks, developers, and city and federal governments for money, jobs and services. Unfortunately, we find ourselves pitted against other oppressed groups who could be our friends but with whom we must fight for scarce resources: labor unions, mental institutions, illegal aliens, and other struggling community groups.

Adopt-A-Building's Goals

We have many plans for carrying through the Adopt-A-Building objectives. Some are just beginning; others are more fully realized. The more important of these are educating and training community residents in essential skills such as bookkeeping, legal matters, plumbing and so forth; sponsoring demonstration projects; keeping land from auction and buildings from demolition; obtaining funds; and organizing tenant, block and neighborhood associations.

There are problems as well. Time, money and resources are limited, and we are not yet adept at choosing among the many demands made on them. Our rapid expansion brings with it more complicated management and a lack of adequately informed, experienced leaders. Due to our insistence on tenant self-help, we now find ourselves pitted against other community groups who are interested in developing our neighborhood through a federal housing program, but are willing to relinquish tenant control.

—Linda Cohen

Over the past nine years, abandonment by landlords has been especially severe, for various reasons, including rising oil costs and lack of investment capital. Low income tenants are left to fend for themselves. When a building is abandoned, the basic services (heat, hallway lights, hot water) stop and families are forced to move. Fires in vacant apartments scare other families. At present, there are nearly 200 vacant structures and many more vacant lots in our neighborhood. The vacant buildings stand open and full of garbage, so there is a bad smell in the streets. Scarce city resources are spent fighting fires and demolishing structurally unsound buildings. Community merchants lose business and leave the area.

There are presently 25,000 residents in Loisaida. Just five years ago there were 75,000—the loss of neighbors, friends and fellow organizers has been truly dramatic! Of those still here, nearly 60% are of Puerto Rican descent, 20% are black, and 20% are a mixture of European, Chinese, Indian and white bohemian. The yearly income for a family of three is estimated at $7,000. Many are unemployed and derive their income from welfare and social security. In addition, 50% of the people here are under 24 years old.

The Struggle

"No heat—NO RENT" is definitely the most popular graffiti slogan in Loisaida. Scrawled across walls and sidewalks, it testifies to the countless battles between landlords and tenants.

In 1971, Interfaith Adopt-A-Building was a small handful of organizers operating out of a storefront. Working with tenant-initiated rent strikes, Adopt-A-Building encouraged a new vision—tenant

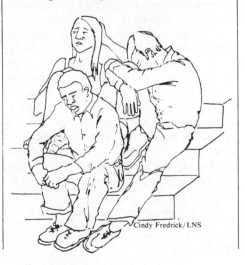

Cindy Fredrick/LNS

control and management of buildings. Tenants could do a better job running a building than a landlord or the city.

The goal of the program was to restore basic services such as heat and hot water and to work with the tenants to develop a strategy to improve building management and maintenance. While some of these efforts ended in failure (properties continued to deteriorate and were eventually vacated by the tenants), there were many tenant groups who were able to restore services and manage and maintain their buildings successfully.

In order to provide assistance to tenant associations, the staff of the program continually worked to develop new ideas and resources. In addition to locating contacts for building repairs and services, the program encouraged city agencies to develop policies which would directly benefit the residential community and obtained professional consultants in the areas of litigation, insurance, and accounting. As more tenant associations began to manage their own buildings as an alternative to abandonment, the staff sought additional resources to provide assistance to a growing number of buildings.

Success with organizing tenants' associations in occupied buildings, however, did not affect the huge problem of many vacant buildings, scheduled for demolition. Adopt-A-Building knew that abandoned buildings were a blight in the neighborhood, but were potentially valuable if they could be renovated to provide low income housing.

519 East 11th Street

519 East 11th Street was chosen as a pioneer project to prove that an organized group of residents could transform a burnt-out, gutted shell into a comfortable, affordable multi-family dwelling cooperative (see *WIN*, 2/3/77).* City bureaucrats were initially contemptuous of the notion.

Even other residents on 11th Street thought that the 519 group was spitting into the wind. But after one-and-one-half years of hard, dirty work, sometimes in weather below 20°, late night meetings, and constant reversals, 519

*[Jane Wholey, "The Story of the USA's First Urban Solar System and Windmill," *WIN* 13, no. 4 (February 3, 1977): 4-9.—eds., *Alternative Papers.*]

became a real vision of what was possible in Loisaida.

The 519 group asked for a $177 thousand loan from the city, to be paid back over 30 years through the future tenants' rents. Only the threat of a sit-in and the support of some local politicians finally pressured the Housing Development Administration to sign the loan.

These tenants worked under an arrangement called "sweat equity homesteading," which means that the tenants' labor reduces the cost of rehabbing (and meanwhile, they get money to pay themselves for the work) and the rents will thus be kept low. Sweat equity has proved to be the only way of producing low-income housing involving either rehabilitation or new construction without massive federal subsidy. The $177 thousand loan to 519 represents a saving of $189 thousand over what a conventional job would have cost, producing rents of only $35 a room, way below any other rehab program. Other people in Loisaida, and groups around the city and country, were inspired by 519's success and now many neighborhood-based groups operate under the same homesteading concepts.

Adopt-A-Building now sponsors and organizes homesteading and tenant takeovers of buildings throughout Loisaida. Although sweat equity worked well in 519, jobs are still a vital missing element in the community.

We now have incorporated into many of our programs a CETA workforce. We have trained 350 workers in construction skills. This has made Adopt-A-Building the largest employer in Loisaida. But CETA funds are running low and are not enough to support many families and supply steady employment. We are presently seeking to develop a construction company that will pay competitive construction wages and provide steady employment to neighborhood residents.

The sum of our experience is that the residents of Loisaida, through tenant management and organizing, can rebuild and manage their own housing stock. A lot has been accomplished. However, for every building saved, ten have been abandoned. And the difficulties of self-management can be discouraging—for example, the tenants may not be able to come up with enough money for fuel.

If there isn't a major campaign against abandonment, we will lose our neighborhood. Adopt-A-Building organizers are

encouraging block groups to devise strategies for survival. A neighborhood council is being formed to develop a comprehensive plan for the neighborhood. To obtain a large influx of development monies, Adopt-A-Building is mobilizing community residents to pressure the city and federal bureaucracies. (Over half of federal community development funds go unspent each year by the City of New York.)

Gentrification of the Lower East Side

A new danger has recently emerged: gentrification. Young, white professionals, forced by the overall city housing scarcity, and drawn by the potential charms and conveniences of a renovated East Village, are seeking apartments in Loisaida. Smelling the big breaks, the landlords of the area are attempting to drive out their low income tenants by withholding services and raising rents. The newcomers, meanwhile, snatch up tiny tenement apartments at absurdly high rents, easily double what they would have been a few years ago.

Even though Loisaida looks like a bombed-out city, it is actually one of the richest pieces of real estate in the country, situated halfway between Wall Street and the midtown business district. The city has been content to let abandonment run its course in order to rid the area of its present population. During the mid 70s, when New York City experienced its famous "fiscal crisis," the city's top housing official, Roger Starr, advanced the theory of "planned shrinkage" which would ignore areas such as the Lower East Side until monies were available to rebuild it for the upper middle class gentry.

The various factors controlling how much money, and for what sorts of people, will come into Loisaida are powerful. But for the people here now, control over the community is a vital and desperate necessity.

We are not going to let ten years of hard, gruelling work be taken away from us overnight. The people of Loisaida will not permit it!

THE RHYTHMS OF THE STREET

A Musician and Activist

"In 1964 I first heard about the Beatles and with that I found a whole new group of people and ideals." Edgard Rivera, then 12, started in music an ideology based on the strength of the group. "Everybody had strong minds—musicians, listeners and followers of rock music, people who didn't understand what the music said, but bought the albums anyway."

In 1971 Edgard formed a band, The People of Time (POT), with some younger musicians in Cayey, Puerto Rico. He came to Loisaida in 1973 and three years later began performing at community block parties, setting to music poetry of local poets and creating songs about the movement. To encourage Loisaida growth and development, he formed A Band Called Loisaida, and Tu Casa, a musicians' rehearsal space. The band set out to play "guerilla concerts," to "empower the people through music. Loisaida is a progressive microcosm of society in which the people (silent heroes) do all the doing," says Edgard.

Edgard is currently with a band, Z. He performed at the September 23 anti-nuclear rally at the Battery Park City landfill and at the October 28 Wall Street Rally. He believes there should be a lot more nuclear teachings, for "as long as people don't know what the dangers are and how it affects all our lives, there won't be any concern. We have to unite, to struggle for a better and safer world and to put aside labels of nationalities. We are one people living on one planet."

—Josie Rolon
Charas cultural organizer

Come Home to East Sixth Street

People are on the move. There is no tradition of people on the sidewalk handing over their attention. The poet has to get out there and project a reality, a volume that stops the crowd and concentrates it into a listening body. The success with which a poet can do this determines his reputation in the community as a poet. . . . The way that the poet makes himself responsible for teaching the people how to think about themselves, and how to put time out for thinking about themselves, is for him to do it, and do it aloud, and do it where people will hear him. . . . It's a responsibility that all poets have.

All of the poetry programs that exist in New York are usually outside of communities like the Lower East Side. Most often the place is a West Village bar, or a library, and that's not where the people we wanted to read to come. . . . So I opened a cafe. . . . I put the price at 50¢ on the wine and the beer. It was the cheapest price in town, and we served a whole mug of beer too.

I didn't know what that economic move had done. I didn't really understand that until later. It meant that at 50 cents we would get street people, and at 50 cents we would automatically knock out the chic. . . . People who buy drinks at 50 cents are dangerous. . . . So what happened in that situation was that I had done something that was very valuable without being aware of it. I had made my place a home for oral poetry.

Poetry is an oral tradition. I think that before this democratic idea of educating everybody, the poet was responsible for telling interesting oral stories. This responsibility was very real then. Poetry is oral and the ear works wonders on language. The average Puerto Rican kid who cannot read or write has one or two poems in Spanish that he can quote for you. These are passed down by the family.

—Miguel Algarin
Co-founder of the Nuyorican Poets' Cafe

This statement is excerpted from Agarin's essay, "The Volume and Value of Breath in Poetry," in *Revista Chicano-Riquena, ano VI, no. 3;* Indiana University Northwest, 3400 Broadway, Gary, IN 46408, $3.

An excellent collection of many of the poets who read at the Cafe and New Rican Village is *Nuyorican Poetry: An Anthology of Puerto Rican Words and Feelings,* eds. Miguel Algarin and Miguel Pinero; Wm. Morrow Press, 1975.

Loisaida Living Rooms

Loisaida, a winter night too cold to hang out in the streets. The hanging out has moved indoors, and if you've an ear for poetry, an eye for the visual arts, and a soul for living theatre, then you're hanging out at the Nuyorican Poets' Cafe and the New Rican Village.

The regulars can't keep away from these salsa cafes. . . . Everyone's here. El templo esta abierto. Willy's at the turntable and the dancing—Latin and disco—begins, dancing the week's tensions away. Baila mas Baila.

The music lowers and Lobo at the microphone introduces the evening's poets, There are many. The musicians sit up in the small, crowded performance space. Photographs create visual histories with slide shows, and artists' work are on the walls.

The cafe hosts a theatre season presenting works by black and Puerto Rican writers and groups. For a minimal charge—barely enough to pay for costuming—El Grupo Cemi charms us with the *Hustle Dance Contest Nine to Five;* and *What is the Lone Ranger's Relation to the Means of Production?* offers us new insights into American worklife; Pinones mystifies us with Puerto Rican magic and teaches unforgettable lessons about racism.

Both Cafe and Village contain a bar, art display and performance spaces. At either, one can buy a beer or two and sit or stand for hours living the cultural life of Loisaida.

The door is always wide open to new faces and new energy at these two Loisaida living rooms. The New Rican Village, hosted by Eddy Figueroa, is located at 101 Avenue A, and the Poets' Cafe has recently moved to larger quarters at East Third between Avenues C and D. Both open at 8:30 and close at about 3 am.

—Susan Friedman
Freelance writer and photographer,
Loisaida resident

Tu Casa Studio: Economic Development Through Art

In the fall of 1978, The Lower East Side Community Music Workshop, Inc., a musicians' cooperative formed in 1972, joined with Tu Casa Studio, the home of "A Band Called Loisaida," to renovate a loft space on Avenue B between East 6th and 7th Streets. Both groups recognized that a primary need of local musicians, and particularly bands, was rehearsal space. Since January, the Studio has booked bands and individual musicians and has provided a space for music workshops for both beginning and semi-professional musicians. Every night of the week there is a group rehearsing at Tu Casa. They pay $5 per hour, providing the Studio with enough money to pay rent and other basic expenses. These bands also make themselves available for community concerts and other events in Loisaida. The team currently responsible for running Tu Casa consists of folk singer/song writer Edgard Rivera, guitarist Edwin (Pupa) Santiago, vibes player Hector Rivera and songwriter/painter Fred Good. In addition to practicing their respective art forms, these men work in the Loisaida community in the movement to help revitalize the neighborhood.

—Fred Good
Director of the Tu Casa Lower
East Side Music Workshop

PEACE & FREEDOM THROUGH NONVIOLENT ACTION

From *WIN* 16, no. 5 (September 15, 1980): 4-7

Out of the Rubble of Broken Promises

by Anne Boggan

"We are encouraged by the effort of the people of the South Bronx to take control of their lives. . . . I wish to say that in our returning the land to the people here and giving them responsibility for the land, that we give that in true, very real solidarity with the people of the South Bronx." With these words, Ted Means of the American Indian Movement, representing the original inhabitants of the land, symbolically turned over Charlotte Street to the local community of New York's South Bronx, officially opening the two-day People's Convention on Friday, August 8.

The Convention, a planned alternative to the Democratic National Convention going on that same week in Manhattan, was a little late in starting as delegates drifted in that morning. Work crews continued to prepare the site, an open stretch of several city blocks which had been completely covered with bricks and rubble as recently as July 4. Representatives of the establishment media, many of whom showed up at 9 am for the announced starting time, grew impatient with the delay, but soon learned that this was a People's Convention and was moving at more of a "people's rhythm" than would the Democratic Convention downtown.

Convention organizer Jose Rivera welcomed delegates to the People's Convention under a large green and red striped tent and gestured to "our Grand Canyon" just outside: the towering shells of abandoned buildings which he said were *not* created by nature. Rivera traced the history of the area since the 50s when he

Reprinted with permission from *WIN: Peace & Freedom Through Nonviolent Action,* 326 Livingston St., Brooklyn, NY 11217.

attended Public School 40, which is no longer standing. "One hundred fifty thousand people have been burned out of their homes and no one investigates why, no one went to jail, no one was indicted. We cannot continue dreaming about the 60s, or let a number be done on the people like in the 70s. We must get together in the 80s and struggle for our own survival."

The slogan for the weekend's activities was "Too many years of broken promises . . . Now we will be heard." And the people were heard throughout the two days, meeting first on Friday afternoon in issue workshops to allow networking among those involved in similar work. Caucuses met at lunchtime bringing together constituencies such as Blacks, Hispanics and Jews; and at the dinner break women gathered to discuss their concerns.

Saturday opened with a panel on "The Economic Crisis and the Quality of Life" where speakers drew the connections among peoples' struggles such as Three Mile Island, the South Bronx, the People's Firehouse in a white working class area of Brooklyn, the welfare movement, industrial plant closings, small farmers, and the disabled movement.

This was followed in the afternoon by a second panel on "War, Militarism and Liberation Struggles" with presentations by Dave Dellinger, Jose Alberto Alvarez of the Puerto Rican Socialist Party, representatives from the African National Congress and the Venceremos Brigade, and Floyd Westerman of the American Indian Movement. This panel helped clarify the relationship between imperialism and the multi-national corporations and the Charlotte Streets of the United States which have been created through misplaced priorities and a war economy.

The third panel "And Justice For All— Struggles for Democratic Rights" was compressed due to lack of time. It dealt briefly with racism, the lesbian movement, southern struggles, New York City cutbacks and the need for independent political action.

The plenary then moved into a discussion of the Unity Statement, the "Declaration of Charlotte Street," which had

been distributed on Friday and was discussed at workshops and caucus meetings over the two days. Revisions were proposed and voted on for acceptance. As the session drew to a close and religious leaders from the South Bronx were on hand waiting to start a prayer service, a fuse blew out and left the tent without lights or a sound system. Jose Rivera spoke to the group in Spanish through a megaphone and kept everyone calm. After a few tense moments, the service based on the theme "The Lord Hears the Cry of the Poor" began in near darkness illuminated only by a strong flashlight. At its conclusion, those attending the service walked out of the tent and across "Pennsylvania Avenue" to the small two-story "White House" where a young tree was planted to symbolize hope for the future.

Over 1500 delegates from small and large groups working for social change throughout the country, together with the South Bronx Coalition, gathered on Charlotte Street to share experiences, link issues and lay the groundwork for building a popular social change action program for the 80s— a People's Alternative. In addition to the political discussions, workshops and plenaries, each evening ended with music, poetry, and theater representing the diverse voices in the coalition.

Charlotte Street became a small city for those two days. Three small houses sprung up in the weeks and days before the Convention, built by members of the local community. Behind them was nestled a campground with brightly colored tents. A daycare center nearby looked after the youngest delegates.

One participant, Dan Horn, a teacher and poet who has lived in New York all his life and works in the anti-nuclear movement, was very moved by the two days. "Although the area is depressing, I also found tremendous optimism there because

CPF/Daily World/LNS

people were willing to work so hard to create something for themselves." Horn saw clearly what Paul Mayer meant when he referred in one of the panels to Charlotte Street as the "other end of the military budget" tracing the lack of human services directly back to the cost of nuclear weapons. "Hearing panelists talk about imperialism and national liberation struggles in the middle of the South Bronx put them into a new context for me," Horn continued, "and made what could have been rhetoric in another setting suddenly seem very real to me. Charlotte Street is imperialism and racism at work."

The idea for the People's Convention was the dream of Jose Rivera, a 43-year-old former carpenter born in Puerto Rico and now executive director of United Tremont Trades (UTT). His 10-year-old organization in the South Bronx places Blacks and Hispanics in jobs in the building trades. Rivera received support for his dream at the People's Alliance conference held in Nashville in November 1979 which endorsed the Convention idea as well as a plan to demonstrate at this year's Democratic Convention.

At about the same time, Mobilization for Survival's national conference in Louisville passed a similar resolution calling for a protest during the Democrats' stay in New York City. A planning conference was jointly called by the two organizations and hosted by Steelworkers Local 1462 in Youngstown, Ohio, on March 15 and 16. Some 100 people from 60 organizations representing peace, labor, Black, Puerto Rican, Native American, tenants, environmental, anti-nuclear, farm labor, women's, lesbian/gay, international solidarity, rural, civil liberties and other left movements joined together to form the Coalition for a People's Alternative in 1980.

It was unanimously agreed to begin building a political alternative for the 80s, one that would effectively oppose the anti-human actions of those in power and lay the foundation for the creation of a society based on justice, peace, freedom and equality. Plans were approved for a convention of unrepresented people to be held in the South Bronx on Charlotte Street, the scene of Jimmy Carter's 1977 visit and his hollow promise to rebuild that devastated area. A day of protest would follow on August 10 outside the Democratic Convention at Madison Square Garden to voice dissatisfaction over the policies of our government and corporate

D.C. Gazette/LNS

"leaders" from both the Democratic and Republican parties.

When the South Bronx Coalition began meeting in early April at UTT, no one quite knew where to start since Charlotte Street presented a challenge unlike most other political events. A landscape architect, Karl Linn, with experience in transforming outdoor community spaces in several cities, joined the South Bronx group and helped people to conceptualize what they wanted to do and what was possible to do with the site.

On July 4, after two months of meeting and working together, activists from around the city and from the local community held the first of many work days to begin clearing the ground. Bulldozers removed the major part of the rubble but left behind a layer of bricks, wood and other debris which had to be raked and then shoveled into wheelbarrows and carted off to a symbolic "Mount Carter," at the far end of the area.

About 150 people showed up to work that first day and stayed to share a roast pig supplied by feminist lawyer Florynce Kennedy and 300 ears of corn from the Coalition. That day was the first of many work days when community residents and political activists worked side by side. Blisters appeared on hands unfamiliar with manual labor and sunburns were epidemic. By the beginning of August, organizers who had no time all summer to sneak off to the beach were sporting healthy-looking tans courtesy of Charlotte Street.

A People's March

The day after the Convention, the Charlotte Street site was cleared and the last remaining conventioneers formed a car caravan into Manhattan. Their contingent led a spirited march starting at 72nd Street and Central Park West going down Seventh Avenue past crowded streets to 42nd Street. As Jose Rivera passed through Times Square he shouted, "This is fantasy island. Go to the Bronx, go to Brooklyn. There, you will see what the politicians have done to us."

The march, which was large and spirited,

stretching some 15 blocks, represented the first multi-ethnic, multi-national, multi-issue march of its kind since the July 4 Coalition marched through the streets of Philadelphia on July 4, 1976.

The Puerto Rican Socialist Party, one of the orginal organizations in the Coalition, was responsible for mobilizing a large, united contingent—the Latin America Anti-Imperialist Pro-Independence Coalition (CAIL)—to bring attention to the oppressive colonial conditions in Latin America as a result of US imperialism.

The crowd numbered over 10,000 and included large contingents from the women's, gay and lesbian, and anti-nuclear movements together with many other organizations and cities. As the marchers filed into the rally site, they were greeted by a booming sound system and a huge stage stretching from Madison Square Garden across to the Statler Hilton Hotel with the canyon of Seventh Avenue behind it.

Speakers at the rally represented local and national issues as well as anti-imperialist and national liberation struggles. The highlight of the cultural program was Bright Morning Star singing "Blame it on the Ayatollah."

Arthur Kinoy of the Coalition for a People's Alternative ended the rally by summing up the "Declaration of Charlotte Street" which calls for a radical turnaround in national priorites to end militarism and interference with countries around the world and to focus on meeting the needs of people.

For most people who attended the Convention or who worked on the site in the weeks leading up to the weekend, they met people different from themselves and came to recognize their shared problems. People felt a commitment to continue working together to help build the kind of movement that is needed for the 80s—a movement which will promote their own survival and that of their communities. The Coalition will be meeting again in the fall to discuss future plans and strategies.

Contact:

Coalition for a People's Alternative, 29 West 21 St., New York, NY 10010; (212) 242-3270.

Anne Boggan is a freelance researcher and producer of television documentaries who works with the People's Alliance in New York City.

dollars & Sense
A Monthly Bulletin of Economic Affairs

From *Dollars & Sense,* no. 59
(September 1980), pp. 14-16

The Fight to Save Youngstown, Ohio

by John Brouder and Carol Greenwald

"When I was young the fire and smoke from the mills could light up the sky for miles around. The glow was always there . . . the steel mills. You saw them, you heard them, you smelled them. They were always there.

—a former resident of Youngstown

The steel mills are an imposing sight: a vast expanse of concrete and steel beams, blackened with age, stretching along the Mahoning River, with a forest of smokestacks reaching high into the pale Ohio sky. Twenty years ago the steel mills were working at full capacity and Youngstown, Ohio was a prosperous city. Today, after two decades of plant shutdowns, only a handful of smokestacks spew smoke skyward, and the city is dying.

Since 1965, 25% of the steelworkers in America—150,000 men and women—have lost their jobs. Landlocked, technologically obsolete facilities like those in Youngstown were the first cut: at least 30,000 jobs lost since 1950; 10,000 just in the last three years.

The impact of these plant closings has been devastating. Municipal revenues plummeted in Youngstown and the neighboring towns of Campbell and Struthers just when more people needed government assistance. In Campbell, the school system went bankrupt and survived only with massive state aid. Alcoholism, domestic violence, mental illness, suicide . . . all increased.

Youngstown's black community, which represents over a third of the city's population, has been particularly hurt by the massive unemployment as white workers are more able to move away in search of work. Fierce competition for the

city's few remaining jobs has exacerbated racial tensions and the city recently lost a sizeable federal grant because of its refusal to build low income housing in a white ethnic neighborhood.

Youngstown's rank and file steelworkers, community groups, religious leaders and politicians have challenged the corporate desertion of their city on a variety of fronts. One of the first moves came in September 1977, when the Lykes Corporation closed Youngstown Sheet & Tube's doors. The Ecumenical Coalition, an interfaith community organization led by local religious leaders, launched a campaign to purchase the facilities and establish a community/worker controlled steel mill.

Lykes, a New Orleans-based conglomerate, bought the Youngstown company in 1969. Never too interested in making steel, Lykes preferred to invest all of its steel profits into other more lucrative enterprises. Nevertheless, Lykes Comptroller William Fogerty found the Ecumenical Coalition's plan naive: "We didn't just shut down those facilities in a haphazard way. We think we're experts in the steel industry. If we couldn't make it go, we don't see how a bunch of uninformed people can make it go."

Assisted by a $300,000 grant from the Department of Housing and Urban Development, the Ecumenical Coalition continued to explore the possibility of buying the company. In conjunction with the National Center for Economic Alternatives, the Coalition developed what it felt was a viable plan for governing the mill and profitably producing steel in Youngstown—possible in Sheet & Tube's case, because, unlike many other area mills, these facilities were still in pretty good shape.

Finally, the Coalition approached the Federal Economic Development Administration (EDA) in March 1979 with a proposal for almost $250 million in federal aid. But the EDA rejected the bid, saying that if it were to fund this proposal it would have no money left for others. Afterwards, many Youngstown residents blamed the Carter Administration for the refusal and in the recent presidential primary Youngstown, previously a staunch Carter town, went overwhelmingly for Kennedy.

On November 27, 1979—Black Monday—the Board of Directors of U.S. Steel ordered thirteen plants across the country shut down, including Youngstown's Ohio Works and McDonald Mills: 3,500 Youngstown steelworkers then got the axe. The company complained of a decline in profitability owing to foreign competition,

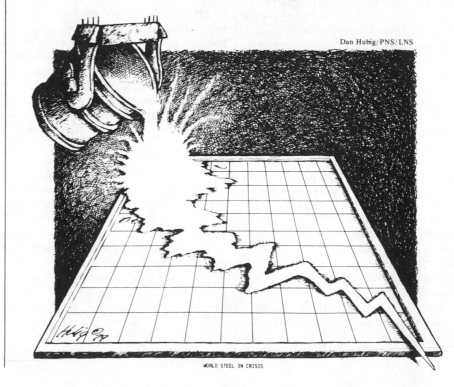

Dan Hubig/PNS/LNS

WORLD STEEL IN CRISIS

government regulations, and excessive wage demands by the United Steelworkers of America.

The response to the latest blow was swift. A thousand steelworkers rallied immediately and within days 300 people drove to Pittsburgh to let U.S. Steel's corporate headquarters know just how they felt.

At a televised news conference Rev. Charles Rawlings, a mainstay of the Ecumenical Coalition, joined with Pittsburgh's Episcopal bishop to denounce the closings, and local congresspeople redoubled their efforts to convene hearings, file legislation, to do something—anything—to prevent the future erosion of their community.

The only real support for U.S. Steel's move came from Lloyd McBride and the Steelworkers' International who agreed with management that the cuts were unfortunate, but necessary. Indeed, many Youngstown rank and filers blame McBride for the plant closings. Youngstown's Steelworkers' Locals have a reputation for rank and file militancy and the district provided strong support for reform candidate Ed Sadlowski when he ran against McBride for the union's presidency four years ago.

The next three months were ones of frantic activity for everyone concerned with saving the mills. The Ecumenical Coalition, after months of inactivity, began again to reach out to the religious community, and the steelworkers continued to organize.

Monday, January 28, 1980, saw 500 people turn out for speeches and a march to U.S. Steel's Youngstown office. After a few circuits around the four-story brick building the marchers surged past guards and quickly occupied the office. While corporation officials hastily called Pittsburgh for instructions, the steelworkers and their supporters set up headquarters in the executive exercise room, complete with pool table, driving range and exercise equipment.

After hours of negotiations, U.S. Steel changed its position and agreed to meet with the workers to discuss a proposal to sell the mills. The occupiers then filed out of the building, though some were clearly upset by the decision to leave. That meeting did eventually take place, but the corporation reiterated its position that it would under no circumstances sell the mills to the steelworkers and community people.

Round two of the battle against U.S. Steel was played out in the courtroom, as radical historian and lawyer Staughton Lynd, along with other attorneys for the local steelworkers, filed a civil suit in Ohio Federal District Court in the last days of 1979. The suit contended the corporation had promised the workers since 1977 that the Youngstown mills would stay open if they remained profitable. In exchange for this promise, the suit argued, workers deferred raises, worked overtime without pay, and made other concessions to management.

At a minimum, the suit asked the court to issue a temporary restraining order forcing U.S. Steel to keep the mills in operable condition until a community/worker controlled corporation, similar to the one proposed by the Ecumenical Council, had the opportunity to purchase the facilities.

A trial date was set for March 17 and presiding Judge Thomas Lambros issued an order forcing the corporation to operate the mills until the trial was over. Throughout the five-day proceedings U.S. Steel's lawyer Charles Clarke maintained that the lawsuit was "close to a sham on this court . . . It has merit only in the fantasy world of the steelworkers and their attorneys." Despite its protests, U.S. Steel was forced to take the proceedings very seriously, and even chairman David Roderick took the stand to testify about the corporation's move and the purchase offer from the workers.

Back on January 31st, Roderick had told reporters in Washington, DC that U.S. Steel rejected outright the idea of selling their facilities to the community because, "We're not ourselves or others of the private enterprise steel industry in favor of pursuing anything involving government subsidies."

This statement had drawn a howl of protest from Youngstown. Within days the Federal Trade Commission had announced an investigation to determine if the giant corporation was acting in restraint of trade; and a House Anti-Trust Subcommittee announced plans to call U.S. Steel to testify. In response to this pressure, Roderick conveniently dropped the competition argument when testifying at the trial, preferring instead to stress the mill's obsolescence and unprofitability.

Profitability *was* an issue on everyone's mind. Even Lynd acknowledged the steelworkers' dilemma when, in his closing remarks, he asked the judge to order U.S. Steel to provide raw materials to worker/community mills as well as to purchase a fixed percentage of the finished products for at least five years. As one steelworker commented: "If that doesn't happen, we'll get squeezed out of the market before we ever get started. We've been dependent on U.S. Steel for raw materials for 80 years. If they can't compete, how can we compete?"

Despite these worries, most of the workers did want to take over the mills and most felt that the judge would rule in their favor. Ronald Jones, a massive and eloquent steelworker in boots and a ten gallon hat told one meeting: "In my heart I know that the judge is going to rule for the men because everyone has a little bit of goodness in them."

But when the verdict finally came down, it was U.S. Steel and not the steelworkers that had won the battle. Judge Lambros rejected the workers' allegations of contract violations, though he did rule that the company was flirting with an anti-trust violation in its adament position not to sell to the workers. Both sides were ordered back into court in late May to take up anti-trust issues. The rank and filers have continued to pursue this despite Lynd's pessimistic appraisal immediately after the verdict that "anti-trust cases are the specialty of the steel company lawyers."

Lynd and others are now also pursuing the idea of getting the city of Youngstown to take over the mills by eminent domain. With each passing day, however, it becomes more difficult to keep up the fight, particularly for the union. According to one leader. "The union is in disarray, especially in the closed plants. People live all over the valley . . . up to 30 miles away. It's hard to keep people fighting. I don't think my mill is ever going to reopen and neither do most of the men."

Lack of investment by the steel companies, a national union more concerned with keeping labor peace than keeping jobs, and a legal system that favors property rights over human rights have so far combined to thwart Youngstown residents' attempts to save their community. Industries fold and communities die: in Lowell yesterday, in Youngstown today,

and who knows, maybe Silicon Valley tomorrow.

Americans are increasingly concerned about the "private" economic decisions which have such a profound impact in human terms. Legislators in ten states are already considering bills to regulate runaways, and the National Employment Priorities Act has 58 sponsors in Congress. In Ohio, the Ohio Public Interest Campaign, a Cleveland-based organization with chapters in several cities in the state, is leading the battle to *prevent* the devastating impact of plant closings.

OPIC's bill—the Community Readjustment Act—has served as a model for progressive activists across the country. The bill requires two years advance notice before a plant can close, severance pay, coverage of health benefits and community assistance funds equal to ten percent of the affected payroll. Corporate lobbying against the bill has been extremely well organized and financed: yet CRA continues to work its way through the legislative mill.

"We have to eventually figure out a way to control investment decisions," says OPIC executive director Ira Arlook, "but that will take years. I'm encouraged by the fact that polls show people overwhelmingly in support of the bill. However, I don't know if it will bring any relief for Youngstown in the near future."

Some people, including some of Youngstown's militant trade unionists, think the steel industry should be nationalized. Another proposal, set forth by the Youngstown Save Jobs Committee, calls for the establishment of a National Plant Closings Administration. Clearly none of these solutions will happen overnight. But the Youngstown residents who've fought so hard to save their city have learned at least two important lessons—that their problem is bigger than Youngstown, and that prevention may well be the only cure for the Youngstowns of the future.

From *Open Road*, no. 11 (Summer 1980), pp. 4-5

Kraakers Explode Over Housing

by Jan Bervoets

For Amsterdam's homeless, househunting doesn't have to mean sitting back, scanning newspapers, patiently waiting and hoping for a liveable, affordable empty space. Instead, they can join in a mass-based, highly-organized anti-authoritarian squatters' movement that has become increasingly militant and capable of defending itself in the squats or in the streets, taking on police and speculators who try to throw them out.

The movement of squatters—or "kraakers" as they're known in Dutch—has a growing consciously anarchist element in it and is prepared and willing to clash head-on with the State for the right to a home.

With the battle-cry of "no housing, no crowning," thousands of the kraakers, for example, recently confronted a security

force of 8,000 and laid siege to the coronation of the new Dutch Queen, protesting the extravagant spectacle at a time of an acute housing crisis.

This battle in itself was no incidental outburst, but the expression of a powerful, self-organized popular movement that has matured over the years and can now draw on an extensive support network throughout Holland.

While not exclusively composed of young people (there are many families and elderly among them), the comparison has been made between the Provos of 1966 (Holland's equivalent of the Yippies!) and today's Kraakers.

The big differences are that today's movement is:

- less intellectual
- more spontaneous
- more conscious of its own interests and therefore, more powerful.

It is no abstraction of the imagination, it is imagination itself, created from the interests of reality: scarcity of dwellings, unemployment of educated scholars, rat-races in schools and universities, militarism and a decrease of income for workers.

In Amsterdam alone there are 53,000

people on waiting lists for accommodation while many buildings destined for demolition or held as investment speculation stand empty. An estimated 10,000 people have now squatted some 5,000 of these buildings.

Support System

Today, the Kraakers are the best organized autonomous movement in Amsterdam and are organizing themselves in many other cities creating their own cafes, meeting centers, defence systems, etc.

To defend their own interests and those of newcomers, in Amsterdam they've organized an "alarm-centre" to defend kraakers against goonsquads (mostly petty gangsters) of the big owners.

They find empty houses for people in need of accommodation, they assist in reparation and upkeep of the houses and collect contributions from the squatting tenants. These contributions to the reparation funds replace rents. Squatters who have been evicted from their dwellings are moved to other dwellings at the expense of the whole squatters movement which has formed a "collective of carrier cycles."

Every committee is basically organized from the quarters. Central contacts are held only for offensive actions in the whole city or for defence actions against the goon squads. The organization's principles correspond to syndicalist movements such as those in France or Spain in the early 1900s and have no connection whatever to any political party. Most squatters, in fact, see their actions as a direct struggle against the State.

Some squatters have organized themselves into "Living-Working" committees in an effort to combat the separation of home life and alienating work. They try to create living-communes which are productive associations. There are also attempts at alternative lifestyles: all gay households, feminist collectives, "hash-communities," etc.

While there are only a few anarchist collectives, anarchist influence and consciousness has grown since the Provo-time. Nobody wants to appeal to any form of parliamentary intervention.

Kraaker History

Squatting has been an ordinary phenomenon since the time of the Provos (1965-1966) when run-away children, drug-dealers and those people who were totally incapable of finding dwellings in Amsterdam began taking refuge in empty buildings. The emergence of an absurd situation where a surplus of office buildings (most of them former private homes) stand empty in a city with an acute housing shortage dates back to 1945, when in rebuilding homes which had been demolished or extensively damaged during the German occupation, speculators found it more profitable to convert homes into offices than provide desperately needed housing.

With the slogan "save a building, kraak a building" a former founder of the Provos set up a "Kraaker Office" in 1967 and an organized squatters' movement was born. The purpose of the office was to establish a support network for squatters and to oppose city-planning by capitalist speculators. It was in this period that many inhabitants of quarters in Amsterdam (as in the centers of other cities) began uniting to reclaim the destiny of their quarters which were mainly slated for demolition.

Need for Self-Organization

The most famous and violent of these actions was the resistance of the Nieuwmarket quarter in Amsterdam against the building of a metro through the whole quarter that meant the demolition of existing dwellings which were to be replaced by offices and luxury apartments.

The quarter committees were supported by the kraakers, but didn't manage to create a decentralized organization for solidarity. Apart from the Nieumarket committee which was autonomous, all the other committees were dominated by Maoist or Communist political parties. And the Communist Party was in the city government of Amsterdam, doing its utmost to prevent solidarity between the quarters.

At first, self-organization of kraakers didn't seem very urgent because in Holland squatting is not an illegal action. Only breaking in can be cause for arrest, so legally kraakers can't be charged unless they are caught at the moment of "kraaking." After the initial kraak, a new lock always replaces the broken one so there is no further illegal action.

However, in 1975 some judges found means to force kraakers to evacuate kraaked buildings. And in 1976 a law against kraaking was introduced to parliament. It was accepted by the second chamber but after a delay of years in the first chamber it has been tabled as a result of the recent squatters' riots.

But house owners have found illegal means to chase kraakers from their dwellings. They're organising goon squads to evict the inhabitants and destroy the interior of their buildings to make them utterly uninhabitable. Basically sound buildings are set on fire, even with the inhabitants inside. They also pretend to have rented their houses—a ploy which could easily be settled in summary procedures. A kraaker might then win the appeal but as a summary judgment has already caused the eviction, it is impossible to get back in. The kraakers found their answer in self-organization.

Action Days Proclaimed

Ater the proposal of the "anti-kraaklaw" in 1976, a national Kraakers committee was formed to proclaim periodic action days. Its effectiveness was demonstrated at the end of 1979 when on the same day in the cities of Amsterdam, The Hague, Rotterdam, Breda, Utrecht, Nijmegen, Leeuwarden, and Amersfoort, important buildings were occupied. Those occupations were sometimes followed by fierce battles with local police, kraakers defending their houses with paint, stones and barricades.

In November 1978 a block of five houses known as De Groote Keizer (The Grand Emperor), were occupied and inhabited by about 50 kraakers. The proprietor, an investment society, sold the buildings for a profit of $190 million on the condition that they be empty. The investment company began proceedings to have the kraakers evicted.

The case was at first lost when the inhabitants couldn't be cited as their names were unknown. But after a year, on October 26, 1979, the Court of Appeal ordered evacuation of the houses which by then held 100 squatters.

The squatters refused to recognize the decision and prepared to resist the bailiffs with all possible means. The floors were barricaded and arms—tar, paint, gas, projectiles and smoke bombs—were stockpiled.

In order to execute sentences of the civil court bailiffs are entitled to appeal to the police. In cooperation with the Kraaker Alarm Centre of the city of Amsterdam, every barrack of the mobile squads of the police was guarded by kraakers. The inhabitants of De Groote Keizer declared they were prepared to defend their living space, to the death if necessary.

The mayor, as chief of police, hesitated in deciding whether the police should intervene at the request of the bailiffs and risk "public disorder" and perhaps even casualties for the profit of the speculators.

The kraakers drew attention to their cause on December 19 by letting off a smoke bomb at a sitting of the towncouncil which was devoting itself to the politics of housing. During January and February tension grew because the mayor could not and would not decide in favour of the bailiff, but also refused to show the police that he refused to intervene.

Police Riot and Make Their Own Laws

Meanwhile, there were new incidents. On February 22, in order to distract the mobile squads from De Groote Keizer, a group of kraakers tried to occupy a building on Vondelstraat that had stood vacant for three years.

They penetrated the building but that evening 70 police from the mobile squad showed up at the house armed with axes and evacuated it within 15 minutes. One squatter had to be taken to hospital with a concussion.

The action by the mobile squads was blatantly illegal as there had been no complaint from the owners and there was no civil court order for evacuation.

The next day, in protest against the police action, the windows of the mobile squad's training centre were smashed. As a result of this a 22-year-old woman, Nanda M., was arrested and kept incommunicado, charged with painting slogans.

The kraakers weren't about to back down. They decided to reconquer the Vondelstraat building.

On Friday February 29, they organized a large group of demonstrators who marched to City Hall apparently to show solidarity with the inhabitants of De Groote Keizer. The mobile squads were distracted by the demonstration and failed to notice a few hundred people who remained behind. At 6:00 p.m. those kraakers again occupied and barricaded the house on Vondelstraat.

"Nanda must be released," "A place to live is our right" resounded as the hoodwinked police units that had followed the larger procession to City Hall thrust their way back to Vondelstraat. Again, without any order, the mobile squad tried to clear the house but finally had to retreat before the thousand people who had come to defend the occupation, armed with street signs and pavement stones. After several assaults of the mobile squads had been repelled, the squatters conquered several streets which they reinforced by building barricades, creating a "free state" of their own.

'Freedom Place'

Barricaded on all sides, the intersection where the occupied house was situated was renamed "Freedom Place." Access was sealed tight; cars no longer passed through, but thousands of Amsterdamers sought out the "free state." Saturday night the crowd continued to grow. Music played all through the night and a theatre group, "Prologue," cancelled their production in a local threatre and came to stage a play at the liberated intersection.

On Sunday the town-council convened and at 3:30 a.m. Monday morning the mayor gave his ultimatum. The barricades had to be removed by 5:00 a.m. or the police would move in.

The squatters had won some important concessions: they would be allowed to inhabit De Groote Keizer and the Vondelstraat and Nanda M. would be released, so they began clearing the barricades themselves but said they would need more time.

The mayor wouldn't wait. He gave the order throughout Holland for police units to gather together. By 6 a.m. about 1,000 mobile squad, military and rural police moved in with armoured cars, personnel carriers and four Leopard tanks with bulldozer blades, and smashed the barricades. In the mayor's combat-order it was made clear that firearms could be used if necessary.

This totally unnecessary display of power and force only increased the hatred against the existing forces of order. The clearing of the barricades was answered by spontaneous riots throughout the city. Police cars were commandeered and overturned; many people were wounded. These riots were the direct result of interference by the mobile squads.

The force used against the squatters was also seen as a preventative measure taken by the State to lessen the possibility of any solidarity action between the kraakers and the trade unions which were planning a major strike against wage controls for the next day.

'No Accommodation—No Coronation!'

The week following the squatters' battle saw increased violence on the part of the mobile squads. At Nijmegen, 11 women from a feminist collective were evacuated by 110 policemen and immediately thrown into an infirmary. At Borssele, a group of non-violent anti-nuke activists who chained themselves to the entrance of a nuke-center, were attacked by police dogs

and clubbed with truncheons. At The Hague, an armoured car and axes were used to force the door of a house inhabited by squatting Turkish labourers.

In answer to the State's obvious support of property speculators and the organized cruelty of the mobile squads, some kraakers printed a leaflet calling for "action" in Amsterdam on April 30th, the coronation day for Queen Beatrix. The leaflet would have passed unnoticed if it had not been seized by the police in Tilburg and Zwolle. The printers were arrested for sedition and within 24 hours the contents were published in all the papers. Now everybody knew the message: "Come to Amsterdam and don't forget your helmet!"

The government acted accordingly. Special riot police were sent for training in the countryside and on the day of the inauguration 8,000 police and soldiers guarded Dam Square where the coronation took place. Many supporters of the monarchy were frightened by the State's preparations for maintaining "law and order" and so stayed away from the coronation.

On this day, half the city was transformed by the State into an armed camp reminiscent of the time of the German occupation of 1940-1945. Anarchists and left-wing autonomists responded by announcing a demonstration to take place on the very spot where the Germans founded the Jewish ghetto, where a monument commemorating the famous February strike of 1941 now stands.

Chanting "No accommodation, no inauguration," several thousand protestors prepared to march to the Dam when the coronation took place at 2 p.m. The mobile squads kept them back with tear gas and high-powered water hoses. However, comrades from outside the city went directly

from the station to Dam Square.

Unmolested they waved red and black flags and banners with circle A's. After the abdication, when the old queen introduced the new, masses of people began not to cheer but to shout; smoke bombs exploded.

More to Come

At the same time, squatters kraaked an office just two kilometers away and prepared for an open air feast. When the mobile squads came uninvited with armoured cars they were greeted by thousands and thousands ready with sticks and stones. After an hour's battle the acting mayor ordered the squads to retreat and a new building was conquered.

Squatting actions were also taking place at Breda, Nijmegen, Gronigen, Leeuwarden, Utrecht (25 houses!), Tilburg, Leiden, Eindhoven. At The Hague, an attempt to occupy the parliament buildings failed.

Pitched battles raged between the mobile squads and nearly the whole youth of Amsterdam far into the night. Schoolboys who had been invited to the Dam to cheer the new queen refused and were now learning spontaneous street-fighting.

The objective: to disturb the impression of a loyal and cheering people in front of the queen, was surpassed.

There were barricades and battles in every street, and the queen herself could see the rising smoke from the burning police cars.

The straight press focussed on the destructive powers of this spontaneous gathering of thousands of people ready to fight the system, refusing to see that they were organized around the serious issue of housing. This was no one day explosion. The squatting continues.

GROUNDSWELL

From *Groundswell* 2, no. 7 (July 1979): 3-4

How to Pass a Transportation Ban

Reprinted with permission from *Groundswell: A Resource Journal for Energy Activists* and the Nuclear Information and Resource Service.

The number of towns asserting authority over radioactive shipments rose again last month when Charleston, S.C. passed strict regulations over the transportation of nuclear materials through the city. Charleston—scarely a hotbed of anti-nuclear fervor—became concerned when the Nuclear Regulatory Commission showed interest in using the city's port as the regular point of entry for weekly shipments of foreign nuclear wastes. The foreign spent fuel, imported under the Atoms for Peace program, goes to the government's Savannah River reprocessing facility to be recycled into nuclear weapons and reactor fuel.

With the number of spent fuel and other waste shipments rising each year, residents of towns and cities around the country are looking into the possibility of passing ordinances regulating transportation of nuclear materials. The Charleston Palmetto Alliance, which played a major role in organizing the Charleston effort, offers some advice on how to pass a municipal transport ban.

1. Collect and publicize accurate information about the nature of shipments through your area. In Charleston, the issue was relatively clearcut. The NRC conveniently solved the problem of public awareness when its inspection team arrived to check out Charleston's port. But in communities where actual or potential shipments are not so well publicized, research and public education must precede any legislative effort to pass an ordinance. Finding out what is actually shipped through your area may be difficult, but you need these facts in order to convince legislators and the public of the need for regulation.

2. Find out which local authority has jurisdiction over the flow of traffic over municipal roadways. This will be the enforcing body for the ordinance: the office in charge of issuing and denying permits, if that is included in the ban, or the body to whom notification of shipments must be made. Usually the town holds the authority; but if it's the county, then the proposed ordinance must be routed through county government.

3. If it is not already common knowledge, find out who is on the local governing body—the City Council or its equivalent—and how that body works. You should know in advance what every step of the legislative process will involve.

In some towns, citizens have the option of putting an issue on the ballot if a certain

Ross Beecher & Ron Richardson/LNS

Follow the Leaders

Some of the other communities which regulate transportation of nuclear materials:

New York City
New London, CT
Plymouth, MA
Wendall, MA
El Paso, TX
39 Vermont towns
Marin County, CA
Wood County, WI
Shaker Heights, OH and 22 other Ohio municipalities

Louisa County, VA
Charlotte, NC*
Huntington, WV*
Wilmington, DE*

*resolution

Miami, FL—port does not accept shipments of nuclear wastes (by decision of Port Authority)

Chicago, IL—bans plutonium and enriched uranium from O'Hare International Airport

For further information contact Nuclear Transportation Project, American Friends Service Committee, P.O. Box 2344, High Point, NC 27261.

percentage of the electorate demands it. A referendum is an alternative route to regulation which you should consider if local law provides for it.

4. Find a sponsor among members of the governing body. If your local legislative process requires the ordinance to be introduced by a Council member, then this step is obligatory. Otherwise, it is optional but definitely a wise move. Needless to say, the more political weight your sponsor pulls, the better off you will be.

5. Draft the ordinance. This requires careful thought. Most of the major municipal transport bans so far have been based on the 1976 New York City ordinance, but the fact that most towns are not New York City makes minor modifications necessary in each case. Charleston, for example, determined that the city's budget would not permit setting up or enlarging an office for the purpose of issuing and denying permits, as was done in New York City. Instead of adopting a permit system, Charleston's ordinance distinguishes between three categories of radioactive shipments: materials banned outright (plutonium, enriched uranium, actinides, and spent fuel in quantities over

20 curies); exempted materials (medical and defense-related shipments); and all other radioactive shipments, which require notification of the Chief of Police.

6. Get the ordinance into the hands of the person who will introduce it, and give a copy to the legal counsel for the City Council as well. The proposed ordinance will almost certainly be debated on the basis of its legality—the town's right to restrict the flow of traffic that may well be part of an interstate transport system. But other towns have done it, and the Department of Transportation's upholding of the New York ban stands as an important precedent. Furthermore, the NRC's new draft regulations on spent fuel indirectly affirm local rights to restrict nuclear shipments, by stating that the existence of local ordinances will affect the NRC's choice of routes. (See: NUREG 0561, "Physical Protection of Shipments of Irradiated Reactor Fuel," June 1979)*

7. Follow the proceedings of the legislative process. The ordinance may be referred to a committee, and hearings may be held. At this stage, it is advisable to line up some expert witness to testify on your side. To begin with, you need someone—a member of the community—who understands the proposed ordinance from a technical point of view. He or she must be able to explain exactly what the ordinance will regulate and why it is necessary in your community. This person will need a fairly good background in nuclear issues, in order to be able to explain what the banned materials are, what a curie is, and so on.

In presenting your case, it's helpful to provide estimates of what the consequences of a radioactive transport accident in your town would be. These estimates can be based on calculations drawn from government studies: simply plug in population and population density figures appropriate to your area. A study useful for this purpose is NUREG 0194, "Calculations of the Radiological Consequences From Sabotage of Shipping Casks for Spent Fuel and High Level Waste."†

---

*[*Physical Protection of Shipments of Irradiated Reactor Fuel: Interim Guidance*, Report no. NUREG-0561 (Washington, D.C.: Nuclear Regulatory Commission, 1979), 38 pp.—eds., *Alternative Papers*.]

†[C. V. Hodge and J. E. Campbell, *Calculations of Radiological Consequences from Sabotage of Shipping Casks for Spent Fuel and High-Level Wastes*, Report no. NUREG-0194 (Washington, D.C.: Nuclear Regulatory Commission, Division of Fuel Cycle and Material Safety, 1977), 23 pp.—eds., *Alternative Papers*.]

(Available from National Technical Information Service, 5285 Port Royal Rd., Springfield, VA. (703) 557-4600. $4.50.) This is the study on which the new spent fuel regulations are based.

Finally, you need someone who can explain how the ordinance would be enforced in the town. This could be a member of the enforcing agency, or it could be any member of the community who can convey the idea that enforcement will be simple and unproblematic, and will not require special technical expertise or a large investment of time and labor.

8. After this, it's basically a matter of lobbying to get the ordinance through. In some places this may depend on public participation and support, and in others, it may be largely a matter of playing local politics. In any case, it is certainly effective to have influential members of local government, such as the mayor, on your side.

Some towns have provisions for public input into the legislative process, such as a segment of time reserved for community members to express their opinions during each Council meeting. If this is the case, marshal all the community support you can get to appear at these sessions.

For further information, contact the Charleston Palmetto Alliance, c/o Susan King Dunn, 37-B Charlotte St., Charleston, S.C. 29403. Also see: "How to Get Nuclear Transportation Curbs Passed in Your Community," *Critical Mass Journal*, January 1979, for a detailed description of organizing strategy.

which need consideration by the whole Alliance are brought to a Coordinating Committee (C/C) meeting where representatives of all the local groups meet. The proposals are then carried back to the local groups for either approval or amendment. At the next C/C meeting, if all the local groups have agreed to the proposal in question, it is then officially adopted by the Alliance.

Short-Circuits in Emergencies?

The above process makes it possible for everyone to participate in decisionmaking, a true commitment to the phrase "power to the people." There is, however, a practical problem with the process, which is that it takes both patience and time to work. When the Three Mile Island accident occurred this spring, people in the Shad office in NYC were faced with a difficult situation. Events seemed to dictate that Shad join with other direct action organizations like Mobilization for Survival in sponsoring the demonstrations which were to occur as immediate expressions of public outrage and concern. Yet, to agree to a course of action using the consensus process would have taken too much time. During those hectic days, people in the NYC Shad office took upon themselves the responsibility of committing Shad as a cosponsor of many activities. Some people expressed mixed feelings about the "process" being left behind in the dust as soon as there was a time pressure to cope with.

An example of where the consensus process worked well is the way in which the Shoreham demonstration and scenario developed, following consensus process, at least in its beginning. Broad outlines of the action, such as the date of the event and the occupation Guidelines were brought to the C/C by the Shoreham Task Force (STF) and were eventually approved by the whole Alliance. However, as the date of June 3rd drew nearer, the STF took upon itself more and more of the decisionmaking. Time pressure again accounted for the trend. Certain decisions had to be made, and there was the real risk that if they were sent out to the whole Alliance as proposals, June 3rd might have come and gone before essential questions were resolved. For instance, should the people doing Civil Disobedience (C.D.) leave from the rally, or enter the construction site from a completely different place? Obviously, this question was an important one, and much discussion of its complexities went on at STF meetings before it was finally

𝕱𝖆𝖑𝖑𝖔𝖚𝖙 𝕱𝖔𝖗𝖚𝖒

From *Fallout Forum* 2, no. 4 (July/August 1979): 11

Where Has All the Process Gone?

by John Breitbart

As the Shad Alliance emerged at its first Congress an unbelievably short ten months ago, participants could only hope for what the future would bring. We began the Shoreham Campaign and knew that lots of hard work and organizing were ahead. At the time no one would have dared imagine that Shoreham was to become one of the largest demonstration/actions in the United States during the June 3rd weekend of International Protest. The ideas that united people in Shad were the principals of Nonviolence, Consensus, and Direct Action—the three themes which the Clamshell Alliance established through its experience as the basis for successful grassroots anti-nuke organizing.

Many of the people who founded Shad had participated in the Clamshell actions at Seabrook and had been touched by the "magic" of Nonviolence in action, and in decision-making as it is expressed in the Consensus process. Through involvement

in the "process," many learned that alternatives to oppression and the violence it entails need to exist on every level of social organization. The destructive methods of the huge corporations and government agencies are represented on a smaller scale by the individuals who use meetings as places to fill personal and emotional needs at others' expense.

Perhaps the secret to the Clamshell success and mystique is the realization that the movement to bring peace and justice must progress on the personal level as well as the larger political plane. At least in those early days, being committed to the anti-nuke movement came to mean a personal desire to struggle against the oppressive and implicitly violent qualities in oneself: egotism, sexism, ageism, paternalism, and all the other selfish motivations most people bring as psychological baggage into their political activities. Nonviolence in its purest form emphasizes the unity between the political and personal sides of living.

Enough with the philosophizing. Back to the specific topic at hand: where has all the process gone?

People who join the Shad Alliance are told that it operates by consensus. Unfortunately, sometimes that is all they are told. What consensus means, in theory, is that everyone who is a member of the Alliance gets to participate in all important decisions. How is this done? Proposals resolved. However, aside from those who attended the open STF meetings, other people in the Alliance only found out this aspect of the demonstration scenario when they were told what had been already decided.

Minutes of Meetings Available to Locals

Were there ways in which these decisions could have been made more in tune with the spirit of the consensus process, if not by using the process literally? One way that Alliance members can be kept in touch with working committees and the decisions they are making is by sending records of the meetings to the local groups. In actuality, minutes of committee meetings were included in the minutes of C/C meetings which were sent out to all the locals. The problem here was that often the C/C minutes were not sent promptly and by the time locals received them, they were badly out of date. As the Alliance has proceeded, it has become apparent that people who go to meetings often do not have the energy or desire to report to the rest of the Alliance what's going on. This is unfortunate, since after the decisions are made, people are heard to say, "When were these decisions made, and who made them?" or "I didn't know this question was being discussed . . ." In all fairness, though, C/C minutes were often not thoroughly read by people in the local groups.

Another situation has arisen where the consensus process has been strained. A proposal was sent out through the C/C minutes from a person in Westchester for a Shad-wide action at Indian Point on or around Hiroshima Day, August 6th. At the next C/C meeting, attendance by local spokespeople was lacking, and not many locals had had the time they needed to discuss the proposal. However, since no locals "blocked" the proposal, according to consensus process, the Indian Point action was approved as a Shad-wide event. Up to the present, the question of what constitutes a quorum at a C/C meeting has not been raised, discussed, or resolved. Nevertheless, the adoption of the important Indian Point proposal at a C/C meeting where no Long Island spokespeople were present did create some bad feelings in the Alliance. The question here seems to revolve around whether or not the previous C/C minutes were mailed out in time for local groups to discuss the proposal. In this instance, it's certainly debatable, since the Shoreham demonstration came between the two C/C meetings and most people were too busy/worried/hysterical to even

consider the thought of the next Shad action.

The second process question raised by the Indian Point demonstration is as follows. The C/C, upon learning of the approval of the Indian Point proposal, set up an Indian Point Task Force to organize the event. At the same time, other organizations expressed an interest in participating as co-sponsors of the event and in setting up a coalition of groups. The first meeting of the Shad Indian Point Task Force spent much of the time trying to figure out the answer to two questions: One, if Shad were to become a member of a coalition of groups, what structure would this coalition have to adopt for Shad to be able to participate and still keep its commitment to the consensus process? The second was, even if members of the Indian Point Task Force figure out an answer to the above quesion, do we have the right to decide to make the Shad Alliance part of a coalition with other groups without the decision being brought before the whole Alliance in the form of a proposal? Needless to say, the meeting was long, sweaty, and highly argumentative.

It was obvious that the whole Alliance should have a chance to review and discuss the situation. However, someone had already taken the liberty of setting up the first meeting of the coalition a mere four days later, on Thursday. If the people at the Sunday meeting could not agree on a proposal setting forth guidelines for Shad participation in a coalition, then Shad would not be able to take part in it and would have to continue with its own solo action. Many people attending the meeting felt that this option was highly undesirable, since Shad would appear to be "snobbish" and "elitist" in its strict adherence to principles which these other organizations consider less important than building a large network of groups fighting (if you haven't forgotten) the evils of nukes.

Finally, a proposal was agreed upon saying that Shad would participate in a coalition which operates according to Shad's basic principles: Nonviolence, Consensus, and Direct Action (including Civil Disobedience). The group also proposed that the Civil Disobedience be organized in affinity groups, and C.D. participants need to receive Nonviolence training.

Several days later, the first coalition meeting took place. Most of the meeting ended up being a discussion of how the coalition would function. A fairly large number of people were not familiar with

consensus. To make a long story a little less long, the group finally arrived at a compromise solution which some called "modified consensus" and others preferred to call "two-thirds majority voting." The idea was that the group would try to attain complete agreement on each of its decisions, but if there were a significant deadlock the group could then revert to a voting system where a two-thirds majority would "win." This proposal was passed in two steps. First a vote was taken to estimate support for this compromise or complete consensus. In the vote, 43 were in favor of the compromise, and either 21 or 23 (two different numbers were arrived at by two different counters) were for consensus. It is interesting to note that even according to the compromise "two-thirds majority" system of decision-making, the vote to adopt it was barely enough. Secondly, it was asked if anyone felt strongly enough to block the compromise proposal's acceptance.

When no one indicated that they felt strongly enough to block the compromise proposal, being a hopeless consensus freak of the thirteenth order, I had to leave the room. I felt that although the group was going through the formality of asking for a consensus, the spirit of respect, tolerance, and trust was missing. Had I chosen to force the group to use consensus by blocking these proposals, I felt it would have been useless, because the most important condition for using consensus is the attitude that the people involved bring to the group. If they do not begin with a desire to trust each other and work together in a non-coercive manner, democratic voting is the only "workable" alternative. How could the Shad "spokespeople" accept the compromise proposal without at least getting together on their own as a "Shad" group and discussing the implications that it has for Shad? Not only had we in Shad taken upon ourselves the decision to commit the Shad Alliance to being a member group of a coalition, but we had also agreed to go against a coalition structure proposal that our Indian Point Task Force had taken six hours to decide upon only four days earlier.

Needless to say, there are many questions to be resolved within the Alliance. Fortunately, there is a place where Shad will have an opportunity to thrash out (please excuse the violent imagery) these issues and heal organizational wounds. It's called a Congress and will take place sometime this September. The Congress is a weekend-long gathering of all interested Shad members who have the devotion, time, and energy to attend about eight or nine marathon meetings in two and a half days. A Congress has the power to make binding decisions for the whole Alliance and is open to all. Its structure is too involved to explain here, but rest assured that in the next issue of *Fallout Forum,* there will be more details on this fascinating Shad institution.

Northern Sun News

From *Northern Sun News* 2, no. 10 (November 1979): 8-9

Northern Sun Alliance: A Conversion Plan: Is Northern Sun Alliance New to You?

Let us introduce ourselves.

We are a locally-based citizen's organization which, like many others rising up across the country, is mounting a grassroots offensive against the unfolding energy disaster.

Lest you be put off by the sharp odor of politics, however, let us explain that our commitment is broader—it is by necessity spiritual as well, because the scope of the crisis not only embraces every citizen but also every creature. It not only reaches into the genetic structure of our bodies but into the marrow of our collective spirit as well.

Look what business-as-usual energy policy has brought us: further assaults on the public health and environment, ballooning prices on traditional fuels, rocketing utility bills, diversion of capital from job-creating alternative technologies into exorbitant projects which produce few permanent jobs, and further anger and hopelessness as tensions mount over threats to fuel supplies, land, health, and income. We will also see more Native American and family farm land swallowed by draglines and power-

lines, and our general sense of powerlessness deepened.

Our response to this state of affairs is an all-out effort to mobilize people at the grassroots level. We are sending out speakers, presenting films, publishing *Northern Sun News*, and distributing a lot of other literature.

We are cooperating with other citizen groups by sharing information and co-sponsoring educational and fundraising events. Furthermore, we are firm believers in the propriety of public demonstrations and even of civil disobedience, when our sense of justice is particularly offended. We invite you to examine both the substance of our positions and the character of our approach.

We are not simply doomsayers. There is still a way out, and one of our principal objectives is to publicize the alternative route. We perceive this alternative route not only in terms of affordable, reliable sources of energy, but in terms too of enhancing grassroots community life.

THE CONVERSION PLAN

While we must continue to draw attention to the violations and failures of present policy—to the acid rain, the locally unneeded powerline, the accelerating nuclear accident rate, etc.—we are also devoting a major effort to an *energy conversion plan* for our region.

This plan features conservation, improved efficiency, and cogeneration, as well as such sources as small fluidized bed coal plants, wind, solar, hydro and our enormously rich biomass potential (particularly for fuel or "farmer's" alcohol and methane). The plan features a great shift to more *local* or decentralized, as opposed to the increasingly remote, centralized systems.

Conservation

As startling as it may sound, waste and inefficiency are of such proportions that

our regional and national economy could continue to grow at a moderate rate through the end of the century *without requiring the building of any more large central electric power plants.* "Technical fixes" such as more efficient appliances, less commercial overlighting, and—in the case of non-electrical energy—thermal insulation, more efficient furnaces and automobile engines, for example, would in the not-too-long run cut energy use down to a third or a fourth of what it is now.

Such technical fixes do not affect lifestyle. Yet certain changes affecting lifestyle, such as drastically improved mass transit, carpooling, and recycling materials would also contribute large net amounts of energy. Such conservation measures as these would also create jobs: Armory Lovins writes, "Even making more energy-efficient home appliances is about twice as good for jobs as is building power stations. . . ."

Cogeneration

Local *cogeneration* potential alone could be developed to a point that would allow the closing of Minnesota's nuclear reactors, should citizens desire to stop increasing our stockpile of radioactive poisons (which, in all likelihood, we'll be stuck with guarding *indefinitely*), or should more breakdowns force their closing.

Cogeneration is essentially the combined production of heat and electricity. Cogeneration involves utilizing the "waste" heat and steam *already* produced by industry to generate electricity. According to one study, "Cogeneration and more efficient use of electricity could together reduce U.S. use of electricity by a third and central station generation by 60 percent."

A REVERSAL: MORE FOR LESS

All of the measures described so far involve great increases in the supply of available energy—without any increase in the consumption of fuel!

The present style of large remote generating plants should be allowed to die the death of the dinosaurs. *The transmission and distribution system they require alone accounts for some two-thirds of our electric bill.* Two-thirds of the BTU's in coal are lost in the big plants; whereas with gas or the relatively new "fluidized-bed" coal technology, which radically decreases pollution, small plants could be located close to the centers of need and their excess heat used for various purposes, such as district heating or alcohol distillation.

All the renewable technologies, in fact, have the considerable advantage of eliminating the need for an expensive distribution system. The need for additional fossil-fuel electric plants would be minimal, indeed, given an aggressive conservation policy as outlined above, and given the availability today of competitive renewable energy technologies.

Solar

Solar heating, especially passive solar (which relies not on pumped fluids and expensive storage systems, but on such simple devices as south-facing windows with insulated drapes)—and soon, solar cooling—head the list of renewable technologies which are both presently available and economically competitive. If passive solar were built into all new houses in the next twelve years, according to a paper published in the *Bulletin of the Atomic Scientists,* the energy saved would be equivalent to what we expect to recover from the Alaskan North Slope.

Wind, Biomass, Hydro

Wind power systems available today can provide cheaper electricity than that to be supplied by the infamous Coal Creek plant and powerline project which has been so stoutly resisted by Minnesota farmers. Moreover, wind can also be used to compress air or pump water, as well as generate electricity.

Liquid and gaseous fuels could in a short time be produced at thousands of sites in enormous quantities, amounting to a major part of the gasoline consumed in this country today, by using agricultural, forestry and urban wastes, often termed "biomass." In addition to using wastes, energy-rich biomass such as cattails could actually be farmed in areas that are not now productive. A Wisconsin citizens' organization is proposing that several small fluidized-bed coal-fired electric plants be built and their excess heat used to distill alcohol, which can then fuel furnaces or engines.

There is even significant untapped hydroelectric potential in our region.

To summarize, the renewable resources plus conservation and cogeneration make it possible to immediately stop building large central-station electric plants, to retire the increasingly unreliable and dangerous nuclear plants, and eventually to shift our economy to a renewable energy base that will have much simpler and cheaper distribution systems, much more flexibility through short construction times, much greater political accessibility at the local level, less vulnerability to massive failure, low initial costs, vastly greater job-creating potential, suitability for mass production, and on and on. The potential for international trade and even for world peace through bottling the nuclear genie is highly compelling.

OBSTACLES

ALL OF THIS IS POSSIBLE AT DRAMATICALLY LOWER LEVELS OF LONG-RANGE INVESTMENT. BY MUSTERING OUR GRASSROOTS POLITICAL WILL POWER. THE OBSTACLES TO ALL THE MEASURES OUTLINED HERE ARE REMOVEABLE: MISPLACED TAX INCENTIVES, ABSENCE OF GRANT AND LOAN FUNDS, BACKWARD RATE STRUCTURES, REGULATIONS AND LAWS TAILORED TO A CENTRALIZED SYSTEM.

If aroused citizens don't counter the plans of the corporations and corporate-minded government officials we face disaster.

- With a cancer epidemic already gripping the country (one out of four of us are being stricken), we don't need to add more sources of cancer by mining uranium and leaving millions of tons of radioactive tailings on the ground to contaminate the water, air and land; or by continuing to burn vast quantities of uranium-bearing coal. We need hardly mention the threat of nuclear plants or the increasingly critical radioactive waste situation.

- More than 50,000 lakes in the U.S. and Canada could be virtually devoid of fish and other life by 1995 as a result of acid rain, caused by coal-burning and automobile exhaust.

- The Coal Creek power plant and 800,000 volt DC transmission line running across central Minnesota will triple the bills of customers of the utilities building the project. Already the residents of Dakota County, Minnesota, have received 40-50% rate increases due to this project. The line has been proven to be unneeded by those customers; it is proving to be the threat to health and safety it was feared to be; it is an economic boondoggle. The power it would deliver would cost more than presently available wind-generated power at pre-mass production prices.

- While fuel shortage stories appear in the headlines, the back pages tell another story. For example, oil companies had an average 18% increase in crude oil exports this year over last year. And fifteen top oil corporations are being "cited" for overcharging the American people some $4.8 billion since 1973.

- Big Oil has been buying up the solar industry. Of the nine major companies making solar cells, eight have been bought up by large corporations, five of them by major oil companies. Exxon and ARCO together will soon control more than half the industry.

- Major corporations are searching for uranium southwest of Duluth. The exploratory drilling itself endangers an underground reservoir which furnishes water to parts of the Twin Cities. Drilling through any uranium ore into the reservoir can lead to contamination of the water with several radioactive elements. Actual mining and milling would be slow but sure suicide, as it is proving in the West and Southwest. Not only do the miners contract lung cancer at extremely high rates, but no safe way has been found to contain the mill tailings, which retain 85% of the original radioactivity after the uranium is removed. The tailings contaminate ground water and are subject to being blown across the land. Uranium should be left safely locked in the ground.

- Contrary to the virtual lie the nuclear industry tells about nuclear power plant waste—that it amounts to only 1% of the military nuclear waste—the quantity of radioactivity in power plant waste has already exceeded the radioactivity of all the military waste so far produced. Industry figures come from measuring the wastes by volume; it happens that the military wastes are highly diluted with water and oil.

- The Black Hills of South Dakota, beautiful and sacred to the Lakota Sioux, and guaranteed to them by treaty, are about to be stripmined for uranium and coal. The Lakota people are about to be robbed by the big corporations on a scale that few of us have ever experienced. In thirty years' time the underground reservoirs in the entire region will be depleted. Millions of tons of radioactive tailings will spread cancer and genetic disease. They will suffer this so that the monopolies can keep depriving the rest of us of cheap, clean energy.

WE'RE FIGHTING FOR A BETTER FUTURE THAN THIS

We think our plan will stimulate growth, and growth of a much better kind. We think it will allow greater social equity and open up many more jobs for poorly and under-employed people. We think it will open the locks to barge loads of small and medium-scale enterprise and inspire the cooperation of communities. But it's going to take quite a fight, much hard labor, lots of working together. And YOUR help!

Won't you contribute to our efforts?

OUR HISTORY AND PURPOSE

Twin Cities Northern Sun Alliance was founded in July of 1977 principally to halt the proliferation of nuclear power and weapons. Our first target was the nuclear plant proposed for Tyrone, Wisconsin, just sixty miles east of the Twin Cities. We are proud to have worked with Wisconsin citizens to achieve the disapproval of the plant by the Public Service Commission this year.

When the struggle of Minnesota farmers against the 800 kilovolt powerline came to our attention in the winter of 1977-78, we could not help but recognize the same themes which drew us into opposing the Tyrone nuclear plant. Both projects cost too much, were not needed locally, presented dangers to health and environment, and brought appalling violations of legal statutes and citizens' rights.

More recently we have become aware of the Lakota's desperate fight to save the Black Hills in South Dakota. The scale of corporate "development" plans is sobering, yes; but we are compelled to stand by the Lakota in their struggle to save the land that is sacred to them and which is guaranteed to them by a constitutionally valid treaty.

In these struggles our philosophy has matured. Except for our call for an end to the nuclear arms race, which has drained physical and spiritual resources beyond imagining, we focus on energy. We want power over energy to be decentralized into units which can be controlled by real communities, whatever the details of organizing those units. We want a virtual crusade for efficiency and conservation, and a mobilization of forces to start the Great Conversion to renewable sources of energy.

Above all, in our focus on energy, we desire equity. We desire equity of op-portunity for basic physical and spiritual satisfaction for all people. The energy policies we call for will address the needs of people on the lower half of the scale of privilege by multiplying jobs that will generate decent income, self-respect, and contribute in a truly constructive way to the welfare of the local community and the larger society.

We further desire the equity which encompasses future generations and the whole, interconnected, living Creation with *respect*. Ultimately, these are the spiritual values behind our political commitments.

WHAT WE DO

With a legion of volunteers and a small full-time staff which is paid bare "survival expenses," we publish *Northern Sun News* (which receives the single largest ex-penditure of the Alliance) and distribute literature on alternatives, nuclear power, powerlines, etc. We provide films and speakers, and we participate in public forums and hearings. We help organize other groups and sustain a communications network in the region. We have organized or supported numerous public demonstrations and have organized legal defense resources for citizens arrested because of protest actions or beliefs.

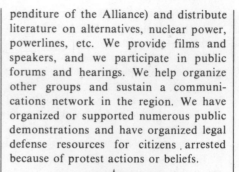

From *Hot Times* 3, no. 1 (February 1980): 4

Citizens to Pay Corporate Electric Bill

The proposed ACORN* rate structure is costbased, promotes conservation, provides a rate for essential needs and is easily understood. It is the first step in the development of a rational energy policy for Austin.

Austin's current electric rate schedule, implemented in 1978, is the creation of the outside consulting firm of Touche Ross. In their 1977 "Electric Cost of Service and Rate Study," Touche Ross proclaimed the need to: "Establish rate structures that are easily understood . . . " (p. 20). Yet Austin residents have testified before the Electric Utility Commission and the City Council that the Touche Ross structure is complex and incomprehensible.

The ACORN rate proposal would

*[Association of Community Organizations for Reform Now.—eds., *Alternative Papers*.]

Reprinted with permission from *Hot Times*, Austin, Texas.

eliminate the complex Touche Ross declining-block-structure (the more you use—the less you pay) and replace it with a simple, uniform system-wide lifeline structure, composed of a flat rate for larger users and a lifeline rate for low consumers. Each month the first 500 kilowatt hours consumed would cost each customer 3¢ a kilowatt hour. For each kilowatt hour consumed beyond the first 500 lifeline hours, the customer would be charged 5.1¢. During the months of May through October, all customers would be charged an extra 2.5¢ for each kilowatt hour consumed above the 500 kilowatt hour lifeline level. Under the terms of this proposed system, the monthly bills of many customers would differ considerably from what they now receive.

Under the lifeline rate structure, the only customer class to be retained is that of Large Primary Service customers. They would continue to receive a 4% discount on block rates and be charged 4.9¢ a kilowatt hour for consumption about 500 kilowatt hour per month, yet May to October they would also pay the extra 2.5¢ charge.

Promoting Conservation

Energy consumption patterns are integrally related to the price of that energy. As the price of a product goes up, the demand tends to decrease. The steady rise in the price of electricity during the last decade has produced a rather consistent reduction in the growth of energy consumption. In 1975, the staff at Austin's Electric Utility Department noted that demand for electricity had increased 13% annually before 1973, and that the annual increase in demand was expected to be 9.5%. In 1978 the Electric Utility Department predicted a growth rate of 6.1%. In 1979, this same department indicated that they expected annual demand to increase only 2.4%. Peak demand on Austin's system has actually decreased since 1977.

This moderate conservation can be attributed to the steady across-the-board rate increase, and to some marginal cost-based components of the Touche Ross rate structure. However, because it is composed of declining blocks, the Touche Ross schedule provides a powerful disincentive to conservation. When a user increases consumption, it is rewarded with lower rates.

The resistance of the Austin Electric Utility Department to conservation measures such as lifeline rates may originate in part in their commitment to replace existing oil and gas units with large nuclear and coal units. Increased consumption is needed to pay for the nuclear and coal plants. In a report from the Center for Energy Studies, Dr. Woodson wrote:

> If load management (i.e. conservation) policies were successfully implemented, the need for new capacity in the future would be reduced. Reduction of new capacity additions would prolong the use of existing capacity, mainly natural gas plants. The short and medium-term result of load management would therefore be a continued dependence on

Peg Averill/Art for the People/LNS

A Comparison of Monthly Bills				
Class	Consumption/ kwh	Month	Touche* Ross/$	ACORN* $
Residential Multifuel	200	May-Oct.	14.38	6.00
Residential Multifuel	300	January	13.73	9.80
Residential Multifuel	1300	October	77.49	75.80
Residential Multifuel	2000	January	75.54	91.50
Residential Multifuel	2000	October	114.50	129.00
All-Electric Residential	1000	January	38.67	40.50
All-Electric Residential	1300	October	72.95	75.90
All-Electric Residential	2000	October	112.36	129.00
General Service Multifuel Non-Demand	1300	October	92.28	75.80
Large Primary Service	3,437,539	†	140,944.00	‡

*Estimated Bill
†May 1978-April 1979
‡175,288

high cost natural gas and oil in existing plants. Rates for electricity must be allowed so that utilities can afford to reduce their high dependence on natural gas. [cited in Rough Draft, p. 24]

In other words, rates should be tailored, and the consumption patterns of consumers should be altered, to fit the requirements of a transition to coal and nuclear-generated electricity.

ED. NOTE: On Friday, Feb. 1, the Austin City Council passed the proposal, 5-2, that forces residential consumers to pay a portion of the five largest user's electric bill: Motorola, IBM, TI, the State offices, and Bergstrom AFB benefit from your high rates. According to the state law, however, Austin officials are required to institute some form of lifeline rates for small users. Write your city council and demand fair rates for all.

From the Hometown of Susan B. Anthony
New Women's Times

From *New Women's Times* 6, no. 15 (July 18, 1980): 3

Health Leaders Win Awards

The National Women's Health Network announced recently the five winners of the 1980 Health Advocate of the Year Awards—individuals and groups whose groundbreaking scientific and legal research has set a national precedent in the fields of environmental and reproductive health.

Recognized for their achievements were Lois Gibbs and Joann Hill (founders of the Love Canal Home Owners Association) who were responsible last year for the public disclosure of health hazards and genetic damage caused by 21,000 tons of abandoned chemical wastes dumped by Hooker Chemical Co., upon which Love

Canal residents built their homes and an elementary school. The Association's "citizen's research" and political pressure prompted the federal government to evacuate over 700 families, in one of the nation's worst chemical dumping disasters.

Making Connections

Award winners were Bonnie Hill and Rose Anna Lee (Citizens Against Toxic Sprays) who first discovered the link between herbicide spraying of forest lands and subsequent miscarriages in the Alsea, Oregon region. Despite personal tragedies—including Lee's daughter developing a rare blood disease—the women successfully pressured the U.S. Environmental Protection Agency to place a moratorium on the further use of 2, 4,5T (a herbicide containing chemical dioxin).

Lawyer Betty Jean Hall and educator Connie White of the Coal Employment Project/Coal Mining Women's Support Team in Tennessee were instrumental in the late 1970's in helping to establish health and safety training programs for the

MARCH 8, 1908: DEMONSTRATION BY WOMEN ON NEW YORK'S LOWER EAST SIDE LEADS TO CELEBRATION OF INTERNATIONAL WOMEN'S DAY.

Peg Averill/LNS

nation's 1,500 women coal miners. Today the Coal Employment Project is staffed by women raised in the coal fields, and works towards the establishment of safety standards based on a male/female workforce. CEP is collecting data on the possible reproductive hazards of coal dust, after learning of birth defects in the offspring of pregnant miners.

Abortion Rights

This summer the U.S. Supreme Court will decide a precedent-setting abortion rights case (*McCrae* v. *Harris*) because of the legal work of award winners Nancy Stearns and Rhonda Copelon of the Center for Constitutional Rights. They argued the *McCrae* case in New York, which resulted in the U.S. Supreme Court's temporary reinstatement of federal Medicaid abortion funds. The Supreme Court case will determine whether the controversial Hyde Amendment, passed by Congress in 1978 to prohibit federal funds for Medicaid abortions, will be declared unconstitutional.

A community-based clinic in Florida—the Tallahassee Feminist Women's Health Center—brought the nation's first anti-trust monopoly lawsuit against the medical profession. This year an out-of-court settlement of $75,000 was reached after the health collective revealed evidence that physicians had conspired to put the clinic out of business by denying it access to the city's hospital and medical staff.

In announcing the awards, National Women's Health Network executive director Belita Cowan explained that "This year American women have taken the lead in efforts to prevent environmental disasters and to preserve reproductive health rights. It is significant that all of the award winners worked directly with community and citizen groups. This appears to be the single most effective way to get results."

In response to the recent setback it suffered at the meeting on infant and child feeding sponsored by the World Health Organization (WHO) and UNICEF in October, 1979, Nestle has initiated a vast public relations campaign aimed at stopping the boycott. At the meeting, it was unanimously agreed that there is a strong need for effective measures to restrict infant formula promotion in Third World countries, as the industry obviously cannot be counted on to monitor itself. The director general of WHO, Dr. Halfdan Mahler, said, "There is no way industry can get away with what they've been doing in the past and say they have our blessing."

But Nestlé contends that its marketing practices are in accord with the recommendations issued at the meeting: Arthur Furer, Nestlé's managing director, stated, "We do not feel restricted in any way in our commercial activities by the WHO recommendations."

Nestlé's strategy has been to remain as ambiguous as possible about the specific demands of the boycott (see box). It refused a formal request by Infant Formula Action Coalition (INFACT) for a meeting in November, 1979, to discuss exactly what changes the corporation is making in its formula marketing practices.

Another boycott leader, the Interfaith Center for Corporate Responsibility (ICCR), maintains that Nestle has not met any of the boycott's demands. The center has documented violations of the company's own weak self-regulatory codes.

The boycott is clearly affecting the corporation. Nestle has hired Hill and Knowlton (the corporate public relations firm responsible for the estrogen replacement therapy cover-up) to prepare the company's response to the boycott. Nestle executives are traveling around the country to talk to churches, college and consumer

From *HealthRight* 5, no. 3 (1979): 9

Nestlé Boycott

Worldwide. The Nestlé boycott is not over! In spite of recent publicity intimating the opposite (for example, the November 1, 1979, *Wall Street Journal* carried an editorial entitled, "The Nestlé Boycott Kills Babies," portraying Nestlé as a poor, beleaguered company doing everything it could to placate the unrelenting boycotters), the boycott is still going strong. In fact, it is being expanded to force a permanent end to the aggressive promotion of infant formula in Third World countries. In areas where conditions prohibit the safe use of formula, bottle feeding is leading to increased illness among infants and even death. Millions of babies who could have been safely breastfed are victims of gastroenteritis and other diseases resulting from the use of diluted or contaminated formula (*see* HealthRight, *Vol. III, Iss. 2*).*

*[Leah Margulies, "Exporting Infant Malnutrition," *HealthRight* 3, no. 2 (Spring 1977): 1, 4.—eds., *Alternative Papers.*]

Reprinted with permission from *HealthRight: A Women's Health Newsletter.*

BOYCOTT NESTLE

Eileen Whalen/LNS

groups, and so far, two huge mailings have gone out to all the nation's churches explaining why the boycott should not be supported.

Global sales of infant formula now total about two billion dollars a year, of which Third World sales account for nearly 50 percent. Nestlé has the largest share of this market, and it is for that reason, as well as its steadfast refusal to make reforms, that the multinational has been targeted for the boycott by ICCR, INFACT and other groups.

A few small gains have been made in the struggle so far, but *now* is a crucial time. Only intensified, continuous pressure will succeed in finally eliminating all promotion of infant formula. Write to Nestlé and tell them why you are boycotting its products at 100 Bloomingdale Road, White Plains, NY 10605. See the accompanying box for a partial list of Nestlé-owned companies and products. The list grows daily.

ICCR is also investigating infant formula marketing practices in the U.S. In many U.S. hospitals, mothers are routinely given drugs to dry up their milk, are not given adequate information about choices they may have in feeding their babies and are given free infant formula samples (a tax deductible activity for infant formula manufacturers). ICCR is trying to document existing conditions across the nation. If you can help, contact ICCR, 475 Riverside Drive, Room 566, New York, NY 10027.

Boycott Nestlé

The Nestlé boycott is aimed at stopping the promotion, not the availability, of infant formula. The boycott's four specific demands are:
- Stop direct promotion of infant formula to the consumer, including mass media promotion and direct promotion such as posters, calendars, baby shows, wrist bands and baby bottles.
- Stop the use of company-employed "milk nurses."
- Stop the distribution of free formula samples to mothers.
- Stop promotion within health care facilities and to health workers.

Nestlé Boycott List

Chocolates
Nestlé's Crunch
Toll House Chips
Nestlé's Quik
Hot Cocoa Mix
Choco'lite
Choco-bake
$100,000 Candy Bar
Price's Chocolates
Go Ahead Bar

Coffee & Tea
Taster's Choice
Nestea
Pero
Decaf
Sunrise
Nescafé

Cheeses
Swiss Knight
Wispride
Gerber
Old Fort
Provalone Locatelli
Cherry Hill
Roger's

Packaged Foods, Soups, Etc.
Libby's
Stouffer Frozen Foods
Souptime
Maggi Soups
Crosse & Blackwell

Hotels & Restaurants
Stouffer
Rusty Scupper

Miscellaneous
L'Orcal Cosmetics
Nestlé Cookie Mixes
Deer Park Spring Water
Pine Hill Crystal Water
Kavli Crispbread
McVities
Keiller
James Keller & Son, Ltd.
Contique by Alcon
Ionax by Owens Labs
Lancôme Cosmetics
Beech-Nut Baby Foods

From *Newspage* 4, no. 1 (January 1980): 3

WAVAW Boycott of Elecktra Records Succeeds!

On November 8th, 1979 Women Against Violence Against Women (WAVAW) and Warner Communications, Inc. (WCI) announced the end of a 2½ year dispute

Reprinted with permission from *Women Against Violence in Pornography and Media Newspage.*

regarding the use of violent images of women in record advertising. David H. Horowitz, office of the President, WCI stated: "The WCI record divisions oppose the depiction of violence, against women or men, on album covers and in related promotional material. This policy expresses the WCI record group's opposition to the exploitation of violence, sexual or otherwise, in any form." Mr. Horowitz further states, "Although this policy is subject to prior contractual restrictions where applicable, the WCI record group has chosen to strongly discourage the use of images of physical and sexual violence against women in these cases as well."

WAVAW, initially a Los Angeles group, joined with California NOW of the National Organization of Women in calling for a boycott of all WCI records (Warner Bros., Atlantic and Elecktra/Asylum) in December of 1976. The Rolling Stones' "Black and Blue" album cover and billboard advertising on Sunset Strip in L.A. precipitated the outcry against the exploitation of women through physically and sexually violent images. "Black and Blue" depicted a woman tied up, bruised, and looking sexy.

In order to counteract the depiction of violence not only in record advertising but throughout the entertainment industry, WAVAW chapters have been formed in over 25 cities to deal with the problem. WAVAW has developed into a serious national movement striving to eliminate all media exploitation of violence against women. The WCI record group policy is a step closer to that goal.

Network
Gray Panther

From *Gray Panther Network*, March/
April 1980, p. 16

Rod Riding Radical: John Thompson

by Chuck Preston

Long before the 1960s there was another free-breathing movement—a revolutionary movement of working people—even in our own country. It was the brotherhood of men who roamed the land, mostly as uninvited guests of freight-trains, and men who roamed the seas doing the work on freighters. And there was with it also a sisterhood, we are reminded by the spirit of Elizabeth Gurley Flynn, calling us to sing the textile strikers' "Bread and Roses."

John Thompson of Portland, Ore., knew Elizabeth Gurley Flynn. John Thompson was a member of the Industrial Workers of the World, called for short the IWW or Wobblies. Hardly more than a boy, he crisscrossed the West and then went to sea. He joined the Communist Party of the U.S.A. and took part in the great struggles of the Depression. He was an example of the figure once seen in many lands—the jaunty, rootless vagabond-seaman, educated by wide and cosmopolitan travel, unfazed by cops and jails, and carrying in his pocket the Little Red Book.

And now? Why now, John Thompson is a Gray Panther. And an active one.

It figures that of the various strands that have gone into the weaving of our organization, one would be a scarlet thread leading back to the Wobblies. I remember how in my youth the Establishment press vilified them as bums, tramps, hoboes, comparable in vileness only to the Russian "Bolshev*iki*"; cartoons showed them unshaven, carrying placards reading "I Won't Work," or with dogs biting at the seat of their pants after being sic'ed on by righteous householders. It was years before I learned the truth: the Wobblies were anarchists or anarcho-syndicalists, which meant they were workers believing in One

Reprinted with permission from the *Gray Panther Network,* 3635 Chestnut St., Philadelphia, PA 19104.

Big Union, through which they hoped to establish a new society of liberty and equality. Meanwhile—unlike some "closet" movements we have had—they lived out their principles in the midst of get-rich-quick America, scorning the middle-class lifestyle as they indeed gathered in hobo camps where the proletarian was king. It might seem strange that no one has likened the Wobblies to a monastic order—say one with vows of poverty and sharing. But then you run into their strong and humorous anticlericalism, which produced such classics as "Pie in the Sky." ("The longhaired preachers come out every night.")

John Thompson was a Wobbly almost from the go. He was born April 9, 1909, at Annabella, Sevier County, Utah. He left home at the age of 12 and, he recalls, tended stock for roundups and rodeos in Salt Lake City, Pendleton, Ore., etc, That "etc." includes more geography than some of us will ever visit. At Cheyenne, Wyo., two railroad bulls attacked him and were working him over (a bull was a private policeman employed by the railroad—the deadly enemy of a freight-hitcher). Three men jumped the police and rescued John. "They were IWW and the best men I have known." John joined the IWW, Local 510 of Marine Transport.

Around 1925-26 he rode many freights and worked many odd jobs, from cleaning theaters to herding and milking goats, all the way from Denver to Las Vegas—Gallup, N.M.—Prescott, Ariz.—Phoenix, Ariz., and to Los Angeles. He worked for the Red Arrow Messenger Service in Los Angeles, hopped bells in Hollywood and

Bülbül/LNS

shipped out as a wiper on the Transmarine Steamship Company; was an extra in "Old Ironsides," "Ben Hur" and other movies. As a seaman he spent time on the beach in Shanghai and Manila and, he says, "lasted three days before being locked up in Kobe, Japan."

John joined the International Seaman's Union in San Francisco in 1926. Conservatives were in power in it, and as he says, "Not anything was happening to better conditions at this time." In 1928 he switched to the more radical International Seaman's Club, which became the left-wing Marine Workers Industrial Union. It was also at this time, as the Great Depression struck, that along with other former Wobblies he joined the Communist Party and launched into a decade of mass struggle. He took part in national Hunger Marches in 1931 and 1932—marches which on Dec. 7 of both years presented demands to the White House, where President Herbert Hoover was holding forth ineffectually. Another march of 1932 was the famed Bonus March, in which World War I veterans encamped in Washington and demanded that Congress pay their war bonuses in full. At President Hoover's orders they were driven out by Army troops under command of Gen. Douglas MacArthur. Not being a veteran, John Thompson could not participate, but he assisted the march by organizing for the Workers Ex-Service Men's League.

In those days there were two principal organizations of the unemployed, the Workers Alliance led by the Socialists and the Unemployed Councils by the Communists. John served as secretary of the Waterfront Unemployed Councils in Baltimore. In 1932 he was agent of the Marine Workers Industrial union in Philadelphia. He was arrested—"I was speaking from a soapbox and was arrested under the criminal syndicalism (Red-hunting) law," he says. On conviction he "enjoyed the hospitality of Moya Mensing (the name of a prison) for a while." On being released he was sent by the Party to Newport News, Va., where he organized marches and demonstrations on behalf of the Scottsboro Boys. This world-known civil rights case, as we would call it today, involved eight Black youths who were taken from a freight train at Scottsboro, Ala., and charged with rape on the perjured testimony of two white women. All the young men were convicted and sentenced to death. A national and even international legal and para-legal struggle ensued, continuing for years. I remember well singing the stirring chant, "The Scottsboro Boys . . . shall not die!" In the end one of the women recanted her testimony and the youths were cleared of the death sentence, although some served years in prison.

The Party next sent John Thompson—in the summer of 1934—to the West Coast, where a longshoremen's strike was going on. When two maritime workers were killed on Rincon Hill in San Francisco, in protest all the workers of the city went out in the historic San Francisco General Strike. After the conclusion of this struggle John was sent—he was a "Party man," and often has use for the word "sent"—to Portland and work with the union.

One incident of this West Coast stay John recalls vividly and with customary few words. "In 1935 a group attacked us in San Pedro, one of them was killed in the fight. Five of us had murder warrants issued against us. None of us were near this man at any time and we surely did not kill him." The charges were dropped in 1939.

The same year saw the signing of the Soviet-German Non-Aggression Pact, which looked like an alliance although it turned out to be a mere lull before the storm. Disillusioned with the Soviet leaders who had "shaken hands with Hitler," John left the Communist Party. His past radical connections pursued him, however, and during the McCarthy repression era his seaman's papers were "pulled." (He is now trying to get his "record" from the FBI through the Freedom of Information Act.) Eventually he got his papers back and sailed until 1974, when he suffered a heart attack and retired. "I got wind of the Gray Panthers, joined, and here I am." He takes part in the Portland Panthers' wide range of activities, serving on their City Energy Task Force.

John Thompson's life has been different from those of most Gray Panthers. Yet "as such, it is my life," he says. Each of our lives is unique, but related to all the others. John has not given up his commitment to a better world. He recalls that the preamble to the IWW membership book contained this sentence: "We shall build a new society within the shell of the old." And he adds: "I believe the Gray Panthers will eventually achieve this goal."

precariousness as a minority in this country, with little chance for involvement in the power structure. Capitalism and anti-Semitism limit our identification with other oppressed groups by pitting one against the other (as in the Black-Jewish conflict in Ocean Hill-Brownsville N.Y.). Nevertheless, many of us began to relate our historical experience of oppression to a feeling of connectedness with other oppressed minorities.

Coming Together

The Six Day War in 1967 was a watershed for many Jews active in the left. The threat of extinction of the State of Israel aroused strong feelings of Jewish identity in people who had considered themselves universalists and had identified primarily as leftists. Anti-Semitism reemerged in the left after 1967. The general denial of Jewish national rights by socialists (and so-called "socialist" countries like the Soviet Union) catalyzed many leftist Jews into forming Jewish support groups, and raised the old question of the importance of an independent Jewish socialist movement.

The Jewish student movement (Jewish alternative, Jewish counter-culture) reached its peak in the late 60's and early 70's. The politics were vaguely leftist. The strength of the movement centered around college campuses. It strongly parallelled the feminist movement, experiencing similar alienation and invalidation from the mainstream left. As the New Left declined after its anti-war focus disappeared, the Jewish alternative movement also lost much of its force. In addition, many of its leaders were socialist-Zionists, and had made aliyah by the early 70's.

The class make-up of the movement was significant. Although there was strong involvement of young working-class Jews, much of the "Jewish student movement" (sic) was made up of middle-class Jews whose parents has the money to send them to college. Upon graduation, many former activists settled back into middle-class roles, becoming doctors, lawyers, and businesspeople. Some channeled their energies into the more personal and spiritual chavurah communities. Many just drifted away. A small minority remained. A small minority remained identified as Jews and as leftists, and continued to define their politics as they struggled through the seventies.

As Time Goes By

With declining economic conditions and the rise of the New Right, the ranks of

CHUTZPAH

From *Chutzpah*, no. 17 (August 1980), pp. 4-7

Progressive Jewish Trends

As we began to look at present trends in the Jewish community in preparation for this issue, we were struck by the preponderance of small groups springing up in different cities. Independent of each other, their work, principles, goals, and styles are strikingly similar. We find an awareness of anti-Semitism, a leftist perspective of our connections as Jews with other oppressed groups, a commitment to democratic principles, a non-hierarchical structure, and a focus on consensual process. These simultaneous and independent developments are significant. These groups originate from the same conditions, are influenced by similar historical forces. These grass-root organizations seem to be the product of our common experience as young Jews.

Who We Are

We are the generation of post-Holocaust American Jews. Born with the existence of a Jewish state, in the shadow of the A-bomb, we grew up in the civil-rights and anti-war movements of the sixties. Many (though not all) of us were college-educated, members of the counter-culture, affected by the feminist movement, and mobilized by the draft. We were highly influenced by the emergence of the black power movement, with its trend toward particularism ("go organize your own") and national pride. The constant questioning of the established order engendered by the Vietnam war and emergent class issues affecting many of us in a permanent way: we stopped believing in the American Dream. We began to distrust assimilation and the middle-class security for which our parents worked so hard. We realized (as so many other progressive Jews had) our

Reprinted with permission from *Chutzpah* and the Jewish Socialist Collective.

Jewish leftists have grown. Some of the older groups (like Chutzpah) have enlarged and increased their activity; several new groups (like BCCAS and Kadimah) have appeared in the past few years. The Jewish Left of the eighties is more seriously aware of anti-Semitism. Its style is strongly influenced by feminism. Issues of process and communications (decision-making, responsibility, ideological discussion) are given priority. For the most part, democratic principles are embraced as a means of promoting consensual decision-making, to allow for the growth and potential leadership of all members of the group, and to prevent feelings of powerlessness and eventual burn-out. This emphasis comes in part from many of our experiences with burnout in the 60's and 70's.

Experiences with anti-Semitism and the dissolution of the New Left into unconnected sectarian groups have contributed to the isolation of these small Jewish groups from the left and from each other. Alienation and isolation have been factors in inhibiting their coalescence into a conscious movement.

Reclaiming Our Tradition

How can we strenghten this scattered community? We in Chutzpah believe that one very important task is to reclaim our progressive Jewish heritage. Recent trends have allowed the right (and, in the Jewish community, the Orthodox) to lay sole claim to tradition. We are led to believe that only conservative forces value tradition. Therefore, only they have a "reliable" view of history. Our goal is to dispel that myth, reclaim our Jewish tradition, and point to our progressive history with pride, and as a foundation for our future.

Many of us did not discover our progressive Jewish tradition until after we called ourselves Jewish leftists. This was certainly not the heritage taught in most Hebrew and Sunday schools. We learned, rather, that the "Jewish Communist Conspiracy" was a malicious anti-Semitic lie. (Just look at Hayim Solomon and Leonard Bernstein; we've always been good Americans!) The general terror during the McCarthy era and the long standing fear of anti-Semitism created a defensiveness in the Jewish community which allowed the middle-class establishment to whitewash the history of Jewish radicalism. The characteristic tendency of young Americans to be embarrassed by the preceding generation also contributed to the loss of contact with the Old Jewish Left, as did the very human tendency of some old leftists to retain old issues without expanding to new ones.

However, some connections remained. It may be easier to point to the phenomenon of "red diaper babies" (children of leftists being raised on their parents' ideology) as the basis of that connection. But many of the forces which radicalized our parents and grandparents still exist today.

It is true that there are many differences between this generation of Jewish leftists and past generations. Our economic situation is generally more comfortable than our grandparents' and even our parents'. We live in a time where the labor movement (which played such a crucial role in the radicalization of the Jewish masses) is sadly diffused. The Holocaust, the existence of a thirty-year-old State of Israel, the rise of the Third World, and the threat of atomic annihilation are all forces which make our responses as Jewish leftists different than the response of previous generations.

But the basic issues of those generations are surprisingly similar to our own. The question of universalism vs. particularism is just as intense: how do we find a place in the struggle of all oppressed peoples without abandoning our own cause? Anti-Semitism is as crucial today as it was twenty-five and fifty years ago. The worldwide rise of fascism, though tempered by the post-Holocaust lull, is as frightening now as it was in the twenties and early thirties. Even our potential allies too often have accepted the anti-Semitic stereotypes prevalent in the society. Frequently we are forced to choose between wider goals and our own people. Though upward mobility has generally improved our people's economic status, Jews are still forced into "middle-person," buffering roles in society, denied both the power of the economic aristocracy and the potential mass power of workers in heavy industry.

Making Connections

To reclaim our progressive Jewish tradition, we need to look to our history to learn from the successes and mistakes of preceding generations of Jewish radicals. We can benefit from an understanding of their struggles to maintain themselves as positive Jewish groups while building ties with the left. We need them as role models, to know that Jewish socialists survived without burning out. We have learned from them that culture is crucial in building and maintaining a mass movement. We recognize that the rise of American middle-class consciousness (the American Dream) encouraged the decline of the power of the working class. At the same time, the power of Jewish culture, especially Jewish socialist culture, maintained a certain critical distance from the values of mainstream middle-class American culture. We in Chutzpah and those of us in Am Chai are influenced by the power of the old cultural clubs, softball teams, camps, and theater groups in holding out against assimilation and contributing to the survival of a socialist movement. Finally, we look to the Jewish socialists who came before us to give us hope and strength. Their courage, their beauty, their humor and insight give us pride and help us to continue the struggle.

What to Do?

Recognizing the importance of connecting to our progressive past, we know that we must connect with other Jewish leftists in the present and also forge connections with potential Jewish radicals of the next generation. We have to realize that we are now cast into the role of educators. Us! It is our job to make the Jewish left a strong, visible presence in the left and in the Jewish community. It is our responsibility to share with others the benefits of our practice as we struggle to establish and maintain ties with both of these communities. In the process, we will increase our theoretical understanding of historical and present conditions.

We must be constantly involved in presenting alternatives to mainstream culture and politics, in demystifying the word "socialism," and offering it as a model and a way of life. Our involvement in issue-oriented coalition building and in the formation of cooperatives and collectives can increase the number of people who experience the power to participate in and control the conditions of their own lives. In cooperative work, we can challenge issues endemic to capitalist society: hierarchy, sexism, racism, individualism, feelings of powerlessness, irresponsibility, alienation. As strong Jewish role models for the next generation, we must be ready to become the teachers and the links to the past generation. Lastly, we must strengthen our own movement with increased communication, ideological debate, and sharing of experiences. Our challenge is to fight the Jewish tendency (a product of our own internalized oppression) to try to become invisible. We have no choice but to continue to speak up and take principled actions. We have a tradition to live up to.

From *In These Times* 4, no. 21
(April 23–29, 1980): 3, 6

Citizens Launch 'Second Party'

by John Judis and David Moberg

Cleveland, Ohio. The convention opened with a taped version of a familiar anthem—"America the Beautiful"—sung in an unfamiliar fashion by blues singer Ray Charles. It was an appropriate theme for the founding meeting of the Citizens Party, which, author Studs Terkel said in his keynote speech, vows to "reclaim the American dream from the predators who have stolen it."

In an exhausting weekend in Cleveland April 11-13, 261 delegates adopted a party platform and nominated Barry Commoner and La Donna Harris as their presidential and vice-presidential ticket.

At the convention, delegates frequently noted the recent poll showing that 58 percent of American voters are dissatisfied with the choice of Ronald Reagan and Jimmy Carter. If they are the major party candidates, then the Citizens Party will probably be able to play a visible role in the election and may even be able to pick up the 5 percent of the vote they need to qualify retroactively for federal election funds.

The strengths of the party are apparent. Commoner, who is known primarily as a foe of nuclear energy, has a remarkable ability to explain difficult ideas to a wide audience. Harris, the wife of former senator and presidential aspirant Fred Harris, is an American Indian activist. She will help the party's following among women and minorities and also among populist Democrats, who rallied to her husband's 1976 campaign.

The party's principal ideas, articulated largely by Commoner and economists Jeff Faux and Gar Alperovitz, emphasize the need for a democratic alternative to corporate power. Where in the past such an alternative has been presented abstractly or in terms of bureaucratic take-

---

Reprinted with permission from *In These Times: The Independent Socialist Newspaper.*

overs, the Citizens Party stresses a decentralized system of production with a maximum of worker and community control. It presents popular control of energy and transportation rather than federal tax breaks or loan credits as the only means of reinvigorating American industry. It stands for the solar transition as the only viable option to the risk of planetary holocaust.

Its strategy from the beginning has been to establish itself as a "second" party—to the peculiar party that the Citizens Party members call the "Republocrats"—not as a "third" party. To this end, it has eschewed both left-wing labels and the usual assumption of left-wing electoral parties that elections are secondary to some other activity—community organizing, building unions, or preparing for armed insurrection. "This group is neither right nor left," former foundation executive and party founder Archibald Gilles said, "It's mainstream. It's just a little further downstream."

The party has also done a remarkable job of organizing, given the tremendous limitations it has been operating under. With Senator Edward Kennedy, the choice of many potential Citizens Party partisans, still in the race, the party was nevertheless able to assemble a membership of 4,000 prior to the convention and functioning organizations in 30 states. Among the individuals recruited to the party were some like Chicago political consultant Don Rose and East Harlem Democrat Yolanda Sanchez, people with considerable political background and clout. Among the organizations was the 4,000-member Consumers Party of Philadelphia, whose membership is 70 percent black and whose mayoral candidate, Lucien Blackwell, won a majority of the black vote in last year's election.

But the party also faces formidable obstacles to its success in the fall. The most important is outside the party's control— the slim possibility that Senator Edward Kennedy could win the Democratic nomination and the more likely possibility that Representative John Anderson will run an independent race. While Anderson's race would legitimate third-party candidacies, it would also deprive the Citizens Party of a moderate protest vote and of

much of its potential middle-class base.

Another obstacle emanates, however, from the party itself. As was apparent at its founding convention, the Citizens Party, no less than other past left efforts, is prey to destructive factional struggles that could divert it from its central purpose and destroy its potential. The founding convention did not wreck the party, but it certainly didn't aid its development.

Faction Fighting

The faction fighting in the Citizens Party began several months before the convention when civil rights lawyer Arthur Kinoy, Marilyn Clement of the Center for Constitutional Rights, and Lucius Walker of the Interfaith Coalition of Community Organizations joined the party's leadership (*ITT*, Apr. 2).* Kinoy, Clement and Walker emphasized a dual strategy of waging a presidential campaign and leading local coalition efforts around immediate issues.

Commoner, businessman Stanley Weiss, staff member Burt DeLeeuw and others opposed the Kinoy proposals as a threat to the campaign's viability and as an invitation for the Citizens Party to become a coalition of the kind of marginal left organizations that Kinoy's miniscule Mass Party of the People and People's Alliance had been populated with.

At the convention, the Kinoy faction muted their political disagreements over the importance of the national campaign. Instead, they challenged Commoner's single-minded anti-corporate thrust, which they believe would make it more difficult for the Citizens Party to reach what Walker described as the "oppressed and hurting." "No political party is worth my time if it doesn't reach out to the people who are oppressed and hurting," Walker said in an interview at the convention. "By and large, you'll find these people in community organizations."

While it was hard to get Kinoy or Walker to spell out their position, they seemed to favor an issues-campaign that would be closely linked to various left groups in the minority and white communities.

Instead of taking their political differences with the Kinoy faction to the convention floor, Commoner, Weiss and DeLeeuw tried to keep Kinoy, Walker and Clement off the elected party leadership by

---

*[John Judis, "Carter-Reagan Race Can Give Citizens Party Space," *In These Times* 4, no. 18 (April 2, 1980): 13.—eds., *Alternative Papers.*]

threats and backroom conniving. This mode of operation further angered the Kinoy faction and created resentment toward Commoner among many delegates who had come to the convention unaware of the factional struggles and unfamiliar with the political differences.

But the Kinoy faction—possibly against Kinoy's own wishes—did its part to abort the founding convention. After the convention had formally adjourned, with about half the delegates departed (including the predominantly black, pro-Commoner Consumers Party delegation), Denise Carty-Bennia, who had been elected party co-chair on a Kinoy slate, announced her resignation. Carty-Bennia was resigning, she said, because the delegates had not elected Lucias Walker to the party's leadership.

There were disagreements among blacks, as well as among whites and Hispanics, about Walker's candidacy. While some doubts focused on Walker's politics, more focused on his political reliability. Several delegates complained that Walker had not performed his past responsibilities as a party leader. And others, perhaps on the basis of Walker's controversial past, claimed they simply didn't trust him. In spite of this, Carty-Bennia attributed Walker's defeat to "rank racism."

Dan Leahy, another defeated candidate on the Kinoy leadership slate, reconvened the convention after a hurried and by no means unanimous voice vote. The remaining delegates then spent a ragged and inconclusive three hours debating what to do about Carty-Bennia's resignation.

While the delegates from the respective factions left the convention bitter and angry, the uncommitted and often politically inexperienced delegates left confused. "It reminds me of the same old political process," Atlanta delegate Janet Lowe complained. "All this faction fighting—it is like having to choose between a Carter and a Reagan."

Besides making it impossible to energize and educate its delegates, the faction fighting also impeded two other functions of the convention: to impress observers from interested organizations with the party's promise and to gain favorable publicity for the party's candidates with the national media. One observer representing several important citizen action groups left the convention saying that he would recommend a "hands off" attitude. And NBC's *Today* show on Monday morn-

ing highlighted Carty-Bennia's walkout.

Campaign Strategy

If the Citizens Party were a traditional left organization that survived on the strength of the collective zeal of a stagnant membership, a convention like the Cleveland one could wreck it. But the Citizens Party is presently riding a historical wave much greater than its present membership or leadership. Regardless of the convention, it could grow rapidly in the next few months.

The debate that underlay the convention's factional fight could easily pop up again—perhaps with the same participants—as the campaign gains momentum. It could re-emerge as disagreement over the essential task of integrating recruits from the Kennedy, Brown or Anderson campaigns into the party's staff and leadership. Or it could re-emerge over the question of campaign strategy.

The party's long-run success depends on its winning over the Democratic Party's blue-collar and minority base, but its initial chances for success in 1980 will probably lie with what Don Rose calls the "new class." In 1980, these middle-income Democrats have supported Anderson, Brown and Kennedy. Their concerns are with the waste and irrationality of American capitalism and with the dishonesty and corruption of politics. They are more concerned about energy conservation and the solar transition than about jobs and welfare spending. They can be won over either by a clean economic conservative/

social liberal like Anderson or by a genuine radical like Commoner.

It will be more difficult for the party to score initial gains among blue-collar workers and minorities. Commoner is not sufficiently well-known, nor is his image right, to reach either constituency over the opposition or indifference of their elected leaders. "Blacks and major labor unions feel they have something now [with the Democratic Party], while we offer just a lick and a promise," Rose said.

Commoner's only chance to attract such voters would be to establish sufficient electoral credibility with his potential "new class" base to begin winning some endorsements from labor and minority leaders.

Kinoy, Clement and Walker have already indicated their disagreement with such a strategy. They are not as concerned about electoral credibility as about the party's links with certain causes and organizations in minority communities. If they have their way in determining the party's strategy, it will more resemble traditional left-wing efforts at community organizing than an attempt to become the "second party."

Commoner and his allies are presently undecided about their campaign strategy, but they are committed to achieving electoral credibility for the Citizens Party and can be expected to adjust their tactics accordingly. If so, and if Anderson doesn't enter the race, the Citizens Party could surprise everyone, including the delegates who left its founding convention disgruntled and bewildered.

Green Revolution

From *Green Revolution* 37, no. 3 (Early Autumn 1980): 20–21

The Politics of Strategic Misrepresentation

by John McClaughry

Reprinted with permission from *Green Revolution: A Voice for Decentralization and Balanced Living*.

The January, 1980, issue of the New England alternative magazine, *New Roots,* carried in its opinion space an argument for the newly-formed "Citizens Party" by Harriet Barlow, one of the new party's founders. Her argument is couched in terms which will appeal to people who consider themselves decentralists. Indeed, when I first heard about the new party from a friend who is now a leading official of the party, I was considerably attracted to the idea. America does need a political movement which will give some form and shape to the many varieties of decentralist thought—a movement that provides some unifying force to groups as diverse as appropriate technology practitioners, organic farmers, small-business advocates, spiritual rebirth devotees, worker self-management groups, the cooperative movement, neighborhood revitalizers, and many others.

But the more I learned about the new Citizens Party, the more I came to the opinion that it is not such a political movement. It is a movement which consciously appeals to the thousand varieties of decentralists in America, but its program is not an honest decentralist program. It is a centralist program, disguised—deliberately, I believe—in decentralist rhetoric. The aim of the Citizens Party is not to build an America where centralized power gives way to decentralized power, but an America where centralized private power is made subservient to centralized government power.

What More Control Does the Citizens Party Want?

"What we are about," reports Mrs. Barlow, "is a deconcentration of economic power and an increase in the number of decision-making points in society—some call it decentralization." The new party, she says, is "trying to build a politics for decentralism. That's what." But inspection of the official "working paper," i.e., platform, distributed by the Citizens Party national office shows that that is not what.

The first plank in the Citizens platform is "public control of the energy industries." Some would observe, with considerable reason, that the energy industry is already about as controlled by the public as an industry can get. What more control does the Citizens Party want? The answer to that seems simple. It wants the government, always in the name of "the public," to actually take over the energy industries. Then the energy industries would be responsive to "the people" in the same way as, say, the Postal Service. In other words, the call for "public control of the energy industries" amounts to nationalization or state socialism. The Citizens Party has shown absolutely no awareness of more subtle decentralist policies, centering around a restructuring of the tax laws, which would truly deconcentrate the energy industries and concentrated corporate power generally.

Then we come to the Citizens Party plan calling for a "guaranteed job for everyone who wants to work" coupled with "national planning." In other words, the new party wants to resurrect the original Humphrey-Hawkins bill, a great favorite of the left in recent years. The national planning issue, it seems to me, is perhaps the primary issue one may use to tell the decentralists from the pseudo-decentralists. Is it reasonable to believe that a decentralist society can be achieved by the Federal Government hiring a horde of experts to develop some kind of national blueprint for decentralism?

If the blueprint is nothing more than that—a mere plan—it will, of course, have little or no effect on society. But suppose there is to be some means of enforcing the "national plan," a supposition essential to treating the proposal seriously. Who, one may ask, is going to finalize this national plan? Oh yes, there may be input from town meetings all over America, but when all is said and done, someone in a position of authority will decide what the plan shall contain, who shall enforce it, and what shall be done with the violators. The Sovietry have already given us one mode which answers those intriguing questions.

Then we come to another interesting item: "stable prices for the basic necessities of life—food, fuel, housing, medical care." And how to assure stable prices? The Citizens Party is not interested in putting a brake to the continual printing of money by the Federal Reserve and the banking system. Nor is it interested in developing a stable commodity-backed currency along the lines advocated by the late Ralph Borsodi. No, its interest is in price controls. Well, Nixon and his economic czar, John B. Connally, were the last to embrace that idea in 1971. And they perhaps ruefully discovered what Hammurabi, Diocletian, and countless other practitioners of the idea found out: that price controls produce shortages, black marketeering, ubiquitous bureaucracies, invasions of civil liberties, and the undermining of public morality. It is, in fact, hard to conceive of a more egregiously anti-decentralist proposal than price controls. Or one that would do more to destroy what is left of the American economy.

Finally, returning to the theme of large corporations, the Citizens Party advocates putting them under "our" control. It cites worker and community ownership as desirable approaches. But even to long-standing advocates of worker ownership and community development corporations (such as myself), it should be evident by now that purely voluntary approaches will not have much more than novelty value in terms of overall contribution to the national economy for the rest of this century. What the Citizens Party really yearns for is government control of large corporations. It apparently clings to the quaint notion that government control of business bears some resemblance to control by the people. We should have learned by now that the threat of government control of corporations leads mainly to corporate efforts to control the government as a matter of self-protection.

What the Citizens Party is, in a nutshell, is a party devoted to a revisionist socialism. This it hopes to bring about by hoodwinking decentralists through shrewd decentralist-oriented appeals, while plunging on toward the centralist goals of national planning, guaranteed jobs, price controls, and state socialism.

I object to the kind of politics which tries to sell a bill of goods with a misleading label. This is the kind of thing which has rightly given the older political parties a bad name.

The right response is not to seek to outdo them in strategic misrepresentation, but to offer a genuine politics of principle.

I have no doubt that most of the people attracted to the Citizens Party yearn for a politics of integrity, built upon honest decentralist principles. The Citizens Party unfortunately fails to meet that need.

It is time for another political movement—not necessarily a party—to shoulder the decentralist cause. It is time for a movement which spurns the dogma of socialism, of communism, of finance capitalism, and of every other -ism with which we are plagued. It is time for a movement devoted to the restoration of civic virtue and the recognition of the benefits of diversity and toleration. The need is great, and the time is ripe.

John McClaughry is president of the Institute for Liberty and Community in Concord, Vermont, and is a member of the School of Living's Advisory Board. He is a longtime decentralist activist.

From *The Wine,* September 1979, p. 3

Declaration of Rights & Goals

by Women Against Violence Against Women

Women of all ages, races, religions, economic statuses, educational backgrounds, sexual preferences, and states of physical and mental health share these basic rights. We unite against violence against women to work towards these goals.

Our concerns lie in four major areas:

I. Personal Awareness and Skills

*Women have the right to love and value themselves in their private and public lives.

*Women have the right and the responsibility to feel strong and assertive, to say and act on what is important to them.

Goals

—That education create an awareness of the historical contributions of women to the world and of the disrespect women have suffered in this society both past and present.

—That quality assertiveness classes be made commonly available in schools and businesses.

—That self-defense classes be provided to women of all ages.

—The adequate resources and services be developed to meet the special needs of women of color, sexual minorities, children, the elderly, the mentally handicapped, and low-income.

II. Neighborhoods

*Women have the right to feel safe in their neighborhoods any time of day or night, in or out of their homes. A woman in danger has the right to a place she can go to for help where she will receive comfort, support and respect.

*Neighborhood residents have the right to know about sexual assaults that are occurring in their area.

***All** neighborhoods have the right to police protection.

Goals

—That active block clubs work on the issues of rape and battering.

—That clearly identified safe houses be established in each neighborhood as refuges for women in fear or in danger.

—That adequate, accessible shelters with secure funding be established for battered women.

III. Women Out in the World

*Women have the right to be seen by themselves and others as intelligent, competent, sensitive, and creative members of society.

*Women have the right to move freely, comfortably, and safely in society both as workers and as consumers of goods and services.

Goals

—That women not be used as sexual objects in advertising and the media.

—That safe transportation be provided for women day **and** night.

—That every work place have griev-ance procedures for any sexual harassment on the job.

—That women be hired, paid, and promoted equally with men.

IV. Supportive Government and Legal Systems

*Women have the right to a government and legal systems that recognize the continuous violence against women and are committed to its elimination.

Goals

—That the scope of state programs addressing violence against women be expanded to emphasize women's safety and rape prevention.

—That institutionalized, on-going funding be continued for rape crisis centers, battered women's shelters and sexual assault services.

—That laws be passed to make sexual assault between husband and wife a crime.

—That laws be passed requiring that a physician, therapist, or counselor give every patient or client a written statement describing their right to be free of sexual abuse by that therapist and the grievance procedure to be used whenever they are sexually approached.

—That laws be enforced to end forced sterilization of women.

—That laws be enforced to prevent the abuse of women in mental institutions and prisons.

—That laws be passed to make sexual harassment on the street a crime.

—That government and legal systems work actively for passage of the ERA.

From *The Wine,* September 1979, pp. 4-6

Women Take Back the Night

by Sarah Young and Sherrie Mentzer

Twin Cities Women Against Violence Against Women (WAVAW) was founded seven months ago by a group of Minneapolis MNS women (Kathy Sharp, Flow Carlson, Laura Jolly, Sarah Young, Sherrie Mentzer and Kendrick Wronski). We have grown to a membership of approximately 60, containing a decision making group of 20-25. We are affiliated with a national network of independent

Reprinted with permission from *The Wine,* the monthly newsletter of Movement for a New Society.

Reprinted with permission from *The Wine,* the monthly newsletter of Movement for a New Society.

WAVAW groups. A Take Back the Night march was the second big project we undertook. We chose to do it because we could involve many people at once in organizing, to seize the time (summer) when outside danger is the highest, to reach many people with a simple, direct message, to reach groups and individuals all over town with the name of our organization, and ideas about what WAVAW could do. The first part of this article describes some successful methods of organizing that we'd like to share with MNS folks, and the second half describes the results, and possible next steps.

ORGANIZING THE MARCH

To Be or Not To Be a Collective

In typical MNS form WAVAW started with a small group of friends. We had plans for months of intensive 'getting to know each other,' working on "isms," forming our politics, etc. To our surprise, our first workshop drew in 60 people, all hot to trot. Being only two weeks old at that point, we quickly thought up a neighborhood survey project, to make use of so much new energy and enthusiasm. We were soon challenged with (GASP . . .) elitism. Did we really think that women would be satisfied to go out and do our work for us? Why were we a "closed group"? Did we think we could stop rape single-handedly? The women were asserting that they had skills and ideas to share, that they wanted to be involved in planning strategy and making decisions.

We decided to take a deep breath and open up our Thursday night meetings to other strongly concerned women. We had to trust that our sense of group process could withstand new people, and that disruptive people could be directly asked to leave. We also realized how important it was to open up and listen to what new people had to offer, especially if we were to attract a wider range of age and race groups.

Our meetings soon expanded by 20 women, about half of whom were ready to take on large chunks of responsibility. All were impressed with our efficiency and warmth and open to what they could see of our MNS approach. We soon realized our original core group could never have begun to accomplish the amount of work this group took over.

Reaching Out to the Community

Seeking help with the march: For the march to have as large an impact as we wanted, we needed lots of help. Our group of 25 sent out recruitment flyers to nearly 100 organizations—those that dealt with women's issues, violence, alternatives, or services for a minority group. Flyers were posted on poles, in stores and women's bathrooms all over town. Our organizational meeting drew in 60 more women. They were met with a well planned agenda, beaming with the power, seriousness and inspiration of our new group. They saw charts of 10 carefully planned and described task groups, and what participation in each would involve. They heard a history of WAVAW, other marches, some of our visions of women reclaiming power, and how the march fit in. We made sure that at least one person from the core group facilitated each task group.

This meeting drew in many women who had never done anything "political" before. We drew in a good cross section of class, present lifestyle, lesbian/straight women. We had representatives from elderly, handicapped, black and chicana communities, but failed (read—didn't get to it) to do enough work on ourselves to make it worth the while of more of these women to become actively involved.

Advertising the march: We started with the same approach, expanding our mailing to about 250 groups and agencies. We had speakers available to go out to anyone who would have us, talking about WAVAW and the purpose behind the march. We made a point to get info into all the Twin Cities community newspapers, and to speak on all local radio stations. We were especially fortunate to get spots on stations serving third world communities. We sent out small news releases to everyone on our mailing list who we knew to have a newsletter. As a fundraising/publicity effort we silkscreened hundreds of tee-shirts with our logo and the date of the march. We invested in a phone answering machine, so that information could go out and come in at all times.

At the time of the march: Detailed lists were posted as to possible actions, and skills and resources people could contribute. Hundreds of women filled out cards, indicating interests and possibilities.

Appreciating Whatever People Could Offer

One very important principle of our organizational meeting was that any amount of time, ideas or money a person could give, was valuable to us. We especially wanted to make WAVAW accessible to women who are working and/or raising children, and to women who are otherwise intimidated by political work. We emphasized that people come to meetings because they **want** to be there (as opposed to should), and that if the workload turns out to be unrealistic for them, that it's fine that they drop out. We found that we did not need rigid guidelines about decision making. We welcomed comments from everyone, and found that the few who cared the most, always had good thinking to offer. Everyone got the feeling that they did make a difference because they were there.

This attitude also carried over to the 200 marshals who were trained for the march, and helped account for the warm, excited and powerful tone that shone out in the face and motions of everyone present.

Learning from Other Marches

Early in the planning, we wrote to MNS people in Boston, and got back a detailed description of problems and successes in a Boston Take Back the Night march. Louise Brille from Putney came through town and gave us a vivid description of a march she attended in Massachusetts. As well as organizing info, we were able to learn from these women about issues that had come up—such as hostility from men, or racism on the part of the marchers. This helped us to do good advance thinking of some difficult issues. We also learned about special flourishes, such as providing banners for women that said **I Survived a Rape**.

On Letting Go of Leadership

Even with such a booming organization, for those of us who were in the core group from the start it was very hard to sometimes lay down our "passion" and trust that others could get the work done. Says Sherrie—time and again . . . "I had to give up being a hot shit indispensable organizer, and see that I wasn't worth anything when I started to get burnt out, desperate, nervous and disconnected from others. I've felt strongly all along that if we had enough energy among us to get 5,000 people out, it would happen, and if we only had enough energy to draw 500, that would be okay too. So I found that times I felt I just couldn't make one more phone call, I would stop. Sure enough, when I really listened to myself and stopped, most everytime someone would call up or appear and say—is there some little thing I can do to help?"

Our results were fabulous! There were 5,000 to 6,000 people marching. The march was led by an all women's groups (about 4/5 of the crowd) followed by a mixed

grouping. Some of the proud banners carried high by groups of women included ex-prostitutes, battered women, the Gray Panthers, women in elected offices, Jewish women's Minyon, and more. Due to some good statewide outreach, women came from as far as 3,000 miles away. We marched through the sleazy heart of Minneapolis late on a Saturday night, singing and chanting. Hundreds of women proudly wore the **I Survived a Rape** banners. It was a joyous example of many people together banishing the fear we all take for granted alone.

Some goals accomplished by the march: hundreds of agencies and thousands of individuals all over town now know who WAVAW is and what we stand for; we got a lot of vital facts and information out to these same people as to the different types of violence against women and the extent to which it happens around us; the 60 women who worked with us feel a lot more powerful as social changers and have considerably more radical insights into the nature of the problems; we developed a strong base of unity among people working with us; many links, and the beginnings of a coalition among the many groups and agencies we contacted; we established ourselves with local press and police; a huge mailing list, and many names of people indicating specific projects they're interested in or skills they have to offer. Not to mention we actually came out $2,000 ahead after expenses, due to generous donations and the tee-shirts selling like hotcakes. Most important, many many women were moved to feel some way in which they feel powerless as women, against violence, and sparked to feel **You bet we don't deserve this and we're going to have to do some things about it.**

What Next?

We are all taking a well deserved vacation after the march, so here in this article I (Sarah) can speak only as an individual in WAVAW, and not for the group. So please keep posted for future *Wine* articles, as our plans and politics develop and get consensed on.

How will our "trust-founded" structure and decision making hold up over time?

How do we find the time to build a solid organization with common principles among so many people, and do actions as well? Can we continue as a diverse group, continue looking so good around town, and maintain a **radical** focus? Many concerns. The flip side of having a huge number of people feeling unified and trusted, was that inexperienced members were known to make (unaware) racist statements in the name of WAVAW, to make big mistakes in handling police, and otherwise misrepresent what those of us in the core feel to be important.

For now, some of us have a vision of WAVAW continuing as a network of task groups each dealing with different aspects of violence against women. Some examples that many women are interested in are: Neighborhood organizing against rape; street actions and community education on porno; street actions on rape (such as confronting known rapists); campaigning against violence in advertising and the media; supporting campaigns of local native american women against forced sterilization and harassment. All of these actions would be starting from the premise that no woman deserves any type of violence against her, under any circumstances. We have a commitment to nonviolence, and to working above ground as an organization.

Sorting priorities and spreading around knowledge and skills are the largest tasks awaiting us. The following are next steps that some of us see as critical to strengthening our organization:

- To develop our understanding of the sources of violence against women; to learn more of the herstorical roots of violence, and its present relationship to the economic conditions of our society.
- To learn more facts about rape, battering, women in prison, etc.
- To share our personal tales of power—success stories that help us to personally become stronger in the world, and to destroy the myths inside us and around us.
- Actively look at and **struggle** with our own racism, classism, and ageism.
- Share leadership organizing, speaking, and writing skills.
- Develop a newsletter for local and national communication.
- Contact the hundreds of women who filled out cards at the march or otherwise showed interest along the way, keeping them updated.

Those of us also in MNS plan to meet occasionally as a caucus within WAVAW. We think it's likely we will someday clear into the network as a collective. We have high falutin' goals (as well as burning personal needs) for effecting changes in individuals and institutions and for of course **ending** the threat of violence against women in our society. We have done several strategy sessions and need to do more. There's a lot of pain in the way of our visions. We see that we can't do it alone, and we see that it will take time and much work to do it well with a big group. We're ready and willing and just aching to kick up some shit!

You'll be hearing more from us. . . .

CASA
THE NEWSLETTER FOR THE
CENTER AGAINST SEXUAL ASSAULT

From *CASA* 7, no. 3 (May/June 1980): 2

Men Who Are Victims of Rape

by Thomas Levine

Reprinted with permission from *CASA: The Newsletter for the Center Against Sexual Assault.*

Most men never give a thought to the possibility of becoming a sexual assault victim. There are many misconceptions and myths about men as victims of rape. In the first part of this two part article, we will explore the realities of men who are victimized by female rapists. Can it happen? Does it happen? And why does it happen? The second part of this article which will appear in the July-August 1980

CASA Newsletter,* will pertain to men who are sexually assaulted by other men outside of the penal institution.

Men as Victims

Can a man be raped by a woman? Most people believe that this is impossible, and yet males can be and are sexually assaulted by females. A major misconception is that a man has to be a willing participant in order for a sex act to be physically possible. In fact, fear can produce an involuntary erection. Susan Brownmiller, author of *Against Our Will*, cites war as an example of a time when men are so terrified that they often go into battle with an erection. A life threatening situation, such as potential sexual assault, can cause the same physical reaction, thus making it possible for a woman to rape a man.

Any man, as well as any woman, can be a victim of this horrifying crime. Between the months of January and March of 1980, CASA had twenty-two (22) calls from males who were victims of sexual assaults. These assaults were committed by both female and male offenders. Although CASA served many more female victims over the same time period, this does not mean we can ignore this problem.

There are men who say they would like to be raped by a woman. Men who state this opinion do not realize just what rape is. The fulfilling of pleasurable sexual fantasies, and the actuality of rape are two completely different things. In a fantasy, one has either conscious or unconscious control over everything that happens. The person imagining the scene can stop the imagery at any time. But in a rape situation, the rapist has complete control. The victim has no idea what the rapist is going to do; he or she may even kill the victim. The rapist enjoys the fact that the victim has no control. Humiliation, degradation, and pain are common tools of the rapist. A female raping a male may use these same tools, or perhaps more subtle forms of coercion. An example of this might be sexual harassment at one's place of employment. More and more women are actively resisting male employer's sexual advances. This type of interaction also takes place between female bosses and male employees. The male in this instance feels intimidated when he is told he will lose his job if he does not have sex with his boss.

*[Thomas Levine, "Men Who Are Victims of Rape," [Part 2] *CASA: The Newsletter for the Center Against Sexual Assault* 7, no. [4] (July/August 1980): 2.—eds., *Alternative Papers*.]

The victim would be afraid to report because he would not only lose his job, but fear no one would believe him. It is commonly believed that men are ever-ready and indiscriminate in regards as to who they have sex with. It is difficult to convince a jury or judge that a man was forced to perform a sex act with a woman. It is understandable that a man would choose not to report to the police. Whereas society might find the aftermentioned incident unbelievable, even laughable, this kind of dehumanizing by employers happens to men and women daily.

The Offender

Who are the women who rape men? No one really knows. There are no general characteristics clearly defined by research, because most assaults are not reported. Many of the women operate in gangs. Several might hold a man down, while each member in turn proceeds to sexually degrade and humiliate him. Victims feel angry and humiliated. They have difficulty believing that anything like this could happen to them. In many instances, gangs of two pick up men. One of them pulls out a gun and holds it on the unsuspecting victim, while the other woman assaults him.

Women do not always operate in gangs, but frequently this is the case; women do not always have full sexual intercourse with the victim, but the elements of power, domination, and fear on the part of the victim are nearly always present.

We can only theorize as to what motivates a woman to sexually assault men. Perhaps it is some sort of misplaced revenge, or an intense hatred of men.

The Law

There are laws to help men who have been victimized in this manner. Revised Arizona State statute, section 13-1406 was written to protect both sexes. It has been in effect since October of 1978. "Sexual assault" has replaced the word "rape" in this new law, and defines sexual intercourse as "penetration of the penis, vulva, or anus by any part of the body or by any object or manual masturbation of the penis or vulva." The law states that both females and males may be victims as well as perpetrators.

Summary

Men are victims of sexual assault. Men who have been raped did not enjoy it, nor do they want it to happen again. One of the most difficult problems male victims have to overcome is embarrassment combined with disbelief. Often they are so humiliated by the incident, that they do not go to a hospital or clinic for treatment of possible venereal disease. A very real need of victims is the desire to talk to someone. To be understood by a sympathetic person who helps the victim deal with his emotions can aid greatly to that person's recovery. CASA is here to offer support and counseling to both male and female victims. Hopefully, as more people learn that sexual assault can happen to men as well as women, it will become less difficult for a male victim and his family to seek out the kind of supportive services they need.

From *Radical America* 14, no. 3 (May/June 1980): 41-47

Battered Women's Refuges: Feminist Cooperatives vs. Social Service Institutions

by Lois Ahrens

Reprinted with permission from *Radical America*.

Refuges for battered women, like rape crisis centers, seem to be undergoing a transformation throughout the United States from feminist, nonhierarchical, community-based organizations to institutionalized social service agencies. The shelter in Austin, Texas provides a typical example of this transformation. As someone who witnessed this process as part of the original Coalition on Battered Women which formed in Austin, Texas in November 1976, and later as one of the shelter's two staff people first hired in May 1977, I have had a long association with the Center, from planning to implementation stages. This experience may help feminists working with battered women avoid the pitfalls we faced.

When we began in November 1976, we were a coalition of twenty women who represented a feminist counseling collective, a women and alcoholism task force, a Chicano group, nurses, social workers, grant writers, a women's center, the local mental health agency, and women who had themselves been battered or who had come from families where mothers or sisters had been battered. We represented a diversity of agencies, ages, ethnicities, and ideologies. Though our differences were abundant, our common goal kept us striving to have everyone's concerns heard. We spent hundreds of hours talking about what we wanted the goals of the group to be because we felt that process to be crucial to creating a non-bureaucratic organization. Through discussion it appeared that we all believed hierarchical models are oppressive to all people, and have historically been especially so to minorities and to women, in particular, battered women. Because of this conviction we believed that the structure of refuges for women should be models for collective work. Each individual should have her own area of expertise and that work should be done in a collaborative manner. We argued that this method would allow for personal growth for staff members and also serve as a model to women living in the Center by showing that women can work together cooperatively, without bosses.

Further, the group ostensibly agreed that when we create bureaucracies each worker's role in the shelter becomes more specialized and fragmented. Such specialization leads to individual involvement in only one area and creates a familiar syndrome. First, workers begin to feel less responsibility and involvement with the entire program. They begin to view work as a "job," lacking political purpose. Second, the individual worker feels less empowered and less capable of working as peers with women who come to the refuge. Women are transformed into 'clients' to be routed from one desk or department to another (and nowhere viewed as complex individuals). In this scheme everyone suffers and feminist hopes for new models of support are dashed.

Phase One: The Formative Stage

In the beginning, our group was singly-focused, and functioned in a collective and task-oriented fashion. At the time, there seemed to be general agreement on issues such as the value of a feminist perspective in the shelter, the inclusion of lesbians as visible members of the collective, and the need for workers and residents in the shelter to share in decision-making and leadership. We viewed ourselves as a collective, and a very successful one. Our Center opened in June 1977, funded by county and private mental health funds.

Phase Two: Significant Changes

Soon after the shelter opened, the twenty coalition members agreed to form a twelve-member Coordinating Committee. The coalition agreed that a smaller number of women was needed to meet more frequently to direct the actual workings of the new Center. They elected twelve of their group according to how much time and energy each could devote to a Coordinating Committee. Three different things began to happen at that point. First, two of the Committee members became paid staff people. Staff was working approximately eighty hours a week and therefore had greater and greater knowledge of the shelter operations. Other Coordinating Committee members began to feel threatened by this shift and started treating the staff as "paid help." Simultaneously, many Coordinating Committee members chose not to work directly in the shelter. A division grew between members with day-to-day knowledge of shelter happenings and those who became more divorced from the daily realities faced by paid and nonpaid staff. Secondly, many of the original Coalition members who identified themselves as radical feminists became involved in other projects instead of continuing with the Center. They felt they had worked to establish the shelter, but were not interested in committing time to its daily operation. This created a definite tilt in ideological perspective on the Coordinating Committee and a significant lessening of support for the few remaining radical feminists. Third, the Center for Battered Women began its own process of incorporating as a nonprofit, tax-exempt organization.

Phase Three: Board Development

Until that point we operated under the tax-exempt status of the Austin Women's Center. Six months after the Austin Center for Battered Women began its own incorporation process, elections were held to choose a board of directors. Unfortunately, the first board was not representative of the community. Ballots were sent to those on the mailing list and to all those who had participated in volunteer training. Individuals who merely "expressed interest in the issue of battered women" composed one part of the electorate. Women volunteered to run for directors. This loose system allowed board members to be selected who had had no previous contact with the Center or whose knowledge of the Center was only through friends of the incumbent board members. Volunteers in the shelter were already working overtime, and most could not be convinced of the necessity of volunteer representation on the board. The majority of volunteers had had little or no previous experience as volunteers or as board members, since they were former battered women who were divorced, working full-time jobs, and caring for their children. Most felt their primary interest was in working directly with battered women in the shelter, not in serving on a board.

This vague and unrepresentative election allowed for board members to be elected who represented no community or group, making them responsible or responsive to no one but themselves. This problem grew when two minority women (both volunteers with a community base), feeling overlooked and misunderstood, resigned from the board. The board, rather than address the issues raised by their resignations or call new elections, replaced them by appointing two personal friends, an Anglo male lawyer and an Anglo woman.

The staff viewed this as a consolidation of power by the board, and challenged the appointment rather than election of new board members. The staff protested a number of issues. First, no attempt was made to fill the vacancies with other Black and Chicano women involved with the shelter. Second, the board was not addressing the issues the two women had raised. Third, there had been no precedent for having men on the board. The staff indicated to the board that it was essential for them to examine their own racism and the Center's credibility in the Black and Chicano communities. Further, we were concerned that the replacement board members had no ties to the daily operation of the shelter. The board responded to our concerns by sending letters to the ex-board members thanking them for their past work. Both women continued to work in the Center.

Further, staff recommendations that all board members participate minimally in the eighteen-hour volunteer training was turned down. Board members were elected and served without prior knowledge of the

Coalition's original plan for the working of the shelter. The board/staff division became sharper as fewer board members maintained contact with battered women at the shelter. This division and the fact that the more strongly feminist women had already left the original group and so did not run for the board, helped to solidify the more professional, liberal feminist block on the board. This segregation of board members from the program paved the way for what was to come.

Phase Four: Administration and Staff

During this time the Center was growing in the scope of services and programming it offered women and children. The number of staff began to expand from the original two. In July 1977 we hired the first full-time counselor, and by October five staff people funded by CETA were hired. During the same month the board decided that the Center needed an administrator who would report to and make contact with the funding agencies, keep track of the finances, and oversee the Center's administration. An administrator was hired in November and the staff of eight women was divided into two work groups: those involved in funding, administration, and the running of the house, and those who came into direct contact with the women and children using the services of the Center. The latter came to be known as direct services or program staff. The direct services staff consisted of myself as director, two counselors, a childcare worker, and a lawyer/advocate. It became clear to those of us in services that the administrator's principal concern and involvement was the board. We, on the other hand, were concentrating on providing good services, training large numbers of volunteers, and expanding our funding, and felt that this focus would speak for the validity of the internal structure of the shelter.

The administrator never had been a battered woman, nor had she been through the volunteer training. She had little or no contact with women residing at the Center. In response to her approach, two groups developed. One camp, composed of the direct services staff and a large number of volunteers, was collectivist and feminist; the other, made up of the board and administrator, placed greater value on those with credentials and on a hierarchical structure. Under the influence of the administrator, the board of the Center for Battered Women was beginning to push for *one* director. The stated rationale for this

was that other agencies would be better able to work with an organizational structure similar to their own, and that funding sources would be reluctant to grant funds to any group with an 'alternative' form of organization. This seemed at the least ironic, since all the funding we had received prior to this organizational change had been granted because of our demonstration of the direct relationship between a nonhierarchical structure and the power issues of violence against women. We had argued that the Center should provide a model of cooperative, nonhierarchical work, and that the one-up, one-down model was counterproductive in working to change women's (and especially battered women's) lives. Nonetheless, in February 1978, the board voted to make the administrator the director.

Phase Five: Disintegration

The first step was to demote and render powerless the staff who had been instrumental in formulating the original program and policies—in this case, the direct service staff. This was accomplished by rewriting job descriptions into jobs containing very specific and fragmented functions. Policy-making power went completely to the director. Staff meetings became little more than lectures by the director, allowing no avenue for staff input. I resigned. Three weeks later the board, with guidance from the director, fired one counselor, the childcare worker, and the lawyer. Two of them were dismissed for 'insubordination'. The Center was left with one counselor, who then resigned, leaving none of the original direct service staff. The task of ridding the Center of the original staff was complete.

There were many reactions to this upheaval. Upon resigning I wrote a letter to all volunteers stating the reasons for my resignation and listing the changes which I thought would be forthcoming. Meetings with staff, a few residents and as many as forty volunteers followed. In these meetings volunteers challenged the right of the board to make the changes. They discussed the composition of the board and the resignations of its two volunteers. Volunteers pressed for more representation on the board. The CETA workers hired lawyers and began to appeal their firing to the City of Austin. Ex-staff and volunteers approached funding sources, warning of changes in policy which would have a detrimental effect on the program.

Volunteers and ex-staff began to pressure the Women's Center (which was still the parent group) to exercise its authority over the Center for Battered Women board. Joint Women's Center and CBW board meetings were held, with as many as sixty people attending. However, the Women's Center board finally opted to not exercise its control, stating that it had not entered into the internal workings of the CBW board prior to this, and would not do so now. Funding sources monitored the events, but felt it was not wise to intervene into intraorganizational disputes. Many volunteers withdrew completely, feeling the situation to be hopeless. The fired CETA staff appeals dragged on for more than a year and finally, after many hearings, the staff decided that the issues had been lost and trivialized in the process. "Winning," they felt, would mean nothing. They dropped their cases. The board emerged stronger than ever. All the opposition staff and volunteers were gone from the Center.

Phase Six: Discrediting and Maligning

The next step was to find a way to discredit the program and policies of the original staff. The most expedient way of doing this was to let it be known through the informal social service network that the director and her allies had prevented a lesbian (translated 'man-hating') takeover. This was said despite the fact that among the five staff and forty volunteers who left the Center perhaps not more than five were lesbian. With this one word—lesbian—no other explanation became necessary. The validity of the charge remained unquestioned since none of the original staff or volunteers remained. Other agencies willingly took the shelter into the social service fold.

Phase Seven: The Aftermath

The following is a summary of events in the Center since the transition from a collective to a hierarchical structure. The progression toward developing a model of a 'professionalized' social service institution divorced from the community it was to service is evident.

The new leadership of the Center for Battered Women has said that it is very important to separate the issue of feminism and sexism from that of battered women. With the new federal emphasis on the nuclear family, the Center chooses to look at battered women as a "family violence problem," but refuses to consider the societal, cultural, and political implications of why women are the ones in the family so often beaten. Soon after the original staff people left the shelter, men began to be trained and to serve as volunteers working directly with the women in the house. In the past, those who felt that men should not work in the house as volunteers compromised with those who felt that positive male role-models are necessary. The result was that men were included in regular volunteer training and received additional training to work with children in the house. Now, however, men are also answering the telephone hot-line and staffing the Center.

In the view of the founders of the Center, it is not a good idea for men to work in a shelter for battered women. Their presence can reinforce old patterns for battered women. Male volunteers and/or staff can easily be cast (or cast themselves) in the role of rescuer, encouraging a dependent role. Just when they need to be developing their own strengths, battered women can focus their attention on a man as the person most likely to solve their problems. This helps to perpetuate a continued cycle of dependence and inequality—two of the causes of battering.

The Center for Battered Women has undergone the transformation to a social service agency by becoming more and more removed from its 'client' population. The feminist ideology brought insights into programming for battered women. This belief demanded that staff and volunteers not make separations between themselves and battered women. We were able to integrate an understanding of the oppression and violence against women with a concern for the individual woman. This same ideology created a shelter based on the opinion that informal worker/resident relationships, self-help and peer-support would be more effective in fulfilling some of the immediate needs of battered women than rigid, bureaucratic structures. For example, women now living at the center must make an appointment to see a counselor days ahead of time. In the past, this type of interaction between the staff and a woman could just as easily have taken place at the kitchen table as in an appointed time in a more formal office setting.

There is now a distancing of staff from women who stay at the shelter. Direct service people complement policy and procedures made by an administrator and board which is divorced from the group they are intending to serve. Little room remains for the less formal, more

supportive sharing which was an original goal.

Preventive Measures

There are some lessons from our experience which may help insure that feminist-based shelters remain places that are responsive to the needs of battered women:

1. It is essential that women who organize shelters have an identifiable feminist analysis, which encompasses an understanding of the ways in which that analysis affects services to battered women. In addition, it is crucial that this specific analysis be part of all board orientations, volunteer training, and public education. This policy is necessary in order to make all who come in contact with the shelter understand that feminist ideology is not a tangential issue, but basic and essential. It will serve the dual purpose of informing possible shelter participants of the ideological basis of the program, as well as continually placing the issue of battered women in a feminist cultural and political context.

2. The issue of lesbianism has lost none of its volatility in recent years. Lesbians have continually taken part in all aspects of the women's movement, and the battered women's movement is no exception. It is therefore imperative that each group or collective initially acknowledge lesbians as a valuable part of their organization as one way of eliminating lesbianism as a negative issue. This can be accomplished by publicly encouraging the active participation of lesbians as staff, board, and volunteers. Further, position papers outlining the ideological framework of the shelter must include the contribution of lesbians in all aspects of the shelter program.

3. As feminists we realize how vital the inclusion of ex-battered women, working class, minority women, and volunteers are in forming a community-based governing board. Too often, these women have little money, little time, and little children! While their inclusion may not guarantee the development of a feminist analysis, it is a step toward keeping services tied to needs.

4. Those of us who have worked developing refuges for battered women know we cannot exist in a service vacuum. In order for a shelter to be effective, we must initiate and maintain working relationships with the police, courts, hospitals, welfare departments, and mental health services. We must also, however,

maintain our own organizational integrity. We can work with the police or welfare, but we also must retain enough freedom to be able to be an effective and strong advocate for women who are beaten. Links are vital, but we must be cautious, and understand the tenuous line between working with existing agencies and being seduced by the 'respectability' and seeming advantages these law enforcement and social service agencies appear to offer, often at the expense of the battered women. The feminist stance and advocacy role must not be diffused.

5. Feminist shelters must join other feminist services and groups in providing a base of support for one another. The roles and functions of each group may be different, but the shared ideological base is of critical importance. This alliance will provide an alternative to the traditional social service network. It is important in terms of referrals, but even more vital because it provides a constituency which can understand the broader implications of the shelter's work. Indeed, should they be needed, other groups can be political allies as well as friends.

Conclusions

The lure of building powerful social service fiefdoms is not gender-based. The shelter movement will attract women (and men) who view these services as stepping stones to personal career goals. It is vital for us to recognize that many in local, state or federal agencies will more easily accept that which is already familiar, those who do not threaten their own beliefs. The community support needed to maintain a feminist-based shelter for battered women requires political sophistication. Self-education, our own raised consciousness, and good faith are not enough. Consensus decision-making works only if everybody is playing by and believes in the same rules. Our unhappy experience shows that battered women's shelters committed to the full empowerment of women will remain feminist in content and approach only by constant discussion, analysis, and vigilance.

Lois Ahrens identifies herself as part of the radical feminist movement. She was a founder and is an active member of Womenspace, a feminist action group and counselling collective in Austin, Texas. She would like to hear from people who have had experiences similar to those described in her article; and she can be contacted through RA.

From *The San Francisco Bay Guardian* 14, no. 20 (March 27, 1980): 5

Rallies Mark the Coming of Age of the New Anti-Draft Movement

IN WASHINGTON
by Allan MacRobert

A new anti-war movement is gathering momentum on college campuses across the country.

The movement began in January, the day after President Jimmy Carter announced in his State of the Union address his intent to have young people registered for the draft. Since that time, the movement has grown far beyond being just a protest of draft registration. Last weekend, in Washington, D.C. and in other cities around the country, the anti-draft movement held its first mass demonstration. They showed that activists have put together a nationwide base and an all-inclusive radical analysis and have developed connections to other issues—surprising in a movement that nine weeks ago did not exist.

Thirty thousand of the new movement's members, mostly college students, marched, chanted and sang their way through Washington on Saturday, yelling themselves hoarse at the White House and gathering at the Capitol for an afternoon of speeches. It was the first time the bulk of the movement has assembled in one place, looked at itself and begun to realize its size.

Thanks to Jimmy

From the stage on the Capitol steps, Norma Becker of the War Resisters League joked to the cheering throng, "Probably the finest thing this country will remember Jimmy Carter for is the resurrection of the student movement in the 80s." Alan Canfora, a student who was shot at Kent State in 1970, recalled "that over 500

SNEAK UP ON EM WITH REGISTRATION THEN WE HIT 'EM WITH THE DRAFT!

campuses were shut down tight in the student strike that year." He promised more of the same if Congress reinstitutes the draft.

David Harris, one of the earliest of the draft resisters, stepped to the microphone. "There are ghosts walking with us today," he said, "55,000 ghosts from the last time."

One of several Congressmen to speak was Ted Weiss of New York City. Like many other speakers, he quoted from the administration's recent report on the need for registration, a report which Carter received a week before his January speech. It concludes that peacetime registration is unnecessary for the rapid mobilization of an armed force, calling it "redundant" and "not cost-effective."

Weiss brought up one of the movements' central themes, that registration is a smoke screen for bringing back the draft itself. "Listen to these words," read Weiss, his voice rising, "from the testimony of Gen. Bernard W. Rogers, Army Chief of Staff for the Senate Armed Services Committee on Feb. 20:

"'Because of the antipathy of so many in this country for the Selective Service System, that system being equated to the draft, and the draft being anathema to so many, is why I suggest the evolutionary approach. First, start to register, and get us accustomed to that . . . Then commence classification . . . Then, third, start to draft for the Individual Ready Reserve.'"

Rev. Barry Lynn, chairman of the Committee against Registration and the Draft, told the crowd of his recent meeting with Selective Service Director Bernard Roskter. "Roskter," said Lynn, "told me there will be no draft cards issued this time

because these cards are a 'hated symbol.' We know that millions of Americans will find plenty of good reasons to hate the new selective service system whether it has draft cards or not."

Carter's registration plan faces an uncertain fate in the next few weeks, but is still very much alive. The registration proposal is now in the House of Representatives, where anti-registration forces estimate they have 180 to 195 members of the House on their side. "But," says one lobbyist, "there's still some shortfall." Sen. Mark Hatfield of Oregon has promised to lead a filibuster against registration on the floor of the Senate, if all else fails. If that effort fails, too, registration could be law as soon as early May.

IN SAN FRANCISCO
by B. J. Norman

It looked much like a scene from the late 60s and early 70s. There were the brightly-painted signs proclaiming "No Draft, No Registration," "I Am Not a Natural Resource" and "War is the Health of the State." The thousands of people mostly young, mostly white, with just a smattering of blacks, Chinese and Hispanics. Here and there an older man or woman could be seen, but they were rare. Hawkers stood on the edge of the crowd, selling small bags of potato chips for almost twice the grocery-store price.

Even the theme was much the same: a halt to U.S. imperialism, self-government for third world countries, an end to U.S. greed and aggression.

The scene, however, was not from a movie about the Vietnam era. The crowd

Mike Konopacki/The Progressive/LNS

'Welcome to a life of crime!'

gathered at the San Francisco Civic Center was there to protest American intervention in yet another war overseas and the reinstitution of draft registration.

Really Glad

The rally began with a late morning march from 5th and Market Streets to the Civic Center. One man, joining the march minutes before it neared its destination, said, "I didn't even know that the rally was taking place. I knew about the one in D.C. and if there'd been any way for me to go there and show how I feel about the draft, I would have. I'm really glad somebody thought to organize something like this here in the city."

Bob Costello, a worker with Mobilization Against the Draft (MAD), reports the rally wasn't organized until late February. "We hadn't even talked about the rally before Feb. 26," he said, "and then it was organized as a support rally for the one held in Washington. I think things went quite well. There were no problems, no violence, no outside groups coming in." As for the next step, Costello says, "The only thing we can do now is to wait and see what's going to happen with Congress."

Congressman John Burton, D., SF, one of many speakers at the rally, told the cheering crowd, "We have a chance to stop the war before it gets started. Our message to the Carter administration is that we want no more wars in our lifetime. We want peace."

Burton also declared that it is a "goddamn disgrace" to talk about spending money to register 23 million people when "they're cutting back on food stamps for the hungry and health care for the sick."

Although politicians may not have to stand in line for food stamps or be concerned about medical care, said Burton, "They hate like hell to be unemployed. We've got to let them know that a vote for the draft is a vote for their unemployment."

Affects the Cities

Early in the rally, San Francisco Supervisor Harry Britt announced that he had failed to get other supervisors to vote for an anti-draft, anti-registration resolution.

"In a vote of 8-3," he said, "the Board of Supervisors said we shouldn't oppose the draft because it doesn't affect the cities. I say Carter's war fever is a cover-up for his inability to solve the problems of the American people and this does affect the cities."

For most of the day one man, a beer can peeking from the top of the brown bag he held in his hand, roamed through the crowd announcing, "Carter is right. If he says we've got to fight, then we've got to fight. That's the system. It's always been that way and it always will." He was largely ignored by the crowd.

After the rally, demonstrators, expressed mixed feelings about its effectiveness. One woman, leaving about an hour and a half after the speeches began, said, "I got really tired of all the talk about imperialism. It just seemed that everybody was there to speak for his organization or his cause, and the anti-draft issue was just an aside."

An older man, a camera hung casually over his shoulder, said he was "encouraged" to see so many people come out in support of the anti-draft movement. "Maybe we can avoid another war by nipping this thing in the bud."

A New England Peace Movement Newsletter

From *Peacework,* no. 90 (October 1980), pp. 10–11

Survival Summer: What's Being Done and What Remains on the Agenda: Help Still Needed

by Jonathan Saxton

This summer a large segment of the peace movement embarked on a massive grassroots education and outreach project called Survival Summer, the goal being to generate informed public debate on key aspects of US domestic and foreign policy so as to lay the ground work for a popular, broad-based movement to effectively reorder our national priorities.

Four basic principles were adopted: No registration, No draft and No war; Stop the nuclear arms race; Implement a sane energy policy; and Redirect the economy from unnecessary military spending to peaceful and socially productive spending. Much of the Summer's focus has been to link these principles with the problems of inflation, unemployment, housing, health care, and other issues of specific and local import.

The Survival Summer effort came none too soon. Our economy and society is being militarized with speed unprecedented in

Reprinted with permission from *Peacework,* a New England Peace Movement newsletter published by the American Friends Service Committee.

"peaceful" times. A new Cold War is upon us. The Carter Administration and the Pentagon have succeeded in confusing the American people and cynically manipulating US national chauvinism, creating a climate conducive to increased military spending, and to the build up of US interventionary capability around the world. It is necessary to understand this process in order to place the Survival Summer effort in perspective.

Three out of four prerequisites for creating the new Cold War have been systematically fulfilled. First, "enemies abroad" have been identified, in the forms of a revolutionary Iranian nation, a "hegemonic" Soviet Union, and growing Third World insurgency. Second, the "enemies at home" have been identified: Iranian nationals, "troublesome" Haitian, Cuban, Puerto Rican, and other "aliens"; as well as "unpatriotic" Americans, such as those who opposed the Olympic boycott, the harassment of Iranians, etc. Third, the US is consistently identifying traditional allies abroad as suddenly less than reliable. Legitimate European and Japanese reservations on the advisability of the Olympic boycott, on sanctions against Iran, and on the appropriateness of US military escalation in both the Middle East and NATO, have all been portrayed as evidence of wavering commitment, perhaps even cooptation, in the face of Soviet and other threats.

Survival Summer was proposed late in 1979 when the first three moves toward militarization were becoming obvious to many. It was then thought that what was needed to stop or at least counter this militarization was an effort which could get out the information and create the local structures necessary to generate informed mass participation in the formation of national policies and goals. It may not be possible to directly affect the Pentagon, but it may be possible to affect and organize enough people in places to build a basis for the formulation of US policy that reflects Americans' basic beliefs in peace, freedom and equality.

The focus of Survival Summer therefore was meant to be, and has been, both local issues while providing a background of national purpose and direction of public policy.

Survival Summer has done this in many ways. By the end of the second week of June, the project which has been co-ordinated nationally by the Mobilization for Survival, had trained nearly 800 volunteer organizers in nine regional training conferences around the country. These people were given orientations to the basic skills of organizing and to the basic interrelatedness of the principal issues. These key organizers then went back into their home communities where they shared their skills and knowledge with others, and participated in or helped establish local outreach. Within weeks, the *Survival Summer News* staffs in Philadelphia and San Francisco were receiving and publishing reports of the formation of organizations and training events from all across the country. Lincoln, Nebraska reported canvassing, peace exhibits, and various educational events. Portland, Oregon reported house meetings and plans for a Hiroshima/Nagasaki commemoration. Albuquerque, New Mexico reported vigils, and a area-wide planning conference. St. Louis, Missouri reported work to save a local black community hospital, for housing and against police brutality, while in Scranton, Pennsylvania, local peace activists were working in peace education around Iran and Afghanistan situations. Similar things were happening in all parts of the country. In Boston, 150 organizers were trained in early June from the Boston area, a newsletter for the region was at the printer, local non-binding referendum campaigns were receiving new impetus, and local draft organizing had spread to the Greater Boston area. The rest of the Northeast, especially New Haven, Providence, Albany, Portland among other locales, were benefiting from the opportunities for sharing skills and information brought to their communities by volunteers.

Survival Summer has placed a great deal of emphasis and faith in the initiative of the many volunteer organizers. It was made clear from the beginnings of the project that only the minimum of coordination was going to be attempted nationally. This was partly because of the limitations imposed by scarce resources and funds, but more significantly, this reflected the idea that people working together in their own communities are capable of developing their own agendas and their own tactics in the light of the specific issues and problems which they face. Central resource centers like the Boston Mobilization for Survival offered whatever ongoing support that they could to local groups around their regions. They asked in return only for the sharing of information, experiences and ideas which could be published for distribution to others. Surprisingly good contacts and communication was engendered in this way, while avoiding the pitfalls of "topdown" administration.

The real test of the effectiveness of this type of organizing was the advent of registration for the draft. For of the four Cold War prerequisites, this was and is the only one which we could directly affect.

Draft registration was effectively resisted in hundreds of communities across the country. By the first week in July, the *Survival Summer News* was reporting the formation of anti-registration groups in almost every one of the areas where Survival Summer volunteers were working. The national Coalition Against Registration and the Draft (CARD) had also been working feverishly to prepare the widest possible resistance to the registration process. In many communities the local organizing around Survival issues merged or cooperated with that most pressing survival issue facing young people in this country. In many, if not most cases

SCHOOL CAREER DAY
JOIN THE MARINES

Bülbül/LNS

WHERE DO WE SIGN UP... FOR .... CONSCIENTIOUS OBJECTOR!

the foothold established by local Survival Summer volunteers helped to facilitate registration resistance. The often times loosely structured and de-centralized community-based organizations were very effective in their peace education. They had grown from within the community.

The point is not that Survival Summer was responsible for the successes during registration weeks, for it was not. However the basic purpose of the project, to engender locally-based peace education and action, has proven effective. The training of core volunteers and their dispersal throughout the country to engage in local struggles is essential to the growth of our movement, and to our success. This effort has shown that almost anywhere we go, there are people who care desperately about our survival, and who are willing to listen, to teach, and to act.

The Survival Summer effort endorsed and encouraged participation in a number of other summer projects including the Black Hills Survival Gathering and The Coalition for a Peoples' Alternative. Each of these was an effort to help consolidate and broaden the movement for peace. The attempt at consolidation is perhaps the most important task at the moment.

Survival Summer is still happening. It will continue through International Disarmament Week, October 24-31. From now till then we will be working to solidify the gains we have made an attempt to revitalize those community groups which have dissolved through student attrition and the inevitable problems of over-work and burn-out. Locally in the Boston area the Survival Project will concentrate on support of the Jobs with Peace referendum, on the revitalization of anti-registration draft network, and on regional communication through the *Survival Notes* newsletter. The Jobs with Peace referendum has special significance for the Summer Project in this area, as it puts the question of "more butter or more guns?" on the ballot in four state senatorial districts. It directly asks the employed and unemployed transportation, health care, construction, and other service sector workers to consider the unavoidable choices between life and death forces. After the November elections, there is the hope that the support can be found to finance an evaluation/strategy conference through which the many people who have worked to build local bases of support can share their successes and failures, and plot a strategy for the months to come.

There's a movement goin' on, but there's

a tidal wave of reaction that is forming against us. The evidence of this is everywhere, and we know it. Our strongest hope for the future is our perseverence in the present. We must strengthen our foundations. We must remain intent upon our goals. We must not be moved.

The Survival Summer effort began on reasonable financial grounds. Funds raised were sufficient to publish the newsletter, conduct trainings, and hire staff both nationally and locally. Thousands of leaflets, booklets and pamphlets were published. In many areas, the money raised for Survival Summer went a long way toward financing the anti-registration resistance. But those initial funds are gone, gone to good purposes, but gone. More, much more, is needed. Election year

campaigning has drawn off significant sources of income. It is clear that there are millions of dollars systematically being raised by the Right in this country. They are banking on that wave, buying property, so to speak. Money can't buy peace, but it can sure buy paper and ink; and maybe, just maybe, some time. Please send donations and inquiries to Survival Summer, c/o Mobilization for Survival, 13 Sellers St., Cambridge, MA 02139. Make checks payable to Mobilization for Survival/Survival Summer. Pay to Survival Education Fund, Inc. for non-profit tax-exemption.

Jonathan Saxton is a staff person at the Mobilization for Survival office.

Obedience is essential for that—and it requires the complete severing of an individual's responsibility for her acts. The dehumanization inherent in military training works very well, as U.S. atrocities in Vietnam showed. The young men who murdered and raped the Vietnamese did not start out as psychopaths. They started out as ordinary, naive, often poor, young men.

I was in high school in 1964, and I saw the rough, innocent, decent working class boys I had grown up with enlist at age 17 because it was the "right" thing to do, or because it was the only way they could get money for college.

And I saw them come home again, those who did come home, as monsters who had butchered old people, who had raped children, who had worn necklaces of human ears about their necks to celebrate their own survival in the hell of Vietnam. I saw the boys I had grown up with come back with shattered minds, full of the shrapnel of despair, and many of them haven't recovered *yet*. Those boys could not resist the dehumanizing efficiency of the U.S. military machine, which took simple, small-town boys and turned them into monsters, and young women will not be able to resist either.

On the Nature of Feminism

Feminism is directly opposed to militarism in two major ways. First, feminism is fundamentally nonviolent, except in matters of immediate self-defense. Second, feminism emphasizes the importance of each individual woman, rejecting the idea that human beings can be a means to an end.

Rejection of violence as a tool for forcing agreement is so basic that it is rarely even discussed. For two feminists of even widely different perspectives to resort to physical violence against each other is unimaginable. We do not have to take time out at our conferences and meetings to agree that we will not beat each other up. We reject assault as instrument of political persuasion.

Likewise, the base of our radical social analysis is the belief that individual women are important, that we as individuals are important, and that we are going to destroy the patriarchal, male-supremacist structure which views women as a disposable commodity. What we are about is taking ourselves and each other seriously, and not giving up our individual power and responsibility to any authority, particularly not to the military.

From *off our backs* 10, no. 4 (April 1980): 4

Women and the Military: A No-Win Proposition

by Janis Kelly

I want to present a radical feminist response to rising militarism, particularly to the specious argument that the price of equal rights is serving in the U.S. military. To do that, I will consider three things: the nature of the military; the nature of international feminism; and what that means for radical feminists in an era of rising nationalism.

On the Nature of Armies

Two factors are common to all armies and distinguish them from other large groups of people, such as symphony orchestras.

First, and most important, an army is an instrument of mass murder, which is approved by the state. Since the inception of the voluntary army, the fact that the essential purpose of armies is to train and provide murderers on a mass scale has been obscured. To hear most liberals talk, you'd

---

Reprinted with permission from *off our backs: a women's news journal*, 1724 20th St. NW, Washington, DC 20009.

think the army was primarily an equal employment opportunity program.

There is a good reason for this confusion, which is that in the past three years the U.S. Dept. of Defense has mounted one of the largest advertising and public relations programs ever seen in this country. Last year the Dept. of Defense spent $128,452,000 on advertising. They have produced the public feeling that the army is a cross between a community college and a summer camp. In fact, the army is a collection of people trained to provide mass murder of other armies and of innocent civilians, upon command of the states.

The picture of military life presented in military advertising is carefully designed to obscure these two primary characteristics of the military: killing and obedience. Ads ignore killing and suggest that the army is just about education, training, and travel. Military propaganda hides the fact that once you're in the army, you are always under orders. Military recruiters suggest that going into the army involves a "contract" between you and them, which obligates them to give you the education and job you want. This is bullshit. Once you're in, you are obliged to do whatever they tell you, and they can do anything they want with you.

And ultimately what the army wants you to do is kill—on demand—unquestioningly—or to provide unquestioning support for others more directly involved in killing.

On Appropriate Action

The change we seek transcends any narrow national interest because it is based on our common oppression as women, in all countries, in all societies. No national interest can override our common sisterhood.

We will not make the mistake of helping the male supremacist military machine murder, rape, and torture our sisters in other lands. We will not help the racist war machine send young colored people to fight old, white men's wars. What we will do is this:

We will expose the military for the murder machine that it is. We will counter military propaganda by talking loud and long about what armies are really for.

We will resist any move to register young people for the draft. If registration comes, we will disrupt it.

If the draft comes, we will actively encourage young people to escape it, and we will help those already inducted to escape the war machine. And especially we will resist any attempt to force our younger sisters into the military.

I say to Jimmy Carter, to the Joint Chiefs of Staff, and to the moral idiots who work in the Pentagon, DON'T EVEN THINK ABOUT DRAFTING WOMEN. If you come after our sisters, we will hide them. They will vanish into our communities like drops of water into the ocean. There are radical feminists in every major city, in every ethnic group, in every profession. And there is no radical feminist who will EVER turn another woman over to the United States Military.

Finally, I say to the War Department, which is now asburdly called the Defense Department: There is no Russian woman with whom I have an argument to the death, and I will not help the U.S. government kill Russian women. There is no Arab woman who has any property I would take by force, and I will not help the U.S. Army seize Arab lands. If you madmen and madwomen who plan U.S. military strategy think the anti-war movement of the sixties gave you trouble . . . if you think Weather Underground attacks on military property were a problem . . . if you think your FBI had trouble getting women to help you find Susan Saxe and Kathy Power.

YOU AIN'T SEEN NOTHIN' YET!

This speech was originally delivered at the Washington, D.C. Women and the Draft Conference on March 1, 1980.

Peacemeal graphics/Win/LNS

over how we use our lives, whether we will kill, and what we will die for, makes any sense. Each person must finally make that choice for himself—though not, we hope, alone. We hope that they will find in their families, neighbors and churches a community of support in whatever decision they make—especially if they make the very difficult decision to refuse to register. Though they act as individuals, we believe they act on behalf of all of us who feel the chances of human survival depend on many individuals asserting the demands of conscience over law.

But here we are talking about the draft, some will object, when the issue at hand is merely registration. Indeed, the administration has gone to great lengths to distinguish between registration—a matter of the "utmost urgency," a "signal to the Soviets," a sign of the willingness of the American people to sacrifice"—and an actual draft, which is, for the moment, still officially considered unfair and unnecessary, the farthest thing from the government's mind. The *New York Times* joined this argument in a recent editorial. "Registration," it declared, "will have no real consequences . . . there is no practical reason to demur; refusing to register risks punishment for no clear reason." The same editorial, which concedes that the law

CATHOLIC WORKER

From *The Catholic Worker* 46, no. 6 (July/August 1980): 1, 3

Buying Time

by Robert Ellsberg

For two weeks in July, young men across the country walked into their local post offices, signed a piece of paper and logged themselves into the computer arsenal of the Pentagon. The Selective Service System estimated in advance that 98% of those eligible would comply with the law. Though final figures are not yet available,

there is every reason to believe that the success of this exercise will fall far short of the government's optimistic figures. If even five percent of those 19- and 20-year-olds have declined to register, that will leave a gap of 200,000 names in the government's lists. If non-compliance reaches as much as ten percent, the whole system might as well be scrapped. Although the law threatens a penalty of five years imprisonment and $10,000 fine, the Selective Service System must ultimately rely on voluntary cooperation.

But no matter how many decide to "sit this one out" and for whatever reasons, in the end each young person must face this issue for himself and decide whether the government's claim to have the final say

is a "hollow, even political exercise" which will "add nothing substantial to preparedness," nevertheless counsels young people to obey the law, to register "and without asking why." For if registration will not enhance our national security by one iota (of course the government won't concede that point) massive non-compliance with the law will damage our security a great deal, and so the merits, even the morality of the law, are by this argument, cast beside the point.

It is an argument which failed to deter three federal judges in Philadelphia from ruling the law unconstitutional. Registration cannot be judged apart from the draft. Otherwise, said the court, the problem would be very simple: "It is absolutely unconstitutional to register citizens for no purpose." (The decision was subsequently stayed by the Supreme Court, pending an appeal in the fall.)

The plain truth is that, if registration goes smoothly, the draft will not be far behind. That is only the least of the very "real consequences" which the *Times* and others have ignored. Even more serious is the question of what a conscripted army is good for and why so many powerful people want us to have one.

No one can seriously suppose that a draft army would ever be used to fight Soviet troops. We have 30,000 nuclear weapons to do that job. A draft army is needed to fight long, drawn-out, high-casualty, non-nuclear wars. A return to the draft is highly favored by those who remember Vietnam with nostalgia, who regret only that our failure there has made us timid and has restricted the choice of means available to enforce our will in the world. If registration proceeds without controversy—in the words of the *Times*—the world may conclude "that Americans are ready again to support a diplomacy that risks military action far from home." We will end up not deterring future "Afghanistans" but "creating" them.

The Catholic Worker has always opposed the peacetime draft, ever since its inception in the 1940's. And, ever since then, members of the Catholic Worker have gone to jail in protest of such a law. We believe that registration and the return of the draft signal the return to a policy of open force in asserting American interests, especially in the division of scarce resources and in the fact of increasing efforts on the part of poor people in the world to control their own destinies. We protest now, not only the draft, but the still uncommitted crimes which lie behind this

door our government is opening, and which may yet be averted. We believe that in a world loaded with nuclear weapons, every concession to a policy which entrusts our security and the peace of the world to stiff-necked competition and blind escalation moves us gradually to a time beyond protesting.

It may be too late to protest when this or the next president sends the first conscripts to Saudi Arabia, South Africa or Central America. It will certainly be too late to protest when our missiles are cruising toward Moscow. But it may not be too late now. All our efforts today rest on that possibility. Young people may never have a chance to do something as important for their country and the prospects of future generations as they can today by contributing to the failure of draft registration. They can buy us time.

From *The Guardian* 31, no. 17 (January 31, 1979): 9

GIs Fight Agent Orange Contamination

by Joe Bangert, Sheila Morfield, and Annie Vercker

Paul Ruetershan of Norwalk, Conn., died Dec. 14 of stomach cancer at the age of 27. Ten years ago, as a helicopter crewman assigned to Vietnam, he regularly flew clouds of the defoliant known as Agent Orange. Shortly before he died, Ruetershan murmured to his fiancee, "We've got to stop. We're poisoning the earth."

Hong Thi Thu also suffers from the aftereffects of Agent Orange. The Vietnamese child has multiple birth defects and is severely retarded. Her mother, living in an area which had been heavily sprayed with Agent Orange for six years, ate a steady diet of rice and tubers contaminated with the defoliants.

Nobody knows how many U.S. troops and Vietnamese were exposed to Agent Orange, named for the orange stripe on the containers, over the nine years it was used in Vietnam. Eleven million gallons were sprayed from planes, trucks and hand-held cannisters during that period. Herbicide-producing firms like Dow Chemical, Diamond Alkali, Uniroyal, Thompson, Monsanto, Ansul and Thompson-Hayward reaped enormous profits from wartime sales to the Pentagon.

Deadly Dioxin

The deadliest ingredient in Agent Orange is dioxin, a byproduct in the manufacture of trichlorophenol. Dioxin has both short- and long-term effects on the body. It causes skin diseases ranging from severe acne to abscesses and shingles. It also causes numbness and pain in the joints, stomach and liver disorders, cancer, nerve damage, personality changes and chronic fatigue. It is responsible for spontaneous miscarriages and birth defects among the children of those exposed.

The toxic effects of dioxin build up over time, so that people, plants, animals and water are affected for years after initial exposure. The chemical is stored in the fatty tissues of people and animals. It also seeps through the soil to pollute underground water, lakes, rivers and streams. The damage dioxin inflicts is cumulative and long-lasting.

When dioxin-based Agent Orange began to be used as a "humane" weapon in the Vietnam war, its extreme toxicity had been known for years.

In 1960, Dow Chemical was forced to close its Michigan plants because 60 workers had developed a disease characterized by chronic fatigue and depression.

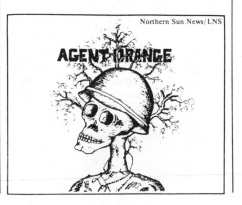

Northern Sun News/LNS

Workers at another chemical firm in New Jersey reported similar symptoms, and many still suffered the effects six years later. These symptoms, along with skin and liver problems, have long been known to occur among farm workers exposed to herbicides.

Throughout the 1960s there were persistent reports that the Vietnamese exposed to the Agent Orange defoliant were suffering health problems, in particular an unusually high rate of birth defects and miscarriages. Although the U.S. government dismissed these reports as "communist propaganda," the National Institute of Health was finally ordered to carry out a secret study of Agent Orange in 1968. The tests showed that the component chemical 2, 4, 5-T caused deformities and stillbirths in mice.

Although the U.S. officially halted the use of Agent Orange in Vietnam in 1970, 2, 4, 5-T is still in use in the U.S. as a herbicide. In fact, 5 million pounds of it were used last year. Dioxin compounds are also used in common household products as Lysol, many detergents, diaper presoak preparations, and lawn and garden weed killers.

VA Denials

According to David Kriebel, research associate at Washington University's Center for Biology of Natural Systems in St. Louis, "Dioxin is one of the most toxic substances known, and it appears to be hazardous to health even when the dioxin-to-2,4,5-T ratio is extremely low, sometimes only a few parts-per-trillion." Yet Dow Chemical cintinues to characterize 2,4,5-T herbicides as totally safe to humans.

The Veterans Administration (VA) is refusing to admit the fatal effects of Agent Orange exposure on Vietnam vets and their families. Not only does the VA refuse to consider dioxin poisoning as a service-connected disability, but it has done its best to sidetrack the efforts of veterans and activists who are trying to get something done.

Maude DeVictor, a VA claims worker in Chicago, had never heard of Agent Orange before she took a 1977 phone call from the wife of a veteran named Charles Owens. Her husband was dying of cancer, Mrs. Owens said, and he blamed it on "those chemicals from Vietnam." Four months later Mrs. Owens called again, to say that her husband had died and that her claim for survivor's benefits had been denied by the VA.

DeVictor began asking her clients, "Have you ever been in Vietnam? Got any kind of a rash? Any children with deformities?" Often they answered, "Yeah, how'd you know?"

In the first two months of 1978, she logged 27 examples of this new disability. Her inquiries at the Veterans' Hospital turned up about 30 more, all from the Chicago area. Then, without explanation, DeVictor's boss ordered her to stop tracing potential dioxin poisoning cases.

DeVictor decided to tell the press what she had learned.

A March 1978 documentary aired by a Chicago TV station brought 300 calls from worried veterans to a local VA hospital.

DeVictor was transferred to a job in which she no longer comes into contact with clients.

The VA has no rating criteria for chemical disabilities in veterans, DeVictor points out. Such cases are either denied outright or filed in a computer and never acted on.

Before his death, Reutershan had filed a $17,000 claim for service-related injuries to cover the medical costs of his long bout with cancer. Two days before he died the VA sent him a check for $1500. But a day after he died, the VA called Reutershan's mother and warned her not to cash the check, since a veteran's death closes all outstanding claims. Reutershan's sister, Jane Dziedzic, said bitterly, "The VA acknowledged his illness was combat-related, but they wouldn't admit dioxin was the cause."

Sounding the Alarm

In the months before his death, Reutershan had organized Agent Orange Victims International. The organization wants to sound the alarm and to pressure the VA to recognize dioxin poisoning as a service-related disability. Until this is recognized, victims cannot hope for any help with the illnesses that result among them and their families. Reutershan had explained. "I'm helping other guys out, and that's all I care about. I'm not doing this for me. My time is up."

Reutershan also filed a $10 million suit against Dow Chemical which manufactured the herbicide. The suit, now pending in the New York Supreme Court, charges that Dow "knew the properties [of dioxin] would cause cancer before selling it for military use."

Activists concerned with the toxic effects of Agent Orange contrast the negligence of the U.S. government with the campaign mobilized by the Vietnamese to combat the devasting aftereffects of the defoliant on their countryside and population.

Michael Uhl, a Vietnam veteran working with Citizen Soldier (a New York-based GI and veterans' rights group) has said he suspects many affected GIs have "kept quiet about their mental and physical ills for so long because they thought it was some kind of personal craziness resulting from the war." But, he continued, "What we have here is a bunch of Vietnam vets,

Cindy Fredrick/LNS

28-34 years old, who are sick. But their doctors don't know what to do about it. These guys should be in the peak of health, but they find their health declining."

In some cases, the decline is drastic. One Vietnam vet who attempted to contact several friends who had served with him was shocked to find that four of them were dead. "One," he said, "of brain cancer, one of 'unknown' causes, one of a heart attack at the unheard-of age of 28, and one possibly of liver cancer."

Children Also Affected

The children of Vietnam veterans are suffering as well. One former Green Beret who had served 10 months in Vietnam became a father last January. His daughter was born without a kneecap or shinbone on one leg, and that leg will eventually have to be amputated, doctors say.

Another veteran who was in base camps repeatedly sprayed with herbicides now has a son whose fingers and toes are either missing or deformed. And one former helicopter pilot who sprayed Agent Orange has no children—his wife has had four miscarriages.

Citizen Soldier has sent out detailed medical questionnaires in an effort to identify and assist Vietnam vets who may be victims of exposure to Agent Orange. In a four-week period last summer, they received over 1000 phone calls from vets suffering from symptoms probably related to Agent Orange exposure.

A group of Massachusetts vets in Cape Cod have formed Vietnam Vets for Self Reliance. They are developing a 6-point program to get the VA moving on the Agent Orange health crisis. Among the program's demands are:

• A comprehensive national study and mass education program for all veterans who had contact with a variety of poisons in the Vietnam war. Comprehensive screening for all vets who worked with radiation in the military;

• Close monitoring of all pregnancies of Vietnam veterans and their spouses;

• Complete psychological counseling and genetic services for affected veterans;

• An official VA invitation to Dr. Ton That Tung, a Vietnamese expert in treating dioxin sickness, to consult with their medical officers on detoxification.

Environmental groups have also joined the fight against the use of dioxin-containing herbicides. In February 1978, representatives from 16 state groups met in Washington, D.C., and formed the Citizens' National Forest Coalition to co-ordinate and direct the fight against uncontrolled use of herbicides. Their goal is to win a national ban on all products containing 2,4,5-T.

For more information, contact: Citizen Soldier, 175 5th Ave., Room 1010, New York, N.Y. 10010. tel. 212-777-3470; Joe Bangert, Vets for Self Reliance. P.O. Box 153, Brewster, Ma. 02631, tel. 617-896-7842; Agent Orange Information Resource Service, P.O. Box 6558, Washington, D.C. 20009.

From *Seven Days* 4, no. 1 (April 1980): 21-23

The 'Me' Generation Says 'Not Me!'

by Dave Dellinger

On February 22, The *New York Times* Quotation of the Day came from Michael Severn, president-elect of Columbia Uni-sity. "In the sixties you had campuses united on . . . race and Vietnam. Nowadays, race issues are a divisive factor. . . .

And I don't see registration provoking widespread protests. There are students who see it as a wise course."

Had I been dreaming, then? The milling angry students at Columbia who just a few days earlier had rallied and marched en masse against the draft—rallied so soon after Carter's call for registration, I was amazed that they had gotten together so quickly.

The ones who have been dreaming are those who thought they could stampede the country into accepting the draft and the Carter doctrine of military interventions thousands of miles from home. Congress, of course, is easier to stampede than the country. The Vietnam war taught us that.

But I don't think Congress will prove so easy this time. Too many members remember the way opposition started small during the Vietnam era and grew year after year until the war abroad became virtually a civil war at home and produced first desertions, then mutinies, in the armed forces.

The real test will come not in Washington, which has been swept off its feet before by presidential manipulations and exaggerated or false information. Congress does not represent the youth, the Blacks and Hispanics, the women, the poor, nor any of the people for whom inflation means a real cut in standard of living. The real test has already begun in the responses of the youth who, if Carter has his way, will be asked to kill and be killed ten thousand miles from home, in defense of "our" vital interests in the Persian Gulf area.

Already the number of protests and protesters against Carter's attempts to put the country on a war footing is greater than at any time during the first five years of the Vietnam war. And while television and the press run pictures of angry Americans burning Iranian flags and announcing their support for armed intervention in faraway places, the Army, Navy, and Marines have all failed to meet their enlistment quotas.

"No outsiders have turned us on," Jane Fischberg, an antidraft organizer at Williams College, told the media. "It's our own paranoia. I really like this country, but I'm scared by what's happening, by talk of war."

A lot of other people have been scared by talk of war. Frightened into their wits by talk of nuclear war. In case anyone felt personally exempt from the risks involved in the Carter doctrine, Pentagon officials let it be known that military conflict in the Gulf area will probably be nuclear. The United States, they say, could not hope to win a conventional war so far from home and so close to the Soviet homeland and supply routes.

More trustworthy analysts have come to the same conclusion. Marcus Raskin, who resigned as special assistant to McGeorge Bundy when he saw where a similar arrogance in the Kennedy administration was leading says, "If the United States uses tactical nuclear weapons in the Persian Gulf, the U.S., as a result of the forces the Soviets have, will probably have to move in a strategic strike, which would be the end of civilization."

The Carter administration has succeeded in building some initial support for its policies, though not nearly so much as it

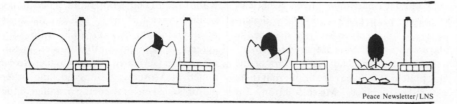

Peace Newsletter/LNS

claims. We should not be misled as to the true attitude of the American people toward foreign interventions and nuclear war. The specific wrongs that have been most visible in recent months have been the taking of hostages in Iran and the Soviet invasion of Afghanistan. For Americans, these invoke a different set of emotions and political questions than were at work in the sixties. It's harder at first to focus indignation and protest on an American overreaction to a Soviet invasion than to build a head of steam against an American invasion. Most people do not want to seem to condone either the taking of hostages or the Soviet military intervention, even though both actions may have been provoked in large part by American actions.

The ambiguities of the situation changed when Carter rushed troops and ships to the Persian Gulf area, announced that "we" were prepared to intervene militarily, called for the draft, and leaked messages that the United States would use nuclear weapons. Suddenly it became a totally different war game.

II

Those who delight in contrasting the "massive protests" of the sixties with the imagined political apathy today consistently underestimated the number of protesters then and insisted that the bulk of the population supported the war. They were wrong in the sixties. And there is no reason to believe them now. Why should anyone think that the people who believed they were winning the hearts and minds of the Vietnamese people understand now what is going on in the hearts and minds of the American people?

Last year these so-called experts tried to tell us that the Shah was loved and supported by the people in Iran. Now they are trying to tell us that we love our leadership and will support their war plans.

The seventies were not wasted. People really did get their heads together more than it sometimes seemed. Now that the issues are becoming clear, more and more people are saying no again. The "me" generation is saying "not me." In fact, it is becoming the "we" generation again.

Having learned from the women's movement and the gay movement that the personal is political, we are now being taught by Jimmy Carter's war talk and the economic crisis that the political is personal.

From the teach-ins, demonstrations, and planning conferences I have attended around the country during the past few months, I am convinced that the movement for peace and justice is not just more numerous but stronger by reason of experience and diversity than it was during the first few years of opposition to the Vietnam war. At the Columbia rally, two prestigious professors spoke out—their counterparts would never have done that in the first several years of protest against the Vietnam war.

The clarity, wisdom, and militance of the people we rarely saw on a podium in the sixties also stands out in my mind. There's a new equality and vitality of public leadership by women. At Yale, 1,100 people repeatedly applauded a woman reading a very militant statement from a lesbian/gay group. And 30 high school students signed up to be on an anti-draft committee; 50 showed up a few days later for the first meeting.

There were tears in the front rows at Temple University when two veterans recounted their personal experiences in the

Army and Marine Corps. Time and again, in fact, the most effective speakers at today's rallies are the Vietnam veterans who speak with a down-to-earth realism and sense of urgency. It should also be noted that the links between Third World and minority resistance movements in this country and the antidraft movement are growing, slowly. A great deal remains to be accomplished against continued governmental efforts to keep the groups apart. I am heartened by groups like the People's Alliance, the Mobilization for Survival, and others that have been holding meetings of Third World and white activists to explore methods of bringing about greater unity.

III

It's hard to say exactly what the government's public-relations experts had in mind when they programmed Jimmy Carter to establish his *macho* qualifications by pulling out all stops in his nuked-up saber rattling. Was the plan to frighten us with forebodings of such cataclysmic death and destruction at home as well as abroad that everyone would breathe a sigh of relief when it turned out that the wars were relatively limited? Limited for Americans, that is, not for the Third World peoples in whose countries they take place. The presidential PR staff may figure that Jimmy will be hailed (like Kissinger before him) as a peacemaker worthy of the Nobel prize if he gets us out of what he's called "the most serious crisis since World War II"—gets us out with a surgical strike here, a CIA coup there, and perhaps a victory or two in our behalf by Egyptian, Israeli, or other surrogates.

CPS/LNS

"WHAT THE HELL, THE SIXTIES ARE OVER — GIVE IT A TUG!"

I had a conversation recently with an astute analyst who represents his Third World country at the United Nations. He describes his country as nonaligned, but the United States calls it a "member of the Soviet bloc." After expressing dismay at the Soviet actions in Afghanistan, he made clear that his country would still refuse to line up with the United States:

The U.S. has decided it needs a good local war. Not for geopolitical reasons so much as to provide a temporary shot in the arm for the economy. Above all, they need to take people's minds off their problems—inflation, unemployment, unrest in the ghettos, crime, corruption, and cynicism. This society is collapsing.

I don't think the U.S. has any intention of tackling the Soviet Union head-on, but it is using the Soviet invasion of Afghanistan as a smokescreen to create a climate of fear and push through military measures. They are preparing to launch a local war.

I told him of my fears, after my recent trip to Lebanon, Syria, Jordan, the West Bank, and Israel, that the United States would initiate an intervention in the Middle East. It would be hard to limit such a war, given the political instability of the area and its proximity to the Soviet Union. Was this the kind of war he was talking about? "It Isn't," he answered. "But think about Central America where there are also significant oil reserves. El Salvador is only a little behind where Nicaragua was when Somoza fell, and Guatemala is not far behind El Salvador. Given America's increased propaganda about its dependence on oil, Central America may be the place where the U.S. is prepared to strike."

Even the most heady supporters of the new policies would have to admit that there are risks involved. Miscalculation, for example, underestimating Third World resistance, computer failure, or perhaps an excess of zeal on the part of an enthusiastic Pentagon general or one of our new Shahs, such as the brutal General Zia in Pakistan. Can we count on the South Africans, Israelis, South Koreans, and Chinese (who still argue that nuclear war is a paper tiger) not to take advantage of the mood of the times? Will they get the message if Carter decides that "we" have accomplished "our" objectives and are ready for restraint? Some things are easier to turn on than off.

What will happen if the Soviet hawks are as foolhardy as the American species and think it possible for the country that strikes first to "win" a nuclear war? American Presidents have a habit of accusing the Soviets of being irresponsible and warlike, then setting up a situation in which the fate of the world depends on the willingness of the Soviets to restrain themselves after being pushed to the wall. Long before the Soviet invasion of Afghanistan, the United States sabotaged SALT II, announced a dramatic increase in the arms budget and a crash program for developing the MX missile. It countered a Soviet offer to withdraw 20,000 troops and 1,000 tanks from Eastern Europe by twisting the arms of its reluctant NATO allies until they agreed to let the United States install missiles in Germany. Those missiles, to be aimed at Moscow, Leningrad, and other major Soviet cities are being installed in the country whose troops and planes left 25-million dead Russians in their wake during World War II. Would it be so surprising if some Soviet Carters, Brzezinskis, Reagans, and Bushes are arguing today that the Soviet Union should respond to Carter's contrived and irresponsible confrontation by beating us to the punch?

Blood being more precious than oil, America's vital interest in the Middle East is peace, not fuel. Air, earth, and water not yet poisoned by a nuclear holocaust—all these are more important than oil.

The present course is leading step by step to catastrophe. We must take matters of life and death into our own hands, as we did in the sixties. We must insist that half the present arms budget be devoted to safe, renewable energy sources. The balance should be used for houses, hospitals, child care, facilities for the elderly, mass public transportation—for meeting human needs and building a just society of equals.

Faced with disaster, but with glimpses of the possibility of human solidarity, we require a new way of relating to our fellow human beings and the universe that is our home.

11 THE MOVEMENT

Remember. Reexamine. Renew. These are the exhortations running through this section, and they are shared by all the alternative movements that constitute The Movement. Behind these exhortations is the shared belief that change must be fundamental if it is to be meaningful or lasting. But these movements also have their own voices. What came out of the 1960s, that era of mass rallies in support of a common goal—the ending of a tragic war—were the many voices of the 1970s, each presenting its separate case, each calling for its distinct goals. This section echoes some of those voices.

"The bad economy is destroying the movement as no agent ever could." So Janet Sergi points out in her look at the "Selfish Seventies" and the economic limits placed on the 1980s and the women's movement. Despite the crunch of inflation and recession on community energies, Sergi sees the new decade as a period for the "humanization" of the economic structure.

Two other articles take a retrospective/introspective look at the preceding decade. In "Remembering Kent State," Taylor Whitney examines the day some say "broke the back" of the anti-war movement. "The war is over and no more far-reaching political goals bind us together," says Whitney. "Yet we remember." From *Sojourner,* Karen Lindsey analyzes the growth of the women's movement.

Growing out of the 1970s and spurred by the "incident" at Three Mile Island was the anti-nuclear movement. In "No Nukes Is Not Enough," Marcy Darnovsky analyzes the strategy of resistance and wonders if the movement will be drained of its radical impulses. She concludes that these impulses are essential, for the basic social and political structure of the country must be changed if the chain from consumer need to corporate greed and nuclear disaster is to be broken.

That any movement has room for the individual is seen in two open letters from *The Black Bartletter* and *Northwest Passage,* both musing about what they see as important.

A back to the earth movement, a return to simple beliefs and a sacred trust, is the subject of "The Rainbow Family Healing Gathering," a description of a communal celebration in West Virginia, and of

"Declaration of Dependence on the Land," a gentle prayer for harmony with Mother Earth by a culture that never really left the land.

The traditions of the alternative press movement—wry, acerbic, tongue-in-cheek pokes at the status quo—are seen in the remaining articles. On the press's hit list are The Moral Majority and the mass media; tactics range from a utopian *TV Guide* to a non-interview with a government official and an anarchist poke at Marxist theory.

The voices of the alternative press are many and varied, but they all speak for action, for continuity, and for growth.

—LD

From *The San Francisco Bay Guardian* 14, no. 25 (May 1, 1980): 36

Remembering Kent State, 1970-1980

by Taylor Whitney

In America. It happened in America. Stunned, we heard the news, ten years ago on May 4, 1970, that four sons and daughters of the white middle-class had been killed on the campus of Kent State University in Kent, Ohio. Nine others were injured—cut down by the gunfire of the Ohio National Guard, called out by the governor to occupy the campus because of anti-war protests.

Watching *The War at Home,* the movie currently showing at the Surf Theatre in San Francisco, not only brings back those events of the Sixties and early Seventies with chilling clarity, but presents yet another of those uncomfortable moments, forcing many of us who lived through those times to assess our lives once again and to examine anew where we are going politically.

Kent State in particular was more than a few frames of film to many of us. It was the culmination, it was the apocalypse. It was also the catalyst.

What happened at Kent State? What happened to you?

Friday, May 1, 1970

There were two peaceful assemblies of students protesting the Cambodian incursion on campus this day. They were without incident. Downtown Kent, however, was the scene of some disorder and trashing. (*And so in Berkeley, in Madison, in New Haven.*)

Saturday, May 2, 1970

The Mayor called the Govenor's office to request the National Guard. By the time the Guard, exhausted after being on duty for several weeks because of a trucking

---

strike, arrived in town, a fire in the ROTC building on campus had almost burned out. (*One, Two, Three, Four, We don't want your Fucking War!*)

Sunday, May 3, 1970

At an informal session at the firehouse, Governor Rhodes directed the National Guard to use any necessary force to disperse any meetings or gatherings of students, declaring that "he didn't want to see any two students walking together."

Later, at a press conference, Rhodes called the people who disrupted the campus and burned the ROTC building "worse than the Brown Shirts and the Communist elements and also the Night Riders and Vigilantes." He said, "No one is safe and I do not believe that people understand the seriousness of these individuals organized in a revolutionary frame of mind, believe me." (*And Vice President Agnew says "these bums" to us all.*)

There was an assembly ban, but most students didn't know of it. On the evening of May 3, many people gathered on the edge of campus. It was a time, all over the country, of daily gathering to discuss, to let our bodies be counted as a measure of our displeasure with the government's policies of war. On this night, in Ohio as elsewhere around the country, the Riot Act was read to demonstrators, and when people failed to disperse, troops marched into the crowd with bayonets bared. At least one person was wounded. (*The anti-riot lights on Shattuck Avenue illuminate the shattered glass of selected banks and stores. The tear gas looks like yellow clouds under them.*)

Monday, May 4, 1970

Around 11 a.m. students began to gather in an open grass area in the center of the campus. The lunch period was approaching, it was a warm spring day and gatherings were commonplace on this spot. The group of students was entirely peaceful. They were ordered to disperse. They did not.

Tear gas only partially dispersed the students, but it did provoke reaction in the form of shouts, gestures and a few rocks. Troops moved out in formation, forcing

the students to move up a hill and effectively dispersing them. The troops did not stop, though. They continued, down the other side of the hill, then turned and raggedly marched back up to the crest of Blanket Hill. The students thought it was all over—that the Guard was returning to its compound. People left for their classes, returning to their dorms, talking, most very far from the troops.

At the top of the hill, the troops turned and faced the practice field and parking lot. An officer kneeled among them, pistol pointed at the sky. His arm descended, and the troops opened up with a continuous barrage of gunfire lasting thirteen seconds. (*"They deserved it," mothers, pinch-faced, said to daughters, stricken. "But mother, I was there, too." "Then they should have shot you."*)

What did it mean, in retrospect? It meant death to Alison Krause, Sandy Scheuer, Jeffrey Miller and Bill Schroeder. It meant death to a girl in a green army jacket whose chest was ripped open, a girl walking between classes whose jugular vein was severed, a boy who may have chanted an obscenity, whose face was splattered, a boy wearing cowboy boots who was shot in the chest and the back and leg. Their parents were bereaved, embittered, politicized. And it put Dean Kahler in a wheelchair for life, severely injured James Russell, made Maoists out of Alan Canfora and Tom Grace and marked forever four other students. Real people, ever so typical and yet how hallowed names. It meant ten years of legal battles, with a pitifully small settlement at the end.

And, as a whole, we did not stop, we could not stop because these four were killed, these nine were injured. Some believe the intensity of the struggle increased. Later, more were killed at Jackson State, black students, in their dorms.

And that war ended. We, the protesters, won. But some say the back of the anti-war movement was broken that day in May because so many could not take the step to armed confrontation that the Government had taken. Some say, yes, the war ended, the draft ended, but it was a dwindling, a slowdown, not a decisive victory for "the people."

And since then, since that day, what has happened to us? Us, the great host of youth that felt unified against the war, unified against Nixon. We are now over thirty and not to be trusted. We are lawyers,

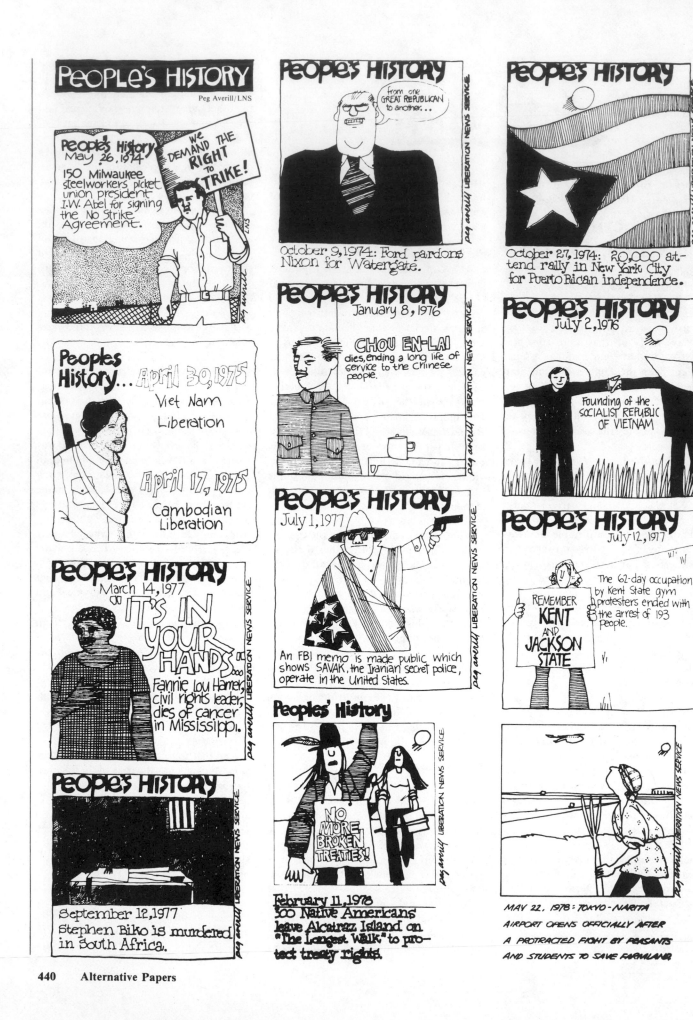

midwives, carpenters, aging hippies and members of the RCP. We work for women's rights, gay rights, the PTA and John Anderson. We feel guilt, we feel rage, we feel complacent. The war is over and no more far-reaching political goals bind us together. Yet we remember.

The War at Home makes us think. Do we have to go through that again? Do more Alisons, Sandys, Jeffs, and Bills have to be caught in the cross-fire? The answer is, probably yes. Because this country is inexorably being drawn into conflict around the world. Not just in the Persian Gulf, not just for oil is the draft again around the corner. It is closer to home. Look to El Salvador and Guatemala, where leftists and students are being killed by the hundreds and revolutions are imminent. And what of the workers here at home, laid-off by the recession? "This country needs a war to get back on its feet," some say. The people in power have not changed.

The gunshots of ten years ago echo in our minds today. We've changed, but too many things are still too much the same. Perhaps it's time to stop (Hey, what's that sound?) and look what's going down. Perhaps it's time to get a thousand people in the streets.

It happened in America, and it will happen again.

Taylor Whitney is a pseudonym for a Bay Area activist who rioted at UC Berkeley in 1970. Since then she has studied the Kent State case closely, and has come to see it as a moral lesson for our time.

The BLACK BARTLETTER

The Black Bartletter, **Winter 1979/ 1980, pp. 1-3**

[Letter]

by Irv Thomas

Dear Friends and Readers:

Always, at this time of year, comes the urge to get in touch again. It's partly the season, per se, partly the postal permit deadline. It's become one of the few regularities we seem to observe. But this season both the energy and the funds are in short supply, so it looks like a newsletter will have to do for it.

No matter, the important things can be said in a few pages. This is the passing of a decade. And it feels to be the entry into a particularly excruciating year. I'd just like to share what insights and perceptions I have, for whatever value they might be to your peace of mind and well-being.

I don't claim any superior pre-cognitive abilities, but I've learned a few things about how the year-cycle functions. There are clues, of a theme or 'mood' sort, in the mid-Fall weeks that often seem to telegraph the year ahead. Anyone can become sensitive to them—although they are easily lost in the coloration of personal bias.

And why should late October and November be harbingers, any more so than other months of the year? For some quite natural reasons. The year is a complete cycle of seeding, quickening, blossoming, fruition and harvest. The seeds of a newly generating round are briefly visible (and *feelable*) for that time between early October's fallow days and Winter's quiet nurturance.

November of '78, for example, presented us with some incredible rapid-fire shocks— the most memorable being the Jonestown experience. Common denominators were suddenness, impact, and their totally off-the-wall character. And the year's spring-time-into-summer, you'll recall, brought a whole series of such events, from the Ayatollah's return to Iran, to the Three-Mile Island accident—and all that has followed in their train.

In the November just past, we've had crisis of an entirely different nature: a drawn-out, high-tension, frustrating struggle between clashing values and realities, which at this writing is still clouded in its month-long fog of uncertainty. Perhaps by the time you read this the Tehran Embassy problem will have reached some resolution, perhaps not. Either way, it promises an expanding whorl of repercussions, and can be seen as the setting of a thematic stage for the coming annular round. I am quite afraid, my friends, that we have a very trying year to look forward to.

On personal levels, too (for they always run parallel), it's being felt as a winter of exceeding discontent and frustration. More than that, an unnerving confusion; for it seems like *nothing* is as it has been, or as it should be. Uneasiness, disconnection, uncertainty, estrangement from self and others, a feeling that some unknowable and scary turns lie just ahead—these are the terms by which I would reference my own recent reality. I leave it to you to reflect upon yours.

But see it in the larger context. The 'seventies are now behind us. When we left the 'sixties we were releasing a decade of turmoil in the streets—over civil rights, over Vietnam, over a range of revolutionary 'Movements' that very much amounted to the demand for a real

Wright/Guardian/LNS

Reprinted with permission from *The Black Bartletter*.

individual freedom in pursuit of life and happiness. These struggles were not fully over (are still not), but we had turned a corner from fighting for a *recognition* of the issues to working toward their implementation.

The 'seventies, accordingly, have been witness to a large-scale turnaround in the national consciousness. We've come through the de-mythification of government, of corporate industry and its once-taken-for-granted contribution to our health and well-being, and of a whole basketfull of time-hallowed American Institutions, such as the glory of Progress and Growth, the work ethic, the reign of science, the role-locked nuclear family, etc. Once again, these struggles with consciousness are not by any means fully worked through—but they are well past the challenges of a visionary minority.

Who could've imagined, just a year ago, that a single nuclear-plant mishap (with no fatalities!) would bring us, within a few months' time, to a full national reconsideration of the wisdom of our nuclear commitment? This newest Movement has that suddenly attained legitimacy!

We are clearly on a path of progression in the remaking of a societal consciousness. That this remaking is *necessary,* in light of such realities as resource limits, pollution, threat of planetary extinction, etc., is hardly to be questioned by any sane and thinking mentality. But that this remaking may be *inevitable,* and a matter of destiny, is something that may not be so easy to grasp. We don't readily give credence to the idea of a 'world consciousness' (to use one among several possible terms) that seeks to heal its own ills. And yet, this is an appropriate description of the rather astounding directiveness with which things have been moving in the past two decades.

In other words, Three-Mile Island was conceivably no 'accident' at all. Nor was the 'loss' of Iran, or the more recent developments in that part of the world. In the course of the consciousness shift, it was certainly *necessary* that the American people find the reason, the strength, and the unity to say, somewhere along the line—"No, we will not pay that price for oil!" Just a token statement, perhaps, at this point—but one which makes its mark on consciousness. And in the course of world events, it was *inevitable* that circumstances should bring it about.

I write these very words on December 7th, the anniversary of another day of inevitable events, 38 years ago. Many pages of written history have thrashed over the question of why Roosevelt 'permitted' Pearl Harbor to be attacked, when he is known to have received hours-prior information and never relayed it to the Hawaiian military command. But America was as divided in consciousness, as apathetic about the trend of world development in that day as she is in this, and the stroke of catalytic violence which happened at Pearl Harbor on that morning was conceivably the *only* kind of event that could have brought us into a clear and common mind. Roosevelt's 'lapse'—intentional or not—was the instrument of an inevitable destiny.

What this all means, as we entertain the probability of a year that is likely to be exceedingly wearing and difficult, is that we can at least look toward its directive destiny. Hard times are a good deal easier to bear if we can develop a confidence in their ultimate necessity and inevitability, and in their promise of a better future at some distant time ahead.

One of the things we also learn, when we come to see life as a spiritually purposeful path of development, is that nothing happens to us which we are not somehow able to cope with—whether this be taken in terms of our material or psychic resources. To be able to cope with the cutback of fuel and energy resources that seems clearly to be our destined lot, we are going to need a strong sense of national unity and determination. It becomes increasingly clear that events such as Three-Mile Island, and the Ayatollah of Iran, are slowly forging in us that sort of will and purpose necessary to such a development of consciousness.

I shall not be at all surprised to see this trend furthered in 1980. It will happen with the tightening of the screws. It is not likely to be a pleasant experience, but the compensation will be a different kind of meaning to our lives and to the austerity which will come to characterize our lives.

I reflect back, once more, to the war years of the 'forties, when we were engaged in a truly monumental worldwide life-or-death struggle; and yet, the spirits were very high, very strong—they were *good* years, right along with their deadly-earnest seriousness. Challenge and stress, in a constructive, positive sense, are qualities which have too long been absent from our national psyche.

From *Big Mama Rag* 7, no. 5 (June 1979): 13

The Exciting Eighties

by Janet Sergi

Happily the selfish seventies are drawing to a close. They need to be analyzed. Introspection, hedonism, and cynicism reached new depths in the 70's. The life style changes of the sixties were coopted into the trendy mentalities of the 70's. What will the eighties be like: Hopefully exciting. This economic overview of the late seventies will sketch the economic boundaries in which feminism will find itself during the coming decade, the exciting eighties.

Jerry Brown calls the coming decade the age of limits. His opportunistic, but skillful exploitation of trends serves to popularize a major motif of the late 70's: limits. We have reached the end of "the sky is the limit" view of America. Just as the "endless" western frontier closed at the end of the last century, the economic "endless" frontier begins to close now. The limitless frontiers of economic imperialism by the multinationals have been reached. The Third World, symbolized by the OPEC oil cartel, is beginning to fight back. We cannot have all the oil we want, at the price we want.

Due to the oil and auto industries' choices after WWII to base the American economy on private cars and trucks we have begun to suffer the consequences of their gasoholic decisions! Present oil reserves are running low. The oil companies' choice of quick profits—sell as much oil as possible as quickly as possible—meant necessary but expensive investment in efficient refinery capacities and produced the present refined oil shortage. Some absolute loss of oil reserves only adds to the basic problem and gives some validity to high oil prices.

The American working people are forced to bear the burden of rebuilding the multinational oil corporations' refineries through high energy prices. This hurts not only at the gas pump. All goods and services will cost more; a pair of shoes will cost more to make, ship, store and sell. Oil profit will also be invested in uranium holdings and nuclear reactor projects owned by the energy companies. General mobility will be severely limited, e.g. fewer mothers received visits from their children on Mother's Day 1979 due to gas shortages and high prices. Also moving from state to state and city to city will be limited due to the accompanying inflation and poor job prospects of a slowed down, recession-prone, energy-short economy.

Inflation is tied to low productivity; productivity is the amount of goods and services produced per woman-hour of work. Lazy workers and high union wages are not the problem. American industry did not invest in enough new efficient machinery since WWII. Western Europe and Japan did. Their goods are cheaper and more competitive. American corporate giants choose quick profits through advertising a wasteful consumer life style. Corporate government chooses defense spending through deficit spending rather than increased taxation due to the political unpopularity of the Vietnam War. Government debt went up: an unbalanced budget.

Kurt Vance/LNS

FREE ENTERPRISE

There was not enough money left over for housing, medical care, education, social welfare and a clean environment. All this makes the American economy slow down, a recession reoccurs and at the same time inflation and unemployment increases. This means salaries don't keep up with prices, and strikes become ineffective due to the large labor reserves of unemployed workers, especially youths, women and minorities. Nuclear families need two jobs to meet basic expenses. People on fixed incomes, such as the disabled and elderly, have to choose between food and heat. Cheap or inflated dollars may hurt the average American but they help corporations. They make American goods cheaper to sell overseas and make foreign goods more expensive here. So, the once cheap VW now costs $6,000 while IBM Computers are cheaper and easier to sell abroad.

The stress of recession, inflation, and unemployment produce instability in family life, make relationships and friendships strained. Hostility is misdirected to the people closest to you instead of onto the responsible multinationals. Despair, desperation and alienation increase in our lives. We take it out on ourselves. Since Americans are purposely ill-informed on economic matters, the complex causes of our own financial troubles are not understood nor easily identifiable. We blame our lovers and friends for making "unneeded" purchases with our or their increasingly worthless dollars.

Another distressing fact, that part-time job of the 60's and early 70's doesn't pay the rent anymore. Therefore, feminist projects such as *Big Mama Rag* can't be staffed as easily. Likewise, the cost of paper, ink, printing and supplies are rising astronomically. The bad economy is destroying the movement as no agent ever could. Still, we blame ourselves for each failure.

As times get tougher, we need each other more. The women's community in which we once sought identity, comfort and social acceptability, now needs to become a survival support system. Already weakened by ideological and personal strife, this new economic burden could break the fragile community structure. As women devote more time to their jobs, community energies will be sapped into the workplace. The economy of the eighties may doom our women's communities. The government knows this.

Jimmy Carter was astute to fire Bella

Abzug when she questioned his economic policies. As the hand-picked presidential candidate of the David Rockefeller chaired Trilateral Commission, Carter cannot allow the corporate domain of economic policy to be attacked, especially by a woman with a mass following. Bella began publicly to define economic policy as a women's issue. Bella is right. The 80's will be exciting if we as feminists take up this battle. Feminists need to tackle the economic ramifications of our present condition. This means continued leadership in the anti-nuclear movement—notice the amount of real power women have in it versus the subordinate role played by women in the anti-war movement.

The whole debate of hard/high technology and centralized nuclear power versus the soft/forgiving and decentralized technology of solar energy are the paradigm male/female views of reality. The feminist critique of the patriarchy with its aggressive and destructive use of rationality holds equally true as a critique of nuclear technology and its destructive probabilities. The feminist vision of a wholistic and humane lifestyle is dependent on an ecological solar-based economy.

Regional planning and decentralized economy would automatically reduce the need to exploit other countries and regions of the world. Likewise, solar technology developed here could rapidly be used to bring the underdeveloped world to self-sufficiency at a decent standard of living without huge capital outlays a nuclear or oil based economy would need.

The eighties have a chance to be the beginning decade of the humanization of the whole economy—a truly exciting prospect. However, we, as feminists, must not succumb to the taunting of the New Right, who are now devouring themselves in hate: see Crane/Reagan cannibalization of each other in the primaries. The New Right is a pesty backlash to the real social victories of the 60's and early 70's: feminism, gay rights, and social programs such as food stamps and welfare reforms.

The New Right is only one part of the ruling class. The monied Yankee establishment who supports liberal reforms like welfare is another enemy of feminists. Jimmy Carter's bosses, the Rockefeller-led Eastern Establishment, are the owners and creators of the high technological/nuclear-based, computer-run 1984 future.

A minute and detailed analysis of how and why these multinationals run the world's economy must be made a feminist task. Feminists must convince ourselves of the necessity to fight this hidden but all encompassing enemy. The fight will take the rest of this century. It will determine the course of human history. The choices are a world-wide humane level of existence or a world-destroying nuclear war. A war started by one big nuclear-armed power or the other over scarce resources such as a Middle Eastern oil field. The choice is ours. An ecological and just world with limitless excitement or death.

A Political Newsjournal for the Anti-Nuclear Movement

From *No Nukes Left!* 1, no. 1 (Summer 1980): 2-6

No Nukes Is Not Enough

by Marcy Darnovsky

Nuclear power and nuclear weapons cannot be faced without understanding how they reflect the organization of current society, without reference to their social political roots. In the anti-nuclear movement, tendencies that obscure those roots are vying with tendencies that reveal them.

Some see nukes as aberrations while others explain them as symptoms of the social order—or as its logical outcome. Some advocates of the single issue approach see themselves as strategically sophisticated pragmatists. Over a beer they'll discuss the necessity of revolutionary change but in public they delimit their critique.

In an effort to open this discussion, several groups in the San Francisco Bay area called a "No Nukes Is Not Enough" conference on November 4, 1979. What follows is a slightly altered version of a presentation given that day on the culture and ideology of the anti-nuclear movement.

Zen Opportunism

My first big anti-nuke demonstration was the Diablo Canyon occupation in August of 1978. A friend and I had

prepared a leaflet that we called "I'd Rather Be Smashing Capitalism (Than Atoms)." The reaction to it was extremely mixed. Of the people who absolutely hated it, the predominant reason was the one given by a woman who told us, "You're trying to reduce a human issue to a political one."

I have no trouble understanding the fear of sacrificing people to some god called "politics," or the individual to a pre-defined collective good. But the "humanists" have spread the worst kind of confusion by taking what is merely one of the more spectacular excesses of the capitalist system and isolating it from the political and economic structures which support it.

Besides, they keep bad company—Jerry Brown, for example, who is fond of saying that "environmental problems are above politics." I've seen him whip up a crowd and yell, "Are you *for* the environment!?" And then only the punks and the nihilists scream back, "No!"

It's ironic that a Zen opportunist like Brown should manage to capitalize on the popular disgust with politics, because that disgust does have some radical seeds. Many people want nothing to do with politics because they see it as a racket, as being concerned with only a very narrow, circumscribed part of life. In contrast, any politics that has a chance of facilitating social transformation must address itself to the patterns of life as a whole, to the structure of society as a whole—how it's organized and how we'd like to see it organized, how we experience daily life, what our imaginations and utopian desires suggest as alternatives, and how we get from here to there.

The Grassroots Alliances

With politics understood in this sense, I don't think many anti-nuke activists would put themselves into the apolitical camp. In fact, the formation of the grassroots anti-nuclear alliances marked a process of intense politicization. The alliances were predicated on the idea that we can't and shouldn't appeal to politicians, the courts or the regulatory agencies to stop nukes for us, but that we must take the initiative ourselves. The anti-nukers insisted from the beginning that decisions about the best way to produce energy were questions for social debate, not agenda items for corporate boardrooms or central committees. As a corollary, the anti-nuclear alliances believe that their members should participate directly in decision-making within the group.

The grassroots alliances took it upon themselves to mount a direct challenge to the direction and priorities of capitalist development. Their criteria of evaluation were social as well as technical, and their vision of the future was of a world free of the domination of nature by humanity and, if only by extension, of social domination as well.

On the other hand, there are cultural and ideological assumptions associated with the anti-nuclear movement (as well as the ecology movement which influences it) which mystify the social system that has spawned both nuclear power and weapons and a population that allows them to continue.

One of these is the notion that "we're all in it together," that radiation and chemicals in our food affect everyone equally, that we're all passengers on "Spaceship Earth." As the German critic Hans Magnus Enzenberger points out, the problem with this metaphor is that it fails to notice that little difference between those who ride first class and those who are down in the hold.[1] And it certainly doesn't distinguish between those who pilot the ship and the rest.

The Culture of Nonviolence

To look at society and fail to see that there are different groups of people—different *classes* of people with very different interests, is myopic. Yet certain tendencies in the anti-nuclear movement encourage this. One of these is often found associated with the culture of nonviolence. This culture, which is influential if not hegemonic in the anti-nuclear movement, fosters a decided reluctance to face the conflicts of society. The concept of "speaking truth to power" assumes that even the heads of governments and corporations can be convinced to give up their interests and act on ours. But the fact is, these people are agents and personifications of the interests of capitalism, and its interests will never be compatible with ours.

The tendency in the anti-nuclear movement strives to avoid conflict at all costs extends itself to intergroup and interpersonal relationships, so that it sometimes becomes hard even to *disagree*. Or worse, you tell someone that you think they're wrong, and they thank you for sharing your concerns. As a result, dialogue is difficult and the development of ideas is stunted.

The culture of nonviolence also nurtures a desire to believe that if only we get the facts out, everyone will come around to our point of view and everything will change. While it is certainly true that the facts of the case are powerful weapons and the dissemination of information a crucial part of our work, it is naive to expect that once we tell people where it's at they'll rise phoenix-like from the ashes of apathy and false consciousness.

All of us make certain psychic adjustments and unconscious compromises in order to tolerate the humiliation of wage labor, the boredom of scheduled leisure, the passivity of fraudulent democracy and the ache of repressed or exploited sexuality. There are entire industries dedicated to manipulating our frustrated and submerged desires. No wonder that many people can't very easily understand their real interests, no matter how logically or earnestly the arguments are presented.[2]

What we have to get across isn't a bunch of facts, but a conceptual shift, a different way of looking at the world, a creative and critical mode of thinking. That's why the culture and ideology of our movement are crucial topics for examination.

The theory of nonviolence, as well as its culture, is open to criticism. Though in the abstract nonviolence seems preferable to violence if only because it appears to lower the likelihood of getting hurt, it isn't useful as a first principle of analysis. In fact, it can be downright misleading. Let me quote from the training handbook for last October's Wall Street Action (an action and certainly a target for which I've got a lot of sympathy.) The handbook states, "Power is not derived from violence, but

Cindy Fredrick/LNS

from the consent of the governed—largely through passive consent." This isn't true. The consent of the "governed" doesn't arise spontaneously, but is conditioned and maintained through economic coercion, psychic manipulation and the threat and use of violence. Those who question the legitimacy of this authority, and begin to act on their answers, will meet with a violent response. And I'm not just talking about a violent police response to a fence takedown around a nuclear reactor construction site, or to an unemployed person who's robbed a bank.

Capitalism is based on violence—from the violence of dictatorial regimes and starvation in the Third World, which are part and parcel of capitalism, to the violence that's been turned loose every decade since the 1870's on strikers who usually are asking only for a bigger piece of the pie.[3]

Indeed, nonviolence can be an effective tactic precisely when it is used to reveal the violence on which this society is based.[4] The relative stability of the social order depends on the myth that the governed have freely given their consent, that you choose to use nuclear electricity or that when you go to work you're freely entering into a contractual agreement with your employer. Whatever threatens to explode this myth threatens to delegitimate the existing society, and delegitimation must be a key element in any strategy for social change.

The Class Composition of the Movement

The existence of this culture of nonviolence doesn't fully explain why the anti-nuclear movement has failed to develop a class analysis. Part of that explanation lies in the fact that the idea of class isn't very widespread in this country or in our experience. Another big reason is the class composition of the movement.

The anti-nuke movement has recognized that it draws predominantly from the young, white and college educated population; in fact, it chastises itself regularly for this state of affairs. But despite all the talk, at anti-nuke rallies the same soft rock—or limp rock—is heard from the stage, at anti-nuke meetings we get "light and livelies," on anti-nuke leaflets and posters we keep seeing smiling suns and nice trees.

At the Seabrook occupation last October a man from California volunteered to buy food for the Western regional group. Everyone gave him $5.00 and he came back with 50 pounds of soy nuts, 50 pounds of tamari and a little wheat germ. Several people grumbled, several people choked over their coffee, but no one said anything.

This is the culture of the New Age and it reinforces the narrow class composition of the movement. To be fair, the New Age approach has some strong points. It tries to deal with the whole of life and refrains from reducing the nuclear problem to an "issue," or the anti-nuclear movement to a pressure group.

But the New Agers seem to think they're on to something new under the sun, as if their ideas had sprung full-grown from the forehead of Zeus. Though they may invoke the civil rights era or the Hopi Indians or the days of Gandhi, none of the other great social uprisings of the last couple of centuries are ever referred to. The barricades, the general strikes are never mentioned.

The anti-nuclear movement's many appeals to the future are always made in the name of "our children and our children's children," as if we should be afraid or ashamed to demand a different world for ourselves. This religious, moralistic tone removes the nuclear issue from the historical realm and from society, making it a matter of right against wrong.

There are also strains in the movement which equate fighting nuclear power and even the whole social structure with "right living." We are still sometimes told to take "personal responsibility" for environmental problems. We are advised to "walk lightly on the Earth" in a way that suggests we ought to feel guilty about our very existence.

In these prescriptions for voluntary simplicity there is an important element of disgust with commodity society and a refusal to dedicate oneself to a "job." And there's no doubt that 6% of the world's population can't go on consuming 30% of its resources, as is the case with the United States today. But voluntary simplicity often implies that we are somehow to blame for the mess that capitalism has made, and that we ought to pay for its crisis. As the economy staggers and our living standards slip, voluntary simplicity becomes a way to make a virtue out of necessity and to hide the fact that the system no longer delivers the material abundance it has always touted itself for.

Soft Energy Planners

The politics of alternative technology have become a mainstay of anti-nuclear culture, and it's to its credit that the anti-nuclear movement has been determined and creative enough to tackle the nitty-gritty of safe, clean energy production. Unfortunately, however, figuring out the "best way to produce energy" often serves to provide capitalism with innovative ideas that it will gobble up on its own terms. We may decide that our survival, our health, or our living standards are at stake and therefore that we do want to support the development and deployment of alternative energy sources even within the existing economic system. But those who shift their focus to solar retrofitting and biomass conversion often undergo a transformation of their own and begin to resemble New Age planners, volunteering to do the work of the utilities for them.

We're not out to make the existing system more efficient and rational, but to replace it with a world of our own making. We're not energy planners, but a movement of opposition.

The alternative technologists believe that a decentralization process will inevitably reduce the control of the state and the corporations over our lives, that it will offer a new way of working and a revitalization of community. Obviously these are worthy goals, but it may be completely wrong to think that decentralized energy production will bring them about. As an East Coast group called Midnight Notes points out, "Decentralization of things does not automatically imply decentralization of command over our lives. If this was true, capitalism would never have admitted the individual car as a means of very "decentralized" transportation and would have

favored the railroads which are more centralized and easier to control."[5]

The *production* of the automobile, of course, is extremely centralized and it's easy to imagine a similar scenario for energy: solar collectors and photovoltaics produced by a few huge corporations and used to provide "decentralized" energy in individual homes, schools and factories. In fact, the centralized production of alternative energy paraphernalia may very well take place in parts of the world like Southeast Asia where labor is cheap and easily exploitable.

The Electoral Swamp

Since Three Mile Island the movement has attracted not only large numbers of people but also politicians of all varieties. This is not to say that every political candidate who has jumped on the anti-nuclear bandwagon was oblivious to the problem before, but that the public outcry following Three Mile Island made the issue politically permissible. Nor is it to imply that politicians are necessarily ineffective.

In fact, the Haydens and Browns may be able to negotiate a nuclear stalemate, since there are growing rifts in high places about the profitability of nuclear power and the advisability of pursuing it.[6] (Of course, it's hard to imagine the powers-that-be agreeing to a slowdown of nuclear weapons development.)

If the politicians succeed in stopping nuclear power, you may be sure they won't credit the anti-nuclear movement with having forced them into it. But even now, the electoral swamp is affecting the movement. It's being transformed by and integrated into an emerging social democratic and left liberal consensus. The representatives of this perspective, like the Citizens Party and the Campaign for Economic Democracy, are pushing "politics" back into its old narrow confines of mass rallies and voting. Questions of fundamental social transformation are always put off until some ever-receding future date.

Barry Commoner and the Citizens Party are an informative case study. They have been actively wooing the anti-nuclear movement, plugging the party at anti-nuke conferences and teach-ins and recruiting anti-nuke activists for their staff. More recently they've gotten involved in the anti-draft movement, recommending, "Don't register for the draft, register to vote for the Citizens Party."

Perhaps Commoner's basic satisfaction with the existing society is best revealed in the Citizens Party's working paper which states, "There is nothing wrong with profit, or with private ownership." Declarations of this sort caused dissension and embarrassment among some Citizens Party members. But despite Commoner's talk about internal democracy in the organization—"We've erected a flagpole, but it's up to whoever joins us to design the flag."—his next draft emphasized these points all the more. One Citizens Party member said, "He wrote a paper showing how entrepreneurial business is what America should be about and tried to push it through."

It's not that Commoner is afraid to mention capitalism. He often refers to the ". . . mistakes (sic) made by capitalists in the interests of improving their profits." He recommends workers' participation—assuming that if workers had a say in the management of capitalism, our economic problems would be solved and we'd have undertaken some fundamental social transformation.

The two times I've heard Commoner speak have been in front of anti-nuke audiences and both times he has exhorted them to "take the moral responsibility of victors—to seize state power." Commoner's listeners haven't seemed to share his assurance that the nuclear industry has agreed to roll over and play dead. And there has certainly been no overwhelming consensus that anti-nuclear or anti-corporate (let alone anti-capitalist) aims can be gained through the only strategy that Commoner recommends—national electoral politics.

If the social democrats or left liberals should come to power, the system they have chosen to defend will severely constrain even their intentions to be a bit more "humane" than our present leaders. The most these politicians will ever do is challenge the *conditions* of production, things like safety and wages. They will

Green Revolution/LNS

never attack the *relations* of production—who's in control, who benefits from the social wealth we produce when we go to work in the morning.

Another part of Commoner's vision is the nationalization of parts of the economy, especially the energy-industry. Assuming such a move to be any improvement over the current state of affairs, how would it be accomplished? When asked, Commoner becomes quite vague. Once he replied, "It'll just fit into the natural scheme of things."

I would argue that any system of production that included profit and the private ownership of factories, natural resources and other means of production will, whatever lesser changes are made in it, merely extend rather than solve our basic social problems. The logic of capitalism, in which production is geared toward profit rather than the satisfaction of overall social needs, makes this inevitable. Its "ills"—chronic unemployment, dangerous and unhealthy working conditions, wasteful production—aren't "mistakes" but methods of profit-making. This holds true whether we're speaking of big businesses or small, privately or publicly owned, as long as the market system remains intact.

And it holds true even when workers are participating on corporate boards of directors. Chrysler's near bankruptcy is a good example. Coming to the aid of the company, the United Auto Workers Union convinced Chrysler workers to accept wages lower than those of other autoworkers. In exchange, UAW president Doug Fraser was given a seat on the board of directors. Shortly after, when the government handed Chrysler a bail-out in the form of a Defense contract for the Army's XM-1 tank, Fraser went along. Is this the kind of socially useful production the Campaign for Economic Democracy has in mind?[7]

The Show Goes On

The mystifying ideological and cultural characteristics described here—the moralism, ahistoricism, ostrich-like avoidance of conflict and the promotion of small-is-beautiful as a panacea—are dulling the radical cutting edge of the anti-nuclear movement. Its most liberatory aspects are being left behind—its challenge to the direction of capitalist production, explicitly anti-hierarchical and anti-authoritarian tone, and attempts at direct democracy.

During the last year, the anti-nuclear movement has grown increasingly distant from the "wholistic" approach to politics that so strongly and refreshingly characterized its earlier, less "respectable" days. For many newly interested people, the huge star-studded rallies held in New York, Washington and San Francisco have come to define the culture of the anti-nuclear movement. Instead of encouraging participation, these rallies turn each protester into a member of an audience, passively watching the little figures on stage. And though we've been careful to prevent the media from singling out some of our own number to turn into "stars," we allow the little figures on stage to speak in our name to the audience and, through the media, to the world.[8]

No media star, whether he or she rises from the ranks or is already famous, can be held accountable to any democratic process or mandate from the group. We may want the rock stars to work with us, but we can't allow them to speak for us.

If the anti-nuclear movement tailors itself to this version of politics, it will be drained of its radical impulses and its vision of a qualitatively different world. Still, I'm not saying that we can afford to ignore electoral politics. But if we must vote, we should make it absolutely clear that it was the grassroots movement which forced the issue, that the initiative came from outside the narrow political structures of bourgeois democracy. We should never plug our movement into those structures or allow it to be defined as a pressure group on them. The anti-nuclear movement should remain independent of parties and join with groups that are willing to look beyond single issues and immediate demands.

Radical Alternatives

Electoral campaigns and pressure-group politics are the easy answer. There's a prescribed way to proceed, with rules and formulae. The alternatives that point beyond capitalist and authoritarian social relations as well as beyond nuclear technology are largely uncharted territory. There are clues from our own experiences and those of others who have fought for a better life in this society or for a different social order altogether, but I know of no blueprint or definitive program.

I continue to support "direct actions" of the more-or-less traditional anti-nuke variety, though I see them as largely symbolic rather than directly effective. And I'm interested in strategies and tactics that use the economy as a lever, such as the proposal for a rate strike that's now being hammered out in the Abalone Alliance. But whatever the tactic, demand, or strategy, there are certain criteria that can be applied, certain questions that can help evaluate their meaning.

First, of course, *will it work?* But then—*does it improve our lives? Does it do that by reclaiming some of the social wealth we have created? Does it clarify the existing social relationships? Does it reveal the exploitation on which the system is based, or does it legitimize the current social order? Is it clear that the change comes from outside the existing political institutions? Does it reveal to the participants their real interests and their collective strength?*

What is crucial in all of this isn't so much *that* we are fighting nukes—we have to do that, if only because we want to be left with a world worth winning. What is crucial is how we fight them. If we see nukes as an isolated evil and are willing to limit our vision of the future to the development of alternative energy sources, then there is no point in thinking about our culture or our ideas—capitalism will define them for us. But if we see nukes both as a symptom of capitalist and authoritarian social relations and as an analyzer of them, then we can continuously evaluate our activities and assumptions to see what points beyond "no nukes."

Footnotes

1. Hans Magnus Enzensberger, "A Critique of Political Ecology." Reprinted in Alexander Cockburn and James Ridgeway, *Political Ecology,* Times Books, 1979.
2. Maurice Brinton, *The Irrational in Politics,* 1975.
3. Jeremy Brecher, *Strike!,* South End Press, Boston, 1977.
4. Harvey Wasserman, "Stopping the Nukes," in *New Age* magazine, March, 1980. This presents a contrary view of nonviolence.
5. Midnight Notes Collective, *Strange Victories: The Anti-Nuclear Movement in the U.S. and Europe,* 1979. Available from the authors for $1.50 at 491 Pacific St., Brooklyn, NY 11217.
6. Robert Stobaugh and Daniel Yergin, *Energy Future, Report of the Energy Project at the Harvard Business School,* Random House, 1979.
7. Steve Stallone, "Business As Usual," in *It's About Times* (the Abalone Alliance newspaper), April, 1980. Subscriptions are $5.00 a year from 944 Market Street, Room 307, San Francisco, CA 94102.

8. Murray Bookchin, "An Open Letter to the Ecology Movement," Special Issue number 1 of *Comment—New Perspectives in Liberatarian Thought.* Available at P.O. Box 371, Hoboken, NJ 07030.

"*I started working with the anti-nuclear movement because it looked like the best alternative to apathy, cynicism, the sectarian left, the bland left, the paralyzed theoretical left, or nuclear war. My relationship to the movement has been one of continuous low-level frustration variously coupled with optimism and despair. The appearance of* **No Nukes Left!** *is a hopeful sign if it can become a goad to as well as a reflection of the anti-nuclear movement—and not just a comfortable niche for congenital critics (like me) to let off steam.*"

BLACK HILLS PAHA SAPA REPORT

From *Black Hills-Paha Sapa Report* 2, no. 1 (August/September, 1980): 1, 12

Declaration of Dependence on the Land

Land is a sacred trust and a precious resource. Together with the water that flows under and through it and the air that flows around it, the land has been created by God, the Great Spirit, and given in sacred trust to all living creatures. The land is one, its water, soil, air elements within and living creatures are a whole, not meant to be divided and abused. Mother Earth nourishes her children, and they are to treat her with respect. They are to live in harmony with her and with each other.

But the sacred trust has been violated. The harmony has been shattered. The land has been desecrated because it has been treated as a commodity. Mother Earth has been violated by individuals and corporations who *abuse* her or *appropriate* her for their own selfish ends.

The *abuses* of the land are many: desecration of sacred Indian lands; strip mining; grassland plowing; soil and water poisoning and depletion through excessive agricultural, industrial and consumer use; lack of land conservation practices; capital and chemical intensive agriculture; overgrazing of pasture lands; displacement of native plant varieties; irresponsible for-

estry practices; and dumping of chemical and radioactive wastes. Many of these abuses result from an economic system that oppresses Native Peoples, farmers and ranchers, taking from their ownership or control of their land base.

The forms taken by *appropriation* of the land include: stealing Native Peoples' land to satisfy the greed of those seeking mineral or agricultural wealth; seizure of rural lands in general through purchase by large corporations, or government exercise of eminent domain on behalf of those corporations, for mining, power plants and lines, urban and suburban development and nuclear missile sites; diversion of water to serve corporate rather than community needs; consolidation of rural and urban lands; and exploitation of Third World nations' lands by U.S.-based transnational corporations to increase their own profits and prop up the failing U.S. economic system. These forms of appropriation are supported by government policies and practices which serve the profit interests of corporations rather than the primary needs of people.

The abuse and appropriation of the land alienate people from their rightful inheritance and their true heritage. They also pose both short and long term threats to the survival of Mother Earth and of all living creatures.

We are meeting near the Black Hills of South Dakota in an International Survival Gathering. We come from 23 Indian nations and 36 other nations of the world. We come to express our outrage at the desecration of the land. We realize that those who violate the earth here in North America do so throughout the world in an international conspiracy to satisfy their greed and deprive all peoples of the lands entrusted to them by the Creator.

1. We call for the restoration of the sacred relationships among all creatures and the earth. We declare our dependence on the land, and urge all peoples to recognize their own dependence on the land for their lives and livelihoods.

2. We call for an end to the abuse and appropriation of the land. We invite all

This document was produced by members of the Forum on Indian Genocide and the Planned Extinction of the Family Farm and Ranch, a work group at the July 1980 Black Hills International Survival Gathering. The ten-day gathering was sponsored by the Black Hills Alliance, Box 2508, Rapid City, SD 57709.

Peg Averill/LNS

concerned peoples to struggle with us to achieve that goal.

3. We call for an end to all genocidal programs which uproot, displace and relocate Native Peoples and other rural peoples.

4. We call for all nations to acknowledge that international law holds that all treaties are binding upon the nations that contract them, and cannot be changed without the consent of all the parties involved.

5. We call for land justice for Native Peoples: recognition of their sovereignty and traditional forms of government, with the 1868 Fort Laramie Treaty as the starting point for the just resolution of differences and the model for honoring all other treaties.

6. We call for the return of federal and state lands in treaty areas to the jurisdiction of Native Peoples as the initial step in treaty resolutions; these areas to be maintained in a manner harmonious with the natural environment.

7. We call for the recognition of the right of family farmers and ranchers to exercise stewardship over family-sized holdings in treaty areas restored to Indian control, as long as they respect and care for these lands, through long term, renewable guarantees.

8. We call for the promotion of family farms and ranches, especially through owner-operator and residency requirements, and parity programs tied to conservation practices that lead to the eventual elimination of agricultural dependence on chemical pollutants of the land.

9. We call for the revision of inheritance, estate and property taxes to benefit family farmers and ranchers.

10. We call for an end to the urban development that misuses rural land, and areas of natural beauty.

11. We call for the right of the people to determine how eminent domain is to be used.

12. We call for control of rural water resources by the consensus of all land-based people, and protection of water quality and quantity for rural and urban needs.

13. We call for support of the labor organizing efforts of farmworkers.

14. We call for the termination of all phases of nuclear energy development, and the promotion of safe and clean energy alternatives.

15. We call for an end to nuclear weapons development and the dismantling of nuclear weapons systems.

16. We call for an end to government's role as a political arm of big corporations, and establishment of a people's government.

17. We call for the expropriation of transnational corporations' agricultural holdings, and their redistribution to indigenous and agricultural people.

18. We call for an end to the manipulation of the world economy by such non-elected bodies as the Trilateral Commission and the Committee on Economic Development.

19. We call for the establishment of a solidarity network with other people engaged in the international struggle for justice on the land.

20. We call for the promotion of sisterhood and brotherhood among peoples of all races and social classes.

21. Finally, we call for the recognition of our responsibility to be stewards of the land, to treat with respect and love our Mother Earth, who is a source of our physical nourishment and our spiritual strength.

We are people of the land. We believe that the land is not to be owned, but to be shared. We believe that we are the guardians of the land. The future of our children, and of all generations to come, will depend on our efforts today to prevent corporate seizure and abuse of the land. We challenge our concerned sisters and brothers throughout the world to unite with us in the struggle to liberate the land and all people from the economic and political domination of the transnational corporations and the governments that serve them.

The Great Spirit will guide our thoughts and strengthen us as we work to be faithful to our sacred trust and restore harmony among all peoples, all living creatures, and Mother Earth.

The Struggle will be long and difficult. So let us begin.

COMMUNITIES *journal of cooperative living*

From *Communities,* no. 45 (October/November 1980), pp. 32-37

The Rainbow Family Healing Gathering

by Allen Butcher

Life flowing with and around us leads each person along a different path. But as we seek a feeling of shared purpose and responsibility, as a family caring for itself, so we can manifest that idea by coming together in community. Welcome Home! Welcome to the Rainbow Family Healing Gathering!

Reprinted with permission from *Communities: Journal of Cooperative Living,* Box 426, Louisa, VA 23093.

A Rainbow Community

Each year in a different state is held the Rainbow Family Healing Gathering. The organization and structure that exists in these temporary communities is that which is minimally necessary to see that people's needs are met, their and the environment's health is protected, and that the general air of celebration keeps flowing.

The 1980 Gathering held in the Monongahela National Forest of West Virginia was the first to be held east of the Mississippi. Of the nine Gatherings held since '72, this year's was the smallest, attracting 3 to 4 thousand people. Last year 5 to 7 thousand people gathered in the White Mountains of Arizona, and before that 20 thousand came together in Oregon.

The West Virginia Gathering was set along the Williams River in a large expanse of rolling meadowland interspersed with groves of trees, all surrounded by six steep tree covered mountains. This meadow was once a company town called Three Forks, its only access being by a railroad built to haul out the timber. When the Great Depression came and the trees were gone, the town left. Now there remains one concrete foundation, a shallow well, numerous apple and cherry trees, and a memory among a few local people. The Forest Service now care-takes the valley, which proved to be of ample size for the number of people attending the Gathering. According to one district ranger quoted in the *Beckley Post-Herald*, "From an aesthetic standpoint, they probably couldn't have found a better site."

Coming into this year's Gathering, folks were first greeted by the Shanti Sena or Peace Keepers who explained that, as there were so many trees around, only unloading could happen at the Front Gate, with parking being at a remote site. A shuttle system into town and the parking area facilitated this system, thanks to the many folks willing to donate their time and vehicles to the service. For many, this was the Gathering's first example of a family providing for its needs. The second experience of family came upon reaching the trailhead where Shanti Sena stationed there welcomed everyone with a hug. Greetings of Welcome Home were shouted to everyone carrying camping gear, and embraces were more common than handshakes. Embraces worked so well in encouraging smiles and good times that Shanti Sena wandering throughout the site were called Hug and Kiss Patrols!

This year the trail into the Gathering site was not long. Just after crossing two shallow forks of the Williams River over stepping stones, people were invited to stop and rest at the Welcome Center. Here food, water and a little shelter was available, and a short orientation session, called Rap 107 was at first read to people, then later played on a tape player:

Howdy Folks, We Love You! Welcome Home!

Protect our watersources and our health—Hygiene, Health, Happiness & Hope, the four H's. Protect our land, kill no plants or animals, harmonize, walk gently, blend in. We are caretakers of the land. Be good neighbors, relate perfectly with all local residents. Build community fires only. **Watch your stuff: Tempt not lest ye be lifted from. Take only photographs, leave only foot prints!**

Volunteer—everyone helps, everything gets done! Everyone sharing the effort makes for a strong human tribe. Discourage these habits: Drinking alcohol, scamming, lifting. Problems? Contact Shanti Sena/Medical Center. Donations: Green energy to take care of your/our home.

Participate in all activities—Experience the Rainbow. Workshops—facilitate, attend, begin sharing, working. Council—alert, speak, listen, facilitate. Kiddie City—guides for our children, mimes, stories, childcare, Parade! Volunteer for Shanti Sena—mellow handling of difficulties, maintain unity, focus, harmony through discussion, truth, love, tribal respect. Welcome Center—Rap 107, greet the folks, Howdy! Welcome Home! Spread awareness, consciousness, and happiness. Firewatch. Shitters. Healing Center. Sweat Lodges. Herb Walkers. Hike Guides. Supply Depot —leave surplus food. Community Kitchens—Ever cook breakfast/dinner for us? Do it! Help us serve you! Info Center. Pitch in on the clean-up. Recycle. Reseed. Other Necessary Community Activities and Projects— We Need You. Please Help, Share, Learn, Enjoy, Celebrate, Communicate and Most of all Love Your Brothers and Sisters.

Down the main path, beyond the Welcome Center. It was a short walk under a canopy of leaves before the forest opened to the meadows. The first meadow, a ways off to the left, was the Healing Meadow where, at noon on the Fourth, people congregated for a contemplative silence during which, as was written for the first Gathering of the Tribes, 1972 in Colorado:

We, the invited people of the world may consider and give honor and respect to anyone or anything that has aided in the positive evolution of humankind and nature upon this, our most beloved and beautiful world—asking blessing upon we people of this world and hope that we people can effectively proceed to evolve, expand, and live in harmony and peace.

This silence ended with an om, then a shout heard and echoed around the Gathering site.

The second meadow, just to the right of the main path, was the Tipi or Lodge Circle. This year about a dozen lodges were erected. The view for those camped around the edges of the meadow made for a most beautiful and peaceful sight; the evening smoke spiraling up, or morning mist encircling and slowly rising above the tall white lodges, multi-colored tents scattered around, the green of grass and trees in the field, and the blue or grey of sky above.

In the early days of the Gathering the entire area that was exposed to the sun was filled with waist-high golden rod. The main path, and all others, were single file trails through these plants. As more people and tents appeared, the paths got ever wider, but the meadows kept their stands of golden rod. Only Center Fire meadow, around the Council Circle, had large groups of people in it which quickly overran the fibrous plants.

The Council Circle was the community center, and the main path went right to it, and beyond to the river where there were sweat lodges, a bucket shower and of course, space for swimming. The activities at the Council Circle were almost non-stop. The morning meal was served around the Center Fire as the people sat in concentric circles. The Main Kitchen was between the circle and the river, and the food, generally a cooked grain and fruit in the morning, and a thick soup, salad and sometimes bread in the evening, was served from large pots. The feeling of family, as people serving each other, was nicely facilitated by this food service system. The variety and quantity of the food was generally quite good, and the clean up system was quite efficient, with hot water and a rinse system done by volunteers. After each meal the councils began, one person speaking at a time, with an eagle feather as totem being passed to succeeding speakers. Access to the feather was open to everyone, and all issues of importance to the community were discussed. Information was given on sanitation procedures, local relations, and media (photographers had to ask permission of their subjects), lost children were connected with their parents, and volunteers were solicited for the many tasks to be done.

Around the periphery of the Council Circle people sat in the shade to talk, or played various games in the sun, including constant, day long volleyball. Much trading also happens here by the Council Circle, usually near the main path, with everything beautiful or useful (and generally small) being exchanged, except money. Anything hinting at commercialism and the use of money is discouraged at Healing Gatherings as the site is considered a temple, and its sanctity is to be respected.

In the evening the predominant social activity at the Gathering centered around the various fire places. Center Fire generally had the largest crowd, with all manner of non-electrical instruments, particularly drums, providing music. The dancing often went on many hours. In addition to the central community fire, there were many other fire places around the camp. At each Gathering there are a lot of individuals who attend as well as many groups or families. These families generally have their own community fires and, here too, there is music played far into the night. These various camps provide a wonderful variety of music for wandering revelers, and one camp, that of the Love Family, set up what served as a stage with candlelight reflectors providing very nice lighting. With rows of people sitting on a small hill side and several bands, soloists and short plays presented, it really resembled a concert. One earlier evening at a different site a fair number of local people came to enjoy a square dance. Thereafter, square dancing became a fairly regular evening attraction.

Music and dancing is always a major activity at the Gatherings with each Gathering site's particular natural setting and particular type of music common to that region of the country providing each year a unique experience.

The last day of each Gathering there is one major celebration that includes an air of pageantry as it is a presentation to the Gathering by the seven major families or service groups present. The number seven is used as it is the number of the primary colors in the rainbow, which symbolizes both the diversity of the human race and, as all the colors together comprise white light, further symbolizes humanity's basic unity.

Metanokett Village, New England community that facilitated the Kiddie City this year, began the pageant by leading the children's parade through the Council Circle. Then after people were seated around an open circle in the center of the meadow, Fantuzzi, a musician acting as master of ceremonies, announced that members of Metanokett Village would do the Dance of Numbers. This was a pantomime and dance adapted from the book, The Kin of Ata Are Waiting For You. Following them was Wavy Gravy of Merry Pranksters and Hog Farm fame doing a "blow-up" skit. Wavy spends much of his time at the Gatherings at Kid Village, and so, having such good rapport with the children, he called them all into the circle and asked, "Have you hugged a grown-up today?!" Everyone in the crowd wanting a hug from a child was then asked to raise a hand and the children ran to hug them all while the assemblage sang a song.

The third color of the rainbow was represented in a special way. All those who had helped by volunteering for any of the work that was done in service to the community, all the rainbow helpers, were asked to come into the center. Of course, soon the center was full, making the whole assemblage one large group. As a poster of the Earth with Saturn-like rings around it painted in rainbow colors was displayed from the center, everyone cheered each other and themselves for our wonderful Rainbow Sharing Energy.

Next Henry the Fiddler with musicians of the Love Family playing guitar and stand-up bass led the group in singing the traditional Gathering theme, "The Lion Sleeps At Night." Then Dramanon a Theatrical Family from Canada performed several songs and dances under a large banner reading "Life Force." Members of the Krishna community of New Vrindaban in southeastern West Virginia led everyone in the Hare Krishna Rama chant. As usual the Krishna folk brought only a few people to the Gathering but enough food to feed a hundred or more times their number. This is part of their faith as they believe that people who chant the names of God or who eat food that has been prepared by members of the faith, will be similarly blessed.

The Love Family made the last presentation, being announced as: New Jerusalem, Family of Peace. For the Love Family, as with each group, music was played and songs were sung. This continued all the way from the end of the morning council until the evening meal, then the music and dancing resumed until long into the night.

The Adversities

As the Rainbow Gatherings are essentially temporary communities, they include much of the same elements as do permanent communities; adversities as well as pleasures.

The weather at this year's Gathering, though not terribly adverse, at least could not be said to be totally in the spirit of things. Generally the temperature was nice, even at night it never was uncomfortably cool, but the skies were grey as often as they were blue. It rained about half of the days that there were a thousand or more people at the site. Usually the rain came down as a drizzle and it often dried up fairly well before the next day's rain, but the storm that came mid-festival really turned parts of the main path into a mud-way.

We first heard the storm coming as a great wind in the trees at the top of the mountain to the north of the site. The sound of the wind in the trees kept growing in intensity. We watched the line of violently swaying tree limbs advance steadily down the mountains until the wind was upon us, picking up everything not tied down, and tearing up things that were tied. Three lodges and a large army tent collapsed, most of the people getting out safely. The conical roof of the medical yurt was picked up and sailed. The parachute covering the Networking Center flew away and the large sheets of plastic protecting the Center's large site map and workshop notice board flapped violently until people who had been reading it cut it all down. Tree limbs snapped and fell and many tents, medium and small were flattened. Most people threw all their gear inside their tents and climbed in to hold them down, but one person was caught with an empty tent and, as it was a model that holds its shape through the tension created by slightly bent poles, the wind caught it and was almost strong enough to drag its owner along behind it. After the wind came the rain and everything exposed was drenched. Later in the afternoon as people rebuilt their shelters, the sun came out to the cheers of the whole camp!

Various other minor adversities cause some problems for some people. One of the problems involved the water which was presumed to be the cause of some mild cases of dysentery. It was summarily decided in council to chlorinate the community water, and suggested that those not wishing to drink chlorine could boil their water. As one woman put it, "make like you're in Mexico for a week."

The more serious problems were probably caused by the fact that this year's site was in a significantly more populated area than any prior Gathering. Being the Fourth of July holiday there were potential congestion problems in a local town due to an annual Pioneer Days Festival, and a potential conflict of use as the Gathering site is a favorite for the area coal miners who have their Miner's Holiday the first two weeks of July. There was one instance of gun shots fired from a vehicle into a camp site near a parking area one night, and earlier, before the Gathering actually started, two young women were found shot to death fifty miles from the Gathering. It was assumed that the two women were traveling to the Gathering as they carried some paper with the Rainbow name on it, so the local and not so local papers picked up and spread the story.

In response to this tragedy, the Council held a prayer vigil, then wrote and released a statement reading:

The Rainbow Family deeply regrets the tragic and senseless deaths of our sisters. We view this incident as one more of a long series of examples from our creator that this world is in dire need of more love and understanding. We stand unified in our purpose here and realize these deaths will only strengthen our resolve to create a world of peace and harmony. We wish to extend this call for unity to the people of the state of West Virginia.

We have visited with and been visited by many local people. The reception has been mutually friendly. The good people of this state, who share in our purposes, are invited to gather with the Rainbow Family. Together we can create a living example of peace and friendship.

Considering that the local people and authorities had little more means to understand who these Rainbow People were than to compare us with the hippy stereotype of more than a decade ago, the apprehension with which the plans for the Gathering were viewed is understandable. West Virginia's Secretary of State James Manchin in the Charleston Gazette termed the Family "derelicts," and Governor Jay Rockefeller said he wished the Family would stay away, but added that the state had no authority to block the Gathering. As a district ranger stated, "Its not a life or death situation where we feel we have to go in there and forcibly remove them." The rangers did, however, issue a few citations to document what was called the uncooperative nature of the Family as a record

for future Gatherings in other national forests. The ranger was quoted in the *Beckley Post-Herald,* "They've got to cooperate. They can't come in here and forcibly take over a forest and thumb their noses at us."

The reference to a thumbing of noses probably came from the disagreement between the Family and the Forest Service. In May the two parties agreed on criteria for deciding a Gathering site, but when the Scouting Council applied for a special use permit for the Three Folks of the Williams River area, the Forest Service declined stating that a more remote Gauley Mountain site would be more suitable. The Forest Service's Environmental Analysis cited poor parking and potential conflict of use at Three Forks site, but the Scouting Council refused to accept the Gauley Mountain site primarily because of poor access. This whole conflict continued right through the Gathering period, complete with media coverage. A permit never was issued, and because of the hassle, it was suggested that next year we not even apply. As it turned out, since less than a quarter of the number of people attended the Gathering as was projected, none of the Forest Service's concerns became a problem. But the Scouting Council will take one of the Forest Service's suggestions, and that is that the Scouting be done earlier, preferably the preceding Autumn.

As all this conflict was being reported in the local papers, more PR work was in order. Two meetings were therefore held. The first was between a few Rainbow spokes-people and members of the State Police, County Sheriff's Department, Forest Service, local City Police and City Council members. This meeting focused on the law enforcement aspects of the Gatherings, and it was explained how the Shanti Sena deals with various problems. Always it is best to deal with problems without using force, but when something unusual happens, the police are notified and the Shanti Sena works to isolate the trouble, moving people away from it. Clearly the folks in uniform were not satisfied, but the local people who attended the public meeting that happened later generally had a better impression. After some fiddle and washboard music, a presentation, slide show, and question and answer period, some of the 150 or so local people joined hands with the Rainbow representatives and sang "Will

the Circle Be Unbroken". The public meeting ended with the Rainbow folk inviting everyone out to a square dance, and two local women being quoted by a Charleston Daily Mail reporter as saying, "I think they're just great. I believe in what they're saying—being neighborly and all that" and, "If those people can get out in the world and make it a better place, then that's great."

Building a Better World

The people who support the Rainbow ideal, and who consider themselves part of the Family, are in many ways people who are optimistic about the possibility of building a society that nurtures the qualities of respect for life, of cooperatively providing for our needs, and of sharing responsibility for all our actions. These are the basics for the building of a family consciousness, an awareness that a society based on love and respect can be so much more harmonious and beautiful than is contemporary American culture.

This family consciousness is the major impression or concept that is conveyed to people as they experience the Rainbow Healing Gatherings. These celebrations are, in effect, much like a week long retreat or seminar in community living. The Gatherings are built by pulling together that which is common among the great diversity of individuals, and among the tribes or communities that attend. Future Gatherings can be a common meeting ground where our diversity can be explored, while we hold to an understanding of our basic unity. This is the potential of Healing Gatherings, and perhaps also a means to build a better world.

For many individuals, just that awareness of a basic unity is a new experience. It is evident that the desire for community is strong, as many people after experiencing a Gathering want to continue living in that form of cooperation. At this year's Gathering, a group split off from one of the Councils to talk about community. For some of the need was to find an existing community to join. For others, there was the idea of establishing a new community from among those present who had the pioneering spirit. This interest speaks of a great opportunity at Gatherings to connect people seeking community with those communities seeking members, and of connecting people with access to land wanting to support the establishment of a community with those people wishing to begin one.

There also exists at the Rainbow Gatherings the opportunity for the many diverse existing communities to share their diversity with each other. To learn of the experiences of the various families and to gain an understanding of the differences, and to perhaps thereby benefit each other. In this too there was interest shown at this year's Gathering. One workshop in particular was held for the sharing of information on child education in community. Some very interesting experiences were shared, and an offer was made by one person to collect addresses and contacts in various communities to begin collecting and distributing information on educational materials used. So much more of this kind of sharing is possible.

It is well known that the diversity among communities is great, even among those few that attend the Gatherings. But surely our diversity need not be threatened by building upon what unifies us. The Rainbow Gatherings could be a common ground for communities to extend their practice of sharing.

So much can be done in the interest of building a better world. So much has already been done, but there is so little awareness of it among the great majority of people. The outreach and consciousness raising that happens as a result of Rainbow Gatherings is certainly of great value to the concept of world betterment.

Finding a basis for unity among the great diversity of peoples inhabiting this land is a primary aspect of Rainbow Consciousness. There are basic truths common to all religions, and the feeling of brotherhood and sisterhood is understood by all. Therein we may find the basis for a social structure that provides for a plurality of lifestyles, and that provides a foundation upon which we may build an understanding of our unity-in-diversity.

How much of the potential for community building , that will be realized through the annual Rainbow Gatherings probably depends on the form of networking activities that are developed through the future. That potential can increase as at this year's Gathering there was interest expressed in the Vision Council of beginning to hold two Gatherings, one in the East, and one in the West. This will probably happen in '82 as it was decided that a Gathering should first be held in the Midwest before splitting the energy. Therefore, look to the upper mid-west for the 1981 Rainbow Gathering site.

idealistic, depending on which sixties analysis you are reading.) Everyone fought the good fight, except, of course, the folks we were fighting against. They didn't know it was the Good Sixties.

By contrast, in the Bad Seventies, there were no major social change movements. In fact, in a recent interview, Abbie Hoffman—and he should know—said that the seventies didn't even exist. In the Bad Seventies, there were only self-awareness movements and the New Narcissism and the Me Generation, and no one cared about anyone else.

This is the gospel of the chroniclers of the past two decades, and they recite it as solemnly and unquestioningly as second graders chanting the Pledge of Allegiance.

As with all mythology, the myth of the seventies and sixties has in it a nugget of truth, and it is this which gives it its terrible power to subvert reality. I expect that there were as many narcissists in 1967 as there were in 1977—some of them the same folks who were burning flags and marching— but they didn't have the institutionalized framework for their narcissism that existed in the seventies. Only the seventies could produce and market a magazine called *Self.*

And it's true that there was, in the sixties, on the part of a large minority (but it was always a minority) an active anger over the oppression of American Blacks and the war against the Vietnamese. (In the latter case, it is useful to remember that much of the impetus of the antiwar movement came from young men who didn't want to get their heads shot off—a wholesome but hardly altruistic motive.) And it's true that their anger eventually helped bring the war to an end.

But there were also other realities in the sixties and seventies, and in these realities can be seen a different and truer myth.

In the sixties, women died from botched abortions and from beatings quietly administered by their husbands and boyfriends, and women were raped, and women had babies they didn't want, and women dutifully prepared cocktail parties for their husbands' bosses or dinners for the men on their communes, and women put out for the sexual revolutionaries who had created yet another morality that left women's needs unheeded. And all the good radicals read Paul Goodman's *Growing Up Absurd,* and learned that men in America

SOJOURNER

From *Sojourner* 5, no. 5 (January 1980): 5, 22

Towards a New Recognition of Reality

by Karen Lindsey

We are, I am, you are
by cowardice or courage
the one who find our way
back to this scene
carrying a knife, a camera
a book of myths

This article first appeared in *Sojourner: The New England Women's Journal of News, Opinions, and the Arts,* 143 Albany St., Cambridge, MA 02139.

in which
our names do not appear.
　　　　　　　—Adrienne Rich,
　　　　　　"Diving Into the Wreck"

And now we leave it behind us, that much-maligned decade, the seventies. It was a bad decade. We know it was a bad decade because the media tell us it was, and the male left tell us it was, and the media and the male left never lie; except about each other.

The Bad Seventies stand in direct opposition to the Good Sixties, which many of us knew when it had not yet become the Good Sixties, but was simply the time we were living through and coping with. In the Good Sixties, everyone cared about civil rights and ending the war; everyone loved each other and hated what was wrong. (This was either naive or

led stifled lives but of course that wasn't true of women (wrote Goodman) because we got to have babies and type men's manuscripts.

And by the end of the sixties a lot of women had gotten fed up and they created a new movement, and in the seventies that movement grew into the strongest and most revolutionary and most magnificent social movement in the history of the world. And it threatened, for the first time in the history of Man, the very foundations of power: it stripped off the masks of history, the history of the left as well as the right; it screamed out that the emperor had no clothes.

And the emperor was scared shitless. The power of this movement was awesome; it was terrifying. It threatened not only men's sovereignty, but, inevitably, women's accommodation to that sovereignty. It threatened the lies we had accepted about ourselves in order to live with the degradation from which we had seen no escape. And the men in power fought the movement with lies, with distortions, with trivialization, and, most effective of all, with cooptation. And this is the story of the seventies that the patriarchal myth has hidden—the story of the rise of this incredible movement, this Goddess/Fury, and of the attempt to destroy it.

One of the sounder bits of wisdom to slip through the patriarchy is Christ's command to "love thy neighbor as thyself." Its wisdom rests in the profundity of the equation: each is necessary. Love for others is rooted in love for the self, love for the self extends to identification with others who are also selves. The women's movement of the late sixties and seventies took that wisdom a step further, from a deeper understanding of love than any male prophet could ever have. The personal, said the movement, is political.

If Christian society needed to pervert the wisdom of its own founder, to change his demand for integration into a dichotomy between self-love and other-love, how much more patriarchy needs to defuse the power of "the personal is political." And so the feminist insistence that women return to their selfhood—a selfhood battered down by centuries of oppression—became interpreted as a call to isolated personal (material, sexual, pseudo-spiritual) advancement, in the male mode, while abandoning all concern for others. In this framework, the feminist attack on the nuclear family was translated into a call to ignore all affection and responsibility toward others; the feminist demand that women respect and cherish their own sexuality was portrayed as a male-style quest for a collection of impersonal orgasms.

In the seventies, as women struggled for liberation (often putting in 24-hour days and seven-day weeks organizing demonstrations and consciousness-raising groups, building shelters for rape victims and battered women, compiling and exposing the hidden statistics of our oppression), the patriarchy invented the Liberated Woman. The Liberated Woman (a.k.a. the Cosmo girl, swinger, lady executive, etc.), is a careful and essential construction of the male power structure (this doesn't mean that it's conscious, only that it's deliberate). Women must be made to perceive this figure as the goal feminists are describing. They must first be seduced by her allure and then disillusioned by her shallowness, and then finally return to the forgiving arm of the patriarchy. This return is the patriarchal agenda for the eighties.

To frame the Liberated Woman, the patriarchy has, with some success, created the New Narcissism, which the media have dutifully expanded out of all realistic proportion, and then righteously condemned. The New Narcissism, though it poses as an androgynous concept, is chiefly a definition tailored to fit the self-absorbed woman: men have always been given the right to be self-absorbed. And there are enough women around to take on the role—out of greed, desperation, lack of imagination, lack of other bearable alternatives. More important, there are many more women to guiltily perceive their own honest efforts at self-definition as the New Narcissism and who, failing to find the instant self-fulfillment the New Narcissism pretends to offer, are prime candidates for a retreat to altruism. The Liberated Woman has been created as a facade covering up true feminism, precisely so that when the facade is knocked down, feminism itself will be destroyed.

Our agenda for the eighties, then, must be to fight the efforts to obliterate our movement. And we must do this simultaneously within ourselves and with the outside world. Patriarchy sustains itself with false dichotomies: if we accept these dichotomies, we embrace our own destruction. The personal is political; the political is personal. Self-love (which is not narcissism) and other-love (which is not altruism) are inseparable, interwoven, life-confirming realities.

It isn't easy to be a feminist, to simultaneously live in the undefined, evolving space of a new world and cope with our existence in a patriarchy that we can destroy only slowly, only over a long and painful period of time. It means lobbying legislatures in which we don't believe, in order that their laws can be made a little less brutal and a few more of our people survive. It means shaking in helpless rage while some of us die of starvation, of battering, of psychological withering, because there's not enough we can do yet to save them. It means creating what shelter we can for those women we can save. It means facing the fact that the woman who is today the shelterer may tomorrow be the victim in need of shelter, or for whom there is no shelter. It means understanding and forgiving our own limitations: knowing that we will face betrayal, trashing, desertion not only from men but from each other, and not being shattered by that knowledge. It means knowing that sisterhood is often a reality but more often a goal: we bring to everything we do the baggage of our patriarchal training, and we will fail each other as often as we nurture each other.

Above all—because the rest is lost without it—being feminists means not allowing the patriarchs to define us. The New Narcissism is their myth, not ours, and we are no more bound to it than we are to the male messiah or the happy housewife or the noble soldier. The seventies saw the growth of the most monumental movement in history, and that is our truth. No matter how bitter, burned-out, frustrated, terrified we are—and we have reason to be all these things—we cannot allow ourselves to lose that knowledge. We must bring with us into the eighties not their myths, but our realities.

Cultural Correspondence

From *Cultural Correspondence*, no. 9 (Spring 1979), pp. 52-53, 57, 59

Toward Emancipatory Culture and Media Politics

by Douglas Kellner

EDITOR'S NOTE: *The following is the first in a series of dicussions by participants in various local media projects. Austin Community Television (ACTV) has begun producing "Alternative News," an hour-long newsmagazine on a community access station, in addition to its other work.*

Given the cultural-political importance of television, the American Left's lack of a theory and practice of media politics is distressing. We must recognize that television is increasingly important as a vehicle of socialization and as a site of political communication and struggle, and devise a strategy to come to terms with this fact. In order to do this, the Left must change its attitude toward the electronic media, especially television, and recognize its potential for communications that might promote social change. Although many radicals have realized the importance of cultural practices, there has been little discussion of cultural politics for the broadcasting media. But let's face it. If we want to communicate with and politically educate/entertain large numbers of people, we must use the broadcasting media, above all television.

Despite the current use of television as a vehicle of hegemonic ideology and political manipulation, it is defeatist and self-defeating to argue that television is in itself evil or regressive. Television is an instrument of unrealized possibilities. It could mobilize people, and entertain and educate on an unprecedented scale. It could democratize culture so that everyone could share in the cultural heritage, undermining the prerogatives of cultural elitism. It could allow people to understand the working of

their society and government. It could help eliminate prejudices and biases of all sorts through communicating a better understanding of minorities and engaging in radical enlightenment. It could be used to reconstruct society and consciousness, and to change the world in ways as yet unforeseen.

There are, of course, risks here. It is sometimes argued that the very form of the electronic media imposes passivity on its audience, and more and better television might simply mean increased passivity and political apathy. Innovations such as electronic voting might create a specious sense of democracy and a facade of participation in societal processes. Further, media technology is now controlled by corporations who will fight uses of the media that contradict its interests. Developing an emancipatory culture and media politics should be connected with an anti-capitalist political movement, and should not suffer any illusions that change in media technology and production will suffice to bring about radical social change.

Nonetheless, these risks must be taken. Many are predicting that cable-satellite TV will break network hegemony and will open new channels of communication that could be used to transmit a more emancipatory culture. More television channels, home video-recorders, video-discs, and the like, give people more choice and control over their cultural environment. Further, citizen-band radio and some new cable TV systems provide for two-way communication, allowing the individual to overcome the passivity imposed by the present media system. We need to be aware that with the proliferating electronic technology and expanding communications markets, more and more electronic media productions will be demanded which will open new channels for emancipatory cultural production.

Unfortunately, many people are not yet fully aware of the tremendous potential of cable and satellite television. There are already operative forty channel cable systems with two-way communication. Cable-satellite TV makes it technically possible for a group producing video programs in, say, San Francisco to show their works in Austin, Columbia, New York or Boston. Already, Home Box Office is showing recent, uncut movies to hundreds of thousands of homes across the country, the Christian Broadcasting Network and the PTL (Praise the Lord) Club programs are shown on many cable systems, porn movies are being regularly shown on many cable systems and local video groups and special interest groups are showing their productions on local cable stations. Important changes are thus taking place in the communications media. Radicals, too, must get into the act, and take advantage of existing media potentials and plan for the future.

Although we should reject the disdain for television that has marked so many radical theories, we must also beware of the sort of technological optimism found in Benjamin, Brecht and to some extent Enzensberger. Hence we need both a critical theory of the culture industry and television ideology, and a coherent radical media strategy based on the technical potentials of the electronic media, and the contradictions in the media industries that might allow emancipatory cultural production to take place.

Some groups have begun taking initial steps in this direction, but their efforts must be supported and stepped up if we are to effectively develop a socialist media politics. For example, socialist media groups have been meeting in Los Angeles and San Francisco to discuss possibilities of emancipatory communication within the existing media. Socialist feminists have been writing for Norman Lear; Cine Manifest has had dramas produced on PBS; a NAM sponsored production *Union Maids* was shown on PBS; Barbara Kopple's academy award winning *Harlan County, USA* was shown on the Home Box Office Network and PBS; different cultural and political groups have been using local public access cable channels and videotape for political education; and groups in Boston and around the country at various Pacifica radio stations have been trying to develop a socialist radio politics. We now have two major independent national radical print journals, and other print media. We must also begin getting into the electronic media, and using them to communicate our critique of capitalist society and vision of an alternative society.

There have been over 500 public access movement groups all over the country, struggling for more public access to the media. It is argued that the first amendment right to free speech contains a right to communicate, and a right to be heard. The "fairness doctrine" stipulates that all sides of an issue should be heard, that the broadcast industries must "devote a reasonable amount of broadcast time to the discussion of controversial issues; and to do so fairly, in order to afford reasonable opportunity for opposing viewpoints." The "first amendment" and "fairness doctrine" thus provide constitutional and legal grounds for radical access to the media. Why not radicals' participation in the public access movement, pushing ideas and cultural productions, testing the political waters and electronic wires, seeing what can be done and what cannot, discovering what works and what doesn't work? Areas which have existing public access channels provide the opportunity for radical groups to make videotapes which can be shown on local TV. For instance, in Austin, when there is an important conference or cultural event it is videotaped and shown on the local public access channel. Eventually, an impressive tape library will be collected and could be exchanged with other groups.

The Austin Television Group has been meeting regularly in Austin, Texas for three years, studying the American communication system, and attempting to develop a theory of media politics. We urge an immediate, short-term strategy for existing radical groups to explore the possibilities of using local media more effectively as instruments of political communication and education. We also support radical cultural production of film, video, and documentaries, and would like to see a national left distribution network emerge so that the producers of emancipatory culture could have a distribution system and large audiences at their disposal. Finally, we want to begin devising a long term strategy to effectively utilize existing and emerging technology, and to map models of future media systems, in which electronic media are used as instruments of education and emancipation rather than of social control. We are currently working on these problems and hope that individuals who share our goals and are interested in this project will communicate with us and share their ideas and struggles. We hope in the future to produce a more detailed program of media politics, as the conclusion to our collective book on American television, based on the existing activities of radical groups and future possibilities for emancipatory media-political action.*

A Symposium: Why We Watch TV

[Two Selected Articles]

EDITOR'S NOTE: *In spite of our appeals, dear readers, few have stepped forward to admit that yes, they watch television, and give us a few reasons why. Guilt anxieties? Befuddlement? "You first"? Whatever the cause, we publish a few contributions below. Reflect like them!*

Sports

by James P. O'Brien

Two years ago this magazine (i.e., *Cultural Correspondence*—ed.)† trained the glaring searchlight of Marxian analysis on the shadowy world of TV football. The historical truth which emerged from this encounter is known to us today as the Falling Rate of Excitement.

At the risk of vulgarizing, the F.R. of E. basically states that professional football has a built-in tendency to become more boring over time. This is so chiefly because a defense can be devised to stop every offense. Various techniques have been used by the owners and the TV people to counteract the Falling Rate (the most notable being the introduction of instant replay in the early '60s), but it keeps making itself felt.

Has this analysis stood the test of time? You bet it has! The inexorable workings of the F.R. can best be seen in the frantic efforts of the moguls to evade its consequences. During the past two years, three major tactics have been employed in the cause of staving off viewer boredom and keeping profits high. These tactics have been: rules changes to allow more scoring, schedule changes to produce more suspenseful games, and cheerleader changes to augment violence with sex in the game's TV appeal. Each of these tactics will be discussed in turn, but it is the third that will be of the most general interest.

Unfortunately I've forgotten what the exact rules changes were this fall, but the major ones were aimed at helping the offense and restricting the defense. *E.g.,* blockers were allowed to use their arms more without being charged with "holding." The object was to make it easier for teams to score points. The Tank McNamara comic strip satirized this goal by having an economist advise the owners simply to declare each touchdown to be worth more points.

In preparing for the 1978-79 season, the owners also manipulated the schedule to produce fewer mismatches. The better a team does one season, the tougher its schedule will be the following year. (Of course you still have to play the other guys in your own division, twice each, but this has to do with the teams you play outside your division.) This seems a little on the socialistic side, but profits have always been more important than ideology, and nothing bores the fans more than one-sided games.

Well, you can lead a viewer to the living room, but you can't make him turn on the TV set. Despite the frantic improvisations, the audience for pro football this fall was 5 per cent smaller than the previous year. Furthermore, in my experience, the non-watchers are getting more aggressive and are starting to ridicule the watchers.

It is when we come to the third tactic, the off-again on-again employment of thinly dressed cheerleaders, that we get a sense of the overall framework in which televised pro football is trapped. Prior to the 1978-79 season, it looked as though pro football would be a full participant in a general TV trend away from violence and toward sex. Last year's Superbowl telecast had included innumerable shots of the Dallas Cowboy cheerleaders, to sustain viewer interest between playing (not that the plays themselves were anything but dull in that game). Over the spring and summer team after team announced that it would hire sexy cheerleaders and give them flimsy uniforms. It looked as though the TV broadcasts would feature the cheerleaders as much as the players, and that pro football would bask in the kind of audience

---

*Those participating in radical media politics should write us and send us material on their efforts and strategy, so we can assemble information on media politics for our forthcoming book. Write c/o Douglas Kellner, Department of Philosophy, University of Texas, Austin, Texas 78712.

†In actuality this is the writer's private joke. Either he missed something or we have.

appeal that "Charlie's Angels" had shown was possible.

Yet by the end of the season the tactic had been all but abandoned. Telecasts were including a mere handful of cheerleader shots per game, and only in the most half-hearted fashion. There was more sex on a recent installment of the Muppets Show (Raquel Welch doing a torrid dance) than in the late-season football telecasts.

Why didn't the tactics work? I would say there were interrelated reasons. First, the cheerleader shots were gratuitous, not an integral part of the game at all. "Charlie's Angels" has a story line, but the cheerleader shots were transparent in having no purpose other than voyeurism. For this reason, they were an embarrassment to those fans whom they didn't annoy. They also were vulnerable to two separate sources of opposition: family-oriented puritanical opposition to any "immorality" on TV, and opposition to the use of women as sex objects. Undoubtedly, given the overwhelmingly male audience for TV football and the nature of the corporate sponsors, the first type of opposition was much more important than the second. But there are straws in the wind that suggests that women's consciousness has pervaded the culture enough to have placed some limits on the way the networks used the cheerleaders. For example, the name of the Dallas cheerleaders was changed this year from Dallas Cowgirls to Dallas Cowboy Cheerleaders; similarly, the Los Angeles Rams' group was at first named the Embraceable Ewes but the name was quickly dropped.

Whatever the reasons, the failure of the cheerleader tactic suggests that pro football will have to rely on its own inherent appeal to keep its audience. And all the scurrying and the gimmickry that the owners have resorted to only suggests the limits of that inherent appeal.

Watchin' the Dream Television . . .

by Paul Buhle

1) Enactment of the *First Surrealist Manifesto* round-the-clock for several weeks. Animated actors include Bugs Bunny, Isadora Duncan, Victoria Woodhull, Little Nemo, André Breton, Harpo Marx and Peetie Wheatstraw ("The Devil's Son-in-Law"). Host Franklin Rosemont, dressed in a large rabbit suit above the waist (ears included) and tuxedo pants, introduces a circle of intimates—Lenora

Carrington as a luminous bird, Aimé Césaire as the sound of wind through the jungle. A.K. El Janaby as Wisdom, Philip Lamantia as the Spirit returning to the origins of human creativity . . .

2) Sports, with Marx Naison, Heywood Hale Broun and Muhammad Ali: Jewish boy meets genteel gent and jive jock. Horses make demands upon their jockeys. Football players (as O'Brien suggests) award the ball to the team that needs it most. Cheerleaders join the Women's Movement. And Lester Rodney is prevailed to come out of retirement as the next commissioner of baseball. Alternates with the New Captain Video, a sitcom (or "civcom," as civilization-comedies will be known) scripted by Naomi Weisstein, with Lily Tomlin as the Captain, Alan Alda and Richard Pryor as Lefttenants in pursuit of extragallactic humor.

3) The Ishmael Reed Hour. Reed regularly blisters Xtianity and Western Civilization as "White Folks Stuff" through a combination of antic memories of American popular culture, crank hints of Cosmic Conspiracy and the best poetry to reach the screen. Millions of white viewers offer to sacrifice themselves to Reed's bad temper. Reed can't decide whether to accept or not, become the world's craziest anarchist or a disciplined Socialist . . . Alternates with Lee Marrs' Women, animated by Trina, Michelle Brand, Aline Kominsky and the rest of the gang . . .

4) Dreamers & Drug Visions, animations with Paul Garon as host and ghost, several frog-like figures as his guests (Froggy the Gremlin, Griffy's Mr the Toad) and part-time dreamers drifting in and out of transparency. Alternates with the Charles Fort Comedy Hour, the slap-

stick version of In Search Of.

5) News of the Future, the program that asks the question: If I could have been happy in any century, why was I born in *this* one? Ursula LeGuin scripts.

6) News of the Present, with Danny Schechter and Todd Gitlin. Real news. Revolutions and non-revolutions from the perspective of the bottom up. Daily life in Milwaukee, Guatemala City and Moscow.

7) Roots Hours. Entertaining comedy variety and drama telling about the origins and continuity of immigrant life in the U.S., with the cultural values under stress, in dissolution and potential revival today. Multilingual sections encourage common use of second, third and fourth languages in the population at large.

8) Native American Television. *Akwesasne Notes* of the air. Poetry, visions, humor, agricultural, ritual, daily life before the White Man.

9) Women's Own. Series featuring the finest comediennes from television's past and present—Eve Arden, Audrey Meadows, Ann Sothern, Jean Stapleton—scripted and directed by themselves and their assistants.

10) Back porch television. Locally produced shows with use of commercial facilities. Stress upon regional and local/neighborhood/ethnic values. Includes Saturday Day Nite Live every night, a return to live television.

11) TV exchange. More foreign shows dubbed in English. Foreign produced shows from American money, beginning with a series of dramatizations of African and West Indian novels.

Other demands? Send 'em in!

A REVIEW OF CONTEMPORARY CINEMA

From *Jump Cut*, no. 20 (May 1979), p. 30

Eyewitless News: An Amusing Aid to Digestion

by Tim Patterson

Reprinted with permission from *Jump Cut: A Review of Contemporary Cinema*.

"O.K., Rex, thank you—too bad the Sox got bombed. Coming up: film of last night's big fire, an update on all those civil wars in South America, Betty Lovely with a consumer report on the best bagel shop in Poughkeepsie, and the Channel 5 Action-cam takes us behind the scenes at—get this!—a co-ed Turkish bathhouse."

Only the names have been changed to protect the guilty. Any night of the week, viewers in most cities can chuckle their way through their own version of local "Eyewitless News."

For the past several years, local news shows have placed an increasing emphasis on turning news into entertainment, turning reporters into celebrities and turning short film clips into a substitute for journalism. As the competition for local ratings has intensified, the rivalry among these public affairs situation comedies has grown accordingly. WLS-TV, the ABC affiliate in Chicago, is generally credited with pioneering the concept of "Happy News" a half dozen years ago. Its success in the ratings led ABC to spread the format to the four other major city stations it directly owns and operates. By now elements of the approach have been picked up and incorporated into local news shows on nearly every commercial station in the country. As if further evidence were needed, the illusion of autonomy on the part of local tv stations is effectively punctured by the remarkable congruence of news formats in different cities.

The local news used to be a disaster area in the ratings, as well as in its content, but at least the former has changed dramatically in the era of happy talk. FCC figures for fiscal 1976 (the latest available) indicate that net profits for local stations jumped an average of 70.7%, the biggest rise for any segment of the tv industry. And the highest ratings (and therefore highest advertising time rates) for locally-originating programming these days are consistently held by the evening local news. While it may be a little depressing to think of happy news as a model of successful media innovation, rather than as an example of pathetic neglect, that's what it is.

Apparently, the audience eats it up. Since the only way viewers can punish their local tv station is by turning it off, the rise in the ratings seems to indicate that the audience has wrested a concession out of the media. In a sense, that is probably true: with most of the people in the U.S. highly skeptical about both public officials and the media, happy news has a considerable advantage over the drier old-fashioned style of delivery. For straight news to be appealing enough to leave the set on, it has to be perceived as at least minimally true and informative; eyewitless news only has to be amusing and an aid to digestion, which is certainly more up the media's alley. So the local news audience has gotten what it wanted in the same narrow sense in which moviegoers have won their demands

for JAWS, STAR WARS and yet another Clint Eastwood epic.

The success of happy news lies in its reflection—even anticipation—of trends in the entertainment programming on tv and in mass commercial popular culture generally in the past few years, including the attempt to turn everyone in sight into a star of at least local magnitude. A major part of the eyewitless strategy is the recruitment and exposure of attractive, photogenic news "personalities", selected on the basis of their sex appeal rather than their journalistic credentials. A premium is placed on the ability to project a fresh, spontaneous image in a contrived atmosphere of informality, and on a newscaster's capacity to provoke a strong, personal audience response.

The extreme of the selection process for choice anchor slots in the larger cities verge on science fiction. Stations can contract with established testing firms which will conduct experiments with mock newscasts on closed-circuit tv to an audience wired with electrodes that measure skin response and the behavior of their sweat glands. More to the point, this bio-journalistic wizardry is at the service of a thriving and very mobile market for newscasters, who circulate through the ranks of the farm-league stations on their way to the majors with maximum fanfare. *Variety,* the leading show business trade paper, devotes a full page every week to reports of how much stations are paying to snap up heralded anchorpeople. Spots on local stations that plug the newscasts emphasize either the current star performer, the infectious collective spirit of the whole newsgang, or both.

The key anchorperson is nearly always a white male in his thirties, with women and minorities confined to supporting roles, to specialized "consumer reports" or similar features, or to the late-night and weekend newscasts that draw considerably smaller audiences. The racist and sexist mold tv news is cast in certainly predates happy news, and the proportion of women and minority faces on the screen has inched upwards in recent years, but the newer format can claim no credit for even these token advances.

And in the case of female newscasters in particular, greater prominence on the evening news has been a decidedly mixed blessing. Women, at least in subsidiary roles, are essential foils for the zippy humor of the happy newsmen, since a dash of sexual innuendo, as every tv producer

knows by now, is definitely good for digestion. Speculation about on- and off-air romances can add voyeurism to the proceedings, and occasional participation by an attractive female newswoman in a wet T-shirt contest can provide an added promotional bonus.

The rise of the photogenic non-journalist has been accompanied by a proliferation of several kinds of non-news filler. "People in the news" segments are common, yet another manifestation of the current super-promotion of celebrities throughout the U.S. media. Consumer advice departments do dispense some useful information, but function primarily as ad campaigns for consumerism in general or as free advertising for specific products. The "action line" segments that many local stations have copied from newspapers do manage to retrieve several lost welfare checks a year and hasten installation of a few traffic signals, but they certainly aren't news; more than that, they encourage political passivity, by turning over the fight against your local bureaucracy to the bureaucracy at your local tv station.

The growing clutter of non-news items has apparently outgrown the bounds of the news shows themselves. NBC has had good results with national distribution of its "Evening Magazine" concept, which is simply an additional half hour of frisbee championships, celebrity profiles and tips on flower arranging, filling the slot after the half hour of national network news. (NBC, in fact, has also been the leader in happifying its national news, with John Chancellor and David Brinkley lounging on the edges of their desks in a revamped set.)

The innovations of eyewitness news are a triumph of form over content. The essential structural strategy of contemporary news programming is making the show as fast-paced as possible, with a higher number of shorter items using the maximum amount of film or videotape footage. Film is highly prized for its visual appeal, which builds in a bias against "dull" stories that require detailed and complex analysis but which do not photograph well. News shows move along at a rapid clip to command continued viewer attention, with a sizeable portion of each brief item often being the transitions to and from the surrounding items. The sequence of items is determined not by their substantive overrelation, but by the conventions of effective program construction—the proper mix and alternation of "light" and "hard" news, film clips and "talking heads," and "good news" and "bad news." The opportunity to draw connections and provide a synthesizing perspective is not only passed up by the stations themselves; it is made prohibitively difficult for the audience, which is presented with a daily bag of jigsaw puzzle pieces with no completed picture as a guide.

One of the most significant improvements in video technology in recent years has been the development of lightweight portable cameras that make on-the-spot coverage considerably easier. Unfortunately, the technology is frequently used by having the "Action-Cam" or "Instant Eye" turn a non-news story into "news", or by giving even greater prominence to police blotter and disaster reports. Demonstrations can provide graphic film clips, but the visual pull is used to neglect or distort why any particular, anonymous crowd has taken to the streets.

Portable cameras and improved remote broadcasting equipment have also enlarged the possibilities for reporters to become participants in the events they cover. There have been numerous instances where tv reporters have served as negotiators in armed confrontations, suicide attempts and similar dramatic incidents while the station suspended normal programming to carry the story live. In such a situation, the "story" becomes the station and its reporter, a remarkable variation on the media's creation of the news.

The combination of pretested personalities, witty banter and rapid-fire action footage amounts to an avoidance of the traditional responsibilities of journalism, even of bourgeois journalism. With items running usually under 30 seconds, with the camera taking precedence over the reporter, with mindless filler given equal billing with hard news, there is no room for serious, in-depth examination of major economic, social and political developments that affect the lives of the viewers. There is almost no investigative reporting done by local news staffs, merely packaging of news from the papers, wire services and official press releases, and it is not simply nostalgia that suggests that there has been a demonstrable decline in the performance of textbook journalistic functions.

The significance of this degeneration of bourgeois standards of professionalism is hard to assess. It is true that the higher ratings for local happy news shows mean that more people are getting at least the

tidbits of "real" news that are sandwiched between the slices of fluff. It is also true that the major electronic and print press outlets have always presented an ideologically distorted version of the news and suppressed a correct analysis of capitalist society. Happy news is surely not by its nature any more conducive to reactionary than to "liberal" content, and the eyewitless trend does not seem also to be a rightward trend. The shift to happy news is a shift in the form of mystification, not a fundamental change in the basic function of the press as an institution of social control and class domination.

At the same time, the eyewitless trend does have important implications, espe-cially when viewed as a microcosmic representation of market-oriented U.S. culture as a whole at the present time. A culture which can't stomach news about itself unless it is disguised as or replaced by entertainment has got to be in some kind of serious trouble.

But where do you get a film clip for that story?

We thank the Guardian *for permission to reprint a revised version of Tim Patterson's article which appeared in their pages last year. The* Guardian *offers the most extensive national and international news coverage on the left from an independent Marxist-Leninist position. Subs: $17/yr and 6-week trials for $1; 33 W. 17th St., New York, NY 10011.*

From *Seven Days* 4, no. 1 (April 1980): 29–31

What George Bush Didn't Say to *Seven Days*

by Barbara Ehrenreich and Annette Fuentes

What would campaign coverage be without in-depth interviews of the major candidates? We felt we owed it to our readers to bring them a close-up, personal view of at least one of the leading candidates. As a challenge we picked George Bush—former U.S. congressman, U.S. delegate to the U.N., special envoy to China under Nixon, head of the CIA under Ford, decorated World War II Air Force pilot and self-styled Horatio Alger of the oil-drilling industry.

But we ran into one obstacle after another. We couldn't afford the plane fare to New Hampshire. We couldn't find Bush's home address anywhere. At the Bush-for-President Headquarters in New York, the staff suggested that we were too young to vote. Undaunted, we assigned Barbara Ehrenreich and Annette Fuentes to do the interview *without* George Bush. It wasn't easy. For weeks they immersed

themselves in a subject that puts most people to sleep in minutes—studying every detail of George Bush's biography. Then, using special computer techniques, they were able to produce a simulated interview, far more accurate than the real George Bush could have given us.

So here it is, the first published interview to probe behind the colorless, vacuous, bland exterior to the real man underneath.

How do you think your experience as director of the CIA has helped prepare you to run the country?

Well, in the CIA we ran *several* countries. Iran for twenty-five years, Chile for about seven now, South Korea—jeez, I can't even remember them all now. One country more or less shouldn't be all that difficult.

We've heard that when the Justice Department was investigating the assassination of Orlando Letelier, you misled them by providing CIA documents on the Chilean Left—even though you knew former CIA agents and Pinochet's boys had pulled the caper . . .

Some caper, huh? Right in the heart of D.C.

Sir, there was nothing illegal in what you did?

Illegal, no! My job was to weaken our enemies, not fink on our friends. And where would I be now if I hadn't covered for the intelligence community? Floating in the Potomac face down for all I know.

There's a rumor that, if nominated you might cross party lines and call on Lyndon LaRouche former head of the National Caucus of Labor Committees as a running mate. Anything to that?

At first I was put off by LaRouche's running as a Democrat, but I have to say in all honesty that he's the only candidate besides myself that the CIA has real confidence in. And he's the only candidate, besides myself, who's had the experience of running a major international intelligence operation. [See box] I don't know if I go all the way with his—what is it? Labor Party's—plan for a preemptive strike at England, but we're only talking about a VP now, and they all mellow in time, Heck, Mondale used to be a liberal.

You told the L.A. Times *that you are convinced that the U.S. could come out of a nuclear war with a "survivability rate" greater than 5 percent. If there were to be a nuclear war in the next few months, how do*

Likeable Lyndon LaRouche

With talk of a Bush-LaRouche GOP/ Democratic ticket in the elections, *Seven Days* takes a brief look at the least-discussed presidential candidate— Lyndon LaRouche.

Best known as ex-chair of the U.S. Labor Party (USLP) and founder of NCLC (National Caucus of Labor Committees), LaRouche is the only candidate who doesn't care if he's elected. He thinks President Carter should appoint him to the vice-presidency and then resign so La-Rouche could automatically ascend to the Oval Office.

Whether elected or appointed, La-Rouche's vast experience in covert intelligence operations here and abroad, and his alleged connections with the CIA and the FBI, make him an ideal partner for ex-CIA director George Bush.

The Citizens for LaRouche campaign headquarters in New York City shares a floor with a press service publications office and the intelligence branch of NCLC. Every day this beehive of intelligence-gathering activity disseminates information, gleaned from periodicals, phone calls, and two international Telex systems, to regional offices and affiliates in 26 European cities.

International contacts in various political parties and foreign governments make LaRouche the best-informed candidate, he claims. He doesn't have to depend on the U.S. news media for information and wouldn't want to because he believes it's controlled by the Carter administration anyway. That's why, LaRouche says in a campaign handout, Americans don't know that the hostages in Iran are under the control of former Attorney General, Ramsey Clark, that a British-Zionist conspiracy to take over the world exists, or that Carter hopes to invade and conquer Mexico.

LaRouche intelligence operatives in Concord, New Hampshire, recently engaged in an "undercover number," impersonating local reporters in order to investigate alleged threats to their candidate's life from the Keene *Sentinel*, the Manchester *Union* and other New Hampshire papers. LaRouche, uniquely able to unveil assassination threats against his life at any moment, defended the espionage as "necessary for security," explaining that "these amateurs are not supposed to play games with people of my rank; otherwise they get chewed up . . . they are going to be lucky to get jobs as ditch diggers [sic!] when I get through with these characters."

Hans Magnus Enzensberger, a left-wing German writer, and unspecified "Iranian terrorists" are others who, for unknown motives, are plotting to murder LaRouche, according to the USLP paper *New Solidarity*.

Does he have a political future with so many people trying to eliminate him? Fortunately, LaRouche's supporters include some fifty antiterrorists security guards, specially trained in martial arts, sniping, and surveillance.

you think it would affect the outcome of the 1980 elections?

It depends, of course, on *which* 5 percent survives. Looking at present ownership of bomb shelters, home decontamination units, etc., I would figure the survivors to be about 92 percent Republicans. There would be a definite impact on the elections, and, from a strictly partisan point of view, I would say a positive one.

What do you say to the rumors we've picked up in Republican circles that you're just a stalking horse for Jerry Ford?

I resent that kind of talk. It is true that Mr. Ford's rehabilitation therapist has recommended that he not campaign in person ever since an injury to his chin, sustained, I believe, at a podium in Cincinnati. But I haven't worked for the man for several years now. In fact I'd like to stress that I've been on my own ever since I left my dad at the age of 24 and went out to Texas to start a few oil companies. I had only $385 and a note from dad. [Bush's father was a director of the oil company he first worked for.]

We're not questioning your independence, but what about the money you received from Nixon's campaign slush fund in 1970?

There was nothing political about that. Before President Nixon gave me that job as U.S. delegate to the U.N., I used to do a few things around the Nixon home—picking up Tricia at the hairdresser's, taking Checkers out, things like that. It was off the books, but that's no reason to castigate a man for life.

If you're elected, where do you see former President Nixon fitting into your administration?

Considering his ground-breaking work in foreign policy, I've discussed with my staff the possibility of offering him a position as Special Envoy to New York. He knows the people, their customs, and frankly there's just no other leading Republican in political life who's actually prepared to live there.

You've served on the board of Eli Lilly, the drug company, which has come under a lot of criticism because of DES. Would you comment on DES?

I have to admit that I'm not familiar with that group. I do support the D.A.R. [Daughters of the American Revolution] wholeheartedly, but DES I just don't know about.

DES is a synthetic hormone which has been found to cause cancer of the vagina in . . .

Listen, if this is not something I would feel comfortable talking about to my wife Barbara and our five children, none of whom, to my knowledge, even knows what the word "premarital" means, I certainly am not going to discuss it with the press.

Maybe this is a good time to get into your stand on homosexuality. You've stated that you would like to see the issue "just go away." What kind of a position is that? Aren't you just evading the issue?

If you're one of those people who's trying to insinuate that I'm not tough enough to be President, I want to go on record right now that I'm very tough. Very, very tough. And ever since I was a kid in prep school it's made me very, very angry when . . .

Could we just get back to your stand on homosexuality?

It is a stand I have never wavered from and one which I will stand by, as President, with firmness and determination and to use an expression we use in Texas . . .

Your New Hampshire campaign literature says that you're a New Englander.

That's right, from Texas.

If You Thought Ford Was An Edsel . . .

We'd almost decided to endorse George Bush, the "company" man, for President when we heard the rumors. "They're talking about Jerry Ford on Wall Street," whispered our contact who makes the rounds of higher circles and knows about these things. "My Washington bookie—who's never wrong—says it'll be Ford over Carter by a hair in November," leaked another insider.

Gerald Ford? Wasn't he the man who, in 1959, was named one of the 25 football players of the previous quarter century who had contributed most to their fellow citizens? But why would anyone want the butt of so many chewing gum jokes for President?

Just when we'd decided it must have been a case of mistaken identity, the real Jerry Ford stood up and announced he'd like to run for President, please. Looking back we found the clues had been there all along. Accompanying his regular column, "The Presidency," in *Time* magazine, Hugh Sidey ran a picture of Ford. Sidey noted a lack of leadership ability among the first round of candidates, Democrat and Republican, and then hit home with his last paragraph: "Jerry Ford [was] perhaps the least imaginative of recent Presidents, but maybe the one with the most common sense. [When] he decided that inflation was the threat of the moment . . . he bludgeoned almost 70 bills sent down from Capitol Hill. That was a negative way to work, but work it did."

Get the message? Only Ford can whip inflation.

The captains of industry are putting their money on Ford because they think that Ronald Reagan is too much of a hard liner to appreciate the subtleties of international trade and finance—and George Bush is just an Eastern establishment version of Reagan (with some Texas dirt rubbed into the polished surfaces to make him more palatable out West). The financial wizards fear that the Reagan-Bush brand of conservatism will bring back "free enterprise" just when they need all the help they can get to see them through the impending economic crisis. So they're looking for Mr. Malleable.

"A sweet person, but . . . a bumbler with very poor judgment." That's the way one Washington lobbyist put it when Ford was appointed Vice-President in 1974. A bumbler who's smart enough to know that he doesn't know what he's doing. One who's willing to take advice. After all, he's the only man to finish a year of the presidency without a single new white hair or wrinkle: he couldn't have been doing much and remain so unscathed.

But Ford might not be so bad. As we teeter on the brink of nuclear annihilation, a man who'll say "Where?" when they tell him to push the button might assure us all a good night's sleep for once. And in the retro spirit of the eighties, he's the closest thing we have to Dwight Eisenhower.

Seriously though, would you mind telling us what exactly is your address?

I don't think, just because a man is running for President, that every aspect of his personal life has to be dragged out into the press.

Well, this may be a little personal too. Does it ever bother you not having an image?

No, in fact it's a distinct advantage. When people vote for me, they know exactly what they're getting—a man who very much wants to be their President. If they know my name too, I am more than gratified, I am deeply honored.

We have a few questions about the incident in World War II when your plane was shot down by the Japanese: you escaped but your two companions drowned. There are still some unanswered . . .

But there is no reason for the press to be talking about the "Chappaquiddick of the Pacific." I get very, very . . .

Yes, of course. Now as we understand the facts, you swam rapidly away from the downed plane and were picked up by a U.S. submarine, leaving the other two men behind to drown. The question is whether you might have reported their situation a little bit earlier or whether you yourself might have been able to help in some way . . .

I can only repeat what I have already explained in detail so many times. This is very painful for me. They were fine, upstanding boys, both of them. When I left them behind in the plane, I had no way of knowing that they couldn't, uh, swim. It was very dark, we'd had a long night . . . and the tide, yes, well, as I've explained in several previous statements, was well . . .

Thank you, George Bush.

Northwest Passage

From *Northwest Passage* 20, no. 9 (May 13-June 16, 1980): 3

Urban Wars: To Whom It May Concern

by Sarah Stearns

There are some things I'd like changed immediately. You see, I've had this headache lately and it keeps getting worse every time I read the paper or listen to the news, and it doesn't respond to aspirin or dope, or appear to be caused by a fatally-enlarging tumor or anything simple like that, so I've decided it's environmentally caused. Therefore, Person(s) in Charge, please address the following non-negotiable demands. There may be more later, depending on the state of my headache. And don't accuse me of demanding action on mere trivia—one person's trivia may be another person's reason to seize an embassy.

Demand 1: The Boeing Company should be made to swear, upon penalty of confiscation of all its profits for the past 20 years, that if it hires ONE MORE out-of-state employee, it will provide living space for that person and her/his family at the private residence of a Boeing vice-president for as long as that person and family remain in the area. And if that person is laid off and wishes to leave Seattle, Boeing will send it's ex-employee away with one year's pay. An alternate housing plan would be for Boeing to convert some 747's into condos, park them on a runway in Everett, and offer them rent-free to out-of-area employees. No more 'most-liveable-city' bullshit advertising, either.

Demand 2: All the former radicals who've left politics behind, gotten into natural foods and 'living lightly,' and are now (often with seed money from capitalist warmonger parents they derided 10 years previously) busily buying up old houses, re-doing them with stripped woodwork and solar acoutrements, and then selling them for tremendous profits, should be made publicly to admit what they are: profit-hungry CAPITALISTS. Who are they selling those $90,000 houses to anyway, welfare mothers? And what's 'alternative' about a solar-heating system that adds $15,000 to the price of a house when it could be done for $10,000 less? And what are these capitalists doing that's really better for society at large than the landlords who are throwing old people out of apartment houses so they can sell a third-floor walkup 'condo' for $60,000? Due to these 're-dos,' a good part of the Central District in Seattle is now lost to people who lived there for years.

Demand 3: A non-profit corporation, administered by elected officials, should be set up to take charge of all rental housing, construction of which would be supported by corporate taxes. (Boeing, for instance.) No one should own a house they do not live in-one person, one house.

Demand 4: The daily newspapers (and some of the weeklies, too) should be forbidden by law (I know, censorship) from printing any more interviews with people flying through town trying to sell their own brand of nonsense—how to be your dog's best friend, how to get women to be corrupt business execs like men are, how to build a solar mousetrap—all those things which only increase the tension load on our brains. Of course, these people don't want to flack their books? The publishers insist on it so the books will sell. Therefore, we will cut off the avenue of propaganda, the worst-offending publishers will go broke, and we can concentrate on serious matters, like:

Demand 5: Dixy, her band of incredibly stupid and unimaginatively crooked supporters, and in fact practically the whole Washington State Legislature should be stood up against any wall that stretches long enough to support them all, and gunned down with long-acting tranquilizers. As a long-time pacifist and mourner of capital-punishment victims back to Caryll Chessman, I can't say 'kill,' but let's at least incapacitate them. We'll save people like McDermott and Becker and a few others. All the rest—drill 'em.

My headache feels better already. That's probably enough for you to start working on, O Person(s) in Charge. Get busy.

Sincerely,

A disgruntled citizen

NO LIMITS

From *No Limits* 5, no. 1 (February/March 1980): 16

Theses on Groucho Marxism

1

Groucho Marxism, the theory of comedic revolution, is much more than a blueprint for crass struggle: like a red light in a window, it illuminates humanity's inevitable destiny, the *declasse* society. G-Marxism is the theory of *permanent revelry*. (Down boy! There, that's a good dogma.)

2

The example of the Marx Brothers themselves shows the unity of Marxist theory and practice (for instance, when Groucho insults somebody while Harpo picks his pocket). Moreover, Marxism is dialectical (isn't Chico the classic dialect comedian?). Comedians who fail to synthesize theory and practice (to say nothing of those who fail to sin at all) are un-Marxist. Subsequent comedians, failing to grasp that separation is "the discrete charm of the bourgeoisie," have lapsed into mere pratfalls on the one hand, and mere prattle on the other.

3

Because G-Marxism is practical, its achievements can never be reduced to mere humor, entertainment, or even "art." (The aesthetes, after all, are less interested in the appreciation of art than in art that appreciates.) After a genuine Marxist sees a Marx Brothers movie, he tells himself: "If you think that was funny, take a look at your life!"

4

Contemporary G-Marxists must resolutely denounce the imitative, vulgar "Marxism" of the Three Stooges, Monty Python, and Bugs Bunny. Instead of vulgar Marxism, we must return to authentic *Marxist vulgarity*. Similarly, rectumfication is in order for those deluded comrades who think the "correct line" is what the cop makes them walk when he pulls them over.

Class-conscious Marxists (that is, Marxists who are conscious that they have no class) must spurn the anemic, trendy, narcissistic "comedy" of comedic revisionists like Woody Allen and Jules Feiffer. Already the comedic revolution has surpassed mere neurosis—it's ludic but not ludicrous, militant but not military, adventurous but not adventurist. Marxists realize that today you have to look into a funhouse mirror to see the way you really are.

6

Although not entirely lacking in glimmers of Marxist insight, socialist (sur)-realism must be distinguished from G-Marxism. It is true that Salvador Dali once gave Harpo a harp made out of fishhooks; however, there is no evidence that Harpo ever played it.

7

Above all, it is essential to renounce and revile all comedic sectarianism, such as that of the equine Trots. As is well-known, Groucho repeatedly proposed sex but opposed sects. For Groucho, then, there was a difference between being a Trot and being hot to trot. Further, the trot slogan "Wages for Horsework" smacks of reform, not revelry. Trot efforts to claim *A Day at the Races* and *Horsefeathers* for their tendency must be indignantly rejected; in truth, *National Velvet* is more their speed.

8

The urgent issue confronting Marxists today is *the Party question,* which—naive, reductionist "Marxists" to the contrary—is more than just "Why wasn't I invited?" That never stopped Groucho! Marxists need their own disciplined vanguard party, since they're rarely welcome at anybody else's.

9

Guided by the Marxist leader-dogmas of *misbehaviorism* and *hysterical materialism,* inevitably the masses will embrace, not only G-Marxism, but also each other.

10

Groucho Marxism, then, is the *tour de farce* of comedy. As Harpo is reliably reported to have said:
"   "

In other words, comedy is riotous or it is nothing! So much to do, so many to do it to! On your Marx, get set—go!

CoEVOLUTION Quarterly

From *CoEvolution Quarterly,* no. 25 (Spring 1980), pp. 128-131

Bop It Out

by R. Crumb

[See pages 464-467.]

SOIL OF LIBERTY

PUT OUT BY NORTH COUNTRY ANARCHISTS AND ANARCHU-FEMINISTS

Soil of Liberty 6, no. 3 (1980): center pp.

We Found It!!! Simple Answers!!!

WE FOUND IT!! THE SIMPLEST ANSWERS IN THE WORLD

Today's world raises a lot of questions. When you see or read about the riots in Miami, sanitation worker strikes, revolutions around the world, and homosexuals marching in the streets you begin to worry about what is going on. Will it creep into your neighborhood? Will it destabilize your children? Will you die of disgust?

You don't have to worry anymore. Fundamental Answers, Incorporated has the answers to your problems. At a nominal $50.00 a month subscription for your whole family, we will provide you with a world view that answers all your questions about life and guarantees to put a stop to any other troublesome questions from entering your mind, or your money back.

LOOK AT WHAT WE HAVE!!

God

God is on our payroll. If you're Pro-God you'll want to subscribe to Fundamental Answers Program. God is a Fundamental Answers exclusive and He will tell you what is right and wrong. No longer will you have to agonize over knotty social problems. God Himself will point you in the right direction. Think of it! You'll always be right! You can say to friends and colleagues, "I'm against abortion, homosexuals, minorities, women, anarchists and other mental defectives," and when they look uneasy you just tell them that God told you this is *the* correct position. Then go on to tell them more about Fundamental Answers, Inc.

Reprinted with permission from *Soil of Liberty*.

Family

Fundamental Answers, Inc. can cement together disintegrating families with its Family Law and Order Program. If you're Pro-family, you'll want to subscribe. The Family Law and Order Program includes a 150 page book of regulations, ranking and uniforms for each family member, and a list of 100 commands that the male head of the household can use to run a tight ship. The Family Law and Order Program puts authority and submission back into the family structure where it belongs. The good old-fashioned values of order-giving and obeying can be easily followed because the program's uniforms, insignias, regulation book, and the 100 commands make everyone know their place and function. You'll be surprised how fast your wife begins to keep a spotless house and have dinner cooked on time. You'll be amazed that the kids catch on quick (or catch heck from you). In days, the Family Law and Order Program will have Jr. and his sister mowing the lawn, picking up their room, and even calling you sir!

Decency

It's getting hard to decide what is decent nowadays. We're bombarded from every

THE PATENTED DECENCY DETECTION DEVICE

DON'T GET CAUGHT WITH YOUR PANTS DOWN. GET THE DECENCY DETECTION DEVICE

---

side by all kinds of people claiming this and that. Fundamental Answers' Decency Detection Device solves all these dilemmas and has public function capabilities. If you're prodecency you'll want to rush your order for a decency detection device for your home. Here are some of the ways you can use it:

A: Hooked up to the T.V., the Decency Detection Device will warn you and your family when profane language or sexually

---

ORDERING INFORMATION

YOU NEED FUNDAMENTAL ANSWERS

To order, first answer these fundamental questions:

Your Name _____

Address _____

    yes *no*
Are you male? ☐ ☐

    yes *no*
Are you white? ☐ ☐

How many children?   8 ☐   9 ☐   10 ☐   11 ☐   12 ☐   14 ☐   15 ☐   16 ☐ More than 16 ☐

How long have you been born again? ☐ 1 year ☐ 2-5 years ☐ ever since I was born

Which organizations do you belong to?
Minute Men ☐   Anita Bryant Brigade ☐
Papal Army ☐   Reagan's Rayguns ☐
John Birch Society ☐   U.S. Gov't. ☐

What is the greatest threat to our way of life?
☐ Anarchism   ☐ Anarchists   ☐ Anarchy

I want to order/subscribe to:

☐ 1. God Provides The Answers. Up to 25 questions for $29.99. Includes a sealed and signed certificate authenticating God's answers.
 ☐ $29.99 for 25 questions
 ☐ $50.00 for 50 questions
 ☐ $100 unlimited questions for a month

☐ 2. Family Law and Order Programs. All you need to whip your family into shape (including the whip!)
 ☐ $45.50 families 2-6
 ☐ $66.60 families 7-18

☐ 3. Decency Detection Device. Keep you and your family's minds clean for only $169.69 ☐

suggestive material is about to be aired, and censor them from your home.

B: Attach the Detection Device to your doorbell and it will tell you if a person calling on you is decent or not. A homosexual is sometimes difficult to discern from decent people, but the Detection Device will tell you what they are. A negro ringing your doorbell at night is difficult to see, but Detection Device will let you know if it's a decent person on your doorstep.

C: Printed materials can be fed through the detection device and it will eliminate all references to indecent ideas, people, and things. Think of it, you can be assured that you and your family can safely read anything without having to self-censor articles on Women's Libbers, Appeasing the Communists, Atheism, Pre-born Murderers or any kind of phoney Equality talk regarding race, sex and creed.

Directory

A list of periodicals, newsletters, and newspapers quoted in *Alternative Papers* follows. Address, telephone, and subscription rates are provided. The frequency of publication, publisher, and availability of back issues and spoken and microform editions are noted whenever possible. A statement of intent culled from the pages of each publication is also included. Publications marked with an * are indexed by the *Alternative Press Index: An Index to Alternative and Radical Publications*, published since 1970 (available from the Alternative Press Center, Box 7229, Baltimore, MD 21218). For the most comprehensive directory to alternative press publications available consult *Alternatives in Print: An International Catalog of Books, Pamphlets, Periodicals and Audiovisual Materials*, now in its sixth edition, compiled by members of the Task Force on Alternatives in Print of the Social Responsibilities Round Table of the American Library Association (available from Neal-Schuman Publishers, 23 Cornelia Street, New York, NY 10014).

Aegis: Magazine on Ending Violence Against Women
Box 21033
Washington, DC 20009
(202) 659-5983

"The purpose of *Aegis* is to aid the efforts of feminists working to end violence against women. To this end, *Aegis* provides practical information and resources for grassroots organizers, along with promoting a continuing discussion among feminists of the root causes of rape, battering, sexual harassment and other forms of violence against women."
Published 4 times a year by the Feminist Alliance Against Rape, the National Communication Network, and the Alliance Against Sexual Coercion.

Subscription rates in the United States are $10.50 a year, $19.50 for 2 years, to individuals; $25 a year, $45 for 2 years, to institutions. Outside the United States $13 a year, $24 for 2 years, to individuals; $30 a year, $50 for 2 years, to institutions.
Back issues available, $2.75 each.

*Akwesasne Notes
Mohawk Nation
via Rooseveltown, NY 13683
(518) 358-9531

"Official publication of the Mohawk Nation at Akwesasne."
"A journal for native and natural peoples."
Published 5 times a year in March, May, July, September, and December by the Program in American Studies at the State University of New York at Buffalo and D-Q University, Davis, Calif.
Subscription rates are $6 a year; $12 a year for the express mailing list, which also includes a subscription to the E.R.I.N. (Emergency Response International Network) *Activity Bulletin*.

*Alternative Media
Box 775, Madison Square Station
New York, NY 10010
(212) 481-0120

"Mass media consumers, beware! Your information is coming from fewer and fewer sources. . . . Read about public-access television, community radio, underground comics, the ever-growing alternative press. Discover news and entertainment overgrown media empires suppress or ignore."
Published quarterly by the Alternative Press Syndicate.
Subscription rates are $7.50 for 4 issues.

Available on microfilm from Bell & Howell, Old Mansfield Road; Wooster, OH 44691.

*Alternative Sources of Energy
107 South Central Avenue
Milaca, MN 56353
(612) 983-6892

"*Alternative Sources of Energy* is . . . concerned with the development and use of renewable resources. Particular emphasis is on alternative environmental technologies which are energy-related. The major thrust of the organization is to publicize and share practical applications of such technologies as a means of attaining some degree of energy independence."

Published bimonthly.

Subscription rates in the United States are $16.50 for 6 issues, $30 for 12 issues, to individuals; $21.50 for 6 issues, $39 for 12 issues, to institutions. In Canada and Mexico $19.50 for 6 issues, $35 for 12 issues. Foreign air mail $33.50 for 6 issues, $62 for 12 issues.

Back issues available.

Available on microfilm from University Microfilms International, 300 North Zeeb Road, Ann Arbor, MI 48106.

Anti-Apartheid News
89 Charlotte Street
London W1P 2DQ Great Britain

"The newspaper of the Anti-Apartheid Movement."

Published 10 times a year.

Subscription rates in the United Kingdom and Europe are £4.50 a year. Outside Europe £4.50 surface mail, £6.50 air mail.

*Big Mama Rag: A Feminist Newsjournal
1724 Gaylord Street

Denver, CO 80206
(303) 322-2010

"We demand control of our reproductive process. We demand free, adequate health care. We demand free, 24 hour day care. We demand the right to the use of self defense. We demand equality in the job market. . . ."

Subscription rates to individuals are $6 a year in the United States, $10 outside the United States. To institutions $18. Free to women in prisons and mental institutions.

The Black Bartletter
Box 48
Canyon, CA 94516

"*Black Bart*:

"Stands for anti-materialism, non-growth, righteous living, faith in the flow, and a Nature consciousness.

"Has no subscription price, but welcomes (and requests) periodic donations. Libraries unable to deal thusly are asked $10/year.

"Rejects advertising, disdains copyright (for ourselves or others), welcomes correspondence and responds personally to all.

"May or may not be published once or twice a year, embellished with occasional newsletters.

"Is done by Irv Thomas."

Black Hills-Paha Sapa Report
Box 2508
Rapid City, SD 57709
(605) 342-5127

"To the people of South Dakota: Energy development, or exploitation (depending on how you look at it) is a reality in many parts of North America—the South-western United States, the mineral belt

[that] runs to Saskatchewan, Canada. We believe that the people should know what is happening to other peoples living in resource-rich areas. There is no race, state or national boundary in resource exploration. From experience and history we should learn."

Published bimonthly by the Black Hills Alliance.

Subscription rates are $7 a year to individuals, $10 to institutions. Free to prisoners.

*Body Politic: A Magazine for Gay Liberation
Box 7289, Station A
Toronto, Ontario M5W 1X9 Canada
(416) 977-6320

"'The liberation of homosexuals can only be the work of homosexuals themselves.' Kurt Hiller, 1921."

Published 10 times a year by Pink Triangle Press.

Subscription rates in Canada are $20 a year for 1st class mail, $10 a year for 2nd class mail. Outside Canada $25 a year for 1st class mail, $12.50 a year for 2nd class mail.

Available on microfilm from MacLaren Micropublishing; Box 972, Station F; Toronto, Ontario M4Y 2N9 Canada.

Broadside: Topical Song Magazine
215 West 98th Street—4D
New York, NY 10025

". . . we have recorded the history of the 60's & 70's in song and comment. We have done this with love and tenderness, yet with hard-hitting honesty."

". . . topical songs, articles relevant to protest music by Phil Ochs, Tom Paxton, Malvina Reynolds, Bob Dylan, Pete

Seeger, Kristin Lems, Carol Hanisch, Sammy Walker, Steve Forbert, many, many more."

"A magazine like ours cannot publish in the U.S. without financial help. All donations are welcome."

Back issues available; complete set of back issues spanning the years 1962 to 1980, $55. Send self-addressed, stamped envelope for information on Broadside LPs.

Broomstick: A Periodical By, For, and About Women Over 40
3543 18th Street
San Francisco, CA 94110
(415) 552-7460

"A monthly periodical with a longer issue every third month."

Subscription rates to individuals are $7.50 a year in the United States, $10 in Canada, $15 overseas. To institutions $15.

*Bulletin of Concerned Asian Scholars
Box R
Berthoud, CO 80513

"If the title of this journal means anything, it surely refers to the concern of everyone of us that we take up the responsibility for breaking the habitual, guilty silence of our profession. . . ."

Published quarterly.

Subscription rates in the United States are $17 a year, $30 for 2 years, $43 for 3 years, to individuals. Outside the United States are $18 a year, $30 for 2 years, $45 for 3 years, to individuals. To students and the unemployed $14 a year; to institutions $23 a year, $65 for 3 years.

Caribbé
Box 20546
Philadelphia, PA 19138

"'Stand firm—live clean—and let your works be seen!' By High Priest of Reggae Peter Tosh."

Ceased publication in 1980.

CASA: The Newsletter for the Center Against Sexual Assault
1131 East Missouri
Phoenix, AZ 85014

"CASA hopes that through community education the public can be informed: that through community awareness the victim, whether male or female, child or adult, can receive sensitive understanding and support: that through community dedication we can someday eliminate sexual assault."

Subscription rate is $5 a year.

The Catholic Worker
36 East First Street
New York, NY 10003
(212) 254-1640

"Organ of the Catholic Worker Movement."

Published monthly, except bimonthly in January/February, June/July, and October/November.

Subscription rates are $.25 a year in the United States, $.30 a year Canada and foreign.

*Changes: Socialist Monthly
17300 Woodward
Detroit, MI 48203
(313) 869-4749

"We stand for: socialism . . . labor action . . . independent political action . . . liberation movements . . . movements for social change . . . solidarity

. . . a revolutionary socialist party . . . unity on the left."

Published monthly except for combined issues in July/August and December/January by the International Socialists.

Subscription rates are $10 a year to individuals, $25 to institutions, $15 foreign surface mail, $30 foreign air mail, $25 for a supporting subscription. Free to prisoners.

*Chutzpah
Box 60142
Chicago, IL 60660

"The Chutzpah Organization is a group of radical Jews, committed to socialism and to positive Jewish identity."

Published erratically.

Subscription rates for 4 issues in the United States are $3.25 to individuals, $6 to libraries and institutions. In Canada $4.75 to individuals, $7.50 to libraries and institutions. Overseas surface mail is $3.25; air mail to Europe $7.50, to Israel and Australia $9. To libraries and institutions overseas add $3.50. Free to prisoners.

Clamshell Alliance News
39 Congress Street
Portsmouth, NH 03801

"Serving Clams everywhere."

The Alliance disbanded and the *News* ceased publication in March 1980.

*CoEvolution Quarterly
Box 428
Sausalito, CA 94966

"Published by the *Whole Earth Catalog*."

Published quarterly by POINT.

Subscription rates in the United States are $14 a year, $25 for 2 years. For 1st class mail in the United States and Canada add $5 a year; for air mail to Mexico and Central America add $9 a year; to South America and Europe add $14 a year; add $18 to all others.

Back issues available.

*Communities: Journal of Cooperative Living
Box 426
Louisa, VA 23093

"Personals: Human beings concerned about planet. How to be human together in small enough groupings to mean anything to each other, large enough to survive. Men and women respecting personhood, sharing insights, urban, rural touching of the universe. Prepared to build political, social, economic, ethical models toward spiritual growth. Please make contact."

Published 5 times a year by Communities Publications Cooperative, a division of Unschool Educational Services Corporation from the offices at Twin Oaks Community.

Subscription rates are $10 a year to individuals, $15 a year to institutions, add $2 for foreign subscriptions. Free to prisoners.

Convoy Dispatch
Box 10728
Detroit, MI 48210

"Voice of the Teamster Rank and File since 1975."

Published monthly by the Teamsters for a Democratic Union.

Subscription rate to nonmembers is $25 a year.

*Co-op Magazine
Box 7293
Ann Arbor, MI 48109

"The only subscription magazine that covers the North American Co-op Movement."

Published quarterly by the North American Students of Cooperation.

Ceased publication in 1981.

*CounterSpy: The Magazine for People Who Need to Know
Box 647, Ben Franklin Station
Washington, DC 20044

"'*CounterSpy* is self-described as a source of analysis and information on the practices, organization and objectives of U.S. intelligence.' Federal Bureau of Investigation."

Subscription rates in the United States are $10 a year to individuals, $20 to libraries and institutions. In Canada and Mexico $13 to individuals. In Central America and the Caribbean $20 to individuals. $25 overseas air mail. $75 to United States government agencies.
Free to prisoners.

Back issues available.

Available on microfilm from University Microfilms International; 300 North Zeeb Road; Ann Arbor, MI 48106.

*CovertAction Information Bulletin
Box 50272
Washington, DC 20004
(202) 265-3904

"Our publication, as you are undoubtably aware, is devoted to exposing what we view as the abuses of western intelligence agencies, primarily, though not exclusively, the CIA; and to exposing the people responsible for those abuses. We believe that our nation's intelligence activities should be restricted to the *gathering* of

intelligence, in the strictest sense. We believe it is wrong, and in the long run extremely detrimental to our democracy, for this country to interfere covertly in the affairs of other countries."

Published 5 to 7 times a year.

Subscription rates for 6 issues are $15 in the United States; $20 in Canada and Mexico; $21 air mail to Latin America, Europe, Mediterranean Africa; $23 air to Asia, Pacific, rest of Africa. Institutions add $5.

Back issues available, $2.50 each; $3 outside North America.

Available on microfilm from University Microfilms International; 300 North Zeeb Road; Ann Arbor, MI 48106.

*Cultural Correspondence
107½ Hope Street
Providence, RI 02906

"Popular culture and revolution."
Ceased publication in summer 1981.
Back issues available.

The DC Gazette
1739 Connecticut Avenue, NW
Washington, DC 20009
(202) 232-5544

"Bucking the system since 1966."
Published 10 times a year.
Subscription rates are $5 a year. $2 to prisoners and low income people.

*Dollars & Sense: A Monthly Bulletin of Economic Affairs
38 Union Square, Room 14
Somerville, MA 02143
(617) 628-8411

"*Dollars & Sense* is edited and produced

by a group of members of the Union for Radical Political Economics. We offer interpretations of current economic events from a socialist perspective to be of use to people working for progressive social change."

Published monthly except in June and August by the Economic Affairs Bureau.

Subscription rates in the United States are $9 a year, $16 for 2 years, to individuals; $18 a year to institutions. Outside the United States add $2 a year for surface mail or $13 a year for air mail postage. Free to prisoners.

Back issues available.

Available on microfilm from Bell & Howell, Old Mansfield Road, Wooster, OH 44691.

*Environmental Action
Suite 731
1346 Connecticut Avenue, NW
Washington, DC 20036
(202) 833-1845

"*Environmental Action* has a reputation for taking stands and uncovering threats to our earth—nationally and locally—while telling what activists are doing to stop them."

Published monthly, except for a combined issue in July/August.

Membership rates are $15 a year to individuals, $18 to a family, $25 to contributors, $50 to sponsors, $100 to patrons; $15 to libraries; $30 to businesses; $10 to students and people 65 and over.

Equal Times
235 Park Square Building
Boston, MA 02116
(617) 426-1981

"Boston's newspaper for working women."

Published biweekly by Eunice West.

Subscription rates are $8 a year to individuals, $14 to institutions.

Fallout Forum: SHAD Newsletter
339 Lafayette Street
New York, NY 10012

"SHAD: Sound and Hudson against Atomic Development is a regional coalition of concerned people. We recognize that nuclear power is a threat to all life. We oppose through education and nonviolent direct actions the proliferation and use of nuclear technologies whether for energy or weapons anywhere in the world."

Publication suspended in 1980.

*Fifth Estate
4403 Second Avenue
Detroit, MI 48201
(313) 831-6800

"NO WAR, NO Ayatollah, NO Shah, NO President, NO Nationalism, NO Militarism, NO Ideology, NO Religion, NO God, NO State, NO Leaders, NO Followers. Destroy That Which Destroys You."

Published bimonthly.

Subscription rates are $4 a year to individuals in the United States; 56 foreign; $10 to libraries, institutions, corporations; an additional $1 pays for half a prisoner's subscription. $100 to governments.

Free For All
Box 962
Madison, WI 53701
(608) 255-2798

"Here? In Madison?"

Published biweekly by the Better World Educational Corporation.

Subscription rates are $8 a year, $15 for 1st class mail. Free to prisoners.

Frontiers: A Journal of Women's Studies
Women's Studies Program
University of Colorado
Boulder, CO 80309

"The continuing goal of *Frontiers* is to publish a journal which bridges the gap between university and community women; to find a balance between academic and popular views on issues common to women."

Published three times a year in association with the Women's Studies Program at the University of Colorado, Boulder.

Subscription rates are $11 a year to individuals; $18 a year to institutions.

Back issues available.

*Gay Community News: The Weekly for Lesbians and Gay Males
22 Bromfield Street
Boston, MA 02108
(617) 426-4469

"*Gay Community News* is dedicated to providing coverage of events and news of interest to the gay community."

Published every week except the first week of January and the last week of August by National Gay News.

Subscription rates in the United States are $6 for 12 weeks, $12.50 for 25 weeks, $25 a year, $43.50 for 2 years, $62 for 3 years; $17.50 a year to low-income people. Outside the United States add 30% for postage. Free to prisoners.

Available on microfilm from the publisher.

*Gay Insurgent
Box 29627
Philadelphia, PA 19144

A Gay left journal.
Published semi-annually by the Lavender Archives.
Subscription rate is $5 a year.
Back issues available.

*Gray Panther Network
3635 Chestnut Street
Philadelphia, PA 19104
(215) 382-3300

"Age and youth in action."
Published bimonthly by the Gray Panther Project Fund.
Subscription rates are $5 a year to individuals; $15 to libraries, organizations, institutions, and foreign addresses. Persons unable to afford a subscription may request *Network* free of charge.

*Green Revolution: A Voice for Decentralization and Balanced Living
Box 3233
York, PA 17402
(717) 755-1561

"*Green Revolution* is the School of Living's voice for reporting on activities of a worldwide movement of the same name, which works for decentralized government, industry, population. It promotes community, community land trusts, balanced living, sufficient and healthy foods, appropriate technology, right education, homesteading, right livelihood, harmonious living on earth, cooperative self-sufficiency, economic reform, spiritual growth."

Published 6 times a year in January, March, May, July, September, and November.
Subscriptions can be obtained by request; institutions and libraries $6 a year.
Back issues available, $1 each.
Available on microfilm from University Microfilms International; 300 North Zeeb Road; Ann Arbor, MI 48106.

Groundswell: A Resource Journal for Energy Activists
1536 Sixteenth Street, NW
Washington, DC 20036
(202) 483-0045

"Capsule news briefs on major atomic energy stories of the month . . . [and reviews of] . . . new publications of use to the safe energy movement."
Published bimonthly by the Nuclear Information and Resource Service.
Subscription rate is $15 a year to individuals and nonprofit citizen organizations. $20 to libraries. $25 to institutions. Life line subscriptions to prisoners are $10.

*The Guardian: Independent Radical Newsweekly
33 West 17th Street
New York, NY 10011

"'The forces of progressive America—Black activists, Marxists, feminists, Hispanics, antinuke advocates, gays and others—need critical information to wage our individual and collective struggles. *The Guardian* has been a major factor in providing that information for decades.' Manning Marable."
Published every week except the first 2 weeks in August.

Subscription rates in the United States are $12 for 6 months, $23 a year, $40 for 2 years; $1 a year to prisoners. Outside the United States add $11 a year.

*Health/PAC Bulletin
17 Murray Street
New York, NY 10007

"No one else offers independent analysis of health policy issues from prenatal care to hospices for the dying; covers medical carelessness for women and on the job poisoning; offers incisive international reports and lively briefs on domestic health developments."
"Remember, nine out of ten radical doctors recommend the *Health/PAC Bulletin* for fast relief of health care policy mystification."
Published bimonthly.
Subscription rates are $14 a year to individuals, $11.20 to students; $28 to institutions.

*HealthRight: A Women's Health Newsletter
41 Union Square, Room 206-8
New York, NY 10003

"Women and children first—that chivalrous expression of patriarchy and sexism—takes on a new meaning in an age of nuclear and industrial hazards. Women and children are the first to manifest the effects of the poisons recklessly spewed into our environment and the first to be advised to flee. For most of us, the realization of the magnitude of the potential disaster that we face is a recent one. We have long recognized that there are no individual solutions to the problems of pollution and contamination, that it is, for example, not enough to be careful about what we eat because it is the sources of food and the water supply that must be cleaned up. But events like the near-miss at Three Mile Island or the contamination of millions of acres of land with dioxin bring home to us with ever more force that there is simply no place to run, no place to hide any more . . . . Collective action, concerted and worldwide, will be only effective means of stopping the headlong destruction of our planet which is, at least for now, the only place we have to live."

Ceased publication in 1979.

*Heresies; A Feminist Publication on Arts & Politics
Box 766, Canal Street Station
New York, NY 10013

"*Heresies* is an idea-oriented journal devoted to the examination of art and politics from a feminist perspective."

Published quarterly.

Subscription rates in the United States and Canada are $15 for 4 issues to individuals; $24 for 4 issues to institutions. Outside the United States and Canada add $2 postage.

Hot Times
2204 San Gabriel
Austin, TX 78705

"Where is the resistance?"

Published by Bread and Roses.

Donations of $5, $10, $15, or assistance with producing, distributing, or selling ad space are requested.

*In These Times: The Independent Socialist Newspaper
1509 North Milwaukee Avenue
Chicago, IL 60622
(312) 489-4444 (in Illinois)
(800) 247-2160 (outside Illinois)

"*In These Times* is an independent newspaper committed to democratic pluralism and to helping build a popular movement for socialism in the United States. Our pages are open to a wide range of views on the left, both socialist and non-socialist."

Published 42 times a year by the Institute for Policy Studies.

Subscription rates in the United States are $23.50 a year, $35 for 2 years to individuals; $35 a year to institutions. Outside the United States $35 a year.

Available on microfilm from University Microfilms International, 300 North Zeeb Road, Ann Arbor, MI 48106.

Intercontinental Press combined with Inprecor
410 West Street
New York, NY 10014

"*Intercontinental Press*" specializes in political analysis and interpretation of events of particular interest to the labor, socialist, colonial independence, Black, and women's liberation movements."

Published each Monday except the first in January and the third and fourth in August by the 408 Printing and Publishing Corporation.

Subscription rates in the United States are $35 a year. In Canada $41 a year in Canadian currency. Inquire for other rates.

*Jump Cut: A Review of Contemporary Cinema
Box 865
Berkeley, CA 94701

"The radical word on Hollywood releases."

Published about 4 times a year.

Subscription rates in the United States are $6 a year to individuals; $9 to institutions. In Canada and abroad $8 to individuals; $11 to institutions.

Back issues available.

Available on microfilm from University Microfilms International, 300 North Zeeb Road, Ann Arbor, MI 48106.

*Labor Notes
Box 20001
Detroit, MI 48220

"A monthly newsletter designed to report on important developments in the labor movement, *Labor Notes* . . . will have a different starting point than other publications that carry labor news. This newsletter will cover events from the point of view of working people. This means not only reporting how a given event will affect ordinary union members; it also means giving extensive coverage to the growing reform movement in many unions."

Published monthly by the Labor Education and Research Project.

Subscription rates are $7.50 a year to individuals, $15 supporting, $15 to institutions.

The Leaping Lesbian
Box 7715
Ann Arbor, MI 48107

"Or, Entertaining Companion, Free for

All Women, Appropriated Solely to their Use and Amusement."
Suspended publication in 1979.

The Lesbian Feminist
243 West 20th Street
New York, NY 10011
(212) 691-5460

"Movement notices . . . Forum . . . Book Reviews."
Published by Lesbian Feminist Liberation.
Suspended publication in June 1979.

*MERIP Reports
Box 1247
New York, NY 10025

MERIP Reports focuses "on the political economy of the contemporary Middle East, the role of imperialism, and popular struggles in the region."
Published 9 times a year by the Middle East Research & Information Project.
Subscription rates in the United States are $15.50 a year to individuals, $26 to institutions. For Canada, Mexico, and overseas surface mail add $4; all air mail add $15.50.
Back issues available, $2-$2.50 each.

Midwest Energy Times
434 West Mifflin Street
Madison, WI 53703

"Serving The Safe Energy Network."
Published by the Alternative Power Alliance.
Ceased publication in 1979.

*The Militant: A Socialist Newsweekly
14 Charles Lane
New York, NY 10014
(212) 929-3486

"Published in the interests of the working people."
"*The Militant* is the voice of the Socialist Workers Party."
Published weekly except 2 weeks in August, the last week in December, and the first week in January.
Subscription rates by 2nd class mail in the United States are $24 a year, $30 a year outside. By 1st class mail in the United States, Canada, and Mexico $60 a year. Inquire for other rates.

*Multinational Monitor
Box 19405
1346 Connecticut Avenue, NW, Room 411
Washington, DC 20036
(202) 833-3932

"Tracking big business across the globe. The seventies: ITT in Chile—Lockheed and the fall of a Japanese government—the rise of the OPEC cartel. The eighties promise even more dramatic developments, as multinational corporations move to expand their power and influence in the global economy. One magazine can bring you up-to-the-minute reporting and analysis each month on the activities of these giant corporations and the governmental and citizen responses to their growing power."
Published monthly by the Corporate Accountability Research Group.
Subscription rates in the United States are $15 a year to individuals, $20 to nonprofit institutions, $30 to business-institutions. In Mexico and Canada add $2.50; elsewhere add $8.
Available on microfiche from Bell & Howell, Old Mansfield Road, Wooster, OH 44691, and on microfilm from University Microfilms International, 300 North Zeeb Road, Ann Arbor, MI 48106.

*NACLA Report on the Americas
151 West 19th Street, 9th Floor
New York, NY 10011

"The North American Congress on Latin America (NACLA) is an independent research organization founded in 1966 focusing on the political economy of the Americas."
Published bimonthly by the North American Congress on Latin America.
Subscription rates to individuals are $13 a year, $24 for 2 years, $34 for 3 years; to institutions $24 a year, $45 for 2 years, $64 for 3 years. Air mail to North America add $6 a year; South American and Europe add $8 a year; Asia, Africa, and Australia add $9 a year.
Back issues available, $1.75-$3 each.
Microfilm available, inquire of publisher.

National Abortion Rights Action League Newsletter
825 15th Street, NW
Washington, DC 20005
(202) 347-7774

"I'm pro-choice . . . and I vote!"
Published monthly.
Membership rate is $15 a year, of which $5 is for the newsletter.

Newspage. See Women Against Violence in Pornography & Media Newspage

New Women's Times
804 Meigs Street
Rochester, NY 14620

"From the hometown of Susan B. Anthony."

Published monthly except in August. *New Women's Times Feminist Review,* a review of literature and the arts, is issued 6 times a year as regular supplement to *New Women's Times.*

Subscription rates to individuals are $15 a year, $28 for 2 years; $30 to institutions.

No Limits
Box 2605
Madison, WI 53701

"Voices of the revolution: Clip & Save. Read nightly."

Published monthly by Dream World Dragon Press.

Suspended publication in 1980.

No Nuclear News: A Monthly Cooperative Clipping Service
595 Massachusetts Avenue
Cambridge, MA 02139

"Each month newspaper clippings and graphics are sent to *No Nuclear News* from all over the United States, Japan, Canada, France, Germany, Spain, England and elsewhere. *No Nuclear News* chooses the most comprehensive clippings and arranges them in nine categories—Uranium, Opposition, International, Government-Industry, Contamination-Accidents, Wastes, Weapons, Breeders-Fusion and Alternatives. . . . We also feature a scoreboard showing, at a glance, all the nuclear accidents reported to us each month."

Published monthly.

Subscription rates in the United States are $7.50 a year regular, $12 sustaining. In Canada and Mexico $10 regular, $15 sustaining. Overseas airmail is $20.

Back issues available $.75 for monthly issues, $1 for special issues.

No Nukes Left!
Box 643
North Amherst, MA 01059

"*No Nukes Left!* is a quarterly journal of internal political discussion, debate and analysis written for and by anti-nuclear activists nationally and internationally. It offers a meeting place for fresh, theoretical thinking about the anti-nuclear power movement and the social-historical context in which it acts."

Subscription rates are $4 a year regular, $10 sustaining, $6 to institutions.

No Nukes News
Box 6625
Chicago, IL 60680
(312) 786-9041

"The movement keeps growing."

Published by Citizens Against Nuclear Power.

Subscription rates are $5 a year; $2 to students and low income people.

Northern Sun News
1519 East Franklin
Minneapolis, MN 55404
(612) 874-1540

"Alternatives for the north country in energy and politics."

Published monthly by the Twin Cities Northern Sun Alliance.

Subscription rates are $10 for 2 years, $14 for 3 years. Free to prisoners.

*Northwest Passage
1017 East Pike
Seattle, WA 98122
(206) 323-0354

"The *Northwest Passage* is an independent radical journal of news and analysis, laid out and printed in Seattle by a regional staff collective every third Monday."

Subscription rates are $8 a year, $15 for 2 years to individuals; $5 to low-income people; $20 to sustainers; $15 to institutions. Free to prisoners.

Nukelessness
Box 7828
Ann Arbor, MI 48107
(313) 996-9277

"The Arbor Alliance is a non-partisan group of citizens opposed to nuclear power and nuclear weapons, dedicated to halting the construction of nuclear power plants in Michigan (and worldwide), to stopping the arms race, and to turning around national priorities to meeting basic human needs."

Published bimonthly by the Arbor Alliance.

Subscription rates are $3 a year, more if you can afford it.

*off our backs: a women's news journal
1724 20th Street, NW
Washington, DC 20009
(202) 234-8072

"We've been a monthly for 10 years now. We've outlived *Life* and *The Saturday Evening Post.*"

Published 11 times a year.

Subscription rates are $7 a year to individuals, $12 contributing, $20 to institutions, $14 foreign.

Available on tape from Womyn's Braille Press, Box 8475, Minneapolis, MN 55408.

*Open Road
Box 6135, Station G
Vancouver, British Columbia V6R 4G5
Canada

"When Emma Goldman decided to start an anarchist publication in 1906 she chose the name *The Open Road*, from a poem about freedom by Walt Whitman. After discovering that another paper of the time already bore the name, however, she switched titles and the renowned *Mother Earth* was born. For more than 50 years, Goldman spoke out, wrote and organized on behalf of the Social Revolution. She fought in the streets, in prison, in union halls, urging people to 'ask for work; if they won't give you work, ask for bread; if they don't give you bread, then take the bread.' In her autobiography, *Living My Life*, Goldman set out the policy of a journal dedicated to human liberation: 'In *The Open Road* they should speak without fear of censor. Everybody who longed to escape rigid moulds, political and social prejudices, and petty moral demands should have a chance to travel with us in *The Open Road*.'"

Suggested subscription rates are 2 hours' pay or more to individuals, $25 to institutions, $50 sustaining. Free to prisoners and people without money.

Back issues available, $1-$2 each.

The Organizer
27 Union Square West, Room 306
New York, NY 10003
(212) 243-8555

"Free all political prisoners."

Published bimonthly by the National Alliance Against Racist and Political Repression.

Membership rates are $5 a year to individuals, $25 for an affiliate. Free to prisoners.

Organizing Notes
201 Massachusetts Avenue
Washington, DC 20002
(202) 547-4705

"The Campaign for Political Rights is a national coalition of over 80 religious, educational, environmental, civic, women's, Native American, black, latino, and labor organizations which have joined together to work for an end to covert actions abroad and an end to political surveillance and harassment in the United States. The Campaign office serves as a clearinghouse providing materials, organizing assistance, press and publicity advice and speaker scheduling to organizations across the country."

Published 8 times a year by the Campaign for Political Rights.

Free to anyone contributing $10 or more to support the Campaign.

The Outlaw: Journal of the Prisoners' Union. See **Prisoners' Union Journal**

*Paid My Dues
Box 6517
Chicago, IL 60680
(312) 929-5592

"A quarterly journal of women in music."

Published by Calliope Publishing.
Ceased publication in 1980.

Peacework: The New England Peace Movement Newsletter
2161 Massachusetts Avenue
Cambridge, MA 02140
(617) 661-6130

"A New England peace movement newsletter."

Published 11 times a year by the American Friends Service Committee, Cambridge, MA.

Subscription rates are $5 a year for 3rd class mail, $8 for 1st class mail.

*Prisoners Union Journal
1315 18th Street
San Francisco, CA 94107

"The Prisoners Union is a non-profit organization of convicts, ex-convicts, and others interested in improving prison conditions of those housed in the California state prisons. The organization started in 1971 and has worked in California since that time toward three goals: (1) the achievement of uniform and equitable sentencing laws; (2) the restoration of civil and human rights to prisoners; and (3) the payment of fair wages for work done, safe working conditions, and compensation for injuries that are work-related."

Published bimonthly. Until 1980, title was *The Outlaw: Journal of the Prisoners' Union.*

Subscription rates are $10 a year regular, $5 or a contribution to families and friends of prisoners, $15 to institutions. Free to indigent California prisoners; $2 to out-of-state prisoners.

*The Public Eye: A Journal of Social and Political Issues Concerning Repression in America
Suite 918
343 South Dearborn Street
Chicago, IL 60604

"*The Public Eye* is a magazine written by investigators, journalists, attorneys, and researchers who specialize in watching government intelligence abuse and right-wing spying and harassment of progressives."

Published by the Public Eye Network, an affiliate of the Campaign for Political Rights, in conjunction with the National Lawyers Guild Committee Against Government Repression and Police Crimes.

Subscription rates are $8 to individuals, $15 to institutions.

Back issues available.

Available on microfilm from Bell & Howell, Old Mansfield Road, Wooster, OH 44691.

*Puerto Rico Libre!
Box 319, Cooper Station
New York, NY 10003
(212) 741-3131

"Puerto Rico is a colony of the United States, as the U.S. was once a colony of the British Empire. The Puerto Rico Solidarity Committee calls for the complete withdrawal of the United States from Puerto Rico and full independence for Puerto Rico."

Published monthly by the Puerto Rico Solidarity Committee.

Subscription rates are $5 a year to individuals, $15 to institutions. Free to prisoners.

Quash: Newsletter of the Grand Jury Project
853 Broadway, Room 1116
New York, NY 10003
(212) 674-6005

"The Project was begun in February 1975 by the New York Women's Union, following the broad FBI/Justice Department attack on women's and lesbian communities across the country. We are co-sponsored by the National Lawyers Guild."

Published every 6 weeks, except during July and August.

Subscription rates are $6 a year to individuals and National Lawyers Guild members; $12 to institutions and lawyers who are not Guild members. Free to prisoners.

*Quest: A Feminist Quarterly
Box 8843
Washington, DC 20003

"*Quest: A Feminist Quarterly* is seeking long-term, in-depth feminist analysis and ideological development. *Quest* is not an end in itself, but a process leading to new directions for the women's movement, possibly including such concrete forms as regional or national conferences, a national organization, or a political party. . . ."

Subscription rates to individuals are $9 for 4 issues in the United States, $10 in Canada and Mexico, $11 overseas surface, $14.50 overseas air. $25 to institutions.

Back issues available, $3.35-$5 each.

*Radical America
38 Union Square
Somerville, MA 02143
(617) 628-6585

"*Radical America* is an independent Marxist journal, featuring the history and current developments in the working class, the role of women and Third World people, with reports on shop-floor and community organizing, the history and politics of radicalism and feminism, and debates on current socialist theory and popular culture."

Published bimonthly by the Alternative Education Project.

Subscription rates to individuals are $12

a year, $22 for 2 years, $8 to the unemployed. Add $3 year to foreign subscriptions. Double rates for institutions. Free to prisoners.

Available on microfilm from University Microfilms International, 300 North Zeeb Road, Ann Arbor, MI 48106.

*Rain: Journal of Appropriate Technology
2270 NW Irving
Portland, OR 97210
(503) 227-5110

"*Rain* is a national information access journal making connections for people seeking more simple and satisfying lifestyles, working to make their communities and regions economically self-reliant, building a society that is durable, just and ecologically sound."

Published 10 times a year by Rain Umbrella.

Subscription rates are $15 a year, $25 for 2 years, $9.50 living lightly rate. Add $2.80 for foreign surface mail; inquire for air rates. Add $5 billing fee if payment is not enclosed.

The San Francisco Bay Guardian
2700 19th Street
San Francisco, CA 94110
(415) 824-7660

"'It is a newspaper's duty to print the news and raise hell.' Wilbur F. Storey."

Published every Wednesday.

Subscription rates in the United States are $31.20 a year; in Canada add $.10 per issue; in foreign countries add $.20 per issue.

Back issues available, $1 each.

*Science for People
9 Poland Street
London W1V 3DG Great Britain
01-4372728

"We believe that science is not neutral. It cannot be separated from politics. It both reflects and helps determine the values of society. Hence to change the social role of science it is necessary to change society. We are committed to fighting for the use of science and technology by and for the benefit of working people, to demonstrating the political content of science, and to furthering the links between scientific workers and the rest of the labour movement."

Published quarterly by the British Society for Social Responsibility in Science.

Subscription rates in the United Kingdom are £4 a year to individuals, £10 to institutions and libraries. Overseas, surface mail is £4 to individuals, £10 to institutions and libraries. Overseas air mail is £6 to individuals, £12 to institutions and libraries.

*Science for the People
897 Main Street
Cambridge, MA 02139
(617) 547-0370

"Science for the People is an organization of people involved or interested in science and technology-related issues, whose activities are directed at: 1) exposing the class control of science and technology, 2) organizing campaigns which criticize, challenge and propose alternatives to the present use of science and technology, and 3) developing a political strategy by which people in the technical strata can ally with other progressive forces in society."

Published bimonthly by the Science Resource Center.

Subscription rates in the United States are $12 a year to individuals, $24 to institutions, $25 member subscription, $15 to low-income people. Outside the United States $16 surface mail; add $4 air mail to Latin America, $6.50 to Europe, $8.50 to Asia and Africa. Free to prisoners.

Available on microfilm from University Microfilms International, 300 North Zeeb Road, Ann Arbor, MI 48106.

*The Second Wave: A Magazine of Ongoing Feminism
Box 344, Cambridge A
Cambridge, MA 02139

"'It may be that a second wave of sexual liberation might at last accomplish its aim of freeing half the race from its immemorial subordination and in the process bring us all a great deal closer to humanity.' Kate Millet."

Subscription rates for 4 issues are $8 to individuals, $16 to institutions, $12 overseas. Free to prisoners and mental patients.

Back issues available, $1-1.50 each.

*Seven Days
206 Fifth Avenue
New York, NY 10010

"Reading *Time* or listening to Walter Cronkite, you might conclude that most people are uninterested in having a say in the questions that affect their daily lives. Reading *Seven Days,* you may discover that lack of interest in speeches, smiles, and families of the candidates reflects not political apathy but the wisdom of people who on the one hand have learned to distrust 'campaign oratory' and on the other hand, at least in many cases, are busily exploring alternate methods of asserting their right to democratic control

over their work, neighborhoods, and environment."

Ceased publication in April 1980.

*Sinister Wisdom
Box 660
Amherst, MA 01004

"Founded in 1976 as 'a journal for the lesbian imagination in all women,' *Sinister Wisdom* has published fresh and daring work in feminist theory, fiction, graphics, poetry, lesbian history, autobiography, literary criticism. . . . We seek material which is visionary and courageous to help us withstand violence, invisibility, silence, indifference and fear."

Subscription rates to individuals are $10 for 4 issues, $18 for 8 issues; $12 for 4 issues foreign, $21 for 8 issues foreign; $15 for 4 issues to institutions. Free to women in prisons and mental hospitals.

Back issues available.

Soil of Liberty
Box 7056, Powderhorn Station
Minneapolis, MN 55407

"Put out by north country anarchists and anarcho-feminists."

Published 4 times a year.

Subscription rates are $4 a year to individuals, $5 to institutions. Free to those incarcerated in prisons and mental hospitals.

Sojourner: The New England Women's Journal of News, Opinions, and the Arts
143 Albany Street
Cambridge, MA 02139
(617) 661-3567

"*Sojourner* was founded on the principle of presenting an open forum for women.

Our goal is to present a space in which all women can speak freely about their concerns."

Published monthly.

Subscription rates in the United States are $8 a year, $15 for 2 years to individuals; $16 a year to institutions. Overseas $16 a year.

Somos
Box 5697
San Bern, CA 92412

"*Somos* Magazine is a training project of the Somos School of Publishing, Los Padrinos of Southern California."

Ceased publication in June 1980.

＊Southern Africa
17 West 17th Street
New York, NY 10011

"OK, so southern Africa is in the news. And you want news on southern Africa. Where do you turn? The *New York Times? The Washington Post?* CBS? Sure you'll get the news. *Their* news. You'll learn of 'riots' in Soweto. A year later you'll learn of more 'riots' on the first anniversary. You'll learn of the death of the black nationalist leader, Steve Biko. But will you hear of the resistance that has continued non-stop since the uprisings in 1976? And that Steve Biko is only one of the twenty-five political prisoners known to have died inside Vorster's jails since the uprisings?"

Published monthly except for a bi-monthly issue in July/August by the Southern Africa Committee.

Subscription rates are $10 a year, $18 for 2 years to individuals; $18 a year, $35 for 2 years to institutions. Add $12.50 a year in Africa, Asia, and Europe; $9 a year in South and Central America for air mail.

Available on microfilm from University Microfilms International, 300 North Zeeb Road, Ann Arbor, MI 48106.

Southern Struggle
Box 10797, Station A
Atlanta, GA 30310

"Fighting to break the chains of all oppression."

Published monthly except October by the Southern Conference Educational League.

Subscription rates are $5 to individuals; $10 to institutions; $6 foreign. Free to prisoners.

Spare Rib
27 Clerkenwell Close
London EC1R OAT Great Gritain

"A women's liberation magazine."

Published monthly.

Subscription rates are £8 a year to individuals, £12 to institutions. Free to prisoners.

third world
Apartado 20-572
Mexico, 20 D.F.
559-3013

"*third world* is part of a large scale project which aims to provide alternative information about the realities and experiences of Third World countries; promote the awareness of Third World peoples on the causes of underdevelopment and the means to overcome it; [and] promote cooperation among progressive sectors throughout the world."

The English edition of *Cuadernos del*

Tercero Mundo, published monthly by Third World Journalists.

Subscription rates to the United States are $12 for 5 issues, $22 for 10 issues.

Back issues available, $3 each.

Undercurrents
27 Clerkenwell Close
London EC1R OAT Great Britain
01-2357303

"We regularly publish features, news reports and book reviews on many aspects of alternative technology, human communities, fringe science, inner technologies, food production, and science and industry generally."

Published bimonthly.

Subscription rate in the British Isles is £4.50 a year. £5.10 for overseas surface mail. US $12.50 to North America. £7.80 air mail to Europe, £9.60 to other countries.

Back issues available.

Union W.A.G.E.: A Working Women's Newspaper
Box 40904
San Francisco, CA 94140

"A paper that puts working women first."

Published bimonthly by the Women's Alliance to Gain Equality.

Membership rates are $15 a year, $7.50 to low-income people. Subscription rates are $4 a year in the United States, $6 in Canada.

The Waste Paper
3164 Main Street
Buffalo, NY 14214
(716) 832-9100

"Published by the Sierra Club Atlantic Chapter Radioactive Waste Compaign."
Published quarterly.
Subscription rate is $6 a year. Free to prisoners.
Back issues available.

Well-Being: The Do-It-Yourself Journal for Healthy Living
Suite 921
41 East 42nd Street
New York, NY 10017
(212) 490-3999

"*Well-Being* starts in the heart. . . ."
Published monthly.
Subscription rates in the United States are $14 a year, $25 for 2 years, $36 for 3 years; Canada and foreign $17 a year, $31 for 2 years, $45 for 3 years.

*WIN: Peace & Freedom Through Nonviolent Action
326 Livingston Street
Brooklyn, NY 11217
(212) 624-8337

"Workshop in Nonviolence."
"Across the country and around the world, people are preparing for peace. Every two weeks, *WIN* Magazine brings you news of disarmament, draft resistance, safe energy, human liberation, and all the places, large and small, where people are making peace."
Published twice a month, except in January and September, when it is monthly.
Subscription rates are $20 a year in the United States and Canada. Overseas surface mail $25 a year. Free to prisoners.

The Wine: A Newsletter of the Movement for a New Society
232 East Limberlost Drive
Tucson, AZ 85705

"Movement for a New Society (MNS) is a nationwide network of activist groups working for basic social change."
"A subscription to *The Wine* won't give you free books on feminism, a trip to Yugoslavia, or 7 old 'Free Sacco and Vanzetti' buttons. But it will keep you in the know, be a forum for your ideas, and help in spreading the word to your friends and coworkers."
Subscription rate is $15 a year, "more if you got it, less if you don't."

Womanews: N.Y.C. Feminist Newspaper and Calendar of Events
Box 220, Village Station
New York, NY 10014
(212) 868-3330

"*Womanews* provides a forum for New York City's feminist community while focusing on issues of interest to women everywhere; our focus is local, national and international."
Published monthly by Women's Focus.
Subscription rates are $8 for 12 issues, $12 or more supporting, $20 to businesses and institutions. Add $8 to sponsor a free subscription to a prisoner.

*WomanSpirit
Box 263
Wolf Creek, OR 97497

". . . I am a proud woman. I am a full woman. I am a sensitive woman. I am a free woman. I am a hopeful woman. . . ."
Published quarterly at equinoxes and solstices.
Subscription rates to individuals are $8 a year in the United States, $9 to other countries, $14 to institutions.
Back issues available, $2 each.

*Women: A Journal of Liberation
3028 Greenmount Avenue
Baltimore, MD 21218
(301) 235-5245

"We are a group of 13 women (sometimes more, sometimes less) who work together collectively. We share all aspects of producing the *Journal* and are as committed to this process as to its end result. Our method of working together requires time; each issue takes several months to complete. There is a diversity of political opinion and lifestyle among us, but we are all committed to an autonomous women's movement and to fundamental social change to eliminate sexism, classism, racism, and imperialism."
Subscription rates are $6 for 3 issues to individuals in the United States, $7 in Canada, $8 overseas, $15 to institutions. Free to prisoners.
Available on microfilm from Bell & Howell, Drawer 'E,' Wooster, OH 44691 (issues to October 1971); from the Women's History Research Center, 2325 Oak Street, Berkeley, CA 94708 (to June 1974); and from University Microfilms International; 300 North Zeeb Road, Ann Arbor, MI 48106.

**Women Against Violence in Pornography
& Media Newspage**
Box 14614
San Francisco, CA 94114
(415) 552-2709

"End media violence now!"
Published monthly.

Membership rates are $50 and up sustaining, $25 supporting, $15 subscribing, $10 low-income, $20 institutional and international.

Back issues available, $.50 each.

*The Workbook
Box 4524
Albuquerque, NM 87106
(505) 262-1862

"*The Workbook* is a fully indexed catalog of sources of information about environmental, social and consumer problems. It is aimed at helping people in small towns and cities across America gain access to vital information that can help them assert control over their lives."

Published bimonthly by the Southwest Research and Information Center.

Subscription rates in the United States are $7 a year to students and senior citizens, $10 to other individuals, $20 to institutions. In Canada $10 to students and senior citizens, $15 to other individuals, $28 to institutions. Inquire for foreign rates.

Index

Compiled by Sanford Berman, Head Cataloger, Hennepin County Library, Edina, Minnesota

NOTE: *All entries are filed alphabetically, word by word. Simple abbreviations (like "CIA" and "FBI") appear at the beginning of each alphabetical sequence, while acronyms and contractions (like "Dr.," "OSHA," and "SWAPO") are treated as whole words. Numbers (like "2, 4-D") are arranged as if spelled out (e.g., "Two, four-D").*

CAIL (Latin America Anti-Imperialist Pro-Independence Coalition), 399
Cal/OSHA, 366-67
Caldicott, Helen, 32, 46
Caldwell, David, 252
Caldwell, Earl, 102
Caldwell, Malcolm, 118
California Agriculture, 202
California Campaign for Economic Democracy, 177
California Department of Corrections, 243-49
California Department of Industrial Relations, 202
California Department of Public Health, 202
California Medical Association, 293
California NOW, 413
California prisons, 247-49, 480
California Public Policy Center, 177
California Rural Legal Assistance, 201-3
California Solid Waste Management Board, 80
Callahan, Sidney Cornelia, 344-45
Calliope Publishing, 480
Caltex, 171
Cambodia. *See* Kampuchea.
Cambodia Year Zero (Ponchaud), 116
"Cambodian Liberation" (graphic), 440
Camp David Accords (1978), 106, 218-19
Camp, William E., 226
Campaign for a Nuclear-Free Philippines, 175
Campaign for Economic Democracy, 446-47
Campaign for Homosexual Equality, 353
Campaign for Human Development, 142
Campaign for Political Rights, 480-81
Campbell, J. E., 405
Campbell Soup Company, 374-76
Campo Libertad (Fort Walton Beach, Florida), 134
Campos Menendez, Enrique, 229
Campos, Sarah, 141
Canada, 224, 332
Canadian Atomic Energy Control Board, 189
Canadian Bill of Rights, 324
Canadian gay community, 323, 338-43
Canadian National Institute for the Blind, 339-40
Canadian uranium exports, 174
Canals, Nelson W., 241
Canby, Vincent, 270
Cancel Miranda, Raphael, 251
Cancer. *See* Bone cancer; Carcinogens; Leukemia; Lung cancer; Muscle cancer; Nuclear power and cancer.
"Cancer in the Earth" (1979), 51-53
Canel, James B., 227-29
Canfora, Alan, 427, 439
Canning industry, 375
Cannon Mills, 365
Cantell, Timothy, 88-89
Cape Town Student Boycott (1980), 97
Capital investment, 379
Capital punishment. *See* Death penalty.
Capitalism, 12-13, 21, 59, 98, 105, 120, 157, 205, 232-33, 253, 272-74, 304, 338, 355, 415, 419, 444-48. *See also* Banks; Corporate power; Free enterprise; Inflation; Literary-industrial complex; Multinational corporations; Recession; Unemployment.

"Capitalism and Plant Breeding" (1980), 203-6
Capitalism & Slavery (Williams), 108
Captain Video, 457
Carcinogens, 32, 37, 47, 49, 51, 53, 57-58, 187-90, 192-93, 198, 409. *See also* Nuclear power and cancer.
CARD (Coalition Against Registration and the Draft), 429
Cargill Corporation, 208
Carribe', 104-5; directory data, 473
Carleton, William Baker, 227
Carlson, Flo, 420
Carolina Brown Lung Association, 364
Carolina Peacemaker, 252
Carrington, Lenora, 457
Carrington, Lord, 103
Carroll, Thomas Edward, 227
"Carrying the Burden of Apartheid" (1980), 98-101
Cartagena, Police Superintendent, 240
Carter Administration, 56, 108-10, 119, 135, 138, 173, 188, 400, 428, 434-36. *See also* Camp David Accords; Iranian hostage "crisis."
Carter Doctrine, 108-10, 434
Carter family, 35
Carter, Jimmy, 29, 50, 52, 54-55, 134, 157, 188, 212, 215, 235, 240, 253, 357, 378, 383, 399, 417, 427-28, 431, 443, 460
Carter-Reagan election. *See* Presidential election (1980).
Cartlege, Sue, 308, 351-54
Carty-Bennia, Denise, 418
CASA, 422-23; directory data, 473
Casa Nicaragua (San Francisco), 132-33
Case, Patricia J., 7, 9, 259-60, 307-8, 391-92
Casey, Leo, 307, 329-30
CAST (Council on Agricultural Science and Technology), 199
Castano, Ciro, 129
Castro, Fidel, 134, 228, 236-38
Catholic Church, 282, 331, 348. *See also* Papal Army.
Catholic Worker, 431-32; directory data, 473
Cattaraugus Indian Reservation (New York), 145
Cauce, Cesar, 252
Caughlan, Robert, 165-67
Cazaux, Jean-Jacques, 115
Cecil, Ruth Ann, 196
Cederberg, Elford, 192
Celanese Corporation, 208
Celebrities, 458
Censorship, 24, 34-35, 39, 101, 138, 218, 230, 270, 319, 323, 325-26, 329-31, 339, 469. *See also* Banning (South Africa); Film censorship; First Amendment; Mass media bias; Music censorship; Prison censorship; Television censorship.
Center Against Sexual Assault (Phoenix, Arizona), 422-23, 473
Center for Alternative Industrial Systems, 385
Center for Career and Occupational Education (New York City), 280
Center for Constitutional Rights, 412, 417
Center for Development Policy, 175
Center for International Environment Information, 58

Center for Maximum Potential Building Systems, 71
Central America, 432, 436. *See also* Latin America; *and names of specific countries (e.g.,* El Salvador; Nicaragua).
Central American Common Market, 119
Central Electricity Generation Board (Great Britain), 60
Central Intelligence Agency. *See* CIA.
Central Soya, 208
Central Workers' Federation (Chile), 123
Centralization, 70. *See also* Bureaucracies; Decentralization.
Cerebral palsied persons, 339-43
Cervantes, Miguel de, 393
Cervical cap (birth control), 285-86
Cesaire, Aimé, 457
Cesium, 32, 47-48
CETA Program, 157, 247, 281, 371, 396, 425
Chacker, Neil, 374-76
Chain gangs, 249
Chamorro, Pedro Joaquin, 130
Chamorro, Xavier, 130
Champion Construction, 41
Chancellor, John, 458
Chandler, David P., 119
Changes, 355, 374-76; directory data, 473
Changing of the Gods (Goldenberg), 298
Chapman, Frances, 19
Chapnick, Ellen, 240-42
Charette, Wilfred J. A., 226-27
Charles Briscoe Committee for Justice, 232-33
Charles Fort Comedy Hour (television program), 457
Charles, Ray, 417
Charleston Palmetto Alliance, 405-6
Charleston (South Carolina) radioactive waste regulation, 404-6
Charlie's Angels (television program), 457
"Charlotte Street Declaration," 398-99
Chase Manhattan Bank, 180, 212, 216
Chavis, Ben, 251
Cheek Pants Company advertisements, 263
Cheerleaders (pro football), 456-57
Chem Nuclear Company, 179
Chemagro Company, 196, 200
Chemical industry, 195-202. *See also* Agrochemical industry; Petrochemical industry.
Chemical Industry Institute of Toxicology, 188
"Chemistry of Risk: Synthesizing the Corporate Ideology of the 1980s" (1979), 186-90
Cheney, Richard, 195
Chesimard, Joanne, 234
Chesler, Phyllis, 352
Chessman, Caryll, 462
Chevron Company, 185
Cheyenne Nation, 143, 185-86
Chicago Journalism Review, 19
Chicago Nazi rallies (1978-1979), 254-57
Chicago Police Department "Red Squad," 236
Chicago Political Surveillance Litigation and Education Project, 236
Chicago Tribune, 271
Chicanas, 138-40
Chicano art, 138-40
Chicano Moratorium (1970), 140
Chicano movement, 140-42

Committee for Women in Non-Traditional Jobs, 281
Committee of 61, 97
Committee on Economic Development, 449
Common Market countries, 207
Commoner, Barry, 417-18, 446-47
Commonwealth Edison (Chicago), 178
Commonwealth Monitoring Force (Zimbabwe), 101-2
Communes, 402, 437, 453
Communication Workers of America, 235
Communism, 419. *See also* Council communism; Marxism; State communism.
Communist Party of Chile, 125
Communist Party of Colombia, 126-27
Communist Party of El Salvador, 119-21
Communist Party of Kampuchea, 115-19
Communist Party of the United States of America, 414-15
Communist Party USA/Marxist Leninist, 234
Communist Workers Party, 214, 251-53
Communists, 348, 414
Communities, 382-85, 449-53; directory data, 474
Community concerts, 397
Community Conservation Centers (Berkeley, California), 82
Community gardens, 393
Community newspapers, 9, 16
Community organizing, 393-97, 481
Community radio, 471
Community Readjustment Act (proposed), 402
Composting, 80-81
Composting toilets, 71, 80
Computers, 94, 379, 443
Con Ed. *See* Continental Edison.
Consensus decision-making, 391, 406-8, 415-16
Concerned About Trident, 50
Concerned Asian Scholars Bulletin. See Bulletin of Concerned Asian Scholars.
Concerned Citizens Against the Klan, 253
Concrete houses, 71
Conditions of the Filipino People under Martial Law (1979), 176
Condominium conversion, 462
Condominiums, 13
Conference of Latin American Bishops (1968), 121
Conference on Church and Society (1967), 17
"Confronting Neo-Nazis in Chicago" (1979), 254-57
Conglomerates, 21, 167, 174, 176, 330, 379, 383. *See also* Corporate power; Literary-industrial complex; *and names of specific firms* (*e.g.,* Exxon Corporation; Gulf & Western Industries; Stevens [J. P.] & Company, Inc.).
Congress, 54, 56, 161, 168, 188, 190-91, 195, 207, 238, 288, 380, 427, 434
Congress of Gay People (1974), 318
Congress To Unite Women (2d), 313
Congressional Research Service, 110
Connally, John B., 419
Connelly, Claude Patrick, 223
Conoco (Continental Oil Company), 165, 178, 184
CONPASO (Consolidated Coal Company-El Paso Natural Gas Company), 185

Conqueror (film), 56-57
Conrad, 21
Conscientious objectors, 429
Consciousness, 441-42
Conservation, 63, 70. *See also* Energy conservation; Forest conservation; Recycling; Soil conservation; Waste resource recovery.
Consolidated and Peabody Coal Companies, 185
Constable, Mike, 431
"Construction Workers Talk About the Monster They're Building at Shoreham" (1979), 39-42
Consumer information, 485
Consumer Products Safety Commission, 187
Consumerism, 12-13, 21, 63, 163, 458
Consumers Federation of America, 207
Consumers Party (Philadelphia), 417
Container Corporation of America, 168
Contemporary Culture Collection (Temple University Library), 5
Continental Edison, 47
Contract concessions, 161, 377, 447
Contract labor systems, 90, 99
Control Data Corporation, 171
Convict labor, 250
Convoy Dispatch, 356, 387-89; directory data, 474
Conyers, John, 154
Coogan, Mark, 103
Coolidge, Calvin, 159
Co-Op Magazine, 71-75; directory data, 474
Cooper, Alice, 309
Cooper, Eleanor, 307, 312-13
Cooperative education, 383-85
Cooperative League of the USA, 72
Cooperative Method of Natural Birth Control (Nofziger), 286
Cooperative Power Association, 72-76
Cooperatives. *See* Electric co-ops; Housing co-ops; Labor cooperatives; Rural co-ops; Women's co-ops; Worker cooperatives.
Copelon, Rhonda, 412
Copley News Service, 228
Copple Decision, 185
Cordova, Jeanne, 315-16
Cornell, Michiyo, 307, 332-33
Corporate Accountability Research Group, 478
Corporate advocacy advertising, 159, 165-69, 187
Corporate bribery, 173-75, 190-202
"Corporate Connections," 159-212
Corporate Information Center, 176
Corporate negligence, 39-42, 180-82, 187, 195-202, 365, 432-34. *See also* Industrial pollution.
Corporate power, 4, 22, 95, 124, 126, 159-212, 417, 419, 443, 446, 449. *See also* Conglomerates; Literary-industrial complex; Mass media ownership; Multinational corporations; Union busting.
Corporate profits, 358, 362, 380-81, 383, 385-86, 400-401, 432, 442-43, 446-47, 456, 458
Corporate research and development, 379
Corporate television funding, 164, 169
Corporations, multinational. *See* Multinational corporations.
Corrada del Rio, Baltasar, 240

Corruption, 1, 20, 418, 436. *See also* Academic corruption; Corporate bribery; Labor union corruption; Pension fund abuse; Watergate scandal.
"Corruption Starts at Home" (1980), 389
Corson, Don, 81
"Cosmo girl" stereotype, 454
Cost of living, 443
Cost-of-living wage increases, 363
Costello, Bob, 428
Costa Rica, 134
Costa Rican gay community, 332
Cottage industries, 90
Cotton dust hazards, 363. *See also* Brown lung disease.
Council communism, 11
Council of Economic Priorities, 184
Council of Europe, 321
Council on Agricultural Science and Technology. *See* CAST.
Counterculture, 2-3, 9, 15. *See also* Communes; Hippies; "New Age."
CounterSpy, 213, 229-31; directory data, 474
Country Joe and the Fish, 15
Court, Robert, 271
Covert action, 480. *See also* CIA covert action; FBI covert action; Police spying.
Covert Action Information Bulletin, 213, 220-29, 236-38; directory data, 474
Cowan, Belita, 412
Coxe, Spencer, 235
Crane, Philip M., 443
Cranston, Alan, 55
Cranz, Roger, 19
Creel, Billy, 365
Creitz, Walter, 28
Crime, 246-47, 249, 436. *See also* Child abuse; Criminal justice system; Violence against gays; Violence against women.
Crimes Against Women (Russell), 280
Criminal justice reform, 245-47. *See also* Prison reform.
Criminal justice system, 152, 154-55. *See also* Police informers; Police terrorism; Racist law enforcement; Racist trials.
Criminal syndicalism laws, 414
"Crisis in Iran—None for Me, Thanks" (1979), 215-17
Critical Mass, 166
Critical Mass Journal, 406
Croall, Stephen, 61
Cronkite, Walter, 482
Crop patents, 206-9
Crosby, Don, 198-99, 202
Cross, Tia, 338
Crow Nation, 185
Crowley, Mart, 324, 326
Crown, Sheryl, 58-61
Crude oil prices, 380
Cruising (film), 270, 307, 322-30
Crumb, R., 463-67
Crusade to Save Vieques, 240
Cuadernos del Tercero Mundo, 483
Cuba, 218, 229, 304, 460
Cuban economy, 135
Cuban exile groups, 236-38

"Energy Conversion Plan" (Northern Sun Alliance), 408-10
Energy costs, 85-86, 379, 443. *See also* Electric utility rates; Oil prices.
Energy demand, 28, 85-86, 411
Energy Department. *See* Department of Energy.
Energy-efficient houses, 70-71
Energy facility siting, 191
"Energy From Waste" (Freeman/Olexsey), 81
Energy Future (Stobaugh/Yergin), 447
"Energy Game" (song), 45
Energy Independence Program, 182
Energy industry, 43, 51, 64, 85. *See also* Electric utilities; Nuclear industry; Oil industry; Solar industry.
Energy industry nationalization, 419, 447
Energy industry reinvestment, 443
Energy policy, 43, 85-88, 408-10, 428. *See also* Nuclear policy.
Energy Policy and Conservation Act (1975), 380
Energy policy and employment, 42-44, 51, 408
Energy prices. *See* Energy costs.
Energy Research Development Agency. *See* ERDA.
Energy resources, 143. *See also* Alternative energy resources; Fossil fuels; Nuclear power.
Energy shortages, 70, 443
Engelmann, Jacques, 115
Englehart, Bob, 287
Enlisted Times, 19
Ensign, Tod, 250
Environmental Action, 53-56, 160, 190-95; directory data, 475
Environmental Action Foundation, 166
Environmental advertising, 167
Environmental Defense Fund, 207
Environmental impact statements, 173, 183, 185, 209
Environmental movement, 43, 89-93. *See also* Anti-nuclear movement; *and names of specific groups* (*e.g.,* EFFE; Sierra Club).
Environmental policy and employment, 42-44
Environmental Policy Center, 53
Environmental protection, 186-95. *See also* Environmental movement.
Environmental Protection Agency, 79-80, 173, 185, 187-88, 191, 193-94, 198-99, 411
Environmental Protection Commission, 186
Environmentalists for Full Employment. *See* EFFE.
Enzensberger, Hans Magnus, 444, 447, 455, 460
Epstein, Beryl, 19
Equal Employment Opportunities Commission, 366, 370
Equal Rights Amendment, 325, 376, 420
Equal Times, 355, 362-64; directory data, 475
Equality, 2, 12-13, 469. *See also* Civil rights movement.
ERDA (Energy Research Development Agency), 182
Erdman, Paul, 87
Erickson, Nancy S., 231
Erlich, Reese, 140-42
Erotic film advertisements, 15
Ervin Committee, 239
Espectador (Colombia), 126
Espejo, Rene Silva, 227-28

Esso, 203
Esterline, Jacob, 229
Estes, Pete, 381
Ethion (pesticide), 200
Ethiopia, 38, 135
Ethiopian women, 275
Ethnicity, 13
Etruscans, 70
Eugene (Oregon) solid waste disposal, 82-83
European Broadcasting Corporation, 320
European environmental movement, 45-47
European Parliament, 46
"Europeans Oppose Nukes" (1980), 45-47
Evans, Rupert Armstrong, 87
Eve (Biblical figure), 300
Evening Magazine (television program), 458
Evening news (television program), 457-59
EVO. See East Village Other.
Ewe women, 275-76
"Exciting Eighties" (1979), 442-44
Executions, 216, 320
Executive Nurse, 374
Exorcist (film), 324, 327
"Exploiting Indians' Lands for the Hard Energy Path" (1979), 184-86
Export-Import Bank, 174-75
Exxon Corporation, 34, 174, 178-80, 182-84, 409
Exxon Foundation, 190
"Eyewitless News: An Amusing Aid to Digestion" (1979), 457-59
Eysenck, Hans J., 206

FALN, 241
FAO. *See* Food and Agriculture Organization of the United Nations.
FAPL. *See* Armed Forces of Popular Liberation (El Salvador).
FBI, 144, 213, 233, 235, 240-43, 431, 440, 460, 474, 481
FBI Charter (proposed), 238-40
FBI covert action, 17, 220, 238
FBI informers, 16, 238-39
FBI raids, 234
FBI records, 415
FCC. *See* Federal Communications Commission.
FDA. *See* Food and Drug Administration.
FDR. *See* Democratic Revolutionary Front (El Salvador).
FHAR. *See* Frente Homosexual de Accion Revolucionaria (Mexico).
FLH. *See* Frente de Liberacion Homosexualle.
FMC-Niagra, 196, 199, 208
FOIA. *See* Freedom of Information Act.
FOIA, Inc., 239
FI Hybrid seeds, 205
FPL. *See* Popular Liberation Forces (El Salvador).
FPS, 163
FSC. *See* Federation of Southern Cooperatives.
FSLN. *See* Sandinista Liberation Front.
FTC. *See* Federal Trade Commission.
Fabar, Al, 380-82
Fabens, Tish, 359-62
Factory speedups. *See* Production line speedups.

"Faggot" (term), 314, 347, 350-51
Fair Employment Practices Commissions, 366
Fairness Doctrine (broadcasting), 166, 169, 456
Falk, Dennis, 156
Fallout Forum, 51-53, 406-8; directory data, 475
Fallout hazards, 26, 51, 54, 56, 60
Fallout shelters, 51-52
Famiglia Cristiana, 116-17
Family Farm Coalition, 207
Family farms, 449
Family Law and Order Program (advertisement), 468
Fanning, David, 148-50
FAPU. *See* Front for United Popular Action (El Salvador).
Far Eastern Economic Review, 117
FARC (Revolutionary Armed Forces of Colombia), 128-29
FARE (Full Access and Rights to Education), 280
The Farm, 294
Farm Labor Organizing Committee, 374-76
Farm women, 376
Farmer, J. S., 316
"Farmer" (1979), 376
Farmland loss, 88-89
Farmworkers, 100, 120, 203, 206, 449. *See also* Farm Labor Organizing Committee; United Farmworkers Union.
FARN. *See* Armed Forces of National Resistance (El Salvador).
Farrell, Warren, 310
Fascism, 12, 17, 357. *See also* Nazis.
Fast Flux Test Facility (Washington), 181-82
Fast Forward (television series), 164
Faux, Jeff, 417
Fedayi Khalq (Kurdish political group), 113
Federal Bureau of Investigation. *See* FBI.
Federal Communications Commission, 164, 458
Federal debt, 443
Federal Prison Industries Board, 250
Federal Reserve System, 419
Federal Resources-American Nuclear, 178
Federal Trade Commission, 166, 168, 401
Federation of Southern Cooperatives, 242-43
Feiffer, Jules, 463
"Fela's Afrobeat *Zombie*" (1979), 104-5
Feldman, Dede, 53
Felice, John, 389
Felker, Clay, 230
Fellowship of Reconciliation, 251
"Female World of Love and Ritual" (Rosenberg), 316
Feminism, 5, 60, 140, 229-31, 259, 284, 297, 300-301, 311, 315, 330, 337, 352, 392, 416, 425, 442-44, 454. *See also* Anarcha-feminism; Indian feminism; Lesbian feminism; Radical feminism; Socialist feminism; Women's movement; Women's resistance.
Feminist Alliance Against Rape, 471
Feminist collectives, 402, 424, 484
"Feminist Economics: A Global View" (1979), 274-80
Feminist Healthworks, 285
Feminist periodicals, 471-73, 475-85

Fuller, John, 60
Fundamental Answers, Inc., 468-69
Fundamentalism, 16, 218, 312, 468-69
Fuqua, Don, 194
Furer, Arthur, 412

GAA. *See* Gay Activists Alliance.
G.E. *See* General Electric Company.
"GIs Fight Agent Orange Contamination"
  (1979), 432-34
GLF. *See* Gay Liberation Front.
GM. *See* General Motors Corporation.
"G-Marxism," 463
Gairy, Eric, 222
Gaitan, Armondo, 337
GALA. *See* Gay and Latino Alliance.
Gall, Norman, 176
Gallardo, Cesar, 131
Gallen, Hugh, 236
Galli, Rosemary, 125-27
Galloway, Bob, 195
"Games-man-ship Spells Defeat" (1979), 373-74
Games Mother Never Taught You (Harragan),
  373-74
Gammage, Bob, 192
Gandhi, Indira, 90
Gans, Herbert, 21
Gara, Larry, 251
Garbage resource recovery. *See* Waste resource
  recovery.
Garbagios (Eugene garbage collection com-
  pany), 82
Garcia, Dick, 197, 202
Garcia Marquez, Gabriel, 126
Garden Products, 208
Garment workers, 136, 163
Garon, Paul, 457
Garret, Banning, 17
Garrison, Jim, 180-82
Garry, Vincent F., 76
Gasohol, 204
GASP (General Assembly to Stop the Power-
  line), 75-76
Gates of Eden (Dickstein), 16
Gay Activists Alliance, 312-13
Gay American History (Katz), 316
Gay and Latino Alliance, 133, 332
Gay bar raids, 331
Gay bars, 323-24, 326-27, 329, 332, 340-41, 368
Gay baths, 342-43
Gay communes, 312
Gay Community News, 3, 5, 132-34, 309-12,
  318-22, 331-38, 346-51; directory data, 475
Gay history, 322. *See also* Gay Holocaust (1933-
  1945); Lesbian history; Stonewall rebellion
  (1969).
Gay Holocaust (1933-1945), 352
Gay households, 402
Gay Insurgent, 7, 332-33; directory data, 476
Gay Liberation Front, 312-13
Gay liberation movement, 5, 307, 309-12, 345,
  399, 472. *See also* Stonewall rebellion (1969);
  and names of specific groups (*e.g.,* Gay
  Activists Alliance; International Gay Associa-
  tion; National Gay Task Force).
Gay men, 309-12, 322-29
Gay Mystique, 339

Gay parents, 344. *See also* Children of gay
  parents; Lesbian mothers.
Gay Parent's Guide to Child Custody (1978), 345
Gay People for the Nicaraguan Revolution,
  132-34
Gay periodicals, 472, 475-78, 482
Gay police, 312, 327
Gay Political Caucus, 264
Gay press, 9, 329-30. *See also* Gay periodicals;
  Lesbian press.
Gay Pride Day, 347, 349-50
Gay Pride Week, 331
Gay prisoners, 321-22
Gay racism, 333-38
Gay radicalism, 311-12
Gay refugees, 320
Gay resistance, 307, 311-12, 328-29. *See also*
  Gay liberation movement; Gay sick-ins;
  Stonewall rebellion (1969).
Gay rights, 269, 307, 311, 318-22, 326, 332, 441,
  443, 460
Gay sadomasochism, 310, 323-24, 326-29
Gay sick-ins, 321
Gay slang, 313-17
Gay soldiers, 312
Gay students, 320
Gay Sunshine, 312
Gay teachers, 312, 349, 351
Gay Theology, 339
Gay women. *See* Lesbians.
Gays, 307-8, 348. *See also* Disabled gays; Gay
  liberation movement; Gay men; Gay press;
  Gay rights; Homophobia; Homosexuality;
  Lesbians; Third World gays; *and names of
  specific communities* (*e.g.,* Dutch gay com-
  munity; Mexican gay community; Nicara-
  guan gay community; New York gay com-
  munity; San Francisco gay community).
"Gays Support the Revolution in Nicaragua"
  (1980), 132-34
General Accounting Office, 81, 161, 182, 243
General Assembly to Stop the Powerline. *See*
  GASP.
General Atomic, 36, 178
General Electric Company, 35-36, 38, 40,
  178-79
General Foods Corporation, 124
General Mills, Inc., 164
General Motors Corporation, 164-65, 169, 171,
  177, 380-81
General Services Administration, 186
General strikes, 415, 445
"Generations: Conflict and the Ethnic Experi-
  ence" (1979), 281-84
"Genetic imperialism," 205
Genocide, 18, 115-16, 143, 157, 174, 449. *See
  also* Jewish Holocaust (1933-1945).
"George Merritt: How Many More Trials? How
  Many More Years?" (1979), 154-55
George, Susan, 206
Germany, West. *See* West Germany.
Geto, Ethan, 325
Getty Oil Company, 178
Giandoni, William B., 229
Giarusso, Edward, 118
Gibbs, Lois, 411
Gidlow, Elsa, 315

Gierek regime, 357
Gilles, Archibald, 417
Gilven, Curtis, 156
Ginsberg, Allen, 17, 186
"Girl" (term), 271
"Girls and the New York City Vocational
  Education System" (1980), 280-81
Gitlin, Todd, 457
Glass Station (Eugene, Oregon), 82
Gleaner. See Jamaica Daily Gleaner.
Gleason, John V., 154
Glenwood (Oregon) Solid Waste Center, 78-79,
  82
*Global Reach: The Power of the Multinational
  Corporations* (Barnet/Muller), 173
God, 468. *See also* Goddess Movement;
  Religion.
Goddess Movement, 296-97
Goesgen (Switzerland) Nuclear Power Plant,
  46
Golden Triangle, 17
"Golden Windfall" (1980), 171-72
Goldenberg, Naomi, 296, 298-99
Goldman, Emma, 480
Goldstein, Richard, 325, 327
Goldwater, Barry, 21
Gomez Hurtado, Alvaro, 129
Gonzalez, Gil, 125-27
Good, Fred, 391, 397
Good, Joyce, 7
Goodman, Bernice, 344-45
Goodman, Paul, 453-54
Goodstein, David, 312
Goodyear Tire & Rubber Company, 178-79
Gordon, Jerry, 43
Gordon, Peter, 101
Gore, Albert, 194
Goree Island (Senegal), 105
Gorleben (West Germany) nuclear waste re-
  processing-storage plant, 45-46
"'Got to Be a Macho Man'" (1979), 309-10
Gould, Sue, 259, 266-69
Government negligence, 53-56, 432-34
Government secrecy, 34-35
Goyo (artist), 131
Grace, Tom, 439
Grace (W. R.) & Company, 164, 178
Graduate (film), 186
Graeb, Margaret, 343
Gay discos, 342
Graffiti, 6
Graham Center Seed Directory (1979), 209
Graham, Katharine, 230
Grahn, Judy, 313
Grain prices, 203
Grand jury, 240-43
Grand Jury Project, Inc., 238, 481
Grass, Randall, 104-5
Grassland Resources, 208
Grassroots movement, 9, 447. *See also* Com-
  munity newspapers; Community organizing;
  People's Convention, South Bronx (1980);
  Powerline resistance; Rank-and-file labor
  movement.
Gray Panther Network, 414-15; directory data,
  476
Gray Panthers, 414-15, 422

Great Britain, 227. *See also* British Broadcasting Corporation; British Information Service; British land policy; British nuclear power development; British productivity; British Rail; London anti-nuclear demonstration (1961).

Great Depression. *See* Depression (1929-1941).

Great Speckled Bird, 3

Greek gay community, 319

Green, Mark, 188

Green Revolution, 173, 203

Green Revolution, 27-28, 418-19, 446; directory data, 476

Green, Richard, 346

Green, William, 234

Greenbaum, Wolff & Ernst, 230

Greene, Graham, 137

Greene, Merle, 184-86

Greens (West German political party), 46

"Greensboro: Long History of Struggle" (1980), 251-53

Greensboro (North Carolina) killings (1979), 251-53

Greenwald, Carol, 391, 400-402

Greenwich Village leather bars, 323-24, 326-27

Gregory, Dick, 235

Grenada, 222

Grier, Barbara, 24, 311

Grievance procedures, 420

Griffin, Leo, 356, 372-73

Griffin, Robert, 192

Griffy's Mr the Toad, 457

Grimes, Willie, 252

Grohnde (West Germany) Nuclear Power Plant, 46

Grossman, Karl, 40

Grossman, Larry, 164-65

Grossman, Richard, 43

"Groucho Marxism Theses" (1980), 463

Groundswell, 404-6; directory data, 476

Groves, Gail, 259, 261

Growing Up Absurd (Goodman), 453

Gruening, Albert, 17

Grupo Cemi, 397

Guard, G. C., 259, 266-69

Guardian (London), 228

Guardian (New York), 118-19, 122-25, 161-62, 177-80, 214, 251-53, 432-34; directory data, 476

Guardian (San Francisco). See *San Francisco Bay Guardian.*

Guatemala, 210, 225, 441

Guatemalan gay community, 332

Guerrilla warfare, 95, 120, 127-30. *See also* Urban guerrillas.

Guevara, Che, 123, 238

"Guide to the Nuclear Bomb Industry" (1979), 179

Guinea invasion (1970), 222

Gulf & Western Industries, 2

Gulf Atomic, 36

Gulf Oil Corporation, 35, 178-79, 182, 184

Gun control, 263

Gust, Larry, 76

Guthion (pesticide), 200

Gutierrez, Andy, 196-98

Gutman, Richard, 236

Gwertzman, Bernard, 357

Guyana, 225

"Gynecological Imperialism and the Politics of Self-Help" (1979), 288-93

Gyorgy, Anna, 25, 45-47

HBO. *See* Home Box Office.

"H-Bomb Recipe" (1979), 34-39

Hadley, Donnell, 156

Hageman, Alice, 279

Haig, Suzanne, 357-58

Haight-Ashbury district (San Francisco), 15

Hains advertisements, 271

Haiti, 225

Haitian Fathers, 137

Haitian refugees, 95-96, 136-38, 218

Hall, Benjamin H., 315-16

Hall, Betty Jean, 411-12

Hall, David, 131

Hall, Darwin C., 202

Hall, Marny, 345-46

Hall, Radclyffe, 352

Hall, Ran, 307, 310-11

Halliday, Fred, 108

Halloween (film), 271

Hamer, Fannie Lou, 440

Hammer, Armand, 194

Hammock, Ron, 181

Hampton, Fred, 220, 233, 239

Hancock, Don, 160, 206-9

Handicappism, 338-43

Hanford Conversion Project, 182

Hanford Nuclear Reservation, 58

Hanisch, Carol, 473

Hanke, Jonathan, 229

Hannon, Gerald, 307, 338-43

Happy Days (television series), 310

"Happy news" concept, 458-59

Harden, Lakota, 55

Hardy, Robin, 323

Hare Krishnas, 451

Hargan, James, 314, 316

Hargett, Daryal, 265

Harlan County, USA (film), 455

Harlem, 153, 232, 234

Harlequin Romances, 2

"Harlequin Syndrome" (cartoon), 38

Harnik, Peter, 191, 195

Harper's Magazine, 20, 167

Harragan, Betty Lehen, 373-74

Harrington, Olbie, 106

Harris, David, 427

Harris, La Donna, 417-18

Harris polls, 151, 168

Harris v *McRae,* 286-88

"Harrisburg Accident: Once in 17,000 Years?" (1979), 28-31

Hart, Gary, 182

Hart, Win, 198

Hartmann, Betsy, 210-11

Harvard Medical School, 289-93

Harvard University, 190

Hassan, Crown Prince, 220

Hatfield, Mark, 182, 427

Hausman, David, 20

Havana Post, 228

"Having Nothing to Say" (1979), 11-14

Hawk, Beverly, 101-2

Hawkes, J. G., 207

Hayden, Tom, 446

Hayes, Floyd, 388

Hayward, Susan, 56

Hazaras, 110

"Hazardous Cargo: Contains Nuclear Wastes" (graphic), 405

Hazardous waste disposal, 79, 187, 190-95, 411, 448

Hazelrigg, George H., 224

He Knows You're Alone (film), 271

Health, 484. *See also* Carcinogens; Occupational health and safety; Stress; Women's health.

Health Advocate of the Year Awards (1980), 411-12

Health Care Employee Union, District 1199, 358-59

"Health Leaders Win Awards" (1980), 411-12

Health/PAC Bulletin, 293-94; directory data, 476

Health policy, 476

HealthRight, 290-91, 293, 391, 412-13; directory data, 476-77

Hecksher, Henry, 229

Hedonism, 442

Heflin, Howell, 193

Heights & Valley News, 230

Helioflores (artist), 132

Heller, Agnes, 382

Helms, Richard, 216, 227-28

Helms, Thomas, 156

"Help Rebuild Nicaragua" (graphic), 134

Hemmings, Susan, 308, 351-54

Henderson, Nicholas, 101

Hendrie, Joseph M., 29

Hendrix, Harold, 229

Henley, W. E., 316

Herbal medicine, 286

Herbal Remedies for Women, 286

Herbicides, 187, 191, 199, 204, 250. *See also* Agent Orange; 2,4,5-T (herbicide).

Herding societies, 67, 113

Heresies, 356, 370-71; directory data, 477

Hereth, Dave, 198

Herkimer (New York) furniture cooperative, 382-83, 385

Herman, Edward, 116

Hernandez, Juan Jacobo, 331-32

Hernandez, Judithe, 138-40

"He's Sick, Homeless and Unloved" (cartoon), 216

Hess, Charles, 196, 204

Heterosexism, 301, 304, 309, 313, 316, 318

Heterosexuality, 343, 351, 353-54

Hidemi, Azuma, 280

"High Court Upholds 'Hyde'" (1980), 286-88

High technology, 51, 78, 82, 443. *See also* Computers; Nuclear power.

High voltage powerlines. *See* Powerlines.

Hildebrand, George, 119

Hill and Knowlton (public relations firm), 412

Hill, Bonnie, 411

Hill, Joann, 411

Hill, Robert, 151

Hill, Walter, 270-71

Labor mobility, 443
Labor Notes, 377; directory data, 477
Labor organizers, 218
Labor organizing, 44, 120, 174, 355, 359-61, 373, 481
Labor periodicals, 474, 477, 483-84
Labor productivity, 355, 358, 377-79, 381, 443
Labor relations consultants, 358-62
Labor solidarity, 359-60
Labor union corruption, 387-89
Labor union pension fund investment, 177
Labor union reform, 387-89
Labor union television funding, 163-65
Labor unions, 120-21, 124, 127, 460. *See also* Rank-and-file labor movement; Strikes; Union busting; *and names of specific unions and labor groups (e.g.,* AFL-CIO; Central Workers' Federation (Chile); Coalition of Labor Union Women; Industrial Workers of the World; International Association of Machinists; United Auto Workers).
Labor unions and nuclear power, 42-44, 180, 183
Labour Party (Great Britain), 387
Lacefield, Patrick, 136-38
Lacey, Louise, 286
Lackner, Jerome, 200
Lacouture, Jean, 116
Ladder, 24, 316
"Lady executive" stereotype, 454
LaFleur, Nathaniel, 155
Laguna Pueblos, 184
Lakota people, 183, 409-10
Lamantia, Philip, 457
Lambda (Mexican gay group), 332
Lambros, Thomas, 401
Lampiao, 332
Lancet, 58
Lancome Cosmetics (Nestlé subsidiary), 413
Land "development," 448
Land grants, 142
Land reclamation, 63, 88-89, 185
Land reform, 113-14, 129, 203
Land Rights Council (Chama, Colorado), 141-42
Land trusts, 89, 476
Land use, 448-49. *See also* Land "development."
Laney, Mary, 267
Landfills, 79, 82
Landis, Fred, 227-29
Lane County (Oregon) solid waste disposal, 78-80
Lane Economic Development Council, 83
Lange, Harry, 196
Language and Responsibility (Chomsky), 150
Language control, 14, 102-3, *See also* Information control.
Language development, 66
Lans, Ken, 49-50
Laos, 17
Lappe, Frances Moore, 211
LaRaque, Frank, 137-38
LaRose, Roy, 342
Larouche, Lyndon, 460
Last House on the Left (film), 271
Latin America, 95, 203. *See also* Central America; Third World; *and names of specific countries (e.g.,* Chile; Nicaragua).

Latin America Anti-Imperialist Pro-Independence Coalition, 399
Latin American women, 277. *See also* Brazilian women; Peruvian women; Puerto Rican women.
LATIN (wire service), 228
Latina Lesbians, 338
Latino gays, 337-38
Latino periodicals, 481, 483
Lauck, Gerhard, 254
Laurie, Peter, 93-94
Lavender Archives, 476
Lavender Menace, 313
Lawrence Livermore Nuclear Weapons Laboratory, 55
Lawrence, Richard, 109
Lawson, Ed, 388
Layoffs. *See* Unemployed workers.
Layzer, Judith, 281
Le Grange, Louis, 97
Le Monde, 116, 126
Leacock, Eleanor, 280
Leadership, 421
League of Conservation Voters, 191
League of Revolutionary Struggle (Marxist-Leninist), 141
League of United Latin American Citizens, 141
Leahy, Dan, 418
Lean Years: Politics in the Age of Scarcity (Barnet), 173
Leaping Lesbian, 317-18; directory data, 477-78
Lear, Bert, 201-2
Lear, Norman, 455
Leary, Timothy, 15
Leaseway (trucking firm), 389
Leather bars, 323-24, 326-27, 329
Lee, Jack M., 76
Lee, Michelle, 251
Lee, Rose Anna, 411
"Left liberalism," 446
Leggett, Elizabeth, 293-94
Leggs advertisements, 271
Leghorn, Lisa, 265, 274-80
LeGuin, Ursula, 457
Leidholdt, Dorchen, 270
Lemoine, Patrick, 137
Lems, Kristin, 356, 376, 473
Lenin, V. I., 370
Leniz, Fernando, 228
Lens, Sidney, 50
Leonard Peltier Defense Committee, 251
Leonard, W. O., 365
Lesbian: A Celebration of Difference (Goodman), 345
Lesbian child custody, 318, 344-45, 348
Lesbian feminism, 23, 312-13, 317, 338, 354
Lesbian Feminist, 312-13; directory data, 478
Lesbian Feminist Liberation, 313, 478
"Lesbian/Gay Rights Now!" (graphic), 319
Lesbian Herstory Archives, 24, 313
Lesbian history, 307, 482
Lesbian Liberation Committee (GAA), 312
Lesbian literature, 310-11
"Lesbian Mothering" (1980), 343-46
Lesbian mothers, 308, 343-51
Lesbian music festivals, 318
"Lesbian Origin" (Cartlege), 351-54
Lesbian periodicals, 477-78, 482

Lesbian press, 23-24. *See also* Lesbian periodicals.
"Lesbian Pride: Ten Years and Beyond: A Personal and Political Perspective" (1979), 312-13
Lesbian Pride Week, 313
Lesbian racism, 333-38
Lesbian rights. *See* Gay rights.
Lesbian separatism, 307, 317-18
Lesbian slang, 313-17
"Lesbian" (term), 314
Lesbian Tide, 313
Lesbian/Woman (Martin/Lyon), 262, 343
Lesbianism, 351-54
Lesbians, 263-64, 285, 301-2, 304, 366-70, 398, 425-26. *See also* Afro-American lesbians; Asian-American lesbians; Gay liberation movement; Gay rights; Homophobia; Latina lesbians.
"Lesbians and Gay Men," 307-54
"Lesbians Struggle with Racism" (1980), 333-37
"Let the Faithful Know the Joys of Poverty" (cartoon), 299
Letelier, Orlando, 237, 459
"Letter from Jordan" (1980), 218-20
"Letter" (1980), 441-42
Leukemia, 32, 38, 47, 49, 51, 56, 58
Levine, Thomas, 392, 422
Levitt, Martin Jay, 358
Levy, Spencer, 219
Lewis, Edmonia, 315
Lewis, Harold, 57
Lewontin, Richard, 205
Libby, McNeil & Libby, Inc., 374-76, 413
Liberalism, 446
"Liberated Woman" stereotype, 454
Liberation League, 256
Liberation News Service, 5-6, 17, 293
Libertarianism, 5
Libraries, 4, 7, 24, 98, 339-40, 397. *See also* Alternative Press Collection (University of Connecticut at Storrs Library); Contemporary Culture Collection (Temple University Library).
Library of Congress, 109, 189
"Libre" (graphic), 240
Libya, 226
Lichauco Paper: US Imperialism in the Philippines (1973), 176
Lichty, Ron, 19
Liebling Counter-Convention (1973), 19-20
Life-line (IGA project), 320
Life Magazine, 2, 20, 479
"Life Supportive Index," 69-70
Lightstone, Ralph, 201-2
Like, Irving, 40
"Likeable Lyndon Larouche" (1980), 460
LILCO (Long Island Lighting Company), 39-42
Lilith (folkloric figure), 300
Lilly (Eli) & Company, 165, 461
Lim Pech Kuon, 118
"Limited Nuclear War" policy, 52
Lincoln, Abraham, 144
"Linda Butcher: Striking While the Iron's Hot" (1979), 367-70
Linden, Robin Ruth, 284-85
Lindsey, Karen, 437, 453-54
Linn, Karl, 399

Marx, Karl, 69, 303, 381

Marxism, 5, 12, 123, 148-49, 205, 217, 438, 463, 481

Marxist (word), 102-3

Mary Reynolds Babcock Foundation, 383

Masango, Reeds, 102

"Masculine Mystique: 'Got to Be a Macho Man'" (1979), 309-10

Mason & Hanger-Silas Mason Company, 179

Mass media, 438. *See also* Alternative mass media; Broadcast journalism; Censorship; Films; Socialist media groups; Television.

Mass media bias, 1-4, 25, 33, 53, 95, 101-4, 115-19, 136, 148-54, 157, 255-56, 328, 357-58, 412. *See also* Homophobic films; Racist films; Sexist advertising; Sexist films.

Mass media control, 163-65, 227-29, 330, 455. *See also* Corporate advocacy advertising; Mass media ownership.

Mass media ownership, 21, 330. *See also* Literary-industrial complex.

Mass media policy, 455-56

Mass media violence, 263, 265, 322-29, 485

Mass Party of the People, 417

Massachusetts Institute of Technology, 189-90

Massage parlor ads, 15

Masterpiece Theater (television series), 150

Masturbation, 248-49, 342-43

Mathews, Mitford, 315-16

Mathis, Weldon, 389

Matriarchy, 67

Mattachine Society, 311

"Matter of Social Justice" (1980), 362-64

May Day Committee, 235

Mayer, Paul, 399

Mazon, Ronald, 161

Mazumdar, Vina, 280

"Me Generation," 2, 12, 453

"Me Generation Says Not Me!" (1980), 434-36

Meadows, Audrey, 457

Means, Russell, 186

Means, Ted, 398

Medea, Andra, 266

Media Access Project, 168

Media bias. *See* Mass media bias.

"Media Politics" (1979), 455-56

Media violence. *See* Mass media violence.

Medicaid abortions, 286-87, 412

Medical education, 288-93

Medieval civilization, 68

Meehan, Tom, 16

Melchior, Fabienne, 280

Melendez family, 135

Mellon Foundation, 190

Mellon Institute, 190

Melnick, Jane, 35

Melnick, Mickus, and McKeown (union-busting consultants), 359-62

Men childcare workers, 372-73

"Men Who Are Victims of Rape," 422

Menjivar, Rafael, 131

Men's consciousness-raising, 309-10

Men's sexuality, 328-29

Mental illness, 14. *See also* Psychoanalysis.

Mental patients' rights, 218

Mentzer, Sherrie, 391, 420-22

Meo people. *See* Hmong people.

Mercado, Jose Raquel, 128

Mercedes Hodgers, Silvia, 131

El Mercurio (Chile), 227-29

MERIP Reports, 95, 108-14, 213, 218-20; directory data, 478

Mermaid and the Minotaur (Dinnerstein), 304

Merrill Lynch, 165

Merritt, George, 154-55

Merryfinch, Lesley, 58-61

Mesquita Neto, Julio, 228

Mesurol (pesticide), 196

Met Ed. *See* Metropolitan Edison.

Metals Recovery Demonstration Project (Corson), 81

Metallurgy, 67

Metanokett Village, 451

Meteorology and Atomic Energy (1968), 49

Metropolitan Community Church, 342

Metropolitan Edison, 27-32

Metropolitan Life, 180

Mexican American Legal Defense and Education Fund. *See* MALDEF.

Mexican-American Legal Defense Fund (San Francisco), 141

Mexican-American relations, 460

Mexican-American women. *See* Chicanas.

Mexican-Americans. *See* Chicanos.

Mexican gay community, 331-32

Mezo, Cliff "Cowboy," 69

Miami Herald, 229

Miami Riots (1980), 136, 155-56, 468

Michigan nuclear power development, 479

Michigan Women's Music Festival, 318

Microwave hazards, 35, 50

Middle class families, 284

Middle East, 95, 174, 205, 436. *See also* Third World; *and names of specific countries (e.g.,* Egypt; Iran; Israel; Saudi Arabia).

Middle East oil reserves, 108, 444

Middle East Research & Information Project, 478

Middle East Task Force, 109

Middletown, Pennsylvania, 32

Midnight Notes Collective, 446-47

Midwest Energy Times, 160, 182-86; directory data, 478

Midwifery, 260, 293-94

Migrant workers, 99, 204, 355, 374-76

Milby, Thomas, 199, 202

Militant, 159, 162-63, 355, 357-58; directory data, 478

Militarism, 215, 259, 392, 399, 428-31. *See also* Draft; Military spending.

Military bases, 173-74

Military policy, 50-53, 108-10, 434-36. *See also* Draft; "Limited Nuclear War" policy; MAD policy.

Military propaganda, 430-31

Military spending, 132, 157, 171, 219, 357, 428, 436, 443

Milk contamination, 32, 49, 60

Milk, Harvey, 326

Millazzo, Connie, 235

Miller, Al, 370

Miller, Jean Baker, 262

Miller, Jeffrey, 439

Miller, John (Coalition for a Non-Nuclear World), 235

Miller, John N. (American College of Obstetricians and Gynecologists), 293

Miller, Marc, 249

Miller, Ralph, 46

Millett, Kate, 309, 482

Milligan, Molly, 56

Milliken, William G., 50

Millstone (Connecticut) Nuclear Power Plant, 41

Millworkers. *See* Textile workers.

Milwaukee steelworkers, 440

Mine Shaft (Greenwich Village bar), 325-27

Mine Workers' Union. *See* United Mine Workers.

Minneapolis "Take Back the Night" March (1979), 391, 420-22

Minneapolis water treatment, 69

Minnesota Department of Health, 76-77

Minnesota Energy Agency, 73

Minnesota Environmental Quality Council, 73, 75

Minnesota powerlines, 71-77

Minorities, 96, 110-14. *See also* Affirmative action; Equality; Ethnicity; Genocide; Racism; *and names of specific groups (e.g.,* Afro-Americans; Azeris; Chicanos; Native Americans; Soviet Jews; Ukrainians).

"Minority Contract" (cartoon), 151

Minority women, 277, 300-302. *See also* Afro-American women; Asian-American lesbians; Chicanas; Latina lesbians.

Mintz, Morton, 202

Minute Men, 468

"Misbehaviorism" dogma, 463

Miscarriages, 191, 199

Misery, 1, 14. *See also* Hunger; Injustice; Poverty.

Miso soup, 57

Miss Gay America contests, 310

"Missing Male" (1980), 372-73

Missouri State Penitentiary, 250

Moberg, David, 391, 417-18

Mobil Oil Corporation, 124, 165-69, 171, 174, 178, 180, 182, 184, 187-88

Mobilization Against the Draft, 428

Mobilization for Survival, 175, 399, 406, 435

Modern Language Association Commission on the Status of Women, 301

Modern Management Methods (union-busting consultants), 359-62

Moffitt, Ronni, 237

Mohawk, John, 63, 65-70

Mohawk Nation, 66

Mohawk Nation at Akwesasne, 471

Mohawk Sovereignty Committee, 146

Mom's Apple Pie, 344-46

Monde, 116

"Mondragon System of Industrial Cooperatives in Spain" (1979), 384

Money, 2

Monsanto Company, 179, 186-88, 190, 204, 432

Montana Power Company, 185

Montgomery, Stephen Elroy, 226

Monthly Review, 377

Moody, Kim, 355, 377

Moore, April, 190-95

Moore, Howard, 243

Moore, Michael, 236

Public Employees Retirement System, 176-77
Public Eye, 213, 231-34; directory data, 480-81
Public Eye Network, 481
Public interest advertising, 167
Public Interest Video Network, 166
Public ownership of utilities, 44
Public radio, 21
Public Service Company of New Hampshire, 33-34
Public television, 21, 148-50, 159, 163-65, 169, 456
"Public Television" (1980), 163-65
"Public Transit: Who Should Pay?" (1980), 162-63
Public transportation, 162-63, 171
Puerto Rican Alliance (Philadelphia), 235
Puerto Rican Day Parade (New York City), 394
Puerto Rican independence movement, 240-42, 393-94, 440
Puerto Rican Socialist Party, 398-99
Puerto Rican women, 264-65, 277
Puerto Ricans (New York City), 393-97
Puerto Rico Libre!, 240-42; directory data, 481
Puerto Rico Rape Crisis Center (Rio Piedras), 264
Puerto Rico Solidarity Committee, 481
Pullman National Standard Car Division, 44
Purex Corporation, 208
Pyongyang Times, 15

Qashqa'i, 110-11, 113-14
"Quality of worklife" committees (GM-UAW), 382
Quarles, George, 280-81
Quash, 238-40, 242-43; directory data, 481
"Que Disem Non a Las Centralas Atomicas" (graphic), 46
Quebec women, 278
Quest, 23, 302-5; directory data, 481
Quest Tavern (Toronto), 342

REA. *See* Rural Electrification Administration.
RN. *See* National Resistance (El Salvador).
RT: Journal of Radical Therapy, 344
Racism, 4, 6, 12, 17, 95-96, 134, 136, 150-54, 157, 214, 247, 253, 259-60, 300-302, 307, 333-38, 348, 366-67, 398, 416, 422, 424, 431, 468-69, 484. *See also* Apartheid; Chinese Exclusion Act (1882); Genocide; Ku Klux Klan; Nazis; Redlining.
"Racism and Women's Studies" (1980), 300-302
"Racism in Public TV" (1979), 148-50
"'Racism is Dead, Long Live Racism'" (1979), 150-54
Racist education, 98
Racist employment practices, 360, 362, 367. *See also* Affirmative action.
Racist films, 270
Racist journalism, 101-4
Racist law enforcement, 155-57, 231-34, 242-43, 251-53, 335, 414-15
Racist television programs, 458
Racist trials, 154-57, 249
Radiation & Health Information Service, 182
"Radiation Exposure Pathways" (graphic), 57

Radiation hazards, 26, 32, 39, 43, 46-49, 51, 53-61, 174-75, 181. *See also* Fallout hazards; Microwave hazards; Radioactive contamination.
Radiation victims, 53-57
Radical America, 355-56, 380-82, 423-26; directory data, 481
Radical feminism, 424, 426, 430-31
Radical professional groups, 9. *See also names of specific groups* (*e.g.,* British Society for Social Responsibility in Science; Social Responsibilities Round Table [American Library Association]).
Radical Science Journal, 206
Radicalesbians, 313
Radicalization of Science (1976), 206
Radio. *See* CB radio; Community radio; Pacifica Radio Network; Public radio; Voice of America; WHUR (radio station).
Radioactive contamination, 32, 49, 58, 60, 182-84, 479. *See also* Fallout hazards.
Radioactive fallout hazards. *See* Fallout hazards.
Radioactive waste, 32-33, 37
Radioactive waste disposal, 56, 58, 60, 448
Radioactive waste transportation, 47-49, 60, 404-6
"Radionuclides Released During Loss of Coolant Spent Fuel Shipping Accident" (table/map), 48
Rain, 78-84; directory data, 481
"Rainbow Family Healing Gathering" (1980), 449-53
Rainbow Societies, 340-41
"Rallies Mark the Coming of Age of the New Anti-Draft Movement" (1980), 427-28
Ramparts, 17
Rand Corporation, 109, 151-52
Randall, Kate, 77
Random House, 230
Rank-and-file labor movement, 5, 124, 356, 387-89, 401, 440
Ransom, David M., 223-24
Rape, 259, 261, 263-65, 277, 310, 329, 332, 420, 430, 453
"Rape and Virginity Among Puerto Rican Women" (1979), 264-65
Rape crisis centers, 278, 420
Rape threats, 92
Rape victims, 287, 329, 392, 422-23. *See also* Rape crisis centers.
Rapid Deployment Force, 108-10
Rarihokwats, 27-28
Raskin, Marcus, 434
Rasmussen Report, 30-31, 49, 189
Rassbach, Elsa, 164
Rastafarians, 218
Rat, 2
Rate hikes. *See* Electric utility rates.
Rates of interest. *See* Interest rates.
Rather, Dan, 104
Raush, Richard W., 226
Rawlings, Charles, 401
Ray, Dixy Lee, 462
"Raza Si Migra No" (graphic), 139
Reactor Safety Study: An Assessment of Accident Risks in U.S. Commercial Nuclear Power Plants (1975), 31, 49

Read, Robin, 236
Reader's Digest, 95, 115-19, 164, 283
Reagan, Ronald, 15-16, 131, 212, 378, 417, 443, 461
Reagan's Rayguns, 468
Real estate taxes, 395
Rearmament. *See* Arms race.
"Rebuilding a Community" (1979), 395-96
Recession, 20-21, 86, 134-36, 377, 379, 437, 441, 443. *See also* Unemployment.
"Recession Imperils Small Press" (1980), 20-21
Rechy, John, 327
Recidivism, 245-46
Recycler Looks at Resource Recovery: The Berkeley Burn Plant Papers (Knapp), 82
Recycling, 63, 79-80, 82-84, 107. *See also* Waste resource recovery.
Red Cloud (Dakota chief), 142
Red Paper on Housing, 386
"Red Squads," 233, 236
Redbook, 23, 365
Redlining, 247, 255
Redstockings, 229
Redwood Alliance, 177
Reed, Ishmael, 457
Reflexology, 286
Refugee camps, 134-36, 219
Refugee policy, 96, 135-38
Refugees, 95, 102, 117. *See also* Cuban refugees; Haitian refugees; Hungarian refugees; "Political refugees"; Vietnamese refugees.
Refuse-derived fuel, 81
Reggae music, 148-49, 473
Regional planning, 443
Rehabilitation hospitals, 246-47
Rehnquist, William H., 286
Reich, Wilhelm, 12, 305
Reid, Coletta, 311
Religion, 13, 66. *See also* Atheism; Christianity; God; Hopi cosmology; Islam; Judaic theology; Theocracy; Women's religion.
"Religion for Women" (Ruether), 296-300
Religious fanaticism, 216-17. *See also* Fundamentalism; "Moral Majority."
"Remembering Kent State, 1970-1980" (Whitney), 439, 441
Renewable energy sources. *See* Alternative energy sources.
Rent strikes, 395
Report on the Americas. See NACLA Report on the Americas.
Repression, 6, 17, 19, 33, 46, 60-61, 96, 111, 122-26, 131, 137, 144, 215-57. *See also* Banning (South Africa); Censorship; Curfews; Criminal syndicalism laws; Genocide; McCarthyism; Martial law; Police state; Police terrorism; Political prisoners; Torture.
"Repression," 213-57
Reproductive freedom, 263, 278, 286-88, 412, 472, 478. *See also* Abortion; Birth control.
Republic (Plato), 303
Republic Steel Corporation, 190-95
Republican Convention (1972), 19
Research and development. *See* Corporate research and development.
Research ethics, 195-202
Reserve Mining Company, 193
"Resist" (graphic), 244

"Sapphist" (term), 314
Saravodaya Movement, 91
Sarris, Andrew, 270
Sasser, Lois, 161
Satellite television, 455
Satire, 34-39, 162, 457, 459-63, 468-69
Saturday Day Nite Live (television program), 457
Saturday Evening Post, 20, 479
Saturday Night, 324
Saturday Review, 270
Saudi Arabia, 38, 108-9, 162, 432
Savage, J. A., 176-77
SAVAK (Iranian secret police), 111, 216, 440
Savell Passive Variant Home, 70
Savoy, Roy, 220-22
Sawyer Air Force Base, 50
Sawyer, Ethel, 314, 317
Saxe, Susan, 431
Saxton, Jonathan, 428-30
Saylor, Louis, 199
Scabs, 359, 364
Schechter, Danny, 457
Scheiner, Charles, 51-53
Schele de Vere, Maximilian, 315, 317
Scherr, Max, 15-16
Scheuer, Sandy, 439
Schlesinger, James R., 52, 73
Schlosser, Francois, 118
Schmertz, Herb, 166, 168
Schneberger, Pete, 309
Schneider Lift Translator, 71
Schneider, Marvin, 196
Schoenfeld, Eugene, 15
Schoessling, Ray, 388-89
School boycotts, 97-98
School busing, 254-55, 334
"School Career Day: Join the Marines" (cartoon), 429
School for the Blind (Brantford), 339
School of Living, 476
Schrader, Paul, 270-71
Schroeder, Bill, 439
Schubert, Conrad C., 223
Schuster, Michael, 101
Schwartz, Charles, 202
Schwartz, Jack, 19
Schwartzman, Andrew, 169
Science, 50, 189
Science for People (London), 203-6; directory data, 482
"Science for Sale" (1980), 195-202
Science for the People (Cambridge, Massachusetts), 3, 159-60, 173-76, 195-206, 288-93, 374; directory data, 482
Science for the People Collective (Ann Arbor), 375
Science News, 58
Science Resource Center, 482
Scientific accountability, 482
Scientific-industrial complex, 195-206
Scipione, Maria, 270
Scorsese, Martin, 270-71
Scottsboro Boys, 414
SCRAM Energy Bulletin, 61
SCRAM system, 32-33
Scurato, Michael, 43, 103, 175, 216, 361

"Seabrook May 24, 1980: Occupation/Blockade" (1980), 33-34
Seabrook (New Hampshire) nuclear power plant, 25, 33-34, 60, 236, 445
Seafarer Project. *See* Project ELF.
Seattle Coalition on Governing Spying, 236
Seattle housing, 462
"Seattle Mirrors Miami: White Justice, White Guns" (1980), 155-57
Seattle Times, 358
Seaweed, 57
"Second Time Around" (1980), 300
Second Wave, 274-80; directory data, 482
Secret Service, 235
Securities and Exchange Commission, 193
Seed industry, 206-9
"Seed Patenting: An Invitation to Famine" (1980), 206-9
Seeger, Pete, 472-73
Seizing Our Bodies (Dreifus), 292
Selectro-Thermo (Dracut, Massachusetts), 71
Self, 38, 453
Self-awareness movements, 453
Self-care, 484
Self-defense, 259, 266-69
Self-reliance, 481
Self-sufficiency, 71, 86, 93-94, 443, 476
Sellers, Cleveland, 253
Sempler, Kaianders, 61
Senate Veterans Committee, 55
Seneca Nation, 145-48
Senegal, 105, 107-8
"Senior Advocacy" (graphic), 414
Seniors' economic conditions, 443
Senner, James M., 226
Sentencing laws, 480
Sentinel, 329
"September 6, 1979, Statement" (*CounterSpy*). 229-31
Sergi, Janet, 437, 442-44
Service Employees International Union, 43
Seven Days, 5, 20, 31-42, 119, 125-27, 150-54, 160, 186-90, 434-36, 459-62; directory data, 482
"*Seven Days* Homemade H-Bomb Recipe" (1979), 34-39
The seventies, 4, 9, 13, 16, 22, 435, 437, 440-42, 453-54. *See also* "Black Monday," Youngstown, Ohio (Nov. 27, 1979); Camp David Accords (1978); Carter Administration; Chicago Nazi rallies (1978-1979); Democratic Convention (1972); Greensboro (North Carolina) killings (1979); International Women's Year Conference, Houston (1977); Iran hostage "crisis" (1979-1981); Jackson State shootings (May 14, 1970); Kent State shootings (May 4, 1970); Nixon Administration; Republican Convention (1972); Soweto Uprising (June 16, 1976); "Take Back the Night" march, Minneapolis (1979); Three Mile Island nuclear accident (1979); Vietnam War.
"Seventies Commemorative Stamps" (graphic), 13, 22
"Severe Effects of Plant Closings on Communities" (1979), 383
Severn, Michael, 434
Sevin (pesticide), 197-98

Sewage resource recovery. *See* Waste resource recovery.
Sex aids, 343
Sex advertisements, 15-16
"Sex, Death and Free Speech: The Fight to Stop Friedkin's *Cruising*" (1979), 322-29
Sex Information and Education Council of Canada. *See* SIECCAN.
Sex Information and Education Council of the United States. *See* SIECUS.
Sexism, 4, 12, 60-61, 274-80, 303, 313, 335-36, 348, 354, 416, 425, 453, 468, 484. *See also* Patriarchy; Violence against women.
"Sexist Ads in Ms." (1980), 271-72
Sexist advertising, 15-16, 218, 259, 263, 265, 269-72, 413, 420
Sexist education, 259. *See also* Sexist vocational education.
Sexist employment practices, 363-64, 367, 369-71. *See also* Affirmative action; Sexist wages; Sexual harassment.
Sexist films, 269-71
Sexist language, 277, 298-99, 310-11
Sexist medical care, 288-93
"Sexist Slang and the Gay Community: Are You One, Too?" (Stanley/Robbins), 314
Sexist television programs, 456-58
Sexist vocational education, 280-81
Sexist wages, 100, 272-73, 275, 277
Sexual Freedom League, 15
Sexual harassment, 263, 265, 267, 356, 365-67, 420, 423
"Sexual Harassment Used to Keep Women in Their 'Place'" (1980), 365-67
Sexual Outlaw (Rechy), 327
Sexual Politics (Millett), 309
Sexual Trauma Services (San Francisco), 263-64
Sexuality, 17, 264, 277, 297, 304. *See also* Disabled persons' sexuality; Heterosexuality; Homosexuality; Masturbation; Men's sexuality; Pornography; Sadomasochism; Sex aids; Women's sexuality.
Shackley, Ted, 229
SHAD Alliance, 51, 406-8, 475
Shaffer, Carolyn, 298
Shaffer, Ellen, 201
Shah of Iran, 108, 111, 113, 212, 215-16, 435
"Shah Was Here" (cartoon), 216
Shahsevan, 110-11
Shake (artist), 254
Shakur, Assata, 234
Sharecroppers Fund, 207-9
Sharman, Brent, 391, 395-96
Sharp, Kathy, 420
Shawcross, William, 118
Shelby, Richard, 243
Sheldon, Robert, 74
Shell Chemical Company, 196, 201-2
Shell Oil Company, 188
Shenk, Janet, 119-21
Shield, William, 234
Shi'i Muslims, 111-12, 114
Shilling, Dana, 285-86
Shippingport (Pennsylvania) nuclear reactor, 32
"Shopfloor Politics at Fleetwood" (Lippert), 382
Shore, Elliott, 1-8, 25-26, 63-64, 95-96, 159-60, 355-56

Xenon gas, 48
Xenophobia, 215
Xhosa, 170

Yankelovich, Skelly and White, 168
"Yellowcake Connection: Or How Nuclear
    Power Ties Suburban Long Island to a Tiny
    Town 2000 Miles Away" (Feldman), 53
Yemen, South. *See* South Yemen.
Yergin, Daniel, 447
"Yes, Admiral—Here's to the Old Days . . ."
    (cartoon), 108
"Yes to Choice" (graphic), 287
YOBU. *See* Youth Organization for Black
    Unity.

Yoming Minerals, 184
Yoriko, Nojiri, 280
York Rainbow Society for the Deaf, 340
Young, Andrew, 137, 222
Young, Bob, 206
Young, Coleman, 161
Young, Sarah, 391, 420-22
Youngstown (Ohio) steel mill closings, 391,
    400-402
Youth Organization for Black Unity, 252
Youth revolts, 14. *See also* Student boycotts;
    Student movement.
Yrurzun, Hugo Alfredo, 131

Z (musical group), 397
Zacharias, Larry, 168

Zaire, 227
Zambia, 227
Zambian women, 276
ZANU (Zimbabwe African National Union),
    101-3
ZAPU (Zimbabwe African People's Union), 101
Zawinski, Andrena, 271
Zimbabwe, 101-4, 171
Zippies, 19
Zirblis, Ray, 45
Zolone (pesticide), 200
Zombie advertisements, 271
Zombie (record), 104-5
Zulus, 170
Zwentendorf (Austria) Nuclear Power Plant, 46